Fundamentals of Private Pensions

Pension Research Council Publications

A complete listing of PRC publications appears at the back of this volume.

Fundamentals of Private Pensions

SEVENTH EDITION

Dan M. McGill
Kyle N. Brown
John J. Haley
Sylvester J. Schieber

Pension Research Council
The Wharton School of the University of Pennsylvania

PENN

University of Pennsylvania Press
Philadelphia

Library of Congress Cataloging-in-Publication Data
Fundamentals of private pensions/Dan M. McGill . . . [et al.] — 7th ed.
    p.   cm.
  Rev. ed. of: Fundamentals of private pensions/Dan M. McGill, Donald S. Grubbs, Jr. 1989
  Includes bibliographical references and index.
  ISBN 0-8122-3380-8 (cloth: alk. paper)
  1. Old age pensions—United States. I. McGill, Dan Mays. II. McGill, Dan Mays. Fundamentals of private pensions. III. Wharton School. Pension Research Council.
HD7105.35.U6M34 1996
658.3′253′0973—dc20   96-15518
                                                    CIP

Contents

Preface

The first edition of this book appeared more than 40 years ago in 1955. It reflected the state of the pension art at that time—or, at least, the author's perception of the prevailing state. The book contained 209 pages of text compressed into five long chapters. During the intervening years, the private pension institution has expanded enormously in scope, diversity, and complexity. The successive editions of this book have mirrored the changes in the field, especially the increasing diversity and complexity. This edition bears little resemblance to the original.

At the time of its publication, the original edition was thought to be a comprehensive and authoritative exposition of existing theory and practice in the design and operation of employer-sponsored retirement programs. It won the coveted Elizur Wright Award of the American Risk and Insurance Association as the outstanding original contribution to pension literature in the year of its publication. Yet by today's standards, the book would be considered relatively elementary and naive, particularly the portions dealing with the actuarial and financial aspects of pensions.

Each revision has been a major undertaking, reflecting interim developments and a refinement of concepts and terminology. The second edition, published 10 years after the first, was necessitated by the evolution of pension practices. As the preface to that edition stated: "Plan provisions have been refined, new types of funding instruments have been developed, investment policies have been expanded, new tax rulings have been issued, and more meaningful terminology has evolved."

A third edition, published in 1975, was necessitated by the enactment of the Employee Retirement Income Security Act (ERISA), even though it would have been justified by other forces and events. The third edition was more than a revision; it represented a recasting and rewriting of most of the materials in the second edition. More emphasis was placed on the rationale for various practices in plan design and financing, including the advantages and disadvantages of the various approaches. The requirements and standards of ERISA were dealt with as appropriate throughout the book. The presentation in this edition was based on the legislative language and history of ERISA since no regulations or interpretive rulings had been issued before the book went to press.

The major thrust of the fourth edition, brought out only four years after its predecessor, was to update the book in the light of the manifold regulations, rulings, and interpretations issued by the Internal Revenue Service, Department of

Labor, and Pension Benefit Guaranty Corporation in explanation of ERISA. The section of the third edition dealing with actuarial considerations was completely rewritten and expanded, with new terminology and a new framework for the analysis of actuarial cost methods. New chapters on profit-sharing plans, thrift plans, and the federal tax treatment of qualified asset accumulation plans were added. Finally, new developments, such as guaranteed income contracts of life insurers, were recognized, and refinements of various sorts were introduced.

In recognition of the mushrooming volume of pension plan assets and the responsibilities associated with their investment, the fifth edition, published in 1984, added chapters on investment policy and operations. This edition also included a discussion on accounting for pension plan costs and liabilities, a subject of growing importance and controversy. Individual account plans of various sorts were given expanded treatment, and this necessitated the addition of a new chapter on individual retirement accounts and voluntary employee contributions. The material on plan benefits insurance was completely rewritten to incorporate the changes introduced by the Multiemployer Pension Plan Amendment Act. A section on stochastic modeling was added to the chapter on forecasting plan costs, liabilities, and cash flow. The material was again updated to reflect changes in applicable law and business practices.

Like the previous revisions, the sixth edition, published in 1989, contained much new material. Repeated rounds of federal legislation during the 1980s had touched almost every aspect of pensions, and the text had to be substantially changed throughout. Court decisions, together with new regulations and guidelines from the regulatory agencies, also necessitated extensive changes. The chapter on accounting was completely rewritten to reflect *Statements of Financial Accounting Standards No. 87* and *No. 88* of the Financial Accounting Standards Board. Further revision had to be made because of changes in the types of contracts used by insurance companies and changes in other areas.

This seventh edition is once again necessitated by the evolution of the pension environment. Since 1989, we have seen the continuing development of new legislative and regulatory initiatives that have affected retirement programs. These include the Technical and Miscellaneous Revenue Act of 1988, the Omnibus Budget Reconciliation Act of 1989, the Omnibus Budget Reconciliation Act of 1990, the Older Workers Benefit Protection Act of 1990, the Unemployment Compensation Amendments of 1992, the Omnibus Budget Reconciliation Act of 1993, the Family and Medical Leave Act of 1993, the Uruguay Round of the General Agreement on Tariffs and Trade, and the Uniformed Services Employment and Reemployment Rights Act of 1994. We have also seen new changes in the structure and design of plans as employers attempt to deal with the needs of workers and the cost of operating their benefit programs. This edition represents a major restructuring of the materials included in the earlier editions. For example, the discussion on the structure of defined benefit and defined contribution plans has been reorganized in a way that should facilitate the understanding of those plans. This edition also includes a great deal of new material. Over the last 10 to 15 years, a substantial economics literature on the operations of employer-sponsored retirement programs has evolved. Chapters have been added that address the economics of the tax incentives provided to retirement programs and evaluate the varying human resource incentives in defined benefit and defined contribution programs. We have also significantly expanded the discussion and development of retirement income adequacy measures that date back to the first edition of the volume.

The current volume is organized into five main sections dealing with a variety of separable pension issues. It is organized in this fashion to enable the reader to use the volume as a text, a research tool, or a general reference. Chapter 1 stands alone as an introductory discussion on the historical evolution of the pension movement and how pensions fit into the patchwork of the whole retirement income security system in the United States. By necessity, this chapter is a very general discussion and many of the issues that are touched upon there are discussed in much greater detail elsewhere in the volume. Section 1 (Chapters 2 through 9) lays out the regulatory environment in which private pension plans operate. Section 2 (Chapters 10 through 15) investigates the various forms of retirement plans that are available to workers to determine how they are structured in practical terms. Section 3 (Chapters 16 through 21) focuses on the economics of pensions. Much of the material covered in this section of the volume did not appear in prior editions and includes discussion of the growing body of economic literature on the operations of employer-sponsored retirement plans that has arisen in recent years. Section 4 (Chapters 22 through 28) explores the funding and accounting environments in which private employer-sponsored retirement plans operate. The concluding section (Chapters 29 through 34) investigates the handling of assets in employer-sponsored plans and their valuation as well as the insurance provisions behind the benefit promises implied by the plans.

The order of the sections in this volume might not be appropriate for some readers. The student coming to the study of pensions for the first time likely will need to understand the regulatory environment and structure of plans before turning to a detailed understanding of why employers sponsor plans or how they fund them. Those with a general knowledge of the regulation and structure of pension plans might want to jump past the first two sections and first turn to the discussions on the economics of pensions in order to understand why employers sponsor plans and operate them in the fashion that they do. Others who are more interested in the actuarial issues important in the operation of defined benefit plans might want to jump to later sections of the volume first. Those interested solely in the regulatory environment might not be interested in the section on the economics of the plans at all. The grouping of the chapters should allow diverse groups of students with widely varied interests to focus most intently on the elements of pension fundamentals that are important to each of them.

The first five editions were developed under the sole authorship of Dan M. McGill. The sixth edition was developed under the coauthorship of Dan M. McGill and Donald S. Grubbs, Jr., who was a collaborator in prior editions. This seventh edition is coauthored by Dan M. McGill, Kyle N. Brown, John J. Haley, and Sylvester J. Schieber.

A number of individuals who provided substantial input into this volume deserve recognition. Alexander Miller and Gordon P. Goodfellow, both of Watson Wyatt Worldwide, were largely responsible for much of the data and modeling work that went into the development of the expanded discussion on retirement income targets and saving. John Sabelhaus of the Urban Institute provided us with a 13-year linked file of *Consumer Expenditure Surveys* that significantly facilitated the development of retirement income targets and saving. We would also like to thank Professors Olivia Mitchell of the University of Pennsylvania and Jack Vanderhei for their helpful comments on various parts of the volume. We also offer our thanks to two anonymous reviewers selected by the University of Pennsylvania Press to assess the desirability of the manuscript for publication and to offer comments on the contents, as appropriate. Our gratitude for help rendered in connection with previous editions carries over to this edition. Robert J. Myers, F.S.A., former Chief Actuary of the Social Security Administration, and Dr. Howard E. Winklevoss, an independent consultant, deserve special recognition for their past help.

We would like to record our very special intellectual debt to a small group of eminent pension actuaries who over the years shared their insight and knowledge and in so doing contributed enormously to the understanding of the private pension institution: Preston C. Bassett; Dorrance Bronson (deceased); Joseph B. Crimmins; John K. Dyer, Jr. (deceased); Frank L. Griffin, Jr. (deceased); Meyer Melnikoff; Ray M. Peterson (deceased); and Charles L. Trowbridge.

Needless to say, the authors take full responsibility for the book and any errors that may remain after all the scrutiny to which the manuscript was exposed.

Finally, we especially want to recognize Susan Prahinski of Watson Wyatt Worldwide for her tireless editing and insightful comments on each of the chapters as they were developed. Nina Droubay of Watson Wyatt also contributed significantly to this seventh edition, handling all final word processing, proofreading, and the assembly of the final manuscript.

We invite all readers to assist us with the next edition by calling our attention to any errors, omissions, or other shortcomings in the book.

Dan M. McGill
Kyle N. Brown
John J. Haley
Sylvester J. Schieber

Chapter 1
Underlying Forces

The private pension movement in the United States is rooted in a combination of significant demographic, economic, social, and political developments during the twentieth century. During this century there has been a progressive increase in the number and proportion of the population considered elderly, by whatever definition. Following trends begun during the late nineteenth century, the continued industrialization and growth in the size of individual firms drove some employers to seek ways to retire superannuated workers in the interest of efficiency of their operations. The growing number of elderly and the increasing perception of their economic obsolescence in the large industrial setting gave rise to organized retirement programs sponsored by individual employers.

The pension movement in the United States began during the latter part of the nineteenth century. The movement expanded slowly until the Great Depression. While the Depression slowed the progress of the pension movement, it raised the public consciousness about the economic security of the elderly. While some older retirees from large industrial firms were receiving a pension, most older people who no longer had job-related income did not. Even some of those fortunate enough to have a pension benefit prior to the Depression found that their plans could not afford to provide the benefits promised as the Depression wore on. Unemployment was particularly prevalent among older segments of the population. Out of this environment, Social Security was born.

The combination of Social Security spurring the general consciousness about retirement income security and the favorable tax treatment of employer-sponsored retirement programs led to rapid expansion of the pension system during the 1950s through the 1970s. In many regards, the employer-based pension system in the United States has been successful at extending income security for many workers into their retirement years. Yet the forces that led to the establishment of employer-sponsored pensions and Social Security have continued to evolve. As they have done so, they have continued to pose significant challenges to both plan sponsors and policymakers. Some conception of the magnitude of the problems can be grasped from the following brief account of the demographic, social, economic, and public policy influences at work.

Motivations Behind the Pension Movement

Population Trends

During the twentieth century both the absolute and relative size of the aged population in the United States has grown significantly. According to census data

TABLE 1-1   Total Population and Population over the Age of 65 for Selected Years, 1900–1990 (thousands of people)

Year	Total Population	Population over 65	Percentage over 65
1900	75,995	3,080	4.05
1910	91,972	3,950	4.29
1920	105,711	4,933	4.67
1930	122,775	6,634	5.40
1940	131,669	9,019	6.85
1950	150,697	12,270	8.14
1960	179,323	16,560	9.23
1970	203,235	20,266	9.97
1980	227,061	25,549	11.25
1990	249,924	31,224	12.49

Source: U.S. Census of the Population for various years; 1900 to 1970 taken from *Historical Statistics of the United States, Colonial Times to 1970,* p. 15; 1980–90 taken from *Statistical Abstract of the United States, 1992* (Washington, D.C.: USGPO, 1992), p. 14.

shown in Table 1-1, the general population of the United States in 1990 was 3.3 times the size of the population in 1900. Over the same period, the number of persons aged 65 and over had grown 10.1 times. In 1900, there were roughly 4.1 million persons aged 65 and over, whereas 90 years later the number had grown to 31.2 million. The increase in the absolute and relative number of older persons in the United States during this century reflects the combined influence of a decline in the birthrate and an increase in life expectancy. Immigration levels have also played some role in the changing age composition of the population.

Birthrate Trends

High birthrates result in an ever growing population, with younger cohorts of the population being larger than older cohorts. Low birthrates, on the other hand, signify slower population growth or even contraction. If a population is growing slowly or contracting, the result will be a general aging of the population compared to a situation where there are high birth rates.

During the early decades of the twentieth century, the birthrate in the United States fell, as it did in most developed economies. The long-run decrease in the birthrate was reversed toward the end of World War II, and the birthrate remained high for a number of years thereafter. During this period, the group of individuals now known as the "baby boomers" were born. But between 1960 and 1975 the birthrate fell sharply and until very recently has remained somewhat below the replacement level.[1]

Between 1984 and 1991 the total fertility rate rose from 1.80 to an estimated 2.06.[2] Although projected fertility rates are important in estimating the future

[1] U.S. Department of Health and Human Services, Public Health Service, *Vital Statistics of the United States, 1988* (Washington, D.C.: USGPO), p. 1.
[2] The total fertility rate for a given year is the average number of children who would be born to a woman during her lifetime if she were to experience the age-specific fertility rates of all women in that year over her lifetime.

TABLE 1-2   Life Expectancy at Birth, Selected Years, 1900–1990

| | Life Expectancy | | |
Year	Total	Males	Females
1900	47.3	46.3	48.3
1910	50.0	48.4	51.8
1920	54.1	53.6	54.6
1930	59.7	58.1	61.6
1940	62.9	60.8	65.2
1950	68.2	65.6	71.1
1960	69.7	66.6	73.1
1970	70.8	67.1	74.7
1980	73.7	70.0	77.4
1990	75.4	72.0	78.8

Source: Data from 1910 to 1960 taken from *Historical Statistics of the United States, Colonial Times to 1970,* p. 55; 1980–90 taken from *Statistical Abstract of the United States,* 1992, p. 76.

relative size of the elderly population, there is no sure way to precisely estimate them, and demographers often disagree on the rates used to project population growth. For example, during 1993 the U.S. Census Bureau, as the chronicler of population growth, revised its assumed long-term fertility rate from 1.8 to 2.1 children per woman. At the same time, the intermediate assumptions used in preparing the 1993 valuation of the Social Security program were somewhat lower. According to the 1993 projections, the long-term fertility rate is expected to again fall to 1.9 children per woman during the first quarter of the next century.[3]

Life Expectancy Trends

In addition to the general decline in birthrates over most of this century, extensions in life expectancy have driven up the number of elderly in both relative and absolute terms. The greatest gains in life expectancy occurred during the first half of the century, as shown in Table 1-2, but gains are still being realized. The tremendous extension in life expectancy in this century is the result of advances in medical science, particularly in the control of infectious diseases and the reduction of infant mortality, improvements in public health services, and a rise in general living standards. Such a rise will probably not be duplicated during the next half-century. However, as medical science devotes more and more resources to the studies of diseases of old age, further gains in life expectancy can be expected. On the other hand, either continued deterioration of the physical environment or some unforeseen catastrophe could reduce life expectancy, but such an occurrence would run counter to a long history of improvements.

Immigration Trends

Another factor affecting the overall age composition of the population is immigration. As Table 1-3 shows, immigration contributed large numbers of people

[3]Social Security Administration, *1993 Annual Report of the Board of Trustees of the Federal Old-Age and Survivors Insurance and Disability Insurance Trust Funds* (Washington, D.C.: USGPO, 1993), pp. 64–66.

TABLE 1-3   United States Immigration, Selected Years,1900–1990

Period	Thousands of Immigrants	Rate[a]
1900–1901	8,795	10.4
1911–20	5,736	5.7
1921–30	4,107	3.5
1931–40	528	0.4
1941–50	1,035	0.7
1951–60	2,515	1.5
1961–70	3,322	1.7
1971–80	4,493	2.1
1980–90	7,338	3.1

Source: Statistical Abstract of the United States, 1992, p. 10.
[a]The annual rate of immigration per 1,000 people of the population.

to the U.S. population during the early decades of this century. The immigrants during this period tended to be younger people looking for career opportunities. After the 1930s immigration declined, but it has picked up again since the mid-1970s, especially most recently. The long-term role that immigration will play in the age structure of the United States will depend heavily on public policy decisions, which are impossible to predict.

Growth of the Elderly Population

Today the population over the age of 65 is increasing by about 650,000 people per year. The fastest growing group includes people over 85. Shortly after the turn of the century, members of the baby boom generation will begin to reach their 60s and a continued expansion of the elderly population in both absolute and relative terms can be expected. Table 1-4 shows recent projections by Social

TABLE 1-4   Estimates and Projections of Total Population and Population over the Age of 65, Selected Years, 1950–2070[a]

Year	Total Population (thousands)	Population over 65 (thousands)	Percentage over 65
1950	159,386	12,752	8.00
1960	190,081	17,250	9.08
1970	214,776	20,920	9.74
1980	235,085	26,143	11.12
1990	259,357	31,918	12.31
2000	285,025	35,476	12.45
2010	305,965	39,945	13.06
2020	325,090	53,322	16.40
2030	339,549	68,282	20.11
2040	348,505	72,456	20.79
2050	354,090	74,276	20.98
2060	359,017	79,148	22.05
2070	364,119	82,458	22.65

Source: 1994 Annual Report of the Board of Trustees of the Federal Old-Age and Survivors Insurance and Disability Insurance Trust Funds, p. 144.
[a]The population counts in this table that overlap with those in Table 1 do not correspond exactly because this estimate was adjusted for net census under counts and increased for other U.S. citizens living abroad and for populations in the geographic areas covered by U.S. Social Security but not included in the U.S. population.

Security actuaries on the portion of the population over 65 for selected future years. Looking back to Table 1-1, we see that during the first half of the twentieth century the population over age 65 increased by approximately 4 percent. The projections for the year 2000 by Social Security's actuaries suggests that the population over age 65 will increase again by about 4 percent during the last half of this century. But the next 4 percent increase in this portion of the population is expected to occur within roughly 20 years after the turn of the century. And we expect another 4 percent increase in the over-65 population in the 20 years after that, between 2020 and 2040. Any discussion about retirement programs and policy has to consider these significant increases in the elderly population.

Declining Labor Force Participation Among the Elderly

The increase in the proportion of old people in the population has been accompanied by a decline in the employment of the aged. In 1900 the aged constituted 4.1 percent of the total population and 4.0 percent of the total labor force. By 1992 the percentage of the population aged 65 and over had more than tripled, but the percentage of the total labor force age 65 and over had declined to 2.8 percent. In 1900, 35.9 percent of all persons age 65 and over were in the labor force, while in 1992 only 11.2 percent were in that category. This decline has taken place chiefly among aged males. In 1900, 63.5 percent of such males were in the labor force, but by 1992 the proportion had shrunk to 16.1 percent. The rate of female participation in the labor force aged 65 and over held relatively steady during that period, measuring 8.3 percent in both years.[4]

Understanding the changes in the labor force participation of the aged requires an understanding of both sides of the market for older workers' services. On the demand side of the market, a significant reorganization of the national economy meant that the services that older workers could provide were often perceived as being less valuable than they would have been earlier. On the supply side of the market, increasing levels of national wealth and productivity meant that workers could enjoy increased levels of leisure. One form of increased leisure that has become prominent during the twentieth century has been the ability of workers to withdraw from the work force at an earlier age than prior generations of workers were able to do.

Employment Opportunities for the Aged

The economy in the United States during the early part of the nineteenth century was predominantly rural or craft-oriented. In this economy, the primary source of income for most families was a farm or small craft business, which in both cases tended to be family owned and operated. Within these small business units, every member of a family was part of the production process. As age limited one's abilities, daily tasks could be adjusted among family members so less demanding tasks could be performed by the older family members.

[4]U.S. Bureau of the Census, *Historical Statistics of the United States, Colonial Times to 1970* (Washington, D.C.: USGPO, 1960), pp. 10, 15, and 131; and *Statistical Abstract of the United States 1993* (Washington, D.C.: USGPO, 1993), Tables 17 and 622.

In addition to providing a basis for constructive employment, the business structure of early-nineteenth-century America also provided older family members with significant control over the family's financial assets, the largest of which was generally the farm or business itself. While the business was often handed down from generation to generation, the transfer generally did not occur until the financial security of the older generation was ensured. As Steven Sass points out: "In 1870, while the economy was still largely organized along traditional lines, the over-65 age cohort controlled more wealth than any other group. They could enjoy a reasonably secure source of income whether they continued to operate their assets, put them up for rent or sold out and banked the proceeds."[5]

During the latter half of the nineteenth century the economy began to change significantly with the growth of large industrial firms. In this changing environment, employers began operating on a much larger scale than ever before. The larger scale meant specialization of tasks and new evolving managerial organizational structures. The power machinery associated with the activities in industrialized firms required performance efficiencies not associated with craft or agrarian activities. As Andrew Achenbaum observes: "Efficiency had become the *sine qua non* of any successful enterprise by the turn of the century. Consequently, impersonality symbolized a bureaucratic order in which functions and procedures, not particular men, were indispensable."[6]

The growth in industrialization and the concurrent drive for efficiency meant that older workers were increasingly subjected to standards of performance they could no longer meet. Some employers found relatively light assignments for long-tenured superannuated workers, but many employers simply put them out of their jobs. To add to the problem, alternative employment was difficult to find. Sass points to a key indicator of this growing phenomenon in the unemployment rate among men over the age of 65, which had been relatively constant throughout most of the nineteenth century. It jumped from 26.8 percent to 31.3 percent between 1890 and 1900.[7] By 1930, 54 percent of the men over 65 were out of work and looking for a job, and another quarter still had jobs but were on layoff without pay.[8]

Agricultural workers to this day continue to work longer than their industrial counterparts. Industrial employees, because of the physical demands of their jobs or employer personnel policy, are simply more likely to retire at a relatively early age. While the overall physical depreciation that workers faced at the beginning of the century has been somewhat ameliorated by various technological innovations, those same technological advances have caused a greater depreciation of human capital than that in earlier generations. In recent years automation and continuing improvements in employer efficiency have led many employers to downsize and restructure their organizations. For many workers this has meant increasingly early

[5]Steven A. Sass, *The History of Private Pensions in America* (Cambridge, Mass.: Harvard University Press, 1997), quotation from preprint manuscript, chap. 1.

[6]W. Andrew Achenbaum, *Old Age in the New Land* (Baltimore: Johns Hopkins University Press, 1978), p. 48.

[7]Sass, *History of Private Pensions*, chap. 1.

[8]Committee on Economic Security, *Social Security in America* (Washington, D.C.: USGPO, 1937), p. 146.

retirement.Throughout most of the twentieth century, employers wishing to lay off older workers because of age could do so somewhat arbitrarily. Legislation passed in 1967 and amended during the 1980s prohibits mandatory retirement by employers because of age.[9] This legislation, however, had little effect on the average retirement age among workers. By the time this legislation was passed and fully implemented, employers were increasingly limited in their ability to control the age composition of their work force by any means other than financial incentives because of the adoption and expansion of age discrimination laws. Most large employers, and many smaller ones as well, built incentives into their retirement programs to entice people to retire who would not do so otherwise.

Growing Worker Interest in Leisure Time

Economists evaluating individual work decisions define time as the period devoted to either work or leisure. In this framework, leisure is any activity not related to one's job; also, economists consider leisure to be an economic good. An individual's decision to work an additional hour versus enjoying an additional hour of leisure is based on the preference between income earned by working, leisure, and the hourly wage rate. In an economic context, an hour of leisure is purchased by forgoing the income that would be earned by working an extra hour. In this context, leisure and work are thought of as competitive goods.

At a given wage rate there is an inverse relationship between earnings (i.e., the wage rate times hours worked) and leisure. The wage rate, then, is important in determining a worker's supply of labor because it determines the tradeoff in goods or services the worker can purchase (i.e., earnings) by giving up an extra hour of leisure. Up to a point, an individual is willing to give up leisure for additional earnings. But for every worker there is also a point at which an additional hour of work and wages will not provide enough goods and services to make it worth while to give up the extra hour of leisure.

Over a range of wage levels, a higher wage is thought to induce a typical worker to work additional hours because the marginal value of the extra goods and services outweighs the extra leisure that must be given up. But as wages continue to rise, they can ultimately reach a level at which a worker can earn all of the nonleisure goods and services desired by working fewer hours than he or she would have to work at a lower wage. In this case, the growth in wage rates will result in increased consumption of leisure time.

One result of the increased industrialization of the economy in the United States over the last century has been to increase the productivity and real wage rates of workers. For example, the data in Table 1-5 show that the average wage rates of all workers (in 1983 dollars) rose from $2.01 per hour in 1890 to $3.32 per hour in 1920; thus the growth rate was nearly 1.7 percent per year. The average wage of union workers grew somewhat slower, at a rate of only 1 percent per year, but it did start from a higher base. Table 1-5 also shows that union workers with higher wage rates worked fewer weekly hours than workers in general. Furthermore, it shows

---

[9]Age Discrimination in Employment Act of 1967 (ADEA) as amended by the Age Discrimination in Employment Amendments of 1986, Pub. Law 99-592.

TABLE 1-5   Average Hours and Average Earnings in Manufacturing, Selected Years, 1890–1920

	All Workers		Union Workers Only	
Year	Weekly Hours	Wage Rate[a]	Weekly Hours	Wage Rate[a]
1890	60.0	2.01	54.4	3.27
1900	59.0	2.57	53.0	4.02
1910	56.6	2.77	50.1	4.29
1920	51.0	3.32	45.7	4.42

Source. Data from 1910 to 1960 taken from *Historical Statistics of the United States, Colonial Times to 1970,* p. 168.

[a]The wage rates reported in the table are the average hourly earnings reported in the source document adjusted by the Bureau of Labor Statistics consumer price index, with the base for 1982–84 = 100.

that in each subsequent 10-year measurement of average wages and weekly hours that the higher wage rates corresponded with reduced hours of work per week.

The information Table 1-6 is similar to that in Table 1-5, except that it covers an extended period beyond 1920 and is calculated on a different basis. Where Table 1-5 refers to unionized and all workers in manufacturing, Table 1-6 includes both union and nonunion workers, but only those workers in production jobs. The wage rates from 1909 (those from 1910 were not available) and 1920 in Table 1-6 are somewhat below the rates for 1910 and 1920 in Table 1.5, but the overall pattern of increasing wage rates and declining work hours over the overlapping period up to 1920 is consistent across the two data sets.

A particularly interesting aspect of Table 1-6 is that while wages continued to grow up until 1980, the average hours worked per week stabilized in the manufacturing industry at around 40 hours during the 1940s. While the reductions in the

TABLE 1-6   Earnings and Hours of Production Workers in Manufacturing, Selected Years, 1909–90

Year	Weekly Hours	Wage Rate[a]
1909	51.0	1.92
1920	47.4	2.75
1930	42.1	3.29
1940	38.1	4.71
1950	40.5	5.98
1960	39.7	7.64
1970	39.8	8.66
1980	39.7	8.82
1990	40.8	8.29

Sources. Data for 1909–1970 taken from *Historical Statistics of the United States, Colonial Times to 1970,* GPO, 169–70. Data for 1970 and 1980 taken from U.S. Bureau of the Census, *Statistical Abstract of the United States, 1993,* pp. 417, 419.

[a]The wage rates reported in the table are the average hourly earnings reported in the source document adjusted by the Bureau of Labor Statistics consumer price index with the base 1982–84 = 100.

average hours worked per week might have come at the instigation of the employers in some instances, the union movement had pushed for the shorter workweek since the 1890s.[10] The reductions in the workweek achieved by the unions for their own workers were passed on to most nonunion workers in due course. The record is fairly clear that during the 50 years leading up to 1940, the real growth in wages allowed manufacturing workers to substitute leisure time for time at work through reduced hours in the workweek.

While the workweek pattern may have been slightly different in other industries, in most cases it was being reduced in a fashion consistent with that occurring in manufacturing over this time period. Beyond the 1940s, however, the continued improvement in real wages in manufacturing and other industries was not reflected in further commensurate reductions in average hours worked per week. It was about this time that large segments of the working population discovered a new way to convert higher real incomes into added leisure time.

The phenomenon we now know as retirement has existed in American society for a long time. The earliest documented records of the prevalence of retirement date back to the late nineteenth century. According to the 1870 U.S. Census, an estimated 65 percent of the men over the age of 60 were in the labor force shortly after the end of the Civil War. Men this age not in the labor force were generally retired. From 1870 through 1930 the prevalence of retirement among men over 60 held relatively steady and actually may have declined slightly. In 1930 about 35 percent of the men over 60 were retired.

In 1935 the Social Security Act was enacted. Social Security tax collections were started in 1937, and the first retirement benefits were paid in 1940. Today nearly 95 percent of all U.S. workers retiring at age 62 or later receive Social Security benefits. In 1940 a sharp increase in federal corporate income tax rates expanded the incentive for employers to establish pension programs. In the late 1940s organized labor won the right to negotiate for pension benefits. Pension plans grew rapidly throughout the 1950s and 1960s, especially among larger firms. At the end of the 1930s there were fewer than 700 pension plans in the United States. Today there are nearly 1 million plans in operation. The overwhelming majority of workers in firms with at least 100 employees are covered by such plans.

With the beginning of Social Security and the growth in pensions, the prevalence of older men in the labor force began to decline, as shown in Figure 1-1, and it has continued to do so, until now. The retirement patterns of women have varied somewhat from those of men because of their different attachment to the formal work force outside of their homes. The labor force participation rates of women over 65 have been relatively constant since 1940. The labor force participation rates of women younger than age 65 have been rising, especially recently, because women have been entering the work force at much greater rates than they did historically. It appears that women with career tenure patterns similar to the typical male tenure patterns are likely to have retirement characteristics similar to those of their male counterparts.

---

[10]John G. Turnbull, C. Arthur Williams, Jr., and Earl F. Cheit, *Economic and Social Security* (New York: Ronald Press, 1968), p. 543.

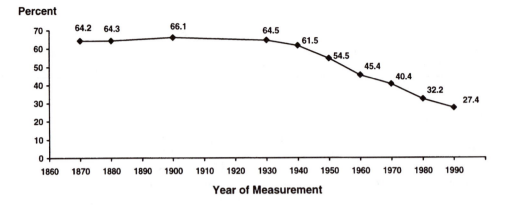

Figure 1-1. Labor force participation of men over the age of 60, 1860–90. Sources: Roger L. Ransom and Richard Sutch, "The Decline of Retirement in the Years Before Social Security: U.S. Retirement Patterns, 1870–1940," in Rita Ricardo-Campbell and Edward P. Lazear, *Issues in Contemporary Retirement* (Stanford, Calif.: Hoover Institution Press, 1988), Table 1.2, p. 12; and Bureau of Labor Statistics, *Employment and Earnings* (Washington, D.C.: USGPO, November 1990), Table A-4, p. 9.

The gradual lowering of retirement ages in American society is not purely the result of some grand scheme dreamed up by employers to get older workers to retire sooner than they would otherwise. To a certain extent, the growth in the retirement phenomenon is merely an extension of workers' pursuit of more leisure that led to the gradual reduction of the workweek over the 50 years leading up to 1940. The difference is that instead of continuing to shorten the workweek, since 1940 workers appear to have been more motivated to shorten the working life. In this regard, the interest of workers has corresponded with the interest of many employers.

Social Factors Affecting Retirement Patterns

Historically, many retirement provisions crept into plans because of changing perspectives on what was a reasonable time to retire. Whether some fundamental change had occurred in workers values and led them to seek more leisure at the expense of reduced labor supply, or whether productivity considerations had affected the demand for older workers, or both, is unclear. The wide acceptance of age 65 as the traditional "normal retirement age" for retirement plans was some-what serendipitous, although it was more related to the selection of 65 as the Social Security retirement age than anything else.

Social Security's early retirement age of 62 was established for women in 1956. The rationale for this change had nothing to do with labor market considerations: rather, it was the social phenomenon that wives tended to be three years younger than their husbands on average, and politicians thought it would be nice to let couples retire together. The decision to change Social Security's early retirement age to 62 for men in 1961 was based on reducing unemployment levels. This latter reduction set the stage for reducing the retirement ages under employer-sponsored pensions.

Given the three-year cycle on major union contract negotiations, it was more than a coincidence that three years after Social Security's early retirement age for men was reduced, the United Auto Workers (UAW) won $400 monthly retirement benefits for workers aged 60 with 30 years of service. These benefits were also payable to workers retiring prior to age 60 or with less than 30 years of service, but they were reduced. Under this arrangement, the normal retirement benefit was reduced to account for the early retirement, but a supplemental benefit brought the combined benefit level up to $400 per month for the 30-year worker. These "supplements" were payable until the age of 65 as long as the retiree did not take another job paying more than $100 per month or become eligible for Social Security disability benefits. Employment income from another job reduced the pension supplement by $2 for each dollar of earned income. Other heavily union-ized industries followed the auto industry patterns in introducing early retirement benefits for union workers.

The early versions of the "30-and-out" provisions linked to age merely whetted the appetites for pure 30-and-out provisions. This trend, coupled with the influx of the baby boom workers, made strictly service-related 30-and-out provisions a nego-tiating priority by the early 1970s. During the auto negotiations on these provisions in 1970, the young workers were as committed to "30-and-out" as older workers, even though the discounted value of the additional benefits would have been relatively small for them at the time. They were concerned not so much about their personal added value of retirement benefits as about clearing the rungs on the position ladders that they could fill as older workers left. During the first half of the 1970s, the 30-and-out plan became common in the steel and auto industries and then spread to other industries as well.

Early-out provisions spread to white-collar plans partly because of the success of organized labor in negotiating these provisions. Unionized companies have always been faced with the possibility that their white-collar workers might unionize if their compensation packages did not move somewhat along parallel tracks. In addition, the expansion of the U.S. work force as the baby boom members entered during the early 1970s placed enormous pressures on the workers nearing retire-ment by increasing the competition for jobs.

Retirement Plans: An Intersection of Interests

The history of the industrial era in the late nineteenth century suggests that many urban workers failed to accumulate adequate financial resources to meet their economic needs in retirement. In earlier days it was not of particular concern if persons reached old age without adequate means of support. The elderly members of a family resided with and were supported by the younger members. In many cases, the elderly persons were able to perform some tasks around the household or farm, thus lightening the burden on the younger people. With increasing urbanization, changes in housing conditions, greater geographical mobility, and many other economic and social developments, the traditional approach to old-age care and support was weakened.

The net result of the inability or unwillingness of workers to save adequate amounts to cover their own retirement needs and the changing concept of filial responsibility was widespread financial insecurity among older Americans. The interests of employers in providing an orderly mechanism to retire superannuated workers and the interests of the larger society in the social welfare of older citizens gave rise to the institutional provision of retirement benefits in the United States. Since the very beginning of the pension movement in the late nineteenth century, American society has looked increasingly to government and employers for old-age support.

Public Pension Programs

Although this story is primarily about private employer-sponsored retirement programs, it would be incomplete without a brief discussion of public plans. The largest of these, Social Security, provides the financial underpinning of the retirement income security system in the United States and is the foundation on which most employer retirement plans build. Public employer pension plans also warrant mention because of their size.

The limitations of the individual approach to old-age financial security and the general lack of employer-sponsored plans led to the establishment of various governmental social insurance and old-age income maintenance programs. The most comprehensive and significant undertaking of this sort is the federal Old-Age, Survivors, and Disability Insurance (OASDI) system. This program has had such a profound impact on private pension plans that careful consideration should be given to its structure and underlying philosophy.

Federal Old-Age, Survivors, and Disability Insurance

Coverage

Federal Old-Age, Survivors, and Disability Insurance is the national program of social insurance created by the Social Security Act of 1935 to cover long-term risks. As such, it is the foundation of all other programs of old-age income mainte-nance.[11] Unlike many national programs of old-age social insurance, including those of Canada and Great Britain, OASDI is not based on the principle of universal coverage of the entire population. Rather, coverage is conditioned on attachment to the labor market. The broad objective of the program is to cover all gainfully employed persons, including the self-employed. With certain exceptions, coverage for all eligible persons is compulsory and immediate. In other words, OASDI is a device by which gainfully employed persons are forced by statute to assume some responsibility for the old-age maintenance of persons who have retired.

The Medicare program, enacted in 1965, is closely associated with OASDI. One part, Hospital Insurance (HI), covers by and large the same employed persons as OASDI; it provides hospital and related benefits for insured persons who are over the age of 65 or have been disabled for at least 2.5 years (actually 29 to 30 months), and certain of their dependents, with financing by payroll taxes. The other part,

[11]For a comprehensive text on social security see Robert J. Myers, *Social Security*, 4th ed. (Philadelphia: Pension Research Council and University of Pennsylvania Press, 1993).

Supplementary Medical Insurance, covers all persons over 65 and all disabled persons covered by Hospital Insurance, on an individual voluntary basis; it provides benefits for physician and related medical services, with financing by individual premium payments and contributions from the federal government.

The program covers people through exclusion, not inclusion. That is, all gainfully employed persons are covered except those specifically excluded. The original legislation, however, excluded some important groups. Thus, 4 out of every 10 gainfully employed persons were ineligible for coverage.

The exclusion of such a large proportion of employed persons introduced serious inequities into the program and, what was even more important, tended to frustrate the basic objective of the program. Therefore, by amendments in 1950, 1954, 1956, and 1983, the coverage was extended to many previously excluded groups. The concepts of elective coverage (for employees of state and local governments) and qualifying conditions as to regularity of employment (for domestics, farm laborers, and casuals) were introduced. Today 9 out of every 10 gainfully employed persons are covered under the system. The principal exclusions are railroad workers (who have their own plan, which is coordinated with OASDI), federal employees hired before 1984 under any federal retirement system, those employees of state and local governments who are not covered by election, irregularly employed farm and domestic workers, and self-employed persons with very low income.

Benefits

A. ELIGIBILITY FOR RETIREMENT BENEFITS   Benefits under the OASDI program are paid as a matter of statutory entitlement and are not generally conditioned on a showing of need. This characteristic of the program avoids the administrative complications of a needs or income test (except for the retirement test and proof of dependency for some categories of beneficiaries) and thus protects the privacy of individuals and preserves their self-respect. Equally important, it encourages individuals to accumulate savings to supplement the benefits of the OASDI program and any other retirement plan of which they might be members. Before the 1983 amendments the statutory retirement age at which unreduced benefits became payable was 65. The statutory retirement age is still 65 for those born before 1938 (who will reach age 65 before 2003) and is graduated upward to 67 for those born in 1960 and later. Retirement benefits are payable upon actual retirement at or after the age of 62 (benefits are permanently reduced for retirement before the statutory retirement age) and the satisfaction of a service requirement. An individual is entitled to retirement benefits only if that individual has been credited with quarters of coverage[12] equal to one-fourth of the calendar quarters that have elapsed since December 31, 1950 (or the year in which the individual became 21, if later), up to age 62 (which requirement will be at most 40 quarters of coverage), subject to a minimum of six quarters of coverage. An individual who has met such

[12]In 1994, an employee earned one quarter of coverage for each $620 of earnings in the calendar year (maximum of four quarters per year). The $620 will increase automatically in future years in proportion to average wages.

service requirements is said to be "fully insured." It might be said that the benefits vest[13] after 10 years of service (the period is shorter for those over the age of 22 on January 1, 1951), with the amount being subject to diminution through periods of noncoverage.

As stated above, benefits are conditioned on actual retirement, the test of which has been substantial withdrawal from covered employment. Under the 1939 act, an otherwise eligible claimant was disqualified for benefits for any month in which the individual earned wages in covered employment of $15 or more. This earnings limit has been increased and moderated from time to time. The earnings limit has been eliminated for persons aged 70 and over, and partial payment of benefits has been made possible when earnings somewhat exceed the limit. In 1996 the law provided for a reduction of $1 in benefits for each $2 of annual earnings in excess of $11,520 for those aged 65 and older and $8,280 for those under 65. In the year that an individual first becomes entitled to benefits, however, benefits are not withheld for any month in which the beneficiary's remuneration as an employee is one-twelfth the annual limit or less, and in which the individual renders no substantial services in self-employment. On the other hand, all earnings, not just covered earnings, are taken into account. The foregoing exempt amounts will be automatically adjusted in future years for changes in the general level of wages in the country.

Incorporated originally in the law mainly as a device for forcing older workers out of a depressed labor market, the earnings limit has been retained primarily to hold down the cost of the OASDI program. Complete elimination of the earnings limit today would increase current outlays under the program. It is politically difficult to justify benefit payments to persons who have not actually retired, particularly in view of the burdensome level that the cost of the program will eventually reach. Furthermore, an earnings limit is thought to preserve the basic character of the old-age element of the program, which undertakes to provide benefits primarily to those workers no longer substantially connected to the labor force.

Opponents of an earnings test argue that such a test discourages persons from continuing to be active, productive members of the labor force, thus depriving society of the goods and services that they might otherwise have produced; that it encourages dishonesty; and that it induces individuals to enter the underground economy, with an accompanying loss of tax dollars.

B. NATURE OF BENEFITS   The OASDI program provides retirement, disability, and survivorship benefits, all based on the insured's "primary insurance amount" (PIA), the derivation of which is described below. The insured's retirement benefit, a life income, is designated the "old-age insurance benefit" and is identical with the primary insurance amount if the individual retires at the statutory retirement age (age 65 for those born before 1938). If the worker delays retirement past that age, the benefit is increased for each year of deferral up to age 70. If retirement takes place at any time between the ages of 62 and the statutory retirement age, the benefit is permanently reduced. For those born before 1938, the reduc-

---

[13]Some persons question whether the concept of vesting can properly be applied to a noncontractual benefit.

tion is 20 percent at age 62 and is proportionate for retirement at any intervening age, being 10 percent at age 63.5, for example. For those born later, the reduction at age 62 will range from 20 to 30 percent.

The wife of a retired worker is entitled to a benefit equal to 50 percent of the primary insurance amount if she is at the statutory retirement age or older or, irrespective of her age, if she has under her care a dependent and unmarried child of the insured under the age of 18 (or a child who has been disabled since age 18 or before); if the wife has no such child, she may claim permanently reduced wife's benefits at any time between age 62 and her statutory retirement age. The percentage reduction is slightly larger than the percentage used in determining early benefits for retired workers. Furthermore, each such child is entitled to a benefit equal to one-half of the primary insurance amount. The husband of a retired worker is entitled to benefits determined in the same way as a wife's benefit, provided the husband is 62 or older. The wife's or husband's benefit is paid only if it is larger than the benefit payable in respect of the spouse's own covered earnings and is subject to the earnings test. A spouse's benefit is currently payable to about 15 percent of all retired workers. The combined family benefits may not exceed prescribed amounts, which generally are about 1.75 times the primary insurance amount.

Social Security provides survivorship benefits and includes a special category of insured status to facilitate the payment of such benefits to orphan children and their mothers. Such survivorship benefits are available if the deceased was "currently insured," a status that can be attained with 6 quarters of coverage, all of which, however, must have been earned within the 13 quarters preceding the date of death, including the quarter in which death occurs. The same survivor benefits are available if the deceased was "fully insured" without being "currently insured." In addition to a lump-sum benefit equal to $255, income benefits are payable to widows and widowers aged 60 and over (aged 50 and over if disabled), mothers of any age who have dependent children of the deceased under their care, dependent children under the age of 18 (or disabled since before age 22) or children aged 18 through 21 if in school, and dependent parents aged 62 and over.[14]

Social Security provides monthly benefits for permanently and totally disabled workers under the age of 65 after a five-month waiting period. Dependents' benefits are payable to the same categories of dependents as for retired workers. The benefit for the disabled worker is the primary insurance amount. To be eligible, the worker must be both fully insured and have 20 quarters of coverage during the last 10 years (fewer quarters are required if one is disabled before the age of 31).

C. LEVEL OF BENEFITS   All benefits payable under the OASDI program are based on the insured's covered earnings. Benefits for individuals attaining age 65 before 1982 (and for many retiring in later years, under a grandfather provision) are based on the "average monthly wage" (AMW). Benefits for individuals attaining age 65 after 1982, unless the grandfather clause is applicable, are based on the "average indexed monthly earnings" (AIME).

---

[14]Mothers whose only children are 18 through 21 and in school are not eligible for survivor benefits.

Starting for those attaining age 65 in 1982 (except for grandfather provisions), or dying or becoming disabled before age 65 in 1982, the primary insurance amount is based upon "average indexed monthly earnings" instead of the average monthly wage. The average indexed monthly earnings are calculated in exactly the same manner as the average monthly wage, except that the worker's earnings in each year before the year of attainment of age 60 (or the second year before death or disability prior to age 62) are indexed to reflect the increase in average nation-wide wages during the intervening years. The formula used to determine the primary insurance amount based upon the average indexed monthly earnings is different from that used under prior law for the average monthly wage.

The resulting "replacement ratios"—the ratio of the primary insurance amount for the initial month of retirement (as of the beginning of the year) to the annual covered earnings for the year just prior to retirement—will remain fairly stable under the amended law and will be about 23 percent lower than the replacement ratios under the prior law for those retiring at age 65 in 1981. The replacement ratios for workers retiring at age 65 in the future are estimated as 37 percent for the average worker, 49 percent for one whose earnings were only half of those of the average worker, and 24 percent for workers whose earnings always equal the taxable earnings base. The survivorship benefits payable to a widow and two or more children run about 70 percent of the covered annual earnings for the average worker, about 90 percent for the low-earnings worker, and 50 percent for the maximum-earnings worker. The benefits are automatically adjusted each year by changes in the cost of living, as measured by the consumer price index.

Financing

Up to the present, the cost of the OASDI program, including both benefits and administrative expenditures, has been borne almost entirely by the covered workers[15] and employers. Almost all funds have been derived from a payroll tax levied in equal proportions on employers and employees and from a tax on covered earnings of the self-employed.

The rate of contribution in 1996 was 6.20 percent each for wage earners and their employers, plus 1.45 percent for Hospital Insurance. For self-employed persons the rate equals the sum of the employer and employee tax rates (twice the employee rate). Since 1990 self-employed individuals have been allowed an income tax deduction for half their Social Security taxes, comparable to the deduction allowed to employers. The OASDI tax is levied on earnings up to a taxable wage base, $62,700 in 1996. This base increases automatically for changes in the general level of nationwide wages. The HI tax is levied on all earnings without limit.

The present system of financing is a modified pay-as-you-go arrangement. The expenditures of the program are approximately equal to the income from contributions and interest earnings. The excess contributions over the years have led to the accumulation in the OASI and DI trust funds of approximately $500 billion as of the end of 1995.

---

[15]The term *workers* includes self-employed individuals.

Billions of dollars

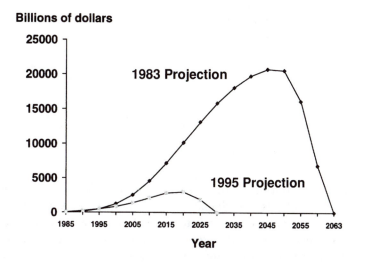

Figure 1-2. Projected OASDI trust fund accumulations in current dollars, 1985–2063. Source: Harry C. Ballantyne, "Long-Range Projections of Social Security Trust Fund Operations in Dollars," Social Security Administration, *Actuarial Notes* (October 1983), no. 117, 2; and *1995 Annual Report of the Board of Trustees of the Federal Old-Age and Survivors Insurance and Disability Insurance Trust Funds*, p. 179.

For some time, policymakers have been aware that the baby boom generation will pose a particular set of challenges for the Social Security program. Traditionally, the Social Security program in the United States had been run largely on a pay-as-you-go basis. The 1983 Social Security Amendments, anticipating the special burden that baby boomers' retirements would place on workers in the future, included provisions for accumulating a substantial trust fund to prefund some benefits promised to the boomers. In other words, the baby boom generation was expected to prefund a larger share of its own benefits than prior generations had prefunded for their own Social Security retirement income. As discussed earlier, the 1983 Amendments also reduced the benefits promised to the baby boom generation by gradually raising the age at which full benefits would be paid to age 67 after the turn of the century.

Shortly after the passage of the 1983 Amendments, the Social Security actuaries estimated that the OASDI trust funds would grow from around $27.5 billion in 1983 to about $20.7 trillion in 2045 (see Figure 1-2). The trust funds were expected to have resources available to pay promised benefits until the youngest of the baby boomers reached 99 years of age. The first projections after the passage of the 1983 Amendments expected OASDI trust funds to be solvent until at least 2063.

In almost every year since 1983, the estimates of the accumulations in the OASDI trust funds have been revised downward. The most recent projection published in April 1995 (see Figure 1-2) suggests that the trust funds will accumulate to only about $3 trillion around 2025 and then decline to zero some time during 2030. At that time the baby boomers will range in age from 66 to 84. Although their numbers will be declining, a good many will still be depending on their Social Security benefits to meet their ongoing needs.

TABLE 1-7   Social Security Income and Cost Rates as Projected Under
Current Law, 1994–2068

Period	Income Rate	Cost Rate	Difference as % of Income Rate
1995–2019	12.68	12.38	2.37
2020–44	13.06	16.95	–29.79
2045–69	13.25	18.22	–37.51

Source: 1995 Annual Report of the Board of Trustees of the Federal Old-Age and Survivors Insurance and Disability Insurance Trust Funds, p. 112.

An alternative way to look at the financing of Social Security is to divide it into periods. Table 1-7 reflects the Social Security actuaries' April 1995 long-term OASDI financing projections broken into three 25-year periods. For the most part, the first 25-year period, from 1995 to 2019, will precede the bulk of the baby boom's claim on the program. The baby boomers will first be eligible for early retirement benefits in 2008, and only about half of them will have attained age 62 by 2019. In addition, if the increases in the actuarial reductions for early retirement benefits and the increases in actuarial adjustments for delayed retirement have any effect, the baby boomers will proceed into retirement at a somewhat slower pace than prior generations. On a purely pay-as-you-go basis, the tax revenues funding OASDI benefits are expected to exceed outgo until some time between 2010 and 2015. Over the 25 years starting in 1995, OASDI's revenues are expected to be about 2 percent above projected outlays.

As the baby boom generation moves fully into retirement, the projected financing situation for Social Security will turn decidedly negative. During the second 25 years reflected in Table 1-7, the period in which the majority of baby boomers expect to get the majority of their lifetime benefits, the projected outlays under OASDI exceed projected revenues by nearly 30 percent. In other words, all evidence available to national policymakers today indicates that Social Security will not be able provide the benefits being promised to the baby boom generation under existing funding legislation. Although it is impossible to anticipate exactly how OASDI projections might change over the next 5 or 10 years, if legislative mandates do not change, the recent 10-year history of continual deterioration in the projected actuarial balances of the program suggests that the future may turn out even worse than policymakers now anticipate.

Federal Staff Retirement Plans

Entirely distinct from the national old-age insurance program, several staff retirement plans have been established under the aegis of the federal government. Designed, with one notable exception, to provide old-age benefits to various categories of federal employees, these plans closely resemble private pension plans. Employees hired before 1984 covered under these plans are not concurrently covered under OASDI, although coordination with OASDI has been achieved in the case of the Railroad Retirement System.

In 1861 the federal government established the first major nondisability program in the United States providing for voluntary retirement of military officers after 40 years of duty. In 1885 nondisability retirement was extended to Marine and Army enlistees, providing voluntary retirement after 30 years of service.[16] This oldest of pension plans in the United States paid benefits to 1.5 million retiree or disabled beneficiaries at the end of 1992. An additional 181,000 individuals were receiving survivors' benefits at that time.[17]

Largest of the federal plans, and, in fact, the largest single employer pension plan in existence, is the Civil Service Retirement System established in 1920, which provides retirement, survivorship, and disability benefits to career employees of the federal government hired before 1984. The new Federal Employees Retirement System covers federal civilian employees hired in 1984 and later, as well as those who were hired earlier and who elect to transfer to the new system. Participation in these systems is compulsory for all eligible employees. At the end of 1991 about 1.6 million persons were drawing retirement and disability benefits from the system, and another 570,000 were receiving survivors' benefits.[18] Federal civilian employees hired after 1983 were included in the OASDI program, as well as about 2.2 million members of the armed forces (who also have a separate noncontributory pension plan, which is primarily of value to career personnel).

In addition to the Civil Service Retirement System and the Federal Employees Retirement System, other retirement plans cover federal civilian employees. Some of the more important plans cover members of the foreign service, employees of the Federal Reserve banks, employees of the Tennessee Valley Authority, and members of the federal judiciary. Most of these plans provide more liberal benefits than those of the Civil Service Retirement System.

On the periphery of federal staff plans is the Railroad Retirement System. This program is unique in the American pension field because it is operated for a group of private employees but is administered by the federal government. It was established by the Railroad Retirement Act of 1937 (and enlarged by the Railroad Unemployment Insurance Act), partly in an attempt to restore financial stability to the various individual railroad plans, which were threatened with insolvency after years of difficulties. Protection is provided against the four major hazards to economic security—old age, disability, death, and unemployment—and benefits are administered by the federal government.

State and Local Retirement Systems

A heterogeneous assortment of public pension plans has been established at the state and local levels. These plans differ widely in their details, but in most jurisdictions separate plans exist for policemen, firefighters, and teachers. All other employees, if covered at all, are lumped together into a general retirement system. Because of the hazardous nature of their work, police and firefighters were the earliest groups of public employees to obtain retirement benefits, and, up to the present, plans for such employees have contained more liberal provisions than

---

[16]Office of the Actuary, Defense Manpower Data Center, *Valuation of the Military Retirement System: Fiscal Year 1992* (Washington, D.C.: OSGPO, 1993), p. B-2.

[17]Ibid., pp., L-8, L-14.

[18]U.S. Bureau of the Census, *Statistical Abstract of the United States 1993*, p. 377.

those for other public employees. As a rule, police and firefighter plans provide for low employee contributions, retirement at an early age after relatively brief service (typically 20 years), liberal survivors' benefits, disability benefits, and retirement benefits based on compensation for the highest grade held. Teacher retirement systems are less liberal than the police and firefighter funds, but even so, they usually accord more generous treatment than the plans maintained for all other employees.

Public Assistance Programs

In addition to retirement programs that are based on periods of employment under them, the federal government sponsors some assistance programs financed entirely from general revenues. The benefits provided under these programs are based on financial need. The best known of these programs is Supplemental Security Income (SSI). SSI applies to those indigent persons aged 65 or over who do not qualify for OASDI benefits, or who do qualify but for one reason or another would not receive adequate benefits, and to needy disabled and blind persons. The federal SSI program is entirely financed and administered by the federal government and is, in essence, a "guaranteed-income" program. Federal SSI benefits are supplemented by additional assistance benefit payments in some states.

   Veterans' compensation for service-connected and nonservice-connected disabilities provided through the Veterans Administration is another federal needs-based program. While these programs are important for those receiving benefits from them, they are not the sort of service-related benefit programs being considered here. Indeed, they act as a safety net for those individuals in need who do not qualify for adequate benefits from work-related retirement programs.

The Private Pension Movement

Rationale

Industrial pensions appeared on the American scene during the last quarter of the nineteenth century, but only within the last 50 or so years have they assumed any significance in the old-age financial picture. In the beginning, private pension benefits were universally regarded as gratuities from a grateful employer in recognition of long and faithful service. The payments were usually discretionary, the employer assuming no legal obligation to provide benefits. In fact, most plans stated in specific terms that no employee rights were being created thereunder and reserved to the employer the right to deny benefits to any employee and to reduce or terminate benefits that had already commenced. A few plans promised to continue benefit payments to retired employees but made no commitment to active employees. These plans exemplified the gratuity theory of pensions.

   As the years went by, certain groups, anxious to encourage and strengthen the pension movement, sought to place on the employer a moral obligation to provide pensions to superannuated employees. As early as 1912, one student of the old-age problem wrote: "From the standpoint of the whole system of social economy, no employer has a right to engage men in any occupation that exhausts the individual's industrial life in 10, 20, or 40 years, and then leave the remnant floating on society at large as a derelict at sea."[19] The subject of widespread debate in the early 1920s, this point of view was frequently expressed during the next few decades. It was adopted by the United Mine Workers and used by that organization in a 1946 campaign to establish a welfare fund. The union's position was expressed by its president, John L. Lewis:

> The United Mine Workers of America has assumed the position over the years that the cost of caring for the human equity in the coal industry is inherently as valid as the cost of replacement of mining machinery, or the cost of paying taxes, or the cost of paying interest indebtedness, or any other factor incident to the production of a ton of coal for consumers' bins. . . . [The agreement establishing the Welfare Fund] recognized in principle the fact that the industry owed an obligation to those employees, and the coal miners could no longer be used up, crippled beyond repair and turned out to live or die subject to the charity of the community or the minimum contributions of the state.[20]

The concept received its most influential endorsement in the report of the fact-finding board in the 1949 steel industry labor dispute. The board wrote, in part:

> As hereinafter amplified, we think that all industry, in the absence of adequate government programs, owes an obligation to workers to provide for maintenance of the human body in the form of medical and similar benefits and full depreciation in the form of old-age retirement—in the same way as it does now for plant and machinery.[21]

And again:

> The steel companies have, with some exceptions, overlooked the fact that the machines and plant on which the industry has prospered, and on which it must depend in the future, are not all made of metal or brick and mortar. They are also made of flesh and blood. And the human machines, like the inanimate machines, have a definite rate of depreciation.[22]

The human depreciation concept has been criticized on various grounds. For example, aging is not so much a result of employment but of physiological processes. If aging is physiological and not employment related, it is not clear that the employer should bear any responsibility for former workers who have become "depreciated" by factors beyond the employer's control. Furthermore, the concept seems to place the obligation of providing retirement benefits entirely on the last employer. Only the terminal employer is accused of casting away the worn-out

---

[19]Lee Welling Squier, *Old Age Dependency in the United States* (New York: Macmillan, 1912), p. 272.
[20]United Mine Workers of America Welfare and Retirement Fund, *Pensions for Coal Miners* (n.d.), p. 4.
[21]Steel Industry Board, *Report to the President of the United States on the Labor Dispute in the Basic Steel Industry*, September 10, 1949, p. 55.
[22]Ibid., p. 64.

human machine, leaving it "floating on society at large as a derelict at sea." The same disapprobation does not attach to an employer who discharges an employee in his or her middle years without providing paid-up pension benefits. Finally, it is agreed that the cost of replacing a human machine is not comparable to that of replacing a physical machine. A human machine can be replaced only with the cost of training a replacement, whereas the purchase price of a new unit must be accumulated to replace a worn-out physical machine.

Conversely, it can be said that the concept does not question the physiological basis of aging, but simply asserts that the cost of maintaining a human machine both during and after an active working life should be a cost of production, analogous, for example, to the economic cost of industrial injuries and disease. The concept is normative; its validity is not negated by the fact that an employer may, as a practical matter, be able to discharge a long-service employee without making any provision for old-age maintenance needs. Depreciation allowances are made for physical equipment even though it is not actually replaced.

In some quarters, the human depreciation concept has been supplanted—or supplemented—by the theory that pensions are essentially deferred wages. The latter concept holds that an employee group has the prerogative of choosing between an immediate wage increase and a pension plan and, having chosen the latter, is entitled to regard the benefits as deferred wages. If the workers choose to receive some share of their wage on a deferred basis, a compensating reduction in current wages will occur. Like the human depreciation concept, this point of view found early expression:

> Theoretically, the simplest way of dealing with labor would be the payment of a money wage, requiring the employee to provide for the hazards of employment and his old age. While here and there an employee does this, by and large the mass of employees do not.
>
> In order to get a full understanding of old-age and service pensions, they should be considered a part of the real wages of a workman. There is a tendency to speak of these pensions as being paid by the company, or, in cases where the employee contributes a portion, as being *paid* partly by the employer and partly by the employee. In a certain sense, of course, this may be correct, but it leads to confusion. A pension system considered as part of the real wages of an employee is really paid by the employee, not perhaps in money, but in the foregoing of an increase in wages which he might obtain except for the establishment of a pension system.[23]

From the standpoint of an individual participant, this concept has validity only if the funds paid into a pension plan in lieu of a personal wage increase are administered to ensure their ultimate payment to the workers or their beneficiaries in one form or the other. This implies either full and immediate vesting of employer contributions on behalf of current participants, a practice rarely encountered among industrial pension plans, or an implicit agreement between the employer and worker that benefits promised will ultimately be paid. From the standpoint of

---

[23]Albert deRhoode, "Pensions as Wages," *American Economic Review* 3 (June 1913): p. 287.

an entire body of employees, such as those represented by a labor union, the concept is valid if, in the aggregate, the employer contributions to a pension plan are precisely equivalent to the cash wages forgone and are held in such fashion as to ensure their use for the exclusive benefit of the employees as a group. With the tendency for the parties to a collective bargaining agreement to express the employer's pension commitment in terms of wage equivalency, such as x cents per hour, and given the safeguards surrounding a formal, IRS-approved pension plan, these conditions would seem to be fulfilled, at least when the benefits are collectively bargained. In the absence of collective bargaining, the relationship between pension contributions and immediate wages forgone is less clear. Nevertheless, the theories of "deferred wages" and "compensating differentials" have become increasingly popular, as discussed at length later in the volume.

The tenuous relationship between wages forgone and pension benefits received in the case of individual participants has caused some to look for another explanation of pensions. Thus, some view old-age retirement benefits as a differential wage payment, similar in nature to a shift differential or other payment in recognition of the unusual or special character of the service. In the case of a pension, the differential payment goes only to those who remain in the service of the employer for a long time (possibly to retirement) and is made in recognition of the special contributions, not reflected in wage payments, that a long-service employee has made to the firm. These contributions include the preservation of the folklore of the industry, the fostering of loyalty to the firm and its traditions, and the transmission of technical skills from older to younger generations of workers. Long service also reduces employers' direct costs for the recruitment and training of workers, thus warranting some differential payment for workers who remain with their employers for long periods.

Still another view of pensions is that they are a device, instituted and nourished by business firms, to meet the social problem of old-age economic dependency. In this view, the part of the business community in a private enterprise society has a duty to provide the mechanism through which gainfully employed individuals, by direct contributions or forgone wages, can provide for their own old-age needs. This obligation can be discharged only through the establishment and operation of plans that measure up to minimum standards of benefit adequacy, benefit security, and financial solvency.[24] According to this view, only if the business community meets this challenge can social insurance schemes be confined to their proper bounds.

Persuasive as some of these theories are, it is doubtful that the private pension movement can be explained in terms of any one social or economic philosophy. Its rationale lies in broad and conflicting forces that do not lend themselves to definitive characterization. One might conclude that the only tenable explanation of the development is "business expediency." Yet this expression is so pervasive that it furnishes only the vaguest of clues to the specific forces that motivate employers to adopt pension plans. It might be helpful, therefore, to examine some of the significant factors and developments that have made it seem expedient to an employer to establish a pension plan.

---

[24]President's Commission on Pension Policy, *Coming of Age: Toward a National Retirement Income Policy* (Washington, D.C.: February 1981), pp. 41–42.

Forces Influencing the Growth of Private Pension Plans

Productivity of the Employee Group

Unquestionably, one of the most compelling employer motives in adopting a pension plan is the desire to attract and retain highly productive employees. This motive is usually mixed with others, including a sincere desire to provide financial security to retired or superannuated employees. Nevertheless, unless the employer believes that the cost of the pension plan can be substantially offset by savings in other areas of the company's operations, including production costs, the employer may not be overly receptive to the idea of pensions.

On balance, there is little doubt that the efficiency of the labor force is enhanced through the establishment of pension plans. American industrial development has reached the stage where most firms of any size now, or soon will, face the problem of dealing with employees whose productivity is perceived to be declining. This problem may be handled in one of three ways. First, the employer can discharge employees without retirement benefits as they become less productive (because of a decline in energy, manual dexterity, and mental agility). With federal OASDI benefits available at subsistence levels, at least, such action would not be as callous as it might otherwise be. Nevertheless, in the present state of social consciousness, most employers shun such an approach, not only for humanitarian reasons but because of the risk of public censure and the constraints imposed by age discrimination laws. Second, the employer can retain superannuated employees on the payroll at full or reduced pay but in a capacity commensurate with their diminished ability and vitality. This policy usually has an adverse effect on employee morale and may prove to be uneconomical in other respects. Third, in the great majority of cases the only approach offering a satisfactory solution is for the employer to establish a formal pension plan. This generally results in the retirement of overage employees from the payroll in an orderly fashion, without adverse employee and public reaction, and enables the employer to replace them with younger, presumably more efficient, workers. The inevitable result is a more productive work force.

Tax Inducements

Related to the foregoing factor, in the sense of a cost-reducing device, are the tax inducements offered by the federal government. The Revenue Act of 1942 is frequently—and erroneously—cited as the genesis of the favorable tax treatment of private pension plans, but the real beginning of such policy is found in much earlier legislation. The provisions of the 1942 act, as subsequently amended, were reenacted in the Internal Revenue Code of 1954 and the Internal Revenue Code of 1986, which, with the refinements and extensions added over the years, still provides the statutory base for the tax treatment of private pension plans.

If a plan meets the requirements of the Code and implementing regulations, it is said to be "qualified."[25] A qualified status carries with it certain economic advantages that result from the tax preferences accorded these plans. The first such

---

[25]IRC §401(a).

advantage is that employer contributions to the plan are tax deductible, within specified limits, as ordinary and necessary business expenses for federal income tax purposes.[26] Second, employer contributions to the plan cannot be included in the taxable income of the participants until actually received by them.[27] Third, investment earnings on the plan assets, including realized capital gains, are not subject to income taxation until disbursed in the form of benefits.[28] Fourth, certain distributions from qualified plans receive favorable income tax treatment. The distributions of a participant's entire individual account balance within one taxable year, upon the participant's death, disability, or separation from service or after age 59.5, is classified as a lump-sum distribution,[29] subject to reduced taxation. Taxation of certain distributions may be deferred by rolling over the proceeds into another qualified plan, an individual retirement account, or an individual retirement annuity.[30] The underlying economic incentives that result from the tax preferences accorded qualified plans are taken up in Chapter 8.

Pressure from Organized Labor

A third broad factor influencing the adoption of pension plans has been the attitude of organized labor. Until the late 1940s or early 1950s, organized labor was, in the main, either indifferent to the pension movement or openly antagonistic to it. Many of the older and well-established craft unions viewed employer-sponsored pensions as a paternalistic device employers could use to wean the allegiance of the workers away from the unions. They also harbored a fear that pensions would be used to hold down wages. Over the years, however, these attitudes changed to such an extent that in 1949, when another round of wage increases seemed difficult to justify, a large segment of organized labor demanded pensions in lieu of wages. The way was paved for such a switch when a federal court ruled that pensions are a bargainable issue.

This case arose out of a union grievance filed with the National Labor Relations Board in 1946, alleging that the unilateral action of the Inland Steel Company in enforcing a policy of compulsory retirement at age 65 constituted a breach of the provision of the general labor contract relating to separation from service. The grievance stemmed from the refusal of the company to negotiate the matter with the union on the grounds that compulsory retirement was an essential part of the company's pension plan and that pension plans did not fall within the scope of collective bargaining. The union did not contend that the provisions of a pension plan were of themselves subject to collective bargaining but argued that the company could not take unilateral action with respect to any provision of a pension agreement that was also a part of the general labor contract and, hence, conceded to be within the scope of mandatory collective bargaining.

In 1948 the National Labor Relations Board ruled in effect that the Labor-Management Relations Act of 1947 imposes a duty on employers to bargain with

---

[26]IRC §404.
[27]Treas. Reg. 1.402(a)-1(a).
[28]IRC §501(a).
[29]IRC §402(e)(4)(A).
[30]IRC §402(a)(5). See Chapter 29 for a fuller description of the tax treatment of qualified pension plans and their benefit distributions.

representatives of their employees on the subject of pensions. This decision was based on the dual premise that the term *wages* as defined in the statute includes any emolument of value, such as pension or insurance benefits, and that the detailed provisions of pension plans come within the purview of "conditions of employment" and therefore constitute an appropriate subject for collective bargaining.[31]

Upon appeal by the company, the Court of Appeals for the Seventh Circuit approved the view of the National Labor Relations Board that the terms of a pension plan are subject to mandatory collective bargaining on the ground that they constitute "conditions of employment," but it expressed some reservation with respect to the wage analogy:

> We are convinced that the language employed by Congress, considered in connection with the purpose of the Act, so clearly includes a retirement and pension plan as to leave little, if any, reason for construction. While, as the Company has demonstrated, a reasonable argument can be made that the benefits flowing from such a plan are not "wages," we think the better and more logical argument is on the other side, and certainly there is, in our opinion, no sound basis for an argument that such a plan is not clearly included in the phrase, "other conditions of employment."[32]

The *Inland Steel* decision established a legal framework within which no employer during the term of an applicable labor agreement can install, alter, or terminate a pension plan for organized workers without the assent of the labor bargaining unit. This obligation rests on the employer, whether or not the plan was installed prior to certification of the bargaining unit and whether or not the plan is compulsory or voluntary, contributory or noncontributory.

Since 1949 organized labor has been a vigorous and potent force in the expansion of the private pension movement. Union demands for pensions have brought old-age economic protection to millions of workers. While there are differences of opinion among the international bodies about the emphasis and reliance that should be placed on private pensions—some would concentrate their energies on liberalization of the federal old-age social insurance program—in general the support of the private pension institution appears to be a "vital trade union aim and function."

Social Pressure

A final factor that has encouraged the spread of pension plans is the social and political atmosphere of the last 60 years. During this period the American people have become security conscious. The economic upheaval of the early 1930s swept away the life savings of millions and engendered a feeling of insecurity that shook the very foundations of the country. Prominent among the proposals for economic reform were those that envisioned social action in the area of old-age

---

[31] *Inland Steel Company v. United Steel Workers of America* (CIO), 77 NLRB 4 (1948).
[32] *Inland Steel Company v. National Labor Relations Board*, 170 F2d 247, 251 (1949). Certiorari denied by the Supreme Court, 336 US 960 (1949).

income maintenance. The federal OASDI program was the outgrowth of these proposals.

Since the federal program was deliberately designed to provide only a "floor of protection," the way was left clear for supplemental benefits to be provided through private measures. In view of the general inability—or unwillingness, as some would have it—of the individual to accumulate through his or her own efforts the additional resources required, society has come to expect the employer to bear a share of the burden. Employers may successfully shift their share of the costs to the consumer, but a great deal of social pressure is exerted on employers to provide the mechanism through which additional funds can be accumulated. If employers choose not to install a formal pension plan, social pressure may force them to take care of their superannuated employees in some other manner. In anticipation of such a development, employers have turned to formal pension programs as the most economical and satisfactory method of addressing the problem.

Approaches to Providing Retirement Benefits

There are two basic approaches to achieving the management, labor, and social objectives that permeate and sustain the private pension movement. One approach is to establish and maintain a pension plan that promises a determinable set of benefits at retirement. Under the typical plan of this type, a unit of benefit—which may be a flat dollar monthly benefit or a specified percentage of compensation—accrues for each year of creditable service. The unit of benefit is set at a level that, with a normal working career and in combination with Social Security and personal savings, will provide the retired individual sufficient income to maintain a comfortable standard of living. The plan sponsor, typically the employer, undertakes to provide the funds, through periodic contributions and investment earnings on the plan assets, that are needed to pay the promised benefits as they become payable. The future cost of the plan is unknown, as it is determined by the rate of mortality, withdrawals from the covered group, pattern of compensation, age of retirement, investment earnings, and other factors. The participants may be required to bear a portion of the cost of the plan through payroll deduction. Quite logically, this type of plan is identified in pension literature as a *defined* benefit plan. It is characterized by definitely *determinable* benefits, by given assumptions as to years of service and level of compensation, and by *indeterminable* future costs.

The other approach is to specify the basis on which contributions will be made to the plan, with no contractual commitment as to the level of benefits that will be provided. Individual accounts are maintained for the participants, the accounts being credited with their allocable share of employer (and employee) contributions and investment earnings. The retirement benefit of a given participant depends upon the balance in the individual's account at the date of retirement. Contributions to the plan, generally expressed as a percentage of compensation, are set at a level designed to produce a satisfactory level of retirement income for a long-service employee. In contrast to the defined benefit approach, the employer's future cost, as a percentage of covered payroll, is known in advance; but the amount of retirement benefit is not determinable in advance, being strongly influenced by investment results. Thus, it may be said that the future cost of the plan is *predictable* but the benefits are *unpredictable*. This approach to retirement planning is known as a *defined contribution plan,* also referred to as an *individual account plan.*

The practical consequences of these two approaches to retirement planning for plan sponsors, plan participants, and society are far-reaching and will be explored in detail throughout the remainder of the book.

Section I
The Regulatory Environment

Chapter 2
Historical Review of Pension Regulation

The Employee Retirement Income Security Act (ERISA), enacted in 1974, was the first legislative act to regulate all aspects of private pensions and savings plans. Before ERISA, there were several attempts to regulate and oversee peripheral aspects of the private pension system, but none was as comprehensive or broad in scope.

Brief Legislative and Regulatory History

The Internal Revenue Code (IRC), the prime statutory source of regulations before ERISA, had only limited regulatory objectives. Congress passed many pieces of legislation throughout the middle of the century, addressing different aspects of private pensions. The Labor-Management Relations Act of 1947 (better known as the Taft-Hartley Act) addressed some peripheral issues related to private pensions: it imposed certain restrictions on collectively bargained multiemployer pension plans, most importantly that they be jointly administered by labor and management trustees.

The Federal Welfare and Pensions Disclosure Act was enacted in 1958 and substantially amended in 1962. This act was intended to provide pension plan participants and their beneficiaries with enough information about their plans to detect any malpractices and to give them a way to seek relief from the wrongdoing. On the whole, however, this act proved largely ineffective and did not approach the scope of ERISA, as will be discussed in greater detail later.

Other pieces of legislation addressed other aspects of private pensions. Plans funded through life insurance companies were partially covered by general insurance regulatory laws, especially those relating to solvency and investments. The assets of plans funded through banks and trust companies were somewhat protected by general trust law, applicable investment statutes, and the supervision of federal and state banking authorities. Theoretically, fiduciary responsibility laws of the various states applied to persons and institutions managing the assets of pension plans, but the reach of the law and the scope of the remedies were considered by most legal experts to be inadequate for pension plans, especially those operating across state boundaries.

Thus before 1974 no single law or body of law was designed to regulate the totality of the private pension institution. This situation was changed by the enactment of ERISA. Some of the major objectives of ERISA were to protect employee benefit rights and to regulate the issues relating to plan qualification, including funding, participation and vesting, reporting and disclosure, and fiduciary responsibility. ERISA also specified which agencies have oversight and jurisdiction and enforcement responsibility over the different areas related to pensions. ERISA established a pension benefits insurance program and an agency, the Pension Benefit Guaranty Corporation, to administer it (ERISA also included other sections that will be discussed later).

After ERISA was enacted in 1974, there was a considerable amount of legislative and regulatory activity dealing with pensions up to the passage of the Tax Reform Act of 1986. The legislative activity included the Multiemployer Pensions Plans Amendment Act of 1980, which primarily focused on the pension system. As tax expenditures for the pension system grew, changes to the pension system began appearing regularly in general tax acts, such as the Tax Equity and Fiscal Responsibility Act of 1982 (TEFRA) and the Deficit Reduction Act of 1984. The Tax Reform Act of 1986 (TRA86), which so significantly revised the Internal Revenue Code of 1954 that it was retitled the Internal Revenue Code of 1986, continued the trend of general tax acts significantly amending the rules affecting pension plans.

While numerous statutes enacted since ERISA have made important changes in the law affecting pension plans, none approach the Tax Reform Act of 1986 in scope. That act significantly revised almost every aspect of the tax code, including most aspects of employee benefits, in enormous detail. Virtually every existing qualified pension, profit sharing, and stock bonus plan needed to be amended because of TRA86.

This chapter describes briefly the nature of pension plan regulation prior to ERISA and the political and legislative process that created ERISA. The development of the Tax Reform Act of 1986 and the development of regulatory guidance from the IRS will be briefly discussed. Finally, some of the causes of the burgeoning complexity of the rules governing pension and profit sharing plans will be explored, as will some of the side effects of the increased plan administration burden.

Nature of Regulation Prior to 1974

This section discusses the Internal Revenue Code and the Federal Welfare and Pension Plans Disclosure Act, the only two statutes that had general applicability to private pension plans prior to ERISA.[1]

Internal Revenue Code

The Internal Revenue Code contained certain provisions specifically directed toward pension plans as early as 1921, but it was not until 1942 that Congress attempted, through the instrumentality of the Code, to lay down general guidelines for the design and operation of private pension plans (along with profit-sharing and stock bonus plans). The primary purposes of the 1942 amendments to

---

[1]For a more comprehensive discussion of federal regulation of private pension plans prior to ERISA, see Edwin W. Patterson, *Legal Protection of Private Expectations* (Homewood, Ill.: Richard D. Irwin, 1960), pp. 85–112.

the Code were (1) to prevent discrimination in favor of shareholders, officers, supervisors, and highly compensated individuals with respect to the coverage, benefits, and financing of private pension plans and (2) to protect the federal revenues against excessive and unjustified tax deductions. Responsibility for enforcement of the Code provisions was placed on the Internal Revenue Service.

Over the next 12 years, the IRS promulgated a voluminous body of regulations and rulings designed to implement the dual objectives of the 1942 amendments. These had a material impact on plan design and some impact on plan financing.

At no time prior to 1974 did the Code impose any obligation on the IRS to be concerned about the actuarial soundness of private pension plans—or their ability to meet their benefit obligations.[2] Nor did the Code provide much protection for the pension rights of individual participants. Except as required to prevent discrimination in favor of people such as officers, there were no requirements relating to the preservation of the accrued benefits of participants terminating employment prior to early or normal retirement, the reporting of information to the participants on the status of their benefit accruals, or the enforcement of individual benefit rights. With a few exceptions, such as the prohibition against certain transactions among parties at interest, and the general mandate that the plan be operated for the exclusive benefit of the participants and their beneficiaries, the Code articulated no standards of fiduciary conduct for those responsible for the administration of the plan and for the management of its assets. There was little or no protection of plan assets against incompetent or dishonest administrators, apart from the remedies in general trust law and the criminal code.

Federal Welfare and Pension Plans Disclosure Act

In 1958 Congress sought to provide somewhat greater protection for the rights of individual participants and protection against mismanagement of plan assets through the enactment of the Federal Welfare and Pension Plans Disclosure Act. As its name suggests, the act was designed to provide plan participants and their beneficiaries with enough information about the nature and operations of their plan to detect any malpractice or wrongdoing and to seek relief for themselves and the plan under existing state and federal laws.

---

[2]The IRS did, however, issue rulings concerning plan funding. One ruling held that, if contributions to a pension plan were suspended, the plan could lose its qualified status if the unfunded liability at that time (or at any time thereafter) exceeded the initial unfunded liability or if the benefits to be paid or made available were adversely affected. To prevent the unfunded accrued liability from exceeding the initial unfunded liability, contributions to the plan had to be at least equal to the normal cost of the plan, plus interest on the initial unfunded liability, plus actuarial losses or less actuarial gains. This rule was widely (but erroneously) interpreted as requiring that plans maintain this level of funding throughout their existence. The IRS did nothing to disabuse plan administrators of this notion, and as a result, the ruling undoubtedly brought about a minimum level of funding.

The IRS also issued a ruling establishing a minimum level of funding for a plan established under a collective bargaining agreement (that expired within a stated period) in order for the plan to meet the requirement that it be intended as a permanent arrangement. However, the IRS had no authority to require a level of funding that would ensure the payment of all accrued benefits in the event of plan termination; because of its emphasis on the prevention of *over*funding, it may well be that, on balance, the IRS had an adverse effect on the financial soundness of pension plans.

To carry out the act, the administrator of any plan covering more than 25 employees was required to file certain information, documents, and reports with the Secretary of Labor. The plan administrator was also required to make available to plan participants and their beneficiaries, upon request, a copy of the plan and the annual reports. The basic purpose of the act was to protect plan assets against fraudulent or criminal behavior of the plan administrator other parties at interest. This purpose was to be accomplished through action against the malfeasors brought by the plan participants under existing state and federal laws, based upon evidence revealed through the annual reports. While the act set forth the type of information to be included in the annual reports, the Secretary of Labor was not authorized to prescribe the forms on which the information was to be submitted nor given any authority or responsibility to enforce the act.

The act was amended in 1962 to give the Secretary of Labor authority to prescribe forms, interpret the provisions of the act, enforce compliance, and conduct investigations where there was reasonable cause to believe that such investigations would disclose violations of the act. Embezzlement, false reporting, bribery, and kickbacks in connection with welfare and pension plans were made criminal offenses, and the Justice Department was given the responsibility, in cooperation with the Labor Department, of bringing appropriate legal action. Thus the burden of protecting the plan assets against maladministration or outright fraud was shifted from plan participants to government agencies. However, the thrust of the law continued to be to protect plan assets rather than to preserve the rights of individual participants to those assets.

Employee Retirement Income Security Act

Gestation of ERISA

ERISA underwent a long period of gestation, including a major study on pension reform by the President's Committee on Corporate Pension Funds created by President John F. Kennedy in March 1962. The Committee ultimately submitted its report to President Lyndon Johnson in early 1964.[3]

President Johnson held the report for almost a year, reputedly because of concern over its recommendations, before releasing it to the public in January 1965. The report concluded that there is a strong *public* interest in *private* pension plans because (1) they represent a major element in the economic security of millions of American workers and their families; (2) they are a significant, growing source of economic and financial power; (3) they affect the mobility of the American labor force; and (4) they are subsidized by the general body of taxpayers by virtue of the special tax treatment accorded them.[4] The report made a number of

---

[3]*Public Policy and Private Pension Programs*, Report to the President on Private Employee Retirement Plans by the President's Committee on Corporate Pension Funds and Other Private Retirement and Welfare Programs (Washington, D.C.: USGPO, 1964).

[4]Many tax experts have taken issue with the Committee's conclusion that the private pension movement is subsidized by special tax concessions. They argue that private pension plans are taxed in accordance with the general principles of tax law. One of the most persuasive treatises on this theme is Raymond Goetz, *Tax Treatment of Pension Plans: Preferential or Normal* (Washington, D.C.: American Enterprise Institute for Public Policy Research, 1969).

recommendations designed to protect the public interest; the principal recommendations proposed a mandatory minimum vesting standard, a mandatory minimum funding standard, a program of pension plan benefits insurance (called pension reinsurance in the report), and a mechanism for pension portability.

Following the release of the Report of the President's Committee on Corporate Pension Funds, an Interagency Task Force was appointed to consider public reaction to the report and to develop legislation to implement the recommendations of the report, which was introduced into both houses of Congress in 1968 but did not get beyond hearings.

Ultimately, the Labor and Tax Committees of both House and Senate developed legislative proposals, reporting their bills out in 1972. Over the next several months, the Senate Finance Committee and the House Ways and Means Committee began to assert jurisdiction over the legislation in their respective chambers, since the Labor Committee bills and a host of others with similar features were largely directed at plans that achieved their legitimacy by compliance with the Internal Revenue Code. Moreover, the administration bill contained some proposals for change in the tax treatment of pension plans. This jurisdictional dispute delayed consideration of pension legislation on the floor of the two houses for more than a year.

During the final stages of the legislative process, the bills of the four committees were largely similar in substance, though differing in detail. The principal difference—and one that was highly charged with emotion—was the choice of a federal agency to administer the new body of law. The two Labor Committee bills called for administration of the law by the Labor Department; the Tax Committee bills gave the Treasury Department exclusive jurisdiction over all provisions affecting the tax qualification of pension plans. The matter was resolved by splitting the agency jurisdiction. ERISA was signed into law by President Gerald Ford on Labor Day, September 2, 1974, almost 10 years after the Report of the President's Committee on Corporate Pension Funds was released and more than 7 years after the introduction of the first pension reform bill.

Structure and Summary of ERISA

The Employee Retirement Income Security Act of 1974 is a massive and exceedingly complex piece of legislation. It is massive because of the scope of the matters covered and the specificity with which the drafters articulated congressional intent in enacting the law. It is complex, partly because of the technical nature of the subject matter and partly because of the numerous compromises that had to be built into it to satisfy the four legislative committees that worked on the legislation as well as their staffs.

The major compromise—one that added length and complexity to the document—gave jurisdiction over private pension plans to both the Labor and Treasury Departments. In some areas the jurisdiction is exclusive; in others it is joint and overlapping. Because of the overlapping jurisdiction, the act legislates with respect to certain important matters in three sections ("Titles") of the statute, not always in the same manner.[5]

---

[5]Title III of the act directed the Secretaries of Labor and the Treasury to establish a Joint Board for the Enrollment of Actuaries to set the standards and qualifications for persons performing actuarial

One major section of the act (Title I) is concerned with the protection of employee benefit rights. This section deals principally with (1) reporting and disclosure, (2) participation and vesting, (3) funding, and (4) fiduciary responsibility. The provisions dealing with reporting, disclosure, and fiduciary responsibility replace and strengthen those heretofore contained in the Federal Welfare and Pension Plans Disclosure Act, which was formally repealed. The Department of Labor has primary jurisdiction over reporting, disclosure, and fiduciary matters, while the Treasury Department has primary jurisdiction over participation, vesting, and funding. However, the Department of Labor is entitled to intervene in any matters or proceedings that materially affect the rights of the participants, even when the matters come under the formal jurisdiction of the Treasury Department. The Department of Labor also can, under prescribed circumstances, enforce the participation, vesting, funding, reporting, and disclosure requirements through civil procedures and criminal proceedings. For qualified plans, the Treasury Department enforces compliance with the participation, vesting, and funding requirements through tax disqualification and excise taxes. The provisions of Title I apply to all pension plans, whether qualified or not, established or maintained by employers engaged in interstate commerce or by employee organizations representing employees engaged in interstate commerce, except governmental plans, church plans, unfunded excess benefit plans (as defined in the law), and plans maintained outside the United States primarily for the benefit of persons who are, for the most part, nonresident aliens.[6] These provisions supersede and preempt all state laws applicable to the covered employee benefit plans except the state laws that regulate insurance, banking, or securities.[7] However, the law explicitly provides that a pension plan is not to be construed as engaging in the insurance or banking business for purposes of this exception.

Title IV of the act establishes a program of pension plan benefits insurance whose purpose is to ensure ultimate fulfillment of the vested rights of participants under defined benefit plans. The program is administered through the nonprofit Pension Benefit Guaranty Corporation (PBGC) located in the Department of Labor, with the Secretary of Labor as chairman of the board.[8] The other board members are the Secretary of the Treasury and the Secretary of Commerce. An advisory committee of seven persons representing management, labor, and the public is appointed by the President. Title IV applies to all qualified defined benefit pension plans, with specified exceptions.

Another major section of the act (Title II) is primarily concerned with tax matters and, in form, is an amendment to the Internal Revenue Code of 1954. Thus it pertains primarily to qualified plans. It contains *essentially* the same require-

---

services for pension plans under the act. The actuarial reports required under the law must be signed by persons, called "enrolled" actuaries, who have met these standards. The actuary must certify annually that the actuarial assumptions and methods used to determine the costs and funding requirements of the plan are, in the aggregate, reasonable and reflect the actuary's best estimate of anticipated experience under the plan.

[6]ERISA §4.
[7]ERISA §514.
[8]ERISA §4002.

TABLE 2-1   Provisions of ERISA and Governing Agency

Title	Governing Agency	Primary Purpose
Title I	Department of Labor	Protect employee benefit rights
Title II	Internal Revenue Service	Address tax matters, primarily those affecting qualified plans
Title III	Internal Revenue Service	Provide standards and qualifications for actuaries
Title IV	Pension Benefit Guaranty Corporation	Provide pension plan benefits insurance

ments with respect to participation, vesting, and funding that are found in Title I, but in the context of conditions that must be satisfied for qualification of a plan. As amended by ERISA, the Code provides for minimum standards of funding for pension plans enforceable through an excise tax. Thus, for the first time, responsibility was placed on the IRS for enforcing the actuarial soundness of plans falling under its jurisdiction.

The IRS is responsible for developing regulations for the participation, vesting, and funding provisions of ERISA, except for certain matters specifically delegated to the Secretary of Labor under the act, but in doing so it must consult and coordinate activities with the Secretary of Labor. By the same token, the Secretary of Labor must consult with the Secretary of the Treasury when developing regulations for matters coming under its jurisdiction.

The term *pension plan* has entirely different meanings in Title I and Title II. In Title II and in the Internal Revenue Code, pension plan refers to one of three types of qualified asset accumulation plans, namely, pension plans, profit-sharing plans, and stock bonus plans. In Title I, however, pension plan includes all three types of qualified plans plus unqualified plans that provide retirement income or result in the deferral of income.[9]

Title II also contains tax provisions not directly related to participation, vesting, or funding. Two of these were designed to expand the coverage of private pension arrangements. The first liberalized the plans for self-employed individuals (generally referred to as Keogh or HR 10 plans). The second permitted individuals not covered by a qualified or governmental plan or a tax-deferred annuity to establish their own individual retirement savings plans and to deferr the tax on the contributions and investment earnings. This type of plan can be funded through an individual retirement account administered by a trustee or custodian or through an individual retirement annuity. Other provisions changed the tax treatment of lump-sum distributions and imposed certain limits on tax-deferred annuities issued under Section 403(b) of the Code. All of these provisions are under the jurisdiction of the Treasury Department (with delegation to the IRS) (see Table 2-1).

Tax Reform Act of 1986

Statutory Impact

The amount of legislative activity on employee benefits is staggering. Prior to the Tax Reform Act of 1986, the legislative acts affecting employee benefits included

[9]ERISA §3(2); IRC §401(a).

TABLE 2-2   Post-ERISA Employee Benefits Legislation

Year	Legislation
1975	Tax Reduction Act of 1975
1976	Tax Reform Act of 1976
1977	Social Security Amendments of 1977
1978	Revenue Act of 1978
1978	Amendments to Age Discrimination in Employment Act
1980	Multiemployer Pension Plans Amendment Act of 1980 (MEPPAA)
	Miscellaneous Revenue Act of 1980
1981	Economic Recovery Act of 1981 (ERTA)
1982	Tax Equity and Fiscal Responsibility Act of 1982 (TEFRA)
1983	Social Security Amendments Act of 1983
1984	Tax Reform Act of 1984, including the Deficit Reduction Act of 1984 (DEFRA)
	Retirement Equity Act of 1984 (REA or REACT)
1986	Tax Reform Act of 1986 (TRA)
	Single-Employer Pension Plan Amendments Act of 1986 (SEPPAA), including the Consolidated Omnibus Budget Reconciliation Act of 1985 (COBRA)
	1986 Amendments to the Age Discrimination in Employment Act
	Omnibus Budget Reconciliation Act of 1986 (OBRA86)
1987	Omnibus Budget Reconciliation Act of 1987 (OBRA87)
1988	Technical and Miscellaneous Revenue Act of 1988 (TAMRA)
1989	Omnibus Budget Reconciliation Act of 1989 (OBRA89)
1990	Omnibus Budget Reconciliation Act of 1990 (OBRA90)
	Older Workers Benefit Protection Act of 1990 (OWBPA)
1992	Unemployment Compensation Amendments of 1992 (UCA)
1993	Omnibus Budget Reconciliation Act of 1993 (OBRA93)
	Family and Medical Leave Act of 1993 (FMLA)
1994	Uruguay Round of the General Agreement on Tariffs and Trade
	Uniformed Services Employment and Reemployment Rights Act (USERRA)

the Revenue Act of 1978, the Multiemployer Pension Plans Amendment Act of 1980 (MEPPAA), the Economic Recovery Tax Act of 1981 (ERTA), the Tax Equity and Fiscal Responsibility Act of 1982 (TEFRA), the 1983 Social Security Amendments, the Deficit Reduction Act of 1984 (DEFRA), the Retirement Equity Act of 1984 (REA), and the Single-Employer Pension Plan Amendments Act of 1986 (SEPPAA). After the Tax Reform Act of 1986, additional legislative changes were made through the Omnibus Budget Reconciliation Act of 1987 (OBRA87), The Technical and Miscellaneous Revenue Act of 1988 (TAMRA), the Omnibus Budget Reconciliation Act of 1989 (OBRA89), the Omnibus Budget Reconciliation Act of 1990 (OBRA90), the Unemployment Compensation Amendments of 1992 (UCA), and the Omnibus Budget Reconciliation Act of 1993 (OBRA93). A more complete listing of the legislative acts affecting employee benefits since ERISA is set out in Table 2-2.

The changes brought by these statutory acts generally were intended to increase equity and benefit security for participants, eliminate tax abuse, and increase tax revenues. As a by-product they have substantially increased the complexity of the requirements and the administrative burden and cost of complying with them, contributing to the termination of small plans and the decline in plan formation by smaller employers.

One objective of the legislative changes affecting pension plans was to raise taxes to offset the revenue loss resulting from lower tax rates and other aspects of tax reform. Changes that increase revenues included both increased taxes on distributions and reductions in the maximum limits on contributions and benefits under plans. Other changes were designed to ensure that benefits would be broadly available by strengthening the requirements concerning coverage, vesting, and integration of pensions with Social Security. Still other changes were designed to stop actual or perceived abuse.

Regulatory Changes

The IRS, as delegated by the Treasury Department, has primary responsibility for enforcing most of the statutory changes mentioned above, including sole authority for enforcing the nondiscrimination requirements for qualified plans. Though the Tax Reform Act of 1986 only slightly changed the statutory language of the basic nondiscrimination requirement, prohibiting discrimination in favor of "highly compensated employees" instead of "officers, shareholders, or [the] highly compensated,"[10] government regulators began to completely restate the regulatory interpretations of the nondiscrimination rule.

In 1991 the Department of the Treasury published regulations[11] substantially changing the long-standing requirements for demonstrating that a qualified plan does not discriminate in favor of highly compensated employees. The package of regulations represent comprehensive guidance providing an integrated framework for demonstrating that a qualified plan does not discriminate in favor of highly compensated employees in the delivery of benefits. Chapter 3 contains an overview of the nondiscrimination requirements for qualified plans, and following chapters examine these rules in more detail.

Burgeoning Complexity

ERISA is a "comprehensive and reticulated" statute,[12] but that fact has not slowed the legislative activity governing employee benefits. At least 22 legislative acts since ERISA affect pension plans, significantly expanding the areas in which rules are promulgated and the scope of the existing rules. Coupled with the growth of regulatory guidance, the resulting increase in the complexity of the rules affecting employee benefit plans is immeasurable. The impact of such complexity on the pension system is similarly immeasurable, but observable.

Impact on Defined Benefit Plans

The growing complexity has significantly increased the cost associated with administering a plan. For defined benefit plans administrative expenses have grown to the point that the administrative costs of a defined benefit plan with 15 participants

---

[10]Tax Reform Act of 1986, Pub. Law 99-514, § 1114(b)(7).
[11]Treas. Reg. 1.401(a)(4).
[12]*Nachman Corp. v. PBGC*, 446 U.S. 359 (1980).

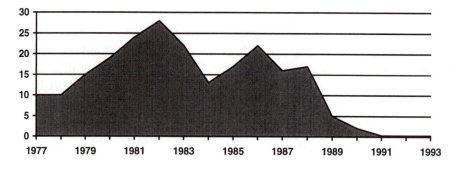

Figure 2-1. Initial applications for determination letters for defined benefit plans, 1977–93 (in thousands). Source: Various IRS news releases, 1976–92.

grew to 33 percent of the cost of participants' annual accruals between 1981 and 1991.[13]

While the possible explanations for the decline in defined benefit plans and the shift toward defined contribution plans are numerous, at least part of the reason is the increasing expense of administering defined benefit plans. As illustrated in Figure 2-1, IRS statistics on the issuance of determination letters for new defined benefit plans indicate that initiation of defined benefit plans has effectively stopped since the late 1980s.[14] Applications for new defined contribution plans have also declined, as noted in Figure 2-2, but not as dramatically.

In addition to requesting determination letters for plan commencements, plan sponsors also request determination letters for plan terminations. Again, requests for determination letters for terminating plans for defined benefit plans have increased since the middle part of the 1980s. Requests for determination letters for terminating defined contribution plans have also increased, especially as some of the new requirements enacted by the Tax Reform Act of 1986 were implemented. A comparison of Figures 2-1 through 2-4, however, clearly indicates that more defined contribution plans are being initiated than terminated, while more defined benefit plans are being terminated than initiated.

While the expense of administering a defined benefit plan grew significantly, defined contribution plans did not escape such additional expenses. For defined benefit plans with 15 or fewer participants, or for defined benefit plans with 10,000 or more participants, the administrative expenses grew at almost 11 percent a year between 1981 and 1991. Administrative expenses for defined contribution plans with similar participant levels grew at a slower rate, but still between 6.3 and 7.1 percent.[15]

As noted above, the increasing administrative cost associated with defined benefit plans is one reason for the declining number of such plans being initiated

---

[13]PBGC, *Pension Plan Cost Study* (September 1990).

[14]IRS determination letters generally provide employers reliance on the plan's qualified status; see Chapter 3 for a complete discussion. Since employers are not required to obtain IRS determination letters, but many do, the rate of determination letter requests may be used as an imperfect, but useful, measure of plan starts and terminations.

[15]PBGC, *Pension Plan Cost Study* (September 1990).

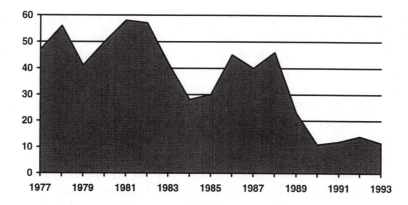

Figure 2-2. Initial applications for determination letters for defined contribution plans, 1977–93 (in thousands). Source: Various IRS news releases, 1977–92.

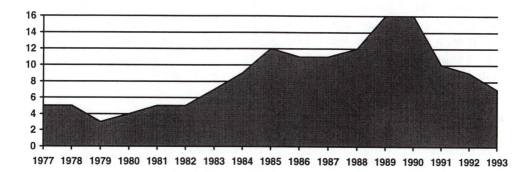

Figure 2-3. Determination letter requests for defined benefit plan terminations, 1977–93 (in thousands). Source: Various IRS news releases, 1976–92.

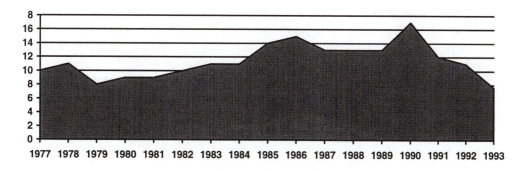

Figure 2-4. Determination letter requests for defined contribution plan terminations (in thousands). Source: Various IRS news releases, 1976–92.

by employers, but other reasons exist for the shift from defined benefit plans to defined contribution plans, and for the cyclical nature of determination letter requests. Other reasons include the volatility of legislative changes and general economic conditions. Because the U.S. economy fared poorly during the first part of the 1990s, many employers were reluctant to assume the financial commitment that a defined benefit plan represents in terms of both administrative costs and benefit commitments.

In addition, the cyclical nature of plan commencements, or at least the cyclical nature of determination letter requests for plan commencements, can be partly explained by changes in the qualification requirements for both defined benefit and defined contribution plans. The drop in initial determination letter requests for both types of plans starting around 1982 and 1988 should be considered in context of the Tax Equity and Fiscal Responsibility Act of 1982 and the Tax Reform Act of 1986. When the various changes to the qualification requirements enacted by those acts became effective, the IRS generally had not completed the process of issuing guidance on the new requirements. The IRS did not open the determination letter program to requests until that guidance was issued. Accordingly, determination letter requests for the period immediately after the effective date of major legislative changes generally drop until the IRS begins receiving such requests on a regular basis again. Finally, the sheer complexity of defined benefit plan administration, separate and apart from the expense of administering such a plan, has hindered the growth of the private pension system.

Impact on Private Pension System

Complexity in the tax code and the resulting impact on tax administration have been a concern for some time. A 1972 report from a New York State Bar Association committee concluded that complexity in the tax code could lead to enforcement difficulties and a reduction in the level of voluntary compliance, possibly threatening the self-assessment nature, or "honor system" of the tax system itself. In addition, because the federal tax system affects every citizen, a reduction in public belief in the fairness and integrity of the system would adversely affect the attitude of the public toward our entire system of government.[16]

But the solution to growing complexity remains elusive. The New York State Bar committee recommended greater elaboration and clarification of ambiguous terms in order to eliminate complexity. Another commentator argues that ambiguity is inevitable, and that the vagueness of simple rules providing guiding principles is preferable to the greater ambiguity of more elaborate rules.[17]

The tax regulators seem to have come around to the latter perception. While the final regulations under §401(a)(4)[18] comprised 62 *Federal Register* pages, the proposed amendments,[19] which completely restated the §401(a)(4) regulations, only

---

[16]Roberts, Friedman, Ginsburg, Louthan, Lubick, Young, and Zeitlin, "A Report on Complexity and the Income Tax," 27 *Tax Law Review*, 325 (1972).
[17]Manning, "Hyperlexis: Our National Disease," 71 *Nw. U.L. Rev.* 767 (1977).
[18]56 Fed. Reg. 47524, Sept. 19, 1991.
[19]58 Fed. Reg. 3876, Jan. 12, 1993.

required 44 pages in the *Federal Register*, a 30 percent reduction. The minimum participation regulations, discussed in Chapter 4, were 19 pages in the *Federal Register* when originally proposed.[20] When finalizing these rules, IRS regulators assumed a completely different compliance strategy, and reduced the regulations to 7 *Federal Register* pages.[21]

Current regulatory efforts appear aimed at providing general objective standards, in order to assure plan sponsors of their plan's qualified status. But, many of the separate elements of the objective standards are left undefined or otherwise subject to a reasonable, good faith standard based on the facts and circumstances of a given situation. This leaves plan sponsors with some uncertainty regarding the plan's qualified status, but greater flexibility in proving the nondiscriminatory nature of the plan.

Whether the pension qualification rules can be simplified sufficiently to revive employer interest in sponsoring plans without jeopardizing the protection for participants or the public fisc remains to be seen.

---

[20]54 Fed. Reg. 6710, Feb. 13, 1989.
[21]56 Fed. Reg. 63410, Dec. 4, 1991.

Chapter 3
Basic Regulatory Environment

Pension plan regulations deal with all issues related to plan design, commencement, administration, benefit dispersal, and plan termination. The most important, indeed fundamental, issue, of course, is plan qualification.

The basic requirements for qualification are found in the Internal Revenue Code of 1986, as amended and elucidated by a series of regulations and rulings. Meeting these requirements is crucial to the employer, since otherwise its contributions could not be deducted from income taxes (unless they are vested in the accounts of individual participants), and the investment earnings on the plan assets would not be exempt from current taxation. The participants also have a strong stake in the tax status of the plan since they would be currently taxed on contributions to the trust for their vested benefits and they would lose favorable treatment on the taxation of distributions if the plan is not qualified. By and large, these requirements are designed to ensure that the plan is operated for the exclusive benefit of a broad classification of employees, and not for any privileged smaller group of executives or for the employer alone.

Securing the Approval of the Internal Revenue Service

While plan sponsors are not required to obtain the approval of the IRS concerning the qualified status of the plan, qualification is of such vital importance that the vast majority of plan sponsors seek approval in the form of a determination letter. A determination letter from the IRS provides the plan sponsor with "reliance" that the IRS will not retroactively challenge the qualification of the plan, even if a disqualifying defect is discovered.[1]

The request for approval may be submitted directly by the employer or an officer representing the employer, or through an attorney, certified public accountant, or pension consultant acting under a power of attorney. For a plan established by joint agreement between a union and one or more employers that will be administered by a joint board, the filing is made by an attorney acting for the board. The form[2] requesting approval must be accompanied by various attachments and by a user fee.

---

[1] Rev. Proc. 93-39, 1993-2 CB 513.

[2] Form 5300 is for a defined benefit plan or a defined contribution plan, Form 5303 for a collectively bargained plan, Form 5307 for an employer who adopts a master or prototype plan, and Form 5309 for an employer stock ownership plan.

Before submitting the request for approval to the IRS, the plan sponsor must provide a "notice to interested parties" prepared in accordance with detailed rules[3] to inform participants and others that the application is being made and to explain their right to intervene in the process. In practice employees almost never intervene in the process, and there is no known instance where such intervention affected the outcome of the request for approval.

The IRS operates several types of letter ruling programs, reflecting the different types of plans that can be adopted by plan sponsors. For plan sponsors who adopt individually designed plans (plans that are customized for that particular company or set of employees), the determination letter ruling program provides an individual review by the IRS of the plan's form and operation. The opinion letter program is available for master and prototype plans that sponsoring organizations (usually a bank, mutual fund, insurance company, or other financial institution) offer employers for adoption. Master and prototype plans are generally plans of simple design intended for smaller employers. Plans using a single funding medium (i.e., a single trust for all employers adopting the plan) are commonly referred to as master plans. Plans using separate funding vehicles (i.e., separate trusts for each employer adopting the plan) generally known as prototype plans. Other types of letter ruling programs (e.g., mass submitter, volume submitter, regional prototype) are generally intended to permit practitioners who draft plan documents for multiple clients to obtain IRS approval of their standard plan language. Because of their distinct nature, individually designed plans take the most time to draft or obtain IRS approval.

If the key district office[4] of the IRS finds the plan acceptable in all respects, it will issue a favorable determination letter. In the event that revenue officials find the plan or related documents unsatisfactory in some respect, they generally give the employer and his or her advisers an opportunity to discuss in conference the objectionable or questionable features. If the employer can overcome the objections of the revenue authorities or, failing that, agrees to any necessary modifications, a favorable ruling will then be issued.

It should be noted that a determination letter does not end the IRS interest in the plan. Moreover, it does not relieve the employer of the responsibility of clearing with the IRS any future changes or modifications in the plan that might affect its qualified status. Nor does it assure the employer that the IRS will not challenge the qualified status of the plan because of problems in its operation, for example, if it discriminates in practice.

General Requirements for Plan Qualification

Written Plan Document Required

The basic requirement for every plan, qualified or nonqualified, is that its terms be set forth in a written document.[5] This requirement's fundamental purpose is to

---

[3]IRC §7476(b)(2), Treas. Reg. 601.201(o)(3)(xiv)–(xvi).
[4]Not all IRS district offices contain revenue agents trained in employee plans or have responsibility regarding employee benefit plans. Those that do are commonly known as key district offices.
[5]ERISA §402(a)(1); Treas. Reg. 1.401-1(a)(2).

ensure that the plan is a formal arrangement, communicated as such to all employees affected, and that it is distinguishable from the informal and unenforceable arrangements that characterized the early years of the private pension movement in this country. On a more operational level, the plan needs to be in writing so participants may examine the document and determine their rights and obligations thereunder. As a part of the disclosure requirements for all plans under the Employment Retirement Income Security Act, the plan administrator must make available to employees copies of the plan, related documents, and a summary of the essential features and provisions.[6]

A qualified plan must comply with the Code's qualification requirement both in operation and in form. That is, the plan document must contain certain appropriate language. Without the appropriate plan language, the plan will be disqualified, even if it plan meets all the qualification requirements in operation.[7]

Permanency

Although not specified in any statute, IRS regulations require that the plan be established with the intent that it be a permanent and continuing arrangement.[8] A plan that is abandoned without a valid business reason a few years after it is set up will be deemed not to have been a bona fide program for the exclusive benefit of employees in general from its inception. In that event, employer income tax deductions for contributions to the plan will be disallowed for all open tax years.[9] To prevent discrimination in the event of early termination, all plans must include a limit on the benefits of the 25 most highly paid employees should the plan be terminated within the first 10 years.[10]

Segregation of Plan Assets

The assets of both qualified and nonqualified plans must be legally separated from those of the employer or other sponsoring organization. This is to comply with ERISA's fiduciary requirements, as well as with the Internal Revenue Code's mandate that the plan be operated for the exclusive benefit of participants and their beneficiaries.

This segregation of plan assets can be accomplished by having them held in trust under a suitably drawn trust instrument[11] or held by a life insurance company under one or more of the various contracts available for this purpose.[12] If a trust is used, the trustee may be an individual (or more likely, a group of individuals) or

---

[6]ERISA §101(a).

[7]*Buzzetta Construction Corp. v. Commissioner*, 92 TC 641; *Basch Engineering v. Commissioner*, 59 TCM 482.

[8]Treas. Reg. 1.401-1(b)(2). Courts have rejected this IRS view that a permanence requirement exists. *Lincoln Electric Co. Employees' Profit-Sharing Trust* (CA-6, 1951 rev'g and rem'g TC) 51-2 USTC §9371, 190 F 2d 326.

[9]Tax years are considered open if the statute of limitations, generally three years from the date the tax return of a year is filed, has not expired.

[10]Treas. Reg. 1.401-4(c) and 1.401(a)(4)-5(b).

[11]ERISA §403(a); IRC §401(a), (f).

[12]ERISA §403(b); IRC §§403(a), 404(a)(2), 401(g).

an institution with trust powers. A trust may be used for convenience or control even when the organization that holds and manages the assets is a life insurance company. In that event, the insurance or annuity contracts serving as the funding receptacles are treated as trust assets. While not required, a trust or custodial account serves a useful purpose if the plan is funded through individual life insurance or annuity contracts.

Coverage

The plan must benefit a nondiscriminatory group of employees, not just a limited number of highly compensated employees, and it must cover a minimum number of participants.[13] These coverage requirements, a fundamental element of plan design, are discussed in detail in Chapter 4.

Nondiscrimination in Contributions or Benefits

A qualified pension plan must not discriminate in favor of highly compensated employees either in its coverage or in its contributions and benefits.[14] This sounds like a simple concept that should be easy to enforce, but in practice discrimination in favor of the proscribed group in a particular arrangement may be difficult and complex to determine. In general, if the benefit structure is deemed equitable, it does not matter if the dollar contributions for the various participants are not equal. By the same token, if the contribution formula is equitable, it is immaterial if the benefits vary among participants.

Variations in contributions or benefits are permissible as long as the plan, viewed as a whole and with all its attendant circumstances, does not favor employees who are highly compensated. The IRS recently finalized detailed and lengthy procedures for of clarifying, revising, and stating the nondiscrimination standards for qualified plans. These rules are discussed in Chapter 5. It is especially significant that contributions or benefits based on remuneration excluded from the Old-Age Survivors, and Disability Insurance taxable wage base may differ from contributions or benefits related to that base, as long as the resulting differences in contributions or benefits do not exceed specified limits.[15] These rules, which integrate qualified plan benefits and Social Security benefits for nondiscrimination testing purposes, are described in Chapter 4.

Participation and Vesting Requirements

As noted above, the Internal Revenue Code and implementing regulations have long contained provisions related to participation (stated in terms of coverage) and the crediting of benefits. These provisions have had the limited and specific purpose of preventing discrimination in favor of certain classes of individuals.[16]

[13] IRC §§410(b), 401(a)(26).
[14] IRC §401(a)(4).
[15] IRC §401(a)(5), (l).
[16] ERISA §§202, 203, 204; IRC §§410(a), 411.

ERISA's participation and vesting requirements (see chapters 4 and 6) are not primarily directed at discrimination and, through Title I (the labor portion of the act), even apply to plans that do not seek tax qualification. They are intended to foster the accrual and preservation of benefits for all classes of actual and potential plan participants.

Definitely Determinable Benefits

Under the Internal Revenue Code, a pension plan must provide definitely determinable benefits.[17] This technical requirement is designed to distinguish a pension plan from a profit-sharing plan, which is subject to many of the same qualification requirements as a pension plan but is required to have a definite formula only for allocating contributions.[18] A plan that provides retirement benefits to employees and their beneficiaries will be deemed a pension plan if either the benefits payable to the employees or the contributions required of the employer can be definitely determined.[19]

Benefits under a defined benefit plan are not definitely determinable if funds may be used to provide increased benefits for the remaining participants, instead of being used as soon as possible to reduce the amount of contributions by the employer. In a defined contribution plan, forfeitures from terminations *may* be allocated among the remaining participants. Benefits that vary with the increase or decrease in the market value of the assets from which such benefits are payable, or that vary with the fluctuation of a specified and generally recognized cost-of-living index, are consistent with the requirement that a pension plan provide definitely determinable benefits.[20]

Communication and Enforcement of Benefit Rights

Communication of Benefit Rights to Plan Participants and Their Beneficiaries

The Internal Revenue Service has long required that a qualified plan be written and communicated appropriately to plan participants and their beneficiaries.[21] The labor portion of ERISA, applicable to all pension and welfare plans (with some exceptions such as certain unfunded executive retirement plans and governmental plans) whether qualified or not, contains much more detailed requirements for informing plan participants of their rights and status under the plan. A plan administrator who willfully fails to comply with these provisions is subjects to both criminal and civil sanctions.[22]

Since the plan document is usually complex and written in legal jargon, the plan administrator is required to furnish each participant and beneficiary with a sum-

---

[17]Treas. Reg. 1.401-1(b)(1)(i).
[18]Treas. Reg. 1.401-1(b)(1)(ii).
[19]IRC §401(a)(8); Treas. Reg. 1.401-1(b)(1)(i).
[20]Rev. Rul. 185, 1953-2 CB 202, Rev. Rul. 78-56, 1978-1 CB 116. *See also* Rev. Rul. 78-403, 1978-2 CB 153.
[21]Treas. Reg. 1.401-1(a)(2).
[22]ERISA §501.

mary plan description (SPD) written in a manner "calculated to be understood by the average plan participant or beneficiary."[23] Detailed regulations specify the content of summary plan descriptions.[24] The summary must include, *inter alia*, the name and address of the plan administrator, names and addresses of the persons responsible for the management of the plan assets, important plan provisions, a description of benefits, the circumstances that may cause disqualification or ineligibility, and the procedures to be followed in presenting claims for benefits under the plan. Summary plan descriptions are to be furnished to participants within 120 days after the plan is established or, if later, within 90 days after an individual becomes a participant.[25] Updated plan descriptions are to be provided to participants every five years whenever there have been plan amendments in the interim.[26] In any case, a plan description, old or revised, is to be provided every 10 years. In addition, participants are to receive a summary of material modifications or an updated summary plan description within 210 days after the end of the plan year in which the change or changes occur. A copy of the summary plan description and summary of any material modifications must be filed with the Department of Labor.[27]

Conflict between plan sponsors and participants may arise when the terms of the summary plan description, the plan document, and, if applicable, the collective bargaining agreement are inconsistent or ambiguous. As a practical matter, the potential economic hardship to retirees, combined with the fact that controversies involving benefits often concern retired employees who no longer depend on the employer for active employment, often results in situations where there is little reason for the participants not to litigate the issue. If participants' benefits or rights under the plan are ambiguous, courts have often decided the issue under a total contract theory,[28] in which the employer is bound by the total contract terms,[29] or a line of conduct theory,[30] in which informal communications to employees may be considered crucial.[31] While these types of cases are usually fact-intensive, the importance to plan sponsors of clear and precise communication with participants cannot be overemphasized.

The plan's principal office (and other such places as may be prescribed by regulations) is also required to make available to the participants the entire plan

---

[23]ERISA §§101(a)(1), 102(a).

[24]29 CFR 2520.102-1,2,3,4.

[25]ERISA §104(b)(1)(A).

[26]ERISA §104(b)(1)(B).

[27]ERISA §104(a)(1).

[28]In which all related plan documents, including the summary plan description and other booklets and announcements, are considered to represent the total contract between employer and employees concerning employee benefits.

[29]*Bachelder v. Communications Satellite Corp.*, 8 EBC 1609 (DC Me. 1987); *Noell v. American Design, Inc. Profit Sharing Plan*, 6 EBC 1833 (11th Cir. 1985); *Musto v. American General Corp.*, 10 EBC 1441 (6th Cir. 1988).

[30]Under a line of conduct theory, ambiguities in an agreement are to be construed in a particular fashion in light of the pattern of conduct of the employer or employees. While cases using other theories may also attempt to bolster their conclusion by reference to a line of conduct, it is not the controlling issue.

[31]*Eardman v. Bethlehem Steel Corp.*, 607 F.Supp. 196 (WDNY 1984); *Bower v. Bunker Hill Co.*, 725 F2d 1221 (9th Cir. 1984); *Local Union 150-A v. Dubuque Packing Co.*, 756 F2d 66 (8th Cir. 1988).

document and any collective bargaining agreement, trust agreement, insurance contract, or other instrument associated with the plan.[32] Upon written request, the administrator must furnish such documents, the plan description, and the latest annual report directly to a participant; a reasonable charge may be made to cover the cost of complying with such a request.[33]

Within seven months after the close of the plan year, the administrator is required to furnish to each participant with a copy of the summary annual report (SAR) containing certain financial information about the plan.[34]

Upon termination of employment, a one-year break in service, or the request of a plan participant or beneficiary, the plan administrator must provide the latest information available on the total benefits that have accrued to the participant, those that have vested, or those that have become nonforfeitable.[35] No more than one request per year may be made by a participant or beneficiary for this information.[36] Once a year, the employer submits to the Secretary of the Treasury a list of employees with vested benefits who terminated during the year, along with the amount of those benefits, and the Secretary must send a copy of this list to the Social Security Administration.[37] The latter will provide this information to participants or their beneficiaries upon request and will do so automatically when application is made for Social Security old-age benefits.

Enforcement of Benefit Rights

If the benefit claim of a plan participant or beneficiary is denied, the plan administrator must inform the claimant in writing of the denial of the claim and must set forth the specific reasons for disapproval in a manner calculated to be understood by the claimant.[38] In addition, the plan administrator is required to give any participant or beneficiary whose claim for benefits has been denied a reasonable opportunity for a full and fair review of the decision by the plan administrator. If still dissatisfied with the administrator's decision, the claimant may bring suit in a federal district court for enforcement of that claim, or under certain circumstances in a state court of competent jurisdiction.[39] If the claimant brings the action in a federal court, he or she must provide a copy of the complaint to the Secretary of Labor and the Secretary of Treasury by certified mail. At their discretion, either secretary, or both, may intervene in the suit.[40]

It is unlawful for the plan administrator or other person to discharge, fine, suspend, expel, discipline, or discriminate against a plan participant or beneficiary for exercising any right under the law or the plan or to interfere coercively through the use of fraud, force, violence, or intimidation with the exercise of any

[32]ERISA §104(b)(2).
[33]ERISA §104(b)(4).
[34]ERISA §104(b)(3); 29 CFR 2520.104b-10.
[35]ERISA §§105, 209; IRC §6057(e).
[36]Prop. DOL Reg. 2520.105-2(c)(1).
[37]IRC §6057; IRS Form 5500, Schedule SSA.
[38]ERISA §503; 29 CFR 2560.503-1.
[39]ERISA §502(a)(1).
[40]ERISA §502(h).

right under the plan or applicable law.[41] Any person who willfully uses fraud, force, or violence or who threatens to restrain, coerce, or intimidate any participant or beneficiary for the purpose of interfering with his or her rights is subject to criminal penalties,[42] in addition to the civil enforcement actions available to prevent any interference.

Reporting Requirements

ERISA requires that certain reports be submitted to government agencies on behalf of all plans. Annual or periodic reports are required, as well as reports on certain events. Certain plans are exempted from the various reporting requirements.

Periodic Reports

For the annual report,[43] plans with 100 or more participants must complete Form 5500, while smaller plans complete the simpler Form 5500-C or Form 5500-R (or Form 5500-EZ for plans with only one participant). The appropriate form must be filed with the IRS within seven months after the end of the plan year unless an extension is obtained. The IRS gives a copy of the report to the Department of Labor and provides certain information from the report to the Pension Benefit Guaranty Corporation.

Form 5500 (and the shorter Form 5500-C) includes identifying information, statistics on participants, a balance sheet, a statement of income and expense, and other information about the operation of the plan. The form must disclose compensation paid from the plan to persons who rendered services to the plan. Plans with fewer than 100 participants generally may file a shorter Form 5500-R in two out of every three years.[44] If the plan had any prohibited transactions involving a party-in-interest, a detailed schedule must be attached. For plans with 100 or more participants, a detailed schedule of all assets must be attached, as well as schedules of any loans or leases in default and a schedule of all transactions exceeding 3 percent of plan assets.

The financial statements and schedules required for the annual report must be examined by an independent qualified public accountant retained by the plan on behalf of all its participants. The accountant must give an opinion on whether the financial statement and supporting schedules are presented fairly, in conformity with generally accepted accounting principles applied in a manner consistent with that of the preceding year. Such an opinion has to be based upon an examination carried out in accordance with generally accepted auditing standards. For purposes of ERISA, a qualified public accountant includes a certified public accountant, a licensed public accountant, and any person certified by the Secretary of Labor as a qualified public accountant in accordance with regulations published by the Labor Department (for people who practice in states that have no certification

---

[41]ERISA §510.
[42]ERISA §511.
[43]ERISA §103; IRC §6058(a).
[44]Form instructions specify when use of Form 5500-R is permitted.

or licensing procedures for accountants). Plans with less than 100 participants are not required to have an audited financial statement.

If plan benefits are provided by an insurance company, Schedule A must be attached to the annual report.[45] Schedule A reports the premiums paid, benefits paid, the number of persons covered, charges for administrative expenses, commissions paid to licensed agents or brokers, dividends credited, and other information. Insurance companies must transmit and certify the required information to the plan administrator within 120 days after the close of the plan year.

If the plan is subject to the funding requirements of ERISA, it must retain an enrolled actuary on behalf of all its participants.[46] The actuary must prepare an annual actuarial statement, Schedule B, which is attached to Form 5500, 5500-C, 5500-R, or 5500-EZ.[47] Schedule B includes an exhibit of the "funding standard account," which shows whether the funding requirements have been satisfied. It also includes additional information from the most recent actuarial valuation. The actuary must attach a statement of actuarial assumptions and methods used and certain other information. The actuary must certify that the actuarial assumptions used to compute plan costs and liabilities are, in the aggregate, reasonably related to the experience of the plan and to reasonable expectations, and that they represent the actuary's best estimate of anticipated experience under the plan. In making this certification, the actuary may assume and rely on the correctness of any accounting matter about which any qualified public accountant has expressed an opinion, if the actuary so states. By the same token, an accountant may rely on the correctness of any actuarial matter certified by any enrolled actuary if the accountant indicates his or her reliance on such certification.[48]

Special Reports

In the event of a merger, consolidation, or transfer of assets or liabilities involving a qualified plan, the plan administrator must file Form 5310-A with the IRS at least 30 days before the event. No Form 5310-A is filed if the amount of assets and liabilities transferred or merged is less than 3 percent of the assets of the larger plan, or if the transfer or merger involves only defined contribution plans.[49] For a defined benefit plan, an actuarial statement must be attached indicating that ERISA's rules concerning such events have been satisfied.[50]

Upon plan termination, the plan sponsor will ordinarily submit the Form 5310 to request a determination concerning the qualification of the plan at that juncture. For a single employer plan subject to plan benefits insurance, the plan administrator of a defined benefit plan must provide advance notification of a plan termination to the Pension Benefit Guaranty Corporation and to participants, as described in Chapter 31.

[45]ERISA §103(e).
[46]ERISA §103(a)(4).
[47]ERISA §103(d); IRC §6059.
[48]ERISA §103(a)(3)(B), (4)(D).
[49]Form 5310-A, Instructions.
[50]IRC §6058(b).

For plans covered by plan benefits insurance, the PBGC must be notified within 30 days of when the plan administrator knows or has reason to know of the occurrence of a specified reportable event. Reportable events include certain decreases in active participants by 20 percent since the beginning of the plan year, or 25 percent since the beginning of the previous plan year, when the present value of unfunded vested benefits is $250,000 or more; the inability to pay plan benefits; certain changes of employer; certain distributions to a substantial owner of $10,000 or more; the bankruptcy, insolvency, liquidation, or dissolution of the employer; and the plan's failure to meet minimum funding requirements or the grant of a minimum funding waiver, when the present value of unfunded vested benefits is $250,000 or more.[51] When a plan is established or amended, the plan sponsor will ordinarily request a determination of the plan's qualified status by submitting appropriate forms and information to the IRS, as discussed earlier in this chapter.

Maintenance of Basic Records

The most routine—and yet extremely vital—function associated with the operation of a pension plan is the maintenance of the basic records necessary to establish eligibility for participation and receipt of benefits, as well as the amount of contributions and benefits under the plan.[52] For defined benefit plans, this includes data required for actuarial valuations to determine the costs and liabilities under the plan. The most basic record has already been alluded to—the one for each participant showing date of birth, date of employment, and earnings. For every defined contribution plan and every plan that includes employee contributions, the record for each employee must reflect current contributions and accumulated contributions with interest or investment earnings. For a defined benefit plan that calls for a unit of benefit for each year of service, the benefits must be recorded as earned in order that the proper amount of benefits will be payable at retirement. For both defined benefit and defined contribution plans, employee data are also needed to produce periodic statements for employees on the amount of their benefits. All the information concerning each participant is not necessarily kept on one form or by the same department. The cost data needed for actuarial valuations for defined benefit plans can be derived from the basic records maintained for the individual participants.

Every person (including the plan sponsor, actuary, and plan auditor) required to file any description or report or to certify any information under ERISA must maintain records sufficient to verify that information for six years.[53] All records of employee information that are used to determine each employee's benefits must be maintained as long as any possibility exists that these records might be relevant in determining those benefit entitlements.[54]

[51]PBGC Reg. 2615.
[52]ERISA §209(a).
[53]ERISA §107.
[54]DOL Reg. 2530.209-2(d).

Fiduciary Responsibility

ERISA imposes fiduciary responsibilities on any person who exercises any discretionary authority or control over the management of a pension plan, its administration, or its assets; or who renders investment advice for a fee or other form of compensation.[55] Under this definition, directors and certain officers of the plan's sponsor, members of a plan's investment committee, and persons who select these individuals are regarded as fiduciaries. A fiduciary status attaches to these persons by virtue of their having authority and responsibility over the matters in question, apart from their formal title. Investment advisers are by definition fiduciaries, and other consultants or advisers may be considered fiduciaries because of the special expertise (and hence authority) that they bring to the management or administration of the plan or its assets. In practice, the determination of who is a fiduciary under the plan depends to a great extent on the facts and circumstances of the case. Although every person who has any official connection with a pension plan may incur some fiduciary obligation, not all persons who become fiduciaries have obligations extending to every phase of the management and administration of the plan. The obligations are governed by the nature of the duties involved.

Named Fiduciaries

In order that participants may know who is responsible for operating the plan, the plan document must identify one or more "named fiduciaries" who jointly or severally shall have authority to control and manage the operation and administration of the plan.[56] Such persons may be identified by name or position in the plan document or be designated by a procedure set out in the document. For example, the plan may provide that the employer's board of directors is to select the person or persons to manage the plan. Under a collectively bargained multiemployer plan, the named fiduciaries would normally be the joint board of trustees selected in accordance with the procedure described in the plan document.[57] The named fiduciaries may serve in more than one fiduciary capacity under the plan. For example, it is not unusual for a named fiduciary to serve also as administrator and trustee of the plan.

Management of Plan Assets

Management of plan assets is an especially critical fiduciary function. Unless the plan is funded through a life insurance company or is a type authorized to use a custodial account without a trustee (as in the case of a Keogh plan or individual retirement account), the assets must be held in trust by individual or corporate trustees.[58] The trustees may be appointed in the plan document, in the trust agreement, or by action of the named fiduciary or fiduciaries. However, to emphasize the importance of this responsibility, the trustees must accept appointment before they can act in that capacity.

[55]ERISA §3(21).
[56]ERISA §402(a)(2).
[57]ERISA §402(c)(1).
[58]ERISA §403(a).

The trustees may be given exclusive control over the investment of the plan assets subject to applicable law, in which event they are fully accountable for the results of their stewardship. However, the plan may provide that the trustees will be subject to the direction of the named fiduciaries.[59] This may be accomplished by placing investment responsibilities in an investment committee appointed under the terms of the plan. (For example, the plan may specify that the investment committee is to consist of the president, financial vice president, and comptroller of the employer firm.) Since investment decisions are basic to plan operations, members of such an investment committee must be named fiduciaries. If the plan so provides, the trustee must follow the directions of the investment committee, unless the actions to be taken under the committee's directions clearly would be prohibited by the fiduciary responsibility rules of ERISA or would be contrary to the terms of the trust or the plan. A trustee who properly follows the instructions of the investment committee, is not legally responsible for any losses that may arise from compliance with the instructions.

Instead of directing that investment decisions be made by the plan trustee or an investment committee, the plan document may authorize a named fiduciary to appoint a qualified investment manager (or managers) to control or manage all or part of the plan's assets.[60] However, the fiduciary must exercise prudence in selecting the investment manager and in continuing to use that manager. In this case, the plan trustee would no longer have any responsibility for managing the assets controlled by the qualified investment manager and would not be liable for the acts or omissions of the investment manager.[61] Also, as long as the named fiduciary had chosen and retained the investment manager prudently, the named fiduciary would not be liable for the acts and omissions of the manager.[62] Investment responsibilities can be legally delegated only to an investment adviser who is registered under the Investment Advisers Act of 1940, a bank (as defined in that act), or an insurance company qualified under the laws of two or more states to provide investment management services.[63] To be qualified, the investment manager must acknowledge in writing its fiduciary responsibility under the plan.

The named fiduciary may allocate plan assets to several investment managers in order to diversify investments, to obtain a wider range of investment philosophy and judgment, to encourage competition in investment performance among the various managers, or to fulfill any business purposes. In that event, each investment manager is responsible for the management of the assets entrusted to it and is not a cofiduciary with the persons or institutions managing the other trusts.[64]

The trustee may hire agents to perform ministerial acts but is expected to exercise prudence in the selection and retention of such agents. A trust is not required for plan assets that consist of insurance or annuity contracts issued by a legally licensed life insurance company.[65] Nevertheless, the person who holds the

[59]Ibid.
[60]ERISA §402(c)(3).
[61]ERISA §405(d).
[62]ERISA §405(c).
[63]ERISA §3(38).
[64]ERISA §405(b)(3).
[65]ERISA §403(b)(1).

contracts is a fiduciary and must observe the ERISA rules of fiduciary conduct with respect to the contracts. For example, he or she must prudently take and maintain exclusive control over the contracts and must use prudent care and skill in preserving the property. To the extent that the law treats assets held by a life insurance company as "plan assets," the insurance company is treated as a fiduciary with respect to the plan and must meet the ERISA fiduciary standards. Although normally insurance companies are considered fiduciaries only with respect to the assets under investment management for the plan, insurers can also inadvertently become fiduciaries with respect to their general assets.

An insurance company may be considered a plan fiduciary with respect to investments in its general asset account if the insurer sells insurance contracts that are not "guaranteed benefit" policies.[66] An insurance contract is a guaranteed benefit policy if either a "component" analysis and a "benefit" analysis considers the contract a guaranteed benefit policy. The component analysis divides the insurance contract into its component parts, each of which must allocate investment risk to the insurer in order for the contract to be a guaranteed benefit policy.[67] The benefit analysis apparently requires the benefits payable under the contract to be guaranteed in amount by the contract, again shifting the investment risk to the insurer, if the contract is to be considered a guaranteed benefit policy.[68]

Nondiversion of Assets

It is illegal for a plan fiduciary to divert any plan assets or income to any purpose other than paying benefits to plan participants and their beneficiaries and defraying reasonable expenses of administering the plan.[69] The trust agreement or other relevant documents must specifically state that no funds can be diverted until all claims against the plan have been discharged. This prohibition is an integral part of the overall regulatory goal of having the plan set up for the exclusive benefit of a broad class of employees, with the employer making nonwithdrawable contributions to the plan and the assets being managed in the interest of, and in a manner protecting the rights of, plan participants and their beneficiaries.

The law intends employer contributions to be generally irrevocable transfers of assets to the plan that cannot be recaptured through plan termination until after the favored participants have been provided for. Under certain circumstances, however, the employer is permitted to recover all or some portion of a contribution that it has made to the pension plan. One such circumstance involves a contribution to a newly established plan based on the assumption and *on the condition* that the plan will be adjudged by the IRS as a tax-qualified plan. Should an adverse ruling be made by the IRS, the employer may recover its contribution if the plan so provides and if claim for recovery is made within one year after denial of qualification.[70]

---

[66]*John Hancock Mutual Life Ins. Co. v. Harris Trust and Savings Bank*, 114 S.Ct. 517 (1993).
[67]*John Hancock, supra; Peoria Union Stock Yards Co. v. Penn Mutual Life Ins. Co.*, 698 F2d (7th Cir. 1983).
[68]*John Hancock, supra.*
[69]ERISA §§403(c)(1), 404(a)(1), 4044(d); IRC §401(a)(2).
[70]ERISA §403(c)(2)(B); Rev. Rul. 60-276, 1960-2 C.B. 150.

A similar circumstance arises when a contribution is made on the condition that it be considered currently deductible for income tax purposes, a condition that is satisfied only if the plan continues to be qualified and the contribution does not exceed the amount that can be deducted currently under the limits of the Code. If all or a portion of the deduction is disallowed, the employer may recover that portion of its contribution that was disallowed, provided the plan allows such a recovery and the claim is made within one year after the deduction is disallowed.[71]

The IRS takes the position that only it can disallow the deductibility of a contribution, even though a plan sponsor or administrator can determine that a contribution is in excess of the plan's deductible limit. The IRS will issue a letter ruling to plan sponsors or administrators on the nondeductibility of a contribution, which will allow the refund of the contributions from the plan. Certain *de minimis* contributions (i.e., under $25,000) can be returned to the plan sponsor without a letter ruling if an actuarial certification that the contribution is nondeductible is obtained.[72]

The employer may also recover a contribution based on a mistake of fact, such as an arithmetical error in the calculation of the amount that was required to be made to the plan or that could be deducted in the current year. The claims for recovery must be filed within one year after the contribution was made.[73]

Finally, if a plan terminates in an acceptable manner and all its benefits and other obligations are fully discharged, the employer may recover any assets that remain, if the plan document so provides.[74] This recovery is permitted only if the surplus arose out of an "erroneous actuarial computation," meaning that the costs to provide the benefits accrued upon plan termination were less than the plan assets. Immediate recovery of the plan surplus is possible only if the administrator purchases from a life insurer single-sum, paid-up annuities for all participants and beneficiaries or makes a lump-sum cash distribution to such persons.

The law also contains provisions designed to prevent the diversion of assets through unwise or improper management. As general guidelines, the cost of acquired assets must not exceed fair market value at the time of purchase; a rate of return on invested assets commensurate with the prevailing rate must be sought; sufficient liquidity must be maintained to meet the cash flow needs of the plan; and the other general standards that would govern the actions of a prudent investor must be observed.[75] In addition, a number of specific transactions involving some measure of self-dealing are completely banned.[76] An important exception to both the diversity and self-dealing rules is that the plan is permitted to invest up to 10 percent, and in some cases 100 percent, of its assets in the securities or real property of the employer.[77]

---

[71]ERISA §403(c)(2)(C).
[72]Rev. Proc. 90-49, 1990-2 CB 620.
[73]ERISA §403(c)(2)(A).
[74]ERISA §4044(d); Treas. Reg. 1.401-2(b).
[75]ERISA §3(18), 404(a).
[76]ERISA §406; IRC §4975(c).
[77]ERISA §§404(a)(2), 407, 408(e).

Delegation of Fiduciary Duties Other than the Management of Plan Assets

The law also permits the named fiduciaries to allocate and delegate fiduciary duties that do not involve the management of plan assets.[78] Upon proper allocation or delegation, the named fiduciaries are not liable for the acts or omissions of the persons to whom duties have been allocated or delegated. However, the plan must specifically authorize such allocation or delegation and must provide a procedure for it. For example, the plan may provide that delegation may occur only with respect to specified duties, such as maintaining participant records or disbursing benefits, and only on the approval of the plan sponsor or on the approval of the joint board of trustees of a so-called Taft-Hartley plan. Also, in implementing the procedures of the plan the named fiduciaries must act prudently and in the interests of participants and their beneficiaries. Prudence must therefore be exercised not only in the initial selection of the person or organization to whom duties have been delegated but also in the surveillance of the manner in which the duties are performed. Depending upon the circumstances, the surveillance requirement may be satisfied by a formal periodic review (by all the named fiduciaries who participated in the delegation or by a specially designated review committee), or it may be met through day-to-day contact and evaluation, or in other appropriate ways.

Like the plan's trustees, named fiduciaries may also allocate responsibilities among themselves. Having properly allocated duties among themselves, the cofiduciaries are not responsible for each other's acts or omissions so long as they are not a party to the breach of rules or do not imprudently contribute to it.

Basic Fiduciary Rules

Each fiduciary of a pension plan, regardless of his or her specific duties and responsibilities, must act "with the care, skill, prudence, and diligence under the circumstances then prevailing that a prudent man acting in a like capacity and familiar with such matters would use in the conduct of an enterprise of a like character and with like aims."[79] This phrasing adapts and enlarges the classic judicial prudent man rule enunciated as a standard for a trustee in managing the assets of a personal trust or an institutional endowment.[80] In contrast, the ERISA statutory standard of prudence attempts to apply the concept to all actions of a fiduciary, whether or not they involve managing plan assets. Thus far, the investment function continues to be the focus of the standard and the target of most regulatory and judicial pronouncements on the subject.

Another important manifestation of congressional concern over fiduciary behavior is a general prohibition in ERISA against business and investment transactions between the plan and parties-in-interest, as defined by law. This approach was adopted in lieu of a requirement that all transactions between the plan and parties-in-interest be conducted at "arm's length," an approach suggested by many

[78]ERISA §405(c).
[79]ERISA §404(a)(1)(B).
[80]*Harvard College v. Amory* (Mass. S. Jud. Ct. 1830), 9 Pickering 446.

groups when ERISA was being developed and still espoused by some as a more efficient way of dealing with this sensitive issue.

The law lists certain transactions that are to be exempt from the general prohibitions and authorizes administrative exemptions for other transactions that are in accord with established business practices and provide adequate safeguards to the plan and its participants.[81] Under these exemptions, a life insurance company may purchase insurance and annuity contracts from itself on behalf of the participants in its own pension plan, and a bank may use its own investment facilities for its pension plan. Moreover, a bank or insurance company is specifically authorized to purchase, on behalf of a pension plan of which it is a fiduciary, investment units in a pooled account that it operates. Other exemptions permit a plan to provide nondiscriminatory loans to its participants at a reasonable interest rate and with proper security, and to purchase services from a party-in-interest under certain conditions.

Under the labor provisions of ERISA, a fiduciary who breaches the fiduciary requirements of the act is personally liable to the plan for any plan losses resulting from the breach.[82] Such a fiduciary must also turn over to the plan any profits made through the improper use of any plan asset. Other relief, including removal of the fiduciary, may be ordered by a court under appropriate civil actions. The fiduciary is not permitted to eliminate or reduce his or her liability for breach of fiduciary responsibilities through exculpatory provisions in the trust agreement or other document.[83] However, a plan may purchase insurance for itself and for its fiduciaries to cover their liability or losses from their imprudent behavior if the insurance contract provides for recourse by the insurer against the fiduciaries for breach of fiduciary responsibility. A fiduciary may purchase insurance to cover his or her own liability, and an employer or union may purchase liability insurance for plan fiduciaries. These policies need not provide for recourse.

The tax provisions of ERISA prescribe civil penalties in the form of excise taxes for "disqualified persons" (roughly equivalent to parties-in-interest under the labor provisions) who engage in prohibited transactions.[84] The tax is levied on two levels. At the first level, the disqualified person is taxed at the rate of 5 percent of the amount involved for each taxable year (or part of a year) in the period that begins with the date when the prohibited transaction occurs and ends on the earlier of the date of collection or the date of mailing of a deficiency notice for the first-level tax.[85] The first-level tax is imposed automatically without regard to whether the violation was inadvertent. At the second level, the tax is levied at the rate of 100 percent of the amount involved and is imposed on the fiduciary if the transaction is not corrected within a limited period.[86]

There is a general requirement that every fiduciary of a pension plan be bonded for an amount not less than 10 percent of the funds handled, subject to a mini-

---

[81]ERISA §408, IRC §4975(c)(2).
[82]ERISA §409.
[83]ERISA §410.
[84]IRC §4975.
[85]IRC §4975(a).
[86]IRC §4975(b).

mum of $1,000 and a maximum of $500,000, or other such amount as may be prescribed by the Secretary of Labor.[87] Banks and insurance companies meeting certain tests are exempt from this requirement. The Secretary of Labor is expected to develop regulations that will provide procedures for exempting plans where other bonding arrangements of the employer, employee organization, investment manager, or other fiduciaries (or the overall financial condition of the plan or the fiduciaries) meet specified standards deemed adequate to protect the interests of participants and their beneficiaries.

Benefits Determinations

One of the most common and important decisions a fiduciary makes is whether a participant is entitled to a particular benefit, such as a disability benefit. When fiduciary benefit entitlement decisions are challenged, the appropriate standard of review must be determined. Courts generally use either a standard that permits the fiduciary's decision to be overturned only if the decision is determined to be arbitrary and capricious or a *de novo* standard that provides no deference to the fiduciary's original determination.

The standard of review becomes critical when there is a potential conflict of interest with the plan fiduciary. For example, any benefits claim determination from an unfunded plan creates a conflict of interest for the plan sponsor, who is likely to be the plan fiduciary, because payment of the benefit in an unfunded plan will come from the general assets of the plan sponsor. A less direct potential conflict of interest occurs when a plan sponsor serving as fiduciary has to make a benefits determination from a funded plan. Though payment of benefits will not be made from the general assets of the employer, the use of plan assets to pay benefits may increase the funding liability of the plan sponsor. This potential liability has not been considered serious enough, however, to create a conflict of interest.

The Supreme Court has ruled that fiduciary decisions regarding benefit claims should be reviewed *de novo*, unless the fiduciary is granted discretion to determine eligibility and construe doubtful terms. In that case, the fiduciary's decision should be overturned only if it is arbitrary and capricious.[88] However, other federal courts have not been following that standard exactly, especially in situations where a potential conflict of interest exists.

Another court has characterized the arbitrary and capricious standard as a "sliding scale of judicial review," in which the fiduciary's decisions are due more or less deference, depending upon the degree to which there is a conflict of interest.[89] While few courts have expressly adopted this standard, it approximates the level of review that courts apply to fiduciary benefit entitlement decisions.

---

[87]ERISA §412.
[88]*Firestone Tire & Rubber Co. v. Bruch,* 489 US 101 (1989).
[89]*Van Boxel v. The Journal Cos. Employees' Pension Fund,* 836 F2d 1048 (7th Cir. 1987).

Chapter 4
Coverage and Participation

A participant or member of a plan is an individual specifically included under the plan. This includes retired employees and terminated employees who are entitled to future benefits under the plan, as well as active employees. Participation usually refers to the inclusion of individuals in the plan as participants.

Coverage refers to participation in the aggregate. Sometimes coverage refers to the classes of employees that are eligible, such as salaried employees. At other times, coverage refers to a group whose members are actually current participants in the plan, excluding, for example, employees who have not yet satisfied a minimum age or service requirement.

Most plans have a minimum age or service requirement, or both, before an employee may become a participant. In addition, in some plans participation can begin only on the first day of a year, quarter, or month.

The significance to the participant of the date participation begins varies from plan to plan. Under a plan that requires employee contributions, participation signals the commencement of the employee's obligation to contribute to the plan. Under a defined contribution plan, participation refers to the change in status of an employee that requires the employer to make contributions on the employee's behalf and credit them to the employee's account. Participation may signify a status under which the employee is eligible for death or disability benefits, if the plan includes these benefits, although many plans defer eligibility for these benefits until a later date. Participation may refer to the time when the employee begins to accrue benefit credits for service thereafter, but many plans accrue benefits for service both before and after the date participation begins. Some plans measure the years of participation to determine when an employee becomes eligible to receive normal retirement or other benefits, but other plans use the entire period of service for this purpose. Under some defined benefit plans with no employee contributions, the date that participation begins has no effect whatsoever upon the benefit entitlement of the individual participant; eligibility for benefits and the amount of benefits would not change if the plan should be amended to increase or decrease the period before employees become participants.

Whether an individual is a participant may have several consequences for the employer or other plan sponsor and for the plan as a whole. It may mark when the plan administrator begins to keep records for the employee in question. It determines whether the individual must receive the disclosures that are required to be made to all participants. For defined benefit plans, a premium must be paid to the

Pension Benefit Guaranty Corporation for each participant, and participation usually marks the point at which the employee is first recognized in the actuarial cost calculations that guide the employer's contributions to the plan.

In addition to these administrative issues, the coverage and participation of the plan raises several compliance issues with which the plan sponsor must be concerned. The plan may specify certain eligibility criteria that must be satisfied for an individual to become a participant in the plan. The plan must also include a nondiscriminatory group of employees. Assuming the eligibility criteria include minimum age or service requirements, how the employer determines that employees have met those criteria must follow specified guidelines. Finally, the plan must benefit, or cover, a minimum number of participants.

Eligibility for Participation

A plan document may define the broad classes of employees who are eligible to participate in the plan, as well as the specific conditions that must be met before participation becomes effective. Not all plans are designed to cover every employee on the payroll at any given time. Some employees may never become eligible to participate in a particular plan, since the plan was not designed to cover that classification of workers. For example, employees working fewer than 1,000 hours per year may be excluded from eligibility. Furthermore, separate plans may be operated for different groups of employees. There may be one plan for workers represented by a collective bargaining unit and another for the employees, both management and clerical, not covered by a collective bargaining agreement. There may be several bargaining units, each with its own plan. There may be a separate plan for each plant of a multiplant firm, and there will almost always be separate plans for foreign subsidiaries or nonresident alien employees. Such eligibility requirements are allowed if the coverage tests described below are satisfied.

Age and Service Requirements

Within a particular plan, the members of a potentially eligible class of employees may have to satisfy a service or age requirement, or both. The purpose of a service requirement is often administrative. Recently hired employees, especially younger ones, tend to experience a high rate of turnover. It is an unnecessary administrative expense to bring such persons into the pension plan, with their attendant records, only to have them withdraw a short time later.

A minimum age stipulation has much the same purpose as a service requirement, with which it may be combined, namely, to exclude high-turnover employees. When the plan is contributory, a minimum age requirement serves the additional function of excluding those employees who, because of their youth, have developed little interest in pensions and would object to contributing to a pension plan.

The service requirement cannot exceed one year of service, unless the plan provides for full and immediate vesting, in which case it may require two years of service.[1] While a plan can permanently exclude employees who never have 1,000

---

[1] ERISA §202(a)(1); IRC §410(a)(1). A three-year eligibility standard was permitted for plan years beginning before 1989.

hours of service in a year (i.e., do not have one year of service), the plan cannot exclude part-time employees.[2] This is so because excluding employees on the basis of their part-time status is viewed as a service-based exclusion, and the only service-based exclusion permitted is that requiring one year of service. A part-time employee might actually work more than 1,000 hours in a year and then be eligible under the permitted service exclusions. The fact that the plan satisfies the nondiscriminatory coverage requirements discussed below does not alter this result.

The distinction between service-based exclusions and job categories is often difficult to discern. For example, while a plan cannot exclude part-time employees, it can exclude either hourly or salaried employees, as many plans do.[3] The difference is that part-time status concerns the amount of service the employee provides to the employer, while hourly or salaried status connotes the manner in which the employee is paid by the employer.

The minimum age cannot be higher than 21, except as noted below.[4] Thus the general rule now is that an employee must not be denied membership in the plan because of age or service whenever he or she reaches age 21 and has a minimum of one year of service. A plan may require both conditions. It may require that the employee be at least 21 and have at least one year of service. If an employee is hired at age 18, for example, he or she may be required to wait three years for plan membership. If an employee is hired at age 20 or beyond, the maximum service requirement is one year.

As an exception to the general rule, any plan maintained exclusively for employees of a governmental or tax-exempt educational organization that provides full and immediate vesting for all participants may have a participation requirement of age 26 and one year of service.[5] An employee who has satisfied the minimum age and service requirements must be permitted to commence participation in the plan at the beginning of the next plan year or, if earlier, within six months after satisfying the requirements.[6] All of these are minimum standards and do not preclude more liberal provisions.

It must be emphasized that these age and service requirements pertain only to the time when the employee will begin to accrue benefits toward retirement. They relate strictly to benefit accruals, not to the service required to determine a participant's place on the vesting schedule, a subject discussed in Chapter 6. The law does not require retroactive recognition of preparticipation service for calculating benefit accruals, but it does for determining the participant's vesting status. Some plans, most of them subject to collective bargaining, have nevertheless provided for retroactive recognition for benefit purposes of some or all service prior to date of membership in the plan.

Many plans impose a maximum age limit, as well as a minimum age requirement. Such a limit excludes from plan membership any individual hired at or above the stipulated age. For plan years beginning after 1987, plans may no longer

[2]Treas. Reg. 1.410(a)-3(e)(2), Example (3).
[3]IRC §401(a)(5).
[4]ERISA §202(a)(1); IRC §410(a)(1).
[5]ERISA §202(a)(1)(B)(ii); IRC §410(a)(1)(B)(ii).
[6]ERISA §202(a)(4); IRC §410(a)(4).

contain maximum age limits,[7] as they are now considered to discriminate against employees on account of age.

Some noncontributory plans do not contain any age or service requirements for membership eligibility. This is particularly true for collectively bargained plans that provide uniform benefits for each year of service. Where no eligibility requirements are stipulated, an employee who comes within the scope of the plan is automatically covered from the first day of employment.

Participation in Contributory Plans

Employers usually sponsor contributory plans, i.e., plans in which an employee's participation in the plan or the accrual of benefits under the plan is contingent on the employee making contributions to the plan, in order to generate a higher sense of employee involvement in the plan. The general thought is that if the employees have to contribute some of their own money to the plan, they will have a greater appreciation for the benefits provided by the plan. If these objectives are to be achieved, maximum participation of eligible employees is imperative. Employees who reach retirement age without entitlement to benefits can be an embarrassment to the employer, even though they voluntarily chose not to participate in the plan. This is less of a problem in a noncontributory plan, since all employees who meet the eligibility requirements are automatically included in the plan.

When employee contributions are included, however, participation in the plan is usually made optional, especially for employees already in service at the inception of the plan. Some plans make participation a condition of employment for new employees, thus ensuring ultimate coverage of all eligible employees. Most plans stipulate that an employee, having once chosen to participate, must continue participation throughout employment. This provision prevents employees from terminating their membership in the plan just to draw down their accumulated contributions. Some plans permit an employee to discontinue contributions while still in service but prohibit withdrawal of accumulated contributions prior to termination of service. Some plans permit an employee to terminate his or her coverage while still in the service of the firm but forbid subsequent reentry into the plan. Increased participation among younger employees is sometimes obtained by making membership in the pension plan a condition for coverage by other employee benefit plans, such as group life and group health insurance, which at their age might be more important to them.

Coverage Requirements

As a part of the general thrust of the Internal Revenue Code to encourage broad coverage and prevent discrimination in favor of highly compensated employees, a qualified pension plan must satisfy certain coverage requirements. This is true whether the plan is multiple employer or single employer in scope or negotiated or unilateral in origin.

The Tax Reform Act of 1986 significantly changed these coverage requirements, making them more stringent. The new requirements, described below, generally apply for plan years beginning in 1989 and later.[8]

---

[7]ERISA §202(a)(2); IRC §410(a)(2).

Highly Compensated Employees

The definition of "highly compensated employee" is central to the new coverage requirements, as well as to other key requirements under the Tax Reform Act. Prior to the Tax Reform Act the Code used different definitions of "highly compensated" for different purposes. For most purposes it depended on the "facts and circumstances," which are very subjective criteria.

A new uniform definition of "highly compensated employee" applies for almost all purposes under the Code.[9] The prior proscription against discrimination in favor of the "prohibited group" of officers, shareholders, and highly compensated employees has been changed to apply only to highly compensated employees.[10] In addition to the basic nondiscrimination and minimum coverage rules, the definition of highly compensated employee is used for purposes of the special nondiscrimination test for section 401(k) cash or deferred arrangements (discussed in greater detail in Chapter 11), the affiliated service group and leased employee rules for determining the size of the employer's work force (discussed in Chapter 21), and the requirement that the rate of benefit accruals for employees not indicate a pattern of abuse. Obviously, the definition of highly compensated employee is integral to plan operation and continued qualification.

A highly compensated employee is an employee who, during the current year or the preceding year,

1. was a 5 percent owner,
2. received more than $75,000 in compensation,
3. received more than $50,000 in compensation and was in the "top-paid group,"
4. received more than $45,000 in compensation and was an officer.

The dollar amounts are to be indexed to inflation, beginning in 1988.[11] After 1994, the dollar amounts are indexed in increments of $5,000, rounded to the next lower increment.[12]

For this purpose the "top-paid group" includes the top-paid 20 percent of employees of the employer, including all businesses in a controlled group with the employer and all businesses under common control. Certain employees may be excluded in determining the number of employees in the top-paid group, but such employees are included in determining which employees are actually in the top-paid group. The top-paid group excludes employees who

1. have less than 6 months of service,
2. normally work less than 17½ hours per week,
3. normally work 6 months or less per year,
4. are under the age of 21,
5. are nonresident aliens.

Shorter periods than the above (or none at all) may be used, if used consistently for all purposes.[13] For example, a nonresident alien is excluded in determining the

[8]The prior requirements were contained in IRC §410(b)(1).
[9]IRC §414(q).
[10]IRC §401(a)(4).
[11]IRC §414(q)(1).
[12]IRC §415(d).
[13]Temp. Treas. Reg. 1.414(q)-1T, Q&A 9.

number of employees in the top-paid 20 percent of the work force, but the nonresident alien can be considered one of the employees in the top-paid group once its size has been determined.

For a plan not maintained under a collective bargaining agreement, collective bargaining employees are excluded when determining the number of employees in the top-paid group and are excluded from being in the top-paid group, but only if 90 percent or more of the employer's work force is collectively bargained.[14]

A highly compensated employee is one who meets the definition for either the current year or the prior year. But for the current year, employees who are not 5 percent owners may be disregarded if they are not among the 100 highest paid employees.[15] This rule is intended to provide relief for large employers, since it gives them time to determine who are the highly paid employees for purposes of imposing any necessary restrictions on highly compensated employees. Any former employee is also treated as a highly compensated former employee if that individual was a highly compensated employee when he or she separated from service or at any time after age 55.[16]

For example, a new employee of the ABC company acquires 25 percent of the stock of ABC during 1996. Prior to 1996 he did not own any ABC stock. The employee is a highly compensated employee for 1996 because of the stock ownership. Assuming the employee sells the stock in 1998, he will still be a highly compensated employee for 1998 and 1999 on the basis of the stock ownership. His status as a highly compensated employee after 1999 will be based exclusively on his compensation and officer status.

As another example, assume an employee is not at any time a 5 percent owner, an officer, or a member of the top 100 but was a member of the top-paid group for each year and is included in or excluded from the highly compensated groups as specified in Table 4-1.[17]

Now assume the same facts as those in Table 4-1, except that A is a member of the top-paid 100 employees for the 1987 year and 1990 year. The results are listed in Table 4-2.

The number of officers that need to be taken into account must be at least the greater of three employees or 10 percent of all employees, but in no case more than 50 officers. If no officer earns over $45,000, the highest-paid officer must still be included in the top-paid group, a rule that ensures that every work force will have at least one highly compensated employee.[18]

In the case of 5 percent owners and the 10 highest-paid employees, the compensation of certain family members is combined with that of the highly compensated employee as though all of them were a single individual.[19] Family members are not aggregated when determining the top-paid group or the top 100 employees. Thus, assuming there are no 5 percent owners, if employees A, B, C, D, E, F, G, H, I, and

---

[14]Temp. Treas. Reg. 1.414(q)-1T, Q&A 9(b)(1)(iii).
[15]Temp. Treas. Reg. 1.414(q)-1T, Q&A 3(a)(2).
[16]Temp. Treas. Reg. 1.414(q)-1T, Q&A 3.
[17]Temp. Treas. Reg. 1.414(q)-1T, Q&A 3(e).
[18]Temp. Treas. Reg. 1.414(q)-1T, Q&A 10.
[19]Temp. Treas. Reg. 1.414(q)-1T, Q&A 11.

TABLE 4-1 Is A a Highly Compensated Employee? Part One

Year	Salary	Status	Comments
1986	$45,000	n.a.	Although prior to 414(q)'s effective date, 1986 constitutes the look-back year for purposes of determining the highly compensated group for the 1987 determination year.
1987	$80,000	Excluded	Excluded because employee was not an employee with salary higher than $75,000, or $50,000 and in the top-paid group, or was not a highly paid officer for the look-back year (1986).
1988	$80,000	Included	Included because A was an employee with more than $75,000 in compensation for the look-back year (1987).
1989	$45,000	Included	Included because A was an employee with more than $75,000 in compensation for the look-back year (1988).
1990	$45,000	Excluded	Excluded because A was not an employee with more than $75,000 in compensation or more than $50,000 and in the top-paid group for the look-back year (1989).

n.a. Not applicable.

TABLE 4-2 Is A a Highly Compensated Employee? Part Two

Year	Salary	Status	Comments
1986	$45,000	n.a.	Although prior to 414(q)'s effective date, 1986 constitutes the look-back year for purposes of determining the highly compensated group for the 1987 determination year.
1987	$80,000	Included	Included because A was an employee earning more than $75,000 for the determination year (1987) and was in the top-paid 100 employees in that year.
1988	$80,000	Included	Included because A was an employee earning more than $75,000 for the look-back year (1987).
1989	$45,000	Included	Included because A was an employee earning more than $75,000 for the look-back year (1988).
1990	$45,000	Excluded	Excluded even though in top 100 employees during 1990 determination year because A was not an employee earning more than $75,000 or more than $50,000 and in the top-paid group for the look-back year (1989) or for the determination year (1990).

n.a. Not applicable.

J are the top 10 highly compensated employees in the 1988 look-back year and employees F, G, H, I, J, K, L, M, N, and O are the top 10 highly compensated employees in the 1989 determination year, then family aggregation would be required in the case of all 15 such employees (i.e., employees A, B, C, D, E, F, G, H, I, J, K, L, M, N, and O).[20] If employees A, B, and C are family members, and employees N and O are husband and wife, then there are only 12 highly compensated

[20]Temp. Treas. Reg. 1.414(q)-1T, Q&A 11(d).

TABLE 4-3 Ratio Percentage Test

	Number of Employees		Percentage Covered
	Total	Covered	
Highly compensated employees	200	100	50
Non–highly compensated employees	1,000	350	35
Total employees	1,200	450	
Ratio of percentages (35% divided by 50%)			70

employees from this group: ABC, D, E, F, G, H, I, J, K, L, M, and NO. For purposes of identifying highly compensated employees, compensation must include salary deferrals under any 401(k) plan, tax-sheltered annuity, simplified employee plan, or cafeteria plan.[21]

Minimum Coverage Tests

Prior to the Tax Reform Act there were two ways to demonstrate that a plan's coverage was nondiscriminatory: the percentage test and the nondiscriminatory classification rule. The act substantially changed the requirements for demonstrating nondiscriminatory coverage.[22] The new rules are generally more difficult to satisfy.

The coverage of a plan must satisfy one of three rules: the percentage test, the ratio test, or the average benefits percentage test. Each rule is based on the figure of 70 percent but uses the percentage differently.

In satisfying any of the rules, an employer may treat two or more plans as a single plan if they provide comparable benefits, that is, benefits that are not discriminatory.[23] If an employer has only highly compensated employees, its plans are presumed to satisfy the coverage requirements.

A. PERCENTAGE TEST   A plan passes the percentage test if it covers at least 70 percent of all non–highly compensated employees of the employer. This is the simplest of the three tests.

B. RATIO TEST   A plan meets the ratio test if the proportion of all non–highly compensated employees who are covered under the plan is at least 70 percent of the highly compensated employees who are covered. Recognizing that the percentage test is merely the ratio test if 100 percent of the highly compensated employees are covered under the plan, the IRS has merged the two tests into the ratio percentage test.[24] An example of a plan that satisfies this rule is shown in Table 4-3.

---

[21]Temp. Treas. Reg. 1.414(q)-1T, Q&A 13.
[22]IRC §410(b).
[23]The IRS was directed to revise the rules of Rev. Rul. 81-202, which it has used to determine whether plans are comparable.
[24]Treas. Reg. 1.410(b)-2(b)(2).

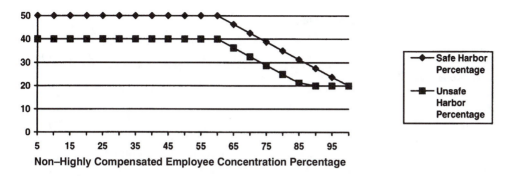

Figure 4-1. Nondiscriminatory classification test. Source: Treas. Reg. 1.410(b)-4(c)(4)(iv).

C. AVERAGE BENEFITS TEST   A plan satisfies the average benefits test only if both of the following requirements are satisfied:

1. The plan covers a nondiscriminatory classification of employees (the "non-discriminatory classification test").
2. The average benefits percentage (the ratio of employer-provided benefits or contributions to the participant's compensation) for non–highly compensated employees is at least 70 percent of the average benefits percentage of highly compensated employees.

The nondiscriminatory classification test is composed of two tests: the reasonable classification test and the nondiscriminatory classification percentage test. Under the reasonable classification test, employees benefiting under the plan must be determined using classifications that are reasonable and in line with objective business criteria. Enumerating employees by name, or a classification that has the effect of enumerating employees by name, will not be considered reasonable. However, groups of employees may be included or excluded on the basis of job category, nature of compensation (e.g., salaried or hourly), geographic location, or other business criteria.[25]

Under the nondiscriminatory classification percentage test, there is a safe harbor (automatic compliance), a facts and circumstances test, and an "unsafe harbor" (automatic failure), depending on the ratio percentage of the plan. The non-discriminatory classification percentage test is essentially similar to the ratio test, in that it compares participation rates of highly compensated employees to participation rates of non–highly compensated employees, except with a lower threshold. A plan satisfies the safe harbor if the ratio percentage equals at least 50 percent, instead of 70 percent, and it may decrease under a sliding scale based on the percentage of non–highly compensated employees in the employer's work force. The higher the percentage of non–highly compensated employees in the work force, the easier it is to pass the safe harbor test. The facts and circumstances test, which is similar to the subjective standard the IRS has been using for many years, applies to the 10 percent corridor between the safe harbor and the unsafe harbor.

As demonstrated by Figure 4-1, when the percentage of non–highly compensated employees in the employer's work force increases, the area of the safe harbor percentage increases. This makes it easier to satisfy the test.

---

[25]Treas. Reg. 1.410(b)-4(b).

TABLE 4-4   Average Benefits Percentage Test

Employee	Compensation ($)	Contributions ($)	Percent
Highly compensated			
A	100,000	25,000	25
B	100,000	15,000	15
Average			20
Non–highly compensated			
C	20,000	2,000	10
D	10,000	1,800	18
Average			14
Ratio of average percentages (14% divided by 20%)			70

For example, assume that an employer has 200 nonexcludable employees, of whom 120 are non–highly compensated employees and 80 are highly compensated employees. The employer maintains a plan that benefits 60 non–highly compensated employees and 72 highly compensated employees. Since 60 percent of the employer's work force is non–highly compensated, the safe harbor percentage is 50 percent and the unsafe harbor percentage is 40 percent. The ratio percentage of the plan is 55.55 percent ($[60/120]/[72/80] = 50\%/90\% = 0.5555$). Accordingly, assuming the plan uses reasonable classification criteria to define eligibility, it satisfies the non–discriminatory classification safe harbor test.

If the plan benefits only 40 non–highly compensated employees, its ratio percentage is 37.03 percent ($[40/120]/[72/80] = 33.33\%/90\% = 0.3703$). Under these facts, the plan's classification is below the unsafe harbor percentage and is thus considered discriminatory. If the plan benefits 45 non–highly compensated employees, the plan's ratio percentage is 41.67 percent ($[45/120]/[72/80] = 37.50\%/90\% = 0.4167$), which is above the unsafe harbor percentage (40 percent) and below the safe harbor percentage (50 percent). The IRS may determine that the classification is nondiscriminatory after considering all the relevant facts and circumstances.[26]

The average benefits percentages do not relate to participants in any particular plan of the employer. Rather the intent is to reveal whether there is nondiscriminatory coverage with respect to the benefits for all employees of the employer (or of a line of business if the line of business exception applies). Thus the average benefit percentages are based on all employees of the employer (or of the line of business, as discussed later), other than the employees specifically excluded, such as nonresident aliens and short-service employees.

To calculate the average benefit percentage one must first calculate the benefit percentage of every employee of the employer (or of the line of business, if applicable), other than the specifically excluded employees. The benefit percentage is the employer-provided contribution or benefit of an employee under all

[26]Treas. Reg. 1.410(b)-4(c)(5).

qualified plans of the employer, expressed as a percentage of compensation. The benefit percentage of every employee must be expressed in terms of either benefits or contributions. Thus if an employer maintains both a defined benefit plan and a defined contribution plan, either the benefits must be converted into a comparable level of contributions or the contributions must be converted into a comparable level of benefits so that there can be a common measure.[27] Table 4-4 provides an example of a defined contribution plan with four participants that satisfies the 70 percent rule of the average benefits percentage test.

Exclusion of Certain Employees from the Tests

In making any of the above tests, nonresident aliens with no earned income from U.S. sources are to be excluded. For a plan not maintained under a collective bargaining agreement, collective bargaining employees are excluded from consideration. Employees not meeting the plan's age and service requirements are also excluded.

Assume an employer maintains three plans. Plan C benefits employees in Division C who satisfy the plan's minimum age of 21 and service condition of 1 year. Plan D benefits employees in Division D who satisfy the plan's minimum age of 18 and service condition of 1 year. Plan E benefits employees in Division E who satisfy the plan's minimum age of 21 and service condition of 6 months. The employer treats Plans D and E as a single plan for purposes of minimum coverage testing. In assessing Plan C under the ratio percentage test or the nondiscriminatory classification test, employees who are not at least age 21 or who do not have at least 1 year of service are excludable employees. In testing Plans D and E, employees who do not satisfy the age and service requirements of either of the two plans are excludable employees. Thus an employee is excludable with respect to Plans D and E only if the employee is not at least age 18 with at least 1 year of service or is not at least age 21 with at least 6 months of service. Thus an employee who is 19 years old and has 11 months of service is excludable. Similarly, an employee who is 17 years old and has performed 2 years of service is excludable.[28]

If a plan includes employees who have not met the minimum age and service requirements permitted by ERISA, the plan may be tested as two plans: a plan benefiting participants who do not meet these legal minimum requirements and a plan benefiting all other employees. Assuming the "plan" benefiting participants that do not meet the age 21 and one year of service requirements passes one of the coverage test detailed above, such employees may be excluded in testing the "plan" benefiting all other employees. However, the employees and their benefits must be included in performing the average benefits percentage test.[29]

For example, an employer maintains Plan J, which does not apply any minimum age or service conditions. Plan J benefits all employees in Division 1 but does not benefit employees in Division 2. Although Plan J has no minimum age or service condition, the employer wants to exclude employees whose age and service are below the permissible minimums. The employer has 110 employees who either do

[27]Treas. Reg. 1.410(b)-5.
[28]Treas. Reg. 1.410(b)-6(b)(4).
[29]Treas. Reg. 1.410(b)-6(b)(3).

not have 1 year of service or are not at least age 21. Of these 110 employees, 10 are highly compensated employees and 100 are non–highly compensated employees. Five of these highly compensated employees, or 50 percent, work in Division 1 and thus benefit under Plan J. Thirty-five of these non–highly compensated employees, or 35 percent, work in Division 1 and thus benefit under Plan J. Plan J satisfies the ratio percentage test with respect to employees who do not satisfy the greatest permissible minimum age and service requirement because the ratio percentage of that group of employees is 70 percent. Thus in determining whether or not Plan J satisfies the minimum coverage requirements, the 110 employees may be treated as excludable employees.[30]

Plan Aggregation and Disaggregation

As mentioned above, two or more plans may be aggregated for minimum coverage testing purposes, as long as the benefits provided by the combined plans are nondiscriminatory. Note that combining the benefits provided by other plans for purposes of performing the average benefits test is not considered "aggregation," which otherwise requires combining the plans for all nondiscrimination testing purposes. Another rule permits an employer to test one plan as two separate plans, to "disaggregate" the plan, in other words. Any plan can be disaggregated at the election of the plan sponsor and tested as two or more separate plans.

Indeed, certain types of plans must be disaggregated. A plan benefiting employees covered by a collective bargaining agreement and employees not included in the bargaining unit must be treated as two separate plans. Furthermore, a plan that includes a qualified cash or deferred arrangement under section 401(k) must be split into the 401(k) plan and the remaining (e.g., profit-sharing) plan. A similar rule applies to plans containing matching employer contributions or after-tax employee contributions tested under section 401(m). Plans that are mandatorily disaggregated cannot be aggregated for testing purposes.[31] An employer sponsoring a profit-sharing plan that covers both collectively bargained employees and non–collectively bargained employees and that also contains 401(k) cash or deferred arrangement and receives matching contributions has six plans for testing purposes: a union profit-sharing plan, a union 401(k) plan, a union 401(m) plan, a nonunion profit-sharing plan, a nonunion 401(k) plan, and a nonunion 401(m) plan. The minimum coverage testing of these six plans is not significantly more complicated, however, than testing the one "actual" plan that the employer sponsors since all the union employees are in all the union plans and all the nonunion employees are in all the nonunion plans. The union and nonunion plans will be considered to satisfy the minimum coverage tests since all nonexcludable employees benefit from each set of plans.

Minimum Number of Participants

Every plan must cover at least 50 participants, or 40 percent of all employees if it has fewer than 50 participants.[32] Employees who are eligible to contribute under

---

[30]Treas. Reg. 1.410(b)-6(b)(4).
[31]Treas. Reg. 1.410(b)-7.
[32]IRC §401(a)(26).

the plan or to have contributions made for them are considered to be covered even if they choose not to participate. For this requirement comparable plans may not be aggregated; each plan must satisfy the requirement separately.[33]

In making the 40 percent test, the employer is to exclude the same groups as in other coverage tests, namely, nonresident aliens, employees not satisfying the minimum age and service requirements, and the like. However, the line of business exception does not apply to the 40 percent test.[34]

For example, an employer has 100 employees and maintains both a defined benefit plan and a defined contribution plan. The defined benefit plan provides that employees who have not completed 1 year of service are not eligible to participate while the defined contribution plan has no minimum age or service requirement. Twenty of the employees do not meet the minimum service requirement under the defined benefit plan. Each plan satisfies the ratio percentage test under the minimum coverage requirements. In testing the defined benefit plan to determine whether it satisfies the minimum participation requirements, the 20 employees not meeting the minimum age and service requirement under the defined benefit plan are treated as excludable employees. In testing the defined contribution plan to determine whether it satisfies the minimum participation requirements, no employees are treated as excludable employees because that plan does not have a minimum age or service requirement.[35]

A defined benefit plan must also have at least 50 employees or 40 percent of the employer's work force with meaningful benefits under the plan. This requirement, which is known as the "prior benefit structure" test and which can also be satisfied if at least 50 employees or 40 percent of the employees are currently accruing meaningful benefits under the plan, is designed to ensure that the plan is not frozen and maintained as essentially an individual account plan for a small number of participants.

Several special rules exist that may assist a plan in satisfying the minimum participation standard. A plan benefiting only non–highly compensated employees and a defined benefit plan subject to PBGC benefit insurance that does not have sufficient assets to terminate are automatically deemed to satisfy the minimum participation requirements. A qualified cash or deferred arrangement under section 401(k) sponsored by employers that include government or tax-exempt entities need allow only 95 percent of those employees who are not precluded from eligibility to participate in the plan. For example, a large tax-exempt hospital with a small for-profit subsidiary clinic or pharmacy may sponsor a 401(k) plan for the for-profit subsidiary. The employees of the tax-exempt hospital are precluded by law from participating in the 401(k) plan, so the special rule allows the hospital to maintain the plan for only the subsidiary.

A transition rule allows plans maintained by employers involved in corporate acquisitions or dispositions sufficient time following the transaction to bring a plan into compliance. A plan that satisfies the minimum participation rules prior to the

---

[33]Treas. Reg. 1.401(a)(26)-2(c).
[34]Treas. Reg. 1.401(a)(26)-6.
[35]Treas. Reg. 1.401(a)(26)-6(b)(2).

corporate transaction is deemed to continue satisfying the rules for the current plan year and the plan year following the corporate acquisition or disposition.

A collectively bargained plan covering only bargaining employees may exclude nonbargaining employees in making the 40 percent test, essentially guaranteeing that such plans will satisfy the minimum participation standard.[36] Multiemployer plans are generally exempt from the minimum participation requirement.[37]

---

[36]Treas. Reg. 1.401(a)(26)-6(b)(4).
[37]Treas. Reg. 1.401(a)(26)-1(b)(2).

Chapter 5
Nondiscrimination Requirements

As a matter of general tax policy, tax incentives are granted to stimulate desired behavior or to deter undesired behavior. The various tax incentives granted to employer-sponsored retirement plans are intended to stimulate the creation of broadly based retirement savings programs for working individuals. A fundamental requirement of a tax-favored retirement plan is that the benefits or contributions under the plan must not favor highly compensated employees. Otherwise employers would be able to provide benefits only to highly compensated employees or could provide significant benefits to such employees and *de minimis* benefits to other employees. This is hardly the behavior Congress intended in establishing the tax incentives for retirement plans. Accordingly, the nondiscrimination rules prohibit plan benefits or contributions from favoring highly compensated employees.

Although the statement that plan benefits or contributions must not discriminate in favor of highly compensated employees appears easy enough to understand, the rules enforcing that requirement are among the most complex in the tax system. The rules are complex because of the multitude of plan designs used by plan sponsors, the variety of retirement income policies adopted by different employers, and the creative ways a small number of benefits professionals and employers have devised to avoid complying with the nondiscrimination standards.

After enactment of the Tax Reform Act of 1986, the IRS commenced a massive and comprehensive revision and reexamination of the nondiscrimination requirements for qualified retirement plans. One purpose of the revision was to provide comprehensive guidance that would allow plan sponsors and pension professionals to determine whether a plan was nondiscriminatory under specific, objective standards. This marked a significant break from the prior nondiscrimination standards, which combined objective criteria with subjective facts and circumstances standards.

A project of such scope consumed more resources, especially time, than any prior pension regulatory effort of the IRS. Owing to the creativity of pension professionals, the disparate needs of employers and other plan sponsors, and the ensuing wide variety of plan designs, attempting to develop objective criteria to cover all types of plans in all types of situations was a herculean task. Only time will tell whether the result was worth the effort.

In addition, establishing exclusively objective nondiscrimination standards proved to be an elusive goal. Even if a plan complies with all the different technical requirements of the nondiscrimination rules, the plan must still pass a final "smell test." The complexity and variety of potential plan designs effectively mandates a final subjective requirement that the plan be implemented without favoring highly compensated employees. Accordingly, the nondiscrimination rules must be interpreted "in a reasonable manner consistent with the purpose of preventing discrimination in favor of highly compensated employees."[1] Though reasonableness is in the eye of the beholder, by associating a reasonable interpretation standard with a nondiscriminatory purpose principle, government regulators seek to limit the use of clever interpretations to circumvent the rules.

As will be seen from a close examination of the various nondiscriminatory benefits standards, the general nondiscrimination rule and the minimum coverage rules discussed in Chapter 4 form a single, coordinated nondiscrimination rule. As a result, in general the same plan year, employer, and group of employees must be used to satisfy both standards.[2]

The nondiscrimination standards have three basic requirements. The best known and most complex requirement is that benefits or contributions must not discriminate in favor of highly compensated employees. Other nondiscrimination standards prohibit offering optional forms of benefits, ancillary benefits, or other rights or features in a discriminatory manner, and that plan amendments and terminations cannot discriminate in favor of highly compensated employees.

The nondiscrimination standards apply not only to active employees but also to former employees. Since the opportunities to favor former highly compensated employees[3] are obviously different from the opportunities to favor active highly compensated employees, separate nondiscrimination testing standards exist for former employees.

If a plan fails to meet one of the nondiscrimination requirements, certain retroactive corrections are permitted. As to be expected in IRS regulations permitting retroactive changes to a plan, there are specific guidelines for the retroactive correction of discriminatory events.

Nondiscrimination in Contributions or Benefits

There are two ways to ensure that a plan's contributions or benefits do not discriminate: by designing a plan formula that satisfies a "safe harbor" rule, or by testing the actual benefits accrued or contributions allocated to participants under the plan. The first method simply looks at the form of the plan, while the second is an ongoing process requiring periodic data collection and testing. Not surprisingly, many employers, especially small and midsized employers seeking to minimize plan administration expenses, prefer to use the safe harbor to demonstrate compliance with the nondiscriminatory benefits requirement.

Safe Harbors

Different safe harbors are available for defined benefit plans using both unit credit and fractional accrual methods and for defined contribution plans allocating

---

[1] Treas. Reg. 1.401(a)(4)-1(c)(2).
[2] Treas. Reg. 1.401(a)(4)-1(c)(4).
[3] The IRS uses the term *highly compensated former employee*. Since this implies the former employee is currently highly compensated, a situation unlikely to occur, the phrase *former highly compensated employee* will be used in this book.

contributions uniformly based on compensation or weighting the allocation for age and/or service. The IRS uses the term *safe harbor* to describe a method of demonstrating compliance with any type of requirement (in this case, the non-discriminatory benefits or contributions requirement) deemed satisfactory. Other methods of complying may be available, but they will either require more onerous testing, such as the general nondiscrimination test discussed later in this chapter, or contain an element of uncertainty, as in the case of a facts and circumstances determination of compliance.

A general requirement under any of the safe harbors is uniform treatment of all participants under the plan. For example, a uniform normal retirement age must be used and any subsidized early retirement benefits or joint and survivor benefits must be uniformly available to substantially all employees.[4]

The first safe harbor applies to unit credit plans, which provide a specific benefit for each year of service under a uniform benefit formula.[5] Benefit accruals should generally be either level (i.e., the same percentage of pay or dollar amount) for all years of service or based on a percentage of pay that varies with years of service in a manner that satisfies the 133⅓ percent accrual rule under section 411(b)(1)(B). The 133⅓ percent accrual rule permits the rate of benefit accrual to increase as participants earn more service, as long as any year's accrual rate under the plan formula does not exceed any prior year's rate by more than 133⅓ percent. For example, a plan benefit formula of 1 percent of a participant's final five times service (maximum 30 years), or a plan benefit formula of .75 percent of pay for each of the first 10 years of service, plus 1.00 percent of pay for each year of service in excess of ten are safe harbor benefit formulas. However, a benefit formula of .75 percent of final five for each year of service prior to age 50, and 1.00 percent of final five for each year of service after age 50 would not be a safe harbor formula, since the change in the accrual rate is based upon age and not service.

The second safe harbor for defined benefit plans applies to plans using the fractional accrual rule, in which participants accrue benefits ratably over their service career.[6] Different types of benefit formulas are eligible for the fractional accrual rule safe harbor, including certain unit credit-type formulas in which no employee can accrue a benefit in a year equal to a rate that exceeds 133⅓ percent of the rate applicable to any other employee (excluding employees with more than 33 years of service). For example, a plan benefit formula under which a participant accrues a benefit of .75 percent of final average compensation for the first 20 years of projected service, plus 1.25 percent of final average compensation for projected service in excess of 20 years, multiplied by the ratio of service to projected service to normal retirement age, satisfies the fractional accrual unit credit safe harbor. While 1.25 percent is more than 133⅓ percent of .75 percent, whether a plan satisfies the safe harbor is determined on the basis of the rate at which employees actually accrue benefits.

As shown in Table 5-1, the lowest benefit that an employee can accrue in any plan year is .75 percent of final average compensation (this is the case for any employee

---

[4]Treas. Reg. 1.401(a)(4)-3(b)(2).
[5]Treas. Reg. 1.401(a)(4)-3(b)(3)(i).
[6]Treas. Reg. 1.401(a)(4)-3(b)(4).

TABLE 5-1   Fractional Accrual Unit Credit Safe Harbor

Employees with 20 years of projected service or less	.75 percent annual accrual rate
Employees with 33 years of projected service	$(.75 \times 20 \text{ years}) + (1.25 \times 13 \text{ years})/33$ years of projected service = .947 annual accrual rate

with 20 or fewer years of projected service to normal retirement age). The greatest benefit that any employee with 33 years or less of projected service to normal retirement age can accrue in any plan year is .947 percent (this is the case for an employee with 33 years of projected service to normal retirement, determined by accruing .75 percent of final average compensation for 20 years and 1.25 percent of final average compensation for 13 years, and dividing the product by 33 years of projected service). Since .947 percent is not more than 133⅓ percent of .75 percent, the formula satisfies the fractional accrual unit credit safe harbor.

An alternative safe harbor is available for plans using fractional accrual flat benefit formulas in which the full flat benefit can be accrued with less than 25 years of service. In such cases, the average accrual rates for non–highly compensated employees must be at least 70 percent of the average accrual rates for highly compensated employees.[7] While this rule is obviously not a "true" safe harbor, since data collection and testing are required, averaging the accrual rates of the highly and non–highly compensated employees can sometimes result in an easier test to satisfy than the general nondiscrimination test. As discussed below, the general nondiscrimination test examines the individual accrual rates of each highly compensated employee, an often precarious testing methodology for plan sponsors. Testing the average accrual rates of employees helps smooth out testing anomalies, such as an unusually high accrual rate in one year for a specific highly compensated employee who, for example, may have satisfied eligibility criteria for a subsidized early retirement benefit.

Two safe harbors are available for defined contribution plans. The first safe harbor covers plans that provide a uniform percentage of compensation (or dollar amount) to every employee under the plan.[8] This is the traditional "plain vanilla" allocation formula of defined contribution plans in which participants receive annual allocations of 1 percent, or 2 percent, or some other fixed percentage of pay. Another safe harbor involves plans (other than employee stock ownership plans [ESOPs]) that weight the allocation for items other than compensation.[9] Each employee's allocation is based on the number of "points" assigned to the employee, which are in turn on the employee's compensation, age, and/or years of service. In addition, the average allocation rate for highly compensated employees cannot exceed the average allocation rate for non–highly compensated employees. Again, the averaging of allocation rates can expedite testing by eliminating testing anomalies.

[7]Treas. Reg. 1.401(a)(4)-3(b)(4).
[8]Treas. Reg. 1.401(a)(4)-2(b)(2)(i).
[9]Treas. Reg. 1.401(a)(4)-2(b)(3)(i).

General Test

A plan that does not satisfy one of the safe harbors must pass the general test to demonstrate nondiscrimination. Under this test, a normal and most valuable rate (for defined benefit plans) or an allocation rate (for defined contribution plans) is determined for each employee. Employees are then grouped according to their accrual or allocation rates, and each such group is tested to see if it covers a nondiscriminatory group. A plan passes the general test if each rate group satisfies the coverage rules.[10]

Separate rate groups exist for each highly compensated participant in the plan. These groups consist of that highly compensated participant and all other participants (whether highly or non–highly compensated) with equal or greater normal and most valuable accrual rates. Employees may be included in more than one rate group.[11]

The normal accrual rate is defined as the increase in the employee's accrued benefit during a measurement period selected by the plan sponsor.[12] This period can be either the current plan year, the employee's total period of service to date, or the employee's total period of service projected to normal retirement age, divided by the employee's service during the period selected.[13] The most valuable accrual rate is the increase in the employee's largest normalized benefit during the selected period, again divided by the employee's testing service during the period.[14]

Both normal and most valuable accrual rates must be determined consistently for all employees for the plan year, including using the same measurement period for all employees. Potential plan benefits cannot be determined by assuming that an employee's compensation will increase or the employee will terminate employment before attaining the testing age.[15]

Allocation rates and normal and most valuable accrual rates can be "grouped" or rounded within a specified range for testing purposes, provided that in general the allocation or accrual rates of highly compensated employees within the range are not significantly higher than the allocation or accrual rates of non–highly compensated employees in the range. Allocation rates that fall within 5 percent of a midpoint or within an increment of .5 percent may be grouped and considered to be equal for testing purposes.[16] Normal accrual rates that fall within 5 percent of a midpoint or within an increment of .1 percent may be grouped and considered to be equal for testing purposes. Most valuable accrual rates that fall within 15 percent of a midpoint or within an increment of .1 percent (assuming accrual rates are determined as a percentage of average annual compensation) may be grouped.[17]

---

[10]Treas. Reg. 1.401(a)(4)-3(c)(1).
[11]Ibid.
[12]Treas. Reg. 1.401(a)(4)-3(d)(1)(ii).
[13]Treas. Reg. 1.401(a)(4)-3(d)(1)(iii).
[14]Treas. Reg. 1.401(a)(4)-3(d)(1)(ii).
[15]Treas. Reg. 1.401(a)(4)-3(d)(2).
[16]Treas. Reg. 1.401(a)(4)-2(c)(2)(v).
[17]Treas. Reg. 1.401(a)(4)-3(d)(3)(ii).

The following examples illustrate these groupings.

Allocation Rates

Grouping Method	Rate
.5 percent increment	4.25 percent $< x <$ 4.75 percent
.5 percent increment	4.75 percent $< x <$ 5.25 percent
5 percent of midpoint	5.25 percent $< x <$ 5.81 percent
5 percent of midpoint	5.81 percent $< x <$ 6.43 percent

Normal Accrual Rates

Grouping Method	Rate
.1 percent increment	.85 percent $< x <$ .95 percent
.1 percent increment	.95 percent $< x <$ 1.05 percent
5 percent of midpoint	1.05 percent $< x <$ 1.16 percent
5 percent of midpoint	1.16 percent $< x <$ 1.28 pecent

Most Valuable Accrual Rates

Grouping Method	Rate
.1 percent increment	.15 percent $< x <$ .25 percent
.1 percent increment	.25 percent $< x <$ .35 percent
15 percent of midpoint	.35 percent $< x <$ .47 percent
15 percent of midpoint	.47 percent $< x <$ .63 percent
15 percent of midpoint	.63 percent $< x <$ .85 percent

As the examples show, the .1 percent increment is the more beneficial grouping method only among very low accrual rates. In addition, grouping most valuable accrual rates using the 15 percent of midpoint method allows for significantly larger groupings of most valuable accrual rates at higher accrual rates.

To better understand how the general test operates and how its accrual rates and grouping rules are determined, consider the following example. An employer has 1,100 nonexcludable employees: N1 through N1,000, who are non–highly compensated employees; and HI through H100, who are highly compensated employees. The employer maintains a defined benefit plan for all of these nonexcludable employees. The normal and most valuable accrual rates for the employees in the plan for a plan year are listed in Table 5-2.

There are 100 rate groups in the defined benefit plan because there are 100 highly compensated employees in the plan. Rate group 1 consists of HI and all those employees who have a normal accrual rate greater than or equal to HI's normal accrual rate (1.5 percent) and who also have a most valuable accrual rate greater than or equal to HI's most valuable accrual rate (2.0 percent). Thus rate group 1 consists of HI through H100 and N101 through N1,000.

TABLE 5-2   Sample General Test

Employee	Normal Accrual Rate	Most Valuable Accrual Rate
N1 through N100	1.0	1.40
N101 through N500	1.5	3.00
N501 through N750	2.0	2.65
N751 through N1,000	2.3	2.80
H1 through H50	1.5	2.00
H51 through H100	2.0	2.65

Rate group 1 satisfies a minimum coverage test because the ratio percentage of the rate group is 90 percent, that is, 90 percent (the percentage of all non–highly compensated nonexcludable employees who are in the rate group) divided by 100 percent (the percentage of all highly compensated nonexcludable employees who are in the rate group). Because HI through H50 have the same normal accrual rates and the same most valuable accrual rates, the rate group with respect to each of those employees is identical. Thus because rate group 1 satisfies the minimum coverage requirements, rate groups 2 through 50 also satisfy the minimum coverage requirements.

Rate group 51 consists of H51 and all those employees who have a normal accrual rate greater than or equal to H51's normal accrual rate (2.0 percent) and who also have a most valuable accrual rate greater than or equal to H51's most valuable accrual rate (2.65 percent). Thus rate group 51 consists of H51 through H100 and N501 through N1,000. Note that even though N101 through N500 have a most valuable accrual rate (3.0 percent) greater than H51's most valuable accrual rate (2.65 percent), they are not included in this rate group because their normal accrual rate (1.5 percent) is less than H51's normal accrual rate (2.0 percent).

Rate group 51 satisfies a minimum coverage test because the ratio percentage of the rate group is 100 percent, that is, 50 percent (the percentage of all non–highly compensated nonexcludable employees who are in the rate group) divided by 50 percent (the percentage of all highly compensated nonexcludable employees who are in the rate group). Because H51 through H100 have the same normal accrual rates and the same most valuable accrual rates, the rate group with respect to each of those employees is identical. Thus because rate group 51 satisfies the minimum coverage requirements, rate groups 52 through 100 also satisfy the minimum coverage requirements.

Accordingly, the employer-provided benefits under this plan are nondiscriminatory in amount because each rate group under the plan satisfies a minimum coverage test.[18]

While this example, taken straight from the IRS regulations, is a good illustration of the mechanics of the general test, it fails to show the true complexity of the general test. The example shows a plan with 1,100 participants, but in effect there are only two rate groups. This result is fairly implausible. The plan in the example clearly does not integrate benefits with Social Security, or there would be

---

[18]Treas. Reg. 1.401(a)(4)-3(c)(4).

significantly more rate groups. As a practical matter, a plan using the general test is more likely to be integrating benefits with Social Security benefits than not.

A better example would be an illustration of a real general test of an actual plan. When a defined benefit plan using the general nondiscrimination test requests a determination letter from the IRS, a demonstration must be submitted that the plan passes the general test as part of the request.[19] As part of this demonstration, the sponsor must indicate the method used for determining accrual rates, whether the plan is imputing disparity, how accrual rates are grouped, the actuarial assumptions used in normalizing the accrual rates, whether accruals after normal retirement age or as part of an early retirement window are taken into account, and the definition of compensation used for determining accrual rates.

Table 5-3 is an example of a demonstration submitted in a determination letter request for a defined benefit plan that covers the employees of one division of a diversified manufacturing and distributing employer. The plan covers 202 employees and imputes disparity in determining accrual rates. The benefits provided by the employer to all employees satisfies the average benefits percentage test, so the rate groups only have to satisfy the nondiscriminatory classification test instead of the ratio percentage test. Since the work force of the employer is highly skewed toward non–highly compensated employees, the non–highly compensated employee concentration is 90 percent. Thus the rate groups are able to pass the nondiscriminatory classification test with a ratio of 27.5 percent. Accrual rates are determined using a 7.5 percent interest rate and the 1983 GAM mortality table.

The normal and most valuable accrual rates have already been determined using these assumptions and grouped to the level that will maximize the number of employees in each grouping. The rate groups are presented in a tabular format, with the ratio percentage of the highly compensated and non–highly compensated employees already determined. The numbers presented in the table are the ratio percentage of each rate group, that is, the percentage of non–highly compensated employees participating in the plan as a percentage of the percentage of highly compensated employees participating in the plan.

In addition to noting the number of rate groups that have to be tested, it is also important to recognize that for this employer only the rate groups based on the highest normal accrual rate are close to the safe harbor threshold. The highest most valuable accrual rate appears reasonably throughout the population, but the highest normal accrual rate is more skewed toward the highly compensated employees than any of the other accrual rates. While not uncommon, this is not always the case. Normal accrual rates often increase for highly compensated employees near the end of their service careers because salary increases augment prior service benefits, and highly compensated employees usually have significantly longer service careers than non–highly compensated employees. The compensation increase for an executive provides for a high accrual rate since the higher compensation not only causes a large benefit to be accrued for the current year, but the increase in prior years' benefit accruals is also counted.

---

[19]Rev. Proc. 93-39, Demonstration 6.

TABLE 5-3   Demonstration of General Nondiscrimination Test for Sample Employer (percent)

	Range of Normal Accrual Rates										
Most Valuable Accrual Rates	0.00 to 0.10	0.10 to 0.20	0.20 to 0.30	0.30 to 0.40	0.40 to 0.50	0.50 to 0.60	0.60 to 0.70	0.70 to 0.80	0.80 to 0.90	0.90 to 1.00	1.00 to 1.10
0.00–0.10	100.0	237.6	237.6	237.6	237.6	237.6	237.6	237.6	237.6	237.6	237.6
0.10–0.20	237.6	237.6	237.6	237.6	237.6	237.6	237.6	237.6	237.6	237.6	237.6
0.20–0.30	237.6	237.6	237.6	238.6	237.6	237.6	237.6	237.6	237.6	237.6	237.6
0.30–0.40	237.6	237.6	237.6	237.6	237.6	237.6	237.6	237.6	237.6	237.6	237.6
0.40–0.50	237.6	237.6	237.6	237.6	237.6	237.6	237.6	237.6	237.6	237.6	237.6
0.50–0.60	237.6	237.6	237.6	237.6	237.6	237.6	237.6	237.6	237.6	237.6	237.6
0.60–0.70	237.6	237.6	237.6	237.6	237.6	237.6	237.6	237.6	237.6	237.6	237.6
0.70–0.80	237.6	237.6	237.6	237.6	237.6	237.6	237.6	237.6	237.6	237.6	237.6
0.80–0.90	237.6	237.6	237.6	237.6	237.6	237.6	237.6	237.6	237.6	237.6	237.6
0.90–1.00	237.6	237.6	237.6	237.6	237.6	237.6	237.6	237.6	237.6	237.6	237.6
1.00–1.35	237.6	237.6	237.6	237.6	237.6	237.6	237.6	237.6	237.6	237.6	237.6
1.35–1.89	237.6	237.6	237.6	237.6	237.6	237.6	237.6	237.6	237.6	237.6	237.6
1.89–2.47	248.8	248.8	248.8	248.8	248.8	248.8	248.8	248.8	248.8	248.8	248.8
2.47–3.35	282.0	282.0	282.0	282.0	282.0	282.0	282.0	282.0	282.0	282.0	282.0

	Range of Normal Accrual Rates									
Most Valuable Accrual Rate	1.10 to 1.21	1.21 to 1.33	1.33 to 1.47	1.47 to 1.63	1.63 to 1.81	1.81 to 2.00	2.00 to 2.20	2.20 to 2.44	2.44 to 2.70	2.70 to 2.98	2.98 to 3.30
0.00–0.10	237.6	237.6	237.6	243.2	261.1	251.9	217.9	190.8	36.3	76.3	28.6
0.10–0.20	237.6	237.6	237.6	243.2	261.1	251.9	217.9	190.8	36.3	76.3	28.6
0.20–0.30	237.6	237.6	237.6	243.2	261.1	251.9	217.9	190.8	36.3	76.3	28.6
0.30–0.40	237.6	237.6	237.6	243.2	261.1	251.9	217.9	190.8	36.3	76.3	28.6
0.40–0.50	237.6	237.6	237.6	243.2	261.1	251.9	217.9	190.8	36.3	76.3	28.6
0.50–0.60	237.6	237.6	237.6	243.2	261.1	251.9	217.9	190.8	36.3	76.3	28.6
0.60–0.70	237.6	237.6	237.6	243.2	261.1	251.9	217.9	190.8	36.3	76.3	28.6
0.70–0.80	237.6	237.6	237.6	243.2	261.1	251.9	217.9	190.8	36.3	76.3	28.6
0.80–0.90	237.6	237.6	237.6	243.2	261.1	251.9	217.9	190.8	36.3	76.3	28.6
0.90–1.00	237.6	237.6	237.6	243.2	261.1	251.9	217.9	190.8	36.3	76.3	28.6
1.35–1.89	237.6	237.6	237.6	243.2	261.1	251.9	217.9	190.8	36.3	76.3	28.6
1.89–2.47	248.8	248.8	248.8	243.2	261.1	251.9	217.9	190.8	36.3	76.3	28.6
2.47–3.35	248.8	282.0	282.0	282.0	282.0	282.0	249.6	214.2	36.3	76.3	28.6

Special Testing Rules

Plan Restructuring

A plan may be restructured into component plans organized around employee groups. If each such component plan satisfies both the minimum coverage requirements and the nondiscrimination rules, the plan satisfies section 401(a)(4).[20] A plan may be restructured into employee groups using any criteria, regardless of whether the classification would satisfy the reasonableness requirement under the nondiscriminatory classification test (see Chapter 3 for more details).[21]

A component plan must independently satisfy either the ratio percentage test or the average benefits test, including both the nondiscriminatory classification test and the average benefits percentage test.[22] This restructuring can provide significant flexibility for the plan sponsor in nondiscrimination testing. One plan can be divided into two or more plans, or two or more plans can be aggregated and then divided into completely new plan configurations. The formal structure of the plans is irrelevant for nondiscrimination testing as long as at least one possible configuration can satisfy the requirements.

Plan Aggregation

If two or more plans are allowed to aggregate to satisfy certain aspects of the minimum coverage tests, they also must be aggregated for nondiscrimination testing.[23] Similarly, plans aggregated for nondiscrimination testing must be aggregated for minimum coverage purposes.[24] It is important to note that merely because plan benefits are being considered in testing another plan under the average benefits percentage test (discussed in more detail in Chapter 3) the plans do not have to be aggregated for nondiscrimination testing.

If the plans that are aggregated are all of the same type (e.g., all defined benefit plans or all defined contribution plans), they are treated as a single plan and are tested under the rules applicable to plans of that type.[25] If the plans that are aggregated contain both defined benefit and defined contribution plans, the aggregate plan must be tested under special "DB/DC plan" rules.[26]

A DB/DC plan is generally tested with the aid of aggregate normal and aggregate most valuable accrual rates or on aggregate allocation rates.[27] In determining accrual rates, special optional rules must be applied consistently to all employees. For example, measurement periods that include future periods, which are not permitted when testing defined contribution plans, may not be used in testing a DB/DC plan on either a benefits or a contributions basis.[28]

---

[20]Treas. Reg. 1.401(a)(4)-9(c)(1).
[21]Treas. Reg. 1.401(a)(4)-9(c)(2).
[22]Treas. Reg. 1.401(a)(4)-9(c)(4)(i).
[23]Treas. Reg. 1.401(a)(4)-9(a)
[24]Treas. Reg. 1.410(b)-7(d)(1).
[25]Treas. Reg. 1.401(a)(4)-9(a).
[26]Treas. Reg. 1.401(a)(4)-9(b)(2).
[27]Treas. Reg. 1.401(a)(4)-9(b)(2)(i).
[28]Treas. Reg. 1.401(a)(4)-8(b)(2).

Conversion of Contributions and Benefits

The rules governing conversion of contributions and benefits are primarily intended for use in aggregating defined contribution plans with defined benefit plans. However, it is also possible to use these principles to test defined contribution plans under defined benefit rules, and vice versa. These rules also apply in the average benefit test, which involves both defined benefit and defined contribution plans.[29]

When testing a defined contribution plan as a defined benefit plan, the basic procedure is to convert contributions (other than contributions to an ESOP, §§401(k) or 401(m) plan) into benefit accrual rates and then test the accrual rates as one would for a typical defined benefit test.[30] The resulting "equivalent benefit accrual rates" are treated as both normal accrual rates and most valuable accrual rates. The basic procedure in determining equivalent accrual rates is to project the increase in the employee's account balance during the measurement period to the testing age (usually age 65) using a standard interest rate[31] (between 7.5 percent and 8.5 percent), and then to convert to a single life annuity using a reasonable mortality table and 7.5 percent to 8.5 percent interest. The result is divided by the employee's testing compensation and, if necessary, the accrual rate can consider integration of benefits by adding the appropriate permitted disparity factor. Often this factor is .65 percent, but it depends on the accrual rate above and the employee's Social Security retirement age. For employees earning more than covered compensation, the rate is reduced in a reasonable fashion.

When testing a defined benefit plan as a defined contribution plan, the annual employer-provided accrual rate generally must be determined by comparing the year-end accrued benefit to the beginning-of-year accrued benefit. Both normal and most valuable accrual rates need to be tested.[32] The present value of each of these accrued benefits for the year divided by compensation is then treated as a normal and most valuable allocation rate. Clearly, the equivalent contribution rates for relatively younger employees will be small and for relatively older employees, contribution rates will be large.

Again, the present value must be calculated using a "standard" mortality table and interest rate (i.e., between 7.5 percent and 8.5 percent). The interest rate used can differ between the preretirement and postretirement periods. The use of a mortality assumption prior to testing age is prohibited.

Nondiscrimination in Plan Amendments

A plan amendment or series of plan amendments is considered nondiscriminatory if the timing of the amendment does not discriminate significantly in favor of highly compensated employees. For this purpose a plan amendment includes the establishment or termination of a plan and any change in benefits, rights, or features under a plan. A plan amendment also includes the grant of past service.[33]

[29]Treas. Reg. 1.401(a)(4)-8(a).
[30]Treas. Reg. 1.401(a)(4)-8(b).
[31]Treas. Reg. 1.401(a)(4)-12.
[32]Treas. Reg. 1.401(a)(4)-8(c)(1).
[33]Treas. Reg. 1.401(a)(4)-5(a)(1).

The focus of this nondiscrimination analysis is whether the *timing* of the plan amendment, rather than its *effect*, discriminates significantly in favor of highly compensated employees. The effect of the amendment, such as the amount of benefits or contributions granted employees, is considered in the other non-discrimination tests discussed in this chapter.

Whether the timing of a plan amendment or series of plan amendments discriminates significantly in favor of highly compensated employees can be determined by examining facts and circumstances. These include (but are not limited to) the following:

- the relative numbers of current and former highly compensated employees and non–highly compensated employees affected by the plan amendment,
- the relative length of service of current and former highly compensated employees and non–highly compensated employees,
- the length of time the plan or plan provision being amended has been in effect,
- the turnover of employees prior to the plan amendment,
- the relative accrued benefits of current and former highly compensated employees and non–highly compensated employees before and after the plan amendment; and
- any additional benefits provided to current and former highly compensated employees and non–highly compensated employees under other plans (including plans of other employers, if relevant).

For an amendment that grants past service, the facts and circumstances also include the benefits that employees and former employees who do not benefit under the plan amendment would have received had the plan, as amended, been in effect throughout the period for which the past service is granted.[34] The timing of an amendment that grants past service is generally deemed not to discriminate significantly in favor of highly compensated employees if the period for which the past service is granted does not exceed the five years immediately preceding the year the amendment becomes effective. However, the safe harbor does not apply if the grant of past service is part of a pattern of amendments that is discriminatory.[35] Note that if an amendment that grants past service does not qualify for the safe harbor, it still may be nondiscriminatory owing to the facts and circumstances of the situation.

Nondiscrimination in Optional Benefits, Rights, and Features

In general, optional forms of benefits, ancillary benefits, and other rights or features under a plan must be tested on the basis of current availability and effective availability. Although each benefit, right, and feature must separately satisfy the nondiscriminatory availability requirements, testing can be done after permissively aggregating two or more benefits, rights, or features. One of the benefits, rights, or features aggregated must be inherently of equal or greater value than the other

[34]Treas. Reg. 1.401(a)(4)-5(a)(2).
[35]Treas. Reg. 1.401(a)(4)-5(a)(3).

benefits, rights, or features. That benefit, right, or feature of inherently equal or greater value must separately satisfy the regulation's requirements.[36]

Because of the inherently greater value requirement, permissive aggregation will apparently only work with benefits, rights, or features that are already substantially identical, such as two lump-sum optional forms of benefits calculated using different interest rates. It is unclear how to prove that a joint and survivor annuity, for example, is inherently more valuable than a plan loan provision.

Current Availability

Generally, the current availability standard requires that the group of employees to whom the benefit, right, or feature is available must satisfy the ratio percentage test or the nondiscriminatory classification test of section 410(b).[37] The average benefits percentage test does not apply for this purpose.[38]

Whether a benefit is currently available to an employee is normally determined on a facts and circumstances basis for each employee. However, age and service conditions are disregarded when testing optional forms of benefits or a Social Security supplement. Therefore, early retirement benefits are considered currently available to all employees who could qualify for such benefits, not just those employees who have already earned the benefit. In addition, employees who will not be able to qualify for the benefit because of age or service limitations, such as an employee who commences participation at age 46 in a plan with an early retirement benefit available only to those employees who attain age 55 with 10 years of service, are considered to have the benefit currently available.

Age or service conditions that must be satisfied within a specified period of time (e.g., early retirement windows) are not disregarded, but the age and service of employees can be projected to the end of the time period. In other words, an early retirement window benefit will be considered currently available to all employees who are or will be eligible to take the early-out benefit.

Status (e.g., death, disability, marital status, hardship) is also disregarded when testing any benefits, rights, or features.[39] A condition stipulating that the value of a participant's benefit must be below a certain amount also may be disregarded in current availability testing.[40] Accordingly, a lump-sum benefit payable for accrued benefits less than $75,000, for example, would be considered available to all participants in the plan.

A special grandfather rule applies for optional forms of benefits and other rights or features that are prospectively eliminated for future benefit accruals. The existing forms of benefits and other rights or features retained with regard to the accrued benefit are considered to automatically satisfy the current availability requirement in future years, assuming they satisfied the current availability requirement on the latter of the amendment's adoption or effective date.[41] So a plan that

[36]Treas. Reg. 1.401(a)(4)-4(d)(4).
[37]Treas. Reg. 1.401(a)(4)-4(b)(1).
[38]Treas. Reg. 1.401(a)(4)-4(b)(1).
[39]Treas. Reg. 1.401(a)(4)-4(b)(2).
[40]Treas. Reg. 1.401(a)(4)-4(b)(2)(ii)(D).
[41]Treas. Reg. 1.401(a)(4)-4(b)(3)(i).

eliminates a lump-sum distribution option for future benefit accruals will be considered to offer the lump-sum option to a nondiscriminatory group if it is currently available to a nondiscriminatory group of participants when the benefit is eliminated. This can be important since the group of employees eligible for the lump-sum option will differ from the total plan population by attrition and new hires.

Effective Availability

The group of employees to whom the benefit, right, or feature is effectively available may not greatly favor highly compensated employees. This is another facts and circumstances test. If as a general matter it is impossible for most non–highly compensated employees to satisfy plan conditions that highly compensated employees will satisfy (e.g., years of service or named disabilities), the effective availability test is failed.[42]

If a benefit, right, or feature is failing or is in danger of failing either current or effective availability, remedial action is required: either its availability should be expanded or the availability of the option for future accruals must be eliminated (the latter alternative solves the problem only if the option currently passes). If an ancillary benefit or other right or feature is failing, it may be removed, since it is not protected by the anticutback rule.[43]

An optional form of benefit is a distribution alternative that is protected under the anticutback rule of section 411(d)(6) and includes early retirement benefits and retirement subsidies. Differences in the terms of distributions (the form, timing, payment schedules, and medium of distribution) will cause different optional forms to exist. Also, differences in any terms that affect the value of an optional form, such as the applicable actuarial assumptions or the method of benefit calculation, will produce different optional forms.[44]

Different benefit formulas, accrual methods, or allocation formulas do not create different optional forms of benefits. For example, different optional forms do not exist when a plan offers the same benefit distribution options to employees of different divisions that have different formulas for determining benefits. Likewise, a lump-sum distribution available to an employee on the greater of two different benefit formulas is only one optional form of benefit. However, different normal retirement ages can create separate optional forms of benefit.[45]

Ancillary benefits include Social Security supplements and "qualified" disability benefits,[46] certain life and health insurance, death benefits in a defined contribution plan, preretirement death benefits in a defined benefit plan, and shutdown benefits not otherwise protected by the anticutback rule of section 411(d)(6).[47] Certain Social Security supplements, which are a form of early retirement benefits

[42]Treas. Reg. 1.401(a)(4)-4(c)(1).
[43]IRC §411(d)(6). The anticutback rule precludes employers from eliminating or reducing a participant's accrued benefit, early retirement benefit or retirement-type subsidy, or optional form of benefit.
[44]Treas. Reg. 1.401(a)(4)-4(e)(1)(i).
[45]Treas. Reg. 1.401(a)(4)-4(e)(1)(ii).
[46]IRC §411(a)(9).
[47]Treas. Reg. 1.401(a)(4)-4(e)(2).

intended to supplement the participants' income until Social Security payments begin, are considered "Qualified Social Security Supplements" (QSUPPs) and are not ancillary benefits.[48] QSUPPs are Social Security supplements that the plan sponsor has contractually agreed are subject to the anticutback rule of section 411(d)(6).[49] A plan sponsor would convert a Social Security supplement into a QSUPP to include the value of the benefit in the participants' most valuable accrual rates under the general nondiscrimination test.

Other rights or features are not optional forms or ancillary benefits, other than rights or features of insignificant value (e.g., administrative details).[50] These include plan loans; the right to direct investments or to a particular form of investment; the right to each rate of elective contributions, matching contributions, and employee contributions under section 401(k) and (m); the right to make after-tax employee contributions to a defined benefit plan that are not allocated to separate accounts; and the right to make rollovers to, or transfers to and from, the plan.[51]

This category appears to be a catch-all for virtually any feature of plan design that is not an ancillary benefit or optional form. Caution should be exercised in any plan provision that is primarily available to highly compensated employees. For example, the right to make each rate of 401(k) elective contributions (e.g., 2 percent, 4 percent, and 6 percent) must be tested for current and effective availability. Also, a plan that imposes a dollar threshold before allowing participants to direct the investment of their accounts (e.g., at least $5,000) must satisfy availability testing. In such cases, effective availability may boil down to a "smell test."

Aggregated Plans

A DB/DC plan must satisfy nondiscrimination standards with respect to the current availability of single-sum benefits, loans, ancillary benefits, and benefit commencement dates (including the availability of in-service withdrawals).[52] All other benefits, rights, and features are deemed to satisfy the nondiscriminatory current availability requirement if either (1) they satisfy the general current availability requirement or (2) any benefits, rights, or features currently available in one type of plan (i.e., defined benefit or defined contribution) included a DB/DC plan that is currently available to all non–highly compensated employees in that type of plan.[53]

In addition, benefits, rights, and features must satisfy the effective availability requirement. In testing effective availability of benefits, rights, and features under a DB/DC plan, one of the factors considered is that a particular type of benefit, right, or feature available under one type of plan may be difficult or impossible to provide under the other type of plan.[54]

[48]Ibid.
[49]Treas. Reg. 1.401(a)(4)-12.
[50]Treas. Reg. 1.401(a)(4)-4(e)(3)(i).
[51]Treas. Reg. 1.401(a)(4)-4(e)(3)(i).
[52]Treas. Reg. 1.401(a)(4)-9(b)(3)(i).
[53]Treas. Reg. 1.401(a)(4)-9(b)(3)(i).
[54]Treas. Reg. 1.401(a)(4)-9(b)(3)(ii).

By imposing the current availability requirements on certain benefits, rights, and features, the nondiscrimination rules make it difficult for those items in DB/DC plans to pass where the plan providing the benefit, right, or feature covers a group that would fail the nondiscriminatory classification test standing in isolation. For example, where a partnership offers only to partners a profit-sharing plan that allows loans and in-service distributions and offers to rank-and-file employees a defined benefit plan, the loans and in-service distribution options would fail the current availability requirement (since they are not allowed or uncommon in defined benefit plans). Except for certain ancillary benefits, most benefits, rights, or features subject to the current availability standard on a DB/DC plan basis are found in defined contribution plans.

Another special rule covers qualified joint and survivor annuities (QJSA) and other spousal benefits. A QJSA, a qualified preretirement survivor annuity (QPSA), and spousal death benefits provided under an aggregated plan satisfy the requirements of current and effective availability if each of the plans included in the aggregated plan satisfy the qualified joint and survivor annuity requirements.[55]

However, if the aggregated plan provides a subsidized QJSA or QPSA, they must satisfy the general requirements of current availability and effective availability. So if a plan with a subsidized QJSA is aggregated with a plan that does not subsidize the QJSA, the plan with the subsidized QJSA would need to independently satisfy the minimum coverage rules. On the other hand, if the aggregated plan is a DB/DC plan, the subsidized QJSA or QPSA is tested under the rules that apply to benefits, rights, and features other than single-sum distributions, ancillary benefits, and benefit commencement dates. Accordingly, a defined benefit plan (with a subsidized QJSA) that is aggregated with a money purchase pension (which cannot subsidize the QJSA) may comply with the nondiscrimination rules even though the aggregated plan may not satisfy the nondiscrimination rules if the money purchase plan were another defined benefit plan. Any reasonable actuarial assumptions may be used to determine whether a QPSA or QJSA is subsidized.[56]

Nondiscrimination Regarding Former Employees

Former employees and active employees are tested separately for purposes of nondiscrimination and coverage. Nondiscrimination testing applies not only to the amount of contributions and benefits but also to the availability of benefits, rights, and features.[57] The amount of benefits or contributions provided under a plan cannot, under all facts and circumstances, significantly discriminate in favor of former highly compensated employees. At the employer's option, the benefits or contributions considered for former employee testing are all contributions or benefits provided to former employees or only those contributions or benefits arising out of a plan amendment.[58]

However, nondiscrimination testing for former employees is a fairly specialized occurrence. Plans under which no former employee currently benefits are deemed

---

[55]Treas. Reg. 1.401(a)(4)-4(d)(5).
[56]Treas. Reg. 1.401(a)(4)-4(d)(5).
[57]Treas. Reg. 1.401(a)(4)-10(a).
[58]Treas. Reg. 1.401(a)(4)-10(b)(1).

to provide nondiscriminatory contributions or benefits.[59] Accordingly, a plan needs to consider whether benefits or contributions are provided on a nondiscriminatory basis to former employees only during years in which former employees accrue benefits, such as when a cost of living adjustment is granted to retirees.

While a former employee's benefit can be integrated when testing for nondiscrimination, the full set of imputed or permitted disparity rules must be followed. Specifically, the cumulative permitted disparity limit (i.e., the cumulative limit on the amount of disparity that can be considered in testing the employee's benefit) applies when testing former employees. The cumulative disparity limit is determined by totaling the annual disparity limit for the employee's total period of service under all plans, up to 35 years of service.[60]

When testing active employees, the cumulative disparity limit is generally not exceeded, assuming the annual disparity limit is not exceeded and the employee has less than 35 years of service. If the participant accrues a benefit after 35 years of service, the cumulative disparity limit can serve to limit the amount of integration taken into account.[61] However, the reason the cumulative disparity limit is rarely an issue is that the limit grows as the employee performs service. But when testing former employees, the individuals receiving the benefits are not increasing their service. An employee who terminated with 10 years of service still only has 10 years' worth of cumulative disparity limit, all of which may have been used accruing benefits during the employee's active career. Accordingly, it may be impossible to impute disparity for such a former employee at all.

The result of the cumulative limit is that integrated plans, which are the plans most likely to need to impute disparity if they have to demonstrate the nondiscriminatory nature of the benefit provided former employees, may be unable to impute any disparity. Such plans may be limited to increasing former employees' benefits by no more than the amount of adjustment in Social Security benefits since the former employees began receiving benefits.[62]

In addition, any change in the availability of any benefit, right, or feature must be applied in a manner that, under all facts and circumstances, does not discriminate significantly in favor of former highly compensated employees.[63] Again, the nondiscrimination rules have a tight focus when examining former employees by only considering changes in the availability of such items.

Enforcement

As the preceding discussion illustrates, the nondiscrimination requirements are a complex series of standards for qualified plans to follow. Almost as complex as the requirements themselves, however, is the enforcement program government regulators have devised to ensure compliance with the nondiscrimination rules. The enforcement policy of the IRS is based on annual tax returns, periodic examination

---

[59]Treas. Reg. 1.401(a)(4)-10(b)(1).
[60]Treas. Reg. 1.401(a)(4)-7(c)(4)(ii)(F) and 1.401(l)-5(c)(2).
[61]Treas. Reg. 1.401(l)-5(c)(1).
[62]Treas. Reg. 1.401(a)(4)-10(b)(3), Example (2).
[63]Treas. Reg. 1.401(a)(4)-10(c).

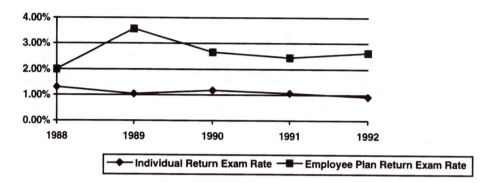

Figure 5-1. Percentage of qualified plans examined by IRS versus percentage of individual tax returns examined by IRS, 1988–92. Source: 1993 Treasury Bulletin.

of selected plans, voluntary compliance, and a variety of programs dealing with plans that have inadvertently failed to meet the requirements.

The foundation of government enforcement is Form 5500, the annual return for qualified retirement plans. Form 5500 requires the sponsoring employer to disclose a significant amount of information concerning the operation and assets of a plan, including information concerning the participation of employees in the plan. Not only is the employer required to disclose information that directly indicates whether or not the plan is complying with certain qualification requirements, but other information on Form 5500 is used by the IRS to determine the plans to be examined by agents.

The IRS examination program is another essential part of the government's enforcement program. IRS field offices around the country engage in examinations of a wide variety of types of qualified retirement plans. In recent years the IRS has attempted to substantially increase its examination activity in response to criticism that government policing of private retirement plans is lax. As indicated by Figure 5-1, the IRS's examination of employee benefit plans has increased, and currently is at a dramatically higher level than the examination rate for individual tax returns. While the number of individual tax returns filed dwarfs the number of employee benefit returns, the difference in the examination rate is indicative of a reallocation of resources at the IRS, with increased emphasis on examination of qualified retirement plans.

The third cornerstone in the IRS enforcement program is the determination letter program discussed in detail in Chapter 3. But even these three programs cannot hope to secure compliance with the myriad requirements applied to qualified plans. Recognizing that voluntary compliance is a vital part of the overall enforcement efforts, the IRS has initiated a series of programs designed to give employers an incentive to perform self-audits and correct their own defects. In addition, the programs provide the IRS with a valuable tool in enforcing qualification requirements. Because the only sanction discussed in the Internal Revenue Code for violation of a qualification requirement is the disqualification of a plan, the IRS has crafted a program with sanctions significantly less onerous on the participants. In addition to disallowing the employer's deduction for contributions to the plan and taxing the trust on trust asset earnings, plan disqualification causes participants to be taxed on their vested account balances.[64] Since the plan participants generally are not involved in the transaction that disqualifies the plan, the IRS has historically been reluctant to actually disqualify plans. In order to develop a meaningful enforcement tool, the IRS created the Closing Agreement program (CAP) and the Voluntary Compliance Resolution (VCR) program.

Closing Agreement Program

Under the CAP, plan sponsors can obtain an agreement that the IRS will not challenge the qualified status of the plan. While the determination letter ruling program provides the plan sponsor with reliance that the IRS will not challenge the qualified status of the form of the plan, the CAP encompasses not only the form of the plan but also the operation of the plan. In addition, the CAP is intended to apply after a potentially disqualifying defect in the plan has been discovered, rather than without the presence of such a defect, as in the case of a determination letter.[65]

When the CAP was introduced on a pilot basis in early 1991, only four types of disqualifying defects were eligible for a closing agreement: (1) failure to properly amend a plan for compliance with the Tax Equity and Fiscal Responsibility Act of 1982, the Deficit Reduction Act of 1984, and the Retirement Equity Act of 1984; (2) improper application of an integration formula; (3) partial termination of the plan; and (4) operational top-heavy violations. The group of eligible defects was eventually expanded to include any disqualifying defect in form or in operation, except for instances in which the following are present:

- Significant discrimination in favor of highly compensated employees.
- Exclusive benefit violations resulting in the diversion of trust assets.
- Repeated, deliberate, or flagrant violations. The deliberate or flagrant violations aspect of this criteria appears to be more significant, since an operational defect that occurs over several years may be eligible for the CAP.[66]

A CAP submission is initiated by a plan sponsor contacting a local IRS office about a potential case for a closing agreement. The case is then assigned to a Closing Agreement Specialist, who is an IRS agent specially trained in closing agreement procedures. Though local office officials have the authority to enter into closing agreements, cases involving 500 or more participants or involving a potential maximum tax sanction of $1 million or more are supposed to be reviewed by the IRS National Office.

In order to obtain a closing agreement, the plan sponsor must make retroactive and prospective correction of the disqualifying defect, as appropriate. In addition, the plan sponsor will be required to pay the IRS a "tax sanction" penalty. The tax sanction penalty is based only on the open tax years of the plan sponsor, although

---

[64]IRC §402(b).
[65]Internal Revenue Manual 7(10)54, §660.
[66]Ibid.

retroactive correction of the disqualifying defect will be required for closed years, if applicable.

The tax sanction penalty is a negotiated figure determined after the case is discussed with the IRS. The IRS begins negotiations using the maximum tax penalty amount, which is the total tax resulting from (1) the disallowance of the plan sponsor's deduction for contributions to the plan, (2) the inclusion of trust income as taxable income, and (3) the inclusion in participants' income of their appropriate shares of plan contributions. The tax sanction penalty is one of the more controversial aspects of the CAP, since the plan sponsor has actual tax liability only for the first item if the plan is terminated.

As noted above, the IRS is in an overpowering negotiating position concerning the tax penalty payment. However, the official position is that the Service will negotiate on the tax penalty payment on the basis of the equities of the situation. Three specific factors are supposed to be viewed by IRS agents as having the greatest impact in determining the amount of the tax penalty payment.

- The nature and extent of the disqualifying defect, including the number of participants affected; the relative dollar amounts involved, if any; the period of time for which the defect went unnoticed or uncorrected; and whether the defect was the result of negligence rising to the level of a possible fiduciary breach of duty.
- The impact of disqualification on non–highly compensated employees. This factor would only apply to disqualifying defects unrelated to the nondiscrimination or minimum coverage rules, since failure to comply with those rules results in the disqualification of the plan having a tax effect only on the highly compensated employees. A disqualifying defect related to the qualified joint and survivor annuity requirements, for example, causes the disqualification to affect every employee in the plan.
- Whether the defects are voluntarily disclosed and corrected. If possible, the defect should be corrected before the plan enters the CAP.

There are no data proving or disproving whether these factors actually influence the stance of the IRS in negotiating the tax penalty payment, but these items should be brought to the agent's attention when they favor the taxpayer.

One factor favoring the plan sponsor during negotiations is the IRS's willingness to consider anonymous negotiations. An agent for the plan sponsor, such as a lawyer or consultant, can contact the Service and commence negotiation on a potential closing agreement without disclosing the name of the plan sponsor or the identity of the plan.

The IRS will negotiate the appropriateness of a closing agreement and the amount of the tax sanction without disclosing the plan sponsor or the plan. Then, the plan sponsor can accept the negotiated settlement, disclose both its identity and the complete facts concerning the case to the IRS, and obtain a closing agreement protecting the qualified status of the plan. However, if the plan sponsor does not approve of the anonymously negotiated settlement, the plan sponsor's negotiator can terminate discussions with the IRS, and no closing agreement will be made.

It is important to remember that disclosure of the plan sponsor and the plan must be made before the IRS will finalize the closing agreement. In addition, if the IRS considers the actual facts of the case materially different from the facts presented during the anonymous negotiations, the IRS may refuse to enter into the closing agreement.

Cases are often initiated under the CAP after a plan defect is found by the IRS. However, plan sponsors can voluntarily submit their plans under the CAP in order to obtain an IRS letter concerning the continued qualification of the plan. The only significant distinction between the general CAP program and the "walk-in" CAP program is the determination of the tax sanction penalty. Plans voluntarily submitted under the CAP program will not be subject to a tax sanction penalty of higher than 40 percent of the maximum tax sanction penalty that could be imposed.[67] Depending on the circumstances of the case, the IRS has indicated its willingness to settle cases for as little as 5 percent of the maximum potential tax sanction penalty, but not for less than $1,000.

Voluntary Compliance Resolution Program

The VCR is an IRS compliance program available only for operational qualification defects and only for plans not under examination or scheduled for examination. Thus nonamenders—plans that have not been amended for the Tax Equity and Responsibility Act of 1982 (TEFRA), DEFRA, and REA—or plans with defects in the plan document are ineligible for the VCR. The defect must be a qualification requirement, so that the sanction for noncompliance is plan disqualification.[68] Operational defects that only have excise tax sanctions, such as prohibited transactions, are not eligible for the VCR.[69]

In order to submit a plan to the IRS under the VCR, one must meet certain other criteria. The plan must have a current determination letter. In addition, the operational defect cannot (1) be an exclusive benefit violation relating to the misuse or diversion of plan assets; or (2) involve repeated, deliberate, or flagrant violations. IRS officials have indicated they expect to view violations as repeated, deliberate, or flagrant only in unusual circumstances. This provision appears to be a safety valve for the IRS, or taxpayers could attempt to use the VCR to correct prior willful misconduct.[70]

The plan sponsor must essentially admit the existence of the operational defect in submitting the VCR request.[71] For this reason, the VCR cannot be used to obtain IRS approval on issues for which the correct response is unclear. A VCR submission cannot set forth a fact pattern and request a determination on whether a disqualifying event has occurred.

---

[67]Rev. Proc. 94-16, §4.
[68]Rev. Proc. 94-62, §4.03.
[69]However, "mixed" violation cases, such as failures to satisfy the nondiscrimination test for elective deferrals into a §401(k) plan and failures to make 401(a)(9) minimum distributions, which have both plan disqualification and excise tax sanctions, are eligible.
[70]Rev. Proc. 94-62, §5.
[71]Rev. Proc. 94-62, §3.04.

TABLE 5-4   VCR User Fees

Participants	Plan Assets	User Fee
No more than 1,000	Less than $500,000	$500
No more than 1,000	At least $500,000	$1,250
More than 1,000, but less than 10,000	n.a.	$5,000
10,000 or more	n.a.	$10,000

n.a. = Not applicable.

The VCR requires payment of a preset "user fee" ranging from $500 to $10,000, which is based on the number of plan participants and amount of plan assets.[72] The user fees are set forth in Table 5-4.[73]

Negotiations with the IRS under the VCR are likely to be quite different from negotiations under the CAP, for at least two reasons. First, different IRS personnel are involved in the different programs. The CAP is administered from the IRS field offices, while the VCR is administered out of the IRS National Office. Second, and more important, there is no tax sanction penalty under the VCR. The user fee under the VCR is preset and not open to negotiation.

With the absence of the tax sanction penalty, the correction mechanism is the only negotiable item under the current VCR procedure. However, in cases where the violation gives rise to excise tax issues, such as the failure to correct an ADP test failure in a timely fashion, the IRS has indicated a willingness to enter into a closing agreement regarding the excise tax issue. Note that correction of the operational defect is not negotiable; what is negotiable is the method or mechanism for correction. As a strategic matter, employers have found it is generally better to propose a correction methodology rather than let the IRS dictate the terms of the correction.

A feature under the CAP was the ability to commence negotiations on an anonymous basis. The VCR does not permit anonymous negotiations, though IRS officials have indicated their willingness to informally discuss potential correction mechanisms on an anonymous basis over the telephone. The telephone conversation will not be binding in any sense on the IRS once the plan has entered the VCR, but can be useful in getting a feel for the kind of position the IRS is likely to take.

Another aspect of the VCR program is the Standard VCR program (SVP). The SVP is a streamlined VCR procedure for certain identified defects.[74] It is a highly restricted program in which certain specified defects have specified corrections already dictated by the IRS. A plan sponsor who files under the SVP simply submits a statement indicating that one of the specified defects occurred, that the mandated correction has been done, and that the IRS will issue a letter approving the correction on an expedited basis. The program is available for the most common types of plan defects:

---

[72]Line 7(f) or (g) of Form 5500 is used to determine the number of plan participants. Line 34f (Form 5500), 31f (Form 5500 C/R), or 9a (Form 5500 EZ) is used to determine the amount of plan assets.
[73]Rev. Proc. 95-8.
[74]Rev. Proc. 94-62, §6.

1. Failure to provide the top-heavy minimum benefit to nonkey employees.
2. Failure to satisfy the nondiscrimination tests for elective deferrals, employee contributions, or matching contributions under section 401(k) and (m) of the Code.
3. Failure to distribute elective deferrals to a 401(k) plan in excess of the maximum dollar limit ($9,240 in 1995).
4. Exclusion of an eligible employee from plan participation.
5. Failure to timely pay the minimum distribution to a participant required under section 401(a)(9).
6. Failure to obtain participant and/or spousal consent for a distribution subject to the participant and spousal consent rules.
7. Failure to satisfy the annual contribution limits to a participant's account in a defined contribution plan.[75]

While both the CAP and VCR are generally well-intentioned programs serving the public good, the existence of these programs has definitely changed the IRS position on plan examinations. Prior to the existence of the CAP, the discovery of inadvertent errors in plan administration on plan examination was not a significant event. The IRS recognized the error was inadvertent, the employer corrected the problem, and the plan examination was closed. Currently, however, the presence of even minor, inadvertent errors will cause the plan to be transferred to the CAP, often with little negotiation on the part of the IRS with regard to the tax sanction penalty. In its zeal to strongly encourage voluntary compliance with the plan qualification requirements, the IRS has turned the examination process into a much more adversarial process than it was previously.

Administrative Policy Regarding Sanctions

In addition to the pilot CAP, the IRS announced the Administrative Policy Regarding Sanctions, a program under which the IRS will "forgive" minor operational disqualifying defects without imposing a tax penalty. While plan sponsors naturally are very interested in this program since it does not entail the payment of a penalty, the scope of the program is exceptionally narrow and of limited utility.

To be eligible for the Administrative Policy, a plan must meet eight criteria must be met.

1. The defect must be an isolated, insignificant instance. This criterion is the most problematic of the group and potentially eliminates all large plans from the Administrative Policy. As a practical matter, large plans experience operational errors on a continuous basis. The existence of an operational defect in more than one year precludes a plan from the Administrative Policy.
2. Either the plan must have a history of compliance or the defect must be discovered and corrected prior to audit. If there is no history of compliance, there must be no evidence of noncompliance in other areas. Therefore the rule

---

[75]Rev. Proc. 94-62, §8.

concerning plans without a history of compliance is aimed at new plans, not plans with a history of noncompliance.

3. The plan sponsor must have established formal or informal procedures to ensure compliance prior to the occurrence of the operational defect, including procedures involving the area in which the defect occurred.

4. The defect must be one that occurred through oversight or mistake even though the plan sponsor's procedures were generally followed.

5. The dollar amount involved must be insubstantial in view of the total facts of the case.

6. The sponsor must make immediate and complete correction so that no participant suffers a substantial detriment. Correction not only requires restoring any adversely affected participants but may also require eliminating any carryover effect that a violation may have for subsequent years, such as correcting an excess annual addition under section 415.

7. The defect cannot be the failure to amend a plan in time for changes in the law. The Administrative Policy is not available to TEFRA, DEFRA, and REA non-amenders. This generally limits the Administrative Policy to operational defects, since a defect in the plan document will likely be either a nonamender or incorrect language that has been in the plan for some time, thereby failing the isolated instance requirement mentioned above.

8. The defect cannot be an exclusive benefit violation.

Correction of Discrimination

Recognizing the complexity of the nondiscrimination regulations, and in an effort to avoid having substantial numbers of plans file under the CAP or VCR, the nondiscrimination regulations contain a mechanism for retroactively correcting noncompliance with the nondiscrimination or coverage requirements. Employers correct a nondiscrimination failure purely on their own—no submission to the IRS is made. Once the correction has been made as permitted by the nondiscrimination regulations, the plan maintains its qualified status. The correction of a nondiscrimination failure is done through a retroactive amendment of the plan increasing the benefits to non–highly compensated employees.

This retroactive amendment must satisfy several criteria. For example, the amendment must be nondiscriminatory when tested separately, and it cannot reduce an employee's benefit. The amendment must be adopted within nine and a half months after the close of the plan year.[76] Retroactive amendments increasing the benefit of terminated nonvested participants will be ignored, since those participants would not receive any economic benefit from the amendment.[77]

The requirement that the retroactive amendment be nondiscriminatory when standing alone is intended to prevent plans from retroactively increasing highly compensated employees' accruals to the maximum amount permitted under the nondiscrimination rules.

---

[76]Treas. Reg. 1.401(a)(4)-11(g)(3)(iv)(A).
[77]Treas. Reg. 1.401(a)(4)-11(g)(1).

The retroactive correction mechanism is not available to cure all noncompliance matters. It is unclear how a benefit, right, or feature can be made retroactively available to an employee in order to meet the availability standards. For example, a loan feature of a plan that was not available during the plan year to certain participants cannot be made retroactively available to those participants. The ability to take a loan during the prior plan year has passed and cannot be recaptured.

However, the retroactive correction mechanism establishes a means for plan sponsors to maintain a plan's qualified status after discovering that some aspect of the plan discriminates in favor of highly compensated employees. Given the potentially volatile nature of nondiscrimination testing, owing to a plan's terms and changing demographics due to a mobile work force, even the most scrupulous plan sponsor could discover that some aspect of its plan has become discriminatory.

Chapter 6
Determination of Benefits

To correctly determine a participant's retirement benefits, one must consider a diverse array of factors. Specific information about the participant must be determined, ranging from age and length of service to marital status and compensation history. Equally important, certain statutorily mandated limits and standards can affect a participant's benefits, such as the vesting rules or the limits on benefits and includable compensation. Consider, for example, the rules governing service crediting: Do all employees who have worked during the past year have to be credited with a year of service for vesting and benefit accrual purposes? The answer to that question can significantly affect the participant's ultimate retirement benefit and the employer's liability under the plan.

Calculating a Participant's Length of Service

Year of Service

A pension plan may use the term "year of service" for three distinct purposes that are subject to ERISA's requirements:[1] (1) to determine eligibility for participation, (2) to determine benefit entitlement through satisfaction of the vesting requirements, and (3) to determine the amount of accrued benefits at any given time.

ERISA and its subsequent regulations provide for two approaches to measuring a year of service for any of the three purposes listed above: the "hours-of-service"[2] approach and the "elapsed-time"[3] approach. Under the hours of service approach, a "year of service" for eligibility and vesting purposes is a 12-month period during which the employee works at least 1,000 hours or is credited with 1,000 hours, whether worked or not. For purposes of benefit accrual, the plan may require more than 1,000 hours of service for a full year of service, but pro rata credit must be given for 1,000 or more hours of service in a 12-month period.[4] The 12-month periods used to determine whether the various requirements have been met are called "computation periods." The eligibility computation period determines whether an employee has fulfilled the service requirements for formal admission

---

[1]"Year of service" may also be used to determine eligibility for normal retirement, early retirement, disability, and other benefits, but this use is not regulated by ERISA.

[2]ERISA §§202(a)(3), 203(b)(2); IRC §410(a)(3); DOL Reg. 2530.200b, 2530.203-2, 2530.204-1,2; Treas. Reg. 1.410(a)-5, 1.411(a)-6.

[3]Treas. Reg. 1.410(a)-7. The elapsed-time method is not specifically described in the statutes.

[4]ERISA §204(b)(3)(B); DOL Reg. 2530.204-2(c).

to plan membership. The vesting computation period defines the participant's place on the vesting schedule and, in most cases, establishes whether or not a break in service has occurred. The accrual computation period determines whether a participant accrues full, partial, or no retirement benefits during a certain time period.

For purposes of the minimum participation requirements, the 12-month eligibility computation period is measured from the date when the employee first enters the service of the employer.[5] Thus the employee has fulfilled the 1,000-hour requirement if he or she has had 1,000 hours of work by the first anniversary of employment.

If the employee does not complete 1,000 hours of service by the first anniversary of employment but is still employed, he or she must start over toward meeting the requirement. For this purpose, the plan can uniformly and consistently provide that the relevant 12-month period is either (a) the year between the first and second anniversary dates, or (b) the first plan year that began after the individual was first employed.[6]

An essential element of this approach is, of course, the definition of "hour of service."[7] The generic definition of an hour of service is an hour for which an employee is paid or is entitled to payment (including back pay) for the performance of duties or an hour during which no duties are performed. Thus hours of service during a given computation period include not only hours actually worked but hours for which the employee is paid, such as holidays, vacation, sick leave, and jury duty.

The regulations permit a plan to measure hours of service in terms of certain "equivalencies" to the basic definition.[8] These equivalencies may be expressed in terms of working time, periods of employment, or earnings. If a plan counts only actual working time, including overtime, it must credit a year of service for 870 hours. The difference between 1,000 and 870 is presumed to represent the hours in the computation period during which no duties are performed but for which employees are paid. If only regular-time hours of work are recognized, excluding overtime, a year of service must be credited for only 750 hours.

Rather than determining actual hours of regular or overtime work, a plan may credit 10 hours of service for each working day, 45 hours for each week, 95 hours for each semimonthly period, or 190 hours for each month.[9] These equivalencies make allowance for the compensable time periods during which no duties are performed. If a plan sponsor chooses this basis, the full number of hours for the period specified must be credited if the individual is employed at least one hour during the period. In other words, if the plan stipulates that hours of service are to be credited on the basis of months of employment, 190 hours would have to be credited for a minimum of one hour of employment during the month in question.

---

[5]ERISA §202(a)(1)(A); DOL Reg. 2530.202-2(a).
[6]DOL Reg. 2530.202-2(b).
[7]DOL Reg. 2530.200b-2(a).
[8]DOL Reg. 2530.200b-3(c).
[9]DOL Reg. 2530.200b-3(e).

If employees are paid on the basis of an hourly rate, their hours of service may be determined by dividing their earnings during the computation period by either (1) their hourly rates of pay in effect from time to time during the period, (2) their lowest hourly rate of pay during the year, or (3) the lowest rate of pay for an employee in a similar job.[10] A plan using this basis of measurement must credit 1,000 hours of service for each 870 hours computed to give equivalent recognition to compensable periods during which no duties are performed. A similar approach may be used for employees who are not paid on an hourly basis if 1,000 hours of service are credited for each 750 hours determined under the method.

Entirely apart from and as an exception to the foregoing rules, a maritime employee who has 125 days of employment during an eligibility or vesting computation period is credited with a year of service.[11]

The other major approach, the elapsed-time method, ignores hours of service altogether.[12] Under this approach, the plan gives credit for an individual's total period of employment, irrespective of the actual number of hours worked or compensated. The period of employment begins on the first day an employee performs an hour of service and ends on the date of severance from service. If employment is terminated, the date of severance from service is the last day worked; but if the employee is absent because of layoff, leave, or disability, the severance date is one year after the day on which the last service is performed. If an employee returns from layoff, leave, or other temporary absence within one year from the last day worked, that employee must be treated for all purposes as though he or she had worked throughout the entire period of absence. However, if an employee returns to work within one year after a quit, discharge, or retirement, the intervening period must be taken into account for eligibility and vesting purposes but not for benefit accruals.

For purposes of participation and vesting, the days of elapsed time in different calendar or plan years must be aggregated to determine whether the service requirements are met. For example, a one-year service requirement for participation would be satisfied with 200 days of elapsed time in employment in each of two successive plan years. For this purpose, a year of elapsed time in employment is 365 days. For purposes of benefit accrual, elapsed time may be measured in terms of years, months, or days, depending upon plan provisions.

A plan may use different methods of measuring years of service for purposes of eligibility for participation, fulfillment of vesting requirements, and computation of the amount of accrued benefits. It may also use different computation periods for different purposes. In addition, it may prescribe different methods for different groups of employees, as long as the methods are reasonable and do not result in any prohibited discrimination. For example, it could use the elapsed-time method for full-time employees and some version of the 1,000-hour method for part-time employees. Or it might use the 1,000-hour method for employees whose regular workweek is less than the standard workweek for their job classification and use the elapsed time method for employees who work the standard week.

---

[10]DOL Reg. 2530.200b-3(f).
[11]ERISA §§202(a)(3)(D), 203(b)(2)(D); IRC §§410(a)(3)(D), 411(a)(5)(D); DOL Reg. 2530.200b-6,7,8.
[12]Treas. Reg. 1.410(a)-7.

Break in Service

ERISA contains specific rules concerning breaks in service for purposes of participation, vesting, and benefit accruals. For participation purposes, a one-year break
in service occurs in any calendar year, plan year, or other consecutive 12-month
computation period (the same computation period used to measure the years of
service) in which the employee has 500 or fewer hours of service.[13] If the plan uses
870 hours or 750 hours to determine years of service, the hours for breaks in service
are reduced proportionately. For plans using elapsed time, a 12-month period of
severance following a severance from service date is treated as a break in service.[14]

In determining whether there has been a break in service, certain periods of
absence for maternity and paternity leave must be treated as though the individual
was actively at work.[15] However, the period so credited need not exceed 501 hours
for plans using the hours method or one year for plans using the elapsed-time
method.

The general rule is that all service with the employer, prebreak and postbreak, is
to be taken into account for purposes of determining whether the participant has
met the participation requirements. If a participant has a one-year break in service,
however, the plan may require a one-year waiting period before reentry, at which
point the participant's prebreak and postbreak service are to be aggregated, and
the employee is to receive full credit for the waiting period service.[16]

A plan that can use a two-year service requirement (because it provides full and
immediate vesting) may stipulate that an employee who has a one-year break in
service before completing the two-year probationary period must start over toward
satisfying that requirement after the break in service.[17]

Determining a Participant's Vesting Status

Basic Vesting Concepts

Vesting provisions differ, within permissible limits, as to the kinds of benefits vested,
the point in time when the eligible benefits vest, the rate at which the accrued
benefits vest, and the form in which the vested benefits may be taken.

The kinds of benefits that are typically vested are retirement, death, and total
disability. All three kinds are vested when they enter a payment status. The traditional approach however, has been to vest only the basic retirement benefit prior to
entering payment status. Before ERISA, a common practice for participants who
terminated their employment prior to retirement was to vest only the normal
retirement benefit. Plans typically specified that the vested benefits of a terminated
participant became payable only at normal retirement, even though active participants were permitted to retire early, possibly with subsidized benefits. Moreover,
the early retirement supplements provided under some negotiated plans were not
vested. Thus, in general, vesting attached only to the normal retirement benefit.

[13]ERISA §202(b); IRC §410(a)(5); DOL Reg. 2530.200b-4; Treas. Reg. 1.410(a)-5.
[14]Treas. Reg. 1.410(a)-7(a)(3).
[15]ERISA §202(b)(5); IRC §410(a)(5); Treas. Reg. 1.410(a)-7T(a).
[16]Treas. Reg. 1.410(a)-7(d)(5).
[17]IRC §410(a)(5)(B).

With the exception of the qualified preretirement survivor annuity benefit described in Chapter 10, it has not been the practice to vest death and disability benefits that are not currently being paid. In other words, protection against the economic consequences of death and total disability is not continued for participants who leave the employer's service. These are considered to be term coverages that should properly extend only to active and possibly retired participants. However, if the participant terminates after becoming vested and dies before his or her annuity starting date (and an eligible spouse survives), a qualified preretirement survivor annuity benefit must be provided.

As to time, vesting may occur immediately or at some future date. The dichotomy here is immediate versus deferred vesting. Immediate vesting is infrequently found among conventional pension plans. Vesting is generally deferred until stipulated service requirements are met. Immediate vesting is more often found in profit-sharing plans, which are considered plans of deferred compensation rather than plans providing retirement income. It is more difficult to justify deferred vesting in a deferred compensation plan since the services that earned the compensation were provided even if the payment of the compensation was deferred to a later date.

As to the rate at which benefits vest, a distinction is made between cliff and graded vesting. Cliff vesting occurs when, upon satisfaction of the conditions laid down for vesting, all benefits accrued to that date vest in their entirety, and all benefits accruing thereafter vest in full as they are credited. Plans have favored the cliff vesting concept, coupled with reasonable service requirements. A small minority of plans have provided for full and immediate vesting. Benefits derived from employee contributions are always required to be fully and immediately vested.

With graded vesting, only a specified percentage of the accrued benefits vest upon fulfillment of specified minimum service requirements. The percentage of vesting increases on a sliding scale as additional requirements are met, until 100 percent vesting is ultimately attained. For example, a plan may specify that 20 percent of accrued benefits will vest after three years of service, with an additional 20 percent vesting each year during the next four years until after seven years of service all accrued benefits are vested. Graded vesting avoids anomalous treatment of employees terminating just before and just after meeting the requirements for full vesting, and it minimizes the danger that employees will be discharged just before their pension benefits vest. In other words, it prevents a situation in which an employee with fairly long service has no vested benefits on a particular day and then, the following day, has all accrued benefits fully vested. On the other hand, graded vesting is more difficult to explain to plan participants, which is a matter of some concern, since the law requires that every participant be furnished with a summary of the plan "written in a manner calculated to be understood by the average plan participant."

Graded vesting is also more difficult to administer. Not only may the plan administrator have to keep track of a relatively insignificant vested benefit for a long period of years for a terminated participant who only had a few years of service, but a participant in a defined benefit plan who terminates and receives a lump-sum distribution while partly vested may reinstate the canceled benefit accruals upon reemployment by paying back that distribution to the plan, plus interest at a prescribed rate.[18] The same rule applies in contributory plans to participants who terminate before their benefits are 50 percent vested, who receive a refund of their contributions, and whose vested benefits are canceled.[19] In this latter case, they do not have to be in the employer's service at the time they seek to restore the benefits that were canceled.

The employer is required by law to furnish the terminated employee with a certificate stating the amount of benefits vested, the form of annuity in which they will be paid, and the time when they will become payable.[20] The form of the vested benefits depends to some extent on the contractual instrument used to fund the benefits.[21] If a defined benefit plan is funded through a trust, the vested terminated employee generally retains a deferred claim against the trust fund in the amount of the vested benefits. The plan may permit or direct the trustee to purchase a deferred life annuity in the appropriate form and amount for the employee from a life insurer.

If a defined benefit plan is funded through a contract with a life insurance company, the vested benefits may take the form of a paid-up insurance or annuity contract or a deferred claim against the plan. Under group deferred annuity contracts, all benefits are funded in the form of paid-up annuities, and when vested employees terminate they are simply given title to the annuities credited to their account. Under a group deposit administration annuity contract, vested employees who terminate may be credited with a paid-up deferred annuity in the proper form and amount, or they may be given a certificate indicating that their benefit claims will remain obligations of the plan to be discharged in the normal manner at retirement. The latter procedure would be similar to the deferred claim arrangement of a trust fund plan. If the plan is funded through individual insurance or annuity contracts (an approach generally confined to small firms), the vested terminated employee may be given the option of taking a paid-up contract in the proper amount or continuing, on a premium-paying basis, at his or her own expense, that portion of the life insurance policy or annuity contract represented by the vested cash values. Some plans permit the terminated employee to continue the contract or contracts in full force by paying the trustee a sum of money equal to the nonvested cash value, a privilege of some significance to a participant whose health has been impaired.

Under defined contribution plans, the vested benefit is the participant's vested account balance, which is usually paid out upon termination of employment, but may be retained until later. Similarly, a defined benefit plan may permit terminating employees to take the full actuarial value of their vested benefits in cash. At their option, the participants may place some or all of the sum withdrawn, except their own contributions and the employer contributions imputed to them, in an individual retirement account (IRA) set up and administered pursuant to applicable law.[22] If carried out within 60 days from receipt, the transfer would be tax free and, in any event, the earnings on the funds in the IRA would be wholly exempt

---

[18]ERISA §204(d),(e); IRC §411(a)(7).
[19]ERISA §203(a)(3)(D); IRC §411(a)(3)(D).
[20]ERISA §105(c), 209(a)(1); IRC §6057(e).
[21]See Chapter 30 for a description of the various funding instruments.
[22]IRAs are described in Chapter 13.

from current income taxation.[23] The employees could leave the funds in the IRA until retirement, or, with the consent of a subsequent employer, they could transfer the funds on a tax-free basis to a qualified pension plan of the new employer. The terminating employees may, with the consent of the successor employer, transfer the "cash-out" value of their vested benefits directly to the pension plan of the new employer, and the transfer will be tax free if carried out within 60 days after receipt from the original plan. Employees are under no obligation to preserve the actuarial value of their vested benefits and may dispose of them in any way that they see fit, except that spousal consent is generally required to receive a benefit in any form other than a qualified joint and survivor annuity.[24] The employer is not under legal obligation to permit a cash out of the vested benefits.

When the actuarial value of the vested benefit of a terminating employee is not greater than $3,500, the employer has the option, without the employee's consent, of discharging the plan's obligation by making a lump-sum cash distribution.[25] This privilege is granted to the employer to avoid the expense of keeping track of a relatively insignificant deferred claim against the plan.

Statutory Vesting Requirements

Before the enactment of ERISA, employers were under no legal obligation to provide vesting of employer-financed benefits prior to retirement, except for unusual circumstances. The law did provide that all accrued benefits of a participant had to vest, to the extent funded, in the event that the plan terminated or the employer permanently discontinued contributions to the plan. In addition to these rules that applied to all plans, the Internal Revenue Service could require any plan to provide reasonable preretirement vesting if it appeared that the plan would otherwise discriminate against the rank-and-file employees in favor of the prohibited group (officers, shareholders, supervisors, and highly paid employees). In certain situations, usually involving small plans, the officers and other favored employees would be likely to remain with the firm until normal retirement, while the rank-and-file employees would tend to terminate their employment and fail to qualify for benefits. Vesting provisions keyed to the expected termination pattern could ensure that the plan would operate for the benefit of the employee group in general, rather than just for the prohibited group.

The minimum vesting standards established by ERISA and modified by TRA are based on the premise that vesting of accrued benefits after a reasonably short period of service is necessary (1) to ensure equitable treatment of all participants, (2) to remove artificial barriers to changes of employment and hence enhance the mobility of labor, and (3) to ensure that private pension plans fulfill their social role of supplementing for a broad segment of the labor force the old-age insurance benefits provided under the Social Security System.[26]

[23]IRC §402(a)(5),(6).
[24]ERISA §205(a),(c); IRC §§401(a)(11)(A), 417(a)(1),(2).
[25]ERISA §204(d),(e); IRC §411(a)(7).
[26]See Dan M. McGill, *Preservation of Pension Benefit Rights* (Homewood, Ill.: Richard D. Irwin, 1972), chap. 2, for a discussion of the public policy considerations involved in the vesting issue. Chapter 5 of that volume provides a detailed analysis of the factors affecting the cost of vesting and the various ways in which the cost of vesting may be measured and expressed.

Under the minimum vesting standards, benefits derived from employee contributions must be fully and immediately vested. For plan years beginning after 1988, they require benefits derived from employer contributions to be fully vested at normal retirement age, and also to meet one of two permissible standards.[27]

1. The simplest standard provides for full vesting of all accrued benefits after the participant has accumulated five years of recognized service, irrespective of attained age. *No* degree of vesting short of five years of service is required under the standard.
2. The second standard, sometimes called the three-to-seven-year standard, embodies the progressive or graded vesting concept. Under this standard, the plan must vest at least 20 percent of a participant's accrued benefits by the end of three years of recognized service, and an additional 20 percent each year during the following four years. This means that the benefits must be fully vested after seven years of recognized service, irrespective of the participant's attained age. A participant's vested percentage at any point in time cannot be less than that provided under the three-to-seven-year standard. Accordingly, a plan using the following vesting schedule does not comply with the vesting requirements:

Years of Service	Vested Percentage	Years of Service	Vested Percentage
1	10	5	50
2	20	6	75
3	30	7	100
4	40		

Even though the participant has a higher vested percentage in years one through four than that required under the statutory schedule, he or she has a lower vested percentage in years five and six, which violates the vesting standard.[28]

An exception applies to collective bargaining employees under multiemployer plans, for which full vesting is required after 10 years of recognized service.

Generally speaking, all years of service, including service rendered before an employee is entitled to participate in the plan and before ERISA was enacted, are to be taken into account in determining a participant's place on the vesting schedule.[29] Accordingly, a plan using the five-year cliff vesting schedule, but based on participation rather than service, fails to satisfy the minimum vesting requirements.[30]

However, the plan may ignore (1) service before the employer maintained the plans or a predecessor plan (so-called past service), (2) service before age 18, (3) service during periods when the employee declined to make mandatory contributions, (4) seasonal or part-time service not taken into account under the rules for determining a "year of service," and (5) service broken by periods of suspension of employment to the extent permitted under the breaks in service rules. It

[27]ERISA §203(a); IRC §411(a).
[28]Treas. Reg. 1.411(a)-3(d)(1), Example (3).
[29]ERISA §203(b)(1); IRC §411(a)(4).
[30]Treas. Reg. 1.411(a)-3(d)(1), Example (2).

TABLE 6-1   Example of Determining Employee's Credited Service

Year	Hours of Service	Status
1	1,000	Year of service
2	800	Neither year of service nor break in service
3	1,000	Year of service
4	400	Break in service
5	1,000	Year of service
6	0	Break in service
7	400	Break in service
8	1,000	Year of service
9	0	Break in service
10	0	Break in service
11	500	Break in service
12	200	Break in service
13	1,000	Year of service

must be emphasized that the foregoing are rules for determining the participant's place on the vesting schedule (i.e., the number of years accrued toward satisfying the service requirement) and not for determining the *amount* of accrued benefits.

For example, assume a participant has a service record like the one shown in Table 6-1. Her years of service and breaks in service are designated next to each year's hours of service. Because the employee does not have five consecutive one-year breaks in service, no prior service is disregarded. Accordingly, at the end of year 13, she has 5 years of service and is fully vested in her benefit.

The pattern of vesting that occurs under the two basic standards is quite dissimilar, but the overall cost impact on a plan with a representative group of participants is remarkably similar. This suggests that they provide about the same amount of vesting, in the aggregate, although the distribution of vested benefits will vary. Young entrants into a pension plan will achieve a fully vested status more quickly under the five-year standard than under the three-to-seven-year standard. A higher percentage of participants will have *some* vesting under the three-to-seven-year standard than under the five-year standard, since vesting commences after three years of service, but fewer participants will have 100 percent vesting.

Top-heavy plans are required to have either 100 percent vesting after three years of service or 20 percent vesting after two years of service increasing 20 percent per year to 100 percent after six years.[31]

The law permits the Internal Revenue Service to require more rapid vesting than that required under the minimum schedules if (a) there has been a pattern of abuse under the plan, such as the firing of employees before their accrued benefits vest; or (b) it appears that there have been, or are likely to be, forfeitures of accrued benefits under the plan that effectively discriminate in favor of highly compensated employees.[32]

[31] IRC §416(b).
[32] IRC §411(d)(1).

It should be recognized that the standards described above are *minimum* standards, and employers are permitted to provide vesting under more liberal rules than those required by law.

Once vested, the benefits are nonforfeitable, except upon the death of the participant before retirement (if there is no provision for joint and survivor annuities), and except for the circumstances noted below.[33] If participants in a contributory plan withdraw their own mandatory contributions before their employer-financed benefits are at least 50 percent vested, the latter can be canceled under a plan provision of general applicability. Moreover, if a participant retires and then returns to work for the same employer, his or her retirement benefits can be suspended during the period of reemployment. Benefits required to be vested can no longer be forfeited in the event of misconduct by a participant or terminated vested participant (the so-called bad boy clause) or in the event that such persons accept employment with a competitor.[34]

Upon request not more often than once per year, or upon termination from the plan, participants must be provided with a statement of their accrued benefits and their vesting status.[35] Information concerning vested deferred benefits of a terminated participant must be furnished to the Internal Revenue Service, which transmits it to the Social Security Administration.[36] The Social Security Administration will provide this information to the participants or their beneficiaries upon request, and automatically when application is made for Social Security old-age benefits.

Determining Benefit Amounts

Limits on Benefits and Contributions

Before the 1974 pension reform legislation, it was not customary for plans to impose an upper limit on the payable benefits other than that implicit in a flat benefit formula. Employers who provided benefits related to compensation felt, by and large, that the economic status that prevailed among their active employees could properly be carried over into retirement. No laws imposed limits on benefits[37] other than the general prohibition against discrimination in favor of certain groups and a specific limit on the benefits that could be paid to the 25 highest-paid employees (at plan inception) in the event of plan termination within a few years after establishment.[38] This state of affairs was changed by ERISA, which added Section 415 to the Internal Revenue Code to impose a limit on the benefits that can be provided under a defined benefit plan and a limit on the contributions that can be made under a defined contribution plan. These limits were further reduced by the Tax Equity and Fiscal Responsibility Act of 1982 and by the Tax Reform Act of 1986.

---

[33]ERISA §203(a)(3); IRC §411(a)(3).
[34]See, e.g., *Vink. v. SHV North America Holding Corp.*, 3 EBC 2172 (SDNY 1982).
[35]ERISA §§105, 209(a)(1); IRC §6057(e).
[36]IRC §6057, Form 5500, Schedule SSA.
[37]There is a general requirement that compensation, including benefits, must be reasonable to be deductible as a corporate expense. In addition, there are limits on the amount of deductible contributions for the plan as a whole. Deductions are discussed in Chapter 7.
[38]Treas. Reg. 1.401-4(c).

Defined Benefit Plan

Under the Code, as amended, the largest annual benefit that can be paid under a defined benefit plan in the form of a straight-life annuity is an amount equal to the lesser of (a) $90,000 or (b) 100 percent of the participant's average compensation during the three consecutive calendar years of highest compensation.[39] The $90,000 limit is adjusted annually after 1987 to reflect changes in the cost of living, pursuant to regulations of the Secretary of the Treasury.[40] These limits need not be scaled down for preretirement ancillary benefits (such as medical, death, or disability benefits) but are subject to actuarial adjustment if the benefit is payable in any form other than a straight-life annuity or a joint and survivor annuity on the lives of the participants and their spouses.

The joint and survivor annuity will be adjusted if the benefit payable to the survivor is greater than the benefit payable during the joint lives of the annuitants.[41] If the survivor portion of the benefit is not greater than the benefit payable during the joint lives of the annuitants, there is no adjustment.[42] Any other form of benefit, however, is based on the participant's single life annuity. Accordingly, a participant entitled to a $75,000 annual single life annuity benefit can receive a lump-sum distribution based on the cost of the single life annuity benefit, even though the plan could also pay the participant a 100 percent joint and survivor annuity of $75,000, a significantly more valuable benefit.

Upward adjustments are permitted to reflect any employee contributions to the plan, including rollover contributions from another qualified plan or from an individual retirement account.[43] An annual benefit of $10,000 may be provided, notwithstanding the salary limit or the required adjustment for postretirement ancillary benefits, if the participant has not also been covered by a defined contribution plan of the employer.[44]

The $90,000 limit is reduced for retirement before the Social Security retirement age and is increased for retirement at any later age.[45] For this purpose "Social Security retirement age" is deemed to be age 65 for those born before 1938, age 66 for those born in the period 1938 through 1954, and age 67 for those born later.[46]

---

[39] IRC §415(b).

[40] IRC §415(d). The adjustments are to be based on the same procedures used to adjust benefits under Social Security and will automatically change if the Social Security basis changes.

[41] Treas. Reg. 1.415-3(c)(2)(i), which references a qualified joint and survivor annuity as defined by IRC sec. 401(a)(11)(G)(iii), which no longer exists. At the time the regulation was released, sec. 401(a)(11)(G)(iii) defined a qualified joint and survivor annuity as "an annuity for the life of the participant with a survivor annuity for the life of his spouse which is not less than one-half of, or greater than, the amount of the annuity payable during the joint lives of the participant and his spouse and which is the actuarial equivalent of a single life annuity for the life of the participant."

[42] Accordingly, a participant entitled to a $90,000 single life annuity can also receive a $90,000 joint and survivor annuity, a potentially significant "increase" in benefits.

[43] Rollover contributions are tax-free transfers of assets from another qualified plan or individual retirement account. To be tax free, the assets must be transferred within 60 days of the original distribution and other rules must be observed. Rollovers and other taxation of distribution issues are discussed in Chapter 7. Individual retirement accounts are discussed in Chapter 14.

[44] IRC §415(b)(4).

[45] IRC §415(b)(2).

[46] IRC §415(b)(8), Notice 87-21, 87-1 CB 458.

The adjustment is made using Social Security early retirement reduction factors for ages between 62 and the Social Security retirement age, and using actuarial equivalent factors at other ages. For participants born after 1954, the result is a limit of $78,000 at age 65 and approximately $35,000 at age 55.

The $90,000 limit is reduced proportionately for participants with less than 10 years of participation in the plan,[47] while the $10,000 limit and the 100 percent of compensation limit are reduced proportionately for participants with less than 10 years of service.[48] So a participant with a salary of $70,000 who retires after 8 years of service but only 7 years of participation has a maximum benefit of $56,000, or 80 percent of her compensation. The higher limit of $63,000, or 70 percent of the $90,000 limit, is ignored since it is higher than the compensation limit.

Defined Contribution Plan

There are corresponding limits on the amounts that may be set aside for a participant in a defined contribution pension plan.[49] The annual addition (as defined) to a participant's account is limited to the lesser of $30,000 or 25 percent of the participant's compensation from the employer. This limit applies to the total annual additions to an employee's account from employer contributions, employee contributions, and forfeitures, but not to additions to the account from earnings. The $30,000 will be adjusted (owing to cost-of-living increases) to equal one-fourth of the dollar limit for defined benefit plans after that limit ($90,000 in 1987) exceeds $120,000.[50]

Two or More Plans

If an employer operates two or more plans of the same type (i.e., defined contribution or defined benefit) and an employee participates in more than one, the aggregate contributions or benefits must be within the limits set forth above, as if only one plan is involved.[51]

If one plan is a defined benefit type and the other is a defined contribution type, each plan is subject to the limits appropriate to its type, and the two must be combined to determine whether they satisfy an overall limit.[52] The benefits and contributions of the combined plans cannot be more than 140 percent of the limits applicable to one plan if the percentage of compensation limits apply, or more than 125 percent if the dollar limits apply.[53] For example, assuming the dollar

---

[47]While the 1986 tax reform legislation also imposed a 10-year participation phase-in on benefit amendments, the IRS has announced it will not enforce the provision, because every plan amendment and benefit increase must be nondiscriminatory—which is the exception to the phase-in requirements.

[48]IRC §415(b)(5).

[49]IRC §415(c). Special rules apply to tax-deferred annuities for certain nonprofit organizations.

[50]IRC §415(c).

[51]IRC §415(f).

[52]IRC §415(e).

[53]To accomplish this, §415(e) defines a *defined benefit plan fraction* and a *defined contribution plan fraction* to be determined for each year. The numerator of the defined benefit plan fraction is the projected

limits do not apply, if the defined benefit plan provides benefits of 80 percent of the limit for a defined benefit plan, the defined contribution plan may provide 60 percent (140 percent – 80 percent) of the limit for a defined contribution plan. If the combined benefits and contributions exceed the overall limit, one or more of the plans is disqualified. The order in which the plans are to be disqualified is determined under regulations, subject to the stricture that no terminated plan may be disqualified until all other plans of the employer have been disqualified.[54]

Top-Heavy Plan

Top-heavy plans are not only subject to certain additional limits, but also must meet certain minimum benefit requirements. Congress developed the top-heavy rules in response to the perception that certain, usually small, plans were focusing too much of their benefits on certain highly compensated employees to justify the various tax advantages given to qualified plans.

In top-heavy plans, the value of accrued benefits for key employees and their beneficiaries exceeds 60 percent of the value of accrued benefits for all employees and their beneficiaries.[55] Key employees include certain officers and owners.[56] Most small plans are top-heavy. Whether a plan is top-heavy is determined each plan year.

If a plan is top-heavy, it is subject to adjustments in the maximum limits on contributions and benefits, more rapid vesting (described later in this chapter), and, for nonkey employees, minimum benefits or contributions.

A top-heavy plan must provide at least minimum benefits or contributions for all participants who are not key employees.[57] As a practical matter, when the requirement applies, most plans will probably apply it to all employees. Under a top-heavy defined benefit plan, the minimum accrued benefit must equal 20 percent of average compensation or, if less, 2 percent of average compensation multiplied by the employee's years of service, excluding plan years when the plan was not top-heavy and excluding all plan years beginning before 1984.[58] For example, an

---

annual benefit, if the participant keeps working at his or her present rate of pay until normal retirement age. The denominator is the lesser of 1.25 times the dollar limit applicable to the year ($90,000, or adjusted amount after 1987) or 1.4 times the participant's average compensation for his or her high three years. For the defined contribution plan fraction, the numerator is the sum for the current year and all prior years of the allocations to the participant's account that are subject to the limits under Section 415. The denominator is the sum for the current year and each prior year of the participant's service with the employer (regardless of whether the plan was in existence during those years) of the lesser of 1.25 times the dollar limit applicable to the year ($30,000 for 1983 and later, other amounts for prior years) or 1.4 times 25 percent of pay for each such year. The sum of the defined benefit plan fraction and the defined contribution plan fraction may not exceed 1.0 in any year. Special transition rules modify these calculations.

[54]Treas. Reg. 1.415-9.

[55]IRC §416(g). Certain plans are aggregated.

[56]IRC §416(i). Key employees include all officers up to a total of 50 employees (or, if lesser, the greater of three employees or 10 percent of the employees). Key employees also include any owners who are among (1) the 10 employees owning the largest interests in the employer, (2) 5 percent owners, and (3) 1 percent owners whose compensation exceeds $150,000.

[57]IRC §416(c).

[58]IRC §416(c)(1).

employer who has sponsored a defined benefit plan for three years must provide nonkey employees who have participated in the plan at all times a benefit of at least 6 percent of average compensation, even if those employees have more than three years of service with the employer. Since the plan was not top-heavy for the years prior to its existence, service prior to the commencement of the plan can be disregarded for minimum benefit accrual purposes.

Average compensation is generally for the five highest consecutive years, with certain years excluded.[59] Under a defined contribution plan, the minimum required contribution is 3 percent of the employee's compensation or, if less, the highest percentage at which contributions are made for any key employee.[60]

A top-heavy plan could not take into account compensation in excess of $200,000 in determining benefits or contributions.[61] This requirement was repealed after 1988, however, when the limit on compensation was extended to all qualified retirement plans.

Under top-heavy plans, if there is both a defined benefit plan and a defined contribution plan, the 125 percent limit for the dollar limit on contributions and benefits under the combined plans is reduced to 100 percent.[62] However, this reduction does not apply to top-heavy plans in which the value of accrued benefits for key employees does not exceed 90 percent of such value for all employees and where certain additional benefits or contributions are provided for nonkey employees.[63]

Assignment, Alienation, and Qualified Domestic Relations Orders

The law requires that a qualified pension plan to contain a general prohibition against the assignment or alienation of vested benefits.[64] To provide a degree of flexibility that would otherwise be lacking, the law permits the plan to give employees the right to make a voluntary, revocable assignment of a portion of their retirement benefits.[65] However, the law specifically prohibits the alienation of any vested benefits for the purpose of defraying the administrative costs of the plan.[66]

The nonalienation provision generally prevents pension benefits from being attached by a court order. An exception to this, however, is the qualified domestic relations order (QDRO).[67]

For the above purpose, a domestic relations order is defined as a court order or court approval of a property settlement agreement that is made pursuant to a state domestic relations law and which relates to the provision of child support, alimony payments, or marital property rights to a spouse, former spouse, child, or other

[59]IRC §416(c)(1)(D).
[60]IRC §416(c)(2).
[61]IRC §416(d).
[62]IRC §416(h)(1).
[63]IRC §416(h)(2).
[64]ERISA §206(d); IRC §401(a)(13).
[65]Treas. Reg. 1.401(a)-13(e)(1).
[66]Treas. Reg. 1.401(a)-13(d)(1).
[67]ERISA §206(d)(1),(3); IRC §§401(a)(13)(B), 414(p).

dependent of a participant.[68] A qualified domestic relations order (QDRO) gives an alternate payee (e.g., the former spouse) the right to receive part or all of the benefits payable with respect to a participant under a plan. In order to be a QDRO, a domestic relations order must meet several requirements. A QDRO must clearly specify certain facts and it may not require a plan to pay any type or form of benefit not otherwise provided under the plan. Complex procedural requirements must be satisfied.

---

[68]ERISA §206(d)(3)(B); IRC §414(p)(1)(B).

Chapter 7
Tax Treatment

For decades, employment-based asset accumulation plans—principally pension and profit-sharing plans—have been accorded favorable treatment under federal tax laws. This favorable treatment has been extended to employers, participants, beneficiaries, and the trust fund or life insurer account holding the plan assets.

This favorable tax treatment is intended to encourage the use of private sector arrangements to meet the economic needs of old age, at least in part. The approach provides maximum flexibility in retirement planning, creates savings for capital formation, and minimizes federal government intrusion into private sector decision making.

Offsetting these advantages is the loss of tax revenues for the federal government. In effect, the private sector is being permitted to allocate for business and personal goals money that would otherwise have flowed into the federal treasury to be spent in ways determined by Congress. This effect is so real that fiscal authorities characterize these tax concessions as "tax expenditures," a concept objectionable to some. In any event, when considering the nature and extent of a particular tax benefit, Congress generally balances the value of the benefit against the amount of lost revenue. This process has led, for example, to restricting the annual amount of tax-favored pensions under defined benefit pension plans to $90,000, a limit that some think should be further reduced, although others think it should be increased or eliminated entirely.

The tax provisions have in part reflected social and philosophical concepts. The difference between taxing monthly pensions and lump-sum distributions, for example, reflects in part considerations of the desirability of encouraging these two forms of payment. Tax provisions also reflect how effectively particular groups have lobbied for their particular goals.

This chapter describes federal tax laws, but state tax laws are also important. State tax treatment is often quite similar to federal tax treatment, but not always.

Taxation of Participants Before Benefits Are Received

Most qualified plans are funded entirely by employer contributions. If employees contribute to the plan, their contributions generally are not tax deductible. But the elective contributions of employees under a cash or deferred arrangement (401(k) plan) are excludable from their taxable income, as described in Chapter 12.

Participants and beneficiaries under a qualified plan generally have no taxable income until benefits are actually received.[1] The doctrine of constructive receipt, applicable in most other situations, does not apply. The doctrine of constructive receipt treats as taxable income amounts set aside for or otherwise subject to the unqualified demand of a cash basis taxpayer, whether or not such income has been actually received. There can be no substantial limitations or conditions on this right.[2]

Without the doctrine of constructive receipt, participants and beneficiaries are only taxed on their actual receipt of benefits. It is immaterial whether the employee could have elected to receive a benefit, so long as he or she does not actually receive it. In certain circumstances, however, taxable income can accrue to a participant before benefits are distributed.

Life Insurance Protection

If a plan purchases life insurance for a participant, and if the proceeds of the policy are not payable to the trust, the cost of the insurance protection is included in the participant's current taxable income. For this purpose, the amount of protection provided equals the excess of the amount of benefit payable upon death over any cash value of the policy. To determine the cost of this protection, one multiplies this amount of protection, technically the "net amount at risk," by cost factors published by the IRS.[3] These costs are often referred to as "P.S. 58 costs," in reference to the IRS publication in which they were originally promulgated.

If a plan is contributory and specifies that costs of insurance are to be paid first from the employee's own contributions, the employee has no current taxable income unless the cost of insurance exceeds his or her own contributions.

A participant has no current taxable income with respect to uninsured death benefit protection provided under a plan.

Loans to Participants

Many defined contribution plans allow loans to participants, usually from their own account balances. A few defined benefit plans allow mortgage loans or other secured loans to participants when fiduciary and party-in-interest requirements are satisfied. Fiduciary requirements are discussed in Chapter 3.

Prior to the Tax Reform Act of 1986, one of the attractive features of plan loans was the deduction of interest paid on the loan, which some considered a deduction for paying interest to oneself. The Tax Reform Act eliminated the deduction of interest for all loans, whether from a qualified plan or any other lender, subject to a four-year phase-out and two generally available exceptions.[4]

Special rules further restrict the deduction of interest on loans from qualified plans.[5] No deduction will be allowed for interest under any loan to a "key em-

---

[1] IRC §402(a)(1).
[2] Treas. Reg. §1.451-2(a).
[3] IRC §72(m)(3); Treas. Reg. 1.72-16(b); Rev. Rul. 55-747.
[4] IRC §163(d),(h).
[5] IRC §72(p)(3).

ployee" made or amended after 1986 (as defined under top-heavy plan requirements). Nor will any deduction be allowed for interest on any loan made after 1986 that is secured by an employee's elective contributions under a 401(k) plan or a 403(b) plan.

Nonqualified Plans

Contributions to an employee's trust that is not part of a qualified plan are included in each participant's taxable income in the first year that the amounts are transferable by the participant or that they are not subject to a substantial risk of forfeiture.[6] This generally applies to all vested benefits to the extent that they are funded. Regulations stipulate how the extent of funding of each participant's benefits is to be determined for this purpose under a defined benefit plan.[7]

If a qualified plan loses its qualified status, all participants may have immediate taxable income equal to the value of their funded vested benefits.

Taxation of Participants Receiving Benefits

Any benefits paid to participants or beneficiaries generally are includable in their taxable income in the year they are received, to the extent that they have not previously been included in taxable income.[8]

Return of Employee Contributions and Other Basis

A participant generally recovers tax-free the amounts that have previously been includable in his or her income. A beneficiary generally recovers tax-free the amounts that have previously been includable in the taxable income of either the participant or beneficiary. These tax-free amounts are called "basis" and generally consist of the employee's after-tax contributions and certain costs of insurance previously included in taxable income. Elective contributions under a 401(k) plan are considered to be employer contributions and thus are not included in the basis. If the recipient has no basis, all payments are taxable in the year they are received.

If in a single tax year a payee receives a total distribution of all amounts to which he is entitled under a plan, he subtracts the basis from the total distribution and the remainder is includable in taxable income. But if he receives only part of the amounts to which he is entitled, as in the case of annuity payments expected to continue over several years or a lump-sum payment of only part of his account, it must be determined how much of the distribution is a return of basis and how much is includable in taxable income.

Every distribution that is not received in the form of an annuity and is received prior to the participant's annuity starting date is generally allocated ratably between recovery of basis and taxable income.[9] However, there are two important

---

[6]IRC §§402(b)(1), 83.
[7]Treas. Reg. 1.402(b)-1(a), 1.403(b)-1(d)(4).
[8]IRS Publication 575, *Pension and Annuity Income*, explains this subject for lay people.
[9]IRC §72(e)(8).

exceptions to this rule. First, a plan may provide that part or all of employee contributions under a defined contribution plan, together with the earnings allocable to them, are treated as though they were in a separate plan, provided the plan separately accounts for the employee contributions and credits them with their share of the trust's investment earnings.[10] Thus a contributory defined contribution plan is treated as if it were two plans, one consisting of all accumulated employee contributions with the earnings thereon and the other consisting of the remainder of the participants' account balances. The benefit of this exception is that an employee's basis is recovered pro rata from an account containing significantly less taxable amounts.

If a defined benefit plan allows *voluntary* employee contributions to be credited with their share of the trust's investment earnings, the accumulated voluntary employee contributions are treated as a defined contribution plan. In order to obtain this separate treatment for employee contributions, the plan must either designate which of the two portions of the plan any distributions are deemed to come from or delegate this designation to the participant. Allowing election by the participant increases administrative work for the plan, which must report the taxable and nontaxable portions of the distribution on Form 1099-R.

The second important exception to allocating every distribution pro rata between recovery of basis and taxable income is a grandfather clause that preserves the treatment of prior law for the basis derived from employee contributions made before 1987 and before 1987 costs of insurance. This grandfather clause applies only if, on May 5, 1986, the plan permitted withdrawal of employee contributions prior to separation from service.[11] Under this rule all distributions are deemed to be paid tax-free from the pre-1987 basis until the pre-1987 basis is exhausted.

To obtain the maximum possible tax deferral, some contributory defined contribution plans that are eligible for this grandfather clause provide that employee contributions made after 1986 and earnings thereon will be treated as a separate plan and that any distributions will be deemed to come first from a pre-1987 basis to the extent that it is sufficient, then from post-1986 employee contributions and earnings thereon, and finally from the remaining balance. For example, assume that a participant has a total account balance of $10,000, that this includes $2,000 of basis derived from pre-1987 contributions (without earnings) and costs of insurance, that the $10,000 also includes $800 of employee contributions made after 1986 and $200 of earnings thereon, and that the participant receives a distribution of $2,500. The first $2,000 of the distribution is deemed to come from the $2,000 of pre-1987 basis, and thus to be excludable from taxable income. The remaining $500 of the $2,500 distribution is deemed to come from the $1,000 of accumulated post-1986 contributions and earnings thereon. Since 80 percent of the $1,000 consists of the employee's own contributions, 80 percent of the $500 distribution, or $400, is excluded from taxable income and only the remaining $100 is taxable.

When annuity payments commence, an exclusion ratio is established to determine what proportion of each payment represents the return of the employee's

---

[10]IRC §72(e)(9), IRS Notice 87-13.
[11]IRC §72(e)(8)(D).

basis. This exclusion ratio is the ratio of the employee's basis to the present value of her expected future benefit payments, determined in accordance with regulations.[12] After the annuity commences, the portion of each payment excluded from taxable income never changes until the amount recovered tax-free exceeds the basis, after which all amounts received are taxable. If the participant and any joint or contingent annuitant die before recovering all of the basis, the remaining unrecovered basis is allowed as a deduction to any beneficiary entitled to a benefit that is in the nature of a refund of employee contributions or a refund of the cost of the annuity. If there is no such beneficiary, the deduction is allowed to the deceased annuitant for the last year of the deceased's life.[13] Thus, in the end, the total of the amounts excluded or deductible exactly equals the participant's basis. Different rules apply to annuities that began before 1987.

Lump-Sum Distributions

Amounts includable in taxable income may be taxed more favorably to the participant if they constitute part or all of a lump-sum distribution.

A lump-sum distribution is a distribution from a plan made to the recipient within one taxable year of the total balance to the credit of the employee that becomes payable because of the employee's death or separation from service or that becomes payable after the employee reaches age 59½.[14] For self-employed individuals, disability is substituted for the separation from service requirement. However, a distribution will only be treated as a lump-sum distribution if the employee has participated in the plan for at least five taxable years before the year of the distribution.[15] For the purpose of determining whether there has been a total distribution, all qualified pension plans of an employer are treated as a single plan, all qualified profit-sharing plans are treated as one plan, and all qualified stock bonus plans are treated as one plan.[16]

Once during a lifetime a taxpayer may elect to have all lump-sum distributions received during that year (but only distributions received after age 59½) taxed under a rule referred to as "five-year averaging."[17]

Under this method, one first determines the *total taxable amount*, which is the amount of the distribution that is includable in income, excluding the net unrealized appreciation on any employer securities included in the distribution. If the total taxable amount is less than $70,000, the total taxable amount is first reduced by a *minimum distribution allowance*. The minimum distribution allowance equals the lesser of $10,000 or 50 percent of the total taxable amount, reduced by 20 percent of the amount by which the total taxable amount exceeds $20,000.[18] The practical effect of this provision of the law is that half of the total taxable amount not exceeding $20,000 may be excluded from the tax computation, the

---

[12]IRC §72, Treas. Reg. 1.72.
[13]IRC §72(b)(3).
[14]IRC §402(d)(4)(A).
[15]IRC §402(d)(4)(F).
[16]IRC §402(d)(4)(C).
[17]IRC §402(d)(1).
[18]IRC §402(d)(1)(C).

allowance diminishing in dollar amount for total taxable amounts in excess of $20,000 and disappearing altogether for amounts of $70,000 or more.

Next, one computes the income tax on one-fifth of this adjusted total taxable amount, determined as though the taxpayer were an individual, not head of a household, with no other income, no personal exemptions, and no deductions. The income tax is five times this amount. The intent and effect of this procedure are to tax the distribution in lower tax brackets than those that would apply if the *total* distribution were added to all other income of the employee in the year of receipt.

A provision under prior law to apply capital gains tax treatment to any portion of a lump-sum distribution that is attributable to participation before 1974 is subject to a five-year phase-out rule.[19] Except in unusual situations, this phase-out rule will not preserve any lump-sum distribution treatment after 1987, since the tax rates applicable to capital gains and ordinary income will be the same after 1987.

A grandfather provision protects part of prior law provisions for any participant who attained age 50 before 1986. Such participants, whether under or over age 59½, may make one election to have either the prior 10-year averaging rule apply in combination with 1986 tax rates or the new 5-year averaging rule apply with the new lower tax rates.[20] The 10-year averaging rule was essentially the same as the current 5-year averaging rule except that 10 years was used instead of 5. Either alternative may produce lower taxes in a particular case, depending on the amount of the distribution.

Participants who attained age 50 before 1986 may also elect to continue to have capital gains treatment apply to any portion of their lump-sum distribution attributable to pre-1974 participation.[21] For those electing this capital gains treatment, a 20 percent tax rate applies to the capital gains portion. In some cases, participants will do better by rejecting this capital gains treatment and having the entire lump sum taxed under the 5-year or 10-year averaging rule.

Rollover Amounts

Several provisions of the law are designed to encourage employees to preserve for retirement the amounts set aside under qualified plans. One of these provisions allows the tax-free rollover of distributions from plans.

Under certain circumstances, if a participant receives a distribution from a qualified plan, she may transfer part or all of the amount received to an individual retirement account or to another qualified plan and exclude it from her current taxable income.[22] Such a transaction has become so common that the term usually used to describe it, *rollover*, has entered the general vocabulary. The ability to roll over the amount to another qualified plan depends upon the other plan's willingness to accept the rollover distribution.

Changes to the rollover rules effective for distributions after 1992 also created two different types of rollovers: the traditional rollover, consisting of a distribution

---

[19]TRA §1122(h)(4).
[20]TRA §1122(h)(5).
[21]TRA §1122(h)(3).
[22]IRC §402(a)(5).

to the participant that is subsequently rolled over into an eligible retirement plan; and a direct rollover, consisting of a transfer of the participant's benefit directly from the distributing plan to an eligible retirement plan.

Distributions eligible for rollover are referred to as "eligible rollover distributions." This term does not apply to minimum required distributions; substantially equal period payments for a specified period of 10 years or more, or for the life (or life expectancy) or joint life (or joint life expectancy) of the participant and beneficiary; or distributions that are not includable in gross income.[23] In addition, the IRS has excluded certain other amounts from the definition of "eligible rollover distribution," and thus from the direct rollover and mandatory withholding requirements. Among these exclusions are the costs of life insurance coverage (P.S. 58 costs) and loans treated as distributions at inception and deemed distributions upon default of participant loans.[24]

Because of the prevalence of plan loans in defined contribution plans, the treatment of plan loans has been a significant concern. If a plan treats a participant's unpaid loan balance as a distribution upon termination of the participant's employment, then such an amount is considered an eligible rollover distribution, if it otherwise qualifies.[25] Accordingly, a plan can distribute the loan (i.e., the promissory note) to the terminated participant along with the remaining balance of the account, in which case the entire amount of the distribution, including the note, would be considered an eligible rollover distribution.[26] Of course, a participant could not roll the note over into an IRA since an extension of credit from an IRA to the owner of the IRA is a prohibited transaction.[27] So the distributed loan can be rolled over, but the participant must use other funds in place of the loan amount.

Distributions of unpaid loan balances are treated like distributions of employer securities.[28] Therefore, although the distributed unpaid loan balance is included in the distribution amount subject to 20 percent withholding, the total amount that must be withheld from the distribution does not exceed the sum of the cash and the fair market value of other (nonemployer security) property received by the participant.[29]

A distribution recipient other than an employee or the employee's surviving spouse (or spousal alternate payee under a qualified domestic relations order) is not permitted to roll over distributions from a qualified plan. A qualified plan is not treated as an eligible retirement plan for a distribution to a surviving spouse.[30] Only an IRA is an eligible retirement plan with respect to the surviving spouse's distribution.[31]

To be treated as a tax-free rollover, the amount received must be transferred to an IRA or another plan within 60 days of receipt.[32] The amount transferred may

[23]IRC §402(c)(4).
[24]Temp. Treas. Reg. 1.402(c)-1T, Q&A 4.
[25]Temp. Treas. Reg. 1.402(c)-2T, Q&A 8.
[26]IRC §402(a)(5) and PLR 8103063.
[27]Technical Advice Memorandum 8849001.
[28]Notice 93-3.
[29]Notice 93-3, § III.b.3.
[30]IRC §402(c)(9); Temp. Treas. Reg. 1.402(c)-2T, Q&A 10(a).
[31]Temp. Treas. Reg. 1.402(c)-2T, Q&A 10(a).
[32]IRC §402(c)(3).

not exceed the amount that would otherwise be included in taxable income; thus it may not include the recovery of the employee's own contributions or other tax basis.[33] If only part of the taxable amount received in a lump-sum distribution is rolled over, the remainder is not eligible to be taxed as a lump-sum distribution.

When a qualified plan makes a distribution that is eligible for rollover, the plan administrator is required to provide the recipient with a written explanation of the rollover requirements.[34] The IRS has published a standard notice that may be used for this purpose.[35]

The plan administrators must provide the written explanation "within a reasonable period of time before the rollover is made," which is generally interpreted to mean no fewer than 30 days and no more than 90 days before the distribution date.[36] The 30-day advance notice requirement generally may be waived, as long as the participant is given the opportunity to consider the rollover decision for at least 30 days after the notice is provided and the plan administrator clearly informs the participant of his or her right to this decision-making period.[37] The plan administrator can use any method reasonably designed to inform the participant of the 30-day period for making the election, such as including the information in the notice discussing the rollover requirements.

In the case of a series of periodic payments that are eligible rollover distributions, the notice requirements are satisfied if the 402(f) notice is provided before the first payment in the series, and also at least once annually for as long as the payments continue.[38] The precise 12-month period (i.e., calendar year or other 12-month period) intended for the annual notice is not specified.

Direct Rollovers

All qualified plans and tax-sheltered annuities must provide for the direct rollover of eligible rollover distributions to eligible retirement plans at the election of the payee.[39] IRAs, defined contribution plans that accept rollovers, and annuity plans described in section 403(a) are "eligible retirement plans."[40] While the statutory definition excludes 403(b) annuity plans,[41] this was corrected by temporary regulations that included such plans as an eligible retirement plan for distributions from other 403(b) annuity plans.[42]Also excluded by the statutory definition are defined benefit plans;[43] this exclusion was not changed by regulation.[44] The exclusion of defined benefit plans from the definition of "eligible retirement plan" does not preclude the transfer of a participant's benefit to such a plan. This exclusion

---

[33]IRC §402(c)(3).
[34]IRC §402(f).
[35]IRC §402(f); Treas. Reg. 1.402(f)-2T and 1.402(c)-2T; Q&A11-15; IRS Notice 92-48.
[36]Temp. Treas. Reg. 1.402(c)-2T, Q&A 12.
[37]Notice 93-26, Sec. II.b.1.
[38]Temp. Treas. Reg. 1.402(c)-2, Q&A 14.
[39]IRC §401(a)(31).
[40]IRC §§ 401(a)(31)(D), and 402(c)(8)(B).
[41]IRC §402(c)(8)(B).
[42]Temp. Treas. Reg. 1.403(b)-2T, Q&A 1.
[43]IRC §401(a)(31)(D).
[44]Temp. Treas. Reg. 1.401(a)(31)-1T, Q&A 2.

merely does not make it a plan qualification requirement to offer a transfer to a defined benefit plan; nor does it consider offering a transfer to a defined benefit plan to comply with the requirement that the plan offer a direct rollover. In addition, the transfer of a participant's account balance or accrued benefit to a defined benefit plan may not be viewed by the IRS as a direct rollover exempt from the 20 percent withholding rules, but as a distribution and rollover subject to mandatory withholding.

As under prior law regarding trustee-to-trustee transfers, a qualified plan is not required to provide that it will accept a direct rollover. Plan provisions should be examined to determine the circumstances (if any) under which direct rollovers will be accepted.

A direct rollover is treated as a distribution and rollover for purposes of a plan's qualification rules and is not considered to be a transfer of plan assets and liabilities. Accordingly, any spousal and participant consent must be obtained before the eligible rollover distribution may be distributed in a direct rollover.[45] However, the rollover is not a transfer of benefits subject to the requirements of section 411(d)(6); therefore, the transferee plan need not protect any optional forms of benefits available under the transferor plan.[46] In this respect, a direct rollover is similar to an "elective transfer," a trustee-to-trustee transfer of plan assets and liabilities that can result in the permitted elimination of protected optional forms of benefits.[47]

Providing the distributee with a check and instructing the distributee to deliver the check to the eligible retirement plan is a reasonable means of accomplishing a direct rollover, provided that the payee line of the check is written so that the check is negotiable only by the trustee or custodian of the recipient plan.[48] Other acceptable delivery methods include wire transfer or mailing the check to the eligible retirement plan.[49]

A plan sponsor is not required to allow a participant to divide a distribution and make a direct rollover to more than one eligible retirement plan.[50] However, a plan administrator may require a participant to elect the direct rollover of all or no part of an eligible rollover distribution, unless the entire amount of the eligible rollover distribution is more than $500.[51] Also, if the participant elects to roll over directly only a portion of an eligible rollover distribution, the plan administrator may require that the portion equal at least $500.[52]

A plan administrator may establish other reasonable procedures for implementing the withholding and direct rollover rules. For example, a plan administrator may require certain information or documentation from a distributee before making an eligible rollover distribution.[53] The plan administrator may also establish

---

[45]Temp. Treas. Reg. 1.401(a)(31)-1T, Q&A 14.
[46]Ibid.
[47]Treas. Reg. 1.411(d)-4, Q&A 3(b)(1).
[48]Temp. Treas. Reg. 1.401(a)(31)-1T, Q&A 4.
[49]Temp. Treas. Reg. 1.401(a)(31)-1T, Q&A 3.
[50]Temp. Treas. Reg. 1.401(a)(31)-1T, Q&A 10.
[51]Temp. Treas. Reg. 1.401(a)(31)-1T, Q&A 9.
[52]Ibid.
[53]Temp. Treas. Reg. 1.401(a)(31)-1T, Q&A 6.

default procedures whereby a distributee who fails to make an affirmative election is treated as having made or not made a direct rollover election.[54] Plan administrators who obtain certain specified information from a participant concerning the plan or account to which a direct rollover is to be made will not be subject to penalties if, in fact, such plan or account is not an eligible retirement plan, provided the administrator reasonably relied on adequate information provided by the distributee. It would not, for example, be reasonable for the administrator to rely on information that was clearly erroneous.[55]

Distribution of Insurance and Annuity Contracts

If a distribution from a qualified plan includes a transferable annuity contract, the value of the contract is includable in taxable income at the time of distribution. But if the contract is nontransferable, generally no amounts are includable in taxable income until actually received. The fact that the annuity contract can be surrendered for its cash-surrender value does not make the annuity contract transferable. The participant will only be taxed on the value of the contract when the contract is actually surrendered or annuity payments are received.[56]

If a distribution from a qualified plan includes a life insurance policy, the entire cash value of the policy is taxable when the policy is distributed, regardless of whether the policy is nontransferable, unless the recipient converts it into a nontransferable annuity contract within 60 days.

Distribution of Employer Securities

If a lump-sum distribution includes employer securities, the net unrealized appreciation of the securities is excludable from taxable income.[57] For this purpose, "net unrealized appreciation" means any excess of the market value of the securities at the time of distribution over the cost or other basis of the securities when the trust acquired them. When the recipient eventually sells the securities, the excess of the sale's price over the original cost or other basis to the trust is includable in the recipient's taxable income.

Minimum Distribution Requirements

Minimum distribution requirements relate to when benefit payments must begin, the minimum amount that must be distributed each year, and the penalties for failure to comply.

For years after 1988, distributions under all qualified plans must begin no later than April 1 of the calendar year following the calendar year in which the participant attains age 70½, regardless of whether he or she has retired.[58]

[54]Temp. Treas. Reg. 1.401(a)(31)-1T, Q&A 7.
[55]Temp. Treas. Reg. 31. 3405(c)-1T, Q&A 6.
[56]Treas. Reg. 1.402(a)-1(a)(2).
[57]IRC §402(a)(1),(e)(4)(J).
[58]IRC §401(a)(9); IRC §4974.

The minimum amount required to be distributed annually must be determined in accordance with regulations. The minimum is determined as though the entire interest of the participant is to be paid as a level annual amount over the life of the employee, or the lives of the employee and a designated beneficiary, or is to be paid in installments over the life expectancy of such person or persons.

The existence of a designated beneficiary can be a significant tax-planning device. Without a designated beneficiary, minimum distributions must be made over the participant's life expectancy, but with a designated beneficiary, the minimum distributions can be stretched over the joint life expectancies, a potentially much longer period of time. Note, however, that if the designated beneficiary is not the participant's spouse, the assumed age of the designated beneficiary for determining the joint life expectancy will be limited to an age 10 years younger than the age of the participant.[59]After the participant's death, payments can continue to be made to the designated beneficiary over the remaining joint life expectancy period or the designated beneficiary's life expectancy. This ruling also stretches the payment of the benefit and defers the taxation of the benefit.

If the participant dies after minimum distributions have commenced, any remaining benefits must be distributed at least as rapidly as under the method in effect at the participant's death.[60] If the participant dies before minimum distributions have begun, the entire plan benefit must generally be distributed by the last day of the year containing the fifth anniversary of the participant's death.[61] If a participant died on January 2, 1995, for example, her entire accrued benefit must be distributed no later than December 31, 2000. The exception to the five-year rule is that benefits can be paid over the life expectancy of the designated beneficiary if they commence within the appropriate time period. For spouses, the benefits must commence by the last day of the later of the year following the participant's death or the year the spouse attains age 70½.[62] For other beneficiaries, the benefits must commence by the last day of the year following the participant's death.[63]

An individual who receives less than his or her minimum distribution requirement in a year will be assessed an excise tax equal to 50 percent of the difference between the required payments and the actual payments during the year.[64] But the IRS may waive the tax if the failure was due to a reasonable error and if reasonable steps are taken to correct the error.

Early Distributions

An additional income tax of 10 percent applies to any distribution before age 59½ unless the distribution meets one of several exceptions.[65] The exceptions include

[59]Prop. Treas. Reg. 1.401(a)(9)-2.
[60]IRC §401(a)(9)(B)(i).
[61]IRC §401(a)(9)(B)(ii).
[62]IRC §401(a)(9)(B)(iv).
[63]IRC §401(a)(9)(B)(iii).
[64]IRC §4974.
[65]IRC §72(t).

1. amounts paid as part of a series of substantially equal periodic payments over the life (or life expectancy) of the employee or the combined lives (or combined life expectancies) of the employee and the employee's beneficiary;
2. amounts paid on or after a separation from service that takes place during any calendar year in which the participant has attained at least age 55;
3. amounts that are used to pay medical expenses that are deductible under Code Section 213, regardless of whether the employee itemizes deductions;
4. distributions upon disability or death;
5. payments under a qualified domestic relations order.

If a participant escapes the tax by beginning to receive payments in substantially equal payments but then changes the distribution method before age 59½ or within five years, the 10 percent tax will be assessed on all amounts received before age 59½.

Payments from IRAs or defined contribution plans will be treated as substantially equal periodic payments if the annual payments are made according to one of the methods set forth below.

*   The annual payments are determined using a method that would be acceptable for the minimum distribution rules. The payment may be determined on the basis of the life expectancy of the employee or the joint life and last survivor expectancy of the employee and beneficiary.
*   The annual payments are determined by amortizing the taxpayer's account balance over a number of years equal to the life expectancy of the account owner or the joint life and last survivor expectancy of the account owner and beneficiary (with life expectancies determined in accordance with the minimum distribution rules) at an interest rate that does not exceed a reasonable interest rate on the date payments commence. At an interest rate of 8 percent, for example, a 50-year-old individual with a life expectancy of 33.1 and having an account balance of $100,000 would receive payments in a series of substantially equal periodic payments by distributing $8,679 annually, derived by amortizing $100,000 over 33.1 years at 8 percent interest.
*   The annual payments are determined by dividing the taxpayer's account balance by an appropriate annuity factor (the present value of an annuity of $1 per year beginning at the taxpayer's age attained in the first distribution year and continuing for the life of the taxpayer). The annuity factor is derived by using a reasonable mortality table and using an interest rate that does not exceed a reasonable interest rate on the date payments commence. If substantially equal monthly payments are being determined, the taxpayer's account balance would be divided by an annuity factor equal to the present value of an annuity of $1 per month beginning at the taxpayer's age attained in the first distribution year and continuing for the life of the taxpayer. For example, if the annuity factor for a $1 per year annuity for an individual who is 50 years old is 11,109 (assuming an interest rate of 8 percent and using the UP-1984 Mortality Table), an individual with a $100,000 account balance would receive an annual distribution of $9,002 ($100,000/11,109 = $9,002).[66]

[66]Notice 89-25, 1989-1 CB 662.

No withholding is required with respect to the 10 percent additional tax.

Excess Distributions

A 15 percent excise tax applies to individuals who receive *excess distributions* from one or more plans in a year.

The tax generally applies to the excess of the total distributions over $112,500 (indexed upward with the $90,000 limit under section 415 beginning in 1988) paid in a year to an individual.[67] However, except in the case of individuals making the grandfather election described below, the $112,500 (indexed) is replaced by $150,000 (not indexed), if larger. This tax is generally based on the total of all distributions that the individual receives under all qualified plans of any of his employers, tax-sheltered annuities, and IRAs, and that are includable in his taxable income.

The following amounts are not subject to the limitation:

- distributions after death (which are subject to a separate tax),
- distributions paid to another person under a qualified domestic relations order,
- amounts attributable to the employee's own after-tax contributions or other tax basis,
- amounts not includable in taxable income because they are subsequently rolled over to an IRA or other plan.

Lump-sum distributions are not aggregated with other payments for this purpose, but are instead subject to a separate 15 percent tax on the excess of the distribution over five times the limit that otherwise applies. Thus lump sums in excess of $562,500 (5 × $112,500, with indexation) may be subject to the tax. A larger limit of $750,000 (5 × $150,000, not indexed) will apply to those who do not make the grandfather election.[68]

The grandfather election applies only to individuals having accrued benefits valued at over $562,500 as of August 1, 1986. These individuals may have elected on their tax returns for years before 1989 to have the portion of all future distributions attributable to the value of their accrued benefits as of August 1, 1986, not subject to the tax.[69]

Suppose that on August 1, 1986, Jane Doe had accrued benefits with a value of $800,000, and she makes a grandfather election. In 1987, when her accrued benefits have a value of $1,000,000, she receives a distribution of $500,000, which is only half of her accrued benefits. Of that amount, 80 percent ($800,000 divided by $1,000,000) of her distribution, or $400,000 (80 percent of her $500,000 distribution), is not subject to the tax. Thus $100,000 is subject to the tax, since her $112,500 tax-free amount is included in the $400,000 exclusion. The additional tax would be 15 percent of $100,000, or $15,000.

---

[67]IRC §4980A.
[68]IRC §4980A(e)(4).
[69]IRC §4980A(e)(4).

It is not always advantageous to make the election, since one must forgo the higher $150,000 annual limit.

Upon death, a similar tax on excess benefits is included in the estate tax. The tax equals 15 percent of the excess of the value of the individual's accrued benefits at the date of death over the value of an annuity for an annual amount equal to the applicable annual limit of $112,500 (indexed) or $150,000 (unindexed).[70]

Neither the unified credit nor the marital deduction, which are normally available under the estate tax, serve to reduce this new 15 percent estate tax.[71] Thus this tax will be payable by estates that would otherwise be completely exempt from estate tax.

Gift Taxation

The transfer of rights or benefits under a pension or profit-sharing plan can be a gift subject to gift taxation under the Code. After the Tax Reform Act of 1986, if the participant irrevocably elects to have benefits paid to another person, the election is a taxable gift.[72] The general $10,000 annual exclusion from gift taxation does not apply unless the benefit is eligible for immediate distribution to the recipient.[73] Note, however, that the spouse's waiver of survivor benefits under a pension plan is not a gift subject to gift taxation.[74]

Taxation of Benefits Paid upon Death

Benefits payable to a deceased participant's beneficiary or estate are generally subject to federal and state income tax. In addition, they may be subject to federal estate tax and to state inheritance or estate tax. Only federal taxes are described in this text.

Income Tax on Death Benefits

Payments to a beneficiary or estate are generally subject to income tax in the same manner as payments to the participant. The beneficiary or estate is entitled to recover tax-free any remaining unrecovered basis of the participant at the time of death. A $5,000 death benefit exclusion also applies to certain payments.[75] If the exclusion applies, the $5,000 is added to the employee's unrecovered basis, resulting in exclusion from income.

The $5,000 exclusion applies to nonqualified as well as qualified plans, and to both funded and unfunded arrangements. The exclusion always applies in the case of lump-sum distributions paid from qualified plans. Otherwise the exclusion does not apply to any amount to which the employee had a nonforfeitable right to receive while living, including any amount to which she would have had a non-

[70]IRC §4980A(d).
[71]Temp. Treas. Reg. 54.4981A-1T, Q&A d-7.
[72]TRA §1852(e)(2)(A), repealing IRC §2517.
[73]IRC §2503(b).
[74]IRC §2503(f).
[75]IRC §101(b).

forfeitable right if she had retired or terminated employment before death.[76] The $5,000 exclusion does not apply to payments to the participant that had already begun or could have begun, or to a qualified preretirement survivor annuity based upon the vested benefit that could have been received by the participant if she had lived. But if a plan provides survivor income benefits that exceed the benefits to which the employee had a nonforfeitable right to receive if she had lived, the exclusion applies to the excess.

If the participant dies after periodic payments have commenced and payments are being continued under a joint and survivor form, the exclusion ratio established when the payments to the participant commenced would continue to apply to the beneficiary. But if payments are being continued to a beneficiary under a period-certain life annuity or under a refund annuity and the basis had not been recovered by the retired employee at the time of death, the beneficiary can exclude all payments from gross income until the sum of the basis recovered by the deceased employee and the payments received by the beneficiary equal the employee's basis; thereafter all payments are taxable income to the beneficiary.

If a death benefit payable under a qualified plan is paid from a life insurance policy, the pure insurance component of the proceeds (that is, the excess of the policy proceeds over any cash value of the policy) is treated as the proceeds of a life insurance policy and is thus excluded from taxable income, while the portion equal to the policy cash value is treated as a distribution from the plan and is subject to the income tax rules.[77] For example, assume that under a noncontributory pension plan a death benefit of $100,000 is paid from a policy with a cash value of $30,000, and the employee had previously had $2,000 of taxable income for pure insurance cost. The taxable income equals the $30,000 cash value, reduced by the $2,000 of basis for the previous cost of insurance, and reduced by the $5,000 death benefit exclusion (provided the exclusion is not applied to other employee death benefits), or a net of $23,000 of taxable income. If the $100,000 of policy proceeds were applied under the policy to provide the beneficiary an annuity, the $77,000 that is not taxable ($100,000 less the $23,000 taxable amount) would serve as the beneficiary's basis to determine the exclusion ratio applicable to future monthly payments.

A lump-sum distribution paid to the employee's beneficiary is entitled to the same favorable treatment as that afforded to lump-sum distributions paid to a participant.

Estate Tax on Death Benefits

The gross estate subject to estate tax includes the value of all payments or annuities receivable by any beneficiary to which the participant had a nonforfeitable right while living.[78] This generally includes the employee's vested account balance under a defined contribution plan. It also includes the value of payments to a joint or contingent annuitant or beneficiary under a joint and survivor annuity, certain

[76]IRC §101(b)(2).
[77]IRC §72(m)(3)(C); Treas. Reg. 1.72-16(c).
[78]IRC §2039.

and continuous annuity, or refund annuity under which payments to the participant began, or could have begun, prior to death.

Any amount payable to the surviving spouse of the deceased, however, is subject to the unlimited marital deduction and thus is not subject to estate tax.[79] In addition, the application of the unified credit under estate tax law eliminates any estate tax unless the taxable estate, after subtracting the marital deduction and other applicable deductions, exceeds $600,000.

A potentially valuable estate planning tool is the qualified terminable interest property (QTIP) trust,[80] which pays the earnings or income on the participant's benefit to the spouse for his or her life and then distributes the remaining benefit to a designated beneficiary. The participant controls the ultimate beneficiary of the plan benefits and defers estate and income taxation on plan benefits. An IRA or qualified plan can serve as the QTIP trust, as long as the plan permits the specialized type of payments scheme, a relatively rare occurrence in qualified plans sponsored by larger employers. The minimum distribution rules and pension plan spousal consent requirements further complicate the application of the QTIP rules to distributions from qualified plans.

A distribution from an individual retirement account can more easily qualify as a distribution from a QTIP trust. In order to qualify for QTIP treatment, the surviving spouse must receive all the income from the IRA annually. For example, assume an IRA distribution option requires that on the owner's death the IRA balance be paid in annual installments to a testamentary QTIP trust along with the income earned on the undistributed balance. Further, the income earned on both the distributed and undistributed portions of the IRA is currently being paid to the decedent's surviving spouse. Because all of the IRA income is being distributed to the surviving spouse, the income earned on the undistributed portion of the IRA is thus payable annually to the spouse, as was required for her or him to receive a qualifying income interest for life in the IRA. Any remaining balance in the IRA, as well as any portion of the balance previously distributed to the trust, would be includable in the surviving spouse's gross estate at death.[81]

As noted earlier, there is also a 15 percent excise tax on excess distributions, which is not subject to relief from either the marital deduction or the unified credit.

Withholding Taxes on Distributions

Tax withholding rules require payors of eligible rollover distributions to withhold an amount equal to 20 percent of the distribution,[82] unless the payee elects to have the distribution directly rolled over to an eligible retirement plan.[83] Payees may not waive withholding on eligible rollover distributions, as permitted under prior law.

---

[79]IRC §2056.
[80]IRC §2056(b)(7)(B).
[81]Rev. Rul. 89-89, 1989-2 CB 231.
[82]IRC §3405(c)(1)(B).
[83]IRC §3405(c)(2).

Other distributions from qualified plans and tax-sheltered annuities and distributions from IRAs that are not eligible rollover distributions remain subject to the prior withholding rules, with periodic distributions subject to withholding based on wage tables, and nonperiodic payments subject to withholding at the rate of 10 percent.[84] The payee continues to be entitled to elect no withholding on such distributions.[85]

The withholding rules do not apply to distributions from IRAs.[86] This means that a recipient of an eligible rollover distribution can avoid mandatory withholding by electing to directly roll over the funds to an IRA and then withdraw the funds from the IRA. Some commentators have described this treatment as eviscerating the mandatory withholding rules, since it allows the participant to avoid mandatory withholding on the distribution with no significant infringement on the individual's access to the funds.

If property (other than employer securities) is distributed in an eligible rollover distribution, the payor or plan administrator must satisfy the obligation to withhold.[87] A rule intended to ensure that payors will not be required to dispose of employer securities in order to satisfy withholding liabilities, however, permits the amount withheld from a distribution consisting of both employer securities and cash not to exceed the value of the cash and nonemployer securities property received.[88]

Taxation of the Trust

The trust of a qualified plan is generally exempt from tax on its income.[89] If the trust engages in an unrelated trade or business, however, it is subject to tax on its unrelated taxable business income.[90]

Taxation of Employers

There are numerous tax consequences to sponsoring a qualified retirement plan, the most evident being the deduction of contributions to the plan. Other potential tax consequences include excise tax liability upon the reversion of excess plan assets to the employer, the failure to distribute excess contributions to a 401(k) plan within certain time limits, or making nondeductible contributions to the plan. Finally, a tax penalty may be assessed if an employer overstates its pension liability.

Deduction of Contributions

Within prescribed limits, employers may deduct their contributions to qualified plans. Not surprisingly, different limits apply for pension plans than for profit-sharing and stock bonus plans.

---

[84]IRC §§3405(a), 3405(b)(1).
[85]IRC §§3405(a)(2), 3405(b)(2)(A).
[86]IRC §3405(c)(3).
[87]Temp. Treas. Reg. 31.3405(c)-1T, Q&A 8.
[88]Temp. Treas. Reg. 35.3405-1, Q&A 29 and 31.3405(c)-1T, Q&A 9.
[89]IRC §501(a).
[90]IRC §§501(b), 511-514.

Deduction of Pension Contributions

The most general rule on deductibility of employer contributions is that the firm may deduct any amounts that were required to meet the minimum funding standards.[91] Beyond this general rule, two specific limits for defined benefit plans have long been part of the tax law on pensions.

Under the first rule, sometimes called the "straight-line" rule, the employer is permitted to deduct any sum necessary to provide all the plan participants with the remaining unfunded cost of their past and current service credits distributed as a level amount, or a level percentage of compensation, over the remaining future service of each such employee. This simply means that each year an employer can deduct such sum, computed in accordance with applicable regulations, as is needed to provide on a level contribution basis (dollars or percentage of covered payroll) the total projected benefits payable under the plan. The calculation can be made with respect to each individual participant or the employee group as a whole.[92]

The second rule, known as the "normal cost" or "normal cost plus ten-year" rule, permits the employer to deduct annually an amount equal to the normal cost of the plan, plus, if there are supplemental liabilities, an amount necessary to amortize such supplemental liabilities in equal annual dollar installments over 10 years. Deductions for contributions toward the amortization of the supplemental liabilities are obviously available only as long as there are unamortized amounts.[93] Both the normal cost contributions and the amortization payments must be determined in accordance with relevant regulations.[94]

If more than 100 employees of an employer are covered under one or more defined benefit pension plans, the maximum deductible limit for each plan of the employer is not less than the plan's unfunded current liability. In some circumstances, this rule results in substantially larger deductible contributions than the rules described above.

A general rule that overrides all the others is that the tax deduction for any particular year cannot exceed the amount needed to bring the plan to a fully funded status.[95] That is, no deductions can be taken for contributions that would raise the plan assets to a level above the actuarial value of plan liabilities. It follows, of course, that no deductions could be taken for contributions made while a plan was in a fully or overly funded condition. Full funding for tax deduction purposes is determined in the same way as full funding under the funding requirements.

Deduction of Profit Sharing Contributions

The deduction rules of the Code generally permit an employer to make tax-deductible contributions to a qualified profit-sharing plan equal to 15 percent of the aggregate compensation of employees covered by the plan. Stated negatively,

[91]IRC §404(a).
[92]IRC §404(a)(1)(A)(ii).
[93]IRC §404(a)(1)(A)(iii).
[94]Treas. Reg. 1.404(a)-14.
[95]IRC §404(a)(1)(A) (last sentence).

tax-deductible contributions are limited to 15 percent of covered compensation in the aggregate.

For taxable years beginning before 1987, a *credit carryover* was created whenever the contribution in a particular year was less than the maximum allowable deduction; namely, 15 percent of covered compensation for such a year. This unused credit was carried forward and applied in any subsequent year in which contributions exceeded 15 percent of the aggregate compensation of the plan participants in that year. Therefore deductions for contributions made in a given year could exceed 15 percent of covered compensation for that year if a credit carryover was available. No limit on the amount of credit carryover could be accumulated, but the most that could be used or applied in a given tax year was 15 percent of covered compensation for that year. The overall deduction that could be taken with a credit carryover was also limited to 25 percent of covered compensation for the year that the credit was used. With an overall limit of 25 percent of compensation, the effective limit on the use of an accumulated credit carryover was 10 percent per year, not 15 percent.

A *contribution* carryover arises whenever the contribution for a given year exceeds the maximum allowable deduction. The maximum allowable deduction in a succeeding year for a contribution carryover is 15 percent of covered compensation less the amount of contribution made for the succeeding year. The 25 percent limit may not be applied to the contribution carryover. Contribution carryovers can be accumulated without limits on time or amount and can be deducted in any subsequent year or years in which contribution payments are less than the maximum allowable deduction. However, as mentioned below, nondeductible contribution carryovers may result in excise tax liability for the contributing plan sponsor.

If the employer covers the same group of employees with both a qualified defined benefit pension plan and a qualified defined contribution plan, the maximum allowable deduction in any one year for the two plans combined is 25 percent of covered compensation.[96] Under these circumstances, the separate limit on deductibility of employer contributions to each of the two plans still applies, as well as the 25 percent combined limit. A carryover provision for combined contributions in excess of 25 percent applies. It is similar to the carryover provision applicable to the profit-sharing plan itself. That is, if the contribution to the pension plan is only 5 percent of covered compensation, the permissible deduction for the contribution to the profit-sharing plan is 15 percent of covered compensation, not 20 percent. Furthermore, if the minimum funding provisions of the Internal Revenue Code require a contribution to the pension plan equal to more than 25 percent of covered compensation, the entire required contribution to the pension plan would be deductible, but there would be no deductible contribution to the profit-sharing plan.

Reversions to the Employer

The opposite of an employer contribution is an employer withdrawal of assets from a plan. Except as noted below for nondeductible contributions, withdrawals are

---

[96]IRC §404(a)(7).

permitted only upon termination, after all liabilities under the plan have been satisfied.

Any reversion of assets to the employer upon plan termination will be included in the employer's taxable income. In addition, a 50 percent excise tax applies to any reversion of assets to the employer at plan termination.[97] The excise tax drops from 50 percent to 20 percent if a portion of the reverting assets is used to improve plan benefits or to fund another qualified plan.

A transfer of a portion of the terminating plan's excess assets to a "qualified replacement plan" reduces the excise tax liability to 20 percent. Such a plan may be a new or existing plan of the employer and may be either a defined contribution or defined benefit plan. Transferred assets must equal 25 percent of the potential reversion. Amounts transferred in excess of 25 percent are arguably still treated as a part of the reversion and subject to the 20 percent excise tax. In addition, the qualified replacement plan must cover at least 95 percent of the active participants in the terminating plan who remain employed with the employer.

Amounts transferred to a profit-sharing plan may be held in a replacement plan for up to seven years and allocated to participants ratably, subject to the limits on allocations under profit sharing plans.

Alternatively, the excise tax is reduced to 20 percent if benefits are increased under the terminating plan. The increase must utilize at least 20 percent of the value of the reverting assets (without regard to excise taxes). Benefits of plan participants (generally including active participants, those in pay status, and those with deferred vested benefits who separated within three years of plan termination) must be increased on a pro rata basis.

Excess Contributions

A 401(k) plan is subject to actual deferral percentage (ADP) tests, which limit the amount of elective contributions on behalf of highly compensated employees.[98] Other plans are subject to similar tests with respect to certain employee contributions and to employer-matching contributions.[99] Contributions that cause a plan to fail these tests are referred to as excess contributions and excess aggregate contributions and may be withdrawn from the plan within two and one-half months after the end of the plan year. The employer is assessed a 10 percent tax on any such contributions not withdrawn within this period.[100]

Excise Tax on Nondeductible Contributions

A 10 percent excise tax is imposed on all employer contributions for a year that exceed the amount that may be deducted.[101] To the extent that any nondeductible contribution is not either withdrawn or deducted during the following year, the

---

[97] IRC §4980.
[98] IRC §401(k)(3),(8).
[99] IRC §401(m).
[100] IRC §4979.
[101] IRC §4972.

10 percent tax is applied again, and this continues each year until no nondeductible contribution remains in the plan. However, the employer is not allowed to withdraw the nondeductible contribution unless it was made by mistake of fact or was originally conditioned on its deductibility.[102] If the full funding requirement has been reached, it may be impossible to deduct the amount for many years, if ever.

Exacerbating the problem is the newly required quarterly contributions to defined benefit plans. One or more quarterly contributions may be due and required before the plan sponsor can determine whether the quarterly contribution is deductible. Accordingly, plan sponsors can easily find themselves in the awkward position of having to make a contribution that is nondeductible (though that may not be known at the time of contribution) and therefore become subject to excise tax liability.

To remedy this situation, the IRS has created a program that issues letter rulings to plan sponsors determining that the contribution was conditioned upon its deductibility and allowing the return of the contribution to the plan sponsor.[103] A letter is not even required for *de minimis* nondeductible contributions of $25,000 or less, providing the terms of the plan specifically allow for the return of nondeductible contributions and an actuarial certification of the nondeductibility of the contribution is attached to the annual return for the plan year in which the contribution is made.[104]

This excise tax on nondeductible contributions does not apply to employers who have been exempt from income tax at all times, even for amounts that would have been nondeductible if the employer had not been tax-exempt.[105]

Penalty on Overstatement of Pension Liability

Upon audit, the IRS may determine that an employer's deduction exceeded the deductible limit because of an error in the actuarial computations or because the actuarial assumptions were too conservative. In such a case, it may redetermine the deductible limit and disallow any contribution in excess of the revised deductible limit. Should that happen, the employer must pay the additional tax due with interest, plus the 10 percent excise tax on nondeductible contributions described above. An additional tax applies when the nondeductible contributions are attributable to the overstatement of pension liabilities.[106] If the resulting underpayment of taxes exceeds $1,000, the employer must pay an additional tax equal to a percentage of the underpayment of taxes. The percentage ranges from 15 percent to 30 percent of the additional taxes due, depending upon the ratio of the deduction claimed to the properly determined deduction.

---

[102]ERISA §403(c)(2)(A),(C); IRC §401(a)(2).
[103]Rev. Proc. 90-49, 1990-2 CB 620.
[104]Rev. Proc. 90-49, sec. 4.
[105]IRC §4972(d)(1)(B).
[106]IRC §6659A.

Chapter 8
The Economics of Tax Preferences for Retirement Plans in the United States

From its very beginning, the U.S. government made a commitment to the retirement income security of its older citizens. Originally the commitment was limited to its own employees, but the commitment was expanded early in this century by encouraging other employers through the federal tax system to offer retirement programs to their own employees. The government broadened this commitment further to the retirement security of the general population in 1935 by directly providing retirement benefits through the Social Security program. Over the years each of these areas of governmental commitment to retirement income security has been amended to account for changing times, needs, and so forth.

Any commitment implies associated costs, and governmental commitments imply the need to pay for them through taxes or borrowing. Today the governmental commitments to retirement income security are coming under increasing scrutiny and criticism because of the burden they place on the current level of government finance, and because they will pose an even larger burden in the future. This chapter examines the nature of the federal government's commitment to employer-sponsored retirement programs from an economic perspective.

The Government's Role in Encouraging Employer-Provided Pensions

The primary mechanism governments use to encourage employers to establish voluntary retirement programs is preferential tax treatment for their plans or the participants in them. In the United States, the preferential treatment arises because employer contributions to the plans are deductible expenses, within limits, at the time the contributions are made to the plans, and neither the contributions nor the investment earnings on the accumulated assets are taxable until benefits are actually paid to the plan participants. While this may be the "American way" of encouraging employers to establish a pension program for its workers, it is not the only way of doing so.

Parts of this chapter draw on previously published research by Gordon P. Goodfellow and Sylvester J. Schieber in "Death and Taxes: Can We Fund for Retirement Between Them?" in Ray Schmitt, ed., *The Future of Pensions in the United States* (Philadelphia: Pension Research Council and University of Pennsylvania Press, 1993), pp. 126–79. To the extent that text from that previous analysis is included verbatim, it is done so with the permission of the Pension Research Council.

TABLE 8-1   Pension Accruals Under Alternative Tax Regimes

	Alternative Tax Regimes			
	(E,E,T)	(T,E,E)	(T,T,E)	(E,T,T)
Earnings	100	100	100	100
Taxes	—	25	20	—
Contribution to fund	100	75	75	100
Net income over 5 years	61.05	45.79	32.67	43.56
Fund at retirement	161.05	120.79	107.67	143.56
Tax on withdrawal	40.26	—	–	35.89
Benefit withdrawn	120.79	120.79	107.67	107.67

Source: Dilnot, "The Taxation of Private Pensions," p. 215.

Andrew Dilnot suggests that pension plans engage in three basic transactions and that each of these can be the object of preferential tax treatment.[1] These transactions consist of contributions made to the plan, income that accrues to the assets in the trust, and the payment of benefits. Dilnot has developed a taxonomy of tax treatments based on each transaction being taxed (T) or exempted (E) from taxation. In this scheme, tax treatment of qualified plans is E,E,T, that signifies that contributions are exempt when made, earnings on the trust are exempt when accrued, and benefits are taxed when paid.

An alternative to the taxing regime used in this country would allow for the taxation of contributions when made to the plan but would exempt earnings on the trust and benefits paid from taxation (T,E,E). Another regime would provide for taxation of contributions and earnings but exempt benefits (T,T,E). A final regime would exempt contributions from taxation but provide for the taxation of earnings on the trust and benefits (E,T,T). Dilnot worked out a simple numerical example to show the outcomes under these four taxing regimes. He assumed a single income tax rate of 25 percent, an annual rate of return on the retirement savings of 10 percent, and a single contribution of 100 to the plan five years before retirement. The results of his calculations are reflected in Table 8-1.

Dilnot's results lead to a number of conclusions. First, the E,E,T and the T,E,E regimes ultimately have the same outcome although they differ somewhat in the timing of the collection of taxes. Second, the E,T,T and the T,T,E regimes likewise lead to the same outcome, and the timing on the taxation is again different. Third, the timing on the taxation should not ultimately be important to the participants in plans under the various regimes, as long as the benefit outcome is the same. On the other hand, the timing may be extremely important to the taxing authority because of various fiscal considerations. Clearly, the first two scenarios would be preferable to potential pension participants over the second two, because the former lead to somewhat larger benefits than the latter. Of course, the provision of greater pension benefits to the participants comes at the cost of net tax revenue paid to the government.

[1]Andrew Dilnot, "The Taxation of Private Pensions," in Zvi Bodie, Olivia S. Mitchell, and John A. Turner, eds., *Securing Employer Based Pensions: An International Perspective* (Philadelphia: Pension Research Council and University of Pennsylvania Press, 1995), pp. 214–16.

Since 1913 the federal government in the United States has depended on the personal income tax for a significant portion of its revenues. In the administration of the tax, regular income is taxed in the year in which it is earned. If a worker saves some of his or her regular income outside of a tax-qualified pension plan, the taxing regime under Dilnot's model is T,T,E. The extent to which pension plans are accorded preferential tax treatment is the measure of the government's commitment to these endeavors. That commitment is significant, and it has become somewhat controversial in recent years.

Forgone Tax Revenues Due to Tax Preferences

For the past 40 years there has been an ongoing discussion in the United States about tax preferences in the federal income tax system. The framework for this discussion was spelled out by Walter Blum when he began developing a concept known as "tax expenditures." Writing in the Joint Economic Committee's 1955 study *Federal Tax Policy for Economic Growth and Stability*, Blum argued that if it was "decided to subsidize a certain activity, we should be hesitant about administering the subsidy by way of a tax preference. Subsidies in this form vary directly in amount with the tax brackets of the recipients; they are invariably hidden in the technicalities of the tax law; they do not show up in the budget; their cost frequently is difficult to calculate; and their accomplishments are even more difficult to assess."[2]

While Blum might be considered the grandfather of the tax expenditure concept, Stanley Surrey was its father. In a 1967 speech delivered in New York while he was serving as the Assistant Secretary for Tax Policy at the Treasury Department, a Surrey said:

> Through deliberate departures from accepted concepts of net income and through various special exemptions, deductions and credits, our tax system does operate to affect the private economy in ways that are usually accomplished by expenditures—in effect to produce an expenditure system described in tax language.
>
> When Congressional talk and public opinion turn to reduction and control of Federal expenditures, *tax expenditures* are never mentioned. Yet it is clear that if these tax amounts were treated as line items on the expenditure side of the Budget, they would automatically come under closer scrutiny of the Congress and the Budget Bureau.[3]

After a slow gestation, the tax expenditure concept was formally defined in law in the Congressional Budget and Impoundment Control Act of 1974, which required that the Treasury make annual estimates of the costs of the various preferences in the federal tax code. The measurement of tax expenditures in the

---

[2]Walter J. Blum, "The Effects of Special Provisions in the Income Tax on Taxpayer Morale," in Joint Economic Committee, *Federal Tax Policy for Economic Growth and Stability*, 84th Cong., 1st sess., 1955, pp. 250–51.

[3]Stanley S. Surrey, a speech to Money Marketeers, New York City, November 15, 1967.

annual federal budgets submitted since the passage of the Congressional Budget Act of 1974 have highlighted the federal revenue implications of the various preferences woven throughout the Internal Revenue Code. Tax expenditures are defined in the act as "revenue losses attributable to provisions of the federal tax laws which allow a special exclusion, exemption, or deduction from gross income or which provide a special credit, a preferential rate of tax, or a deferral of tax liability."[4] The U.S. Treasury Department has estimated that the federal government incurred a $48.8 billion loss in tax revenues in fiscal 1994 because of the preferences in the tax code favoring employer-sponsored retirement plans. It is estimated that the special treatment accorded individual retirement accounts (IRAs) resulted in an added $5.4 billion loss of revenues, and that Keogh plans accounted for another $3.7 billion loss in revenues.[5]

The loss in federal tax revenues has received particular attention in recent years because the federal government's deficit reached a historic peak in fiscal years 1982 through 1994. As the deficit has mounted, there has been a growing clamor to cut back on some of the direct and preferential commitments included in our fiscal system, including those providing retirement income security. In some analysts' minds, the concern about the federal deficit indicates that the tax preferences afforded employer-sponsored retirement plans need to be reconsidered. Alicia Munnell, for one, has argued: "In an era of large budget deficits and a future that includes the rising costs of an aging society, it is difficult to understand why such a large source of potential revenue is allowed to go untapped."[6] While the short-term budget needs to be considered in justifying any government endeavor, a number of other points have been raised about our public commitment to retirement income security programs.

Reassessing Our Commitments

In 1974 ERISA established funding standards for tax-qualified pension and profit sharing plans. In 1978 only 25 percent of large defined benefit pension plans had sufficient assets to cover benefits already accrued under their existing provisions. A similar portion had assets that were less than half their accrued obligations, and 52 percent had assets that would cover less than 75 percent of their accrued benefits. By 1993 only 3 percent of plans held assets that were less than 75 percent of their accrued benefit obligations, and 85 percent had assets that would cover at least accrued benefits.[7]

Despite the improved funding of pension obligations by private pension sponsors, the federal government has become increasingly concerned about the Pension Benefit Guaranty Corporation's exposure to underfunded plans. President

---

[4]Office of Management and Budget, *Special Analyses, Budget of the United States Government for Fiscal Year 1990* (Washington, D.C.: USGPO, 1989), p. G-1.

[5]Office of Management and Budget, *Analytical Perspectives, Budget of the United States Government for Fiscal Year 1995* (Washington, D.C.: USGPO, 1994), p. 55.

[6]Alicia H. Munnell, "It's Time to Tax Employee Benefits," *New England Economic Review* (Boston: Federal Reserve Bank of Boston, July/August 1989): p. 49.

[7]Watson Wyatt (formerly the Wyatt Company), *1983 Survey of Actuarial Assumptions and Funding* and *1993 Survey of Actuarial Assumptions and Funding* (Washington, D.C., 1983 and 1993).

George Bush's 1993 budget pointed out that "between 1989 and 1991, . . . the present value of benefits it must pay in excess of the value of assets—grew 127 percent to $2.5 billion. . . . The agency's exposure to 'reasonable possible' losses has grown approximately $10 billion since 1989."[8] The Clinton administration's concern about the PBGC's "vulnerability" have led it to propose faster amortization of pension underfunding, freezing of guaranteed benefits with respect to plan amendments for structurally underfunded plans, and improvement of the PBGC's status in bankruptcy claims. While the PBGC exposure must seem to make the government's ongoing insurance program vulnerable, it is but one small element in the larger set of considerations about the government's proper role in our retirement income security system.

The issues connected with maintaining existing commitments to our retirement income security system are focusing more and more on equity. The concerns about fairness come from across the political spectrum and target virtually every element of the U.S. retirement income security system. With regard to Social Security, existing questions about whether people can get a reasonable return for the taxes they pay to finance the program will be heightened as policy makers are forced to deal with the fact that the OASDI programs are underfunded by as much as 30 to 40 percent for the baby boom generation's retirement (see Chapter 1). The central concern about federal pension programs is how the overall generosity of their benefits compares with the retirement benefits provided by other employers in combination with Social Security.[9] The central concern about state and local government pensions is whether some governments are not satisfactorily funding their future obligations to current workers.[10] And the central concern about private sector employer pensions is the inequity in the tax system, which provides preferences for pensions that are not universally available, and the potential obligation that a relatively small number of underfunded plans present to the federal government's pension insurance program.[11]

As the issues related to our ability to sustain the commitments we have made to provide retirement income security become clearer, the concerns over equity will increase. Because of the long time horizons required in providing for individual retirement income security, it is imperative that any changes in national retirement policy be anticipated as far in advance as possible. Then such changes in policy can be implemented gradually to provide the maximum opportunity for people to adjust their own expectations and behavior accordingly. Before striking off piecemeal to fix this or that component of our retirement systems, we must give some careful thought to how we might coordinate policy adjustments to achieve

---

[8]Executive Office of the President of the United States, *Budget of the United States Government Fiscal Year 1993* (Washington, D.C.: USGPO, 1992), pt 1, p. 276.

[9]See for example, Barber Conable, "A Formula with a Future," *U.S. News and World Report*, September 30, 1985, p. 80; Hastings Keith, "Fairness Is One Thing: Pigs at a Trough Another," *Los Angeles Times*, January 29, 1992, pt. B, p. 7.

[10]Olivia S. Mitchell and Ping Lung Hsin, "Public Pension Governance and Performance," National Bureau of Economic Research Working Paper 4632 (Boston: NBER, January 1994).

[11]Alicia Munnell, "Current Taxation of Qualified Pension Plans: Has the Time Come?" paper prepared for American Law Institute-American Bar Association, Pension Policy Invitational Conference (Washington, D.C., October 1991).

our long-term goals most affordably and most efficiently. In order to do this, we must first understand how the current components of our retirement system operate separately, and then together in the delivery of retirement income security.

Until recently, Social Security has been run largely on a pay-as-you-go basis. This has generally meant that expansions in benefits have been linked fairly directly to increases in payroll tax rates. In the case of Social Security, the conflict between the desire to expand benefits and the need to raise taxes to support them has been clear. In the case of employer-sponsored retirement programs, the relationship between benefits provided and the role of tax policy has not been nearly as well understood. Even though the relationship is not as direct, the conflict between retirement policy and tax policy as they apply to qualified plans has been far more contentious than in the case of public pensions or Social Security. In this case, the fundamental disagreement between pension advocates and critics is over two issues. The first is how to measure "tax expenditures" in the federal budget as they apply to pension and savings programs. The second is whether the distribution of the benefits provided by the tax incentives is equitable.

The Theory Behind Pension-Related Tax Expenditures

In theory, a true measure of a person's "income" during any given period is his or her level of consumption plus the increase or decrease in wealth during that period. If this theoretical concept of income were applied to tax-qualified income deferral plans, the tax expenditure during any period would be the forgone taxes on the increase in the real present value of benefits rights during the period.

Under the existing tax code, the preferential treatment of qualified retirement programs makes part of the tax system operate more as a consumption tax system than a pure income tax system. Contributions to the plans are deductible from income for tax purposes at the point the contribution is made, and the contributions and interest returns on the contributions are not taxable until benefits are actually paid out. The concept in federal budgeting that gives rise to the tax expenditures related to employer-sponsored pensions is that our tax system should operate more purely as a comprehensive income tax, as Blum and Surrey suggested many years ago. If it did so, contributions to retirement trusts would be immediately taxed and investment returns to the trusts would be continuously taxed—that is, by moving from the current E,E,T taxing regime to a T,T,E regime.

The underlying premises in support of a comprehensive measure of income for purposes of tax administration are that it would simplify the administration of the tax system and allow taxes to be applied equitably to individual taxpayers who are equally situated. Moving away from the comprehensive measure complicates the system and introduces horizontal inequities. The comprehensive base is also thought to create an environment of economic neutrality, because high tax rates and variable rates for different kinds of income lead to distortions in economic decisions that are eliminated when all income is treated equally. To the extent that certain kinds of income can gain preferential treatment, it results in variations between statutory tax rates and the rates actually incurred by taxpayers. When this occurs, it gives rise to public concern about the overall equity of the taxing system and undermines taxpayer morale. Finally, to the extent that some groups can garner special consideration for certain kinds of income, this makes it politically more difficult to put off other requests for special tax consideration, all of which are costly to the public fisc.[12]

The implications of moving from the current tax treatment of pensions toward a more comprehensive income tax treatment can be demonstrated algebraically. Consider a simple case in which no taxes are applied against income. Here, a consumer can enjoy a level of consumption (C) equal to his or her entire income (Y) in the time period in which it is earned (P):

(8-1) $$C_P = Y_P.$$

Alternatively, the consumer can invest his or her income and earn interest at a rate (i), and enjoy future income as follows:

(8-2) $$C_F = Y_P (1 + i).$$

The consumer can trade off current versus future consumption at the rate

(8-3) $$C_P/ C_F = Y_P/[Y_P (1 + i)] = 1/(1 + i).$$

Under this model, the consumer is paid an interest premium for deferring consumption. The way the income tax system works at present, an individual is faced with a slightly different scenario than that laid out in Equations (8-1) to (8-3). Under the current federal tax system, if an individual consumes current income, taxes have to be paid on that income first. That is,

(8-4) $$C_P = (1 - t) Y_P$$

where t is the income tax rate. Under the IRC provisions favoring retirement plans, workers have an opportunity to save out of current income before taxes, but they have to pay taxes on the amount distributed at retirement. In this case, future consumption can be specified as

(8-5) $$C_F = (1 - t) [Y_P (1 + i)]$$

If a comprehensive income tax is introduced into this world, the special treatment of retirement plan contributions would no longer be allowed. Future consumption in this regime would be

(8-6) $$C_F = (1 - t) Y_P [1 + i (1 - t)].$$

Under this regime, the consumer would trade off current versus future consumption at the rate

(8-7) $$C_P/ C_F = 1/[1 + i(1 - t)].$$

[12]Treasury Department Report to the President, *Tax Reform for Fairness, Simplicity, and Economic Growth* (Washington, D.C.: USGPO, November 1984), vol. 1, pp. 25–26.

TABLE 8-2   Alternative Taxes and Benefit Accumulations Under Normal Savings and
             Tax-Deferred Accounts at 25 Percent Tax Rates (dollars)

	Normal Savings Account			Tax-Deferred Account	
	Net Value	Tax Liability	End Value of Taxes	Net Value	Tax Liability
	(1)	(2)	(3)	(4)	(5)
Pretax income	1,000.00	250.00	648.44	1,000.00	0.00
Investment net of taxes paid	750.00	n.a	—	1,000.00	n.a.
End of year:					
1	806.25	18.75	44.21	1,100.00	0.00
2	866.72	20.16	43.21	1,210.00	0.00
3	931.72	21.67	42.22	1,331.00	0.00
4	1,001.60	23.29	41.27	1,464.10	0.00
5	1,076.72	25.04	40.33	1,610.51	0.00
6	1,157.48	26.92	39.41	1,771.56	0.00
7	1,244.29	28.94	38.52	1,948.72	0.00
8	1,337.61	31.11	37.64	2,143.59	0.00
9	1,437.93	33.44	36.78	2,357.95	0.00
10	1,545.77	35.95	35.95	2,593.74	0.00
Gross benefits paid	1,545.77	0.00	—	2,593.74	648.44
After-tax benefits paid	1,545.77	—	—	1,945.31	—
Accumulated value of taxes paid plus interest	—	—	1,047.97	—	648.44

Source: Calculated by the authors.

The application of the "comprehensive" income tax to qualified retirement plans would equalize the tax treatment of pension savings with the tax treatment of a regular savings account under current tax laws. A comparison of Equations 8-5 and 8-6 shows that tax-free earnings for retirement savings enhance the efficiency of the tax-qualified plan. The difference between the two is that in the former the effective tax rate on the interest accruals in the account is zero, whereas in the latter it would be the statutory rate.

To demonstrate the difference in the two tax treatments of savings, assume that an employee is 10 years from retirement, is facing a marginal tax rate of 25 percent, and expects to face the same tax rate in retirement. Assume further that the employee can either receive $1,000 of current wages in cash or have it contributed to a tax-deferred account payable at retirement. Finally, assume that the worker can either invest the money in a traditional savings account at 10 percent interest compounded annually or in a tax-deferred account at the same rate.

Any saving in the regular savings account can only be accomplished after taxes are paid on the income, while saving in the retirement vehicle is done with pretax dollars. In addition, the interest income that accrues to the saving in the regular account is fully taxed in the year the interest is earned, while the interest accruing to the tax-deferred account is not taxed until the benefit is ultimately distributed during retirement. The timing and payment of the tax obligations under the two scenarios are shown in Table 8-2.

After 10 years, the net after-tax distribution from the tax-deferred account is $1,945.31, while that from the regular account is $1,545.77; the tax-deferred account pays $399.54 more than the regular account. In other words, the tax-deferred account would deliver benefits 17.5 percent greater than the regular account under the assumptions postulated. The differential in the two accounts is strictly due to the different tax treatments of the accounts. There is definitely a higher benefit accrual in the tax-deferred account because of the deferral. Column (3) in Table 8-2 shows the value of taxes paid on the regular account at the end of year 10, with interest compounded at the 10 percent rate assumed for the example. The value of the taxes paid on the initial earnings at the end of 10 years would be $648.44, exactly equal to the actual tax payments that would be made on the tax-deferred account when the distribution was made at retirement. In other words, the taxes on the original earnings are ultimately collected if the tax rates are equivalent before and after retirement. The $339.54 difference in the disposable income paid out of the two accounts is equal to the cumulative value of taxes on the interest income of the deposit in a regular saving account. This difference in the tax treatment of regular savings and tax-deferred savings is the theoretical basis of the measure of tax expenditures attributed to tax-qualified plans that is included in the annual federal budgets submitted to Congress each year.

Practical Issues in the Measurement of Retirement Plan Tax Preferences

The Treasury staff do not actually estimate the annual tax expenditures related to employer-sponsored retirement plans by directly applying the theoretical basis for these expenditures as just detailed. Instead they estimate the taxes that would be paid on contributions to the trusts, if such contributions were paid as regular income. They add to that amount an estimate of the taxes that would be paid on the earnings accruing to the trusts if they were treated as regular income. They subtract from that sum their estimate of the taxes paid on benefits currently being paid through the plans. For several reasons, this method of estimating the tax expenditure related to deferred income programs exaggerates the size of the stated tax expenditure with respect to the concepts on which it is built.

Changes in Pension Coverage

Robert Clark and Elisa Wolper have developed a simple example to show that during periods when a pension system is maturing the current method of calculating tax expenditures would result in an increasing and relatively large estimate.[13] They assume that everyone lives for two periods: during the first one they work and during the second one they are retired. They assume that there are 100 individuals in each birth cohort and that each individual earns a salary of $1,000 during the period in which they work. Some workers join firms that sponsor a pension plan,

---

[13]Robert L. Clark and Elisa Wolper, "Pension Tax Expenditures: Magnitude, Distribution and Economic Effects," in Sylvester J. Schieber and John B. Shoven, eds., *Public Policy Towards Pensions* (Cambridge, Mass.: MIT Press, 1997).

TABLE 8-3   Impact of Pension System Growth on Tax Expenditures

Features of Pension	Year						
	1	2	3	4	5	6	7
Number of workers	100	100	100	100	100	100	100
Number of retirees	0	100	100	100	100	100	100
Coverage rate (%)	0	15	30	40	50	50	45
Number of participants	0	15	30	40	50	50	45
Number of beneficiaries	0	0	15	30	40	50	50
Tax expenditure per participant ($)	0	89.04	89.04	89.04	89.04	89.04	89.04
Taxes paid per beneficiary ($)	0	0	47.70	47.70	47.70	47.70	47.70
Total tax expenditure ($)	0	1,336	1,956	2,131	2,544	2,067	1,622

Source: Clark and Wolper, "Pension Tax Expenditures," p. 64.

where they are paid $700 in cash wages and where the remaining $300 is invested in a pension trust that earns 6 percent interest. Thus when workers retire they are paid $318. Persons with incomes above $500 per period are subject to a 28 percent income tax and those with incomes below $500 are taxed at a rate of 15 percent. Finally, the pension coverage rate grows at first, stabilizes, and then declines. Pension recipiency rates lag behind the coverage rate by one period. The Treasury method of calculation results in a tax loss of $89.04 during the working period, or $84.00 on the contribution (i.e., 0.28 · $300) and $5.04 on the interest (i.e., 0.28 · $18), but a gain of $47.70 (i.e., 0.15 · $318) in taxes during the retirement period. Thus the per capita lifetime tax benefit for workers who participate in pension plans is $41.34.

The results of Clark's and Wolper's exercise are shown in Table 8-3. In their model, the aggregate tax expenditures rise during periods 2 through 5, while the coverage rate exceeds the recipiency rate, but it falls as the system moves into a stable equilibrium. If the system were to continue to operate at the levels attained in period 6, the total tax expenditures would remain constant in subsequent periods. The authors show, however, that if the pension coverage rate were to fall below the recipiency rate, as it does in period 7, the total tax expenditure as measured by the Treasury's methodology would result in a significant decline in the estimated aggregate benefits accruing to pension participants.

This analysis is important in the context of the current maturity of the employer-based pension system in the United States. Today's retirees worked during periods when pensions were much less prevalent, and the current prevalence of pensions has little effect on their retirement income levels. A retiree who is 85 years old today worked in an economy in which the average pension participation rate among private sector wage and salary workers averaged less than 30 percent throughout his or her career. Most retirees today over the age of 85 are women. These women had extremely low labor force participation rates in comparison with women today. Most women in this age group are getting only a small survivor pension, if any. Retirees currently between the ages of 75 and 84 worked in an economy where the average pension participation rate was between 30 and 35 percent throughout their career. Many retirees in this age group retired prior to ERISA's passage, and virtually all did so prior to the passage of the Retirement Equity Act. A retiree who is 65 today spent a career with average pension participation rates around 40 percent. Only 40 percent of today's retirees over the age of 65 are receiving a pension. Today's private sector wage and salary workers, on the other hand, work in an environment in which more than half can expect to receive a pension, generally one that is much larger than that being paid today to current retirees. By offsetting current contributions based on today's high level of worker participation in pensions by relatively low amounts of taxable benefits based on low pension participation rates of former workers, the U.S. Treasury underestimates the taxes that will ultimately be recouped when pensions currently being earned today will be paid as benefits and taxed in the future.

Tax Treatment of Social Security

Social Security benefits have been accorded preferential treatment for years. Until 1984 Social Security benefits were not taxed at all. Between then and 1994 only half the annual Social Security benefit was included in the computation of adjusted gross income (AGI) for determining whether Social Security benefits were to be taxed. Starting in 1994 as much as 85 percent of the Social Security benefit may be taxable for individuals whose "adjusted base" income is $34,000 or higher, and for couples filing jointly with "adjusted base" incomes over $44,000. The tax preferences for Social Security lower the marginal tax rates some pension recipients face, and thus the estimated tax collections on current pension benefits do not reflect the ongoing operation of the tax system. The current treatment of Social Security exaggerates the effects of pensions on federal revenue collections. If the tax preferences for employer-sponsored retirement programs are reduced now because of this exaggeration, it will only be future pensioners who will be penalized, even though they will not get current Social Security preferences

Age Composition of the Population

Today pension plans cover many workers, including the baby boom workers, and a few retirees. Because pension plans are funded on a benefit accrual basis during the covered workers' lifetimes, one should expect pension trusts to grow even more rapidly than in Social Security, which is only partly prefunded. The Treasury methodology now calculates tax expenditures when contributions are abnormally high and benefit payouts are abnormally low because of the age composition of society. By calculating the tax expenditures the way it does, completely ignoring the demographic effects of the baby boomers, the Treasury significantly underestimates the taxes that will ultimately be recouped when pensions being currently earned will be paid as benefits and taxed.

As shown in Table 8-4, Clark and Wolper have also developed a simple example to show how varying demographics can affect the estimated tax expenditure using

TABLE 8-4   Impact of Changing Demographics on Tax Expenditures

Demographic Feature	Year					
	1980	*1990*	*2000*	*2020*	*2040*	*2060*
Ratio of workers to retirees	5.1	4.8	4.6	3.5	2.6	2.5
Number of workers	100	100	100	100	100	100
Number of retirees	20	21	22	29	38	40
Coverage rate (%)	50	50	50	50	50	50
Number of participants	50	50	50	50	50	50
Number of beneficiaries	10.0	10.5	11.0	14.5	19.0	20.0
Total tax expenditure ($)	3,975	3,951	3,927	3,760	3,546	3,498

Source: Clark and Wolper, "Pension Tax Expenditures," p. 64.

the Treasury's calculation method. The ratio of workers to retirees in this example reflects the projected ratio of workers to retirees developed by the Social Security actuaries in valuing the OASDI programs. Using a constant work force and applying the projected ratio of workers to retirees, the authors estimate the number of retirees in future years. They assume that current pension coverage rates in the United States (approximately 50 percent) will continue to into the future. According to their analysis, a stable 50 percent coverage rate will ultimately result in 50 percent of retirees getting a pension benefit.[14] Keeping the assumptions used for Table 8-3, the authors have estimated the tax expenditures in this hypothetical economy over time. Specifically, they have assumed that covered workers would have $300 deferred during their working career, that workers would earn a 6 percent return on this amount, and that beneficiaries would be paid $318 during their retirement period. Also, workers would be subject to a 28 percent marginal tax rate, and retirees would pay taxes on retiree benefits at the 15 percent rate specified earlier. In this example, if pension participation rates among workers remain stable, the aging of the work force, which drives up the dependency ratio over time, drives down the total tax expenditure estimates.

Inclusion of Government Workers in the Calculations

Another problem with the current estimates is that employees covered by the pension programs sponsored by governmental and tax-exempt employers are

[14]In fact, a 50 percent coverage rate could end up in more than 50 percent of future retirees receiving benefits because at any point in time some of the 50 percent of the work force not covered by a plan would have previously vested in a plan sponsored by a prior employer. For example, when Goodfellow and Schieber focus on workers and their spouses between the ages of 45 and 64, ages where workers are approaching retirement, as many as 60 to 70 percent of them are directly or indirectly participating in a pension program. Gordon P. Goodfellow and Sylvester J. Schieber, "Death and Taxes: Can We Fund for Retirement Between Them?" in Ray Schmitt, ed., *The Future of Pensions in the United States* (Philadelphia: University of Pennsylvania Press, 1993), pp. 161–63.

TABLE 8-5   Per Capita Tax Expenditures for Employer-Sponsored Retirement Plans, 1991

	Active Participants (millions)	Tax Expenditures (billions of dollars)	Tax Expenditures per Active Participant
Civil Service Retirement System	1.826	3.5	1,917
Federal Employees Retirement System	1.136	2.2	1,936
Military Retirement System	2.130	4.0	1,877
Federal Thrift Savings Plan	1.419	2.7	1,902
State and local retirement systems	11.357	13.1	1,152
Private defined benefit plans	28.000	8.2	292
Private defined contribution plans	29.000	19.3	665

Source: Dallas Salisbury, "Pension Tax Expenditures: Are They Worth the Cost?" *Issue Brief,* no. 134 (Washington, D.C.: Employee Benefit Research Institute, February 1993), p. 9.

included in calculations. While it can be argued that employees of such organizations accruing future income rights should be treated exactly the same as private sector employees, it is incongruous to include these plans in the "tax expenditure" estimates but exclude them in specific "revenue enhancement" measures. The problem is, no deduction issues are raised when the nontaxable employers contribute to their pensions. The contributions would not be taxable anyway. In fact, looking at the largest of these programs—those sponsored by the federal government—the funding of employee retirement is largely a mirror game. For its civil service and military pensions, the government funds benefits by issuing government securities. In other words, the federal government can increase the general level of tax expenditures by issuing additional IOUs to its pension plans.

Furthermore, including public workers' pensions in the aggregate measure of tax expenditures has a much greater effect on the estimates than the relative numbers of covered workers would suggest. Table 8-5 shows a split of the retirement plan tax expenditures for public and private sector plans and estimated the per capita value of the benefits that are accruing under the various major types of plans. Assuming that the typical worker participating in a private sector retirement plan is participating in both a defined benefit and a defined contribution plan, the average combined value of the tax expenditure is about $960. By comparison, the tax expenditure related to the defined benefit plans covering federal workers is twice that amount. On top of that, the estimated value of the tax expenditure related to the thrift-savings plan for federal workers is nearly the equivalent of the tax expenditure related to the defined benefit plans covering them. The value of the tax benefits accruing under the Military Retirement Systems (MRS) are shown to be slightly less than those that accrue to federal civilian workers under their defined benefit plans. However, Table 8-5 includes only $4.0 billion of the $5.5 billion in total tax expenditures related to the program. If the full $5.5 billion is used in the calculation, the MRS per capita tax benefit would have been $2,582 for 1991. State and local plans would appear to be providing benefits that are more in line with the benefits being provided by private sector employers than those offered by the federal government.

An earlier conclusion suggested there is an inconsistency between federal policy that implies people should save during their working years so they will have an adequate income in retirement, in accordance with the American standard of living, and a policy that would doubly tax the savings they laid aside to meet the first policy goal. There is also an incongruity between including nontaxable entities' pension plans in the tax expenditure calculations and not treating them a source of federal revenue when considering alternative tax treatment for these plans. For example, the Tax Reform Act of 1986 (TRA86) accorded governmental and other nonprofit employer-sponsored plans special provisions that increase the tax expenditure estimates under them. Specifically, TRA86 reduced the maximum benefits that private plans could fund for anyone retiring prior to Social Security's normal retirement age. TRA86 also specifically exempted public employees, including members of Congress, and those working for tax-exempt organizations, because these benefit reductions applied to private sector plans would not raise any additional revenues if they were applied to nontaxable entities.[15] Thus, the tax laws are being written to grant special treatment for government and nonprofit employees because the exemptions do not have revenue effects, but then the tax expenditure calculations are increased as though the exemptions do have revenue effects.

The evidence suggests that workers employed in the governmental bodies legislating and regulating pensions are benefiting to a greater extent, on average, from the preferential tax treatment accorded pensions than are the individuals being regulated. While it is possible to cite examples of rich plans providing generous benefits in the private sector, the limits on benefits and discrimination standards that apply to private sector plans limit the extent of benefits that can be provided to higher-income private sector workers. The fact that federal lawmakers have exempted themselves from these regulations, because they would limit benefits under federal pension plans or limit contributions to their savings programs, also suggests that the biggest beneficiaries of these preferences are the bureaucrats who are setting the rules for everyone else while exempting themselves.

Today more than half of the tax preferences accorded retirement plans are accruing to less than 15 percent of the work force, namely public sector workers. Deliberations on public policy regarding retirement programs, especially policies directed specifically at private sector plans, would be better served if the tax expenditure issues and estimates were delineated separately for public sector and private sector plans. If half of the estimated tax expenditures related to pensions can be attributed to returns on assets related to inflation (see below) and if half of the remainder has nothing to do with plans sponsored by taxable entities, full elimination of the preferential tax treatment accorded private pensions would raise significantly less federal revenue than implied by the tax expenditure estimates included in the annual federal budgets. It would do so at a significant cost for the retirement income security of a large segment of the work force in the private sector. Singular curtailment of the retirement benefits that private sector workers can accrue under their plans without addressing the preferential

---

[15]Similarly, the federal government as an employer is exempted from having to meet the actual deferral percentage (ADP) tests for its own 401(k)-type savings plan that it requires all private sector employers to meet.

treatment accorded public sector workers under the Tax Reform Act of 1986 will merely exacerbate the existing inequities.

Policy Conflicts and Pension-Related Tax Expenditures

While the measurement of the tax expenditures related to employer-sponsored retirement plans raises several methodological issues, an even more fundamental problem with the estimates is that the theoretical concept is inconsistent with other stated public policies. One of the stated goals of public policy of the U.S. federal government, as specified in the Older Americans Act of 1965, is that the older citizens of this nation should enjoy "an adequate income in retirement in accordance with the American standard of living."[16] One of the problems with the Older Americans Act is that it is not specific about the levels of income that would satisfy "the American standard of living." Some other conventional measures of adequacy might be considered in this context, however. At the lower end of the income spectrum, absolute measures of adequacy are implied by the federal government's official poverty line. At income levels above these minimalist measures, adequacy of retirement income is often measured against the ability to maintain preretirement living standards.

An analysis of the measures usually used to assess the adequacy of benefits provided through retirement programs shows that Social Security benefits by themselves are inadequate to finance consumption levels commensurate with the American standard of living across most of the income spectrum (see Chapters 18 and 19). This means that in order to attain adequate retirement income to sustain the American standard of living, individuals must accumulate other resources during their working careers by deferring consumption until their retirement. This public policy goal as stated in law is not consistent with the concept of the comprehensive income tax and its application to tax deferrals on retirement plan accumulations.

Current measurements of tax expenditures based on the concept of the comprehensive income tax overlook the fact that some portion of the returns on assets over time do not reflect real economic return for deferring consumption but rather make up for the decreased purchasing power of money resulting from price inflation. That is, the interest rate i in Equation (8-6) above is composed of two elements:

$$(8\text{-}8) \qquad\qquad i = (dP/P) + r$$

where P is the price level in the current period, dP is the change in prices from the current period to the future period, and r is the real rate of return on assets in excess of inflation. In other words,

$$(8\text{-}9) \qquad\qquad C_F/C_P = 1/[1 + (dP/P)(1 - t) + r(1 - t)].$$

In order for deferred consumption to at least be of equal value to present consumption, the rate of return on deferred consumption has to at least equal the rate of inflation. Since the return defined by the factor (dP/P) is merely maintain-

---

[16]Public Law 89-73, USC.

TABLE 8-6   Relative Value of Money in a Normal Savings Account Paying a Rate of Return Equivalent to a 5 Percent Inflation Rate and Subject to 25 Percent Tax Rates

Year	Nominal Value of Constant Purchasing Power	Nominal Value of Savings	Gross Interest	Net Interest	Purchasing Power of Savings as Percentage of Original Earnings	Effective Tax Rate on Original Earnings
0	1,000.00	750.00	37.50	28.13	75.0	25.0
1	1,050.00	778.13	38.91	29.18	74.1	25.9
2	1,102.50	807.30	40.37	30.27	73.2	26.8
3	1,157.63	837.58	41.88	31.41	72.4	27.6
4	1,215.51	868.99	43.45	32.59	71.5	28.5
5	1,276.28	901.57	45.08	33.81	70.6	29.4
6	1,340.10	935.38	46.77	35.08	69.8	30.2
7	1,407.10	970.46	48.52	36.39	69.0	31.0
8	1,477.46	1,006.85	50.34	37.76	68.1	31.9
9	1,551.33	1,044.61	52.23	39.17	67.3	32.7
10	1,628.89	1,083.78	54.19	40.64	66.5	33.5
20	2,653.30	1,566.11	78.31	58.73	59.0	41.0
30	4,321.94	2,263.10	113.16	84.87	52.4	47.6

Source: Watson Wyatt.

ing the purchasing power of income across periods, taxing that factor subjects income to an added tax if it is not consumed immediately. This conception of a "comprehensive tax," where the return on assets that covers inflation is taxable, is the theoretical basis for measuring tax preferences for retirement and savings plans. Under this model, income deferred for retirement purposes outside of a tax-qualified plan is subjected to a higher tax than it would be if used for immediate consumption purposes if there is any inflation at all in the economy.

Consider the extreme case in which the total return on assets equals the inflation rate. Suppose an individual has $1,000 in earnings that can either be consumed today or saved for future retirement consumption purposes. This individual is subject to a marginal tax rate of 25 percent, so the $1,000 in earnings will yield $750 in disposable income. It is actually only the $750 that the individual can use for current consumption or invest for future purposes. For the sake of simplicity, assume that inflation is steady at 5 percent per year and that the individual can invest in a risk-free bond that pays a nominal rate of return of 5 percent per annum, a zero yield in real terms.[17]

Table 8-6 shows that deferring consumption under this type of regime results in a gradual deterioration of the purchasing power of money saved in relation to the

[17]Using an interest rate that merely equals the rate of inflation in the economy is meant to show the effects of the tax system on inflationary gains on savings. It is not meant to suggest that savers cannot realize positive real rates of return. The effects reflected in this example, where the interest rate equals the inflation rate, are equally applicable to situations where the interest rate exceeds the rate of inflation in the economy, as is shown later.

TABLE 8-7   Effective Tax Rates on Current Versus Future Consumption When Consumption Is Deferred Through a Regular Savings Account at 5 and 10 Percent Interest and Inflation Rates

	Effective Tax Rate	
	25 percent	*33 percent*
Consumption time frame at 5 percent interest and inflation rates		
Immediate	25.0	33.0
After 10 years	33.5	42.8
After 20 years	41.0	51.2
After 30 years	47.6	58.3
Consumption time frame at 10 percent interest and inflation rates		
Immediate	25.0	33.0
After 10 years	40.4	50.6
After 20 years	52.6	63.6
After 30 years	62.4	73.1

Source: Watson Wyatt.

purchasing power of the income originally earned. If the earnings are consumed the year earned, the taxpayer can consume 75 percent of the value of earnings. If consumption is deferred just one year, the purchasing power drops to 74.1 percent of the value of the initial earnings. This loss in purchasing power results because the inflationary return on the asset is taxed. No added income accrues to the account holder under the assumptions, just added tax, because of the decision to defer consumption. If the savings are held in this environment for 10 years, the effective tax on the original earnings rises to 33.5 percent. After 20 years it is 41.0 percent, and after 30 years it is up to 47.6 percent. Further analysis of this phenomenon shows that the effective tax rate on earnings not immediately consumed varies in relation to a number of factors, as shown in Table 8-7. Here the effective tax rate varies with the underlying statutory tax rate, the duration of time that consumption is deferred, and the economy's underlying inflation rate.

Thus far it has been assumed that the inflation rate and the rate of return on deferred consumption are identical. In the situation shown in Table 8-8, the savings account has a 10 percent nominal rate of return during a period with 5 percent inflation. The statutory tax rate is assumed to be 25 percent for the calculation. In this case, the after-tax return on the savings can be broken into its component elements to show the effective yield on savings after the effects of inflation on the purchasing power of money are taken into account. Under these assumptions, 50 percent goes to keep up with the eroding purchasing power of money, and 25 percent of the gross interest goes to pay taxes. The effective yield on the deferred consumption in this case implies a 50 percent tax on the real return, which is double the statutory tax rate assumed in the development of this example. In other words, the concept of the comprehensive income tax behind the measurement of tax expenditures related to tax-qualified retirement plans would penalize

TABLE 8-8   Relative Value of Money and Returns in a Normal Savings Account Paying a
10 Percent Rate of Return with a 5 Percent Inflation Rate and Subject to
25 Percent Tax Rates

Year	Nominal Value of Constant Purchasing Power	Nominal Value of Savings	Gross Interest	Net Interest	Inflation Return on Savings Balance	Real Return in Excess of Inflation
1	750.00	750.00	75.00	56.25	37.50	18.75
2	787.50	806.25	80.63	60.47	40.31	20.16
3	826.88	866.72	86.67	65.00	43.34	21.67
4	868.22	931.72	93.17	69.88	46.59	23.29
5	911.63	1,001.60	100.16	75.12	50.08	25.04
6	957.21	1,076.72	107.67	80.75	53.84	26.92
7	1,005.07	1,157.48	115.75	86.81	57.87	28.94
8	1,055.33	1,244.29	124.43	93.32	62.21	31.11
9	1,108.09	1,337.61	133.76	100.32	66.88	33.44
10	1,163.50	1,437.93	143.79	107.84	71.90	35.95
20	1,895.21	2,963.62	296.36	222.27	148.18	74.09
30	3,087.10	6,108.11	610.81	458.11	305.41	152.70

Source: Watson Wyatt.

people who deferred consumption during their working career in order to attain
the federal policy goal of having a consumption level in retirement commensurate
with the American standard of living, since that standard of living cannot be
attained in most cases without such deferred consumption. The two policies are
simply incompatible and irreconcilable.

Some policy analysts suggest that it would be desirable to eliminate the inflation
component of return on capital under the tax system on theoretical grounds, but
that the actual tax expenditure calculation related to pensions should still consider
them, since indexing is not part of the tax system.[18] They argue that it does not
make sense to single out pensions for special treatment in the measurement of tax
expenditures. But the annual federal budget documents themselves create considerable confusion about what should be considered a tax expenditure for purposes
of developing budgetary estimates. This confusion arises because the Congressional Budget Act of 1974, which requires that a list of such expenditures be
included in the budget, failed to specify the baseline provisions of the tax law
against which they could be estimated. The 1993 budget observed that decisions
on whether specific provisions of the tax law are preferential exceptions to the
baseline provisions "is a matter of judgment."[19] The Fiscal 1993 budgetary document specifically addressed the issue of taxing the inflationary return on savings: "A
comprehensive income tax would adjust the cost basis of capital assets and debt for

---

[18]For example, see Alicia H. Munnell, "Comments," in Ray Schmitt, ed., *The Future of Pensions in the
United States* (Philadelphia: Pension Research Council and University of Pennsylvania Press, 1993),
p. 188.

[19]Executive Office of the President, *Budget . . . Fiscal Year 1993*, pt. 2, p. 23.

changes in the price level during the time the assets or debt are held. Thus, under a comprehensive income tax baseline the failure to take account of inflation in measuring . . . interest income would be regarded as a negative tax expenditure (i.e., a tax penalty)."[20]

If including the inflation component of interest earnings on retirement assets results in a "negative tax expenditure," it should exactly offset the positive inflation component of returns on pension assets that is built into the annual estimates of these tax expenditures included in the annual federal budgets. In other words, the tax expenditures related to tax-qualified retirement plans included in the annual federal budget estimates are not only inconsistent with other federal policy, they are exaggerated by the amount of inflationary return on assets in all of the respective plans. If the inflationary return on pension assets is not part of the calculations, the magnitude of the tax preferences accorded employer-sponsored retirement plans declines significantly.

No serious analyst would consider inflationary returns on pension assets as real income. The budget documents themselves have indicated in the past that the inclusion of certain items is judgmental. Furthermore, the budget documents have also specifically indicated in the past that the failure to take inflation into account in considering interest income issues is wrong. Each of these points raises questions about why the inflationary return on pension assets is included in the calculation of pension-related tax expenditures. Finally, if attaining federal government policy goals implies that individual workers have to save some of their lifetime wages to help meet their own retirement needs, why would it impose a "tax penalty" on them for doing so?

Gordon Goodfellow and Sylvester Schieber developed a modified calculation procedure that is more consistent with the concept of having workers defer consumption from the period of their lives when they are working in order to help meet their consumption needs during their retirement years. This concept of tax expenditure is based on only the tax preference accorded to real returns on pension assets. Using the alternative measurement methodology, the average tax expenditure estimate for the first four years after tax reform would have been $27 billion, or about half the estimated tax expenditure calculated by the traditional method.[21]

Retirement Program Tax Effects from a Broader Perspective

Much of the literature analyzing the preferential tax treatment of employer-sponsored retirement plans is written purely from the perspective of the federal income tax. Federal taxing and retirement policy, however, extends well beyond the income tax. The critics of tax preferences for employer-based retirement plans have thus far ignored the interaction of the tax incentives accorded pensions and the taxation and benefit elements of Social Security. In order to assess the interaction of pensions and Social Security, Goodfellow and Schieber calculated the present value of Social Security benefits and taxes and the tax advantage of

[20]Ibid.
[21]Goodfellow and Schieber, "Death and Taxes," p. 153.

qualified pension and savings plans.[22] They noted that many workers covered under Social Security as it is currently configured face the prospect of receiving benefits in retirement with a significantly lower economic value than the value of the payroll tax contributions they and their employers will make over their working careers. They argued that looking at the combined taxation and benefit effects of Social Security and pensions would give a more complete picture of the net winners and losers under federal retirement policy. They based their analysis on estimated benefits and taxes calculated for 25 hypothetical employees. These persons were assumed to be 30, 35, 40, 45, or 50 in 1991 and to have earnings in 1991 equal to $10,000, $20,000, $30,000, $50,000, or $100,000.

For purposes of Social Security, the hypothetical employee was assumed to enter covered employment at age 22 and to work continuously until retirement. Earnings were assumed to increase at 5 percent per year before 1991, and to continue to increase at 5 percent beyond that point until retirement.[23] All employees were assumed to retire at age 65. Qualified plan benefits were based on the hypothetical employees' last jobs. Ultimate tenure in these final jobs was 35, 30, 25, 20, and 15 years. Social Security benefits were calculated for age 65 retirement under Social Security and tax laws as they existed in 1992, projected into the future. In the projections of benefits, national average wages were assumed to increase by 5 percent per year after 1990. The inflation rate was assumed to be 4 percent per year.

Unlike previous estimates of money's worth, the computations here were based on an after-tax Social Security benefit. Taxable retirement income was assumed to consist of benefits from the qualified plans, other income, and 50 percent of the Social Security benefit. Other income was calculated by assuming that the hypothetical employees have additional income in retirement equal to a percentage of final earnings that varies with earnings. Persons with $10,000 of starting earnings were assumed to have no other income. The assumed percentage of final earnings is 5 percent at $20,000, 7.5 percent at $30,000, 10 percent at $50,000, and 15 percent at $100,000.

Total income at retirement was compared to the $25,000 threshold amount for a single person, and the excess up to 50 percent of the Social Security benefit was taxed under law as it existed at the time the analysis was calculated. The income tax rate used in the computations was 15 percent for hypothetical employees whose starting wages in 1991 were $10,000, $20,000, and $30,000; it was 28 percent for employees whose starting wage was $50,000; and it was 31 percent for employees whose starting wage was $100,000. Income tax rates were not assumed to vary over the working and retired life of the employee.

Once Goodfellow and Schieber calculated after-tax Social Security benefits, they estimated the lump-sum equivalents using 1984 unisex pension mortality rates, with a 6 percent interest rate and a 4 percent cost-of-living increase. The analysis

---

[22]Ibid., pp. 126–79.

[23]In their analysis, Goodfellow and Schieber actually used a 6 percent wage growth factor, but Alicia Munnell in her comments on their work criticized their using a higher wage growth factor for the pension-covered work force than for the work force in general. She asserted that this assumption resulted in larger losses under Social Security than would result if pension-covered wages grew at the same rate as general wages across the national economy. See her "Comments," p. 191.

presented here deviates from the earlier projections in that it accounts for future improvements in life expectancy. Social Security actuaries project future improvements in life expectancy that imply the baby boom generation will live about 1.6 years longer than current retirees. Payroll taxes earmarked for OASI benefits were calculated using the current law rates applicable to employees and employers. Interest on taxes accumulated to retirement at the rate of 6 percent, and there was no taxation of interest earnings. No preretirement mortality was assumed.

In analyzing the value of the tax preferences accorded to pension participants, Goodfellow and Schieber used detailed information Watson Wyatt Worldwide had gathered on the pension and savings plan benefits for about 675 companies.[24] Of these companies, 308 had a 401(k) arrangement for employee tax-deferred savings and provided a defined benefit plan for employees. For each such company, the retirement annuity under the defined benefit plan was calculated as the terms applied to new hires. The defined benefit annuity was converted to a lump-sum equivalent. The lump-sum account balances for the 401(k) arrangements of the companies were calculated using reported actual employee contribution rates and the employers' matching rates.

Employee contribution rates to the defined contribution plan for non–highly and highly compensated employees were assumed to be equal to the current Actual Deferral Percentage (ADP) rates reported by companies for such employees. If the company did not report its ADP rates, the average of all companies that did report rates was used. The income level at which employees were considered to be highly compensated was $60,535 in 1991. For computational simplicity, once a hypothetical employee was placed in the non–highly compensated group, he or she did not switch to the highly compensated group, even if future earnings exceeded the indexed threshold. This calculation procedure affects hypothetical employees whose starting wage was $50,000 in 1991 and whose tenure in the last job was more than 11 years. Thus the hypothetical employees whose starting wages were $50,000 remained in the non–highly compensated group, although wage growth at 5 percent per year would have resulted in earnings larger than the crossover income level in a future year. Contributions accumulated with 6 percent interest until retirement.

The tax advantage of qualified plans was calculated in three steps. First, the lump-sum equivalent of retirement benefits under the qualified savings and pension plans was calculated for each hypothetical employee for each defined contribution and defined benefit plan of the companies in the data base. Second, the lump sum was used to calculate a level contribution rate as a percentage of earnings such that annual contributions at the calculated contribution rate, accumulated at 6 percent interest, equal the actual lump sum calculated for each employee and plan. In effect, each plan was treated as if it were a money purchase plan that was not coordinated with Social Security. Finally, the contribution rates calculated above was used to determine the lump sum that would accrue by retirement under two taxation schemes. The difference between the after-tax

---

[24]In 1995, the Wyatt Company allied with R. Watson & Sons and both firms now operate under the name Watson Wyatt Worldwide. We will use the term "Watson Wyatt" in all references to the company.

actual lump-sum equivalent benefit and the lump sums calculated under the two alternative taxation schemes represents the tax benefits for qualified plans.

Qualified plan benefits accumulate without current taxation. To estimate the tax benefits that accrue to participants in qualified plans, the annual contribution amounts made to the plans were estimated and then the taxes that would be paid on contributions and the yield on account balances were estimated under two scenarios. In the first scenario, all contributions and earnings were assumed to be taxed as they accrued. The difference between the after-tax lump sums of the qualified plans and the lump sum that would accrue if contributions and earnings were fully taxed each year is the estimated tax benefit of the tax treatment of qualified plans at the time of the analysis. Under the estimated alternative tax benefit contributions to the plan and only that portion of the annual yield on the account balance in excess of the inflation rate were considered.

The estimated tax benefits show that workers with higher-paid jobs derive greater benefits from the pension system than lower-paid workers. Workers who have longer tenures under their pension plans derive greater benefits than those with shorter service. Under the method of estimating the tax benefits, however, only real returns on assets were considered to be taxable and the resulting tax benefits were only about one-third the level of those estimated using the underlying methodology usually applied. Still, calculations done in this fashion revealed the same general pattern of tax-related benefits.

As Table 8-9 shows, combining the tax benefits from an employer-sponsored retirement plan with Social Security gains and losses gives a more complete picture of the net effects of the combined payroll and income tax systems on retirement savings than just looking at these benefits separately. The results presented here are substantially different from those presented earlier. The reduction in the rate of growth of wages for pension-covered workers did have a slight marginal effect on the results, but it was not as significant as one might expect. For the worker in the highest wage category, this change had no effect at all, because the worker's wage level exceeded the maximum covered wages under Social Security in every year of both projections. For other workers, the reductions in the rate of growth of their wages reduced their overall lifetime tax obligations, but it also reduced the benefits that they can expect to receive in retirement. While the reduction in the tax obligations was on average somewhat larger than the benefit reductions, the combined effect was rather small. The far larger change in these projections is the result of considering improvements in life expectancy. Although increased life expectancy had no effect on the accumulated value of contributions, because the model did not consider preretirement mortality, it had a significant effect on the value of benefits, because it cumulatively extended the benefit periods for each successive cohort of retiring workers.

The essence of the findings is that above middle earnings levels, expected economic losses from participating in Social Security generally overwhelm the benefits provided through the tax incentives accorded employer-sponsored retirement programs. Under the more restrictive definition of the tax preference, the tax benefit accorded the pension completely offsets Social Security loss for the long-tenured worker in the $100,000 pay category. Such a person would be unique, however, in that he or she would already be earning $100,000 at age 30 or

TABLE 8-9   Gains and Losses from Social Security, Average Pension Accrual Gains, and Net Gains and Losses Combined

1991 Wages ($)	Years in Last Job	Social Security Gains or Losses	Pension Accrual Gains		Net Gains or Losses	
			All Yield Taxed	Real Yield Taxed	All Yield Taxed	Real Yield Taxed
10,000	15	42,384	1,689	578	44,073	42,962
	20	37,648	3,113	1,075	40,761	38,723
	25	35,359	5,069	1,766	40,428	37,125
	30	29,840	7,634	2,685	37,474	32,525
	35	21,705	10,841	3,849	32,546	25,554
20,000	15	41,064	3,389	1,159	44,453	42,223
	20	27,135	6,334	2,187	33,469	29,322
	25	15,038	10,394	3,622	25,432	18,660
	30	3,972	15,696	5,521	19,668	9,493
	35	−7,149	22,248	7,899	15,099	750
30,000	15	29,790	5,184	1,773	34,974	31,563
	20	6,153	9,665	3,336	15,818	9,489
	25	−8,796	15,815	5,511	7,019	−3,285
	30	−20,745	23,839	8,385	3,094	−12,360
	35	−36,432	33,746	11,982	−2,686	−24,450
50,000	15	−31,894	14,089	4,924	−17,805	−26,970
	20	−66,867	25,868	9,197	−40,999	−57,670
	25	−97,514	41,785	15,110	−55,729	−82,404
	30	−131,514	62,003	22,802	−69,511	−108,712
	35	−163,122	86,545	32,431	−76,577	−130,691
100,000	15	−44,314	34,673	12,177	−9,641	−32,137
	20	−78,944	63,743	22,834	−15,201	−56,110
	25	−112,367	103,327	38,019	−9,040	−74,348
	30	−150,160	153,778	58,126	3,618	−92,034
	35	−186,643	214,965	83,762	28,322	−102,881

Source: Watson Wyatt.

35 and would have to work under the same plan until retirement at age 65. The pension accrual gains shown in Table 8-9 are the average of those estimated for all of the plans for which we could estimate benefits. Even the tax benefits provided by the most generous plans could not overcome the Social Security losses at the higher income levels under the definition of the tax preference that would consider the real yield on retirement savings as receiving a tax benefit.

The overall system appears to be somewhat progressive up to the Social Security maximum taxable income level, where the stabilization of Social Security losses is gradually offset by increased benefits provided through the pension system. There is a limit, though, to the extent to which high-salaried workers can derive added benefits through the tax preferences afforded pensions because of the section 415 limits that cap them. In the calculations, the youngest individual considered at the 1991 wage level of $100,000 per year (i.e., the 30-year-old) would have his or her benefits capped by the section 415 limits in slightly more than half of the plans for which benefits were estimated. In any event, results under the combined pension and Social Security systems suggest that younger workers in the middle through the highest income ranges can expect no subsidization of their lifetime retirement savings even though they may participate in fairly generous pension programs.[25]

---

[25]The picture detailed in Table 8-8 is not fully current because it does not take into account the tax changes that were implemented in the Omnibus Budget Reconciliation Act of 1993 (OBRA93). OBRA93 would have the effect of increasing the value of the tax preference for the employer-sponsored benefit for the individuals in the highest income brackets, but it would also have the effect of increasing the Social Security losses since more of the Social Security benefits would be subjected to taxation and at higher rates than under prior law.

Chapter 9
Organizational Structure and Flexibility

Given the complexity of designing, implementing, and maintaining a private retirement plan, the additional complexity of considering the sponsoring employer's organizational structure may appear daunting at first glance. But an examination of the various issues considered by and potentially affecting different employers reveals a logical consistency.

It must be pointed out that in today's business environment the size and form of an employer are dynamic, rather than static. Various types of organizational transactions, including business mergers and acquisitions as well as plan mergers, can affect the employer's compliance strategy and plans. When examining a plan's structure, it is vital to consider not only the various changes in the demographics of the plan's participation but also the different types of compliance transition rules intended to allow plans to comply before, during, and after an organizational transaction.

Organizational Structure

Whether the business sponsoring the retirement plan is organized as a corporation, partnership, or sole proprietorship can have an impact on plan design and compliance. While the Tax Equity and Fiscal Responsibility Act of 1982 eliminated many of the differences between retirement plans sponsored by corporate employers and those sponsored by noncorporate employers, some distinctions still remain. In addition, determining exactly who the "employer" is can be far more complicated than it appears at first glance.

The Internal Revenue Code defines employer in terms of the "controlled group" of corporations, trades, or businesses.[1] So the employer of an employee working for a subsidiary corporation also includes the parent corporation and any other subsidiary corporations, also known as brother-sister corporations.

The controlled group rules apply not only to corporations but include noncorporate businesses connected by common ownership. Determining the scope of the controlled group is often the first step in determining the compliance of a retirement plan, since the coverage and benefits provided under a retirement plan are tested against the entire work force of the controlled group, and not just the employees of the specific business entity sponsoring the plan.

[1]IRC §414(b) and (c).

A notable exception to the concept of controlled group, is the separate line of business rules (SLOB), which allow certain, usually diversified controlled groups to test the retirement plans sponsored by separate lines of business as if they were sponsored by separate employers. The rules for determining whether a controlled group has separate lines of business are among the most complex of the retirement plan rules, with several potential hurdles that must be overcome before an employer can take advantage of the SLOB rules.

Choice of Business Entity

In determining the appropriate entity in which to do business, an employer almost never considers how this choice will affect the employee benefit plan. Whether a business is organized as a corporation, S-corporation, partnership, or sole proprietorship depends on the number of owners, the type of business, and other legal and tax considerations. The employee benefit plan does not enter into these considerations. While this is unarguably the appropriate prioritization of the issues when selecting a form of business entity, the employer's choice of how it will organize to do business can have a substantial impact on the design of retirement and benefit plans.

Corporate versus Noncorporate Employers

As noted earlier, the Tax Equity and Fiscal Responsibility Act of 1982 eliminated many of the differences between retirement plans sponsored by corporate employers and plans sponsored by noncorporate employers. Nevertheless, some important distinctions still remain. For an employee, whose compensation is based on wages,[2] the determination of compensation or earned income is obviously different from that for self-employed individuals, whose income is measured as self-employment earnings or earned income.[3] Although substantial owners of a normal corporate employer who participate in the company's pension plan may be eligible for a plan loan on that basis of their account balance, certain substantial owners of S-corporations or members of partnerships may not be eligible for such loans.[4] Finally, while generally not an issue for qualified retirement plans, many owner-employees of noncorporate businesses may not be considered "employees" and therefore may not be eligible to participate in certain types of welfare benefit plans. This is generally not an issue for retirement plans, since owner-employees are considered employees for purposes of pension and profit-sharing plans.[5]

While these distinctions between corporate and noncorporate employers may be important to certain businesses or owner-employees, in general they do not determine the form of doing business. In fact, one of the more important issues usually considered in choosing a business form, namely, the personal liability of the owners, is generally not an issue for qualified retirement plans. Whether a plan

---

[2] IRC §414(s).
[3] IRC §401(c).
[4] IRC §4975(d).
[5] IRC §401(c)(1)(A).

sponsor is a corporate or noncorporate employer, the plan's liability to partici-pants and beneficiaries is generally limited to the amount of plan assets. While the Pension Benefit Guaranty Corporation can seek general assets of the employer in situations involving termination of an underfunded plan, the amount of assets that the PBGC can reach is not governed by the business form of the plan sponsor.[6] In addition, the personal liability that a plan fiduciary may be liable for under a breach of fiduciary duty to a qualified retirement plan is unaffected by whether the plan sponsor or fiduciary is an individual, corporation, or noncorporate business form.[7]

Accordingly, the issue relating to the business form of the plan sponsor that occupies most of the time of an employee benefit plan professional is not the appropriate business form for the employer but the businesses that comprise the employer. Given the myriad types of business structure, determining which busi-nesses are and are not part of the "employer" for retirement plan sponsorship purposes can often be perplexing. The tax code generally defines the employer in terms of the controlled group of businesses under common control, a concept that includes not only parent-subsidiary groups and brother-sister groups but also affiliated service groups.

Controlled Groups of Businesses Under Common Control

The Treasury has not adopted separate regulations on the one-employer rule for controlled groups of corporations[8] on the one hand, and for businesses under common control[9] on the other. The same set of regulations[10] applies to both. As mandated by Code sections 414(b) and (c), these regulations are primarily based on the provisions of Code section 1563 (and the regulations thereunder), which set forth the definition of a "controlled group of corporations" for purposes of the corporate income tax.

Three kinds of businesses are under common control: (1) the parent-subsidiary group, (2) the brother-sister group, and (3) the combined group. The organiza-tions that can be constituents of any of these groups are sole proprietorships, partnerships, trusts, estates, and corporations.[11]

The definition of corporations or trades or businesses under common control used for retirement plan sponsorship purposes is generally the same as it is for corporate income tax purposes. Accordingly, a good rule of thumb is that busi-nesses that file a consolidated tax return for income tax purposes can generally be considered a controlled group of trades or businesses for employee benefit plan purposes. A notable exception to this rule, however, is that while foreign corpora-tions are generally not considered members of a controlled group for U.S. corpo-rate income tax purposes,[12] they will be considered members of the controlled

[6]ERISA §4062(a).
[7]ERISA §409.
[8]IRC §414(b).
[9]IRC §414(c).
[10]Treas. Reg. 1.414(c)-1 through 1.414(c)-4.
[11]Treas. Reg. 1.414(c)-2(a).
[12]IRC §1562(b)(2)(C).

group for employee benefit plan purposes.[13] This means that while foreign companies, including foreign parent organizations, may not be represented on the consolidated income tax return, they must still be considered part of the controlled group for employee benefit plan purposes. The true impact of this rule is fairly limited, however, since nonresident alien employees (i.e., the employees of foreign corporations) are excluded from consideration in nondiscrimination testing.[14]

As mentioned earlier, two or more trades or businesses will be considered under common control if they compose either a parent-subsidiary group of trades or businesses, a brother-sister group of trades or businesses, or a combined group of trades or businesses under common control.

Parent-Subsidiary

A parent-subsidiary group of trades or businesses under common control is generally one or more chains of businesses connected through ownership by a common parent organization. The common parent organization, and each succeeding organization in the hierarchy, must own a controlling interest in its subsidiaries, generally defined as stock ownership with at least 80 percent of the total combined voting power of all classes of stock.[15]

For example, assume L Corporation owns 80 percent of the only class of stock of T Corporation, and T, in turn, owns 40 percent of the capital interest in the GHI Partnership. L also owns 80 percent of the only class of stock of N Corporation, and N, in turn, owns 40 percent of the capital interest in the GHI Partnership. L is the common parent of a parent-subsidiary group of trades or businesses under common control consisting of L Corporation, T Corporation, N Corporation, and the GHI Partnership.[16]

Alternatively, assume ABC Partnership owns 75 percent of the only class of stock of X and Y Corporations; X owns all the remaining stock of Y, and Y owns all the remaining stock of X. Since interorganization ownership is excluded (that is, treated as not outstanding) for purposes of determining whether ABC owns a controlling interest of at least one of the other organizations, ABC is treated as the stock owner possessing 100 percent of the voting power and value of all classes of stock of X and Y. Therefore, ABC is the common parent of a parent-subsidiary group of trades or businesses under common control consisting of the ABC Partnership, X Corporation, and Y Corporation.[17]

---

[13]Treas. Reg. 1.414(b)-1(a). The definition of controlled group for income tax purposes excludes foreign corporations from being "component members" of the controlled group. The retirement plan definition of controlled group, however, determines the scope of the controlled group without consideration of whether a business unit is a component member of the controlled group, thereby bringing foreign corporations into the fold.
[14]IRC §410(b)(3).
[15]Treas. Reg. 1.414(c)-2(b).
[16]Treas. Reg. 1.414(c)-2(e), Example 2.
[17]Treas. Reg. 1.414(c)-2(e), Example 3.

TABLE 9-1   Example of Controlled Group Rules (percent)

Owners	A	GHI	M	W	X	Y	Z
A	100	50	100	60	40	20	60
B	—	40	—	15	40	50	30
C	—	—	—	—	10	10	10
D	—	—	—	25	—	20	—
E	—	10	—	—	10	—	—
—	100	100	100	100	100	100	100

— = Zero ownership percentage.

Brother-Sister Group

A brother-sister group of trades or businesses under common control is a more complicated entity consisting of two or more businesses in which the same five or fewer persons own a controlling interest in each organization. If the ownership of each such person is taken into account only to the extent such ownership is identical for each such organization, such persons are in effective control of each organization.[18]

For purposes of a brother-sister group of trades or businesses, a controlling interest is still considered to be ownership of stock possessing at least 80 percent of the total combined voting power of all classes of stock. Effective control of an organization is obtained by owning stock possessing more than 50 percent of the total combined voting power of all stock of the corporation. In determining whether the group of individuals have effective control of the trades or businesses, however, each individual's stock ownership is considered only to the extent that it is identical for all the trades or businesses, which is essentially the lowest ownership percentage in each business by each individual.

For example, assume unrelated individuals A, B, C, D, E, and F own an interest in sole proprietorship A, a capital interest in the GHI Partnership, and stock of corporations M, W, X, Y, and Z (each of which has only one class of stock outstanding) in the proportions noted in Table 9-1.

Under these conditions, the following four brother-sister groups of trades or businesses under common control exist: GHI, X, and Z; X, Y, and Z; W and Y; and A and M. In the case of GHI, X, and Z, for example, A and B together have effective control of each organization because their combined identical ownership of GHI, X, and Z is greater than 50 percent. (A's identical ownership of GHI, X, and Z is 40 percent because A owns at least a 40 percent interest in each organization. B's identical ownership of GHI, X, and Z is 30 percent because B owns at least a 30 percent interest in each organization.) A and B (the persons whose ownership is considered for purposes of the effective control requirement) together own a controlling interest in each organization because they own at least 80 percent of the capital interest of partnership GHI and at least 80 percent of the total combined voting power of corporations X and Z. Therefore, GHI, X, and Z comprise a

[18]Treas. Reg. 1.414(c)-2(c).

TABLE 9-2   Example of Controlled Group Rules (percent)

Individuals	U	V
A	12	12
B	12	12
C	12	12
D	12	12
E	13	13
F	13	13
G	13	13
H	13	13
Total	100	100

brother-sister group of trades or businesses under common control. Y is not a member of this group because neither the effective control requirement nor the 80 percent controlling interest requirement are met. (The effective control requirement is not met because A's and B's combined identical ownership in GHI, X, Y, and Z—20 percent for A and 30 percent for B—does not exceed 50 percent. The 80 percent controlling interest test is not met because A and B together only own 70 percent of the total combined voting power of the stock of Y.) A and M are not members of this group because B owns no interest in either organization and A's ownership of GHI, X, and Z, considered alone, is less than 80 percent.[19]

Alternatively, assume the outstanding stock of corporations U and V, which have only one class of stock outstanding, is owned by the following unrelated individuals, as detailed in Table 9-2. Any group of five of the shareholders will own more than 50 percent of the stock in each corporation, in identical holdings. However, U and V are not members of a brother-sister group of trades or businesses under common control because at least 80 percent of the stock of each corporation is not owned by the same five or fewer persons.[20]

A combined group of trades or businesses under common control is a group of three or more organizations if each such organization is a member of either a parent-subsidiary group of trade or businesses or a brother-sister group of trade or businesses and at least one such organization is the common parent organization or a parent-subsidiary group and is also a member of a brother-sister group of trade or businesses.[21]

Ownership Attribution

In determining a person's ownership interest, certain stock or partnership interests or other ownership interests not directly owned by an individual or person will be attributed to that person from other entities. For example, an interest owned, directly or indirectly, by or for a corporation shall be considered as owned by any person who owns 5 percent or more of the corporation's stock in

---

[19]Treas. Reg. 1.414(c)-2(e), Example 4.
[20]Treas. Reg. 1.414(c)-2(e), Example 5.
[21]Treas. Reg. 1.414(c)-2(d).

that proportion that the value of the stock that the person owns bears to the total value of all stock of such corporation.[22]

In addition, stock owned by a spouse, other than a spouse who is legally separated from the individual, shall be attributed to the individual, and stock owned by an individual's children who have not attained the age of 21 years will be attributed to the individual.[23] Similarly, stock owned by a parent will be attributed to a child who has not attained the age of 21. If a person owns 50 percent of an organization without regard to any attributed stock, then that person will also be said to own any ownership interest in the organization owned by that person's parent, grandparents, grandchildren, and children who have reached the age of 21.[24]

For example, assume that Frank directly owns 40 percent of the profits' interest of the DEF Partnership. His daughter, Barbara, 20 years of age, directly owns 30 percent of the profits' interest of DEF, and his son, Anthony, 30 years of age, directly owns 20 percent of the profits' interest of DEF. The 10 remaining percent of the profits' interest and 100 percent of the capital interest of DEF are owned by an unrelated person.

Frank directly owns 40 percent of the profits' interest in DEF and is considered to own the 30 percent profits' interest owned directly by Barbara. Since, for the purposes of the effective control test, Frank is treated as owning 70 percent of the profits' interest of DEF, Frank is also said to own the 20 percent profits' interest of DEF owned by his adult child, Anthony. Accordingly, Frank is said to own a total of 90 percent of the profits' interest in DEF.

Barbara directly owns 30 percent of the profits' interest in DEF and is considered to own the 40 percent profits' interest owned directly by her father, Frank. However, Barbara is not considered to own the 20 percent profits' interest of DEF owned directly by her brother, Anthony, and constructively by Frank, because an interest constructively owned by Frank by reason of family attribution is not considered to be owned by him for purposes of making another member of his family the constructive owner of such interest. Accordingly, Barbara is said to own a total of 70 percent of the interest profits of the DEF Partnership.

Anthony owns 20 percent of the interest profits in DEF directly. Since, for purposes of determining whether Anthony effectively controls DEF, he is treated as owning only the percentage of profits' interest he owns directly, and his father's profit interest in DEF is not attributed to him, Anthony is said to own only the 20 percent profits' interest in DEF that he owns directly.[25]

Affiliated Service Groups

Some organizations that are not members of a controlled group of trades or businesses may still be considered a single employer for employee benefit plan purposes if they are members of an affiliated service group.[26] The affiliated service

---

[22]Treas. Reg. 1.414(c)-4(b)(2).
[23]Treas. Reg. 1.414(c)-4(b)(5), (6).
[24]Treas. Reg. 1.414(c)-4(b)(6).
[25]Treas. Reg. 1.414(c)-4(b)(6)(iv).
[26]IRC §414(m).

group rules are a complex set of antiabuse requirements intended to prevent certain types of service businesses from organizing their business structure so that the service professionals might be considered a separate business entity from the rank-and-file employees.

An affiliated service group is defined as a group consisting of a service organization, nominally referred to as a First Service Organization, and one or more "A Organizations" or "B Organizations."[27] An A Organization is a service organization that is a partner or shareholder in the First Service Organization that regularly performs services for the First Service Organization or is regularly associated with the First Service Organization in performing services for the public.[28]

A substantial portion of the business of a B Organization consists of performing services for the First Service Organization, for one or more A Organizations with respect to the First Service Organization, or for both. The services provided by the B Organization must be of the type historically performed by employees in the service field of the First Service Organization or the A Organization, and 10 percent or more of the B Organization must be owned by the First Service Organization or an A Organization.[29]

Whether a service organization regularly performs services for the First Service Organization or is regularly associated with the First Service Organization in performing services for the public depends on facts and circumstances, and takes into account the amount of earned income that the organization derives from performing services for the First Service Organization or from performing services for the public in association with the First Service Organization.[30]

Whether a significant portion of the B Organization's business consists of performing services for a First Service Organization or an A Organization is also determined by facts and circumstances but generally will be considered to be the case if 5 percent or more of the B Organization's revenue from the provision of services is from either the First Service Organization or an A Organization.[31] If 10 percent of the total revenue, not just the services-based revenue, of the B Organization is from the performance of services for the First Service Organization or an A Organization, this will generally be considered a controlling fact in whether a significant portion of the B Organization's business is from providing services to a First Service Organization or an A Organization.[32]

A business that provides health, law, engineering, architectural, accounting, actuarial science, performing arts, consulting, or insurance service will generally be considered a service organization.[33]

Affiliated Management Service Groups

An affiliated service group will also be considered to include an organization whose principal business is performing, on a regular and continuing basis,

[27]Prop. Treas. Reg. 1.414(m)-2(a).
[28]Prop. Treas. Reg. 1.414(m)-2(b).
[29]Prop. Treas. Reg. 1.414(m)-2(c).
[30]Prop. Treas. Reg. 1.414(m)-2(b)(2).
[31]Prop. Treas. Reg. 1.414(m)-2(c)(2)(ii).
[32]Prop. Treas. Reg. 1.414(m)-2(c)(2)(iii).
[33]Prop. Treas. Reg. 1.414(m)-1(c).

management functions for another organization.[34] Note that, in contrast to the rules governing groups of trades or businesses under common control and the affiliated service groups, there is no requirement of cross-ownership between an affiliated management service group and the organization receiving the management service.

IRS proposed regulations on affiliated management services initially defined management services as any professional services including health, law, and other consulting services. This requirement had the unintended result of making many small professional service organizations members of the same controlled group as major clients. After substantial negative public comment on the proposed regulations, the IRS has withdrawn this provision and is currently reconsidering the definition of management services.

Separate Lines of Business

The task of identifying the employer sponsoring the plan does not always the end with the determination of the controlled group of trades or businesses sponsoring the plan. Many employers have diverse lines of business requiring disparate benefit programs for employees. One or more retirement plans may not satisfy the minimum coverage or nondiscrimination requirements when tested against the employer's total work force. Recognizing that employers may have legitimate business reasons for sponsoring different employee benefit plans for different business units, Congress enacted the separate line of business rules. When an employer is treated as operating qualified separate lines of business (QSLOBs), the employer is permitted to apply the minimum coverage, nondiscrimination, and minimum participation requirements applicable to qualified plans separately for the employees of each QSLOB.[35]

The QSLOB rules, however, are difficult administrative and substantive hurdles for employers to overcome in determining QSLOB status. An employer must prove that the business entity at issue is successively a "line of business" (based on businesses or services), a "separate line of business" (based on separation in business organization, finances, work forces, management, and assets), and finally a "qualified separate line of business" (based on demographic and other requirements). In addition, an employer must allocate employees to different business units on two occasions using completely different allocation methods on each occasion. Given the complexity of the QSLOB regulations, employers may well question whether the effort is worth it. For employers with certain organizational structures, however, treating different parts of the employer as QSLOBs can mean all the difference in designing the employer's retirement plans in the desired manner.

Even if the employer operates QSLOBs, certain provisions of the Code must be applied on a controlled group basis. For example, an employer's highly compensated employees may not be determined on a QSLOB basis.[36]

---

[34]IRC §414(m)(5)(A).
[35]IRC §414(r)(1).
[36]Treas. Reg. 1.414(q)-1T, Q&A 6(c).

In order to treat an employer as operating QSLOBs, all property and services provided by the employer to its customers must be allocated to a QSLOB. No portion of the employer may remain that is not included in a QSLOB. In addition, after allocating employees to QSLOBs, every employee must be treated as an employee of a QSLOB, and no employee may be treated as an employee of more than one QSLOB.

An acquired part of an employer is deemed to satisfy the QSLOB requirements, other than the requirement that the IRS be notified that the employer is electing QSLOB status, for the "transition period" during which the plans of the employer are deemed to satisfy the coverage requirements according to the special merger and acquisition rule of Code section 410(b)(6)(C).[37] The transition period runs until the end of the plan year following the plan year of merger or acquisition, or until the coverage under the plans is significantly changed, whichever occurs first.[38]

Under this rule, acquired portions of the employer may automatically be treated as a QSLOB without regard to products, separateness, employee allocation, or the like. The plans in which such acquired employees participate would be treated as maintained by QSLOBs, whether they were transferred by the seller or originally maintained by the buyer.[39]

Line of Business

An employer is permitted to determine a line of business by designating the property or services that each of its lines of business provides to customers of the employer. A line of business is not required to provide only one type of property or service. Nor is there any requirement stipulating that a line of business must provide solely property or solely service. Finally, there is no requirement that all property or services of related types or the same type be provided by a single line of business (e.g., two business units that sell or produce the same product in different geographic locations may be considered two lines of business).[40]

Even though an employer is permitted to designate two or more lines of business that provide related types of property or services, an employer is not permitted to unreasonably designate different lines of business.[41] An employer's designation would be unreasonable if it separated two types of property or services:

- one that the employer did not provide separately from another to its customers; or
- one in which the provision of one type of property or service is merely ancillary or incidental to, or regularly associated with, the provision of the other type of property or service.[42]

The unreasonable designation requirement is apparently aimed at situations in which the employer's business structure could comply with the QSLOB requirements,

---

[37]Treas. Reg. 1.414(r)-1(d)(4).
[38]IRC §410(b)(6)(C).
[39]Treas. Reg. 1.414(r)-1(d)(4).
[40]Treas. Reg. 1.414(r)-2(b).
[41]Treas. Reg. 1.414(r)-2(b)(3)(iii).
[42]Ibid.

but it would be considered "abusive" to treat the business units separately. An example of an unreasonable designation includes designating as lines of business (1) the production of a product and (2) the labor and parts supplied in connection with a warranty of the product.[43]

Separate Line of Business

A separate line of business is a line of business that is organized and operated separately from the remainder of the employer.[44] To be classified as a separate line of business, a business unit must satisfy all of the following four criteria:

- Separate organizational unit. The business unit must be formally organized as a separate organizational unit (or units) within the employer, such as a corporation, partnership, division, or other unit having a similar degree of organizational formality.[45]
- Separate financial accountability. The business unit must be a separate profit center (or centers). The employer must maintain books and records that provide separate revenue and expense information for each profit center composing the line of business. The separate information must be used for internal planning and control for each profit center.[46]
- Separate employee work force. The business unit must have its own separate employee work force. At least 90 percent of the employees who provide any services to the business unit must provide their services exclusively or almost exclusively to the business unit.[47]
- Separate management. The business unit must have its own separate management. At least 80 percent of the top-paid employees who provide services to the business unit must provide substantial services to the business unit. The top-paid employees are the top 10 percent, by compensation, of all employees who provide services to the business unit.[48]

It appears that in general separate management is the most difficult condition to satisfy. The existence of even a moderately sized central headquarters can cause a business unit to fail the separate management requirement.

For example, assume that ABC Corporation has three divisions—A, B, and C—along with a separate corporate headquarters. Table 9-3 presents employee counts for each division and the corporate headquarters summarized by highly compensated employees (HCEs) and non-highly compensated employees (NHCEs).

No headquarters employee provides substantial services for any single division, and each headquarters employee provides at least some service to all divisions. Each division's separate management determination is noted in Table 9-4. The

[43]Treas. Reg. 1.414(r)-2(c)(2), Example 7.
[44]Treas. Reg. 1.414(r)-3(a).
[45]Treas. Reg. 1.414(r)-3(b)(2).
[46]Treas. Reg. 1.414(r)-3(b)(3).
[47]Treas. Reg. 1.414(r)-3(b)(4).
[48]Treas. Reg. 1.414(r)-3(b)(5).

TABLE 9-3   Employee Count

Employee	HQ	A	B	C	Total
HCE	10	20	20	10	60
NHCE	15	300	950	400	1,665
Total	25	320	970	410	1,725

TABLE 9-4   Separate Management

Division	Some Services	Top-Paid 10 Percent	Substantial Services	Separate Management Ratio (%)
A	345	35	25	25/35 = 71.4 fail
B	995	100	90	90/100 = 90.0 pass
C	435	44	34	34/44 = 77.3 fail

headquarters employees in the top-paid 10 percent are the headquarters 10 highly compensated employees. No headquarters non-highly compensated employee was included in the top-paid 10 percent providing service to the divisions.

Under both the separate work force and separate management requirements, employees must be allocated to different business units in accordance with the services provided. The factors to consider in making this determination are whether an employee provides service to a business unit, which employees may be excluded, and what services are performed.

An employee provides services to a business unit if more than a negligible portion of the employee's services contributes to the property or services provided by the line of business to customers of the employer.[49] An employee provides services to a business unit exclusively if the employee provides services to the line of business and no more than a negligible portion of the employee's services contributes to providing the property or services provided by any other business unit to customers of the employer.

In general, the employer is permitted but not required to exclude all non-resident aliens who receive no source of income in the United States.[50] However, there is a special restriction: the employer must include any nonresident alien who does not provide services exclusively to any line of business of the employer. If the nonresident alien employee provides more than negligible services to two or more lines of business, she must be considered in determining whether any line of business for which she does not provide 75 percent of her time passes the separate management and separate work force test. For example, if a nonresident alien employee provides 75 percent of her services to one line of business and 25 percent of her services to another line of business, the employer can disregard the employee when testing the first line of business but must include the employee when testing the second line of business.[51]

[49]Treas. Reg. 1.414(r)-3(c)(5).
[50]Treas. Reg. 1.414(r)-3(c)(3)(ii).
[51]Ibid.

This rule may be problematic for a foreign parent with U.S. subsidiaries. For example, a foreign president who oversees all lines of business must be included. Foreign managers that are included will further complicate the separate management determination. In addition, collecting and maintaining service records for foreign operations is very difficult and expensive. This not only increases compliance costs for employers but also makes tax administration more difficult for the IRS. IRS officials have indicated that the purpose of the rule is to place foreign multinational companies (e.g., headquarters) on equal footing with domestic corporations. How the IRS intends to enforce or administer this rule is unknown.

Another issue concerns the provision of services to a line of business for employers that have business units whose primary "customers" are other business units of the employer instead of outside consumers. While the operations of such business units could be very different and otherwise might qualify for treatment as a QSLOB, it would be almost impossible to prove that two such business units had separate work forces or separate management.

Accordingly, an optional rule is provided to assist an employer who has two lines of business that are "vertically integrated" with one another. Two business units are vertically integrated if one of them (the "upstream line of business") provides the property or service to the other (the "downstream line of business"), and the upstream line of business provides the same type of property or service to customers of the employer.[52]

Two vertically integrated business units qualify for the special rule only if

1. at least 25 percent of the property or services provided to all customers (including outside customers of the employer, the downstream line of business, and all other lines of business of the employer) by the upstream line of business are provided to outside customers or, alternatively, the property (not services) provided to the downstream line of business is also produced by business entities outside the employer's controlled group to unrelated customers;

2. the downstream line of business uses, consumes, or substantially modifies the property or service in the course of providing property or services to outside customers or, alternatively, provides the property or service to customers of the employer at a different level in the chain of commercial distribution than the upstream line of business (e.g., retail versus wholesale).[53]

Under the special rule for vertically integrated lines of business, an employee of an upstream line of business who would otherwise be considered as providing services to the downstream line of business is excluded from consideration when determining whether the lines of business have separate work forces or separate management or 50 employees.[54]

One of the problems with the vertical integration rule is that it applies separately to each property or service of the employer. If the upstream line provides more than one property or service to the downstream line, one property or service

[52]Treas. Reg. 1.414(r)-3(d)(1).
[53]Treas. Reg. 1.414(r)-3(d)(2).
[54]Treas. Reg. 1.414(r)-3(d)(3)(i).

might meet the rule, while the other property or service does not. It appears that the rule could still be useful to such an employer, but in many cases it would not.

The regulations contain an example in which an employer's upstream line of business provides oil, gasoline, and other petrochemical products to wholesale customers and also to the downstream line of business. The downstream line provides oil and gasoline products to retail customers. During the testing year, the upstream line provides 25,000 gallons of oil and 250,000 gallons of gasoline to the downstream line and 75,000 gallons of oil and 515,000 gallons of gasoline to wholesale customers of the employer. Thus, both products pass the 50 percent test because the upstream line provides 75 percent of its oil products and 67 percent of its gasoline products to customers of the employer. Also, the upstream and downstream lines provide oil and gasoline products to customers at "different levels in the chain of commercial distribution." So, the upstream and downstream lines satisfy the vertical integration rule for both oil and gasoline products for the testing year. If employees of the upstream line only provide services to the downstream line by contributing to providing oil and gasoline products to the downstream line, such employees will not be treated as providing services to the downstream line.[55]

If the facts above were the same except that the upstream line only provides 20 percent of its gasoline products to outside customers, then the upstream and downstream lines would satisfy the vertical integration rule with respect to oil products but not gasoline products. If employees of the upstream line of business contribute to providing both oil and gasoline to the downstream line, the employees are treated as providing services to the downstream line. In this case, unless the oil and gasoline portions of the upstream line can be separated into different lines, the vertical integration rule will be of no help. This could be particularly frustrating if, for example, the upstream line had 10 products and 9 passed the vertical integration test.

"Qualifying" the Separate Line of Business

After separateness is determined, each business unit must satisfy three additional statutory requirements in order to be a qualified separate line of business: (1) there must be at least 50 employees in the unit; (2) the employer must notify the IRS that QSLOB treatment has been elected; and (3) each unit must pass "administrative scrutiny" by satisfying any one of four different tests or, alternatively, obtaining an individual determination from the IRS.[56]

In determining whether a business unit has at least 50 employees who provide their services exclusively to the unit, all employees, including collectively bargained employees, may be counted, other than (1) employees who have completed less than six months of service by the end of the testing year, (2) employees who have not attained the age of 21 by the end of the testing year, (3) employees who normally work less than six months in a testing year or less than $17\frac{1}{2}$ hours per week, and (4) nonresident aliens with no U.S. source of income.[57]

---

[55]Treas. Reg. 1.414(r)-3(d)(4), Example (2).
[56]Treas. Reg. 1.414(r)-1(b)(2)(iv).
[57]Treas. Reg. 1.414(r)-4(b) and 1.414(q)-1, Q&A 9(g).

The IRS notice requirement was waived for years before 1994.[58] Since 1993, however, the employer has had to notify the IRS that it elects to be treated as operating qualified separate lines of business.[59] QSLOB notification is given by filing Form 5310-A, Notice of Merger, Consolidation, or Transfer of Plan Assets or Liabilities. A schedule attached to each Form 5310-A must identify each qualified separate line of business operated by the employer, each plan maintained by the employer, the qualified separate lines of business that have employees benefiting under each such plan, and the plan qualification requirements for which the employer is testing on a qualified separate line of business basis (i.e., minimum coverage or nondiscrimination).[60]

Notice for a testing year must be given on or before the later of October 15 of the year following the testing year or the 15th day of the 10th month after the close of the plan year of the plan of the employer that begins earliest in the testing year.[61] After the date for filing the notice, notice cannot be modified, withdrawn, or revoked, and it will be treated as applying to subsequent testing years unless the employer takes timely action to provide new notice.[62]

The requirement that a business unit pass administrative scrutiny is satisfied by either passing a statutory safe harbor (the "50 percent/200 percent" test), passing any one of several safe harbors created by the IRS in the QSLOB regulations (based on industry categories, FAS 14 reporting, or minimum/maximum plan benefits), or obtaining an individual IRS determination.[63] All units of an employer are not required to use the same method to satisfy IRS scrutiny. In addition, it appears that a unit may pass using a different testing method from year to year.

The statutory safe harbor (so-called because it is explicitly prescribed at section 414(r)(3) of the Internal Revenue Code) requires that the "HCE (Highly Compensated Employees) percentage ratio" of a business unit for the testing year be at least 50 percent and no more than 200 percent.[64] The 50 percent HCE percentage ratio threshold is treated as satisfied automatically if at least 10 percent of all HCEs of the employer work exclusively for the business unit. However, the 200 percent limit may not be exceeded.[65]

The HCE percentage ratio is the ratio of the percentage of HCEs among all employees providing services to the *business unit* compared with the percentage of all HCEs to all employees of the *employer*:[66]

$$\frac{\text{HCE \% of Unit}}{\text{HCE \% of Employer}}.$$

The employee count, as well as HCE status, is based on the employees taken into account and their status under the minimum coverage rules. Collectively bargained employees, certain airline pilots, and nonresident aliens with no U.S.

---

[58]Notice 90-57, 1990-2 C.B. 344.
[59]Rev. Proc. 93-40.
[60]Rev. Proc. 93-40, Sec. 3.04.
[61]Rev. Proc. 93-40, Sec. 3.05.
[62]Rev. Proc. 93-40, Sec. 3.06.
[63]Treas. Reg. 1.414(r)-1(b)(2)(iv)(D).
[64]IRC §414(r)(3).
[65]Treas. Reg. 1.414(r)-5(b)(4).
[66]Treas. Reg. 1.414(r)-5(b)(2).

TABLE 9-5   Allocation of Employees

	All EEs	HCEs	HCE Percent	HCE Percentage Ratio
Sub 1	500	20	4	40% fail[a]
Sub 2	1,000	130	13	130% pass[b]
Employer-wide	1,500	150	10	

[a]4%/10% = 40% (<50%).
[b]13%/10% = 130% (<200%).

source of income are excluded. Also, employees failing to meet plan minimum age or service requirements are excluded, but based solely on the lowest minimum age or service requirement of all of the employer's plans.[67]

For example, an employer has a headquarters and two subsidiaries. The employer first determines the employees excludable from testing, and allocates employees among Subs 1 and 2. After allocation, the demographics are as indicated in Table 9-5.

Although Sub 1 fails the 50 percent threshold, it still passes under the special 10 percent rule because more than 13 percent of the employer's HCEs (20/150) are employed by Sub 1.

A business unit passing the 50 percent/200 percent safe harbor in a year (year 1) will automatically pass in the next year (year 2) if

1. the same "line of business" designation is used in each year (i.e., product/ service),
2. either (a) the HCE percentage ratio for the business unit in year 2 does not deviate from that in year 1 by more than 10 percent, or (b) at least 95 percent of the employees of the unit in year 2 were employees of such unit in year 1 *and* no more than 5 percent of employees in year 1 ceased to be employees in year 2.[68]

A 10 percent deviation for the HCE percentage ratio only helps where a unit would otherwise fail by a small percentage (i.e., 10 percent on either side of 50 percent/200 percent (45 percent or 220 percent)). The 95 percent/5 percent alternative does not help an employer pass the administrative scrutiny tests unless the business unit has virtually no turnover or expansion in employees from year to year.

Another safe harbor for the administrative scrutiny test is available for a business unit that is the only one of the employer's units falling into one or more specific industry categories.[69] The 12 industry categories specified by the IRS are derived from the government's Standard Industrial Classification (SIC) codes arranged by two-digit major groups.[70]

[67]Treas. Reg. 1.414(r)-5(b)(3).
[68]Treas. Reg. 1.414(r)-5(b)(5).
[69]Treas. Reg. 1.414(r)-5(c).
[70]Rev. Proc. 91-64.

Certain industry categories (e.g., health services, legal services) are not included. However, the fact that one or more of an employer's business units are outside the prescribed industry categories would not jeopardize safe harbor treatment of a business unit that is the sole unit in one or more categories.

Satisfying the SEC's Form 10-K annual reporting requirements (Securities Exchange Act of 1934), in which an employer may be required to report a business unit as one or more reportable industry segments under FAS 14 (*Financial Reporting for Segments of a Business Enterprise*), can also lead to satisfying another safe harbor. A business unit will pass administrative scrutiny if the unit's property or services designated for QSLOB purposes are identical to those identified under FAS 14 for the reportable industry segment(s) reported on the Form 10K filed for the employer's fiscal year ending latest in the testing year.[71] FAS 14 describes the identification of reportable industry segments thus:

> Each industry segment that is significant to an enterprise as a whole shall be identified as a reportable segment. For purposes of this Statement, an industry segment shall be regarded as significant—and therefore identified as a reportable segment—if it satisfies one or more of the following tests:
> a) Its revenue (including both sales to unaffiliated customers and intersegment sales or transfers) is 10 percent or more of the combined revenue (sales to unaffiliated customers and intersegment sales or transfers) of all of the enterprise's industry segments.
> b) The absolute amount of its operating profit or operating loss is 10 percent or more of the greater, in absolute amount, of:
>   i) the combined operating profit of all industry segments that did not incur an operating loss, or
>   ii) the combined operating loss of all industry segments that did incur an operating loss.
> c) Its identifiable assets are 10 percent or more of the combined identifiable assets of all industry segments.[72]

Some leeway may be available under this safe harbor. FAS 14 also provides that the "determination of an enterprise's industry segments must depend to a considerable extent on the judgment of management."[73] Of course, this safe harbor is only available to public companies.

The final safe harbor has two alternative requirements:

1. The HCE percentage ratio for the business unit is less than 50 percent in the testing year, and a minimum level of benefits (accruals or contributions) is provided to NHCEs of the unit (the NHCE Minimum Benefits Rule).
2. The HCE percentage ratio for the business unit in the testing year exceeds 200 percent and no more than a maximum level of benefits (accruals or contributions) is provided to HCEs in the unit (the HCE Maximum Benefits Rule).[74]

---

[71]Treas. Reg. 1.414(r)-5(c).
[72]Financial Accounting Standard 14, *Financial Reporting for Segments of a Business Enterprise*, para. 15.
[73]Ibid., para. 12.
[74]Treas. Reg. 1.414(r)-5(g)

The intent of the maximum/minimum benefit safe harbor is to qualify SLOBs that fail the statutory safe harbor but provide benefits at a level at which the deviation from the safe harbor percentages does not result in any discriminatory effect. For business units with HCE percentage ratios of less than 50 percent, the business unit has a disproportionately larger percentage of non–highly compensated employees than the total work force of the employer. But providing a minimum benefit ensures that the non–highly compensated work force of the business unit receives a sufficient retirement benefit. Similarly, a business unit with an HCE percentage ratio greater than 200 percent contains a disproportionately larger percentage of the highly compensated employees of the work force. But the maximum benefit limit ensures that benefits are not being skewed toward the business unit full of highly compensated employees.

The defined benefit minimum is based on a normal accrual rate of at least 0.75 percent of high five-year average compensation, with the minimum benefit percentage reduced to 0.70 percent for plans using a high three-year average compensation. The minimum generally must be satisfied on the basis of the nondiscrimination regulations general test methodology using an annual measurement period, subject to certain modifications. No adjustment is made for early retirement subsidies, disability or other ancillary benefits, or integration of the plan benefit with Social Security benefits.[75]

The defined contribution minimum is an allocation rate of at least 3 percent of compensation for the plan year. Only employer contributions and certain forfeitures are included; section 401(k) elective contributions, section 401(m) matching contributions, forfeitures allocated on the basis of employee and elective contributions, and any adjustments for Social Security integration are ignored.

Where the HCE percentage ratio exceeds 200 percent, no highly compensated employee in the unit may accrue an employer-derived benefit exceeding the maximum benefit. The defined benefit maximum is an employer-derived accrued benefit based on a normal accrual rate equal to 2.5 percent of high five-year compensation (determined in the same manner that is used for minimum benefits above). The maximum is reduced to 2.33 percent if high three-year compensation is used. Adjustments must be made for early retirement or joint and survivor benefit subsidies that exceed the value of a normal retirement benefit or single life annuity, respectively.[76]

The defined contribution maximum is an allocation rate of 10 percent of compensation for the plan year. Allocation rates are generally determined as provided in the minimum contribution rules (above) except that section 401(m) matching contributions (including forfeitures allocated based on employee or elective contributions) are included.

A unit that fails all of the safe harbors may only satisfy administrative scrutiny by obtaining a favorable IRS determination for the year.[77] The IRS determination procedure requires that the employer requesting the individual determination satisfy one of several "standard access alternatives." The standard access alternatives include the following:

---

[75]Treas. Reg. 1.414(r)-5(g)(2).
[76]Treas. Reg. 1.414(r)-5(g)(3).
[77]Rev. Proc. 93-41.

- The separate line of business would have satisfied the statutory safe harbor using a 40 percent/250 percent threshold.
- Ninety percent of the gross revenues of the separate line of business result from providing property or services that fall exclusively within one or more of the specified industry categories, and no more than 10 percent of the gross revenues of any of the employer's other separate lines of business result from property or services that fall within the same industry category or categories.
- The separate line of business would satisfy the reportable industry segment safe harbor if the employer were publicly traded and subject to SEC reporting requirements, including the Form 10-K.
- The separate line of business would have satisfied either the minimum/maximum benefits safe harbor or the average benefits safe harbor if the applicable threshold under those tests had been reduced or increased (as appropriate) by one-third.
- The separate line of business manages a government facility pursuant to a government contract that specifies the benefits to be provided under a qualified plan.[78]

If the separate line of business does not satisfy one of the standard access alternatives, an individual IRS determination can still be requested, but it is anticipated that in these cases the IRS will determine that the separate line of business satisfies administrative scrutiny only in exceptional circumstances. Thus an additional burden rests on the employer to demonstrate that relevant facts and circumstances unique to the employer support a determination that the separate line of business meets administrative scrutiny.[79]

QSLOB Employees

Each employee of the employer must be assigned to one, and only one, of the employer's QSLOBs for the administrative scrutiny test and for application of the nondiscrimination, minimum coverage, and minimum participation tests. The assignment of current employees is as follows:

1. Employees who provide "exclusive services" to a business unit are assigned to that unit.
2. "Substantial service" employees (employees who provide substantial services to a unit) are assigned to that unit. An employee provides substantial services if
   a. at least 75 percent of the employee's services are for a given unit,
   b. at least 50 percent of the employee's services are for a given unit, and the employer elects to treat the employee as a substantial service employee.[80]
3. The remaining unassigned employees, called "residual shared employees," are allocated using one of four allocation methods known as the dominant line of business method, the pro rata allocation method, the HCE percentage ratio

[78]Rev. Proc. 93-41, sec. 3.03(4).
[79]Rev. Proc. 93-41, sec. 4.04.
[80]Treas. Reg. 1.414(r)-11(b)(2).

method, and the small group method. Once a method has been selected, it must be used for all purposes for a given testing year.[81]

If an employer has a "dominant line of business," then all residual shared employees may be assigned to the dominant line. To use this method, at least 50 percent of an employer's exclusive service or substantial service employees must be assigned to a business unit. The 50 percent may be reduced to 25 percent if the business unit produces 60 percent of the employer's gross revenue or contains 60 percent of the employer's total work force, or passes certain other administrative tests.[82]

Alternatively, employees are allocated pro rata on the basis of the substantial service or exclusive service employees previously allocated. The pro rata allocation is calculated on the basis of all substantial service employees allocated to a business unit but is applied separately to highly compensated residual shared employees and to non-highly compensated residual shared employees. But, once the appropriate number of employees is determined, the employer may determine which specific employees are allocated to the various business units. If possible, the allocated employees should provide at least some services to the unit.[83]

The HCE percentage ratio method allocates residual shared employees to each business unit by taking the percentage of employees previously allocated to the line who are highly compensated and dividing by the percentage of all highly compensated employees previously allocated to any unit. If any business unit has an HCE percentage ratio less than 50 percent, a highly compensated residual shared employee must be allocated to the unit with the lowest such percentage. If any business unit has an HCE percentage ratio in excess of 200 percent, a non-highly compensated residual shared employee must be allocated to the unit with the highest such percentage. The HCE percentage ratios are then recalculated and the process is repeated. As soon as all the ratios fall in the 50–200 percent corridor the process is continued, one employee at a time, until all employees are allocated without violating the 50–200 percent boundaries. If possible, employees are allocated to units where they provide at least some services.[84] The HCE percentage ratio method can effectively be used to allocate all headquarters employees or other residual shared employees to one business unit. As long as the HCE ratio percentage remains within the 50–200 percent corridor, employees can continue to be allocated to one business unit.

Finally, if the residual shared employees comprise 3 percent or less of the employer's non-collectively bargained work force, the small group method permits the use of any reasonable method as long as the QSLOB satisfies the 50–200 percent test after the employees are allocated.

For example, ABC Corporation has three separate divisions it wishes to treat as QSLOBs—A, B, and C—along with a separate corporate headquarters (HQ). Each division maintains a qualified plan.

[81]Treas. Reg. 1.414(r)-7(c)(1).
[82]Treas. Reg. 1.414(r)-7(c)(2).
[83]Treas. Reg. 1.414(r)-7(c)(3).
[84]Treas. Reg. 1.414(r)-7(c)(4).

TABLE 9-6 Employee Count

Employee	HQ	A	B	C	Total
HCE	10	20	20	10	60
NHCE	15	300	950	40	1,665
Total	25	320	970	410	1,725

Employee counts are summarized in Table 9-6 by division and by HCEs and NHCEs. No HQ employee provides services exclusively for any single division. All HQ employees provide at least some services to each division.

Each of the 25 HQ employees must be allocated to one division or another. ABC Corporation first determines which, if any, of its 25 HQ employees are "substantial service employees." The allocation of such HQ employees is summarized in Table 9-7.

ABC Corporation is able to allocate all residual shared employees to Division B under the "dominant line of business" method. Allocation of all HQ employees using this approach is illustrated in Table 9-8.

Alternatively, ABC could allocate pro rata. The results are shown in Tables 9-9 and 9-10. Under the HCE percentage ratio method, HCE percentages are determined for each division thus:

Division A's HCE percent initially is $(22/323)/(55/1708) = 211.5\%$

Division B's HCE percent initially is $(22/973)/(55/1708) = 70.19\%$

Division C's HCE percent initially is $(11/412)/(55/1708) = 82.91\%$

Non-highly compensated employees must first be allocated to Division A. If all residual shared highly compensated employees could be allocated to Division C and all residual shared non-highly compensated employees to Division A. After allocation, the redetermined percentages would be as follows:

Division A $(22/335)/(60/1725) = 188.81\%$

Division B $(22/973)/(60/1725) = 65.01\%$

Division C $(16/417)/(60/1725) = 110.31\%$

A divisional employee summary is detailed in Table 9-11.

TABLE 9-7 Allocating HQ Employees (Substantial Service Employees)

Employees	HQ Employees	HQ Employees Who Provide Substantial Services to			Total
		A	B	C	
HCEs	5	2	2	1	10
NHCEs	12	1	1	1	15
Total	17	3	3	2	25

TABLE 9-8 Allocating HQ Employees (Residual Shared Employees—
Dominant Line Method)

Employee	A	HQ(A)	B	HQ(B)	C	HQ(C)	Total
HCE	20	2	20	7	10	1	60
NHCE	300	1	950	13	400	1	1,665
Total	320	3	970	20	410	2	1,725

TABLE 9-9 Calculation of Percentages

Division	Exclusive Employees		Substantial Service Employees		Total	Percentage of Total
	HCEs	NHCEs	HCEs	NHCEs		
A	20	300	2	1	323	18.91
B	20	950	2	1	973	56.97
C	10	400	1	1	412	24.12
Total	50	1,650	5	3	1,708	100.00

TABLE 9-10 Residual Shared Allocation

Division	Percentage	HCE Allocation	NHCE Allocation	Grand Total HCEs	Grand Total NHCEs	Total
A	18.91	1	2	23	303	326
B	56.97	3	7	25	958	983
C	24.12	1	3	12	404	416
Total		5	12	60	1,665	1,725

TABLE 9-11 Divisional Employee Summary

Division	Exclusive Employees		Substantial Service Employees		Residual Shared		Total		Total
	HCEs	NHCEs	HCEs	NHCEs	HCEs	NHCEs	HCEs	NHCEs	
A	20	300	2	1	0	12	22	313	335
B	20	950	2	1	0	0	22	951	973
C	10	400	2	1	5	0	16	401	417
Total	50	1,650	5	3	5	12	60	1,665	1,725

Averaging

Some of the tests mentioned above can be performed on an average basis by using data from more than one year, rather than separately testing each year's data. This special rule allows an employer to continue testing its plans on a QSLOB basis even though the current year's data would not satisfy the QSLOB requirements.

Averaging is permitted only if the applicable percentage for each testing year in the averaging period falls within 10 percent of the target percentage. For example, averaging is permitted for the statutory safe harbor for administrative scrutiny only if the highly compensated employee percentage ratio for each testing year in the averaging period is at least 45 percent (within 10 percent of the 50 percent minimum) or no more than 220 percent (within 10 percent of the 200 percent maximum).

In addition, averaging is permitted only if the following conditions are satisfied:

- The employer calculates the percentage for the preceding testing year in the same manner as the employer calculates the percentage for the current testing year.
- Each testing year in the averaging period begins after 1991.
- The employer is treated as operating QSLOBs for the preceding testing year.
- The employer designated the same lines of business in the preceding testing year as in the current testing year.

The following tests can be calculated on an average basis:

- 90 percent separate employee work force requirement;
- 90 percent separate management requirement (if the employee work force requirement is averaged, the separate management requirement must be averaged, and vice versa);
- 50 percent minimum and 200 percent maximum highly compensated employee percentage ratios (but not the special 10 percent rate) under the statutory safe harbor;
- 50 percent of products or services provided to customers requirement under the vertically integrated business rule;
- dominant line of business method of allocating residual shared employees;
- percentage of substantial service employees assigned to a QSLOB for the pro rata method of allocating residual shared employees.

Separate Application of Nondiscrimination and Coverage Requirements

Normally, the coverage rules, nondiscrimination rules, and the minimum participation rules are applied to an employer's plans on an employer-wide basis. Testing an employer's plans on the basis of those employees in a QSLOB is, of course, the purpose of having the separate line of business rules in the first place. However, merely satisfying the QSLOB rules is not by itself sufficient to allow the employer to test its plans on a separate line of business basis.

A plan first must show that it benefits a nondiscriminatory class of employees on an employer-wide basis, but treating only QSLOB participants as benefiting under the plan. This requirement will be met if the plan, when tested on a QSLOB basis, satisfies one of the minimum coverage tests: specifically, the plan satisfies the ratio percentage test,[85] or the plan satisfies the nondiscriminatory classification test.[86]

A plan that satisfies the unsafe harbor standard (i.e., falls within the facts and circumstances area between the safe harbor and unsafe harbor areas) will generally be considered to satisfy the nondiscriminatory classification test. In examining the facts and circumstances, the IRS has indicated that the fact that the employer has satisfied the QSLOB rules will, except in unusual circumstances, be considered determinative.[87]

Once each plan satisfies either of these tests, the employer is entitled to apply the minimum coverage rules to each QSLOB separately, treating the employees of each other QSLOB as excludable employees.[88] As a general matter, plans that are shared by different QSLOBs will be "disaggregated" and tested on a QSLOB-by-QSLOB basis.

The nondiscrimination rules (including nondiscrimination testing for employee deferrals or matching contributions to a 401(k) plan) also must be satisfied by a QSLOB's plan solely by reference to the QSLOB's employees. In particular, where restructuring is used to satisfy nondiscrimination, each component plan must satisfy the ratio percentage or nondiscriminatory classification rules on an employer-wide basis, in addition to passing the nondiscrimination and minimum coverage requirements on a QSLOB basis.

Normally, the minimum participation requirement is applied on an employer-wide basis. However, the employer may elect QSLOB treatment and test each QSLOB separately. In testing the employees of one QSLOB, employees of the other lines are considered as excludable. If an employer elects QSLOB treatment in testing for minimum participation, then such treatment is also required in testing for coverage and nondiscrimination for each QSLOB plan.

Organizational Transactions

Organizational transactions not only affect the demographics of the employer's work force and the plan's participation, but they also subject the plan to several sets of rules. Transactions involving the business entity sponsoring the plan, such as a merger or acquisition, offer different transition rules for the different compliance requirements for qualified plans. Transactions involving the plan, such as the merger or spin-off of part of the plan's assets and liabilities, have their own set of compliance requirements. Finally, beyond the consideration of the different sets of rules that may apply to different types of transactions, the practical consequences of organizational transactions must be considered by the plan sponsor.

Organizational Mergers and Acquisitions

When an employer acquires another business through a merger or acquisition, several decisions will have to be made concerning the integration of the new

---

[85]Treas. Reg. 1.410(b)-2(b)(2).
[86]Treas. Reg. 1.410(b)-4.
[87]Treas. Reg. 1.414(r)-8(b)(2)(ii).
[88]Treas. Reg. 1.410(b)-6(e).

employees into the employer's retirement income policy. The first key question that has to be answered is what retirement benefits will be provided to the employees of the acquired business unit. Will the acquired employees receive the same retirement benefits as other employees of the employer, or should they receive a different level of benefits, either higher or lower?

The answer to that question will often affect the answer to the next issue to be resolved—determining which plan is to provide the benefits. If the acquired employees are to receive the same retirement benefits as other employees of the employer, the existing plan will simply usually be expanded to cover the new employees. However, if a different level of retirement benefits is desired, then the employer must decide whether to bring the employees into the existing plan and establish a separate benefit structure in that plan for the acquired employees or to establish a new plan for the new employees.

This decision can be influenced not only by issues of plan administration and employee communication but also by nondiscrimination requirements for qualified plans. If the acquired group of employees is especially small or highly paid, for example, establishing a separate plan for such employees may not be possible because of the minimum participation or minimum coverage requirements discussed in Chapter 4.

Accounting Implications

Each year, employers incur an expense on their income statements for pension benefits, defined contribution plan benefits, and other benefits that they provide for their employees. Any change in the structure of the business organization that could change those promises or the number or demographics of the employees covered by the promises will have a corresponding change in the expense reflected in the financial statements. In addition, employers include certain disclosures in their financial statements with respect to pension liabilities. These disclosures will also be affected.

Although it is very difficult to specify the impact on periodic expense or financial disclosure associated with any business organizational restructuring, the following principles apply:

- If the employer continues to be responsible for providing benefits for employees who are already terminated or retired, the liability with respect to those benefits will continue to be reflected on the employer's financial statements.
- Similarly, any assets that have already been set aside by the employer to provide these benefits are generated income that offsets the periodic expense associated with these benefits. To the extent that those assets continue to be held by the employer, the income statement will continue to reflect those earnings.
- Generally, consolidated financial statements can be prepared including any business organization of which an employer owns at least 50 percent. Thus, to the extent a liability for a benefit moves from one entity to another included in the consolidated financial statement, the expense for that liability will remain in the consolidated income statement. The amount of the liability may change

however since calculations of the financial statement must be made separately for each plan.

- The periodic expense is derived, in part, by spreading anticipated projected obligations over the remaining working lives of the active employees in the plan. To the extent that an employer's work force remaining in the plan is altered so that its demographics are substantially different, the periodic expense associated with the group may change. For example, if the remaining group is older than the existing work force before the restructuring, the per employee expense each year should increase because the higher obligation for older employees will be spread over shorter working lives.
- If a significant group is removed from continued participation in the plan, special accounting rules for settlements and curtailments may result in a significant extra pension expense or income item for the year.

Transferring Employees

Whenever an employee transfers from one business unit to another and, as a result, ceases to participate in one tax-qualified retirement plan and becomes a participant in another, questions arise as to whether the benefits and associated assets under the first plan should be transferred to the new plan. Whenever a transfer occurs, the amount to be transferred must be determined and certain administrative filings are required to comply with the tax rules. These filings are required whether the plans are sponsored by the same employer or different unrelated employers.

If, on the other hand, several business units within the same controlled group maintain the same pension plan under which an employee is given credit for service with the different business units, no benefits or assets need be transferred as the employee moves from one unit to another. Moreover, a single benefit check representing the benefits from all the units can be paid to the employee upon retirement. The same result can be achieved even if several plans are maintained by several employers and are subject to independent coverage and nondiscrimination testing. The key is that the assets of the plans are consolidated within a single trust from which benefit payments are paid.

To limit administrative complexity, most employers generally try to avoid having frequent transfers of assets and liabilities from one plan to another plan. If frequent transfers are likely, many employers prefer to have a single plan or to provide for a transfer only once, if at all, when the employee retires and benefits become payable.

Plan Mergers and Spin-offs

In any business organization structuring, questions may arise as to whether an employee's old employer or new employer will be responsible for certain promises made in the past to that employee. Quite often, the benefit promises made to an employee must be resolved in some manner. Occasionally, the resolution of which employer will be responsible for prior benefit promises will be prescribed by law, and in other situations the question will be resolved by the employers involved.

Any assets already set aside to provide retirement benefits should also be considered, and, perhaps, divided among the employers involved. Tax laws and ERISA do not mandate any particular transfer or division of assets.

Federal laws and regulations use the terms *merger* and *consolidation* interchangeably. Both terms refer to the combining of two or more plans into a single plan. Whether the surviving plan is one of the precombination plans or a new plan is generally irrelevant for ERISA purposes. Also note that the merger or combination of plans is an event that does not necessarily occur in conjunction with a merger or consolidation of the employers who sponsor the plans. A single employer who is not undergoing any sort of business reorganization or similar transaction can merge two or more retirement plans for any number of reasons.

The definition of a single plan is generally controlled by the asset pool available to satisfy benefit liabilities. The use of one trust by two or more plans is not a combination of plans if the assets owned by one of the plans are available only to provide benefits for the participants and beneficiaries of that plan.[89]

Accordingly, multiple plans are not created merely because a single plan has several distinct benefit structures that apply to participants, several employers (whether or not members of the same controlled group of trades or businesses) contribute to the plan, plan assets are separately invested in individual insurance or annuity contracts or by separate investment managers, or separate accounting is maintained for purposes of cost allocation but not for purposes of providing benefits.

If a plan merges with another plan, each participant must be entitled to a benefit as if the plan terminated right after the merger that is at least equal to the benefit the participant would have received had the plan terminated immediately before the merger.[90] If the sum of the assets of all plans is not less than the sum of the present values of the accrued benefits of all plans, the statutory requirements will be satisfied merely by combining the assets and preserving each participant's accrued benefits. However, if the sum of the assets of all plans is less than the sum of the present values of the accrued benefits (whether or not vested) in all plans, a special schedule of benefits must be maintained.[91]

In such situations, for some participants the benefits provided on a termination basis from the plan as merged would be different from the benefits provided on a termination basis in the plans prior to the merger. Some participants would receive greater benefits on a termination basis as a result of the merger, and other participants would receive smaller benefits. Accordingly, the distribution of benefits on a potential plan termination must be modified in some manner to prevent any participant from receiving smaller benefits on a termination basis as a result of the merger. Under the special schedule of benefits, distributions would be made to participants on the basis of the funding of different priority categories under section 4044 of the ERISA schedule of guaranteed benefits.

Statutory Requirements

A fundamental requirement for the spin-off of a retirement plan is that the assets attributable to participants' benefits cannot be diminished by the spin-off, al-

[89]Treas. Reg. 1.414(l)-1(b)(2).
[90]Treas. Reg. 1.414(l)-1(a)(2).
[91]Treas. Reg. 1.414(l)-1(e)(1).

though this rule is stated slightly differently for defined benefit and defined contribution plans, to reflect each type of plan's unique characteristics. For a defined
contribution plan, the sum of the account balances for each of the participants in
the resulting plans must equal the account balance for the participant in the plan
before the spin-off, and the assets in each of the plans immediately after the spin-off
must equal the sum of the account balances for all participants in that plan.[92]
When spinning off a defined benefit plan, all accrued benefits of each participant
must be allocated to only one of the plans spun off, and the value of the assets
allocated to each of the plans after the spin-off cannot be less than the sum of the
present value of the benefits on a termination basis in the plan before the spin-off
for all participants in that plan.[93]

Benefits on the termination basis are those benefits that would be provided
exclusively by plan assets under §4044 of ERISA if the plan terminated. Under
§4044, the assets of a terminating defined benefit plan must be allocated to
participants and benefits of the plan in a specified order of six categories of
benefits. These six categories include all of the participants' benefits under the
plan, whether forfeitable or nonforfeitable.[94]

In determining benefits on a termination basis, plan sponsors must keep in
mind that upon termination of a defined benefit plan, both the fixed and contingent liabilities of the plan to employees and beneficiaries must be satisfied before
the employer may recover any assets of the plan.[95] A plan's contingent benefit
liabilities include subsidized early retirement benefits to which a participant may
become eligible after plan termination. For example, if a plan offered a subsidized
early retirement benefit for employees attaining the age of 55 and completing
30 years of service, the plan must make provision to satisfy that subsidized early
retirement liability if the employee were to "grow into" the benefit. Accordingly,
the employer would either have to purchase annuity contracts that provide for the
early retirement subsidy in the event that participant satisfied the age and service
conditions, or the plan could be amended prior to termination to provide that all
participants received the subsidy.[96]

Ratable Allocation of Excess Assets

A new requirement for spin-offs of overfunded defined benefit plans added by
the Technical and Miscellaneous Revenue Act of 1988 requires that excess assets in
the plan be ratably allocated to each of the spun-off plans. If the spun-off plan will
be maintained by an employer who is not a member of the same control group as
the employer who maintained the original plan, ratable allocation of the excess
assets is not required to be made to the spun-off plan. The ratable allocation of
excess assets is also not required for spin-off out of a multiple employer plan or a
multiemployer plan. Finally, ratable allocation of excess assets is not required if the
spun-off plan will be terminated by the employer maintaining it. These exceptions

[92]Treas. Reg. 1.414(l)-1(m).
[93]Treas. Reg. 1.414(l)-1(n)
[94]Rev. Rul. 86-48, 1986-1 C.B. 216.
[95]Treas. Reg. 1.401-2.
[96]Rev. Rul. 85-6, 1985-1 C.B. 133.

essentially require ratable allocation of assets only when one employer is spinning off a plan from an existing plan with the intent to operate both plans in the future.

Since the above exceptions to the ratable allocation requirement describe the majority of situations in which a plan spin-off occurs, an analyst must keep in mind the reason for the ratable allocation requirement in order to understand its application. When the funding rules were tightened by the Omnibus Budget Reconciliation Act of 1987, federal regulators and legislative staffers became concerned about the potential for employers to shift excess assets between different plans in order to generate deductible contributions. Accordingly, the ratable allocation requirement severely restricts employers' ability to shift assets between their plans in order to create deductible contributions.

Reporting Requirements

When spinning off or merging retirement plans, the plan sponsor must notify the IRS at least 30 days prior to the plan transaction.[97] After determining that prior notification of such a plan transaction was necessary only in the event that certain actuarial bases would have to be maintained after the transaction, such as when an underfunded plan is merged with another plan, the IRS has waived the reporting requirement for the most common types of transactions.

Accordingly, prior notification of a plan spin-off or merger is not required when two or more defined contribution plans are merged, or if there is a spin-off of a defined contribution plan. Furthermore, prior reporting is not required if two or more defined benefit plans are merged and the present value of benefits, whether or not vested, that are merged into the larger plan is less than 3 percent of the assets of the larger plan. All previous mergers (including transfers from another plan) occurring in the same plan year are taken into account in determining the percentage of assets described above.

For example, assume that a merger involving less than 3 percent of the assets of the larger plan occurs in the first month of the larger plan's plan year. In the fourth month of the larger plan's plan year, a second merger occurs involving liabilities equal to 2 percent of the assets of the larger plan. The total of both mergers exceeds 3 percent of the assets of the larger plan, and, as a result of the second merger, both mergers must be reported to the IRS.[98]

In addition, the IRS will take into account mergers occurring in previous plan years if it is determined that the series of mergers are, in substance, one transaction with the merger occurring in the current plan year. Finally, the larger plan's document must provide that, in the event of a spin-off or termination of the plan within five years following the merger, plan assets will be allocated first for the benefits (on a termination basis) of the participants in the smaller plan.

Prior reporting of a spin-off of a defined benefit plan into two or more defined benefit plans is not required if for each plan that results from the spin-off, other than the spun-off plan with the greatest value of plan assets after the spin-off, the

---

[97]IRC §6058(b).
[98]IRS Form 5310-A.

value of the assets spun off is not less than the present value of the benefits spun off (whether or not vested). In addition, the value of the assets spun-off to all the resulting spun off plans plus all assets previously spun off during the plan year in which the spin-off occurs must be less than 3 percent of the assets of the plan before the spin-off as of at least one day in that plan's plan year.

Transfers of Assets and Liabilities

As discussed earlier, it may be advisable for an employer to transfer an employee's benefits from one plan to another in order to simplify administration of the employee's benefit payments. There are also numerous other situations in which one participant's benefit should be transferred from one plan to another, such as when the employee is transferred to another employer as part of an organizational transaction. An employer transferring an employee's benefit between plans must consider several issues including compliance with various plan qualification requirements.

If the assets or liabilities of one plan are transferred to another plan that existed before the receipt of the assets, two transactions are considered to have taken place: a spin-off from the first plan and a merger of the spin-off plan with the transferee plan. Each transaction—that is, the spin-off and the subsequent merger—are independently subject to the legal requirements of the Internal Revenue Code. This discussion focuses on issues specific to the transfer of assets and liabilities.

Statutory Requirements

The Internal Revenue Code contains certain restrictions on the manner in which plan assets and liabilities can be transferred to another plan. There is a transfer of assets or liabilities when one plan acquires or assumes the assets or liabilities of another plan. The shifting of assets or liabilities under a reciprocity agreement between two plans, in which one plan assumes a liability of another, is a transfer of assets or liabilities, but the shifting of assets between several funding media used by a single plan is not.[99] If a transfer of assets or liabilities results in a single plan being split into two or more plans, the transaction is referred to as a spin-off.[100]

Protection of Benefits

When benefits are transferred from one qualified retirement plan to another qualified retirement plan, the transfer is generally initiated by the plan sponsor, and the participant's consent is not obtained. In these kinds of benefits transfers, any optional forms of benefits accrued by the employee must be protected and provided for under the recipient plan.[101] In certain situations, however, a plan

---

[99]Treas. Reg. 1.414(l)-1(b)(3).
[100]Treas. Reg. 1.414(l)-1(b)(4).
[101]IRC §411(d)(6).

sponsor may wish to transfer an employee's benefits from one plan to another and not have to maintain all the different benefit options payable under the transfer of plan.

In addition, since the IRS considers the defined benefit feature of an employee's benefit under a defined benefit plan and the separate account feature of an employee's benefit under a defined contribution plan as protected benefits,[102] employer-initiated involuntary transfers of a participant's benefit from a defined benefit plan to a defined contribution plan are prohibited. As a rule, transfers of a participant's account balance from a defined contribution plan to a defined benefit plan would be permitted only if the defined benefit plan established a separate account to hold the benefit from the defined contribution plan.

The IRS has provided "elective transfer rules" to allow the transfer of benefits between defined benefit and defined contribution plans and permit the elimination of benefit options payable under the transferor plan.[103] The elective transfer rules require that the transfer of benefits between qualified retirement plans be made pursuant to the participant's voluntary election. In order to ensure that the participant's election is voluntary, the plan sponsor must make available an alternative that retains the employee's protected benefit options. Thus if the transferor plan is terminating, the employee must be able to transfer his benefits into an annuity contract that provides for all the protected benefit options, or, if the transferor plan is not terminating, the participant must be given the option of leaving his benefit in the ongoing plan.[104] In addition, spousal consent to the elective transfer must be obtained if the participant's benefit is otherwise subject to the qualified joint and survivor annuity requirements.

The amount of the benefit transferred must equal the entire vested benefit under the transferor plan, calculated to be at least the greater of the single-sum distribution provided for under the plan for which the participant is eligible (if any) or the present value of the participant's accrued benefit payable at normal retirement age. Furthermore, the participant must be fully vested in the transferred benefit in the transferee plan. In a transfer from a defined contribution plan to a defined benefit plan, the defined benefit plan must provide a minimum benefit for each participant whose benefits are transferred, equal to the benefit, expressed as an annuity payable at retirement age, that is derived solely on the basis of the amount transferred with respect to participant.

Finally, and potentially the issue most difficult to comply with in the elective transfer rules, the participant whose benefits are transferred must be eligible, under the terms of the transferor plan, to receive an immediate distribution from such plan.[105] The distributability requirement is often a challenging issue for proposed transfers from a defined benefit plan to a defined contribution plan. Because defined benefit plans generally prohibit in-service distributions to participants prior to normal retirement age,[106] an elective transfer from a defined benefit

[102]Treas. Reg. 1.411(d)-4, Q&A 3(a)(2).
[103]Treas. Reg. 1.411(d)-4, Q&A 3(b).
[104]Treas. Reg. 1.411(d)-4, Q&A 3(b)(1)(i).
[105]Treas. Reg. 1.411(d)-4, Q&A 3(b)(1)(ii).
[106]Treas. Reg. 1.401-1(b)(1)(i).

plan is normally not available unless the participant has attained a normal retirement age, is separating from service, or the defined benefit plan is terminating.

Distribution of Benefits

In many different types of organizational transactions, it is unclear whether benefits can or cannot be distributed to participants. Quite often, the employees return to work the day after the organizational transaction, returning to the same desk and performing the same work as they did before the transaction, yet are now employed by a different control group that potentially sponsors a completely different set of qualified and nonqualified plans. The IRS has developed a doctrine known as the "same desk rule" to deal with such situations. There are, in fact, two same desk rules, one governing the available tax treatment for any distribution and the other governing whether or not a plan can make a distribution of benefits to the participant at all.

The difference between the two rules stems from the requirement under the special favorable lump-sum distribution tax treatment rules that an employee incur a "separation from service." After much apparent internal deliberation and external litigation, the IRS eventually enunciated the current same desk rule that it applies to the taxation of distribution of benefits, namely, that no separation from service occurs when an employee continues to work in the same capacity for a different employer as a result of a liquidation, merger, or consolidation of the former employer. This is the case even if the change of employer is not merely technical but is accompanied by a meaningful change of beneficial ownership. The underlying rationale behind this requirement is apparently that since the tax treatment of the distribution is a determination made on an employee-by-employee basis, then the determination of whether the employee has suffered a separation from service is something that should be judged from the perspective of the employee. From the employee's perspective, returning to the same desk and performing the same work does not constitute a separation from service from the employer, even if the legal entity serving as the employer has changed. Accordingly, the favorable tax treatment for lump-sum distributions upon separation from service should not be available in that situation.

A completely different analysis is used in determining whether a qualified plan can make a distribution to an employee in the event of certain organizational transactions. The issue here stems from the fundamental regulatory definition of a pension plan, which considers that distributions from a pension plan generally will be made upon or after retirement.[107] The IRS has interpreted this definition to mean that, apart from distributions upon death or disability, a pension plan will not be qualified if it permits the participants, prior to any severance of their employment or the termination of the plan, to withdraw all or a part of the funds accumulated on their behalf.[108] The IRS has also determined that the term *severance from employment*, as used in Revenue Ruling 56-693, does not have the same meaning as *separation from service*, as used in determining whether a distribution is

---

[107]Treas. Reg. 1.401-1(b)(1)(i).
[108]Rev. Rul. 56-693, 1956-2 C.B 82.

eligible for favorable lump-sum tax treatment. A determination as to whether a severance from employment has occurred should be made on the basis of whether the employee continues to be employed by the employer maintaining the plan rather than on the basis of whether the employee continues to work in the same job for a different employer as a result of a liquidation, merger, or consolidation.[109]

In determining whether the employment relationship with the employer maintaining the plan has been severed, the term *employer* includes all members of any control group of trades or businesses under common control. Consequently, if the employer of an employee changes from the employer maintaining the plan to another member of the control group, no severance from employment will be treated as having occurred allowing distribution of benefits from a pension plan.

In addition, severance of employment with the employer maintaining the plan does not occur even where the common-law employer of an employee changes to an employer that is not part of the original control group, if the new employer is substituted as the sponsor of the former employer's pension plan. The same result occurs if the employee is employed by a subsidiary now under the control of a new parent corporation and the subsidiary retains the plan, or if there is a transfer of plan assets and liabilities relating to any portion of the employee's benefit under the pension plan to a plan being maintained or created by the new employer.

Finally, there are situations in which the common-law employer of an employee does not change and yet there can be a severance of employment with the employer maintaining the plan. This most often occurs in certain types of stock acquisitions or dispositions, where a subsidiary corporation is sold to another control group of trades or businesses under common control. Although the common-law employer of the employee (the acquired subsidiary corporation) has not changed, a severance of employment with the employer maintaining the plan has occurred if three conditions are met: the pension plan continues to be maintained by the original parent corporation but is no longer maintained by the subsidiary in the hands of its new owner; no assets or liabilities are transferred to the subsidiary in the hands of the new owner; and the subsidiary in the hands of the new owner is not treated as the same employer as the original parent under the control group of trades or businesses under common control rules.[110]

Consequences of Organizational Transactions

Service Crediting

The acquisition of a group of employees through an organizational transaction also brings up questions concerning whether the new employer should credit service with the prior employer for purposes of the new employer's retirement plans. While an employer could voluntarily credit such prior service, it is often still necessary to determine when such prior service must be credited.

Prior service by an employee with a predecessor of his or her current employer is treated as service for the current employer, provided that the current employer

---

[109]GCM 39824.
[110]Ibid.

maintains the predecessor's plan.[111] This rule affects participation and vesting, because the application of these rules depends upon an employee's years of service. The rule does not affect service credited for benefit accrual, since benefit accrual is based on an employee's years of participation.

However, for a rule that can have such profound significance for plan administration or an employee's ultimate retirement benefit, it offers a surprising lack of guidance. The single most important issue in determining whether to grant prior service—identifying who is a "predecessor employer"—is completely undefined in the existing rules. In general, prior business units acquired through stock acquisitions are considered prior employers, but businesses acquired through asset purchases are usually considered prior employers requiring past service grants if the prior employer's benefit plan is merged into the new employer's benefit plan.

Merger Transition Rules

The key legal and tax issues to be considered with respect to qualified retirement plans in developing changes to an employer's corporate structure include nondiscrimination, the restrictions on distributions from such plans because of reorganization, and the rules for transfers of benefits and liabilities between plans. In addition, the implications for vesting and prohibited benefit cutbacks, the application to limits on benefits and contributions from qualified plans, the issues surrounding plan termination, and the possibility of creating "top-heavy" plans for small business units should be understood. Each of these topics is discussed below.

Nondiscrimination Rules

The tax law requires that the benefits of a qualified retirement or savings plan cannot disproportionately favor highly compensated employees. These rules are complex and interrelated but in practice provide a great deal of flexibility for employer plan design (see Chapter 5). A summary of the basic principles underlying major nondiscrimination provisions follows. These rules govern whether enough employees participate in the plan and whether the "right" proportions of highly compensated and non–highly compensated employees of a *testing employer* benefit under the plan.

The "testing employer" is the employer who maintained the plan and each other organization under common control, with the employer using an 80 percent control test. For example, a parent corporation and an 80 percent–owned subsidiary corporation would be considered a single testing employer.

In addition, an organization that is not 80 percent owned may sometimes be treated as part of an affiliated service group and, thus, as part of a testing employer. The affiliated service group rules are discussed later in this chapter.

In certain situations, different business units of a single employer can be treated as separate lines of business (SLOBs) even though they are commonly controlled and would otherwise be treated as a single testing employer. This can enable each SLOB to design its own benefits without concern for the employees or benefits in

---

[111]IRC §414(a).

the other SLOBs. The requirements to treat different business units of the same employer as SLOBs are discussed later in this chapter.

Minimum Participation Requirements

The minimum number of participants required for either a retirement or a savings plan to be qualified is the lesser of 50 employees or 40 percent of a testing employer's employees. The critical terms for determining compliance with this rule are *testing employer*, as defined above, and *plan*. Plan for this purpose refers to the asset pool available to provide benefits. Normally, all the benefits that are provided by one asset pool are considered one "plan."

The following examples illustrate some situations that might arise after a corporate restructuring:

- Several business units that are considered one testing employer might contribute to one trust or asset pool, which would be available for all benefits. The benefits for employees of the different business units may even be computed under separate formulas. There is only one "plan" for applying the minimum participation rules.
- Several business units that are considered one testing employer might contribute to different trusts or asset pools for their own employees. Each asset pool will be considered a separate "plan" for minimum participation even if the benefit formulas and plan provisions are identical.
- Several business units that are not considered one testing employer might contribute to one trust or asset pool with one formula crediting service for all participating business units. Because they are separate testing employers, what would normally be considered a single plan must be tested separately for each testing employer.
- Different testing employers might maintain separate trusts or asset pools to provide benefits for their own employees. Each asset pool will be considered a separate "plan" for applying the minimum participation rules.

Minimum Coverage Requirements

The minimum coverage requirements (discussed in greater detail in Chapter 4) do not call on all the testing employer's employees to participate in the same plan, or indeed in any plan. They do require that each plan independently satisfy one of two coverage tests indicating that the plan covers a nondiscriminatory group of employees. Thus a testing employer could maintain many different plans for different business units or other employee groups as long as each plan satisfied one of these coverage tests.

Nondiscriminatory Benefits or Contributions

A plan must also provide benefits or contributions that do not discriminate in favor of highly compensated employees covered by the plan. (For further discussion of the nondiscrimination rules, see Chapter 5.) The complex rules in this area allow for great variability in benefits so that one plan may be able to provide different benefit or contribution levels for different groups of employees. The variance can be based on business units, age, service, or other factors. After a corporate reorganization, for example, an employer could modify its retirement plan so that the current benefit level would apply only to employees in certain business units. Employees and other business units might earn a lower level of benefits or a higher level of benefits or might be excluded from future participation under the plan.

Cutbacks in Vesting or Benefits

A participant must vest in his or her plan benefits after completing a certain period of service with the testing employer, typically five years. As with the nondiscrimination rules, a testing employer includes all 80 percent controlled organizations as well as certain service organizations under less control. The special exception for SLOBs does not apply, however.

In general, all service with a testing employer must be counted toward vesting any benefits under a plan maintained by that testing employer. In addition, service with a prior employer must be counted toward vesting benefits with a new testing employer if the new testing employer continues a plan of the prior employer or the new plan receives a transfer of assets and liabilities from the prior employer's plan. Merely accepting a rollover distribution from another employer's plan does not, however, require an employer to recognize the employee's prior service with that employer, if the employers are otherwise unrelated.

Another rule requires vesting of plan benefits in the event of termination or partial termination of a plan. Thus if an employer were to terminate its retirement plan in conjunction with the reorganization of its structure, all participants in the plan would become vested in their benefits earned to date. This rule also applies in the event of a partial termination, which is where a substantial number of employees, such as 20 percent, are eliminated from participation in the plan or from earning future service with the employer. In this case, although the rules for determining when a partial termination occurs are somewhat subjective, only the employees who had their service terminated would have to become vested. A partial termination would not occur, however, if the employees' benefits were transferred to another plan under which future benefits were being earned.

Another important rule is that earned benefits cannot be reduced or eliminated by a plan change. This rule applies to benefits whether they continue to be maintained in the same plan in which they are earned or whether they are transferred to another plan maintained by the same or a different employer. Thus a reduction in benefits should not occur as a result of any restructuring. Note, however, that this applies only to benefits already earned, not to future benefits. Thus a plan formula can be changed to lower or raise future accruals.

Early retirement provisions, such as an unreduced benefit after 30 years of service, and benefit options are treated as part of the earned benefit. Therefore this type of feature could not be eliminated with respect to benefits already earned.

Limits on Contributions or Benefits

Tax rules limit the amount of benefits that can be paid from a qualified defined benefit plan or the amount of contributions that can be made on behalf of any participant in a qualified defined contribution plan. In addition, there are rules that apply a combined limit to a participant in both types of plans. As with the nondiscrimination rules, these limits apply to all plans maintained by a testing employer. In contrast to discrimination, where an 80 percent controlled test is applied, a 50 percent controlled test is applied for the limits on contributions or benefits. Thus the benefits provided by a parent corporation and a 60 percent–owned subsidiary must both be subjected to the limits as though they are provided by a single testing employer. Under this rule, 50 percent ownership does not result in aggregation, whereas any ownership greater than 50 percent does.

Distribution or Transfer of Benefits

An issue that arises in any corporate restructuring or disposal of a portion of a company what should happen to the benefits that have already been earned by the participants being transferred. For example, a company may choose to distribute earned benefits to transferred participants or to offer to transfer those amounts over to another plan. Several restrictions can influence these decisions.

A pension plan can be disqualified if it makes a distribution to a participant unless the participant has attained retirement age, separated from service with the testing employer, or the plan has been terminated. Thus if a participant reaches normal retirement age under a pension plan, benefit distributions may commence even if the participant continues working. However, a younger participant may not begin receiving benefits until separation from service.

If a participant transfers from the parent organization to a new business unit that is at least 80 percent owned by the parent organization, benefits under the employer's pension plan cannot be paid unless the participant is age 65 or older. Similarly, benefits cannot be paid from the pension plan of a controlled subsidiary simply because a participant transfers back to the parent organization. In many business reorganizations, it may be unclear whether a participant has separated from service even when the participant ends up working for a different employer. For example, if a participant continues working at the same desk, performing the same job, it may be unclear whether the participant has a separation from service even though the business unit in which the participant works has been sold to another employer.

A participant is considered to have separated from service and a distribution can be made if the division is purchased by an independent employer, the pension plan remains with the seller, and the assets and liabilities of the transferred participants are not transferred to a plan maintained by the purchaser. A distribution would not be permitted, however, if the division for which the participant works was transferred to a separate business unit 80 percent controlled by the selling business organization, even if the controlled business does not maintain the prior plan.

A distribution from a 401(k) qualified cash or deferred arrangement will raise the same types of issues in a business reorganization as distributions from a pension plan. Unless a participant is eligible for a hardship distribution, the participant's pretax contributions may not be distributed unless the participant has attained age 59½, the plan is terminated and a successor defined contribution plan is not established, or the business organization disposes of 85 percent of the assets used in a particular trade or business or the participant is transferred to the purchaser, and the purchaser does not establish a similar plan.

Transfers to Another Plan

The parent business organization may wish to transfer the liabilities for the benefit earned with the employer as well as the accompanying assets to the new business entity for which the participant will work after a business reorganization. There are important restrictions in this context. These restrictions can be problems for defined benefit plans, but generally are not troublesome for defined contribution plans.

When a liability is transferred from one plan to another, certain assets must also be transferred. If a liability is transferred from a defined benefit plan maintained by an employer to a different defined benefit plan maintained by a business entity that is not 80 percent controlled by the employer, assets equal to liabilities must be transferred to provide that benefit. Transfers of any surplus assets in the transferor's defined benefit plan (i.e., the assets in excess of the amount necessary to provide all the benefits currently earned in the plan) can be subject to negotiation. But if the liability is transferred to another plan maintained by the same employer or controlled group, a portion of the surplus assets must also be transferred to the recipient plan.

Top-Heavy Rules

The tax rules include some additional rules that require minimum benefits or minimum contributions in small plans that benefit primarily a small group of key employees. Although these rules generally do not concern large employers, a small business unit that is created by a business reorganization may have to provide these minimum benefits or contributions. This is so regardless of whether or not the small business unit is 80 percent owned by the parent business organization after the reorganization.

Section II
The Structure of Private Retirement Plans

Chapter 10
Defined Benefit Plan Design: Retirement Benefits

An underlying purpose of a pension plan is to enable employers to remove superannuated employees from the payroll in a manner that is morally and socially acceptable. In practical terms, this means that a life income in some amount must be made available to an employee who has reached the end of his or her economically productive life. The plan may provide benefits in the event that the employee dies or becomes permanently and totally disabled before retirement, but such benefits are collateral and secondary to the fundamental objective of providing an income after retirement. Chapter 15 discusses how to set appropriate retirement income objectives. The next two chapters review the two types of pension plans and their features.

Types of Pension Plans

The obligation assumed by an employer in establishing a pension plan may take one of two forms: (1) a promise to provide benefits according to a specific schedule, or (2) a promise to contribute on a specified basis. The first approach is referred to as a *defined* benefit plan, and the second is called a *defined* contribution plan. Under either approach, employees may contribute toward the cost of the plan.

Defined Benefit Plan

In a defined benefit plan,[1] benefits are established in advance by a formula, and employer contributions are treated as the variable factor. The formula for establishing the benefits may provide that the amount of monthly pension after retirement is fixed, or it may provide that the amount varies after retirement in accordance with some fixed standards (e.g., the consumer price index). The latter formula is discussed in Chapter 21, which deals with variable annuities and other devices for protecting pension benefits against loss of purchasing power. This chapter only examines plans that provide fixed-dollar benefits, which are the most prevalent type.

[1] ERISA §3(35); IRC §414(j).

Benefit Formulas

Benefit formulas of defined benefit plans vary greatly, but basically they may be classified into two categories: (1) unit benefit and (2) flat benefit.

Unit Benefit Formula

In a unit benefit formula, an explicit unit of benefit is credited for each year of recognized service with the employer. The unit of benefit may be expressed as a percentage of compensation—the usual procedure under a plan for salaried employees—or as a specific dollar amount.

DEFINING COMPENSATION   When the benefit unit is expressed in terms of compensation, the plan must clearly indicate which parts of compensation will be included in the earnings base. Overtime pay, holiday pay, sick pay, bonuses, and commissions must be specifically excluded or included. The definition of compensation used must satisfy requirements established by the Tax Reform Act.[2] It is always permissible to define compensation as that portion of compensation received that can be currently included in gross income for tax purposes, that is, earnings included on Form W-2. Such taxable compensation may also be increased by any elective salary deferrals under a 401(k) plan, tax-sheltered annuity (403(b)), simplified employee plan (SEP), or cafeteria plan (125). Unless such salary deferrals are included in the definition of compensation, participants who elect to defer salary will have their compensation as defined under the pension plan effectively reduced, and thus their pension benefits will also be reduced. Regulations also allow the use of other definitions, such as basic or regular compensation (excluding special compensation and overtime) in situations where such definitions do not tend to discriminate in favor of highly compensated employees. For plan years beginning after 1993, no qualified plan may take account of compensation in excess of $150,000.[3] This amount is to be adjusted for inflation.

DEFINING BENEFIT FORMULAS   After compensation has been defined, the plan must decide how to credit benefits earned each year: in terms of the compensation earned in that year, or in terms of the average compensation for a few years close to retirement. When the unit of benefit credited during any particular year of employment is based on the employee's compensation during that year, the benefit formula is called a *career average* formula. This term means that except as noted later, the pensioner's retirement benefit is in effect based on his or her average earnings during the entire period of the pensioner's recognized, or credited, service. However, if recognition is given to service prior to the establishment of the plan, as is customary, benefit credits for such periods are usually based on compensation at the inception of the plan to avoid the necessity of tracing past wage histories. In that event, a lower percentage of compensation may be credited, as

---

[2]IRC §414(q).
[3]IRC §401(a)(17).

compared with future service, in recognition of the fact that the level of compensation is likely to be higher when the plan was established than during the years when the past service credits were accruing. Under a contributory plan, the lower past service benefits may also be because no employee contributions were made in past years.

The following example shows how to calculate the pension under a career average plan that provides a benefit of 1 percent of pay for each year. This example calculates the pension for an individual assumed to start in year 1 with a salary of $20,000 and who receives annual raises of 5 percent. The pension accrual in year 1 is

$$\$20,000 \times 1\% = \$200.$$

The pension accrual in year 2 is

$$\$21,000 \times 1\% = \$210.$$

The total compensation accrued after two years of service is the sum of the accruals in the first two years:

$$\$200 + \$210 = \$410.$$

Thus if the individual's pay in year t is Pay_t, and the accrual rate credited for year t is b_t, then the total pension at retirement under a career average plan for an individual hired at age H and retiring at age R is

$$\sum_{t=H}^{R-1} b_t \cdot \text{PAY}_t .$$

If b_t is a constant, b, for all years, this can be rewritten as

$$\sum_{t=H}^{R-1} b \cdot \text{PAY}_t = b \sum_{t=H}^{R-1} \text{PAY}_t = b \cdot (R - H) \cdot \frac{\sum_{i-H}^{R-1} \text{PAY}_t}{(R - H)} .$$

The retirement benefit is the product of three factors: (1) an accrual rate, b, (2) years of service, $(R - H)$, and (3) the average pay over the individual's entire career,

$$\frac{\sum_{t=H}^{R-1} \text{PAY}_t}{(R - H)} .$$

It is this viewpoint that gives rise to the name *career average*.

This example points out one of the flaws of a career average plan: even with salary increases consistent with modest inflation, the pay base used for calculating a career average benefit can be quite far removed from the individual's pay in the

TABLE 10-1   Illustration of Career Average Pension Accrual

Year (1)	Pay (2)	Annual Pension Accrual (3)	Total Pension Accrued (4)
1	$20,000	$200	$ 200
2	21,000	210	410
3	22,100	221	631
4	23,200	232	863
5	24,400	244	1,107
6	25,600	256	1,363
7	26,900	269	1,632
8	28,200	282	1,914
9	29,600	296	2,210
10	31,100	311	2,521
11	32,700	327	2,848
12	34,300	343	3,191
13	36,000	360	3,551
14	37,800	378	3,929
15	39,700	397	4,326
16	41,700	417	4,743
17	43,800	438	5,181
18	46,000	460	5,641
19	48,300	483	6,124
20	50,700	507	6,631
21	53,200	532	7,163
22	55,900	559	7,722
23	58,700	587	8,309
24	61,600	616	8,925
25	64,700	647	9,572
26	67,900	679	10,251
27	71,300	713	10,964
28	74,900	749	11,713
29	78,600	786	12,499
30	82,500	825	13,324

Assumptions: (1) Pension formula equals 1 percent of each year's pay; (2) pay increases of 5 percent per year.

period immediately prior to retirement, as may be seen in Table 10-1. On the basis of the assumptions underlying Table 10-1, the individual's career average pay is $44,400, while the final year's pay is $82,500.

A second type of benefit formula is the final average formula. In pure form, the final average formula benefits are accrued on the basis of the participant's average compensation during a specified period, such as the 3, 5, or 10 years immediately preceding retirement. This formula can be modified to use the consecutive years of an individual's highest average compensation, whether or not that period fell immediately before retirement. Another alternative is to use the highest *m* years in the final *n* years of employment, where *m* is less than *n*. Also, some formulas use months rather than years—for example, highest 36 consecutive months out of last 60 months of employment. Under a final average formula, the amount of annual benefit earned with each year of credited service is not known until the participant reaches retirement,[4] and this creates uncertainties about the magnitude of the employer's undertaking. The principal appeal of this approach is that it automatically provides benefits appropriately related to the participant's compensation during the years close to retirement.

Table 10-2 shows how the pension would be calculated under a final five-year average plan that provides a benefit of one percent of final five years' average pay for each year of service. This sample calculation is for the same individual used in the career average illustration: someone with a starting salary of $20,000 and annual pay increases of 5 percent. The final five-year average pay at the end of any given year is simply the sum of the current and prior four years' pay, divided by five. For example, the final five-year average pay at the end of year 15 is

$$F5PAY_{15} = \frac{(32{,}700 + 34{,}300 + 36{,}000 + 37{,}800 + 39{,}700)}{5} = 36{,}100$$

The pension accrued at the end of year 15 is then:

$$F5PAY_{15} \times 1\% \times \text{Years of Service} = \$36{,}100 \times 1\% \times 15 = \$5{,}415.$$

This year-end accrued pension is shown in column 4 of Table 10-2. The pension at retirement for an individual with an accrual rate credited in year *t* of a_t under a final five-year average pay plan is

$$\text{Pension at Retirement} = \left(\sum_{t=H}^{R-1} a_t \right) \cdot \frac{\sum_{t=R-5}^{R-1} PAY_t}{5}$$

Again, if a_t is a constant (say, *a*), this simplifies to

$$a \cdot (R - H) \cdot \frac{\sum_{t=R-5}^{R-1} PAY_t}{5} .$$

Note that although each of the sample plans provides a benefit of 1 percent of pay for each year of service, because the final five-year average earnings are so much larger than the career average earnings, the final pay plan provides a benefit almost

---

[4]Most of these plans provide that in the event of an employee's withdrawal from covered employment prior to retirement, any vested benefits will be based on the average salary for the years preceding the date of termination of service.

TABLE 10-2   Illustration of Final Average Pension Accrual

Year (1)	Pay (2)	Annual Five-Year Average Pay (3)	Year-End Pension Accrued (4)
1	$20,000	$20,000	$ 200
2	21,000	20,500	410
3	22,100	21,000	631
4	23,200	21,575	863
5	24,400	22,140	1,107
6	25,600	23,260	1,396
7	26,900	24,440	1,711
8	28,200	25,660	2,053
9	29,600	26,940	2,425
10	31,100	28,280	2,828
11	32,700	29,700	3,267
12	34,300	31,180	3,742
13	36,000	32,740	4,256
14	37,800	34,380	4,813
15	39,700	36,100	5,415
16	41,700	37,900	6,064
17	43,800	39,800	6,766
18	46,000	41,800	7,524
19	48,300	43,900	8,341
20	50,700	46,100	9,220
21	53,200	48,400	10,164
22	55,900	50,820	11,180
23	58,700	53,360	12,273
24	61,600	56,020	13,445
25	64,700	58,820	14,705
26	67,900	61,760	16,058
27	71,300	64,840	17,507
28	74,900	68,080	19,062
29	78,600	71,480	20,729
30	82,500	75,040	22,512

Assumptions: (1) Pension formula equals 1 percent of high-five-year average pay; (2) pay increases of 5 percent per year.

70 percent larger than the career average plan. One way to address this discrepancy is to provide for a larger percentage accrual under the career average plan. For example, if the career average plan had provided an annual accrual equal to 1.7 percent of each year's pay, the hypothetical employee would have had a total benefit at retirement of $22,651, compared with the final average plan benefit of $22,512. This is not a particularly attractive solution since the specific accrual rate needed under a career average plan to equal a given final pay plan is a function of (1) the salary increases experienced over the individual's career and (2) the length of service of the employee.

TABLE 10-3   Annual Career Average Accrual Rate Necessary to Provide Benefit Equal to 1 Percent Final Five-Year Average Benefit

Annual Salary Increase Rate (%)	Service				
	15	20	25	30	35
2	1.10	1.15	1.21	1.26	1.32
5	1.25	1.39	1.54	1.69	1.85
8	1.40	1.63	1.87	2.13	2.40

This dilemma can be seen in a simplified context by setting out the expression for the career average plan and the final average plan at retirement with constant accruals equal to each other:

$$b \cdot (R-H) \cdot \frac{\sum\limits_{t=H}^{R-1} PAY_t}{(R-H)} = a \cdot (R-H) \cdot \frac{\sum\limits_{t=R-5}^{R-1} PAY_t}{5}$$

$$\frac{b}{a} = \frac{\sum\limits_{t=R-5}^{R-1} PAY_t}{\sum\limits_{t=H}^{R-1} PAY_t} \cdot \frac{(R-H)}{5}.$$

The left-hand side of this expression is the career average accrual rate as a multiple of the final average accrual rate. The right-hand side is the product of two factors, the first of which is a function of salary increases and the second of which is a function of length of service. Table 10-3 shows the multiple of a given final average accrual rate that a career average formula must use to produce an equivalent benefit for various salary increases and service contributions. Thus, if a career average accrual rate of 1.7 percent is developed to produce the correct final pay replacement ratio for an individual with 5 percent pay increases and 30 years of service, the plan will provide too rich a benefit for an individual with 2 percent salary increases and too small a benefit for an individual with high salary increases. Similar effects occur for different service combinations than the ones shown in the preceding examples. This wide range of results means that it is impossible to reproduce the final average plan benefits for a plan that has employees with various service and salary characteristics. For this reason, many plan sponsors who are attracted by the limited inflationary commitment inherent in a career average plan use the *modified career average* approach instead, a third type of benefit formula.

In the modified career approach, the promised benefits are based on career average earnings, but they are periodically reviewed to determine whether salary increases have been such that the pay base for past service benefits is out of date, and whether the plan sponsor can afford to update past service benefits. If the answer to both questions is yes, then the plan will be amended to update the pay

Table 10-4   Illustration of Modified Career Average Pension Accrual

Year (1)	Pay (2)	Annual Pension Earned (3)	Sum of Prior Year-End Accrued Pension and Current Year Accrual (4)	High-Five-Year Average Pay (5)	Year-End Pension Update (6)
1	$20,000	200	$200		
2	21,000	210	410		
3	22,100	221	631		
4	23,200	232	863		
5	24,400	244	1,107	$22,140	$1,107
6	25,600	256	1,363		
7	26,900	269	1,632		
8	28,200	282	1,914		
9	29,600	296	2,210		
10	31,100	311	2,521	28,280	2,828
11	32,700	327	3,155		
12	34,300	343	3,498		
13	36,000	360	3,858		
14	37,800	378	4,236		
15	39,700	397	4,633	36,100	5,415
16	41,700	417	5,832		
17	43,800	438	6,270		
18	46,000	460	6,730		
19	48,300	483	7,213		
20	50,700	507	7,720	46,100	9,220
21	53,200	532	9,752		
22	55,900	559	10,311		
23	58,700	587	10,898		
24	61,600	616	11,514		
25	64,700	647	12,161	58,820	14,705
26	67,900	679	15,384		
27	71,300	713	16,097		
28	74,900	749	16,846		
29	78,600	786	17,632		
30	82,500	825	18,457	75,040	22,512

Assumptions: (1) Pension formula equals 1 percent of each year's pay; (2) pension formula is updated by Plan Amendment every five years to base past service benefits on most recent five-year pay; (3) pay increases of 5 percent per year.

base for past service benefits to the most recent five-year period. Table 10-4 illustrates this approach for the sample employee hired at $20,000. Column 3 shows the pension earned under the career average promise in each year. Note that the pension is the same as in Table 10-1. The difference under the modified career average plan is shown in columns 4 and 5. In years 5, 10, 15, 20, 25, and 30, a plan amendment updating prior service is assumed to be made. This plan amendment provides that the *past service benefit* will be at least equal to

$$1\% \times \text{Past Service} \times \text{5-Year Average Pay at Date of Plan Amendment.}$$

For example, after 15 years of service, the amendment provides for a past service benefit at least equal to

$$1\% \times 15 \times \$36,100 = \$5,415.$$

Note that this is the same benefit that an individual would have accrued under our sample final average plan after 15 years of service. Indeed, the total benefit after 30 years of service is the same as that for the final average plan *assuming that the modified career average plan is continually updated.* This assumption is critical since the plan sponsor has not committed to future plan updates. This provides financial protection for the plan sponsor but means that the employee cannot be sure that the pension at retirement will reflect final average earnings. In practice, there are relatively few pure career average plans; most provide past service updates at some point.

Once the earnings base is defined, the percentage to be credited for each year of service must be selected. With a unit benefit formula, the percentage usually falls within the range of 1 to 2 percent, with 1½ percent tending to predominate. The percentage of compensation reflected in the benefit formula may vary with the level of earnings, with several earnings classifications sometimes being employed. Because Social Security provides benefits that are a larger percentage of compensation for lower-paid workers than for higher-paid workers, it is customary to apply a lower percentage to earnings up to some stated level called the "integration level" than to those earnings in excess of that integration level. In this case, the plan is said to be integrated with Social Security, a subject treated in Chapter 15. There may be a distinction between past and future service, with lower percentages being applicable to the past service.

The *specified dollar benefit formula* is a type of formula that provides a stated amount of benefit—unrelated to compensation—for each year of service. It is popular among negotiated plans, cases in which the range of hourly wage rates is generally relatively narrow. With continual increases in prices and wages and greater emphasis in the collective bargaining process on pension benefits, the stipulated monthly benefit in many industries is now $30 or more for each year of credited service. Some employers using this benefit form, however, may have a range of hourly rates for workers covered under their plans. The specified dollar benefit may vary by job classification of the workers covered under the plan or by job location apart from job classification. Thus benefits will vary in relation to covered pay although not as directly as in a plan that calculates the benefit directly from pay.

The basic appeal of the specified dollar benefit is its simplicity. The concept is easily grasped by the parties to the collective bargaining process, and the benefits are easily communicated to the plan participants. For a time, the approach seemed to offer employers a way of freezing pension benefits for service already rendered, in contrast to the escalating effect of the final average salary approach. The freeze was to be accomplished by limiting increases in the unit benefit to years of service rendered after the change (in some ways, this is the opposite of the modified career average approach). However, continuing inflation has made it desirable to give retroactive recognition to benefit increases, thus nullifying the contemplated advantage to the employer. In other words, the benefit amount negotiated in a new labor contract is often applied to all years of credited service, including those rendered prior to the change. But under multiemployer plans, employers often strongly resist any increase in the benefits for prior years to avoid increases in potential withdrawal liability (discussed later). As a further safeguard against the erosive effect of inflation, some unions have sought and obtained a minimum benefit expressed in terms of final salary. In periods of rapidly escalating wages, this type of minimum benefit can become the basic benefit.

Virtually all plans that relate benefits to years of service recognize service performed before the plan was established to provide adequate benefits to persons nearing retirement. Many plans, however, place some limits on the amount of past service that will be recognized. Various forms of limits are used. The most common exclude (1) all service performed before a specified age, (2) the first year or few years of service, or (3) all service over a maximum number of years, such as 10, 15, or 25, or before a specified date. The first two types of exclusion are often set equal to the age and service required for participation in the plan, thus treating old employees the same as new employees. The primary purpose of the type (3) exclusion is to limit the cost of past service benefits, an accrued liability that is almost invariably borne by the employer. This type of exclusion is becoming less common, especially among collectively bargained plans.

Flat Benefit Plans

The second broad category of benefit formulas—flat benefit plans—is based upon the philosophy that, beyond a minimum period of service, retirement benefits should not be related to the length of service under the plan.

This type of formula may provide a benefit at retirement equal to a specified percentage of compensation, without regard to years of service. The compensation base is normally the average earnings during a specified period before retirement, but the career average earnings may be used. A wide range of percentages is used, the benefit typically being 30, 40, or 50 percent of compensation. The percentage applicable to that portion of compensation below the integration level may be lower than that applied to the portion in excess of the integration level. The same percentage applies to all employees who satisfy a minimum period of service, such as 15 or 20 years. Past service may be credited against the minimum requirement. Employees who fail to satisfy the minimum period of service have their benefits reduced proportionately. As is true of the "final average" type of unit benefit formula, the benefit payable to a particular employee cannot be definitely ascertained until he or she reaches retirement.

The distinction between unit benefit plans and flat benefit plans may be only cosmetic. A flat benefit plan of 60 percent of pay reduced one-thirtieth for each year less than 30 is identical to a unit benefit plan of 2 percent of pay per year of service with a maximum of 30 years credit, if the same definition of pay is used for both.

Another type of flat benefit formula ignores differences in both compensation and length of service and provides a flat dollar benefit to all employees who satisfy a minimum period of credited service. This type of formula was typical of the early negotiated plans but is relatively rare today, and where it is used it often serves to provide a minimum benefit in cases where an alternative benefit formula would provide less.

Definition of Year of Service

Implicit in all of the foregoing formulas is the concept of a "year of service." There is no restriction as to how a plan measures years of service for purposes of calculating the amount of accrued benefit at normal retirement age. However, there are restrictions on how years are measured to determine the amount of accrued benefit that is vested upon termination before normal retirement age. These restrictions are described in the section "Withdrawal Benefits" in Chapter 11. In practice, most plans choose to use the same method for measuring years in determining the accrued benefit upon normal retirement as they use for withdrawal benefits.

Pattern of Benefit Accruals

A pension plan need not provide the same benefit accrual for each year of service. Depending upon the employer's conception of the equities involved or the personnel policy to be served, the plan may provide one scale of benefits for the first portion of total service, such as the first 10, 15, or 20 years, and a *higher* or *lower* scale for service thereafter. If the employer wants to encourage and reward long service, he may provide a higher scale of benefits for the later years of service than for the earlier years. This practice is sometimes called "back loading." A mild form of back loading is contained in the federal pension plan covering civil servants hired before January 1, 1984. The Civil Service Retirement System (CSRS) provides for an annual benefit accrual of 1.5 percent for the first five years of service, 1.75 percent for the next five years, and 2 percent for all service beyond the first ten years. The percentage in each case is based on the participant's average salary for the three consecutive years of highest compensation. The new Federal Employee Retirement System (FERS) provides a constant accrual rate of 1 percent for each year of service under the plan.[5] FERS, however, does keep some element of back loading in that workers who stay on beyond age 62 accrue benefits at a rate of 1.1 percent per year. The reason for this back loading in FERS related to age is to encourage federal workers to work beyond age 62.

On the other hand, if the employer wishes to encourage early retirement or at least discourage excessively long service, he may reduce the rate of benefit accrual after some period of service, such as 30 years, or eliminate further accruals altogether. That is, the plan may limit the number of years of service that will be recognized for benefit purposes. In a recent study of the retirement plans offered

---

[5]Civil servants covered under CSRS do not accrue Social Security benefits based on their federal service, whereas those covered under FERS do.

by 50 of the largest companies in the United States, 20 were found to have used a service maximum somewhere in their pension formula.[6] The most prevalent maximum by far was 35 years. The practice of providing more liberal benefits for the early years of service is known as "front loading."

Prior to ERISA, the employer had complete discretion as to the pattern of benefit accruals to build into the company's plan, as long as the plan's operation did not favor officers, shareholders, and highly compensated employees. Concerned that employers might try to undermine the new mandatory vesting standards by back loading the benefit formula, Congress regulated back loading by incorporating three alternative tests that set limits on the extent of back loading permitted in computing vested benefits under defined benefit plans.[7] Since these tests have primarily affected the benefit accruals of terminated vested participants, they are described in the section "Cash Option at Retirement" later in this chapter.

Minimum Benefits

Many plans provide a floor of protection through a minimum benefit provision that operates independently of the normal benefit formula. It is very common for unit benefit plans that base benefits on compensation to stipulate that the annual benefit accrual will not be less than a specified amount. For example, a plan that provides an annual benefit accrual (payable in monthly installments) of 1.5 percent of current compensation might stipulate that the annual benefit for any year of service is not to be less than $120. This is tantamount to saying that the minimum annual wage or salary for benefit purposes is $8,000 (1.5% of $8,000=$120). There may be a minimum benefit for each year of service or a minimum for the total benefit. The minimum may be restricted to participants having a minimum period of service.

Some plans whose normal benefits are based on career average compensation provide a minimum benefit that is expressed as a percentage of final compensation or a percentage of compensation as of some specified date. This type of provision is motivated by the same factors that lead some sponsors to adopt a modified career average approach; it is designed to ensure that the career average salary base bears a reasonable minimum relationship to the participant's earnings during the years immediately preceding retirement. Although the dollar benefit minimum is general and applies to all participants, the percentage of compensation minimum is specific to the individual participant. The latter is generally conditioned on a minimum period of service, such as 20 or 25 years, with reduced minimum benefits being payable for shorter periods of service.

Time of Payment

A second broad aspect of retirement benefits is the time of payment. Under the great majority of plans, participants are entitled to receive the full amount of their accrued benefits upon retirement on or after reaching a specified age, called the

---

[6]See Watson Wyatt.
[7]ERISA §204(b); IRC §411(b).

normal retirement age. This entitlement is a contractual right and can be exercised without the consent of the employer. In some plans, however, the age requirement is supplemented by a minimum service requirement, such as five years. The plan may provide full or reduced benefits upon retirement prior to the normal retirement age. The Age Discrimination in Employment Act (ADEA), passed in 1967, and amended several times since, generally prohibits mandatory retirement at any age.[8]

Normal Retirement Age

The normal retirement age has traditionally been considered to be the earliest age at which eligible participants are permitted to retire with full benefits. However, ERISA defined normal retirement age simply as the normal retirement age specified in the plan, but not later than age 65 with 10 years of participation.[9] For plan years beginning after 1987, the 10-year requirement was reduced to 5 years for any employee who becomes a participant within 5 years of the normal retirement age.

There are three essential components in the definition of a benefit accrual: the *dollar amount* of the benefit, the *age of the participant* at which the benefit is payable in full (i.e., the normal retirement age), and the *annuity form* under which the benefit is payable. No benefit definition is complete without all three of these components. The annuity form of the benefit can be a single life annuity, a joint and survivor annuity, or a single life annuity with a refund feature. The dollar amount of prospective retirement benefits to be paid to two participants of the same age and sex under two separate pension plans may be identical, but the actuarial value of the accrued benefits (and, hence, their cost) can be quite different if they do not become payable at the same age and under the same annuity form.

Thus the normal retirement age should be viewed more as an element in the definition of the retirement benefit than as a statement of when participants are expected to retire. In actuality, participants may retire over a wide range of ages, with appropriate adjustments in their benefits. Most plans permit retirement before the normal retirement age, usually subject to specified age and service restrictions, and most permit deferment of retirement beyond the normal retirement age.

Many retirement plans have linked retirement age to 5 or 10 years of service or participation, but some have a much longer period if the minimum age is under 65. For example, the normal retirement age may be the earlier of age 65 with 5 years of service, 60 with 20 years of service, or 55 with 30 years of service. Discontinuities in benefit entitlement may be avoided by providing benefits unreduced by the employee's age whenever his or her age and service equal a specified number, such as 90. A provision of this sort is referred to as the "Rule of 90," although the concept may also be applied in establishing eligibility for vested benefits. Under the Rule of 90, such combinations as age 60 and 30 years of service would entitle participants to full benefits for their credited years of service. The

[8]ADEA §12(a),(c).
[9]ERISA §3(24); IRC §411(a)(8).

rule may, of course, be stated in terms of other numbers, such as 85 or 95. Some plans with a nominal normal retirement age permit retirement before that age, subject to minimum service requirements, with full benefits for the years of accrued service. Under some collectively bargained plans, participants are permitted to retire with full accrued benefits after a specified amount of service, such as 30 years, irrespective of age. Some plans have alternative criteria for normal retirement age, such as the earlier of age 65 or the completion of 30 years of service. Under all the foregoing arrangements, it would have to be said that there are *multiple* normal retirement ages, which depend on the related service requirement and the participant's age of entry into the plan.

In addition to its actuarial function, the normal retirement age serves as an instrument of personnel policy. In most companies, it indicates the age at which most employees would be expected to retire—or certainly the age by which most employees would have retired. Some plans previously specified an age, usually 70, at which retirement was to be mandatory, but mandatory retirement is generally no longer permitted.[10]

Ideally, from the standpoint of the personnel policy of an individual employer, the normal retirement age should be the age beyond which the service of employees would be uneconomical. This point, of course, is not easy to determine. In theory, multiple retirement ages should be adopted in many cases, since a retirement age that would be suitable for one class of employees might be completely inappropriate for another group. In the airlines industry, for example, flight personnel should—and do—have a lower retirement age than nonflight employees. Jobs that require physical strength and endurance may call for a lower retirement age than those that emphasize mental agility. Within particular job classifications, moreover, differences in individual employees should, ideally, be recognized. Nevertheless, the practice, subject to certain exceptions, is to have a normal retirement age that applies to all employees, with provisions for adjustments to particular situations through optional retirement arrangements, which are discussed below. Since the ADEA generally does not allow an employer to discharge an employee on the basis of age, the mental and physical fitness of the individual for continued employment may have to be evaluated before any discharge of an older employee.

Under ERISA, the normal retirement age for vesting purposes cannot be later than age 65 or, if later, the 10th anniversary of the participant's entry into the plan (5th anniversary for those hired after age 60). Age 65 is designated as the normal retirement age for all employees in the large majority of plans. At one time, some plans stipulated a lower retirement age for female employees, but that is now forbidden under the rules of the Equal Employment Opportunity Commission. An exception to the normal retirement age is sometimes made for employees who are beyond a specified age at the time the pension plan is established. This applies to employees over 55 or 60 on the effective date, for whom the normal retirement age may be set in terms of completion of 5 or 10 years of participation or attainment of

---

[10]An exception applies where age is a bona fide occupational qualification reasonably necessary to the normal operation of the particular business. For example, special rules apply to law enforcement officers and firefighters. ADEA §4(f),(i). *Western Airlines, Inc. v. Criswell*, 472 US 400(1985).

age 70, whichever occurs first. This approach is primarily used for plans funded through individual insurance or annuity contracts. The purpose of this staggered retirement is primarily to spread the cost of the benefits, composed principally of past service credits, over a longer period than would otherwise be available. Other reasons for staggered retirement at the inception of the plan are to permit high-age, low-service employees to accumulate larger pensions and to cushion the personnel impact.

Early Retirement

It is customary to provide that an employee may retire earlier than the normal retirement age, subject to attaining a specified age, typically 55, and possibly fulfilling a minimum period of service, such as 10, 15, or 20 years. At one time, some plans required employer consent for early retirement, but IRS regulations no longer permit this.

Some plans permit early retirement only in the event of total and permanent disability, which is discussed later in this chapter. In such plans, age and service requirements are also imposed. Some of the plans provide a special disability benefit, while others pay only the same percentage of the regular accrued benefit that would normally be paid on early retirement.

Calculating an early retirement benefit involves two steps. The first is to determine the amount of benefit that would be payable at normal retirement age based on the participant's service and compensation at the date of *early* retirement. This determination is made in the same manner as the computation of the vested benefit. The second step is to multiply the *accrued* benefit payable at normal retirement age by an early retirement factor reflecting the fact that benefit payments begin earlier than contemplated and, therefore, extend over a longer time; the assets supporting the benefits earn less investment income before payments commence; and there will be no gains to the plan from the participant's dying before benefit payments commence (the benefit of survivorship).

When the accrued retirement benefits are reduced by a scale of percentages that reflect the foregoing factors, they are said to be "actuarially reduced" or "actuarially equivalent." The expression "full actuarial reduction" is frequently applied to the process that fully recognizes the longer payout period and loss of investment earnings (and benefit of survivorship) to distinguish it from the results obtained by applying a higher scale of percentages to the accrued benefits. Some plans now link eligibility for unreduced benefits to Social Security's age at which a full benefit is payable. Thus one set of reductions applies for workers born before 1938, another for those born between 1938 and 1954, and a third for those born after 1954.

The reduction in the accrued benefits for early retirement depends upon the mortality and interest assumptions that underlie the calculation of the actuarial value of the normal retirement benefits. The greater the assumed rates of mortality and the higher the interest rate assumption, the greater the reduction for each year of early retirement. The percentage reduction in the accrued benefits for each year of early retirement slopes downward. When the actuarial value of the normal retirement

TABLE 10-5   Proportion of Accrued Normal Retirement Income
Available at Early Retirement at Various Ages under a
Plan with Normal Retirement Age 65

Age at Retirement	Benefit Percentage
64	89.6
63	80.5
62	72.5
61	65.5
60	59.3
59	53.8
58	48.9
57	44.5
56	40.6
55	37.1

Note: These percentages apply to the benefits earned to the date of early
retirement and not to the benefits that would have been payable had the
employee continued working to age 65.

benefits is computed on the basis of the UP-94 Table[11] and a 7 percent interest
assumption, the accrued normal retirement benefit is reduced about 10 percent
per year, expressed as a percentage of the benefit for the next higher age. For
example, the benefit payable at age 64 is about 90 percent of that payable at age 65;
that payable at age 63 is about 90 percent of that payable at age 64; and so on. This
relatively uniform progression continues down to at least age 55.[12]

The proportion of the accrued normal retirement benefit that would be payable
at early retirement at ages 55 through 64, under the mortality and interest assumptions set forth above, are shown in Table 10-5. It must be emphasized that the
percentages are applied to the benefit credits accrued to the date of early retirement and not to the benefits that would have been paid at age 65 if the employee
continued working to that age. No distinction is allowed between male and female
employees because of differences in their life expectancy.[13] Since retirement at age
55 results in a benefit of less than half the normal accrued benefit under any scale
that purports to reflect actuarial reductions, most plans do not permit retirement
more than 10 years prior to the normal retirement age.

Most plans have moved away from actuarially precise early retirement factors
and instead provide for a stipulated percentage discount for each month by which
actual retirement precedes the normal retirement date. These monthly factors
may approximate the annual factors that are geared to a full actuarial reduction,

[11] *Society of Actuaries*, Exposure Draft, 1994 Uninsured Pensioner Mortality Table; Society of Actuaries
UP-94 Task Force, January 1995.
[12] It is interesting to note that the Social Security Administration reduces the normal old-age insurance
benefit by a uniform 6⅔ percent for each of the first three years prior to the Social Security
retirement age, and 5 percent for each additional year between the Social Security retirement age
and age 62.
[13] *Arizona Governing Committee v. Norris*, 463 US 1073 (1983); *Long v. State of Florida*, Nos. 86-3282 and
86-3410, December 19, 1986, 11th Cir.

TABLE 10-6   Age and Service Requirements for Reduced Early
Retirement

Retirement	Percentage of Plans
Less than age 55	8
Age 55, service less than or equal to 10	69
Age 55, service more than 10	14
Age 60	2
Age 62	<0.5
Service requirement only	4
Other age requirement	1
No response	2

Source: Watson Wyatt, 1993 Watson Wyatt COMPARISON data base.

or, more commonly, they may be clearly designed to produce a smaller reduction than if full weight were being given to actuarial considerations. Employee groups are generally quite interested in more liberal early retirement benefits or, conversely, in early retirement discounts that are smaller than the full actuarial reduction. More and more plans are using an arbitrary scale of early retirement discounts unrelated to the actuarial scale and frequently the same for each month or year by which actual retirement precedes normal retirement. Typical discounts are one-half of 1 percent per month (6 percent per year) or 1/180 per month (6⅔ percent per year). Some plans use a uniform scale of discounts, such as 1/180 per month, down to a specified age, such as 60, and a smaller scale, such as 1/360 per month, thereafter down to the youngest age at which early retirement is permitted. The arbitrary scale, particularly the one-half of 1 percent reduction per month, is easier to explain to participants than the full actuarial reduction. The

TABLE 10-7   Age and Service Requirements for Unreduced Early
Retirement

Retirement	Percentage of Plans
Less than age 55	<0.5
Age 55	10
Age 60, no service requirement	1
Age 60, with service requirement	13
Age 62, no service requirement	1
Age 62, with service requirement	26
Other requirement, less than age 65	2
Service requirement only	2
Age 65	43
No response	2

Source: Watson Wyatt, 1993 Watson Wyatt COMPARISON data base.

scale may provide for full accrued benefits for retirement not earlier than a specified age, such as 62, and then percentage discounts of different patterns for early retirement factors when they are not based on the full actuarial reduction.[14] The collective bargaining process generated many of the initial early retirement liberalizations. Liberal factors are frequently designed to encourage early retirement, when it is coordinated with the overall personnel policy of the employer. The general practice of using early retirement factors more favorable than the actuarially equivalent ones is referred to as "subsidized early retirement." Tables 10-6 and 10-7 show the results from a large study of pension plans using various age and service requirements for reduced and unreduced early retirement. Special provision may be made for employees who retire early because of poor health. These arrangements are described in the discussion of disability benefits at the end of Chapter 11.

Deferred Retirement

As indicated earlier, under ADEA and many state laws, employers must generally allow employees to continue working beyond the normal retirement date, which is usually the end of the month in which the employee reaches the normal retirement age. Employees may want to continue working beyond that date to earn additional benefit credits, to enlarge the salary base of the benefit formula, to spread the liquidation of the accumulated assets over a shorter period of years (and thus increase the amount of the periodic payments), or to continue receiving their salary. There may also be nonfinancial reasons for wanting to continue on the job.

When an employee delays his or her retirement beyond the normal retirement date, retirement benefits are usually withheld until the actual date of retirement. Benefits credited upon deferred retirement generally may not be less than the amount of monthly benefit computed as if the employee's actual retirement date were the normal retirement date. The critical feature of this calculation is that benefits continue to accrue in the normal manner for service beyond normal retirement, and any changes in the compensation base are recognized in the benefit formula. The result is that if two employees, one age 45 and the other age 50, for example, are hired at the same time and both work for 20 years at equal salary rates, retiring at age 65 and 70, respectively, they will receive equal monthly payments under this method. Other methods in use prior to 1987 when this law was last changed generally produce unequal benefits. The benefits determined under this approach are sometimes greater and sometimes smaller than the normal retirement benefits adjusted to their actuarial equivalence. One permissible alternative to the continuing accrual approach, which has been used by a few plans, is to provide both continuing accrual for the additional service and an actuarial increase of all accrued benefits as of the normal retirement date for the period of deferral.

All participants are generally required to begin receiving their pensions no later than April 1 following the year they attain age 70½, regardless of whether they

---

[14]This, of course, is tantamount to reducing the normal retirement age for individuals going directly from active service to retirement to the lowest age at which no early retirement factor is applied.

have actually retired.[15] When coupled with the requirement to continue accruing benefits, the result is curious. An employee who continues working past age 70½ must begin receiving his pension and also must continue accruing benefits. Presumably the amount of pension being paid in this case must be increased periodically to reflect the continuing accruals.

Manner of Payment

The implicit promise of most pension plans is that they will pay a retirement benefit throughout the remaining lifetime of the retired employee.[16] The plan may provide various collateral benefits, but underlying the whole scheme must be that promise of a life income to the participant upon his or her retirement. If this promise is underwritten or guaranteed by a life insurance company, the life income will be provided in an annuity contract of some type. If the plan is funded through a trust, the benefits may be provided through an annuity contract purchased from an insurance company, probably at the time of the employee's retirement, or they may be paid directly from the trust fund. A series of annual or monthly payments is referred to as an "annuity" or "annuity benefit," whether or not it is insured by a life insurance company.

Types of Annuities

Several forms of annuities are available for the disbursement of pension benefits. Classified broadly, life annuities may be single life or joint life, and within that classification they may be either of the pure or refund type. As indicated by its title, a single life annuity is one that is based on only one life, that is, it is only for one person. The pure form of single life annuity, usually referred to as "straight-life annuity," provides periodic, usually monthly, income payments that continue as long as the annuitant lives and that terminate upon his or her death. The annuity is considered fully liquidated when the annuitant dies, and no guarantee is given that any particular number of monthly payments will be made. Because this benefit will end at death, this type of single life annuity provides the largest monthly income per dollar of purchase price outlay.[17]

As an alternative to the straight-life form, the annuity may promise that a certain number of monthly payments will be made whether the annuitant lives or dies. Under this form, payments continue if the annuitant lives beyond the guaranteed period. In insurance circles, this type of annuity is referred to as a "life annuity certain and continuous," and the annuitant may elect 60, 120, 180, or 240 guaranteed installments.[18] The cost of the annuity increases with the number of

[15]IRC §401(a)(9)(C).

[16]The Internal Revenue Service requires a qualified pension plan to make benefits available in the form of an annuity, either a life annuity or an annuity for a period of years. Treas. Reg. 1.401-1(a)(1)(i).

[17]In this generalized description of annuities, the funds committed to the annuity will be called the price or purchase price, following insurance terminology. Under a pension plan, assets equal to the actuarial reserve for benefits payable to a retiring employee are set aside, in theory or in fact, to be liquidated in accordance with a stipulated form of annuity.

[18]Such a range of options is not usually provided under a pension plan.

guaranteed installments, since life contingencies are not involved during the guaranteed period.

The refund type of single life annuity includes any annuity that guarantees to return in some manner a portion or all of the purchase price of the annuity. An "installment refund annuity" promises that, if the annuitant dies before receiving monthly payments equal to the annuity's purchase price, the payments shall be continued to the annuitant's beneficiary until the full cost has been recovered. If the contract promises, upon the death of the annuitant, to pay to the annuitant's beneficiary in a lump sum the excess (if any) of the purchase price of the annuity over the sum of the monthly payments, it is called a "cash refund annuity." The only difference between the "cash refund annuity" and the "installment refund annuity" is that, under the former, the unliquidated purchase price is refunded in a lump sum when the annuitant dies; in the other, monthly installments are continued until the purchase price has been recovered. These two types of annuities are more costly than the straight-life annuity, and the "cash refund annuity" is somewhat more costly than the "installment refund annuity" because of the loss of any potential interest. A "modified cash refund annuity" promises to refund only a portion of the purchase price, usually the accumulated employee contributions.

The joint and survivor annuity provides periodic payments as long as either of two persons shall live. For most combinations of ages, this is the most expensive of all annuity forms. This type of contract is primarily designed to provide old-age income to a husband and wife. The income may be reduced upon the death of either annuitant to either one-half or two-thirds of the original amount, on the theory that the survivor does not require as large an income as do the two annuitants. Under some plans, the reduction is made when either annuitant dies. Under others, the reduction is made only if the retired participant dies first. This latter arrangement is often called a "contingent annuitant option."

Normal and Optional Annuity Forms Under Pension Plans

The benefits under a pension plan, and their cost, are calculated on the assumption that the benefit payments will conform to a particular pattern. This pattern, the third component of the benefit formula, is known as the "normal annuity form." The normal annuity form specified in most noncontributory plans is the straight-life annuity, although it is not unusual to guarantee a certain number of installments. Contributory plans usually adopt a modified cash refund annuity. This form promises that, should the employee die before receiving retirement benefits equal to the accumulated value at retirement of contributions made to the plan, with or without interest, the difference between benefits and this accumulation will be refunded in a lump sum to the participant's estate or to a designated beneficiary. Some contributory plans prescribe a life annuity with payments guaranteed for 5 or 10 years, either form of which will usually ensure that the employee's accumulated contributions are returned.

Pension plans have traditionally given the participant the option of electing, before or at retirement, and at his own expense, an annuity form different from the normal form prescribed in the plan document. The range of options has differed, some plans offering a wide choice and others being more restrictive; but it has been customary to offer some form of joint and survivor annuity so the participant might assure his or her spouse a life income in some amount. The amount of benefit payable under an optional annuity form is usually calculated to be actuarially equivalent to the amount payable under the normal form. The factors used, or the actuarial assumptions used to compute them, must be specified in the plan or defined by reference to some independent source, such as insurance company annuity purchase rates or interest rates published by the PBGC.[19]

All pension plans must provide that retirement benefits that are payable as a life annuity to an employee married to his or her current spouse for at least one year will be automatically paid in the form of a "qualified" joint and survivor annuity unless the participant elects otherwise with the consent of the spouse. The spouse's consent must be in writing and must be witnessed by a plan representative or a notary public.[20] A "qualified" joint and survivor annuity is a type of annuity that provides income to the surviving spouse in an amount equal to at least one-half of the income payable when the employee and spouse are both alive. The participant must be given a reasonable time before the annuity starting date to elect in writing not to have the retirement benefits provided under a joint and survivor annuity.

In the absence of a provision to the contrary, the spouse would lose any interest in the joint and survivor annuity if the participant were to die before retirement. This is considered a peculiarly inequitable consequence, if the participant dies after becoming eligible for early retirement but before entering on the joint and survivor annuity. In the past, many plans have voluntarily embodied a provision making a presumption that any participant who dies after the early retirement date, but before actual retirement, had entered on a joint and survivor annuity of a specified type (or some other kind of refund annuity) on the day of his or her death. A qualified pension plan must provide a "qualified" preretirement survivor annuity benefit to the spouse of any participant who dies after becoming entitled to a vested benefit but before the annuity starting date. This benefit is described later in Chapter 11 in the section "Death Benefits."

The law permits the employer to recoup the cost of the joint and survivor annuity by reducing the benefits for the participant and his or her spouse (compared with the benefits paid to a participant without a beneficiary). The actuarial reduction usually depends on the age of the individuals and on the assumptions used. Under typical assumptions, the reduction in benefits provided upon retirement under a joint and one-half survivor annuity is 10 percent for an employee age 65 with a spouse age 65, when compared with the benefits under a comparable straight-life annuity payable only to a participant. Many plans use an approximate factor, such as 10 percent, which applies in every case regardless of age.

The benefits can be further reduced under present law to reflect the cost of the preretirement survivor annuity protection enjoyed by the spouse before retirement. Some plans reduce the pension payable at age 65 by one-half percent for each year of preretirement survivor annuity coverage. The participant is required to receive notice, and to have the right to elect, with the spouse's consent, not to have the protection of the preretirement survivor annuity. But most plans make no

[19]Rev. Rul. 79-90.
[20]ERISA §205; IRC §401(a)(11).

charge for the preretirement protection and provide it to all participants automatically, avoiding the cumbersome notice and election requirements.

It may be only a matter of time before organized employees and other groups demand that some type of joint and survivor annuity benefits be provided at no cost to the participants as the normal annuity form under the plan. Some groups have already protested against the cost (in the form of reduced benefits) of joint and survivor annuity benefits and have negotiated the use of benefit reduction factors that are less than those actuarially equivalent. This is comparable to the negotiation of subsidized early retirement factors.

Under the joint and one-half survivor annuity, most plans use the type of joint and survivor annuity that reduces the income only if the spouse is the survivor. If the employee survives his spouse, he or she continues to receive the same income that was payable when both annuitants were alive. Some plans, generally those that utilize the settlement options of individual insurance or annuity contracts, use the type that reduce when either spouse dies. Either type of joint and survivor annuity may be made available under ERISA. Some plans provide a "pop-up" option such that the joint and survivor reduction is restored if the spouse dies before the annuitant.

An option that is available only in the case of early retirement is the so-called Social Security adjustment option. The purpose of the option is to make the benefit from the pension plan plus Social Security a level benefit throughout retirement, even though the full Social Security old-age insurance benefit is not available until age 65 or later. To accomplish this, the original amount of annuity payable upon early retirement is replaced by two other annuity amounts that in the aggregate are actuarially equivalent to the original amount. One of these annuity amounts is a temporary annuity payable to age 65 equal to the expected Social Security benefit, while the other is an annuity payable for life.[21]

If the benefit is provided in any form other than the normal form, the amount of monthly payment will be adjusted to be actuarially equivalent to the payments under the normal form, so that the present value of the expected payments will be the same as if the normal form had been elected. Table 10-8, which is based on one particular set of actuarial assumptions, shows the amount of monthly income under some of the commonly used annuity forms for each $100 of monthly income that would have been provided under the normal form for a participant retiring at various retirement ages. As shown by Table 10-9, a life only annuity is the normal form of benefit in the vast majority of plans, though some plans prefer to use an annuity benefit as the normal form of benefit that has a guaranteed payment feature. All plans are required to include in the plan document either the actuarial factors used or the assumptions upon which they are based.[22] The factors may not differ by sex.

---

[21]Consider the example of an employee eligible to receive a monthly benefit of $600 from the plan at age 60 and a $500 monthly benefit from Social Security at age 65. A benefit of $500 per month from age 60 to age 65 would have the same actuarial value as a lifetime benefit of $200 per month from age 60. Therefore, to provide a level lifetime benefit, the plan's lifetime benefit is reduced by $200 to $400, making possible a $500 monthly supplement from age 60 to age 65.

[22]IRC §401(a)(25).

TABLE 10-8   Monthly Benefits Provided at Various Retirement Ages Under Commonly Used Annuity Forms for Each $100 Provided Under a Straight Life Annuity (dollars)

| Age at Retirement | Life Annuity | | | 100 Percent Joint and Survivor Annuity[a] | 50 Percent Joint and Survivor Annuity[a] |
	No Period Certain	5-Year Certain	10-Year Certain		
55	100.00	99.16	96.84	86.54	92.79
60	100.00	98.55	94.69	84.23	91.44
65	100.00	97.43	91.16	81.83	90.01
70	100.00	95.62	85.91	79.59	88.64

Note: Rate basis: UP-94 Table and 7 percent interest.
[a]Contingent or joint annuitant assumed to be the same age as the employee in each case.

TABLE 10-9   Normal Form of Benefiit

Plan Provision	Percent of Plans
Life only annuity	85
Five-year certain and life annuity	5
Ten-year certain and life annuity	6
Other form	3
No response	1

Source: Watson Wyatt, 1993 Watson Wyatt *COMPARISON* data base.

Cash Option at Retirement

A perennial issue in plan design is whether participants upon reaching retirement should be permitted to take the actuarial value of their retirement benefit in a lump sum, rather than in monthly payments spread over their remaining lifetime. There may be a certain amount of pressure from employees for this cash option, and some plans permit employees to make a full or partial withdrawal of the commuted value of their pension benefits.

The cash option is generally justified as being more flexible for financial planning. It is argued that some employees have a more urgent need for a lump sum than for a life income. They may need the money for medical treatment or to buy a retirement home. Some may want to invest in a business of their own. Others may feel that they can invest their share of the plan assets more profitably than the investment manager or in a way that will provide more protection against inflation. Rollover of the lump-sum value into an IRA may be especially attractive. In some cases, the pension benefit may be too small to justify installment payments, while in others it may be so large that the participant should be permitted to draw some of it in a lump sum. Under some plans, the cash option may be the only way that an employee in poor health can preserve his or her pension for the protection of a spouse or other dependents.

There are several primary arguments against the lump-sum option:

TABLE 10-10   Benefits Payable in a Lump Sum

Plan Provision	Percentage of Plans
Yes, with no dollar limit	29
Yes, but with a fixed limit	8
No	52
No response	11

Source: Watson Wyatt, 1993 Watson Wyatt *COMPARISON* data base.

1. Employees might squander the lump sum or invest it unwisely and thus be left dependent upon society.
2. Employees would give up the benefit of a life annuity that would protect them against outliving their retirement resources.
3. The distribution is based on book value, rather than on the more proper and equitable market value.
4. The plan would be exposed to adverse selection by healthy persons electing a life income and those with health impairments electing a lump sum.[23]

The issue of outliving retirement resources is particularly important. Many retirees facing a choice between taking a lump-sum or an annuity do not realize that if all actuarial assumptions prove to be accurate and the lump sum is drawn down at the same rate as the life annuity, 58 percent of those electing a lump-sum will live to see the fund reduced to zero.

The basic issue is whether a pension plan is to be regarded as a general savings program, with all the flexibility that one would want in such a program, or as an instrument of business and social policy designed to ensure a dependable source of income throughout the remaining lifetime of retired workers.

Under a defined benefit plan, when a vested benefit is to be paid in a lump sum, its value must be determined on the basis of assumptions regarding interest and mortality. The mortality table is specified by the IRS. The interest rate is the annual yield on 30-year Treasury securities the month before the date of distribution.[24] Table 10-10 shows the results of a study of lump-sum benefit availability in pension plans.

---

[23]Some plans that permit a full withdrawal of the actuarial value of the accrued benefits attempt to protect themselves against adverse selection by requiring the participant to elect the cash option some years in advance of retirement.

[24]ERISA §203(e)(2); IRC §§411(a)(11)(B), 417(e)(3).

Chapter 11
Defined Benefit Plan Design: Ancillary Benefits

Most participants in a pension plan on any given date will not remain in the service of the employer until retirement. Some will die, some will become mentally or physically incapacitated, some will have their service terminated by the employer, while others, for various reasons, will voluntarily sever their connection with the firm. These contingencies have to be dealt with in the plan document. Benefits paid out in connection with one of these contingencies rather than retirement are referred to as *ancillary benefits*. This chapter deals with these benefits. The first section discusses the rights of plan participants whose services are terminated prior to retirement for reasons other than death or disability. The second section discusses the impact of death and permanent disability on benefit rights.

Withdrawal Benefits

Benefits Attributable to Employee Contributions

One of the basic rules of pension plan design is that participants must be assured that they or their beneficiaries will ultimately recover, in one form or the other, all the contributions that they make to the plan. This rule applies not only to voluntary contributions but also to those that are required under the terms of the plan. Such a rule is a pragmatic necessity if participation in the plan is optional, since few employees would be willing to have their contributions forfeited upon death or withdrawal from the plan. Even if participation is a condition of employment, equity dictates that the contributions be returnable in the event that the participant does not survive in the employer's service until early or normal retirement.

The law provides that employees' rights in that portion of their accrued benefits derived from their own contributions are nonforfeitable,[1] which is the generic term used in the Employment Retirement Income Security Act of 1974 to refer to a vested status. Since no qualifying conditions were imposed, the benefits are vested immediately and fully. Furthermore, they are vested in the event of death, since no exception was made for that contingency, as it was for benefits attributable to employer contributions.

Before ERISA, virtually all contributory plans provided that if a terminating employee exercised his or her right to withdraw his or her own contributions, with

[1]ERISA §203(a)(1); IRC §411(a)(1).

interest, if any, that employee would forfeit all rights to any pension benefits attributable to employer contributions. This was true, even though the employee had acquired a vested interest in the accrued benefits financed by employer contributions. In legal terms, the withdrawal of the contributions divested the benefits that had been previously vested. Nevertheless, terminating employees, attracted to a lump-sum distribution, almost invariably withdrew their own contributions, in many cases relinquishing rights to deferred pensions having an actuarial present value greatly in excess of the employee contributions recovered.[2]

ERISA continues to grant terminating employees the privilege of withdrawing their own contributions, but it denies employers the right to cancel the benefit accruals that they had previously vested.[3] An exception is made for employees whose benefits are less than 50 percent vested. In such cases, an employer may cancel the vested benefits of those terminating employees who draw down their own contributions. However, if a plan cancels such benefits, it must contain a "buy-back" provision under which the employee's forfeited benefits will be fully restored if he or she repays to the plan the withdrawn contributions. For defined benefit plans, the repayment must include interest, compounded annually. The interest rate must be 5 percent for plan years after ERISA's vesting requirements apply and before 1988, and thereafter must be 120 percent of the federal midterm rate in effect for the first month of the plan year.

Having decided to preserve the employer-financed benefits of employees who cash out the benefits financed with their own contributions, Congress found it necessary to develop rules for determining the respective proportions of an employee's accrued benefits allocable to employer and employee contributions. For purposes of dividing the accrued benefit into employer- and employee-financed portions, the law presumes that all benefits are financed by the employer, except those that can be attributed to employee contributions. Thus the statutory rules pertain only to the calculation of the benefits that can be attributed to employee contributions; the difference between this amount and the total accrued benefits is thus attributable to employer contributions.

Under a defined *benefit* plan, the amount attributable to the employee's own contributions is derived by multiplying the employee's accumulated contributions by a "conversion factor" specified by statute or regulations.[4] The conversion factor is the reciprocal of the actuarial present value at the normal retirement age of a single life annuity of $1 per annum. The statute stipulates that the conversion factor for a normal retirement age of 65 shall be 10 percent, which means that under the mortality and interest assumptions being used, a sum of $10 would have to be on hand at age 65 to provide a single life annuity of $1 per annum. Multiplying the accumulated contributions by the conversion factor is the same as dividing the accumulated sum by the annuity factor of 10, the more conventional

---

[2]Under the contribution schedules and actuarial cost methods of some plans, employees at younger ages contribute in excess of the annual actuarial cost of their currently accruing benefits. If these employees terminate—and the highest rates of termination occur among younger employees—there are no employer-financed benefits to be canceled.

[3]ERISA §203(a)(3)(D); IRC §§401(a)(19), 411(a)(3)(D).

[4]ERISA §204(c); IRC §411(c).

approach. For this computation, the accumulated contributions are assumed to equal the sum of the employee's actual contributions to the date of the computation, with interest, at the prescribed rate described above, compounded annually to the normal retirement date.

The conversion factor would be different for a normal retirement age other than 65. Moreover, the Internal Revenue Service requires adjustments in the factor if the pension benefit is payable other than monthly or is in a form other than a single life annuity. The adjustments[5] are designed to produce actuarially equivalent benefits. The Secretary of the Treasury is authorized to adjust the conversion factor by regulation from time to time, as he or she may deem necessary.[6] However, no such adjustment has ever been made. Under the UP-94 Mortality Table, an interest rate of 6.1571 percent leads to an annuity factor of 10.0000.

These rules for determining the accrued benefits attributable to employee contributions apply only to mandatory contributions. The accrued benefits attributable to voluntary employee contributions are determined in the same manner that they would have been under a money purchase plan.[7]

If the terminating employee receives a refund of his or her contributions in a lump sum under a defined benefit plan, it must include interest at the prescribed rate described above. If this amount would exceed the value of the total accrued benefit, however, the minimum required distribution is the greater of the value of the total accrued benefit or the employee's own contributions without interest.[8]

Benefits Attributable to Employer Contributions

The rights of a terminating employee to the benefits provided by the contributions of the employer depend upon the vesting provisions in the plan. In a defined benefit pension plan, vesting refers to the right of participants to receive their accrued pension benefits at normal or early retirement whether or not they are still in the service of the employer at that time. It is a narrower concept than the strict legal concept of a vested right, since the right to a pension is contingent upon the employee's survival to the earliest date on which he or she can validly claim a pension. Thus a vested pension benefit is usually terminated by the participant's death prior to normal or early retirement.[9] The vesting of a benefit simply removes the obligation of the participant to remain in the plan until the date of early or normal retirement.

Basic Vesting Concepts

Vesting provisions differ, within permissible limits, in the *kinds of benefits vested*, the *time* when the eligible benefits vest, the *rate* at which the accrued benefits vest, and the *form* in which the vested benefits may be taken.

---

[5]Rev. Rul. 76-47.
[6]ERISA §204(c)(2)(D); IRC §411(c)(2)(D).
[7]ERISA §204(b)(2)(A),(c)(4); IRC §411(b)(2)(A),(d)(5).
[8]ERISA §204(c)(2)(E); IRC §411(c)(2)(E).
[9]ERISA §203(a)(3)(A); IRC §411(a)(3)(A); Treas. Reg. 1.411(a)-4(b)(1). A defined contribution plan is also allowed to provide for forfeiture of amounts not yet paid upon death, but very few such plans do so.

The kinds of benefits that can be vested are retirement, death, and total disability benefits. All three kinds are vested when they enter a payment status. If a benefit is not already in payment, the typical approach is to vest only the basic retirement benefit. Before ERISA, a common practice was to vest only the *normal* retirement benefit for participants who terminate their employment prior to retirement. That is to say, the vested benefits of a *terminated* participant became payable only at normal retirement, even though active participants were permitted to retire early, possibly with subsidized benefits. At present, the early retirement supplements provided under some negotiated plans are not vested. Thus in general vesting attaches only to the normal retirement benefit.

With the exception of the qualified preretirement survivor annuity benefit described in Chapter 8, it has not been the practice to vest death and disability benefits not already in payment status. In other words, protection against the economic consequences of death or total disability is not continued for participants who leave an employer's service. These kinds of benefits are considered term coverages that should properly extend only to active and possibly retired participants. However, if the participant terminates after becoming vested and dies before the annuity starting date (and there is an eligible surviving spouse), a qualified preretirement survivor annuity benefit must be provided.

Regarding time, vesting may occur immediately or at some future date. The dichotomy here is between *immediate* and *deferred* vesting. Immediate vesting is infrequently found among conventional pension plans. Vesting is generally deferred until stipulated service and (sometimes) age requirements are met.

As for the rate at which benefits vest, a distinction is made between full and graded vesting. Vesting is said to be *full* when a participant satisfies all the conditions laid down for vesting. All benefits accrued to that date vest in their entirety, and all benefits accruing thereafter vest in full as they are credited. Most plans favor the full vesting concept, coupled with reasonable age and service requirements. A small number of plans provide for *full* and *immediate* vesting; that is, a participant is automatically and completely vested in the plan when participation commences. For example, the individual retirement annuity contracts issued by the Teachers' Insurance and Annuity Association and College Retirement Equities Fund (TIAA-CREF) for the faculty and staffs of institutions of higher learning provide for full and immediate vesting. All plans require benefits derived from employee contributions to be fully and immediately vested.

Graded vesting is the term applied to an arrangement under which only a specified percentage of the accrued benefits vest as specified minimum requirements are fulfilled. The percentage of vesting increases on a sliding scale as additional requirements are met, until 100 percent vesting is ultimately attained. For example, a plan may specify that 20 percent of accrued benefits will vest after three years of service, with an additional 20 percent vesting each year during the next four years so that after seven years of service all accrued benefits will be vested. Graded vesting avoids anomalous treatment of employees terminating just before and just after meeting the requirements for full vesting, and it minimizes the danger that an employee will be discharged just before his or her pension benefits vest. In other words, it prevents a situation in which an employee with fairly long service has no vested benefits on a particular day and then, the following day, has all accrued benefits fully vested. On the other hand, graded vesting is more difficult to explain to plan participants. This is a matter of some concern since the law requires that every participant be furnished with a summary of the plan "written in a manner calculated to be understood by the average plan participant." It is also more difficult to administer. Not only may the plan administrator have to keep track of a relatively insignificant vested benefit for a long period of years, but a participant in a defined benefit plan who terminates and receives a lump-sum distribution while partly vested may reinstate the canceled benefit accruals upon reemployment by paying back his or her distribution to the plan, plus interest at the prescribed rate described above.[10] The same rule applies to participants in contributory plans who terminate before their benefits are 50 percent vested, who receive a refund of their contributions, and whose vested benefits are canceled.[11] In this latter case, participants do not have to be in the employer's service at the time they seek to restore the benefits that were canceled.

The employer is required by law to furnish the terminated employee with a certificate stating the amount of benefits vested, the annuity form in which they will be paid, and the time when they will become payable.[12] The form of the vested benefits depends to some extent on the contractual instrument used to fund the benefits (see Chapters 31 and 32 for a description of various funding instruments). If a defined benefit plan is funded through a trust, vested terminated employees generally retain a deferred claim against the trust fund in the amount of their vested benefits. The plan may permit or direct the trustee to purchase a deferred life annuity from a life insurer in the appropriate form and amount for the employee.

If a defined benefit plan is funded through a contract with a life insurance company, the vested benefits may take the form of a paid-up insurance or annuity contract or a deferred claim against the plan. Under group deferred annuity contracts, all benefits are funded in the form of paid-up annuities, and when vested employees terminate they are simply given title to the annuities credited to their accounts. Under a group deposit administration annuity contract, vested employees who terminate may be credited with a paid-up deferred annuity in the proper form and amount, or they may be given a certificate indicating that the benefit claim will remain an obligation of the plan to be discharged in the normal manner at retirement. The latter procedure would be similar to the deferred claim arrangement of a trust fund plan. If the plan is funded through individual insurance or annuity contracts (an approach generally confined to small firms), vested terminated employees may be given the option of taking a paid-up contract in the proper amount or continuing, on a premium-paying basis, at their own expense, that portion of the life insurance policy or annuity contract represented by the vested cash values. Some plans permit terminated employees to continue the contract or contracts in full force by paying the trustee a sum of money equal to the nonvested cash value, a privilege of some significance to participants whose health has been impaired.

10ERISA §204(d),(e); IRC §411(a)(7).
[11]ERISA §203(a)(3)(D); IRC §411(a)(3)(D).
[12]ERISA §§105(c), 209(a)(1); IRC §6057(e).

A defined benefit plan may permit terminating employees to take the full actuarial value of their vested benefits in cash. At their option, participants may place some or all of the sum withdrawn in individual retirement accounts (IRAs) set up and administered according to applicable law (see Chapter 14). If completed within 60 days from receipt, transfers would be tax-free and, in any event, the earnings on the funds in an IRA would be wholly exempt from current income taxation.[13] Employees could leave the funds in the IRA until retirement, or, with the consent of a subsequent employer, they could transfer the funds on a tax-free basis to a qualified pension plan of the new employer.[14] Terminating employees may, with the consent of the successor employer, transfer the "cash-out" value of their vested benefits directly to the pension plan of the new employer, and the transfer will be tax-free if completed within 60 days after receipt from the original plan. Employees are under no obligation to preserve the actuarial value of their vested benefits and may dispose of them in any way that they see fit, except that spousal consent is generally required to receive a benefit in any form other than a qualified joint and survivor annuity.[15] The employer is not under legal obligation to permit a cash-out of the vested benefits.

When the actuarial value of the vested benefits of a terminating employee is not greater than $3,500, the employer has the option, without the employee's consent, of discharging the plan's obligation by making a lump-sum cash distribution.[16] This privilege is granted to the employer to avoid the expense of keeping track of a relatively insignificant deferred claim against the plan. The rules governing the actuarial assumptions used in calculating such lump sums for terminated vested participants are the same as those described in Chapter 10 with regard to lump-sum payments upon retirement.

Statutory Vesting Requirements

Before ERISA was enacted, employers were not legally obligated to provide for the vesting of employer-financed benefits prior to retirement, except for unusual circumstances. The law did provide that all accrued benefits of a participant had to vest, to the extent funded, in the event that the plan terminated or the employer permanently discontinued contributions to the plan. In addition to these rules that applied to all plans, the Internal Revenue Service could require any plan to provide for reasonable preretirement vesting if it appeared that the plan would otherwise discriminate against rank-and-file employees in favor of the prohibited group (officers, shareholders, supervisors, and highly paid employees). In certain situations, usually involving small plans, the officers and other favored employees would be expected to remain with the firm until normal retirement, while the rank-and-file employees would tend to terminate their employment and fail to

---

[13]IRC §402(a)(5),(6).

[14]IRA funds from qualified rollovers cannot be commingled with other IRA funds and later transferred to another tax-qualified employer plan. To be eligible for transfer to another employer plan, the IRA rollover funds must be segregated.

[15]ERISA §205(a),(c); IRC §§401(a)(11)(A), 417(a)(1),(2).

[16]ERISA §204(d),(e); IRC §411(a)(7).

qualify for benefits. Vesting provisions keyed to the expected termination pattern could ensure that the plan would operate for the benefit of the employee group in general, rather than just for the proscribed group.

The minimum vesting standards established by ERISA and modified by TRA86 were premised on the grounds that vesting accrued benefits after a reasonably short period of service is necessary to (1) ensure equitable treatment of all participants, (2) remove artificial barriers to changes of employment and hence enhance the mobility of labor, and (3) ensure that private pension plans fulfill their social role of supplementing for a broad segment of the labor force the old-age insurance benefits provided under the Social Security System.[17]

The minimum vesting standards require benefits derived from employee contributions to be fully and immediately vested. For plan years beginning after 1988, benefits derived from employer contributions must be fully vested at normal retirement age and must also meet one of two permissible standards.[18]

1. The simpler standard provides for full vesting of all accrued benefits after the participant has accumulated five years of recognized service, irrespective of attained age. No degree of vesting short of five years of service is required under the standard. Roughly 75 percent of defined benefit plans in existence today provide full vesting after five years of service.[19]
2. The second standard, sometimes called the three-to-seven-year standard, embodies the progressive or graded vesting concept. Under this standard, the plan must vest at least 20 percent of a participant's accrued benefits by the end of three years of recognized service, and an additional 20 percent each year during the following four years. This means that the benefits must be fully vested after seven years of recognized service, irrespective of the participant's attained age.

An exception applies to collective bargaining employees under multiemployer plans, for which full vesting is required after 10 years of recognized service.

Generally speaking, all years of service, including service rendered before a participant is eligible to participate in the plan and before ERISA was enacted,[20] are to be taken into account in determining a participant's place on the vesting schedule. However, the plan may ignore (1) service before the employer maintained the plan or a predecessor plan (so-called past service); (2) service before age 18; (3) service during periods when the employee declined to make mandatory contributions; (4) seasonal or part-time service not taken into account under the rules for determining a "year of service"; and (5) service broken by periods of suspension of employment to the extent permitted under the breaks in service

[17]For a discussion of the public policy considerations involved in the vesting issue see Dan M. McGill, *Preservation of Pension Benefit Rights* (Homewood, Ill.: Richard D. Irwin, 1972), chap. 2. Chapter 5 of that volume provides a detailed analysis of the factors affecting the cost of vesting and the various ways in which the cost of vesting may be measured and expressed.

[18]ERISA §203(a); IRC §411(a).

[19]U.S. Department of Labor Bureau of Labor Statistics, *Employee Benefits in Medium and Large Private Establishments, 1991* (Washington, D.C.: USGPO, May 1993), p. 100.

[20]ERISA §203(b)(1); IRC §411(a)(4).

rules. It must be reemphasized that the criteria listed in this section are rules for determining the participant's place on the vesting schedule (i.e., the number of years accrued toward satisfying the service requirement) and are not for determining the *amount* of accrued benefits.

The pattern of vesting under the two basic standards (the five-year or the three-to-seven-year) is quite dissimilar, but the overall cost impact on a plan with a representative group of participants is remarkably similar. This suggests that they provide about the same amount of vesting in the aggregate, although the distribution of vested benefits will vary. Young entrants into a pension plan will achieve a fully vested status more quickly under the five-year standard than under the three-to-seven-year standard. A higher percentage of participants will have *some* vesting under the three-to-seven-year standard than under the five-year standard, since vesting commences after three years of service, but fewer will have 100 percent vesting. Top-heavy plans are required to have either 100 percent vesting after three years of service or 20 percent vesting after two years of service, which is to increase 20 percent per year to 100 percent after six years.[21]

The law permits the Internal Revenue Service to require more rapid vesting than required under the minimum schedules if (a) there has been a pattern of abuse under the plan, (e.g., employees have been fired before their accrued benefits vest; or (b) it appears that there have been, or are likely to be, forfeitures of accrued benefits under the plan that have the effect of discriminating in favor of the highly compensated employees.[22]

The standards described above are *minimum* standards, and employers are permitted to provide vesting under more liberal rules than those required by law. Once vested, the benefits are nonforfeitable, except upon the death of the participant before retirement (and in the absence of a provision for joint and survivor annuities), and except for the circumstances noted below.[23] If a participant in a contributory plan withdraws his or her own mandatory contributions before the employer-financed benefits are at least 50 percent vested, the latter can be canceled under a plan provision of general applicability. Moreover, if a participant retires and then returns to work for the same employer, the retirement benefits can be suspended during the period of reemployment. Benefits already vested can no longer be forfeited in the event of misconduct by a participant or terminated vested participant (the so-called bad boy clause) or in the event that such persons accept employment with a competitor.

Upon request but not more than once per year or upon termination from the plan, the participant must be provided with a statement of accrued benefits and their vesting status.[24] Information concerning vested deferred benefits of a terminated participant must be furnished to the Internal Revenue Service, which transmits it to the Social Security Administration.[25] The Social Security Administration will provide this information to the participant or beneficiary upon request, and automatically when one applies for Social Security old-age benefits.

[21]IRC §416(b).
[22]IRC §411(d)(1).
[23]ERISA §203(a)(3); IRC §411(a)(3).
[24]ERISA §§105, 209(a)(1); IRC §6057(e).
[25]IRC §6057, Form 5500, Schedule SSA.

Pattern of Benefit Accruals for Vested Participants

For defined benefit plans, ERISA set out three tests, designed to limit the extent of back loading in benefit formulas, against which benefit accruals for vested participants must be measured.[26] The tests are defined in terms of a retirement benefit payable at normal retirement age, which cannot be later than age 65 or the tenth anniversary of the date on which the participant entered the plan (the fifth anniversary for employees who become participants within five years of the normal retirement age), whichever occurs last.[27] Ancillary benefits are excluded from the tests, as well as early retirement supplements that do not continue beyond the participant's normal retirement age.[28] The tests were developed to determine the minimum benefit amount that must be credited to a participant who terminates from the plan in a vested status. They are not intended to require that a terminated vested participant always receive the same benefit at normal retirement age that he or she would have received with the same credited service and same compensation had he or she been in service at the time of retirement. For purposes of the tests, Social Security benefits and all other relevant factors affecting benefits under the plan are assumed to remain constant, at current year levels, for all future years. The plan must satisfy only one of the three tests.

1. The first alternative, called the *3 percent rule*, requires that each participant's accrued benefit at least equal the product of his years of participation under the plan times 3 percent of the benefit that would have been payable if participation had commenced at the earliest possible entry age and had service continued to age 65, or the normal retirement age under the plan, whichever is earlier (maximum 100 percent after 33⅓ years). The projected benefit at age 65 must be computed on the assumption that the participant's future compensation equals actual average salary over a period of not more than 10 consecutive years. The test is applied on a cumulative basis, which means that any amount of front loading is permitted. A plan that provides exactly $10 monthly per year of participation with no maximum years of participation and no minimum entry age would not satisfy the 3 percent rule, because the minimum monthly accrued benefit would have to be $19.50 per year of participation (3 percent times $10 times the theoretical maximum of 65 years of participation from entry age 0). The test is also cumulative when the benefits of the plan are increased retroactively. For example, assume that during the first 10 years of an individual's participation the plan provided a flat benefit of $200 per month payable at age 65 and was then amended to provide a flat benefit of $400 a month. The participant's accrued benefit at the end of his eleventh year of participation must be at least $132 (3% × $400 × 11).
2. The second alternative, called the *133⅓ percent rule*, states that the benefit accrual rate for any participant for any future year of service may not be more than one-third higher than the accrual rate for the current year. Like the first

---

[26]ERISA §204(b)(1); IRC §411(b)(1).
[27]ERISA §§3(22),(24),204(c)(2)(B); IRC §411(a)(7)(A),(8),(9).
[28]Treas. Reg. 1.411(a)-7(c)(3).

test, this one also permits an unlimited amount of front loading. The benefit accruals under this test may be expressed in the form of dollar amounts or a specified percentage of compensation. If the plan is amended to increase the rate of benefit accrual, it is assumed (for the purposes of this test) that the new benefit schedule was in effect for all previous plan years. For example, if the plan has been providing an annual benefit accrual of 1 percent of compensation and is amended to provide 2 percent for future service only, it will continue to meet this test, even though 2 percent is more than one-third greater than 1 percent. Also, if the plan has a scheduled increase in the rate of accruals that will not take effect for any participant until future years, as may be the case under collective bargaining, the scheduled increase is not taken into account for purposes of the back loading restrictions until it goes into effect. This 133⅓ percent rule governs all plans using a career average formula.

3. The third alternative is known as the *fractional rule*. It provides for proration of the projected normal retirement benefit over the years of plan participation. The benefit accrual for any particular year of service is based upon the assumption that the participant will continue, until normal retirement age, to earn the same rate of compensation that would have been taken into account under the plan had the employee retired in that year (but not more than the last 10 years). For example, if the normal retirement benefit is based upon five-year final average pay, it is assumed that the participant will continue to earn until retirement her average pay for the past five years. The plan must first determine the projected benefit that would have been payable at normal retirement age if the participant's service had continued to that date at the compensation indicated above. The minimum accrued benefit required under the fractional rule equals this projected benefit multiplied by a fraction whose numerator is the number of years that the participant actually participated in the plan and whose denominator is the number of years of participation that he or she would have had if he or she had continued in the plan until normal retirement.

Instead of the three foregoing tests, the accrued benefit of a participant in a plan funded exclusively through level premium life insurance or annuity contracts is the cash value of the contracts, determined as though the funding requirements of the plan had been fully satisfied. Alternative rules are available for benefits accrued before the effective date of ERISA's vesting requirements.[29]

Early Retirement Benefits for Terminated Vested Participants

ERISA provides that a terminated vested participant must be permitted to receive early retirement benefits based on the same age and service requirements that apply to an active participant.[30] This provision was designed to prohibit the practice of requiring a terminated vested participant to wait to normal retirement age for benefits to commence, when active participants were permitted to retire early, subject to age and service conditions. The benefit payable to a terminated vested

---

[29]ERISA §204(b)(1)(D); IRC §411(b)(1)(D).
[30]ERISA §206(a); IRC §401(a)(14).

participant starting at an early retirement age must be at least actuarially equivalent to the vested benefit he or she could have received at normal retirement age. However, if a plan uses subsidized early retirement factors for active employees who retire early, it need not use the subsidized factors for terminated vested participants.[31]

Break in Service

Benefit accruals that have not vested may be lost—temporarily or permanently—through a break in service. *Years of service* and *breaks in service*—or *periods of service* and *periods of severance* if the elapsed-time method is used—are generally subject to the same rules for vesting requirements as they are for participation requirements (see Chapter 4). No benefit accrues for the period or periods during which a break in service occurs or exists. The crucial issues for the reemployed worker are whether prebreak service is counted in determining eligibility for vesting after the break and whether the benefit accruals that were credited before the break in service are forfeited.

All service before and after the break is aggregated in determining years of service, unless a particular exception applies.[32] Service before a one-year break in service can be disregarded until the participant has completed one year of service after the break.[33] If the participant had no vesting before the break, service before the break can be disregarded if the number of consecutive one-year breaks in service equals the greater of five years or the years of service before the break.[34]

The aggregated service just described is used to determine eligibility for vesting for benefits accrued after the break. In a defined benefit plan, if the participant was not fully vested before the break, his aggregated service will also be used to determine eligibility for vesting of benefits accrued before the break, but only if he repays any distribution he has received.[35]

Many plans use more liberal rules than the requirements described here, partly to simplify the plan.

Death Benefits

An employer may provide death benefits through group life insurance, a pension plan, a profit-sharing plan, or some combination of these. In addition, death benefits are provided by Social Security. Benefits from all these sources should be considered when designing an overall death benefit program.

Prior to ERISA, a plan was not required to offer death benefits. Now the law requires the plan to make a qualified preretirement survivor benefit available for vested married participants, and if the plan is contributory it must return the participant's contributions with interest in the event of his or her death before

---

[31]Treas. Reg. 1.411(c)-1(e)(1).
[32]ERISA §203(b)(1); IRC §411(a)(4).
[33]ERISA §203(b)(3)(B); IRC §411(a)(6)(B).
[34]"Rule of parity," ERISA §203(b)(3)(D); IRC §411(a)(6)(D).
[35]ERISA §204(e); IRC §411(a)(7).

retirement. In considering death benefits of a pension plan, one should distinguish between the benefits payable upon the participant's death before retirement and those payable upon his or her death after retirement.

The IRS has a long-standing rule that the death benefit of a pension plan, other than the required joint and survivor benefit and preretirement survivor annuity benefit, must be incidental to the primary purpose of the plan, which must be to provide systematically for the payment of definitely determinable benefits to the participants over a period of years, usually for life, after retirement.[36] This constraint has been imposed in recognition of the special tax status accorded pension plans.

Postretirement Death Benefits

Postretirement death benefits may take the form of lump-sum payments or income benefits. Lump-sum benefits tend to be modest in size and are often designed to meet the last illness and funeral expenses of the deceased employee. They are regarded as incidental to the retirement benefit if they are not greater than one-half of the participant's salary at the date of retirement and account for less than 10 percent of the cost of the plan exclusive of the death benefit.[37] They often range from $1,000 to $3,000. Some plans provide a lump-sum benefit upon the death of the *spouse* of the retired employee to relieve him or her of the financial burden of paying the last illness and funeral expenses. Most plans provide no postretirement lump-sum death benefit.

The postretirement income death benefit is strictly a function of the annuity form under which the retirement benefits are payable. As indicated earlier, the retirement benefits of noncontributory plans have traditionally been stated in terms of an annuity form that did not provide a benefit to survivors. Contributory plans have used annuity forms that assured participants that they or their beneficiary would receive benefits that in the aggregate would at least equal their contributions. Most plans have permitted the participant to elect annuity forms that would provide death benefits of varying magnitude, instead of the retirement benefits.

The law now requires that every qualified defined benefit plan provide a qualified joint and survivor annuity that pays the participant's surviving spouse an income for life at least 50 percent, but not more than 100 percent, of that payable during the joint lives of the participant and his or her spouse and that meets certain other requirements.[38] The qualified joint and survivor annuity must be the most valuable form of benefit. This means that at a minimum the amount payable must be actuarially equivalent to the single life annuity that would have been payable to the participant. If the amounts are actuarially equivalent the cost of this survivor income is borne by the participant and his or her spouse through a reduction in the retirement benefits that would otherwise be payable. If a married participant (married at least one year) retires and does not elect any other form of annuity with the consent of the spouse, the benefit must be paid as a qualified joint and survivor annuity, unless the benefit would otherwise have been payable in a

---

[36]Treas. Reg. 1.401-1(b)(1)(i); Rev. Rul. 74-307.
[37]Rev. Rul. 60-59.
[38]ERISA §205; IRC §401(a)(11).

form other than a life annuity. Many plans have extended this provision to apply to all married participants, regardless of the length of the marriage. The participant must have the opportunity to elect, with the spouse's consent, not to have the retirement benefits provided under a joint and survivor annuity. The employee must be supplied with a written explanation of the joint and survivor annuity, couched in layman's language, that points out the effect on the participant and the spouse of a decision to accept or reject the provision. The election must be in writing but is subject to revocation. Regulations specify timing limitations for notification, election, and revocation.[39]

Preretirement Death Benefits

Preretirement death benefits may take the form of a refund of employee contributions or an explicit benefit embodied in the plan for the specific purpose of providing protection to the dependents of participants who die before retirement. The first type of benefit is available only under a contributory plan. It is generally paid in a lump sum to a designated beneficiary or to the estate of the deceased participant. It used to be the custom of contributory plans to refund the contributions of a deceased participant, but the practice is now mandatory.[40] Accumulated mandatory employee contributions under a defined benefit plan must include interest.[41] Accumulated voluntary employee contributions must reflect their share of the plan's total investment return, positive or negative. The explicit death benefit may, in turn, be broken down into two types: lump-sum payments and income payments.

Lump-Sum Benefits

A lump-sum death benefit may be provided under a plan funded through one or more life insurance or annuity contracts or one funded through a trust. Most defined benefit plans funded through trusts or group annuity contracts provide no preretirement lump-sum death benefit, other than a refund of employee contributions. On the other hand, plans funded through individual or group permanent life insurance contracts typically provide a preretirement death benefit. A contract form often used in the past, the "retirement income" (or "income endowment") policy, provides a face value of $1,000 for each $10 of monthly income at retirement. Under this contract, the cash value eventually exceeds the face amount and becomes payable in the event of the participant's death before retirement. Some plans use a contract form that provides only a $1,000 death benefit for each $10 unit of monthly income payable under the plan. To permit the use of these contract forms, which have served as the funding instrument for tens of thousands of small pension plans, the Internal Revenue Service has held in a series of rulings[42] that a lump-sum death benefit provided through a life insurance contract

[39]Treas. Reg. 1.401(a)-11(c), 1.401(a)-11T, 1.417(e)-1T.
[40]ERISA §203(a)(1),(3)(A); IRC §411(a)(1),(3)(A).
[41]ERISA §204(c); IRC §411(c)(2),(d)(5).
[42]Rev. Rul. 61-121.

is "incidental" to the principal purpose of the plan if it does not exceed a sum equal to 100 times the expected monthly pension benefit or, if greater, the reserve for the pension benefit. This constraint is patterned after the benefit structure of a retirement income contract.

Alternatively, the life insurance feature is deemed to be incidental if the aggregate of the premiums paid for the life insurance on any particular participant is less than one-half of the aggregate contributions allocated to his or her account at any given time.[43] It is assumed, somewhat arbitrarily, that only one-half of a life insurance premium, irrespective of the issue age or the plan of insurance (except term), is applied to the cost of protection and that the other half goes into the policy reserve. In essence, this rule states that no more than 25 percent of the funds available may be used to provide pure life insurance protection.

These limits have been extended by administrative interpretation to lump-sum death benefits provided under any type of pension plan, whether or not life insurance contracts are used. In other words, the death benefit must not exceed the greater of 100 times the monthly annuity or the reserve for the pending benefit or, alternatively, its cost must not exceed 25 percent of the total cost of the plan.[44] Operating under this authority, pension plans funded through a trust frequently provide lump-sum death benefits. The benefit may be a stated amount, such as $5,000, or a multiple of the deceased employee's annual compensation. A benefit equal to one or two times salary is fairly common.

All of the incidental death benefit limits described above include the value of any qualified preretirement survivor annuity benefit payable. Thus the maximum limit on lump-sum death benefits that would otherwise apply must be reduced by the value of any qualified preretirement annuity benefit payable.

Survivor Income Benefits

Before ERISA, there was increasing interest in an income type of benefit payable to the surviving spouse or other dependents of a deceased participant. Recognition of the need to protect a wife's inchoate interest in her husband's pension during a period when he was eligible to retire and elect a joint and survivor annuity was the initial stimulus for this type of benefit. Under the usual plan provisions, the joint and survivor annuity option would only be paid if the participant retired before dying. If a participant continued in employment beyond the point of eligibility for early or normal retirement, the spouse's potential annuity benefit was jeopardized. Before ERISA, some plans attempted to deal with this problem by stating that if a participant were to die before retirement but during the period when eligible for early or normal retirement benefits, the surviving spouse would receive a benefit equal to the amount that would have been payable had the participant retired and elected a joint and last survivor annuity option immediately prior to death.

Reflecting the concern for the spouse's interest in the participant's accruing pension rights, the law now requires that a plan include a qualified preretirement

[43]Rev. Rul. 74-307.
[44]Ibid.

survivor annuity benefit.[45] However, no survivor annuity is generally required for a profit-sharing plan or stock bonus plan that pays the vested account balance to the spouse upon death.

The qualified preretirement survivor annuity benefit must be available to a married participant from the time that he or she becomes vested in any accrued benefit until the annuity starting date. The benefit is not required unless the participant has been married at least one year at the date of death. In the case of a participant who dies while eligible for early retirement, the benefit payable to the spouse is the amount that would have been payable if the participant had retired under the plan's early retirement provision on the day before dying and had elected the qualified joint and survivor annuity. Thus the benefit amount reflects the reduction of the accrued benefit by the early retirement reduction factor, further reduction by the actuarial factor of the joint and survivor form, and finally, if the plan uses the customary 50 percent joint and survivor annuity, multiplication by 50 percent.

If the participant dies before becoming eligible for early retirement, the qualified preretirement survivor annuity payments are computed on the basis of the benefits accrued to the date of death but do not begin to be paid out until the date that the participant would have reached the earliest retirement age stated in the plan, that is, the age of eligibility to retire under the plan's early or normal retirement provision. In this case the amount of survivor annuity is determined as though the participant had terminated employment immediately prior to the actual date of death, had survived to the earliest retirement age in the plan, had then elected to retire under the qualified joint and survivor option, and had then died.

Plans have a choice of providing this qualified preretirement survivor annuity automatically to all married participants who are vested in an accrued benefit or of allowing any such participants to elect, with the consent of the spouse, not to have this protection. If automatic, the plan sponsor bears the cost of the survivor annuity benefit. If elective, the cost is borne by electing participants in the form of reductions in their benefits otherwise payable at normal or early retirement. Some plans reduce the accrued benefit by ½ to 1 percent for each year the protection is provided.

Regulations[46] provide complex and cumbersome requirements about notifying participants eligible to make the election, about the periods for making elections and revocation, and about the elections themselves. These requirements are avoided if the survivor annuity is provided automatically. In part to avoid the administrative requirements of election, and in part to avoid inequities between electing and nonelecting participants, the majority of defined benefit plans provide the benefit automatically.

As indicated earlier, some plans provided ERISA-type survivor annuity benefits before ERISA. Some such plans had extended this provision to cover all participants who had accumulated a specified period of service, such as 20 or 25 years, and had reached a stipulated age, such as 50. In the next stage of development,

---

[45]ERISA §205; IRC §§401(a)(11), 417.
[46]Treas. Reg. 1.401(a)-11(c), 1.401(a)-11T, 1.417(e)-1T.

some plans provided an explicit benefit not related to a joint and survivor annuity that applied to all participants or to all who meet certain service requirements.

Formerly, many plans provided survivor benefits to widows but not to widowers. However, the Equal Employment Opportunity Commission (EEOC) ruled that a survivor income benefit payable only to the surviving widow or other dependents of a male employee constitutes discrimination against female employees and hence violates Title VII of the Civil Rights Act, which prohibits discrimination on the basis of sex.[47] By force of this ruling, employers have had to convert the surviving *widow's* benefit into a surviving *spouse's* benefit. Some employers, reluctant to provide a lifetime benefit to an able-bodied widower of a female employee, attempted to limit the survivor benefit to a spouse who was financially dependent on the deceased employee at the time of his or her death. The EEOC has taken the position that a dependent spouse's benefit also violates Title VII of the Civil Rights Act inasmuch as there is a higher *probability* that the surviving widow of a male employee will be dependent than that the widower will be dependent. The survivor annuity mandated by ERISA must be provided irrespective of sex or dependency.

It was often necessary to coordinate the qualified preretirement survivor annuity required by law with a previously existing spouse's benefit. Some plans maintain the two benefits separately and others combine them. In some cases, the existing spouse's benefit already provided benefits as liberal as those required by law, and no addition was required. In other cases, the spouse's benefit provision was modified so that it would meet the requirements for the new survivor annuity. In yet other cases, the qualified preretirement survivor annuity benefit was added separately, with a provision that benefits under the earlier spouse's benefit would be offset by any benefit payable under the new survivor annuity provision.

Today any spouse's benefit in excess of the mandated qualified preretirement survivor annuity tends to be an explicitly stated benefit, as described below, payable to the surviving spouse as long as she or he lives, but sometimes it is subject to termination in the event of remarriage prior to a stipulated age, such as 60. The mandatory survivor annuity may not be terminated upon remarriage. The spouse's benefit is often restricted to a surviving spouse who had been married to the deceased employee for a specified period, such as one year, or who is the parent of a child of the deceased. If there is no surviving spouse, the benefit may be payable to dependent parents. Recognizing that unmarried employees may not have dependent children, some plans permit the survivor benefit to be paid to any dependent relatives of the deceased, including, especially, brothers and sisters and parents. The benefit is usually payable for all participants, but it may be restricted to those with long service or those eligible to retire.

The amount of a nonmandatory survivor benefit may be determined by examining the participant's compensation at the date of death or the accrued or projected pension benefit. If the former approach is used, the amount of the benefit is usually set at about 20 to 25 percent of the participant's monthly compensation rate. The monthly amount tends to be the same irrespective of the spouse's age. The present value of future benefits tends to be higher for the younger annuitant,

---

[47]See *Arizona Governing Committee v. Norris,* 463 US 1073 (1983).

except that the remarriage rate is much higher at the younger ages, reducing the actuarial value of the annuity if benefits cease on remarriage. There may be additional benefits for dependent children, in the order of 10, 15, or 20 percent of compensation. The overall benefit allowance may be subject to adjustment for Social Security survivor benefits (see Chapter 15 for a discussion of Social Security integration).

The more common approach is to relate the spouse's nonmandatory benefit to the pension of the deceased employee. This may be done in terms of the pension accrued to date of death or the pension that would have been payable had the employee survived in employment until normal retirement age. In neither case is the amount of the benefit reduced because of the spouse's age at the commencement of the income payments, except in some plans when the spouse is younger than the employee by more than a specified number of years, commonly 5 but sometimes 20. An upward adjustment may be made if the spouse is older than the employee.

The benefit based on the accrued pension may be illustrated in terms of an employee who dies at the age of 55, leaving a spouse aged 50. The spouse's benefit would be a specified percentage of the pension that would have been payable at the employee's normal retirement age, on the basis of the benefit credits accumulated to date of death. There would be no reduction to reflect the fact that the spouse is only 50 and that the benefits will thus be paid over a longer time than was originally contemplated. Under Treasury rules, the maximum spouse's benefit may be expressed in terms of the deceased's *accrued* pension benefit or *projected* pension benefit.

The qualified preretirement survivor annuity benefit mandated by law is always deemed to be an incidental death benefit. In considering the limits that might logically be imposed on any other benefit for a spouse, the Internal Revenue Service took as its guide an earlier ruling on money purchase pension plans, which stated that for any individual the cost of the death benefit must not exceed 25 percent of the total cost. The IRS made a series of actuarial calculations to determine what limits should be imposed to keep the cost of the spouse's benefit from exceeding 25 percent of the total cost with respect to the individual participants. The limits might logically have been related to the age of the spouse at the time the income commences. Instead, since the Internal Revenue Service was considering a test case that reduces the benefit actuarially if the spouse is more than five years younger than the participant, it chose to impose limits in terms of the earliest age at which the participant could qualify for the spouse's benefit. It developed one set of limits for plans that express the benefit as a percentage of the *accrued benefit* and another for plans that provide benefits based on the *projected benefit*. The limits that were promulgated by the IRS are shown in Table 11-1.[48]

It should be noted that the full amount of the participant's projected pension can be paid only if the participant must be age 55 or more to qualify for the benefit. On the other hand, half of the projected benefit, the percentage generally used today, can be provided if eligibility is established at age 25.

---

[48]Rev. Rul. 70-611.

TABLE 11-1   Maximum Percentage of Participant's Accrued or Projected Pension That
May Be Considered an Incidental Death Benefit

Earliest Age at Which Participant Becomes Eligible for Spouse's Benefit	Maximum Percentage[a]	
	Accrued Pension	Projected Pension
20 or younger	75	45
25	75	50
30	80	55
35	80	60
40	85	66⅔
45	90	75
50	100	90
55 and older	100	100

[a]These percentages apply only to a unit benefit pension plan providing a spouse's benefit in the form of a straight-life annuity commencing immediately upon the participant's death, with the benefit being actuarially reduced if the spouse is more than five years younger than the participant.

The scale allows a larger percentage when the spouse's benefit is based upon the participant's *accrued* pension benefit. The full accrued benefit can be provided if eligibility for the benefit is not established before the participant is age 50. The scale grades down to 75 percent for an eligibility age of 25 years or less.

While the qualified preretirement survivor annuity itself is always deemed to be incidental, the above limits apply to any combination of this mandatory benefit and an additional spouse's income benefit. Thus any spouse's income benefit that supplements the qualified preretirement survivor annuity is not allowed to cause the combination to exceed the above limits.[49]

Relative Advantages and Disadvantages of Providing
Preretirement Death Benefits from a Pension Plan

Preretirement death benefits other than the mandated qualified preretirement survivor annuity can be provided outside the pension plan through a conventional group term life insurance contract or a group survivor income contract. A policy decision therefore has to be made on whether death benefits are going to be provided through the pension plan or through a group insurance contract. There are both advantages and disadvantages in using the facilities of a pension plan to provide preretirement death benefits, as compared with using a separate group insurance plan.

A. ADVANTAGES   First, a pension plan is not subject to state laws that impose a limit on the face amount of group term life insurance that may be placed on any one employee. These limits, once common, now apply only to policies delivered in California, Texas, and Wisconsin.

Second, the preretirement death benefit can be coordinated with the pension benefit with somewhat more facility and precision. Group survivor income con-

[49]Rev. Rul. 85-15.

tracts generally express the benefit in terms of the employee's current compensation, which offers certain advantages but may bear little relationship to the accruing pension benefit. If the survivor benefit under a pension plan is expressed as a percentage of the participant's *projected* pension, the preretirement and postretirement survivor benefit can be very similar, since there is no discontinuity.

The third advantage is that the assets of the pension plan can be invested with more latitude than the reserves under a group insurance contract, which presents the possibility of a higher rate of investment return and, hence, lower costs. The assets backing the reserves of a life insurer must be held in the company's general account, which must by law be invested predominantly in fixed-income instruments, while the assets of a pension plan can be held in a separate account of a life insurer, devoted entirely to equity investments, or in a trust whose manager can be given virtually unlimited investment authority, subject to fiduciary requirements.

The other two advantages involve tax considerations. First, there are no state premium taxes on contributions to pension plans, while group life insurance premiums are generally taxed.[50] Second, employer contributions to a pension plan are not taxable to the participants (except when applied to the cost of death benefits under individual or group life insurance contracts), but employer premium payments on the portion of group term life insurance on the life of one employee that exceeds $50,000 are taxable income to the employee to the extent that they exceed the employee's own contributions.

B. DISADVANTAGES   There are disadvantages to providing preretirement death benefits from a pension plan. The first is that the death benefits must be incidental to the main purpose of the plan: the payment of retirement benefits. This may rule out the use of a particular formula for death benefits. For example, it would not be permissible to provide a surviving spouse's benefit equal to the participant's accrued pension if the benefit becomes payable in the event of the participant's death before age 50. A separate group life or survivor income plan would not be subject to this constraint.

A second disadvantage is that lump-sum and income death benefits payable from a pension plan are subject to federal income taxation, while benefits paid through life insurance proceeds are fully excludable from federal income taxation. The first $5,000 of a death benefit paid as a lump-sum distribution from a pension plan is free of federal income tax,[51] and the excess is taxable on a favorable basis as a lump-sum distribution (see Chapter 7). The income benefits are taxed under the so-called annuity rule that permits annuitants to recover the cost over their life expectancy without income tax liability (see Chapter 7). If an annuitant made no contributions to the plan, no investment in the contract would exist and, therefore, all benefits would be taxed in full.[52] Large death benefits under a pension plan

---

[50] There will be premium taxes on premiums paid through individual or group permanent life insurance contracts, and in some states group annuity considerations are subject to the premium tax.
[51] IRC §101(b).
[52] The survivor is permitted to consider up to $5,000 as her or his investment in the annuity contract to the extent that the deceased employee's rights to this amount were nonforfeitable and the exclusion was not applied against a lump-sum benefit payment. Rev. Rul. 71-146.

are subject to a special 15 percent estate tax in addition to the regular estate tax.[53] A group survivor income contract is treated as group life insurance,[54] but the monthly payments would be taxed under the annuity rule, so the interest component of each monthly payment would be treated as fully taxable ordinary income, and the remainder would be treated as a refund of principal and hence would not be taxable.

A third problem is that pension plan death benefits substantially larger than the accrued liability for pensions can cause substantial fluctuations in the employer's cost, particularly for smaller plans. In addition, both pension plans and group life insurance are subject to the pervasive prohibition against discrimination in favor of highly compensated employees. In various situations one or the other of these bodies of restrictions may prove more troublesome, making this either an advantage or disadvantage for pension plans. Of course, a group life insurance plan can be provided that does not satisfy the nondiscrimination requirements, but in that case highly compensated employees lose the benefit of exclusion of the cost of the first $50,000 of insurance.[55]

Disability Benefits

All well-designed pension plans contain provisions that protect the accrued benefits of participants who are temporarily unable to work because of illness or injury. Temporary disability is a type of break in service that must be considered in any plan document. A more serious problem is presented when a participant becomes permanently unable to work because of injury or disease. As a minimum, the plan may vest the accrued benefits of a permanently disabled participant, irrespective of the normal vesting requirements. If the participant has reached the early retirement age, some plans provide an immediate annuity based upon benefits accrued to date, without reduction for age. Some plans provide for early retirement benefits at an earlier age and with fewer years of service than would apply to an able-bodied participant.

The most direct way to deal with the disability contingency is to provide a separately identified disability benefit. Like the survivor income benefit, the disability benefit may be expressed as a percentage of the participant's compensation at the onset of disability or as a percentage of the accrued or projected pension benefit. In choosing among these three alternatives, the plan designer is faced with the same considerations as those pertaining to the spouse's benefit. For example, there is the question of coordination with the retirement benefit and also the question of benefit adequacy for the participant who becomes permanently and totally disabled at a young age. The probability of total disability at the younger ages is very low, but the economic consequences to the participant and family can be catastrophic. This has led many employees to base the disability benefit on the participant's projected pension, without actuarial reduction for age. If the benefit is expressed as a percentage of the accrued pension benefit, a minimum benefit may be provided.

[53]IRC §4981(d).
[54]*Helvering v. Legierse,* 312 US 531 (1941).
[55]IRC §89(a)(1).

Some special considerations are involved in providing a permanent and total disability benefit. Because of the possibility of adverse selection and abuse, some thought must be given to the problem of entry into the plan by an individual who knowingly or unknowingly is afflicted with a health impairment. If the employer requires a preemployment physical examination, the problem is ameliorated but not necessarily eliminated. Three ways to deal with this problem are to (1) withhold the protection of the disability provision for a period of years after entry into the plan, such as three to five years or longer; (2) exclude benefit payments for disability arising out of a preexisting condition that manifests itself within a specified period, such as one or two years after the participant enters the plan; or (3) exclude permanently from the coverage of the disability clause any disability arising out of a preexisting condition. Of course, these approaches do not solve the problem for the employee who becomes disabled without benefits, nor for the employer faced with the difficult choice of providing ad hoc benefits or providing no assistance whatsoever.

A second consideration that arises when the disability is a percentage of compensation at the onset of disability is whether the disability benefit should continue throughout the individual's remaining lifetime (assuming there is no recovery) or only to normal retirement age, at which time the disabled person would become entitled to a retirement benefit. This again is a question of coordination of benefits, that is, the relationship between the disability and retirement benefits. If the disability benefit is to terminate at normal retirement age, the plan usually provides that the disabled person will continue to accrue pension credits on the regular basis, but based on compensation at the onset of disability, to normal retirement age. Under these circumstances, the disabled participant will receive the same retirement benefit, except for the frozen wage base, to which he or she would have been entitled if the disability had not occurred.

A third consideration involves the relationship between the disability benefit and the early retirement benefit. If the disability benefit is a percentage of compensation or a percentage of the projected pension, it may be a more attractive benefit to a person contemplating early retirement than the nondisability benefit, since the latter reflects only accrued pension benefits. Thus there would be an incentive for participants beyond the early retirement age to seek a disability status, and at that stage it is easier to establish a disability claim than in earlier years. To counteract this tendency, a plan can stipulate that if a participant becomes disabled after having met the requirements for early retirement, the plan will pay only the regular early retirement benefit.

Finally, it is vital that the total benefits received by a disabled participant and the family be less than the wages that would be paid if the individual continued to work. Otherwise, there might be a tendency for some participants to seek a disability status, and there would certainly be no economic incentive for the disabled workers to try to rehabilitate themselves. This suggests that the disability benefit formula must take into account, by offset or otherwise, the disability benefits provided under Social Security, workers' compensation, and possibly veterans' legislation.

Long-term disability income benefits may be provided under a separate group insurance contract. The tax treatment of the benefits is the same whether they are paid from a pension plan or a group insurance contract. The total benefit package can perhaps be better coordinated if all benefits are provided by one plan. The limitations on integration of disability benefits under a pension plan may be more restrictive than desired, both in the amount of disability benefit and in the definition of disability. Integration of pension plan disability benefits with benefits payable under Social Security, worker's compensation, and other programs is discussed in Chapter 14. Group long-term disability benefits are subject to non-discrimination requirements, which may be difficult to satisfy. Some employers choose to insure the long-term disability benefit in order to transfer the risk to the insurance company and to reap the advantage of the insurer's experience and objectivity in disability claims administration. Employers who provide benefits before 65 under long-term disability insurance often provide a benefit from the pension plan beginning at age 65, determined as though employment had continued employment to age 65.

Chapter 12
Defined Contribution Plan Design Features

The other distinctive type of retirement plan is the *defined contribution*, or individual account, plan. This type of plan, in sharp contrast to the defined benefit plan, provides an individual account for each participant and bases benefits solely on the amount contributed to the participant's account and on any expense, investment, and forfeitures allocated to that account.

A defined contribution plan defines the amount of contribution to be added to each participant's account. Some plans do this directly by defining the amount the employer will contribute on behalf of each employee (e.g., 10 percent of pay). Other plans do not define the amount of contribution to be made, leaving that completely to the employer's discretion; but these plans define how whatever contributions are made will be allocated among the accounts of participants (e.g., in proportion to compensation).

The individual accounts must receive, at least annually, their share of the total investment return, including investment income received and the realized and unrealized appreciation of market values.[1] Some plans allocate investment returns quarterly, monthly, or even daily; in fact, daily valuation of participants' accounts is rapidly becoming standard practice. Most types of assets fluctuate in market value, although some, such as bank savings accounts and certain annuity contracts, are maintained on a book value basis and hence do not drop in value. Since market values can decline, individual account balances can either decrease or increase.

Ordinarily, the total plan assets are completely allocated to individual accounts. The sum of all of the account balances on any valuation date usually equals the total market value of the plan assets. If a participant terminates employment before he or she is vested, the account balance is forfeited and is applied either to reduce future employer contributions or to increase the account balances of other participants.

When a participant becomes eligible to receive a benefit, the benefit equals the amount that can be provided by his or her account balance. It may be paid in the form of a lump-sum distribution, a series of installments, or an annuity for the lifetime of the participant or the joint lifetimes of the participant and his or her beneficiary.

The principal types of defined contribution plans are

- profit-sharing plans
- money purchase pension plans
- thrift and savings plans

[1]Rev. Rul. 80-155.

- stock bonus plans
- employee stock ownership plans.

Profit-Sharing Plans

A *deferred* profit-sharing plan, which is similar in many respects to a qualified pension plan, may be utilized by an employer to provide retirement income to employees. A *deferred* profit-sharing plan should be differentiated from a *cash* profit-sharing plan, under which the employer makes periodic, usually annual, distributions of a defined portion of profits to employees in cash or in stock in the firm. Cash profit sharing is a form of current compensation designed to provide a direct incentive to productivity and will not be dealt with further in this text. Deferred profit sharing, on the other hand, falls into that classification of employer-sponsored financial arrangements known as *asset or capital accumulation* employee benefit plans and shares many characteristics with them. Other plans of this genre include pension plans of all types and deferred compensation arrangements, qualified and nonqualified.

Profit-sharing plans are one of the three basic types of qualified plans under the Internal Revenue Code, along with pension plans and stock bonus plans. Profit-sharing plans are a type of defined contribution plan. Profit-sharing plans are common among both large and small employers. Smaller employers in particular favor profit-sharing plans if they feel that they cannot afford a pension plan, want to avoid the financial commitment and actuarial complexities associated with a defined benefit pension plan, or recognize that such plans are significantly cheaper to administer, as discussed in Chapter 16. While many large employers operate a profit-sharing plan as a supplement to their pension plan, deferred profit sharing, as the dominant source of employee old-age security, is primarily the province of small and medium-size employers.

Plan Design

Deferred profit-sharing plans can have the same fundamental objective as pension plans and historically have been subject to regulation under the Internal Revenue Code and IRS in much the same manner as pension plans, with any differences being attributable to the peculiar characteristics of the two types of arrangements. As in the case of defined benefit pension plans, many pertinent provisions of the Employment Retirement Income Security Act of 1974 apply to profit-sharing plans to the extent that they seek to obtain and maintain a qualified status. Indeed, many provisions of ERISA will apply to such plans regardless of whether they seek tax-qualified status.

Qualification under the Internal Revenue Code and Internal Revenue Service regulations bestows the same tax treatment on profit-sharing plans and their distributions as on pension plans. Consequently, profit-sharing plans that seek a qualified status must meet most of the general qualification requirements that apply to qualified pension plans. The most significant exception to the general requirements, though, is that the benefits of a pension plan must be definitely determinable. Since contributions to a profit-sharing plan may depend upon the profits of the plan sponsor, neither the contributions nor the benefits under the plan are definitely determinable. This is the principal distinction between a profit-sharing plan and a pension plan. In addition, forfeitures can be, and usually are, allocated to participant accounts, and investment earnings and losses similarly have a direct bearing on the amount distributed to plan participants. If there are large accumulations, adequate retirement income benefits can be provided. If such accumulations sharply decline, because of investment experience or otherwise, the amount of retirement income may be relatively small. In short, the amount of retirement income in a profit-sharing plan is not determinable in advance.

A qualified profit-sharing plan must be established and operated for the exclusive benefit of employees and their beneficiaries. Moreover, it must not discriminate in favor of stockholders, officers, and highly compensated employees as to coverage, benefits, contributions, or otherwise. This pervasive nondiscrimination requirement and the myriad regulations that implement and embellish the requirement exert a strong influence on the design of profit-sharing plans, just as they do on pension plans.

Contributions

All required contributions to a conventional profit-sharing plan are made by the employer; but it is no longer a condition of qualification that the contributions be related in some tangible way to the firm's accumulated or current profits, in terms of the *amount* and the *source* of the contributions. If employee contributions are required as a condition of employer contributions, the plan is technically a profit-sharing *thrift* plan. Pure profit-sharing plans and thrift plans sometimes permit voluntary employee contributions.

A. *Contribution Commitment*

The Internal Revenue Code does not require, as a condition for qualification, that a profit-sharing plan contain a definite predetermined contribution formula. However, IRS regulations require that contributions to a qualified profit-sharing plan be "recurring and substantial."[2] This requirement is designed to demonstrate that the plan was set up in good faith and was intended to be permanent.[3]

To be currently deductible by the employer, the contribution for a particular fiscal year may be made at any time up to the due date for filing the employer's tax return for that taxable year (including extensions), provided the contribution is designated as being on account of that taxable year.[4] The same deductibility rules apply to contributions made by both accrual and cash basis taxpayers.

For the employer, the obvious advantage of the discretionary approach to determining the employer's contribution to the profit-sharing plan is flexibility. The amount of the contribution can be based on the firm's profit for the year and

---

[2]Treas. Reg. 1.401-1(b)(2).

[3]The court rejected this concept in *Lincoln Electric Co. Employees' Profit-Sharing Trust* (CA-6 1951, reversing and remanding Tax Court), 51-2 USTC 9371, 190 F2d 326.

[4]IRC §404(a)(6).

its working capital needs, and the contribution can be adjusted from year to year to reflect changing circumstances. Indeed, the employer can select, in a *loss* year, to make a substantial contribution. The degree of flexibility is constrained somewhat, however, by the IRS requirement that the contributions be substantial and recurring.

There are certain disadvantages to the discretionary formula approach. It may undermine the participants' confidence in the plan and in the employer, especially if the contributions are below the expectations of the participants. Under the best circumstances and with the best intentions on the part of the employer, the discretionary approach has an adverse effect on the financial planning of the participants. Moreover, in an apparent effort to promote the use of a pre-determined formula, the Wage-Hour Division of the Department of Labor has ruled that contributions to a profit-sharing plan under a discretionary formula must be added to regular pay rates in computing overtime pay, except under certain circumstances.[5] If employer contributions are allocated to participants on a basis that recognizes overtime pay or the plan provides for full and immediate vesting, discretionary contributions are not taken into account in calculating overtime pay rates. Since many employers aim to provide the equivalent of one month's salary (or about 8 percent of regular compensation) through the profit-sharing plan, recognition or nonrecognition of profit-sharing contributions in overtime pay rates is not an inconsequential matter.

These disadvantages of the discretionary approach have caused most large sponsors to include a definite, predetermined formula in their plans. Most small employers, keenly concerned with financial flexibility and believing that they can retain the confidence of their work force without a binding, advance contribution commitment, have elected to follow the discretionary approach or a hybrid ap-proach, whereby the plan will provide for both a minimum fixed contribution from profits and a discretionary additional contribution.

B. Contribution Formulas

A plan sponsor who makes no advance contribution commitment may deter-mine annual contributions in any manner. The sponsor may apply a formula of some type, or he or she may determine the amount to be contributed in a completely arbitrary manner, taking into account all relevant financial and person-nel considerations. On the other hand, the plan sponsor who decides to make an advance contribution commitment and incorporate it in the plan document must state clearly and precisely how each annual contribution is to be determined. This statement or description is referred to as the *contribution formula.*

While there are many variations, there are only three *basic* or *conceptual* ways of expressing an advance contribution commitment: (1) as a percentage of profits, (2) as a percentage of covered compensation, and (3) as a percentage of employee contributions. Employer contributions as a percentage of employee contributions are a feature of thrift or savings plans, to be discussed later in this chapter.

---

[5]29 CFR 549.1(e). Opinion Letter no. 404 of Wage-Hour Administrator, May 23, 1966.

A contribution formula that expresses the commitment in terms of profits must carefully define the terms to avoid ambiguity, disputes, and distrust. The definition must obviously be consistent with the accounting system and the terminology used by the employer. The definition should lend itself to an objective determination of profits, by technically proficient outsiders if necessary. When management and the covered employees are in dispute about the amount of "profits" in a particular year or period, it should be possible for an arbitrator, court-appointed expert, or other impartial person to make a reasonably accurate determination of what the profit-sharing contribution should have been.

The plan document must specify whether contributions are to be based on profits before or after federal and state income taxes are deducted. In theory, after-tax profits are the better measure of the funds available for sharing with the employee group. However, inasmuch as employer contributions to a profit-sharing plan are deductible for income tax purposes, after-tax profits cannot be determined until the contribution for the fiscal year is ascertained. If the contribution itself is expressed in terms of the after-tax profit, it will be necessary to apply an algebraic formula to determine the amount of the contribution. This adds a bit of unnecessary complexity to the contribution formula, since the same result can be achieved by applying an appropriately reduced percentage to the before-tax profit. To avoid these problems, many plans express the contribution formula in terms of after-tax profits determined without regard to the contribution to the plan. In addition, profits are sometimes defined to exclude nonrecurring items, such as sales of property.

The contribution formula may call for a flat percentage of profits, however defined, across the board, or the percentage may apply to only that portion of profits in excess of an amount deemed to be a reasonable return on invested capital. For example, a plan might provide that there would be sharing of only that portion of profits in excess of an amount equal to 10 percent of the net worth of the firm. The breakpoint may be stated in terms of a specified dollar amount of profit or a specified dollar amount of dividends. Such a provision ensures that the profit-sharing plan will not operate to reduce earnings to a point below that needed to attract new capital or to meet the ongoing financial needs of the firm. The formula may call for an increasing percentage of profits to be paid to the plan as profits rise. A few plans decrease the contribution percentage as profits expand. The precise formula adopted will reflect the sponsor's long-range goal for the plan, as well as the sponsor's perception of the impact of the plan and its contribution formula on employee morale and productivity. As noted above, many employers adopt a contribution formula that is designed to produce plan contributions in normal years equal to one month's covered compensation.

The formula may call for contributions equal to a specified percentage of the compensation of covered employees. As under a pension plan, the compensation base would have to be defined, particularly in terms of overtime, vacations, sick leave, and so forth. For plan years beginning after 1993, compensation in excess of $150,000 (indexed) may not be recognized.[6] The plan may state that the compensation-based contributions will be made only to the extent that they can be

---

[6]IRC §401(a)(17).

TABLE 12-1   Sample Contribution Schedule

Profits	Contribution as a Percentage of Covered Compensation
Less than $100,000	None
$100,000–$199,999	5
$200,000–$299,999	6
$300,000–$399,999	7
$400,000–$499,999	8
$500,000–$599,999	9
$600,000 or more	10

financed out of current profits (or accumulated profits, if the plan sponsor is so minded), or the contribution percentage may be linked to the level of current profits. An example of a contribution schedule is illustrated in Table 12-1. Whether the contribution is expressed as a percentage of profits or as a percentage of covered compensation, there is generally an overriding provision that the employer's contribution for a given year will not exceed the amount that can be deducted in that year for income tax purposes. This limit is 15 percent of covered compensation per year.[7] There is a limit on the amount of employer and employee contributions and reallocated forfeitures that can be added to the account of an individual employee in any year (see Chapter 5),[8] and that limit can reduce the contribution that the employer would otherwise make.

The plan sponsor reserves the right to change the contributing formula at any time. This would involve a plan amendment, and if the change involved a reduction in contributions, employee morale would probably be adversely affected. Nevertheless, employers have from time to time curtailed their contribution commitment to adapt to changing business circumstances. If such amendment is a clear curtailment of benefits, which is viewed by the Internal Revenue Service as a partial termination of the plan, full vesting may need to be provided. The entire plan may be abandoned; but if this occurs within a few years after inception, there may be adverse tax consequences. (Plan termination is discussed later in this chapter.)

C. Limits on Deductibility of Employer Contributions

Section 404(a)(3) of the Internal Revenue Code imposes certain limits on the deductibility of employer contributions to a qualified profit-sharing plan. This section of the Code permits an employer to make tax-deductible contributions to a qualified profit-sharing plan equal to 15 percent of the aggregate compensation of employees covered by the plan. Stated negatively, tax-deductible contributions are limited to 15 percent of covered compensation in the aggregate.

For taxable years beginning before 1987, a *credit carryover* was created whenever the contribution in a particular year was less than the maximum allowable deduction, namely, 15 percent of covered compensation for that year. This unused credit

---

[7]IRC §404(a)(3).
[8]IRC §§415, 416.

is carried forward and may be applied in any subsequent year in which contributions exceed 15 percent of the aggregate compensation of the plan participants in that year. Therefore, deductions for contributions made in a given year can exceed 15 percent of covered compensation for that year if a credit carryover is available. There is no limit on the amount of credit carryover that can be accumulated, but the most that can be used or applied in a given tax year is 15 percent of the covered compensation for that year. There is also a limit (of 25 percent of covered compensation for the year in which the credit is utilized) on the overall deduction that may be taken when a credit carryover is used. With an overall limit of 25 percent of compensation, the effective limit on the use of an accumulated credit carryover is 10 percent per year, not 15 percent. While such credits may not be created after 1986, many plans have large credits from prior years that may still be used.

A *contribution* carryover arises whenever the contribution for a given year exceeds the maximum allowable deduction. The maximum deduction allowed for a contribution carryover in a succeeding year is 15 percent of covered compensation less the amount of contribution made for the succeeding year. The 25 percent limit may not be applied to the contribution carryover. Contribution carryovers can be accumulated without limit as to time or amount and can be deducted in any subsequent year or years in which contribution payments are less than the maximum allowable deduction.

If an employer covers the same group of employees with both a qualified defined benefit pension plan and a qualified defined contribution plan, the maximum allowable deduction in any one year for the two plans combined is 25 percent of covered compensation.[9] Under these circumstances, the separate limit on deductibility of employer contributions to each of the two plans still applies, as well as the 25 percent combined limit. A carryover provision for combined contributions in excess of 25 percent applies, as in the case of the profit-sharing plan itself. That is, if the contribution to the pension plan is only 5 percent of covered compensation, the permissible deduction for the contribution to the profit-sharing plan is 15 percent of covered compensation, not 20 percent. Furthermore, if the minimum funding provisions of the Internal Revenue Code require a contribution to the pension plan equal to more than 25 percent of covered compensation, the entire required contribution to the pension plan would be deductible, but there would be no deductible contribution to the profit-sharing plan.

The Internal Revenue Code imposes a 10 percent excise tax on all nondeductible contributions that remain in a plan as of the due date for the tax return for the year in which the contributions were made.[10] However, the employer may not be allowed to withdraw any nondeductible contributions unless they were made by a mistake of fact or were conditioned upon deductibility.[11] Government regulators take a fairly restrictive view of when a contribution was made as a mistake of fact, and will not accept the mistaken belief that the contribution was deductible from that category. In addition, in order for a contribution to be withdrawn from a plan because it was conditioned upon deductibility, either the plan document must

---

[9]IRC §404(a)(7).
[10]IRC §4972.
[11]ERISA §403(c)(2)(A); IRC §401(a)(2).

condition all contributions upon deductibility or contemporaneous documentation specifically conditioning the contribution upon its deductibility must exist.[12]
Here again, government regulators are fairly restrictive; in their view, plan language that contributions *may* be returned to the employer is insufficient without
contemporaneous documentation. The excise tax does not apply to contributions
made by governmental and tax-exempt employers that would have exceeded the
deductible limit if the employer were subject to income tax, on the condition that
the tax-exempt employer has "been exempt from tax at all times."[13] The application of the nondeductible contribution excise tax has therefore been unclear for
tax-exempt employers with unrelated business income tax or for-profit subsidiaries,
although the IRS has recently indicated that it will adopt a very restrictive reading
of this language.

Allocations

Employer contributions to a profit-sharing plan may be made in bulk, without
reference to the individual participants, especially when the contribution formula
is expressed in terms of net profits. Moreover, the accumulated plan assets are
usually commingled for investment purposes, and the trust is credited with the
investment earnings. Since the plan is operated for the exclusive benefit of participants and their beneficiaries, there must be a mechanism for serving the interests
of the individual participants in the commingled pool of assets. This is done by
establishing and maintaining a set of individual accounts, one for each participant
in the plan. Each account is credited with a share of the plan assets in accordance
with the *allocation* provisions of the plan. These provisions pertain to the allocation
of employer contributions, investment earnings, and the account balances forfeited by employees who leave the plan before their interests are fully vested.[14]

A. Employer Contributions

Employer contributions are the most significant source of income to a conventional profit-sharing trust, and they must be allocated to plan participants in a
manner that does not discriminate in favor of highly compensated employees if
the plan is to meet the qualification standards of the IRS.[15] Although, as noted
earlier, a profit-sharing plan is not required to include a fixed formula for determining contributions to the plan, it must set forth the basis on which the contributions will be allocated to individual participants. This description is generally
referred to as the *allocation formula*, even though it may apply only to contributions.

The most common basis for allocating employer contributions is the compensation of the employees. Under this arrangement, each covered participant receives
that proportion of the employer contribution that his or her annual compensation
bears to the total annual compensation of all participants. For this purpose,

[12]Rev. Proc. 90-49.
[13]IRC §§4972(d)(1)(B), 4980(c)(1)(A).
[14]Although employee accounts are maintained, employees usually do not have any specific interest in
particular plan assets.
[15]IRC §401(a)(4).

compensation may include only base earnings, or it may be defined to include base earnings, overtime pay, bonuses, and other forms of cash emolument. If total taxable compensation is not used, the definition must be shown not to discriminate in favor of highly compensated employees.[16] If the plan does not contain a definite, predetermined *contribution* formula, it must, for federal labor law purposes, include overtime earnings in the compensation base for *allocating* contributions if the allocations themselves are not to be added to base pay rates for purposes of computing overtime pay.[17]

Allocations are usually made only to those employees who were in the plan on the last day of the plan year, which is usually the employer's fiscal year. Some plans credit terminated employees with a pro rata share of the annual allocation. In other words, an employee who was in the plan for three months during a plan year and then terminated would receive one-fourth of the share of contributions that he or she would have received had he or she remained in the plan for the entire year at the same earnings level. This is especially true where the employee's termination is due to retirement, death, or disability. Pro rata allocation of contributions has sometimes become an issue under collectively bargained plans when a collective bargaining unit withdraws from the plan at any time other than at the end of the plan year.

While equitable in terms of current service, allocating of employer contributions on the basis of current compensation, gives no weight to length of service. Some employers believe that the allocation formula should recognize and reward length of service. If length of service is not recognized in some appropriate way and the employer does not operate a pension plan in tandem with the profit-sharing plan, employees with many years of service and in middle age or beyond when the plan is established will not accumulate a sufficient balance in their accounts to provide adequate retirement income. Whatever the motivation, some plan sponsors adopt an allocation formula that recognizes service rendered prior to inception of the plan.

The most common approach to recognizing length of service is the "unit" system. Units of participation in employer contributions are credited to the employees according to both compensation and length of service. The weights assigned to these two components may vary to suit the preference of the plan sponsor, as long as the results do not discriminate in favor of highly compensated employees. For example, one unit of participation may be credited for each $300 of annual compensation and another unit for each year of service with the employer, whether rendered before or after the plan is established. Under such a formula, an employee who had 10 years of service with the employer on the date the plan was established and earned $15,000 in the first year of the plan's operation would be credited with 11 units of participation in the first round of allocations for service and another 50 units for compensation. A plan sponsor who wants to give more weight to service, for example, might assign two units to each year of service or, conversely, require $600 of compensation for each unit based on earnings. At the end of each plan year, the number of units credited to the various employee accounts is tabulated and the sum total is divided into the employer's contributions to determine the value of each unit.

[16]IRC §414(s).
[17]See footnote 5 in this chapter.

The major advantage of the unit system is its flexibility. The plan sponsor can use innumerable combinations of years of service and compensation in setting the basis for participation in the profit-sharing contribution. Its major disadvantage is that the relationship between service and compensation is distorted as compensation levels increase in response to inflationary pressures, or for any reason. If a combination of one unit of participation for each year of service and one unit for each $300 of annual compensation is appropriate when the average annual compensation is $15,000, it will clearly not produce the same results if the average compensation rises to $20,000, $25,000, or $30,000. The original relationship can be restored by plan amendment, but this would involve certain legal or other costs and could prove unsettling to the employee group as they see their respective shares in the profit-sharing "melon" changing. Another approach is to base the unit of participation on earnings, by linking the amount of annual compensation required for a unit to changes in average earnings, or to some other value.

Length of service may be recognized without resorting to the unit system simply by determining an employee's share of employer contributions in accordance with a schedule that varies the percentage of compensation to be received by years of service. Under such an approach, an employee with 5 years of service might receive an allocation equal to 5 percent of compensation, while one with 10 years of service might receive 10 percent of compensation. There is also great potential flexibility in this approach through the choice of gradations in the schedule of percentages. Needless to say, the overall level of the percentages is controlled by the amount of the employer contributions to be allocated.

Any allocation formula that recognizes years of service will receive special scrutiny by the Internal Revenue Service to determine whether it discriminates in favor of highly compensated employees. Since highly compensated employees will generally have the longest period of service when the plan is established (and each year thereafter), weighting of service in the allocation formula could cause the IRS to consider the formula discriminatory and hence unacceptable. In fact, in most situations the IRS will not approve the unit system because of its potentially discriminatory effect.[18]

Under some older profit-sharing plans, the same dollar amount is allocated to all employee accounts. This is quite logically called the *per capita* basis of allocation. It is appropriate only when the earnings of the various plan participants vary within a very narrow range. This basis of allocation is rarely used in newer plans.

The annual addition, including employer contributions, forfeitures, and employee contributions, if any (see below), that can be allocated to an employee's account in a given year is subject to the limits of Sections 415 and 416 of the Internal Revenue Code, described in Chapter 6.

B. Investment Earnings

The title to the assets of a profit-sharing plan is held by the trustee, but for accounting purposes shares in the composite pool of assets are allocated to the individual accounts of the plan participants. These assets generate investment

---

[18]Rev. Ruls. 68-652, 68-653, 68-654.

earnings, which in turn must be allocated to the participants. The only logical approach to allocating investment earnings is in terms of the individual account balances. Presumably, the assets theoretically assigned to each account contribute on a pro rata basis to the total flow of investment earnings and should participate on a pro rata basis in those earnings.

The investment earnings of a profit-sharing plan are measured on the basis of total return. Under this concept, the return includes dividends, interest, realized capital gains and losses, and unrealized capital appreciation and depreciation. In other words, the total return recognizes actual investment income plus or minus changes in the market value of the underlying assets during the measurement period. This means that the assets of the plan must be valued on a market basis from time to time.[19]

The Internal Revenue Service requires that the assets of a profit-sharing plan be valued at least once a year.[20] To provide more flexibility in plan administration and more equitable treatment of plan participants, many plans call for more frequent valuation;[21] some have monthly or daily valuations. Allocations to individual employee accounts are based on total investment earnings for the accounting period, including changes in the market value of the assets, that the balance in the account bears to the sum of the balances in all accounts.

The more frequent the asset valuations and the associated allocations of investment earnings, the less troublesome is the accounting for transactions with the plan that occur between valuation dates. Normal transactions of this type would be total withdrawals by employees terminating membership in the plan and partial withdrawals by continuing members under the terms of the plan. The policy question is whether these accounts should be credited with investment earnings and increases and decreases in market values for the interim between the last valuation date and the date of withdrawal. If annual valuations are prescribed, the gain or loss could be substantial if interim allocations are not authorized. Alternatively, some plans provide for annual valuations and delay all or a portion of the distribution until the annual valuation date. This is especially true if the employee is entitled to a pro rata share of the employer's contribution for the last fiscal year of employment.

Some profit-sharing plans permit employees to direct part or all of their accounts to two or more investment options, such as a common stock fund and a fixed income fund. In this case each subaccount of an employee shares in the investment experience of the particular fund in which it is invested.

C. Forfeitures

A participant who withdraws from a profit-sharing plan before the balance in his or her account is fully vested forfeits the nonvested portion of the account. Under

---

[19]An exception exists when all the assets of the plan are vested in a contract backed by the general asset account of a life insurance company. Transactions with plan participants under such a contractual arrangement take place on a book value basis, and interest is credited to individual accounts in accordance with the accounting procedures of the life insurer.

[20]Rev. Rul. 80-155.

[21]Ibid.

some plans, amounts forfeited by terminating employees are credited against the employer's required contribution, as under a pension plan; but the prevailing practice is to reallocate the forfeitures among the remaining participants. The basic policy question here is whether the forfeitures should be reallocated on the basis of compensation or account balances, keeping in mind the IRS stricture against any plan provision that will tend to discriminate in favor of highly compensated employees.

For many years, plans frequently specified that forfeitures were to be reallocated among remaining participants on the basis of account balances, with forfeitures and investment earnings being treated in the same manner. Over time, the IRS concluded that this basis of reallocation tends to favor highly compensated employees, since their account balances will have been accumulated over a longer period (because of lower turnover) than those of other employees and hence will be entitled to a disproportionately large share of the forfeitures. The IRS does not flatly prohibit the reallocation of forfeitures on the basis of account balances, but if it concludes that the plan in practice is favoring highly compensated employees, the plan may lose its qualified status.

Money Purchase Pension Plans

A money purchase pension plan is a defined contribution plan that may be used by an employer to provide retirement income to employees. The primary difference between a money purchase pension plan and a profit-sharing plan is that contributions to the former must be based on a fixed formula specified in the plan document. A profit-sharing plan can have discretionary employer contributions, since it is not subject to the definitely determinable benefit rule. A money purchase plan, since it is a *pension* plan, is subject to the definitely determinable benefit rule, and therefore contributions must be fixed.

Since it is also a defined contribution plan, a money purchase pension plan is subject to many of the same requirements for profit-sharing and stock bonus plans. Money purchase pension plans are more common among small employers who want to offer their employees the benefit security of a pension plan but do not want to assume the financial responsibility of a defined benefit plan.

Plan Design

Money purchase pension plans have the same fundamental objective as defined benefit pension plans, namely, to provide retirement income to employees. Since money purchase plans are defined contribution plans like profit-sharing or stock bonus plans, however, they must comply with Internal Revenue Code and IRS standards for both pension plans and defined contribution plans. In addition, as a pension plan, a money purchase plan must abide by the various ERISA regulations.

A money purchase pension plan is quite different from a defined benefit plan in its approach to providing retirement income for employees. A defined benefit plan uses a determinable benefit formula, and employer contributions are made as required to provide that benefit. In contrast, a money purchase pension plan follows a contribution formula, and the ultimate retirement benefit is based upon the accumulated employer contributions and earnings and losses thereon. The fixed contribution formula is said to satisfy the definitely determinable benefit requirement for pension plans.[22]

Like a defined benefit pension plan, a money purchase plan is subject to the minimum funding requirements of section 412[23] and the qualified joint and survivor annuity requirements.[24] Like a defined contribution plan, a money purchase plan is subject to the annual limit on contributions to the plan[25] and the annual valuation of plan assets. This duality of requirements significantly affects the design of money purchase plans.

A. Traditional Money Purchase Pension Plan Design

The contribution formula for a traditional money purchase pension plan is usually quite straightforward, requiring the employer to contribute a fixed percentage of employees' compensation, such as 5 percent or 10 percent, each year. In fact, the contribution formula for a money purchase plan can so strongly resemble the contribution formula for a profit-sharing plan that the repeal of the requirement that profit-sharing plan contributions be made out of employer profits has blurred the distinction between a money purchase plan and a profit-sharing plan with a nondiscretionary contribution. For that reason, when the profit contribution requirement was removed from the Internal Revenue Code, a new requirement was added mandating that money purchase plans and profit-sharing plans designate which type of plan they intend to be in the plan document.[26]

One of the most common differences between money purchase plans and other defined contribution plans is the presence of annuity options in a money purchase plan. The rules governing qualified joint and survivor annuities exempt only defined contribution plans that are not subject to the minimum funding standards of section 412.[27] As a pension plan subject to the minimum funding requirements, a money purchase plan must offer participants a QJSA benefit option. Since participants' benefits are individual accounts, annuity benefits from a money purchase plan are usually provided through the purchase of annuity contracts from an independent annuity carrier.

B. Target Benefit Plan

A target benefit plan is a money purchase plan designed to more closely emulate a defined benefit plan. Employer contributions are actuarially determined as those necessary to achieve a targeted benefit for the employee based on various reasonable assumptions. So while a target benefit plan has a benefit formula, as does a defined benefit plan, rather than a contribution formula, as in a profit-sharing plan, the actual benefit ultimately delivered to employees is based on their individual

[22]Treas. Reg. 1.401-1(b)(1)(i).
[23]Treas. Reg. 1.412(a)(1)(A).
[24]IRC §401(a)(11)(B)(ii).
[25]IRC §415(c).
[26]IRC §401(a)(27).
[27]Treas. Reg. 1.401(a)-20, Q&A 3.

accounts and will fluctuate with the earnings and losses of that account. In other words, the difference between a target benefit plan and a traditional money purchase plan or profit-sharing plan is that the target plan bases contributions on a benefit formula, while the difference between a target benefit plan and defined benefit plan is that the employee still carries the risk of investment loss in a target benefit plan.

Target benefit plans are a relatively rare type of plan design, that has gained little favor among either large employers or small employers. A large employer who desires to provide a specified retirement income benefit for employees is more likely to adopt a defined benefit plan. A target benefit plan does make larger annual contributions for older employees than for younger employees, a feature often coveted by small business owners, but the annual contributions to each employee's account are still limited to 25 percent of compensation or $30,000.[28]

Contributions

The employer makes all required contributions to a money purchase plan according to a fixed and determinable formula.

A. Contribution Commitment

In addition to being contractually obligated to follow the fixed contribution formula in the plan document, an employer is required to contribute the proper amount each year under the contribution formula in order to satisfy the plan's minimum funding standards. The funding standard account for a money purchase plan is essentially each year's specified contribution.

To be currently deductible by the employer, the contribution for a year may be made at any time up to the due date for filing the employer's tax return for that taxable year (including extensions), provided the contribution is designated as being on account of that taxable year.[29]

The requirement for making quarterly contributions to a pension plan does not apply to a money purchase plan.[30] The quarterly contributions are added to the funding standards in order to improve cash flow for defined benefit plans and thereby reduce in some small manner the underfunding of defined benefit plan liabilities. Since underfunding of benefit liabilities is generally not possible in a money purchase plan (the account balances are the benefit liabilities), Congress recognized that there was no need to apply the quarterly contribution requirements to money purchase plans.

B. Contribution Formulas

Except for target benefit plans discussed earlier, contribution formulas in money purchase plans are expressed as a percentage of covered compensation. The definition of compensation is subject to the same concerns as are present in

---

[28]IRC §415(c).
[29]IRC §404(a)(6).
[30]IRC §412(m)(1).

deferred profit-sharing and defined benefit plans, including the requirement that compensation in excess of $150,000 (indexed) may not be recognized after 1993.[31]

C. Limits on Deductibility of Employer Contributions

Employers are allowed to make tax-deductible contributions to a qualified money purchase pension plan equal to the contribution required under the minimum funding standard for the plan year. Since the contribution required under the plan's contribution formula is the normal cost for the plan under the minimum funding standards, all required contributions to a money purchase plan are normally deductible in the year made, subject to the limits on allocations to participants' accounts in defined contribution plans.[32] In effect, this allows a maximum deductible contribution of 25 percent of the covered participants' compensation.

In addition to the excise tax on all nondeductible contributions discussed earlier, a 10 percent excise tax applies for any failure to meet the plan's contribution formula. Such a failure means that the plan has also failed to meet the minimum funding standards. An additional excise tax equal to 100 percent of the accumulated funding deficiency can be assessed, but it is waived by the IRS if the employer makes the delinquent contribution to the plan.[33]

Withdrawal Benefits

Profit Sharing, Stock Bonus, and ESOPS

The primary purpose of many, if not most, profit-sharing plans is to accumulate funds to enhance the old-age economic security of the employee participants. The plan may be the sole mechanism maintained by the employer for this socially desirable objective, or it may supplement a pension plan sponsored and supported by the employer. In either event, it might be assumed that the funds credited to the individual accounts of the employees could not be withdrawn prior to the employee's retirement or death prior to retirement. Such is not the case. As conceived under IRS regulations and reflected in the provisions of most plans, a deferred profit-sharing plan is a much more flexible instrument of asset accumulation than a pension plan, and distributions are permitted under a greater variety of circumstances.

A. Circumstances

Regulations[34] permit distributions from a qualified profit-sharing plan "after a fixed number of years, the attainment of a stated age, or upon the prior occurrence of some event such as layoff, illness, disability, retirement, death, or severance of employment." If there is to be any meaningful distinction between a *cash* or *current*

[31]IRC §401(a)(17).
[32]IRC §§415(c), 404(j)(1)(B).
[33]IRC §4971.
[34]Treas. Reg. 1.401-1(b)(1)(ii).

profit-sharing plan and a *deferred* profit-sharing plan, employer contributions to the latter must be held by the trust for some period after they are made. The controlling regulation indirectly requires that the funds be held for a "fixed number of years," unless one of the other designated events occurs in the meantime. The IRS has interpreted the expression a "fixed number of years" quite literally in ruling that the minimum holding period is two years.[35] This requirement applies to each individual account. That portion of an employer's contribution allocated to a particular employee's account must remain in the account, along with the investment earnings associated with it, for at least two years. If the plan calls for annual contributions by the employer, no distribution can be made from a particular account until the third allocation is made, and at that time an amount equal to the first allocation plus investment could be withdrawn. After the fourth allocation is made, the second allocation could be withdrawn, and so on. If allocations are made monthly, the first distribution from an individual account could be made two years from the date of the first allocation. However, after an employee has participated in the plan for five years he or she may, if the plan permits, withdraw all employer contributions, including those made within the preceding two years.[36]

The plan is under no obligation to make distributions under all the circumstances mentioned. The only affirmative requirement of the regulation in this respect is that the funds credited to an employee's account be made available to him or her at retirement. Between the two extremes of sequestering the allocations for a minimum of two years and making them available in some form at retirement, the plan sponsor is free, if collective bargaining is not involved, to determine the conditions under which distributions will be made.

The distribution provisions are greatly affected by the concept of vesting and the vesting requirements set forth in ERISA and IRS rulings. Profit-sharing plans are subject to the same vesting standards that apply to qualified pension plans under ERISA (see Chapter 6). Vesting pertains to the retention of forfeiture through termination of employment prior to receipt of the vested benefit. But a benefit derived from employer contributions is not treated as forfeitable solely because it is forfeited upon the participant's death, with the narrow exception of the qualified preretirement survivor annuity.[37]

In practice, profit-sharing plans vest account balances much more liberally than required by law. This is partly due to the attitude of the IRS, which has traditionally required faster vesting for profit-sharing plans. Under most plans, account balances are fully vested upon death, total disability, and normal retirement age, the latter being required by law. Moreover, the account balance is distributed to participants or their beneficiaries when these events occur. Upon termination of employment, other than by death, disability, and retirement, the *vested* portion of the account is often distributed immediately, although participants must consent to any immediate distribution[38] and although plans may prohibit any immediate distribution before some stipulated age.

---

[35]Rev. Rul. 71-295.
[36]Rev. Rul. 68-24.
[37]ERISA §203(a)(3)(A); IRC §411(a)(3)(A).
[38]ERISA §203(a)(3)(A); IRC §411(a)(3)(A).

The portion of the account vested will depend, of course, upon the vesting provisions of the plan and the amount of service of the terminating employee. Graded vesting is much more common under profit-sharing plans than under pension plans. It is not uncommon for a plan to vest 20 percent of employer contributions (and the associated investment earnings) for each full year of service, so the account balance would be fully vested after five years of service. Few plans defer full vesting beyond five years. Because forfeited account balances are typically reallocated among the remaining participants, the IRS is more concerned (as noted above) with the vesting provisions of a profit-sharing plan than a pension plan.

The distributions of the account balance of a participant in a qualified profit-sharing plan are made on four general occasions: death, total disability, retirement, and other severance of employment. In the first three cases, the entire account balance may be distributed, whereas at the severance of employment, only the vested portion of the account balance would be distributed.

One of the most difficult policy questions in plan design is whether a participant should be permitted to withdraw all or a portion of his or her vested account balance while still in the active service of the employer. This issue depends on the fundamental objective of the plan. If it is designed to serve as a long-term savings medium, perhaps for old-age economic support, withdrawals during active service to meet current needs should not be permitted. On the other hand, if the plan is viewed as a general savings program that uses the deferred compensation concept and that can meet either current or long-term needs, then periodic withdrawals during active employment are entirely appropriate and consistent with the aim of the program. Some plans allow withdrawals only for unusual hardships or certain specific purposes, such as the purchase of a home.

A participant is subject to tax only on the amount actually distributed from the plan.[39] Prior to 1982 participants were also subject to tax on amounts "made available" under the constructive receipt concept. Many profit-sharing plans still contain penalties for withdrawal that were originally designed to prevent the IRS from applying the constructive receipt doctrine. Perhaps the most common such penalty is to deprive the employee of membership rights for a specified period, such as six months. Another approach to avoiding the constructive receipt problem is to require approval of all withdrawal requests by a duly constituted committee, using some ascertainable standard. Usually, this approach permits withdrawals only for emergencies such as illness or layoff, or to meet such commendable objectives as home ownership or education of the children. The taxation of distributions is discussed in Chapter 7.

B. Form

Distributions from a qualified profit-sharing plan may take several forms. Distributions to employees in active employment or to those terminating employment through voluntary or involuntary withdrawal generally take the form of lump-sum

---

[39]IRC §402(a)(1).

payments. Distributions at retirement may take the form of lump-sum payments, installment payments, or a life annuity, possibly with a survivor income feature. If a profit-sharing plan permits a life annuity form of payment, then it must satisfy the rules of ERISA relating to joint and survivor annuities. Some plans permit participants to elect the form of distribution, within prescribed limits, and the choices sometimes include a variable annuity. Distributions upon death or disability may be in a lump sum or in installments, subject to the survivor annuity requirements described in Chapter 10. Participants may be permitted to elect a life income option or other installment settlement of their account to be payable to a designated beneficiary or beneficiaries upon their death during service. If a life annuity is provided, this is almost always done by purchasing an annuity from a life insurance company.

If a participant has been given the opportunity to allocate a portion of his or her account to individual life insurance, a distribution of the account at retirement or at an earlier separation from service would include the life insurance policy or its cash value. At death, the distribution would encompass the proceeds of the life insurance contract, payable in a lump sum or in installments, at the option and direction of the participant.

Under many profit-sharing plans, some or all of the assets are invested in the common stock or other securities of the plan sponsor. Under those plans, a distribution may include securities of the employer. If a total distribution of the employee's account is made under conditions qualifying for favorable tax treatment, the value of the securities of the employer for the purpose of determining the employee's gain is the cost to the trust and not the fair market value of the securities at the time of the distribution.[40] In other words, the employee is not taxed on the unrealized appreciation at the time of the distribution. The cost to the trust becomes the employee's cost basis should the securities be sold at a later date. Employer securities are accorded the same treatment under qualified pension plans.

C. Loans

Many profit-sharing plans allow a participant to borrow part or all of his or her vested account balance. All loans are subject to ERISA's fiduciary requirements.[41] Loans to participants are exempt from the restriction against alienation and assignment and from the restriction concerning prohibited transactions if they are adequately secured. Loans also bear a reasonable rate of interest, are available to all participants and beneficiaries on a reasonably equivalent basis, and must meet certain other requirements.[42]

A participant who borrows from the plan usually agrees to make periodic payments of interest at an agreed-upon rate and to make payments to amortize the principal of the loan. Payments of interest and principal amortization are often made through payroll deduction. A loan to a participant is usually secured solely

[40]IRC §401(E)(4)(j).
[41]ERISA §404.
[42]ERISA §§206(d)(2), 407(b)(1); IRC §§401(a)(13), 4975(d)(1); Treas. Reg. 1.401(a)-13(d)(2).

by the participant's vested account balance. If the participant terminates employment or otherwise makes a withdrawal, the outstanding balance of this loan is subtracted from the amount otherwise available to him or her. If the loan is considered to be part of the total unsegregated assets of the plan, the plan will account for the loan in the same manner that it accounts for purchasing a bond or a mortgage or for a loan to a disinterested person. Under this approach, the unsegregated plan assets include the outstanding balance of the loan. Interest payments on the loan are included in investment income. Repayments of principal are treated as such and reduce the outstanding balance of the loan. Interest on the loan, together with all other investment income of the plan, is allocated among the accounts of all participants. The account balance of the borrowing participant is treated in the same manner as if he or she had received no loan. If the participant terminates employment or otherwise withdraws his or her account balance, the payment is reduced by the outstanding balance of the loan. In the plan's accounting, this withdrawal is treated as if the entire account balance had been paid to the participant and he or she immediately repaid the loan. Since the individual's account balance under this approach fluctuates with the market value of the plan's assets, it would be imprudent for the plan to lend the participant an amount equal to the entire account balance, lest the fluctuating account balance fall below the outstanding balance of the loan and provide inadequate security for the loan. Depending upon the volatility of plan assets, the plan may restrict loans to one-half or two-thirds of the individual's vested account balance.

Under the alternative approach, the loan is treated not as part of the unsegregated assets of the plan, but as a separate investment of a portion of the assets attributable to the borrowing participant's account. After the loan, the account is divided into two parts, one consisting of the outstanding balance of the loan and the other part consisting of the share of the remaining unsegregated assets of the plan. If the participant makes a $60 payment of interest, it is interest income attributable to his or her own account and increases the account balance by $60. This $60 interest payment is added to the unsegregated assets of the plan available for reinvestment, and the individual participant's share of the unsegregated assets is increased by $60; the loan account balance is unaffected. If the participant makes a $100 payment to reduce the balance of his or her loan, the $100 is added to the unsegregated assets of the fund and the share of the unsegregated assets is increased by $100. In the latter case, however, the outstanding balance of the loan is reduced by $100 and the portion of the account balance represented by the loan is reduced accordingly.

Table 12-2 illustrates the loan and first month's payment on a loan of $6,000 made from a $10,000 account balance with interest of 1 percent per month. The example ignores other transactions and investment income on the unsegregated assets.

Under this method, the loan asset always exactly equals the outstanding balance of the loan. Therefore the plan can safely lend 100 percent of the participant's vested account balance. Every payment of principal or interest increases the participant's own net amount available for distribution.

A loan has an effect similar to a distribution, in that it makes money currently available for use by the participant. But unlike a distribution, a loan is not taxable

TABLE 12-2 Accounting for a Loan to a Participant (dollars)

	Participant's Account Balance				Net Available for Distribution
	Unsegregated Assets	Loan Assets	Total	Outstanding Balance of Loan	
Before loan	10,000	0	10,000	0	10,000
Loan	–6,000	–6,000	–6,000	–6,000	–6,000
After loan	4,000	6,000	10,000	6,000	4,000
Loan	+60	+0	+60	+0	+60
After payment	4,060	6,000	10,060	6,000	4,060
Principal payment	+100	–100	0	–100	+100
After payment	4,160	5,900	10,060	5,900	4,160

income to the participant if certain conditions and restrictions are satisfied.[43] The loan terms must provide for repayment by level installments (quarterly or more frequently) within five years, or within a "reasonable" time in the case of loans taken out to acquire the principal balance of any other loans from the plan; also the loans may not exceed the greater of $10,000 or one-half of the participant's vested account balance. However, the limit may never be more than $50,000, less any principal repayment made during the preceding 12 months. Loans in excess of these amounts, or loans that do not satisfy the repayment requirement, are treated as distributions and are included in the participant's gross income for tax purposes.

The Tax Reform Act of 1986 eliminated the deduction of interest paid for all loans, whether from a qualified plan or any other lender, with only three generally available exceptions.[44]

1. the four-year phase-in of the interest disallowance, which temporarily preserved part of the deduction during the years 1987 through 1990;
2. deduction of certain mortgage interest;
3. deduction of certain investment interest incurred to purchase investments.

In addition to these restrictions, which apply to interest deductions in general, new rules further restrict the deduction of interest on loans from qualified plans.[45] No deduction is allowed for interest under any loan made after 1986 to a "key employee" (as defined under top-heavy plan requirements). Nor is any deduction to be allowed for interest on any loan made after 1986 that is secured by an employee's elective contributions under a 401(k) plan or a 403(b) plan. To alleviate this problem, some 401(k) plans provide that plan loans will not be secured by accounts attributable to elective contributions unless the loan balance exceeds the balance of the participant's vested accounts that are not attributable to

[43]IRC §72(p).
[44]IRC §163(d).
[45]IRC §72(p) (3).

elective contributions. Even if a participant may not deduct the interest paid on a plan loan, the interest paid does not increase the participant's tax basis in his or her account.

There are several advantages to offering a loan provision in a plan. It makes money available to meet the current needs of employees, perhaps on more favorable terms than the employee could obtain elsewhere, and under more favorable tax treatment than a distribution from the plan. In addition, all of the interest paid by the employee benefits that employee. There are also potential disadvantages to such a provision. If the purpose of the plan is to provide for retirement needs, loans that are not repaid can defeat the purpose, just as distributions can. For this reason, some plans limit loans to hardship situations. The administrative work and expense are another disadvantage. Some employees may object to paying interest on their "own money." And if loans are made from the unsegregated assets, the investment earnings of the trust may be diluted if the loan interest rate is less than the rate of return on other trust assets.

Vesting

The vesting provisions of profit-sharing plans cover two types of vesting: *membership vesting* and *class system* vesting. Membership vesting is found in pension plans and is attained by meeting requirements couched in terms of plan participation or service with the employer. Once the participant has satisfied this participation or service requirement, he or she is fully vested (except for graduated vesting) in all accumulated employer contributions and all employer contributions made thereafter. Membership vesting must occur within the period of membership service permitted under the minimum vesting standards prescribed by ERISA. To encourage employee participation, the membership vesting provisions of defined contribution plans tend to be more liberal than ERISA minimum standards. The most common period required for full vesting is five years of service; a large number of plans provide for immediate vesting.

Class system vesting is unique to defined contribution plans. Under this system, the required period of membership service applies separately to each class of contributions. Employer contributions made in a single month, quarter, one-half year, or year (periods of class formation) constitute a class and vest at a designated time following the close of the class formation period. Plans that utilize class system vesting generally vest employer contributions in full in three years or less after they are made. Under this system, a participant would never be *fully* vested except in the case of death, disability, and retirement. Should employment terminate for any other reason, the participant would forfeit some portion of the employer contributions credited to his or her account.

Class system vesting is much more difficult to administer and explain to employees than conventional membership service. Nevertheless, it has been widely used. Some employers adopted the approach in the belief that it is a deterrent to employee turnover, since some forfeiture is involved in every voluntary separation from service. A plan year is by far the most common period for class formation. In other words, plans using class system vesting typically treat the contributions of a given plan year as a class.

For plan years beginning after 1988, the vesting of all plans must satisfy one of two requirements, either 100 percent vesting after five years of service or 20 percent vesting after three years of service graded up to 100 percent vesting after seven years of service.[46] For top-heavy plans, more rapid vesting is required. Years in which an employee declines to contribute while eligible to do so need not be counted. A plan under which vesting is based solely on the class year method will not satisfy these requirements. Therefore such plans must be restructured, either by replacing the class year vesting with a vesting schedule based solely on service or membership or by superimposing such a vesting schedule in addition to the class year vesting schedule. For example, it would be possible to retain three-year class year vesting if the plan also provided that every participant with at least five years of service would nevertheless be 100 percent vested in all of his or her accounts. To avoid the additional complexity of administration and communication of such an arrangement, most employers have completely replaced class year vesting with vesting based on years of service or membership, with a grandfather clause to protect existing classes that might otherwise have more rapid vesting.

In the majority of plans using the membership vesting approach, full vesting is to be achieved in steps; this is called *graduated* or *graded* vesting. A simple example of graduated vesting would be a schedule calling for 20 percent vesting after one year of service and 20 percent increments for each of the next four years. Many plans vest one-third of the accumulated employer contributions for each year of plan membership. A more liberal schedule found among many plans is 50 percent vesting after one year of membership and 25 percent incremental vesting for each of the next two years of plan membership. Graduated vesting is used by plans with class vesting systems, although less frequently than by plans using membership vesting. Graduated vesting is slightly more complex to administer than the type that provides for full vesting at a particular time and none before that time, sometimes called "cliff" vesting. Regardless of the vesting system utilized, some plans provide for full and immediate vesting of employer contributions in the event of certain specified contingencies (in addition to death, disability, and retirement), such as plant shutdown, layoff, involuntary termination of employment without cause, and military service.

Allocation of Forfeitures

Termination of employment, other than that occurring in a specified manner (death, disability, retirement, layoff, and so on), may produce a forfeiture unless the plan provides immediate vesting. Thus the plan must provide for the disposition of any forfeitures.

The most common disposition by far is to apply the forfeitures to reduce the employer's contributions to the plan, thus lowering the costs of sponsoring a plan. Another, much less common approach, is to apply the forfeitures as additional employer contributions, the allocation being made on the same basis as the employer's matching contributions. These additional allocations are subject to the

---

[46]ERISA §203(a)(2); IRC §411(a)(2).

same vesting provisions as regular employer contributions. Some plans allocate forfeitures in proportion to account balances, a procedure normally discouraged by the IRS in the belief that it tends to favor the highly paid and other favored employees. Various other bases for allocating forfeitures may be found, including allocation in equal shares.

Distributions

Upon the death, disability, or retirement of thrift plan participants, their entire account balances are distributed in a lump sum or in some other form elected by the participants, or if applicable, by their beneficiaries, whether or not the account had previously been fully vested. The full amount in the account may be distributed under certain other circumstances, such as layoff or involuntary termination without cause, irrespective of the normal vesting provisions. Upon termination of employment, regardless of the circumstances, the participant ordinarily is entitled to receive immediately the vested portion of his or her account. This will include the participant's contributions, with accumulated investment earnings, and that portion of the employer contributions plus investment earnings that has vested under the normal vesting provisions of the plan and any special vesting provisions that might apply.

Virtually all plans also provide for distributions from individual employee accounts while participants are still in the active service of the employer. Such distributions are subject to the statutory mandate, discussed earlier in this chapter, that the contributions made by the employer on behalf of a particular employee be accumulated and held for a "fixed number of years."[47] The IRS has interpreted this requirement to mean that employer contributions must be held for a minimum time. Since withdrawal provisions for defined contribution plans qualified as pension plans are quite stringent, as discussed above, most thrift plans are qualified as profit-sharing plans instead.

Provisions of thrift plans relating to distributions to individuals still in active service vary widely, reflecting the desires, biases, and objectives of the plan sponsor, tempered by relevant collective bargaining considerations. These provisions may be broadly classified as to whether they relate to normal (or periodic) distributions or to voluntary withdrawals.

A. Normal Distributions

Normal distributions are periodic disbursements to plan participants of a portion of their accounts on a regularly scheduled basis and without penalty. Plans that have such a provision generally have used a class system of vesting and usually have linked normal distributions to the time period required for each year's contribution to "mature," or vest fully. At some point prior to the time a particular class was to mature, each participant was given the opportunity to indicate whether all or a portion of his or her share of the class should be distributed at the end of the period or be withheld for later distribution. This allows the participant, at his

[47]Treas. Reg. 1.401-1(b)(ii).

or her option, to increase current income or to accumulate funds for retirement or for other purposes. The funds that he or she elects to accumulate can be withdrawn subsequently, in accordance with the plan provisions relating to voluntary withdrawals.

In a 1991 survey of large and medium-size firms, 50 percent of the savings and thrift plans permitted withdrawals of employer contributions prior to disability, retirement age, or termination of employment. Among the plans covered in the survey, 26 percent allowed withdrawals for hardship reasons only, but 24 percent allowed them for any reason. At retirement, 30 percent of the plans provided the option to take benefits in the form of a lifetime annuity, including joint-and-survivor forms, 52 percent provided the option of paying the benefits out in a series of periodic installments, and 99 percent of the plans provided the option of taking the benefits as a lump sum.[48]

B. Voluntary Withdrawals

As its name suggests, a voluntary withdrawal is one that takes place at the participant's initiative in accordance with the general rules or conditions laid down in the plan document. A voluntary withdrawal differs from a normal periodic distribution in three ways: (1) it may be made at any time during the year, rather than on a class maturity date; (2) it is not limited to the contributions of any one year but may involve the entire vested account balance; and (3) it often invokes a penalty of some type.

Most plans permit a voluntary withdrawal only on a plan asset *valuation* date, since a withdrawal typically involves a redemption of units of participation in a commingled asset account valued at market. The great majority of large plans are valued at least as often as quarterly and many are valued daily. To provide more flexibility, some plans permit partial withdrawals at any time, subject to minimum notice, such as 10 days. The funds made available to the participant are taken from the money that is being paid over to the plan by the employer. The market value of the employee's account is adjusted on the next valuation date.

The majority of plans permit voluntary withdrawal of all employee contributions and all vested employer contributions, along with the associated investment earnings. Some plans allow only a portion of the vested employer contributions to be withdrawn. A few make no provision for voluntary withdrawals.

Some plans provide more liberal withdrawal terms when the withdrawal is occasioned by *hardship*. For example, a plan that permits withdrawal of only employee contributions under normal circumstances may permit withdrawal of vested employer contributions as well under hardship conditions. In some cases, no penalty is assessed if the withdrawal is due to hardship, provided such hardship is established to the satisfaction of the administrator of the plan. Some plans provide withdrawal privileges only in hardship cases.

Withdrawal provisions of some plans are linked to length of membership, with longer service employees receiving the most liberal treatment. The treatment may

---

[48]U.S. Department of Labor, *Employee Benefits in Medium and Large Private Establishments, 1991,* Bureau of Labor Statistics Bulletin 2422 (Washington, D.C.: USGPO, May 1993), p. 117.

differ as to the dollar amount that can be withdrawn, the availability of partial withdrawals, and the severity of the penalty for a withdrawal.

In the past, the withdrawal of employer contributions and investment earnings on employee and employer contributions had to be subject to a meaningful penalty to avoid assessment of federal income tax liability on the participant in the year in which the amounts were credited to his or her account, on grounds of constructive receipt. Many plans still have such penalties. The types of penalties that may be assessed, listed in order of *increasing* severity, are (1) a *suspension of membership* in the plan, whereby the employee loses the right to contribute to the plan for a specified time and thereby loses the right to the matching employer contribution for that period; (2) a *termination of membership* in the plan, whereby the employee not only ceases participation in the plan for a time but also loses credit for past years of membership accrued to date for purposes of higher employer-matching contributions, membership requirements for voluntary withdrawals, or other provisions related to length of membership; and (3) forfeiture of all or a portion of the nonvested employer contributions. The third type of penalty is subject to an ERISA prohibition against the imposition of a forfeiture penalty if at the time of withdrawal the participant is 50 percent or more vested in his or her employer contribution account.

Some plans impose no penalty if the withdrawal is a result of a hardship. In general, the determination of whether a hardship exists is left to the discretion of the employer committee that administers the plan. The committee must apply the hardship provision in a uniform, nondiscriminatory manner. Although there is no longer a constructive receipt tax problem, an employer may assess a penalty upon withdrawal to discourage withdrawals and encourage long-term thrift.

C. Forms of Distribution

Distributions from thrift plans have traditionally taken the form of lump-sum payments and, where applicable, employer securities. As a matter of fact, until recently profit-sharing thrift plans usually made no provision for any other type of distribution. But in recent years there has been a growing interest in, and emphasis on, using thrift plan accumulations to help meet the financial needs of employees during their retirement years. This had led a significant number of newly established and amended plans to provide alternative forms of distribution, at the election of employees or their beneficiaries.

The most common alternative forms are installment payments over a specified period of years, a life annuity contract purchased from a life insurance company (again, if annuity options are provided, the plan must comply with the rules of ERISA relating to joint and survivorship annuity), and the purchase of an additional monthly retirement benefit through the employer's pension plan. The latter is accomplished through a lump-sum transfer of the employee's thrift plan accumulation to the pension plan at the time of the employee's retirement. In this type of transfer, employer contributions and associated investment earnings lose their identity for federal estate and gift tax purposes. Pursuant to ERISA, any life annuity benefits offered to a married employee through either a separate annuity contract or the pension trust must be payable in the form of a qualified joint and survivor annuity unless the employee elects otherwise.

D. Death and Disability Benefits

As pointed out in the preceding section, defined contribution plans typically provide for payment of the entire account balance upon the death or total disability of the participant. The only other death benefit found in the plans is the diversion of a portion of the account balances to purchase life insurance.

Purchase of Life Insurance

On Participants

A qualified profit-sharing plan may give participants the option of having a portion of their account balances applied to the purchase and maintenance of either term or permanent life insurance, purchased under a group contract or individual policies. This is accomplished by including in the profit-sharing trust agreement a provision that grants each participant the right to direct the trustee to purchase life insurance, and sometimes other specific investments, for his or her account. If the trust agreement authorizes the trustee to purchase investments earmarked for the accounts of the various participants (and all participants have the right to so direct the trustee), then any participant can instruct the trustee to purchase life insurance on his or her life without disqualifying the plan.

An insurance contract purchased on the life of a plan participant is owned by the trust. The premiums for the insurance are charged directly to the account of the individual. The portion of the periodic premium allocable to the pure insurance or protection component of the contract (i.e., the face amount less the cash value) is viewed as a current distribution from the trust and is therefore taxable in the year in which it is paid.[49] The amount of reportable income is calculated by multiplying the pure protection component of the contract by the one-year term insurance premium rate for the participant's attained age.[50] That portion of the periodic premium allocable to the cash value component of the contract is considered an investment of the trust and is not currently taxable as a distribution from the trust. Upon the death of the participant, the insurance proceeds, depending upon the terms of the plan, are either credited in full to the account of the deceased employee or paid directly to the beneficiary designated by the employee. The latter is the more common procedure.

Upon the employee's retirement, the trustee may surrender the contract and pay the cash value to the participant; or the trustee may distribute the contract to the participant or permit the participant to exchange the cash value of the contract for a single-sum life annuity. If the insurance contract is turned over to the participant, he or she may keep the contract in force by continuing to pay the premiums required under the contract.

The disposition of the contract upon severance of employment before retirement depends upon the vesting provisions of the plan. If the participant's vested interest in his or her account balance exceeds the cash value of the contract, the trustee will normally release the contract to the participant, who may keep the

---

[49]Rev. Rul. 56-634.
[50]Rev. Ruls. 55-747, 66-110.

contract in force by continuing the required premium payments. If the vested value of the account is less than the cash value of the insurance contract, the participant can acquire the contract by paying the trustee the nonvested portion of the cash value; the trustee can take out a policy loan equal to the nonvested portion of the cash value and assign the contract subject to the loan, to the participant; or the trustee can surrender the contract for its cash value and pay the participant's vested interest in cash.

If a life insurance contract is part of a distribution from a profit-sharing plan, the cash value, less the employee's cost basis, will be considered taxable income in the year in which the employee receives the contract, even though the contract is not then surrendered for its cash value.[51] Like any other distribution, the distribution will qualify for favorable tax treatment as a lump-sum distribution or as a tax-free rollover to an individual retirement account or to an individual retirement annuity, if all the necessary conditions are met (see Chapter 29). The employee may also avoid any current tax liability by making an irrevocable election, within 60 days of the distribution, to convert the contract to a nontransferable annuity containing no element of life insurance.[52] If current tax liability is avoided by such an election, the employee will not incur any tax liability until payments are made from the annuity contract. At that time, the payments will be taxable in full as ordinary income.

When premium payments for life insurance on plan participants are made by the trustee from funds that have been accumulated for more than two years, the cost of insurance is treated as an allowable distribution, and restrictions or "incidental" death benefits do not apply.[53] Irrespective of the period of fund accumulation, if the insurance is provided through single-premium endowment or retirement income contracts, the incidental restrictions are satisfied.[54] However, if premiums are to be paid out of funds that have accumulated in the participant's account for less than two years *and* the insurance is to be in the form of whole life insurance (ordinary life and limited-payment life), IRS regulations limit the portion of the employee's account balance that can be allocated to premium payments. These limits are designed to ensure that the death benefits under the profit-sharing plan are incidental to the primary purpose of the plan. The concept of limiting death benefits to amounts deemed incidental to the primary purpose of the plan is also applicable to qualified pension plans, as was noted in Chapter 11.

The basic premise of the IRS is that no more than 25 percent of the contributions and forfeitures allocated to the employee's account should be used to maintain pure life insurance on a participant in the plan. On the arbitrary but simplifying assumption that over time about one-half of the gross premium for whole life insurance is applied to the protection component of the contract and the other half is used to build up the reserve, the IRS has ruled that aggregate

---

[51]Treas. Reg. 1.402(a)-1(a)(2).
[52]It should be noted that, if an employee is entitled to a distribution in cash but has the option under the plan of electing, within 60 days, to receive a nontransferable annuity in lieu of the cash payment, he or she may avoid current tax liability through timely exercise of this option.
[53]Rev. Rul. 60-83.
[54]Ibid.

premiums for whole life insurance for any particular employee must be less than one-half of the total contributions and forfeitures that have been allocated to his or her account.[55] In practice, the sum set aside as premiums on whole life insurance generally does not exceed 25 to 33⅓ percent of anticipated average annual contributions to the employee's account. A margin is often provided to avoid violation of the legal limit if contributions should fall off in future years. For the same reason, some plans do not permit insurance to be purchased until the employee has been a member of the plan for several years. The accumulation in the employee's account provides a cushion in the event that contributions decline in future years.[56] Separate rules apply to the purchase of health insurance.[57]

For whole life insurance on a participant to be incidental to the main purpose of the profit-sharing plan, the premium must not only fall within the limit described above, but the plan must require the trustee to convert the entire cash value of the life insurance contract at or before retirement into cash, or to distribute the contract to the participant, or to provide periodic income so that no portion of the cash value may be used to continue life insurance protection beyond retirement.

There are several reasons why it may be advantageous to plan participants to allocate a portion of their account to the purchase of life insurance. During the early years of participation in a profit-sharing plan, accumulations tend to be rather modest. The sum of the accumulations, plus any group insurance and Social Security, may not be sufficient to meet the need for death benefits for a young participant with heavy family responsibilities. Over a long time, however, the balance in the employee's profit-sharing account may reach a substantial sum and is, of course, distributable upon the employee's death. Thus life insurance makes it possible to provide substantial death benefits at all stages of an employee's participation in the plan. Moreover, automatic payment of premiums by the trustee from the employee's profit-sharing account is a convenient and relatively painless way of maintaining life insurance protection.

On Key Personnel

A profit-sharing trust has an insurable interest in the lives of officers, stockholder employees, and key employees of the corporation. Contributions to the plan depend on the continued profitability of the firm. The future profitability of a business, especially a small or medium-size one, may well depend on the performance of a few key employees. Therefore the plan sponsor may regard it to be in the best interests of the plan participants to purchase life insurance to protect the

---

[55]Rev. Ruls. 54-51, 57-213, 66-143.

[56]Another approach to avoid violating the 50 percent limit when profits decline or disappear, presumably for a temporary period, is to surrender the contract for paid-up insurance and then reinstate it when subsequent employer contributions permit.

[57]Rev. Rul. 61-164. No more than 25 percent of the contributions and forfeitures allocated to the employee's account can be used to pay premiums on this type of insurance. If both whole life and accident and health insurance contracts are purchased, the amount spent for accident and health insurance premiums plus *one-half* (presumably the half allocable to pure insurance protection) of the amount applied to whole life insurance premiums may not, together, exceed 25 percent of the unseasoned funds allocated to the employee's account. This means that no more than 25 percent of the employee's account can be used to provide a current protection type of insurance coverage.

trust against reductions in future levels of contributions arising out of the death of such key employees. If this is to be done, it is advisable that the plan document and the trust agreement specifically authorize the trustee to purchase the insurance.

The purchase of insurance on key personnel of the plan sponsor is an investment of the trust for the benefit of all participants. The trustee applies for the insurance, owns the contracts, and is designated as the beneficiary under the contracts. The premiums for the insurance are paid by the trustee out of plan assets and, in effect, are charged ratably to the accounts of the individual participants. Upon the death of an insured individual, the insurance proceeds are paid to the trust and are allocated among the participants on the basis of their account balances. If the plan so provides, the account of the deceased key employee will be credited with its proportionate share of the proceeds.

The purchase of life insurance on key employees creates no current tax liability for the participant. Likewise, the tests regarding the incidental nature of the insurance are not applicable. Since the purchase is for the benefit of the trust and thus the premium payments are not distributions, the limits on the use of funds accumulated in the trust for less than two years do not apply. As a practical matter, of course, the trust is not likely to invest the bulk of contributions in such insurance contracts. ERISA imposes a fiduciary responsibility on plan trustees to demonstrate that key employee insurance is prudent and in the best interest of participants and that it meets asset diversification requirements.

Thrift and Savings Plans

An arrangement under which a nondiscriminatory grouping of employees of a common employer make voluntary contributions to a defined contribution plan is generically called an employee *savings* plan or a *thrift* plan (the two terms are used interchangeably). If the employer makes no contributions to the plan, the arrangement is commonly referred to as a *pure* thrift plan. Such a plan provides employees with a convenient mechanism for indulging their instincts for capital accumulation along with with certain tax advantages and other attractive features, discussed below. In a pure thrift plan, the employer usually absorbs all relevant administrative expenses, thus providing an additional incentive for the employee to save. Most thrift plans provide for employer-matching contributions as a specified percentage of employee contributions. The Internal Revenue Code has no separate provisions for thrift plans. To obtain favorable tax treatment under the Code, a thrift plan must qualify as either a pension plan, a profit-sharing plan, or a stock bonus plan.

There are important differences between thrift plans that qualify as profit-sharing plans and those that qualify as pension plans, owing to the differences in the Code's requirements for the two types of plans. Under a pension plan, employer contributions must be definitely determinable, whereas a profit-sharing plan can be flexible in determining contributions. A profit-sharing plan may make distributions to active employees, while a pension plan generally may not. A pension plan must make distributions *available* in the form of an annuity (a life annuity or an annuity certain), while a profit-sharing plan is not required to provide annuities at all. Finally, a profit-sharing plan can be used as a cash or deferred arrangement (CODA or 401(k) plan), whereas this treatment is not allowed for a pension plan. The great majority of thrift plans are qualified as profit-sharing plans. Many thrift plans are cash or deferred arrangements. Some were originally designed as 401(k) plans and others were modified to become 401(k) plans. Such plans are discussed in the next section.

Advantages of a Thrift Plan

All of the objectives sought by the employer in establishing and maintaining a profit-sharing plan can be achieved through a thrift plan. An all-encompassing objective is to attract and retain a competent, productive, and loyal work force. The motivating power of a thrift plan depends upon its features, the dominant ones being the basis of employer contributions to the plan and the vesting provisions. Whatever the reason, some employers have found that they can match the motivating power of a conventional deferred profit-sharing plan with a thrift plan that costs less as a percentage of payroll. This has something to do with the fact that participants appreciate the clearly defined employer contribution commitment under a thrift plan, in contrast to a profit-sharing commitment that produces variable contributions from year to year and in some years may yield no contribution at all. Also, it seems that employees have a special attraction to a plan that (in the absence of capital losses) ensures an initial rate of return on their contributions (but not on reinvested earnings) at least equal to the employer-matching percentage, which is generally not less than 25 percent of the amount contributed by employees. Plans with employee contributions tend to provide more withdrawal flexibility, at least with respect to the employee's own contributions, and this is a popular feature with the participants. All in all, thrift plans tend to be a popular form of employee benefit plan, resulting in capital accumulations for retirement and materially enhancing employee morale.

A thrift plan offers a number of advantages to employees. The first advantage is the convenience and discipline of saving through payroll deductions. If an employee elects to participate in the plan, the amount that he or she wishes to set aside can be automatically deducted from one's pay each pay period without any further action. This is a great spur to systematic saving. Second, the funds set aside receive the benefit of professional investment management, often at no cost to the employee because such fees are absorbed by the employer. There are several further advantages associated with this feature of a thrift plan. The small periodic savings of the individual participants are combined into one or more large pools of assets that are invested in a diversified group of equity and fixed-income securities. The participants thus enjoy a high degree of diversification and have access to a wide range of investment opportunities, similar to those in a mutual fund. Unless one or more of the investment alternatives happens to be a "load" mutual fund or insurance or annuity contracts, there is no front-end load, so the entire amount of the savings goes into the investment pool. Furthermore, some employers pay the investment management fee out of corporate assets, giving the employees the benefit of the full investment return. Thus employees' savings are given the benefit of professional asset management without any charge for participation and frequently without any charge for the investment services provided.

The third major advantage is related to the second. If the plan meets the qualification requirements of the IRS, the investment income credited to the individual accounts of the employees is not currently taxable to them. It will be taxable as ordinary income when withdrawn, unless it is withdrawn under circumstances that entitle it to favorable tax treatment as a lump-sum distribution, as applicable to profit-sharing distributions in general. If the employee views the thrift plan as a long-term savings mechanism and in fact lets investment earnings accumulate until death, retirement, or earlier separation from service, the earnings will enjoy a net tax advantage, including deferral of tax on the appreciation of employer securities forming a part of the distribution. This, coupled with the payroll deduction feature and professional management of the accumulated assets, makes the thrift plan a very attractive savings medium quite apart from any employer contributions.

In practice, virtually all thrift plans involve employer contributions, which form the foundation of the fourth and undoubtedly most appealing advantage of the thrift plan from the standpoint of the employees. The employer typically contributes at least 50 cents for each dollar set aside by the employee, subject to certain limits, and this practically ensures a handsome return on the employee's "investment" in the plan. Even 25 percent matching by the employer, which is at the lower end of the contribution scale, starts the employee's deposit off with a significant increment. The employer can deduct contributions to a qualified thrift plan, and the contributions are not currently taxable to the employees even when fully vested. When withdrawn, they and their associated investment earnings are taxable as ordinary income, unless the withdrawal satisfies the conditions for favorable tax treatment discussed later. The employee is not taxed when his or her own contributions are returned.

This is an impressive array of favorable features, and employees have responded predictably. A well-constructed thrift plan can be one of the most popular employee benefit plans offered by an employer, and the appeal is often disproportionate to the employer's investment in the arrangement, which is commonly 3 percent of payroll or less.

Plan Design

A qualified thrift plan must meet the general requirements laid down in the Internal Revenue Code and ERISA. Thus the plan must be designed with these statutory and regulatory constraints in mind.

Coverage

The majority of thrift plans cover all or substantially all employees of the sponsoring firm. If all employees are not covered, the excluded group is usually the hourly and part-time employees (those with fewer than 1,000 hours of annual service). Employees who are members of a collective bargaining unit are usually covered only if the bargaining unit accepts the plan. Some plans limit membership to those employees who participate in the employer's pension plan (contributory or noncontributory) or group life insurance program.

A. Eligibility for Participation

The rules governing eligibility for participation in thrift plans have traditionally been very liberal because of the employer's desire to attract new employees and to retain and motivate present employees. The eligibility provisions of the great majority of plans are more generous than those required by ERISA. Most plans have only a service requirement, typically one year or less. Those plans that combine a service and age requirement generally use age 21. Some plans have no age or service requirement, so newly hired employees are immediately eligible for participation. There is no upper age limit on participation, since this would not be permissible under ERISA.

B. Actual Participation

Participation in a thrift plan is always voluntary on the part of the eligible employees. Nevertheless, a remarkably high percentage of eligible employees generally elect to participate. Half of the plans included in a recent survey have an enrollment of 91 percent of eligible highly compensated employees and 70 percent of non–highly compensated employees.[58]

Employee response to the opportunity to participate in a thrift plan is strongly influenced by the formula for employer-matching contributions, the vesting provision, and the availability of investment options. The existence of employer contributions is the most influential factor. Using 1992 survey data, we found that the participation rate among non–highly compensated employees was 46 percent in plans that offered no match, but 72 percent in plans that matched employee contributions at a rate of 75 percent or higher.[59] The same survey also found that the participation rate was significantly higher when going from plans with no match to plans with a 25 percent match than that observed when going from plans with a 75 percent match to plans with a 100 percent match. Among all plans, general economic conditions have an effect on participation that extends beyond plan design.

Thrift plans must satisfy the coverage requirements applicable to all qualified plans, described in Chapter 4. Low levels of participation could cause a plan to fail to meet these requirements.

Contributions

A. Employee Contributions

It is customary for a thrift plan to set forth a permissible range of contributions, with the employee choosing the rate at which he or she will contribute. This, in turn, determines the amount that the employer will contribute on behalf of the employee. The employer may base contributions on the total employee contribution or only on a portion of it. The proportion on which the employer match is based is the *employee basic contribution*, while the remainder, if any, is the *employee additional voluntary contribution*.

---

[58]Watson Wyatt, *1992 Wyatt COMPARISON Survey.*
[59]Ibid.

Among the plans surveyed by Watson Wyatt in a 1993 study, the permissible range of employee basic contributions is 2 percent to more than 10 percent of compensation; 6 percent is both the median and the most common rate. There is a definite trend away from basic contribution rates higher than 6 percent of compensation, because of an IRS rule that an employer permitting them has to prove to the IRS that such a provision will not be discriminatory.[60]

In some plans, the maximum basic contribution rate is related to the employee's service or age, or both, with the older or longer-service employee being permitted to contribute at a higher rate. Such a provision is designed to permit the employee at midpoint (or beyond) in his or her career to accumulate greater balances during the shorter-than-average period to retirement. There is a trend away from this type of provision also because of the necessity of demonstrating to the IRS that it does not discriminate in favor of highly paid employees.

Some plans impose a maximum dollar limit on employee basic contributions, in addition to the maximum percentage limitation. Such a limitation may take one of two forms: (1) a specified flat dollar ceiling on basic contributions, such as $2,000 per year, applicable to all employees irrespective of compensation level or rate of contribution; or (2) a specified level of recognized annual compensation, up to which the elected rate of contribution is applied. While the limits in a few plans effectively restrict basic contributions of almost all employees, most dollar limitations are designed to restrict the contributions that may be made—and have to be matched—by higher-paid employees. Such restrictions are clearly permissible under IRS regulations. For plan years beginning after 1993, plans may not recognize annual compensation in excess of $150,000 for any purpose.[61]

Most plans permit additional voluntary contributions that are not matched by employer contributions. There is an incentive for an employee to make additional contributions, if he or she can afford them, because of the attractive investment features (described earlier) and the advantageous tax treatment of the investment income. The IRS imposes a limit of 10 percent of compensation on additional voluntary contributions to which employer contributions or benefits are not geared.[62] Thus in a plan providing for employee basic contributions of 2 to 6 percent of compensation, the total employee contribution would be limited to 16 percent of compensation, which is the maximum basic contribution of 6 percent plus a maximum of 10 percent of additional contribution. Where the employer maintains more than one qualified plan to which the employee is eligible to contribute, the maximum aggregate annual voluntary contribution to the plans remains 10 percent of the employee's compensation.[63]

As with basic contributions, the employee chooses the rate of additional contributions from a range specified in the plan. The *maximum* additional contribution rates range from 2 to 10 percent, the median maximum being 6 percent. Some plans permit "makeup" voluntary contributions (i.e., if the employee does not contribute the maximum of 10 percent in any one year he or she can contribute

---

[60]Rev. Rul. 72-58.
[61]IRC §401(a)(17).
[62]Rev. Ruls. 59-185, 70-658; IRS Publication 778, Part 4(h).
[63]Rev. Rul. 69-627.

the "shortfall" plus 10 percent in the following year).[64] Such makeup contributions are subject to the limits of Section 415 of the Internal Revenue Code. The maximum limits on allocations under a defined contribution plan include not only employer contributions and forfeitures but also employee contributions. An employee's contribution in a given year becomes a part of the maximum annual addition that may be made to the individual account of an employee under ERISA.[65] Because of the difficulty of satisfying the nondiscrimination tests applicable to employee contributions and employer-matching contributions (described later in this chapter), many employers no longer allow voluntary employee contributions.

To provide even greater flexibility, a thrift plan generally permits a participant to change the rate of contribution from time to time, as his or her circumstances change. By the same token, the participant is usually granted the privilege of suspending contributions to the plan for a period, most often a year, without losing membership in the plan. The participant continues to accrue plan membership for vesting and other purposes during the period of the suspension, but the employer makes no contributions on his or her behalf. The right to change contribution rates or to suspend contributions may usually be exercised, after reasonable notice, at various times during the plan year, and in some plans at *any* time. Some plans restrict the exercise of this right to the beginning of each quarter; others permit change at the beginning of any pay period following the required notice. To minimize administrative expense and complexity, most plans impose some type of limit on the number of times changes may be made. For example, the participant may be permitted to change or suspend contributions only once in any 12-month period. Along the same line, most plans stipulate that a suspension of contributions must remain in effect for a minimum period of time, such as six months or a year, the former being more common.

As noted above, some plans allow employees to contribute lump-sum amounts in excess of the otherwise applicable limits to make up for prior years during which they did not contribute at the maximum rate permitted. In most plans, the makeup contribution is related to the additional voluntary contribution rate that is not matched by the employer; but in some plans, it is related to the basic contribution rate and is matched by the employer.

Some plans permit participants to "roll over" their accumulated contributions from other qualified plans into the thrift plan. Also, when a contributory defined benefit pension plan is converted into a noncontributory plan, the employer may refund the accumulated employee contributions by transferring them to the employees' thrift plan accounts. There may be special restrictions on the withdrawal of such one-time contributions. Needless to say, the employer does not match this special employee contribution.

B. Employer Contributions

The contribution that an employer makes on behalf of a particular employee is typically determined by the amount that the employee contributes. The general

---

[64]Rev. Rul. 69-217.
[65]IRC §415(c)(2).

approach is to match the employee's basic contribution at a rate specified in the plan. The employer match is usually a single uniform percentage of each employee's contribution. In some plans, however, a range is set forth and the match varies with additional factors, such as the employee's length of service or plan membership, or the level of corporate profits. A small number of plans use a different approach and contribute an aggregate amount computed in accordance with a prescribed profit-sharing formula. This amount is then allocated among the participants in proportion to their own contributions, their compensation, or a combination of their contributions and their compensation.

For plans that base the employer's contribution on the employee's basic contributions, the typical matching contribution is 50 percent of the employee's basic contribution rate. In nearly 25 percent of plans, the employer contributes 50 cents for each dollar that the employee contributes up to a maximum of 6 percent of pay.[66] The employer match ranges from 10 percent to 150 percent for plans that matched employee contributions up to 6 percent of pay. While the range is extremely wide, relatively few plans call for employer contributions in excess of 100 percent of the employee's basic rate or less than 25 percent. As noted earlier, there is a positive correlation between the employer-matching contribution rate and the rate of employee participation.

A substantial proportion of plans provide for additional employer contributions (over and above the basic matching contributions) on the basis of corporate profits. In these plans, the employee is assured of a minimum employer contribution, and the amount (and timing) of the additional contribution may be mandatory and specified in a formula related to the level of profits, or it may be optional and occur only on action of the board of directors. There is a strong tendency for plans that match employee contributions at less than 50 percent to provide for additional contributions. This approach is attractive for both the employee, who can receive a larger contribution when the firm has had a good year, and the employer, who can achieve some cost flexibility.

A not insignificant number of plans have a *graduated* employer contribution formula. In those plans the employer's matching contribution, as a percentage of the employee's contribution, varies with the employer's profits and the employee's length of service, years of membership, investment choice, own contribution rate, or the size of the unwithdrawn employer contribution account. In some of these plans, the employer contribution rate is related to a combination of the employee's service and contribution rate.

The cost of a thrift plan to the employer, as a percentage of payroll, is a function of (1) the proportion of eligible employees who elect to participate; (2) the rate at which the participants elect to contribute; (3) the rate at which the employer matches the employees' basic contributions; and (4) the amount of forfeitures applied to reduce employer contributions. If it is assumed that all participants contribute at the maximum permissible rate that will be matched by the employer and that there are no additional employer contributions, the before-tax cost to the employer of a typical thrift plan is approximately 2 percent of payroll. Despite this

---

[66]Watson Wyatt, *1992 Wyatt COMPARISON Survey.*

relatively small cost to the employer, such plans have had wide appeal to employees.

Contribution Percentage Requirement

The contribution percentage requirement, described in Chapter 6, limits the average percentage of employee contributions and employer-matching contributions for highly compensated employees. If a plan has a high level of participation by employees who are not highly compensated, the requirement may have no actual effect on a plan. But if there is a low level of participation by lower-paid employees, the contributions of highly compensated employees may be severely restricted. To encourage greater participation by lower-paid employees, an employer may decide to increase the matching percentage, provide earlier vesting, add more attractive investment alternatives, or improve communication of the plan.

Investment of Contributions

The contributions that a participant makes to a thrift plan, along with those made on his or her behalf by the employer, are credited to an individual account maintained in his or her name by the plan administrator. Legal title to the contributions, however, is vested in the plan trustee, who must invest them in accordance with the instructions contained in the trust agreement and any applicable plan provisions. ERISA requires separate accounting for the employee's contributions and the earnings thereon, which must be 100 percent vested at all times.

A. Investment Media

For the most part, early thrift plans directed the plan trustee to invest both employee and employer contributions in securities, typically common stock, of the sponsoring firm. This was in accordance with the generally held view that the participants would feel greater allegiance to the company and would be more productive if they acquired an ownership interest in the company. Such plans had to register with the Securities and Exchange Commission (SEC). Under some plans, only employer contributions had to be invested in employer securities, and alternative investment avenues were available for employee contributions. Even today many thrift plans require that some portion of the individual account balances attributable to employer contributions be invested in common stock of the employer, and many plans still require that all such contributions be invested in that manner. Investment in employer stock is not feasible for small companies with no established market for their stock. Of course, proprietorships and partnerships have no stock.

In recent years, there has been a growing sentiment that plan participants should be given a voice in the investment of their account balances, especially that portion attributable to their own contributions. It is believed that participants will have a keener interest in, and greater appreciation of, the plan if they participate in the investment process. Employers are partly motivated by the desire to have employees share the responsibility for the investment decisions. In the face of rising interest rates, employees in general have become more interested in investment performance and have become more critical of unsatisfactory results. To many employers it thus seems wise to many employers to let plan participants make their own investment decisions. To the extent that the account balances are vested, the employee is, in effect, investing his or her own money.

In the evolution of investment policy for thrift plans, some employers have questioned the wisdom of requiring or even permitting investment in the securities of the employer. The crucial question is whether an employee should depend on the same firm for both job security and financial security. The same economic forces that produce layoffs may reduce or even seriously undermine the value of the employee's stockholding in the company. There is also concern about possible fiduciary liability under ERISA should the value of the employer's stock decline. Also, ERISA's emphasis on the diversification of plan investments has probably influenced some employers' attitude toward investing plan assets in their own securities. Finally, if a participant has the option of investing any portion of his or her account in employer securities, it may be necessary to register the plan with the Securities and Exchange Commission and issue a prospectus to the employees.[67] Despite these concerns and questions, many plans provide participants with the opportunity to invest in employer securities on an elective basis. A small but increasing percentage of plans prohibit investment in securities of the employer, despite the fact that ERISA permits such plans to provide for unlimited investment in such securities *if it is prudent to do so.*

The typical thrift plan today provides participants with a number of investment alternatives, at least for their own contributions. More than 70 percent of medium and large plans in a 1993 survey offered four or more options for investment of employee contributions. Sixty percent of plans with an employer match offer four or more investment choices for the employer contributions. Only 19 percent of such plans require that the employer's contributions be invested in employer securities.[68] As a minimum, a plan is likely to offer participants the opportunity of investing in a commingled pool of fixed-income securities and a commingled pool of equity securities, with each participant having the right to designate the proportion of his or her individual account balance to be allocated to each pool. There is no obligation to allocate to both pools; the participant may direct the trustee to invest the entire account balance in one or the other of the two funds. This permits each participant to determine the mix of fixed-income and equity securities to be held in his or her individual account. There may be the constraint, noted above, that the portion of the participant's account balance attributable to employer contributions be invested in company stock.

Some plan sponsors offer a balanced fund, composed of designated percentages of fixed-income and equity investments. This approach avoids the complexities associated with operating two separate investment funds, but it restricts the participants' freedom of choice between the two broad classes of investments. Some plans sponsor two or more equity funds, each with its own investment objectives and risk parameters. If prudent, a plan may offer a pooled fund invested

---

[67]If the amount of money involved is small, it may be possible, upon application, to receive an exemption from registration with the SEC, pursuant to Regulation A.

[68]Watson Wyatt, *Wyatt COMPARISON,* May 1994.

exclusively in obligations of the federal government or government agencies. To provide almost complete investment latitude, some plans permit participants to allocate their account balances to one or more mutual funds whose shares are available in the open market. Plans of this type, which permit unlimited investment selection, were popular for a short time, but they involved increased administrative expense, and employees often had difficulty (as everyone does) in selecting the best investment vehicle.

If a participant allocates a share (or all) of his or her account balance to an investment fund operated exclusively for the plan, he or she acquires units of participation in the fund. These units are valued at market levels, and the participant bears the risk of adverse investment experience and, conversely, enjoys the benefits of favorable investment experience. To avoid these investment risks, particularly those associated with fluctuations in the market value of a fixed-income fund owing to changes in prevailing interest rates, many plans in recent years have offered participants the opportunity of placing money in a guaranteed income contract (GIC) of a life insurance company. Under this type of contract, developed primarily for profit-sharing in a thrift plan, the life insurer guarantees an annual rate of return for a specified period of years. Implicit in a guaranteed rate of return is a guarantee of principal, which places the whole transaction on a book value basis. These contracts have proved to be extremely attractive to plan participants, in part because of the volatility of common stock prices. In recent years, however, it has become apparent that these plans carry some of their own risk of default and potential follow-on lawsuits against employers to make the guarantees whole.

Some plans, instead of making guaranteed income contracts of life insurers available, guarantee a minimum rate of return on contributions invested in a fixed-income portfolio. The employer then makes good on any deficiency in the actual rate of return as an additional contribution.

Other plans guarantee participants that they will receive, as a minimum, a sum equal to all or a specified portion of their own contributions. In effect, this is a guarantee of the principal sum of money that the employees contributed to the plan. In most such plans, this guarantee is something of a delusion, since any capital losses that must be made good by the employer may be charged to the employees' nonvested employer contribution accounts. Thus, what an employee gains in one account, he or she loses in another. However, this guarantee has gained in popularity because where the employee's contribution and the 25 percent employer-matching contribution (or lower percentage) are invested in equities, the amount returned to the employee can be less than his or her own contributions, owing to market fluctuations. Any such loss defeats the concept of capital accumulation and is bitterly resented by employees. In many plans, this guarantee, such as it is, is limited to certain circumstances and to specified amounts.

B. Changes in Investment Instructions

An important aspect of the investment latitude plan participants enjoy is the right to change investment instructions to the plan trustee. It is routine for plans that give the participant investment direction over his or her own or employer contributions, or both, to change his or her instructions about *future contributions* at least once a year. Some plans permit a change every six months, and some permit even more frequent change. In the past, however, there has been a general reluctance to permit participants to change their investment instructions as to *accumulated contributions* for fear that they might attempt to "play the market" or simply display poor or unfortunate judgment in the *timing* of their switch. More and more plans, however, are permitting participants to transfer past accumulations from one fund to another, irrespective of the investment risk involved. This is part of a general trend toward giving participants more control over the investment of their account balances, with the concomitant responsibility for investment outcomes. The change in attitude also represents a growing recognition that employees have different needs, aspirations, and financial sophistication. As an employee approaches retirement, for example, he or she may wish to see his or her "nest egg" invested in fixed-income securities, rather than chancing the timing vagaries of the equity market. Another factor is that computer systems have become sophisticated enough to overcome the administrative problem attendant upon changes in investment instructions and transfers of accumulated funds.

Most plans limit transfers from one investment fund to another to once a year. A few permit them more often than once a year, while others impose a limit per career, such as three transfers. Some plans require the consent of the administrative committee, a heavy responsibility for that group of individuals. A sizable percentage of plans permit a transfer of accumulated contributions only as the participant approaches retirement or has been in service for a substantial time.

Vesting

As might be surmised, a participant's own contributions to a thrift plan and the associated investment earnings are fully and immediately vested for all purposes. Furthermore, the employer's contributions on the participant's behalf, and their associated investment earnings, are fully vested upon the participant's death, disability, or retirement.[69] Thus the conventional vesting provision is concerned with the participant's entitlement to the employer's contributions and their earnings upon termination of employment for reasons other than death, disability, and retirement, or upon exercise of withdrawal privileges while still in the service of the employer.

Cash or Deferred Arrangement (401(k) Plan)

In any sizable employee group, some individuals would prefer a cash profit-sharing plan and others would prefer a deferred profit-sharing plan. Younger employees with more limited income and heavier family responsibilities tend to prefer a profit-sharing plan that makes annual cash distributions (in the nature of a bonus or salary supplement), whereas the older and higher-paid employees, with the financial pressures of a growing family behind them and conscious of the need to

---

[69]Governing tax law requires vesting of employer contributions upon the participant's normal retirement age but not upon death or disability. ERISA §203(a); IRC §411(a).

accumulate a fund for old-age maintenance, tend to favor a deferred distribution plan. The needs and preferences of both groups can be met by a profit-sharing plan that permits the employees the option of taking cash or having their share of the employer's contribution accumulated in a deferred account. Such a plan is called a "cash or deferred arrangement" (CODA) or "401(k) plan" (for the Internal Revenue Code subsection that regulates them). The earliest 401(k) plans operated in precisely the same manner as a conventional deferred profit-sharing plan, except for the participants' option as to the mode of the allocation.

Because direct compensation is currently taxable, even though there is no current taxation under a profit-sharing plan of either the employer contributions or the investment income they earn, deferral is very attractive, particularly to employees in the higher tax brackets. While the earliest CODAs were established out of employer contributions that were made in addition to regular compensation, it was soon recognized that the underlying concept could be applied to the regular compensation itself. Motivated by the potential tax savings, employees could arrange with their employer to reduce their regular compensation and to make an *employer* contribution to the profit-sharing plan in the amount of the reduction. To the extent allowed, this is far more favorable than withholding salary to make *employee* contributions. Withholding for *employee* contributions does not reduce taxable income; the employee contributes after-tax dollars. In contrast, under a salary reduction arrangement the employee's taxable income is reduced and the *employer* makes a contribution of before-tax dollars on behalf of the employee. While the salary reduction arrangement effectively allows employees to contribute pretax dollars to the plan, the Federal Insurance Contribution Act (FICA) tax under the Old-Age, Survivors, and Disability Insurance program up to the wage base and under hospital insurance on all earned income is still applicable to deferrals.

The most common type of 401(k) plan allows salary reductions by employees and some amount of matching contributions by the employer. For example, the plan may allow employees to make elective contributions not exceeding 10 percent of compensation and may provide for employer contributions equal to half of all elective contributions that do not exceed 6 percent of compensation.

Special Qualification Requirements

Some policy makers were concerned that only higher-paid employees, who can afford to defer their salary or their share of the employer's profit-sharing contribution and who stand to gain the most from the tax-deferral feature of a qualified profit-sharing plan, would elect to defer their allocations. To minimize the potential "abuse" of the elective feature of the CODA, Congress added Code Section 401(k) to ensure that lower-paid employees would participate to a significant extent.

A CODA must satisfy the requirements of Section 401(k) in order for the plan to be qualified and for the elective contributions to be treated as employer contributions and thus be excluded from taxable income. Section 401(k) in effect allows a plan that otherwise would be a qualified profit-sharing plan or stock bonus plan to be treated as a qualified plan even if it discriminates somewhat in favor of the highly paid, provided it meets the requirements of a "qualified cash or deferred arrangement."

A qualified cash or deferred arrangement is a *type* of profit-sharing plan or stock bonus plan. It is a plan under which an employee can elect to receive employer payments in cash or to have them paid as elective contributions to the plan.

An employee's right to his or her accrued benefit derived from these elective contributions must be nonforfeitable (i.e., it must be fully and immediately vested). Unlike an ordinary profit-sharing plan, however, a 401(k) plan may not distribute any accrued benefit derived from the elective contributions while the participant is still an active employee, except after age 59½ or upon a showing of financial hardship.[70] Hardship distributions arc rcstricted to elective deferrals, excluding income allocable to the elective deferrals.

A 401(k) plan may not require more than one year of service for eligibility for participation, even if it has full and immediate vesting. In determining whether the *coverage* of a 401(k) plan satisfies the Internal Revenue Code, it is only necessary to consider the employees *eligible* to participate, not the employees who *actually* elect to participate in the deferred arrangement. The employees eligible to participate must be a group that satisfies the coverage requirements of the Code.

Actual Deferral Percentage (ADP) Tests

To determine whether *elective contributions* under a 401(k) plan for a plan year are discriminatory, the "actual deferral percentage" must first be calculated for each employee eligible to participate. An employee's actual deferral percentage is a fraction whose numerator is the actual elective contributions paid to the trust on his or her behalf, and whose denominator is the individual's compensation for the plan year. If no elective contribution is made for an employee, his or her actual deferral percentage is 0 percent.

The elective contributions are not discriminatory if the 401(k) plan passes either one of two tests. For purposes of both tests, all eligible employees are divided between "highly compensated employees"[71] and the remainder. The average of the individual actual deferral percentages is calculated for each of these two groups and the two averages are compared.

The first of the two tests is passed if the average deferral percentage for the high-paid employees is not more than 1.25 times the average deferral percentage for the low-paid employees. For example, if the average deferral percentage for the low-paid is 10 percent and that for the high-paid is not greater than 12.5 percent (1.25 times 10 percent), the first test is passed.

The alternative test is met if the average deferral percentage for the high-paid is not more than 2 times the average deferral percentage for the low-paid and the difference between the two percentages is not more than 2 percent. For example, if the average deferral percentage for the low-paid employee is 2 percent and the

---

[70]Financial hardship has not yet been defined by the IRS at the time of this writing. Proponents of 401(k) arrangements are urging that the purchase of a home and payment of college expenses for dependents be explicitly recognized as a source of financial hardship.

[71]Highly compensated employees are defined in IRC §414(q), which is discussed in Chapter 4.

TABLE 12-3 Average Contribution Percentages for Non–Highly Compensated Employees (Non-HCEs) and Maximum Allowable Contribution Percentages for Highly Compensated Employees (HCEs) Participating in 401(k) Plans

Average Contribution Percentage for Non-HCEs	*Maximum Allowable Average Contribution Percentage for HCEs*	*Ratio of Maximum HCE to Non-HCE Contributions*	*Percentage Difference*
1.00	2.00	2.00	1.00
2.00	4.00	2.00	2.00
4.00	6.00	1.50	2.00
8.00	10.00	1.25	2.00
10.00	12.50	1.25	2.50

Source: IRC §401(k).

average deferral percentage for the high-paid is 4 percent, the test would be passed, since 4 percent is 2 times 2 percent and the difference (4 percent less 2 percent) does not exceed 2 percent. These requirements are illustrated in Table 12-3. The same rules apply whether the elective contributions are extra employer payments in addition to regular compensation or are salary reduction contributions.

A 401(k) plan may include both elective and nonelective contributions.[72] If it does, it may satisfy the 401(k) nondiscrimination requirement by subjecting the combined contributions to the 401(k) plan requirements (percentage tests, nonforfeitability, and restrictions on distributions), provided the nonelective contributions also satisfy the general nondiscrimination rules. Alternatively, such a combination plan may satisfy the requirement if the elective contributions satisfy the 401(k) plan percentage tests, while the nonelective contributions satisfy the general rules for nondiscrimination, or if the combined contributions satisfy the general rules for nondiscrimination. Employer-matching contributions are subject to the separate but similar "contribution percentage requirement" described in Chapter 16.[73]

Most plans that include employer-matching contributions have been able to attract a high percentage of participation among lower-paid employees, thus satisfying the tests. Increasing the percentage of employer match and providing immediate or very early vesting generally increases employee participation, making it easier to pass the percentage tests.

For a plan financed solely by employer profit-sharing contributions, an employer might decide to contribute 4 percent of pay for all employees, including 2 percent of pay as nonelective contributions paid automatically to the trust for all eligible employees and 2 percent of pay as elective contributions, which the employee could either receive in cash or direct into the trust. Under this approach, even if all low-paid employees elect cash and thus have a 2 percent average deferral percentage, while all high-paid employees elect deferral and thus have a 4 percent

---

[72]In a proposed regulation, the IRS refers to this arrangement as a "combination plan."
[73]IRC §401(m).

average deferral percentage, the percentage test would be satisfied. But if this employer instead allowed elections for the entire 4 percent, it is possible that the average deferral percentages for the low-paid and the high-paid would be 0 percent and 4 percent, respectively, and the plan would fail the test.

Determining in advance whether the percentage tests will be passed can be a problem under 401(k) plans. Prior experience with the same plan or similar plans may provide reasonable assurance, but for a new plan there may be uncertainty. The employer can almost always assume that at least some low-paid employees will elect deferral, and some high-paid will elect cash. An employer who allows all eligible employees to make elective contributions of up to 6 percent of pay and makes matching employer contributions equal to 50 percent of the elective contributions, with one-third immediately vested and the remainder becoming vested during the following two years, could ordinarily expect the average elective contributions by non–highly compensated employees to exceed 4 percent, so that the test would be satisfied even if all highly compensated employees were to contribute 6 percent. Some employers find that the tests can still be satisfied if all eligible employees are allowed to contribute as much as 10 percent.

Another type of safeguard is to reserve the right to reduce the deferral percentage for the high-paid employee and to observe the experience during the year. In the previous example, if the employer observed halfway through the year that its expectations for elective contributions for the low-paid were overly optimistic, it could then reduce the allowable elective contributions for the high-paid for the remainder of the year in order to pass the test.

It is possible to treat only part of a plan as a 401(k) plan. For example, if a thrift plan allows employees to make basic contributions of 6 percent of pay to be matched by employer contributions and to make additional unmatched contributions of 4 percent of pay, it might treat the basic 6 percent employee contributions as elective contributions under a 401(k) plan (and hence as items excludable from taxable income), while treating the 4 percent unmatched contributions as non–401(k) contributions (and thus as items includable in taxable income), along with the matching employer contributions. Only the 401(k) portion would be subject to the 401(k) rules. This strategy might be followed if the combined plan could not satisfy 401(k) rules.

Correction of Excess Contributions and Penalties

A plan may pay out to highly compensated employees any "excess contributions," that is, any elective contributions higher than the maximum amount that would satisfy the ADP tests, together with income allocable to the excess contributions.[74] Such excess contributions may be paid out without any restriction or penalty. Instead of paying out the excess contributions, a plan may correct them by treating them as if they had been paid to the employee and then recontributed to the plan by the employee as after-tax contributions. The employer must pay a 10 percent tax on any excess contribution not paid out (or treated as paid out) within $2\frac{1}{2}$ months

---

[74] IRC §401(k)(8).

after the end of the plan year.[75] The excess contributions and income paid out are included in the participant's income for the year of deferral. If excess contributions are not corrected by the end of the plan year following their deferral, the plan may be disqualified.

Limit on Elective Contributions: $7,000

The amount of an individual's elective deferrals is limited to $7,000 per year.[76] This limit includes all elective deferrals of an individual during a year under all 401(k) plans, tax-sheltered annuities (Section 403(b)), and simplified employee plans (SEPs). To the extent that any elective deferrals are contributed under a tax-sheltered annuity, the $7,000 limit is increased to $9,500. The $7,000 limit is indexed beginning in 1988, but the $9,500 is not indexed. In 1996 the cumulative indexing raised the $7,000 limit to $9,500, so the difference between these two limits has now disappeared.

If an individual exceeds his or her limit during the tax year (the calendar year for almost all individuals), the excess deferral, together with any income allocable to it, may be paid out to the individual with no penalty or restriction not later than the following April 15, and it will generally be treated as though it had never been made. In such a case the income allocable to the excess deferral will be taxable income in the year the excess deferral was originally made. If the individual has made deferrals under more than one program, he or she can decide which one the excess applies to. If any excess deferral is not paid out to the individual by April 15, the excess deferral will be included in the individual's taxable income in the year it was deferred and again in the year it is eventually paid from the plan.

Social Security Taxes

Compensation deferred under a Section 401(k) arrangement is subject to Social Security payroll taxes and is so recognized for Social Security benefit computation purposes, to the extent that the sum deferred in combination with the individual's cash compensation falls within the Social Security tax base. If the individual's cash compensation equals or exceeds the Social Security tax base, the deferred compensation would not be recognized for Social Security purposes. The HI portion of the FICA tax that is applicable to all earned income applies to all deferrals. Also, a qualified defined benefit plan may, but is not required to, recognize as compensation amounts set aside under 401(k) arrangements in determining benefit accruals.[77] However, sums deferred are not recognized for unemployment insurance and workers' compensation purposes.

Stock Bonus Plans

Section 401(a) of the Internal Revenue Code recognizes three types of qualified plans: pension plans, profit-sharing plans, and stock bonus plans. Treasury Regula-

---

[75]IRC §4979.
[76]IRC §402(g).
[77]Rev. Rul. 83-89.

tion 1.401-1(b)(1)(iii) defines a stock bonus plan as "a plan established and maintained by an employer to provide benefits similar to those of a profit-sharing plan, except that . . . the benefits are distributed in stock of the employer company." Under a stock bonus plan a participant must generally have the right to have the benefits distributed in the form of employer securities.[78] A choice of cash may also be offered. But if the employer's charter or bylaws restrict the ownership of substantially all of the outstanding employer securities to either employees or a qualified plan trust, the plan may provide that distributions will be in cash instead of employer securities.

If the employer securities distributed are not readily tradable on an established market, the participant must have the right to sell the securities to the employer at a fair price (the "put option").[79] Without this requirement, a distribution of stock might have little value to an employee.

Unless the participant elects otherwise, distribution of the benefits must begin within one year following the plan year of retirement at normal retirement age or later, disability, or death or within six years of any other separation from service.[80] Unless the participant elects otherwise, the distribution of the benefits must be in substantially equal periodic payments over a period of five years or less (longer if the account balance exceeds $500,000).[81]

The typical contribution formulas under a stock bonus plan express the contribution commitment as a flat percentage of covered payroll or require the employer to contribute X percent of profits but not less than Y dollars a year. The latter type of formula can also be used under a profit-sharing plan that retains its identity as long as distributions do not have to be made in employer stock.

Employee Stock Ownership Plan (ESOP)

The term *employee stock ownership plan* has been used to describe a wide variety of defined contribution plans that invest in employer stock. In addition to providing a benefit plan with stock ownership for employees, ESOPs have been used to meet a wide variety of financial and other objectives of the employer. The laws governing ESOPs have been the subject of frequent amendments, significantly changing the nature of ESOPs and their uses.

Requirements to Be an ESOP

To be a qualified ESOP, a defined contribution plan must meet a number of requirements.[82] First, it must be a qualified stock bonus plan, or a combination of a qualified stock bonus plan and a qualified money purchase pension plan.[83] An ESOP is therefore subject to all requirements that apply to stock bonus plans and,

---

[78]IRC §409(h).
[79]IRC §409(h)(1)(B),(2).
[80]IRC §409(o)(1).
[81]IRC §409(o)(1)(C).
[82]IRC §§4975(e)(7), 409; Treas. Reg. 54.4975-7,11.
[83]IRC §4975(b)(7).

if applicable, money purchase pension plans. An ESOP may be a designated portion of another plan.[84]

Second, an ESOP must be designed to invest primarily in qualifying employer securities.[85] "Primarily" means at least half. Employer securities must be common stock or preferred stock of the employer or of a corporation in the same controlled group, and they must meet certain statutory requirements.[86] Common stock is almost always used, and most ESOPs are invested solely in employer securities, except for temporary cash positions.

Third, an ESOP must be specifically designated as such in the plan document.[87] In addition, an ESOP must satisfy the following four requirements for stock bonus plans, regardless of whether the ESOP is a stock bonus plan or a combination of a stock bonus plan and a money purchase pension plan.

First, an ESOP participant must generally have the right to have the benefits distributed in the form of employer securities.[88] A choice of cash may also be offered. But if the employer's charter or bylaws restrict the ownership of substantially all of the outstanding employer securities to either employees or a qualified plan trust, the plan may provide that distributions will be in cash instead of employer securities. Second, if the employer securities distributed are not readily tradable on an established market, the participant must have the right to sell the securities to the employer at a fair price (the "put option").[89] Third, unless the participant elects otherwise, the distribution of benefits must begin within one year following the plan year of retirement at normal retirement age or later, disability, or death or within six years of any other separation from service.[90] Fourth, unless the participant elects otherwise, the distribution of his or her benefits must be in substantially equal periodic payments over a period of five years or less (longer if the account balance exceeds $500,000).[91]

A *leveraged ESOP* is an ESOP that borrows money with which to purchase employer securities. Additional requirements apply to leveraged ESOPs. Additional requirements also apply to any ESOP if the employer has a registration-type class of securities. A *tax-credit ESOP* or *TRASOP* (so called because the tax credit was enacted by the Tax Reduction Act of 1975) was an ESOP for which an employer formerly received a tax credit rather than a deduction for its contributions. Such tax credits were eliminated by the Tax Reform Act of 1986.

Operation of a Simple ESOP

A simple ESOP (not leveraged) functions very much like a profit-sharing plan. The amount of contributions may be based on a formula or determined at the employer's discretion. A formula may be based on profits or the compensation of

[84]Treas. Reg. 54.4975-11(a)(5).
[85]IRC §4975(e)(7); Treas. Reg. 54.4975-11(b).
[86]IRC §409(1).
[87]Treas. Reg. 54.4975-11(a)(2).
[88]IRC §409(h).
[89]IRC §409(h)(1)(B),(2).
[90]IRC §409(o)(1).
[91]IRC §409(o)(1)(C).

participants. The contribution commitment is often expressed as a flat percentage of covered compensation. Some employers use an ESOP for the employer-matchingcontributions under a 401(k) plan or a thrift plan.

Contributions to an ESOP may be made in cash or in employer securities. If contributions are made in cash, part or all of the cash is used to purchase stock, either from the employer or in the market. Stock and any contributions not applied to purchase stock are allocated to employee accounts. Any dividends on the stock may be paid in cash to participants or may be used as additional contributions to buy more shares to be added to employee accounts.

Distributions can be made at the same times as under a profit-sharing plan. Distributions may be in cash or stock, in accordance with the requirements summarized above. Distributions of employer securities receive favorable tax treatment, as described in Chapter 7.

Code Section 415(c) limits the amount of contributions and forfeitures that may be allocated to an individual under a defined contribution plan. The dollar limits are increased for a qualified ESOP if not more than one-third of the employer contributions are allocated to highly compensated employees. This special rule increases the $30,000 limit on allocations to $60,000, but not to more than the amount of stock allocated to the participant under the ESOP.

Operation of a Leveraged ESOP

Except as noted below, a leveraged ESOP functions in the same manner as an unleveraged ESOP (described above). Under a leveraged ESOP, the trustee of the trust created under the plan arranges for a loan from a lending institution and uses the loan to purchase employer stock. The employer stock acquired is held by the trustee and gradually allocated to participants as cash contributions are made on their behalf under the plan. The stock is pledged as collateral for the loan, which is customarily also guaranteed by the employer or some other party. Since the trust cannot generate income on its own other than dividends on the stock, the employer corporation or other outside party is usually required to guarantee the loan.

The loan, including interest, is repaid by the trustee from the cash contributions of the employer; and the plan requires the employer to contribute an amount sufficient to repay the loan. As loan payments reduce the principal of the loan, part of the stock is released as collateral for the loan. The plan may provide for allocation of the stock to employees only as the stock is released as collateral, or stock may be allocated to employee accounts at an earlier time.

Distributions to employees are made as under an unleveraged ESOP. However, if a participant becomes entitled to a distribution before all of the stock allocated to his or her account has been released as collateral, he or she will receive only those shares that have been released from the collateral assignment, with the remaining number of vested shares being distributed at a later date as they are released from assignment.

Uses of ESOPs

ESOPs may be viewed as a variation of profit-sharing plans. As such they are an employee benefit that may be adopted for all of the reasons that a profit-sharing plan would be adopted. Many believe that ESOPs are especially useful in boosting employee morale, giving employees a sense of involvement, and motivating employees to make the business more profitable. But if the value of the stock falls, the effect on morale may be negative.

ESOPs are also adopted to meet a wide range of financial and other objectives of the employer. By purchasing outstanding shares, an employer can use an ESOP to convert a publicly owned company into one owned by the trust and a few major stockholders (this is known as "going private"). It may be used to put stock into friendly hands to avoid a corporate takeover. A leveraged ESOP can be used to sell a division of a corporation to the division's management or others. (The selling corporation would organize a new corporation that would establish a leveraged ESOP for the purpose of raising capital used in purchasing the division.) An ESOP can provide liquidity to a major stockholder by agreeing to purchase his or her shares at death. An ESOP can be used to buy out the interest of a deceased or retiring stockholder in a closely held corporation. Newly issued stock can be sold to an ESOP with less expense and complexity than it can be through a public offering.

Estate Tax Deduction for Sale to an ESOP

Under certain conditions, if an estate sells employer stock to an ESOP, 50 percent of the proceeds of the sale are excluded from the gross estate for estate tax purposes. For estates subject to estate tax, this deduction can result in very substantial tax savings. The ESOP can bargain with the estate to share the tax savings and thus get a very favorable purchase price. In some situations the bargain sale by the estate, in combination with the other advantages of an ESOP, may be a reason for establishing an ESOP where none now exists, particularly in connection with the acquisition of the interest of a deceased major stockholder of a closely held corporation.

Deduction for Dividends on ESOP Stock

A corporation ordinarily receives no deduction for dividends paid to stockholders. But an exception allows an employer a deduction for dividends paid on the stock owned by an ESOP. This exception applies whether the dividends are paid to participants or are applied by a leveraged ESOP to repay ESOP loans.[92] Thus the dividends on stock held by the ESOP that has been allocated to participants can be paid to the participants and the dividends on unallocated stock can be used to repay the loan, with all of the dividends being deductible.

Interest Earned on ESOP Loans

The Code allows banks, insurance companies, and certain other lending institutions to deduct half of the interest received on a loan used by an ESOP for acquisition of securities.[93] As a result, lending institutions are often willing to make

[92]IRC §404(k).
[93]IRC §133.

loans at lower interest rates to the ESOP than they would to the employer. The ESOP transfers the money received to the employer in exchange for company stock. This may in effect allow the employer to raise capital at lower cost than it would have had otherwise. The employer has had to bear the cost of providing the employee benefit, a cost incurred indirectly by having more stock outstanding, which tends to lower earnings per share. But the ESOP may be a substitute for a pension or profit-sharing plan for which the employer would have had both expense and cash outlay.

Diversification of Investments

The Code requires that each ESOP participant have the right to diversify his or her investments during the 5-year period following the first plan year that he or she has both attained age 55 and completed 10 years of participation.[94] Except as noted below, the plan must offer three investment alternatives other than employer securities. During each of the 5 years the employee must be allowed to make transfers from employer securities to the investment alternatives to whatever extent necessary to raise the alternative investments to 25 percent of the participant's total account. In the fifth year 50 percent replaces 25 percent. An employer will be deemed to satisfy the requirement if it makes a cash disbursement of the amount that could have been diversified under an election.

Fiduciary Requirements and Prohibited Transactions

An ESOP is generally exempt from the 10 percent limitation on holding employer securities.[95] But ESOPs are not exempt from the general fiduciary requirements of ERISA. If stock is purchased for more than its fair market value, for example, fiduciaries may be liable.

The loan transactions into which leveraged ESOPs enter would ordinarily be classed as prohibited transactions under both ERISA and the Internal Revenue Code,[96] if there were no applicable exemption. To solve this problem, Congress provided an exemption for ESOPs that satisfy a statutory definition of an employee stock ownership plan as well as other statutory requirements. For this purpose, an employee stock ownership plan is a plan that is either a stock bonus plan or a combination of a stock bonus plan and a money purchase pension plan, which is designed to invest primarily in qualifying employer securities and which satisfies detailed regulatory requirements.[97] For purposes of the Code's definition, additional requirements apply. A loan to such an ESOP is exempt from the prohibited transaction rules if the loan is primarily for the benefit of participants and beneficiaries, if the interest rate is reasonable, and if any collateral given by the plan consists only of qualifying employer securities.[98]

[94]IRC §401(a)(28)(B).
[95]ERISA §407(d)(3).
[96]ERISA §406, IRC §4975.
[97]ERISA §407(d)(6); IRC §4975(e)(7); Treas. Reg. 54.4975-11.
[98]ERISA §408(b)(3); IRC §4975(d)(3).

Independent Appraiser

Fair market value of the employer stock plays a critical role in the operation of an ESOP. If participants receive their distributions in cash, the amount must equal the fair market value of the stock allocated to their accounts. By the same token, the ESOP may not pay more than fair market value for any stock that it purchases. If the stock is regularly traded on an established securities market, fair market value is readily ascertainable. If the stock of the corporation is closely held or not publicly traded, the Code requires valuation by an independent appraiser.[99]

Advantages and Disadvantages

As indicated above, an ESOP offers several potential advantages to an employer, in addition to its value as an employee benefit. ESOPs also have disadvantages. They often involve more administrative expense than other qualified plans. They may have to be registered under securities laws. There may be great employee dissatisfaction if stock values decline sharply.

There may be additional disadvantages with a leveraged ESOP. In the first place, no portion of the stock purchased with borrowed funds and held in the unallocated trust account can revert to the employer if the trust is terminated prematurely. Second, there is a greater risk that the plan will at some point be disqualified by the IRS on the grounds that it is oriented more strongly toward employer objectives than to the "exclusive benefit" requirement of the law. Finally, if the employer stock held in trust appreciates in value, the employer forgoes a tax deduction that it could have otherwise taken by contributing the appreciated stock to the trust rather than cash to repay the loan. Simply stated, through the trust the employees, rather than the employer, enjoy the benefits of future appreciation in the value of the pledged stock.

The participants in an ESOP enjoy the advantage of employer contributions and all benefits associated with stock ownership. The primary disadvantage of the arrangement from their standpoint is that their financial security may be too closely linked with the fortunes of the employer. Thus, as noted above, a base pension plan may be desirable in connection with such an arrangement.

Other Stock Ownership Plans

In addition to stock bonus plans and ESOPs, many other plans involve stock ownership. Many profit-sharing plans include substantial investment in employer securities. Two other tax-favored forms of stock ownership are qualified employee stock purchase plans[100] and incentive stock options (ISOs).[101] There are also many types of nonqualified stock option plans and stock purchase plans. Qualified employee stock purchase plans must be made broadly available to employees, but ISOs and nonqualified plans are usually designed for the exclusive benefit of management employees.

[99]IRC §401(a)(28)(C).
[100]IRC §423.
[101]IRC §422A.

Chapter 13
Hybrid Plans

A defined benefit plan cannot be said to have clear-cut superiority over a defined contribution plan, or vice versa. Each plan type has advantages that may be preferred by a particular plan sponsor. Indeed, many times a plan sponsor wants to combine the advantages of each type of plan (e.g., the ease of communication of a defined contribution plan coupled with employer's assumption of investment risks and rewards in the defined benefit plan). Hybrid plans attempt to combine the advantages of each of the pure types of plans into a single plan. Although hybrid plans can be composed of both defined benefit and defined contribution plans (see "floor Plans" later in this chapter), they are often just a repackaging of one plan type so that it looks like the other plan type (see "Cash Balance Plans" below).

Cash Balance Plans

Basic Benefit Formula

Probably the most significant and common hybrid plan is the cash balance plan. Introduced by Bank of America in the early 1980s, the cash balance plan is a defined benefit plan that looks and feels like a defined contribution plan. In contrast to traditional defined benefit plans, a cash balance plan defines its basic benefit not as an annuity payable at retirement, but as a lump-sum account. It does this by providing (in much the same manner as a defined contribution plan) an annual allocation to the participant's account. This allocation would normally be expressed as a percentage of pay. The difference between a cash balance plan and a defined contribution plan shows up in the annual earnings credited to the participant's account: defined contribution plan accounts grow because of the actual earnings of the plan, but cash balance plan accounts grow because of a predetermined formula.

Consider this sample cash balance plan:

Years of Service	Pay Credit Percentage
0–9	6%
10+	8%
Investment earnings	7

TABLE 13-1   Cash Balance Plan Accruals (dollars)

Year	Pay	BOY Account Balance[a]	Annual Pay Credit	Annual Interest Credit	EOY Account Balance[b]
1	20,000	0	1,200	0	1,200
2	21,000	1,200	1,260	84	2,544
3	22,100	2,544	1,326	178	4,048
4	23,200	4,048	1,392	283	5,723
5	24,400	5,723	1,464	401	7,588
6	25,600	7,588	1,536	531	9,655
7	26,900	9,655	1,614	676	11,945
8	28,200	11,945	1,692	836	14,473
9	29,600	14,473	1,776	1,013	17,262
10	31,100	17,262	2,488	1,208	20,959
11	32,700	20,959	2,616	1,467	25,042
12	34,300	25,042	2,744	1,753	29,539
13	36,000	29,539	2,880	2,068	34,487
14	37,800	34,487	3,024	2,414	39,925
15	39,700	39,925	3,176	2,795	45,895
16	41,700	45,895	3,336	3,213	52,444
17	43,800	52,444	3,504	3,671	59,619
18	46,000	59,619	3,680	4,173	67,472
19	48,300	67,472	3,864	4,723	76,059
20	50,700	76,059	4,056	5,324	85,440
21	53,200	85,440	4,256	5,981	95,676
22	55,900	95,676	4,472	6,697	106,846
23	58,700	106,846	4,696	7,479	119,021
24	61,600	119,021	4,928	8,331	132,280
25	64,700	132,280	5,176	9,260	146,716
26	67,900	146,716	5,432	10,270	162,418
27	71,300	162,418	5,704	11,369	179,491
28	74,900	179,491	5,992	12,564	198,048
29	78,600	198,048	6,288	13,863	218,199
30	82,500	218,199	6,600	15,274	240,073

[a]BOY = beginning of year.
[b]EOY = end of year.

This plan produces the following benefit accrual for our sample employee in Table 13-1. Note that the annual pay credit to the participant's account is merely the appropriate pay credit percentage times the participant's earnings in that year. For example, the allocation for year 5 is

$$6\% \times \$24,400 = \$1,464$$

and the allocation for year 15 is

$$8\% \times \$39,700 = \$3,176.$$

Note also that the interest credits on the account are a flat 7 percent, regardless of the actual fund earnings. This independence of the interest credits and the actual fund earnings is critical since it means that the employer, not the employee, bears the investment risks (and reaps the investment rewards). This feature is what makes the cash balance plan a defined benefit plan rather than a defined contribution plan. As explained below, the interest credit need not be a constant but may be tied to a variable standard (e.g., the consumer price index) as long as it does not depend on actual fund investment results.

If the individual's pay in year t is PAY_t, the pay credit percent in year t is p_t, and the interest credit for year t is i_t, then the allocation for year t will have accumulated to the following amount at retirement:

$$p_t \cdot PAY_t \cdot \prod_{S=t+1}^{R}(1 + i_s)$$

and the total account balance at retirement will be

$$\sum_{t=H}^{R-1}\left(p_t \cdot PAY_t \cdot \prod_{S=t+1}^{R}(1 + i_s)\right).$$

If we let p_t be a constant, p, then we can rewrite this as

$$\sum_{t=H}^{R-1}\left(p_t \cdot PAY_t \cdot \prod_{S=t+1}^{R}(1 + i_s)\right) = p \cdot \sum_{t=H}^{R-1}\left(PAY_t \cdot \prod_{S=t+1}^{R}(1 + i_s)\right)$$

$$= p \cdot (R - H) \cdot \frac{\sum_{t=H}^{R-1}\left(PAY_t \cdot \prod_{S=t+1}^{R}(1 + i_s)\right)}{(R - H)}.$$

In this form, the cash balance plan is an *indexed* career average plan, in which the index is the interest credits accrued annually.

Annuity Options

A cash balance plan develops and communicates an account balance that will normally be available as a lump sum at retirement. However, the normal form of benefit for a married employee must be a "qualified joint and survivor annuity." The plan also provides annuity options for single employees, by dividing the account balance at retirement by the appropriate annuity value. Table 13-2 shows annuities at 8 percent, UP-84.

One question that arises in developing the annuity conversion factors is the extent to which the plan sponsor wishes to subsidize early retirement. Although in a traditional defined benefit plan early retirement is typically subsidized by the plan sponsor, as long as there is any degree of (albeit heavily subsidized) early retire-

TABLE 13-2   Cash Balance Plan, Annuity Conversion Factors

Age	Annuity Factor	Percentage of Account Balance Paid as Annual Benefit
55	9.9552	10.04
56	9.8010	10.20
57	9.6415	10.37
58	9.4769	10.55
59	9.3076	10.74
60	9.1331	10.95
61	8.9537	11.17
62	8.7698	11.40
63	8.5818	11.65
64	8.3903	11.92
65	8.1958	12.20

ment reduction, participants are likely to complain of the "early retirement penalty." This occurs because the reduction is visible and communicated clearly to the employee. In contrast, a cash balance plan hides the early retirement reduction in the annuity factor. Some plans have converted from a traditional defined benefit plan to a cash balance plan as a painless way of eliminating or substantially reducing early retirement subsidies.

Annual Pay Credits

The annual pay credits will typically be a percentage of pay. This percentage can be flat or can be graded by age and/or service. Graded percentages are more common since cash balance plans tend to have a larger early career buildup than traditional defined benefit plans, even with a graded approach. This early career buildup occurs when the interest crediting rate outstrips the salary increase rate. The annual pay credit can also be integrated with Social Security (e.g., 4 percent of pay up to the Social Security–covered compensation level, and 6 percent of pay above that level). Integrated cash balance plans are fairly common.

Interest Credits

The plan must specify the formula used for interest credits. This formula can be a fixed percent, or it can be tied to an external variable standard. Common external standards used are Pension Benefit Guaranty Corporation rates, the CPI, Treasury-bill rates, the prime rate, or guaranteed income contract rates under the employer's defined contribution plan. Theoretically, one would not expect to see the PBGC rate used since an interest credit that is revised annually should be based on short-term rates. The interest credit can be equal to the external standard or have some margin over it (e.g., T-bill rates plus 2 percent).

It is possible to provide ad hoc amendments to the interest crediting rate. For example, a plan sponsor might promise rates of only 4 percent but periodically review the interest rate environment to see if higher rates should be credited for the next year or so. Any such change to the specified interest rate in the plan can only be accomplished by a plan amendment.

Conversion of Existing DB Plans to Cash Balance

When an existing defined benefit plan is converted to a cash balance plan, an employer has to deal with two issues:

1. How to develop the opening account balance.
2. What transitional or grandfather benefits to grant to existing employees.

These two issues are related since a more generous approach to defining the opening account balance can reduce or eliminate the need for transition benefits. The most natural approach to item 1 is to develop the present value of the accrued benefit under the existing defined benefit plan and use this as the opening account balance. This is a minimal approach. A key question in this situation is how to factor in early retirement subsidies. If early retirement subsidies are not provided under the cash balance plan, an employee who retires early a year or two after conversion can have a benefit under the cash balance formula that is significantly lower than the employee's accrued early retirement benefit would have been under the prior defined benefit plan. More elaborate administration by the plan sponsor is required to ensure that the plan complies with all "anticutback" rules.

If the value of early retirement subsidies at the time of conversion is included in the opening account balance, an employee who is close to early retirement on the conversion date and who continues working for several years can realize a windfall. Basically, the problem is that the plan sponsor would like to give the prior early retirement subsidies only to those employees who actually retire early. However, at the date of conversion the plan sponsor must include or exclude the early retirement subsidies for everyone. Often it will be prudent to exclude the early retirement subsidies from the initial balance and use a grandfathering approach to ensure that nobody suffers. This problem exists mainly for those close to or above early retirement age on the date of conversion.

Another common approach is to give employees a balance equal to what they would have had if the cash balance plan had always been in effect. This is particularly helpful for midcareer employees who, under the prior defined benefit plans, have had a relatively small accrued benefit and were just about to enter the steepest part of the benefit accrual slope. If nothing special is done, these employees could end up with the traditional defined benefit plan for the early part of their career (when that is less generous than a cash balance plan) and the cash balance plan for the latter part of their career (when that is less generous than a traditional defined benefit plan).

TABLE 13-3   Sample Transition Pay Credits for Converting
Defined Benefit Plan to Cash Balance Plan

Age at Conversion Date	Special Pay Credits (%)
45–49	6
50–54	3
55–59	2
60+	1

As indicated, employees close to retirement and midcareer employees can be protected in other ways. A common grandfather provision is to offer any employee within five years of retirement a benefit at least as large as the prior plan benefit. This type of provision ensures that employees who made near-term retirement plans on the basis of the prior plan will have their expectations satisfied. The midcareer employee problem can be resolved by applying a special scale of transition pay credits (over and above the general pay credits in the plan) to existing employees on the conversion date. A sample table for this situation is illustrated in Table 13-3.

These special pay credits will be designed to make up, in whole or in part, the loss due to conversion to the cash balance plan.

Pension Equity Plan

Basic Benefit Formula

As noted in the previous section, cash balance plans are actually a form of the indexed career average plan and thus share many of its characteristics. In particular, if designed to produce a benefit equal to that under a traditional final-pay defined benefit plan for an average employee, the cash balance plan will produce a smaller benefit for a "fast-tracker" (who has high salary growth). This is merely the phenomenon noted in Chapter 10, which discussed the defined benefit plan and benefit formulas. To deal with this issue, but to preserve other desirable features of cash balance plans, the pension equity plan (PEP), also called a "life cycle plan" by some, was invented. The PEP provides for an accrual each year of a certain percentage of final average pay that is added to an employee's account balance. At retirement, the total percentages accrued over the employee's entire career are added together and applied to final average pay to develop the total account balance. A sample plan formula is illustrated in Table 13-4.

This PEP formula produces the following benefit for our sample employee in Table 13-5. The total PEP credits are applied to the employee's final average pay. Thus after 10 years the employee has accrued an account balance equal to 110 percent (5 × 10 percent + 5 × 12 percent) of his or her final average pay, giving an account balance of

$$110\% \times \$28,280 = \$31,108.$$

After 30 years the employee has accrued an account balance equal to 390 percent (5 × 10 percent + 5 × 12 percent + 20 × 14 percent) of his or her final average pay, giving an account balance of

$$390\% \times \$75,040 = \$292,656.$$

TABLE 13-4   Sample PEP Accrual Formula

Age	Credit (%)
Under 30	7
30–34	8
35–39	10
40–44	12
45+	14

TABLE 13-5   PEP Plan Accruals

Year	Pay ($)	Final Average Pay ($)	Annual PEP Credit (%)[a]	Total PEP Credit (%)[a]	EOY Account Balance ($)[b]
1	20,000	20,000	10	10	2,000
2	21,000	20,500	10	20	4,100
3	22,100	21,033	10	30	6,310
4	23,200	21,575	10	40	8,630
5	24,400	22,140	10	50	11,070
6	25,600	23,260	12	62	14,421
7	26,900	24,440	12	75	18,086
8	28,200	25,660	12	86	22,068
9	29,600	26,940	12	98	26,401
10	31,100	28,280	12	110	31,108
11	32,700	29,700	14	124	36,828
12	34,300	31,180	14	138	43,028
13	36,000	32,740	14	152	49,765
14	37,800	34,380	14	166	57,071
15	39,700	36,100	14	180	64,980
16	41,700	37,900	14	194	73,527
17	43,800	39,800	14	208	82,784
18	46,000	41,800	14	222	92,796
19	48,300	43,900	14	236	103,604
20	50,700	46,100	14	250	115,250
21	53,200	48,400	14	264	127,776
22	55,900	50,820	14	278	141,280
23	58,700	53,360	14	292	155,811
24	61,600	56,020	14	306	171,421
25	64,700	58,820	14	320	188,224
26	67,900	61,760	14	334	206,278
27	71,300	64,840	14	348	225,643
28	74,900	68,080	14	362	246,450
29	78,600	71,480	14	376	268,765
30	82,500	75,040	14	390	292,656

[a]PEP = pension equity plan.
[b]EOY = end of year.

Note that there is not a separate interest credit, as there is in a cash balance plan. The salary growth, plus to some extent the larger annual percentage credits, compensates for the interest credit. While a cash balance plan benefit is indexed according to the interest credits, a PEP plan benefit is indexed according to increases in the participant's final average pay.

Other Features

Most other features of a pension equity plan (annuity options, development of annual credits, transition issues) will resemble those in a cash balance plan.

Floor Plans

Rather than redesigning one type of plan so that it looks like other plan types, some hybrid plans are composed of both defined benefit and defined contribution plans to try to provide participants with the best features of both plan types. Such plans, usually known as floor offset plans or floor plans, provide the defined benefit plan accrual as a minimum benefit (thus ensuring some benefit, the best feature of defined benefit plans), while giving employees the potentially positive investment performance on amounts being accumulated in a defined contribution plan.

A floor plan is actually two separate plans, with two separate funds and two separate documents. Although the benefit provided participants is combined between the two plans, all other aspects of the plans are maintained separately. The offset plan is a defined contribution plan of any type, including a 401(k) cash or deferred plan. The floor plan is a defined benefit plan that provides an umbrella benefit, a minimum or "floor" benefit, to all participants. To the extent that participants' account balances in the defined contribution plan produce a larger benefit (through positive investment results), participants can experience the benefit of the investment performance in the defined contribution plan.

The floor plan pays a benefit only if there is a shortfall in the defined contribution plan. This way, the floor plan can correct for conditions that cause inadequate retirement benefits from the defined contribution plan, such as low employer profits (which resulted in lower employer contributions to the defined contribution plan), poor investment returns of the participants' accounts, or any shortage in the defined contribution plan accumulation for the early retirement of the participant.

The defined contribution plan account must be converted into an equivalent pension benefit: the plan sponsor can use various bases for the conversion, including annuity rates, a stated actuarial equivalent basis, or actual insurance costs of purchasing an annuity contract. The method used for this conversion must be stated in the defined contribution plan.

The amount of the defined contribution account considered for purposes of the offset must reflect the growth of the participant's account due to different investment choices, prior withdrawals, or employee voluntary contributions. While an employer may limit the investment choices of participants, to the extent such choices are made, the actual growth of the account due to the performance of those investment choices must be fully reflected in the offset calculation.

Because the actual benefit delivered from the defined benefit plan depends on the participants' account balances, it is almost always necessary to create an imputed account for defined benefit actuarial valuation purposes. In addition, since the floor plan is a defined benefit plan, any benefit subsidies desired by the employer can be provided easily and automatically from the defined benefit plan.

The establishment and maintenance of a floor offset plan can provide participants with the best features of both defined benefit and defined contribution plans. The employee will get the benefit of any investment windfalls, while also accruing the guaranteed minimum retirement benefit under the defined benefit plan. However, the combination of the two plans is sometimes difficult to communicate to participants prooperly, so they will understand that the offset is part of a combined, unified plan design and does not reduce or take away any benefit that has already accrued.

floor plans can be used for a variety of purposes and thus give plan sponsors the flexibility to ensure that several otherwise mutually exclusive goals can be met. While allowing employees to reap the benefits of any windfall profits in their defined contribution accounts, a floor plan also provides minimum benefits in case of poor defined contribution plan investment experience. Furthermore, floor plan allows an employer to offer benefit subsidies at early retirement, a provision not permitted by sponsoring just a defined contribution plan.

A floor plan can also be designed as a wraparound arrangement with a defined contribution plan after plan termination, or a plan sponsor can add the defined benefit floor plan several years after sponsoring the defined contribution plan as a stand-alone operation. In addition, the defined contribution plan does not have to be a profit-sharing plan dependent upon employer contributions but can be a 401(k) plan allowing employee elective deferrals. In such an arrangement, while elective deferrals arguably create a situation in which an employee is contributing his or her own money to reduce the employer's potential defined benefit plan liability, the elected deferrals provide beneficial tax deferrals for the employee and create the potential for an investment windfall not found in the defined benefit plan.

The defined benefit floor plan's funding is subject to ERISA requirements, as with any other defined benefit plan. The anticipated defined benefit plan benefit is funded through any of the permitted actuarial cost funding methods, using regular actuarial assumptions. Special assumptions are needed to project future account balance growth in the defined contribution offset plan.

Chapter 14
Individual Retirement Plans, Simplified Employee Pensions, Tax-Sheltered Annuities, and Keogh Plans

To encourage personal thrift and to provide an opportunity for persons not participating in tax-favored retirement programs to make their own arrangements for retirement income on a tax-favored basis, the Employment Retirement Income Security Act of 1974 authorized the establishment of *individual retirement plans* with limited tax-deductible contributions. Under the original legislation, the privilege of establishing individual retirement plans was confined to persons not already participating in an employer-sponsored qualified plan or other tax-favored arrangement. Thus it could be said that the primary purpose of the legislation was to narrow or even close the existing gap in coverage of the private sector work force by tax-favored retirement programs.

Individual Retirement Plans

The Economic Recovery Tax Act (ERTA) of 1981 broadened the eligibility provisions to permit employees and self-employed individuals already covered by other retirement programs to establish individual retirement plans, and it increased the maximum annual tax-deductible contribution for one person from $1,500 to $2,000. The impetus behind the ERTA amendments was the desire to emphasize nongovernmental arrangements for the economic needs of old age and to stimulate capital formation through personal savings.

The Tax Reform Act of 1986 retreated somewhat from ERTA. All employees and self-employed individuals are still permitted to contribute to an individual retirement plan, but those who participate in a qualified plan and have incomes above certain levels may not claim a deduction for their contributions. This cutback in deductions was part of the effort to keep the Tax Reform Act from leading to a net loss of revenue while reducing tax rates. Tax-deductible saving for individuals who were already covered by qualified plans and who did not have low incomes was not considered a high-priority item.

General Features

Any employee, sole proprietor, or self-employed person can establish an individual retirement plan and contribute to it. This privilege is available to persons participating in staff retirement plans of the federal government and of state and local governments, as well as those in the private sector. The contributions may be accumulated in a trust or custodial account managed by a bank, trust company, or other eligible financial institution; or they may be deposited with a life insurer under a flexible premium individual retirement annuity.

Contributions

If penalty excise taxes are to be avoided, contributions to the plan must be limited to the maximum permissible amount. The maximum annual contribution for one person is the lesser of $2,000 or 100 percent of the individual's compensation.[1] Compensation includes earned income of self-employed individuals.[2] No contribution is allowed for the tax year in which the individual reaches the age of 70½.[3]

A married person whose spouse has no compensation or elects to be treated as having no compensation is allowed to contribute to a separate plan for his or her spouse if the couple files a joint return.[4] The combined contribution for a worker and spouse may not exceed the *lesser* of $2,250 or 100 percent of the working spouse's compensation. The total contribution can be divided between the two plans in any proportions, so long as not more than $2,000 is attributed to either one.

Although all employees and self-employed persons may contribute the amounts described above to an individual retirement plan, not all may claim a deduction for the amounts contributed. A deduction for contributions not exceeding the above limits is allowed unless (1) the individual (or the individual's spouse in the case of a married couple filing jointly) was a participant in a qualified plan at any time during the plan year ending within the individual's tax year, and (2) the adjusted gross income (AGI) of the individual for the tax year (or of the individual and spouse if filing jointly) exceeds the "applicable dollar amount." The applicable dollar amount is $40,000 for married couples filing jointly, $0 for married individuals filing separately, and $25,000 for unmarried individuals. If the excess of the adjusted gross income over the applicable dollar amount is less than $10,000, individuals (or couples filing jointly) may still claim a deduction of a fraction of the allowable contribution. For example, a single person with an adjusted gross income of $28,000 ($3,000 over the $25,000 applicable amount) could still deduct up to $1,400 (70 percent of the $2,000 limit). Thus no deduction is allowed for plan participants if the adjusted gross income exceeds $50,000 in the case of married couples filing jointly, $10,000 in the case of married individuals filing separately, or $35,000 in the case of unmarried individuals.

An individual can claim a tax deduction for a particular tax year if the contribution is made by the due date (including extensions) for that year's tax return, whether or not the plan was established before the end of the year.

[1] IRC §§219(b)(1), 408(o).
[2] IRC §219(f).
[3] IRC §219(d)(1).
[4] IRC §219(c).

Certain amounts distributed from qualified pension and profit-sharing plans (or other individual retirement plans) may be contributed (rolled over) to an individual retirement plan (see Chapter 7 for information on rollover from qualified plans). Such rollover contributions are not limited to $2,000.[5] Nor do they reduce or eliminate the allowable deduction for a regular contribution to the plan for the year of the rollover. No deduction is allowed for a rollover contribution since it is a tax-free transfer.[6]

An employer may contribute to an individual retirement plan for an employee, in which event the amount paid is treated as compensation of the employee. The employee, however, may take a deduction as if he or she had contributed the amount directly.[7]

If an individual's contribution (other than a rollover contribution) to an individual retirement plan exceeds the allowable amount, a nondeductible excise tax of 6 percent is imposed on the excess contribution.[8] The excise tax is not imposed, however, if the excess contribution, together with the net income attributable to it, is returned to the individual by the funding agency before the tax-filing date (including extensions), and only the net income paid is taxable income.[9] The excise tax on an excess contribution is levied for each year that it remains in the plan. To avoid continuing excise taxes, the individual must either withdraw the excess contribution or offset it against contributions that could otherwise be made in future years.

Investment Earnings

The investment earnings of an individual retirement plan, except for unrelated business income, are fully exempt from federal income taxation while held in the plan.[10] The earnings are taxed as ordinary income without benefit of the special five-year forward averaging rule upon distribution to the individual, unless they are a part of a tax-free rollover to another plan.

Timing of Distributions

Since Congress intended that individual retirement plans be used to provide income support in old age, it introduced tax penalties for distributions made outside a corridor bounded at the lower end by age 59½ and at the upper end by age 70½, except in the case of death or disability. A distribution prior to age 59½, except in the case of death or disability, is termed an *early distribution* and is subject to a nondeductible excise tax of 10 percent.[11] On the other hand, under minimum distribution requirements, distributions from the plan must not be delayed beyond

---

[5]IRC §408(a)(1).
[6]IRC §219(d)(2).
[7]IRC §219(f)(5). Deductions for employer payments to SEPs are dealt with in the section "Contributions" in this chapter.
[8]IRC §4973.
[9]IRC §408(d)(4).
[10]IRC §408(e).
[11]IRC §72(p).

April 1 following the calendar year in which the individual reaches age 70½. Early distributions and the minimum distribution requirements are discussed further in Chapter 7.

If the individual (or the surviving spouse) dies before receiving the entire interest in the plan, the remaining interest must be distributed to his or her (or the surviving spouse's) beneficiaries within five years after death.[12] However, if benefit payments are payable to a designated beneficiary, payments may be made over the lifetime or the life expectancy of the designated beneficiary.

Types of Plans

In terms of the funding instruments that may be used, individual retirement plans consist of two types: the individual retirement account and the individual retirement annuity. An individual retirement plan is commonly called an IRA, regardless of which of the two approaches to funding is used. The Code[13] describes with some specificity the characteristics that must be associated with each major type of funding instrument if it is to qualify as a receptacle for IRA contributions. These requirements are intended to implement the broad purposes of the program and effectuate the various restrictions outlined above. It should be noted, in particular, that the sponsor of each type of instrument is put on notice not to accept any contribution that is not permissible under the applicable rules.

Individual Retirement Account

An individual retirement account is a domestic trust or custodial account created by a written instrument for the exclusive benefit of an individual or his or her beneficiaries. Only banks and other financial institutions falling within the scope of applicable regulations are permitted to offer and operate such an account.[14] In practice, commercial banks, trust companies, mutual savings banks, federally insured credit unions, savings and loan associations, broker-dealers, mutual funds, and life insurance companies sponsor and vigorously promote IRAs. Many of these institutions have developed one or more prototype IRAs and have obtained IRS approval of the documents employed in the establishment and operation of the prototype accounts.

To meet the requirements of existing law and regulations, the legal instrument creating an IRA trust or custodial account must stipulate that

- Except for rollover contributions and simplified employee pensions (SEPs), only cash contributions will be accepted and no more than $2,000 will be accepted on behalf of any one individual in any given tax year of the individual.
- The assets of the account will not be commingled with other property, except in an approved common trust fund or common investment fund.
- None of the account assets will be invested in life insurance contracts.

[12]IRC §401(a)(9).
[13]IRC §7701(a)(37).
[14]Treas. Reg. 1.408-2(b)(2)(ii).

- An individual's interest in his or her account balance is nonforfeitable.
- Distributions must begin by April 1 following the year the individual attains age 70½ and must satisfy the minimum distribution requirements.

An individual retirement account may generally be invested in any type of asset. However, any investment in collectibles (art works, stamps, rugs, antiques, certain coins, and other types of tangible property) is treated as a taxable distribution and thus is prevented for all intents and purposes.[15] The fiduciary statutes of some states also may constrain investments.

Individual retirement plans are subject to the same rules and penalties for prohibited transactions that apply to qualified pension plans. These are designed to prevent self-dealing by "disqualified persons" who exercise control over the individual retirement plan. The trustee cannot make a loan from the IRA to the individual for whose benefit it is maintained. If an individual violates this prohibition and borrows money from his or her account, it will cease to be an IRA from the first day of the taxable year in which the loan was made. Disqualification of the account triggers a *constructive* distribution to the individual equal to the fair market value of all the assets of the account as of the first day of such taxable year. The constructive distribution is considered taxable income and is taxed as ordinary income. The prohibited transactions excise tax will not be imposed, but a 10 percent penalty tax will be assessed on the constructive distribution if the individual is not disabled or is not 59½ on the first day of such taxable year. If an IRA is part of any type of employer-sponsored pension plan, it is subject to ERISA's fiduciary standards.

Despite the general absence of restrictions on the investment of IRA assets, as a practical matter the small size of most IRAs militates against certain types of investments. Most IRA assets are invested in certificates of deposits or in passbook savings accounts of commercial banks, mutual savings banks, and savings and loan associations. A considerable sum is invested in mutual fund shares, including those of growth stock funds, income stock funds, balanced funds, and money market funds. Some individuals establish custodial accounts and direct the investment of their own accounts within the usual range of marketable securities.

Individual Retirement Annuity

The second instrument that can be used to fund an individual retirement plan is an individual retirement annuity. Such an annuity is purchased directly from a life insurance company and does not involve a trust or custodial account.

The following restrictions apply to an annuity used for this purpose:[16]

- The contract must not be transferable by the owner.
- The premiums must be flexible, not fixed.
- Dividends must be applied to pay future premiums or to purchase additional benefits, rather than being distributed in cash.
- The entire interest of the owner must be nonforfeitable.

---

[15]IRC §408(m).
[16]IRC §408(b).

- The insurer must not accept more than $2,000 in annual premiums, except for SEP-IRAs.
- Distributions must be made within the same period as for an individual retirement account.

The owner's interest in the annuity may be distributed as a lump-sum payment, through installments over a period of years, in a single life annuity on the life of the owner, or in a joint and survivor annuity on the lives of the owner and his or her spouse. The owner cannot borrow on the annuity or use it as collateral for a loan. These would be prohibited transactions that would cause the fair market value of the contract to be taxed to the individual as ordinary income on the first day of the year in which the transaction occurred. There would also be a penalty tax of 10 percent on the constructive distribution if the individual was not disabled or was not 59½ or older.

Rollover Contributions

Amounts distributed from qualified pension and profit-sharing plans are ordinarily taxable when distributed.[17] But if an individual receives a "eligible rollover distribution" from a qualified plan and transfers part or all of the amount to an IRA within 60 days of receipt, the amount rolled over is excluded from that individual's gross income.[18] Requirements for such rollovers are described in Chapter 7.

IRA-to-IRA tax-free rollovers are also allowed, if the entire amount received from an IRA is rolled over into another IRA within 60 days.[19] Such a tax-free rollover, however, may be made only once in any 365-day period.

Except as noted, any amount distributed from an IRA is taxable as ordinary income to the payee.[20] The amount received in excess of the individual's tax basis is included in gross income. A lump-sum distribution from an IRA is not entitled to the special five-year forward averaging rule.

If an IRA consists entirely of contributions that were rollover contributions from a qualified plan, and if the entire amount is distributed from the IRA and rolled over into another qualified plan within 60 days, the amount rolled over is excluded from gross income. Rollovers from and to tax-deferred annuities receive the same treatment.

The transfer of an individual's interest in an IRA to a former spouse, incident to a divorce, is not a taxable transfer. The former spouse will pay no tax until he or she receives a distribution from the IRA.[21]

Payroll Deduction IRAs

In 1982 IRAs first became available to employees who are participants in qualified plans. A number of employers decided to offer a payroll deduction facility for

[17]IRC §§402(a)(1), 403(a)(1).
[18]IRC §§402(a)(5), 403(a)(4).
[19]IRC §408(d)(3).
[20]IRC §408(d).
[21]IRC §408(d)(6).

employees to contribute to IRAs, both as a service to employees and to encourage thrift. Some employers who provide payroll deductions for IRAs allow the employee to designate any bank, insurance company, mutual fund, or other entity sponsoring an IRA to receive the withheld sums. Other employers limit the choice to a single funding medium or to a very limited number.

Allowing the choice of any funding medium gives the employee the ultimate flexibility to choose an IRA to fit his or her own desires and needs. It does not, of course, guarantee a good choice. Allowing complete freedom increases the amount of administrative work. Limiting the choice to a single funding medium, or to a few that the employer has carefully selected, does not necessarily result in favorable investment experience. If the experience is unfavorable, the employee may blame the employer.

By the time many employers considered the question, most employees who were interested in IRAs had already made their own arrangements. In any event, all employees are free to arrange for their own IRAs without the assistance of the employer. For these reasons, and because of the administrative expense and the disadvantages of each of the two possible approaches, most employers have not offered payroll deduction for IRAs.

Simplified Employee Pensions (SEPs)

Many small employers have been discouraged from establishing a qualified plan because of the expense and administrative burden involved in developing plan documents, obtaining IRS approval, and preparing summary plan descriptions, annual reports for regulatory agencies, and summary annual reports for participants. To encourage small employers to establish pension plans for their employees and reduce the gap in coverage of the private sector labor force, Congress made provision for a simplified form of employer-sponsored pension plan, called logically enough, *simplified employee pensions*. Since a SEP is essentially an arrangement under which an employer can establish and finance an IRA for each of its eligible employees, this approach is often referred to as a SEP-IRA. Not only does a SEP avoid the expense and complexity of a qualified plan, it permits the owner of a small business to set aside more money for herself on a tax-deferred basis than she could under a regular IRA. Since in the absence of restrictions the arrangement would lend itself to discrimination in favor of the owner and a few favored employees, a SEP must meet certain requirements designed to prevent such discrimination.

Participation

If a principal owner or self-employed employer contributes to a SEP for himself or any one employee in a given year, he must contribute on behalf of every employee who has attained age 21 and has worked for the employer during at least three of the preceding five years.[22] However, no contributions are required for employees

---

[22]IRC §408(k)(2).

covered under a collective bargaining agreement, if good faith bargaining occurred over retirement benefits.

The employer may choose the funding instrument and agency for the individual IRAs or may permit each employee to choose his or her own IRA or type of IRA. If the employer selects, recommends, or otherwise influences employees to choose a particular IRA or type of IRA, and that IRA imposes any restrictions on withdrawals (e.g., a penalty for early withdrawal other than the penalty assessed by the IRS), the plan administrator must, once a year, provide each employee with a clear explanation of the restrictions and a statement that other IRAs may not have such restrictions.

Contributions

The employer's contributions to a SEP are based on the participants' compensation. Employers need not commit themselves to contribute to the plan every year, nor must they commit themselves in advance to contribute a specified percentage of compensation. The governing document for the SEP must contain a formula for allocating the aggregate employer contributions to the various employee accounts.[23] The maximum amount that an employer can contribute to a SEP for an employee in any one tax year is the lesser of $30,000 or 15 percent of covered compensation.[24] The deduction for contributions to SEPs reduces the employer's maximum deduction for other tax-qualified plans.[25] Employer contributions to a SEP are viewed as contributions to a defined contribution plan and are aggregated with employer contributions made on behalf of an employee to any other defined contribution plan in computing the amount that can be added annually to the employee's account (the lesser of 25 percent of compensation or $30,000).[26]

Employer contributions to a SEP are not subject to Social Security Federal Insurance Contributions Act (FICA) taxes and unemployment (FUTA) taxes if the employer has reason to believe that the employee will be entitled to deduct the employer contributions under the SEP rules.[27] Similarly, no federal income tax need be withheld by the employer for payments to an employee's SEP.[28]

Employer contributions generally will be deemed discriminatory unless they bear a uniform relationship to the first $200,000 of each individual's compensation.[29] However, a SEP may be integrated with Social Security if the employer does not maintain another integrated tax-qualified plan. Integration of a SEP with Social Security is subject to the same integration rules that apply to qualified defined contribution plans.

SEP contributions on behalf of any one individual may not exceed $30,000. This limit will be subject to upward adjustment on the same basis as for qualified defined contribution plans. As in the case of qualified defined contribution plans, the limit

[23]IRC §408(k)(5).
[24]IRC §402(h).
[25]IRC §404(h).
[26]IRC §415(e)(5).
[27]IRC §§3121(a)(5), 3306(b)(5).
[28]IRC §3401(a)(12); Treas. Reg. 31.3401(a)(12)-1(d).
[29]IRC §408(k)(3).

may make SEPs more attractive to a small employer than a qualified plan. Employer contributions to a SEP are included in the employee's taxable compensation but are deductible in full by the employee.[30] The maximum employer contribution allowed as a deduction by an employee is the lesser of $30,000 or 15 percent of compensation.[31] This limit is in addition to the $2,000 deduction that an employee may take for an IRA maintained outside the SEP arrangement. There is no deduction for employer contributions on behalf of an employee's spouse.

Elective Contributions

A SEP may allow elective salary reduction contributions by employees, similar to elective contributions under a 401(k) plan.[32] Employees may elect to have the employer reduce their compensation otherwise payable and contribute the amount to a SEP. These elective deferrals are excluded from the employees' taxable income. They are subject to the same limit as elective deferrals under a 401(k) plan. In addition, the elective deferrals plus any other employer contributions under a SEP are subject to the regular SEP limitation of the lesser of $30,000 or 15 percent of compensation.

Elective deferrals are not permissible under a SEP unless the employer had 25 or fewer employees throughout the preceding year and unless at least 50 percent of the employees of the employer elect to make salary deferrals. The elective deferral percentage of each highly compensated employee cannot exceed 125 percent of the average deferral percentage of all non–highly compensated employees. Elective deferrals are not permitted for employees of governmental employers or of tax-exempt organizations.

Withdrawals

Like a regular IRA, an individual's SEP account is fully vested from the beginning. The employer cannot impose any restrictions on withdrawals from the account at any time. The funding agency (i.e., the financial institution sponsoring the IRAs purchased under the plan) may, however, impose penalties for early withdrawal. Moreover, withdrawals from an employee's account before he or she has reached age 59½ are subject to a nondeductible federal excise tax, unless the withdrawal was a consequence of the employee's death or disability or unless rolled over to another IRA. As with a conventional IRA, there is also a penalty tax for failure to commence distributions by April 1 following the year age 70½ has been reached and for insufficient distributions thereafter.

IRS Form 5305-SEP

In an effort to help employers establish a SEP with minimum expense and trouble, the Internal Revenue Service has developed a form, designated Form 5305-SEP

---

[30]IRC §219(f)(5).
[31]IRC §219(b)(2).
[32]IRC §408(k)(6).

and called the Simplified Employee Pension—Individual Retirement Accounts Contribution Agreement. By using this form, an employer can be assured that the form of its contribution agreement is in compliance with IRS requirements. All eligible employees must participate in the SEP established by that form. That form may not be used if the employer currently maintains any other qualified plan. Form 5305-SEP is not submitted to the IRS. The IRS will not issue an advance determination of compliance on the basis of Form 5305-SEP, but none is needed. Form 5305A-SEP is the comparable form used when the plan has a salary reduction feature. At the time of this writing, neither form can be used if employer contributions are to be integrated with Social Security.

A request can be filed with the IRS by sponsoring banks, federally insured credit unions, insurance companies, regulated investment companies, or trade or professional societies or associations wanting to obtain an opinion letter that a proposed prototype SEP agreement, which is to be used by more than one employer, is acceptable in form. An employer may, of course, develop and obtain IRS approval of its own SEP agreement.

Reporting

Simplified reporting requirements apply to employers using model Form 5305-SEP.[33] At the time an employee becomes eligible to participate, the administrator (generally the employer) must provide a copy of the completed and unmodified Form 5305-SEP. At the end of each calendar year, the administrator must provide each participant with a written notice of the amount of employer contributions allocated to his or her account. If an employer does not use model Form 5305-SEP, the reporting requirements are much more rigorous.[34]

Voluntary Employee Contributions

Employee contributions to qualified plans may be classified as *mandatory* or *voluntary*. The Internal Revenue Service considers contributions to be mandatory if they are required as a condition of employment, as a condition of participation in the plan, or as a condition for obtaining benefits attributable to employer contributions.[35] All other employee contributions are classified as voluntary. The code treats elective contributions under cash or deferred arrangements, even if they result from salary reduction, as *employer* contributions rather than as *employee* contributions.

Many defined contribution plans make provision for voluntary employee contributions. These include contributory plans that allow voluntary contributions in addition to mandatory contributions and "noncontributory" plans that allow only voluntary contributions. Some defined benefit plans also allow voluntary employee contributions.

[33]29 CFR 2520.104-48.
[34]29 CFR 2520.104-49.
[35]Treas. Reg. 1.411(c)-1(c)(4).

If voluntary employee contributions are included in a defined benefit plan, the voluntary employee contributions are treated as if they were made to a defined contribution plan.[36] For purposes of determining account balances, the assets must be valued at least annually on a market basis. This adds a type of recordkeeping not otherwise present in a defined benefit plan and is one reason for not allowing voluntary employee contributions in a defined benefit plan.

Voluntary employee contributions receive the same tax treatment as mandatory employee contributions. Such contributions are made with after-tax dollars and are not tax deductible. Even though voluntary employee contributions receive no tax benefit at the time of contribution, they enable the participant to invest on a tax-deferred basis, which means the resulting income is not taxable until distribution. Upon distribution, the investment return earned may be subject to favorable taxation as part of a lump-sum distribution or may be eligible for a tax-free rollover to an IRA.

In most plans that have allowed voluntary employee contributions, few participants have used them. One current reason for the low use of voluntary employee contributions is the competition for savings dollars from tax-deductible IRAs and tax-excludable elective contributions under 401(k) plans, as well as from non-qualified investments, some of which have attractive tax advantages.

For plan years beginning after 1986, voluntary employee contributions under both defined benefit plans and defined contribution plans are subject to contribution percentage requirements under the nondiscrimination tests for employer-matching contributions and employee contributions. These requirements were described in Chapter 12. Because highly compensated employees tend to make much higher voluntary contributions than other employees, these tests are difficult to satisfy if voluntary contributions are allowed under the plan. The problems posed by the percentage tests, the work and expense of administration and communication of voluntary employee contributions, the low rate of utilization by employees, and the availability of investment alternatives have led many employers to conclude that they should not allow traditional voluntary employee contributions.

Tax-Sheltered Annuities

Another retirement savings vehicle is a tax-sheltered annuity, also referred to as a 403(b) annuity after the section of the Internal Revenue Code that regulates it. Tax-sheltered annuities are purchased by public school systems and certain tax-exempt organizations for their employees. While such employers are not concerned with deducting the contribution to the plan, since the employer is exempt from taxation anyway, the contribution and any earnings on the contribution are not taxable to the employee until actually received. Since tax-exempt employers normally would have less interest in the various administrative burdens that accompany establishing a qualified retirement plan, tax-sheltered annuities allow such employers to reduce the administrative requirements of sponsoring retirement savings plans for their employees while still offering them compensation deferral for retirement purposes and the security of a funded retirement plan.

[36]ERISA §204(c)(4); IRC §411(d)(5).

Not every tax-exempt employer can sponsor a tax-sheltered annuity. The only ones to quality are tax-exempt entities organized and operated for religious, charitable, scientific, testing for public safety, literary, or educational purposes.[37] The only type of government operation or facility that qualifies for tax-sheltered annuities is the public school system. This can lead to perceived inequities. For example, publicly owned and operated hospitals may not qualify to sponsor tax-sheltered annuities unless they are affiliated with a public school system, but private tax-exempt hospitals (which generally are exempt from tax as either a religious or charitable organization) can sponsor tax-sheltered annuities.

General Features

In order to receive favorable tax treatment, tax-sheltered annuities must satisfy essentially the same nondiscrimination, coverage, and participation rules that apply to qualified plans. These rules did not apply to tax-sheltered annuities until the Tax Reform Act of 1986. The IRS has indicated that employers can use a reasonable, good faith interpretation of these requirements, instead of following the regulations, until further guidance is released, in order to consider and potentially accommodate the wide variety of tax-sheltered annuity designs that originated under the prior regulatory regime.

Certain employees can be excluded when testing the tax-sheltered annuity for nondiscrimination and coverage, just as certain employees can be excluded when testing a qualified plan, but the employees excludable under the tax-sheltered annuity rules are different. Employees participating in an eligible deferred compensation plan[38] or a 401(k) cash or deferred plan are excluded, as are students working for a university or college and employees who normally work less than 20 hours per week. Nonresident aliens, who are excludable when testing qualified plans, are likewise excludable when testing tax-sheltered annuities.[39]

Salary Reductions

Some tax-sheltered annuities allow participants to defer an amount from their salary into the annuity or account. The maximum amount of elective deferrals an individual may make to a tax-sheltered annuity in a year is $9,500. The maximum amount will increase with the dollar limit for elective deferrals to a section 401(k) plan, when the cost-of-living adjustment for that limit reaches the $9,500 limit.

Distributions of employer contributions from a custodial account cannot occur before the employee dies, attains age 59½, separates from service, or becomes disabled. Distributions of employee contributions to a custodial account are permitted before one of those events occurs if the employee has a financial hardship. Distributions from a tax-sheltered annuity may be made because of the employee's death, disability, separation from service, attainment of age 59½, or financial

---

[37]IRC §501(c)(3).
[38]For government and tax-exempt employers, there are limits on the amount of nonqualified deferred compensation payable to employees. Plans meeting these limits, which are contained in § 457 of the Code, are called eligible deferred compensation plans.
[39]IRC §403(b)(12)(A).

hardship.[40] However, income attributable to employee contributions under a salary reduction agreement may not be provided upon hardship.

Employees are not permitted to make more than one salary reduction agreement with the same employer during any taxable year. However, the salary reduction agreement may be expressed as a percentage of compensation rather than a fixed dollar amount. Thus while the percentage cannot be changed for the rest of the year, the dollar amount actually contributed may change owing to changes in compensation.[41] In addition, a salary reduction agreement is said to continue in place into the next taxable year instead of being considered a new agreement at the start of each year. Therefore the employee can change the agreement during the middle of subsequent years.

The nondiscrimination test for elective deferrals to a section 401(k) plan is not required for salary reduction contributions to a tax-sheltered annuity, though the nondiscrimination test for matching contributions does apply to tax-sheltered annuities. The same employees who can be excluded when testing the tax-sheltered annuity for coverage and nondiscrimination can be excluded from deferring.[42] The employer can require employees to make at least a $200 deferral.

Exclusion Allowance

Employer contributions to a tax-sheltered annuity or custodial contract are excludable from the employee's income only to the extent of his or her "exclusion allowance." The exclusion allowance is generally the excess of an amount, determined by multiplying 20 percent of annual includable compensation by the employee's years of service, over the total of excludable employer contributions in all prior years.[43] As an additional limit, employer contributions to a tax-sheltered annuity generally may not exceed the lesser of 25 percent of compensation or $30,000 annually.

If a participant's interest in a tax-sheltered annuity changes from nonvested to substantially vested during a tax year of the participant, such amount is treated as a contribution made by the employer during that year.[44] For this reason, tax-sheltered annuities do not generally use vesting schedules or cliff vesting. Instead, they normally rely on immediate vesting. Since the exclusion allowance pertains to the full amount vested in one year rather than the amounts actually contributed during the current year and prior years, it is easier to exceed the exclusion allowance in a plan that does not use immediate vesting. Plans with immediate vesting merely consider the contribution each year under the exclusion allowance, without taking into account prior year's contributions.

ERISA Status

Tax-sheltered annuities are subject to the same ERISA requirements as qualified deferred compensation plans, unless the tax-sheltered annuity is exempt from

[40]IRC §§403(b)(7)(A)(ii); 403(b)(11).
[41]Rev. Rul. 68-58, 68-1 C.B. 176.
[42]IRC §403(b)(12)(A)(ii).
[43]IRC 403(b)(2).
[44]Treas. Reg. 1.403(c)-1.

ERISA. While the general exemption from ERISA for plans sponsored by governmental employers excludes a significant portion of tax-sheltered annuities, another provision excludes a substantial number of tax-sheltered annuities
sponsored by private employers.

Because of the unique nature of a tax-sheltered annuity program—the retirement asset is owned by the employee and not the employer—it might be argued
that this is not a retirement program established and maintained by the employer.
Plans in which the only contributions are based on salary reduction agreements
and the employer essentially serves as a mere conduit for the employee's contributions to the various annuity contractors are not considered to be established and
maintained by an employer and therefore are not governed by ERISA.[45]

Keogh Plans

A Keogh plan is simply a tax-qualified retirement plan for an individual earning
income from self-employment activities, such as income from a business owned by
the individual as a sole proprietor or with a partner. Though most such plans are
currently subject to the same rules as a corporate-maintained retirement plan, that
has not always been the case.

Prior to 1962, only employees could participate and benefit in retirement plans.
Since sole proprietors and partners are not considered "employees" under the tax
law, they could not participate in or benefit from a pension or profit-sharing plan,
even if they sponsored a plan for their employees. The Self-Employed Individuals
Retirement Act of 1962, which created Keogh plans,[46] changed that by permitting
the coverage of self-employed individuals, but with substantially more severe limits
than those imposed on corporate employer-sponsored plans. For example,
contributions for self-employed individuals was limited to $2,500 even though
there was no limit on contributions to corporate plans until the passage of ERISA.
One result of this disparate treatment was that many self-employed individuals,
especially professional service providers, incorporated themselves in order to take
advantage of the greater benefits available for corporate-sponsored retirement
plans.

Parity between self-employed and corporate plans was enacted by the Tax Equity
and Fiscal Responsibility Act of 1982 (TEFRA), which eliminated almost all the
distinctions between plans sponsored by the two different types of employers.
Deductions for contributions and the limits on contributions and benefits are now
the same for self-employed plans as they are for corporate plans. In addition, the
coverage of employees under a Keogh plan and the benefits or contributions
provided by such plan are subject to the same nondiscrimination standards as
other plans. Currently, when the law has specific limits or restrictions for participants who have a proprietary interest in the employer, it does so without regard to
whether the owners are shareholders, sole proprietors, or partners.

---

[44]DOL Reg. 2510.3-2(f).

[46]This legislation, also known as SEIRA, was assigned the bill number H.R. 10 and was sponsored by
Representative Eugene Keogh of New York. As a result, in retirement plans sponsored by self-
employed individuals are often referred to as "H.R.10 plans" or "Keogh plans."

ERISA Status

While Keogh plans are now subject to the same qualification requirements under the tax code as corporate plans and the self-employed individual sponsoring the plan is generally treated as an employee for the various limits and restrictions for qualified plans, the self-employed individual is still not considered an employee under ERISA. A Keogh plan that covers only the self-employed individual sponsoring the plan is therefore an employee benefit plan that does not cover employees.

Since ERISA was enacted in order to protect the rights of employees in employee benefit plans, the lack of employees excludes many Keogh plans from the requirements of ERISA.[47] Under ERISA, the spouse of the self-employed individual is not considered an employee either, even if the spouse does not have an ownership interest in the business.[48] If it were to cover one other employee, however, the plan would become subject to ERISA.[49]

Without the application of ERISA, the fiduciary responsibility, reporting, and disclosure rules do not apply. Since in order to obtain tax-qualified status the plan must meet the participation, vesting, and funding rules, some of the restrictions of ERISA will apply to the plan via the tax code if tax-qualified status is sought for the plan. While many plan sponsors might think they would enjoy escaping ERISA's requirements, the exemption from ERISA also means that the trustees or custodians handling the plan assets are not subject to the fiduciary standards of ERISA. Thus the self-employed individual cannot make a claim against the trustee for a breach of fiduciary duty under ERISA.[50] Of course, virtually every state has standards for trustees, but they generally do not rise to the standard of care required under ERISA.

Another consequence of not being considered an employee under ERISA has to do with prohibited transaction rules. As discussed in more detail in Chapter 3, ERISA prohibits certain transactions between a plan and certain parties related to the plan.[51] However, the description of the transactions prohibited are so broad that virtually any contact between a plan and a participant could be viewed as prohibited under ERISA. So several exceptions are also specified for standard transactions between a plan and an employee covered under the plan.[52] Probably the most notable transaction that is permitted between a plan and an employee but is prohibited between a plan and a self-employed individual sponsoring a plan is a loan from the plan to the individual secured by an interest in the participant's account balance.[53] For plans featuring participant loans, usually section 401(k) plans, this inability to take plan loan secured by the participant's account balance substantially restricts the self-employed individual's access to the account balance, even if only as a loan.

---

[47]DOL Reg. 2510.3-3(b).
[48]DOL Reg. 2510.3-3(c)(1).
[49]ERISA Opinion Letter no. 74-01.
[50]*Schwartz v. Gordon*, 761 F2d 864 (2d Cir. 1985).
[51]ERISA §406.
[52]ERISA §408.
[53]ERISA §§408(b)(3), 408(d).

Deduction Limits

One of the few areas of the tax code that affords Keogh plans different treatment is the deduction rules, but the differences generally relate to the differences between self-employment income (or earned income) and wages. A self-employed person can contribute up to the lesser of $30,000 or 25 percent of his or her compensation to a defined contribution plan. The amount of the contribution that can be claimed as a deduction depends on the type of Keogh plan. If the plan is a money purchase plan, the deduction is limited to 25 percent of compensation; if the plan is a profit-sharing plan, the deduction is limited to 15 percent of compensation. These contribution and deduction limits are the same for corporate plans.

For Keogh plans, compensation is defined as net self-employment earnings less deductions for contributions to the retirement plan and one-half of the self-employment tax paid by the individual. This adds complexity to the determination of the limits, since the contribution itself must be subtracted from the individual's earnings in order to arrive at the base for determining the limit. Accordingly, most benefits professionals use a "rule of thumb" for determining the limit.

To determine 25 percent of self-employment earnings less Keogh plan contributions, which is both the limit on contributions to any defined contribution plan and the deduction limit for money purchase pensions, 20 percent of net self-employmentincome without reduction suffices. Deductions to a Keogh profit-sharing plan is generally limited to 15 percent of self-employment earnings, or 13.0435 percent of net self-employment income. Of course, the contribution to the Keogh plan also reduces the individual's self-employment earnings for SECA taxes.

Other Forms of Retirement Savings

There are a number of other employer-sponsored programs that may serve to build retirement savings. Most of them fall outside the scope of this book and are not discussed here. These programs are listed below, with the Internal Revenue Code reference, where applicable.

1. Deferred compensation plans with respect to service for state and local governments and tax-exempt employers (Code §457)
2. Incentive stock options (Code §422A)
3. Employee stock purchase plans (Code §423)
4. Nonqualified stock options
5. Nonqualified stock purchase agreements
6. Excess benefit plans to provide benefits in excess of those allowed under Code section 415 (ERISA §3(36))
7. Shadow stock plans
8. Other nonqualified plans and deferred compensation agreements.

Chapter 15
Integration of Pension Plans with Social Security

A well-designed pension plan will often take into account the contributions or benefits under the federal Old Age, Survivor's, and Disability Insurance program, described in Chapter 1. Employers, employees, and self-employed individuals all pay taxes under the Federal Insurance Contributions Act (FICA) to fund the OASDI program and the Hospital Insurance program.[1] The taxes are a percentage of pay based on compensation up to the taxable wage base, which was $62,700 in 1996. The basic Social Security benefit, the so-called primary insurance amount (PIA), is based upon the average indexed monthly earnings (AIME), which is an average of earnings not exceeding the taxable wage base for certain past years, indexed to reflect increases in average wages and inflation. The PIA is computed by applying a higher percentage to the first portion of the worker's average indexed monthly earnings than to later portions. The average indexed monthly earnings are divided into three segments, and a downward sloping scale of percentages is applied to the three segments. In 1996 the PIA was 90 percent of the first $437 of AIME, 32 percent of the next $2,635, and 15 percent of any excess.[2] Earnings above the taxable wage base are excluded in determining the AIME and the PIA.

Purpose of Integration

The general objective of some employers will be to provide combined benefits (Social Security plus the employer's plan benefits) that constitute approximately the same percentage of the employee's disposable income irrespective of his or her position on the pay scale. In other words, the goal is for higher-paid employees to enjoy a retirement income from Social Security and the pension plan that amounts to about the same percentage of their disposable income as lower-paid employees receive. The objective of other employers may be to make the combined employer contributions for Social Security and the plan about the same percentage of pay for all levels of employees.

---

[1]The Federal Insurance Contribution Act is contained in IRC §§3101–3127. Taxation of self-employment income is contained in IRC §§1401–1403.
[2]The bend points and the taxable wage base are subject to upward revision annually in accordance with movements in the general level of earnings.

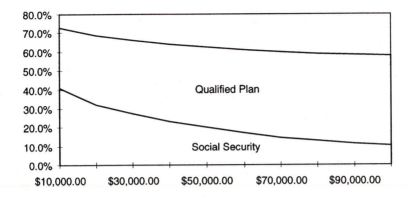

Figure 15-1. Sample of benefits under model integrated pension plan. Source: Authors' calculation.

Contributions and benefits under the OASDI program are both more heavily weighted toward lower-paid workers. The integration of pension plans with Social Security offsets this weighting by having contributions or benefits under the pension plan more heavily weighted toward the higher-paid employees, as a tactic to achieve the objectives described above.

This approach to plan design not only serves the plan sponsor's concept of equitable treatment of participants at all income levels but in operation it reduces the cost of the plan, offsetting to some extent the Social Security taxes the employer pays for participants. When a plan's benefit or contribution formula is set up to achieve these objectives, the plan is said to be integrated with Social Security.[3]

Figure 15-1 shows the interaction of benefits from Social Security and from the final average pay PIA offset plan for employees hired at age 30 and retiring at age 65 over a range of salary levels. At the lowest salary level, 41 percent of final earnings is replaced by Social Security and 32 percent is replaced by the qualified retirement plan. At the highest salary level, 10 percent of income is replaced by Social Security benefits and 48 percent is replaced by the qualified retirement plan. The combined replacement rates from both plans are not precisely uniform along all compensation levels, ranging from a 73 percent replacement ratio at the lowest salary level to a 58 percent replacement ratio at the highest. Although the combined retirement income benefit from both plans is not exactly uniform along all compensation ranges, the integration of the qualified plan with the Social Security benefits goes a long way toward equalizing the treatment of employees across all salary ranges. This offset plan design reduces the benefit variation from 31 percent of final average earnings for Social Security benefits alone at the lowest salary level to 15 percent of final average earnings for the combined benefit at the highest salary level.

---

[3]"Correlation" is perhaps a more descriptive term for the concept and process, but the word "integration" is too deeply embedded in pension literature and regulatory language to change the terminology. As noted below, however, the nomenclature is already changing, with Congress and the IRS adopting "permitted disparity" as the new term.

Underlying Concepts of Regulatory Requirements

As indicated above, integration means weighting pension plan benefits and contributions in favor of highly compensated employees. If there were no limitations on this weighting contributions and benefits could discriminate in favor of the highly compensated and private pension plans could provide little or no benefits for the low-paid. Provisions of the Internal Revenue Code are designed to prevent these two consequences.

Integration must strictly conform with applicable statutory requirements. The Tax Reform Act of 1986 (TRA86) substantially changed these requirements.[4] In general, the new requirements, which form the basis of the discussion in this chapter, apply to benefits accruing for plan years beginning after 1988.[5] Earlier requirements can be found in the apropriate IRS revenue rulings.[6]

One purpose of the requirements, both before and after the Tax Reform Act, has been to ensure that the combined benefits or contributions of the pension plan and the portion of Social Security funded by employer taxes will not constitute a higher percentage of compensation among the more highly paid employees than among the less-favored employees. This is accomplished by limiting the "permitted disparity"[7] (i.e., the amount of disparity, in the form of an offset to a participant's accrual or an excess accrual rate, which is permitted by the Code) between contributions or benefits for the high paid and those for the low paid.

A second new purpose under the Tax Reform Act is to prevent plans from providing little or no contributions or benefits for the low-paid. A related purpose is to provide incentives to increase the contributions or benefits for the low-paid.

General Approaches to Integration

There are three general approaches to integrating plan contributions or benefits with Social Security. For defined contribution plans, employer contributions are integrated with employer FICA taxes for retirement benefits. For defined benefit plans, two approaches to integration are available: the excess plan approach and the offset approach. Under an excess plan approach one layer of benefits is based upon all compensation and a second layer of benefits is added for compensation in excess of a specified dollar amount called the "integration level." Under an offset plan the benefit is first calculated on the basis of total compensation, and then an "offset" is deducted to reflect the fact that Social Security benefits are payable.

Additionally, there are two different methodologies that a plan can use to integrate benefits or contributions with Social Security for nondiscrimination testing purposes. These methodologies correspond to the two different methodol-

---

[4]IRC §401(a)(5),(l) as amended by TRA §1111.

[5]Later for certain collectively bargained plans. TRA §1111(c).

[6]Rev. Ruls. 71-446, 72-276, 72-492, 75-480, 78-92, 83-53, 83-97, 83-110, 84-45, and 86-74.

[7]One consequence of the TRA86 was the adoption of the phrase "permitted disparity" to describe the weighting of pension benefits and contributions in favor of highly compensated employees. Some commenters have viewed this as a first step toward the elimination of the practice entirely. It is conceptually easier, the argument goes, to eliminate an amount of disparity that is currently permitted than to prohibit the integration of plans.

ogies by which a plan demonstrates compliance with the nondiscrimination rules. As discussed in Chapter 5, a plan can demonstrate that its benefits or contributions are nondiscriminatory either by using a safe harbor, which is based on the plan's design, or by passing the general nondiscrimination test, which tests the benefits accrued by plan participants.

For plans using a safe harbor, the plan benefit formula must comply with the permitted disparity rules, which restrict the amount of integration that can be taken into account when accruing benefits. For plans that use the general non-discrimination test, there are no limits on the amount of integration that can be considered by the plan's benefit formula. However, when testing the benefit accruals of employees under the general test, only a certain amount of disparity can be imputed to the employees. The rules limiting the amount of disparity that can be imputed to employees are almost identical to the rules limiting the amount of disparity permitted in a plan's benefit formula. Accordingly, the following discussion will focus on the permitted disparity rules for designing safe harbor pension and profit-sharing plans.

Defined Contribution Plans

As was pointed out earlier, a defined contribution plan is one under which contributions of the employer or employees or both, and possibly forfeitures, are allocated to individual accounts for participants. In an integrated defined contribution plan the allocation of contributions and any forfeitures with respect to compensation above the integration level exceeds the percentage below the integration level. The percentage applied below the integration level is called the "base contribution percentage," and the percentage applied above the integration level is called the "excess contribution percentage." The permitted disparity between these two percentages may not exceed either 5.7 percent or the base contribution percentage.[8]

The integration level, commonly called the "breakpoint," must generally be set equal to the Social Security taxable wage base in effect at the beginning of the plan year ($62,700 for 1996). A higher integration level is not permitted. A lower integration level is permitted only if it is nondiscriminatory. As a practical matter, any lower limit that satisfies the nondiscrimination requirement may not meet employer or employee objectives. The application of these requirements to a defined contribution plan is illustrated by Table 15-1.

Regulations allow the integration of a target benefit plan if the target benefit satisfies the requirements for integration of a defined benefit plan, even though a target benefit plan is actually a defined contribution plan.

Under a profit-sharing plan, allocations are made for all participants in proportion to the sum of their total compensation plus their compensation in excess of the integration level, which is not to exceed 5.7 percent of that sum (which would amount to 5.7 percent of compensation below the integration level plus

---

[8]If the portion of FICA taxes attributable to old-age benefits ever rose above 5.7 percent, the allowable percentage would increase, but no such increase is currently scheduled or even contemplated for the future.

TABLE 15-1   Model Integrated Formulas for a Defined Contribution
             Plan (percent)

Base Contribution	Maximum Permitted Disparity	Excess Contribution
3.0	3.0	6.0
4.0	4.0	8.0
5.0	5.0	10.0
6.0	5.7	11.7

11.4percent above). Any remainder to be allocated is allocated in proportion to total compensation.

Defined Benefit Plans

Regardless of whether the defined benefit plan is integrated using the excess plan approach or the offset plan approach, several concepts apply in similar fashion.

Average Annual Compensation

TRA86 states that integrated defined benefit plans must base benefits on "average annual compensation."[9] The Code defines average annual compensation as the greater of the participant's average compensation for his or her final three years (or all years if less) or the participant's highest average annual compensation for any other period specified in the plan of at least three consecutive years. This would mean that an integrated defined benefit plan would generally be required to base benefits upon the average compensation during the last three years (or all years if less), but a plan could elect to use some alternative definition, such as the average for the highest 5 consecutive years in the last 10 for any participant for whom this would produce a higher average. Such an alternative might be desirable where pay fluctuates up and down from year to year, in order to protect employees from benefits based upon a few low years.

In addition, IRS regulations allow average annual compensation to be determined over the employee's entire compensation history, without limiting the compensation history period to any specific number of years, such as 10 years. This allows plans to use the high three-year average compensation out of the final 3 years of a participant's career as average annual compensation. Furthermore, IRS regulations allow the substitution of compensation for the current plan year or for a 12-month period ending within the plan year for average annual compensation if the plan is an "accumulation" or career average plan. These regulatory provisions permit plans to continue the common pre-TRA86 practice of using a final average compensation or plan year compensation.[10]

The year the employee terminates employment or any 12-month period in which the employee performs less than half-time service can be disregarded for

[9]IRC §401(l)(3).
[10]Treas. Reg. 1.401(a)(4)-12, 1.401(a)(4)-3(e)(2).

purposes of both the averaging period and the compensation history. A special rule also permits the exclusion of certain months for plans that use a rolling average for determining benefits (e.g., final 36-month average).[11] These rules permit a plan to disregard periods of low compensation, which otherwise might result in lower benefits for employees.

Integration Level

The integration level may be set at "covered compensation" as defined by the Code or at any lower level. A higher integration level may be used, but in that case the allowable integration percentage must be reduced. The integration level may never exceed the taxable wage base. No change in the allowable integration percentage is made if the integration level is less than covered compensation.

Covered compensation is defined as the average Social Security taxable wage base for the 35 years ending with the participant's normal retirement age under Social Security (i.e., 65, 66, or 67). Under a transition rule intended to accommodate a different definition under prior law, the 35 years ending prior to the year Social Security normal retirement age is attained may be used for plan years beginning prior to 1995. In making this determination for a participant who has not yet reached the Social Security normal retirement age, a plan must assume that the taxable wage base will remain the same in future years.

Table 15-2 shows a schedule of covered compensation as defined under TRA86. This schedule is based on the 1995 taxable wage base of $61,200, the last year for which the IRS has released a covered compensation table.[12] Note that while the Social Security Administration phases in the different retirement ages on the basis of individuals' month of birth, the IRS uses the year of birth. Accordingly, under the IRS definition there are two gaps (in years 2003 and 2021) in which no one appears to attain Social Security retirement age.

As under prior law, a plan can use a schedule of covered compensation that varies with age, as does the one shown above, or can use for all participants the amount allowable for the oldest possible participant. Similarly, a plan can either freeze the table for all years or can adjust it automatically each year or every five years to reflect increases in the taxable wage base by including in the plan document the appropriate definition of covered compensation rather than specific dollar amounts. Theoretically, the best approach is to use integration levels that vary by age and to change the levels annually, keeping up with changes in the taxable wage base and allowing more integration. But many employers use a single fixed-dollar amount as the integration level for all participants in order to simplify administration and communication of the plan.

Early Retirement

The permitted disparity factor must be reduced if benefits commence before the normal Social Security retirement age. Before the Social Security Amendments of

---

[11]Treas. Reg. 1.401(a)(4)-3(e)(2)(ii).
[12]Rev. Rul. 95-30.

TABLE 15-2   1995 Covered Compensation Table

Year of Birth	Year Attain Social Security Retirement Age	Covered Compensation
1930	1995	25,920
1931	1996	27,528
1932	1997	29,148
1933	1998	30,756
1934	1999	32,364
1935	2000	33,972
1936	2001	35,532
1937	2002	37,092
1938	2004	40,152
1939	2005	41,676
1940	2006	43,200
1941	2007	44,688
1942	2008	46,128
1943	2009	47,508
1944	2010	48,852
1945	2011	50,160
1946	2012	51,432
1947	2013	52,680
1948	2014	53,772
1949	2015	54,780
1950	2016	55,680
1951	2017	56,608
1952	2018	57,240
1953	2019	57,900
1954	2020	58,524
1955	2022	59,568
1956	2023	60,024
1957	2024	60,408
1958	2025	60,684
1959	2026	60,912
1960	2027	61,080
1962	2029	61,176
1963 or later	2030	61,200

Source: Rev. Rul. 95-30.

1983, 65 was the age at which unreduced old-age benefits under Social Security could commence for all covered workers (the Social Security normal retirement age). Under the 1983 Amendments, the normal Social Security retirement age for those born in 1937 and earlier is 65, but it is gradually increased to age 67 for those born in 1960 and later. In contrast, a pension plan's normal retirement age may not be later than age 65 or five years of participation, if later.[13] Most pension plans provide unreduced pensions at age 65 (many plans earlier) and allow early retirement with reduced benefits at earlier ages.

---

[13]ERISA §3(24) and IRC §411(a)(8) as amended by the Omnibus Budget Reconciliation Act of 1986 Pub. Law 99-509.

TABLE 15-3   Simplified Table of Early Retirement Reduction Factors

Age at Which Benefits Commence	Permitted Disparity Factor
70	1.048
69	0.950
68	0.863
67	0.784
66	0.714
65	0.650
64	0.607
63	0.563
62	0.520
61	0.477
60	0.433
59	0.412
58	0.390
57	0.368
56	0.347
55	0.325

Source: Treas. Reg. 1.401(l)-3(e)(3), Table IV.

Thus for participants born after 1937 the permitted disparity factor for any benefits commencing at age 65 must be reduced, and for all participants the permitted disparity factor for any benefits commencing before age 65 must be reduced. IRS regulations supply four tables for reducing the permitted disparity factor: three are for plans that use the normal Social Security retirement ages of 65, 66, and 67, and the other is a simplified table for a plan that uses a single disparity factor of .65 percent for all employees at age 65. The tables contain adjustment factors from age 55 to age 70. Adjustments before age 55 and after age 70 are based on a reasonable interest rate and mortality table.[14]

The simplified table, Table 15-3, is based on a reduction of one-fifteenth per year for the first five years prior to the normal Social Security retirement age, and one-thirtieth for each of the five years before that. For participants with a normal Social Security retirement age of 67, the factors are sometimes greater than and sometimes less than the factors for the table, so the benefits of using the simplified table depend on the plan's early retirement benefit structure.

Defined Benefit Excess Plans

An excess plan is an integrated defined benefit plan that provides a higher percentage of benefits with respect to pay above the integration level than with respect to pay below the integration level. Under prior law it was permissible to have a pure excess plan with no benefit below the integration level; such plans are no longer

[14]Treas. Reg. 1.401(l)-3(e)(1), 1.401(l)-3(e)(3).

permitted. Under TRA86 all excess plans must be "step-rate" excess plans with a base benefit percentage based upon compensation below the integration level and an excess benefit percentage based on pay in excess of the integration level.

Under an excess plan the maximum permitted disparity factor may not exceed any one of three limits:

1. The base benefit percentage,
2. 0.75 percent of excess compensation for benefits attributable to any particular year of service,
3. 0.75 percent of excess compensation times years of service for total benefits (maximum 26.25 percent for 35 year or more).

For the above rule, only years of service during which benefits accrue may be counted. Thus, if a plan uses the fractional rule for determining accrued benefits by prorating projected benefits over years of participation, then years of service during which the employee was not a participant may not be counted.

The determination of the maximum excess allowance can be illustrated as follows:

Base Benefit Percentage	Permitted Disparity Factor (%)
0.5 times years	0.5 times years, max. 26.25
1.0 times years	0.75 times years, max. 26.25

Unlike the rules under prior law, the present rules do not reduce the maximum excess allowance because of death benefits or disability benefits. Prior law requirements for excess plans were different in many respects. They generally allowed more integration. Most excess plans that satisfied the prior requirements would require the benefit formula to be amended to satisfy the new requirements.

Defined Benefit Offset Plans

TRA86 defines an offset plan as "any plan with respect to which the benefit attributable to employer contributions for each participant is reduced by an amount specified in the plan." The maximum allowable offset is no longer directly related to Social Security. In a contributory plan, the benefit may not be reduced below the benefit derived from employee contributions.

The permitted disparity factor may not exceed any one of three limits:

1. Half of the benefit before the offset,
2. For benefits attributable to any particular year, 0.75 percent of the participant's average annual compensation,
3. For total benefits, 0.75 percent of the participant's three-year-final-average compensation times his or her years of service during which benefits accrue (maximum 26.25 percent after 35 or more years).

In calculating the final average compensation, any year's compensation in excess of the taxable wage base must be disregarded. Table 15-4 is used to adjust the

TABLE 15-4   Permitted Disparity Factors for Integration Levels Other than Covered Compensation: Reduction Table at Social Security Normal Retirement Age

Integration or Offset Level as a Percentage of Covered Compensation	Disparity Factor
100	0.75
125	0.69
150	0.60
175	0.53
200	0.47
Taxable wage base or final average compensation	0.42

Source: Treas. Reg. 1.401(1)-3(d)(9)(iv)(A).

disparity factor for integration or offset levels other than covered compensation at the normal Social Security retirement age. The adjustment may be applied on a planwide basis for plans using a single dollar amount as the integration level for all participants, as determined by the covered compensation for an employee attaining the normal Social Security retirement age in the current year, or on an individual-by-individual basis for plans using separate integration levels for each employee in accordance with his or her covered compensation.[15] The disparity factor may be determined by rounding the percentage of covered compensation to the next higher percentage in the table or by straight-line interpolation.[16]

The permitted disparity factor is reduced for each year that benefit commencement precedes the normal Social Security retirement date, in the same manner as for excess plans. No adjustments are required or permitted for other factors.

Under prior rules the offset at times completely eliminated any benefit for lower-paid employees. Limiting the offset to half of the benefit prevents this from occurring.

The new requirements for offset plans under TRA86 are very different from prior rules. Under prior law the maximum offset was defined as a percentage of the PIA. The stated reasons for basing the offset on final average earnings rather than the PIA were to eliminate the need to determine the employee's actual Social Security benefit and to provide for parity between offset plans and excess plans. However, the public outcry at the elimination of the most common integrated plan design caused the IRS to try to craft two different special rules for PIA offset plans: the "PIA replica" plan and the "401(1) overlay" plan.

PIA Replica Plans

In an attempt to "replicate" a PIA offset plan's benefits, IRS regulations permit the reduction for integration or offset levels greater than covered compensation to be applied on an individual-by-individual basis.[17]

[15]Treas. Reg. 1.401(1)-3(d)(9)(iv)(B).
[16]Treas. Reg. 1.401(1)-3(d)(9)(iv).
[17]Treas. Reg. 1.401(1)-3(d)(3).

TABLE 15-5   Permitted Disparity Factors for Compensation in Excess
                of Covered Compensation (dollars)

Final Average Compensation	Covered Compensation	Offset Factor
50,000	17,000	$0.42\% \times 65/75 = 0.36\%$
50,000	25,000	$0.47\% \times 65/75 = 0.41\%$
25,000	17,000	$0.60\% \times 65/75 = 0.52\%$
25,000	25,000	$0.75\% \times 65/75 = 0.65\%$

Source: Author's calculations.

For example, assume an offset plan provides a benefit of 2.00 percent of average annual compensation less 0.65 percent of final average compensation, and the plan satisfies certain demographic requirements in the regulations. The plan could provide that for employees whose final average compensation is greater than covered compensation, the 0.65 percent factor is reduced in accordance with the reduction table, depending on the relationship of final average compensation to covered compensation. This reduction table is illustrated by Table 15-5. Under this approach, the offset factors will be lower for the older or more highly compensated employees.

Unfortunately, while it may be possible to replicate benefits provided through an offset plan for employees currently reaching age 65, the resulting formula will not replicate benefits for employees reaching normal Social Security retirement age in future years. Thus deferred benefits for different generations of terminating employees in the current year will not approximate the PIA offset benefits. Plan sponsors who want to consider this approach must decide whether the changes in benefits and complexities of this type of formula are less troublesome than annual testing.

401(l) Overlay Plan

The IRS regulations also establish a safe harbor for certain PIA offset plans if the offset is the lesser of a specified percentage of the employee's PIA or an offset that otherwise satisfies section 401(l) (a "401(l) overlay").[18] For example, a plan that offsets a participant's benefit accrual by the lesser of 50 percent of the participant's PIA amount or 0.75 percent of average annual compensation up to covered compensation would satisfy the 401(l) overlay and meet the PIA offset safe harbor.

The PIA offset safe harbor was not well received by the pension industry and plan sponsors. Commenters requested a "true" PIA offset safe harbor (e.g., a safe harbor for plans that only offset the participant's benefit by a percentage of PIA). They pointed out that not only will a PIA offset plan usually satisfy the general nondiscrimination test (and therefore plan sponsors should not have to incur the expense of testing), but the 401(l) overlay safe harbor does not describe any plan existing today. In the view of government regulators, the 401(l) overlay is necessary in order to give substance to the statutory provisions of section 401(l).

[18]Treas. Reg. 1.401(l)-3(c)(2)(ix).

Comparison of Excess Plans and Offset Plans

Even when the maximum permitted disparity is fully used in the benefit formula under either an excess plan or an offset plan, the combined benefits under the plan and Social Security will replace a lower percentage of after-tax pay for higher-paid employees than for lower-paid employees, and may thus not fully accomplish the objective of replacing the same percentage of after-tax pay for all. But either method will come far closer to that objective than if no integration had been used at all.

Section III
The Economics of Pensions

Chapter 16
Overall Objectives in Designing a Retirement Program

Discussions about employer-sponsored retirement programs often focus on the level of benefits or retirement income security that is delivered to the participants in the plans. Less often do such discussions focus on what the plan sponsor is attempting to achieve in establishing and maintaining a plan. Chapter 1 examined some of the underlying motivations that led to the establishment of early employer-sponsored retirement plans. This section of the volume considers what can be accomplished with a retirement plan and how plan sponsors can go about structuring their plans to meet the diverse goals behind them. This chapter provides an overview of employer motivations in establishing a plan. Some of the issues touched on are taken up in much greater detail in the rest of the section. Since this volume focuses on private pensions and retirement savings plans, the analysis of employer motivations tends to concentrate on private employers, although their motivations for setting up plans are much the same as those of public and not-for-profit employers.

Paternalism is sometimes identified as a significant motivation for the employer-based pension movement. While paternalism may indeed play some role in the creation of retirement plans, it cannot solely explain the widespread prevalence of plans across the range of employer sponsors that maintain these plans today. From the nature of these plans, it seems their widespread existence must be due to some intersection of employers' and workers' interests. Otherwise it would be hard to explain why so many workers would entrust such a significant portion of their retirement security to these plans.

From the employer's perspective, the widespread existence of plans indicates that they somehow fit into an overall framework that supports the strategic interests of the sponsoring organization. From the employee's perspective, the prevalence of participation in plans, especially where participation is voluntary, suggests that these are powerful vehicles for helping workers secure their retirement goals. While Chapter 8 showed there is considerable economic value in the tax incentives plans provide for participants, the marginal tax benefits that accrue to young workers with relatively limited contributions to defined contribution plans are quite small. Likewise, the marginal tax benefits that accrue to young or even middle-aged workers participating in defined benefit plans are minimal compared with those that accrue just before retirement. Yet many young and middle-aged workers actively seek out employment situations in which they will be covered by a pension or retirement savings plan.

This chapter briefly discusses how the employer-sponsored retirement plan can support the strategic interest of the sponsor and how retirement income security is actually delivered. It also explains what plan sponsors need to do in order to gain the maximum benefit from having set up the plan, while at the same time minimizing the burden that support of the plan poses to the organization.

Supporting the Larger Strategic Interests of the Sponsor

The principles of economics teach that workers are a fundamental factor of production and that workers are attracted to a firm by the wages they can earn. In rudimentary economic models, wages are simply the cash that an employer pays to a worker to buy some of his or her productive time. In the somewhat more complicated real world, "wages," or the more comprehensive concept "compensation," are an amalgam of cash and benefits that employers provide to their workers. The mix of benefits can have important ramifications in terms of an employer's ability to attract and maintain the kinds of workers that are needed to sustain an organization. The pension or retirement savings plan creates a cost that is related to attracting and maintaining workers. These plans might be financed and operated in a variety of ways having different financial ramifications for the sponsoring organization.

Human Resource Issues

An employer is viable in the long term only to the extent that it can attract workers to produce the goods or services it is in business to provide to its consumers. An employer can attract necessary workers in a marketplace where there are multiple employment opportunities only by offering a combination of cash wages, other elements of compensation, and other amenities that are perceived to be equal to or more valuable than what other employers are offering. For many of today's workers, retirement plans are an important part of the "other elements of compensation." In 1991, 78 percent of all full-time workers and 40 percent of all part-time workers employed in private sector firms with more than 100 employees were participating in one or more employer-sponsored retirement plans.[1] In 1992, 45 percent of all full-time workers and 12 percent of part-time workers employed in private sector firms with fewer than 100 employees were participating in one or more employer-sponsored plans.[2] Virtually all larger employers in the United States today—that is, those with 1,000 or more workers—provide some kind of retirement benefit for their workers.

In 1992 the average cost of retirement and savings benefits offered by private sector employers as a group was $0.46 per hour worked. This figure represents 4 percent of wages and salaries and nearly 3 percent of total compensation. For employers with fewer than 100 workers, the average cost of retirement and savings

[1]U. S. Department of Labor, Bureau of Labor Statistics, *Employee Benefits in Medium and Large Private Establishments, 1991* (Washington, D.C.: USGPO, May 1993), pp. 5, 127.
[2]U.S. Department of Labor, Bureau of Labor Statistics, "BLS Reports on Employee Benefits in Small Private Industry Establishments, 1992," *Compensation & Working Conditions*, March 1994, p. 9.

TABLE 16-1 Average Replacement of Final Earnings by Defined
Benefit Plans in Operation in 1993 for Individuals
Retiring at Ages 55 or 65 with 20 Years of Service

Final Annual Earning (dollars)	Age 55 (%)	Age 65 (%)
15,000	23.4	32.6
25,000	21.9	31.4
35,000	21.8	33.0
45,000	22.1	34.7
55,000	22.7	35.8
65,000	23.3	36.6

Source: Watson Wyatt.

plans was $0.31 per hour, or 3 percent of cash wages. For employers with more than 500 employees, the average cost of these plans was $0.80 per hour, or 5.5 percent of wages.[3] Because participation in the plans is not universal, the average contributions to the plans mask the importance of these benefits to the employees participating in them. A better sense of the delivery of benefits under these plans is reflected by the average replacement of final earnings that large private employer defined benefit plans generate for workers with 30 years of service under them and retiring at either age 55 or 65, as shown in Table 16-1.[4] The table indicates the average replacement of final earnings in a sample of 424 large defined benefit plans in operation during 1993. A retirement plan that replaces between 20 and 40 percent of final earnings for career employees will encompass a significant portion of their retirement portfolios in many cases.

Many, if not most, large employers compete in a national labor market for significant segments of their work force. The prevalence of retirement plans being offered by large employers makes it virtually imperative for all employers competing in this marketplace to offer some form of retirement program. While large employers may compete in a national labor market for workers, the jobs they offer are in local communities. Intermediate and smaller firms compete in these same local labor markets for workers who have individual characteristics that would make them attractive to larger employers. Thus the effects of large employers offering retirement plans in their national labor markets force smaller employers operating in more restricted markets to offer plans as well.

While offering a plan may be a necessity in many cases, the overall generosity of benefits offered through the plans varies considerably, even among companies that

[3]U.S. Department of Labor, Bureau of Labor Statistics, "Employer Costs for Employee Compensation, March 1992," *Compensation & Working Conditions*, August 1992, p. 10.
[4]The results in Table 16-1 may seem somewhat inconsistent with what one would expect as the normal plan structure. Specifically, it may seem counterintuitive that the replacement rates at the $15,000 final income level would be higher than the rates at higher income levels. The reason this result occurs in the table is that many of these defined benefit plans have minimum benefit levels for individuals with long service under them. The practical reality is that in many cases the benefits that are calculated at the lowest income level would be extremely rare because virtually all workers retiring with 30 years of service under these plans would have final salaries in excess of $15,000.

compete directly. Consider the case of the nine oil companies on the *Fortune* list of the largest 50 companies in the United States in 1994. None of these companies totally dominates the market in which they operate. Each of them must compete with other companies in some area of the market in virtually every aspect of their business. They must compete with each other for chemical engineers, marketing and sales people, production staff, and so forth.

For comparison purposes, we developed a projection of the retirement benefits these nine companies would provide to a worker starting for each of them in 1994 at age 30 at a starting salary of $60,600 per year.[5] We assumed that the workers would retire at age 60 after 30 years of service under their current plans. The combined benefits provided by the various companies' defined benefit and defined contribution plans range from 90.9 percent of final salary to 50.6 percent. Two companies' plans would pay benefits of 90 percent or more, one would pay a benefit of 85 percent, two would pay benefits in the 71 to 76 percent range, two would pay benefits in the 62 to 68 percent range, and two would pay a benefit between 51 and 58 percent of final pay.[6] Presumably all of these companies are successful at attracting the necessary workers to support their operations or they would not make the elite *Fortune* list. While their retirement plans are an important part of their attractiveness to workers, the variation in retirement plan benefit levels suggests that other factors are also important.

Chapter 20 includes a lengthy discussion about the human resource incentives embedded in both defined benefit and defined contribution plans that may help to explain why different kinds of workers are attracted to companies with alternative plan designs or levels of generosity. For years there has been a sense that defined benefit plans can act as "golden handcuffs" that help employers retain workers in whom they have made considerable training investments. In this regard, the defined benefit plan can contribute to the overall productivity of the firm by reducing expensive turnover. Chapter 20 also discusses the possibility that both defined benefit and defined contribution plans have embedded incentives that encourage worker sorting; that is, more productive workers will be attracted to firms that offer retirement plans than to ones that do not. But not all workers necessarily want to be in a firm with the highest retirement benefit level, because there are tradeoffs that employers must make in offering benefits. High levels of pension benefits may come at the cost of not receiving retiree health benefits or at the cost of reduced wages during the working career. Still, the structure of the retirement plan and its overall level of generosity can play a significant role in

---

[5]The benefits were calculated by assuming that pay increased 5.5 percent per year, the Social Security wage base grew at 4.5 percent per year, and CPI grew at 4.0 percent. We also assumed that the workers would participate in the company defined contribution plans up to the maximum level the employer would match employee contributions, that the account balances in the defined contribution plans would accumulate at 7.0 percent per year, and that at age 60 the balances would be converted into an annuity using an 8 percent interest rate.

[6]Much of the variation in the aggregate benefits is due to variations in the defined contribution plans sponsored by these companies. If the defined benefit plans sponsored by the firms were considered separately, their replacement of final earnings would range from 34.1 percent to 41.9 percent. The defined benefits in each case depend on employee contributions in order to generate the employer-matching contributions.

attracting and keeping committed and productive workers. Being able to attract more productive workers and to retain them once they are employed can be critical in highly competitive markets.

Today, much is being written about the changing nature of the relationship between employers and their workers. There is some indication that the pattern of career-long jobs with single employers that many workers enjoyed in the past may be changing. If that is the case, and we are not convinced that it is, it may imply that the characteristics of retirement plans currently being offered to workers will have to be changed if employers want to maintain their competitive position for workers. The traditional defined benefit plan is well suited to career-long holders of single jobs, but not nearly as effective for more mobile workers. Chapters 10 through 15 analyzed the characteristics of various types of plans, the way their benefit structures treat alternative kinds of workers, and the measures some traditional forms of plans are taking to adapt to perceived changes occurring in the commitments that employers and their workers are making to each other today.

Another element of retirement plans that serves the interests of the sponsoring organizations is flexibility. That flexibility can come in a variety of forms. In recent years the growth of defined contribution plans as supplemental plans in firms already sponsoring defined benefit plans has allowed employers to offer greater opportunities for retirement saving to individuals inclined to save at higher rates than implied by the defined benefit plan's generosity. Also, in many instances, the new defined contribution plans have reduced the pressure to enhance defined benefit plans, which by their nature require that such plan enhancements be offered to all workers covered under them. The restructuring phenomenon that has swept across American business over the last decade has highlighted the value of the types of retirement plans that can be marginally augmented to encourage workers to voluntarily terminate employment and help accomplish restructuring without the painful process of mandatory terminations. As Americans move into the next century and face the prospect of Social Security's normal retirement age increasing to age 67 or possibly higher, many employers may have to rely increasingly on their own retirement plan incentives to maintain the orderly retirement of older workers on the basis of their strategic business interests. While it may be in the interest of our national retirement program to encourage workers to extend their working lives into their late 60s or early 70s, it is unlikely that companies operating in an environment of rapidly changing technologies will have the same perspective.

Financing Issues

The financial commitments that sponsors and participants in the various kinds of plans make are the subject of Chapter 17. If an employer's retirement programs are to serve the long-term strategic goals of the organization, they clearly have to be sustainable. One factor affecting sustainability is the overall cost of the programs. Dismissing, for the time being, the issue of whether employer contributions to their retirement plans are part of the wage bill, it is clear that the cost of these plans is a cost of employing workers. Those costs plus other labor-related costs ultimately have to be borne by the prices that can be charged for the goods and services provided to consumers, or the profitability of the sponsoring organization will be threatened. If that happens for any extended period of time, the long-term viability of the organization becomes questionable.

Not only is the overall cost of retirement programs important, but the timing of the costs can be equally important. For example, one of the touted features of profit-sharing plans is that the employer can contribute to the plan when the sponsoring organization is doing well but is not similarly committed during periods of unsuccessful economic performance. To a certain extent, defined benefit plans offer sponsors similar flexibility in that they do not require that maximum contributions be made to the plan every year. Again, contributions can be larger in successful years and smaller in less successful ones, although the range of flexibility in this regard has been considerably restricted in recent years by changes in the laws governing pension funding partly in response to the Pension Benefit Guaranty Corporation's growing concern about its exposure to the underfunding of insured pension plans.

Providing Retirement Income Security

The very fact that these plans are widely considered to be "retirement" plans indicates that the saving that goes on through them is for a special purpose, namely, to provide income during the years after the working career. For a retirement system to be considered successful, it must provide retirement benefits that allow retirees to maintain a standard of living that is widely considered acceptable. Employer-sponsored plans are only one part of the retirement system in this country and must take into consideration the responsibilities of the other elements of the system, but in many cases the employer-based retirement plans will be the most important element of a retirement portfolio. One of the greatest risks that workers face over their life cycle is that they will reach retirement and find they have not made adequate economic provision for their remaining years. While it is important for workers to take some individual responsibility for the accumulation of their retirement nest egg, myopia on the part of individuals and the favorable characteristics of organized retirement plans make the employer plans a more effective retirement savings device than individual savings in many cases.

Assessing the Delivery of Retirement Benefits

The level of income required to sustain living standards after retiring is discussed in Chapter 18. Two kinds of standards are examined: an absolute level of income needed to maintain minimal consumption levels in retirement, and a relative measure of the income needed to maintain the preretirement life style. Defining reasonable but adequate targets is extremely important for several reasons. First, the targets are a good planning device that employers can use in developing their overall plan offerings. Second, they can be used as a communications device to help workers understand the various elements of their retirement saving program and their personal responsibility for participating in it. Third, the combination of the absolute and the relative standards can be used to evaluate the overall effectiveness of the total retirement accumulation process.

Ultimately, the success or failure of the retirement program is going to be judged by the delivery of retirement benefits to a broad cross section of the elderly. Chapter 19 assesses the delivery of retirement benefits under the current configuration of public and private retirement programs in combination with individual provisions. This analysis suggests that Americans are not doing as good a job as they should in tracking the overall effectiveness of their retirement programs. The problem is that policy makers are often forced to consider options and make policy decisions with incomplete or completely erroneous information. In this area as in most, it is difficult to make good decisions on the basis of bad data.

Dynamics of the Environment in Which Plans Are Offered

One of the major challenges that employers face in designing and maintaining a retirement program that meets the retirement security needs of workers is the fluid nature of the environment in which plans are offered and utilized. At least three major sets of forces are at play here. The first of these is the public policy environment. The second is the changing social patterns and pressures they create. The third is the business environment in which the plan sponsors have to operate.

Public Policy Environment

As discussed in Chapter 1, the long-range outlook for Social Security is uncertain. In 1983 major amendments to the Social Security Act were adopted that were meant largely to see the baby boom generation through their retirement. Subsequent projections have not been as optimistic as those developed after the 1983 Amendments. The 1995 projections suggest that during the baby boomer's retirement, Social Security revenues will fall 40 percent short of benefits, as defined in current law. The combined Old-Age, Survivors, and Disability Insurance systems are expected to run out of money in 2030, when the remaining baby boomers will be ages 66 to 84 and when many of them will still be alive.

In the past when Social Security was amended because of serious financial shortfalls—for example, in 1977 and 1983—some of the adjustments to the system were in the form of increased taxes and others in the form of reduced benefits. Certainly the system again requires significant adjustments to support the baby boomers' retirement. It is likely that some of the adjustment will be in the form of benefit reductions. Whether these reductions will consist of further increases in the retirement age, general reductions of benefits, or selective benefit cuts, such as those flowing from means testing, remains to be determined. Whatever form the future cuts to Social Security might take, they are likely to expose employer-sponsored plans to two problems.

The first problem or risk is that employers might be forced to modify retirement provisions in their plans to support the larger public policy goals. For example, if Social Security's retirement ages are raised in order to keep workers in the labor market longer, employers may be required to raise retirement ages in their own plans to increase the effectiveness of the Social Security changes. This could be a particular problem for employers operating in rapidly changing technical areas where the depreciation of human capital is more accelerated than in more traditional manufacturing or service industries.

The second risk that plan sponsors face is that benefit reductions in one part of the retirement system place a greater burden on other parts of the system because of objective retirement accumulation standards. If Social Security benefits are reduced, the only way overall retirement security can be maintained is by greater saving through employer-sponsored plans, individual saving, or extended working careers. From the perspective of many workers and many employers, none of the options can be achieved without a certain amount of pain. The longer policy makers wait to make the necessary adjustments to Social Security, the larger the challenge that plan sponsors and workers are going to face in implementing adequate changes to the remainder of their retirement portfolios.

The conflict between federal tax policy and retirement policy was noted in Chapter 8. Since the early 1980s, pensions have been subjected to repeated changes from legislative initiatives and the regulatory structure supporting the legislative changes. While some progress has been made in reducing the federal deficit in recent years, there is still a widespread feeling that further reductions are imperative. As long as that is the case and as long as there is a perception that reductions in the tax preferences accorded private pensions can be a major part of the solution to the deficit problem, Americans face the prospect of more changes in the regulatory environment. Delivering adequate retirement income to the expected wave of baby boom retirees in the face of reduced Social Security and more restrictive tax policies will be no small challenge.

Changing Social Patterns and Pressures

There is a general perception that the work force has become much more mobile in recent years than it was 20 or 30 years ago. This perception has led some analysts to conclude that defined benefit plans are not as effective in the delivery of retirement benefits as they used to be. Interestingly, disaggregation of the historical data on worker tenures does not support the general notion that workers have become inherently more job mobile in recent years. Figure 16-1 shows the median tenures of men in the work force over the last 40 years at various ages. The long-term trend of the tenure lines at various ages is somewhat positive since World War II. The decline in the 1960s may be more related to a change in the way the question was asked in ascertaining this information than to an actual decline in workers' tenures at that time.[7]

Figure 16-2 shows the same trend information by age group for women over the period 1951 to 1991. Again, the long-term trends show that at each age group tenures today are higher than they were 20, 30, or 40 years ago. To the extent that these trends continue, defined benefit plans would seem to be as appropriate as ever.

Although Figures 16-1 and 16-2 do not seem to support the perception that the work force has become more mobile in recent decades, they can help explain the perception. The reason the work force appears more mobile can be found in its

---

[7]The original question was "How long ago did you start working for your current employers?" It was changed to "How long have you been working for your current employer?" The change seems subtle, but such changes can account for different responses on these types of surveys.

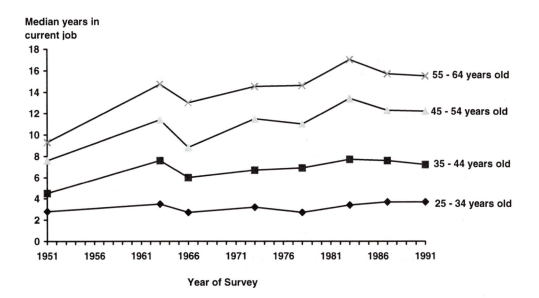

Figure 16-1. Median tenures of male workers by age, selected years. Sources: U.S. Department of Labor, Bureau of Labor Statistics, *Monthly Labor Review*, September 1952, October 1963, January 1967, December 1974, and December 1979. The 1983 and 1987 data are unpublished data from the U.S. Department of Labor, Bureau of Labor Statistics. The 1983 and 1991 data are from the U.S. Department of Labor, *Employee Tenure and Occupational Mobility in the Early 1990s,* Bureau of Labor Statistics News Release USDL 92-386 (Washington, D.C.: USGPO, June 26, 1992).

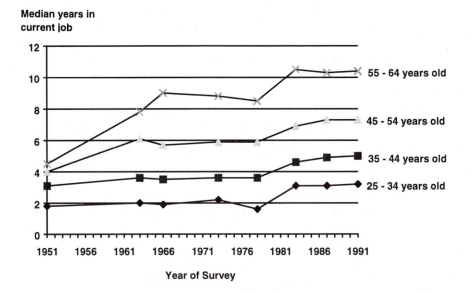

Figure 16-2. Median tenures of female workers by age, selected years. Sources: U.S. Department of Labor, Bureau of Labor Statistics, *Monthly Labor Review*, September 1952, October 1963, January 1967, December 1974, and December 1979. The 1983 and 1987 data are unpublished data from the U.S. Department of Labor, Bureau of Labor Statistics. The 1983 and 1991 data are from the U.S. Department of Labor, *Employee Tenure and Occupational Mobility in the Early 1990s.*

TABLE 16-2 Percentage Change in Numbers of Workers by Age for
Selected Decades and Projected to the Year 2000

| Age | Change from | | |
	1970–1980	1980–1990	1990–2000
16–19	30.6	–21.3	14.9
20–24	50.0	–12.6	–0.7
25–34	72.4	22.2	–10.3
35–44	23.6	56.4	21.6
45–54	0.0	21.3	53.7
55–64	5.3	0.0	20.2
65 and older	–6.1	12.9	8.6

Sources: Derived by the authors from annual summary estimates in the U.S.
Department of Labor, Bureau of Labor Statistics, *Employment and Earnings,*
January issues, 1971, 1981, 1991; and *Monthly Labor Review,* November 1991.

demographic composition. To a large extent, it was the magnitude of the baby
boomer cohorts of workers and their youth in the 1970s and 1980s that gave the
impression that workers had inherently become more mobile. That was because
the mass of the baby boomers was concentrated on the lower two lines of
Figures 16-1 and 16-2 during the years when they were inherently mobile. Table 16-
2 shows the percentage changes in the number of workers by age category over
each of the last two decades, and the projected change over the current decade.
From 1970 to 1980 the number of workers aged 25 to 34 increased 72 percent,
while the number aged 45 to 54 did not change at all, and the number aged 55 to
64 increased only 5 percent. By comparison, from 1990 to 2000 the number of
workers aged 25 to 34 is expected to decline by 10 percent, while the number of
workers between the ages of 45 and 54 is expected to increase by 54 percent and
the 10-year older age group is expected to increase by 20 percent. During this
decade and into the next, the mass of the baby boom is moving up to the upper
tenure lines, as shown in Figures 16-1 and 16-2. Unless there are some remarkable
changes in the employment patterns of workers in the next few years, it appears
that perceptions on worker mobility in the 1990s will change significantly from
those of the 1970s and 1980s.

Another social phenomenon that is having important ramifications for the
retirement system and the role of employer plans in it is the increased labor force
participation rates of women. Figure 16-3 shows the labor force participation rates
of men and women at various ages in 1950. The difference in the participation
rates at ages 20 to 24 was 41 percentage points. By ages 25 to 34 the difference
increased to 62 percentage points as men had by and large finished their education
and military commitments and some women who had entered the work force
initially had withdrawn to start families. Across the middle age groups, the difference ranged between 55 and 60 percentage points. The highest level of women
working outside the home in 1950 was among women aged 20 to 24, where
46.0 percent did so. It appears that once women quit work to have children only
about half of them returned.

Percent
Participating

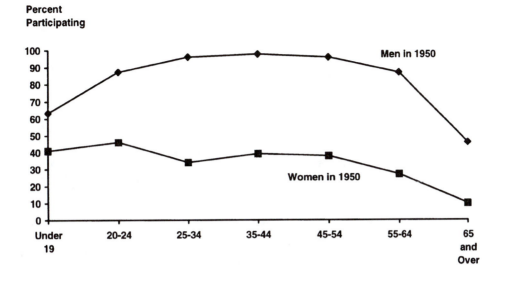

Figure 16-3. Labor force participation rates for men and women at various ages, 1950. Source: U.S. Department of Labor, *Handbook of Labor Statistics*, Bureau of Labor Statistics Bulletin 2340 (Washington, D.C.: USGPO, August 1989), pp. 13, 14, 19, 20.

Women who were 35 to 44 in 1950 are in their 80s today. To the extent they receive pensions today, most are receiving them because their husbands were covered under a plan during his working career. Prior to the Retirement Equity Act of 1984, the beneficiary of a pension benefit could unilaterally choose whether to accept a joint and survivor benefit, and apparently many did not. The combination of low labor force participation rates for older women, shorter life expectancy of men, and failure to select the joint and survivor form of benefits means that many women over age 80 today are not getting pension benefits.

Figure 16-4 juxtaposes the labor force participation rates of men and women in 1990 and the rates shown earlier for 1950. The differentials between male and female labor force participation rates have narrowed markedly. Now, far more women enter the work force initially and the pattern of withdrawal to take up homemaking is no longer apparent from the data. Over almost all of the age spectrum the differential participation rates of men and women are less than 20 percentage points, about one-third the differentials in 1950. The implications of these changes for retirement income security are going to be significant. Many more women today are earning pensions in their own right than did their mothers or grandmothers. In addition, they are also much more likely to benefit from survivor benefits from their husbands' pension plans than did earlier generations of women because they now personally have to sign away their joint and survivor rights. These changes in the social fabric will make the role of employer-sponsored plans significantly more important in the future than they have been in the past.

One last social phenomenon that cannot go unnoticed is the decline in the retirement age that has been occurring for some decades now. The labor force

Percent
Participating

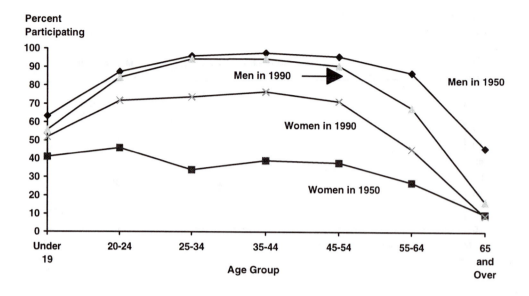

Figure 16-4. Labor force participation rates for men and women at various ages, 1950 and 1990. Source: U.S. Department of Labor, *Handbook of Labor Statistics*, pp. 13, 14, 19, 20; and *Employment and Earnings*, January 1991, p. 164.

participation rates of men over age 60 declined steadily from 1940 through 1990 (see Figure 1-1 in Chapter 1). While women's labor force participation rates at higher ages have been rising somewhat in recent years, that is the result of the phenomenon shown in Figure 16-4 relating to the overall increase in labor force participation rates of women. The pattern in Figure 16-4 suggests that as women take on working career patterns that resemble the traditional pattern of men, they will likely take on similar retirement patterns as well.

As already discussed, the potential burden that the baby boom poses to Social Security may result in higher retirement ages. Higher retirement ages under Social Security imply a greater burden on employer-sponsored plans, which may lead some plan sponsors to coordinate retirement age increases with national policy. The size of the baby boom cohort in relation to the cohorts of workers that will replace it when the baby boomers retire suggests that some employers may wish to extend the working lives of the baby boomers in order to fill personnel needs. The analysis in Chapter 20 suggests that coordinated increases in Social Security and pension retirement ages may be a potent force in keeping workers in the labor market for an extended period of time. The historical trends discussed in Chapter 1 that first led to shorter and shorter working hours per day down to a seven- to eight-hour average for most workers, then shorter and shorter hours per week down to an average of 35 to 40 hours for most workers, and then shorter periods in the work force as exhibited by the trend toward early retirement, suggest some strong historical preferences inherent in American society for reducing periods of work in relation to leisure. Raising the retirement age of the baby boom generation will require the reversal of trends that date back more than 100 years and may be resisted vigorously by those affected.

Changing Business Environment

A great deal has been written lately about the restructuring of American business and the implications that restructuring might have on the basic nature of the relationships between employers and their workers. Without doubt, there is a great deal of restructuring going on within the economy at the present time, but to some extent such restructuring has always been part of the process of economic development. The prospect that some businesses that have been a predominant part of the economy in the past are reorganizing the way they do business does not imply that employer-sponsored retirement plans will be any less important or less available in the future. Indeed, the roots of the private pension movement in the United States are tied to the railroad industry of the late nineteenth century. The reorganization of that industry during this century has meant tremendous increases in productivity and reductions in the relative numbers of workers. But as the railroad industry has reduced its dependence on workers, other industries have sprung up to take useful advantage of the excess labor created by the increased railroad worker productivity.

If anything, the economic restructuring that has been occurring highlights the importance of employer-sponsored retirement plans, especially for workers caught in these restructurings relatively late in their careers. In many cases the reorganizations that have been going on have resulted in employment reductions within the firms undertaking them. Getting thrown out of a job at any point in a career may not be pleasant, but toward the end of one's career it can be particularly devastating. Older work applicants are inherently more expensive for many potential employers than younger ones. Not only are their affiliated benefits costs usually higher, but if the job requires any training or development costs, the employer has a shorter period over the remaining years of the worker's life to amortize the human capital investment needed to utilize the worker's talents. Because employers often perceive older job applicants to be inherently more expensive than younger applicants, the older person is at a natural disadvantage in the labor market. While legislation can limit age discrimination, the economic realities of the marketplace are still an extremely potent force making it difficult for many older displaced workers to find the kinds of jobs they might like to have.

Many of the downsizings that have been going on among larger businesses in recent years have been accomplished through the utilization of "retirement window" benefits that help ameliorate the transition from work to retirement for workers late in their careers. In implementing these special benefit plans, employers often grant older workers additional service or age credits under their regular retirement plan if they will voluntarily take early retirement. While the outcome may not be optimal in every case, the alternative of being thrown out of a job with no benefit until normal retirement age would be far worse.

Maximizing the Perceived Value of the Benefit

Retirement plans ultimately pay out benefits in the form of cash, but they often do so long after the period in which the benefit is actually earned. The extent to which a person considers future income financed by a dollar contributed this year to the pension or saving plan as being less valuable than receiving the dollar today will depend on his or her personal discount rate. Chapter 20 examines the variation in personal discount rates and the way in which the combination of discount rates and plan characteristics can affect worker behavior. However, given that retirement benefits may be perceived as less valuable than the cost of providing them and given that they are not cheap to provide, it is important that plan sponsors share information with their workers so they can make informed assessments about the value of the benefit that is being provided. Ultimately, if workers covered by a retirement plan do not appreciate the value of benefits being provided, the plan sponsor may not be getting much value from the plan. Also, to the extent that the plan requires employee contributions, failure to get widespread participation in the program reduces its effectiveness in providing retirement security for non-participants especially, but possibly for participants as well. Participants in a contributory plan can sometimes be affected by nonparticipants because of the discrimination tests that limit what higher-paid workers put into the plan on the basis of the participation rate of the lower-paid rank-and-file workers.

Perceptions of Participants

One of the factors that will drive the perceptions about retirement plan offerings will be the characteristics of the workers themselves. A young worker who is in her first job and many years from retirement may find little value in a generous defined benefit plan. If she is like most career workers, she may change jobs several times before settling into a long-tenure job. The prospect of vesting under the plan at the time she begins employment may be limited, but the prospect of ever getting to the point of receiving a benefit 30 or 40 years down the road would seem remote in most cases. But a profit-sharing plan or a 401(k) plan with employer matching of contributions might seem like a real windfall to such a worker. An older worker, on the other hand, looking toward the completion of career employment in a few years would likely have a very different attitude toward the two plans. For her, the defined benefit plan will pay the annuity that will be a regular source of income after she retires. The saving plan, while it will make a contribution to her retirement needs, will more likely be used to supplement shortfalls in the regular income stream, or to finance special consumption that arises periodically such as vacations, the replacement of broken appliances, or whatever.

During April 1993 the Census Bureau conducted a survey of workers' participation in employer-sponsored retirement plans as part of its regular *Current Population Survey* (*CPS*), which it conducts for the Bureau of Labor Statistics. The purpose of the regular monthly survey is to measure the levels of employment and unemployment in the economy. The survey is conducted each month on a sample of households representing the noninstitutional population of the country. The April 1993 supplemental questions on retirement plans were directed at workers over the age of 16 in the sample households. Respondents were asked if their employer sponsored a retirement plan or plans, and if so whether they participated in it or them. If they indicated yes to the latter question, they were asked whether the plans were of the type where "your benefit is defined by a formula usually involving your earnings and years on the job" or whether they were of the

TABLE 16-3   Indication of Most Important Retirement Plan by
Individuals Covered by Both Defined Benefit and Defined
Contribution Plans, by Age

| | | Plan Identified as Most Important | |
Age	Total Reporting Both Plan Types (thousand)	Defined Benefit Plan (percent)	Defined Contribution Plan (percent)
21–24	115.3	27.9	72.1
25–34	1,437.1	35.6	64.4
35–44	1,991.9	46.1	53.9
45–54	1,407.8	52.4	47.6
55–64	644.8	71.5	28.5
65 or older	41.4	93.6	6.4
Total	5,638.3	47.9	52.1

Source: Watson Wyatt tabulations of the April 1993 Current Population Survey.

type where "money is accumulated in an individual account for you."[8] If the respondent indicated they were included in a "defined benefit formula plan" or the "individual account" plan, they were asked how many of each type covered them. In addition, respondents could indicate if they were covered by some other type of plan, or that they were included but did not know the type of plan in which they were participating. Respondents who indicated that they were participating in multiple plans were asked which of the plans they had identified was their "most important plan." Table 16-3 shows the results for those who responded that they were covered by both a defined benefit plan and a defined contribution plan.

In most cases where an employer sponsors both a defined benefit and a defined contribution plan, the defined benefit plan would provide higher employer-financed benefits than the defined contribution plan for people reaching retirement under the two plans. Respondents to the survey included 5.6 million workers who indicated that they were covered by both a defined benefit and defined contribution plan sponsored by their employer and who specified which of the plans was most important to them. Among the youngest group of workers included in the table, those between the ages of 21 and 24, only 28 percent indicated their defined benefit plan was the most important of the plans under which they were covered. With each successively older class of workers, there is a significant shift toward identifying the defined benefit plan as the most important plan.

A somewhat correlated way to look at the preference for the type of plan is to consider the relative preference for each type of plan according to how long the individual has been employed by the sponsor and how long he or she has been covered under the plan. In most cases there is little difference between employment tenure and length of plan coverage, so Table 16-4 shows the preferences by

[8]U.S. Department of Commerce, Current Population Survey, Bureau of the Census, Form CPS-1 (Washington, D.C.: USGPO, April 1993), question 42.

TABLE 16-4   Indication of Most Important Retirement Plan by
Individuals Covered by Both Defined Benefit and Defined
Contribution Plans, by Tenure

Tenure	Total Reporting (thousands)	Defined Benefit Plan (%)	Defined Contribution Plan (%)
<1 year	116.0	57.2	42.8
1–2 years	262.5	22.3	77.7
3–4 years	626.1	30.1	69.9
5–9 years	1,519.8	39.1	60.9
10–14 years	1,090.6	45.2	54.8
15–19 years	776.0	54.1	45.9
20–24 years	573.9	67.0	33.0
25–29 years	434.0	70.5	29.5
30+ years	207.2	83.8	16.2
No response	32.2	45.7	54.3
Total	5,638.3	47.9	52.1

Source: Watson Wyatt tabulations of the April 1993 *Current Population Survey.*

tenure with employer. There clearly is some correlation between tenure and age, so the pattern in the table is not particularly surprising. The one interesting anomaly in the table is the relatively high appreciation of the defined benefit plan for workers in their first year of employment with their firms. In many cases, such employees might not yet have benefited from the employer's contributions to the defined contribution plan so the defined benefit plan would seem to be the major benefit that is offered. But as one moves past the first year of employment into the next year, the percentage of workers identifying the defined benefit plan as the most important of their plans drops from 57 percent to only 22 percent. This suggests that early in a worker's tenure relatively small accumulations in the defined contribution plan must have a very strong monetary effect on the perceptions of the relative values of the two plans. But as tenure increases there is a consistent pattern of increasing appreciation of defined benefit plans.

Some interesting implications can be drawn from Tables 16-3 and 16-4 when they are considered in combination with the earlier analysis of the aging of the work force and its potential impact on tenures of workers in coming years. Considering the youth of the work force during the late 1970s and through the 1980s, it is little wonder that there seemed to be a strong growing desire among workers for defined contribution plans. As the baby boomers move into the higher ages and tenures of their working careers, there may well be a strong renewed interest in the overall characteristics that underlie defined benefit plans.

In the final analysis, participants' perceptions about employer-sponsored retirement plans are driven by their belief that the plans provide something of worth to a significant cross section of the work force and allow long-tenured workers to maintain a reasonable standard of living in retirement. There are various ways that participants' perceptions on these matters can be developed. Some plan sponsors are rather lax about providing workers with straightforward statements of plan benefits and annual statements of accruals under the plans. Others are far more aggressive, literally developing public relations campaigns around their programs. What many employers have found as they have moved to "empower" their workers by giving them more freedom and responsibility in accumulating their retirement resources is that they have had to become more aggressive in selling their retirement programs to get the levels of participation required for the plans to be judged a success.

Communicating the Plan

Thus far it seems that a retirement plan can support the strategic interests of the sponsor by attracting and maintaining a productive work force at a reasonable cost over time. Furthermore, the plan will be a vital element in the retirement portfolio of many workers and may become even more important under some Social Security policy scenarios. As also pointed out, workers of different ages have varying perceptions of plans, which can be seen in a general comparison of the value of the retirement benefits these plans generate. In the environment that existed 20 or 30 years ago, it was relatively easy to lead employees through the maze of options facing them and help them achieve retirement security. The maze itself was much simpler then. In most cases, the retirement plan was a stand-alone defined benefit plan, or one supplemented with a relatively modest profit-sharing or thrift/saving plan. Social Security benefits were dependable, because there was a steady history of stable or increasing benefits. Private savings rates were extremely stable for nearly four decades after World War II.

Today the world is infinitely more complicated. While Social Security will undoubtedly survive in some form, it may not provide the next generations of retirees with the same level of replacement income that it provides the current one. While defined benefit plans are still a significant element of workers' retirement programs, defined contribution plans have more or less replaced defined benefit plans in some segments of the employer community and have partly done so in most segments that have not gone completely to them. The challenge in sponsoring a defined contribution program is to help workers understand the implications of their saving behavior in terms of their retirement security. Workers often underestimate the level of capital accumulation they will need to sustain their standard of living in retirement. Furthermore, they often save at rates that will not even get them to their low targets.

Empowerment is one of the new concepts leading workers to rely more on defined contribution plans. The concept is that workers should be given greater control of their own destiny. One of the risks in giving individuals greater responsibility in the accumulation of their retirement assets is that they might badly misjudge what they need to do to make adequate provision for their needs. Given the direction that society is moving in this regard, it is imperative for employers to provide workers with the information they need to understand what the plan provides and why they must participate in it and save outside of it if they wish to achieve a reasonable standard of living in retirement. Given the diversity of age, education levels, and cultural backgrounds of employees that employers face today, this is no small task.

The communication packages available today are a far cry from the standard plan documents that ERISA requires employers to provide to workers covered by qualified plans. Communications programs cut across a variety of media, including printed materials, video and audio presentations, automated voice-response systems sometimes backed up with live operators, and computer retirement planning and simulation models. Employers use employee surveys and focus groups in designing communications programs to make sure that they understand workers' interests and appreciation for retirement programs so they can effectively communicate with those needing program information. It is clear that well-articulated communications programs can affect the behavior of plan participants. It is not uncommon to measure significant increases in worker participation in plans and increases in deferral percentages by those already participating after an effective communications program is implemented.[9]

Designing a plan and implementing it is not enough. Once the program is in place a structural evaluation should assess the program's overall effectiveness. Again, it is important to utilize participant surveys, focus groups, and the like to determine what participants have learned from the program and how they have changed their behavior. The most important thing to ascertain is that the program is generating the kind of understanding and participation that will ensure that the program is working for a large majority of the target group. While some employers have made effective strides in this direction, the overall measures of participants' knowledge of how their retirement programs are working is disappointing.

Olivia Mitchell has compared what a sample of older workers told interviewers about their retirement plans with what their employers' plan descriptions indicated. She found that participants in defined contribution plans tend to be less well-informed about their plans than defined benefit plan participants. This is a disturbing finding when one considers the contributory character of defined contribution plans. In assessing covered workers' knowledge about their defined contribution plans, she found that only about half of those workers whose employers contribute to the plans believed that they did so.

More recent data from the April 1993 CPS also suggest that retirement plan participants know little about their plans. In the data compiled to develop Tables 16-3 and 16-4, when workers were asked to identify their most important plan if they were covered by both a defined benefit or defined contribution plan, 10 percent either did not respond or responded that they did not know which of the plans was more important to them. Even more serious is the discrepancy between those reporting that they were covered by both types of plans on the CPS survey and administrative data. In total, the CPS estimates suggest that only 6.2 million workers, including government workers, are covered by both a defined benefit and defined contribution plan. Yet a Department of Labor analysis of Form 5500 disclosure forms suggests that nearly 14 million private sector nonagricultural wage and salary workers were covered by both types of plans, according to 1990 plan year filings.[10]

---

[9]See, for example, Norman W. Snell and Burkett W. Huey, "Designing a Retirement Education Program for Today's Employees," *Compensation and Benefits Review*, March–April 1994, pp. 47–53; and Shari Caudron, "Target: Future Shock," *Industry Week*, July 20, 1992, pp. 42–46.

[10]U.S. Department of Labor, Office of Research and Economic Analysis, *Private Pension Plan Bulletin*, no. 2 (Washington, D.C.: USGPO, Summer 1993), p. 6.

The potential for harm is much greater when workers covered by defined contribution plans do not understand what their employer offers than when workers are covered by defined benefit plans. A worker who fails to grasp the fundamentals of a defined benefit plan can still end up with a satisfactory retirement income because the sponsor took care to worry about adequacy goals, benefit accumulation, and other such details. In this regard, if workers are not told about the operations of their defined contribution plans they can end up with inadequate incomes in retirement. While low participation rates in defined contribution plans may reduce sponsors' costs in the short run, in the long run it may not serve employers' interest to have significant numbers of workers getting to normal retirement ages without adequate retirement resources. Furthermore, the widespread lack of understanding about coverages and benefits provided by employer plans can affect national survey results and thereby make the employer-based retirement programs seem ineffective. This outcome can lead to public policy changes that add further to employers' cost of running plans.

Minimizing Administrative Implications

For plan sponsors, the plan is one of the facts of doing business that is not directly related to the business itself in most cases. Since sponsorship of a plan implies the need to keep records, pay benefits, and so on, there are some costs associated with plans that would not be incurred if the sponsor merely passed on the equivalent of the value of the benefit in the form of higher wages to workers while they were employed. Add to that the legal requirements spelled out in the previous section of the volume with which plans have to comply and it is clear that some care is needed to operate plans efficiently.

In the early 1990s the Pension Benefit Guaranty Corporation commissioned a study to estimate the administrative costs associated with administering defined benefit and defined contribution plans of various sizes. Estimates were developed of units and costs of services that would be required by plans with 10,000, 500, 75, and 15 participants. The units of services estimated in the study included in-house administration time actuarial, legal, and auditing services. The cost of the services was estimated for the period 1981 through 1991 on the basis of one consulting firm's fee schedules over the period, their past experience, and explicit discussions with clients as they were working on the project. The analysis looked at the routine costs of the ongoing administration of the plans but also considered special one-time costs of implementing plan changes required to stay in compliance with new regulatory provisions covering the respective plans.[11]

Table 16-5 shows the results of this analysis for defined benefit plans. The 1991 figure represents the estimated ongoing cost of administering these plans under an assumption that no additional plan modifications would be required to stay in compliance with new regulations. Several conclusions can be drawn from the table. First, very large companies can achieve tremendous economies of scale in administering a defined benefit plan, in comparison with small companies. On an

---

[11]Hay/Huggins Company, Inc., *Pension Plan Cost Study* (Washington, D.C.: Pension Benefit Guaranty Corporation, September 1990), p. 31.

TABLE 16-5   Per Capita Costs of Administering a Defined Benefit Plan for Plans of Various Sizes, 1981–91 (dollars)

Year	10,000 Participants	500 Participants	75 Participants	15 Participants
1981	19.40	56.45	115.61	161.93
1982	19.44	57.52	118.32	165.95
1983	20.83	64.52	145.92	255.31
1984	20.73	64.43	135.97	204.05
1985	27.19	79.61	198.65	399.59
1986	37.26	112.09	349.02	565.35
1987	37.68	106.57	205.07	337.68
1988	48.48	121.02	245.23	480.65
1989	54.11	142.21	339.88	686.57
1990	55.50	161.73	464.48	805.45
1991	53.64	133.21	259.78	455.35

Source: Hay/Huggins Company, Inc., *Pension Plan Cost Study,* p. 31.

ongoing basis, the estimated per capita cost of plan administration for a plan covering 15 participants exceeded the per capita cost for the 10,000-participant plan by eight to nine times. With 500 lives in the plan the advantage of the largest plan dropped to about 2½ times. Second, the costs of the plan modifications required to stay in compliance with the regulatory environment are relatively more expensive for small plans than bigger ones. For example, in comparing the change in costs from 1988 to 1989, it seems the 10,000-participant plan's per capita cost rose by 11.6 percent (i.e., $48.48 to $54.11) versus 42.8 percent for the smallest plan (i.e., $480.65 to $686.57). Finally, the administrative cost burden for smaller plans is so large that it significantly dampens the tax advantages of setting up a tax-qualified plan. A 15-participant plan that has a normal cost of 4 percent of payroll would generate a $1,200 contribution for a $30,000 salaried worker. Assuming that worker is in the 15 percent marginal tax bracket for federal tax purposes, the $1,200 pretax contribution would generate only $180 in tax savings on the contribution in the year it was made. As pointed out in Chapter 8, however, the tax on that contribution would ultimately be paid anyway, when the benefit was actually distributed. The tax saving for an individual on the accumulated interest on a contribution of this magnitude that was left in a plan for 20 years would be approximately $1,000, but only at a cost of the annual plan administration equal to about one-quarter of the value of the tax benefit if the plan can be operated without frequent modifications. If the plan has to be modified on a fairly continual basis because of changing regulations, as much as half the tax benefit in this hypothetical case would be wasted on administrative charges.

Table 16-6 shows the cost of administering a defined contribution plan in the same four sizes of firms. In this case, there are still considerable economies of scale for the participants in the larger plans; the difference in the steady-state per capita cost of administering the smallest plan, shown for 1991, is 5.75 times the cost of the largest plan. In addition, the cost of implementing changes to plans at the smallest

TABLE 16-6   Per Capita Costs of Administering a Defined
Contribution Plan for Plans of Various Sizes, 1981–91
(dollars)

Year	10,000 Lives	500 Lives	75 Lives	15 Lives
1981	21.39	54.76	95.96	114.13
1982	21.81	55.96	98.36	117.20
1983	23.40	55.31	99.80	143.47
1984	24.20	61.66	110.45	141.00
1985	28.38	64.18	133.48	243.27
1986	30.46	96.05	305.25	463.07
1987	31.69	91.12	166.49	257.40
1988	32.50	70.09	116.69	191.80
1989	37.74	88.16	189.43	344.87
1990	39.91	120.58	363.02	585.40
1991	39.58	85.32	144.42	227.47

Source: Derived by authors from Hay/Huggins Company, Inc., *Pension Plan Cost Study.*

firm level is still fairly expensive. Again, with respect to the changes in the cost of administration from 1988 to 1989, the 10,000-participant plan had a net administration cost increase of 17 percent, while the smallest plan realized an 80 percent rise.

Another way to look at the relative costs of operating a defined benefit or defined contribution plan in firms of various sizes is to consider the difference between Tables 16-5 and 16-6. These differences in administration costs are shown in Table 16-7. While the cost of running a plan and another complications that one

TABLE 16-7   Differences in the Per Capita Cost of Administering a
Defined Contribution versus a Defined Benefit Plan for
Plans of Various Sizes, 1981–91 (dollars)

Year	10,000 Lives	500 Lives	75 Lives	15 Lives
1981	−1.99	1.69	19.65	47.80
1982	−2.37	1.56	19.96	48.75
1983	−2.57	9.21	46.12	111.84
1984	−3.47	2.77	25.52	63.05
1985	−1.19	15.43	65.17	156.32
1986	6.80	16.04	43.77	102.28
1987	5.99	15.45	38.58	80.28
1988	15.98	50.93	128.54	288.85
1989	16.37	54.05	150.45	341.70
1990	15.59	41.15	101.46	220.05
1991	14.06	47.89	115.36	227.88

Source: Derived by the authors from Hay/Huggins Company, Inc., *Pension Plan Cost Study.*

type of plan or the other create might be important in determining what kind of plan to offer workers, these are not the only considerations. The plan ultimately has to support the overall goals of the organization. It can do that by fulfilling the goals that have been laid out in general terms in this chapter, several of which will be examined in greater detail in the remainder of this section.

Chapter 17
Financing of Employer-Sponsored Retirement Plans

Tax-qualified retirement plans are primarily funded by periodic contributions, which may be made monthly, quarterly, or annually. Contributions may be made by the employer, the employees, or both. As described in earlier chapters, employee contributions may be mandatory or voluntary. Employee contributions are considered mandatory if they are required as a condition of employment, as a condition for participation in the plan, or as a condition for obtaining any benefits under the plan attributable to employer contributions.[1] A plan that includes mandatory employee contributions is characterized as contributory. If only the employer contributes to the plan, it is described as noncontributory.

Source of Contributions in Defined Benefit Plans

Early defined benefit plans were predominantly noncontributory. Murray Webb Latimer surveyed approximately 400 existing plans in the United States and Canada during 1928 and found that roughly 22 percent had contribution provisions at that time. Among the 86 companies with contributory plans in that survey, 22 required contributions from all employees while another 20 mandated contributions for all employees hired after the introduction of the contribution provision but made them voluntary for workers already in service at that time. In the remaining 44 plans, contributions were mandatory as a provision of participating in the plans, but the plans themselves were voluntary since workers were not required to participate.[2] Jay Strong, who surveyed 923 firms sponsoring various types of employee benefits programs between 1947 and 1949, reported that contributory plans became popular during the 1930s but that this trend shifted decidedly back toward noncontributory plans during the 1940s.[3] The move to noncontributory plans during the 1940s prevails to the present. A 1993 survey that included 494 large employer-sponsored defined benefit plans found that only 7 percent required employee contributions.[4] Several explanations may account for the shift to noncontributory plans that has persisted until the present.

---

[1]Treas. Reg. 1.411(c)-1(c)(4).
[2]Murray Webb Latimer, *Industrial Pension Systems* (New York: Industrial Relations Counselors, Inc., 1933), pp. 572, 583.
[3]Jay V. Strong, *Employee Benefit Plans in Operation* (Washington, D.C.: BNA Incorporated, 1951), p. 67.
[4]Watson Wyatt, *Wyatt COMPARISON* (1993 Statistical Supplement), p. 30.

In the early days of the pension movement, employers viewed their contributions to the pension plan as a gratuity. If the cost of the gratuity was controlled at affordable levels, the resulting benefit was not always sufficient to meet the retirement needs of the participants in the plan. Employee contributions were a way to enlarge benefits provided through the plan while keeping the sponsor's costs at reasonable levels. Both Latimer and Strong reported that contributory provisions were included in plans as a cost-control measure. Over the years, an alternative theory about plan costs evolved that suggested pensions were not a gratuity, but rather a deferred wage payment made after the termination of employment due to old age or disability. In this context, it made less sense for the employer to pay out money to workers as cash wages and then require that they pay part of their wages back to the plan if the partial amount could merely be withheld from the cash wage in the first place.

Entirely apart from the philosophical or direct financial aspects of the question, there are strong practical reasons for having noncontributory defined benefit plans. Employee contributions greatly complicate the administration of a plan. Unless participation is a condition of employment, all participants must apply for membership in the plan and authorize the employer to deduct the required contributions from their pay. An individual account must be established and maintained for each participant. Under defined benefit plans, the interest rate credited to mandatory employee contributions generally must be 5 percent for plan years after the Employment Retirement Income Security Act's vesting requirements apply and before 1988, and thereafter it must be 120 percent of the federal midterm bond rate in effect for the first month of the plan year.[5]

Policies must be developed and enforced to deal with participants who initially reject participation but later decide they want to join the plan. A policy is also needed to deal with temporary or permanent discontinuance of a participant's contributions. And if long-service employees who failed to join the plan reach an age when they can no longer work effectively, it may be very difficult for an employer to dismiss them with no pension, even if it was their own election. Under contributory plans, the accrued benefit must be divided between employee-derived and employer-derived portions.[6] Thus buy-back provisions are required for employees who quit and later return. All these and similar problems can be avoided by making the plan noncontributory.

If the plan is noncontributory, all eligible employees are automatically enrolled. This facilitates the achievement of the employer's business objectives. Furthermore, funding and investment policies are somewhat more flexible when no employee contributions are involved. Finally, the contributions that an employer makes toward a qualified pension plan are deductible as an ordinary business expense for income tax purposes while mandatory employee contributions are not deductible and as a consequence are made from net income after taxes.[7] Dollar for dollar, therefore, mandatory employee contributions are more burdensome than

---

[5]ERISA §204(c)(2)(C),(D); IRC §411(c)(2)(C),(D).

[6]ERISA §204(c); IRC §411(c).

[7]But elective contributions by employees under cash or deferred arrangements are excluded from taxable income.

employer contributions. An employer with a contributory plan who is considering an across-the-board pay increase can boost take-home pay more by reducing employee contributions than by adding the same number of dollars to wages.

In a defined benefit plan, an employee's contribution rate is often set at a multiple of his or her retirement benefit. The most common practice has been to establish employee contributions at two to three times the rate at which future service benefits accrue. If annual future service benefits accrue at the rate of 1 percent of each year's compensation, for example, the employee contribution rate would usually be set at 2 to 3 percent of each year's compensation. The portion of retirement benefits that such contributions will provide varies with the attained age of the employee and other factors, and the employer then contributes the remainder of the cost of the future service benefits as well as the full cost of the past service benefits.

Mandatory employee contributions to a qualified pension plan generally cannot be withdrawn before normal retirement as long as the participant is in the service of the employer.[8] A plan may allow a participant to recover his or her mandatory contributions, with interest, upon withdrawal from the plan, upon termination of the plan itself, or at the time of retirement. Many plans allow "cash-out" upon withdrawal or plan termination, but not upon retirement. The law permits participants to recover all past contributions, with interest, if the plan is converted from a contributory to a noncontributory plan.[9] The plan would rarely, if ever, refer to such a contingency, so in practice the disposition of accumulated employee contributions is a matter of employer policy or of negotiation between the employer and employees. Some plans have returned the contributions in cash, while others have transferred them to the employees' accounts in profit-sharing or thrift plans. Usually the elimination of employee contributions is prospective only, and prior employee contributions are not returned at the time of the change.

Source of Contributions in Defined Contribution Plans

Money Purchase Plans

One of the oldest forms of defined contribution plans is the money purchase plan, wherein the employer's contribution is usually a certain percentage of earnings. The benefits provided at retirement under these plans are simply the amount that the accumulations in the plan will purchase when the worker begins to draw on them. These plans have been particularly popular among nonprofit institutions. Indeed, the Teachers' Insurance Annuity Association (TIAA), which is a money purchase plan, has grown to be the largest private retirement plan in the country and one of the most popular. For an employer sponsor, the money purchase plan has the advantage that the cost of the plan is strictly defined by the contribution rate specified in the plan's benefit formula. The splitting of the contribution between the employer sponsors and covered workers varies considerably, but the accumulation of a personal account that accrues investment income significantly simplifies the administration issues raised by employee contributions in defined

---

[8]Rev. Ruling. 56-693.
[9]Rev. Ruling 70-259.

benefit plans. Money purchase plans are relatively limited in their coverage of private employees from the for-profit sector of the economy, covering between 6 and 7 percent of such workers.[10] There are a couple of reasons for this. Money purchase plans were established during the early phases of the pension movement in the United States as an alternative to setting up a defined benefit plan. While the cost of the money purchase plan was defined by the employer's commitment on contributions, the benefits provided by the plan were not defined. Since many early retirement plans were established by employers dealing with relatively proximate issues of retiring superannuated workers then on staff, the defined benefit plan was far more accommodating in providing adequate retirement benefits because service credits could be granted for service prior to the establishment of the plan. As the pension phenomenon began to take hold, alternative forms of defined contribution plans became more popular.

Deferred Profit-Sharing Plans

One alternative that also dates back to the earliest days of the pension movement in the United States is the deferred profit-sharing plan. Some employers found the profit-sharing plan more attractive than a money purchase plan because the plan sponsor did not have to commit to a fixed annual contribution. Under these plans, contributions are made only in those years that the company makes a profit, and the size of the contribution can vary according to the level of profits. This feature made these plans particularly attractive to companies concerned about the overall commitment to a defined benefit plan or the invariable commitment to a money purchase plan. This feature also made them attractive to employers interested in establishing supplemental plans to augment the benefits provided through their defined benefit plans. The allocation of the contributions to the plan among the plan participants can be based on compensation levels or, if the plan is contributory, they can be based on employees' own contributions to the plan. Profit-sharing plans cover between 15 and 16 percent of the work force in the private, for-profit sector of the economy.[11]

Thrift-Savings Plans

Another form of defined contribution plan dating back to the 1950s is the thrift-savings plan. Under these plans the employee could choose whether or not to contribute to the plan, and if he or she did, the employer would match the contribution on some basis. Although the employee contributions were made on an after-tax basis, the employers sponsoring the plans often would match 50 percent of an employee's contributions up to 6 percent of salary. The employer contribution was made on a pretax basis, and the income on the assets in the plan

[10]U.S. Department of Labor, *Employee Benefits in Medium and Large Private Establishments, 1991,* Bureau of Labor Statistics Bulletin 2422 (Washington D.C.: USGPO, 1993), p. 108; and U.S. Department of Labor, *Employee Benefits in Small Private Establishments, 1990,* Bureau of Labor Statistics Bulletin 2388 (Washington D.C.: USGPO, 1993), p. 79.

[11]U.S. Department of Labor, *Employee Benefits in Medium and Large Private Establishments, 1991,* p. 108; and *Employee Benefits in Small Private Establishments, 1990,* p. 79.

was not taxed until distribution. These plans were popular because they garnered relatively large participation rates at a relatively low cost to the plan sponsor. Today, 10 percent of workers in large and medium firms and 29 percent of workers in small firms are covered by thrift-savings plans.[12]

Section 401(k) Plans

The Revenue Act of 1978 added section 401(k) to the Internal Revenue Code, allowing workers to make voluntary contributions to defined contribution plans on a tax-deferred basis. Being able to contribute pretax money has provided a strong incentive for employees to contribute to their own retirement. One result has been the widespread adoption of cash or deferred arrangements by private employers, as allowed under section 401(k). In many cases, existing defined contribution plans have been modified to include 401(k) provisions. Sections 403(b) and 457 provide similar incentives to not-for-profit organization and governmental employees. During 1991, 71 percent of all participants in defined contribution plans sponsored by large and medium-size private sector employers could contribute to their plans through voluntary salary reductions. For participants in savings or thrift plans, 98 percent could contribute; for those in deferred profit sharing plans, 28 percent could; and for participants in money purchase pension plans, 17 percent could.[13]

Employer and Employee Contribution Practices and Procedures

Employers contribute to their defined contribution plans in one of two ways: by making "matching" contributions that are based on employees' contributions or by making "nonmatching" contributions that do not depend on employees' contributions. Some plans of both the contributory and noncontributory type allow voluntary employee contributions to the plan. These contributions are accumulated in individual employee accounts, credited with their share of the plan's investment return, including any appreciation and depreciation of market values,[14] and at the employee's option they may be used to provide additional pension benefits at retirement. The contributions and their investment earnings thereon are nonforfeitable and can be withdrawn by the participant at any time, pursuant to the administrative rules of the plan, without prejudice to any other rights or benefits that may have accrued under the plan. Voluntary contributions may not exceed 10 percent of current or cumulative compensation, a limit imposed because of the deferral of taxes on the investment income the contributions generate.[15]

Overall, employee contributions are far more prevalent in defined contribution plans than in defined benefit plans. The 1991 Department of Labor survey of employee benefits in medium and large private establishments found that

[12]U.S. Department of Labor, *Employee Benefits in Medium and Large Private Establishments, 1991*, p. 105; *Employee Benefits in Small Private Establishments*, 1990, p. x.
[13]Ibid., p. 105.
[14]ERISA §204(c)(2)(A),(4); IRC §411(c)(2)(A),(d)(5).
[15]Rev. Ruling 59-185.

95 percent of participants in defined benefit plans were in noncontributory plans. By comparison, 35 percent of participants were in defined contribution retirement plans and 23 percent of the participants were in capital accumulation plans in which all contributions to the plans were made by the employer.[16] A similar survey done a year earlier measuring benefits provided by small firms found that nearly 60 percent of participants in defined contribution retirement plans had all the contributions made by the employer.[17]

A Watson Wyatt survey of 520 plans in 1991 found that nearly 60 percent of companies that make nonmatching employer contributions have no defined benefit plan, while less than 20 percent of those that make only employer-matching contributions have no pension plan. Employers make larger contributions, on average, to plans that are the sole retirement vehicle than to those defined contribution plans that supplement a pension plan. Employer contributions were 6 percent of pay or more for 12 percent of the firms also offering a defined benefit plan, while 14 percent contributed between 4 and 6 percent. By comparison, 34 percent of firms that did not offer a pension plan contributed 6 percent of pay or more, with 21 percent contributing between 4 and 6 percent.[18]

Effects of Employer-Matching Contributions

Plans with matching contributions provide a strong financial incentive for employees to save for their own retirement. In most cases, the employer contribution to a defined contribution plan is made only to match employee contributions. In the majority of cases, the employer's contribution to a matching plan is determined by the maximum employee contribution that will be matched by the employer and the rate of that match. Some plans vary the matching rate on the basis of service, age, or compensation. In some plans, the employer-matching rate varies from year to year, depending on profits or some other measure of firm performance. The most typical match rate found in plans is a 50 percent match on contributions up to 6 percent of pay. Match rates range from 25 percent to more than 100 percent. Matching contributions up to 6 percent of pay are most common, with 43 percent of plans that provide matching contributions matching up to this level.[19]

No objective standards can serve as a basis for splitting pension contributions between the employer and the employees. The capacity and willingness of the employer to support the anticipated level of contributions through good times and bad, and through periods of greater and lesser tax incentives, must be taken into account in determining the type of plan to be established. The allocation of contributions to participants in plans must be made in the light of the circumstances surrounding the particular case, with an eye to the practices in other

---

[16]U.S. Department of Labor, *Employee Benefits in Medium and Large Private Establishments, 1991,* pp. 85, 105. The distinction that the Labor Department report draws between the "retirement" plans and "capital accumulations" plans is that retirement plans do not allow withdrawal of employer contributions prior to retirement, death, disability, termination of employment, age 59½, or hardship, whereas the capital accumulation plans have less stringent restrictions on withdrawal.

[17]U.S. Department of Labor, *Employee Benefits in Small Private Establishments, 1990,* p. 73.

[18]Watson Wyatt, "Employer Contributions to Defined Contribution Plans," *Wyatt COMPARISON,* November 1991, p. 14.

[19]U.S. Department of Labor, *Employee Benefits in Medium and Large Private Establishments,* p. 113.

TABLE 17-1   Employee Participation Rates at Various
Employer-Matching Rates of Employee Pretax and
After-Tax Contributions to 401(k) Plans During 1992
(percent)

Employer-Matching Rate	Average Participation Rate		
	Match Pretax Only	Match Pretax and After-Tax	All Plans Combined
No match	46.2	46.2	46.2
1–25	67.7	63.4	66.3
26–75	73.1	65.8	69.9
76+	72.4	63.7	69.0

Source: Watson Wyatt, 1994.

similar cases. The employee contribution rate should be set with a view to both equity and the desirability of achieving a high degree of participation. Under any plan, the objectives of the program and its qualification[20] can be defeated by inadequate participation.

Although a number of other factors undoubtedly come into play, an employer's willingness to match employee contributions to defined contribution plans can affect overall participation in the plans. Table 17-1 shows the rates of participation in 160 section 401(k) plans during 1992 distributed by the level of matching contributions on the part of the plan sponsors. As the table suggests, employer policies vary in their approach to matching employee contributions under these plans. Some employers provide no match on employee contributions at all; some match only pretax contributions made by workers; and some match both pretax and after-tax contributions. Among those that match, there is considerable variation in the matching rates.

Most employers in the 1 to 25 percent category, shown in the table, match 25 percent of employee contributions; those in the 26 to 75 percent category mostly match at the 50 percent level; and those in the 76 percent and higher category tend to match at the 100 percent level. The plans that do not match any employee contributions have participation rates ranging from 20 to 25 percent below those that do match. Interestingly, matching above the 25 percent rate does not appear to have incrementally larger effects on overall participation in these types of plans.

Limits on the Employer's Commitment

It is customary for the sponsor of a single-employer, nonbargained pension plan to hedge its commitment under the plan by including certain provisions that have become fairly standardized. The first provision, not found in all plans, makes it a matter of record that neither the establishment of the plan nor participation in the plan by a particular employee shall create any obligation on the part of the

---

[20]Mandatory contributions in excess of 6 percent of pay are presumed burdensome and hence discriminatory. Treas. Reg. 1.401-3(d); Rev. Rul. 59-185.

employer to provide continued employment to the employee in order that he or she may qualify for proffered benefits. In addition, while not often mentioned in plan provisions the employer's liability on plan termination is limited to benefits accrued to the date of plan termination. There is no obligation to fund or distribute benefits that the employee would have earned with future service to the normal retirement date after the date of plan termination.[21]

The second provision, which is found in almost all plans, gives the employer the unilateral right to alter, modify, or terminate the plan at any time. However, no action under the authority of this provision can operate to curtail, modify, or terminate any accrued benefit,[22] except as may be necessary under IRS regulations to prevent discrimination in favor of the 25 most highly paid employees upon early plan termination.[23] Reserving the right to amend, modify, or terminate the plan at any time in "the Company" is sufficient; specifically identifying the individual or group with amendment authority is unnecessary since the principles of corporate law govern who has authority to act on behalf of the company.[24] Moreover, the IRS may attempt to retroactively disqualify the plan for termination during the first few (possibly as many as five) years of the plan's existence for a reason other than "business necessity."[25]

A third provision, more critical in some respects than the foregoing, either gives the employer complete freedom to decide whether and how much to contribute or reserves to the employer the right to suspend, reduce, or discontinue contributions to the plan at any time and for any reason. During the first five years, the reason for a complete discontinuance of contributions must be "business necessity" if retroactive tax penalties are to be avoided. Implicit in this provision is the right of the employer to discontinue contributions to the plan, even though the accumulated assets may not be sufficient to provide all the benefits already accrued. For plans subject to ERISA's minimum funding requirements, the freedom to determine the amount of contributions or to suspend contributions is limited.

A fourth clause in defined benefit plans implements the third by stating that in the event of termination of the plan, or the discontinuance of contributions thereunder, the employer shall have no liability for the payment of accrued benefits beyond the contributions already made. In other words, to satisfy their claims if the plan were to be terminated, the participants and their beneficiaries would have to look to the assets in the plan, including any annuities that may have been purchased from life insurers. The employer might voluntarily contribute more to the plan—or pay the benefits out of its own resources—but it would have no legal obligation to do so. If the plan assets proved to be inadequate—as they are likely to be for years after the plan is established or retroactively liberalized—the benefits of all claimants would have to be scaled down or priorities established, with the possibility that some participants would receive nothing. Some plans do not contain an express limit on the employer's liability; instead they rely on the

---

[21] *Blessit v. Dixie Engine,* 848 F2d 1164 (11th Cir. 1988).
[22] ERISA §204(g); IRC §411(d)(6). Restrictions also apply to any change in the vesting schedule. ERISA §203(c); IRC §411(a)(10).
[23] IRC §411(d)(3); Treas. Reg. 1.401-4(c)(2).
[24] *Schoonejongen v. Curtiss-Wright Corporation,* 115 S.Ct. 1223, 131 L.Ed.2d. 94 (1995).
[25] Treas. Reg. 1.401-1(b)(2); *Howard S. Davis Est.* (1954) 22 TC 807(Acq.) Rev. Rul. 69-24.

employer's reserved right to discontinue contributions. Plan benefits insurance guarantees certain benefits and restricts the employer's ability to limit its liability (see Chapters 31 and 32 for the details of the pension plan benefits insurance program).

A final limit on the employer's undertaking that is of a general nature and not found in all plans is a statement that, except in the case of willful misconduct or lack of good faith, no legal or equitable rights against the employer shall be created or shall exist under the plan. The primary purpose of such a provision is to protect the firm and its agents against legal or equitable action arising out of the administration of the plan; but the language seems broad enough to be invoked against a participant or beneficiary seeking to compel the employer to make good on the benefit rights accrued under the plan.

The employer usually does not have all the foregoing rights under a pension plan subject to collective bargaining. A bargained plan cannot be altered, modified, or terminated without the consent of the bargaining agent, unless such rights have been reserved to the employer—an unlikely situation[26]—or to a joint board of trustees. As a matter of fact, the employer's legal commitment under these plans is not always clear. Generally, however, the employer commits itself to one of two types of undertakings: (1) to maintain the plan with specified benefits during the period of the labor agreement, or (2) to make contributions to the plan—a single-employer plan or a multiemployer plan—at agreed upon rates, usually expressed in cents per hour worked. The first type of agreement is often supplemented by the employer's commitment to fund the plan on some acceptable basis, but under both undertakings ERISA's minimum funding requirements apply. Under both arrangements, it is always tacitly assumed that the pension plan will be continued indefinitely through successive labor contracts. The basic legal question is what would be the effect of terminating of the plan, or of the labor agreement(s) under which it was established and operated, on the benefit rights that were created during the term of the labor contract or contracts.

Under a single-employer plan, if the collective bargaining agreement expires without being renewed, the employer generally has the right to continue, modify, or terminate the plan, just as under a nonbargained single-employer plan. Under a multiemployer plan, upon expiration of the collective bargaining agreement the employer stops contributing, and employees accrue no further benefits; in some cases, accrued benefits credited for past service before employer contributions began are canceled.[27] Upon withdrawal from a multiemployer plan or upon termination of a single-employer plan or a multiemployer plan, the employer may be liable for substantial additional payments (see Chapters 31 and 32).

A few prominent companies do not attempt to limit their pension obligations to funds already contributed and promise to pay the accrued pension benefits out of general corporate resources, if necessary. In some cases, this guarantee applies to all classes of accrued benefits, whereas in others it is limited to vested benefits,

[26]An employer does not need a provision in a collectively bargained plan giving it the right to alter, modify, or terminate the plan or to suspend, reduce, or discontinue contributions, since the continued existence of the plan depends upon the continued existence of a related collective bargaining agreement.

[27]ERISA §203(a)(3)(E); IRC §411(a)(3)(E).

benefits in payment status, or some other restricted category. Most of these employer guarantees were unilaterally assumed, one going back to 1904 and another to 1913; but a few were undertaken in response to collective bargaining in exchange for employer control of funding policy.[28]

Recent Trends in Employer-Sponsored Plans

As Chapter 16 discussed, one advantage of defined contribution plans over defined benefit plans for smaller employers administrative costs. An additional advantage over defined benefit plans is that there is greater sharing of the financing of the retirement benefit accumulation in defined contribution plans. Because defined benefit plans do not generally require employee contributions whereas the majority of defined contribution plans do have contributory features, there is often a perception that financing retirement accumulations through the latter plans is less expensive for employers than through defined benefit plans.[29] While there may be some confusion regarding who actually pays for the benefits delivered by the respective retirement plans, there is a clear sense that contributory defined contribution plans including an employer match allows employers to direct contributions toward those workers who most highly value them.

In recent years, some retirement policy analysts have become concerned that the perceived cost advantages of defined contribution plans have led to a substantial decline in the sponsorship of defined benefit plans. Figure 17-1 shows the number of each type of plan with more than one active employee for each year from 1975 through 1991. The number of plans reflected in the figure were derived from the Form 5500 disclosure filings required of plan sponsors. Starting in 1975, just after the passage of ERISA, there were approximately twice as many private defined contribution plans in operation as defined benefit plans. The number of defined benefit plans increased from an initial level of slightly more than 100,000 plans in 1975 to roughly 175,000 in 1982 and 1983. From this peak in the early 1980s, the number of defined benefit plans began to decline gradually, and then more rapidly to the point that there were slightly less than 100,000 plans in operation in 1991. Over this period the number of defined benefit plans declined by more than 75,000, but the number of private defined contribution plans grew by more than twice that amount.

The reasons for the rise and fall in the number of defined benefit plans since the passage of ERISA can be found in the analysis in Chapter 16. Figure 17-2 shows the number of defined benefit plans with fewer than 100 participants as well as the number with more than 100 participants for the years 1975 through 1991. From this latter figure it is clear that most of the variation in the number of defined benefit plans over the period was due to the change in the number of smaller plans. In 1975 there were roughly 80,000 defined benefit plans with fewer than 100

[28]Employer guarantees of pension benefits are discussed at some length in Dan M. McGill, *Employer Guarantee of Pension Benefits* (Homewood, Ill.: Richard D. Irwin, 1974), pp. 19–35.

[29]Most economists have an alternative perspective that the cost of financing retirement benefits is part of the overall compensation bill and that to the extent an employer makes a contribution to a retirement plan, it reduces other elements of the compensation package. A detailed discussion of the theory of "compensating differentials" is presented later in this chapter.

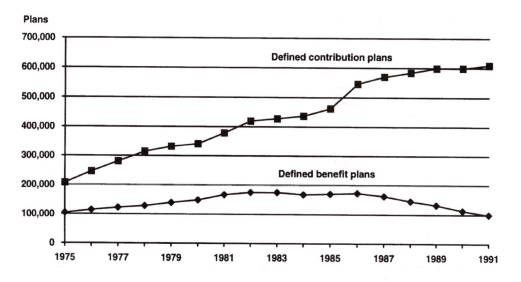

Figure 17-1. Number of private retirement plans by plan type, selected years. Source: U.S. Department of Labor, Pension and Welfare Benefits Administration, *Private Pension Plan Bulletin no. 2, Abstract of 1990 Form 5500 Annual Reports* (Summer 1993), p. 69; and *Private Pension Plan Bulletin no. 3, Abstract of 1991 Form 5500 Annual Reports* (Summer 1994), p. 4.

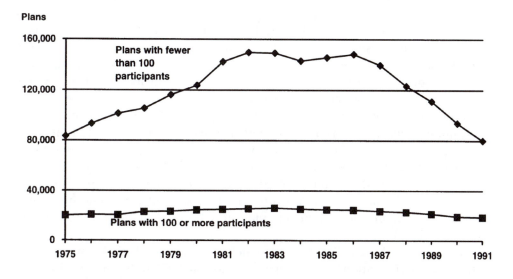

Figure 17-2. Number of private defined benefit plans by plan size, selected years. Source: U.S. Department of Labor, *Abstract of 1990 Form 5500 Annual Reports*, pp. 70–71; and *Abstract of 1991 Form 5500 Annual Reports*, p. 15.

Thousands of participants

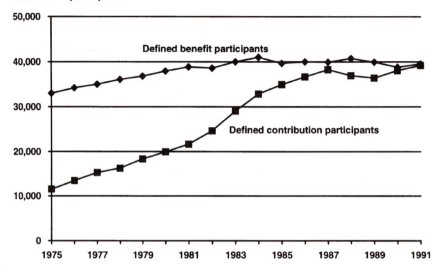

Figure 17-3. Number of private retirement plans by plan type, selected years. Source: U.S. Department of Labor, *Abstract of 1990 Form 5500 Annual Reports*, p. 72; and *Abstract of 1991 Form 5500 Annual Reports*, p. 18.

participants. These plans increased to nearly 150,000 by 1986 but then declined to roughly 80,000 by 1991. By comparison, there were about 20,000 defined benefit plans with 100 or more participants in 1975. This number grew to about 26,000 by 1983 and declined to roughly 19,000 plans by 1991. There was certainly some variation in the number of larger plans, but it was quite moderate in comparison with the variation in the number of smaller plans over the period. As noted in Chapter 16, the relative increase in the administrative costs of defined benefit plans was much greater for smaller defined benefit plans than for larger ones during the 1980s. Undoubtedly the burden of administrative cost accounted for some of the shift away from defined benefit plans toward defined contribution plans that became so apparent during the latter part of the 1980s.

Another way to assess the shift in the prevalence of defined benefit and defined contribution plans is to consider the number of participants covered in the alternative types of plans. During 1975 there were approximately three times as many participants in private defined benefit plans as defined contribution plans. Figure 17-3 shows that the number of participants in defined benefit plans grew gradually, from 33 million to 41 million between 1975 and 1984. Since that time, participation in larger defined benefit plans has declined slightly, to 39.5 million participants in 1991.

In the case of the smaller defined benefit plans, those with fewer than 100 participants, participation grew from 1.6 million in 1975 to 2.2 million in 1981, where it held steady until 1983. In 1984 participation in small defined benefit plans began to decline, gradually at first but on an accelerating basis after 1987. Between 1987 and 1991 participation in small, private defined benefit plans dropped from

2.0 million to 1.2 million. Among plans with more than 100 participants, participation grew from an initial level of 33.0 million in 1975 to 41.0 million in 1984. Since that time, reported participation has varied slightly from year to year, ranging from 39 to 41 million participants.[30] The variation in participation in larger defined benefit plans is more reflective of variations in employment levels in the sponsoring firms than in any specific changes in the availability of the plans themselves.

Overall, some smaller employers made a move to offer defined benefit plans immediately after the passage of ERISA. The growing complications in the regulatory environment during the 1980s made these plans more expensive to administer for smaller employers and less attractive in comparison with defined contribution plans. Larger employers have not experienced the same shift away from defined benefit plans that is apparent in the smaller employer market.

Undoubtedly the regulatory effects during the 1980s resulted in some substitution of defined contribution plans for defined benefit plans among workers employed by smaller employers. Over the period 1975 to 1991, participation in defined contribution plans with more than 100 participants nearly tripled, growing from 2.5 million to 7.4 million. Among larger employers, participation in defined contribution plans grew from 9.0 million participants in 1975 to 31.8 million in 1991.[31] In other words, the absolute growth in participation in larger defined contribution plans was between four and five times the growth in participation in small plans. The relative growth in participation in defined contribution plans also was greater among larger employers than it was for smaller ones, even though the incentives for substituting defined contribution for defined benefit plans was much greater in the latter case. What happened in the case of larger employers was that the introduction of the section 401(k) plans in the early 1980s led to a virtual explosion in the use of supplementary defined contribution plans by larger employers during the 1980s. Between 1981 and 1984, there was a 60 percent increase in the number of participants covered by private defined contribution plans in plans with more than 100 participants.[32] Much of the growth in defined contribution coverage during this period was experienced by workers who were already participating in defined benefit plans.

While much of the recent growth in defined contribution plans might be attributable to the rise in supplemental plans among larger employers, that does not change the fundamental fact that there has been a decided shift toward contributory plans in recent years. As a result, much of the responsibility for the direct financing of retirement saving has shifted from employer sponsors of plans to participants in them. It is not clear, however, that this shift has lowered the total compensation costs that employers incur in attracting and maintaining their work force or that workers are actually having to save more of their compensation in order to meet their retirement needs. Who actually pays for the benefits that are provided by the plans is taken up in Chapter 20.

---

[30]U.S. Department of Labor, *Abstract of 1990 Form 5500 Annual Reports*, p. 72; and *Abstract of 1991 Form 5500 Annual Reports*, p. 18.
[31]Ibid.
[32]Ibid.

Chapter 18
Total Retirement Income: Setting Goals and Meeting Them

Chapter 1 made the case that in an evolving world when workers could no longer support themselves directly through earned income or indirectly through extended family support during their later years of life, the need arose to find mechanisms to provide income security in these years. In a world of free markets and individual responsibility, individual workers would be held responsible for saving enough during their working years to make sure their retirement needs would be met. Economists have developed a theoretical life-cycle model to explain work and saving patterns of individuals at different ages in such a free market economy.[1]

The Concept of Income Needs in Retirement and Providing for Them

The life-cycle model suggests that individuals will borrow against the expected stream of future earnings during the early phases of their life to start their families, buy their homes, and so forth. During the middle phase of their working life, they will pay off their early career debts and begin to accumulate excess assets by regularly consuming less than they earn. The accumulating assets can be laid away at interest, to be reclaimed and used later in life when the ability or inclination to "earn" a living is greatly diminished. The life-cycle model can be enhanced by allowing the family unit, as opposed to a single individual, to define the time horizons for borrowing, saving, and retiring. It can also allow for the possibility of one generation bequeathing some share of its lifetime accumulation to subsequent generations.

Leslie Hannah observes that the life-cycle model provides a reasonable description of how the business and professional classes funded their retirement during the late eighteenth century. In essence, workers saved part of their earnings during their robust years in anticipation of retirement needs during the later part of their lives. Of course, to accumulate savings during their working years workers

---

[1]Franco Modigliani and Richard Brumberg, "Utility Analysis and the Consumption Function: An Interpretation of Cross-section Data," in Kenneth K. Kurihara, ed., *Post-Keynesian Economics* (New Brunswick, N.J.: Rutgers University Press, 1954); Albert Ando and Franco Modigliani, "The Life Cycle Hypothesis of Savings: Aggregate Implications and Tests," *American Economic Review*, vol. 53 (March 1963): pp. 55–84.

had to trade current consumption in favor of consumption deferred until later in life. The willingness of workers to make such trade-offs depended on the nature of their time horizons, the returns they could expect on their saving, and the extent to which they favored the immediate gratification of current consumption over the potential gratification of deferred consumption.

Regrettably, hunger and other needs that many low-income workers experienced during their working years in the late 1800s and early 1900s led them to discount the value of future consumption to the point that little retirement provision resulted. As Hannah points out: "The savings ethos of the mass of the population remained quite sharply differentiated from the patterns established by the Victorian bourgeoisie, and this severely constrained their retirement options."[2] And as Chapter 1 suggests, this environment gave rise to organized retirement plans.

With the growth of organized retirement plans, it became important to set defined goals that these plans would achieve in terms of providing a stream of income that would allow the recipients to maintain acceptable living standards in retirement. In the early evolution of retirement systems there was little discussion of the development of these goals, although the goals themselves were sometimes quite specific. For example, the Committee on Economic Security that developed the Social Security Act for Franklin Roosevelt's administration in 1935 felt that "payment of benefits at a rate . . . approximating 50 percent of previous average earnings is socially desirable,"[3] although there was no justification for reaching that particular threshold. Over the last 25 or 30 years, considerable effort has been devoted to developing retirement income goals by which retirement plans can be judged.

These goals can be separated into two classes: absolute levels of income required in retirement to provide for minimal levels of need and the level of income required to maintain the preretirement standard of living during retirement. This chapter first looks at how each of these measures of need are derived and how they are used when designing retirement income security programs and evaluating the adequacy of the benefits provided by them. The second section of the chapter examines absolute standards of need. Although these are not often considered by employers in the design of their retirement programs, from a public policy perspective they are extremely important to the effectiveness of the retirement system. The third section of this chapter reviews the historical development of the relative standards of need that have been used in plan design and evaluation for the past several years. The derivation of these measures has generally been flawed either because of conceptual inconsistencies underlying them, or because of imprecision in their actual derivations. The fourth section of the chapter examines the development of an alternative derivation of the relative needs standard. It begins with the development of a straightforward conceptual model based on the goal that income in retirement should allow the retiree to maintain the preretirement

---

[2]Leslie Hannah, *Inventing Retirement: The Development of Occupational Pensions in Britain* (London: Cambridge University Press, 1986), p. 5.
[3]Committee on Economic Security, *Social Security in America* (Washington, D.C.: USGPO, 1937), p. 202.

standard of living. It also presents an estimation of various expenditures that are peculiar to the periods before and after retirement, which is crucial for measuring consistent standards of living in the working and retirement periods. Next, it presents several sets of retirement targets, which are based on several scenarios under which workers actually accrue their retirement savings and retire. Then the discussion turns to the interrelationship between the absolute and relative standards of need and the potential of employer-based retirement plans to satisfy the minimalist absolute standard for low-wage workers. The chapter concludes with a brief summary of the implications of the analysis for employers in designing their retirement programs.

Absolute Standards of Need

The concept of minimal economic needs goes back at least two centuries to Adam Smith, who classified consumer goods as "either necessaries or luxuries." Under necessaries he listed "not only the commodities which are indispensably necessary for the support of life, but whatever the custom of the country renders it indecent for creditable people, even of the lowest order, to be without."[4] While this concept of minimal need is absolute, it is not universal. For example, Smith explained that in late-eighteenth-century England leather shoes had become an absolute necessity, and that no creditable person would be seen in public without them. Yet in Scotland, custom had rendered them a necessity for men but not for women. Thus women could still walk about barefooted without embarrassment. And in France they were a necessity to neither men nor women. So Smith's concept includes not only the minimum level of goods needed to survive, "but those things which the established rules of decency have rendered necessary to the lowest rank of people."[5]

Minimal Needs Standards in the United States

Jumping forward to the latter half of the twentieth century, President Lyndon Johnson's War on Poverty in the early 1960s required some measure of families' minimal needs against which the "war" could be assessed. The 1964 *Report of the Council of Economic Advisers* (CEA) set the poverty line at $3,000 in pretax annual money income for families, and implied a poverty line of $1,500 for single individuals: "The $3,000 figure was a consensus choice based on consideration of such factors as the minimum wage level, the income levels at which families began to have to pay Federal income taxes, and public assistance levels."[6] At about the same time as the CEA was devising its poverty line, Mollie Orshansky, an analyst at the Social Security Administration, was developing a statistical measure to assess the relative risk that various demographic groups would be in a low economic status characterized as poverty.

---

[4]Adam Smith, *The Wealth of Nations* (New York: Random House, 1994), pp. 938–39.
[5]Ibid., 939.
[6]Gordon M. Fisher, "The Development and History of the Poverty Thresholds," *Social Security Bulletin*, vol. 55, no. 4 (Winter 1992): p. 4.

Orshansky based her work on a survey done by the Department of Agriculture that showed that families with three or more persons in the mid-1950s spent approximately one-third of their pretax money income on food. She then used an "economy food plan" developed by the Agriculture Department to estimate what it would cost to provide the food in these plans for 58 nonfarm family categories using 1964 price levels. The "economy" food plan was "essentially for emergency use" when funds were low.[7] Orshansky assumed that the family could reasonably cut back its food budget to the level of the economy food plan where expenditures on food would be minimal, but if carefully managed, the budget could still provide adequate nutrition. She further assumed that such a household also could cut back its other expenditures in proportion to its food expenditures. Thus, holding constant the one-to-three ratio of food expenditures to other household expenditures that prevailed among family units of three or more people, she could derive poverty thresholds for households of varying compositions by multiplying the economy food budget for the family by three.

Orshansky derived separate measures for single individuals and couples that accounted for the higher fixed costs of setting up and maintaining a household—for example, it does not take three times the space or rental cost to house three people as it does to house one. For single- and two-person households, she also distinguished between units headed by a person over age 65 as opposed to one headed by a younger person. Combining the four classifications of smaller households to the 58 classes of families with three or more people in them gave a total of 62 poverty thresholds that varied by family size and composition.

Finally, through the technique just described Orshansky adjusted the poverty measures that she derived to develop a separate set of poverty measures for farm families in which housing on average tended to be part of their farm operations and the household produced 40 percent of its own food. Thus, considering the farm and nonfarm thresholds, she ended up with 124 different thresholds. In addition to the poverty measures that she developed, Orshansky used an alternative "low-cost" food plan developed by the Agriculture Department to derive a parallel set of measures to identify people who were living at income levels designated to be near poverty.

Aged persons living in family units whose combined income fell below their respective thresholds were considered to be in poverty. The poverty level for a single person over age 65 in 1963, by Orshansky's calculation, was $1,470, which was 7.0 percent below the rate for a single person under 65. For a couple in a household headed by an elderly person, the poverty threshold was $1,850, which was 9.8 percent below the threshold for a couple under the age of 65.[8] The reason that the elderly poverty budgets were lower in her derivation was that the elderly need less food to maintain themselves than younger people, which converted into smaller allocations in the food budgets developed by the Department of Agriculture. Given that the food budget was the basis for the poverty measure, it merely carried through to the final thresholds.

---

[7]Mollie Orshansky, "Counting the Poor: Another Look at the Poverty Profile," *Social Security Bulletin*, vol. 28, no. 1 (January 1965): pp. 3–29.

[8]Gordon M. Fisher, "The Development and History of the Poverty Thresholds," *Social Security Bulletin*, vol. 55, no. 4 (Winter 1992): p. 6.

The underlying concept supporting Orshansky's poverty thresholds was that families whose income equaled the thresholds would be able to maintain a minimal but adequate standard of living. Orshansky's original goal in developing her thresholds was to devise statistical measures to estimate the extent and distribution of poverty in the United States. These thresholds were not meant to be applied individually to determine who was poor, for as Orshansky herself knew, in "deciding who is poor, prayers are more relevant than calculation because poverty, like beauty, lies in the eye of the beholder. Poverty is a value judgment; it is not something one can verify or demonstrate, except by inference and suggestion, even with a measure of error."[9] But Orshansky's statistical measure of poverty was published just as the Economic Opportunity Act of 1964 was being implemented. The research division at the Office of Economic Opportunity adopted her measure for budgeting and planning purposes, making it the quasi-official government measure of poverty. In 1969 a slightly modified version of Orshansky's poverty measure was adopted by the Bureau of the Budget (which later became the Office of Management and Budget) as "an attempt to specify in dollar terms a minimum level of income adequacy for families of different types in keeping with American consumption patterns."[10]

After 1980 additional changes to the poverty thresholds were introduced that eliminated the differences between farm and nonfarm family units, eliminated separate thresholds for households headed by a female and for a catchall category, "all other" families, and an extension of the thresholds to families with seven, eight, and nine or more members. For all practical purposes, though, the major changes to the poverty levels since they were first derived reflect their annual indexation by the annual average consumer price index.[11] By 1993 the poverty thresholds for persons over 65 living alone had risen to $6,928, and to $8,738 for two-person households headed by a person over the age of 65.

Minimal Needs Standards Revisited

The use of the official poverty standards as a measure of minimally adequate income has been criticized by many analysts over the years. One criticism is that the standards are based on cash income available to families and do not include measures of the value of in-kind income provided through programs like the food stamp program, Medicaid, Medicare, housing assistance, and so forth. Another criticism is that they are based on food consumption patterns that persisted nearly four decades ago. Along with the criticisms of the poverty measures has come a series of proposed alternatives. Patricia Ruggles has shown the implications of using a number of alternative measures of poverty on the overall levels of the thresholds, as shown in Table 18-1. While her presentation was developed on the

[9]Mollie Orshansky, "How Poverty Is Measured," *Monthly Labor Review*, vol. 92, no. 2 (February 1969): p. 37.

[10]Office of the Assistant Secretary for Planning and Evaluation, Department of Health Education and Welfare, *The Measure of Poverty: Technical Paper II, Administrative and Legislative Uses of the Terms "Poverty," "Low-Income," and Other Related Items* (Washington, D.C.: USGPO, September 1976), p. 8.

[11]Social Security Administration, *Annual Statistical Supplement, 1993 to the Social Security Bulletin* (Washington, D.C.: USGPO, 1993), pp. 346–47.

TABLE 18-1   Alternative Poverty Thresholds for a Three-Person Family at Five-Year Intervals, 1967 to 1987 (dollars)

Year of Dollar Value	Official Threshold	Threshold Indexed by Growth in Median Income	Relative Threshold, Four-Person Standard[a]	Housing Consumption Standard[b]	Updated Multiplier Standard[c]
1967	2,661	2,661	3,098	n.a.	3,379
1972	3,339	3,729	4,341	n.a.	4,241
1977	4,833	5,370	6,252	2,008	6,380
1982	7,693	7,860	9,152	11,386	11,540
1987	9,056	10,317	12,094	13,977	15,195

Source: Patricia Ruggles, Drawing the Line: Alternative Poverty Measures and Their Implications for Public Policy (Washington, D.C.: Urban Institute, 1990), p. 53.

[a]Poverty threshold for four-person families set at 50 percent of the median income, and all other thresholds adjusted accordingly, using equivalence scales implicit in official thresholds.

[b]Based on fair market rents and housing affordability guidelines used in the Section 8 subsidized housing program. Data on fair market rents not available before 1975, when the Section 8 program was established.

[c]Calculated using the same general methods as the original Orshansky standard, but with a "multiplier" updated to reflect the changing share of food in family budgets.

basis of a three-person family, the relative variations would be comparable if the different approaches to calculating the various thresholds were applied to the elderly thresholds as well.

The first alternative to the official threshold would simply apply a different indexing basis to the 1967 base-year thresholds shown in Table 18-1, using the rate of growth in median income rather than the CPI as the annual indexing factor. The "relative" poverty threshold is set at 50 percent of median income in each year of measurement. Under this approach, as society becomes better off the minimum acceptable level of income would move up on a pro rata basis. Under the "housing consumption standard," Ruggles applies essentially the same methodology as that used in deriving the official poverty threshold, except that she uses housing expenditures rather than food expenditures as the basis for developing the multiplier, and she uses Fair Market Rental rates from the Department of Housing and Urban Development's Section 8 housing program for low-income families as the basis for minimum rental levels. The updated multiplier standard uses the same calculation methodology as the official index, except that it is updated to reflect more current food consumption patterns than those underlying the current poverty measure. Looking at the indices based on the housing consumption standard and the updated food multiplier, Ruggles concludes that "they strongly imply that a realistic consumption-based standard would be considerably higher than our current official [poverty] thresholds."[12] Given the range of alternative estimated needs standards that Ruggles considered, the official poverty index is the lowest of the

[12]Patricia Ruggles, Drawing the Line, Alternative Poverty Measures and Their Implications for Public Policy (Washington, D.C.: Urban Institute, 1990), p. 52.

TABLE 18-2   Alternative Elderly and Nonelderly Poverty Measures for Single Persons
and Couples in 1993 (dollars)

	Elderly Households		Nonelderly Households	
	Single Persons	Couples	Single Persons	Couples
Official poverty line	6,930	8,741	7,517	9,726
Updated multiplier standard	12,716	16,039	13,293	17,846

Source: Official poverty line from Social Security Administration, Office of Research and Statistics.
The updated multiplier standard was calculated by the authors as described in the text.

group and the "updated multiplier standard" is the highest. If Table 18-1 were
updated through 1993, the alternative needs measures for a family of three would
range from $11,521 to $21,140.

By 1993 the official poverty index for a family of three had reached $11,521.[13]
The 1992 *Consumer Expenditure Survey* done by the U.S. Department of Labor
estimated that average income before taxes for all consumer units in the country
was $28,671.88 and that average total expenditures for food was $4,358.66,[14] which
would yield a "multiplier" of 6.578 rather than the 3.0 multiplier that Orshansky
had used in the derivation of her poverty measures. The Human Nutrition Information Service of the U.S. Department of Agriculture developed two "thrifty food
plan" budgets for two-parent families with two children that can be used to derive
a measure comparable to the updated multiplier standard shown in Table 18-1.
One of the families has one child aged 1 to 2 and another aged 3 to 5; the other
family has one child aged 6 to 8 and another aged 9 to 11. The annual cost of the
thrifty food budget in 1993 for the younger family was $3,840.20 and the cost for
the older family was $4,396.60, yielding an average of $4,118.40.[15] Applying the
updated multiplier to the average thrifty food budget for 1993 would yield a
four-person needs standard of $27,091 for 1993. Using an equivalent adjustment
between three- and four-person families as that inherent in the official poverty line
(i.e., $11,521/$14,764 = 0.78034) would yield a three-person "updated" measure of
$21,140 (i.e., 0.78034 × $27,091) for 1993.

Table 18-2 shows that in 1993 the poverty line for individuals over 65 and living
alone was $6,930. The poverty line for two-person families in which the head of the
household was over 65 was $8,741. By comparison, the poverty threshold for single
individuals under the age of 65 was $7,517 in 1993, and, for two-person families in
which the head of the household was under age 65, it was $9,726. Using Ruggles's
"updated multiplier standard" to calculate the poverty rates for single elderly
persons in 1993 would yield a poverty threshold of $12,716, and for elderly couples
$16,039. Using the updated multiplier to calculate the poverty rates for nonelderly

[13]Social Security Administration, Office of Research and Statistics.
[14]Division of Consumer Expenditure Surveys, Bureau of Labor Statistics, "1992 Interview Survey
Public-Use Tape Documentation" (Washington, D.C.: USGPO, November 24, 1993), p. 120.
[15]Estimate derived from monthly budget costs published by U.S. Department of Agriculture, Human
Nutrition Information Service, "Cost of Food at Home Estimated for Food Plans at Four Cost Levels,"
HNIS Adm. 329 (Washington, D.C.), for each month of 1993.

individuals would yield a threshold of $13,293, and $17,846 for nonelderly households including two people.

Ruggles questions the appropriateness of poverty thresholds for elderly persons that are lower than those for their younger counterparts. Although the elderly may need less food than younger people and may have lower housing costs because they tend to have their homes paid for, they typically have higher expenditures in other areas, especially health care. She concludes: "Based on the evidence on consumption patterns, it would be easier to make a case for differential [i.e., lower] poverty thresholds for units headed by those under age 25 than for units headed by those age 65 and over."[16] Even if one were to move to the higher thresholds that result from using more contemporary consumption patterns, these would still be minimalist income levels to consider when designing a comprehensive retirement income system across much of the income spectrum. The absolute standards of need are valuable, however, because they establish floor targets below which public policy and public programs should not allow retirees to fall.

Preretirement Living Standards of Need

Even if precise definitions of minimal need within the range of income levels specified in Table 18-2 could be agreed upon, many people would still find such income levels to be woefully inadequate to meet their needs in retirement. Indeed, policy analysts and public policy makers have prescribed a retirement income objective that would be significantly higher for many retirees than that implied by the concepts of minimum absolute need inherent in the various poverty thresholds. These largely began to evolve at about the same time as the basic poverty standards were being developed. In 1964, in the second edition of the *Fundamentals of Private Pensions*, Dan McGill wrote that "it might be argued that a pension plan in conjunction with OASDI should provide a spendable pension (gross pension less income tax) approximately equivalent to the worker's spendable wages (gross wages less income tax and deductions for OASDI and private employee benefit plans) prior to retirement."[17]

In 1965 Congress enacted the Older Americans' Act, which listed first among ten objectives for the older people of the nation that they enjoy "an adequate income in retirement in accordance with the American standard of living."[18] While federal lawmakers established this lofty goal, they failed to define it concretely. Public policy analysts have helped to define what has become a widely accepted standard against which retirement income levels can be judged. For example, in a working paper developed for the President's Commission on Pension Policy in the early 1980s, Elizabeth Meier, Cynthia Dittmar, and Barbara Torrey implicitly embraced the standard that McGill had laid out a decade and a half earlier. They suggested: "The implicit or explicit goal is the maintenance of preretirement standards of living."[19]

---

[16]Ibid., p. 71.
[17]Dan M. McGill, *Fundamentals of Private Pensions*, 2d ed. (Homewood, Ill.: Richard D. Irwin, Inc., 1964), p. 59.
[18]Pub. Law 89-73, July 14, 1965.
[19]Elizabeth L. Meier, Cynthia C. Dittmar, and Barbara Boyle Torrey, *Retirement Income Goals*, Report prepared for the President's Commission on Pension Policy (Washington, D.C.: March 1980), p. 1.

The goal set out by McGill and then by Meier, Dittmar, and Torrey was ultimately endorsed by the President's Commission on Pension Policy in 1981. The Commission's final report indicated that "preretirement living standards should be measured in terms of preretirement disposable income. . . . Although preretirement disposable income is difficult to quantify precisely, estimates can produce reliable ranges of income that would need to be replaced for different income groups."[20] While maintaining preretirement living standards has become generally accepted as a public policy goal over the years, it does not mean that the federal government has assumed, or intends to assume, the responsibility of providing retirement income levels that maintain every worker's preretirement standard of living during their retirement years.

The Concept of Maintaining Living Standards in Retirement

Before looking at the relative roles of various players in attaining the goal of maintaining preretirement standards of living, it is important to understand the goal itself. In order to do so, consider a simple conceptual model of a worker's outlook on the future. Assume the worker lives in an economy with no taxes or formalized retirement savings programs. Further, assume this worker has reached age 30 and has just finished paying off all the liabilities related to her years of educational development, and that she has no other assets than her human capital. Also assume that she is in a job that will provide her with employment throughout her career and, for the sake of simplicity, that she will receive a constant real wage until her retirement at age 65. Finally, assume that she remains single throughout her life and has perfect foresight, anticipating her death at age 80, and assume that she can save some portion of her annual wages at a nominal interest rate equal to the inflation rate, which will finance her consumption during her retirement years.

Figure 18-1 represents the worker's outlook over the remainder of her lifetime under the assumption that she will save enough of her lifetime earnings to maintain her preretirement standard of living in retirement. The height of the larger rectangle, AB or CD, represents the worker's annual wage level and the area of the rectangle, ABCD, represents her total expected cumulative lifetime earnings. The worker's challenge is to spread her income, earned over a period of 35 years, over a period of 50 years of consumption needs based on her life expectancy. In other words, she needs to accumulate savings in the amount EBCF during her working career in order to finance her retirement consumption, DFGH. In retirement, the annual spend-down of the retirement savings will equal DF or HG in the figure. The relationship DF/DC is the equivalent of what retirement plan analysts refer to as the replacement rate of preretirement income by a retirement annuity funded by the accumulated savings.

Figure 18-1 grossly simplifies the actual operation of formal retirement programs. In most cases, workers will realize some real wage growth over significant parts of their careers. In addition, money that is laid aside for funding future consumption should generate real returns in most cases. Further, workers gener-

---

[20]President's Commission on Pension Policy, *Coming of Age: Toward a National Retirement Income Policy* (Washington, D.C.: USGPO, 1981), p. 42.

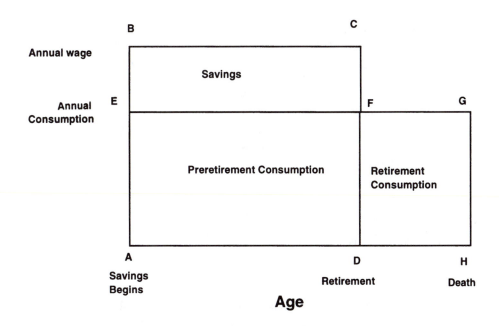

Figure 18-1. Conceptual model of lifetime earnings, savings, and consumption.

ally cannot anticipate their life expectancy with any real precision. Also, the model does not recognize the possibility that workers may incur special expenses during their working life specifically related to working that will not persist during retirement, or that special expenses might arise during retirement that are specifically related to aging. Finally, the existence of a noncontributory retirement program might generally be perceived as part of the overall compensation package, but annual contributions to the plan would not be part of a worker's wages when considering the replacement of preretirement earnings by retirement annuities.

While the model implied by Figure 18-1 may be an oversimplification, it captures the essence of a retirement program or system that would maintain workers' preretirement standards of living during their retirement years. Much of the analysis of appropriate replacement targets that has been developed to date extends the basic concepts captured by the figure. These analyses usually take account of the growth in wages over the career, by considering that retirement savings should be gauged against earnings during the period shortly before retirement. Consideration of the earnings on retirement plan assets are part of the cost and funding issues that are crucial to designing a retirement plan that will aid in maintaining the preretirement living standard. These models usually recognize that taxes are higher for many workers during their working careers than during retirement, and that other special expenses are incurred by workers. Typically, the "replacement rates" that these studies develop are calculated on the basis of cash wages paid prior to retirement.

Deriving the Retirement Income Targets

In many cases the analyses of retirement program maintenance of preretirement living standards is based on models that take into account differences in tax rates

TABLE 18-3   Retirement Income Equivalent to Preretirement Income
for a Person Retiring in 1980, by Marital Status

Gross Preretirement Income (dollars)	Equivalent Retirement Income Ratio (%)	
	Single Person	Married Couple
6,500	0.79	0.86
10,000	0.73	0.78
15,000	0.66	0.71
20,000	0.61	0.66
30,000	0.58	0.60
50,000	0.51	0.55

Source: Preston C. Bassett, in Elizabeth L. Meier, Cynthia C. Dittmar, and Barbara Boyle Torrey, *Retirement Income Goals,* Report prepared for the President's Commission on Pension Policy (Washington, D.C.: USGPO, March 1980), pp. 9–10.

before and after retirement and make certain assumptions about other special expenses related to either of the two periods. For example, Preston Bassett, an actuary working for the President's Commission on Pension Policy in 1980, developed such an analysis by basically quantifying the retirement goal standard that McGill had laid out in 1964. Bassett's derivation of retirement income goals was included in the presentation by Meier, Dittmar, and Torrey and is shown in Table 18-3.

Bassett estimated the necessary retirement income to maintain preretirement standards of living at six wage levels ranging from $6,500 to $50,000 per year. He began by deriving preretirement disposable income by subtracting estimated federal income taxes at each wage level, and an additional 19 percent to represent state and local income taxes because state and local income tax receipts were 19 percent of federal income tax receipts in 1978. He postulated that work-related expenses were 6 percent of disposable income at each income level, and that the savings rate ranged from 0 percent of disposable income at the lowest salary rate and incremented up 3 percentage points at each of the successively higher pay levels, reaching 15 percent at the highest. Subtracting work-related expenses and preretirement savings from disposable income gave net preretirement income that would need to be replaced in retirement. Because retirees at the higher income levels would face federal, state, and local income taxes, these had to be added back in to get to the income amounts that would sustain an equivalent standard of living in retirement. The results of Bassett's analysis are presented in Table 18-3.

Michael Dexter, an analyst working for the National Committee on Public Employee Pension Systems, developed one of the early empirically based measures of earnings replacement targets that was intended to estimate somewhat more precisely the extent to which retirement benefits actually maintained preretirement living standards. He defined the retirement income target as a ratio of retirement income to preretirement earnings. He defined the target ratio as

(18.1)
$$RR = \frac{P_r RPG - P_r RT - P_r RS \pm NCCR + P_o RT}{P_r RPG}$$

TABLE 18-4   Household Income Required in Retirement to Maintain
            a Preretirement Standard of Living (dollars)

Preretirement Income	Postretirement Income Needed to Maintain Living Standard	Preretirement Income Replacement Ratio (%)
10,000	8,175	0.818
25,000	18,028	0.721
50,000	28,999	0.580
75,000	29,657	0.395

Source: Dexter, *Replacement Ratios*, pp. 42–43.

where RR is the target replacement ratio; P_rRPG is preretirement gross pay; P_rRT is preretirement taxes; P_rRS is preretirement savings; NCCR is net changes in consumption requirements from preretirement to postretirement; and P_oRT is postretirement taxes. His derivation was based on the fact that for most people income tax obligations are lower during retirement than while working; that before retirement an individual should save to provide for the retirement period, but that the need for savings should decline in retirement if the individual has made proper provisions while working; that prior to retirement there are work-relatedexpenses that are eliminated during retirement; that some other expenditures, such as health care and education, may vary significantly between the working and retirement stages of life; and that individuals tend to give more gifts and contributions prior to retirement than after.[21] What distinguishes Dexter's work from earlier replacement rate targets was a detailed estimate of how the variables in Equation (18-1) change across a fairly broad spectrum of earnings levels. He used the 1973 *Consumer Expenditure Survey* to estimate the level of various expenditures that were related strictly to the working and retirement periods of life. A summary of his analysis is presented in Table 18-4. He concluded that the amount of income needed at upper income levels to maintain preretirement standards of living dropped off steeply. He reached this conclusion because he found that high-income retirees engaged in significant gifting, which he did not consider to be a necessary retirement expenditure.

Professor Bruce Palmer updated the Dexter study in 1988, taking into consideration the potential effects of the Tax Reform Act of 1986, updated information on consumption levels, and several other methodological considerations.[22] In 1991 and 1993 he updated his 1988 study after taking into account further changes in tax laws and consumer behavior.[23] In his studies, Palmer has developed two basic sets of replacement rate targets. The first of these dropped the variable NCCR, net change in consumption requirements, that Dexter included in his analysis, as

[21]Michael K. Dexter, *Replacement Ratios: A Major Issue in Employee Pension Systems* (Washington, D.C.: National Committee on Public Employee Pension Systems, 1984).

[22]Bruce A. Palmer, *The Impact of Tax Reform on Wage Replacement Ratios* (Atlanta: Georgia State University, Center for Risk Management and Insurance Research, 1988).

[23]Bruce A. Palmer, *1991 Georgia State University/Alexander & Alexander Consulting Group RETIRE Report* (Atlanta: Georgia State University, Center for Risk Management and Insurance Research, 1991); and Palmer, *1993 Georgia State University/Alexander & Alexander Consulting Group RETIRE Report* (Atlanta: Georgia State University, Center for Risk Management and Insurance Research, 1993).

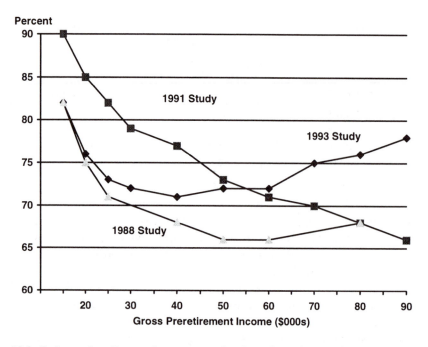

Figure 18-2. Estimate baseline replacement ratios for selected years. Source: Alexander & Alexander Consulting Group Inc., *Replacement Ratios, Important New Pieces to the Puzzle* (Atlanta: Alexander Consulting Group Inc., 1994), p. 2.

reflected in Equation (18-1). In his second set of replacement targets, Palmer conceptually divided this variable into two component elements—work-related expenses and net change in age-related expenditures—although he did not separate them when estimating them. Palmer's two measures of the postretirement levels of income needed to maintain a preretirement standard of living attempt to estimate two variants of Dexter's model. The first is the equivalent of the model as Dexter conceived it. The second does not consider preretirement expenses related to working or special consumer expenses incurred by the elderly.

In his three studies, Palmer developed baseline estimates of the income required in retirement to maintain preretirement living standards for a married couple in which only the husband is employed and retires at age 65. He assumes that the homemaker spouse is three years younger than the husband. The results of this baseline case for the model in which he considers differences in expenditures before and after retirement are shown in Figure 18-2. These results would seem to be problematic for a couple of reasons. First, the shape of the replacement rate targets in 1988, and to a greater degree in 1993, suggests that as workers go from middle to upper income levels their income replacement needs actually increase, which contradicts traditional estimates of such replacement targets and begs for some explanation. Second, the substantial variation in the replacement rates from one study to the next suggests that replacement rate targets are unstable.

The concept of replacement rate targets loses virtually all value for employer sponsors in designing their retirement programs if such instability is truly reflective

TABLE 18-5   Estimated Saving Rates from Three RETIRE Project Studies
(percent)

Preretirement Salary in Nominal Dollars	1988 Study	1991 Study	1993 Study
15,000	3.4	−8.0	2.4
20,000	6.2	0.1	2.8
25,000	8.0	1.1	3.2
30,000	9.5	1.9	3.5
40,000	10.5	3.8	4.2
50,000	11.7	5.8	4.7
60,000	12.3	7.7	5.4
70,000		10.0	6.1
80,000	13.0	12.0	6.8
90,000		14.4	7.4

Source: Palmer, *The Impact of Tax Reform on Wage Replacement Ratios*, p. 33; Palmer, *1991 Georgia State University/Alexander & Alexander Consulting Group RETIRE Report*, p. 11; and Palmer *1993 Georgia State University/Alexander & Alexander Consulting Group RETIRE Report*, p. 13.

of the short-term variations in income required to maintain retiree living standards. If it takes 20, 30, or 40 years to accrue an adequate benefit, it would be impossible to design a plan that would consistently hit a target that varies by as much as 10 percent over a period of a couple of years. For a worker in the middle-income ranges, such variation could equal as much as $50,000 or more of the required accrued benefit at retirement. An analysis of Palmer's three studies suggests that the pattern of replacement rates that emerges in Figure 18-2 is partly due to the basic methodology he uses and partly due to his measurement of expenditures before and after retirement.[24]

One of the major reasons that the target replacement rates in these studies vary so much from year to year is related to the volatility in savings rates. Table 18-5 shows the savings rates as a percentage of after-tax income from Palmer's three studies. The 1988 study was based on the 1984 *Consumer Expenditure Survey*, the 1991 study was based on the 1988 CES, and the 1993 study on the 1990 CES. In other words, the data were collected over a six-year span. In the four years between the collection of the data for the first and second study, savings rates declined markedly at all but the very highest income levels. In the two years between the collection of the data for the second and third studies, Palmer found an improvement in the savings levels of workers earning up to $40,000 per year, but a deterioration at all income levels above that. At the highest income levels, the results suggest that between 1988 and 1990 the savings rates of high-wage workers were cut in half. The volatility in the savings rates is important because of its relationship to the estimated replacement rate targets. Palmer notes in the 1988

[24]For a detailed discussion of the various methodological and measurement issues raised by these analyses see Sylvester J. Schieber, "Conceptual and Measurement Problems in Contemporary Measures of Income Needs in Retirement," in *Benefits Quarterly* (Fourth Quarter, 1995): pp. 57–70.

report that "the current study's higher gross replacement ratios at the low to upper-middle salary levels, to a large extent are the result of the differences in savings rates between the two studies."[25] The significant drop in saving rates of workers in the upper half of the income distribution between the 1991 and 1993 studies accounts for the significant increases in the replacement rate targets for this group between the two studies.

Conceptually, the treatment of savings in these studies is inconsistent with the model depicted in Figure 18-1. There the problem a worker faced was figuring how to spread her cumulative lifetime earnings to cover her cumulative consumption during the period she expects to be working as well as the period she expects to be retired. In that model, the worker's decision to consume more or save less during her working career would reduce her consumption level during retirement. In Palmer's conceptualization of the model, just the opposite occurs. If the worker increases her consumption during her working career, it raises her target level of consumption during her retirement. But the only way higher consumption in retirement can be financed is through a higher rate of saving during the working career. By raising the replacement rate targets in the face of reduced savings, Palmer creates a scenario that cannot, on average, be achieved.

If one thinks of formal retirement programs as one part of workers' total savings programs for their retirement, then it is important to measure individual savings to make sure that sum of total savings will indeed allow workers to maintain their living standard in retirement. But a reduction in one part of the savings portfolio has to be matched either by introducing an offsetting increase in saving elsewhere in the portfolio or by adjusting the living standard in retirement, assuming that retirement age, life expectancy, and so forth, are the same. Palmer's measured reductions in personal savings rates during the latter 1980s might imply that employer-sponsored retirement programs or Social Security need to become more generous to meet current workers' retirement needs. But such increases in the aggregate would add to the total compensation of workers and would have to be offset by reductions in their current compensation or increases in the prices of goods and services that they produce. If it is the former, the workers have not gained disposable income during their working life by reducing personal savings because the reduction in personal savings is matched by an increase in retirement plan saving at the cost of reduced wages. If the increased retirement plan saving is financed through a general increase in the prices of products and services, the workers as consumers of goods and services will not realize any "real" increase in consumption over their lifetime by reducing savings during their working lives. One could argue that one generation might be able to reduce their savings and yet maintain their retirement income through increased transfers from a program like Social Security. But even in that case, workers have to give up consumption in order to pay the higher payroll taxes implied by higher benefits.

Barry Bosworth, Gary Burtless, and John Sabelhaus have analyzed survey data, including the CES, to assess the decline in savings rates in the United States.[26] They

---

[25]Palmer, *1991 Georgia State University/Alexander & Alexander Consulting Group RETIRE Project Report*, p. 19.

[26]Barry Bosworth, Gary Burtless, and John Sabelhaus, "The Decline in Saving: Evidence from Household Surveys," *Brookings Papers on Economic Activity*, no. 1 (Washington, D.C.: Brookings Institution, 1991), pp. 183–256.

noted that the *National Income and Product Accounts* (NIPA) developed by the Department of Commerce indicated that the savings rate in this country averaged 8 percent of national income from the end of World War II up until 1980, but that the rate fell precipitously during the 1980s. Looking at the NIPA data over the decades of the 1950s through the 1970s also suggests that there was not much variation in the savings rate from year to year. These authors compared the *Surveys of Consumer Finances* (SCF) done in 1963 and again between 1983 and 1985 and found that the personal savings rate had declined 4.5 percentage points over the period. Comparing the *Consumer Expenditure Surveys* from the periods 1972 to 1973 and 1982 to 1985, they found a decline in the personal savings rate of 4.3 percentage points. In their detailed analysis of the decline in savings rates, however, they found that the declines in savings rates were much greater among households headed by a person 45 years of age or older than in younger households. Among households headed by a person aged 25 to 34, they found the drop in the savings rate to be about one-quarter of the national average using the SCF, and no drop at all using the CES. They speculate that "the trend in real interest rates over the period provides a possible explanation for the age pattern of the saving decline. The real corporate bond rate averaged 2.6 percent in 1963 and 3.3 percent in the 1972–1973 period but then jumped to 7.5 percent between 1982 and 1985."[27] Another factor that could be of equal importance is that there was a very substantial increase in the market values of savings held in the form of equities and in the value of the housing stock that occurred during the late 1970s and throughout much of the 1980s. If workers are target savers attempting to save enough to maintain their standard of living in retirement, an increase in the yield on their assets should lead them to conclude that they would need to save less to provide for their retirement needs. This analysis points back to the importance of considering the yield on assets.

The analysis of changes in savings behavior also suggests that younger workers were not reducing their savings rates nearly to the degree that people nearing or in retirement were lowering their rates. Palmer's measure of preretirement savings rates focuses strictly on workers between the ages of 50 and 64, the single age group with the biggest decline in savings rates in the analysis of the CES developed by Bosworth, Burtless, and Sabelhaus.

Developing an Empirically Based Needs Standard

In the case of middle- and higher-income individuals, it is clear that absolute standards of need that are generally considered in the context of minimal living standards are not particularly useful. Therefore the alternative is a relative measure of retirement needs along the lines captured in Dexter's conceptual model. The question is whether such a measure can be derived that could be applied across relatively large segments of the work force. In order to do so, begin with a modified version of the conceptual model discussed earlier, as shown in Figure 18.3. In this case earnings are still shown by the rectangle ABCD, but the

[27]Ibid., p. 200.

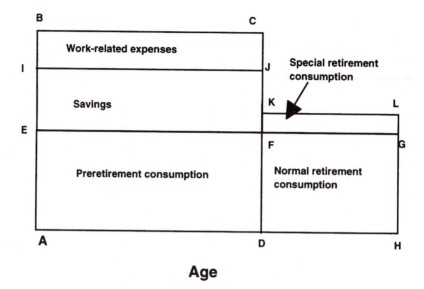

Figure 18-3. Modified conceptual retirement-needs model.

rectangle IBCJ represents expenses specifically related to working that will not be necessary in retirement. The rectangle AEGH shows the constant level of normal consumption before and after retirement shown in Figure 18-1, but FKLG shows special consumption expenditures related only to the retirement period. The savings and returns implied in the modified figure shown by the rectangle EIJF have to be large enough over the working life to finance total consumption during retirement, DKLH. The individual whose life is represented by the figure would work from ages A to D and be retired from ages D to H.

In its simplest form, the savings rate and lifetime consumption levels might be derived assuming that there was no other form of retirement savings than personal savings. We can assume that the only income the worker earns each year while working is Y_T and that income is either consumed (Y_C) or saved (Y_S). In this case, Y_S accumulated to retirement has to equal the retirement income level payable for life. If we set $Y_C + Y_S = Y_T = 1$, then Y_S equals the rate of saving for the worker. If we assume that the worker experiences no salary growth and saves for n years then we can derive the savings rate as

$$(18\text{-}2) \qquad Y_s = \frac{A \cdot (i)}{(1 + i)^n - 1 + A \cdot (i)}$$

where A is a life annuity payable at retirement age on a single or joint life basis at the assumed interest rate j, where j may be equal to i, the assumed interest rate on accumulated savings during the working period. If we allow for salary growth, then

$$(18\text{-}3) \qquad Y_s = \frac{(1 + k)^{n-1} \cdot A \cdot (i - k)}{(1 + i)^n - (1 + k)^n + (1 + k)^{n-1} \cdot A \cdot (i - k)}$$

where k is the assumed rate of salary growth during the working career. The model can accommodate the salary level growing and then peaking in either nominal or real terms, but that is merely a refinement of the basic model.

As Figure 18-3 suggests, the real world is somewhat more complicated than the simple model of retirement savings. While working, workers pay certain taxes they no longer are required to pay once they retire and incur explicit expenses related to working. In other words, Y_T includes Y_S and Y_C, as above, but also includes Y_F, which includes the taxes that are peculiar to earned income, and Y_W, which are the expenses related to working. Another refinement of the model has to consider the existence of Social Security and employer-sponsored pensions. The existence of these programs means that the workers do not have to accumulate personal savings sufficient to maintain their preretirement consumption levels in retirement. In this case, we can derive a Y^* which is the portion of Y_{RC}, income deferred for consumption during retirement—that is, savings, that must be provided out of the accumulated savings in Y_S to meet the preretirement living standard and where

(18-4) $$Y^* = Y_T - Y_F - Y_W - Y_O - Y_{SS} - Y_P + Y_M$$

and where Y_O is any other special expenditure related to the period prior to retirement and that is not carried into retirement; Y_{SS} is Social Security income; Y_P is pension income; and Y_M are medical expenditures in retirement that are expected to be higher than during the working period. All of the parameters in Y^* must be known for a given population as a percentage of Y_T, where $Y_T = 1$. If that is the case, then we can restate Equation (18-2) from above as

(18-2′) $$Y_s = \frac{Y^* \cdot A \cdot (i)}{(1 + i)^n - 1 + A \cdot (i)}$$

where we assume there is no salary growth over the working career and that the worker saves for n years and where all of the variables are defined as above. In the case where we allow for salary growth, we can restate Equation (18-3) as

(18-3′) $$Y_s = \frac{Y^* \cdot (1 + k)^{n-1} \cdot A \cdot (i - k)}{(1 + i)^n - (1 + k)^n + (1 + k)^{n-1} \cdot A \cdot (i - k)} \ .$$

The model will accommodate a variety of salary patterns, although variable growth assumptions over the career do complicate the calculations. Inflation can be accommodated in the relationship between salary growth and assumed investment return. Postretirement inflation can be factored into the choice of the annuity interest rate. Special expenses that are incurred during the working career or during retirement that would adjust the overall goal of having retirement consumption Y_{RC} exactly equal Y_C can also be accommodated. In order to estimate the savings rates that workers have met in order to maintain their preretirement standards of living, we have to develop estimates of the various special expenses related to working and retirement. The savings rate, of course, will depend on the generosity of the pension plan that a worker is covered under, the date that worker begins saving, and the expected date of retirement.

Treatment of Social Security and Related Taxes in the Estimation of Needs Standards

In the context of the retirement income security system in the United States, some retirement consumption is financed with Social Security benefit payments, some is financed with pensions or retirement plan savings, and some is financed out of personally accumulated assets.[28] This means that the rectangle representing saving in Figure 18-3 is segmented into a number of separate elements for many workers. The treatment of Social Security in this model, though, is not as straightforward as it might seem. Referring back to the last part of Chapter 8, note that Social Security no longer provides every worker with the accumulated economic value of his or her contributions to the plan. Many current middle- and upper-income workers will not get back as much as they put into the system, although lower-income workers will get back more than they contribute. In other words, for some, Social Security is a work-related tax but for others it is a very effective retirement savings plan.

As long as the contributions during the working career are segregated and the benefits provided during retirement are considered in developing the replacement and savings targets, it makes virtually no difference if the payroll tax is treated as savings or a work-related expense in the model. The Social Security payroll tax paid by workers during their careers effectively reduces their disposable wages and does not need to be replaced in retirement to maintain a preretirement standard of living. In addition, the worker's share of the payroll tax is itself subjected to federal and state and local income taxes. If the federal marginal income tax rate is set equal to "t_F" and the state and local marginal income tax rate is set equal to "t_S" then a worker can have an income in retirement that is less than earnings by an amount equal to $(1 + t_F + t_S)$ times the payroll tax and still have the same post-tax income in retirement as he or she earned prior to retirement.

Effective tax rates for Social Security contributions were calculated by estimating the amount of federal and state income taxes that are due on Social Security contributions and adding those taxes to the basic Social Security tax for the selected income levels shown in Table 18-6. Federal income taxes were calculated for taxable income using the tax rates and bend points for 1994. Taxable income was estimated by calculating the average deductions for single and joint filers with no aged or blind personal exemptions from a data base of tax filers. Average deductions were calculated for ranges of adjusted gross incomes that spanned the median income levels shown in Table 18-6. The average deductions and adjusted exemptions for each income and filing status group were subtracted from income to get taxable income. We assumed that married filing units contained two persons and that single filing units contained one person. A filing unit's state taxes were assumed to be the same percentage of the filing unit's federal income taxes as average state income taxes are to average federal income taxes in the National Income and Product Accounts for the period 1990 to 1993. The table shows the effective average rate of tax due to FICA at various income levels. The rates increase

---

[28]Empirical evidence indicates that many households receiving retirement benefits still report receiving wage income. Sometimes this income is attributable to a worker gradually transitioning into full retirement. In other cases it is attributable to a spouse who has not yet retired. Wage income could also be factored into the model but for this analysis we consider that a worker moves directly from active work status into full retirement. Although some workers may continue to work for some time after they leave their main career employment, most spend their retirement years in full retirement where Social Security, pension, and other asset income are the sole means for sustaining their retirement consumption.

TABLE 18-6 Effective Tax Rates in 1994 on Earnings Due to FICA and
Related Income Taxes at Specified Income Levels

Income (dollars)	Single Filers		Married Filers	
	Rate (%)	Amount (dollars)	Rate (%)	Amount (dollars)
8,500	9.07	771	9.07	771
12,500	9.06	1,133	9.06	1,133
17,500	9.06	1,586	9.06	1,586
22,500	9.07	2,040	9.07	2,040
27,500	9.07	2,493	9.07	2,493
35,000	10.10	3,543	9.07	3,173
45,000	10.14	4,563	9.06	4,076
55,000	10.17	5,594	10.07	5,538
65,000	9.63	6,261	9.55	6,210
75,000	8.81	6,610	8.56	6,419
85,000	8.02	6,816	7.79	6,621
95,000	7.39	7,023	7.18	6,824
110,000	6.67	7,332	6.48	7,126

Source: Calculations by the authors. To calculate the effective marginal rate due
to income taxes, divide the amount of the tax shown below by actual FICA taxes
due on the amounts in the income column and subtract one.

as income increases at the lower income levels because of the progressivity in the
income tax. They fall at higher income levels because the payroll tax is not applied
to all earnings.

Work-Related Expenses

In addition to the FICA and attendant taxes related to wage income, the mere
process of going to work creates certain expenses that do not persist after retirement. For one thing, workers have to travel back and forth between their home
and their place of work. Some people work in their homes and others can walk
back and forth to work, but for the overwhelming majority, getting to work and
back home involves commuting by personal automobile or on public transportation. Both of these forms of transportation generate an expense. Retirees do not
have to undertake the regular commute that most workers do. Another work-
related expense is clothing. Some workers can do their jobs in casual clothes that
are no different from the clothes they wear in their leisure time, but most workers
dress more formally or in uniform when at work, and they incur some added
expense in buying and maintaining their work wardrobe. Retirees can spend most
of their time in informal attire, which is usually less expensive than more formal
work clothes.

Yet another expense that many workers incur that can be reduced in retirement
is the cost of meals. This added cost is not incurred because workers necessarily eat
any more than nonworkers do, although that is undoubtedly the case for workers
who engage in physically demanding activities, but because the cost of their food is

higher. Some workers "carry their lunch" and do not incur any added expense, but many eat their mid workday meal at a restaurant or buy it at a carryout facility at some added expense. For those who dine out for one meal a day because they are away from home, the cost of eating includes both the cost of the food itself and the cost of preparing it. Retirees can organize their schedule so they do not have to regularly incur the preparation costs associated with eating out.

It is conceptually easy to describe expenses related to working that are not incurred after retirement. Measuring these expenses is far more complicated. In an ideal world one would be able to monitor workers during their careers and calculate how much they spend on gasoline, oil, upkeep, and depreciation for automobiles and apportion the relative share of total costs that relates to work trips. For workers taking public transportation, one would want to monitor the cost of getting back and forth to work. For clothing one would want to measure the cost of the wardrobe worn to work and the percentage of time the clothes were worn in work-related activities. For food expenditures, one would want to measure the cost of food eaten while on the job and calculate how that cost differs from the cost if comparable meals were prepared and eaten at home. The problem is that such monitoring of specific work-related expenditures would be expensive and time-consuming, and no one has developed such estimates. An alternative approach would be to monitor a group of individuals for some period before and after their retirement and measure how their expenditures for these items changed from their working period to their retirement period. Again, following specific individuals over a number of years is expensive, and those panel survey efforts undertaken thus far that have followed individuals for a number of years have focused on measuring income before and after retirement and the retirement decision rather than work-related expenses.

The lack of appropriate data leaves researchers in the position of developing ways to compare expenditures on work-related goods and services by workers and retirees under the assumption that the differences are attributable to the work status. As noted earlier, Palmer has utilized various annual versions of the *Consumer Expenditure Survey* in developing his analysis of comparative expenditures by workers versus retirees. The CES is an ongoing survey conducted by the Census Bureau for the Department of Labor. It surveys sample households selected on a probability basis to represent the general noninstitutionalized population. Once a household is selected, the residents of the household are interviewed quarterly for one year. In addition, the survey units are asked to complete a diary of expenses for two consecutive one-week periods. The interview survey is estimated to collect detailed data on an estimated 60 to 70 percent of total household expenditures. In addition, expense patterns for a three-month period are obtained for food and other selected items that account for an additional 20 to 25 percent of total expenditures. Finally, the diary is used to estimate expenditures on smaller items.[29]

While the CES is released by the Bureau of Labor Statistics in annual components, a single-year survey file does not include participants over identical periods. The Census Bureau selects survey households on a rolling basis. It selects a sample

---

[29]U.S. Department of Labor, *Consumer Expenditure Survey, 1990-1991*, Bureau of Labor Statistics Bulletin 2425 (Washington, D.C.: USGPO, September 1993), p. 1.

of households during the first quarter of a calendar year, and those households are in the survey for that calendar year. But it selects another sample during the second quarter of the year, and that sample is in the survey for three quarters in the calendar year in which they were chosen, and in the first quarter of the subsequent year. Each household is in the survey for four quarters, but only one-quarter of the participants are in for single calendar years.

One of the problems that we encountered in analyzing the CES data was that some respondents had provided incomplete income or expenditure information. In an analysis that is comparing expenditures to income levels, it is important to have complete reporting. So we restricted our analysis only to cases where there was complete reporting on the survey.[30] After imposing this restriction, subsets of the annual samples drawn to look at workers nearing retirement or just past retirement often provided very small numbers of individuals at various levels of income, combinations of marital status, and so forth, that were working or retired. It is inappropriate to develop representative analyses on the basis of such small samplings. In order to deal with the problem of small numbers of respondents in various age, work status, marital status, and income-level categories, we worked with a data set that consisted of pooled CES files from 1980 to 1992. For comparability, we converted income and expenditure data from each of the years into 1993 dollars using the CPI for urban consumers.

We developed a series of separate regressions on food, clothing, and commuting expenditures for consumer units where either the householder or the spouse reported they were working full time and for consumer units where neither the householder nor the spouse worked but instead reported that they were retired. For the "worker" regressions we restricted the analysis to units where the householder was between the ages of 50 and 64 because we wanted to capture expenditures of workers as they approached retirement age. For the "retiree" regressions we restricted the analysis to units where the householder was between the ages of 60 and 74 because we wanted to look at a segment of the retiree population that had retired relatively recently and wished to avoid including a large cross section of the oldest elderly where consumer patterns might be quite different than among the younger elderly because of mobility restrictions or other factors related to advanced age. Given the categories of expenditures we were considering in this portion of the analysis, we thought it highly likely that expenditures would be falling at such advanced ages rather than increasing. Such reductions would not be related to the status of working versus retirement, but purely to the conditions related to advanced aging.

One final restriction that we imposed on the analysis was to choose only consumer units that reported annual incomes of at least $7,000 in 1993 dollars. We did this for two reasons. First, a number of "working" consumer units reported significant negative income where their expenditure patterns were more similar to higher-income units than truly low-income units. We believe these cases reflect low income in an accounting sense more than they reflect a "real" low permanent

---

[30]We still cannot assure absolutely complete reporting because even though the respondents selected may have responded to each of the questions on the survey about their income and expenditure levels, they may have underreported actual income and expenditures in many cases. We believe, however, that we have minimized the underreporting problem to the extent possible.

income level. Including these cases in estimating the consumption behavior of low-income workers would bias the results. Second, we are focusing on relative adequacy measures in developing this analysis and, at annual incomes below $7,000, replacement of final earnings would have to equal or exceed 100 percent to provide income in retirement at the lowest absolute adequacy measures discussed at the beginning of this chapter. We ended up with 5,333 observations of working units and 4,148 observations of retired units.

The results of the regression on food expenditures (FE_W) for consumer units that include workers are shown in Equation 18.5. The results for the retired units (FE_R) are shown in Equation (18-6). In the equations, marital status (MARSTAT) equals one if the consumer unit includes a married couple with both spouses present and it equals zero otherwise. The presence of people other than the householder and spouse in the consumer unit (OTRPEOPLE) is equal to one if such persons are present and zero otherwise. The numbers in parentheses below the equations are the *t statistics* for the estimated coefficients. These equations were used to calculate food expenditures at various income levels for worker units and retired units. The expenditures for other people that might be present in the household were handled on a probabilistic basis in that we multiplied the coefficient by the probability that other people were present in the household. The probability of other persons being in the household was 0.55 for the worker units and 0.23 for the retiree units.

(18-5) $FE_W = 1907.64 + (0.032 \cdot \text{INCOME}) + (1503.55 \cdot \text{MARSTAT}) + (1443.00 \cdot \text{OTRPEOPLE})$

      (21.54)   (23.77)   (16.86)   (18.56)

      Adjusted R-square = 0.398

(18-6) $FE_R = 1867.58 + (0.038 \cdot \text{INCOME}) + (1341.92 \cdot \text{MARSTAT}) + (864.42 \cdot \text{OTRPEOPLE})$.

      (29.13)   (18.16)   I(19.27)   (11.12)

      Adjusted R-square = 0.361

The estimates of food expenditures and the differences in food expenditures between working units and retiree units are shown in Table 18-7. The results at first appear to be counterintuitive. Reductions in food consumption expenditures among the lowest-income retirees are greater than they are among the higher-income retirees. At the highest income levels the reduction in food expenditures attributed to retiring is relatively small. If we had extrapolated to even higher income levels, the model suggests that the effects of working on food costs would vanish. In measuring food expenditures we used the survey file data from the CES and accounted for food expenditures on food consumed at home as well as that consumed outside the home. We did not augment the survey data with the diary data and thus may have missed some food expenditures that workers failed to account for in their survey responses. An alternative explanation is that at the lowest income levels, incomes for low-income individuals after retirement are so marginal that medical and rental expenditures and other necessities crowd out food expenditures. From around $15,000 to $40,000 the food expenditures among retiree units consistently average about $60 to $70 per month less than they do for

TABLE 18-7   Estimated Food Expenditures for Worker Units with Householders Aged 50–64 and Retired Units Aged 60–74 (1993 dollars)

| | Food Expenditures | | |
Income	Worker Units	Retired Units	Difference
8,500	4,034.61	3,204.05	830.56
12,500	4,163.29	3,355.89	807.40
17,500	4,324.14	3,545.69	778.45
22,500	4,484.99	3,735.49	749.50
27,500	4,645.84	3,925.29	720.55
35,000	4,887.11	4,209.99	677.12
45,000	5,208.81	4,589.59	619.22
55,000	5,530.51	4,969.19	561.32
65,000	5,852.21	5,348.79	503.42
75,000	6,173.91	5,728.39	445.52
85,000	6,495.61	6,107.99	387.62

Source. Authors' estimates based on an analysis of the combined *Consumer Expenditures Surveys* from 1980 to 1992.

comparably situated worker units. Above that, though, the differences diminish. One might expect such a pattern if food expenditures and leisure are complementary goods at upper-income levels.

Mean and median food expenditure patterns are well behaved within this data base in that at each higher level of income both worker units and retiree units spend more than lower-income units. Given that people can only eat a finite amount of food, the data suggest that as income increases people eat more expensive foods or food that is delivered in a more expensive fashion. If upper-income people naturally eat more expensively, additional leisure time in retirement gives them a greater opportunity to either get more involved in creative culinary activities or to go out to eat more often than when they were working. Maintaining the preretirement standard of living, however, does not mean increasing the quality of food consumption in retirement or shifting to more expensive preparation and delivery methods.

Given the consistently lower estimated expenditures for food between the incomes of $17,500 and $35,000, we used an average of the differences at these income levels ($731) and applied it at each income range as the cost of extra food expenditures attributed to working. A logical case can be made that we should be applying higher food cost reductions at upper income levels than we have. High-wage workers may have greater "socialization" requirements in their jobs than lower-wage workers, requiring that they eat out more often or at more expensive restaurants. On the other hand, an argument could be made that the positive relationship between food expenditures and income both before and after retirement suggests that higher-wage workers do not spend more on food because they are working but because of their inherent taste for socializing and eating away from home. At the higher-wage levels we are considering here, the added food expenses

TABLE 18-8   Estimated Clothing Expenditures for Worker Units
with Householders Aged 50–64 and Retired Units with
Householders Aged 60–74 (1993 dollars)

	Clothing Expenditures		
Income	Workers	Retireds	Difference
8,500	731.27	489.15	242.12
12,500	805.59	545.45	260.14
17,500	898.49	615.82	282.67
22,500	991.39	686.20	305.19
27,500	1,084.29	756.57	327.72
35,000	1,223.64	862.14	361.50
45,000	1,409.44	1,002.89	406.55
55,000	1,595.24	1,143.64	451.60
65,000	1,781.04	1,284.39	496.65
75,000	1,966.84	1,425.14	541.70
85,000	2,152.64	1,565.89	586.75

Source: Authors' estimates based on analysis of the combined *Consumer Expenditures Surveys* from 1980 to 1992.

attributed to workers is relatively minor, and by using a conservative number we will tend to bias the target retirement income level upward rather than downward. Biasing it upward provides extra insurance against unforeseen contingencies.

The results of the regression on clothing expenditures (CE_W) for worker consumer units are shown in Equation (18-7). The results for retired units (CE_R) are shown in Equation (18-8). The specifications of the independent variables in this case are the same as in the food expenditure equations discussed above. We used these regression equations for estimating clothing expenditures by worker and retired units in the same fashion that we used food equations presented earlier. The results of that estimation are presented in Table 18-8. In this case the estimates follow a pattern of gradually increasing differences with increasing income. We used the estimated amounts developed here in developing our overall estimates of work-related expenses.

(18-7) $CE_W = 315.49 + (0.019 \cdot \text{INCOME}) + (164.12 \cdot \text{MARSTAT}) + (257.91 \cdot \text{OTRPEOPLE})$

   (6.80)   (26.20)   (3.51)   (6.33)

   Adjusted R-square = 0.256

(18-8) $CE_R = 303.36 + (0.014 \cdot \text{INCOME}) + (79.13 \cdot \text{MARSTAT}) + (78.17 \cdot \text{OTRPEOPLE})$.

   (12.02)   (17.10)   (2.89)   (2.55)

   Adjusted R-square = 0.155

In estimating commuting expenses related to working, we began with national data on commuting patterns. The 1990 decennial census indicated that 73.2 percent of workers go to work in single-occupant vehicles; another 13.4 percent by carpool; 3.9 percent by walking; 3.0 percent of workers work at home; and 1.3 percent go by motor bike, bicycle, or other means.[31] The average length of journeys to

[31]U.S. Department of Transportation, *Journey-To-Work Trends in the United States and Its Major Metropolitan Areas 1960-1990* (Washington, D.C.: USGPO, 1991), p. 2–6.

work was 10.7 miles.[32] In 1993 the Internal Revenue Service allowed employers to reimburse workers for auto expenses related to work travel at a rate of $0.28 per mile, which might be used to estimate the average cost of operating an automobile. The Congressional Budget Office developed estimates of the per passenger mile cost of various forms of public transportation in 1985. Their estimate in 1985 monetary values was $0.65 per mile for commuter rail costs and $0.35 for bus costs. Updating these to 1993 values using the CPI would raise these costs to $0.87 per mile for commuter rail and $0.47 for bus. The American Public Transit Association (APTA) estimates that transit fares in 1992 covered an average 37.5 percent of operating costs for public transit systems nationwide.[33] If one assumes that workers commuting by rail pay between one-quarter and one-third of the cost of their public transportation, their costs would average between $0.21 and $0.28 per mile, which is similar to the cost allowed by IRS for motor vehicle expense reimbursement. While workers commuting by bus or carpools might experience lower average costs of commuting than single-occupancy vehicle or rail commuters, a reasonable estimate of the modal cost of commuting might be set at $0.28 per mile in 1993 dollars.

Assuming that most employers focus on full-time workers in developing their retirement programs, the $0.28 per mile can be the basis for estimating an annual commuting cost for average workers. Since the typical workweek is five days with a trip to work and returning home, an average worker would have a work-related commute of 107 miles per week. If one assumes the typical worker commutes 48 weeks per year—to allow for vacation, holiday, sick time, and so forth—total annual work-related commuting would amount to 5,136 miles. At $0.28 per mile this would result in average annual work-related commuting costs of $1,438.

Our analysis of the CES data suggests that higher-income workers have higher variable expenditures for auto and local public transit expenses than lower-income workers. The results of the regression on commuting expenditures (TE_W) for worker consumer units are shown in Equation (18-9). Again the specification of the independent variables is consistent with the earlier derivation as explained in the discussion surrounding Equation (18-5).

(18-9) $TE_W = 1113.72 + (0.020 \cdot \text{INCOME}) + (895.38 \cdot \text{MARSTAT}) + (987.55 \cdot \text{OTRPEOPLE})$.

$\qquad$ (15.58) $\qquad$ (18.88) $\qquad\qquad$ (12.43) $\qquad\qquad\qquad$ (15.37)

$\qquad$ Adjusted R-square = 0.293

In Table 18-9, total commuting expenses are estimated using Equation (18-9) and controlling for household composition, as discussed earlier. When we considered the prevalence of consumer units at the various income levels represented in the table, we found that the average commuting expenses for the whole sample corresponded with a total income of approximately $40,000. This may seem a high income level, given the somewhat lower average incomes that generally prevail in

---

[32]U.S. Department of Transportation, *1990 Nationwide Personal Transportation Survey Databook* (Washington, D.C.: USGPO, 1991), p. 6–20.

[33]American Public Transit Association, *Transit Fact Book* (Washington, D.C.: American Public Transit Association, 1993), p. 15.

TABLE 18-9   Estimated Commuting Expenditures for Worker Units
with Householders Aged 50–64 (1993 dollars)

Income	Total Commuting Expenses	Work-Related Commuting Expenses
8,500	2,463.87	1,140
12,500	2,546.37	1,178
17,500	2,649.51	1,226
22,500	2,752.64	1,273
27,500	2,855.78	1,321
35,000	3,010.48	1,393
45,000	3,216.75	1,488
55,000	3,423.02	1,583
65,000	3,629.29	1,679
75,000	3,835.56	1,774
85,000	4,041.83	1,870

Source: Total commuting expenses are based on the authors' analysis of the
combined *Consumer Expenditures Surveys* from 1980 to 1992. The derivation of
the work-related commuting expenses is discussed in the text.

the economy, but we have excluded consumer units with annual incomes below
$7,000 in the analysis. In developing our final estimates of work-related commuting
expenses, we assumed they distribute similarly to total commuting expenses and
derived a distribution of work-related expenses that varies across the income
spectrum. In other words, the work-related commuting expenses estimated in
Table 18-9 vary in direct correspondence with the total commuting expenses of
working units as estimated from the regression model.

Age-Related Expenses Unrelated to Working

While work-related expenses are eliminated at retirement, expenditures on a
number of other major consumption items may change significantly at about the
same time. If there are any children in the family, frequently they will be completing their education some time before their parents' retirement or shortly thereafter. Many people pay off their home mortgage before retiring, relieving the
budget of monthly house payments. In the other direction, retirement often
means the loss of employer-provided health insurance, or a shift in the cost of
coverage. At age 65, however, Medicare coverage helps to cover the cost of medical
expenses.

In our analysis of education expenditures, we focused on expenditures for
tuition payments and did not consider room and board charges related to going to
college. In some regards, money spent on children, regardless of what the expenditure is financing, is a consumption expenditure and is made on the basis of the
consumer's own personal preferences. The extent to which workers or retirees are
willing to continue to feed, clothe, and provide housing for their children as they
reach young adult ages is a matter of negotiation and agreement between the
parents and the children and should not be a concern of an employer. Tuition
expenditures covering the cost of higher education can be thought of as an

investment or intergenerational transfer. In 1990 the typical worker with a bachelor's degree had average monthly earnings that were 96 percent greater than the earnings of a typical worker with only a high school diploma.[34] The commitment to make such investments is typically of limited duration. While some students can take a long time to complete a college degree program, most do so in four or five years. The commitment to let adult children live in the parents' home can go on indefinitely. In our analysis of the CES population we found significant differences in the prevalence of other persons in the household than the householder and spouse between working and retired households at the lowest income levels, but smaller differences at higher levels. For example, at income levels between $7,000 and $10,000 the difference ranged from 51 percent for working households to 15 percent for retired households. At the $60,000 to $70,000 income level, the difference was 60 to 46 percent, and at the $70,000 to $80,000 level it was 67 to 50 percent.

In developing the analysis of education financing we were surprised at the relatively low levels of expenditures reported by the participants in the CES. Even at the highest income class that we considered, working households with incomes above $80,000 per year, we found the mean expenditure by couples to be only slightly above $1,300 per year, and single-headed units only about $750 per year. In all but the highest two income categories, the median expenditure on higher education was zero. When we focused only on working households reporting education expenditures, at the 70th percentile the reported expenditure was only $1,309; at the 80th percentile it was $2,179; at the 90th percentile it was $4,734; and the maximum reported expenditures were less than $31,000 per year. While the expenditure at the top end is quite significant, it is not inconsistent with having two children in Ivy League or other prominent universities at the same time today. Press accounts of the high and growing cost of higher education often focus on such private schools.[35] But the majority of students attending college today are not in such institutions. In 1991, 78 percent of the total enrollment in institutions of higher learning was in public schools.[36] All around the country, these public institutions offer significantly lower tuition rates than their private counterparts. In Table 18-10 we compare the tuition and fees for the 1994–1995 academic year charged at a number of prominent public and private institutions of higher learning paired by the state in which they are located. The cost of sending someone to one of the state universities listed in the table is not inconsistent with the reported expenditures in the CES. The one case in which the public and private university costs are closest, at the University of Massachusetts and Harvard, arises because such a large fraction of the student body at the former school is from out of state and those students are charged a tuition rate more in line with the private rates than is charged for in-state students. Another thing apparent in

[34]Robert Kominski and Rebecca Sutterlin, *What's It Worth? Educational Background and Economic Status: Spring 1990* (Washington, D.C.: U.S. Department of Commerce, Bureau of the Census, December 1992), p. 5.

[35]For example, see Geeta Anand, "In Picking a College, Bottom Line Often Comes First," *Boston Globe*, April 15, 1994, Metro Section, p. 1.

[36]Bureau of the Census, U.S. Department of Commerce, *Statistical Abstract of the United States, 1993*, 113th ed. (Washington, D.C.: USGPO, 1993), p. 175.

TABLE 18-10   Number of Students by Residency Status, Published Tuition Rates for the 1993–94 Academic Year, and Average Tuition Rates Net of Aid at Selected Universities

	Number of Under-graduates	Portion from In-State	Portion from out of State	In-State Tuition and Fees (dollars)	Out-of-State Tuition and Fees (dollars)	Average Tuition Net of Aid (dollars)
University of Massachusetts	17,086	0.54	0.46	5,467	11,813	7,508
Harvard University	6,799	0.16	0.84	18,745	18,745	12,761
University of Connecticut	12,059	0.84	0.16	4,290	11,410	4,129
Yale	5,236	0.10	0.90	18,630	18,630	13,766
SUNY Albany	9,215	0.92	0.08	2,961	6,961	3,180
Columbia-Barnard	2,190	0.42	0.58	17,756	17,756	11,811
University of North Carolina	15,674	0.80	0.20	1,419	8,461	2,606
Duke University	6,008	0.14	0.86	19,050	19,050	15,514
University of Georgia	22,301	0.84	0.16	2,250	5,940	2,755
Emory University	4,920	0.19	0.81	16,820	16,820	12,340
University of florida	22,301	0.84	0.16	2,250	5,940	2,755
University of Miami	8,352	0.51	0.49	16,665	16,665	14,683
Indiana University	26,243	0.73	0.27	3,252	9,927	5,042
University of Notre Dame	7,600	0.09	0.91	16,145	16,145	13,756
University of Illinois	26,333	0.92	0.08	3,406	8,438	3,588
Northwestern University	7,495	0.25	0.75	15,804	15,804	11,881
University of Texas	35,206	0.91	0.09	1,460	4,860	969
Rice University	2,674	0.47	0.53	10,775	10,775	10,441
UCLA	22,892	0.94	0.06	3,549	11,248	2,237
Stanford University	6,573	0.42	0.58	17,775	17,775	13,354

Source: Compiled by the authors from *Peterson's Four-Year Colleges, 1995* (Princeton, N.J.: Peterson's Guides, 1994).

the table is that the private universities discount their tuition rates considerably. They do this primarily by providing aid to lower-income applicants, although some of the schools do provide limited merit scholarships as well. National data on tuition and fees at all institutions of higher learning for 1989 indicate an average tuition rate of $2,505 per enrolled student. About 38 percent of the enrolled students were in two-year institutions at an average cost of $712, and those at

TABLE 18-11   Estimated Expenditures on Higher-Education Tuition
Paid by Working Households in the Years Prior to
Retirement (1993 dollars)

Income	Single	Married
8,500	19	80
12,500	45	106
17,500	77	137
22,500	108	169
27,500	140	201
35,000	188	248
45,000	251	312
55,000	315	375
65,000	378	439
75,000	442	502
85,000	505	566

Source: Estimated by authors on the basis of the *Consumer Expenditure Surveys*
from 1980 through 1992, as discussed in the text.

four-year institutions had an average tuition rate of $3,584. The combination of
low tuition rates in public colleges and universities, the prevalence of school-
administered aid from private schools, and the availability of government-insured
loans for college students make the reported data from the CES palpable.

For purposes of our analysis, we assumed that the education expenses incurred
by worker units prior to retirement would not be expenses that they would have to
cover during their retirement. Our estimated costs of education expenses attributed to worker units at various income levels are shown in Table 18-11. While the
averages seem relatively low, keep in mind that these are averages of all working
households where the head of the household is between the ages of 50 and 64. In
many cases children are no longer in the household or those that still reside there
have already completed their education. As we reported earlier, the median expenditure in most income categories was zero.

Another expense that many workers dispose of prior to retirement is the home
mortgage. If they pay it off prior to retirement, they eliminate much of the
month-to-month cash cost of providing shelter for themselves. They still have
maintenance costs, property taxes, and so forth, but the largest month-to-month
cost for most home owners is the servicing cost on the mortgage. Among the
retired population between the ages of 60 and 74 that we analyzed from the pooled
CES files, 62 percent of those with annual incomes between $7,000 and $10,000 in
1993 dollars owned their own home. The percentage owning their own homes
gradually increased to 96.5 percent at incomes over $80,000 per year. The data
suggest somewhat lower rates of home ownership among worker households at the
lower end of the income spectrum that we considered but very comparable rates at
the upper-income end of the spectrum. Table 18-12 shows the difference in the
prevalence of workers units and retiree units with mortgages. Even though the
worker units are somewhat less likely to own their own home at the lower income
levels, they have a greater likelihood of having a mortgage. In order to estimate the

TABLE 18-12   Home Ownership and Prevalence of Homes Without Mortgages for
Worker and Retiree Households

Income in 1993 Dollars	Workers with Mortgages (%)	Retirees with Mortgages (%)	Difference (%)	Average Cost of Servicing Mortgage (1993 dollars)	Expecvted Value of Lower Cost (1993 dollars)
$ 8,500	25.4	10.2	15.2	3,465	527
12,500	25.2	13.3	11.9	3,545	422
17,500	26.0	14.6	11.4	3,768	430
22,500	37.6	19.4	18.2	3,396	618
27,500	40.5	19.9	20.6	3,642	750
35,000	42.3	20.0	22.3	3,783	844
45,000	49.5	23.0	26.5	4,268	1,131
55,000	59.8	28.7	31.1	5,119	1,592
65,000	67.2	32.7	34.5	5,176	1,786
75,000	69.6	33.3	36.3	5,528	2,007
85,000	75.7	37.9	37.8	8,866	3,351

Source. Estimated by authors on the basis of the *Consumer Expenditure Surveys* from 1980 through 1992, as discussed in the text.

difference in the cost of housing between workers on the threshold of retirement and retirees, we multiplied the difference in the probability of having a mortgage in each of the income classes times the cost of servicing the mortgage. The results are shown as the expected value of the lower cost of housing in Table 18-12.

The major change in expenditures that many people will experience in retirement is from the consumption of medical goods and services. Not only do these expenses typically increase at older ages, at retirement many workers lose their employer-provided health insurance or have to pay considerably more for it than they did prior to retirement. This major expenditure category has experienced much higher rates of inflation in recent years than most other classes of consumption. Finally, the individual policy health insurance markets have not functioned efficiently in recent years because often the people who purchase health policies have a higher risk of being sick than those not purchasing such policies, forcing the issuers of policies to charge extra risk premiums for them. Some employers continue to provide health insurance, some are moving to curtail these benefits on a prospective basis, some are eliminating retiree health benefits altogether, and some have never provided them and are not about to start providing them now voluntarily. It is somewhat difficult in this environment to establish hard and fast rules about the implications of health care costs and insurance variations in retirement.

In developing this analysis, we assumed that employers could either offer benefits on much the same grounds they do today, where they do offer them, or that they could act as an insurance broker so that retirees could buy insurance on the basis of expected utilization under the plans by a population that was not adversely selecting against the plans. We estimated the claims under a plan that has a $200 deductible for individual coverage and $400 for couples, where the plan covers 80 percent of the claims up to $1,500 per year for single coverage and $3,000 for a couple. We based our estimates on existing plan characteristics of sample plans currently provided by large employers and a microsimulation model we have developed to simulate claims under alternative plans by various populations. In this analysis, we focused on the claims that would arise from covering a cross section of the general population aged 55 and older. In addition to the claims that would be paid under the plan, we also provided for an administrative loading to account for the administration costs of operating the plan. In 1994 dollars we estimated that such a plan would cost $4,300 for an early retiree not yet eligible for Medicare, and $1,370 for a person eligible for Medicare. The presence of a spouse would double the annual costs of health care coverage for a consumer unit's total budget. The implications of health expenditures on retirement accumulations will depend on what the employer offers to retirees, inflation of health costs relative to other costs of living, age at retirement, and the number of years before a worker retires.

Estimating Savings and Replacement Rates

We have developed a set of estimated savings and replacement rates at various income levels under a variety of assumptions that permit an evaluation of alternative approaches to providing retirement income. We have assumed that work-relatedexpenses and other special age-related expenditures would grow over time at the same rate as the rate of growth assumed for wages. The initial analysis examines the case of a hypothetical single worker using a variety of assumptions about the age at which the worker began to accumulate retirement savings and at several potential retirement ages.

Baseline Estimates

The initial results are shown in Table 18-13. In this case we assumed that the worker begins saving at age 35 and is covered under a pension plan that provides a benefit equal to 1 percent of final pay. We assumed that the inflation rate in the economy would persist at 4 percent per year, that the worker's wages would grow at 5 percent per year until peaking in real terms at age 55, and then grow at the inflation rate thereafter. We assumed that the rate of return on savings accumulations would be 6 percent per year, and that the savings would be converted to an annuity at retirement using a 6 percent interest rate. We assumed the annuity would be indexed in retirement to account for inflation. Finally, we assumed the retiree would receive a retiree health benefit provided by his or her former employer.

The results in Table 18-13 suggest that for a worker retiring at age 65 the replacement rates would decline from a high of roughly 82 percent at a starting salary of $8,500 per year to a low of approximately 72 percent for the worker starting at $85,000. For individuals wishing to retire earlier, the model suggests that they would have considerably lower replacement of final earnings. One of the main reasons for that can be seen on the savings side of the table. For the lowest-wage

TABLE 18-13   Replacement Rates at Various Retirement Ages and the Saving Rates
Required to Maintain Preretirement Standards of Living in Retirement

Starting Pay Level When Saving Begins (1993 dollars)	*Replacement Rate*			*Saving Rate Required*		
	Age 65	*Age 60*	*Age 55*	*Age 65*	*Age 60*	*Age 55*
8,500	82.3	64.4	57.9	0.0	0.0	6.6
12,500	73.0	66.2	58.8	0.0	6.8	14.3
17,500	75.6	66.7	59.0	1.9	10.9	18.6
22,500	75.3	66.5	58.6	3.9	12.7	20.6
27,500	75.2	66.5	58.5	5.2	14.0	22.0
35,000	75.9	67.0	58.6	5.9	14.9	23.3
45,000	74.6	65.9	57.5	7.9	16.6	25.1
55,000	73.5	65.0	56.6	9.1	17.6	26.1
65,000	73.6	65.0	56.3	10.2	18.9	27.6
75,000	73.5	64.9	56.0	11.6	20.2	29.1
85,000	72.4	64.0	55.2	12.3	20.8	29.6

Source. Watson Wyatt.

worker retiring at age 65, the model suggests that no saving beyond Social Security and the pension would be required. The combination of Social Security and pension benefits paid to this worker will exceed his or her preretirement income net of work- and age-related expenditures and the worker's standard of living will rise in retirement. We do not allow the savings rate to fall below zero for purposes of calculating the replacement rate for such a worker. As the income levels increase, the required savings rates increase because the relative decline in Social Security benefits requires that higher-wage workers save on their own for retirement. For retirements at age 55, the model suggests the lowest-wage worker would have to save a larger portion of preretirement income than a high-wage worker who is willing to put off retirement until age 65. The savings rates required by workers at all income levels if they wish to retire at 55 are relatively high and are the primary factor driving down the computed replacement rates at this age and service combination. It may seem counterintuitive that a worker retiring at an earlier age would need a lower replacement of final earnings than one retiring later. But the higher savings rate during the working years for a worker determined to retire early means such an individual is willing to live at a lower level of consumption relative to earnings before retirement. Thus, the standard of living to be maintained, measured in terms of consumption, is lower.

Implications of Alternative Returns on Investments

Table 18-14 shows the postretirement income replacement rates and the preretirement savings rates required to achieve them under three alternative assumptions about the rate of return on assets. In this case we use the same pension formula and other assumptions as stated in the development of Table 18-13 for a worker retiring at age 65, except we compare the implications of realizing a

TABLE 18-14 Replacement Rates at Two Real Rates of Return and the Saving Rates
Required to Maintain Preretirement Standards of Living in Retirement

Starting Pay Level When Saving Begins (1993 dollars)	Replacement Rate at Age 65 with Real Rate of Return			Savings Rate Required with Real Rate of Return		
	2 Percent	4 Percent	6 Percent	2 Percent	4 Percent	6 Percent
8,500	82.3	82.3	82.3	0.0	0.0	0.0
12,500	73.0	73.0	73.0	0.0	0.0	0.0
17,500	75.6	76.0	76.3	1.9	1.5	1.2
22,500	75.3	76.1	76.8	3.9	3.1	2.4
27,500	75.2	76.3	77.2	5.2	4.2	3.3
35,000	75.9	77.1	78.2	5.9	4.7	3.7
45,000	74.6	76.2	77.6	7.9	6.3	4.9
55,000	73.5	75.3	77.0	9.1	7.3	5.6
65,000	73.6	75.7	77.5	10.2	8.2	6.3
75,000	73.5	75.8	77.9	11.6	9.3	7.2
85,000	72.4	74.9	77.1	12.3	9.9	7.7

Source: Watson Wyatt.

2 percent real rate of return on savings with 4 and 6 percent real rates of return. At the lowest two income levels, the increased rate of return has no effect because the model implies the worker does not save outside of Social Security and the pension plan. At each successively higher income level there is a greater replacement of preretirement income at a higher rate of return than under a lower one. The net result of the higher return is that the worker could attain a higher standard of living across his or her whole life at the higher rate of return while generally reducing the savings rate required at the lower interest rates.

Under the basic set of assumptions used in developing Table 18-14, replacement rates become flatter over the income spectrum at the higher rates of return analyzed. Two underlying forces at play result in the relatively flat replacement rates across the income spectrum. First, Social Security benefits decline at progressively higher income levels, which would tend to decrease the replacement profile for higher-wage workers. Second, saving becomes increasingly important at higher wage levels, but higher rates of return on savings reduce the amount that needs to be saved or increase the amount that is consumed during the working periods. Maintaining this higher level of consumption progressively increases the income needed in retirement—that is, it increases the replacement rate. These results show the potential benefit that more aggressive investment decisions by retirement savers can have on consumption levels both before and after retirement.

Implications of Alternative Tenures

Table 18-15 shows the effects of alternative tenures or starting dates at accumulating retirement savings. In this case the underlying assumptions are that the pension formula provides a benefit equal to 1 percent of final pay at retirement with retirement occurring at age 65 and that retirement savings will accrue interest at a

TABLE 18-15   Replacement Rates at Three Career Starting Points and the Savings Rates Required to Maintain Preretirement Standards of Living in Retirement

Starting Pay Level When Saving Begins (1993 dollars)	Replacement Rates at Age 65 with Age When Retirement Saving Begins			Savings Rates with Age When Retirement Saving Begins		
	30	40	50	30	40	50
8,500	82.0	81.1	74.1	0.0	0.0	0.0
12,500	72.9	73.1	73.2	0.0	0.0	0.1
17,500	75.9	74.8	70.7	1.5	2.8	7.0
22,500	75.9	74.1	69.0	3.2	5.1	10.4
27,500	76.1	73.8	67.9	4.3	6.7	12.7
35,000	76.9	74.4	68.3	4.9	7.5	13.7
45,000	75.9	72.7	65.5	6.5	9.9	17.2
55,000	75.1	71.4	63.6	7.5	11.3	19.2
65,000	75.3	71.2	62.9	8.5	12.6	21.1
75,000	75.4	70.8	61.8	9.6	14.3	23.4
85,000	74.5	69.6	60.2	10.2	15.2	24.7

Source: Watson Wyatt.

rate of 6 percent per year, or at 2 percent over the assumed rate of inflation. Table 18-15 shows the calculations for workers beginning their retirement accumulations at ages 30, 40, and 50. The results show that the earlier a worker starts saving for retirement, the greater the level of retirement income that is provided at successively lower rates of personal savings. In cases where workers start to accumulate savings relatively early in their careers, the replacement rate profile is flat over most of the income spectrum. In cases where they wait until later in their career, the profile is somewhat steeper, with higher-income workers being required to ante up higher savings levels while working and ending up with lower replacement of preretirement earnings in retirement. The worker with an annual salary of $85,000 at age 50 who waits until then to start retirement accumulations would have to save $21,000 at age 50 and progressively more each year as the wage level grows. The pattern is clear: delaying retirement savings extracts a price on consumption levels both before and after retirement. Looking back to Table 18-13, an alternative to such reduced levels of living for workers who delay saving for their retirement is to merely work additional years.

Implications of Alternative Benefit Formula Generosity Levels

Table 18-16 shows the effects of alternative levels of generosity of benefit formulas on saving requirements and the replacement of preretirement earnings. In this case, we assumed that our worker begins the accumulation process at age 35 and works until age 60 and that savings will accumulate at a 2 percent real rate of return. We assumed there would be no actuarial reduction in the benefit at that age and again we assumed that the employer provides a retiree health benefit. We compare the situation the worker faces under three alternative benefit formulas that respectively pay 1.0, 1.5, or 2.0 percent of final earning for each year of service

TABLE 18-16   Replacement Rates at Three Benefit Formulas and the Savings Rates
Required to Maintain Preretirement Standards of Living in Retirement

Starting Pay Level When Saving Begins (1993 dollars)	Replacement Rate at Age 60 with Defined Benefit Plan Accrual Rate			Personal Savings Rate Required with Defined Benefit Plan Accrual Rate		
	1.0 Percent	1.5 Percent	2.0 Percent	1.0 Percent	1.5 Percent	2.0 Percent
8,500	64.4	64.4	72.6	0.0	0.0	0.0
12,500	66.2	69.4	72.6	6.8	3.6	0.5
17,500	66.7	69.8	73.0	10.9	7.7	4.5
22,500	66.5	69.7	72.9	12.7	9.5	6.4
27,500	66.5	69.7	72.8	14.0	10.8	7.7
35,000	67.0	70.1	73.3	14.9	11.7	8.5
45,000	65.9	69.1	72.2	16.6	13.5	10.3
55,000	65.0	68.2	71.3	17.6	14.5	11.3
65,000	65.0	68.1	71.3	18.9	15.7	12.5
75,000	64.9	68.1	71.2	20.2	17.0	13.8
85,000	64.0	67.2	70.3	20.8	17.6	14.4

Source: Watson Wyatt.

under the plan. At each given income level, the more generous the pension plan, the higher the replacement of earnings during retirement and the lower the personal savings required to get there. The implication of the information in this table is that once an employer has established a benefit structure for the defined benefit plan and considers the age at which typical workers are hired and the age at which people are retiring, it is possible to estimate and communicate what the personal savings rates of various workers should be in order to meet the retirement targets.

Implications of Providing Retiree Health Benefits

Table 18-17 shows the effects of having an employer-provided retiree health benefit compared with not having such a benefit. In this case we assumed that the worker would begin pension coverage and retirement accumulation at age 35 and would retire at age 60. We assumed he or she was covered by a pension plan that provided 1.5 percent of final salary at retirement. The only difference in the two cases is the provision of retiree health benefits. In developing the analysis we assumed that health premiums would increase at a rate of 6 percent, 1.5 times the rate of general inflation assumed in developing the estimates. The results suggest that the lack of a retiree health benefit reduces the replacement of final earnings in retirement for other consumption needs by more than 10 percentage points at the lower wage levels but by less than 2 percentage points at the highest starting salary considered in the analysis. If we had used a higher rate of health cost inflation it would magnify the differences that are reflected in the table.

The reason the effects of not receiving retiree health benefits generally decline at higher income levels is that the health insurance is assumed to cost all retirees

TABLE 18-17   Replacement Rates Without and with Retiree Health Benefits, and the
Savings Rates Required to Maintain Preretirement Standards of Living in
Retirement (percent)

Starting Pay Level When Saving Begins (1993 dollars)	Replacement Rates and the Provision of Retiree Health Benefits		Savings Rate Required with and Without Retiree Health Benefits	
	With	Without	With	Without
8,500	64.4	59.1	0.0	17.4
12,500	69.4	57.8	3.6	17.7
17,500	69.8	59.8	7.7	17.7
22,500	69.7	61.9	9.5	17.3
27,500	69.7	63.3	10.8	17.2
35,000	70.1	65.1	11.7	16.7
45,000	69.1	65.2	13.5	17.4
55,000	68.2	65.0	14.5	17.6
65,000	68.1	65.5	15.7	18.4
75,000	68.1	65.7	17.0	19.4
85,000	67.2	65.1	17.6	19.7

Source: Watson Wyatt.

the same regardless of their income levels. It may seem strange that the worker whose starting salary was $8,500 would not be as adversely affected by not receiving retiree health benefits as someone at a starting salary of $12,500 or even higher. The reason is that the value of the pension and Social Security benefits are such that they would provide a lifetime inflation-adjusted benefit in retirement that would exceed the lowest-wage worker's preretirement wage level net of working expenses and taxes. In other words, this worker's standard of living would go up in retirement if his or her employer provided retiree health benefits. When retiree health benefits are not offered, the extra Social Security and pension benefits in excess of the preretirement standard of living are used to purchase health care insurance.

In developing the analysis, we assumed that retirees whose employers did not pay for their health insurance could get such insurance at group rates that reflected the general needs for health care among retirees. As noted earlier, the health insurance markets have not been operating efficiently in recent years, and many retirees whose former employers do not provide them with health insurance have found that they have to pay significant risk premiums in order to purchase health insurance. If this phenomenon persists into the future, the results in Table 18-17 would significantly underestimate the implications of employer-provided health insurance.

Probably the most significant implication of the story told by Table 18-17 is the increase in personal savings that is required for workers who will not receive retiree health benefits. The lack of retiree health coverage basically flattens out the savings targets over the income spectrum. Under the scenario without employer-sponsoredretiree health insurance, the savings targets for low-wage workers are generally beyond the ability or willingness of most workers to save.

Implications of Being Single Versus Being Married

Table 18-18 shows the effects of being single versus being married and having a spouse who is a homemaker. In this case we assumed the worker would begin pension coverage and retirement accumulation at age 35 and would retire at age 65. We assumed that the worker was covered by a pension plan that provided 1 percent of final salary at retirement. The only difference in the two cases is that one worker is married and has a homemaker spouse and the other is single. In the married household we assumed that the worker and spouse were both the same age, that the worker would choose a joint and survivor benefit at retirement that would pay the surviving spouse 75 percent of the joint and survivor benefit after the death of the worker. Finally, we assumed that the worker would not receive a retiree health benefit although he would be covered by Medicare at age 65 and that the cost of securing insurance for the couple would equal 1.75 times the rate for single coverage under a plan that would supplement Medicare.

The results in Table 18-18 may appear to be counterintuitive. The target savings rate for the married worker is less than that for the single worker in every case. At the lowest pay levels the savings rates for the married worker would be about 5 to 7 percent of annual wages less than for the single person. Even at the highest wage levels reflected in the table, the saving rate by the married couple would be 2.5 percent of wages less than for the single worker. The reason for this is the significant value of Social Security benefits for a dependent spouse. A spouse's benefit that is equal to 50 percent of the worker's basic Social Security benefit represents a substantial claim on resources during retirement for which the married worker does not have to save additionally in comparison with the single worker. On the replacement rate side, the combination of the nonworking

TABLE 18-18   Replacement Rates for a Single Worker and a Married Worker with a Nonworking Spouse, and the Savings Rates Required to Maintain Preretirement Standards of Living In Retirement (percent)

Starting Pay Level When Saving Begins (1993 dollars)	Replacement Rate at Age 65		Savings Rate Required	
	Single Worker	Married Worker with Nonworking Spouse	Single Worker	Married Worker with Nonworking Spouse
8,500	60.2	65.7	4.7	0.0
12,500	66.2	73.8	7.3	0.0
17,500	68.9	75.9	8.6	1.2
22,500	70.0	73.5	9.2	2.4
27,500	71.0	74.4	9.5	3.3
35,000	72.5	76.5	9.3	4.2
45,000	72.0	75.4	10.5	6.5
55,000	71.4	74.3	11.2	7.0
65,000	71.8	74.3	12.0	8.3
75,000	71.9	73.9	13.1	10.2
85,000	71.0	72.6	13.7	11.2

Source: Watson Wyatt.

spouse's benefit under Social Security and the lower personal savings required during the working career result in higher income replacement rates for the married worker compared to the nonmarried one at every point on the income spectrum.

We do not show a separate analysis for married households where both of the spouses are employed. If both of the spouses have full-career jobs, their individual work expenses and work-related taxes are going to parallel those of individual workers. If each of them participates in a retirement program and saves in accordance with a plan that will allow each of them individually to maintain their living standard in retirement, then their combined retirement incomes should allow them to maintain their combined preretirement standards of living. For married couples where one spouse, typically the wife, only works part-time for a period of normal working ages in order to cover special expenses that arise—such as the college expenses of the children—it hardly seems appropriate to include such income as part of the normal preretirement standard of living. If, on the other hand, one or the other of the spouses works throughout a career but does not receive the benefits of an employer-sponsored pension, the model suggests such households should have markedly higher savings rates. But that should be the concern of the household. Any particular employer in designing its pension or retirement savings program for its own workers should not have to cover the contingencies that all other employers are not developing adequate programs of their own.

The Relationship Between Absolute and Relative Retirement Income Targets

In the earlier discussion about absolute standards of need, Table 18-2 showed that the 1993 official government poverty line for a single elderly person was around $7,000 and that the poverty level for a couple was around $9,000. That discussion also indicated that for a variety of reasons one could conclude that a true measure of poverty among the elderly would put these minimal income measures at much higher levels. Table 18-2 showed, for example, that simply updating calculations using exactly the same methodology used to derive the original poverty measures back in the 1960s would nearly double the current poverty lines for the elderly.

In the preceding section of this chapter, the discussion on estimating savings and replacement rates considered a number of alternative scenarios whereby workers could accumulate sufficient retirement income to maintain their pre-retirement standards of living. In deriving these measures, we considered expenses that workers could expect to incur because of working as well as special taxes related to working and other special expenses that they might incur before or after their retirements. In developing those scenarios, we tended to consider workers with relatively long tenures under a variety of pension programs. In evaluating the effectiveness of employer-based plans it makes sense to consider tenures ranging from 15 to 35 or 40 years because such tenures are common under the retirement plans sponsored by many if not most employers.

While the typical tenures under employer-sponsored retirement plans generally follow the scenarios that we have examined, the typical tenures of low-wage workers are not at all in accordance with the tenures that we have considered here. Indeed the tenures that we have considered here would tend to be the rare exception for a low-wage worker and, in that regard, the results of our analysis should be considered to be the most generous outcome that many low-wage workers could hope to achieve. In most of the cases that we considered, the lowest-wage workers in the analyses would end up with combined Social Security and pension benefits that would raise their standard of living in retirement above the level achieved during their working lives. Yet in a number of cases our results suggest that these lowest-wage workers would end up with replacement of their final earnings in the 60 to 70 percent range. Such replacement of final earnings will not get the lowest-wage workers in our society up to the most conservative standards of absolute need discussed earlier, much less up to the even higher standards that some analysts suggest are more realistic.

For most low-wage workers the situation is even worse than our analysis suggests. These workers tend to jump around from job to job. When they are covered by a pension program they are often not covered long enough to get vested under the plan, despite the significant reductions in vesting periods that have occurred over the last 25 years. When they are covered by a tax-qualified savings plan, they often have insufficient resources to save on their own and, to the extent the plans are noncontributory, they often cash out their accumulated benefits when they do move from job to job.

The combination of pensions, personal savings, and Social Security can get many workers a secure retirement where they can maintain a lifelong lifestyle that is generally perceived as satisfactory. But employer-based retirement programs are unlikely to ever be a mechanism to meet the minimal level of needs of the lowest-income members of our society. Even with long exposure, these plans do not throw off adequate levels of resources in an absolute sense, and long exposure to these plans by low-wage workers is rare. Meeting low-wage career workers' needs is the challenge of our social programs. If that challenge is not being met, we have to restructure our social programs if we hope to be successful in addressing the situation of the lowest-income retirees.

Implications of Savings and Replacement Rate Targets

In some regards, the earlier efforts to define a set of income replacement rate targets at various income levels has been an extension of the absolute measure of needs that is embodied in the poverty line measures discussed at the beginning of this chapter. Instead of measuring the absolute minimal level of income needed to survive, these earlier measures of replacement rates have attempted to set minimal incomes needed in retirement to match a range of preretirement consumption levels. These analyses have proven unsatisfactory, though, because they have failed to consider the reality of accumulating sufficient assets to meet the standards they were setting out to define. The model that has been laid out here provides a more realistic approach to defining a set of targets for workers of given characteristics. In doing that, however, it generates a variable set of target measures that depend on the age at which a worker begins to accumulate retirement assets, the age at which he or she decides to retire, and a host of other factors, as already discussed.

In the abstract it may seem desirable to develop an absolute set of income targets that define what an adequate income will be in retirement across the income spectrum. In reality, however, different employers and their employees bring a different set of circumstances to the challenge of accumulating an adequate retirement income. If we are to have a model that can help those unique employers and their workers develop a successful retirement accumulation process, it has to take into account their variability. As explained in Chapter 20, employers do look for workers with certain characteristics, and the nature of the retirement programs that the employer sponsors can help to attract and retain the kinds of workers being sought. Some hire workers early in their career and attempt to keep them throughout much of their career, maybe 30 or 40 years. Others hire workers later in their careers and may have an employment association that typically lasts only 15 or 20 years. Some have much less enduring relationships with their workers but still feel obligated to help in the accumulation of retirement assets.

Given that each employer tends to seek out workers with some set of relatively common traits, this approach to developing retirement benefit targets and the implied savings rates that support them give them the flexibility to design a retirement and savings program with the potential to deliver retirement benefits that will allow retirees to maintain preretirement standards of living. The approach will also help the sponsor of a retirement benefit plan more clearly delineate the relative responsibility of the formal retirement plan and the individual worker in providing the retirement benefit. Finally, the model provides a structure around which communications and measurement programs can be developed.

While most workers aspire to a happy retirement in which they can live at least as well as they lived during their working lives, most are incapable of pulling together all of the information on financial markets, costs of living, and life contingencies that are crucial in providing for their aspirations. In a work-oriented society, one of the main focal points of many people's lives is the employer. In the design and provision of retirement programs, employers have taken on some responsibility in helping workers sort out these complicated factors that they cannot sort out for themselves. Employers do not do this purely out of benevolent motivations, but because it serves the personnel interests of their organizations. Employers can best serve these personnel interests if their personnel understand the program and take appropriate advantage of it. This means the employer must successfully communicate the goals of the retirement accumulation program and the individual's responsibility to participate in achieving it. The evidence discussed in Chapter 16 suggests that employers generally are not as successful in communicating to workers as they need to be if they expect their retirement income programs to work. This is a challenge that clearly requires further effort.

The public policy debate about the adequacy of the baby boom generation's savings behavior is important in the context of the issues that have been covered in this chapter. On one side of that debate are a group of economists who believe the baby boomer's savings behavior is woefully inadequate.[37] On the other are analysts who believe the baby boomers are ahead of the savings trajectory that their

---

[37]See for example, B. Douglas Bernheim, "Is the Baby Boom Generation Preparing Adequately for Retirement?" Technical Report prepared for Merrill Lynch & Co., Inc. (August 1992).

parents' generation followed at a comparable stage in their lives.[38] No employer can be expected to resolve the debate about the adequacy of the baby boom generation's retirement savings behavior, but each employer sponsoring a pension or retirement saving program can monitor the participation in the plans and assess the adequacy of its own employees' retirement savings patterns within the context of the benefits that Social Security and employer-financed programs can realistically be expected to deliver.

---

[38]See for example, Joyce Manchester, *Baby Boomers in Retirement: An Early Perspective* (Washington, D.C.: Congressional Budget Office, September 1993).

Chapter 19
Delivery of Retirement Benefits

Chapter 18 focused on the development of retirement targets using both absolute and relative measures of retirement income adequacy. It explained the underlying theory behind the measures of retirement income adequacy and how those levels of adequacy might be achieved under various scenarios and assumptions. While such an analysis is important in understanding the measures of adequacy, by itself it tells very little about the actual performance of the American retirement income security system. This chapter looks at the structure of existing plans in operation across large segments of the economy and their potential delivery of retirement income to try to determine how the retirement system actually works. Some important information can also be obtained by comparing the economic status of the elderly population today with the working-age population and assessing the standard of living achieved by contemporary retirees and the role that pensions play in helping achieve that standard of living.

The next section of the chapter evaluates the level of benefits generated by a combination of defined benefit and defined contribution plans that currently exist in the national economy. The discussion opens with the benefits generated by defined benefit plans alone and then turns to the benefits generated by a set of defined contribution plans sponsored by employers who do not offer defined benefit plans. Also discussed are the benefits generated by a large cross section of employers offering defined benefit plans in combination with a defined contribution plan. The analysis is conducted within the framework of the savings and retirement targets developed in Chapter 18.

The last section of this chapter is concerned with the levels of income actually being delivered to the elderly population and the sources of that income. In some regards, the story told in this section of the chapter is inconclusive in its assessment of the performance of the American retirement income security system and the role that pensions play because the evidence shows that the measures of the delivery of pension benefits are inconsistent across the data sources typically used for analyses of this sort. A firm conclusion of the chapter is that one of the more popular sources of information used to assess the retirement income security system is coming up significantly short in the reporting of pension income.

Potential Benefits Generated by Contemporary Retirement Plans

To understand the level of potential benefits that existing retirement plans generate, one must look at a distribution of existing plans. In our analysis, we used a group of actual plans that were surveyed during 1993 by Watson Wyatt. Approximately 560 firms are included in this data base. The firms surveyed were predominantly larger firms, most having more than 1,000 employees and half having more than 5,000 employees. Larger firms often have multiple plans because they have different benefits across different operating units, classes of workers (i.e., union versus nonunion), and so on. For that reason, the respondents in this survey were asked to identify the retirement plans that best represented the benefits provided to nonunion, salaried workers in their companies. The respondents to the survey do not constitute a random sample of plans offered by all companies, or even large companies, but they and their retirement plans represent more or less the range and type of plans offered by private employers today. Because the participants in the survey are predominantly larger firms, there is a greater prevalence of defined benefit plans in our sample than firms generally offer.

In developing the analysis that follows, we used a consistent set of economic assumptions. We assumed that the inflation rate would remain at 4 percent per year; that workers' wages would grow at 5 percent per year until the workers attained age 55, and at 4 percent per year thereafter; and that the interest rate would be 6 percent per year for calculating returns on retirement plan assets and for calculating annuities. Throughout the analysis we calculated benefits on a projected basis, by assuming that current plans and Social Security will continue to provide benefits in accordance with current formulas. In order to give a sense of the distribution of benefits generated by existing plans, we developed calculations for plans at the 15th, 40th, 65th, and 90th percentiles of benefit generosity. In comparing the results across varying retirement scenarios, the plan selected for one scenario might not be the same one chosen for an alternative scenario. For example, a plan that provides a 15th-percentile benefit at age 65 with 30 years of service might not provide any retirement benefit at all for a worker retiring at age 55 with 30 years of service. So the plans representing the 15th-percentile level of generosity under these two scenarios would be different.

Defined Benefit Plans

In assessing the level of benefits provided by defined benefit plans, we used all of the defined benefit plans that were recorded in the survey whether or not they were supplemented by a defined contribution plan. We did this because most employers would consider the defined benefit plan the primary plan for providing a "career" benefit for long-service workers, even when they offered a combination of plans. Also, estimating the benefits generated by the defined benefit plans allowed us to derive the savings rate required to meet the goal of accumulating adequate resources to allow retirees to maintain their preretirement standard of living after they withdraw from the work force. The calculations presented here cover 455 plans.

The level of benefits generated by the defined benefit plans alone at three retirement ages with 30 years of service is shown in Table 19-1. The benefit levels provided by the plans are reflected as replacement rates relative to final annual wages for a single life annuity. The general pattern of benefits in Table 19-1 is one in which each of the plans pays a somewhat higher benefit at higher income levels

TABLE 19-1   Replacement of Final Earnings by Defined Benefit Plans for Workers
Retiring with 30 Years of Service at Three Retirement Ages

Retirement Age	Plan Ranking by Generosity (percentile)	Ultimate Replacement Rates at Three Initial Salary Levels (%)		
		$20,000	*$50,000*	*$80,000*
65	15	24.1	27.3	28.4
	40	30.2	34.3	36.9
	65	36.1	39.4	42.2
	90	47.2	50.0	52.0
60	15	17.8	19.9	22.1
	40	26.0	28.7	31.3
	65	33.2	35.1	37.2
	90	45.6	47.2	49.1
55	15	12.1	13.3	14.5
	40	17.8	19.4	21.1
	65	24.1	25.9	27.5
	90	38.2	39.2	40.8

Source: Watson Wyatt.

because the pension benefit is integrated with Social Security. Of course, plans at higher percentile levels replace a greater portion of preretirement income than those at lower levels. Finally, workers who retire at younger ages receive a lower benefit than those retiring at older ages, owing to the actuarial reductions that are common in defined benefit plans for workers retiring prior to the normal retirement age specified in the plan.

For workers retiring at age 65 under these plans, the benefits provided range from slightly less than one-quarter up to slightly more than one-half of final earnings. For workers retiring at age 60, the low-end plan reflected in Table 19-1 provides a benefit relative to final salary that would be between 74 and 78 percent of the benefit provided to a worker retiring at age 65. By comparison, taking the benefit at age 60 in the 90th-percentile plan would produce a benefit that was 94 to 97 percent of the benefit payable at age 65. In this case the greater relative reduction in benefits for the less generous plan relates to the earlier or more steep actuarial reductions for early retirement in comparison with the more generous plans. Moving to retirement at age 55 would result in a pension benefit that was 50 to 51 percent of the age 65 benefit at the 15th-percentile plan and 78 to 81 percent of the age 65 benefit at the 90th-percentile plan level.

As the analysis in Chapter 18 suggests, once the benefits provided by Social Security and the pension are defined, the age at which the individual starts to accumulate a pension and to save for retirement is known, and the retirement age target is set, it is possible to estimate the appropriate savings rate that will allow the worker to maintain his or her preretirement standard of living in retirement. Table 19-2 shows the savings rates that would be required for a worker who begins to accumulate retirement savings other than Social Security at age 35 and who would work until age 65 under the four defined benefit plans described earlier. In

TABLE 19-2   Levels of Defined Benefit Plan Generosity, Savings Rates Required to Maintain Preretirement Standards of Living, and Replacement of Final Earnings from All Retirement Income Sources for Workers Aged 65 with 30 Years of Service (percent)

Salary When Pension Coverage and Saving Begin (dollars)	Required Personal Savings Rate Associated with the Pension Plan				Retirement Income Replacement of Preretirement Earnings			
	15th Percentile	40th Percentile	65th Percentile	90th Percentile	15th Percentile	40th Percentile	65th Percentile	90th Percentile
12,500	0.0	0.0	0.0	0.0	73.0	73.0	75.1	83.7
15,000	2.1	0.9	0.0	0.0	75.5	76.6	77.5	79.4
20,000	4.8	3.5	2.3	0.0	75.5	76.8	78.0	80.3
25,000	6.1	4.8	3.6	1.3	75.2	76.5	77.7	79.9
30,000	6.9	5.6	4.5	2.2	75.2	76.5	77.7	79.9
40,000	8.2	6.8	5.8	3.6	75.8	77.2	78.3	80.5
50,000	9.5	8.1	7.1	4.9	74.7	76.1	77.2	79.4
60,000	10.4	8.9	7.8	5.7	73.7	75.2	76.2	78.4
70,000	11.5	9.8	8.8	6.7	73.5	75.1	76.2	78.3
80,000	12.6	10.9	9.8	7.8	73.4	75.1	76.2	78.2

Source: Watson Wyatt.
Note: Sources of income include employer plan benefits, Social Security, and personal savings.

this analysis, we assumed that the employer would provide a retiree health benefit for the retired worker.

At the lowest starting salary level in this terminal job, the model suggests that the combination of Social Security and the pension benefit would be sufficiently generous that the worker would not have to save additional funds to achieve the goal of maintaining the preretirement standard of living after withdrawing from the work force. At the $15,000 starting salary level, a worker covered by the pension plan at the 15th-percentile level of generosity among all plans would have to save 2.1 percent of pay each year. The required savings rate would increase at each higher initial salary level up to 12.6 percent at the $80,000 level. At the 90th percentile of generosity, workers with a starting wage up to $15,000 would not have to save outside of Social Security and the pension program. At the $80,000 starting salary level, a worker in the 90th-percentile plan would be required to save roughly 7.8 percent of his or her wages per year.

Under the scenario of workers joining a single firm offering a defined benefit plan and spending the last 30 years of their career leading up to retirement at age 65, most plans appear to offer benefits that, in conjunction with Social Security, would put workers within reasonable reach of attaining a retirement income consistent with maintaining the preretirement living standard. While saving on a $15,000 salary under the 15th-percentile plan might seem daunting, the saving implied by the results would be around $6 per week for such a worker at age 35. Also, the 12.6 percent saving rate may seem a little steep for a worker at $80,000 but a 401(k) plan that allows a worker to save up to 6 percent of earnings with a 50 percent employer match would get the worker within $240 per month of the target savings level.

TABLE 19-3   Levels of Defined Benefit Plan Generosity, Savings Rates Required to Maintain Preretirement Standards of Living, and Replacement of Final Earnings from All Retirement Income Sources for Workers Aged 55 with 30 Years of Service (percent)

Salary When Pension Coverage and Saving Begin (dollars)	Required Personal Savings Rate Associated with the Pension Plan				Retirement Income Replacement of Preretirement Earnings			
	15th Percentile	40th Percentile	65th Percentile	90th Percentile	15th Percentile	40th Percentile	65th Percentile	90th Percentile
12,500	13.3	12.0	10.6	7.1	59.6	60.9	62.4	65.8
15,000	15.9	14.6	13.1	9.7	61.5	62.8	64.3	67.7
20,000	18.1	16.8	15.3	12.0	62.2	63.5	65.0	68.3
25,000	19.1	17.7	16.2	13.0	62.1	63.5	65.0	68.3
30,000	19.8	18.4	16.9	13.7	62.3	63.7	65.2	68.4
40,000	21.3	19.9	18.4	15.2	62.7	64.1	65.6	68.8
50,000	22.2	20.8	19.2	16.1	62.0	63.4	65.0	68.1
60,000	22.7	21.2	19.7	16.6	61.3	62.8	64.3	67.5
70,000	23.7	22.1	20.6	17.5	61.3	62.8	64.3	67.5
80,000	24.5	22.9	21.4	18.3	61.5	63.0	64.5	67.7

Source: Watson Wyatt.

Note: Sources of income include employer plan benefits, Social Security, and personal savings.

In calculating the replacement rates shown in Table 19-2, we used the estimated taxes and other work-related expenses as derived and modeled in Chapter 18. The range of replacement rates is at a level that most people involved in the design of pension plans would consider reasonable to generous—73 to 75 percent replacement of preretirement earnings for the 15th-percentile plan and 78 to 84 percent earnings replacement by the 90th-percentile plan. These replacement rates assume that Social Security will continue to provide the benefits that are implied in the benefit formula specified in law as it existed in late 1994. If the imbalances in Social Security discussed in Chapter 1 result in reductions in these benefits in the future, either pension benefits or individual savings would have to increase to make up the difference. Such an increase in either pension savings or individual savings would imply a reduced standard of living before and after retirement from that shown here.

Table 19-3 shows the savings rates and replacement of preretirement income for a worker who wishes to retire at age 55 with 30 years of service. In this case, the savings rates required suggest that this is not a viable scenario for many workers. In the 15th-percentile plan, the required savings rates vary from 13.3 percent of preretirement pay at the lowest salary levels up to slightly more than one-quarter of pay at the highest levels. Some workers with a strong disposition to withdraw from the work force as early as possible might be willing to endure such savings rates over a significant portion of their career, but the overwhelming majority would not. Even under the 90th-percentile plan, the required savings rates from about 7.1 percent of pay at the lowest salary level up to 18.3 percent at the highest level would present many workers with a challenge that they would not be willing to meet. The higher savings rates and longer retirement periods under this scenario also suggest significantly lower replacement of preretirement earnings than under the scenario where the workers work to age 65. The combination of the higher savings rates during the working career and relatively low replacement rates in retirement imply lower standards of living than many workers would be willing to accept. However, those with a strong preference for leisure time over other forms of consumption could attain an acceptable standard of living in many cases. At lower wage levels, the replacement rates implied by this scenario almost certainly would result in retirees living out their nonworking years with incomes below the official poverty line.

Stand-Alone Defined Contribution Plans

In assessing the potential level of benefits provided by defined contribution plans, we used plans in firms where the employer sponsored only defined contribution plans. We did this because then we could be relatively certain that the plan we were dealing with was not a supplemental plan meant to augment a more generous retirement benefit. In this case, we had a group of 107 plans for which we could calculate benefits and compare them.

Defined contribution plans are much more likely to require employee contributions than defined benefit plans. For years, thrift plans have had provisions that permit employers to match employee contributions to the plan. Since the early 1980s, the growth of 401(k) plans has made these employer-matching provisions much more common. In a 1991 U.S. Labor Department survey of private sector firms with more than 100 employees, for example, 48 percent of the full-time employees in the firms were found to be participating in one or more defined contribution plans sponsored by their employer. The same survey also found that 44 percent of the full-time workers were enrolled in a plan with a cash or deferred arrangement—that is, a 401(k) plan. The employer made all of the contributions to the retirement or savings program for only about 16 percent of all of the workers covered by a defined contribution plan in these medium-size and larger establishments.[1]

The Profit Sharing Council of America does an annual survey of profit-sharing and 401(k) plans to gather information on the characteristics of plans offered by employers. In its survey for the 1993 plan year, which covered 557 firms, the Council found that 31 percent of the responding firms offered plans in which all contributions were made by the employer. Among larger firms (those with more than 1,000 employees), however, only 14 percent of the firms offered plans with only employer contributions. Thirty-seven percent of all respondents, but 41 percent of the larger ones, indicated that they offered combination plans, in which the employer contributions were made on a variable matching basis depending on employee contributions. In the remaining plans, all contributions were made by the participants, or the participants' contributions were matched on a fixed basis by the employer.[2]

[1]U.S. Department of Labor, *Employee Benefits in Medium and Large Private Establishments,* Bureau of Labor Statistics Bulletin 2422 (Washington, D.C.: USGPO, May 1993), p. 104.
[2]Profit Sharing Council of America, *37th Annual Survey of Profit Sharing and 401(k) Plans Reflecting 1993 Plan Year Experience* (Chicago, Ill.: Profit Sharing Council of America, 1994), p. 6.

The Profit Sharing Council's survey also reported average employer contributions in cases where the employer did not offer a defined benefit plan. In those companies in which all contributions were made by the employer, the average contribution rate was 8.5 percent of annual payroll. In the combination plans, the average was 5.8 percent of payroll, and in the cases where there was no employer contribution or where the employer contribution was fixed, the average was 3.4 percent of payroll.[3] The interesting aspect of the matching requirements under the 401(k) arrangement is that full participation by workers can significantly augment the benefits provided by the employer. Variations in matching rates also cause some confusion in scaling the overall generosity of plans. For example, different workers might reach different conclusions about the relative generosity of two 401(k) plans, one providing a 100 percent match of employee contributions up to 3 percent of pay and the other providing a 50 percent match of up to 8 percent of pay. For the employee who wants to contribute less than 6 percent of pay to the plan, the 100 percent match is clearly superior, because it generates a greater employer contribution than the 50 percent match, even though the marginal contributions above 3 percent of pay are zero. For the employee who wants to contribute more than 6 percent of pay, however, the plan offering the 50 percent match would be more generous because it generates higher employer contributions—between 6 and 8 percent of pay—than the 100 percent match of 3 percent of pay would generate.

In assessing the potential retirement income available from employer-sponsored defined contribution plans in cases where no defined benefit plan is available, we assumed that employees would contribute at a level that would generate the maximum employer contributions to the plans. In this regard, we are exaggerating the benefits that these plans are likely to provide to many workers because not all of them participate at a level that generates a maximum employer match. In addition, there is some leakage of contributions and accumulated assets in these plans over time as some workers cash out some of their retirement savings to finance consumption prior to retirement. On the other hand, we assumed that employees would not contribute to their plans if there was no employer match. In some cases, there is no employer match at all, and in many cases where there is an employer match, many workers contribute more than the level at which contributions are matched. Thus in cases where contributions going into a 401(k) plan were unmatched, we attributed no accumulating value to the employee's unmatched contributions to the plan. In this regard, we are underestimating the value of the benefits that these plans are likely to provide to many workers. Even in cases where there is no 401(k) match we know that half of eligible workers regularly participate in the plans (see Chapter 16). Table 19-4 shows the calculated replacement of final earnings that would be generated by an inflation-indexed annuity purchased with the savings that would be accumulated under the sample of defined contribution plans analyzed according to the assumptions that have been spelled out here.

In Table 19-1, which is comparable to Table 19-4 but focuses on defined benefit plans, we showed the results on the basis of a range of starting wage levels. That is

[3]Ibid., p. 8.

TABLE 19-4   Replacement of Final Earnings by Defined Contribution
              Plans for Workers Retiring with 30 Years of Plan Savings
              at Three Retirement Ages (percent)

Retirement Age	Replacement Rates from Plans with Percentile Ranking by Plan Generosity			
	15th	40th	65th	90th
65	21.4	28.8	37.6	50.2
60	18.6	25.0	32.5	43.4
55	16.4	22.0	28.7	38.3

Source: Watson Wyatt.

unnecessary in the case of contemporary defined contribution plans because the potential contribution rates tend to be much more consistent across the range of wages than the accrual patterns in defined benefit plans. Because of the higher participation rates by higher-wage workers in comparison with those at lower wage levels, however, the pattern of benefits delivery by defined contribution plans is similar to that of defined benefit plans. At the same time, under the assumptions of full participation in the plans up to the maximum contribution by the employer, the results are not affected by beginning salary level.[4]

The results in Table 19-4 and Table 19-1 suggest that the potential retirement income generated by plans in firms that sponsor only defined contribution plans is comparable to that provided by the cross section of defined benefit plans analyzed earlier. For workers retiring at age 65 after 30 years of participation in the plans, the defined contribution plans tend to generate slightly less retirement income at each of the percentile rankings than the defined benefit plans at comparable levels. For those retiring at age 60, the benefits are quite close to each other. For those retiring at age 55 with 30 years of participation, the defined contribution plans generate slightly higher income than the defined benefit plans. The reader should keep in mind that we are assuming that the 25-year-old is as focused on saving in this example as the worker who begins saving at age 35. That probably is not the case in most instances and is a concern that does not arise for most defined benefit plans since the employee generally does not directly contribute to the plan.

In the earlier analysis of defined benefit plans, we looked at the level of individual savings required to augment the pension benefit so workers can maintain their preretirement standard of living in retirement. Given that the defined contribution plans that have become so popular today require a significant amount of individual savings, it may seem strange to separately identify the individual savings that must be accumulated to meet the retirement income targets we evaluated in the earlier context. The defined contribution plans that we have been evaluating,

[4]At very high salaries, 401(k) contribution limits would come into play. They have not been factored into this analysis. Also the section 401(a)(17) pay limit of $150,000 may limit the contributions of lower-paid "highly compensated employees" if the contributions by all highly compensated individuals have to be reduced as a result of the pay limit. If such limits come into play, employers would either have to make up the difference through a nonqualified arrangement or the workers affected would have their overall benefits reduced.

TABLE 19-5   Levels of Potential Defined Contribution Plan Generosity, Savings Rates Required Beyond Employer Matching in the Plans to Maintain Preretirement Standards of Living, and Replacement of Final Earnings from All Retirement Income Sources for Workers Aged 65 with 30 Years of Service (percent)

Salary When Pension Coverage and Saving Begin (1994 dollars)	Required Savings Rate Beyond Employer Matching in the Capital Accumulation				Retirement Income Replacement Rate for Preretirement Earnings			
	15th Percentile	40th Percentile	65th Percentile	90th Percentile	15th Percentile	40th Percentile	65th Percentile	90th Percentile
12,500	0.0	0.0	0.0	0.0	70.0	70.9	77.0	85.8
15,000	1.7	0.0	0.0	0.0	72.8	73.5	72.7	81.5
20,000	4.5	2.6	0.2	0.0	72.9	73.7	74.1	76.7
25,000	5.9	4.1	1.7	0.0	72.4	73.2	73.6	73.8
30,000	6.9	5.1	2.7	0.0	72.2	73.0	73.4	74.1
40,000	8.4	6.6	4.2	1.0	72.7	73.5	73.9	75.1
50,000	9.9	8.1	5.7	2.5	71.4	72.2	72.6	73.7
60,000	10.8	9.0	6.6	3.4	70.2	71.1	71.4	72.6
70,000	12.0	10.2	7.8	4.6	70.0	70.8	71.2	72.4
80,000	13.1	11.3	8.9	5.8	69.8	70.6	71.0	72.2

Source: Watson Wyatt.

Note: Source of income include employer plan benefits, Social Security, and personal savings.

however, are merely an alternative vehicle for accumulating retirement income. There is no reason to believe that defined contribution plans by themselves would be any more likely to generate adequate retirement income without supplemental savings than defined benefit plans. Indeed, many of the plans analyzed here provide workers with the opportunity to save additional amounts on a tax-preferred basis, although these amounts would not be further subsidized by employer-matching contributions. In this regard, these plans would require additional savings by workers, just as defined benefit plans do.

Table 19-5 shows the savings rates required beyond the rate at which the employer matches employee contributions in the defined contribution plan for a worker who begins to save for retirement at age 35 and retires at age 65. The table shows the savings rates for the defined contribution plans representing four levels of benefit generosity. These are cases in which the firm sponsors one or more defined contribution plans but no defined benefit plans. The savings rate required beyond employer matching of employee contributions at the lowest starting pay rate shown in Table 19-5 is zero at all four levels of plan generosity. At the $15,000 starting pay level, the worker would be required to save 1.7 percent of salary beyond what the employer would match in the savings plan at the 15-percentile level of plan generosity. At this level of generosity, the typical employee would receive a 100 percent match on his or her contributions of up to 3 percent of pay. So the worker in this case would be contributing only 1.7 percent of pay that was not matched by the employer, plus another 3 percent that was matched in order to meet the retirement target of being able to maintain the living standard after retiring from the work force. Moving up the starting wage scale in the table, the rate of saving beyond the worker's matched savings in the plan increases to 13.1 percent of pay for the worker with a salary of $80,000 per year at age 35. At the 90th-percentile level of generosity, workers with a salary of up to $30,000 per year would not have to save beyond what the employer matches in the plan. Even at the $80,000 starting wage rate, the worker would need to save only 5.8 percent of pay beyond the level of the employer match. At this level of plan generosity, however, the worker would be contributing 8 percent of pay inside the plan on which he or she would be receiving a 75 percent match from the employer.

The replacement rates under this scenario have to take into account that the worker is saving some of his or her potential disposable wages as a plan participant. From the discussion in Chapter 18, we know preretirement savings rates directly affect postretirement replacement rates. The savings rates required to meet target retirement income levels reflected in Table 19-5 match up fairly consistently with the savings rates required under the defined benefit plan analysis reflected in Table 19-2. For example, a worker in a 15th-percentile defined benefit plan with a starting salary of $15,000 would be required to save an additional 2.1 percent of pay to meet the target rate. The same worker covered under a 15th-percentile defined contribution plan would have to save 1.7 percent beyond the savings matched by the employer. At the $80,000 pay level, the tables are slightly turned in that the defined benefit participant is required to save 12.6 percent but the defined contribution participant being required to save 13.2 percent of pay.

The replacement rates in Table 19-5 do not compare quite as favorably with the earlier results presented in Table 19-2, which showed the calculations for participants in defined benefit plans. The primary reason is that the defined contribution participant is saving from actual cash wages in order to generate the employer match in the tax-qualified plan. This lowers preretirement disposable income and thus the target replacement rates. If this analysis were being carried out within the context of total compensation where employer contributions to the defined benefit plan were considered part of the preretirement wage of the worker and the contributions were saving by the workers, then the two analyses would be more parallel. The difference between the scenario considering stand-alone defined contribution plans and the earlier one is that in this case the worker almost always has to contribute directly to the retirement plan in order to make the scenario come true; in the overwhelming majority of defined benefit plans, employee contributions are not involved. Since we know many workers are not willing to make even moderate contributions, even when the employer provides a generous match, the potential of this defined contribution scenario is roughly equal to that of the earlier one, but it is often less successful.

Table 19-6 shows the savings rates and replacement of preretirement income for a worker who wishes to retire at age 55 with 30 years of service. In this case the worker in the 15th-percentile plan would be required to save 11.2 to 22.9 percent of pay beyond matched savings across the pay spectrum shown in the table. Considering that plans at this level would also typically require an employee contribution of 3 percent of pay, a worker earning $20,000 per year at age 25 would have to be saving 14.2 percent of his or her wages for retirement purposes to make this scenario come true. At the upper end of the wage distribution shown

TABLE 19-6   Levels of Potential Defined Contribution Plan Generosity, Savings Rates Required Outside the Plan to Maintain Preretirement Standards of Living, and Replacement of Final Earnings from All Retirement Income Sources for Workers Aged 55 with 30 Years of Service (percent)

Salary When Pension Coverage and Saving Begin (1994 dollars)	Required Savings Rate Beyond Employer Matching in the Capital Accumulation Plan				Retirement Income Replacement of Preretirement Earnings			
	15th Percentile	40th Percentile	65th Percentile	90th Percentile	15th Percentile	40th Percentile	65th Percentile	90th Percentile
12,500	11.2	9.5	7.2	4.1	58.8	59.4	59.8	60.8
15,000	13.8	12.1	9.8	6.7	60.7	61.4	61.7	62.7
20,000	16.0	14.3	12.0	9.0	61.3	62.0	62.3	63.3
25,000	17.0	15.3	13.0	10.0	61.2	61.9	62.2	63.2
30,000	17.8	16.1	13.8	10.8	61.3	62.0	62.3	63.3
40,000	19.4	17.7	15.4	12.4	61.6	62.3	62.6	63.6
50,000	20.3	18.7	16.3	13.3	60.9	61.6	61.9	62.9
60,000	20.9	19.3	16.9	13.9	60.1	60.8	61.1	62.1
70,000	22.0	20.3	18.0	15.0	60.0	60.7	61.0	62.0
80,000	22.9	21.2	18.9	15.9	60.0	60.7	61.1	62.1

Source: Watson Wyatt.

Note: Sources of income include employer plan benefits, Social Security, and personal savings.

in Table 19-6, the required savings rate would increase to more than one-quarter of cash wages. While some workers might save at these rates, they are significantly higher than the real savings rates reported for typical working-age individuals. For example, survey data from the mid-1980s suggest that homeowners aged 22 to 45 saved around 8 percent of income. For nonhomeowners the estimates range from 7 to 15 percent.[5] In any event, the average savings rates appear to fall far short of the savings targets suggested by the 15th-percentile defined contribution plan scenario for a worker wishing to retire at age 55.

In the 90th-percentile plan, the required savings rates outside the plan become somewhat more plausible. At this plan level, however, the employee would be required to put 8 percent of his or her wages into the plan in order to get the employer match that would maximize the employer contribution to the plan. In other words, at the lower starting wage levels shown in Table 19-6 the worker would have to contribute 12.2 percent of pay over his or her career. At the upper wage levels, the total savings required to meet the retirement accumulation goals by the individual worker would fall between 23 and 24 percent of pay if he or she were to be able to retire by age 55.

The replacement rates reflected in Table 19-6 are generally in the lower range of what plan designers would consider reasonable. Note that these are lifetime annuities that include a provision to cover increases in the cost of inflation. However, in

[5]Barry Bosworth, Gary Burtless, and John Sabelhaus, "The Decline in Saving: Evidence from Household Surveys," *Brookings Papers on Economic Activity,* no. 1 (Washington, D.C.: Brookings Institution, 1991), p. 210.

our baseline assumptions we have assumed that the retiree would be provided with an employer-sponsored retiree health benefit. While such benefits might be common for retirees receiving defined benefit pensions, they are fairly rare in cases where the employer sponsors only defined contribution retirement benefits. The reason is that a retiree health benefit is an in-kind defined benefit. The employer who is not willing to make the commitment to a defined benefit pension that can be funded over the working lives of covered employees is generally not inclined to commit to one that cannot be prefunded, especially one whose cost is highly inflationary, as health costs have been in recent decades.

Factoring in the additional individual savings required to have sufficient resources to pay for retiree health insurance, as outlined in Chapter 18, would increase the target savings rate by as much as 10 to 20 percentage points at the lower wage levels and up to 2.5 percent of pay at the higher levels. In other words, the relatively difficult task of being able to retire by age 55 suggested by Table 19-6 would be even more difficult than the table implies because it does not take into consideration the special health consumption costs associated with retirement, especially retirement prior to Medicare eligibility.

Defined Benefit Plans in Conjunction with Defined Contribution Plans

In the early evolution of defined benefit plans, employers set up the plan and generally considered it the mechanism through which they would meet the retirement security of the participants. The plan was often coordinated with Social Security, but in most cases it was the single vehicle sponsored by the employer. With the passage of ERISA in 1974 establishing the section 415 contribution and funding limits for tax-qualified plans, there was some financial advantage for higher-paid workers to be covered under both a defined benefit and defined contribution plan. During the 1970s people grew increasingly aware that traditional defined benefit plans did not meet the retirement needs of all workers covered under them although in many cases these plans were the most effective vehicle for meeting the needs of workers. Another growing concern during the 1970s was the effect of inflation on retirement annuities. Employers sponsoring defined benefit plans wanted to give employees a mechanism to insure against the loss of retirement income purchasing power but were extremely reluctant to unreservedly commit to underwriting this risk over which they had absolutely no control. The combination of these forces led many sponsors of defined benefit plans to introduce supplemental defined contribution plans for their workers. The establishment of section 401(k) of the Internal Revenue Code in 1978 and the promulgation of regulations for plans established under this section of the code in the early 1980s led to a significant proliferation of supplemental plans and a reconfiguration of many supplemental plans that had been established earlier.

The retirement program offered by most large employers in the mid-1990s is a defined benefit plan supplemented by a defined contribution plan that generally includes a 401(k) feature. In order to assess the levels of benefits being provided in this environment, we analyzed the retirement benefits being provided by 313 employers sponsoring both a defined benefit and defined contribution plan. We looked at the total potential benefits under the combined arrangements. Again

TABLE 19-7   Replacement of Final Earnings by Defined Benefit and Defined Contribution Plans Combined for Workers Retiring with 30 Years of Service at Specified Ages

Retirement Age	Plan Ranking by Generosity (percentile)	Ultimate Replacement Rates at Three Initial Pay Levels (%)		
		$20,000	$50,000	$80,000
65	15th	51.0	54.4	55.5
	40th	59.9	63.3	66.5
	65th	67.2	70.0	73.1
	90th	80.0	82.8	86.3
60	15th	42.7	44.2	46.3
	40th	50.8	52.7	54.9
	65th	59.4	61.0	63.8
	90th	71.6	73.8	77.4
55	15th	33.8	34.7	36.2
	40th	40.1	41.2	43.2
	65th	48.4	49.6	50.9
	90th	63.2	63.9	65.4

Source: Watson Wyatt.

many of the defined contribution plans analyzed provide for employer matching of employee contributions but also allow for additional contributions above the level at which the employer match is provided. In this case, as in the earlier one, we assumed that the participants would contribute at the rate that would maximize the employer contribution but would not contribute above that amount. We did not include employers who provided no contribution, nor did we include employers who make discretionary profit-sharing contributions only.

Table 19-7 shows the replacement of final earnings under the combined plans for workers retiring with 30 years of service at three ages. As in the earlier cases, the replacement rates are estimated on the basis of a single life annuity compared with the final annual wage. The results here are similar to those reported earlier on defined benefit plans alone in that each of the combined plans pays a somewhat higher benefit at higher income levels because of the integration of the pension benefit with Social Security.

Table 19-8 shows the savings rates beyond savings matched by the employer in the combined plans that would be required in order to meet the retirement income target that would allow participants at various pay levels to maintain their standard of living after they stop working. Needless to say, these savings rates appear quite attainable. In the majority of cases the workers would have to do little or no saving beyond what the employer matches or provides in the employer-sponsored plans. In most instances, however, they would be required to save 6 percent of their pay inside the plan in order to attain the levels of replacement income indicated in the table. The replacement rates in this instance, which also take into account matched savings inside the savings plan, are so high that only partial participation in the defined contribution plan would result in a living standard in retirement that was equal to or higher than the standard achieved during the working career in some cases at low wage levels in the most generous plans.

TABLE 19-8   Levels of Potential Combined Retirement Plan Generosity, Savings Rates Required Outside the Plan to Maintain Preretirement Standards of Living, and Replacement of Final Earnings from All Retirement Income Sources for Workers Aged 65 with 30 Years of Service

Salary When Pension Coverage and Saving Begin (1994 dollars)	Required Savings Rate Beyond Employer Matching in the Combined DB and DC Plans				Retirement Income Replacement of Preretirement Earnings			
	15th Percentile	40th Percentile	65th Percentile	90th Percentile	15th Percentile	40th Percentile	65th Percentile	90th Percentile
12,500	0.0	0.0	0.0	0.0	86.5	92.2	97.5	106.7
15,000	0.0	0.0	0.0	0.0	82.1	88.0	93.3	102.3
20,000	0.0	0.0	0.0	0.0	77.3	83.5	88.6	97.5
25,000	0.0	0.0	0.0	0.0	75.3	81.2	86.2	95.1
30,000	0.0	0.0	0.0	0.0	76.1	79.9	84.8	93.7
40,000	0.9	0.0	0.0	0.0	77.2	78.1	81.1	90.0
50,000	2.2	0.4	0.0	0.0	76.0	77.8	78.2	86.6
60,000	3.1	1.1	0.0	0.0	75.0	76.9	78.1	84.6
70,000	4.2	2.1	0.7	0.0	74.8	76.9	78.3	82.4
80,000	5.3	3.0	1.7	0.0	74.7	77.0	78.3	80.4

Source: Watson Wyatt.

Table 19-9 reflects the required savings rates that will not be matched in the employer-sponsored retirement plans and the replacement of final earnings for workers retiring at age 55 after 30 years under their combined defined benefit and defined contribution plans. In the less generous plan settings the required savings rates would be a bit of a stretch for many workers, but still reachable. At the upper

TABLE 19-9   Levels of Potential Combined Retirement Plan Generosity, Savings Rates Outside the Plan to Maintain Preretirement Standards of Living, and Replacement of Final Earnings from All Retirement Income Sources for Workers Aged 55 with 30 Years of Service (percent)

Salary When Pension Coverage and Saving Begin (1994 dollars)	Required Savings Rate Beyond Employer Matching in the Combined DB and DC Plans				Retirement Income Replacement of Preretirement Earnings			
	15th Percentile	40th Percentile	65th Percentile	90th Percentile	15th Percentile	40th Percentile	65th Percentile	90th Percentile
12,500	5.9	4.4	2.4	0.0	61.0	62.5	64.5	66.9
15,000	8.5	7.1	5.1	1.6	62.9	64.4	66.4	69.8
20,000	10.8	9.3	7.3	3.8	63.5	65.0	66.9	70.4
25,000	11.8	10.3	8.3	4.8	63.5	65.0	66.9	70.4
30,000	12.5	11.0	9.0	5.6	63.6	65.1	67.1	70.5
40,000	14.0	12.5	10.6	7.2	64.0	65.5	67.5	70.9
50,000	14.9	13.4	11.4	8.0	63.3	64.8	66.8	70.2
60,000	15.4	13.8	11.9	8.5	62.6	64.2	66.1	69.5
70,000	16.3	14.7	12.8	9.4	62.6	64.2	66.1	69.5
80,000	17.1	15.5	13.7	10.3	62.8	64.5	66.3	69.7

Source: Watson Wyatt.
Notes: Sources of income include employer plan benefits, Social Security, and personal savings.

end of the generosity spectrum, they appear to be more easily attainable assuming that covered workers participate to the fullest extent in the subsidized benefits offered by their employers. It is important to keep in mind that this is an inflation-adjusted benefit payable from age 55.

Reservations about the Results

The general conclusion in this section is that workers covered by both a typical defined benefit and a defined contribution plan can achieve a reasonable retirement standard of living by their mid- to late 50s with 30 years of participation in their employer-sponsored plans. Most workers covered by both types of plans who are willing to work into their 60s can acquire sufficient retirement resources to maintain their preretirement standard of living with only partial participation in their supplementary defined contribution plans. For workers who are covered only by a defined benefit plan or only a defined contribution plan, reaching an adequate retirement income is somewhat more of a challenge, albeit one that can be met given steady and full participation in existing retirement plans. It is much more likely in the stand-alone plans that workers will have to work later in their lives than in the cases where they are covered by the combination of defined benefit and defined contribution plans, but still very adequate retirement income levels can be achieved.

At this point, it is important to note some caveats about the outcomes that are potentially achievable under the existing retirement income security system. Thus far this chapter has focused on the benefits achievable by 30 years of continuous participation in a set of retirement plans that are currently available. The prospect of this scenario playing out for current workers is somewhat doubtful.

When employers design their retirement plans, they often assume that the typical worker will spend a relatively full career under their programs. While the analysis in Chapter 16 showed that today's workers are not inherently more mobile than similar workers have been historically, the analysis of median tenures presented there suggests that many workers retire with less than 30 years of service under a single retirement plan. Under the traditional defined benefit plan, changing jobs in midcareer can be a costly experience in view of the potential loss in retirement benefits, as discussed in Chapter 20. The greater prevalence of defined contribution plans and their increasing importance even in the retirement portfolios of defined benefit participants helps to ameliorate the problem of midcareer job changes for workers counting on their employer-sponsored retirement benefits. Participating in supplemental defined contribution plans does not completely eliminate the problem because the defined benefit plan is still a more substantial part of the retirement package in most cases and because defined contribution assets are not always rolled into another retirement account when workers change jobs. Letting defined contribution assets escape the retirement portfolio in mid-career is as bad as not having had any retirement plan in the first place.

Another development that is helping to ameliorate the problem of midcareer job shifting among defined benefit plan participants is the shift toward new types of defined benefit plans, as discussed in Chapter 13. But again, the overall effectiveness of these solutions to the problems associated with job shifting and defined benefit plans depends on the extent to which accumulated retirement assets are rolled into another retirement account when a worker terminates a covered job and moves on to another one. The decision to keep retirement assets dedicated to the goal of retirement security is largely in the hands of the worker and just as some workers are conscientious about participating in their employer-sponsored retirement plans when they require employee contributions, many are not so conscientious.

Another concern about these results is that they assume that the current elements of the retirement portfolio will remain intact as they are configured today. As pointed out in Chapter 1, the financing situation facing the Social Security program in the United States today is such that taxes would have to be increased significantly, benefits would have to be reduced significantly, or some combination of the two would have to occur to keep the program financially viable as a retirement resource for the baby boom generation. If Social Security benefits are reduced, either employer-sponsored benefits or personal savings will have to be increased to achieve the level of benefits suggested by this analysis.

The aging of the baby boom generation also portends that the cost of defined benefit plans will increase significantly for many employers in this decade and into the next century.[6] Some employers will continue to support their defined benefit plans despite rising costs, but some, undoubtedly, will not. If there are substantial curtailments of the plans now offered to workers, many workers in midcareer today will not realize the level of benefit generosity that the analysis here suggests the system is currently offering. If employer benefits from defined benefit plans are curtailed for the same workers threatened with Social Security reductions, the imperative challenge of personal savings will be accentuated. In other words, the current system is holding out a respectable promise to current workers, but there is a substantial probability that the promise will not be realized in many instances.

Reported Retirement Income Delivery in the Current Environment

In addition to what current workers might receive from the retirement system, another aspect of the delivery of retirement benefits should be considered, namely, the benefits now being paid to individuals who are already retired. Analyses of the adequacy of current retiree income levels come in two general forms. The first looks at the overall income levels among the elderly in comparison with the level of income of the nonelderly. Looking at the income of the elderly from a broad cross-sectional perspective, however, is not exactly the same as looking at the income of retirees. Being elderly, in many cases, may be more a state of mind than a chronological age, and it certainly is not a precondition for being retired. Since there is no precise chronological age at which people either become elderly or retire, the analyses that fall into this first class generally consider the incomes of people over age 65 with the incomes of those who are younger. In analyses of this type, some of the income that the "elderly" receive is wage-related because some people over age 65 continue to work, or they are married to someone who does.

[6]See Laurene A. Graig and Sylvester J. Schieber, *The Sleeping Giant Awakens: Retirement in the 21st Century* (Washington, D.C.: Watson Wyatt, 1995).

Also, some of the income that the "nonelderly" receive is from pensions and Social Security because many of them retired before age 65 or other arbitrary ages that are used in these types of studies.

The second type of analysis looks at the sources of income among the older segments of the population and assesses the overall efficiency of each element of the retirement income security system. Analyses of this type often look at segments of the population that indicate they are receiving some retirement income. In some cases, however, this type of analysis also concentrates on people over age 65 because the data are too limited to focus solely on people who are truly retired. Some of these analyses concentrate on the income levels and sources of income of those receiving retirement benefits. Others attempt to estimate the extent to which retirement income actually replaces preretirement earnings in accordance with the concepts of the replacement rate discussions above. These two types of studies share a common goal, which is to determine whether the retirees' incomes meet one or both of the kinds of adequacy measures that are used in evaluating retirement programs. These adequacy measures are briefly examined below.

The Economic Well-Being of the Aged

Studies that compare the economic well-being of the elderly and the nonelderly focus on the relative consumption levels among the two groups. These studies typically make a number of adjustments to money[7] income received by individuals or households in each of the groups because money income across the groups does not necessarily represent their true claim on economic resources.[8] The results of one such comparison along with the adjustments is shown in Table 19-10. The source of the data for this analysis is the *Current Population Survey,* a monthly survey done by the Census Bureau for the Department of Labor. This survey is the source of the monthly estimates of employment and unemployment in the national economy. The March version of the survey each year is the source of the annual estimates of the prevalence of poverty in the United States. The March survey solicits information from each of the sample households on the sources and levels of money income available to the household members over the prior calendar year. The reported money income data from this survey are used to develop the poverty estimates among the population. The survey is also widely used to analyze the sources and levels of money income to various subgroups of the population.

Column 3 of Table 19-10, which shows the ratios adjusted for family size, takes into account the composition of the households when deriving the measures. The adjustments were made using the Census Bureau's poverty line equivalence scale applied to the unadjusted or reported income from the survey. As discussed at the beginning of Chapter 18, the national poverty line is a weighted average of the poverty thresholds for family units of various compositions weighted by the preva-

---

[7]Money income is income received in cash as opposed to in-kind income such as health insurance, food stamps, and subsidized housing.

[8]See, for example, Joseph F. Quinn and Timothy M. Smeeding, "The Present and Future Economic Well-Being of the Aged," in Richard V. Burkhauser and Dallas L. Salisbury, eds., *Pensions in a Changing Economy* (Washington, D.C.: Employee Benefit Research Institute, 1993), pp. 5–18.

TABLE 19-10   Ratios of Incomes of Elderly Households to All Households in 1991

Income Concept	Unadjusted for Size of Family	Adjusted for Size of Family
A. Ratios of means		
Money income before taxes	0.70	0.85
Expanded income	0.81	0.99
Expanded income plus implicit rents	0.86	1.05
B. Ratios of medians		
Money income before taxes	0.60	0.74
Expanded income	0.78	0.95
Expanded income plus implicit rents	0.83	1.02

Source: Quinn and Smeeding, "The Present and Future Economic Well-being of the Aged," p. 7, based on data in U.S. Department of Commerce, *Measuring the Effects of Benefits and Taxes on Income and Poverty: 1979 to 1991,* Bureau of the Census Current Population Report, Series P-60, no. 182-RD (Washington, D.C.: USGPO, 1992).

lence of those types of family units. The equivalence scale used to adjust income in this case is an index derived from the poverty thresholds for the various household compositions. In 1991, for example, the average household size for all families was 2.63 persons compared with 1.65 persons for all households headed by a person aged 65 or older.[9] The theory behind these adjustments is that since the elderly households have fewer people on average, a lower cash income is required to provide an equivalent level of consumption. A straight per capita adjustment of income, though, would not take into consideration the economies of scale from people living together—for example, two people do not require twice as much housing as a single person because certain characteristics of a residence can be easily shared up to a point.

The expanded income measure in the table includes the estimated value of realized capital gains, the value of employer-provided health insurance, the value of noncash transfers from Medicare and Medicaid, and the values of food stamps and public housing. It subtracts federal and state income taxes and the payroll tax. Medicare and Medicaid are counted on the basis of their "fungible value" or the extent to which they free up resources that could be spent on medical care. If family income is not sufficient to cover basic food and housing requirements, Medicare and Medicaid are treated as having no income value. If income exceeds the cost of food and housing requirements, the value of Medicare and Medicaid is equal to the amount income exceeds food and housing requirements up to the market value of the medical benefits programs.[10] Since the elderly, on average, are somewhat greater beneficiaries of government in-kind transfer programs than the nonelderly, the expanded income measure improves the income distribution of the elderly in comparison with the nonelderly.

[9]Ibid., p. 7.
[10]U.S. Department of Commerce, *Measuring the Effects of Benefits and Taxes on Income and Poverty: 1979 to 1991,* Bureau of the Census Current Population Reports, series P-60, no. 182-RD (Washington, D.C.: USGPO, 1992), p. viii.

The expanded income plus the implicit rent measure includes an estimate of the implicit rental income on the value of the net equity in owned homes and subtracts property taxes owed on the home for homeowners. The assumed rate of return for developing this calculation was 6.89 percent. Since the elderly are more likely to have their mortgages paid off or of being closer to having them paid off than the nonelderly population, the attribution of the implicit rental income raises the elderly population's income in comparison with that of the nonelderly by this measure.

The ratios in Table 19-10 are different from the replacement income targets that were derived in Chapter 18, but they are a comparison of the income available to the elderly (defined as the population over age 65 in this case) and to the remainder of the population, which largely consist of employed persons or dependents of the employed. The ratios in the table suggest that in relative terms the money income of the elderly falls within the proximity of the target replacement rates derived earlier. The adjustments for expanded income take into account the very valuable Medicare benefit, but that benefit largely covers the extra age-related health needs of the elderly, so that while the benefit is of definite monetary value, whether it truly represents an improvement in the standard of living as measured against a preretirement level is not clear. Adding in the considerations of the value of an accumulated housing asset and adjusting for family size suggests that, on average, the retirement income position of the elderly is quite comparable to that of the working-age population. Other evidence on the income levels of the elderly suggests that their poverty rates are about the same as those of other adults between the ages of 18 and 64 and only slightly more than half the poverty rates among children under the age of 18.[11] The problem with these measures is that they do not give a clear indication of the role that pensions play in providing for retirees' income security after they quit working.

Pensions as Income for Today's Retirees

Analyses of retirement income adequacy often focus on people age 65 and over because the overwhelming majority of workers have retired by this age. Thus it is possible to look at the sources and levels of income available to people over 65 to get some sense of the standards of living that are achievable in retirement. Table 19-11 shows the percentage of elderly units receiving income from a variety of sources for a number of years from 1976 to 1990. An elderly unit is a family in which at least one person is 65 years of age or older. The table shows that by 1990, 44 percent of the elderly units were receiving some pension income, up from only 31 percent in 1976. The receipt of private pensions over the period grew considerably more than the receipt of public pensions. To a certain degree this was the result of the participation and vesting standards that had become mandatory with the passage of ERISA in 1974. It was also the result of the maturing of the pension system that had grown rapidly during the 1950s and 1960s but did not provide retirement benefits to many retirees until the plans in the system had been in operation for several years.

[11]Quinn and Smeeding, "The Present and Future Economic Well-Being of the Aged," p. 8.

TABLE 19-11   Percentage of Elderly Units Receiving Selected Sources of Income, Selected Years

Source of Income	1976	1980	1984	1988	1990
Social Security	89	90	91	92	92
Pensions, total	31	34	38	42	44
Public	13	14	16	16	17
Private	20	22	24	29	30
Earnings	25	23	21	22	22
Income from assets	56	66	68	68	69

Source: Susan Grad, *Income of the Population 55 and Older, 1990* (Washington, D.C.: U.S. Department of Health and Human Services, Social Security Administration, 1992), as reported in Virginia P. Reno, "The Role of Pensions in Retirement Income," in Richard V. Burkhauser and Dallas L. Salisbury, eds., *Pensions in a Changing Economy* (Washington, D.C.: Employee Benefit Research Institute, 1993), p. 20.

Table 19-12 shows the shares of aggregate income for these same elderly households that came from the various income sources. The story behind this table is that Social Security is the largest source of income for the elderly, although its importance declined moderately over the period from 39 to 36 percent of total income. Earnings as a share of income were declining substantially over the period, from 23 to 18 percent of total income, but even though the focus here is on the elderly over age 65, employment-based earnings were still an important source of income for the population that is generally considered to be retired. Income from other assets rose sharply over the period, from 18 to 24 percent of total income. While the percentage of retirees receiving a pension increased substantially over the period, the share of income coming from pensions had risen only modestly, from 16 to 18 percent of total income. The sharp increase in pension recipiency suggests that ERISA's participation and vesting standards were having a beneficial effect. The modest increase in the level of income generated from pensions suggests that the new pensioners were receiving rather small benefits.

Pension Income Underreporting on National Surveys

The information presented in Tables 19-11 and 19-12 was derived from data in the March *Current Population Surveys* gathered over several years. The prevalence of

TABLE 19-12   Shares of Aggregate Income of the Elderly, Selected Years

Source of Income	1976	1980	1984	1988	1990
Social Security	39	39	38	38	36
Pensions	16	16	15	18	18
Earnings	23	19	16	17	18
Income from assets	18	22	28	25	24
Other	4	4	3	3	3

Source: Grad, *Income of the Population 55 and Older, 1990,* in Burkhauser and Salisbury, *Pensions in a Changing Economy,* p. 21.
Note: The shares do not sum to exactly 100 percent in all years because of rounding.

pension coverage at middle and lower income levels noted in Chapter 8 and the potential benefits generated by contemporary retirement plans as suggested by the analysis presented earlier in this chapter might lead one intuitively to conclude that employer-sponsored retirement plans are generating greater retirement income than the CPS respondents are reporting. Indeed, the *National Income and Product Accounts* (NIPA) developed by the Bureau of Economic Analysis on the basis of administrative and disclosure data suggest that pensions are paying benefits equivalent to those being paid by Social Security. NIPA estimates indicate that the benefits paid by federal retiree programs in 1990 totaled $53.9 billion; those paid by state and local government retiree programs were $40.6 billion; and those paid by private pension and profit-sharing plans were $148.8 billion. In aggregate, employer-sponsored retirement programs paid out $243.3 billion during 1990. According to the NIPA data, the Old-Age, Survivors, and Disability Insurance program paid out $244.1 billion in benefits during 1990.[12] In other words, during 1990 employer-sponsored retirement plans paid out benefits that were almost precisely equal to Social Security benefits. Yet the CPS suggests that retirees over the age of 65 are only getting half as much from these plans as from Social Security. There are some potential explanations for the discrepancy.

As noted earlier, some people participating in employer-sponsored retirement plans do not roll their accumulated retirement assets paid in a lump sum into new retirement plans when they change jobs throughout their careers. When an individual takes a lump-sum benefit from a retirement plan, the plan administrator issues an Internal Revenue Service Form 1099-R to the beneficiary and to the IRS stating the total amount of the distribution and the reason for the distribution. The IRS has tabulated these forms for the tax years 1987 through 1990. In 1990, the aggregate lump-sum benefits paid were $125.8 billion. Of this amount, $43.0 billion covered normal distributions, that is, payments to individuals who were qualified to begin receiving retirement benefits. These lump sums could be rolled over into an IRA and drawn down periodically by the recipient or used to purchase an annuity. Six percent of the lump sums were tax-free exchanges of insurance contracts, so while they were technically a distribution, in fact they were merely exchanges of one form of insurance for another. Fourteen percent of the lump sums were excess contributions and earnings on them, so these were amounts that should not have been in the plans in the first place. And finally, 7 percent of the distributions resulted because of the death of the participant. Rollovers accounted for $71.4 billion of the distributions, but some of this amount overlaps with the payments as normal distributions.[13]

It is unlikely that the lump sums being reported on the Form 1099-R are also being fully reported as benefit payments. If they were, more than half of all pension benefits paid during 1990 would have been in the form of lump-sum payments. According to U.S. Department of Labor tabulations of Form 5500 disclosure data,

[12]U.S. Department of Commerce, Bureau of Economic Analysis, *Survey of Current Business*, vol. 74, no. 7 (Washington, D.C.: USGPO, July 1994), pp. 77, 92.

[13]Paul Yakoboski, "Retirement Program Lump-Sum Distributions: Hundreds of Billions in Hidden Pension Income," *EBRI Issue Brief*, no. 146 (Washington, D.C.: Employee Benefit Research Institute, February 1994).

slightly more than half of all the benefits paid by private retirement plans in 1990 were paid by defined benefit plans.[14] These would have been paid predominantly in the form of annuities. In addition, some of the defined contribution benefits would have also been paid as annuities. Among public plans, the overwhelming majority of the benefits would have been paid in the form of annuities because public plans have historically been predominantly defined benefit plans in which the only benefit form is an annuity. Public employers' experience with supplemental defined contribution plans is relatively recent and the benefits being paid out of these plans in 1990 would have been dwarfed by the annuities paid out of their defined benefit plans.

Another possible explanation for the discrepancy between the NIPA pension estimates and the CPS estimates is that many retirees receive their benefit checks from third-party plan administrators or insurance companies. It is possible that the annuity check coming from the ABC insurance company is not reported as a pension when respondents report income on surveys like the CPS. Also, when individuals take lump-sum payments and put them in self-managed IRA accounts with banks or mutual fund companies, periodic distributions from such accounts might not be reported as coming from employer-sponsored retirement plans.

The problem in reconciling the discrepancy between the NIPA and CPS pension estimates is that there is no large source of administrative data that captures total income and its components for the whole population. The closest thing to it is the Internal Revenue Service's Annual Tax Files, which are part of the Statistics of Income (SOI) files that the IRS develops for research purposes. These files, which have been produced since 1960 and which are referred to here as the IRS Tax File, are an annual sample of tax filer records that have had all personal identification information deleted. The primary purpose of these files is to simulate the revenue and administrative impact of tax law changes and to provide general statistical information on the sources of income and taxes paid by individuals. One problem with the IRS Tax Files is hardly any information in them describes the characteristics of tax filers other than the financial information that relates to the filing of federal income taxes. Another problem is that below certain income levels, potential tax filing units are not required to file income tax statements with the IRS, and thus the Tax Files do not cover the lowest income segments of the population.

Despite their drawbacks, the IRS Tax Files may be a better indicator of the level of pension payments from employer-sponsored plans than any other potential source of such information. If pensions contribute to retirement income security, people receiving a pension in retirement should, on average, have higher levels of income than people who do not. Of course, higher levels of income trigger the responsibility to file a tax return. This responsibility is enforced by the threat of potential fines and even imprisonment for the failure to file and to do so accurately. In addition, in the past individuals who received retirement annuities during 1990, as an example, received a Form W-2P in early 1991 stating the amount of annuities they received during 1990 to help in the accurate reporting of

---

[14]U.S. Department of Labor, Pension and Welfare Benefits Administration, "Abstract of 1990 Form 5500 Annual Reports," *Private Pension Plan Bulletin*, no. 2 (Washington, D.C.; USGPO, 1993), pp. 81, 83.

TABLE 19-13   Receipt of Pension and IRA Income by Total Income Deciles During 1990 for Federal Income Tax Filers Aged 65 or Older (dollars unless otherwise noted)

Income Decile	Income Range	Percentage with Pension Income	Mean Pension Income	Percentage with IRA Income	Mean IRA Income	Percentage with IRA or Pension Income	Mean Retirement Plan Income
1	0–8,232	45.2	3,595	3.5	2,976	48.1	3,595
2	8,233–11,810	54.7	5,202	8.2	2,433	57.4	5,310
3	11,811–14,982	56.6	6,022	9.5	2,553	60.0	6,093
4	14,983–18,054	69.6	6,583	8.5	3,217	72.3	6,718
5	18,055–21,762	69.0	8,093	9.6	3,650	72.0	8,243
6	21,763–27,357	73.2	9,098	13.2	3,847	77.1	9,296
7	27,358–34,644	73.6	10,711	12.1	3,321	77.4	10,709
8	34,645–44,450	72.3	13,444	15.7	3,579	77.2	13,314
9	44,451–62,080	71.9	16,785	18.2	5,170	76.6	16,971
10	62,081+	65.6	34,939	22.7	10,079	72.3	34,832
Total		65.2	11,864	12.1	4,845	69.0	12,050

Source: Authors' tabulations of the IRS 1990 Tax Files.

income for the purposes of filing tax returns. Also, although the IRS Tax File has little personal information on tax filers it does include information on whether the filer and spouse, if there was one, were over the age of 65 or blind. The coding of this information is such that filing units containing a person over 65 can be identified as long as that person was not also blind. Blind filers over 65 cannot be separated from younger blind filers. In addition to information on annuity income, the IRS Tax Files provide information on a host of other income categories.

Table 19-13 shows the reporting of pension, annuity, and IRA income for elderly tax filers as computed from the IRS 1990 Tax File. It shows the percentage of filing units reporting to have received such income and the average amount reported by those who received the income. The population is split into 10 groups of equal size (i.e., deciles) based on their 1990 income. The table also shows the combined total income provided from the various sources. We include the IRA distributions in the analysis because IRA accumulations receive comparable tax treatment to employer-sponsored tax-qualified plans and because many workers roll employer-sponsored retirement accumulations into IRAs when they terminate employment with an employer and receive a lump-sum distribution.

Nearly two-thirds of the elderly tax filing units indicated that they had received pension or annuity income during 1990. The average pension or annuity income was a significant portion of the total income reported by the elderly on their tax filings. In the lower half of the income spectrum, benefits account for one-third or more of reported income. As one leg of a retirement system composed of private savings, Social Security, and employer-sponsored plans, pensions provide a substantial base of retiree income security. At higher income levels pensions take on less relative importance but provide progressively higher benefits.

TABLE 19-14   Prevalence and Level of Pension Income by Income Decile for Single Persons and Couples over Age 65 During 1990 as Computed from the 1991 *Current Population Survey* and the IRS 1990 Tax Files (dollars unless otherwise noted)

Income Decile	Current Population Survey			IRS Tax File		
	Income Range	*Percentage with Pension Income*	*Mean Pension Income*	*Income Range*	*Percentage with Pension Income*	*Mean Pension Income*
1	0–5,000	5.1	1,906	0–8,232	48.1	3,595
2	5,001–7,080	13.9	1,864	8,233–11,810	57.4	5,310
3	7,081–9,338	25.1	2,347	11,810–14,982	60.0	6,093
4	9,339–11,892	38.1	3,100	14,983–18,054	72.3	6,718
5	11,893–14,980	50.7	4,173	18,055–21,762	72.0	8,243
6	14,981–18,614	60.4	5,755	21,763–27,357	77.1	9,296
7	18,615–23,621	67.7	7,098	27,358–34,644	77.4	10,709
8	23,622–30,736	67.9	9,248	34,645–44,450	77.2	13,314
9	30,737–44,688	73.3	13,159	44,451–62,080	76.6	16,971
10	44,689+	62.0	20,883	62,081+	72.3	34,832
Total		46.4	8,919		69.0	12,050
Total reporting units	21.3 million			13.5 million		
Total pension benefits	88.1 billion			112.1 billion		

Source: Authors' tabulations of the March 1991 *Current Population Survey* and the IRS 1990 Tax Files.

Across the whole income spectrum the receipt of pension income is much more prevalent than the receipt of IRA income. There is also considerable overlap between pension and IRA recipiency since 12.1 percent of tax filers reported receiving IRA income that only raised total receipt of retirement income from 65.2 percent of all filers who reported receiving pension or annuity income to 69.0 percent of those filers indicating that they were receiving one or the other or both forms of retirement benefit. In most cases the average level of benefits provided from the IRA were significantly less than the income that was paid from pensions or annuities, although the average benefits being paid from IRAs were sizable enough to make having them worthwhile to those retirees who did. Even at the lowest income levels, the average individual reporting an IRA distribution would have realized benefits of nearly $250 per month in income. In the upper income ranges, the average IRA distribution would have been the equivalent of $300 to $400 per month in retirement income. In the uppermost decile, the average IRA would have generated an income of $800 per month.

Table 19-14 compares the reporting of pension and annuity income from the March 1991 *Current Population Survey* and from the IRS 1990 Tax File. Both data sets cover calendar-year 1990. Again, the population in each case is split into 10 groups of equal size based on their 1990 income. Using the CPS, the population was distributed on the basis of total reported income in the survey. With the 1990 Tax Files, the filing population was distributed on the basis of adjusted gross income. While the 1990 Tax Files use a different measure of income than the CPS and do not include low-income elderly units, the income deciles have somewhat more correspondence across the two data sets than one might expect. From the CPS, we estimate there were 21.3 million single persons or couples in which at least one of the two was over the age of 65 during 1990.[15] From the Tax Files we estimate that there were 13.5 million filing units that included a person over the age of 65. In other words, roughly 63.4 percent of the potential tax filing units with a person over 65 filed a tax return in 1990.

In virtually every income decile shown in Table 19-14, the prevalence of pension or annuity income is significantly higher in the Tax Files than in the CPS. If it is assumed that most people in the bottom three deciles of the CPS population would not be represented in the tax-filing population because of their low incomes, the pension and annuity recipiency rate at the bottom end of the income distributions might be somewhat closer than the table suggests. But at the middle- and upper-income ranges the data on income tax filing suggest that pension and annuity receipt is far more widespread than the CPS evidence would lead one to believe. Indeed, the total pension and annuity income going to elderly units as indicated by estimates from the tax files is 27 percent higher than the estimate based on CPS reporting, even though 37 percent fewer elderly units are represented in the tax files.

In a separate tabulation, we did not include the respondents in the CPS representing the 7.8 million aged units with the lowest reported incomes because we assumed that they would be the least likely to have filed income tax returns for 1990. By deleting 37 percent of the aged units, we were left with two samples of the same size. We deleted slightly less than 1.5 million pension-receiving units, or 15.2 percent of all the units that reported they received a pension during 1990. Eliminating these low-income units, however, only reduced the aggregate estimate of pension income paid to the population over 65 by 4.1 percent. At this level, the CPS respondents would have had to report one-third more pension income than they did to equal the aggregate pension income reported in the 1990 Tax Files.

In another set of tabulations we estimated the total pension and annuity income paid to all individuals in our two sets of data. These tabulations included the payments being made to individuals who had not yet reached age 65, as well as those who had. In this case the CPS file generated aggregate estimated pension and annuity payments of $154.5 billion for 1990, compared with $231.9 billion from the IRS Tax Files. The tax file estimate is much closer to the NIPA estimate of $243.3 billion cited earlier than is the CPS estimate. One would not expect the Tax Files to be less than an estimate of total pension benefits paid in any year because there will always be some pension beneficiaries whose incomes are low enough that they are not required to file an income tax return. The bottom line here is that the

[15]Note this is a slightly different definition of filing unit than Susan Grad used in developing the information reported in Tables 19-11 and 19-12. In her work, Grad also included people over 65 who were living in extended family arrangements where the elderly person was not the head of the family unit or married to the head of the family unit. She also considered the income available to other members of the family unit in these cases as providing support to the elderly person in the extended family.

TABLE 19-15   Percentage of Elderly Pension Recipients and
Nonrecipients Categorized by Reported Income Deciles
Based on 1990 Tax Filings

Income Decile	Percentage of Pension Nonrecipients	Percentage of Pension Recipients
1	16.8	7.0
2	13.8	8.3
3	12.9	8.7
4	8.9	10.5
5	9.0	10.4
6	7.4	11.2
7	7.3	11.2
8	7.4	11.2
9	7.6	11.1
10	8.9	10.5
Total	100.0	100.0

Source: Authors' tabulations of the IRS 1990 Tax Files.

Current Population Survey, which is widely used for retirement policy analytic purposes, is significantly underreporting the actual provision of retirement benefits by
the employer-based pension system.

The income deciles presented in the tax file analysis were developed using all the
tax filer units that could be identified as having a person over age 65 on the basis of
total reported income on Form 1040 for 1990. While each of the aggregate deciles
contained 10 percent of the tax filers, the distribution of the pension recipients
and nonrecipients across the deciles was somewhat different. Table 19-15 shows the
distribution of the pension recipients and nonrecipients separately. Nonrecipients
are disproportionately concentrated in the lowest three income deciles and are
generally underrepresented above that level, with the greatest underrepre-
sentation in the sixth through the ninth deciles. The distribution of pension
recipients is strikingly different in that they are underrepresented in the lowest
three deciles and overrepresented in the remaining ones, with their greater over-
representation falling in the sixth through the ninth deciles. Undoubtedly a
pension helps those retirees who receive them to achieve a relatively higher
income level than those who do not. However, many of the elderly who do not
receive a regular payment from a formal tax-qualified retirement program do have
a number of alternative sources of income that provide substantial income for
them in their older years.

The Current Population Survey is the most widely used data base for assessing
the income status of the aged. It is used to estimate the official measures of poverty,
including the extent of poverty among the aged, and to assess the overall effectiveness of the various elements of the retirement income security system, including
pensions. One of the common conclusions of such analyses is that pensions
contribute to a minority of retirees' income security, and even there the contribution

is either minimal or concentrated among the well-off. The analysis presented here suggests that the CPS is widely underestimating the overall contribution that pensions are making to retirees' income security. It significantly underestimates the prevalence of the receipt of pension benefits and the magnitude of those benefits when they are available.[16]

---

[16]For a more detailed discussion of the reporting of pension income on the *Current Population Survey* and on federal income tax forms see Sylvester J. Schieber, "Why Do Pension Benefits Seem So Small?" *Benefits Quarterly* (Fall 1995).

Chapter 20
Human Resource Incentives in Employer-Sponsored Retirement Plans

This chapter examines a number of the important human resource incentives embedded in employer-sponsored retirement programs, their effects on the compensation of workers during their working lives, and their impact on workers' behavior. The first topic of concern is the role that employer-sponsored plans play in attracting and keeping workers that employers find desirable. The second is whether or not workers pay for their pension or retirement savings accruals through reduced wages during their working careers, as one might expect under competitive labor market conditions. The final topic is the role employer-sponsored pension and retirement savings plans play in facilitating the timely retirement of older workers.

Chapter 1 outlined a number of competing theories behind the early development of employer-sponsored pensions. One theory is that human capital, like its physical capital counterpart, depreciates over time and that employers should lay aside resources during the period over which workers' human capital is exhausted so retirees will have a means of sustenance at the end of their industrial life. An alternative theory is that a pension is merely deferred compensation and that the cost of the retirement program is paid for through the reduction in cash wages during the working career. Yet another theory is that pensions represent an attempt by employers to provide for the economic security of the older citizens in an economy dominated by private enterprise.

While each of these theories might capture some of the underlying motivations for establishing private pensions, from their beginnings employer-sponsored plans were understood to affect employee behavior. One of the earliest motivations for establishing a pension was to provide a mechanism to retire superannuated workers. Early in the history of these programs, however, plan sponsors also realized that pension plans could be instrumental in attracting workers and encouraging them to remain with a firm. In recent years, the literature on pensions has begun to investigate the role that employer-sponsored retirement plans play in attracting, keeping, and compensating workers during their careers, and the role that they play in encouraging the retirement of workers. While there are still unanswered questions about the incentives and motivations underlying these plans, a substantial body of economic theory and considerable empirical evidence has emerged in recent years to explain the incentives underlying employer-sponsored retirement programs.

The Role of Retirement Plans in Attracting and Keeping Workers

When looking at the motivations underlying employer-sponsored retirement plans, it is important to keep in mind that both workers and employers have created the environment in which these plans are established and maintained. While both employers and workers have an interest in the plans, each represents a different perspective.

Workers' Perspectives on Retirement Plans

Tax Incentives in Plans

Chapter 8 discussed the tax preferences accorded tax-qualified plans under the federal tax code. Under the existing tax code, in the period in which a contribution is made to the plan a dollar of tax-qualified savings is cheaper for the saver than a dollar of nonqualified savings. The forgone taxes on original contributions are ultimately collected from individuals who have the same marginal tax rate in retirement as they had during their working careers. But many workers face reduced tax rates in retirement, which yield significant tax savings over one's lifetime because of participation in these plans. In addition, the after-tax returns on retirement plan savings are greater than nonqualified savings for the overwhelming majority of people who participate in these plans.

A characteristic of the American tax system that greatly affects workers' motivations for supporting these plans is its progressivity. This feature of the income tax system makes a dollar of tax-qualified savings cheaper for higher-wage workers than for their lower-wage counterparts. In a broader federal taxing context, the extra generosity of the federal income tax system toward tax-qualified plan accumulations is offset by the contribution and benefit structure of Social Security,[1] but the underlying incentives for retirement plan savings are significant, and somewhat more pronounced at higher wage levels than lower ones.

In addition to the tax incentives accorded retirement plans, economic theory suggests that the marginal utility of additional consumption declines as income rises, leading higher-income individuals to have a greater propensity to save. This is especially true in cases where consumption can be transferred to a period when expected income will be lower and the marginal utility of consumption will be higher. Employer-sponsored plans are attractive to workers because they possess a number of characteristics other than the pure tax incentives discussed earlier in this volume.

---

[1]For a full discussion of this issue see Gordon P. Goodfellow and Sylvester J. Schieber, "Death and Taxes: Can We Fund for Retirement Between Them?" in Ray Schmitt, ed., *The Future of Pensions in the United States* (Philadelphia: Pension Research Council and University of Pennsylvania Press, 1993), pp. 126–79, and Sylvester J. Schieber, "Public Policy Schizophrenia: The Conflict Between National Retirement Goals and Federal Budget and Tax Policies," presented at a conference, "Retirement Policy in America: Is It Time for Change?" John F. Kennedy School of Government, Harvard University, Cambridge, Mass., April 19, 1994.

Pensions as Retirement Income Insurance

Another reason employees wanting retirement plans is that they provide several kinds of retirement income insurance. Zvi Bodie has described five kinds of risk that threaten the retirement income security of workers:[2] replacement rate inadequacy, Social Security retrenchment, longevity, investment risk, and inflation. In essence, Bodie argues that individual workers face a great deal of uncertainty, and that by sponsoring retirement plans employers can use the law of large numbers to do things that each worker covered by the plans cannot.

REPLACEMENT RATE INADEQUACY   The risk of replacement rate inadequacy arises because of the complexity of estimating the level of income that is required in retirement to maintain preretirement living standards. Most people do not have the resources to do the kinds of calculations presented in Chapter 18, nor do they have the ability to calculate the level of savings required during the working career to finance that level of living even when they might know what their target retirement income level should be. Some hire a financial planner to help them with these calculations, but even then some people believe they do not have enough money left at the end of the month to adequately finance their retirement needs.

Employer-sponsored retirement plans can help to ameliorate the risk individual workers face when trying to save an inadequate amount for retirement. For workers covered under employer-sponsored retirement plans, often the employer has designed a retirement program that will provide adequate retirement resources, especially in conjunction with Social Security. The extent to which the plan provides a relatively generous or parsimonious benefit becomes well known across the covered work force and gives those workers a strong signal as to whether they need to save more outside the plan to attain a reasonable standard of living in retirement.

SOCIAL SECURITY RISK   Employer-sponsored plans also help ameliorate the risk that the basic underpinning of retirement security—Social Security—might be changed in ways that are not anticipated. There is a considerable skepticism that Social Security will provide the benefits that are embedded in current law as implied promises to current workers. In a national survey aimed at measuring the confidence in the Social Security system, only 30 percent of the respondents were confident that Social Security benefits would be there when they needed them, and 42 percent were not confident.[3] The prevalence of employer-sponsored defined benefit plans that are integrated with Social Security through an offset formula acts as insurance against reductions in future Social Security benefits because such reductions would be at least partly offset by employer-sponsored retirement benefits. To the extent that this form of insurance is important to workers, its value has been significantly diminished in recent years because of changes in laws and regulations limiting the extent to which retirement benefits can be integrated with Social Security.

---

[2]Zvi Bodie, "Pensions as Retirement Income Insurance," *Journal of Economic Literature*, vol. 28 (March 1990): pp. 28–49.
[3]Robert B. Friedland, *When Support and Confidence Are at Odds: The Public's Understanding of the Social Security Program* (Washington, D.C.: National Academy of Social Insurance, May 1994), p. 5.

CONCERNS ABOUT LONGEVITY   The longevity risk that people face is that they usually cannot predict their life expectancy at retirement with any precision. If people live longer than they anticipate, they will deplete their retirement savings before dying if the regularly scheduled payments from their accumulated wealth reflect their own assumptions as to future longevity. To deal with this problem, individuals can purchase annuities, but private annuity markets are characterized by adverse selection. As a result, there is a pricing premium on such annuities, in addition to the administrative cost and profit loading that issuers include in the pricing of these vehicles. One estimate has placed the combination of these premium loadings on individual annuities at between 32 and 48 percent of the cost of an actuarially fair annuity.[4]

The mere fact that some individuals who can successfully anticipate that they are not going to live very long after retirement do not buy annuities, however, does not necessarily mean that the annuity markets are being unfair to the remainder of the retirees who purchase annuities. If the annuity markets can properly evaluate the life expectancy of the remaining pool of people purchasing annuities, those individuals will have to pay a premium for their annuities relative to a pool of annuitants that would include all retirees, but it is not necessarily an unfair premium, given the risk characteristics of the people who are actually in the pool.

In general, defined benefit plans and some defined contribution plans can overcome the adverse selection problem by mandating participation in the plan and only providing benefits in the form of an annuity. In addition, employers who set up their own trusts for funding and administering their retiree benefit programs do not include profit loadings or other commission charges in calculating the value of annuities under their benefit programs. The combination of adverse selection and the neutralization and reduction (and possibly elimination) of administrative and profit loadings on annuities under employer-sponsored retirement plans makes them particularly effective in dealing with this concern.

INVESTMENT RISK   Employer-sponsored retirement programs can also ameliorate the financial risk that individuals face in investing their own liquid assets. Even in the case of defined contribution plans, virtually all plans that allow participant-directed investment options offer at least one relatively risk-free investment choice, and often they offer more than one. In the case of defined benefit plans, participants in the plans face none of the investment risk. As Bodie points out, the defined benefit plan implies "that the combination of plan contributions and investment income will be enough to provide a promised benefit level at retirement."[5]

EXPOSURE TO INFLATION   Bodie suggests that pensions can also provide insurance against the risk of eroding income levels because of the effects of inflation on nominal annuities. Since the early 1970s, Social Security has provided benefits fully

---

[4]Benjamin M. Friedman and Mark Warshawsky, "Annuity Prices and Saving Behavior in the United States," in Zvi Bodie, John B. Shoven, and David A. Wise, eds. *Pensions in the U.S. Economy* (Chicago: University of Chicago Press, 1988), p. 73.
[5]Bodie, "Pensions as Retirement Income Insurance," p. 35.

indexed for increases in the cost of living as measured by the consumer price index. The federal government indexes the retirement benefits for many of its former employees by the CPI. Many state and local governments provide regular cost-of-living adjustments for retirement annuities, although virtually all of them place limits on the extent of indexation they provide. In contrast, virtually no private sector plans provide for automatic increases in retirement benefits to cover the erosive effects of inflation, but many do provide periodic ad hoc increases that partly cover increases in the cost of living. While most plans do not fully insure against inflation in retirement, many employer-sponsored plans are structured to provide some inflation protection for individuals up to the point that employment is terminated, as discussed in Chapter 21.

Other Efficiency Considerations

In addition to their tax incentives and insurance characteristics, other efficiencies make tax-qualified plans attractive. For many individuals, the process of sorting out the risk characteristics of various classes of investments, accumulating market information on specific investment options, and actually investing assets is expensive in time costs, if not financial outlays. As a plan sponsor, an employer can sort out many of the issues relevant to covered workers so as to yield significant economies of scale to participants. When retirement assets for investment are placed in large pools, administrative and management fees are usually lower than when investments are disaggregated and placed individually. Finally, the expertise that professional managers bring to the investment of retirement assets usually means greater risk-adjusted returns over the long term than many individual investors would realize on their own.

Employers' Perspective on Retirement Plans

Defined Benefit Plans

Defined benefit plans are often characterized as creating "golden handcuffs" that restrain workers' job mobility. The reason that employers might want to restrict workers' mobility relates to the investment that they make in their workers and the desire to minimize labor costs over time. If a company has to invest a substantial amount in specific training for workers in order for them to do their jobs, retaining workers once they have been trained minimizes the cost of such investment. Since employers cannot indenture workers, alternative means of retaining them can be highly desirable in many instances.

The pattern in which benefit entitlements accrue under typical defined benefit plans encourages workers to remain in their jobs over a significant portion of their possible careers. This is largely accomplished by letting the salary just prior to the termination of employment play a predominant role in determining benefits under these plans. The majority of defined benefit plans today base retirement benefits on average pay levels in the three to five years immediately prior to employment termination. Moreover, many plans that base retirement benefits on average pay over the working career adjust their benefit formulas periodically to

TABLE 20-1   Pay Levels and Retirement Benefits Based on Current and Career Terminal Salary for a Hypothetical Worker at Selected Ages (dollars)

Age at End of Year Worked	Salary for Year	Benefit Based on Current Salary	Benefit Based on Terminal Salary
25	20,000.00	0.00	1,340.95
35	31,026.56	3,102.66	13,409.50
45	50,539.00	10,107.80	26,819.00
55	82,322.71	24,696.81	40,228.51
64	134,095.02	53,638.01	53,638.01

Source: Calculated by the authors.

actually operate the plan as though it was a final average pay plan. And even when this is not done, the typical pattern of wages rising over the worker's career will give added weight to years just before job termination in comparison with earlier years of employment in determining average wage levels over the whole period of tenure with an employer.

In order to understand how the incentives in defined benefit plans operate, assume that a worker takes her first job on her twenty-fifth birthday at an annual salary of $20,000 per year. Assume further that this worker will receive pay increases of 5 percent per year throughout her career up through her 64th birthday, regardless of whether she stays with her first employer or moves on to other employers at various times during her career. Next, assume that she will retire on the occasion of her 65th birthday at the completion of a 40-year working career. Finally, assume that the employer this woman joins in her first job has a pension plan in which she earns a vested benefit after five years of service under the plan, and that the plan provides a retirement benefit payable at age 65 that is equal to 1 percent of her final annual salary under the plan for each year that she is in the plan sponsor's employ.

Table 20-1 reflects this worker's perspective on the pension plan that her initial employer offers. If she stays with her employer for only the first year of her career, the value of her benefit based on her current salary will be zero because she has to stay with the employer at least five years to vest in any benefit under the plan.[6] If she stays with her first employer until retirement, however, she will ultimately be paid a benefit of $1,340.95 per year based on her first year of employment, or 1 percent of her final salary during the year immediately prior to her retirement.[7] In actuality, the worker would not consider the current value of the benefit to be the full $1,340.95 because the benefit will not be paid until many years in the future, and there is some probability that her job might not last until retirement or that she

[6]This value is sometimes characterized as the "quit" value of the pension benefit. In actuarial terms, the quit value is the discounted present value of the accumulated benefit that would be payable at retirement solely on the basis of service to date and not anticipating any further service under the plan.
[7]This value is sometimes characterized as the "stay" value of the pension benefit. In actuarial terms, the stay value is the discounted present value of the accumulated benefit that would be payable at retirement solely on the basis of service to date but anticipating that the worker will continue to be covered by the plan until retirement and that benefits will be based on the career terminal earnings.

might die before attaining retirement eligibility. Thus the worker will discount the value of a benefit that she would be paid if she stayed until retirement, but even after discounting there is clearly some economic value to staying covered under the plan.

Continuing with the example, if the worker takes a new job on the date of her thirty-fifth birthday, she would ultimately be paid a benefit of $3,102.66 per year out of her first employer's retirement plan—that is, 1 percent of her terminal salary with her first employer for each of 10 years of service, as shown in Table 20-1. If she stays until retirement, however, she will receive an annual benefit of $13,409.50 because she will receive 1 percent of her career terminal earnings for each of her first 10 years of service rather than 10 percent of her earnings during the year in which she was 35 years old. Looking at the difference between the two benefits from the perspective of a 35-year-old worker deciding whether to change jobs, the prospect of receiving roughly an additional $10,000 per year in retirement income 30 years in the future would be discounted somewhat. At an 8 percent discount rate, the difference in the annual benefit values would only be about $1,000 per year, but over a normal life expectancy, it would be valued at more than $10,000. By age 45 the potential difference in the value of the two benefits would be about three times the difference at age 35. Thus the plan imposes significant penalties on workers who terminate their jobs prior to retirement eligibility.

The magnitude of the penalties that typical defined benefit plans impose on workers whose coverage is terminated can be estimated under a range of assumptions. To do so, we calculated accumulated and projected benefits that would be provided to a set of hypothetical workers by 431 large, traditional defined benefit plans that were included in a 1993 survey of employer-sponsored benefit plans done by Watson Wyatt. In developing the calculations, we assumed a 4 percent inflation rate over the calculation period, a 5.5 percent rate of growth in salary levels, and an 8 percent discount rate applied backward from age 65.[8] We developed calculations for workers at three pay levels in 1993—one-half the Social Security wage base, at the Social Security wage base, and at twice the Social Security wage base—and at different starting ages with their terminal employers. After calculating the amounts in each year for each of the hypothetical workers under the 431 plans, we calculated average accumulated and projected benefits under all the plans for each of the workers during each year of hypothetical coverage. In this regard, the results represent the average structure of benefit accruals under the set of plans analyzed.

---

[8]The assumptions used in this case and throughout the analysis in much of this chapter imply much higher rates of return on assets than in the most common assumptions used in Chapters 18 and 19. In those two chapters we were considering rates of return on assets in defined contribution plans, generally in 401(k) type plans. In most cases, the investment of those assets will be directed by the plan participant. Empirical evidence indicates that self-directed investment of retirement assets results in somewhat more conservative investment patterns and lower long-term rates of return than for assets managed professionally, as defined benefit assets are. Thus the higher implied real rates of return in this analysis of defined benefit plans is appropriate. In addition, in the earlier chapters we were estimating savings rate targets so workers would be able to maintain preretirement standards of living after they leave the work force. It is entirely appropriate to be somewhat conservative in positing assumptions about rates of return on retirement savings when developing such estimates.

Multiple of salary

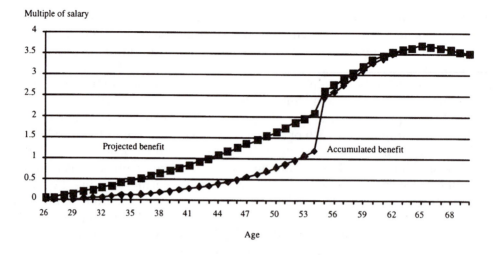

Figure 20-1. Accumulated benefits and projected benefits as a multiple of current salary.
Source: Watson Wyatt.

Figure 20-1 shows the results of the projections for an individual beginning a job at age 25 in 1993 at a starting salary of $28,800 per year, half the Social Security wage base in that year. The accumulated and projected benefit values in each year are shown as a multiple of the salary that the worker would receive in that year. Initially, the difference in the two values is relatively small, but by the time the worker has been in the job for 10 years, the projected benefit is one-third of a year's earnings larger than the accumulated benefit. The difference continues to increase steadily until it reaches nine-tenths of a year's earnings just prior to early retirement eligibility at age 55, when the discrepancy between the two values diminishes to about the equivalent of two month's earnings and continues to diminish until the two values are equivalent at age 65. The other hypothetical workers for whom we calculated benefits showed that the differences in the accumulated and projected benefits tend to be somewhat larger for workers who have a higher wage level than those with lower wages. Also the discrepancies are smaller for workers who become covered under a plan later in their career compared with those who are covered earlier.

One theory about the incentives in defined benefit plans is that the differential in the value of the accumulated and projected benefits under the plans is the equivalent of a bond that a worker accepts from the employer as a condition of employment. In essence, the existence of a defined benefit plan forces workers to accept such bonds. Upon reaching retirement eligibility, the bond can be fully redeemed. Theoretically, only people who ultimately expect to realize the benefit of accepting such a bond would be willing to do so. To realize the benefit, a worker has to accumulate considerable tenure under the pension program and stay in the employ of the sponsor until attaining at least early retirement age. In this way, defined benefit plans can act as a screening device that attracts workers who expect to stay in their positions for considerable duration—in other words, the type of workers in whom employers would be willing to make an investment and form an enduring relationship.

Bonding theory also suggests that workers covered by defined benefit plans would be less likely to shirk on the job and would require less supervision than workers not willing to accept such a bond. The logic in this case is that shirking or participating in other behavior that might result in the termination of a worker would result in the forfeiture of the bond. A worker who has accepted such a bond and does not want to forfeit it should be naturally inclined to avoid behavior that might cause employment and the benefit rights it entails to be terminated.

Over the years a number of studies have noted that pension coverage is strongly correlated with lower worker turnover. On the surface, the differences can be quite impressive. For example, Alan Gustman and Thomas Steinmeier, analyzing a group of males between the ages of 31 and 50 who were employed 30 hours or more per week in private sector, nonagricultural firms during 1984, found that the probability of moving to a new job was more than three times higher for workers with no employer-provided retirement coverage—19.5 percent versus 6.0 percent—compared with workers covered by a defined benefit plan.[9]

The problem with the surface-level results is that they point to a number of other differences between pension-covered workers and those that are not covered. Using an empirical model to sort out the factors affecting turnover, Gustman and Steinmeier found that pension-covered workers received higher cash wages than similar workers in nonpension jobs. They concluded that these higher wages were more important in explaining the greater stability of workers in pensioned jobs than the characteristics of the pensions themselves.[10] In addition, they found that turnover among workers covered by a defined contribution plan, where the capital loss issues related to defined benefit plans do not exist, was almost identical to the turnover among workers covered under defined benefit plans: 6.2 and 6.0 percent, respectively.[11]

Steven Allen, Robert Clark, and Ann McDermed attempted to sort out the effects of pensions and bonding on worker tenure over the period 1975 to 1982 using panel survey data on a sample of private sector wage and salary workers employed in 1975. They found that 61 percent of the workers not covered by a pension in 1975 had changed jobs by 1982, compared with 39 percent of those covered by a pension in 1975. Again, on the surface the relationship between pension coverage and tenure is impressive. In this case, the authors developed a three-equation model to empirically sort out the various characteristics of pensions that could account for their observed difference in turnover among this population of workers. They concluded that the capital loss incurred by terminating employment and coverage under a plan accounted for about 41 percent of the difference in turnover between the two groups. They also found that a number of worker characteristics associated with low turnover were related to the probability of moving into jobs covered by a pension. Men, whites, union members, and married workers had lower turnover than women, blacks, nonunion members, and single workers. While sex, race, union membership, and marital status were

---

[9]Alan L. Gustman and Thomas L. Steinmeier, "Pension Portability and Labor Mobility, Evidence from the Survey of Income and Program Participation," *Journal of Public Economics*, vol. 50 (1993): p. 304.
[10]Ibid., pp. 299, 315.
[11]Ibid., p. 304.

important in explaining pension coverage and turnover in general, they were not important in explaining turnover within the covered and noncovered populations separately. Finally, these authors concluded that it was higher overall pay levels rather than the level of "pension compensation" that lead to lower turnover.[12]

In an article summarizing the literature on the role of pensions in the labor market, Alan Gustman, Olivia Mitchell, and Thomas Steinmeier suggest that this topic merits additional research.[13] They indicate that the research done to date on turnover patterns under defined benefit plans has not taken into consideration the wage opportunities that workers face when they consider moving from one job to another. If a worker can move to a new job that pays 2 or 3 percent more per year than an existing job, where the two jobs have comparable nonwage compensation, such a cash wage increase might more than offset the capital loss many workers would face in terminating employment and coverage under a defined benefit plan. They suggest that the incentive effects in defined contribution plans deserve more research attention.[13]

Defined Contribution Plans

Traditionally, advocates of true profit-sharing plans have argued that they link the interests of the workers covered by them to the profitability of the plan sponsor, although empirical research has not found that companies sponsoring these plans have greater profitability as a result of the plan. Other forms of defined contribution plans have generally been treated as savings accounts, and their incentive effects have received little attention until recently. Richard Ippolito has constructed a theoretical model that suggests defined contribution plans might also play a significant role in sorting out undesirable workers from an employer's work force.[14]

Ippolito bases his model on the argument that the rate at which a worker discounts future consumption in relation to current consumption depends on his or her marginal productivity. In order to understand how this might be the case, assume that an individual either has an infinite discount rate or a discount rate of zero. The person with an infinite discount rate would never save anything for the future. It is also unlikely that such an individual would be willing to make a significant investment in his or her own human capital through intensive or extended schooling, because such an investment would suggest deferring the good life—that is, current consumption—until some future time, a prospect incongruous with an infinite discount rate. One would not expect such a person to make any significant personal investment to become a more productive worker even in cases where the employer facilitated such investments. An employee of this sort would likely require considerable monitoring to make sure that he or she was not taking

[12]Steven G. Allen, Robert L. Clark, and Ann A. McDermed, "Pensions, Bonding, and Lifetime Jobs," *Journal of Human Resources* (1992): pp. 463–81.

[13]Alan L. Gustman, Olivia S. Mitchell, and Thomas L. Steinmeier, "The Role of Pensions in the Labor Market: A Survey of the Literature," *Industrial and Labor Relations Review*, vol. 47, no. 3 (April 1994): pp. 430–31.

[14]Richard A. Ippolito, "Discount Rates, Imperfect Information and 401(k) Pensions," draft paper (Washington, D.C.: Pension Benefit Guaranty Corporation, November 1993).

advantage of work rules to maximize personal consumption of leisure and income at the unfair expense of the employer.

The person with a zero discount rate, on the other hand, would be indifferent between consumption today or in the future. An investment of today's income that would reap additional returns in the future absolutely would be pursued because the deferral of current consumption would result in added lifetime consumption later and greater lifetime consumption value. Such a person would jump at the opportunity to take advantage of an employer's offer of training, because a little investment sacrifice now brings with it the prospect of future added income. It is unlikely such a worker would take advantage of work rules, sick leave, and so forth, for fear of losing his or her job and ending up with lower lifetime consumption.

Few people may have discount rates that put them at either end of the discounting spectrum, but across any group of potential workers there is likely to be substantial variation in their internal discount rates. It is also likely that those with relatively high discount rates will be less disposed to engage in activities that most employers would consider adding to their overall productivity than workers with relatively low discount rates. In other words, under this model a worker's quality as an employee is inversely correlated with his or her internal discount rate. Even though a potential worker's discount rate might be a good indicator of his or her value as an employee, employers can do only limited screening of workers' attitudes and background when they apply for jobs and, once workers are hired, monitoring their behavior in the workplace can be expensive. In this environment employers clearly need to establish efficient ways of sorting out undesirable workers and encouraging them to leave the firm while providing incentives for the desirable workers to stay.

Many defined contribution plans sponsored by employers today provide incentives that encourage workers with high internal discount rates to terminate employment relatively early in their tenure. Frequently, they also allow employers to provide special rewards to low discounters. In order to understand how this is accomplished, consider a 401(k) plan where the sponsor makes some initial contribution to the plan for all workers covered under it and provides for additional employer contributions by matching voluntary employee contributions. In this case, the gradual buildup of the assets in the accounts of the high discounters is going to provide an economic enticement for them to get at these resources. But the only way the plan can provide a distribution to the high discounters is to do so coincident with their termination of employment. Thus the defined contribution plan includes economic incentives that effectively work as a sorting device, bidding out undesirable workers. At the other end, the matching rate on voluntary contributions will act as an added incentive for low discounters to put money into the plan. Thus the employer has identified highly desirable workers and provided them with added benefits through the plan matching rate.

Retirement Benefits and Current Compensation

In a competitive economic environment, economic theory suggests that workers with equal productivity will receive equal compensation. If that is not the case, an employer will substitute workers willing to accept lower compensation for those demanding more. As workers who have been demanding higher wages see they are being replaced by other similar workers, they will have to reduce their acceptance wage or go without jobs. Economic theory also suggests that in a competitive environment employers will be willing to pay workers up to their marginal contribution to the productivity of the firm. If the worker is paid more than his or her marginal product, the employer will suffer an economic loss by employing that worker. If the employer offers the worker less than his or her marginal product, the worker will take an alternative job with an employer willing to pay a wage equal to the marginal product.

To determine the relative cost of each worker to the organization, employers must consider all elements of the compensation package. The theory of "equalizing differences" suggests that workers will trade cash wages for noncash elements of the total compensation package.[15] The theory implies that in competitive labor markets, firms providing retirement benefits should pay lower cash wages than firms that do not offer retirement benefits to workers doing similar jobs. In other words, workers can be thought of as paying for their own retirement benefits through reduced cash wages during their working years.

This model of competitive wages and equalizing differences led Jeremy Bulow to challenge the concept of the "stay value" or projected benefit value of defined benefit plans as a meaningful concept in workers' valuation of their pension accruals.[16] He observed that workers renegotiate their salaries at many points throughout their working careers and suggested that at each of the renegotiations a firm should be willing to pay a worker his or her marginal product. In other words, he assumed that wages were being set at each of the renegotiations as though labor was being bought and sold in a spot market. If the concept of a spot labor market is correct, in cases where employers sponsor retirement plans, the provision of a pension should lower the payment of cash wages by the amount of the accruing quit value of the pension in each year.[17]

The alternative measure of pension accruals, the stay value, implies that employers compensate workers for their marginal product over their working lives, although they do not necessarily compensate them for their marginal product in any given year. Bulow considered the accrual patterns under defined benefit plans and employers' explicit benefit obligations under ERISA. He observed that ERISA only requires that an employer pay an employee the present value of accrued benefits at the point of termination—that is, the quit value of the pension. He argued that if workers place a value on the pension equal its stay value in the spot labor market, employers will undercompensate them during the early part of their tenures and overcompensate them during the latter part if they stay until retirement eligibility. Figure 20-2

---

[15]C. Brown, "Equalizing Differences in the Labor Market," *Quarterly Journal of Economics*, vol. 94 (February 1980): pp. 113–34.

[16]Jeremy I. Bulow, "What Are Corporate Pension Liabilities?" *Quarterly Journal of Economics* (August 1982): pp. 436–52.

[17]While human resource professionals might consider it unlikely that workers would renegotiate their wages with current employers periodically as though they were in a spot market, Bulow's analysis is important because it set economic studies on a whole new direction that has led to a better understanding of the economic incentives embedded in employer-sponsored retirement and savings plans.

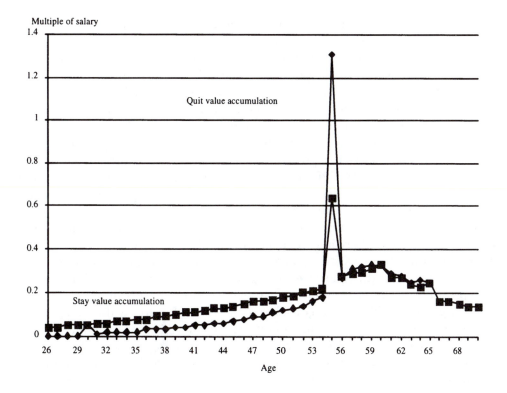

Figure 20-2. Average change in quit values and stay values as a multiple of salary. Source: Watson Wyatt.

shows annual accrual patterns under the pension plans considered in Figure 20-1 for the worker joining a firm at age 25. In this case, the year-to-year change in the present value of the accrued and projected benefit—that is, the annual quit and the stay values, respectively—is a multiple of annual salary.

During the early years of the career referred to in Figure 20-2, the annual change in the stay value of the pension is about 10 percent more of cash wages than the annual change in the quit value. The narrowing in the difference at age 30 reflects the five-year vesting standard that is common among defined benefit plans, under which the value of the first five years of accumulated benefits becomes an explicit obligation only if the worker gets to the fifth anniversary of the plan. Beyond the year of vesting, the annual difference in the two accumulations is still roughly 10 percent of cash wages initially, but narrows as the worker approaches early retirement age. In the first year of early retirement eligibility, there is a considerable jump in the quit value of the benefit, and for the next few years, the quit value of the benefit exceeds the stay value. This is the result of early retirement subsidies that are common in defined benefit plans today.

The implications of Figure 20-2 are important if workers consider the combination of cash wages and the value of their retirement benefits in their periodic renegotiations of compensation with their employers. If workers negotiate compensation on the basis of their marginal product and consider pension accruals on the basis of stay values, while the employer is only obligated to pay accrued benefits calculated from quit values, employers can pay workers less than their marginal product early in their careers but must overcompensate them late in their careers. Workers might be willing to accept such a "wage tilt" because of the various benefits that employer-sponsored pensions provide, as discussed earlier, but only if they felt they would ultimately be paid the value of their marginal product over their career with an employer. Employers would want to offer such lifetime compensation profiles because they provide the incentives for attracting good workers and reducing costly mobility. In this case, the theory of equalizing differences suggests that the existence of a pension should lower total cash wages over a career, although there might be little or no difference in cash wages between a pension-covered job and one without such coverage in any given year.

Bulow argues, however, that workers should only consider the stay value of the benefit in cases where there is an actual contractual obligation to ultimately pay it. Such contracts do not exist except where there is an employment agreement between a worker and employer ensuring that the employment relationship will last up until retirement eligibility. Since explicit contracts of this sort are rare, Bulow argued that if workers considered the stay value to be the appropriate measure of their pension accumulation it suggests the existence of "implicit labor contracts overpaying older workers at the expense of younger ones."[18] He posed a number of theoretical challenges to the existence of such implicit contracts, adding that the mere fact that accruals late in the career were higher than early in the career was not itself proof that such contracts existed because one has to consider the entire compensation package of the worker. In other words, equalizing differentials could mean that higher pension benefit accruals late in the career could be offset by reductions in other elements of the compensation package. He suggested that his theoretical discussion of these issues could be subjected to empirical tests.

Evidence of a Wage-Pension Trade-off

During the 1980s a number of economic studies using different data bases attempted to determine whether workers with pensions paid for their benefits through reduced wages. Olivia Mitchell and Silvana Pozzebon have summarized the results of several of these studies.[19] They first looked at nine cross-sectional studies of the effect of pension generosity on cash wage levels. These studies had attempted to prove that the spot market model was appropriate in explaining the dynamics of wage-pension trade-offs. Mitchell and Pozzebron concluded that the cross-sectional evidence in these studies does not provide strong support for the spot market theory of equalizing differences. Next, they reviewed ten studies that investigated whether pensions affected the shape of the earnings profile over the career and thus whether the implicit contract model or the spot market model was

---

[18]Bulow, "What are Corporate Pension Liabilities?" p. 440.
[19]Olivia S. Mitchell and Silvana Pozzebon, "Wages, Pensions and the Wage-Pension Tradeoff," Department of Labor Economics, unpublished paper, New York State School of Industrial and Labor Relations, Cornell University, July 1987.

more appropriate in explaining the financing of pension accruals. Again, the empirical evidence did not support the conclusion that the existence of a pension resulted in a reduction of cash wages from the perspective of either the spot market or the implicit contract models.

Mitchell and Pozzebon went on to develop their own analysis of the wage-pension trade-off using the *1983 Survey of Consumer Finance* (SCF), a somewhat richer data base than those used in a number of the earlier studies. Prior studies had relied on data bases that had relatively scanty information on plan generosity or pension accruals. The SCF was unique in that if a worker participating in the survey indicated that he or she was covered by a pension plan, the surveyors approached the worker's employer and gathered the necessary administrative information on the plan or plans covering the worker to estimate benefits, accruals, and so on.

The authors used the SCF data to test both the spot market and implicit contract models. Their analysis was restricted to nonagricultural wage and salary workers. Following their analysis of potential wage reductions relating to pension coverage in the spot market context, they concluded that "workers do not appear to receive lower wages for more generous pension provisions such as lower eligibility criteria and earlier retirement ages, nor are wages higher for those required to contribute to their pension plans."[20] Their results were consistent for both defined contribution and defined benefit plans. In relation to the implicit contract model they concluded that "workers covered by a pension prove to have higher earnings profiles than do workers without pensions, and their wage/tenure trajectories run parallel to those of noncovered workers. . . . In general, there is only weak evidence that workers with pensions pay for benefit improvements in the form of reduced wages."[21] Again, the results were consistent for workers covered by either defined contribution or defined benefit plans.

Mitchell and Pozzebon's results were consistent with those of Alan Gustman and Thomas Steinmeier, who used the same SCF data to analyze the effects of pension coverage and other factors on labor mobility. Gustman and Steinmeier restricted their analysis to nonagricultural, private sector, full-time male workers between the ages of 30 and 50. They found that workers covered by pensions receive higher levels of cash compensation than those without pensions. Indeed, they concluded that the "wage premium" paid to workers with pensions was more important in explaining the lower labor mobility of workers with pensions than the pensions were themselves.[22] Gustman and Steinmeier again reached this conclusion in a later study using the *Survey of Income and Program Participation* (SIPP) data reported earlier in this chapter.[23]

While most of the economic research suggests that providing a pension does not lead to offsetting reductions in cash wages, Edward Montgomery, Kathryn Shaw, and Mary Benedict came to a somewhat different conclusion in their analysis of the SCF data on workers covered by defined benefit plans. The authors estimated the

[20]Ibid., pp. 19, 21.
[21]Ibid., p. 25.
[22]Alan L. Gustman and Thomas L. Steinmeier, "Pensions, Efficiency Wages, and Job Mobility," NBER Working Paper, 2426 (Cambridge, Mass.: National Bureau of Economic Research, November 1987).
[23]Gustman and Steinmeier, "Pension Portability and Labor Mobility," pp. 299–323.

expected present value of wage income and pensions for these workers. They used plan provisions and the expected retirement date ascertained in the survey to estimate the expected present value of the pension. They estimated the expected present value of wages by projecting forward and backward wages reported on the survey using growth rates estimated from a regression model in which wage growth between 1982 and 1985 was a function of work experience. Separate wage growth regressions were developed for men and women by educational grouping. The results of the analysis suggest that pension accruals offset cash wages dollar for dollar over a worker's lifetime and thus support the implicit contract and compensating differential theories discussed earlier.[24]

Montgomery and his colleagues reached significantly different conclusions from the researchers investigating the relationship between cash wages and pension accruals. Indeed, when Gustman and Steinmeier used the same data set to run a simple regression of the natural log of lifetime pension wealth on the natural log of lifetime earnings for workers covered by a defined benefit or combination plan, they found a positive relationship,[25] in contrast to the dollar-for-dollar offset reported by Montgomery and his associates. Another possible reason for this discrepancy in results based on the same or comparable data sets is that other studies focused on a wider population, comparing the cash compensation of those covered by retirement plans to those not covered by them. Montgomery and his associates focused only on individuals participating in defined benefit plans and measured the relationship between expected pension accruals and expected cash earnings for this much narrower population. On the basis of information outside the study itself, Gustman and others observed that Montgomery and his associates had "found both positive and negative correlations between pension and pay depending on which other variables were controlled."[26]

For now, at least, the empirical evidence supports the proposition that workers covered by employer-sponsored retirement plans receive a cash wage premium in addition to their retirement benefits when compared with workers not covered by such retirement plans. Montgomery and his colleagues do not refute that finding. Their results merely suggest that among the population covered by a defined benefit plan, more generous in relation to less generous retirement benefits suggest offsetting wages during the working life. This conclusion does not invalidate the widely recognized finding that defined benefit participants receive cash wages during their working careers that are generally higher than those paid to similar workers without such pension coverage.

Pensions as a Compensation Premium

The implicit contract theory of pensions is appealing because it provides a strong intuitive explanation of the sorting characteristics of pensions and their ability to

[24]Edward Montgomery, Kathryn Shaw, and Mary Ellen Benedict, "Pensions and Wages: An Hedonic Price Theory Approach," *International Economic Review*, vol. 33, no. 1 (February, 1992): pp. 111–28.

[25]Alan L. Gustman and Thomas L. Steinmeier, "An Analysis of Pension Benefit Formulas, Pension Wealth, and Incentives from Pensions," in Ronald Ehrenberg, ed., *Research in Labor Economics* (Greenwich, Conn.: JAI Press, 1989), p. 62.

[26]Gustman, Mitchell, and Steinmeier, "The Role of Pensions in the Labor Market," p. 425.

encourage worker stability. But it leaves unresolved two important questions. First, if workers perceive the value of their benefit on a projected basis but employers perceive it on a quit basis, would employers not be inclined to implement policies that would allow them to realize the difference between the two when they reach their maximum? Second, if pensions are an element of compensation, why do cash wages for workers covered by them seem to be too high in relation to workers without pension coverage?

The first of these questions, which applies primarily to defined benefit plans, is raised because employers can terminate workers prior to their retirement eligibility.[27] Looking back to Figure 20-1, assume that the hypothetical worker has concluded that she is being compensated on the basis of her projected pension accrual but that her employer can terminate her prior to retirement eligibility and is legally obligated to pay only the accumulated benefit. At age 50, the difference in the implicit contract value of the benefit and the legal obligation of the employer is the equivalent of nearly three-fourths of the worker's annual cash wage. In other words, an employer could reduce the defined benefit obligation to the worker by terminating her before the significant narrowing of difference in the two benefit obligations at the point of early retirement eligibility. It seems obvious that if employers manifested a discernible pattern of terminating workers prior to significant increases in the accumulated value of benefits—for example, just before vesting or becoming eligible for an immediate benefit—the workers would either come to understand there was no implied contract between them and their employer or would take their employer to court for systematic wrongful dismissals.

The logic of discerning workers notwithstanding, the passage of the Employment Retirement Income Security Act was, at least in part, a response to a public policy concern that employers were taking advantage of workers participating in their retirement plans.[28] Empirical evidence, however, does not support the conclusion that employers take advantage of their workers through some sort of systematic cheating on implied contracts. Christopher Cornwell, Stuart Dorsey, and Nasser Mehrzad statistically evaluated the hypothesis that workers with pensions are more likely to be discharged than workers without them.[29] They used data on a group of males workers who were aged 45 to 55 in 1966 and who were interviewed periodically in the *National Longitudinal Survey* (NLS) between 1966 and 1981. The data allowed the researchers to track workers over time and to determine those who were terminated involuntarily, those who retired, and those who continued to work.

In general terms, Cornwell and his colleagues hypothesize that employers would be inhibited in their exploitation of the implied contracts with workers because they would damage the companies' reputations in the communities in which they

---

[27]Technically, the same issue applies to defined contribution plans prior to vesting. It is much less a problem in defined contribution plans, however, because vesting schedules tend to be shorter under them than under defined benefit plans, and because the problem goes away once the worker becomes vested in the defined contribution plan.

[28]Richard A. Ippolito, "A Study of the Regulatory Effect of the Employee Retirement Income Security Act," *Journal of Law and Economics*, vol. 31 (April 1988): p. 85.

[29]Christopher Cornwell, Stuart Dorsey, and Nasser Mehrzad, "Opportunistic Behavior by Firms in Implicit Pension Contracts," *Journal of Human Resources*, vol. 26, no. 4 (1991): pp. 704–25.

operate. In their aggregate analysis, they found that pension-covered workers were 4.6 percent less likely to be discharged than those without coverage, and that among covered workers the probability of termination did not increase for workers with greater potential losses in relation to those with smaller ones. One of their most interesting findings was that nonunion workers benefited more than union members, who might generally be expected to have greater protection against exploitative behavior by employers. Their conclusions do not support the notion that being covered by a pension plan increases the risk of termination for older workers.

In a more refined set of estimates, the authors broke the pension loss estimates into two categories: fully anticipated pension losses and unanticipated losses. They noted that during a period of increasing inflation, the pension loss from early termination will be greater because the higher inflation will typically be associated with higher nominal wage growth. They calculated anticipated pension losses by assuming that the inflation rate when a worker joined a firm would persist in perpetuity. The actual pension loss was calculated using the inflation rate that prevailed at the point of termination. The unanticipated loss was the difference in the actual and the anticipated pension loss. On the basis of this analysis, the authors concluded that *higher expected losses* do not increase the risk of involuntary termination but that *higher unexpected losses* do. The explanation of this latter phenomenon in light of the underlying theory that employers guard their reputation is that the unexpected gain from early terminations during periods of high inflation more than offsets the expected damage to the employer's reputation from implementing such a program.

In yet a third formulation of their analysis, the authors analyzed the effects ERISA had on opportunistic behavior by firms. Specifically, they isolated the group of workers who had been participating in a pension plan for 10 years or more but had not vested prior to the passage of ERISA. Since ERISA required that these workers be vested, the prospect of employer gains from early termination diminished significantly immediately after the implementation of the new vesting requirements, which should have reduced the probability that the workers affected would be terminated involuntarily. In this case, the authors were unable find any negative impact from ERISA on the rates of terminations of workers affected by its vesting standards.

Ippolito conducted a similar analysis, using the Retirement History Survey, a longitudinal survey of older men, including workers aged 59 to 63 in 1969. The participants in this survey were reinterviewed every other year for 10 years. He used these data to test whether pension participants on the verge of retirement were denied a pension prior to ERISA. Prior to ERISA's passage, vesting occurred at retirement for 40 percent of the covered workers. Ippolito hypothesized that if employers were engaging in opportunistic behavior, the data should show an increase in pension receipt by covered workers after the passage of ERISA. His results did not support the conclusion that employers had been taking unfair advantage of their workers prior to the passage of ERISA by terminating their employment before they became eligible to collect benefits.[30]

---

[30]Ippolito, "A Study of the Regulatory Effect of the Employee Retirement Income Security Act," pp. 97–98.

The findings of both Cornwell and his associates and Ippolito suggest that employers share the implied contract theory of pensions with their workers. Still, these results do not explain why workers covered by employer-sponsored retirement plans appear to have higher cash wages than do workers not covered by such plans. One theory is that certain employers pay "efficiency wages" or premium wages above what the market would normally dictate because workers are more productive when they receive such a premium. The arguments for paying such premiums parallel the arguments for offering retirement plans. One argument is that paying a worker a premium discourages shirking on the job, because a worker caught shirking and losing the job would be faced with the prospect of lower-payingalternative employment. Another argument is that a firm might pay an efficiency wage in order to minimize turnover costs. If a firm can minimize turnover by paying a higher wage than the market would dictate, it might be able to also minimize its investment in worker training. Yet another argument is that premium wages act as a worker-sorting device, because workers observing wages in the marketplace would expect the jobs paying relatively high wages to be for relatively high-quality and productive workers. Finally, efficiency wages might be paid in cases where productivity is related to morale, and higher wages might induce a greater sense of commitment to the employer on the part of workers.[31]

While the efficiency wage theory offers a credible explanation for relatively high wages in some firms or industries, the strong correlation between wage premiums and the prevalence of employer-sponsored retirement programs suggests that employers are offering a double premium in many cases. Gustman and Steinmeier found that turnover among workers with defined benefit plans, which are the plans attributed with turnover inhibiting characteristics, was as high as that among workers with defined contribution plans, which are not said to have such turnover inhibiting characteristics.[32] Their analysis also showed that the wage premium was the predominant factor in explaining lower turnover among pensioned workers. Their results lead one to ask why many employers would offer both a wage premium and a retirement plan. Richard Ippolito has attempted to theoretically reconcile this widely observed phenomenon.[33]

Ippolito begins with the assumption that some firms are more productive if they can establish enduring relationships with their workers. The prospect of increased productivity generates excess demand for workers with certain characteristics, which thus enables them to command a wage premium in the labor market. If a firm wishes to engage such workers in a long-term contract, it must compensate them for forgone alternative job opportunities. The firm could establish a compensation program whereby it always waited until a worker received an alternative job offer and then renegotiated pay to keep the worker, but that would create potential

[31]For a more complete discussion on efficiency wages, see William T. Dickens and Lawrence F. Katz, "Inter-Industry Wage Differences and Theories of Wage Determination," NBER Working Paper, 2271 (Cambridge, Mass: National Bureau of Economic Research, June 1987); and Alan Kreuger and Lawrence Summers, "Efficiency Wages and the Wage Structure," *Econometrica*, vol. 56 (1988): pp. 259–94.

[32]Gustman and Steinmeier, "Pension Portability and Labor Mobility."

[33]Richard A. Ippolito, "Pensions and Indenture Premia," *Journal of Human Resources*, vol. 29, no. 3 (Summer 1994): pp. 795–812.

problems. A worker who is crucial to a company's operations might negotiate—or extort—an excessive premium for staying at the firm. So the task is to design a compensation scheme that pays the worker his or her lifetime expected wage, but in a fashion that discourages premature employment termination. This is where a defined benefit plan can play an important role. In order to do this, it must meet a number of conditions.

The first condition is that lifetime compensation offered by the firm has to at least equal the expected lifetime pay a worker can receive outside the firm, or the worker will take alternative employment. The second condition is that the cash wage the firm pays a worker early in his or her career will be less than total compensation, or workers covered by defined benefit plans would not face a capital loss for leaving the firm. The third condition is that once a worker has some tenure in a job, the combination of expected future cash wages plus expected pension benefits has to equal or exceed alternative compensation offers, or the worker will leave the firm. In this context, the defined benefit plan acts as an indenturing device. But the only way a firm can get workers to accept such indenturing is by paying a sufficiently high cash wage to attract them into it.

Once a worker is covered by a defined benefit plan, the plan alone can deter some workers from taking alternative jobs where marginal increases in lifetime compensation would be small. For example, looking back at Figure 20-1 one notes that within five years of employment under a typical defined benefit plan, a worker could lose 15 percent of a year's pay by terminating employment prematurely. The wage tilt, discussed earlier, increasingly raises the cost of quitting well into the worker's career. But by itself, the pension plan may not be sufficiently inhibiting to stifle job changing by high-quality workers. Such workers enjoy sufficiently high probabilities of alternative job offers at premium cash wages that would more than offset the losses in their pension accruals caused by premature terminations. For example, Gustman and Steinmeier found that many workers can overcome their pension loss by realizing a 2 or 3 percent increase in their lifetime wage levels through a job change. Thus, even firms with defined benefit plans that wish to maintain long-tenure relationships with workers are forced to pay efficiency cash wages in addition to the indenture premiums embodied in their pension systems. This necessity may account for the widely observed phenomenon of pensions and generous cash wages.

At the limit, a firm could pay high enough efficiency wages in combination with indenture premiums in a defined benefit plan to eliminate turnover. That is not very practical, though, nor would most employers consider it desirable. Rather, a firm would want to balance the cost of workers quitting against the cost of deterring quitting and would structure the combination of efficiency wages and their retirement programs accordingly. This creates an interesting optimization problem because of the interactions between the incentives in the efficiency wages and the indenture premiums in defined benefit plans leading workers to stay in their jobs or take alternative offers. In cases where the probabilities of alternative job offers are relatively high, but at only marginally better wages, the indenturing characteristics of defined benefit plans would be highly effective in reducing turnover.

Where the probability of alternative job offers is relatively low, but there is a likelihood of significantly higher pay being realized when jobs are offered, the defined benefit plan would provide a negligible effect on turnover in comparison with a higher efficiency wage. Increases in cash wages would be more effective in keeping workers in situations of this sort than providing a generous defined benefit plan. Indeed, a firm in an industry with a work force facing this kind of prospect would probably find that a defined contribution plan would be at least as effective in inhibiting turnover as a defined benefit plan, if not more so. The accumulation of the cash balance and the lack of the indenture premium would make the defined contribution plan a closer substitute for cash wages than the defined benefit plan would be. If firms with work forces that have few job alternatives naturally tend to offer defined contribution plans, it is not surprising to find that worker turnover under defined contribution plans is comparable to that under defined benefit plans, as noted earlier, even though the incentive effects in the two kinds of plans are quite different.

This theory of pensions and wages has not been directly tested empirically. But the theory does conceptually reconcile a number of the other empirical inconsistencies that have been identified above. For example, it suggests that a combination of premium wages and retirement benefits is compatible, which is wholly consistent with the broad body of empirical research that finds little evidence of compensating reductions in cash wages among employers offering retirement plans in comparison with those not offering them. It also suggests that the seemingly inconsistent findings of Montgomery and his associates make sense because they limited their analysis to firms offering only defined benefit plans. The other research suggests that this limited subset of firms offers premium compensation packages, but Ippolito's theoretical construct suggests there should still be trade-offs between retirement benefits and cash wages within the total compensation package. Finally, it even offers a rationale for why different firms might offer defined benefit versus defined contribution plans and why observed turnover under them might be comparable. It is hoped that further empirical research will probe the validity of this theoretical explanation of the trade-offs between pensions and wages.

Employer-Sponsored Retirement Programs and the Retirement of Older Workers

One of the important reasons many employers maintain their defined benefit programs is that these programs are generally perceived to contain more effective retirement incentives than defined contribution programs. Most of the defined benefit plans in operation in the United States today include incentives that encourage workers to retire, many before they reach the normal retirement ages specified in the plans. In a recent survey of more than 900 employers, two-thirds of the respondents sponsored defined benefit pension plans and 70 percent of them subsidized early retirement.[34] A subsequent survey found that virtually all of the defined benefit plans sponsored by larger employers provide reduced early retirement benefits, and that the majority provide unreduced early retirement benefits

---

[34]Watson Wyatt, *Retirement Policy Schizophrenia: Does America Want Its Elderly to Work or Retire?* (Washington, D.C.: Watson Wyatt, 1991), p. 4.

under various specified age or service conditions.[35] In other words, the value of benefits paid on a lifetime basis by the majority of defined benefit plans will be higher for many workers who retire prior to the normal retirement age specified in their plan than if they were to retire at the normal retirement age or later.

Retirement Incentives in Typical Retirement Plans

Laurence Kotlikoff and David Wise used the *1979 Level of Benefits Survey* done by the U.S. Department of Labor to develop an analytical presentation showing how defined benefit accruals late in the career can provide strong incentives for workers to retire.[36] They began by postulating that the annual accrual in the pension at age a, $I(a)$, is equal to the difference between the pension wealth based on the accrued vested benefit at age $a + 1$, $Pw(a + 1)$ and pension wealth at age a, $Pw(a)$, accumulated to age $a + 1$ at the nominal interest rate r. This might be written as

$$(20\text{-}1) \qquad\qquad I(a) = Pw(a + 1) - Pw(a)(1 + r).$$

In this conception, $Pw(a)$ is the equivalent of a "pension bank account" and the pension accrual is the increment to pension wealth in excess of the annual return on the previously accumulated bank account. This amount can be represented as we represented the accrued and projected benefits earlier, namely as a fraction of annual wages. Figure 20-3 shows the average accrual pattern under 513 defined benefit plans included in Kotlikoff and Wise's data base for a worker beginning coverage under these plans at age 30. The plans selected in this case provided for normal retirement at age 65 but had provisions allowing early retirement benefits to commence as early as age 55.

Kotlikoff and Wise's derivation of accruals shows a significant accrual in the tenth year of employment, the date of initial vesting under the plans that was common back in the late 1970s, gradual growth in the accrual up to the early retirement date, a somewhat reduced but relatively flat accrual between the ages of 55 and 60, a gradual decline in accruals between the ages of 60 and 65, and decidedly negative accruals after age 65. A worker continuing employment up to age 70 would realize a decline in $I(a)$ that would be almost the equivalent of 20 percent of annual cash wages. The negative pension accrual would act as a damper on cash wages and would be a significant penalty for continuing to work. When Alan Gustman and Thomas Steinmeier examined the *1983 Survey of Consumer Finances* data discussed earlier, they found a similar pattern of accruals and retirement incentives under defined benefit plans.[37]

In fact, defined benefit plans do not work exactly as Kotlikoff and Wise analyzed them. First, most plans do not pass on early retirement supplements to workers

---

[35]Watson Wyatt, "Early Retirement Provisions and Incentives," *Wyatt* COMPARISON, no. 1 (September 1991): p. 19.

[36]Laurence J. Kotlikoff and David A. Wise, "The Incentive Effects of Private Pension Plans," in Zvi Bodie, John B. Shoven, and David A. Wise, eds., *Issues in Pension Economics* (Chicago: University of Chicago Press, 1987), pp. 283–36.

[37]Gustman and Steinmeier, "An Analysis of Pension Benefit Formulas, Pension Wealth, and Incentives from Pensions," pp. 53–106.

Multiple of salary

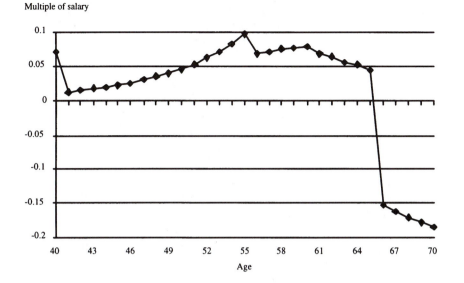

Figure 20-3. Accrual rate as a multiple of salary with early retirement at age 55 and normal retirement age of 65. Source: Kotlikoff and Wise, "The Incentive Effects of Private Pension Plans," pp. 290–91.

terminating prior to early retirement eligibility. Thus the benefits for premature terminations should be discounted from the normal retirement age, not the early retirement age. In addition, most plans do not provide the terminating worker with the opportunity of taking a lump-sum distribution prior to retirement eligibility unless it is a relatively nominal amount. If a lump sum is not available under a plan, it would not accrue interest income between the point of termination and the commencement of benefit payments, and indeed this is often a criticism of defined benefit plans. At the point of benefit commencement, however, many plans provide the option of a lump sum or an annuity, taking into account future interest returns on the accumulated value of the benefit over the life expectancy of the beneficiary. Either payment of a lump sum or eligibility for an annuity would make the analysis more relevant to the actual operation of these plans.

Using Kotlikoff and Wise's accrual measure, we analyzed the retirement incentives in three actual defined benefit levels selected to show how the incentives might vary across plans with different levels of generosity. The assumptions in this analysis are similar to those used in developing Figures 20-1 and 20-2, except that we varied the wage growth assumptions beyond early retirement eligibility. Specifically, we assumed the worker begins employment in 1993 at age 25, earning an annual salary of $28,800 per year—that is, half the Social Security wage base. We assumed that inflation was constant at 4 percent per year, and that the worker would realize wage increases of 5.5 percent per year until early retirement eligibility. We employed an 8 percent interest and discount rate in the calculations. We used slightly different assumptions on pay increases after early retirement eligibility than we used in the earlier calculations. Here we assumed that after age 55 pay

TABLE 20-2   Accrual Rate as a Fraction of Earnings for Three Defined
Benefit Plans in 1993, with Decreasing Pay Increases
After Age 55 (percent)

Age	Generosity of the Plan as Defined in the Text		
	Lowest	Middle	Highest
55	0.56	0.79	1.61
56	0.06	0.19	0.02
57	0.05	0.18	0.00
58	0.03	0.17	−0.01
59	0.02	0.15	−0.03
60	0.00	0.13	−0.05
61	0.09	0.03	−0.07
62	0.08	0.02	−0.08
63	0.06	−0.07	−0.09
64	0.04	−0.08	−0.10
65	0.03	−0.09	−0.11
66	−0.19	−0.18	−0.21
67	−0.23	−0.23	−0.26
68	−0.23	−0.25	−0.31
69	−0.27	−0.30	−0.36
70	−0.30	−0.34	−0.40

Source: Watson Wyatt.

increases would drop to 4 percent per year, the rate of inflation, until age 65 and would drop to zero beyond that age. Under these assumptions, at age 55 the least generous plan would generate an accrued benefit equal to 1.71 times salary. The plan with middling generosity would generate a benefit that is 2.01 times salary, and the most generous plan would generate a benefit 3.10 times salary.

Slowing the growth in wages prior to retirement is consistent with the underlying motivations that employers would have for implementing defined benefit plans. If employers are structuring their plans to encourage termination at certain ages, it must be tied to their perceptions about declining productivity, as discussed in Chapter 1. Assuming that employers attempt to pay workers in accordance with their marginal productivity, giving a worker wage increases that exceed the inflation rate would be consistent with increasing productivity. Wage increases that just match the inflation rate would be consistent with productivity having reached a plateau and stabilized. Giving a worker no wage increases in an inflationary environment would be consistent with an employer's perception of declining productivity on the part of a worker.

Table 20-2 presents the interactions of the assumptions that we have postulated here and the three defined benefit plans we analyzed. The most generous plan provides the biggest bonus for retiring at age 55 and the strongest disincentives to continue working much beyond the early retirement age. The midlevel plan we have chosen continues to provide significant accruals up to age 60, but they fall off quickly after that. The lowest-level plan offers some positive, although moderate,

Table 20-3   Accrual Rate as a Fraction of Earnings for Three Defined Benefit Plans in 1993, with Pay Increases of 5.5 Percent a Year (percent)

Age	Generosity of the Plan as Defined in the Text		
	Lowest	Middle	Highest
55	0.56	0.79	1.61
56	0.06	0.19	0.02
57	0.05	0.19	0.01
58	0.04	0.18	0.01
59	0.04	0.17	0.00
60	0.13	0.17	−0.01
61	0.12	0.08	−0.02
62	0.11	0.08	−0.02
63	0.09	−0.01	−0.03
64	0.08	−0.02	−0.04
65	−0.13	−0.02	−0.05
66	−0.13	−0.11	−0.17
67	−0.10	−0.11	0.03
68	−0.10	−0.10	−0.14
69	−0.11	−0.10	−0.15
70	−0.11	−0.11	−0.15

Source: Watson Wyatt.

incentive to continue working up until age 65. But all three of the plans provide strong disincentives to work beyond 65, with the generosity in the plan from the perspective of early retirement accruals accentuating the disincentives. For an individual working to age 70, the decline in the pension value would offset 30 to 40 percent of the cash wages earned in the last year of employment, a significant discount of the wage paid for working an additional year. Thus the typical defined benefit plan actually can penalize the worker who stays "too long" at a covered position. The penalties can be quite significant and act as a strong disincentive for a worker who does not terminate employment on a timely basis, and they get more severe the longer he or she works. If the structure in the pension benefit formula is coupled with other unsubtle compensation signals to the older worker—for example, no pay raises—they can convey an economic message to the worker that it is time to move on to other activities.

While the defined benefit pension plan allows the sponsor to provide strong incentives for workers to retire at certain ages, they also allow for differential incentives. For example, an employer with a retirement incentive structure of the sort just described might not want to provide such strong incentives to older workers perceived to be highly productive for the firm. Table 20-3 is developed on the same basis as Table 20-2, except that we assumed our hypothetical worker would continue to receive 5.5 percent per year pay increases beyond age 55 up until age 70. In this case, not only does the worker see continued immediate reward from staying in the firm in the form of annual wage increases, but in each instance, an additional year of work is rewarded with a greater accumulated retirement benefit or less of a penalty than in the earlier case. Of course, larger wage increases would have even a greater effect.

The ability to provide incentives to encourage the retirement of older workers might not have been so important a number of years ago when many employers with pensions had mandatory retirement provisions, but they have taken on increased importance over the last decade as the ability to retire workers on the basis of age has been essentially eliminated. In today's litigious world, the ability to get older workers to retire on a systematic and predictable basis is important. Defined contribution plans do not offer plan sponsors even the limited flexibility that defined benefits have in terms of building in economic incentives to encourage retirement. In providing an incentive to retire, the defined benefit plan has the advantage that each year a benefit is forgone is a year's worth of benefits that will not be paid. In the case of a defined contribution plan, a year in which a benefit is not paid out of the plan simply means the accumulated benefit accrues interest for another year, and the larger accumulation will be paid out over a shorter remaining life expectancy at retirement. In other words, delaying retirement under defined benefit plans often means the depreciation of the retirement asset, whereas under defined contribution plans it means just the opposite. To understand the difference in the retirement incentives provided by the two types of plans it is helpful to look at a set of actual plans and see how they operate in real life.

A Case Study of Retirement Incentives in Higher Education

The majority of public institutions of higher learning either offer their faculty the option of participating in a defined benefit plan or require that they be covered under such a plan.[38] In addition to, or instead of, their public defined benefit plan, many faculty members can participate in the Teachers Insurance Annuity Association–College Retirement Equity Fund (TIAA-CREF) program, a defined contribution plan. Also, in recent years many public employers have gone the same direction as industrial employers and offered their employees the opportunity to participate in supplemental defined contribution savings programs. In the private institutions, on the other hand, the overwhelming majority of faculty, 89 percent, and the majority of clerical and service workers are covered under TIAA-CREF. As with the plans sponsored by industrial employers, the defined benefit and defined contribution plans sponsored by academic employers have different incentives for workers to continue active employment or retire once eligible.[39]

Most college and university employees enrolled in public plans are covered under a retirement system for public employees in general or one specifically targeted at teachers. In some states, all public workers are covered under a single plan. In many cases where there are separate plans for teachers and other public workers, the formulas for determining benefits are identical or quite similar. The

---

[38]For a more detailed analysis of retirement programs in institutions of higher education from which this is drawn, see Sylvester J. Schieber, "Retirement Programs and Issues," in Sigmund G. Ginsburg, ed., *Paving the Way for the 21st Century: The Human Factor in Higher Education Financial Management* (Washington, D.C.: National Association of College and University Business Officers, 1993), pp. 133–78.

[39]Ibid.

majority of plans provide benefits that are not integrated with Social Security. Most of the benefit formulas range between 1.5 percent and 2.0 percent of final average pay for each year of service covered under the plan. A handful of states provide benefits below these levels, and a similar number provide benefits in excess of the upper end reported here. This latter group largely, if not totally, comprises states whose public employees are not covered under Social Security. Most of these plans require contributions from plan participants, typically around 5 percent of pay.[40]

The colleges and universities using TIAA-CREF as a retirement vehicle make regular contributions to the plans based on the covered employees' pay levels. A recent analysis published by TIAA-CREF indicates that for 85 percent of the faculty participating the contributions are set at a fixed rate, depending on the institution where the individual is employed. In approximately 15 percent of the institutions, a step-rate contribution is made. Under the step-rate plans, the contribution on one portion of the salary, generally related to the Social Security earnings base, is less than the contribution on the other portion. For example, the contribution may be 10 percent on earnings up to the Social Security wage base and 14 percent on earnings above that level. Contributions are above 10 percent on all covered earnings in 87 percent of the institutions. In about 27 percent of the schools some portion of the contribution is set at 15 percent or more of covered earnings. In 16 percent of the schools all of the contributions are 15 percent or more. In 25 percent of the institutions the employer makes the full contribution. In another 47 percent the school makes the larger contribution, and in 28 percent it is the other way around.[41]

In order to show the differences in retirement incentives in these various plans, we estimated extra retirement benefit accruals under a range of plans that reasonably represent the range of offerings across higher education. For this exercise we chose two individuals who turned age 55 in 1993. We assumed that these individuals had been employed at their respective academic institutions for 20 and 30 years. We assumed that both of them earned $57,600 in 1993—that is, the Social Security wage base—if they chose to work. While this earnings level is significant for purposes of determining the relative value of Social Security in retirement, it is not significant in comparing the relative value of the benefits provided by the various employer-sponsored retirement plans considered in this analysis.

Further, we assumed that as the workers approached retirement they would have received pay increases of 4 percent per year over the recent past, and would continue to receive pay increases in this amount in the future. We also assumed that future inflation would occur at a rate of 4 percent per year, meaning that their real cash wages would be constant in future years. This is a reasonable assumption for workers at retirement age. If we had assumed that wages grow slightly in real terms, it would slightly depress the growth of retirement plan balances in relation to wages in comparison with the estimates presented here. If nominal wages grow less than inflation, the opposite would be true. In neither case would small

[40]For a description of the plan formulas used in determining public retirement plan benefits see State of Wisconsin Retirement Research Committee, "1988 Comparative Survey of Major Public Pension Plans," Staff Report, no. 78 (1988), photocopy; and Workplace Economics, Inc., *1992 State Employee Benefits Survey* (Washington, D.C.: Workplace Economics, Inc., 1992).

[41]TIAA-CREF, Summary of Retirement Plan Provisions, August 1, 1989 (New York: TIAA-CREF, 1989).

differences in wage growth and inflation have a significant effect on the analysis. Of course, as the earlier discussion suggested, larger increases in wages can have a considerable ameliorating effect on the declining value of the benefits provided through the pension.

We assumed that accumulations in defined contribution accounts would realize an 8 percent rate of return. Over the 1960s, TIAA provided an annual compound return of 4.75 percent in excess of the inflation rate; during the inflationary 1970s, it dropped to 1.34 percent; it rebounded to 5.19 percent during the 1980s. From 1960 to 1991 the compound growth rate was 3.77 percent. Of course, CREF offers participants in the program the chance to invest in equities and was established to give participants in the program an opportunity to realize the greater return potential they offer, in relation to the TIAA program. During the 1960s CREF yielded a real compound return of 7.07 percent per year, during the 1970s it was 5.92 percent, and during the 1980s, 11.60 percent. For the period 1960 to 1991 it was 7.86 percent per year in excess of inflation. The access to equity investment has not been unlimited, though, because funds originally invested in TIAA, or transferred from CREF to TIAA could not flow back the other way until recently, and still there are some limitations.[42] On the whole, participants in defined contribution plans do not take advantage of the long-term added returns for investing in equities that the potential gains in their retirement benefits would imply. That notwithstanding, it seems appropriate to assume a slightly higher return than that provided from investing solely in TIAA.

We calculated the present value of the hypothetical workers' retirement benefit accruals on the assumption that they continued to work between the ages of 55 and 70. In order to calculate the present value of the annuity benefits that would be paid under the pension plans, we used an 8 percent discount factor and used a blended mortality rate that reflects the average life expectancy of men and women. From our estimates of accrued benefits, we could calculate the change in the present value of benefits under the various plans we considered and could compare these changes with the hypothetical workers' cash pay. In the case of the value of defined benefit plan accruals, we used the same method of calculating them as discussed earlier and as reflected in Equation (20-1). The value of the defined contribution accruals was calculated on the same basis.

Figure 20-4 shows the results of the first simulation. In this case the results reflect the situation faced by the individual with 20 years of service at age 55. The various lines on the figure reflect the change in the value of the retirement benefit accumulated by working beyond age 55 under four retirement plans. They do not include the interest that would be earned on the prior accruals because that is not a direct return for working an additional year. The changes in values earned from each additional year of work are presented as a percentage of salary in the year prior to each attained age. As the workers decide to work or retire, one thing they must consider is the potential value of an added year of work. They undoubtedly do so by considering the extra income they would earn from an added year of employment, including the extra accumulation of pension wealth.

---

[42]Elias Clark, "Additional Opinion," in Oscar M. Ruebhausen, ed., *Pension and Retirement Policies in Colleges and Universities: An Analysis and Recommendations* (San Francisco: Jossey-Bass, 1990), pp. 105–6.

Percent

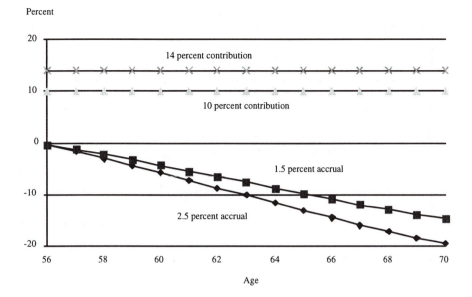

Figure 20-4. Employment-related retirement benefit accruals at selected ages as a percentage of annual pay for a worker with 20 years of service at age 55 under various plans. Source: Watson Wyatt.

The lowest line in Figure 20-4 shows that if this worker, covered by the pension plan that provides a benefit of 2.5 percent of final average salary, stays employed during the year in which he or she is 55 years of age, the accumulation of extra value in his or her pension from an additional year of work will be negligible. If this worker stays employed under the plan beyond age 55, the negative pension accrual in relation to salary increasingly penalizes extended work to the point that it reaches 20 percent of pay at age 70 for a worker who began the covered job at age 35. The second line from the bottom in the figure shows the accrual pattern under a pension formula that provides 1.5 percent of the average of final three years' earnings for each year of covered service. This plan with the less generous benefit formula does not impose as stringent a penalty on the extended career as the more generous plan, but it reflects the same pattern over the potential period of extra work. We chose these two formulas because they band the benefits provided by roughly two-thirds of all state and local pension programs. Other formulas that are more or less generous would reflect similar patterns, just at different levels.

The top two lines in the figure reflect the increase in the present value of the work-related retirement benefit as a percentage of annual earnings in defined contribution plans in which contributions are being made at two rates. Again, we chose these rates because they encompass the vast majority of contribution rates in operating plans. The pattern of growth in the value of the retirement benefits under these plans is quite different from the defined benefit plans. For each additional year that the individual stays in position, the retirement accumulation as a percentage of earnings remains constant. If one stays beyond age 70, accumulations continue to grow on the basis of annual earnings.

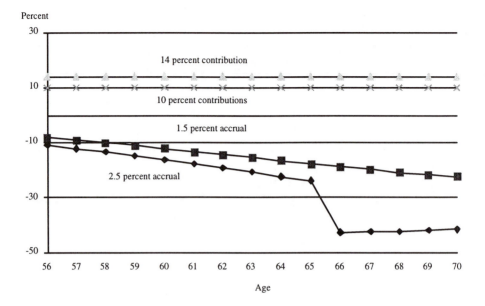

Figure 20-5. Employment-related retirement benefit accruals at selected ages as a percentage of annual pay for a worker with 30 years of service at age 55 under various plans. Source: Watson Wyatt.

Figure 20-5 is similar to Figure 20-4, except that it reflects the accrual patterns of the worker who has 30 years of service under the retirement plans at age 55. The participants in the defined benefit plans will have 10 years more of accrued service under the benefit formulas in the plans than in the earlier examples. The dip in the accrual line for the 2 percent defined benefit formula is the result of the worker capping out on the replacement of final average earnings at 80 percent. A service or percentage-of-pay cap on benefits is a common feature of defined benefit plans. In this case, the annual penalty imposed on pension accruals is equal to about 42 percent of annual salary for a worker who stays on beyond age 65. For the defined contribution plan in this case, the accruing benefits that are attributable to extra years of work are identical to those depicted in the earlier case for the shorter-tenured worker.

Figure 20-6 looks at the accumulation of pension wealth in these defined contribution plans from a somewhat different perspective. The two lines in the figure reflect the increase in the present value of retirement plan accumulations, including the interest that accrues to the account balance each year, as a percentage of prior year earnings in defined contribution plans in which contributions are being made at the two contribution rates being considered. In estimating these benefits, we started with an accumulation at age 55 that would provide the worker with an annuity equivalent to 50 percent of earnings during the year in which he or she turned age 60. From this accumulation we could estimate the value of the accumulated benefits in earlier and later years, given our assumptions. We chose this particular amount because it corresponded somewhat with the lower boundary of

Percent

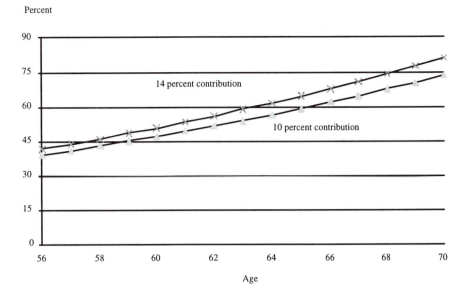

Figure 20-6. Retirement benefit accruals at selected ages as a percentage of annual pay for a worker with 20 years of service at age 55 under various plans. Source: Watson Wyatt.

benefits of recent faculty retirees from the University of Chicago.[43] The relatively small difference between the 10 and 14 percent contribution accrual lines is related to the assumption that the accumulated benefit in both cases would provide a potential replacement of 50 percent of final earnings at age 60. If we had assumed that contributions had been made at the two rates over a full career, the difference between the two lines would have been much greater.

The bottom line reflects total accumulations in plans with contributions of 10 percent per year, and the top line reflects contribution rates of 14 percent. Again, we chose these rates because they encompass the vast majority of contribution rates under TIAA-CREF at universities around the country. The levels of growth in the value of the retirement benefits under these plans is significant. For each additional year that the individual stays in position, the total retirement accumulation as a percentage of earnings actually increases. If individuals continue to work beyond their late 60s, accumulations grow to 60 percent of annual earnings, a tremendous supplement to delay retirement.

The Faculty Committee on Retirement at the University of Chicago analyzed a sample of 21 recent retirees to see what level of preretirement income was being provided by their basic retirement program. The years of service at retirement across the sample ranged from 16 to 48 years, with a median of 30 years. They found that the percentage of preretirement income received as an annuity, not including Social Security or any Supplementary Retirement Accounts, ranged

[43]Report of the Faculty Committee on Retirement, University of Chicago (Chicago: University of Chicago, 1990), p. 4.

Percent

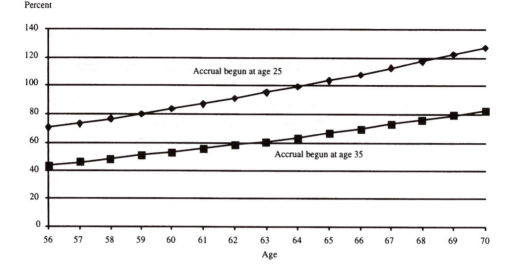

Figure 20-7. Total retirement benefit accruals at select ages as a percentage of salary for a worker with 12 percent annual contributions, starting at ages 25 and 35. Source: Watson Wyatt.

from 53 to 122 percent, with a median of 76 percent.[44] A sample of 21 individuals is too small to permit broad conclusions. But the variation and median years of service seem quite reasonable in comparison with other retirement programs sponsored by larger employers. The contributions to TIAA-CREF at the University of Chicago amount to 12.5 percent of salary, which is somewhere in the middle of the pack among the contribution rates to TIAA-CREF cited earlier.

Figure 20-7 shows the total retirement benefit accrual rate as a percentage of salary under a defined contribution plan in which contributions are 12 percent of salary per year over the whole covered career. We show two levels of accumulation. The bottom line in Figure 20-7 reflects an accumulation of benefits by a worker who participates fully in the plan, beginning at age 35. The top line reflects an accumulation for a worker whose coverage begins at age 25. This figure would give a reasonable representation of the range of retirement accumulation incentives that employers sponsoring TIAA-CREF or similar defined contribution benefits would be offering to older workers with fairly long tenures around the ages normally associated with retirement. For workers who started their teaching careers and retirement savings in their mid-20s, working past their early 60s means that each additional year of work allows them not only an additional year of pay but also an increase in their accumulated retirement wealth that is equivalent to their pay. There is tremendous remuneration from staying in the work force for an added year in these circumstances, especially in cases where faculty members are facing relatively light teaching loads. It is in the more prestigious universities character-

[44]Ibid., pp. 6–7.

ized by light teaching loads and significant research opportunities that faculty members tend to work the longest.

Retirement Plan Incentives and Retirement Behavior

The accrual patterns under defined benefit and defined contribution plans are clearly different. The earlier discussion about the incentive effects that industrial employers embed in their defined benefit plans indicated that these plans are used to achieve desirable retirement patterns. Given that defined contribution plans do not have the same kinds of incentives, it is likely that retirement patterns under the two kinds of plans will be different. A number of years ago when the age at which mandatory retirement could be imposed was raised from 65 to 70 for faculty members in institutions of higher learning, there was a sharp change in faculty retirement behavior at the University of Chicago. "Indeed, the median age at which faculty actually retired also went from 65 to 70."[45] While this anecdote might lead one to conclude that workers covered under defined contribution plans might never retire, that is not the case.

Gregory Lozier and Michael Dooris provide some evidence that higher education faculty retirement patterns are affected by the basic structure of the retirement program offered by academic employers. Evidence taken from their study is presented in Table 20-4, which shows average retirement ages of faculty at 101 colleges and universities over seven academic years.[46] On average, faculty retirement ages in institutions with a defined benefit plan are two to two-and-one-half years younger than at institutions with only a defined contribution program.

There are several reasons that workers who enjoy relatively strong financial incentives to continue working might choose to retire even though they are physically and mentally able to continue in their career. One reason is that even many prestigious jobs include some amount of disutility. The evidence on faculty member retirement patterns in higher education suggests that it is those colleges and universities where faculty members have relatively light teaching loads and spend a considerable amount of time doing research that retirement ages are the highest. Those professors who have heavier teaching loads, which entail more class preparations, grading of exams and papers, and so forth, tend to retire earlier.

Another reason is that under plans like TIAA-CREF, participants can ultimately accumulate sufficient resources to maintain or increase their standards of living while being able to enjoy increased leisure. Being able to enjoy increased leisure activities requires at least partial withdrawal from the commitment of full-time employment. Figure 20-8 converts the potential retirement plan accumulations in Figure 20-7 into replacement of final earnings ratios. For workers with long tenures under these plans, the potential retirement income levels are more than sufficient to meet the income standards developed in Chapter 18. Keep in mind that the replacement rates reflected in Figure 20-8 do not include Social Security benefits.

---

[45]Ibid., 4.
[46]G. Gregory Lozier and Michael J. Dooris, *Faculty Retirement Projections Beyond 1994: Effects of Policy on Individual Choice* (Boulder, Colo.: Western Interstate Commission for Higher Education, 1991).

TABLE 20-4   Average Age at Retirement by Type of Retirement Plan,
1981–88

| Academic Year | Average Age of Retiring Faculty | | |
	Defined Benefit Plans Only	Defined Contribution Plans Only	Both Types of Plan
1981–82	62.7	65.1	63.2
1982–83	64.0	65.1	63.1
1983–84	62.8	65.4	62.7
1984–85	63.2	65.4	62.1
1985–86	62.6	65.3	62.5
1986–87	64.0	65.1	62.9
1987–88	62.4	65.6	62.9
Overall	63.1	65.3	62.7

Source: Lozier and Dooris, *Faculty Retirement Projections Beyond 1994*, p. 18.

Yet another reason that workers covered by defined contribution plans retire somewhat earlier than they might otherwise be expected to do so is related to Social Security. Social Security includes its own set of retirement incentives. It offers an income stream that is itself conditional on work reductions for most people who might work between the ages of 62 and 70. While Social Security has long had full actuarial reductions for people who retired prior to the normal retirement age of 65 under the program, it has not equally rewarded people who delayed retirement beyond that age. Retirement patterns under the program have

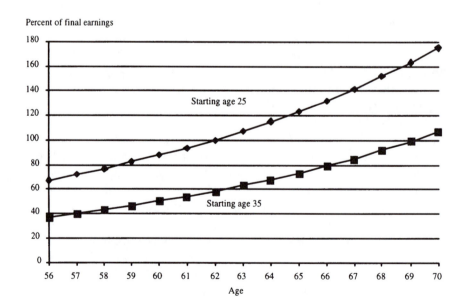

Figure 20-8. Potential replacement of final earnings under defined contribution plan with 12 percent annual contributions, starting at ages 25 and 35. Source: Watson Wyatt.

shown a strong tendency toward retirement at age 62 and 65, with most of the remaining retirements falling between those two ages.

On January 1, 1994, the special provisions that allowed academic institutions to mandate faculty retirements at age 70 expired. Concerned about their ability to get older faculty members to retire voluntarily in this new environment, a number of academic employers have implemented early retirement incentive programs to encourage older faculty members to retire voluntarily. In this regard, these institutions of higher learning were following a well-established pattern of providing such incentives in other sectors of the national economy, but the structure of their incentives was different because of the reliance on defined contribution plans in academic institutions. Typically, these plans offer to continue to pay for some period of time a share (often 100 percent) of the salary of faculty members meeting the age and service eligibility requirements.[47]

A number of studies have looked at changes introduced into employer-sponsored defined benefit plans over a period of years.[48] In general, these studies have found that the early retirement incentives in these plans were broadly strengthened during the late 1960s and throughout the 1970s. A couple of theories have been proposed to explain why employers would have begun to provide stronger financial incentives encouraging early retirement during this period. One is that the baby boom generation entering the work force provided employers with an ample supply of workers who generally were paid less than older workers but who could often easily be substituted for them. One way of getting these older, more expensive workers to relinquish their jobs was to persuade them to retire voluntarily, and the early retirement incentives were thought to help accomplish that end. Another theory is that the limitations on mandatory retirement made it more difficult for employers to systematically retire older workers and that the early retirement incentives grew up as a substitute for the outlawed retirement requirements that many employers had utilized. Certainly, the demand for early retirement on the part of workers, as discussed in Chapter 1, should not be overlooked in considering this phenomenon.

Whatever the reason that moved employers to provide earlier retirement incentives in their defined benefit plans, a significant change in the participation of the targets of those incentives corresponded with their availability. For example, Richard Ippolito notes that the labor force participation rates of men between the ages of 55 and 64 had held relatively steady for the 15 years prior to 1970, dropping from 86.4 percent to 83.0 percent. But by 1980 they had fallen to 72.1 percent and by 1985, to 67.9 percent. Ippolito concluded that part of the decline in the labor force participation of men prior to age 65 was attributable to significant increases

[47]For example, see Judy Greenwold, "Stanford Offers Early Retirement Bonus," *Business Insurance*, May 9, 1994, p. 6, describing a two-year salary continuation program for Stanford professors age 60 or older with at least 15 years of Stanford service who would voluntarily retire under the program.

[48]See, for example, D. Bell and W. Barclay, "Trends in Retirement Eligibility and Pension Benefits, 1974–1983," vol. 110, *Monthly Labor Review* (April 1987): pp. 18–25; Edward Lazear, "Pensions as Severance Pay," in Zvi Bodie and John B. Shoven, eds., *Financial Aspects of the United States Pension System* (Chicago: University of Chicago Press, 1983), pp. 57–89; and Olivia S. Mitchell and Rebecca A. Luzadis, "Changes in Pension Incentives Through Time," *Industrial and Labor Relations Review*, vol. 42, no. 1 (1988): pp. 100–108.

in Social Security benefits, but that pension rule changes could also be responsible for the move toward earlier retirements.[49]

When an employer provides a subsidy to a worker for retiring at a given point in time, it implies that the worker will suffer a penalty—that is, lose the subsidy—for working beyond that point in time. Empirical studies of the behavioral responses to retirement incentives embedded in pension programs have been generally consistent in finding that these incentives are effective in encouraging retirement.[50] One particularly interesting approach to analyzing retirement behavior under defined benefit plans has been developed by Robin Lumsdaine, James Stock, and David Wise. In their model they postulate that an employee compares the expected present value of retiring currently with the value of retiring at future ages. They call the maximum of the expected values of retirement at future ages minus the expected value of retiring currently the "option value" of delaying retirement. If the option value is positive, the worker does not retire; if it is negative, he or she does. They estimated this model using data from a large corporate employer for a period prior to the company's offer of an early retirement window. They then used the results of their estimates to predict the response to the early retirement incentive program, and did so fairly effectively.[51]

More recently the same authors used the option value model to assess the interaction between pension incentives, Social Security, and retiree health benefits on retirement. They concluded that the changes in the 1983 Social Security Amendments raising the normal retirement age to 67 after the turn of the century and increasing the benefit of delaying retirement will have only a modest effect on retirement behavior. They estimated that increasing the early retirement age from 55 to 60 in the firm they analyzed, however, would reduce cumulative retirements by age 59 from 29 to 4 percent. Further, they estimated that if the early retirement age in the firm were coordinated with Social Security's early retirement age and if normal retirement ages in both plans were raised to 67, that cumulative retirements by age 61 would be reduced from the current 51 percent to 8 percent, and that cumulative departure rates at 65 would be reduced from 86 percent to 64 percent.[52]

The evidence suggests that the structure and generosity of employer-sponsored retirement programs are important in determining the retirement patterns of

[49]Richard A. Ippolito, "Toward Explaining Earlier Retirement after 1970," *Industrial and Labor Relations Review*, vol. 43, no. 5 (July 1990): pp. 556–69.

[50]In addition to some of the research cited earlier throughout this chapter, see, Richard V. Burkhauser, "The Pension Acceptance Decision of Older Workers," *Journal of Human Resources*, vol. 14, no. 1 (1979): pp. 63–75; Roger H. Gordon and Alan S. Blinder, "Market Wages, Reservation Wages, and Retirement Decisions," *Journal of Public Economics*, vol. 14 (October 1980): pp. 277–308; Joseph F. Quinn, "Microeconomic Determinants of Early Retirement: A Cross-Sectional View of White Married Men," *Journal of Human Resources*, vol. 12 (Summer 1977): pp. 329–46; and Rebecca A. Luzadis and Olivia S. Mitchell, "Explaining Pension Dynamics," *Journal of Human Resources*, vol. 26, no. 4 (1991): pp. 679–703.

[51]Robin L. Lumsdaine, James H. Stock, and David A. Wise, "Three Models of Retirement, Computational Complexity versus Predictive Validity," in David A. Wise ed., *Topics in the Economics of Aging* (Chicago: University of Chicago Press, 1992), pp. 21–57.

[52]Robin L. Lumsdaine, James H. Stock, and David A. Wise, "Retirement Incentives: The Interaction Between Employer-Provided Pensions, Social Security, and Retiree Health Benefits," NBER Working Paper, no. 4613 (Cambridge, Mass.: National Bureau of Economic Research, January 1994).

plan participants. The desirability of any particular retirement pattern depends on the nature of the activities in which the plan sponsor engages. Some employers might be able to operate efficiently with workers who stay at their job well beyond age 60 or 65. Others might find that the ability of older workers to stay abreast of changing technology requirements or the physical demands of certain jobs dictate that retirement should occur at or before age 60. In any event, a carefully crafted retirement program can help to meet the needs of both the employer and workers participating in it.

Chapter 21
Adjustment of Retirement Benefits for Inflation and Productivity Gains

Inflation of consumer prices is a persistent phenomenon in most market economies, certainly in the United States. The cost of living, as measured by the consumer price index, has increased in 64 of the last 80 years in this country. Over this period, the annual increase in the CPI has averaged 3.4 percent per year. Over the last 20 years, the CPI growth rate has averaged 6.1 percent per year. The persistence of inflation in modern times has focused attention on the need to protect retirement benefits against the loss of purchasing power.

There are two areas of concern about the erosive effects of inflation. The first is protecting the value of the accruing benefit during the worker's career. For workers who terminate a job some years prior to retirement eligibility and receive a benefit at retirement based on a salary paid many years earlier, this is a particular problem. The other concern is protecting the purchasing power of benefits during retirement. Some policy makers and analysts believe both issues need to be addressed.

The Inflation Problem and Retirement Benefits

Retirement benefits may accrue over a period of 40 to 45 years and may be paid out for another 30 years or more. In a period of steadily rising prices, benefits may lose much of their purchasing power between the time they are earned and the time when final payments are made to retired employees or their beneficiaries. Even at 2 percent inflation, a fixed nominal annuity will lose 45 percent of its annual purchasing power over a 30-year period.

Concurrently, improvements in technology and production processes usually create productivity gains that enhance the standard of living of the working population through wage levels that increase more rapidly than prices. In some years, prices rise faster than wages, but most economists expect that the historic relationship between these two economic variables will prevail in the long run. In the absence of a special adjustment feature, retired individuals do not share in the productivity gains that are realized after their retirement, except through the impact of such gains on consumer prices. Thus, during their retirement years, retirees' standard of living generally declines in relation to that of the working age population.

Some observers believe that the retired population should share fully in the productivity gains in the economy, in addition to having their pension benefits protected against the ravages of inflation. In other words, retired individuals should be able to improve their standard of living over their retirement. Other observers would settle for provisions or procedures to preserve the relative standard of living of a pensioner as it existed at the time of retirement. This approach would limit adjustments in postretirement benefits to those associated with cost-of-living changes.

Many, if not most, plan sponsors reject the proposition that the purchasing power of their pension plan benefits should be fully preserved, and possibly enhanced through productivity gains, on the grounds that the inflationary threat to the benefits of retired people comes from governmental fiscal and monetary policies that are the underlying causes of inflation, and thus the solution must come from the public sector. On strictly pragmatic grounds, most plan sponsors believe that they could not afford to preserve the purchasing power of their pension plans.

A number of approaches have been developed to protect against the loss of purchasing power; some have the further objective of making it possible for the retired population to share in the productivity gains that would normally benefit only active employees. These approaches may pertain to either the accruing benefits of active participants or to the benefit payments to retired employees or their beneficiaries.

Protection of Accruing Benefits in Defined Benefit Plans

Final Average Salary Formula

A common and reasonably effective approach to protecting the purchasing power of accruing pension benefits under defined benefit plans is to compute the benefits at retirement on the basis of the employee's average annual compensation over the last few years immediately preceding retirement. The shorter the averaging period, the closer the benefits will reflect the employee's earnings status at the point of retirement. Earnings are seldom averaged over a period longer than 10 years, the modal period being 5 years. Some plans are using a 3- or 4-year average. Some public employee retirement systems base benefits on the earnings for the last year of employment, and a few use the earnings on the last day of employment.[1]

Earnings tend to reflect inflationary forces, usually with some lag. Hence a final average salary formula usually produces a pension benefit that is protected against the erosive effects of inflation *up to the point of retirement.* Moreover, to the extent that wages embody realized productivity gains, the employee's pension will likewise be enriched by this component up to retirement. However, this approach provides no protection against the loss of purchasing power that may occur during retirement. Nor does it channel to retired employees any part of the productivity gains that may have emerged after their retirement. Hence this approach needs to be supplemented by some other method to provide reasonably effective protection against inflation for the employee's total period of participation.

---

[1]Those systems that base benefits on the earnings of the last year of employment may include overtime and unused sick leave.

Ad Hoc Adjustments of Salary Base or Flat Benefit Accruals

A second approach to protecting the accruing benefits of active participants under defined benefit plans is to make ad hoc adjustments in the salary base of a career average formula plan or the benefit accruals of a plan that provides a specified dollar benefit for each year of credited service. The chief characteristic of this approach is that the employer or other plan sponsor is not committed in advance to making adjustments in the accrued benefits. The sponsor observes the trend of events and then makes whatever modifications tht seem justified. To the extent that the compensation levels or the flat dollar derivatives reflect productivity gains in the economy, this approach is consistent with the twin objectives of protecting purchasing power and enhancing the standard of living.

The underlying premise of a career average formula is that the benefit accrual for any particular year of service will be based on the employee's actual compensation in that year, rather than on the average salary for the last few years of employment. The main reason that an employer chooses a career average formula instead of a final average salary formula is to avoid making a benefit commitment in terms of an unknown future salary base. Yet when wages are rising sharply in response to inflationary pressures, benefits based on the earnings of previous years become hopelessly out of date, especially in cases where a long earnings history is used.[2] The longer the service of the employee the worse the predicament, a result that cannot be reconciled with sound personnel and social policy. A solution to the problem that does not involve a future commitment of indeterminate magnitude is to amend the plan to recompute all benefits for service prior to that date based on the compensation levels in effect at that time or on some stipulated basis that represents an updating of the salary. This is analogous to granting past service benefits at the inception of the plan on the basis of the compensation levels then in effect. This procedure may be repeated as often as conditions seem to warrant. If the salary base is updated systematically, the benefit (and cost) results could approach those of the final average formula, but without the advance commitment.

The same principle is involved in updating the benefit accruals of a flat benefit plan. This type of plan is generally subject to collective bargaining, and any change in the benefit accruals would tend to result from the collective bargaining process. The updating may take the form of an upward adjustment in the yearly benefit accruals for future years of service or an adjustment in the benefit accruals for all years of credited service, past and future. Periodic retroactive adjustments in the flat dollar benefit accruals may approximate the results obtained through the use of a final average formula, again without the advance commitment. Each ad hoc adjustment involves a formal plan amendment, an administrative inconvenience avoided by the final average formula approach.

---

[2]For example, if the compensation of a plan participant were to increase at an annual compounded rate of 3 percent, a modest assumption by today's standard, over a covered period of 35 years a pension benefit based on career average earnings would be only 67 percent of that based on a 5-year final average formula and only 65 percent of that based on a 3-year final average formula. If the compounded rate of salary increase were 5 percent, the respective percentages would be 54 and 52 percent.

Automatic Index Adjustments

The benefit accruals of active participants in defined benefit plans may be automatically adjusted in accordance with changes in a specified price or wage index. Thus far, plans using this approach have designated the CPI of the Bureau of Labor Statistics as the measuring rod; but an appropriately constructed wage index could serve equally well, although it would produce different results.[3] Beginning in January 1978 the Bureau of Labor Statistics established two new CPIs: the CPI for all urban consumers (designated CPI-U) and a revised CPI for urban wage earners and clerical workers (revised CPI-W). Both new CPIs tie into the value of the old CPI (unrevised CPI-W), which was discontinued after June of 1978. Plans now need to designate which CPI is intended. Adjustments based on the CPI would be designed to protect accruing pensions only against a loss of purchasing power, while wage index adjustments would have the additional purpose of reflecting productivity gains.

When a plan provides for index adjustments before retirement, the benefit that accrues during any particular year of service is adjusted at retirement to reflect the changes that have taken place in the specified index since the benefit was credited. For example, the benefit that accrued when a participant was age 35 would be adjusted to reflect the net cumulative change in the index over the next 30 years. The benefit accrual for the following year would be adjusted for the index movement over the next 29 years and so on. The percentage adjustment for each year of the intervening period may be limited.

The index adjustment technique is primarily designed for defined benefit plans that provide a flat dollar benefit for each year of service or a benefit based on career average compensation. It may also be used with a final average formula to adjust the compensation for the years entering into the defined salary base. For example, if the plan formula bases benefits on the average earnings of the last 5 years of employment, the participant's actual compensation for the fifth, fourth, third, and second years prior to retirement would be adjusted to reflect the changes in the index from those years to the date of retirement. No change would be made in the compensation for the year in which retirement occurs. This procedure makes it possible to base the benefits of a retiring employee on compensation immediately prior to retirement, if there were no merit increases during the preceding 5 years, without the risk of salary manipulation that would be present if benefits were expressed in terms of the individual's actual compensation during his or her final year of employment. This type of adjustment would be especially advantageous to a participant in a plan that bases benefits on average compensation during the last 10 years of employment or the average compensation during the 5 consecutive years of highest earnings, wherever they happened to fall. In the latter case, of

---

[3]In 1977 the Social Security Act was amended to provide for the indexing of wages (and the earnings of self-employed persons) in the calculation of an individual's average monthly earnings. The wages or earnings of an individual for any particular year are multiplied by a factor reflecting the percentage increase in average covered earnings for all covered persons from that year to the year of entitlement. The average monthly earnings of an individual adjusted in that manner is called the average *indexed* monthly earnings.

course, the earnings of each of the 5 years would be adjusted by the appropriate index factors to the year of retirement.

Annual increases in the accrued benefits of active participants on the order of 3 percent would elevate the long-run cost of the plan by about 75 percent, not counting the cost of adjusting benefits after retirement. These adjustments would be in lieu of ad hoc updating of past benefit accruals that would have about the same cost consequences.

Linkage of Benefits to Asset Values

A fourth approach to protecting the accruing benefits of active participants and giving retirees an opportunity to share in the productivity gains of the economy is to provide a direct linkage between the dollar value of the benefit accruals and the market value of the assets accumulated to pay the benefits. All defined contribution plans, as well as some defined benefit plans, use this approach. The composition of the asset portfolio is immaterial to the concept. It may be composed entirely of equities (e.g., common stocks and real estate), entirely of fixed-income instruments (e.g., bonds and mortgages), or of a combination of equity and debt instruments (i.e., a so-called balanced fund). For this approach to meet its objectives, however, the market value of the assets must over time keep pace with increases in the cost of living (and the standard of living), and the participants must be permitted to share fully and directly in the growth of the asset values. But for many plans that link benefits to investment performance, the objective is to credit the participant with the total rate of return on the portfolio investments, whether it be more or less than the rate of inflation.

Asset Portfolio(s)

Economists and investment experts disagree about what type of asset portfolio is most likely to provide a hedge against inflation and pass along productivity gains. Indeed, there is no certainty that any type of portfolio can meet that test in all situations. Until recent years, it was generally believed that the total investment return (dividend income, net realized capital gains, and net unrealized capital appreciation) on a wisely selected portfolio of common stocks would over time be at least equal to the rate of growth in consumer prices over the same period.[4] In fact, since capital's share of productivity gains should be reflected in the price of common stock, the long-term growth of common stock values should be greater than the rise in consumer prices. A risk premium in the common stock return would increase the differential.

---

[4]This view was expounded by Dr. William C. Greenough in a book entitled *A New Approach to Retirement Income* (New York: Teachers Insurance and Annuity Association, 1952). Dr. Greenough, who later became chairman of the board of TIAA-CREF, studied the relationship between common stock prices and the consumer price level over the period 1880 to 1950. This study showed that over long periods the market value of a representative group of common stocks conformed faithfully to changes in the consumer price level. He did find periods of several years' duration when these two variables moved in opposite directions. He therefore recommend the use of both equity and fixed-income investments in any pension plan that links benefits to investment performance.

Uncertainty over the long-term performance of common stock had led some observers to espouse the use of a portfolio of marketable bonds and other fixed-income securities.[5] The presumption behind such a proposal is that market yields on bonds will reflect the inflationary expectations of investors and thus will serve as a reasonably satisfactory hedge against inflation, without the greater risks believed to be associated with common stock investments. The market value of a bond portfolio would, of course, move inversely to changes in the level of interest rates (i.e., falling when interest rates rise and rising when interest rates fall), thus influencing the total rate of return on the portfolio. The total rate of return might go down during an inflationary period and go up during a deflationary period—the exact opposite of the desired results. A fund invested in money market debt instruments would tend to reflect inflation, but the rate of return might or might not be satisfactory in the long run.

In view of the uncertain relationship between consumer price behavior and the total rate of return on different types of asset portfolios, many experts recommend the use of a balanced portfolio, or, alternatively, an appropriate distribution of assets between two different portfolios, one invested wholly in equities and the other entirely in long-term fixed-income instruments. A balanced portfolio has the capability of smoothing or moderating the short-term fluctuations in the equity component and stabilizing the long-term results by combining negatively correlated returns on the two components of the portfolio. In other words, the return on the equity component should in theory be high when the yield on the fixed-income component is low and vice versa. During many periods over the last hundred years, the consumer price level and common stock prices moved in opposite directions, and the undesirable consequences of this configuration of prices are greatly moderated by a substantial component of fixed-income investments. The same moderating influence would be operative if consumer prices and bond yields should move in opposite directions or in the same direction at different rates.

Participation Mechanism

The process by which the individual participants share in the total return on the investment portfolio or portfolios differs from plan to plan. In all cases, however, the investment experience of the plan is reflected fully and directly in the individual account balances of the participants or, under some plans, in the accumulated benefit accruals. The accounts of the participants may be kept in dollars or, because of the greater convenience in accounting for changes in the market value of the plan assets, in "units." In the case of unit accounting, the value of the "unit" at the time of valuation of the participants' stake in the plan is determined by dividing the market value of the portfolio assets by the aggregate number of units credited to the accounts of participants. The unit may be valued monthly or daily. The value of the unit must be recomputed as of each date on which additional units are purchased or existing units are cashed out or converted into annuities. At

---

[5]Marketable bonds would probably have to be used to avoid the problem of valuing directly placed securities and real estate mortgages, which would not have a readily ascertainable market value. Avoidance of the latter instruments would undoubtedly reduce the overall yield on the portfolio.

retirement, participants may be given the option of taking their pensions in the form of a conventional fixed-income annuity or an annuity whose income varies with the investment performance of an associated asset portfolio.

Under a defined contribution plan, *contributions* are converted into units, whereas, under a defined benefit plan, the accruing *bene*fits are converted into units. The conversion of defined benefit accruals into units may be accomplished in two ways. Under one procedure, the actuarial present value of the benefit accruing for an individual participant in a given year is divided by the current value of an accumulation unit. For example, if a participant is credited with a benefit of $10 a month payable at age 65, the then actuarial value of that $10 benefit accrual is divided by the value of an accumulation unit, and the result is the number of accumulation units to be credited to the participant. At the same time, a sum of money equal to the actuarial value of the original benefit accrual will be paid to the plan and credited to the participant. The plan then operates on a defined contribution principle with respect to that benefit accrual and any later benefit accruals so converted and funded. With each year of service, the participant will be credited with additional accumulation units, whose total value at any time is the product of the number of units times the value of the unit computed in the conventional manner. At retirement, the total dollar value of the aggregate accumulation units can be converted into variable annuity units or a fixed-income annuity, depending upon the terms of the plan.

Protection of Accruing Benefits in Defined Contribution Plans

Twenty or more years ago, the majority of defined contribution plans were traditional money purchase or profit-sharing plans. The assets held by these plans fell into two broad categories. In many profit-sharing plans the plan sponsor provided shares of its own stock to fund the promised benefits. In the typical money purchase plan and some profit-sharing plans, the assets in the plan were managed by a life insurance company, a bank trust department, or other professional investment manager. The funding instruments in this latter group of plans were generally individual or group annuity contracts of a life insurance company, trust agreements with banks, trust companies, or individual trustees, or shares in a mutual fund. While the plans provided periodic updates of the individual's accrued benefits in the plan, in most instances the assets were invested and managed through arrangements dictated by the plan sponsor.

With the establishment of section 401(k) and section 403(b) plans, which became so prevalent during the 1980s, employee contributions to defined contribution plans took on a greater role in their funding. This factor, coupled with the immediate vesting schedules typical in these plans, created a much greater sense of individual ownership of the assets in the plan than had prevailed under the earlier traditional defined contribution plans. Because of the growing sense of individual ownership, plan sponsors gave plan participants more direct control over the investment of plan assets.

The growth of the self-directed investment of defined contribution assets resulted in the issuance in October 1992 of final regulations relating to section 404(c) under the Employment Retirement Income Security Act. These set forth conditions that must be satisfied if employers are to limit their fiduciary responsibility in participant-directed individual account plans. The regulations provide general rules concerning the characteristics of investment options that would have to be offered to participants if plan fiduciaries are to be relieved of certain fiduciary responsibilities related to participants' investment choices. The regulations require that participants be able to choose from at least three diversified investment options. Profit-making entities cannot count company stock as one of the three investment choices. Under the regulations, if a participant exercises independent control over the assets in his or her account, then no plan fiduciary is liable for any losses that occur because of choices made by the participant.

The potential problem that has arisen as defined contribution plan participants have taken over the management of their qualified plan assets is that they may not be managing them as effectively as professional managers would. For example, a 1992 survey of larger employers sponsoring section 401(k) plans found that over half of the assets of these plans are invested in guaranteed insurance contracts and one-quarter are invested in employer stock.[6] The importance of employer stock as an investment option is due in part to employee choice, but the more significant factor may be the number of plans with a provision requiring that employer-matching contributions be invested in company stock. Over one-quarter of the plans in the survey provide only one type of investment option for employer-matching contributions and, for most, it is company stock.

The problem with the concentrated investment in GICs or other low-yielding investments is that the assets laid aside for retirement purposes generate low, if any, real returns. Over time, the potential economic horsepower of defined contribution plans can only be realized if the assets are generating significant returns above the underlying rate of inflation in the economy. The problem that workers face with significant investment in company stock is that it directly links their retirement security to their job security. In many cases, factors leading to the job insecurity and job loss also adversely affect the value of an employer's stock. Forcing workers to invest in their employers' stock does not allow them to diversify their economic risks.

Many investment advisers and financial planners helping individuals plan for retirement caution against precisely the investment pattern that is often seen for assets in defined contribution plans, that is, investing a large part of savings in typically lower-yielding investments like GICs. For plan participants hoping to use the assets in their defined contribution plans to provide a significant part of their retirement income, a higher level of investment in indexed equity and growth funds than GICs over an extended period of years is required to provide a more satisfactory level of retirement income.

The Dilemma of Early Leavers

Terminated Vested Benefits in Defined Benefit Plans

Loss of Benefit Formula Adjustments

There are many ways that defined benefit formulas can provide inflation protection for the accruing benefits of workers who spend most of their careers with the

---

[6]Watson Wyatt, "Investing for the Future in Defined Contribution Plans," *Wyatt COMPARISON* (Washington, D.C.: May 1993), pp. 13–18.

same company. For a worker whose career is broken into significant segments under different plans, however, the inflation protection is not so generous. Consider the case of a worker who begins her career job at age 25 at an annual salary of $25,000. Assume that this young woman will work to age 65 and receive nominal pay increases of 5 percent per year. Assume further that this woman's employers and all other employers for whom she might work sponsor defined benefit plans that pay a benefit equal to 1 percent of final annual pay under the plan for each year of coverage.

In this case, the woman's final earnings for her last year of employment would be $175,999.72. If she works all 40 years for one employer, her annual pension will be $70,399.89 (i.e., 40 years × 1 percent per year × final pay). If, on the other hand, she works for 20 years for her first employer and then works the final 20 years for another employer, her pension at age 65 will be only $48,466.43 per year or 55.6 percent of what it would be if she works her whole career for one employer. The reason the pension is reduced in this case is that half her pension is based on her final salary in her original job, which she left as she was turning age 45. Under the assumptions we set, that final salary would have been $66,332.44, not the $175,999.72 that was her ultimate terminal salary.

Considerations on Sharing Productivity Gains

Under the typical defined benefit plan, benefits are not indexed between the termination and commencement of retirement benefits. While wage growth provides indexing protection for workers who stay under the typical defined benefit plan up until retirement, providing similar protection for workers who terminate prior to retirement eligibility would significantly increase the cost of these plans. Indeed, one of the attractions of defined benefit plans for employers is that they include financial incentives that discourage turnover.

Tying retirement benefits to earnings immediately before retirement rewards workers for productivity increases related to their period of employment under the plan. From the perspective of a plan sponsor, indexing benefits for early leavers would be passing on the benefit of productivity increases to a group of individuals who did not contribute to the increases. Paying a higher lifetime benefit to the early leavers would come at the expense of reduced lifetime benefits for the long-tenured career employee.

Public Policy Considerations Regarding Retirement Income Security

Policy makers have granted pensions their preferential tax treatment in order to help provide retirement income security to workers through the private provision of retirement benefits. In the public policy context of providing retirement income security, the fact that some workers are more mobile during their careers than others does not justify their getting less generous "publicly subsidized" retirement benefits.

Concerns about the portability of pension benefits have increased in recent years partly because of the improved vesting provisions legislated since the passage of ERISA, especially under the Tax Reform Act of 1986. With all defined benefit plan participants now vesting with 5 years of covered service or less, in comparison with the 10 years common before TRA86 or even before the enactment of ERISA, many more workers are qualifying for and benefiting from terminated vested benefits. As more workers have benefited, there has been a growing awareness of the temporarily declining value of terminated vested benefits leading up to retirement eligibility. The growth in vesting coupled with the broadly held perception that workers are more mobile than earlier generations of workers has led some policy analysts to conclude that preserving the value of terminated vested benefits is of paramount importance.

Although public policy analysts have been concerned for some time about the problem of early leavers under defined benefit plans, they have been ineffective in devising public policies to ameliorate the problem. Given the significant variation in benefit formulas and other plan provisions, transferring credits and funding from one plan to another when workers change jobs is impossible. Until recently it seemed the only way to ensure that mobile workers would have the opportunity to accumulate equivalent tax-qualified retirement benefits as their more stable counterparts was to shift more and more plan accumulations into defined contribution plans. Now plan innovations among employers are beginning to change that.

RJR-Nabisco recently implemented a new form of defined benefit plan that may address the concerns about the accrual patterns and portability. The "pension equity plan" provides employees with a percentage of their final average salary for each year they work, expressed as a lump-sum amount.[7] The percentage accrued each year increases with age. The normal retirement benefit is the lump-sum amount derived by multiplying the sum of the percentages accrued over the worker's career by final average salary. At termination, the accumulated benefit can be cashed out, rolled into an individual retirement account, or used to purchase an annuity. The advantage of this type of plan is that short-term workers can earn more substantial benefits than they normally would. In fact, a worker who participated in such plans with several different employers over a span of a career would accumulate a benefit comparable to one who was covered by a single plan throughout a whole career. The characteristics of this plan and its portability are discussed in more detail in Chapter 13.

Rolling Over Preretirement Distributions

Although the typical defined benefit plan does not provide any compounding of benefits for early leavers between the termination of employment and retirement benefit eligibility, many large employers provide lump-sum distributions for workers when they terminate their employment. One 1993 survey of large employers found that among 440 plans where complete information was provided, 41.6 percent provided some lump-sum benefits, and 32.6 percent provided lump sums with no limit on the amount.[8] In addition, most defined contribution plans provide a lump-sum distribution option for covered workers terminating employment prior to retirement.

---

[7]Hillary Durgin, "RJR Modernizes Pension Plans," *Pensions & Investments*, September 28, 1992, p. 1.
[8]Watson Wyatt, *Wyatt COMPARISON: 1993 Statistical Supplement*, p. 36.

Nonretirement Leakages

One problem with preretirement distributions is that not all of them are rolled over into tax-preferred retirement accounts. If they are not rolled over, the lifetime accumulation of retirement benefits can be eroded significantly. Consider the case of a worker who begins a job on her 30th birthday earning $30,000 per year. Assume this worker participates in a defined contribution plan to which her employer annually contributes 5 percent of her pay on her behalf. Assume that her wages grow at an annual rate of 5 percent per year over her career, and that the accumulated balance in her plan earns an annual return of 4 percent per year. If she stays in her job until her 65th birthday, she will have accumulated $240,199 in her defined contribution plan at retirement, an amount equal to 1.52 times her final annual salary.

Now assume this woman stays in this first job only until her 40th birthday and then changes to a new job for the remainder of her career, where she is covered by an identical retirement plan and receives the same salary she would have earned if she stayed in the first job. In this case, she could take a sum of $22,744 out of the first employer's plan. If she rolls it over into another tax-qualified plan that earns her a 4 percent annual return, she will still end up at retirement with $240,199. If, on the other hand, she decides to take the $22,744 as regular income so she can buy a new car, or go on vacation, or the like, she will end up with an accumulation of only $179,568 in her retirement savings account. If she had stayed in the first job until age 45, she would have been able to take a cash distribution from her retirement savings plan of $42,532 when she changed jobs, but would only end up with $147,007 at retirement.

According to Internal Revenue Service tax filing information, in 1990 there were 10.8 million lump-sum distributions from tax-qualified plans. The total amount distributed in this fashion was $125.8 billion. By comparison, private pension plans paid $141.2 billion in annuity benefits in 1990. Of the 10.8 million lump-sum distributions in 1990, 8.2 million came from regular tax-qualified plans, while the remaining 2.6 million were from IRA accounts or simplified employer plans. The 8.2 million distributions from regular employer plans were down from 8.8 million in 1987, but the total amount distributed rose from $65.9 billion in 1987 to $107.2 billion in 1990.[9]

Some of the lump-sum distributions from tax-qualified retirement programs are paid to people who are actually retiring. The IRS data on lump-sum payments suggests that 39 percent of the distributions in 1990, encompassing 62 percent of the total funds distributed, went to people aged 59½ or older. While much of the lump-sum money is going to people eligible to retire, significant amounts are not.[10] Workers who cash these benefits out prematurely lose the benefit of the tax-deferred accumulation of earnings in their retirement accounts. Those who spend the money on immediate consumption lose all aspects of the retirement security the accumulations were meant to support in the first place.

---

[9]Paul Yakoboski, "Retirement Program Lump-Sum Distributions: Hundreds of Billions in Hidden Pension Income," *Issue Brief* (Washington, D.C.: Employee Benefit Research Institute, February 1994).

[10]Ibid.

Withholding Penalties

With the growth of defined contribution plans during the 1980s and of lump-sum distributions from defined benefit plans, policy makers became increasingly concerned about the premature distribution of tax-qualified retirement savings. To discourage these premature distributions, TRA86 established a 10 percent excise tax on premature distributions in addition to the regular income tax rates applied to them. Beginning in 1993, nonperiodic qualified plan distributions that were not directly transferred to another eligible retirement plan were subject to automatic 20 percent withholding taxes.

The growth in defined contribution plans has been partly a response to the greater perceived value that younger and more mobile workers place on a portable account balance. Mechanisms are available that can help mobile workers maintain the value of their benefits as they change jobs during their careers. But any early consumption of retirement savings will ultimately diminish the retirement income security that portable benefits can provide.

Protection of Annuity Payments During Payout Stage

While protecting the purchasing power of retirement benefits leading up to retirement is important, many policy analysts have been equally, if not more, concerned about maintaining the purchasing power of annuities during the period of retirement itself. On average, benefits will be paid to a retired participant for 15 years or more, and the purchasing power of the benefits can be seriously impaired by cost-of-living increases over such a long period. The recipient of an annuity that is fixed in nominal terms faces considerable uncertainty about future growth in price levels. In this regard, nominal annuities make real income levels uncertain during retirement.

In addition to the effects that general price inflation might have on retirees' absolute standard of living, technological changes may be enhancing the earnings and standards of living of the working population, eroding the relative economic status of the retired population. Some policy analysts advocate that the relative standard of living of retired participants should be maintained over time.

Other analysts suggest that not all retiree income deserves the benefit of full indexation. They hold that some basic level of benefits should be indexed because these benefits represent a basic standard of living that should be maintained for retirees. This line of reasoning suggests that benefits above this level, however, do not warrant indexation because inflationary effects on other members of society are not insured against the effects of inflation. Following this reasoning, Hastings Keith, a former Republican congressman from Massachusetts, argues that the full benefits provided to federal retirees should not be indexed. He argues that it is unfair for lower- and middle-class taxpayers whose earnings have not been protected against inflation in recent years to have to pay added taxes to support full federal annuity indexation for individuals who are getting much larger federal annuities, ranging up to more than $100,000 per year. He advocates that federal annuities up to the maximum Social Security benefit should be fully indexed, but that amounts above that level should not be indexed at all, or should be indexed at something less than the annual increase in the CPI.[11] Whether annuities are fully indexed or only partly indexed, some of the same techniques used to protect accruing benefits can be used to protect the benefit payments of retired individuals.

Linking Benefits to Asset Values

When benefit accruals have been linked to the value of an associated asset portfolio, it is a natural progression to continue the linkage into the retirement of the participants. As a matter of fact, the whole arrangement is usually set up in anticipation that the retirement benefits will be linked to the same asset portfolio that regulated the value of the benefits during the accrual stage. However, a participant reaching retirement may be given the option of converting asset-linked benefits to a conventional fixed-income annuity, and a participant in a conventional defined benefit plan may be given the option of taking retirement benefits in the form of an asset-linked annuity.

The potential advantage to a participant in a pension plan that links benefit accruals and payments to the performance of a portfolio of assets is that he or she is credited with the total investment earnings on the assets allocable to the account or benefits. This is true whether the plan operates on a defined contribution or defined benefit basis. Under a defined benefit plan, benefits are *increased* only if the actual investment return exceeds the assumed investment return (AIR). In any event, after the number of annuity units has been fixed, the participant receives the full investment earnings on the associated assets.

In many cases the employer's expectation (or, at least, hope) in setting up an asset-linked pension plan is that the total long-term investment return will at least equal the rate of increase in the consumer price level. If this expectation were to be realized, even over the long term, the asset-linked annuity would be a powerful force for protecting the purchasing power of an employee's pension benefits.

An equity portfolio holds out the possibility that capital's share of productivity gains in the economy may be passed along to the plan participants, thus enabling them to improve their standard of living in retirement. Common stock prices may also reflect a reward for risk-taking on the theory that equities embody a higher degree of investment risk than debt instruments. Thus, there is a chance that the total return on an equity-based portfolio will more than offset the rate of increase in the prices of consumer products and services. One disadvantage of an asset-linked pension plan is that the participant must assume the investment risk. In some years, the return on the invested assets has been less than the AIR, and the monthly benefits have dropped below the level originally contemplated.

The employer, on the other hand, may find an asset-linked pension plan advantageous, in that there will be less pressure from participants to provide cost-of-living supplements or other types of inflation hedges. This advantage will exist only if the arrangement proves to be reasonably effective in coping with inflationary price movements. Another advantage to the employer is that the plan sponsor is relieved of the investment risk. Employer contributions to the plan are not affected one way or the other by deviations of actual from assumed investment results. The

---

[11]William M. O'Reilly, *Federal Deficit Reduction and COLAs* (Washington, D.C.: National Commission on Public Employee Pension Systems, 1989), p. 3.

primary disadvantage of an asset-linked pension plan to an employer is the loss of contribution credit for excess investment earnings. Under a conventional fixed-annuity pension plan, the employer takes credit against future contributions for the excess investment earnings over the rate used in the actuarial calculations. This can be a potent cost-reducing factor, as will be apparent from a later discussion of cost factors. The plan sponsor sacrifices this source of cost savings for the asset-linked component of a pension plan.

This feature of the plan will not be an unmitigated disadvantage to the employer if it eliminates or reduces the need to provide cost-of-living supplements, the burden of which is almost always borne by the employer. As a matter of fact, in plans without automatic adjustments many employers expect to finance cost-of-living supplements out of inflation-induced excess investment earnings. It may be a matter of indifference to the employer whether the cost of benefit adjustments due to inflation are met through ad hoc adjustments in the benefits of retired employees, added sponsor contributions, or the advanced allocation of all investment earnings to the individual accounts of the plan participants, as exemplified by the asset-linked approach.

A potential disadvantage of the asset-linked approach is employee disenchantment with the performance of the investment portfolio. Since the employer sponsored the plan and selected the investment manager, he or she will have to take a large degree of responsibility for the outcome. When investment experience is poor, a certain amount of employee ill will may be inevitable. This had led a number of employers to abandon variable annuity plans and make up the previous losses suffered by participants.

Some policy analysts, realizing the variation in the risk and return characteristics of certain investment strategies to underwrite variable annuities, have sought to identify specific investment strategies that would minimize the likelihood of adverse investment experience yet provide a real return on retirement assets to allow some indexation of benefits. One such analysis, by Zvi Bodie and James Pesando, evaluated variable annuities backed by Treasury bills, long-term bonds, common stocks, and a mixed portfolio of investments. Their analysis concluded that Treasury bills or equivalents would provide the most stable real retirement incomes.[12] The problem with investing a retirement portfolio in T-bills is that the stability of the investment return is attained at the expense of a very low real rate of return.

Some policy analysts have gone so far as to suggest that the federal government should create a series of bonds with returns and principal indexed to inflation. These investment instruments would be made available to private individuals or retirement plans to underwrite real annuity payments.[13] The essence of such bonds would be to more fully transfer the risk of uncertain inflation to taxpayers. From an investment perspective, such bonds would pay an extremely low real return over time and would not be a suitable investment for plan sponsors seeking higher risk-related returns on their retirement portfolios.

---

[12]Zvi Bodie and James E. Pesando, "Retirement Annuity Design in an Inflationary Climate," and Franco Modigliani, "Comment," both in Zvi Bodie and John B. Shoven, eds., *Financial Aspects of the United States Pension System* (Chicago: University of Chicago Press, 1983), pp. 291–316.

[13]Susan M. Wachter, *Inflation and Pensions* (Homewood, Ill.: Richard D. Irwin, Inc., 1987), p. 340.

Automatic Cost-of-Living Adjustments

The most direct and responsive method of adjusting the pension benefits of retired persons to changes in the price level is to stipulate in the plan that benefits will be modified in accordance with a prescribed procedure to reflect variations in a specified index of consumer prices. Thus far, plans adopting this approach have designated the consumer price index as the measuring rod, but some advocate constructing a more specialized index that would show changes in the prices of items affecting the budget of retired persons. However, a 1982 study by the General Accounting Office concluded that "existing indexes would have provided a reasonable indicator of the impact of inflation on retirees."[14] Some argue that the CPI-U is more appropriate than the CPI-W, since the CPI-U includes retirees in its underlying data, while the CPI-W is based solely upon active workers.

The prescribed procedure may provide for both upward and downward adjustments, but the principal plans using the approach provide only for upward adjustments. An adjustment is made only when the change (increase) in the CPI over the base period exceeds a specified percentage. For example, the plan may provide that benefits will be adjusted upward on a specified date, such as June 1, if during the preceding calendar year the CPI increased by 3 percent or more, the adjustment in plan benefits being for the full amount of the CPI increase, rounded to the nearest 0.1 percent.

The benefits of the Social Security program are subject to adjustment on the basis of changes in the CPI from the third quarter of one calendar year to the third quarter of the succeeding calendar year. More precisely, the adjustment in benefits is based upon the change in the arithmetic average of the CPI for each third quarter of the two calendar years involved. Benefits are adjusted effective on December 1 of the year in question. The benefits of the Railroad Retirement System are subject to cost-of-living increases in accordance with the Social Security formula.

More than half of the states provide for automatic cost-of-living increases for some or all of their public retirement systems. They all use changes in the national CPI as the basis for benefit adjustments, except California, which uses the average of the CPI for the Los Angeles–Long Beach area and the San Francisco–Oakland area. The Commonwealth of Puerto Rico uses the CPI for the San Juan metropolitan area. The retirement plans of New York City and certain other municipalities tie the benefits of retired employees to the CPI. Few businesses provide for automatic adjustment of benefits on the basis of changes in the CPI.

A plan may limit the amount of benefit increases on any one adjustment date. The limit is usually 3 to 5 percent. Plans that revise benefits downward make such adjustments only if the CPI falls substantially below the base, namely, 10 percent below. As with ad hoc adjustments, these automatic increases (or decreases) may apply to all benefits that are being paid out, including death and disability benefits.

As its name implies, a cost-of-living adjustment is designed only to protect the purchasing power of the benefits payable under the plan. It does not attempt to provide the retired employees a stake in the expanding economy. Nevertheless, it

---

[14]General Accounting Office, "A CPI for Retirees Is Not Needed Now but Could Be in the Future," GAO/GGD-82-41 (Washington, D.C.: USGPO, 1982).

can be a very costly feature of a pension plan. If it produces annual increases in the benefits of retired employees at the compounded rate of 3 percent, for example, the long-run cost of the plan may be increased by about 25 to 30 percent. The cost would be commensurately higher if the benefit adjustments were greater than 3 percent per year.

Formula Escalation Factor

A technique sometimes used to provide at least partial protection against the loss of pension purchasing power is a formula escalation factor. Under this approach, the plan stipulates that the benefits of all retired individuals will be automatically adjusted upward each year by a specified percentage, such as 2 or 3 percent. Such an escalator is built into the formula in anticipation of future price increases, but the percentage adjustment is automatic and not linked to any cost-of-living index. This approach avoids the complexity of the index adjustment and limits the obligation of the employer to predetermined benefit increases. Moreover, the annual percentage increase normally applies to the original retirement benefit, rather than to the augmented benefits. This, of course, avoids the compounding effect of the index-related adjustments, reducing the cost somewhat.

A number of states use the fixed escalator approach, some requiring the employees to share the cost of the escalator with the employer. The approach is also used to a limited extent in the plans of private employers. Under one type of arrangement, the retiring participant is permitted to elect, at his or her own expense, an annuity option with a fixed annual increase factor. The pension benefit that the participant would otherwise receive is actuarially reduced and then grows each year at the compound rate selected. For example, a male participant retiring at age 65 with a regular pension of $400 per month would start with a monthly benefit of $270.40 if he elected a 5 percent annual increase. By the ninth year of retirement, his benefit would have grown to its original amount and would continue to grow at a compound rate of 5 percent. If the same participant had elected a 3 percent growth factor, his initial pension would be $319.20, and it would regain its original level within eight years. Where such an election is allowed, most employees elect an unreduced level annuity.

Ad Hoc Adjustments

Another approach to protecting the purchasing power of benefits in a pay status is ad hoc adjustments. The ad hoc adjustment of benefits of retired employees has become a common practice among plans with no other method of preserving the purchasing power of benefit payments. Many plans have increased the benefits of retired employees every two or three years, and the amount of the increase is sometimes keyed to changes in the CPI since the date of the last adjustment (or the date of retirement). If several years have elapsed, there may be a series of percentage changes, the percentages varying with the number of years since the employees have retired. If these periodic adjustments reflect the appropriate changes in the CPI, and the benefits were computed originally on the basis of final average compensation, the retired employees enjoy reasonably effective protection against inflation, even though they have no formal assurance that the employer will continue to keep the benefits in line with cost-of-living increases. The protection is not fully effective because of the time lag in the adjustments, which tends to be greater than that under automatic adjustment techniques. Because of cost considerations, most such ad hoc adjustments have been less than the CPI increase.

Some plans apply these periodic adjustments to the vested benefits of terminated employees, but the practice is not at all common. If the plan provides disability and survivor income benefits, the periodic adjustments may be made applicable to these benefits as well. There is no reason, in theory, why the adjustments should not apply to all benefits in process of payment.

During periodic declines in common stock prices over the last several years, some plans with asset-linked benefits have provided temporary benefit supplements on an ad hoc basis. The supplements have been roughly equal to the decline in benefits.

Supplementation Contingent on Actuarial Gains

Another method of augmenting benefits, largely confined to the public sector, is to provide annual or periodic supplements from actuarial gains, primarily excess investment earnings. This method has been applied primarily to defined contribution pension plans under which it is customary for the governing statute to specify the interest rate to be credited to employer and employee contributions and is to be used in converting accumulated funds into annuity benefits. The rate is usually set at a conservatively low level, so that high-quality portfolio management is likely to produce earnings in excess of the statutory interest assumption. This excess provides a source of funds that can be used for a number of purposes, including supplements for retired employees. The supplements may be payable for life or for one year at a time. In most state employee retirement systems employing this strategy, the actuarial gains are used to provide an additional benefit payment for the year in question, the supplement sometimes being termed the "thirteenth benefit check."

The strength of this method is its flexibility. No advance commitments are made and supplements are granted on the basis of realized experience. The supplementation method has a number of disadvantages: It is not easily understood by the participants; it offers no assurance about the size of future supplements; and a portion of the funds for the supplements comes from investment earnings on the contributions of the active employees, which it can be argued, should be credited to their individual accounts.[15] Active employees might also argue with some validity that the excess earnings of the employer contributions should be applied to the liquidation of unfunded actuarial liabilities (for past service benefit credits or retroactive benefit liberalizations). Finally, the ERISA requirement that the plan actuary use "best-estimate" actuarial assumptions may reduce actuarial gains for plans subject to its jurisdiction.

[15]Some systems credit investment return in excess of a low guaranteed rate to both active and retired employees and thus eliminate this objection.

Wage Indexation

Another method of dealing with inflation and productivity gains is to link the benefits of retired individuals and other income recipients to changes in a specified wage index. The index can be one for the whole labor force or a specified segment of the labor force, such as those employed in a given profession, industry, or locality. Under the recomputation approach, described in the next section, the index may be constructed in terms of the salary associated with a given position or rank with a particular employment or employee group. Recognition may be given to changes in the index after the crediting of each benefit unit or only the changes that have occurred since retirement.

Because wages reflect not only inflationary forces but labor's share of productivity gains, the adjustment of pension benefits based on a general wage index would enable the retired population to maintain its relative position on the economic scale. That is, if there are real gains in the gross national product and they are reflected in wages on which the index is based, retired employees would receive their pro rata share of the gains and thus enhance their standard of living. A more specific index would pass along the productivity gains, if any, associated with the wages entering into the index. Some public employee retirement systems adjust the benefits of retired employees in accordance with changes in an index of salaries currently being paid to the active employees. Thus far, the wage index concept is rarely used by private employers in the United States. An application of the wage index adjustment technique to broad segments of the working population is found in the so-called *repartition* approach that has been used in France since the close of World War II.[16]

Recomputation

The wage index concept can be applied to a limited segment of the working population through an approach called *recomputation*, which is literally what takes place. It is appropriate only for employee groups with rigidly structured and formally recognized job classifications, as exemplified by the military services and uniformed civilian services.

The principle underlying recomputation is that the pension benefits of the retired members of the group should bear a constant relationship to the current

---

[16]For a detailed description of the repartition scheme and the institutional framework within which it operates, see Tony Lynes, *French Pensions*, London School of Economics and Political Science Occasional Papers on Social Administration, no. 21 (London: G. Bell & Sons, 1967). For a succinct summary of the system, see Dan M. McGill, *Preservation of Pension Benefit Rights* (Homewood, Ill.: Richard D. Irwin, 1972), pp. 280–94. The philosophical basis of the repartition principle is the doctrine of social solidarity. This doctrine was first enunciated in the second half of the nineteenth century, its principal spokesman being Leon Bourgeois, and it became the ideological basis of the French social security system. In that context, the doctrine connoted the obligation of society to ensure a minimum subsistence to all of its members who, by reason of age or infirmity, are physically or mentally incapable of maintaining themselves by their own efforts. It has taken on a more specialized meaning in connection with the *repartition* scheme. Here it means that each generation of workers undertakes to support the preceding generation of workers in the expectation that it will be accorded the same treatment by the succeeding generation. It is solidarity *between* generations rather than within one generation.

compensation levels for the rank or job classification that they held when they retired. In other words, the pension benefit of a retired member should be expressed in terms of the base compensation, as defined, of an active member of the same rank, or in the same job classification, as that held by the retired individual at retirement. In the military service, this would mean, for example, that a person who retired at the rank of colonel would receive a pension throughout retirement equal to the appropriate percentage, reflecting his or her years of service, of the base compensation of a colonel still on active duty. If the regular pay scale of the active members of the military services were to be raised, the pension benefits of all retired members would be recomputed in terms of the new scale applicable to their retired rank. The process would be repeated each time there was a pay increase.

Recomputation was a feature of the military retirement system until 1958, when it was replaced by cost-of-living adjustments. Benefits of retired military personnel are now subject to automatic cost-of-living adjustments in accordance with the formula applied under the Civil Service Retirement System. The military services were not pleased with the removal of the recomputation feature, an economy measure on the part of the Congress, and have attempted several times to have it restored.

In the meantime, recomputation continues to be a feature of many retirement plans for police and firefighters, which tend to be liberal in other respects, frequently including no age requirement for retirement. The principle seems to be fairly well accepted in that specialized segment of public pensions.

It would seem that recomputation, like a general wage index, would bestow productivity gains on the retired population, in addition to protecting this group against a loss of purchasing power. It might be questioned whether the concept of productivity gains can be applied to government employees, especially to members of the Armed Forces, but the benefits associated with the concept tend to spill over into plans using the recomputation technique through another principle of governmental personnel policy known as "comparability." This term refers to the concept of keeping governmental pay scales, including those of the military services, in line with the pay in comparable job classifications in the private sector. There are obvious difficulties in applying the concept, of course; but, to the extent that governmental pay scales do reflect the general wage structure of private industry, the recomputation technique would probably keep benefit levels somewhat higher than they would be with only cost-of-living adjustments. The fact that the affected groups put up a strong fight to retain (or to reacquire) the recomputation feature would suggest that this is the case.

Section IV
Pension Funding and Accounting

Chapter 22
Actuarial Cost Factors

As pointed out earlier, under a pension plan an employer's obligation may be to set aside funds on a specified basis (the defined contribution approach) or to provide benefits according to a stipulated formula (the defined benefits approach). In a defined contribution plan, the employer's obligation is discharged fully and completely with the payment of the stipulated sum of money; if all previous payments were made at the proper time and in the proper amount, the employer's cumulative obligations are at all times fully and unconditionally met. Measuring the employer's obligation for accruing benefits does not present a problem because the present value of the benefits at any given date is, by definition, the exact equivalent of the funds on hand.

On the other hand, when the employer undertakes to provide a predetermined benefit, there is no necessary equivalence between the monetary value of the benefits that have been credited at any given point and the sums that have been accumulated to pay the benefits. A liability—moral or legal—of measurable value is created with the crediting of each dollar of future benefit, entirely apart from any financial or budgetary arrangements that may have been made to meet the obligation.

If the plan is to operate on an acceptable basis, however, the accrual of benefit credits must be offset, over time, by setting aside funds estimated to be sufficient, with cumulative investment earnings, to provide the benefits credited under the plan. To guide the funding policy of the employer, it is necessary to estimate the amount and timing of benefits that will eventually be paid under the terms of the plan. Because the benefits will be paid over many years, and funds set aside for the payment of such benefits will earn interest until finally disbursed, it is necessary for proper financial planning to convert the anticipated benefit payments into a single sum value through the discounting process. The process of deriving the actuarial present value of future benefit payments, which involves other actuarial concepts not yet considered, is referred to as the *valuation of the liabilities* of the plan.

Actuarial valuations are undertaken for a number of purposes. The most common are listed below:

1. To estimate the long-term cost of a pension plan or any proposed changes in the plan (Chapter 25).

2. To ascertain the level of benefits that can be provided from a series of stipulated contributions (Chapters 23 and 24).
3. To indicate the contributions needed to fund a given set of benefits (Chapters 23 and 24).
4. To determine the proper charge to be made against the firm's operating revenues for expense accounting purposes (Chapter 28).
5. To determine the maximum contribution that the firm can deduct in any one year for federal income tax purposes (Chapter 27).
6. To determine the minimum annual contribution to the plan under federal law (Chapter 27).
7. To prepare actuarial reports required under federal law (Chapter 27).
8. To establish plan costs and liabilities in connection with corporate mergers and spinoffs (Chapter 9).
9. To provide a basis for allocating the assets of a terminated plan (Chapters 33 and 34).
10. To determine the withdrawal liability for an employer withdrawing from a multiemployer plan (Chapter 34).
11. To inform plan participants of the funding status of plan benefits (Chapter 3).

There are two main types of valuations: static and dynamic. A *static* or *closed group* valuation takes into account only the accrued or prospective benefits of a person currently affiliated with the plan as an active participant, a terminated vested participant, or a retired participant or beneficiary. This type of valuation is required under federal law for validating tax deductions and establishing minimum funding levels. Some plans also employ a *dynamic* or *open group* valuation, which takes into account the accrued and prospective benefits of not only the current group of participants but also those who may enter the plan during some finite future period. The *dynamic* or *open group* valuation is primarily designed to inform an employer about the future costs, funding obligations, and cash flow of its pension plan.

A distinction is also made between a valuation that is based on the assumption that the plan will continue in operation and one based on the assumption that the plan is being terminated on the valuation date. The former is routinely required under the Employment Retirement Income Security Act and is known as a *plan continuation* valuation. The latter may be performed to indicate the effect of a plan termination and is called a *plan termination valuation*. The overall valuation process can be better understood by examining some basic concepts concerning plan population.

Basic Concepts of Plan Population

A pension plan that has operated for a number of years will be made up of four major components or subsets:

- active participants (employees still in the active service of the employer),
- terminated vested participants (former employees who terminated with vested benefits),

- retired participants,
- beneficiaries of retired or deceased participants.[1]

Together these four segments constitute the *plan population.*

The broad characteristics of the plan population that significantly affect plan costs, and therefore affect the actuarial liabilities of the plan, are

- the number of participants (and beneficiaries),
- the male/female mix,
- the attained age distribution,
- the distribution by years of service,
- the distribution of the population by age of entry into the plan.

If the benefits of the plan are related to compensation, the level and distribution of salaries are also relevant characteristics.

The plan population and its characteristics are determined by the flow of persons into and out of the plan. A particularly crucial factor is whether the population is increasing, decreasing, or remaining constant. If the number of people leaving the plan—through withdrawals, deaths, disabilities, and retirements—is constant, and a constant number of new entrants flow into the plan population in a fixed pattern of entry ages, in theory the number of persons in the population and their attained age and service distribution will eventually become constant and will remain so as long as the basic assumptions are realized. Such a population is described quite aptly as a *stationary population.* If the basic conditions are fulfilled, a stationary population will be reached within a period of years equal to the difference between the age of the oldest possible person in the population and the age of the youngest entrants. If, for example, no retired participant or beneficiary lives beyond 95 and the youngest age at which a person can enter the plan is 21, it will take no more than 74 years from the time the first group enters for a stationary population to be achieved. Once a plan population has become stationary in this sense, its normal cost and accrued liability will remain the same year after year, with no change in the benefit structure or other factors that would affect the cost. In practice, no plan will ever have an exactly constant flow of new entrants or an exactly stationary population. The stationary population concept is applicable to each segment or subpopulation of the plan population.

Closely akin to the concept of the stationary population is that of the *mature population.* In fact, a stationary population is a type of mature population. In a mature population, the attained age and service distributions remain constant from year to year but the *size* of the population does not necessarily remain constant.

A population is considered to be *undermature* when the proportion of the participants at younger ages and with the shorter periods of service is greater than that within a mature population. Conversely, an *overmature* population is one that

---

[1]If the plan provides disability benefits, disabled participants would constitute another distinct subset of the population.

contains a greater proportion of older participants and participants with longer periods of service than is true of a precisely mature population.[2]

Pension plans characteristically begin their operation with an undermature population, since most participants were hired at younger ages and spill over into the higher attained ages and service categories over many years.[3] If no new employees were hired after the plan went into operation, the population would gradually move through the various age and service cells, eventually reaching an overmature state without ever satisfying the precise criteria of a mature population. In the normal situation, of course, new employees would be hired from time to time, which would slow down the maturation process.

If the growth *rate* were to continue to decline, the population would continue its aging process, passing through the mature state into an overmature state.[4] If at some point additions were no longer being made to the employee group, the population would ultimately die out, and the various subpopulations would disappear from the scene within the same period of years that it would have taken a plan population to mature if it had had a constant rate of increments and decrements.

The natural tendency is for a plan population is to mature. Generally speaking, the only population that would not move toward a more mature state each year would be one growing at an *increasing* rate. No plan population, of course, can grow indefinitely at an increasing rate, since it would ultimately swallow up the entire labor force. However, if a population is to mature systematically in accordance with the time parameters mentioned earlier, persons must enter it at a constant rate or in constant numbers; the additions at the various ages of entry (i.e., the hiring ages) must take place at a constant rate or in constant numbers; and the decrements at the various attained ages in each of the subpopulations must conform to a fixed pattern. If any one of these three broad conditions is not satisfied, the maturation process will be erratic. Changes in hiring patterns, mass layoffs or plant closings, and alterations in retirement practices, for example, would disrupt and distort the process.

Cessation of growth in the active employee population would have an important and enduring effect. If the active life population were to remain constant in number, each person leaving the group by death, disability, retirement, or voluntary withdrawal would have to be replaced; but in all likelihood, they would not be replaced by a person of the same age. That being the case, the additions at the various entry ages would not be constant, one of the conditions of a mature population. The net effect of deviations from the prescribed conditions would be

---

[2]It should be recognized that there are an infinite number of possible plan populations, reflecting past hiring practices and varying rates of decrement from the labor force. In fact, there are as many potential plan populations as there are possible combinations of age and service distributions. Thus in reality plan populations do not fit neatly into categories here characterized as undermature, mature, or overmature. These categories themselves do not have sharply defined boundaries, since the whole maturing process is in the nature of a continuum.

[3]Some plans start with a reasonably mature active participant population, that being the primary impetus for establishing the plan. Likewise, a firm with a dormant, overmature group of active employees might start a pension plan in recognition of the cohorts quickly approaching retirement.

[4]In the long run, the rate of growth of most plan populations must decline, even down to zero or near zero. In practice the growth rate (*positive or negative*) varies from year to year.

to slow down the maturation process and to make it more erratic. As will be seen later, the maturity of the population has a material effect on the accrued liability of a pension plan and, depending on the actuarial cost method, may have an impact on the normal cost.

Valuation Assumptions and Factors

An essential step in the valuation of a pension plan is to determine the *actuarial present value* of the accrued or projected benefits of the plan. The determination must be made for each type of benefit provided under the plan and for each participant in the plan.

The amount of a participant's accrued benefit can be determined from the provisions of the plan and data for the participant. If the valuation is based upon projected benefits, however, projected compensation, years of service, and other relevant factors must first be determined.

The actuarial present value as of a specified date of any given benefit amount payable thereafter is equal to the benefit amount (1) multiplied by the probability of occurrence of the event on which the benefit payment is conditioned and (2) discounted at a stipulated rate or rates of interest. The aggregate amount derived from these individual determinations constitutes the actuarial present value of the benefits of the plan as a whole.

To fully appreciate the valuation process, it is necessary to examine in detail the factors that enter into all components of the computations. To sharpen the focus of the discussion, only retirement benefits will be considered in this chapter and in Chapters 23 and 24. The valuation of death, disability, and withdrawal benefits is treated in Chapter 26. However, it is essential to remember that most of the actuarial cost factors discussed in the context of retirement benefits are also involved in the valuation of other benefits under the plan.

ERISA's minimum funding requirements include rules concerning the actuarial assumptions and methods to be used in valuations.[5] For single-employer plans the valuation must be based on actuarial assumptions and methods, each of which is reasonable (taking into account the experience of the plan and reasonable expectations), or which, in the aggregate, result in total contributions equivalent to those that would be determined if each assumption and method were reasonable. Thus one assumption that is too conservative may offset another assumption that is not conservative enough. For multiemployer plans the methods and assumptions used are required to be reasonable in the aggregate. For all plans the methods and assumptions used must in combination offer the actuary's best estimate of anticipated experience under the plan. Valuations done for purposes of Financial Accounting Standard No. 87 must be based on assumptions that are all "best estimates." Special rules that apply to the interest assumption used are described elsewhere in this text.[6]

---

[5]ERISA §302(c)(3); IRC §412(c)(3).

[6]For rules concerning the interest assumptions required to be used for determining (1) the current liability, (2) unfunded vested benefits for purposes of determining PBGC premiums, or (3) values for generally accepted accounting principles, see Chapters 27 and 28.

The assumptions used are generally classified as *demographic assumptions* and *economic assumptions*. Demographic assumptions concern changes in the various components of the plan's population, while economic assumptions concern rates of investment return, wage and salary patterns, future levels of inflation, and other monetary factors.

For purposes of this discussion, retirement benefits are said to include only those benefits payable to individuals who enter retirement status from an active participant status. They will *not* include benefits payable to individuals who enter retirement status from either a terminated vested or disabled status. This distinction is made to illustrate and emphasize the calculation of the expected cost of the different benefit components of the plan.

Population Decrements

Retirement benefits, as defined above, are payable only to those participants who survive in the service of the employer to early or normal retirement age. Thus the first step in the valuation of a retirement benefit is to determine the probability that the participant will survive with the employer to early or normal retirement age. This probability is usually expressed as a decimal, such as .70. The probability of surviving equals one less the probability that the person will not survive. The probability of *not* surviving involves the *forces of decrement.* These forces are death, disability, retirement, and other terminations of employment (voluntary and involuntary). The reductions in the plan population that they generate are called *decrements.* The probability that a participant will leave the active life subpopulation because of one of these decremental forces is not independent of the probability associated with the other three forces, and a valuation may take this factor into account.

Terminations

Terminations, other than by death, disability, and retirement, tend to be the most important decremental force operating within the active life component of a pension plan population. Typically, they overshadow the decrements attributable to preretirement mortality and disability.

Terminations are accounted for through a schedule of termination rates (also called "turnover" or "withdrawal" rates) contained in a *termination table.* A termination table purports to reflect the rate of termination that can be expected to occur each year at each age in the active life subpopulation from the earliest age of entry into the plan to the youngest age at which retirement with immediate benefits can take place. There may be one set of rates for male participants and another for female participants. Separate schedules may be used for hourly rated employees and salaried employees or for any subset of the active employee population that may be subject to a distinctive pattern of terminations.

Since termination rates tend to vary inversely with length of service, the termination table may portray termination rates not only by attained age but also by duration of service—up to 5 or 10 years of service. Such a table is described as a *select and ultimate* table: select rates vary with the duration of service and ultimate rates apply after the select period, according to the terminology of mortality tables. Some tables extend the select period all the way to retirement.

Termination rates should not reflect the proportion of *participants* terminating but rather the proportion of actuarial *liabilities* terminating. Terminations among long-service employees with large accrued benefits have far more effect on costs than terminations among short-service employees. Therefore if select and ultimate rates are *not* used, the aggregate rates used for each attained age should be heavily weighted by ultimate experience. Termination rates may be combined with disability rates to determine the combined decrements from the active life population age by age resulting from causes other than death or retirement.

The termination rates used in the valuation of a particular plan should ideally reflect the expected experience of the plan population involved. Usually no reliable experience data on past employment terminations exist at the inception of the plan, and the actuary, consulting with the employer, selects a hypothetical schedule of termination rates considered appropriate for the plan population involved. The rates may reflect the observed experience of an existing plan with population characteristics similar to the plan being valued. Over time, a large plan will develop a body of experience that can serve as the basis for the termination schedule, with due allowance for changing circumstances.

Many plans, including most small and medium-size ones, continue to use the original hypothetical scale of terminations, or replace it with another hypothetical scale that appears more reasonable in the light of experience. Many of these scales show no terminations after age 50 or 55. Select and ultimate rates are not usually used, since they introduce a degree of complexity into the calculations that may not be justified by the crudeness of the termination assumptions employed by many plans. Termination rates vary with company culture, the fortunes of the individual employer, the fortunes of the general industry, and the fortunes of the entire economy.

Failure to take anticipated terminations into account overstates the actuarial liabilities of a pension plan at any given time, unless all liabilities represent fully vested benefits, or unless it is assumed that the plan terminates at that point and all benefits vest in full. Moreover, the condition is not corrected as terminations occur and liabilities are canceled, since, in the normal course of events, offsetting liabilities will have been created with the entrance of other participants who also will ultimately terminate their membership in the plan before achieving a fully vested or retirement status.

Death

A second decremental force within the active life subpopulation is death. Retirement benefits are paid only to those participants who live to early or normal retirement, even when the benefits of the deceased participant had vested prior to death. Thus to estimate pension cost it is necessary to predict the survival rates of the participants with an appropriate mortality table. A mortality table reflects the probabilities of death and survival at the various ages of the human life span. An annuity mortality table is a type of mortality table used to reflect mortality under annuity contracts and pension plans.

A mortality table can be constructed from the observed experience of any group of lives, adjusted to smooth out irregularities and possibly to provide margins of safety. It typically depicts a death rate per 1,000 for all ages from birth to the oldest age that people are presumed to live. The terminal age of the mortality table is not intended to reflect the actual extremity of the human life span but the age by which, for all practical purposes, the last survivors of a group of lives will have died. The death rates are applied to the survivors of an arbitrary number of persons, called the *radix*, assumed to be alive at the youngest age in the mortality table. From the number of persons in the original group assumed to be alive at each attained age, it is possible to predict the probability that an individual alive at any given age will survive to any later age. A mortality table clearly lends itself to predicting the proportion of active participants in a pension plan who will live to early or normal retirement, as well as calculating the actuarial value of the lifetime benefits payable to persons who reach retirement.

Since mortality rates vary among different segments of the general population, a mortality table used for a particular purpose should reflect the body of mortality experience most appropriate for that purpose. It has been found, for example, that mortality among individuals who purchase life insurance tends to be higher, age for age, than that of persons who purchase annuities. Insurance companies thus adopt a mortality table for underwriting annuities different from that used for writing life insurance. This practice is dictated not only by the lower death rates among annuitants but by the necessity or desirability of providing a margin of safety in the mortality assumptions. Such a margin is provided in a life insurance mortality table by using death rates that are higher than those likely to be experienced, while the converse is true with respect to an annuity mortality table. That is, a conservative annuity mortality table shows lower death rates than those normally expected. Thus the same table cannot be conservative for both life insurance and annuity purposes. The need for a margin of safety in annuity mortality tables is heightened by the secular improvement in longevity that has recently occurred in varying degrees at all ages and among virtually all elements of the population. This demographic phenomenon operates to reduce the safety of an annuity mortality table, while it enlarges the original margin of safety in an insurance mortality table.

It has also been found that mortality among most employee groups is lower than that of the general population. This is attributable to the fact that the general population embraces persons in varying conditions of health, including a substantial percentage in an impaired state of health, while a minimum standard of health is required for participation in the active labor force. This superior vitality presumably carries over into retirement, which suggests that an annuity mortality table used for the underwriting or valuation of retirement benefits should lean heavily on the mortality experience of employed lives and of those retired from active employment.

Finally, females live longer, on average, than males. The lower female mortality rates occur at all ages, including the first week of life, and this superior longevity appears to flow from a better biological heritage. The superiority of female longevity has been so pronounced in recent decades that the annuity values for female lives at any particular age have tended to conform rather well to those for male lives five or six years younger. As a result, it is possible to use the same annuity table for male and female lives by assuming that the female is five or six years younger than her stated age, a device known as an age setback or "rating down."

For the most part, mortality assumptions for the valuation of pension plan benefits have been based upon mortality tables developed by life insurance companies for writing individual or group annuities. Some actuarial consulting firms have constructed their own mortality tables from the observed experience among pension plans that they service.

The pattern of mortality among group annuitants is markedly different from that among individual annuitants. The Group Annuity Mortality Table for 1951 (Ga-51),[7] developed by Ray M. Peterson, was the first published table to be based entirely on the mortality experience of group annuitants. Male and female death rates were tabulated separately; but many actuaries found it more convenient to use the male table for both male and female lives, with the death rates for females at various ages equated to the male rates for ages five years younger. To provide a margin for future improvement in mortality, Peterson developed a projection scale (designated projection scale C) that reduces the death rate at all ages with each passing calendar year. The table can be used in its basic, static form without the projection factors. If the projection factors are used without limitation, the expected mortality rate at any given age will vary with the calendar year of birth. The 1951 Group Annuity Table is no longer generally used.

By 1971 the continued decline in death rates had virtually wiped out the safety margin in the Ga-51 Table at the significant ages. As a consequence, a new table, the 1971 Group Annuity Mortality Table (1971 GAM) was constructed[8] from mortality data generated under certain group annuity contracts. Two sets of projection factors were developed: scale D for both male and female lives (with separate percentages), and scale E for male lives only. When only the male table is used, female ages are set back six years.

In 1976 William W. Fellers and Paul H. Jackson published the UP-1984 Table.[9] "UP" stands for "unisex pension." The UP-1984 Table is based on the mortality experience of pension plans funded through trusts, with mortality improvement projected to 1984. This table represents the combined experience of males and females; about 20 percent of the experience is for females. It was the first published unisex table and is intended to be used for groups containing both male and female lives or for groups containing only males or only females. Because it is based upon the experience of groups with a particular sex distribution (the composite mix was 80 percent male and 20 percent female), it may not represent the experience of groups with significantly different sex distribution. Fellers and Jackson recommend that the table be used with a four-year setback for a group made up of female lives exclusively, and that it be used with a one-year setforward for a group of male lives.

---

[7]Ray M. Peterson, "Group Annuity Mortality," *Transactions of the Society of Actuaries,* vol. 4 (1952): pp. 246–307.

[8]Harold R. Greenlee, Jr., and Alfonso D. Keh, "The 1971 Group Annuity Mortality Table," *Transactions of the Society of Actuaries,* vol. 23 (1971): pp. 569–604, and discussion on pp. 605–22.

[9]William W. Fellers and Paul H. Jackson, "Noninsured Pensioner Mortality—The UP-1984 Table," *The Proceedings, Conference of Actuaries in Public Practice,* vol. 25 (1976): pp. 456–502.

The Group Annuity Mortality Committee of the Society of Actuaries found that rates of mortality had decreased during the 1970s and that the 1971 GAM Table no longer provided an adequate mortality basis for the valuation of group annuity benefits. On the basis of data from several sources, the Committee constructed the 1983 Group Annuity Mortality Table (1983 GAM).[10] The 1983 GAM Table was designed as a valuation basis for group annuity contracts. Many pension actuaries have also adopted it for the valuation of pension plans. The Committee also developed Projection Scale H to project improvement after 1983. While separate tables were developed for males and females, the Committee determined that annuity values calculated using the male table with a six-year setback can reasonably approximate annuity values using the female table.

In November 1994 the 1994 Group Annuity Mortality Table and 1994 Group Annuity Reserving Table were released in exposure draft form by the Society of Actuaries Group Annuity Valuation Table Task Force. In January 1995 the 1994 Uninsured Pensioner Mortality Table was released in exposure draft by the Society of Actuaries UP-94 Task Force. A separate exposure report issued in January 1995 compared the 1994 Group Annuity Reserving Table (GAR94) and the Uninsured Pensioner 1994 Table (UP94). Both tables are based on the same underlying mortality: Civil Service Retirement System mortality for lives under age 66 and group annuity mortality experience for benefits in payment status at 11 large life insurance companies for ages over 65. (Mortality rates at the extreme ages [1 to 24 and 96 to 115] were based on general population statistics.) The basic difference between the tables is that the GAR94 is intended as a reserve standard, for which a degree of conservatism is appropriate, and the UP94 is intended as a "best-estimate" valuation table.

Specifically, the GAR94 table takes the underlying mortality rates and incorporates a 7 percent reduction at all but the oldest ages. This 7 percent reduction is composed of a 5 percent reduction to cover random deviations in mortality and a further 2 percent reduction to cover the risk of nonhomogenous populations. The GAR94 has an allowance for continuing mortality improvements built directly into the table.

The UP94 Table does not incorporate any mortality margin. In addition, no future mortality improvements have been put directly into the table. However, it does include a projection scale, and the authors recommend that actuaries consider using this projection scale to create a projected version of the UP94 Table that is appropriate for their particular valuation. This gives the actuary a choice between two types of mortality table: (1) a *static* table, which uses mortality rates that are constant over time; and (2) a *generational* table, which assumes that mortality rates will be subject to continuous improvement. Under a static table, the mortality rate for any given age, say, age 50, is the same whatever the current age of the individual. In contrast, under the generational approach the mortality rate at age 50 for an individual currently age 30 is lower than the mortality rate at age 50 for an individual currently age 40. The static table can still take account of expected future improvements in mortality, for example, by using a projection

---

[10]Committee on Annuities, "Development of the 1983 Group Annuity Mortality Table," *Transactions of the Society of Actuaries*, vol. 35 (1983): pp. 859–99.

TABLE 22-1   Increases in the Value of Deferred Annuities at Various
Sex/Age Combinations

Age	Sex	Percentage Increase from UP94@1994 to UP94G@1994	Percentage Increase from UP94 @1994 to UP94G@2004
32	Male	12.4	15.5
32	Female	4.6	5.8
47	Male	7.3	10.7
47	Female	2.7	3.9
62	Male	2.5	5.0
62	Female	1.2	2.1

scale to project mortality improvements to, say, the year 2005. However, the resulting mortality rates will be applicable for all years, both before and after 2005.

The authors have suggested notation that helps to distinguish the various possible ways that a projection scale can be used. The basic static table using 1994 mortality is referred to as the UP94 Table. The basic generational table with 1994 mortality and assumed future mortality improvements is referred to as UP94G. Projections of either the static or generational tables to future years are then denoted using the @ sign. Thus the static table based on mortality improvements to 2005 is denoted as UP94@2005. The generational table that would be applicable for valuations in the year 2005 is denoted as UP94G@2005.

The data in Table 22-1 are taken from the exposure report comparing the two tables and show the percentage increase at various age/sex combinations in the value of a deferred annuity payable starting at age 62. The largest percentage increases arise at the youngest ages. This suggests that the issue of future mortality improvements is most critical for a pension valuation composed largely of active employees. The increases for males are also much more significant than the increases for females.

For very large plans a separate mortality table may be developed on the basis of the plan's own experience. Separate mortality tables are often used for disabled individuals to reflect their higher mortality rates.

Disability

The third source of decrements in the active life population of a pension plan is disability. This decremental force operates just like the other two in preventing plan participants from qualifying for a retirement benefit. Many plans provide disability retirement benefits that differ from the retirement benefits available to nondisabled participants. Disablement rates are used to estimate both the number of participants who will receive disability benefits and the number who will *not* receive regular retirement benefits.

Tables are available that show the probability of becoming disabled at various ages within the active life group. The rates depend on the definition of disability used and the time period the individual must be so disabled before any benefits become payable. The more liberal the definition and the shorter the waiting period, the higher the rate of becoming disabled. The rates are also influenced by how the definition is interpreted and administered—strictly or loosely. In addition, disability rates are affected by the level of benefits provided (the more generous the benefit the higher the disability rate) and the general level of economic activity.

Disability experience of Social Security and the Railroad Retirement System is used by many pension actuaries. The experience of a large plan can be tabulated over a period of years and safely used, with adjustments for changed circumstances and provisions, to estimate terminations from disability and determine the actuarial value of the benefits payable to a person who becomes disabled.

Disabled status may terminate because of either death or recovery. To simplify the computations, actuaries ordinarily ignore the possibility of recovery, and this has very little effect on the overall calculated costs of the plan.

Retirement

Under most pension plans, a participant may retire within a range of permissible ages, from the youngest age at which early retirement is permitted to the oldest age at which employees actually do retire. Retirement age may affect the amount of monthly benefit payable, the period during which contributions are made to the plan, and the number of years during which the retired participant will receive his or her pension. Each of these variables is a cost consideration. Therefore it is necessary to estimate the age or ages at which plan participants will retire.

A precise procedure is to assume rates of retirements over the full range of ages when retirement may take place. A high rate usually occurs at the normal retirement age. Relatively high rates also often occur at the first age that individuals are eligible for early retirement, at age 62 (when Social Security benefits are first available), and at age 65, even if this is not the normal retirement age. As an approximation to the distribution, the actuary often assumes that all participants retire at normal retirement, or at some estimated average retirement age that may be earlier or later than the normal retirement age.

Population Increments

If the retirement benefits of a closed group of active life participants are being valued, no population *increments* are involved. In fact, it would be contradictory to talk about population increments in a closed group valuation. On the other hand, introducing population increments into an existing group of plan participants is essential to carrying out an open group valuation.

Two separate assumptions are usually made concerning new entrants. The first is the change, if any, in the size of the total active labor force. Even if it is assumed that the firm has reached a stable condition and there will be no growth in the active labor force, it will be necessary to add enough new participants to replace those who will disappear through termination, death, disability, and retirement. If there is to be some growth in the firm's overall labor force, the increments must exceed the decrements. There would probably be some increments even if the overall labor force of the firm was declining.

The second type of assumption is the distribution of new entrants by age, sex, and salary level. An open group valuation is rather sensitive to the assumption about the distribution of the new participants brought into the plan. It would be unrealistic to assume that each person leaving the active life population would be replaced by a new participant of the same age, sex, and salary. Rather, it is assumed that the distribution of new participants will reflect the hiring practices of the employer. In the typical situation, most new participants would be hired at younger ages and lower salaries; but there may be some additions throughout the full range of employment ages and salaries. For ease of computation, it may be assumed that all new participants in any year are hired at a few of the younger ages and at the same starting salary.

Economic-Based Factors

One set of actuarial cost factors is primarily based on broad economic forces and reflect predictions about future economic behavior. They are frequently referred to as "economic assumptions." Cost factors falling within this general category are those relating to salary progression, consumer price levels, and investment earnings. In adopting assumptions about these factors, the plan actuary may seek input from the plan sponsor, the investment manager or managers, economists, and others with special insights into economic phenomena.

Cost of Living

Expectations concerning future levels of inflation indirectly affect all economic assumptions used by the plan. In addition, a direct assumption concerning future increases in the cost of living must be made for a number of purposes.

The $90,000 maximum limit on benefits under Code section 415 and the $150,000 maximum limit on compensation that may be recognized under Code section 401(a)(17) are both adjusted annually for increases in the cost of living. These expected future increases may not be taken into account for purposes of determining the minimum required contributions or maximum deductible contributions,[11] but they must be recognized for accounting purposes.

For integrated plans that offset benefits by a percentage of benefits payable under Social Security, a cost-of-living assumption is also needed to project the age 65 primary insurance amount under Social Security.

A cost-of-living increase assumption must be made for the minority of plans that provide postretirement cost-of-living increases. If cost-of-living increases in the plan are subject to a maximum limit, such as 3 percent per year, this limit will be reflected in valuing projected benefits—even if a higher cost-of-living assumption is used in projecting Social Security benefits or is used for other purposes. Cost-of-living increase assumptions in current use generally range from 4 percent to 6 percent.

[11]IRC §404(j), (l).

Salary Progression[12]

If the retirement benefits of a pension plan are expressed in terms of final average or highest average earnings, it is necessary to project the current earnings of plan participants to the level expected to prevail during the period of service that will establish the formula salary base—usually the years immediately preceding retirement.[13] If the plan valuation is based on total prospective benefits, as contrasted with accrued benefits, it is essential to project earnings even when a career average benefit formula is employed.

In addition, an assumption must be made about future increases in the Social Security taxable wage base if the plan is integrated by utilizing the level of covered compensation[14] or by offsetting by actual Social Security benefits (see Chapter 15). The Social Security taxable wage base increases automatically by the percentage increase in average earnings of those employees subject to Social Security.

Compensation for an individual participant (in contrast to the entire group) is projected through an assumption about the annual rate at which the individual's compensation will increase over his or her future working lifetime. The series of projected compensation increases is called a "salary scale." Either explicitly or implicitly, the salary scale usually consists of three elements: cost-of-living increases, the increase in *average* salary levels in excess of the cost-of-living increases, and merit increases.

Cost-of-living increases were discussed above. Compensation levels tend to reflect the cost-of-living increases to allow employees to maintain their standard of living, to respond to the demands of collective bargaining, and to compete for employees in the marketplace.

During most periods in the past, salary levels have increased more rapidly than price inflation. These salary increases are typically manifested both in an increase in the average salary of all employees covered by the plan and in an increase in starting salary rates for new employees. Increases in average compensation in excess of average price increases are generally attributable to productivity gains. The amount of this excess has varied greatly over time. In some recent years, price increases have exceeded compensation increases. While there is considerable uncertainty about the magnitude of future productivity gains in the American economy—and some concern that there may be no such gains in the foreseeable future—a good deal of evidence suggests that there should be some labor-hour productivity gains over the long term. If this forecast is correct, and it is assumed that a portion of these gains will find their way into wages over a time period, the wage scale of a firm should increase from this factor. Actuaries usually assume that increases in average compensation will exceed the assumed increase in prices by 0 to 2 percent.

[12]For a provocative and enlightening discussion of the impact of salary changes on pension plan costs, see William F. Marples, "Salary Scales," *Transactions of the Society of Actuaries*, vol. 14 (1962): pp. 1–30, and discussion contained in pp. 31–50.

[13]Salary projections are also essential in the valuation of the prospective benefits of participants who will terminate with vested benefits prior to retirement, and here the need is to project current earnings to the level that will prevail during the few years prior to termination.

[14]IRC §401(l)(5)(E).

Where a specific assumption is made concerning future increases in the Social Security wage base, the same assumption is usually used to represent increases in average compensation levels for plan participants, since, in the long run, average increases in compensation for a particular employer will usually be close to the average increases for all workers of all employers.

In addition to the increases in average compensation, salary scales should also reflect merit increases: those that reward a participant for acquiring greater skills, assuming broader responsibilities, or simply rendering additional years of loyal service to the employer. These increases in earnings occur within a wage or salary structure existing at a given time and are independent of changes that may occur as the whole wage structure is adjusted upward in response to broad economic forces. The majority of employees commence their employment with salary levels less than the average salary for all employees of the employer, and many of them rise to above average salaries. Merit salary increases are usually more rapid at younger ages than at older ages.

The proper way to construct a merit salary scale is to examine the historical relationship between the average compensation of employees at various attained ages from 20 to 65 and the average compensation of the entire covered group of employees of the firm. For example, if in 1995 the average compensation for 26-year-old participants with at least one year of service is 52 percent of the average compensation of all participants in that year, and if in 1994 the average compensation of these same individuals (who were then age 25) was 50 percent of the average compensation of all participants, then the rate of merit salary increase during 1994 for 25-year-old employees was 1.04 (52/50). This would mean that in 1994 the average 25-year-old employee had a compensation increase of 4 percent more than the average increase for all participants. If this was a stable relationship, established by historical observation of compensation rates within the employing firm, the merit salary scale would show 1.04 for age 25.

An actuary may use more than one salary scale in valuing the liabilities of a plan. One scale may be used for male employees and another for females. Also, special scales may be constructed for executives and other employees whose pattern of compensation growth is likely to vary from that of the rank-and-file employees. This type of salary scale is very important when valuing excess plans or SERPS.

Table 22-2 shows a hypothetical salary scale for illustrative ages that assumed 3.5 percent inflation and 0.5 percent increases in average wages resulting from productivity, and merit increases that vary by age. The merit increase schedule is taken from Appendix Table A-5. Instead of using a merit salary scale that varies by age, many plans assume a level annual increase at all ages to simplify the valuation. For example, Table 22-3 presents a salary scale similar to the one used in deriving Table 22-2, but it assumes merit increases of 2.3 percent at all ages, and a total expected salary increase of 8 percent at all ages. This results in somewhat lower total wage increments at lower ages, somewhat higher wage increments at higher ages, but a final salary that is roughly the same multiple of the beginning pay level across a full career. An integrated plan using these assumptions likely would assume a 4.0 percent increase in the Social Security wage base under a 3.5 percent increase for inflation and 0.5 percent increase for productivity.

TABLE 22-2   Salary Scale

	Annual Increase				Ratio of Salary at Attained Age to Salary at Age 20
Age	Inflation	Productivity	Merit	Total	
20	.035	.005	.068	.108	1.000
21	.035	.005	.066	.106	1.108
22	.035	.005	.064	.104	1.225
—					
—					
64	.035	.005	.003	.043	15.831
65					16.512

Often the actuary does not explicitly identify the separate elements of the salary scale. In an open group valuation, salary scales should be used with any type of benefit formula, including one that provides a flat dollar benefit for each year of service. The usual purpose of an open group valuation is to estimate the cost and the liabilities of a pension plan over some future period, such as the next 10 or 20 years. The level of initial compensation for new employees should be assumed to increase each year to reflect the increase in the cost of living plus the increase in average salaries resulting from productivity gains. A similar assumption should ordinarily be made regarding the plan's benefit formula in a plan that provides a flat dollar benefit for each year of service, since flat dollar benefit formulas are likely to be adjusted upward to keep pace with rising wages. The actuary should also consider what assumptions should be used regarding future increases in benefits for retired participants that will be made on either an automatic or ad hoc basis. As might be surmised, salary scale assumptions have a potent influence on cost and liability estimates.

TABLE 22-3   Salary Scale

	Annual Increase				Ratio of Salary at Attained Age to Salary at Age 20
Age	Inflation	Productivity	Merit	Total	
20	.035	.005	.023	.063	1.000
21	.035	.005	.023	.063	1.063
22	.035	.005	.023	.063	1.129
—					
—					
64	.035	.005	.023	.063	15.304
65					16.260

Interest Rate

The present value of a series of future contingent payments is a function of the rate of investment return, or of interest at which the payments are discounted. The higher the interest assumption, the smaller the present value. Pension plan costs and liabilities are extremely sensitive to the interest assumption in the valuation formula because of the long time-lapse between the accrual of a benefit credit and its payment. The precise impact of the interest assumption depends upon the plan population characteristics, the rates of decrement, the salary scale, and the assumption as to the pattern of cost accruals (as determined by the actuarial cost method); but it is a fairly sound generalization that, for a typical plan, a change (upward or downward) of 1 percent in the interest assumption (e.g., an increase from 7 to 8 percent) alters the long-run cost estimate by about 25 percent.[15] This relationship seems to hold within any reasonable range of interest assumptions.[16]

Because cost estimates are sensitive to the interest assumption, the rate must be chosen with great care. Consultation with the employer and the agency investing the plan assets concerning present and future investment policy may assist the actuary in estimating the future investment return. The rate should represent the expected rate of return on plan assets over the long term. It should not be changed to reflect fluctuations in the financial market that appear to be transitory or short-term. The concept of what investment return to employ must be considered. It should be the total expected long-term return on invested assets, including expected changes in market value.

The treatment of unrealized gains or losses on the equity portion of the investment portfolio is of perennial concern, and there is no consensus on how such gains or losses should be handled. To enforce funding standards, the law requires that common stocks and other equity investments be valued on a reasonable actuarial basis that takes into account fair market value (see Chapter 30 for discussion of asset valuation).[17] There is no direct comparable requirement for measuring investment return, but in the long run, investment return will include any appreciation and depreciation of assets, so changes in asset values should be reflected in the interest assumptions.

As noted earlier, for purposes of the minimum funding requirements the valuation must be based on actuarial assumptions and methods that are all reasonable (taking into account the experience of the plan and reasonable expectations), or that in the aggregate result in a total contribution equivalent to what would be determined if each assumption and method were reasonable. Thus in minimum

---

[15]For a mathematical demonstration of this relationship and the constraints that must be observed, see Warren R. Adams, "The Effect of Interest on Pension Contributions," *Transactions of the Society of Actuaries*, vol. 19 (1967): pp. 170–83, and discussion, pp. 184–93. See also M. T. L. Bizley, "The Effect on Pension Fund Contributions of a Change in the Rate of Interest," *Journal of the Institute of Actuaries Students' Society*, vol. 10 (1950): pp. 47–51.

[16]It should be understood that the impact on the *actual* cost of the plan depends upon the rate of contributions to the plan, the extent to which the accrued liabilities have been funded, and the rate of actual investment return on the invested assets. The suggested relationship is based on the tacit assumption that the ultimate fund of plan assets is 25 times the ultimate annual contribution.

[17]ERISA §302(c)(2)(A); IRC §412(c)(2)(A).

funding valuations one assumption that is too conservative may offset another assumption that is not conservative enough.

In the past, in the interest of conservatism actuaries often used an interest assumption somewhat lower than the expected long-term rate of return. This would be contrary now to the statutory requirement unless the effect of the conservative interest assumption is offset by some other assumption that is not sufficiently conservative.

In today's economic environment, the basic issue involved in the choice of interest assumption is what allowance should be made for future inflation. In theory, there is a "pure" rate of interest for a risk-free investment, reflecting only the lender's time preference; and, in the absence of inflation, the long-run return on a portfolio of assets should be a rate equal to the pure rate of interest plus whatever premium is demanded by investors for the possibility of loss of principal or income. For a particular portfolio, the risk premium would reflect the quality mix of the individual holdings. Under inflationary conditions, prudent investors can be expected to demand an investment return that will include an allowance for anticipated price increases during the term for which they relinquish control over their capital.

Economists have widely differing views about the pure rate of interest on risk-free investments. For the period 1926 through 1994, the annual rate of return on long-term U.S. Treasury bills exceeded the rate of inflation by only 0.5 percent. The inflation-adjusted return for this period was 1.7 percent for long-term government bonds, 2.2 percent for long-term corporate bonds, and 6.9 percent for large capitalization common stocks.[18] The risk premium for the type of portfolio held by the typical pension plan is probably about 3 to 5 percent. Many actuaries currently assume an interest rate of 1 to 4 percent above the assumed cost-of-living increase. Whether or not the cost-of-living increase assumption is explicitly stated, the total interest assumption currently used for funding is typically 7 to 9 percent. The Internal Revenue Service has disallowed deductions based on interest assumptions it considers unreasonably conservative.

If benefits are related to compensation, the allowance for price inflation should be the same in the interest assumption and the salary scale. However, the two inflation increments do not "wash out" or neutralize each other in a valuation of liabilities. The salary scale applies only during the period of active employment, while the interest assumption affects the estimated cost of benefits for all segments of the plan population, including retiree participants and the future retirement period of those now active. For each one percentage point added to both the interest and salary scale assumptions for inflation, the estimated cost of a representative plan without cost-of-living adjustments goes down about 10 percent.[19] For example, if the assumed rate of inflation is increased by 1 percent per year and is added to both the interest and salary scale assumptions, the projected cost of the plan would be reduced about 10 percent. If there are cost-of-living adjustments after retirement, an increase of one percentage point in the interest, salary scale, and cost-of-living assumptions would have little effect upon the cost of the plan.

---

[18] *Stocks, Bonds, Bills and Inflation: 1995 Yearbook* (Chicago: R. G. Ibbotson Associates, Inc., 1995).

[19] This percentage will vary with a variety of factors.

Additional statutory constraints that apply to the interest assumption used for certain special purposes are discussed later in connection with those uses.

Immediate Annuity Factors for Retired Participants

The valuation of retirement benefits requires the use of immediate annuity factors. As used here, an *immediate annuity factor* is the actuarial present value of an amount of one dollar per annum payable monthly from a specified age to a retired participant under the normal annuity form or any of the unsubsidized optional annuity forms available under the plan. An immediate annuity factor or rate must be computed for each age at which retired persons or their joint annuitants may be found. Specifically, there must be a factor for each age in a spectrum that begins with the earliest age at which retirement can occur and ends with the attained age of the oldest annuitant. For each age, there is usually one factor for male annuitants and another for female annuitants, the latter factor being larger because of the longer life expectancy of females.

The immediate annuity factor usually reflects only two assumptions: the probability of survival from age to age and a rate of interest for discounting future contingent payments.[20] Both assumptions are critical since they operate during the crucial payout stage. Overstating the rates of decrement during this period, or the rate of return on the underlying assets, could have serious cost consequences. The mortality assumptions are usually taken from the same annuity mortality table used to predict the probabilities of survival among the active life population, although separate tables are sometimes used for the two subsets of the population. If separate mortality rates are to be used for male and female lives, they may be taken from separately developed sex distinct tables, such as those prepared in connection with the 1983 GAM Table. Alternatively, female rates may be assumed to equal male rates for setback ages. The interest rate used for computing annuity factors is generally the same as the rate used in discounting the projected retirement benefit back to the valuation date.

Usually there is no separate actuarial assumption regarding immediate annuity factors, since these factors typically result from computations based on the mortality and interest assumptions. But sometimes a separate assumption is made concerning the immediate annuity factors with no explicit statement concerning the mortality or interest assumptions underlying them. Where used, the immediate annuity factors are usually set equal to guaranteed annuity purchase rates of insurance or annuity contracts used to fund the plan.

Annuity factors must be computed for each optional form of annuity paying benefits to retired participants and beneficiaries. If the benefits payable under the optional forms of annuity are the actuarial equivalent of the normal retirement benefit, no allowance need be made for active participants who may choose an optional annuity form. On the other hand, if the optional annuity forms are subsidized, special annuity factors must be computed for each form of subsidized annuity, and the percentage of the retiring participants that will elect each of the

---

[20]For plans with automatic cost-of-living adjustments, a cost-of-living assumption is also used. An expense assumption may be used.

options must be estimated. A more detailed description of the process of computing the annual cost of the plan must be deferred until actuarial cost methods are considered.

Expenses

The foregoing factors are concerned only with the valuation of the *benefits* under a pension plan; if an estimate of the total *cost* of the plan is to be derived, expenses must be taken into account.

The expenses associated with a pension plan may be broadly classified as (1) developmental, (2) legal, (3) actuarial, (4) financial, (5) general administrative, and (6) premiums payable to the Pension Benefit Guaranty Corporation. They may be incurred originally by a number of different agencies, but the cost ultimately falls upon the employer (and possibly the employees, if employer contributions are fixed by collective bargaining or if the plan is contributory).

Investment expenses may be considered an offset to investment income, in which case the interest assumption reflects this reduction. Other expenses paid directly from plan assets may be recognized by a specific expense assumption, either as a fixed dollar amount or as a percentage of some other account (e.g., a percentage of other costs or contributions). If expenses are paid directly by the employer, rather than from the plan assets, no expense assumption will be used in the actuarial valuation. Often no expense assumption is made, even when expenses are paid by the plan assets, particularly if the expenses are relatively small. Any excess of actual expenses over those assumed results in an actuarial loss.

If the plan is insured, the bulk of the expense may be borne by the insurance company. Under some types of annuity contracts, the insurer recovers part or all of its expenses by a direct charge to the individual plan's account balance. Under other contracts, the insurer recovers its expenses by deductions from the investment income otherwise payable or from the margins in premiums charged under the contract.

Chapter 23

Benefit Allocation Actuarial Cost Methods

The preceding chapter described the factors and types of assumptions that enter into the valuation of the benefits (and expenses) of a defined benefit pension plan. It also described the general procedures used to determine the actuarial present value of the accrued or prospective retirement benefits. This chapter defines some fundamental terms and concepts involved in the valuation of a defined benefit pension plan. It also describes the basic actuarial cost methods associated with one generic approach to apportioning the actuarial present value of benefits to the years of service of the plan participants. The other generic approach and its associated cost methods are considered in Chapter 24.

Terminology

As the literature demonstrates, a great variety of terms are used to express actuarial concepts. The most widely used terms are found in the Employer Retirement Income Security Act, the Internal Revenue Code, and IRS publications (which are not always internally consistent). Another set of terms appears in the 1981 report of the Joint Committee on Pension Terminology; this set was adopted by the American Academy of Actuaries, the American Society of Pension Actuaries, the Conference of Actuaries in Public Practice, and the Society of Actuaries. In addition, many other terms not contained in either of these two sets are widely used. For the most part, this text follows the terminology of ERISA, the Code, and IRS publications when applicable but otherwise follows the Joint Committee terminology. Alternative terms are identified when they arise. A comparative summary of the terminology is found in Table 24-1 in Chapter 24. Still different terminology is used for accounting purposes, as discussed in Chapter 28.

Fundamental Concepts

The actuarial present value of future benefits is the amount that, together with future investment earnings, is expected to be sufficient to pay those benefits. The term *actuarial present value*[1] is intended to connote that the derivation of such a

---

[1]ERISA §3(27).

value involves population decremental factors, salary scales, and other functions, in addition to an interest discount for the time value of money.

Normal Cost

For funding, accounting (see Chapter 28), and tax purposes, it is necessary to assign or allocate—in a systematic and consistent manner—the expected cost of a pension plan for a group of participants to the years of service that give rise to that cost. The technique used for this assignment or allocation is called an *actuarial cost method* (or sometimes *funding method*).[2] The general objective of an actuarial cost method is to assign to each fiscal or plan year the cost assumed to have accrued in that year. The portion of the actuarial present value of benefits assigned to a particular year for an individual participant or the plan as a whole is called the *normal cost.*[3] Since the various actuarial cost methods allocate benefits and actuarial present values according to different patterns, the normal cost of a plan is a function of the actuarial cost method employed. The term *normal cost* originated because under some methods, the normal cost is defined as the cost that would be assigned to a given year of the plan's operation if, from the earliest date of credited service, the plan had been in effect and costs had been accrued in accordance with that actuarial cost method—and all actuarial assumptions had been exactly realized. The significance and implications of this definition will be more fully grasped as actuarial cost methods are examined in greater detail. The normal cost is usually determined for the year following the valuation date.

Actuarial Liability

Actuarial cost methods generally (but sometimes imprecisely) divide the present value of future benefits into two parts, the part attributable to the past and the part attributable to the future. The part attributable to the past is called the *actuarial liability* while that attributable to the future is called the *present value of future normal costs.*

From a retrospective point of view, the cumulative normal cost of the plan—increased by the valuation rate of interest, decreased by benefit and expense disbursements, and adjusted for actuarial gains and losses (explained below)—equals the *actuarial liability* of the plan.[4] Viewed prospectively, the actuarial liability is the actuarial present value of future benefits less the actuarial present value of future normal cost accruals. The actuarial liability of a plan increases each year until the plan population reaches a mature state, if ever, after which it would remain constant if the population and benefit distribution were to remain stable.

The terms *accrued liability*[5] and *actuarial accrued liability* are synonymous with *actuarial liability* (the latter being favored in this text). The term *initial actuarial*

---

[2] ERISA §3(31).
[3] ERISA §3(28).
[4] The pension plan obligation described here as an actuarial *liability* is not necessarily a legal or accounting liability of the plan or its sponsor; accounting liabilities are discussed in Chapter 28, legal liabilities upon plan termination in Chapters 33 and 34.
[5] ERISA §§3(29), 302(c)(1),(7); IRC §412(c)(1),(7).

liability or *initial accrued liability* refers to the actuarial liability existing at the inception of a plan if past service credits must be provided. It equals the normal costs, increased by interest at the valuation rate, that would have accrued for that service had the plan been in continuous operation from the date of the earliest credited service. The term *past service liability*[6] or *past service cost* is frequently used to refer to the initial actuarial liability, and it is sometimes used to refer to (a) any additions to the actuarial liability brought about by retroactive benefit increases after the plan has been in operation, or (b) (erroneously) the actuarial liability at the current date. The terms *prior service liability* or *prior service cost* may be used synonymously with actuarial liability or may be used to indicate the actuarial liability on the valuation date attributable to benefits credited for service prior to the effective date of the plan. These terms with ambiguous meanings are avoided in this text.

That portion of the liability offset by plan assets is referred to as the *funded* actuarial liability, and the ratio of assets to liabilities is called the *funded ratio*. The portion of actuarial liability not offset by plan assets is quite naturally called the *unfunded actuarial liability* or *unfunded accrued liability*,[7] and is an item of significance and concern.

The actuarial liability may be divided into two segments: the *normal cost liability* and the *supplemental cost liability*, although this differentiation is not usually made in practice. The normal cost liability is retrospectively the sum of all normal cost accruals *since the inception of the plan*, increased by interest at the valuation rate and decreased by benefit and expense disbursements allocable to the normal cost accruals.[8] Prospectively, the normal cost liability equals the actuarial present value of future benefits minus the actuarial present value of future normal cost accruals and supplemental cost accruals. The supplemental cost liability is equal to the difference between the actuarial liability and the normal cost liability. In other words, it is the residual or balancing item in the equation. It is present whenever the actuarial cost method establishes future normal cost accruals whose actuarial present value is less than the actuarial present value of the total projected benefits of the plan.

A significant source of supplemental cost liability is the benefit credits granted for service prior to inception of the plan. These credits are expensive because there were no normal cost accruals for years prior to establishment of the plan. The supplemental cost liability attributable to past service benefits is equal to the actuarial accumulation of the normal costs that would have accrued for such benefits had the plan been in operation from the earliest date of credited service. This means that at the inception of the plan the *actuarial liability*, the *supplemental cost liability*, and the *initial past service liability* are all equal. By the end of the first plan year, the actuarial liability will have increased by the normal cost for the year

---

[6]ERISA §302(b)(2)(B); IRC §412(b)(2)(B).

[7]ERISA §3(30).

[8]This description applies to the normal cost liability for the plan as a whole. The normal cost liability for an individual participant must also recognize the benefit of survivorship in service. It should also be pointed out that the normal cost accruals in question are those that would be applicable under the current plan design and current actuarial assumptions, which might be different from those originally determined.

plus interest at the valuation rate on the supplemental cost liability and less benefit payments; while the supplemental cost liability will have increased only by an amount equal to interest at the assumed rate, less benefit payments attributable to the supplemental liability. Never again will the two values be the same, the disparity becoming larger with each passing year.

Another component or layer of supplemental cost liability is created when the benefits of the ongoing plan are retroactively liberalized. The characteristics of this layer of liability are identical to those of the initial supplemental liability, since they represent the actuarial accumulation of the *additional* normal costs that would have accrued from the inception of the plan had the new level of benefits been in effect from the beginning. The actuarial liability would increase by the amount of the additional layer of supplemental cost liability *plus* the normal cost for another year of all actuarial liabilities. Additional layers of supplemental cost liability are created by the adoption of actuarial assumptions more conservative than those that underlie the prior cost accruals. (A *negative* supplemental liability is created by the adoption of less conservative actuarial assumptions.)

Funding the Supplemental Cost Liability

Supplemental cost liability must be funded in accordance with various schedules laid down in ERISA (the schedules are discussed in Chapter 27). Each layer of supplemental cost liability has its own amortization schedule; however, the plan sponsor may merge the various schedules into one, with proper weighting of the actuarial values and remaining time periods involved, after regulations regarding this are issued.[9]

The annual cost accrual associated with amortization of the plan's supplemental cost liability is called the *supplemental cost* (also called amortization payment by the Joint Committee). This cost parallels the normal cost that is associated with the benefit accruals for the current year of a plan's operation. For purposes of ERISA's minimum funding requirements this supplemental cost is called an *amortization charge* if positive or an *amortization credit* if negative. The normal cost and supplemental cost together constitute the *annual cost* of the plan.

Actuarial Gains and Losses

Only by coincidence will the actual experience of the plan conform to the assumptions that underlie the actuarial cost estimates. If the experience of the plan is financially more favorable than the underlying assumptions, *actuarial gains* emerge. If the experience is financially less favorable than that assumed, *actuarial losses* emerge. These concepts are applicable to each of the underlying assumptions, as well as to the assumptions taken as a whole. For example, if fewer participants die than were expected to do so according to the underlying mortality assumptions, there is an actuarial loss for the retirement benefits but an actuarial gain for any death benefits in the plan, and the net effect would be uncertain. On the other hand, if there were more withdrawals than expected, there would be an

---

[9]IRC §412(b)(4).

actuarial gain for retirement benefits and a partly offsetting loss for the benefits of terminated vested participants. An inadequate salary scale would produce an actuarial loss, while an investment result that was more favorable than the valuation interest rate would create an actuarial gain. There may be actuarial gains for some factors and actuarial losses for others in the same year. The experience status of the plan as a whole for a given year of operations reflects the net balance of actuarial gains and losses among the various actuarial cost factors. Actuarial gains and losses arising out of the deviation of actual from expected experience are frequently referred to as *experience gains and losses*, to distinguish them from gains or losses resulting from a *change in the underlying actuarial assumptions*.

Some actuarial cost methods, called *spread gain* methods, automatically spread all gains and losses over the normal cost for the current and future years. Under all other actuarial cost methods any actuarial gain or loss results in a change in the unfunded actuarial liability of the plan, which may be amortized over a period of years. The choice of amortization period may be influenced by legal and accounting requirements, the actuarial cost method, the funding instrument, plan provisions, collective bargaining agreements, and the fiscal objectives of the plan sponsor. For purposes of determining compliance with minimum funding standards (described in Chapter 27), the law now requires that experience gains and losses be amortized over 15 years for multiemployer plans or over 5 years for other plans. Changes in the unfunded liability arising out of modifications in the actuarial assumptions must be amortized over 30 years for multiemployer plans, or over 10 years for other plans. To determine the maximum deductible limit for income tax purposes, actuarial gains and losses can be amortized over 10 years.[10]

Desirable Characteristics of an Actuarial Cost Method

Pension plan sponsors or administrators may seek various properties or characteristics in an actuarial cost method. Some would want the method to develop a normal (or annual) cost that would be a level percentage of covered payroll over the years, assuming no change in the benefit formula or other substantive features of the plan, and assuming actual experience would precisely conform with the underlying actuarial assumptions. Some would want the method to generate an actuarial liability that would be at least equal to the actuarial present value of all accrued benefits, vested and nonvested, that would be payable in the event of plan termination. Some—and this is related to the second characteristic—would want the method to generate an actuarial liability that is not grossly in excess of the plan termination liability, to avoid what they contend is a distortion in the allocation of total plan costs over time. Finally, there are those who would want the method to provide sufficient flexibility to meet the short-term fiscal needs of the employer or other plan sponsor. In other words, they would want some room for varying the year-to-year contributions in response to the firm's earnings and cash flow situation.

These four objectives are inherently contradictory, and no actuarial cost method yet devised can satisfy all four. The rest of the chapter examines the extent to which the various cost methods can satisfy these objectives. Note that flexibility may be

[10]IRC §404(a)(1)(A)(iii).

provided through the creation of a supplemental cost component and through the treatment of actuarial gains and losses.

Classification of Actuarial Cost Methods

Actuarial cost methods may be classified in various ways, depending upon the particular characteristic of the methods that one wishes to emphasize in the classification. From both a conceptual and operational standpoint, one of the most fundamental bases for classification is whether the method allocates the *benefits* of the plan to various plan years and then determines the actuarial present value associated with the benefits themselves, or whether it allocates the *actuarial present value* of all prospective benefits to the various plan years without allocating the benefits themselves. Thus to calculate the actuarial liability under a *benefit allocation* actuarial cost method one first determines the amount of each future monthly pension payment (together with any other potential payments such as death benefits) that each participant may become entitled to and that is attributable to service prior to the valuation date; then one determines the actuarial present value of those benefits. But to calculate the actuarial liability under a *cost allocation* actuarial cost method, the actuarial present value of all projected future benefits under the plan is allocated among the periods before and after the valuation date without determining the portion of the specific monthly benefits attributable to service before and after that date.

Those methods that allocate the *benefits* to particular plan years may be further divided on the basis of whether they allocate the benefits according to the plan's provisions describing the benefit that accrues each year or whether they project the total benefit to become payable at normal retirement age and then allocate the projected benefit to each year of a participant's service in portions that constitute either a level dollar amount or a level percentage of pay. Likewise, those methods that allocate *costs*, rather than *benefits*, may be further classified as to whether the portion of the total projected cost (actuarial present value) assigned to each year of a participant's service is a level dollar amount or a level percentage of pay.

Other classifications focus on whether the method develops a supplemental cost liability, which, as noted earlier, is usually related to past service benefits or to plan amendments that increase accrued benefits. If a method does not generate a supplemental cost liability, then the actuarial present value of all benefits, including past service benefits and other retroactively granted benefits, must be assigned to particular years of service in the form of normal costs.

Another basis for classification is whether the accruing costs of the plan are computed with reference to the entry ages or to the attained ages of the various participants. If normal costs are computed on the basis of the participants' actual or assumed entry ages, a supplemental cost liability will be produced by past service and other retroactively granted benefits. If all costs are apportioned from the participants' attained ages to the year of retirement, the annual (normal) cost charges may meet the total cost of the plan, in which case no supplemental liability will develop.[11]

---

[11]It will be noted later that actuarial present values under benefit allocation cost methods are computed as of the participants' attained ages, but a supplemental cost liability is typically developed from past service benefits and retroactive benefit increases.

Yet another basis for classification is whether the normal cost and actuarial liability for the plan are determined separately for each participant or for the group of participants as a whole without reference to the individual participants. Under an *individual* actuarial cost method, the normal cost and actuarial liability are calculated for each participant, and the values for the entire plan are simply the sum of the respective values for all the participants. Under an *aggregate* method, the costs (but not necessarily the actuarial liability) are determined for the group as a whole in such a manner that the cost for an individual participant cannot be separately identified. As will be noted later, the cost of the plan determined on an aggregate basis is not the same as the sum obtained by adding the individually determined costs for the various participants. However, under an individual method it would be possible (although laborious, perhaps) to determine the costs for each participant, whereas it would be completely impossible (in theory and in fact) to do so under an aggregate method.

Finally, actuarial cost methods can be distinguished according to how they determine and deal with actuarial gains and losses. Under some actuarial cost methods, actuarial gains and losses are directly and explicitly computed as the difference between the actual unfunded actuarial liability as of the date of current valuation and the unfunded actuarial liability that would have existed at that date if all actuarial assumptions had been exactly realized. A gain or loss so determined is then amortized over a period of years. This is quite logically known as the *direct* method of determining and dealing with actuarial gains and losses. Under other actuarial cost methods, especially those characterized as aggregate methods, gains and losses are not directly computed. In effect, actuarial gains and losses are automatically, and without separate identification, spread over the future working lifetimes of all active participants as a component of the normal cost. This approach is referred to as the *spread* method of dealing with gains and losses and will be more comprehensible after the structure of aggregate cost methods has been examined.

Those features of actuarial cost methods that have been described in this section as *basis* for classifying cost methods may also be termed *characteristics* of actuarial cost methods. Any one method may have several of these characteristics and thus the dichotomous classifications overlap. The cost method being employed for a given pension plan cannot be conclusively identified until its principal characteristics are given. It is not enough in itself to know whether the plan's costs and actuarial liabilities are computed on the basis of *benefit* allocations or *cost* allocations. It is also necessary to know whether benefits or costs are assigned to plan years in quantities that constitute level dollar amounts or level percentages of payroll, whether or not supplemental cost liabilities are generated, whether entry ages or attained ages are used, whether the computations are made on an individual or aggregate basis, and how actuarial gains and losses are handled. If there is a supplemental cost liability, there needs to be a statement about the way it is being handled and, if appropriate, the period over which it is being amortized.

A full identification of one widely used actuarial cost method would indicate that it is an individual, level percentage, entry-age cost allocation method with supplemental liability and with immediate recognition of actuarial gains and losses. Some authorities would also indicate whether it is a closed-group or open-group valuation. Which of these approaches is used would seem to be more a matter of actuarial assumptions than a cost method characteristic. It is undeniably a vital piece of information about the overall valuation process. Except where otherwise indicated, all descriptions and illustrations of actuarial cost methods in this text assume a closed group of participants.

Benefit Allocation Cost Methods

A number of actuarial cost methods are commonly used, each generating a different normal cost and actuarial liability for the same set of underlying data and actuarial assumptions. For pedagogical purposes, this text divides them into two broad classes, classifying them according to whether *benefits* or *costs* are assigned to the various plan years. Those methods that allocate benefits and then derive the actuarial present value of the benefits are called *benefit allocation cost methods* (also called accrued benefit cost method by ERISA, unit credit method by ERISA, unit credit actuarial cost method by the Joint Committee, single premium method, and step-rate method).

Those methods that compute the actuarial present value of the total benefits to be paid and then assign a portion of that value (or cost) to each plan year are called *cost allocation cost methods*. These two approaches are quite distinctive, from both a philosophical and computational standpoint. Benefit allocation cost methods are described in this chapter, and cost allocation methods are discussed in Chapter 24.

The distinctive characteristic of any benefit allocation cost method is that a discrete unit of retirement benefit is allocated to each year of credited service of a plan participant, and the actuarial present value of that unit of benefit is separately computed and assigned to the year during which it accrued or is presumed to have accrued. The benefit allocation and actuarial value are determined for each participant, and the resulting values are summed to determine the annual cost and actuarial liability for the plan as a whole. In other words, the aggregate approach by which plan costs and liabilities are determined directly and without specific reference to individual participants is not applicable to benefit allocation cost methods. The actuarial value is always determined as of the participants' *attained* ages, but a supplemental cost liability may be—and typically is—developed.

Two types of benefit allocation cost methods are in common use. They differ only in how they determine the unit of benefit assigned to a participant's given year of service. In all other respects, they are identical. Both are called the *accrued benefit cost method* or the *unit credit method*.

Traditional Accrued Benefit Cost Method

Under the traditional accrued benefit cost method, the benefit assigned to a participant's given year of credited service is determined by directly applying the plan's benefit formula. The traditional accrued benefit cost method is sometimes called the *traditional unit credit* method. This method is often used when the annual benefit accrual is expressed as a flat dollar amount or a specified percentage of the participant's *current* compensation for each year (which, of course, means a *career average* formula). It is technically possible to use the traditional accrued benefit cost method in connection with a final average pay plan, but Internal Revenue Service regulations do not permit its use for *funding* such a plan.[12] However, to help readers grasp the differences among the various actuarial cost methods, it seems desirable to show the application of all methods under the same hypothetical plan; so all actuarial cost methods are illustrated in this text by a final average pay plan.

Under the traditional accrued benefit cost method, the benefit assigned to a given year of credited service is defined as the expected *increase* in the participant's accumulated plan benefit during the year. Under a final average pay plan, the increase in a participant's accumulated benefit during a given year of service is a combination of that year's benefit accrual and the adjustment of all previous years' accruals to reflect the moving (presumably upward) salary base. In other words, each year the benefit accruals for all previous years are recomputed in terms of the new salary base, such as the average for the last five years, including the current year.

The plan accrued benefit must be ascertainable at all times. Even if the plan provides a composite benefit at normal retirement that is subject to a minimum period of service, equal to a specified percentage of defined compensation (such as 40 percent of the participant's average salary during the last five years of service) or a specified dollar amount, the total prospective benefit must be arbitrarily assigned by the plan document to the participant's potential years of service. It will be recalled that for purposes of determining *vested* benefit accruals, ERISA requires that such a composite benefit be prorated over the total potential years of service or be apportioned in such a fashion that it does not create excessive back loading.

Normal Cost

The first step in deriving the normal cost for a given participant under the traditional accrued benefit cost method is to determine the dollar amount of benefits allocated to the participant during the year in question. This amount is the *increase* in the participant's accumulated plan benefit during the year, as defined by the plan document. Needless to say, an increase in the participant's accumulated benefit because of a plan amendment would not be a part of the normal cost calculation but would lead to an increase in the actuarial liability.

The second step in deriving the normal cost for a given participant is to multiply the dollar amount of benefit allocated to the participant for the year in question by the actuarial present value factor for a benefit of one unit payable commencing at normal retirement age. The actuarial present value of a unit of benefit at any given attained age is equal to the present value (at normal retirement age, here assumed to be age 65) of a life annuity commencing immediately in the amount of one unit per year payable monthly, multiplied by the probability that the participant will survive in service to normal retirement age and discounted back to the participant's current age at the valuation rate of interest. The probability of survival takes into account decrements from death, disability, and withdrawal.[13]

---

[12]Treas. Reg. 1.412(c)(3)-1(e).

[13]For present purposes, withdrawal of vested participants is treated as a decrement, since the examples are concerned with calculations of the actuarial value of a retirement benefit. Benefit accruals preserved

The actuarial present value of a unit benefit increases with each advance in age, since the probability that the participant will survive in service is enhanced and the discount period is shortened.

On the basis of the UP-94 Table and interest at 7 percent, the actuarial present value at age 65 of a straight life annuity due one unit per year payable monthly to a male participant is 9.41.[14] In other words, the plan would have to have assets of $9.41 on hand for a male participant at age 65 to pay him a lifetime benefit of $1 per year; the first monthly payment would be due upon retirement. According to the mortality, disability, and withdrawal assumptions employed in the derivation of survivorship functions (in Appendix A), the probability that a male participant now age 30 will survive in service until age 65 and hence become entitled to a retirement benefit is .2874, and the present value at age 30 of one unit payable at age 65 at 7 percent is .0937. Thus for a male participant aged 30, the actuarial present value factor of a lifetime benefit of one unit per year payable monthly from age 65 under a 7 percent interest assumption is $9.41 \times .2874 \times .0937 = 0.2534$. With interest at 7 percent and the benefit of survivorship in service, this amount would accumulate to 9.41 when the participant reaches age 65. If a male participant aged 30 should be credited for his year of service at that age with a benefit of $100 per year payable monthly from age 65, the actuarial present value of that benefit at age 30 would be $0.2534 \times \$100 = \$25.34$. This would be the normal cost for this participant in this year under this particular cost method. The normal cost for the same benefit credited to a female participant of the same age would be about $30, since the actuarial value of her benefit at age 65 would be about 20 percent larger and her probability of surviving in service from age 30 to 65 would be greater than that of a male participant of the same age, if withdrawal rates for females are assumed to be the same as those for males.[15]

If the foregoing male participant should be credited with another $100 of annual benefit during his next year of service at age 31, the actuarial present value or normal cost of the benefit would be $29, reflecting the slightly higher probability of survival to normal retirement and a one-year shorter discount period. Again, this sum invested at 7 percent interest and improved by the benefit of survivorship in service would accumulate to $927 at age 65, the amount that would have to be on hand at that time, according to the mortality and interest assumptions, to provide a life income of $100 per year payable monthly from age 65.

---

through vesting have their own cost and must be separately valued. Some actuaries do not make this distinction and include the cost of terminated vested benefits with the cost of retirement benefits. Under this procedure, terminations of vested participants are not treated as decrements. When the traditional accrued benefit cost method is used by life insurers in connection with group deferred annuity contracts, no allowance is made for terminations by disability and withdrawal. All participants are assumed to remain in service until retirement, or their earlier death, and all terminations of nonvested participants, other than from death, result in actuarial gains whenever they occur. This same procedure is often used by trust fund plans.

[14]The cost illustrations in this text assume that all participants retire at age 65. In practice, the actuary will typically assume that a percentage of participants retire at each age at which retirement is possible.

[15]Using different withdrawal rates and salary scales for females in some instances may cause the normal cost for a female to be lower than for an equally compensated male of the same age.

TABLE 23-1   Calculation of the Normal Cost for an Individual Male Participant at Various Attained Ages Under the Traditional Accrued Benefit Cost Method

Attained Age (1)	Benefits Allocated to Attained Age (dollars) (2)	Probability of Surviving in Service to Age 65 (3)	Interest Discount from Attained Age to Age 65 (%) (4)	Annuity Factor at Age 65 for 1 unit per Year Payable Monthly for Life (5)	Normal Cost (dollars) (6)
30	250	0.2874	0.0937	9.4131	63
40	685	0.5040	0.1842	9.4131	599
50	1,508	0.6547	0.3624	9.4131	3,368
60	2,752	0.8227	0.7130	9.4131	15,195

The foregoing process for determining the normal cost under the traditional accrued benefit cost method for an individual participant with a normal retirement age of 65 may be illustrated where normal cost equals[16]

$$\begin{pmatrix} \text{Benefits allocated} \\ \text{to attained age} \\ \text{for current year} \end{pmatrix} \times \begin{pmatrix} \text{Probability of} \\ \text{surviving in} \\ \text{service to age 65} \end{pmatrix} \times \begin{pmatrix} \text{Interest discount} \\ \text{from attained} \\ \text{age to age 65} \end{pmatrix} \times \begin{pmatrix} \text{Annuity factor at} \\ \text{age 65 for 1 unit} \\ \text{per year payable} \\ \text{monthly for life} \end{pmatrix} .$$

The same formula can be used to derive the normal cost under all benefit allocation cost methods; the only difference among the methods is the dollar value of the benefits allocated to the participant in the current year.

The values involved in determining *future* normal costs of the retirement benefits of a male participant entering the plan at age 30 (under the assumptions employed in Appendix A) are set out in Table 23-1.[17] The retirement benefit is assumed to be 1 percent of the participant's average salary during the last five years of service for each year of credited service, with no explicit integration with Social Security. The participant's salary, currently $25,000, is assumed to increase in accordance with the merit scale (shown in Appendix Table A-5, part of which was reproduced in Table 22-2), plus an annual compound rate of increase of 4 percent to reflect inflation and real wage gains. The total projected benefit at normal retirement age is $49,995.

Note that the normal cost for this participant, expressed in dollar terms, increases in astronomical proportions over time. This is due to three factors, as may be clearly seen from the table: the dollar benefit allocated to each attained age increases many times because the salary base grows, the probability of surviving in service to age 65 improves, and the period over which the prospective benefit is

---

[16]All the cost illustrations in this chapter are in terms of normal retirement benefits only. It would unduly complicate the discussion to demonstrate how the cost of withdrawal, death, and disability benefits is derived or how multiple retirement ages would affect plan costs. It should be kept in mind, however, that the normal cost and actuarial liability for the plan as a whole reflect the cost and actuarial value of all benefits under the plan, not just retirement benefits.

[17]The figures in this chapter may not total because of rounding.

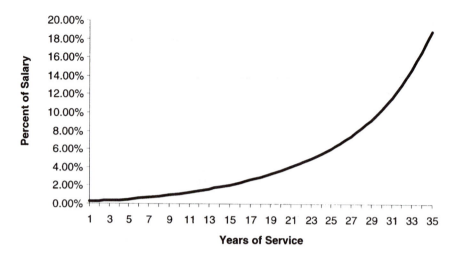

Figure 23-1. Normal cost curve as percentage of the salary of a male participant entering the plan at age 30 under the traditional accrued benefit cost method.

discounted shrinks, leading to a smaller discount. The annuity factor at age 65 remains constant, of course.

The increase in the individual participant's normal cost is not quite so shocking when expressed as a percentage of the participant's growing salary. The normal cost curve of a male participant entering the plan at age 30 and remaining to age 65, under the set of actuarial assumptions used in this text, is depicted in Figure 23-1. The normal cost is only 0.25 percent of the participant's salary at age 30, but it rises each year, eventually reaching 18.8 percent of current salary. The annual increase is especially sharp after about age 45. Because of such sharply increasing costs, regulations do not permit using the traditional accrued benefit cost method for minimum funding requirements for final average pay plans.[18]

The normal cost of retirement benefits for the plan as a whole is the sum of the separately computed normal costs of the benefits allocated to the individual participants at the various attained ages. Since the actuarial value of each unit of benefit for a particular participant goes up each year, for reasons previously noted it might appear that the normal cost for the plan as a whole must also increase from year to year. This is not necessarily so. The normal cost of benefits for the participants in any given attained age cohort increases from one year to the next only by an amount reflecting the one-year shorter period of interest discount and the increased probability of surviving to retirement age, and, of course, any increase in benefit accruals. The annual increase in the normal cost from the discount factor is equal to the interest rate assumed in the valuation formula. In a particular case, the entry of new participants into the plan with their relatively low normal cost, and the retirement of the oldest participants with their relatively high normal cost, might offset, or more than offset, the increased cost associated with surviving participants. As the plan population matures, however, the normal cost for the

[18]Treas. Reg. 1.412(c)(3)-1(e)(3).

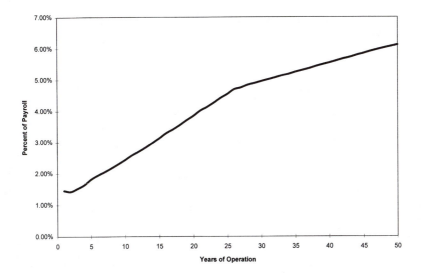

Figure 23-2. Normal cost as a percentage of covered payroll of a hypothetical pension plan over a 50-year period under the traditional accrued benefit cost method.

whole group *tends* to increase in absolute dollar amounts and as a percentage of covered payroll.

The normal cost curve under the traditional accrued benefit cost method for a hypothetical pension plan is shown in Figure 23-2. The normal cost as a percentage of covered payroll was simulated on an open-group basis over a 50-year period, beginning with a relatively immature plan population. The population was assumed to grow from an initial level of 1,000 to 1,895 by the end of 25 years, and to decline thereafter to the original number of 1,000 by year 50. New entrants to replace those leaving active service were introduced at various realistic entry ages. The average age of the participants increased from 40.2 to 46.6 years during the period, and the average period of service increased from 6.7 years to 13.8 years. This change in the attained age and service composition of the plan population caused the normal cost of the plan to increase during the period, from 1.46 percent of covered payroll to 6.12 percent of covered payroll, or 319 percent overall. The normal cost, *as a percentage of payroll*, was not affected by the increase in the dollar amount of benefit accruals arising from growing salaries. The covered payroll grew at the same rate as the benefit accruals, the relationship remaining constant. Differing assumptions could, of course, produce quite different results.

Actuarial Liability

The actuarial liability for a given participant under the traditional accrued benefit cost method is at all times precisely equal to the actuarial value of the cumulative benefit allocated to the participant on the date of the valuation. The process for determining the actuarial value of a participant's accumulated plan benefit is identical to that employed in the calculation of the normal cost, the only difference being the use of the *total* accumulated plan benefit rather than the annual *increase*

TABLE 23-2   Calculation of the Actuarial Liability for an Individual Male Participant at Various Attained Ages Under the Traditional Accrued Benefit Cost Method

Attained Age (1)	Benefits Allocated (dollars) (2)	Probability of Surviving in Service to Age 65 (3)	Interest Discount from Attained Age to Age 65 (%) (4)	Annuity Factor at Age 65 for 1 unit per Year Payable Monthly for Life (5)	Actuarial Liability (dollars) (6)
40	4,737	0.5040	0.1842	9.4131	4,140
45	9,216	0.5871	0.2584	9.4131	13,161
50	15,801	0.6547	0.3624	9.4131	35,290
55	24,956	0.7156	0.5083	9.4131	85,447
60	37,423	0.8227	0.7130	9.4131	206,634
65	49,995	1.0000	1.0000	9.4131	470,608

in the accumulated plan benefit. Thus if only retirement benefits are considered, the basic calculation is as follows:

If a male participant age 40 with a salary of $48,394 at the inception of the plan described above had been credited with 10 years of service and if his past salary increases had followed the assumed rates, he would have a composite annual benefit of $4,737 beginning at age 65 standing to his credit. Each dollar of this benefit would have the same actuarial value at age 40 as a dollar of benefit accruing at that age. Thus the actuarial liability associated with this one individual at plan inception would be:

$$\$4,737 \times .5040 \times .1842 \times 9.4131 = \$4,140.$$

The actuarial liability in respect of this participant would be $5,310 at age 41. The increase of $1,170 would represent the combined effect of the normal cost of the benefit allocation for age 40, interest on the initial actuarial liability of $4,140 at the valuation rate, and the benefit of survivorship in service.

The computation of the actuarial liability for this individual participant at quinquennial ages beginning at age 40 is shown in Table 23-2.

The actuarial liability for the plan as a whole is the sum of the separately computed actuarial liabilities for all the participants, including the retired and terminated vested participants. The actuarial liability for the entire plan is at all times precisely equal to the actuarial present value of all benefits actually credited to date. The traditional accrued benefit cost method is the only actuarial cost method that produces such an equality.

If the plan should terminate, or for some purpose is assumed to terminate, the benefits would be valued on the basis of the traditional accrued benefit cost method. This would be known as a *plan termination liability*. Depending upon the purpose to be served, this type of valuation may be based on all accrued benefits, all vested accrued benefits, or all guaranteed accrued benefits. A plan termination valuation differs from a plan continuation in that the termination valuation does not take the following areas into account: future decrements from disability or withdrawal, future salary increases, or future death and disability benefits that are not part of the accrued benefit payable after plan termination. In other words, a plan termination valuation assumes that benefits under the plan are fixed in amount for all time and are fully vested. The plan termination liability may be larger or smaller than the ongoing plan liability, depending upon the relative cost impact of the differences in treatment of the various cost factors.

Supplemental Cost

Supplemental cost or *amortization charge* was defined earlier as the annual cost accrual associated with amortization of the plan's supplemental cost liability. This definition needs to be refined at this point to recognize that under some plans the supplemental cost liability is not amortized. The objective of the plan sponsor may be limited to preventing the *unamortized* (or *unfunded*) portion of the supplemental cost liability from growing by crediting interest to it at the rate assumed in the actuarial valuation. In this situation, the interest credited to the supplemental cost liability (and paid to the plan) may be regarded as a form of supplemental cost. Counting the crediting of interest only as a method, there are three general approaches to determining the supplemental cost for a given year of pension plan operation. These approaches apply to the supplemental cost liability generated under any actuarial cost method and should not be uniquely associated with the traditional accrued benefit cost method.

A. Interest-Only Supplemental Cost

This is the simplest method of dealing with the supplemental liability and is usually the least costly method in the early years. The aim is not to amortize (and fund) the supplemental liability but only to prevent the dollar amount of its unfunded component from growing. The only pension expense recognized under this procedure is the interest credited to the account and funded. Specifically, the expense or cost is precisely equal to the original amount of supplemental liability, possibly adjusted for actuarial gains and losses, multiplied by the discount rate used to determine the present value of plan benefits. This is known (and has been previously referred to) as the *valuation rate of interest*. Technically, this interest payment is due at the end of the plan year. If it is paid at the beginning of the plan year, the amount is discounted for one year at the valuation rate of interest.

Over time, several layers of supplemental liability may develop from retroactive benefit liberalizations, actuarial losses, and changes in actuarial assumptions, each with its own original value and its own valuation rate of interest. The various layers of supplemental liability may be dealt with differently. Some may be funded on an "interest-only" basis, with some being amortized over a period of years. For example, the initial supplemental liability, which is created at plan inception when past service benefits were granted, may be administered on an interest-only basis, with all future layers of supplemental liability being amortized over a period of years.

The principal weakness of the approach is that the plan never becomes fully funded, and in the event of its termination the accrued benefits of plan participants and their beneficiaries cannot be paid in full. To combat this weakness and to protect the plan benefits insurance program (which is discussed in Chapter 33), ERISA prohibited the interest-only approach for pension plans subject to the minimum funding standards (see Chapter 27). It can still be used by governmental plans, church plans, and other plans not subject to the funding requirements of ERISA.

B. Level Dollar Supplemental Cost

A second method (which is the one usually used) for deriving the supplemental cost of a pension plan is to determine the level dollar amount that would have to be expensed (and presumably funded) each year to fully amortize the supplemental liability over a given number of years, recognizing that the liability is a discounted value and hence bears interest. This is accomplished by dividing the original dollar amount of the supplemental liability by the present value at the valuation rate of interest of an annuity certain of one unit per year for the period over which the liability is to be amortized. The value of one unit per period payable for a specified number of periods without reference to death or any other contingency is an *annuity certain.*

For example, if the supplemental liability is derived in the first instance on the basis of a 7 percent interest assumption and is to be amortized in 30 equal annual installments payable at the beginning of each year, the divisor is the present value of 1 payable immediately plus 29 subsequent annual payments of 1, all discounted to the present at a 7 percent rate of interest. This value can be obtained from a conventional compound interest table that gives the present value of 1 per annum for varying periods and at varying rates of interest. The amortization process is precisely analogous to repaying a mortgage on a home. Each annual installment is part principal and part interest, with the interest component dominating in the early years. The proportion of the annual installment representing repayment of principal increases each year.

During a period of expanding payrolls, each level annual charge against (or contribution toward) the supplemental liability constitutes a declining percentage of covered payroll. This is graphically illustrated in Figure 23-3, which shows the level dollar supplemental cost as a percentage of covered payroll for the simulated pension plan used for illustrations in this text when the supplemental liability is assumed to be fully amortized over a 30-year period. (The dollar amount of the supplemental liability and the manner in which it was derived are immaterial for the purposes of this illustration.) This is the maximum amortization period permitted under ERISA for future increases in the unfunded actuarial liabilities arising from the establishment or amendment of a plan or from a change in actuarial assumptions. ERISA prescribes level dollar amortization of supplemental liabilities as the minimum standard.

The dominance of the interest factor in a long-term amortization schedule is strikingly displayed in Figure 23-4. This figure portrays the unamortized portion of the supplemental liability of the illustrative pension plan from year to year as a percentage of the original value of the liability under a 30-year amortization schedule. The amount of amortization is modest through the first 15 years.

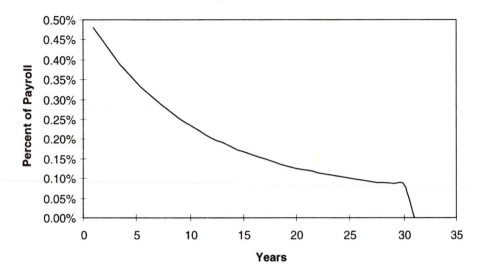

Figure 23-3. Supplemental cost as a percentage of payroll under 30-year level dollar amortization.

C. Level Percentage Supplemental Cost

A third method of deriving the supplemental cost of a pension plan is to amortize the supplemental liability over a period of years in annual installments that constitute a level percentage of the covered payroll. The procedure for determining this amount is somewhat more complicated than that involved in deriving the level dollar amount to be amortized. It is necessary to determine the present value of the future covered payroll expected to be paid during the amortization period. The future covered payroll may be projected by using an open

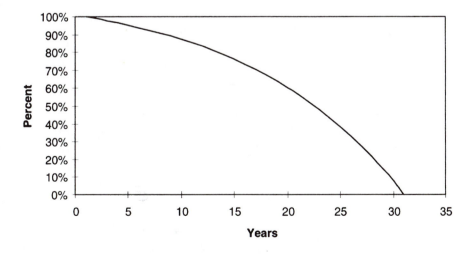

Figure 23-4. Unamortized supplemental liability as a percentage of the original dollar value under a 30-year level dollar amortization schedule.

group method that reflects new entrants, or it may merely be assumed to equal the current payroll increasing by a fixed percentage annually.

The present value of the future covered payroll for the amortization period is then divided into the supplemental liability to determine the supplemental cost as a percentage of payroll. The percentage so derived is applied to the projected payroll for each of the years in the amortization period, to determine a fixed schedule of annual supplemental cost charges (and funding contribution) for the amortization period. The dollar amount of the annual charge will rise with the assumed increase in payroll, but the percentage charge will be level. The initially derived percentage may be applied to the *projected* payroll, rather than to the *actual* payroll that emerges in the future to ensure that the scheduled dollar charges (and contributions) will actually amortize the supplemental liability over the period desired. Otherwise, if the actual payroll turned out to be smaller than the projected one, there would be a shortfall in the future charges and contributions, and the supplemental liability might never be fully amortized without an upward adjustment in the percentage charge. Contrariwise, if the actual payroll were to grow more rapidly than assumed, the supplemental liability would be amortized over a shorter period than planned, which is not necessarily an undesirable result.

Since the covered payroll is assumed to increase over time, the level percentage supplemental cost will be smaller than the level dollar supplemental cost during the early years of the amortization period and greater during the later years. Moreover, depending on the length of the amortization period, the assumed rate of growth in covered payroll, and the valuation rate of interest, the level percentage supplemental cost may be *less than the interest-only* supplemental cost during the early (or possibly during a substantial) portion of the amortization period, in which event the unfunded component of the supplemental liability would grow for a time. For this reason and others, pension plans subject to the minimum funding standards of ERISA are not permitted to use the level percentage supplemental cost method. The method continues to be used by some plans not subject to ERISA's funding standards.

Figure 23-5 shows the supplemental cost under the level dollar and level percentage methods for the illustrative pension plan under a 30-year amortization schedule. The two curves are actuarially equivalent, but as pointed out earlier, amortization proceeds at a faster pace under the level dollar method during the early part of the amortization period.

Figure 23-6 delineates the unamortized portion of the supplemental liability from year to year as a percentage of the original value under the level dollar and level percentage supplemental cost methods, when the amortization period is 30 years. Note that with a 7 percent interest assumption, which underlies all actuarial illustrations in this text, the *unfunded* component of the supplemental liability *increases* for about 10 years under the level percentage method. In fact, the unfunded component of the supplemental liability in year 17 is about the same as it was in year 1. Thereafter, it declines rapidly to zero.

Even though the *dollar* value of the unamortized portion of the supplemental liability increases for a time under the level percentage method, its *relative* value declines throughout the period. That is, as a percentage of the total actuarial

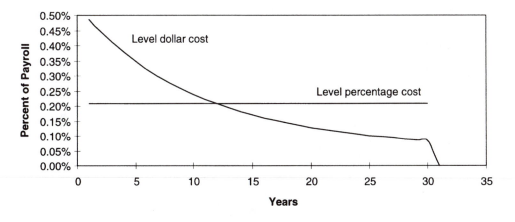

Figure 23-5. Supplemental cost as a percentage of payroll under 30-year level dollar and level percentage methods.

liability for the plan, the unamortized supplemental liability declines steadily. This may be observed in Figure 23-7, which shows the actuarial liability and unamortized supplemental liability under the traditional accrued benefit cost method.

Projected Accrued Benefit Cost Method

The traditional accrued benefit cost method fails to satisfy the criteria of an "ideal" actuarial cost method postulated earlier, because (1) the normal cost of the plan is likely to rise from year to year, and (2) the actuarial liability may fall short of the plan termination liability. Both of these shortcomings are moderated by the projected accrued benefit cost method. A modification of the traditional accrued benefit cost method described later in this chapter *ensures* that its actuarial liability will equal the plan termination liability.

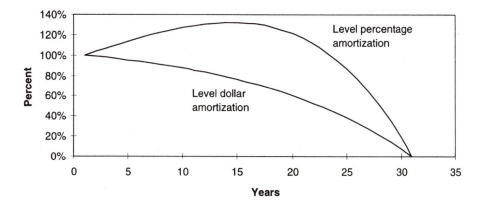

Figure 23-6. Unamortized supplemental liability as a percentage of the original dollar value under 30-year level dollar and level percentage amortization schedules.

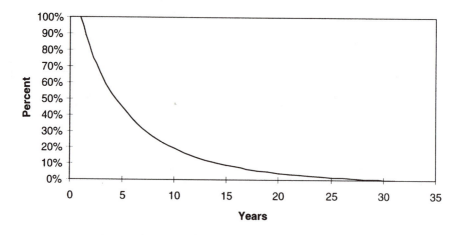

Figure 23-7. Unamortized APBM supplemental liability as a percentage of the total accrued liability under 30-year level percentage amortization schedule.

Normal Cost

The normal cost under the projected accrued benefit cost method (also called the projected unit credit method) is computed by the same formula that is used for the traditional accrued benefit cost method. The only difference between the two methods is the manner in which the annual benefit accrual is determined. Under the projected accrued benefit cost method, a total prospective retirement benefit is projected for each participant in the plan, and a salary scale is used if the benefit is based on the participant's compensation. It is necessary to project the participant's current salary, whether the benefit is based on career average or final average salary. This is especially important if the plan is integrated with Social Security. Once the total prospective benefit has been estimated, a pro rata portion is allocated to each year of service. This is done by dividing the prospective retirement benefit by the number of years for which benefits are credited.[19] If benefits are related to compensation, this results in a larger allocation of benefits to the earlier years of service and a smaller allocation to the later years of service than occurs under the traditional accrued benefit cost method. The total prospective benefit, which reflects the effect of rising earnings from merit, inflation, and real wage gains, is simply leveled out over the participant's entire period of credited service. If benefits under the plan do not accrue uniformly, as is the case when the benefit formula applicable to years of prior service is less than that for future service, the allocation of the projected benefits must be adjusted to reflect the difference.

The benefit allocations that occur under the previously illustrated hypothetical pension plan at selected ages and the manner in which their normal cost is derived are shown in Table 23-3. With a salary of $25,000 at age 30 and an annual growth rate of approximately 5 percent, a benefit of 1 percent of the participant's average salary during the last 5 years of service for each of the 35 years of service would add up to a total annual benefit of $49,995. This amount divided by 35 produces a

[19]Treas. Reg. 1.412(c)-1(e)(3).

TABLE 23-3   Calculation of the Normal Cost for an Individual Male Participant at
Various Attained Ages Under the Level Dollar Benefit Method

Attained Age (1)	Benefits Allocated to Attained Age (dollars) (2)	Probability of Surviving in Service to Age 65 (3)	Interest Discount from Attained Age to Age 65 (%) (4)	Annuity Factor at Age 65 for 1 unit per Year Payable Monthly for Life (5)	Normal Cost (dollars) (6)
30	1,428	0.2874	0.0937	9.4131	362
40	1,428	0.5040	0.1842	9.4131	1,248
50	1,428	0.6547	0.3624	9.4131	3,190
60	1,428	0.8227	0.7130	9.4131	7,887

benefit allocation of $1,428 to each year of credited service. The actuarial values in columns 3, 4, and 5 are identical to those in Table 23-1. The normal cost of the benefit allocated to any of the attained ages is obtained by multiplying the benefit times the values in columns 3, 4, and 5. Thus, the normal cost associated with the benefit allocation at attained age 30 is $1,428 × .2874 × .0937 × 9.4131 = $362.

Note that the normal cost rises from $362 at age 30 to $7,887 at age 60, compared with $63 and $15,195, respectively, under the traditional accrued benefit cost method. The moderation of the cost incline produced by the projected accrued benefit cost method is graphically depicted in Figure 23-8, which shows the normal cost as a percentage of salary under both the projected accrued benefit cost method and the traditional accrued benefit cost method. The normal cost, as a percentage of salary, starts at 1.45 percent and rises to 7.75 percent at age 64, the comparable percentages for the traditional method being 0.25 and 18.81 percent, respectively.

A more meaningful measure of the cost characteristics of the projected accrued benefit cost method is the normal cost curve for an entire plan over a period of years. Figure 23-9 presents such a 50-year curve based upon the same hypothetical pension plan and actuarial assumptions as those underlying Figure 23-2. For purposes of comparison, the normal cost pattern for the traditional method is juxtaposed with the projected accrued benefit cost method curve.

Note that the projected accrued benefit cost method normal cost curve is flatter than that of the traditional method, rising from 2.71 percent of covered payroll to 4.39 percent over the 50-year period.

Actuarial Liability

Like the normal cost, the actuarial liability under the projected accrued benefit cost method is calculated in precisely the same manner as under the traditional method, except for the determination of the benefits allocated to the date of valuation. The benefit allocated to date under the projected accrued benefit cost method for an individual participant, when early retirement and ancillary benefits are ignored, is determined as follows.

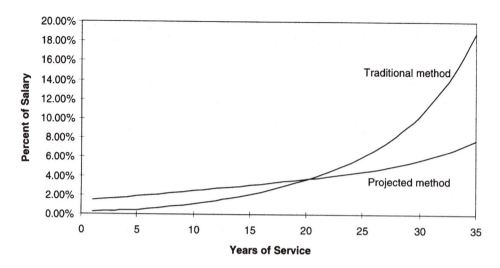

Figure 23-8. Normal cost as a percentage of the salary of a male participant entering the plan at age 30 under the projected and traditional accrued benefit methods.

Using again the example of the male participant who entered the plan at age 30 and expects a retirement benefit of $31,903 per year at age 65, the benefit allocated up to his age 40 would be

$$\$49,995 \times 10/35 = \$14,284.$$

The actuarial liability in respect of this illustrative participant at his attained age 40 would be

$$\$14,284 \times .5040 \times .1842 \times 9.4131 = \$12,483.$$

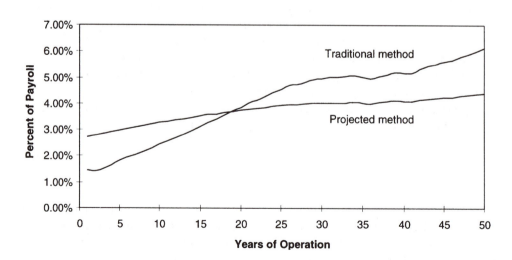

Figure 23-9. Normal cost as a percentage of payroll of a hypothetical pension plan over a 50-year period under the LDBM and APBM.

This is a larger actuarial liability than would have been developed under the traditional accrued benefit cost method, since a greater cumulative benefit has been allocated to the participant's first 10 years of service.

In the following year's actuarial valuation the projected benefit for this participant would be recalculated on the basis of his then-current salary rate and the salary scale, and the portion of the projected benefit based on service to this new valuation date would be determined as in the prior year. To whatever extent this new cumulative benefit differs from the sum of the cumulative benefit calculated the prior year plus the benefit allocated for the intervening year, an actuarial gain or loss will result.

Projected Accrued Benefit Cost Method with Level Percentage Allocation

The total prospective benefit can be allocated to a participant's year of service in dollar amounts that represent a level percentage of the participant's pay in the year in which the benefit allocation is made, rather than in level dollar amounts as described above. This approach has strong theoretical justification, being based on the concept that a participant's annual benefit accruals should reflect his or her current economic worth to the employer. If it is assumed that the cash compensation of employees is a rough measure of their worth to the firm, then it may be argued that their annual benefit accrual should bear a constant relationship to their current compensation.[20] A unit of benefit that constitutes a level percentage of the participant's current cash compensation meets this test.

Since an employee's cash compensation usually increases each year, this method of benefit allocation would produce annual benefit accruals that increase in *dollar* amount from year to year, or at least periodically. If an employer's funding contributions should follow the pattern of benefit allocations, the rate of funding would be slower than that which occurs under any of the cost methods approved for final pay plans. Believing that the method would produce an unacceptably slow rate of funding, the IRS has prohibited the method for funding purposes. Moreover, in developing Statement 87, the Financial Accounting Standards Board rejected the method, despite its theoretical underpinning, in favor of the more pragmatic method that allocates the total prospective benefit in level *dollar* amounts. In view of the fact that the method is not currently being used for any purpose, its manner of generating the normal cost and actuarial liability of a pension plan will not be described here.[21]

Plan Termination Cost Method

In some instances, it is appropriate and meaningful to compare the actuarial liability under any actuarial cost method calculated on a plan continuation basis

[20]This rationale and a set of cost accounting principles based on it were developed by William D. Hall and David L. Landsittel in *A New Look at Accounting for Pension Costs* (Homewood, Ill: Richard D. Irwin, 1977); see especially pp. 47–48.
[21]The method is described in detail on pp. 291–96 of the fifth edition of this text.

with the liability that would exist if the plan should be terminated on the valuation date. The two sets of values will be different. As pointed out earlier, a plan termination valuation omits salary projections, withdrawal assumptions, and ancillary benefits that would not be paid in the event of a plan termination. Whether a plan termination liability will be larger or smaller than a plan continuation liability depends upon the interaction of several opposing cost factors. There is a greater probability that the plan continuation liability will be less than the plan termination liability under a benefit allocation cost method than under a cost allocation cost method, since the latter, to produce level annual costs, *implicitly* allocates larger benefit accruals to service to date than a benefit allocation cost method. Since the smallest cumulative benefit allocations are made under the traditional accrued benefit cost method, this method has the greatest probability of producing an ongoing plan liability smaller than the plan termination liability.

This undesirable result can be avoided by defining the normal cost in terms of the progression of year-to-year values of the actuarial liability determined on a plan termination basis. This modification of the traditional accrued benefit cost method is called the "plan termination cost method."[22] The plan termination cost method defines normal cost in a different way from all other cost methods, which assume the normal cost is an independent quantity derived by applying appropriate actuarial present values to an assumed pattern of benefit allocations. The normal cost at any age under the plan termination cost method is the liability for accrued benefits at the next higher age less the actuarial accumulation of the current year's liability for accrued benefits to the next year. If there are no gains and losses, this formulation is equally applicable to an individual participant and the plan as a whole.

In effect, the normal cost for the plan or an individual participant in any given year is the actuarial value of the benefits accruing in that year plus the increase in the actuarial value of all previously accrued benefits attributable to a rise in the salary base—with all actuarial values ignoring future withdrawals and ancillary benefits that would not be paid in the event of a plan termination. Previous benefit accruals are updated only when the plan uses a final average benefit formula. If the plan provides benefits on the basis of the average salary during the last five years preceding retirement, the plan termination cost method calculates the accrued benefits of each participant annually on the basis of his or her average salary for the preceding five years.

---

[22]First developed in Dan M. McGill and Howard E. Winklevoss, "A Quantitative Analysis of Actuarial Cost Methods for Pension Plans," *Proceedings of the Conference of Actuaries in Public Practice*, vol. 23 (1974). This is not one of the six methods listed in ERISA §3(31) as acceptable for minimum funding requirements.

Chapter 24
Cost Allocation Actuarial Cost Methods

Cost allocation actuarial cost methods are built around a completely different principle from the one behind benefit allocation methods. Rather than assign benefits to specific years of service, as under the benefit allocation methods, the cost allocation methods view the total cost of the benefits, however accrued, as an amount to be allocated equally to all years of service. This is done in a two-step process. First, through the use of salary projections (if the benefits are salary-related), the participant's total prospective benefit at retirement is estimated and the actuarial present value of that benefit at the participant's entry age or attained age (depending upon the method) is determined. Second, this present value (or cost) is allocated to each year of the participant's total prospective service (from entry age or attained age) in an amount that is constant in dollars or a constant percentage of the participant's estimated salary from year to year. Costs are generally allocated as a percentage of salary when a salary projection scale has been used to project plan benefits. Under all other circumstances, costs are typically allocated in level dollar amounts.

The cost may be computed for the individual participants and summed to obtain the normal cost and actuarial liability for the plan as a whole, in which event the cost method is referred to as an *individual* method. Or the cost may be computed directly for the entire plan without attribution on any theoretically precise basis to the individual participants, in which event the approach is called an *aggregate* method. Finally, under both the individual and aggregate approaches, there are methods that develop a supplemental liability and others that do not. Thus a full identification of these methods must indicate whether they are *with supplemental liability* or *without supplemental liability*.

Individual Cost Allocation Methods

Level Dollar Cost Method

The individual level dollar cost method is typically used for pension plans that provide a flat dollar benefit for each year of service. It is not considered appropriate for a plan that provides benefits on the basis of final average salary. As before, a distinction must be made between the derivation of the normal cost and the actuarial liability. The procedure for calculating the normal cost determines whether or not there will be a supplemental liability.

Normal Cost

Four steps are involved in deriving the normal cost for retirement benefits under the individual level dollar cost methods. The first is to estimate the participant's total prospective benefit at retirement. This is done in exactly the same way as it is under the projected accrued benefit cost method, salary projections being used if the benefit is salary related. The second step is to determine the actuarial present value of the total prospective benefit of the participant. If the individual entered the service of the plan sponsor after the plan had been established, this present value calculation would be made as of the individual's entry age (which in the first year would, of course, also be his or her attained age). If the plan has just been established and this is the first valuation, or if a newly created set of retroactive benefits is being valued for the first time, a decision must be made as to whether a supplemental liability is to be generated. If so, the actuarial present value calculation will be as of the employee's entry age into the plan (in a newly established plan, the age from which past service benefits are credited), the method being called the *entry-age normal cost method*. If not, the calculation will be as of the participant's attained age, the method being called the *individual level premium cost method*.[1]

The verbal formula for the second step of the entry-age calculation is as follows:

$$
\begin{pmatrix} \text{Actuarial present} \\ \text{value of} \\ \text{projected benefit} \\ \text{at participant's} \\ \text{entry age} \end{pmatrix} = \begin{pmatrix} \text{Projected} \\ \text{annual} \\ \text{benefit at age 65} \end{pmatrix} \times \begin{pmatrix} \text{Probability of} \\ \text{surviving in} \\ \text{service from} \\ \text{entry age to} \\ \text{age 65} \end{pmatrix} \times \begin{pmatrix} \text{Interest discount} \\ \text{from entry age} \\ \text{to age 65} \end{pmatrix} \times \begin{pmatrix} \text{Annuity factor} \\ \text{at age 65} \\ \text{for 1 unit per} \\ \text{year payable} \\ \text{monthly for life} \end{pmatrix}.
$$

This is the same formula that is used to compute the normal cost under the benefit allocation cost methods, except that here the total projected benefit is inserted in column 2 and the values in columns 3 and 4 are computed as of the participant's entry age, rather than his or her attained age. It should be noted that the actuarial present value of the participant's projected benefit is frequently referred to as the "present value of future benefits" and abbreviated as PVFB. Although this formula has been expressed in terms of the retirement benefit, conceptually the same formula applies to all other benefits. The expression PVFB generally includes all benefits to which participants or their beneficiary might become entitled, rather than just the retirement benefit.

The same formula is used for an attained age valuation of the projected benefit, except that the values in columns 1, 3, and 4 reflect the participant's attained age at plan inception or amendment.

The third step in the normal cost calculation is to determine the actuarial present value factor for a *temporary employment-based life annuity* of one per year payable from the participant's entry age or attained age. This is an annuity assumed to be paid at the beginning of each year that the participant is alive and still in the service of the plan sponsor. Its present value reflects the probability

---

[1]The individual level premium cost method is called the *individual level actuarial cost method* by the Joint Committee.

(involving life contingencies and withdrawal rates)[2] that the participant will survive in service from year to year all the way to retirement, with the annual probabilities being discounted back to the participant's entry or attained age at the valuation rate of interest. Again, the choice of entry age or attained age depends upon whether a supplemental liability is desired.

Finally, as a fourth step the actuarial PVFB is divided by the actuarial present value factor for the temporary employment-based life annuity of 1 per year. This is a matter of simple proportion. If the value of $1 per year payable as long as the participant is in service is known, then the number of dollars that would have to be paid in that manner to have a present value equal to another previously determined quantity, the PVFB, is obtained by dividing the unit value of the temporary employment-based life annuity into the PVFB. The result is the normal cost for the participant in question. It is assumed that this cost will remain fixed and level up to the participant's normal retirement age, but it may be recomputed from time to time to reflect changing circumstances.

The process for computing the normal cost under the individual level dollar cost methods can be illustrated in terms of a male participant in the hypothetical pension plan postulated earlier. That is, his current salary is $48,394 and his attained age is 40, but since he has 10 years of credited past service, his entry age is 30. It is assumed that the plan has just been established and that this is the initial valuation. The first example calculates the individual level premium cost method normal cost as a level dollar cost from *attained age* to retirement age.

A. ATTAINED AGE CALCULATION   The projected benefit of the participant at retirement is $49,995. Each dollar of projected retirement benefit has an actuarial present value of $0.8739 at the participant's *attained age 40*, the product of columns 3, 4, and 5 of the formulation set out below.[3] Thus the actuarial present value, or PVFB, of the total benefit is $49,995 × 0.8739 = $43,690. The actuarial values and process employed in arriving at this PVFB are as follows:

$$
\begin{matrix}
\text{PVFB at} \\
\text{participant's} = \\
\text{attained age}
\end{matrix}
\begin{pmatrix}
\text{Projected} \\
\text{annual} \\
\text{benefit at age 65}
\end{pmatrix}
\times
\begin{pmatrix}
\text{Probability of} \\
\text{surviving in} \\
\text{service from} \\
\text{attained age to} \\
\text{age 65}
\end{pmatrix}
\times
\begin{pmatrix}
\text{Interest discount} \\
\text{from attained age} \\
\text{to age 65}
\end{pmatrix}
\times
\begin{pmatrix}
\text{Annuity factor} \\
\text{at age 65} \\
\text{for 1 unit per} \\
\text{year payable} \\
\text{monthly for life}
\end{pmatrix}
$$

$$= \$49,995 \times .5040 \times .1842 \times 9.4131$$
$$= \$43,690.$$

Note that the values shown in columns 3 and 4 are *attained age* values.

Under the actuarial assumptions used for the hypothetical plan, the actuarial present value factor of a temporary employment-based life annuity of one per year for a 40-year-old male is 11.8338. Thus the

---

[2]In the valuation of smaller plans, the actuary may use only the mortality decrement and discount factor because of the unpredictability of withdrawals. If the plan is very small (e.g., less than 10 participants), even the mortality decrement may be omitted.
[3]Figures in this chapter may not total because of rounding.

$$\text{Normal cost} = \begin{pmatrix} \text{Attained age} \\ \text{PVFB} \end{pmatrix} \div \begin{pmatrix} \text{Temporary employment-based} \\ \text{life annuity of 1 unit per year} \\ \text{from age 40 to age 65} \end{pmatrix}$$

$$= \$43,690/11.8338$$
$$= \$3,692.$$

As before, the normal cost for the plan is the sum of the normal cost values calculated for each of the participants.

There is no supplemental liability under this attained age derivation of costs, since all prospective benefits are taken into account, and at the establishment or amendment of the plan the actuarial present value of future benefits is offset fully and precisely by the actuarial present value of future cost accruals. Neither is there any *initial* actuarial liability, for the same reason. After the first year of the plan's operation, there is an actuarial liability that retrospectively is the actuarial accumulation of past annual cost accruals less benefit disbursements and that, prospectively is the actuarial present value of total prospective benefits (the PVFB for the plan) less the present value of future cost accruals.

The normal cost under this method is not solely attributable to benefit accruals after the attained age, since it includes a component for the amortization of past service benefit costs that under certain other actuarial cost methods would be separately identified as a supplemental cost. Over time, the proportion of the annual cost attributable to past service will decrease under the individual level premium cost method, since for new entrants the annual level cost is determined on an entry-age basis. As will be illustrated later, the annual cost under the individual level premium cost method, in the absence of retroactive benefit liberalizations, will merge into the entry-age normal cost and thereafter be identical to it, after the youngest participant with past service or other retroactive benefit credits has retired. In this sense, the individual level premium cost method is a transitional cost method. The long-run or ultimate level dollar cost method normal cost is that derived on an entry-age basis.

Because the level dollar cost method normal cost is computed as a level annual dollar cost, it is larger than the normal cost developed under benefit allocation cost methods during the early years of a participant's service. If there are past service or other retroactive benefit credits, however, the actuarial liability under the individual level premium cost method may be less than the plan termination liability for all benefits accrued under the terms of the plan. This is so since the *implicit* supplemental liability created by the past service or retroactive benefit credits under this method is not fully amortized until the participant reaches normal retirement age. There is little funding flexibility under this method, since there is no *explicit* and *separately amortized* supplemental liability. The only element of flexibility is found in the treatment of actuarial gains and losses, which may be recognized immediately or spread over a period of years.

The individual level premium cost method is sometimes used in combination with the traditional accrued benefit cost method to provide a supplemental liability and, hence, more flexibility. Under this combination approach, the initial actuarial liability (and supplemental liability) is determined under the traditional accrued benefit cost method. Similarly, any increase in actuarial liability arising out of subsequent benefit improvements is determined under the traditional accrued benefit cost method. Then, the excess of the PVFB over this supplemental liability is amortized in equal annual accruals (constant dollar amount or level percentage of pay) over the participant's future service lifetime, as determined by the individual level premium cost method. This combination is sometimes referred to as the *attained age normal cost method*,[4] a term also used, confusingly enough, for a similar approach utilizing an *aggregate* method.

B. ENTRY AGE CALCULATION   The individual entry-age normal cost calculation differs from the attained-age calculation only in the use of the participant's entry age in computing the PVFB and the actuarial present value factor for a temporary employment-based life annuity of one per year. The projected benefit for the illustrative male participant at age 40 with 10 years of past service is still $49,995, and the actuarial present value factor at age 65 of each unit of benefit is still 9.4131. However, since the intent of the calculation is to determine what the normal cost of the participant's accruing benefits would have been had the plan been in operation at the beginning of his credited service and had the normal cost been recognized each year thereafter, it is necessary to ascertain the actuarial present value of the participant's total projected benefit, or PVFB, as of the participant's theoretical age of entry into the plan. Moreover, since the objective is to amortize the entry-age PVFB in level annual dollar amounts over the participant's total years of credited service, it is necessary to compute the actuarial present value factor for a temporary employment-based life annuity of one per year payable from the participant's earliest date of credited service and divide that sum into the PVFB.

The actuarial values that would be used in this illustrative entry-age computation are as follows:

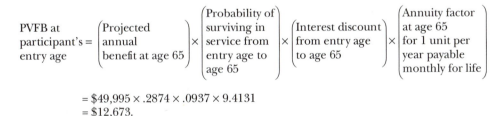

$$= \$49{,}995 \times .2874 \times .0937 \times 9.4131$$
$$= \$12{,}673.$$

The entry-age PVFB is smaller than the attained-age PVFB, since the probability of the participant's surviving in service to normal retirement age is lower at age 30 than at age 40, and the period over which the prospective benefit is discounted is 10 years longer. The actuarial present value factor for a temporary employment-based life annuity beginning at entry age of one per year, 13.2211, is larger than its attained-age counterpart, since the annual payments are assumed to continue over a period 10 years longer than that under the attained-age calculation. The net result is a smaller normal cost than the attained-age normal cost:

---

[4]ERISA §3(31).

$$\text{Normal cost} = \left(\frac{\text{Entry-age}}{\text{PVFB}}\right) \div \left(\begin{array}{l}\text{Temporary employment-based} \\ \text{life annuity of 1 unit per year} \\ \text{from age 30 to age 65}\end{array}\right)$$

$$= \$12,673/13.2211$$
$$= \$959.$$

The lower annual cost accruals under this method are due solely to the fact that the total projected cost is spread over a longer period of years, resulting in more accruals, more interest credits, and greater benefit of survivorship in service. Another way to view the matter is that the individual level premium cost method includes in each annual cost accrual a pro rata portion of the cost that is treated as a supplemental cost under the entry-age normal cost method.

Actuarial Liability

The actuarial liability under the individual level dollar cost methods can be determined retrospectively or prospectively. Retrospectively, the actuarial liability *for the plan as a whole* is the sum of all normal cost accruals to date plus interest at the valuation rate of interest and less all benefit disbursements, the total being adjusted for actuarial gains and losses. *For an individual participant* still in the active service of the plan sponsor, the retrospective actuarial liability is the sum of normal cost accruals to date plus interest at the valuation rate of interest and the benefit of survivorship in service. The latter increment is the participant's pro rata share of the cumulative normal cost accruals "forfeited" by those participants who entered the plan at the same age and in the same year as the participant but who died or terminated with nonvested benefits prior to the valuation date. For the plan as a whole and the individual participants, the normal costs that are accumulated are those that *should have accrued* on the basis of circumstances existing at the date of valuation and not necessarily those that were initially computed. In other words, if in the interim the benefits, actuarial assumptions, or actuarial cost methods have changed, the actuary constructs a new schedule of normal costs from the participants' various entry ages, and these revised normal costs are accumulated to determine the retrospective actuarial liability. For all cost and liability illustrations in this book, it is assumed that the original cost calculations remain valid.

It can be demonstrated mathematically and logically that the actuarial present value of a participant's total prospective benefit at any date is equal to the actuarial value of his or her normal cost accruals to date plus the actuarial value of the normal cost accruals that will be allocated to future years of service. This is so because the normal cost allocations must add up to the total cost of the projected benefits. This is true for the plan as well as the individual participant. This relationship is shown below:

$$\begin{array}{l}\text{Actuarial value} \\ \text{of projected} \\ \text{benefits (PVFB)}\end{array} = \left(\begin{array}{l}\text{Actuarial value of normal} \\ \text{costs allocated to date} \\ \text{(actuarial liability)}\end{array}\right) + \left(\begin{array}{l}\text{Actuarial value of future} \\ \text{normal cost accruals}\end{array}\right)$$

If the dollar value of items 1 and 3 is known, then the dollar value of item 2 can be easily derived. Transposing items, the following relationship is obtained:

$$\begin{array}{l}\text{Actuarial value}\\\text{of normal costs}\\\text{allocated to date}\\\text{(actuarial liability)}\end{array} = \begin{pmatrix}\text{Actuarial value of}\\\text{projected benefits}\\\text{(PVFB)}\end{pmatrix} - \begin{pmatrix}\text{Actuarial value of future}\\\text{normal cost accruals}\end{pmatrix}$$

This happens to be the verbal formulation of the prospective approach to the valuation of a pension plan. The formula is usually shortened to read as follows:

$$\text{Actuarial liability} = \begin{pmatrix}\text{Present value of}\\\text{future benefits}\\\text{(PVFB)}\end{pmatrix} - \begin{pmatrix}\text{Present value of future}\\\text{normal costs}\end{pmatrix}$$

In this formulation, future benefits include benefits credited for service to date, benefits to be credited for future service, benefits of terminated vested participants, and benefits payable to retired participants. If the valuation is for the plan as a whole it will also include, if appropriate, benefits payable to disabled participants and beneficiaries of deceased participants. Because of computational advantages, the prospective valuation formula is generally used.

A. ATTAINED AGE CALCULATION   Under the individual level premium cost method, the present value of future normal cost accruals at the inception of the plan is precisely equivalent to the present value of future benefits; hence there is no actuarial liability at that point. For the same reason there is no supplemental liability. The actuarial present value of future benefits at age 40 for a male participant entering the plan at age 30 is $49,995 \times 0.8739 = \$43,690$. The normal or annual cost for such a participant is $3,692. The actuarial present value factor for a temporary employment-based life annuity of one per year is 11.8338. The actuarial liability in respect of the illustrative participant is

$$(\$49,995 \times 0.8739) - (\$3,692 \times 11.8338) = 0.$$

There will be an actuarial liability at the end of the first year, representing for the male participant now age 41 the normal cost for the year, plus interest and the benefit of survivorship in service. At the participant's age 41, the PVFB has moved up to $48,373 ($49,995 x 0.9676), the temporary employment-based life annuity factor has decreased to 11.6381, and the normal cost remains $3,692. The actuarial liability thus becomes:

$$(\$49,995 \times 0.9676) - (\$3,692 \times 11.6381) = \$5,407.$$

The actuarial liability for the individual participant and the plan as a whole increases from year to year, not only because of additional normal cost accruals but because the group of participants moves ever closer to the normal retirement age. This upward movement in attained ages increases the probability of surviving in service to retirement and shortens the period over which future benefit payments are discounted at compound interest.

On the other hand, no supplemental liability ever arises under the individual level premium cost method, since the costs associated with retroactive benefit increases, changes in actuarial assumptions, and so forth continue to be amortized on an attained age basis. The actuarial present value of the benefit changes will be exactly offset by the present value of the future normal costs associated with those changes.

B. ENTRY AGE CALCULATION The situation is different whenever the normal cost accruals are computed on the assumption that the accruals were initiated prior to the establishment or amendment of the plan, as is the assumption under the entry-age normal cost method. In the example of the male participant aged 40 at the inception of the plan, with 10 years of credited past service and total projected benefits of $49,995 per year, the PVFB at plan inception is $49,995 × 0.8739 = $43,690. The present value of future normal cost accruals is $959 × 11.8338, or $11,349, with $959 representing the annual cost accrual and 11.8338 the actuarial present value of each unit of cost charges to be made annually for as long as the participant survives in service between that date and the participant's normal retirement age. The difference, $32,342, is the initial actuarial liability (and supplemental liability) attributable to this one participant. In terms of the formula, this would appear as follows:

$$(\$49,995 \times 0.8739) - (\$959 \times 11.8338) = \$32,342.$$

It should be apparent that the initial actuarial liability (and supplemental liability) is derived by using in the formula the annual cost accrual for age 30, rather than the one for age 40. All other figures in the two equations (one for the attained-age individual level premium cost method and one for the entry-age normal cost method) remain the same.

Retrospectively, the initial actuarial liability in this particular case is the sum of the annual cost accruals of $959 for the 10-year period of credited past service, improved at 7 percent interest and with the benefit of survivorship in service. There is a theoretical presumption that these cost accruals were actually made, but it is clearly a presumption contrary to fact. No cost accruals could have been made prior to the establishment of the plan, although some provision with respect to the supplemental liability may be made at the date of plan inception.

Both the actuarial liability and the supplemental liability in respect of the participant in question will increase from year to year. Ten years after establishment of the plan, the actuarial liability for the individual, then age 50, would be

$$(\$49,995 \times 2.2334) - (\$959 \times 9.1844) = \$102,851.$$

The projected benefit and the normal cost accrual would remain the same, the present value of each dollar of benefit would be larger (since retirement is closer), and the actuarial present value factor for the employment-based temporary life annuity would be smaller (since fewer payments remain). The result is an actuarial liability that is $70,509 greater than at the inception of the plan. In the meantime, the supplemental liability would have increased by $50,303 as a result of interest and the benefit of survivorship in service.

The nature of the initial actuarial liability (and supplemental liability) under the entry-age normal cost method can perhaps be more fully grasped by comparing it with the initial actuarial liability (and supplemental liability) under the traditional accrued benefit cost method. In the discussion of the latter method, it was pointed out that the initial actuarial liability at plan inception for a male participant aged 40 with cumulative benefit credits of $4,737 per year payable monthly at age 65 is $4,140. It was further pointed out that this sum represents the present value at aged 40 of a projected benefit of $4,737 per year—the precise amount of benefits credited under the plan for 10 years of service prior to establishment of the plan. In contrast, the initial actuarial liability for the same participant under the entry age normal cost method is $32,342. Thus it is larger than the value of the benefits attributable to service prior to inception of the plan. The explanation of this difference lies in the leveling of cost accruals under the entry-age normal cost method. Since for any particular individual, the cost of each $1 of benefits at age 65 (or any other designated age) goes up with each increase in age, the level costs are more than the cost of benefits accruing in the earlier years and less than the cost of benefits accruing in the later years. Hence the costs allocated to past service benefits are always greater than the present value of past service benefits at the effective date of the plan. Since retrospectively the initial actuarial liability (and supplemental liability) is merely the sum of the normal cost accruals for the years of credited past service, plus interest and the benefit of survivorship in service, it follows that the entry-age normal cost method will produce a larger initial actuarial liability (and supplemental liability), other things being equal, than the traditional accrued benefit cost method.

The initial actuarial liability (and supplemental liability) for the entire plan is the sum of such liability attributable to each of the participants in the plan. Yet the liability need not be computed in terms of the specific periods of service of such individuals. Rather than compute the annual cost accrual from a participant's earliest date of credited service, some actuaries use an arbitrary age at which the participant is assumed to have entered the plan. For example, the cost calculations may be based on the assumption that all individuals enter the plan at age 28. If this assumption had been made in the case of the hypothetical male aged 40 with 10 years of actual credited service, the costs would have been leveled from age 28, producing a lower normal cost and a larger initial actuarial liability. In lieu of *one* assumed entry age, the actuary may use an assumed entry age for each quinquennial grouping of ages. Thus all individuals entering the plan at ages 25 to 29 may be assumed to have entered at 27. The assumed entry age or ages may be based on the observed or anticipated experience of the group—or may be rather arbitrary in nature, particularly if the group is small. However, the assumption about the entry age or ages must be reasonable. Such uses of an assumed entry age were developed to reduce the computational burden before modern computers. Their use is gradually disappearing, although they are still used by some actuaries.

The use of assumed or average entry ages will produce a supplemental liability for individuals entering the plan after its establishment at ages above the assumed entry age. Hence, the concept of a supplemental liability should not be associated exclusively with the process of establishing a plan. Individuals entering the plan at ages lower than the assumed entry age bring with them a *negative* actuarial liability, offsetting the positive actuarial liability of those entering at higher ages. A supplemental liability may also arise out of a retroactive increase in benefits (identical in principle to granting past service credits at plan inception); a class of benefits, such as disability benefits or a minimum retirement benefit, not envisioned or properly provided for by the normal cost accruals; an unfavorable deviation of actual from expected experience not offset by an increase in the normal cost accruals; a change in actuarial assumptions; or a change in the method by which costs are computed.

Unless modified by actuarial gains and losses, a given layer of supplemental liability increases each year by an amount equal to the assumed rate of interest, reduced by expected benefit payments. For the entire group of participants whose benefit accruals give rise to the supplemental liability, the probability of survival in service has already been discounted. Thus the aggregate value of the supplemental liability does not increase because of the benefit of survivorship in service if the actuarial assumptions are realized.

Level Percentage Cost Methods

The individual level *percentage* cost methods differ from the individual level *dollar* cost methods only in that the normal cost is defined (and derived) as a level percentage of salary (or payroll) rather than as a level dollar amount. It is suitable only for plans that express the benefit as a percentage of salary. In contrast, the level dollar cost methods are used mainly for plans that express the benefit as a flat dollar amount for each year of credited service.

The level percentage cost methods can function on either an attained-age or entry-age basis. In practice, they are usually structured on an entry-age basis, thus generating a supplemental liability. The term *entry-age normal cost method* refers to individual cost allocation methods based upon entry age regardless of whether the normal cost is determined as a level dollar amount or as a level percentage amount. Both approaches are widely used.

Normal Cost

In deriving the level percentage to be used in the normal cost calculation under the entry-age normal cost method, the actuary, once again, starts by estimating the total cost of the participant's projected annual retirement benefit as of the participant's entry age. This value, the PVFB, is determined in exactly the same manner as it is under the level dollar entry-age normal cost method and, in fact, is the same value. However, rather than dividing the PVFB by the actuarial present value for a temporary employment-based life annuity of one per year payable from entry age to retirement age, the actuary divides by the actuarial present value of such an annuity payable from entry age to age 65, with an amount beginning at one and increasing each year at a rate equal to the assumed rate of salary increase for the participant. The actuarial present value of this annuity is divided into the PVFB to determine the normal cost at entry age. The participant's entry-age salary (i.e., his or her current salary divided by the salary increase ratio expected under the actuarial assumptions)[5] is divided into the first-year normal cost to determine the *normal cost percentage*. For each year of subsequent service, the normal cost for the

---

[5]The actual salary at entry age is not used, and indeed should not be used even if known, since it would in all likelihood contradict the stated salary-scale assumption.

participant is obtained by multiplying the participant's attained-age salary by the normal cost percentage.

This process is summarized below and illustrated in terms of the familiar male participant aged 40 at plan inception with 10 years of credited service:

$$(\text{PVFB}) \div \left(\begin{array}{l}\text{Present value of a temporary}\\ \text{employment-based life annuity of}\\ \text{1 unit at entry age increasing}\\ \text{annually at salary scale to age 65}\end{array}\right) = \text{Normal cost at entry age}$$

$$(\text{Current annual salary}) \times \frac{\text{Salary scale factor for entry age}}{\text{Salary scale factor for attained age}} = \left(\begin{array}{l}\text{Participant's assumed annual}\\ \text{salary at entry age}\end{array}\right)$$

$$\left(\begin{array}{l}\text{Normal cost}\\ \text{at entry age}\end{array}\right) \div \left(\begin{array}{l}\text{Participant's assumed annual}\\ \text{salary at entry age}\end{array}\right) = \text{Normal cost percentage}$$

$$\left(\begin{array}{l}\text{Normal cost}\\ \text{perecentage}\end{array}\right) \times \left(\begin{array}{l}\text{Participant's annual}\\ \text{salary at attained age}\end{array}\right) = \begin{array}{l}\text{Normal cost for}\\ \text{each subsequent year}\end{array}.$$

An alternative approach is to ascertain the normal cost percentage directly by determining the actuarial present value at entry age of the participant's future salary earnings and dividing that quantity into the entry-age PVFB. One way of determining the present value of the participant's future salary is to multiply his assumed entry-age salary by the actuarial present value factor for a temporary employment-based life annuity of one, increasing annually by the projected salary scale. Another approach is to compute the actuarial present value at entry age of the salary expected to be received by the participant during each year of credited service, taking into account the probabilities of death and termination and the passage of time before the salary is received. The sum of these seriatim present values is the actuarial present value of the participant's career salary.

The level percentage individual level premium cost method would be computed in the same manner as the level percentage entry-age normal cost method, except that all values would be computed as of the participant's attained age. In this case, the actual salary at attained age would be used, with no need to calculate the salary at entry age. Since the attained-age normal cost would fully amortize the expected cost of all benefits, there would be no supplemental liability and, of course, no supplemental cost.

The normal cost for the entire plan that would develop under several cost methods over a 50-year period under the previously described hypothetical pension plan is shown in Figure 24-1. The normal cost curve of the traditional accrued benefit cost method is repeated to show the contrast with the level percentage entry age normal cost method and other cost allocation methods. Several significant relationships may be observed in Figure 24-1. As might be expected, the lowest normal cost, as a percentage of payroll, during the first several years of the hypothetical plan simulation is that generated by the traditional accrued benefit cost method; true to the characteristics of the method, however, the plan normal cost rises during each year of the 50-year simulation and eventually exceeds by a wide margin the normal cost under any other method.

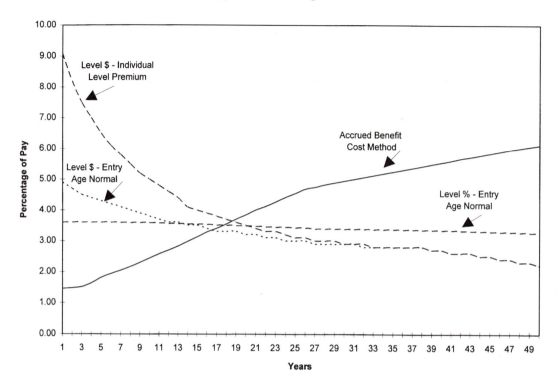

Figure 24-1. Normal cost curves for hypothetical pension plan under individual cost allocation methods and the accrued benefit cost method

The individual level premium cost method using the level dollar approach generates the largest initial normal cost because, among other reasons, it amortizes the *implicit* supplemental liability as a component of the normal cost. The normal cost declines over time as participants with past service benefits retire, eventually becoming identical with the entry-age normal cost method using the level dollar approach. The latter represents the true long-run normal cost of the plan when expressed as a level dollar amount. Its ultimate level is lower than the entry-age normal cost method using the level percentage approach, since it generates a larger actuarial liability than the level percentage approach and, hence, the investment earnings on the plan assets (real or theoretical) assume a larger share of the total cost burden than under the level percentage approach.

The entry-age normal cost method using the level percentage approach represents the long-term normal cost of the plan when measured as a percentage of payroll. It develops an initial normal cost (under the illustrative plan) lower than that of the level dollar approach under either the entry-age normal cost method or the individual level premium cost method, but its ultimate normal cost is second only to that of the traditional accrued benefit cost method. Because its initial entry-age normal cost is smaller using a level percentage approach than using a level dollar approach, it develops a smaller actuarial liability, as can be appreciated on a retrospective look. The normal cost declines until a stable plan population has been achieved, after which it continues as a level percentage of payroll but on a higher plane than the level dollar cost methods because of smaller investment earnings.

Actuarial Liability

The actuarial liability under the entry-age normal cost method using the level percentage approach is derived in the same manner as that under the level dollar cost methods. It can be derived either retrospectively or prospectively, the latter being the standard approach. The initial actuarial liability (and supplemental liability) in the example of a male participant at age 40 with 10 years of credited service is computed prospectively as follows:

$$PVFB = \$49{,}995 \times 0.8739 = \$43{,}690$$

$$\text{Present value of future normal costs} = \$48{,}394 \times .0172 \times 19.9644 = \$16{,}618$$

$$\text{Actuarial liability} = PVFB - \text{present value of future normal costs}$$

$$= \$43{,}690 - \$16{,}618$$

$$= \$27{,}072.$$

Note that this is a smaller actuarial liability than that developed under the entry-age normal cost method using the level dollar approach. The difference is accounted for entirely by the substitution of a larger normal cost for future years in the formula. All the other values are the same as those for the other individual level cost methods and will be in each future valuation. It should be remembered that after the first inception-of-plan valuation all the values in the formula are *attained-age* values, except the normal cost rate, which is always determined on the basis of the participant's entry age.

The actuarial liability that develops under the entry-age normal cost method using the level percentage approach and the other individual level cost methods under the previously illustrated hypothetical pension plan is given in Figure 24-2 as a percentage of payroll. As with the normal cost, the traditional accrued benefit cost method is included to give further perspective. The plan termination liability curve is given to indicate whether the actuarial liability under each method is deficient or excessive, compared with that particular standard of adequacy.

There are no surprises here. The lower the ultimate normal cost developed by a plan, the larger the actuarial liability. The greater the actuarial liability, the larger the portion of the total cost borne by investments on the real or assumed plan assets. Both approaches to the entry-age normal cost method generate an actuarial liability that greatly exceeds the plan termination liability. In a sense, this is the price that has to be paid for their level normal cost. The traditional accrued benefit cost method actuarial liability conforms closely to (but in this example is lower than) the plan termination liability, but does so at the expense of a normal cost that tends to rise over time.

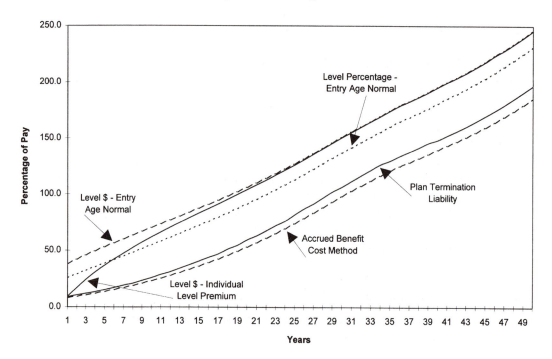

Figure 24-2. Accrued liability curves as a percentage of payroll for a hypothetical pension plan over a 50-year period under individual cost allocation methods and the accrued benefit cost method, as compared to the plan termination liability.

Aggregate Cost Allocation Methods

The second broad approach to determining the annual cost of a pension plan through an allocation of the total projected cost is the *aggregate method*. The portion of the total projected cost to be allocated to each plan year is generally expressed as a percentage of covered payroll if benefits are related to pay, and as a stipulated dollar amount per active participant if benefits are not related to pay. The annual cost accrual (normal cost plus supplemental cost) can be computed with or without supplemental liability.

It is one of the peculiarities of this approach that no actuarial liability ever directly emerges.[6] The normal cost is defined and derived in such a way that the present value of future benefits, less plan assets and any unfunded liability, is always fully and precisely offset by the actuarial present value of future normal cost accruals. If the plan sponsor desires a supplemental liability, it must be computed under one of the individual forms of actuarial cost method. In its pure form, the aggregate method is simply incapable of producing its own supplemental liability.

[6]Some argue that the aggregate method develops an actuarial liability that is precisely equal to the present value of future benefits less the present value of future normal costs, which also equals the

Level Dollar Cost Method

The basic concept underlying the aggregate cost method without supplemental liability is that the remaining *unfunded* projected cost of the pension plan is to be amortized over the remaining service lifetimes of the active participants in level annual dollar amounts or in annual amounts that constitute a level percentage of covered payroll. The dollar or percentage cost accrual so determined would accomplish this purpose only if there were no new entrants into the plan, no benefit changes were made, and actual experience conformed precisely to the projected experience. In fact, there are new entrants to any sizable plan every year, there are likely to be actuarial gains and losses, and there may be other developments that affect the cost of the plan. Consequently, it is necessary to recompute the annual cost accrual every year, the sum derived always being the amount expected to be required to amortize on a level basis the then *unfunded* cost over the remaining service lifetimes of the new "closed" group. The process can be viewed as one in which a series of temporary annual cost accruals must be determined for a succession of closed groups.

As its name suggests, the aggregate level dollar cost method determines the level annual *dollar* cost accrual that would be needed to amortize the unfunded projected cost of the plan if the postulated conditions were to be realized. The first step in the overall computation for the first year is to determine the actuarial present value of future benefits, the PVFB. If there is to be no supplemental liability, this calculation takes into account all projected benefits, irrespective of their type or the period of service to which they are attributable. The actuarial present value is determined exactly as it would be under any of the individual level cost methods. The second step is to determine the actuarial present value of a temporary employment-based life annuity of one per year for each active participant, the values being computed as of the participants' attained ages.[7] The third step consists of dividing the *sum* of the individual participant unit annuity values into the PVFB. This step yields the dollar amount of cost that must be accrued or amortized for each active participant. It is a weighted average cost per participant and does not represent the actual annual cost for any particular individual. The process is summarized below and illustrated with values derived from the hypothetical pension plan used in previous examples.

$$\begin{pmatrix} \text{Annual cost per} \\ \text{active participant} \end{pmatrix} = \begin{pmatrix} \text{Present value of} \\ \text{future benefits at} \\ \text{participant attained} \\ \text{ages (PVFB)} \end{pmatrix} \div \sum \begin{pmatrix} \text{Temporary employment--based life} \\ \text{annuity of 1 unit per year for each} \\ \text{participant attained age to age 65} \end{pmatrix}$$

---

assets plus the unfunded liability. The IRS has said that under the aggregate cost method the actuarial liability is not *directly* calculated.

[7] In theory, the remaining unfunded cost at any point in time could be amortized through any pattern of assumed cost accruals that would meet the fiscal needs of the employer and the funding requirements of federal law. This concept was explored in C. L. Trowbridge, "The Unfunded Present Value Family of Pension Funding Methods," *Transactions of the Society of Actuaries*, vol. 15 (1963): pp. 151–69. The aggregate cost method is a special case of the unfunded present value family of methods.

$$\$3,611 = \$32,282,946 \,/\$8,940$$

First-year total cost = (cost per employee) × (number of employees)

$$\$3,611,000 = \$3,611 \times 1,000.$$

After the first year, the formula must be modified to reflect the asset values that have been accumulated to offset the cost accruals for the first and subsequent years. Hence, as of any date after establishment of the plan, the level dollar cost accrual is derived by dividing the present value of future benefits (including those payable to retired participants), *less any plan assets*, by the sum of the individual participant unit annuity values. This amount must be recalculated annually, and with a stable group and no change in the benefit structure or the actuarial assumptions it will decline from year to year until the implicit cost of any past service benefits has been completely amortized. Indeed, whether or not there are any past service benefits, the ratio will tend to fall as new participants enter the plan at the younger ages, the cost amortization period being thereby lengthened. The cost of past service benefits, retroactive benefit increases, or any other plan development that would normally lead to a supplemental liability is amortized over the remaining service lifetimes of the active participants.

Actuarial gains and losses are not explicitly recognized under this type of cost method. Like any element of cost, they are merged indistinguishably into the remaining unfunded cost to be amortized over the remaining service lifetimes of the active participants.

A supplemental liability can be created under the aggregate level dollar (or level percentage) cost method in a variety of ways, the most common being to assume the recognition of cost accruals prior to the effective date of the plan. The approximate effect of this is to make no allowance in the regular or normal cost accrual for benefits attributable to past service. This can be accomplished by excluding past service benefits from the present value of future projected benefits. In practice, the actuary may assume a supplemental liability equal to that produced under the accrued benefit cost method or one of the individual level cost methods.[8] Regardless of how it is arrived at, the unfunded portion of the supplemental liability is subtracted (along with plan assets) from the present value of future benefits in calculating the annual cost. Thus the annual cost accrual under the aggregate level dollar cost method with supplemental liability is derived by dividing the present value of future benefits, less *the unfunded liability and plan assets*, by the sum of the individual participant unit annuity values. Like the aggregate level dollar cost method without supplemental liability, this method allocates costs over the remaining service lifetimes of the active participants.

After the first year, the unfunded liability is not calculated directly but is determined as if the actuarial assumptions had been exactly realized. That is, the unfunded liability for any year after the first is assumed to equal the unfunded

---

[8]Under the aggregate cost approach, the actuary frequently computes the first-year cost accrual on the basis of the entry-age normal cost method. The supplemental liability would thus be available as part of the regular costing procedure.

liability for the previous year plus interest for one year and the annual cost for the current year, less contributions to the plan during the current year. Thus actuarial gains and losses are not reflected in the unfunded liability but are automatically spread over the remaining service lifetimes of the active participants.

When the supplemental liability was calculated to be precisely equal to the present value at plan inception of the past service benefits, this procedure is known as the "attained-age normal" cost method, like its individual counterpart.[9] When the supplemental liability was derived by techniques that assumed an average age of entry into the plan, or a set of assumed entry ages, the method is identified as the frozen initial liability method.[10]

Level Percentage of Payroll Method

This form of aggregate cost method differs from the one described in the preceding section only in that the annual cost accrual is defined and derived as a level percentage of payroll, rather than as a dollar amount per participant. This form of aggregate cost method is used by plans that have salary-related benefits.

The cost accrual percentage for the first year of a plan's operation under this method, assuming no supplemental liability, is determined by dividing the aggregate present value of future benefits by the present value of the estimated future earnings of the active participants in the plan at the time of the valuation. The present value of future salaries is obtained by summing the present value of the future salary of each individual in the "closed" group. The latter value is derived by multiplying the participant's current salary times the actuarial present value factor for a temporary employment-based annuity beginning at the participant's *attained age* and continuing as long as the participant survives in service to age 65; this value increases each year at a rate equal to that at which the participant's salary is assumed to increase. This is the same procedure used to value future salaries under the individual level premium cost method using the level percentage approach.

Dividing the present value of future salaries into the present value of future benefits yields a percentage called the *normal cost percentage* or *annual cost accrual rate*. This percentage is multiplied by the current covered payroll to obtain the annual cost (in dollars) for the plan.

This process and illustrative amounts are set out below:

$$
\text{Annual cost accrual rate} = \left(\begin{array}{l} \text{Present value of} \\ \text{future benefits at} \\ \text{participant attained} \\ \text{ages (PVFB)} \end{array} \right) \div \sum \left(\begin{array}{l} \text{For each participant,} \\ \text{temporary employment-based life} \\ \text{annuity of 1 unit per year, increasing} \\ \text{annually at salary scale, from attained} \\ \text{age to age 65, times current salary} \end{array} \right)
$$

$$.0498 = \$32,282,946\ /\$648,466,368$$

First year normal cost = current covered payroll × cost accrual rate

[9]ERISA §3(31). The Joint Committee terminology is *frozen attained-age actuarial cost method.*
[10]Ibid. The Joint Committee terminology is *frozen entry-age actuarial cost method.*

$$\$2,101,321 = \$42,159,202 \times .0498.$$

The cost accrual rate must be recomputed each year, taking into account the growing plan assets and other changed circumstances, and applied to the then current payroll.

A supplemental liability can be created in the same manner and with the same consequences as under the aggregate level dollar cost method.

Individual Aggregate Cost Method

The *individual aggregate cost method,* as the name suggests, blends some of the characteristics of an individual cost method and an aggregate cost method. This method is widely used for small plans.

Under the individual aggregate cost method, sometimes referred to as the *individual spread-gain cost method,* the PVFB is first calculated for each individual participant. The total plan assets, if any, are allocated (see later discussion) among all the participants. The assets allocated to each participant are subtracted from his or her PVFB to obtain the present value of future normal costs for the individual. Since this present value of future normal costs must be paid by the normal costs of future years, it is divided by a temporary employment-based life annuity of one per year from attained age to age 65 to obtain the individual's normal cost. If a level percentage approach is used rather than a level dollar method, the temporary employment-based life annuity will be for one per year, increasing annually in accordance with the salary scale.

At the inception of the plan, when there are no plan assets, this method is identical to the individual level premium cost method. Because the PVFB is expected to be funded entirely by future normal costs, there is no supplemental liability under this method. Like the aggregate cost method without supplemental liability, the individual aggregate method never has an unfunded liability. The individual aggregate cost method automatically spreads actuarial gains and losses over the future working lifetimes of participants through the normal cost.

Various methods are used to allocate plan assets among participants for purposes of the method. If the method is first applied to a plan at some point after the plan's effective date, plan assets are usually allocated in proportion to each participant's PVFB.[11] Thereafter regulations require only that the allocation be "reasonable." One commonly used approach is to increase the amount of assets allocated to each participant on the prior anniversary by the individual's normal cost for the intervening year, and then to allocate the total plan assets in proportion to this adjusted total. If the plan includes participants or beneficiaries who are not active employees, this approach may be modified to first allocate assets to such participants and beneficiaries equal to their PVFB, and then to allocate the remaining plan assets in accordance with the previously described procedure.

Summary of Actuarial Cost Methods

The characteristics of the principal actuarial cost methods are presented in schematic form in Figure 24-3. Actuarial gains and losses can be determined on either

---

[11]Treas. Reg. 1.412(c)(3)-1(c)(5); Rev. Proc. 80-50.

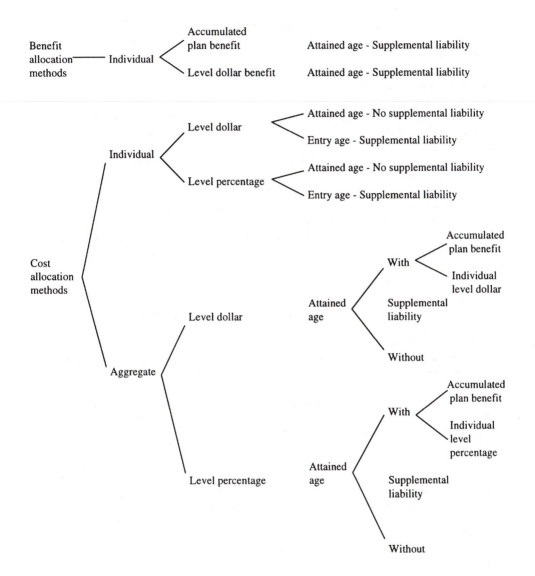

Figure 24-3. Schematic summary of characteristics of the principal actuarial cost methods.

TABLE 24-1   Classification and Comparative Terminology of Actuarial Cost Methods

Classification	ERISA	Joint Committee
Benefit allocation cost methods		
Accumulated plan benefit method	Accrued benefit cost method or unit credit method	Unit credit actuarial cost method
Level dollar benefit method	Same as above	Same as above
Cost allocation methods: individual		
Level dollar cost method		
Attained age, no supplemental liability	Individual level premium cost	Individual level actuarial cost method[a]
Entry age, supplemental liability	Entry-age normal cost method	Entry-age actuarial cost method
Level percentage cost method		
Attained age, no supplemental liability	Individual level premium cost method	Individual level actuarial cost method[a]
Entry age, supplemental liability	Entry-age normal cost	Entry-age actuarial cost method
Cost allocation methods: aggregate		
Level dollar cost method		
With benefit allocation cost method supplemental liability	Attained-age normal cost method	Frozen attaine-age actuarial cost method
With entry-age normal cost supplemental liability	Frozen initial liability cost method	Frozen entry-age actuarial cost method
Without supplemental liability	Aggregate cost method	Aggregate actuarial cost method
Level percentage cost method		
With benefit allocation cost method supplemental liability	Attained-age normal cost method	Frozen attained-age actuarial cost method
With entry-age normal cost supplemental liability	Frozen initial liability cost method	Frozen entry-age actuarial cost method
Without supplemental liability	Aggregate cost method	Aggregate actuarial cost method
Mixed methods		
Attained-age benefit allocation cost method supplemental liability	Attained-age normal cost method	Attained-age actuarial cost method or frozen attained actuarial cost method

[a]If spread gain, individual spread-gain actuarial cost method.

a *direct* or *spread* basis under any of the cost methods except the aggregate, which always spreads such gains and losses.

Table 24-1 compares the classification used to describe the principal actuarial cost methods in this text with the terminology of Employment Retirement Income Security Act and the terminology of the Joint Committee on Pension Terminology.

Chapter 25
Pension Cost Illustrations and Forecasts

The dynamics of a pension plan and the long-run characteristics of the various actuarial cost methods can be portrayed by simulating the plan's operations over successive generations of participants, with appropriate assumptions about future experience. Such a simulation of an actuarial plan, with alternative assumptions about future experience, can provide the plan sponsor with valuable insights about the potential normal cost, actuarial liability, cash flows, and asset accumulations under various scenarios. It can also indicate the potential financial consequences of any plan changes that might be under consideration, taken individually or collectively. Large pension plan sponsors have shown increasing interest in projections of pension costs and associated cash flows. These projections can extend far into the future, but because of the difficulty of predicting the behavior of the various cost factors, especially the size and characteristics of the participant population, salary levels, and rate of investment return, the results become less reliable the further they project into the future. This is especially true of the dollar values obtained.

This chapter presents a 50-year simulation of a hypothetical pension plan in order to demonstrate the dynamics of three basic actuarial cost methods and to illustrate the types of financial information that plan sponsors can obtain from long-term actuarial forecasts. The period of the simulation is much longer than would usually be used for an actual plan. A typical forecast would extend about 5 to 10 years into the future; in special circumstances some might forecast as far as 25 years. A 50-year simulation is used in this example to carry the plan through the 30-year amortization of the supplemental liability and into a time frame in which long-term cost characteristics come to the surface. The forecast component of the illustration can be said to constitute the first 10 or 15 years of the simulation. After the supplemental liability has been amortized, the simulation shows only normal costs. With an actual plan, additional layers of supplemental liability are almost certain to be created during a period of 50 years, and their amortization would add to the plan's annual costs.

Pension Cost Illustrations

The pension costs and liabilities generated in this simulation are based on a plan that begins with a relatively immature population of 1,000 male participants, with no retired participants, and grows at the rate of 5 percent during the first year of the plan's operation. The rate of growth declines to zero in year 25. Beginning in year 26, the population starts to decline at the same rate at which it was assumed to grow in year 25, with the annual decline mirroring the assumed annual growth during the first 25 years and reaching the original population of 1,000 at the end of year 50 of the forecast. With this pattern of growth and decline, the plan population moves in continuous progression from a relatively immature state to a fully mature state and eventually to a relatively overmature state.

The plan is assumed to provide a retirement benefit at age 65 of 1 percent of the participant's average annual compensation during the last five years of employment multiplied by the years of credited service, with no explicit integration with Social Security. Retirement benefits are assumed to vest in full after 5 years of credited service. The normal annuity form is the single life annuity, and in the interest of simplicity it is assumed that there are no death, disability, or early retirement benefits.

The benefits under the plan are valued in accordance with the actuarial functions and values set forth in Appendix A, all present values being derived on the basis of a 7 percent interest assumption. For simplicity it is assumed that the actual experience during the 50-year simulation conforms in all respects to the actuarial assumptions, there being no actuarial gains or losses.[1] The supplemental liability under the traditional accrued benefit cost method and entry-age normal cost method is assumed to be amortized in equal annual dollar installments over a 30-year period, the maximum period permitted for single-employer plans established after January 1, 1974. It is also assumed that the annual cost (normal cost plus the allocable portion of the supplemental liability, if any) is funded currently, the contributions being made at the beginning of the year in which the cost is incurred. The assets are assumed to earn interest at the rate of 7 percent per year compounded.

The 50-year simulation is, in essence, a series of 50 closed-group valuations based on the plan population, benefit accruals, and asset accumulations pertaining to the years in question. The deferred benefits of terminated vested participants and the benefits payable to retired participants are also reflected in the successive valuations.

Table 25-1 provides some data that serve as points of reference for a pension cost forecast. It shows, for example, the number of retired participants year by year, starting with 2 at the beginning of the second year of operation and rising to 925 at the beginning of year 51. Thus, by the end of the period there are 9 retired

[1]In producing a simulation, the actuary must decide not only what valuation assumptions to use for each year of the simulation, but also whether or not to assume that each year's experience during the period of the simulation will match the valuation assumptions. In many if not most simulations, experience economic assumptions may differ from those used for valuation purposes, producing actuarial gains and losses. Indeed, best-estimate economic assumptions may be used for both valuation (simulation only) and experience purposes, again eliminating actuarial gains and losses but possibly projecting a markedly different financial scenario. Often, the most realistic and satisfactory approach is to assume that contributions to the plan during the forecast period, typically from 5 to 20 years depending on the purpose of the simulation, will be made in accordance with the actuarial assumptions currently used for valuation purposes but to also assume that experience gains will emerge in consonance with a less conservative set of economic assumptions, producing year-to-year adjustments or corrections in the cost and cash flow projection.

TABLE 25-1   Background Data for Pension Cost Simulation

Year of Plan Operation	Number of Active Participants at Beginning of Year	Number of Terminated Vested Participants at Beginning of Year	Number of Retired Participants at Beginning of Year	Salary at Beginning of Year (dollars)	Benefit Payments During Year (dollars)	Plan Termination Liability at Beginning of Year (dollars)
1	1000	0	0	42,195,202	7,328	0
2	1050	14	2	46,005,806	14,622	3,315,757
3	1100	37	3	50,040,384	22,514	4,143,722
4	1151	47	5	54,371,037	31,033	5,306,019
5	1202	66	6	58,984,406	40,202	6,421,383
6	1252	86	7	63,861,954	50,059	7,944,478
7	1302	110	8	69,051,308	75,081	9,812,048
8	1352	134	11	74,508,376	101,931	11,832,265
9	1400	158	14	80,233,794	130,657	14,417,627
10	1448	182	16	86,313,388	163,330	16,923,952
11	1494	206	19	92,675,040	198,117	20,341,783
16	1699	327	44	128,556,923	690,052	45,071,356
21	1839	443	94	169,599,728	2,033,750	88,538,564
26	1895	549	176	212,336,924	5,044,163	157,051,348
31	1839	624	317	249,226,758	11,502,368	247,019,025
36	1699	640	520	278,400,833	21,181,242	344,430,273
41	1494	615	709	300,595,629	29,948,194	429,966,746
46	1252	575	843	312,701,180	37,543,520	506,573,330
51	1000	515	925	310,855,133	45,423,984	582,657,478

participants for each 10 active participants, a very high ratio reflecting the advanced maturity of the group. In addition, there are 515 terminated vested participants with deferred claims against the plan. Thus by the end of the period there are more inactive participants with claims against the plan than there are active participants.

The total of the annual salaries for all active participants rises from $42 million to $310 million, reflecting a per capita rate of growth in excess of 4 percent per year.[2] Benefit payments to retired participants start off slowly because of the small number of persons in that subset of the plan population. By the tenth year of the plan, benefit payments are approximately $160,000 per year and thereafter increase rapidly, reaching $45 million after 50 years. It is interesting and instructive to compare these yearly cash outflows, which of course are not affected by the actuarial cost method, with the yearly contributions under the three actuarial cost methods employed in this simulation. Throughout the first 30 years, when supplemental costs are being funded, contributions under all three cost methods are well in excess of benefit payments. Benefit payments eventually overtake contributions,

---

[2]The salary of each participant is assumed to grow in accordance with a merit scale plus 4 percent per year for inflation and productivity increases. Per capita average salaries rise at a rate more than 4 percent per year because of the maturing of the population.

but investment income from accumulated plan assets is available to absorb the deficiency. In each year of the simulation, investment income must be added to contributions to arrive at the total flow of funds into the plan. Under all three cost methods plan assets continue to grow throughout the period.

The plan termination liability measures the adequacy or redundancy of the asset accumulations under the various actuarial cost methods if the plan were to terminate. The plan termination liability purports to reflect the actuarial present value of all retirement benefits accrued to date,[3] with no allowance for future salary increases or employee withdrawals. If the accumulated assets, properly valued, equal the plan termination liability, the plan could on the date of valuation discharge all of its obligations for accrued benefits without further contributions.

The projection of costs, liabilities, and assets under the traditional accrued benefit cost method (see Chapter 23) is portrayed in Table 25-2. Projections under this method are shown for instructional purposes only, since in practice the traditional accrued benefit cost method would not be used for a plan with benefits based on final average compensation. In absolute terms, the normal cost increases from $614,917 in year 1 of the plan's operation to $19,109,532 in year 51. As a percentage of salary, however, the growth in normal cost is much less spectacular, going from 1.46 percent to 6.12 percent. This represents a fourfold increase over the 50-year period. The supplemental liability is amortized in 30 equal annual installments of $205,655, which because of rising salary levels constitute a declining percentage of payroll. The supplemental cost ranges from 0.49 percent of payroll in the first year down to a relatively insignificant 0.08 percent in year 30, when the final installment is paid. The normal and supplemental costs combined range from 1.94 percent in year 1 to 6.12 percent in year 51. These costs are lower than they would have been had ancillary benefits been provided by the plan.

The assets accumulate rapidly during the period in which the supplemental liability is being amortized and funded. As would be expected, by the end of the amortization period the plan assets are precisely equal to the actuarial liability and will remain in that relationship until another layer of supplemental liability is created or actuarial gains and losses emerge. At all durations, however, the plan assets fall short of the plan termination liability. Such a deficiency is to be expected until the supplemental liability has been fully funded, but in the example there is still a deficiency at the end of 30 years and thereafter to the end of the simulation. After 30 years of the plan's operations the plan termination liability is $267 million, whereas the plan assets amount to only $243 million, a deficiency of 9 percent. A deficiency of 6 percent remains after 50 years. This indicates the cost-inflating impact of omitting employee withdrawal assumptions in the derivation of the plan termination liability.[4]

---

[3]This exceeds the plan termination liability under Title IV of ERISA, which is based on that portion of accrued benefits guaranteed by the Pension Benefit Guaranty Corporation. See Chapter 24.

[4]Whether the actuarial liability under the traditional accrued benefit cost method would be more or less than the plan termination liability for any particular plan may depend upon the plan provisions and the actuarial assumptions used. In addition, in the case of an actual plan termination the liability might be redetermined on the basis of actuarial assumptions different from those used for an ongoing plan. The percentages would then differ from those shown.

TABLE 25-2. Annual Cost, Liability, and Asset Accumulation Under the Traditional Accrued Benefit Cost Method

Year	Normal Cost In Dollars	Normal Cost As Percentage of Salary	Supplemental Cost In Dollars	Supplemental Cost As Percentage of Salary	Annual Cost In Dollars	Annual Cost As Percentage of Salary	Assets In Dollars	Assets As Percentage of Actuarial Liability	Assets As Percentage of Plan Termination Liability
1	614,917	1.46	205,655	0.49	820,572	1.94	0	0	0
2	656,984	1.43	205,655	0.45	862,639	1.88	870,432	24	21
3	762,662	1.52	205,655	0.41	968,317	1.94	1,839,261	41	35
4	890,917	1.64	205,655	0.38	1,096,572	2.02	2,980,820	53	46
5	1,072,784	1.82	205,655	0.35	1,278,439	2.17	4,330,709	62	55
6	1,240,701	1.94	205,655	0.32	1,446,356	2.26	5,960,204	70	61
7	1,416,153	2.05	205,655	0.30	1,621,808	2.35	7,873,238	76	67
8	1,617,469	2.17	205,655	0.28	1,823,124	2.45	10,082,035	80	70
9	1,845,286	2.30	205,655	0.26	2,050,941	2.56	12,633,082	84	75
10	2,102,073	2.44	205,655	0.24	2,307,728	2.67	15,576,752	87	77
11	2,393,699	2.58	205,655	0.22	2,599,354	2.80	18,967,444	89	79
12	2,682,744	2.70	205,655	0.21	2,888,399	2.91	22,871,540	91	80
13	3,009,936	2.83	205,655	0.19	3,215,591	3.03	27,273,288	92	82
14	3,377,676	2.98	205,655	0.18	3,583,331	3.16	34,242,498	94	83
15	3,779,425	3.13	205,655	0.17	3,985,080	3.30	37,856,020	95	84
16	4,232,629	3.29	205,655	0.16	4,438,284	3.45	44,177,791	96	85
17	4,658,327	3.41	205,655	0.15	4,863,982	3.56	51,305,405	96	86
18	5,135,076	3.55	205,655	0.14	5,340,731	3.69	59,158,560	97	86
19	5,662,586	3.71	205,655	0.13	5,868,241	3.84	67,828,449	97	87
20	6,204,195	3.85	205,655	0.13	6,409,850	3.98	77,412,131	98	87
21	6,809,309	4.01	205,655	0.12	7,014,964	4.14	87,924,132	98	88
22	7,359,002	4.13	205,655	0.12	7,564,657	4.24	99,481,106	98	88
23	7,966,117	4.27	205,655	0.11	8,171,772	4.38	111,911,836	99	88
24	8,629,190	4.42	205,655	0.11	8,834,845	4.53	125,313,088	99	89
25	9,266,060	4.55	205,655	0.10	9,471,715	4.65	139,787,319	99	89
26	9,964,922	4.69	205,655	0.10	10,170,577	4.79	155,237,664	99	89
27	10,468,318	4.75	205,655	0.09	10,673,973	4.84	171,769,095	99	90
28	11,014,507	4.83	205,655	0.09	11,220,162	4.92	188,843,349	100	90
29	11,501,282	4.89	205,655	0.09	11,706,937	4.98	206,502,382	100	90
30	12,006,335	4.95	205,655	0.08	12,211,990	5.04	224,686,647	100	91
31	12,486,539	5.01	0	0.00	12,486,539	5.01	243,154,311	100	91
32	12,963,824	5.07	0	0.00	12,963,824	5.07	261,637,567	100	91
33	13,460,225	5.13	0	0.00	13,460,225	5.13	280,185,239	100	92
34	13,906,785	5.19	0	0.00	13,906,785	5.19	298,784,686	100	92
35	14,386,615	5.25	0	0.00	14,386,615	5.25	317,352,971	100	92
36	14,779,926	5.31	0	0.00	14,779,926	5.31	335,419,717	100	92
37	15,164,661	5.37	0	0.00	15,164,661	5.37	352,803,571	100	92
38	15,646,205	5.43	0	0.00	15,646,205	5.43	370,282,615	100	93
39	16,086,158	5.49	0	0.00	16,086,158	5.49	387,954,353	100	93
40	16,494,016	5.55	0	0.00	16,494,016	5.55	405,781,696	100	93
41	16,864,077	5.61	0	0.00	16,864,077	5.61	423,093,844	100	93
42	17,214,232	5.68	0	0.00	17,214,232	5.68	439,776,322	100	93
43	17,565,973	5.73	0	0.00	17,565,973	5.73	456,702,450	100	94
44	17,938,088	5.79	0	0.00	17,938,088	5.79	473,897,238	100	94
45	18,217,813	5.85	0	0.00	18,217,813	5.85	490,955,886	100	94
46	18,495,219	5.91	0	0.00	18,495,219	5.91	507,777,686	100	94
47	18,712,006	5.97	0	0.00	18,712,006	5.97	524,276,689	100	94
48	18,883,963	6.02	0	0.00	18,883,963	6.02	540,548,036	100	94
49	19,015,384	6.07	0	0.00	19,015,384	6.07	556,543,072	100	94
50	19,109,532	6.12	0	0.00	19,109,532	6.12	572,168,787	100	94

TABLE 25-3   Annual Cost, Actuarial Liability, and Asset Accumulation under the Entry-Age Normal Cost Method

Year	Normal Cost In Dollars	As Percentage of Salary	Supplemental Cost In Dollars	As Percentage of Salary	Annual Cost In Dollars	As Percentage of Salary	Assets In Dollars	As Percentage of Actuarial Liability	As Percentage of Plan Termination Liability
1	1,518,796	3.60	718,018	1.70	2,236,814	5.30	0	0	0
2	1,655,758	3.60	718,018	1.56	2,373,776	5.16	2,385,811	20	58
3	1,801,160	3.60	718,018	1.43	2,519,178	5.03	5,077,633	35	96
4	1,957,303	3.60	718,018	1.34	2,675,321	4.92	8,105,299	46	126
5	2,123,433	3.60	718,018	1.22	2,841,451	4.82	11,503,163	55	145
6	2,298,750	3.60	718,018	1.12	3,016,768	4.72	15,307,151	62	156
7	2,477,832	3.59	718,018	1.04	3,195,850	4.63	19,554,812	68	165
8	2,670,703	3.58	718,018	0.96	3,388,721	4.55	24,265,544	73	168
9	2,873,006	3.58	718,018	0.89	3,591,024	4.48	29,484,625	76	174
10	3,086,100	3.58	718,018	0.83	3,804,118	4.41	35,255,792	80	173
11	3,309,908	3.57	718,018	0.77	4,027,926	4.35	41,625,154	82	173
12	3,531,295	3.55	718,018	0.72	4,249,313	4.28	48,643,862	84	171
13	3,767,934	3.55	718,018	0.68	4,485,952	4.22	56,305,850	86	169
14	4,015,186	3.54	718,018	0.63	4,733,204	4.17	64,666,626	88	166
15	4,268,018	3.53	718,018	0.59	4,986,036	4.13	73,780,200	89	164
16	4,533,492	3.53	718,018	0.56	5,251,510	4.08	83,687,687	90	161
17	4,785,909	3.50	718,018	0.53	5,503,927	4.03	94,451,145	91	158
18	5,056,074	3.50	718,018	0.50	5,774,092	3.99	106,009,242	92	155
19	5,332,777	3.49	718,018	0.47	6,050,795	3.96	118,422,375	93	152
20	5,600,506	3.48	718,018	0.45	6,318,524	3.92	131,742,965	94	149
21	5,882,096	3.47	718,018	0.42	6,600,114	3.89	145,960,405	94	146
22	6,144,741	3.45	718,018	0.40	6,862,759	3.85	161,138,028	95	143
23	6,425,082	3.44	718,018	0.38	7,143,100	3.83	177,131,572	95	140
24	6,709,019	3.44	718,018	0.37	7,427,037	3.80	193,997,526	96	137
25	6,973,872	3.42	718,018	0.35	7,691,890	3.77	211,773,313	96	135
26	7,251,775	3.42	718,018	0.34	7,969,793	3.75	230,358,264	96	133
27	7,473,159	3.39	718,018	0.33	8,191,177	3.72	249,793,298	97	130
28	7,716,479	3.39	718,018	0.32	8,434,497	3.70	269,672,655	98	129
29	7,961,200	3.38	718,018	0.31	8,679,218	3.69	290,009,078	99	127
30	8,164,236	3.37	718,018	0.30	8,882,254	3.66	310,799,152	100	126
31	8,384,782	3.36	0	0.00	8,384,782	3.36	331,731,873	100	124
32	8,581,091	3.35	0	0.00	8,581,091	3.35	352,026,679	100	123
33	8,793,133	3.35	0	0.00	8,793,133	3.35	372,212,065	100	122
34	8,995,963	3.35	0	0.00	8,995,963	3.35	392,259,601	100	121
35	9,137,722	3.34	0	0.00	9,137,722	3.34	412,116,550	100	120
36	9,293,362	3.34	0	0.00	9,293,362	3.34	431,200,431	100	119
37	9,488,848	3.36	0	0.00	9,488,848	3.36	449,418,312	100	118
38	9,656,212	3.35	0	0.00	9,656,212	3.35	467,587,267	100	118
39	9,808,681	3.35	0	0.00	9,808,681	3.35	485,661,039	100	118
40	9,898,065	3.33	0	0.00	9,898,065	3.33	503,610,950	100	117
41	9,995,161	3.33	0	0.00	9,995,161	3.33	520,713,478	100	117
42	10,128,223	3.34	0	0.00	10,128,223	3.34	536,879,590	100	117
43	10,210,412	3.33	0	0.00	10,210,412	3.33	553,020,917	100	116
44	10,249,810	3.31	0	0.00	10,249,810	3.31	569,087,547	100	116
45	10,285,401	3.30	0	0.00	10,285,401	3.30	584,583,059	100	115
46	10,293,403	3.39	0	0.00	10,293,403	3.29	599,471,081	100	115
47	10,298,527	3.29	0	0.00	10,298,527	3.29	613,612,678	100	114
48	10,274,146	3.28	0	0.00	10,274,146	3.28	627,135,121	100	113
49	10,220,157	3.26	0	0.00	10,220,157	3.26	639,978,749	100	113
50	10,158,246	3.25	0	0.00	10,158,246	3.25	652,034,068	100	112

The trend of costs, liabilities, and asset accumulations under the individual entry-age normal cost method using the level percentage approach (see Chapter 24) is shown in Table 25-3. In absolute terms the normal cost rises from $1,518,796 in year 1 to $10,158,246 in year 51. As a percentage of salary, however, the normal cost declines from 3.60 percent to 3.25 percent, reflecting a downward shift over time in the average entry age of the plan participants.[5] The supplemental liability is amortized in 30 equal annual installments of $718,018, which because of rising salary levels constitute a declining percentage of payroll. These annual charges are much larger than under the traditional accrued benefit cost method, since the supplemental liability itself is much larger. In year 1 the supplemental cost is 1.70 percent of salary, declining to 0.30 percent in year 30. The combined normal and supplemental costs range from 5.30 percent of payroll in year 1 to 3.66 percent in year 30. Thereafter the normal cost drifts downward to 3.25 percent of payroll, as compared with 6.12 percent under the traditional accrued benefit cost method. In other words, since the entry-age normal cost method allocates a larger proportion of the total prospective cost of the plan to the supplemental liability component, the normal cost ultimately becomes smaller in absolute terms than the traditional accrued benefit cost method normal cost.

Assets build up much more rapidly than under the traditional accrued benefit cost method. By the end of the supplemental liability amortization period, the actuarial liability and asset accumulation are in balance and remain so thereafter. After three years, the asset accumulation surpasses the plan termination liability and the margin increases in absolute terms with each passing year. By year 30, the assets have grown to over $331 million while the plan termination liability is only $267 million, an excess of 24 percent. With the completion of the supplemental liability amortization, the percentage margin of plan assets over the plan termination liability declines, dropping to 12 percent by the end of the period. This excess results from the leveling of future costs that is characteristic of individual level cost methods.

The annual cost and asset accumulation under the aggregate level cost method without supplemental liability (see Chapter 24) are depicted in Table 25-4. There is no actuarial liability in the conventional sense under this method since the accumulated assets plus the present value of future annual costs at all times equal the present value of future benefits. Under this method, the adequacy of the asset accumulation may be measured against the plan termination liability.

The annual cost under the aggregate method is higher than the traditional accrued benefit cost method in the early years and lower than the entry-age normal, with this position eventually reversing. This relative relationship to entry-age normal stems from the fact that for this particular plan population (relatively young) and this set of actuarial assumptions the unfunded future costs during the early years of the forecast are being amortized over a period significantly greater

---

[5]Under the individual entry-age normal cost method, the normal cost percentage for a particular participant remains constant throughout his or her active membership, barring changes in assumptions, but the normal cost percentage for the plan as a whole may move upward or downward in response to changes in the entry-age distribution of the active participants, as occurred in the present simulation.

TABLE 25-4   Annual Cost and Asset Accumulation Under the
Aggregate Cost Method Without Supplemental Liability

| | Annual Cost | | Assets | |
| | In Dollars | As Percentage of Salary | In Dollars | As Percentage of Salary |
Year				
1	2,101,321	4.98	0	0
2	2,240,483	4.87	2,240,833	5
3	2,391,930	4.78	4,779,883	10
4	2,555,439	4.70	7,650,551	14
5	2,725,080	4.62	10,888,309	18
6	2,912,105	4.56	14,524,741	23
7	3,100,404	4.49	18,605,644	27
8	3,308,172	4.44	23,147,807	31
9	3,514,240	4.38	28,202,459	35
10	3,737,370	4.33	33,801,715	39
11	3,975,759	4.29	39,997,871	43
16	5,283,690	4.11	81,292,244	63
21	6,733,109	3.97	143,078,719	84
26	8,238,673	3.88	227,464,411	107
31	9,470,617	3.80	329,618,761	132
36	10,412,191	3.74	434,975,891	156
41	11,152,098	3.71	532,716,984	177
46	11,601,214	3.71	623,605,058	199
51	11,594,896	3.73	705,582,348	227

than the 30 years being used under entry-age normal.[6] By year 15 the annual cost rises above the combined normal and supplemental costs of the entry-age normal cost method and remains so to the end of the 50-year period. The annual cost under the aggregate method moves below the traditional accrued benefit cost method *normal* cost around year 21 (this is also the first year it crosses below the combined costs of the traditional accrued benefit cost method).

Consistent with the characteristics of this cost method, the growth in assets initially lags slightly behind the entry-age normal cost method but is much more vigorous than under the traditional accrued benefit cost method. After one year the plan assets are more than one-half of the plan termination liability, and after three years they exceed the plan termination liability, the margin reaching 67 percent after 25 years. The excess declines thereafter, being 15 percent by the end of the simulation.

In addition to their use in projecting costs, assets, and liabilities for funding purposes, forecasts can be used to project amounts for accounting purposes.

---

[6]The period over which the remaining unfunded costs are amortized declines as the average attained age of the plan population increases.

Forecast as an Actuarial Cost Method

A long-term forecast of the plan's liability can determine the amount of pension cost to be recognized and funded each year. Such a cost determination would not be carried out through a series of annual closed-group valuations, as in the foregoing simulation, but through a form of open-group valuation.

The first step might well be to select a funding objective. The length of the forecast period, say, 25 years, is a key element of the funding objective. One possible objective might be to accumulate assets equal to the actuarial liability on an ongoing plan basis by the end of the forecast period. Another objective might be to accumulate assets equal to the plan termination liability within a specified time, possibly shorter than the forecast period. The funding objective might include a contribution pattern for reaching the ultimate objectives, such as contributions that are a level percentage of salaries during the forecast period.

The second step in the process would be to project the existing plan population ahead to the end of a selected period, using best-estimate assumptions as to increments and decrements, especially the age and sex distribution of the new entrants. This projection would include the active participants and their compensation for each year, as well as the terminated and retired participants and beneficiaries and the amounts of their benefit payments.

The third step would be to calculate the amount of the funding objective at the end of the forecast period. For example, if the funding objective were to accumulate assets equal to the actuarial liability under the entry-age normal cost method at the end of 25 years, then such a liability would be determined on the basis of the projected population of active, terminated vested, and retired participants and beneficiaries as of that date. Such a valuation would be made using the same methods previously described.

The final step would be to determine the amount of contributions required to meet and satisfy the funding objective. The assets of the plan at the beginning of the forecast period plus the contributions paid during the forecast period must be sufficient, together with investment earnings, to provide the benefits projected to be paid during the forecast period and to accumulate a balance of assets at the end of the forecast period equal to the funding objective at that time. The present value of future contributions can be determined by first determining the present value, as of the beginning of the forecast period, of the respective items, as follows:

$$\text{Present value of future contributions} = \left(\begin{array}{l}\text{Present value of}\\\text{benefit payments}\\\text{during forecast period}\end{array}\right) + \left(\begin{array}{l}\text{Present value of}\\\text{forecast objective}\end{array}\right) - (\text{Initial plan assets})$$

If it is important for future contributions to be a level percentage of compensation, this percentage can be determined by dividing the present value of future contributions by the present value of future compensation during the forecast period. This determination is illustrated for an employer whose funding objective is to accumulate the actuarial liability under the entry-age normal cost method at the end of 25 years by a level percentage of compensation. The data and assumptions are those shown earlier in this chapter. The benefit payments for certain years were shown in Table 25-1. The total benefit payments during the 25-year period are

$23,958,190. The present value of these payments, discounted at 7 percent interest to the beginning of the period, is $6,261,385.

The actuarial liability under the entry-age normal cost method at the end of the 25 years, based on the projection shown in Table 25-3, is $239,105,088. The present value of this amount, discounted at 7 percent interest for 25 years, is $44,054,916. In the example the initial plan assets were assumed to be $0. Thus the present value of future contributions is $50,316,301 ($6,261,385 present value of benefit payments plus $44,054,916 present value of funding objective less $0 assets).

The projection of future salaries for certain years is shown in Table 25-1. The total projected salaries to be paid during the 25-year period come to $2,815,362,036. Discounted at 7 percent interest, the present value of this amount is $1,086,668,219. The contribution percentage required to satisfy the funding objective equals the present value of future contributions ($50,316,301) divided by the present value of future compensation ($1,086,668,219), which is 4.63 percent.

The employer could not actually contribute this amount unless it satisfied the minimum funding requirement but did not exceed the maximum deductible limit during each year. Table 25-3 shows that 4.63 percent contributions would not be sufficient to satisfy the minimum funding requirement in the early years if the entry-age normal cost method were used for the funding requirements. This would force the employer either to modify the initially proposed funding pattern or to adopt a different actuarial cost method to determine the minimum funding requirements.

One or more years after the initial forecast a new forecast can be made, which can take into account the then current asset values and participant data and an updated forecast of anticipated experience. It would not be necessary to make annual forecasts, but they could be undertaken every few years, or whenever there are significant new developments.

This technique of establishing cost accruals and funding contributions might come close to satisfying the four objectives of an actuarial cost method postulated in Chapter 9, if actual experience follows the projections. The annual cost and funding contributions could be calculated as a level percentage of covered payroll or level dollar amounts, whichever is desired. The actuarial liability and associated assets would not need to exceed the plan termination liability. In fact, the accumulation of assets equal to the plan termination liability after a reasonable period of years could be the central funding objective, which would satisfy the third objective mentioned. There would be flexibility in the choice of the period over which the funding objective is to be accomplished, and the method could accommodate modification of the costing and funding schedule in the event of fiscal exigencies. On the other hand, it can be argued that assumptions regarding new entrants over a long future period are likely to be too unreliable to serve as a basis for a plan's funding.

The forecast actuarial cost method, as it might be termed, is not one of the approved cost methods for determining the maximum tax-deductible limit on contributions or for complying with the minimum funding standards. Indeed, some persons believe that the approach is too unstructured even to justify calling it an actuarial cost method. It is clearly a management tool that properly used could provide useful insight into both the near-term and long-term fiscal implications of a pension plan. In some circumstances it would seem practicable, and perhaps highly desirable, to have cost forecasts made for the guidance of plan sponsors, while still using conventional and officially recognized cost methods to determine funding requirements and income tax deductions.

Stochastic Forecasting

The simulations set forth above are *deterministic* in nature (i.e., the results are determined by a single set of economic experience assumptions).[7] If there is a high probability that the assumptions will be realized over time, a deterministic forecast with one set of assumptions can be a useful management tool. But financial forecasts can also be developed using various combinations of plan specifications, economic and demographic assumptions, actuarial cost methods, and funding policies. However, great uncertainty surrounds any assumptions that purport to reflect future economic developments, especially the rate of inflation. The rate of *expected* inflation is a component of the salary scale and the rate of investment return, and it serves as the basis of postretirement benefit adjustments.

Recognizing the uncertainty of future economic events, the plan actuary may prepare several deterministic simulations, each based on a separate set of economic experience assumptions. For example, he or she may prepare projections based upon three sets of economic assumptions, characterized as optimistic, pessimistic, and most probable. Nevertheless, for each projection the assumptions are fixed throughout the forecast period or follow a predetermined pattern, such as a downward graded schedule of interest rate assumptions.

On the other hand, the simulation may be made on a basis that reflects the observed variability of the economic forces that form the foundation of the economic assumptions. Such a simulation employs Monte Carlo techniques and is generally referred to as a *stochastic forecast*. Since in theory economic forces are infinitely variable, it is necessary to construct and parameterize a model that will track the behavior of the forces shaping the economic experience assumptions.

The most basic economic assumption for a pension plan pertains to the annual rate of investment return. Unfortunately, the rate of return on the portfolio of a given pension plan can vary greatly from year to year, reflecting broad market forces as well as forces specific to the individual portfolio holdings. For instance, during one recent 20-year period, the aggregate annual rate of return on the 500 common stocks making up Standard & Poor's Composite Index ranged from a high of 32.4 percent to a low of –4.9 percent. The total annual rate of return on portfolios of intermediate and long-term bonds has also displayed considerable volatility.

---

[7]It will be recalled that a forecast of pension plan costs, liabilities, cash flow, and asset accumulations usually utilizes two sets of actuarial assumptions: (1) the *valuation* assumptions, which establish the plan's actuarial liabilities, cost, and funding contributions (and hence the employer's tax deductions for the plan) before adjustment for experience gains and losses; and (2) the *experience* assumptions, which produce annual adjustments in costs and contributions through actuarial gains flowing from more realistic assumptions, especially those of an economic character. Stochastic forecasting is concerned with experience assumptions and their variability.

To generate a pattern of returns, the portfolio of a particular pension plan must be partitioned into various broad classes of assets, such as equities, intermediate and long-term bonds, and cash equivalents (money market instruments). Each component of the portfolio has its own distribution of returns, but there is no extant probability distribution that precisely describes the historically observed pattern of return for any class of assets. Experience suggests, however, that the pattern of annual returns on a portfolio, or any of its major components, can be modeled by a log normal distribution (in statistical terms). The various portfolio components vary in the mean and dispersion of their normal distribution. For example, the normal distribution of possible returns on debt instruments is characterized by a smaller expected return and narrower dispersion than that for common stock. Once these distributions have been quantified, Monte Carlo techniques can be used to create sequences of random returns for the portfolio and any of its components.

The distribution of returns for any portfolio, or subset thereof, is determined by assumptions about its *mean* return and its *standard deviation* or other measure of dispersion. These two values are derived from observation of historical experience, tempered by judgment as to the course of future events. The area beneath the curve of the probability distribution is partitioned into, say, 100 segments of equal area, with the segments being assigned numbers from 1 to 100. For each year in the forecast, a large quantity of random numbers from 1 to 100 is generated and then associated with their corresponding segment, thereby establishing a pattern of random returns. Typically, 400 to 500 expected returns are generated for each year of the forecast, with a full gamut of related values, such as asset accumulation, being projected with each of the random returns. These randomly generated returns take the place of the fixed, predetermined rate (or rates) of return associated with a deterministic simulation model. The net effect is that a stochastic forecast can be characterized as a set of deterministic forecasts in which the economic assumptions of each forecast are determined randomly by statistical technique, rather than by subjective judgment.

More realism can be introduced into the simulation if the variability of inflation is taken into account. As indicated above, inflation affects benefit payouts through the salary scale and cost-of-living adjustments and through both nominal and real rates of return. Expected inflation can be built into the projections on a deterministic and judgmental basis, but *unexpected* inflation is a disruptive influence. Unexpected inflation can be randomly generated in a manner similar to the random generation of expected returns, based on assumptions about the potential range of unexpected inflation. Also, serial correlation may be involved in the year-to-year inflation rates, and appropriate weights must be assigned to the randomly generated annual rates of inflation and the assumed long-run rate to develop the expected rate of inflation for successive years. An algorithm based on historical relationships must be developed to measure the impact of simulated inflation on the *real* and *nominal* rates of return on the various subsets of the portfolio and, through an assumed *mix* of asset classes, on the real and nominal rates of return on the entire portfolio. This impact is, of course, created through the process of randomly generated unexpected rates of inflation.

Once a stochastic forecast has been developed, it can be analyzed to ascertain statistical probabilities of various results and to assess the volatility of those results. For example, in contrast to the deterministic forecast illustrated in Table 25-3, which projects an asset accumulation of $41,625,154 at the end of 10 years, a stochastic forecast would have the capability of indicating the statistical probability that the assets of the plan at that time would be greater or smaller than that amount or would fall within a range of, for example, $37 million to $47 million.

The primary function of a stochastic simulation is to make the plan sponsor aware of the potential range of outcomes over the forecast period, while indicating the probabilities and volatility involved, in contrast to predicting a specific future result. The simulations may vary greatly as to the scope and sophistication of the assumed relationships among the economic cost factors and their impact on other elements. Needless to say, the results of a stochastic forecast are no more reliable than the validity of the assumed relationships among the relevant variables and the potential range of the fluctuations, as constrained by the parameters.[8]

---

[8]For a fuller and more general treatment of stochastic processes, the interested student should consult Frederich S. Hillier and Gerald J. Lieberman, *Introduction to Operations Research* (San Francisco: Holden-Day, 1967), pp. 439–76.

Chapter 26
Valuation of Ancillary Benefits, Employee Contributions, and Small Plans

Chapters 22–25 were concerned with the valuation of the retirement benefits of a defined benefit pension plan. However, by law all plans must provide withdrawal benefits and survivor benefits and, at the option of the employer or other plan sponsor, disability benefits and additional death benefits. The cost of these ancillary benefits must be recognized in the valuation process. This chapter discusses procedures for determining the cost of these benefits, and it examines the special problems associated with contributory plans and small plans.

Ancillary Benefits

Withdrawal Benefits

Withdrawal benefits are benefits that are payable to participants who leave the plan before early or normal retirement age.[1] They are payable only to participants who had achieved a fully or partly vested status prior to termination, which in the case of a contributory plan encompasses all participants, in respect of benefits attributable to their own contributions. The benefits may be payable in the form of cash (sometimes limited to a refund of employee contributions or to small benefits with present value below some threshold amount) or a deferred claim to income payments commencing at early or normal retirement age. The following discussion focuses primarily on income benefits.

The valuation of the withdrawal benefits of a pension plan must recognize the expected or actual benefits of three subsets of the plan population: active participants, terminated vested participants, and retired participants. Valuing the benefits of the active population is by far the most complex task.

Active Participants

The valuation of withdrawal benefits is basically the same as the valuation of retirement benefits except that one uses the present value of withdrawal benefits

---

[1]For a detailed discussion of the cost of withdrawal benefits, see Dan M. McGill, *Preservation of Pension Benefits Rights* (Homewood, Ill.: Richard D. Irwin, 1972), pp. 141–76; and Dan M. McGill and Howard E. Winklevoss, "A Quantitative Analysis of Actuarial Cost Methods for Pension Plans," *Proceedings of the Conference of Actuaries in Public Practice*, vol. 23 (1974): pp. 212–43.

instead of the present value of retirement benefits when determining both the normal cost and the actuarial liability.

The first step in calculating the present value of the expected withdrawal benefits of an active participant is to calculate the annual amount of projected accrued benefit for each age at which the participant can terminate with vested benefits. This projection will ordinarily reflect future years of credited service and projected salary increases up to the potential termination date. But if the traditional accrued benefit cost method is used instead of the projected accrued benefit method, the benefit accrued to the valuation date and the benefit to be accrued during the year following the valuation date are determined for purposes of the actuarial liability and the normal cost, respectively.

The second step is to calculate the vested accrued benefit for each age at which the participant can terminate with vested benefits. This is done by multiplying the accrued benefits determined in the preceding step by the vesting percentage applicable to each age.

The third step is to determine what the value of such benefits would be at each age if the participant were to terminate at such age. This value is calculated by multiplying the amount of annual vested accrued benefit by the value of a deferred annuity of $1 beginning at the normal retirement age. This value of a deferred annuity equals the value of an immediate annuity as of the normal retirement age discounted to the age of possible termination by interest and by the probability of surviving in the interim years.

The fourth step is to discount, with interest, back to the date as of which the present value of withdrawal benefits is to be determined, the values found in the third step (which were as of the dates of possible termination). This provides the value, at the date as of which the present value of withdrawal benefits is to be determined, of the vested accrued benefit potentially payable at each age at which the participant can possibly terminate with vested benefits.

The fifth step is to multiply this potential value, with respect to each age at which the participant might terminate, by the probability that he or she will actually do so. This probability equals the probability that the participant will (1) survive in service to that age,[2] and (2) terminate service during that age. The first component of that probability reflects the impact of the three decremental forces discussed earlier (in connection with retirement benefits), and the same assumptions about the rates of termination, death, and total disability would be made. The second component involves only the probabilities of withdrawal and death for the year in question.

The sixth step in calculating the present value of the expected withdrawal benefits of an active participant is to sum for the participant the values just computed of withdrawal benefits payable upon termination at each possible age. While this process has been described as a series of steps, the computer of course can accomplish them successively in moments, producing the final result for the individual and combining it with the results for all other active participants.

The foregoing discussion assumed that benefits were payable only at normal retirement (or actuarially reduced for earlier commencement). Some plans pro-

---

[2]For a participant who has already achieved a vested status, this probability for the *current* year is 1, or certainty.

vide subsidized early retirement benefits to terminated vested participants (usually only those with significant service, e.g., 15 years). This can be handled by adjusting appropriately the percentage in step two and the deferred annuity in step three. For example, if the plan provided benefits commencing as early as age 55, reduced 3 percent per year before age 65 to terminated vested participants with 15 or more years of service, then for projected years prior to age 55 when the employee would terminate with this amount of service, the percentage in step two would be 70 percent $(100\% - [3\% \times 10])$ and the step three amount would be a deferred annuity to age 55.

The actuarial present value of withdrawal benefits in respect of active participants can be, and usually is, allocated to the participants' years of service in accordance with the same actuarial cost method that is used to allocate retirement benefits. When an individual cost allocation cost method is used, the actuarial liability for withdrawal benefits may be negative for many active participants and, indeed, the actuarial liability for the entire group of active participants may be negative. The explanation for this seemingly anomalous result is that the probability of termination decreases with age and a level normal cost may be less than the actual annual cost at the younger ages. This negative actuarial liability for withdrawal benefits will automatically decrease the actuarial liability for the plan as a whole, if the cost of retirement benefits and the cost of withdrawal benefits are computed in a single operation, as they frequently are. If separate calculations are used, any negative actuarial liability for withdrawal benefits is subtracted from the positive actuarial liability for retirement benefits. This negative liability can be avoided by computing the level annual cost for each slice of benefit to the age at which the decrement occurs.

When the traditional accrued benefit cost method is used, and the benefit that accrues in a particular year is a definitely fixed quantity, it is not necessary to calculate the cost of withdrawal benefits separately. The cost can be accurately reflected in the cost of retirement benefits by assuming no terminations among the participants whose benefits have fully vested. If a vested participant should, in fact, terminate, the actuarial value of his or her withdrawal benefit generally would be precisely the same as the actuarial value of the accrued retirement benefit at the moment before termination. Thus the termination would have no effect on the actuarial liability of the plan. Since it is expedient to use the same termination rates for all participants who are at the same attained age, regardless of their entry age, the termination assumption may be eliminated at all ages above the *average* age at which full vesting is achieved. Of course, this shortcut yields only the approximate cost of vesting. An even less precise, but more conservative, approach would be to assume that there will be no withdrawals at any ages, in which case an actuarial gain would be produced whenever a participant terminates with a non-vested accrued benefit. This technique is especially associated with allocated funding instruments, since it is impracticable to use termination assumptions with individual allocation of funds.

The technique of assuming no withdrawals among fully vested participants is also sometimes used in connection with the projected accrued benefit cost method or with cost allocation cost methods, but the cost of vesting (or withdrawal benefits) is overstated. If a participant were to terminate after having achieved a fully vested status, the actuarial liability for this vested benefit would be less than his or her actuarial liability as an active participant just prior to termination, and the result would be an actuarial gain of the difference.

Terminated Vested Participants

The valuation of the vested benefits payable to terminated participants is somewhat simpler. These individuals have already satisfied two of the requisite conditions for benefit entitlement. They survived in service to vesting and then later severed their employment relationship. The only remaining requirement is that they survive to early or normal retirement. Moreover, the amount of their benefits is fixed, unless subject to cost-of-living adjustments. The actuarial present value of the benefits of a terminated vested participant is derived by (1) multiplying the benefit amount by the probability of survival to normal retirement age, (2) multiplying the sum so derived by the annuity factor for the normal retirement age, and (3) discounting the value obtained in (2) to the date of valuation. All the factors and assumptions are identical to those used for active participants. In effect, the valuation is accomplished in accordance with the principles of the benefit allocation cost method.

Retired Vested Participants

The valuation of the benefits of terminated vested participants who have begun to receive income payments is the simplest procedure of the three. The actuarial liability associated with a particular individual is determined by multiplying the dollar amount of the individual's benefits by the annuity factor for his or her attained age. This is done for each individual in the retired group, using the annuity factor appropriate for the participant's sex and attained age. Terminated vested participants who have retired later are usually combined with all other retired participants for valuation purposes. The sum of the actuarial liability of the withdrawal benefits associated with active, terminated vested, and retired vested participants constitutes the actuarial liability for withdrawal benefits for the plan as a whole.

Death Benefits

The actuarial present value of preretirement death benefits provided under a pension plan is usually determined in accordance with the principles governing the net single premium of an individual life insurance contract. There is one important difference. The net single premium takes into account *only* the probability of death and an assumed rate of interest, but the actuarial present value of pension plan death benefits must *also* recognize the probability that the participant may withdraw from the plan and no longer be exposed to the possibility of death in service.

Preretirement Lump-Sum Benefit

The actuarial present value of a preretirement lump-sum benefit is determined by multiplying the amount of the benefit by the separate probabilities that the participant will die in service in each year from the date of valuation to retirement age and discounting the expected value of the benefit for each year back to the date of valuation at an assumed rate of interest. The sum of the discounted yearly values represents the actuarial present value of the benefit. The calculation for each year must reflect the probability that the participant will survive in service to that year and then die in that year. This means the computation must take into account the combined probabilities of death, withdrawal, and total disability prior to each year. As with retirement benefits, this is accomplished by applying the yearly probabilities of these occurrences to the plan population cells and showing the survivors year by year. Then the appropriate death rate is applied to the surviving members of the cell. The rates of decrement are usually assumed to be the same as those used in the valuation of retirement and withdrawal benefits.

When the retirement benefits of a plan are being valued on the basis of a cost allocation cost method, the actuarial present value of the preretirement death benefits will be allocated to years of service in the same manner as the cost of retirement benefits. However, if the basic benefits are being valued on the basis of a benefit allocation cost method, a special procedure may be used for the valuation of the death benefit. Under this procedure, a portion of the lump-sum death benefit is assumed to accrue each year, and the single premium cost of that "piece" of death benefit is charged to expenses for the year. If the death benefit does not vary with years of service, the unit of benefit accrued each year is arbitrarily determined and an actuarial loss will ordinarily occur in the year of death, since the full cost of the death benefit will not have accrued.

Another general approach to the valuation of a preretirement death benefit is the so-called one-year term insurance method. Under this method, the current year's cost for death benefits is assumed to be an amount equal to the death benefits expected to be paid during the year, discounted back to the beginning of the year at the valuation rate of interest. There is no actuarial liability under this method. If actual benefit disbursements exceed those expected, there will be an actuarial loss; and if the disbursements are less than expected, there will be an actuarial gain. Under a modification of this method, all actuarial gains are accumulated in a special reserve for future adverse experience.

In some plans, the preretirement death benefit is approximately or precisely equal to the actuarial liability for retirement benefits. In this case the additional cost of the death benefit may be obtained indirectly by omitting the mortality assumption in the valuation of the pension benefit. There is no additional cost or loss upon death, since the benefit paid equals the actuarial liability for retirement benefits, which is released. In those small plans where no preretirement mortality is assumed in the valuation of pensions (see below), it is considered appropriate to ignore the cost of uninsured preretirement death benefits if they do not significantly exceed the actuarial liability.

Preretirement Income Benefit

Preretirement income death benefits may include both the survivor annuity required under the Employment Retirement Income Security Act and other survivor income benefits. They are valued in the same way as lump-sum death benefits

TABLE 26-1   Yearly Probabilities of Remarriage of Widows Under the Railroad
Retirement System, According to the 1980 Railroad Retirement Board
Remarriage Table

Age at Widowhood	Number Per 1,000 Remarrying During Year						Attained Age[a]
	0	1	2	3	4	5	
20	76.00	131.82	86.31	73.35	66.58	40.70	25
25	58.58	115.40	77.03	67.83	62.23	36.11	30
30	39.27	97.45	71.44	64.02	58.61	34.09	35
35	28.78	74.22	61.40	41.03	36.55	25.85	40
40	15.20	47.15	41.91	26.32	24.87	14.00	45
45	8.35	23.22	23.89	17.61	13.80	6.29	50
50	5.03	9.94	12.43	8.56	5.85	4.06	55
55	3.56	7.60	7.56	6.78	5.06	3.95	60

[a]Remarriage rates for the attained ages above are those shown for the fifth year of widowhood. Attained age rates, known as "ultimate" rates, are the ones used by actuaries in valuing benefits subject to a remarriage provision.

except that the value of the income benefit changes each year. The lump-sum benefit for a given year is a known quantity, but the amount at risk under an income benefit in any given year is the present value of an immediate or deferred life annuity in the amount stipulated. Survivor annuity benefits not required by ERISA sometimes terminate with the remarriage of the spouse before a specified age. Benefits to children usually cease at a stated age, such as 18. The present value of the immediate or deferred life annuity is calculated in the same manner as the value of any other annuity. This reflects the yearly probabilities of survival and discounts each benefit payment; but if benefits cease on remarriage, the value must be reduced by the yearly probabilities that the income recipient will remarry before a stipulated age. Many actuaries use the remarriage rates of female income beneficiaries of the Railroad Retirement System. The yearly probabilities of remarriage, by years since widowhood, for quinquennial ages at widowhood 30 through 55 are shown in Table 26-1.[3]

An assumption may be made concerning the proportion of participants who are married, since only these will be covered for benefits payable to a spouse. Experience can be helpful in setting this assumption, but the effect of changing societal trends (such as the increasing percentage of married women in the work force) must be taken into account. Note that the percent married assumption is not for current status but for marital status at death. Usually the spouse's age is not known for the pension valuation, so an assumption must be made for this factor also. An assumption may be made that all participants are unmarried. That would in effect eliminate the valuation of survivor benefits for living participants; such an assumption may be justified if other actuarial assumptions are conservative in nature and the resulting combination of assumptions satisfy the "reasonable in the aggregate" requirement. If survivor benefits are payable to children, an assumption may be made concerning the number and ages of children.

[3]U.S. Railroad Retirement Board, *Sixteenth Actuarial Valuation*, Table S-7. See also Francisco Bayo, "Mortality and Remarriage Experience for Widow Beneficiaries Under OASDI," *Transactions of the Society of Actuaries*, vol. 21, part 1 (1969), pp. 59–80.

For purposes of computing the annuity factor, remarriage (if relevant) is treated as a decremental factor, having the same effect as death. Thus each payment is contingent upon the annuitant being alive in an unmarried state. Most plans that have a restriction on remarriage remove it after the annuitant reaches age 60.

Survivor Income Benefits for Deferred Vested Participants

ERISA requires survivor income benefits to be provided upon the death of terminated participants entitled to deferred vested benefits. The value of such benefits needs to be determined for all individuals who have already attained such status. This involves computations similar to the computation of the value of survivor income benefits for active participants.

In addition, the value of such survivor benefits payable upon the death of a terminated vested employee who was eligible for a deferred vested pension must also be computed for all active employees, since all active employees may enter deferred vested status with such accompanying survivor benefit coverage. The valuation of these benefits combines the techniques of valuation for active participants of the deferred retirement benefits payable upon withdrawal and the valuation of survivor income benefits payable with respect to those who have already withdrawn.

The valuation of survivor benefits related to death during the period of entitlement to deferred vested benefits is quite complex, while the magnitude of the value of the benefits may be so small as to be of little significance. This has led some actuaries to adopt one of the several alternative simplifications:

1. Assume no deaths among terminated participants during the period of deferral (increasing the value of deferred pensions while eliminating the value of survivor benefits). This is a conservative approach.
2. Assume that all terminated employees will be immediately paid in a lump-sum distribution (eliminating the value of survivor benefits payable upon death after the termination of employment).
3. Assume that all participants are unmarried (eliminating the value of survivor benefits both before and after retirement). This is an unconservative approach that may be justified if other actuarial assumptions are conservative.

Postretirement Death Benefits

Postretirement lump-sum death benefits are valued in the same manner as preretirement lump-sum benefits, except that there is no possibility of loss of coverage through withdrawal or total disability. The only probability taken into account is death, and it increases with each increment in attained age, reaching 1, or certainty, with the last age in the annuity table. The costs are recognized and they accrue during the working lives of the participants.

Postretirement income death benefits are a function of the annuity form under which the retirement benefits are being paid and are reflected in the calculation of the annuity factor for that type of annuity.

Disability Benefits

Disability is one of the three decremental forces taken into account in the valuation of retirement, withdrawal, and death benefits. If an explicit, independently determined benefit is payable under the plan in the event of total disability, it too must be valued as part of the overall valuation of the plan.

Valuation of Disability Benefits for Active Participants

There are three steps in the valuation of a disability benefit for active participants. The first is to determine the yearly probabilities of the occurrence of disability as defined in the plan. These probabilities are not independent of the probabilities of death and withdrawal and must be combined with them to form a multiple decrement table, as in the valuation of the other types of benefits under the plan. The disability rate increases with attained age and varies by sex.

The second step is to determine the present value of the benefits that would be payable should a participant become disabled. The amount of monthly benefit that would be payable is multiplied by a disabled life annuity factor for an annual benefit of $1 payable monthly. The value of a disabled life annuity is usually computed on the basis of a mortality table that reflects higher rates of mortality than those associated with active lives. In theory, it should also reflect the probability that the disabled person will recover from the disability. However, since the cost reduction associated with recovery would be partly offset by the cost of restoring the accrued benefits of the individual as an active participant, the probability of recovery is often ignored in the interest of simplicity. Even if the recovery probability is recognized, the cost of restoring the accrued retirement benefits may be ignored. A disabled life annuity factor must be computed for each age at which a participant could qualify for disability benefits under the plan. In this regard, it is similar to the survivor annuity described in the preceding section. Like the probability of disablement, the value of a disabled life annuity varies with the attained age and sex of the disabled person.

The third step is to multiply the disability benefit that would be payable at each potential age of disablement by the probability that the participant will survive in employment to that age and *then become disabled at that age.* The result is then multiplied by the value of a disabled life annuity at that age and discounted back to the valuation date at the same interest rate used for other valuations. These calculations are made for all active participants and summed.

Disability benefits for active participants can be, and frequently are, valued on the basis of the same actuarial cost methods and assumptions (except for mortality after disablement) as those used for the normal retirement benefits. The normal cost and actuarial liability for disability benefits may be independently determined, or they may be derived in combination with the other benefits under the plan. If the latter procedure is used, the present value of disability benefits expected to be paid in the future is added to the present value of all other benefits, and the combined values are assigned to years of service in accordance with the characteristics of the actuarial cost method employed in the valuation. If a benefit allocation cost method is used, an allocation of disability benefits can be made to particular years, similar to the allocation of normal retirement benefits. If a disabled participant continues to accrue retirement benefits, the actuarial present value of these accruals can be recognized annually as they occur or in their entirety at the time of retirement.

Disability benefits can also be valued on a one-year term insurance basis. Under this method, the current year's cost is assumed to equal the actuarial present value of all disability benefits ultimately to be paid to all participants who are expected to become disabled during the year. No actuarial liability is set up for participants not disabled. If the present value of future disability benefits for those participants who actually become disabled is greater than the expected present value, an actuarial loss is sustained. If the actual present value is less than the expected value, there would be an actuarial gain. There could also be actuarial gains or losses in the future in respect of the disablements of a given year if the duration of the disabilities (reflecting deaths or recoveries) is different from the actuarially predicted durations. In other words, actuarial gains and losses may emerge in connection with either the *expected rate of disability* or the *expected value of the disabled life annuity*. Actuarial gains may be accumulated in a reserve for future adverse experience with respect to either the rate or duration of disability.

Some plans, especially those so small that no one is likely to become disabled in a particular year, do not use a disability decrement in valuing normal retirement benefits and do not calculate any cost for disability benefits for active participants. If and when a disability actually occurs, the actuarial present value of the benefits payable to the disabled participant is set up as an actuarial liability, creating an actuarial loss in that amount in the year of disability. This loss, like other gains and losses, may be amortized over a period of years.

Valuation of Disability Benefits in Payment Status

The actuarial present value of the benefits payable to a participant in a disabled state at the time of valuation is derived by multiplying the amount of the benefit by the disabled life annuity factor for the participant's attained age, sex, and (sometimes) duration of disability. This calculation is carried out for all disabled persons, and the sum of the present values constitutes the actuarial liability for benefits in payment status.

Valuation of Employee Contributions

Employees may contribute to a pension plan on a mandatory basis, as a condition for participation and possibly even as a condition of employment, or on a voluntary basis. Voluntary contributions present no valuation problems since they accumulate in the participant's individual account and are administered on the money purchase principle. The funds in the account are withdrawable in the event of the participant's death, disability, or termination prior to retirement and are payable to the participant at retirement in the form of a lump-sum distribution or supplemental retirement income. On the other hand, mandatory employee contributions may necessitate special valuation procedures because of the employee's right to a refund of contributions, usually with interest, upon termination or death before retirement.

Mandatory employee contributions create no valuation problems when the contributions are administered on the money purchase principle and applied to provide retirement benefits supplemental to those financed by employer contributions. However, special valuation procedures must be used when employee contributions are applied to the reduction of employer costs. The new dimension added to the valuation process under this circumstance consists of (1) estimating the probability that a refund of an employee's contributions will have to be made in each of the future years that the employee participates in the plan and (2) then determining the amount of each potential refund. The employer's cost is obviously reduced by employee contributions, but the gross savings are reduced by the refunds that have to be made. The basic purpose of this valuation procedure is to determine the *net* effect of employee contributions on the employer's cost. Thus the employee's right to a refund of contributions is considered an additional benefit of the plan.

In determining the present value of future benefits for active employees, the actuary generally assumes that a refund will be made if an employee dies when no survivor annuity is payable, or if an employee terminates employment before becoming eligible for a vested pension attributable to employer contributions. But if an employee dies when a survivor annuity is payable or terminates employment with a vested pension, it is usually assumed that no refund will be paid, and the entire vested pension or survivor annuity is valued accordingly.

The crucial actuarial function in this valuation procedure is the actuarial present value of the employee's right to a refund of $1, plus accumulated interest, in any future year in which he or she might die or terminate employment and receive a refund. The actuarial present value of the refund right for each such future year is the probability of payment (i.e., the probability that the employee will continue in the plan to the beginning of such year and then terminate and receive a refund during the year) times the amount of the payment times the interest discount factor.

An actuarial liability is associated with past employee contributions. Under all actuarial cost methods, this liability is equal to the actuarial present value of the employee's right to a refund of all his or her prior contributions with interest. If the interest rate credited to employee contributions is the same as the interest rate used in the interest discount factor, the two interest rates offset each other and the present value of any potential refund of $1 is simply the probability of payment times $1. In this case, the present value of the refund of past employee contributions for all future years combined is the accumulated employee contributions with interest as of the valuation date times the probability that the employee will die or terminate employment when a refund is payable. For example, if a 35-year-old employee has $1 of accumulated employee contributions and the probability that he or she will receive a refund is 60, the present value at age 35 of his or her right to a refund of the $1 contribution is $1.00 \times 60 = $0.60. This simplifies the calculations to such a degree that offsetting interest is sometimes assumed as an approximation even when the two interest rates differ.

Under the traditional accrued benefit cost method, the normal cost should include the value of refunds associated with the current year's contribution. This is calculated in the same manner as the value of refund of past employee contributions, using the current year's contribution in place of the accumulated employee contributions. The total normal cost, including the value of future refunds of the current year's employee contributions, is reduced by the amount of employee contributions for the current year to determine the employer's normal cost for the year.

Under cost allocation cost methods, employee contributions for all years, past and future, and the cost of refunding them are taken into account. In the valuation equation, the present value of future benefits includes the present value of refunding both accumulated *prior* contributions and *future* contributions. The amount of refund potentially payable in each future year must be projected, multiplied by the probability that it will be paid, and multiplied by the interest discount factor to determine the present value of future refunds. The actuarial liability for the plan equals the present value of future benefits (including a refund of employee contributions) minus the present value of future employee contributions and the present value of future employer normal costs. In effect, the present value of future benefits is reduced by the present value of future employee contributions in determining the actuarial liability and the present value of future employer normal costs. Instead of adding the cost of refunding employee contributions to the present value of future benefits, one might offset such cost against the present value of future employee contributions on an exact or approximate basis.

There is a hybrid valuation method under which a cost allocation cost method is used for all items except future employee contributions. In this case, the actuarial liability is determined as if there were no future employee contributions, and the calculated normal cost is reduced by the current year's net employee contributions (contributions less the related cost of refund). The refund cost for prior accumulated employee contributions would be included in the present value of future benefits.

The normal annuity form for most contributory plans is a modified cash refund annuity, which ensures ultimate payment of an amount not less than the accumulated contributions of the employee, with interest. The present value of the refund feature can be determined directly and precisely for each employee under such an annuity. However, the additional cost of the refund feature can be approximated by calculating an average ratio of death benefits to monthly income at normal retirement and by using this ratio for all employees, irrespective of their particular circumstances.

Valuation of Small Plans

The great majority of pension plans cover fewer than 25 employees, and the valuation of such small plans involves certain special considerations. In the first place, the experience of the plan is less predictable than that of a larger plan. A plan with 10,000 active participants, for example, may, depending upon the age and sex distribution, experience about 50 deaths per year, or a composite death rate of 0.5 percent, with relatively little annual variation. The number of deaths within an active population of 100 participants would normally be either none, one, or two per year, constituting 0 percent, 1 percent, or 2 percent, respectively, of the active life group. On the other hand, there would normally be no deaths among an active life group of 10 persons; but if a death were to occur, the death rate for that year would be 10 percent. There may be equally large variations in the year-to-year rates of withdrawal. Not only will the smaller plan have wider variations in the death and withdrawal rates, but for the very small plan the most probable assumption for any given year may be that there will be no deaths or withdrawals.

Second, it is important to minimize the cost of actuarial valuations for a small plan. The cost of actuarial services should constitute only a small part of the overall cost of the plan. Through the use of computers, complex methods and assumptions may be applied to a large plan at a low cost per employee, whereas using the same methods and assumptions for a small plan may produce burdensome costs per employee.

Third, the actuarial valuations for many small plans (but by no means all) are carried out by persons with limited actuarial skills who may not be qualified to use the more complex methods and assumptions.

Any or all of the foregoing considerations may affect the actuary's choice of actuarial methods and assumptions. The actuary may decide to assume no deaths, no withdrawals, and no disablements prior to retirement, or to assume no deaths but some withdrawals, or vice versa. Even when benefits are based on final average earnings, the actuary may use the individual level premium cost method with no salary scale, accruing the cost of actual salary increases on a level annual cost basis from the participant's attained age to normal retirement age. He or she may use a simplified approach to determining the cost of withdrawal, death, or disability benefits or may ignore such costs altogether. The actuary may be conservative with respect to some assumptions (e.g., no deaths and no withdrawals and a low interest rate) and unconservative with respect to others (e.g., no salary scale with a final average salary formula), expecting the gains from one source to offset the losses from another. However, for even the smallest plans, the assumptions must be reasonable and must represent the actuary's best estimate of future experience.[4]

---

[4]ERISA §302(c)(3); IRC §412(c)(3).

Chapter 27
Approaches to Meeting the Financial Obligations of a Defined Benefit Plan

The dominant function of an actuarial cost method is to apprise the employer of the rate at which the obligations under a defined benefit plan are accruing, so that appropriate financial arrangements may be made to meet such obligations. Unless satisfactory arrangements are made to discharge the obligations of a plan, the benefit rights created by the plan may not be attainable. This chapter analyzes the various approaches that may be utilized to meet the obligations of a defined benefit pension plan as they accrue or become due.

Current Disbursement Approach

The simplest approach that can be used to meet the financial obligations of a pension plan is for the employer to disburse the benefits as they become due. This is commonly referred to as the pay-as-you-go approach, but throughout this volume the more accurate expression "current disbursement approach" is used to describe the arrangement.

Under the current disbursement arrangement, retirement benefits are paid directly to the pensioner by the employer in the same manner as payroll. Such benefits, if reasonable in amount, are deductible from the employer's gross income as a necessary business expense and are taxable to the recipient as ordinary income. For this purpose, no distinction is made between past service and future service benefits, since under this arrangement such a distinction would be meaningless.

The outlay under this method is normally low during the early years of an employer's existence, or at the start of the pension program, since the number of retired employees is relatively small and no provision is being made to meet the accruing benefits of those employees who are still working. As the employee group matures, however, constantly increasing numbers of persons are added to the retired rolls until retirement benefits eventually constitute a significant percentage of the payroll cost. In fact, the annual outlay under this arrangement, expressed as a percentage of payroll, ultimately reaches a level that is considerably higher than that of any other financing method.

To anticipate the heavy drain on cash resources that this method ultimately entails, an employer may set up a special reserve for pensions. To this end the employer may earmark specific assets to pay pension benefits or may only place a restriction against surplus, similar to a reserve for depreciation. Whatever the nature of the action taken, it does not place any assets beyond the control of the employer and therefore fails to insulate the pension benefits against the financial vicissitudes of the employer. Moreover, the reserve is usually not established or maintained on the basis of actuarial estimates of the liabilities of the plan. An unattractive feature of the special reserve arrangement from the standpoint of any taxable employer is that the sums transferred to the reserve are not deductible as an ordinary and necessary business expense.[1] To be deductible, such sums would have to be placed beyond the control of the employer, as by transfer to a trustee under a suitably drawn trust agreement or by payment to an insurance company for the purchase of benefits. The benefits, nevertheless, are deductible in the tax year in which paid.

Prior to the Employment Retirement Income Security Act of 1974, there were no restrictions on the current disbursement approach to financing, and it was used by a substantial number of plans. Many, if not most, of these plans provided benefits that supplemented a basic underlying plan. However, with specified exceptions, the approach can no longer be used for pension plans subject to ERISA's funding requirements.[2] This is true whether or not the plan seeks a qualified status under the tax provisions of the law administered through the Internal Revenue Service. Hereafter the current disbursement approach can be used within interstate commerce only for (1) plans maintained by an employer primarily to provide deferred compensation for a select group of management and highly paid employees, (2) supplemental plans that provide benefits or contributions in excess of the limits imposed by law, (3) plans that have not provided for any employer contributions since the enactment of ERISA (i.e., plans of unions funded exclusively by member contributions), (4) governmental and church plans, (5) nonqualified plans of employers not engaged in interstate commerce or plans of employee organizations whose membership is not interstate in character,[3] and (6) plans for certain other organizations and classes of employees.

Funding

The conventional approach to financing pension benefits is for the employer (and employees, if the plan is contributory) to set aside the necessary funds with a trustee or insurance company before the benefits become payable. This practice is known as *funding*, a term frequently used throughout this book. The amount of funds set aside each year usually bears a definite relationship to the pension costs assumed to have accrued in that year. As a matter of fact, most employers prefer to set aside enough funds each year to meet the costs attributable to that year, plus a portion of the initial actuarial liability, with a view to having all obligations fully funded at the earliest practicable date. The effect of recent legislation has made it

---

[1] In some countries—Germany, for example—sums set aside in a balance sheet reserve are deductible for income tax purposes.
[2] ERISA §§3(31), 4,301; IRC §412(a),(h).
[3] Courts have interpreted "interstate commerce" extremely broadly to include almost all business and industry.

much more difficult to follow such a funding policy, as discussed at the end of this chapter.

Pension plans have traditionally been funded through cash contributions, and that is still the dominant practice. In recent years, however, some large firms, to conserve their working capital and reduce their liquidity requirements, have met some or all of their funding requirements by transferring real property or property rights to the pension plan. Some firms have contributed shares of common or preferred stock in their own companies to the pension plan. This type of funding is permissible if the assets transferred constitute *qualifying* employer real property or *qualifying* employer securities, if it is prudent for the plan to hold such assets, and, in the case of defined benefit plans and most money purchase pension plans, if the securities and real property of the plan sponsor do not constitute more than 10 percent of the pension asset portfolio (see Chapter 3 for fiduciary requirements).[4] Other firms have transferred mineral rights or royalty interests to their pension plans. Some commercial airlines have transferred their aircraft to their pension plan and then leased back the aircraft. Assets of this type do not fall within the 10 percent limit, as they are not in the form of employer securities or real estate.

These transactions would normally be prohibited, since they involve parties in interest (see Chapter 3 for prohibited transactions).[5] The plan sponsors, however, have been able to obtain exemptions from the Department of Labor. To procure the exemption, the plan sponsor usually agrees to buy back the property at any time at a price equal to the value at which it was transferred to the plan. In addition, the sponsor may agree to indemnify the plan against any loss of principal that it might suffer from holding the asset. Naturally, the repurchase and indemnity agreements are no more secure than the fiscal viability of the firm. Indeed, holding employer stock and relying on employer repurchase and indemnity agreements do not insulate the pension plan against the financial vicissitudes of the plan sponsor. If held in moderation, however, they pose no serious threat to the well-being of the plan and lend an element of flexibility to the firm's financial management.

Under some plans no assets are set aside for active participants, but as each participant reaches retirement his or her benefits are funded in full. This practice is known as *terminal funding* and is usually a compromise between no funding (as represented by the current disbursement approach) and approximate full funding.[6] Terminal funding can be accomplished through the purchase of an immediate annuity in the appropriate amount for each employee as he or she reaches retirement or by the transfer to a trustee of a principal sum actuarially estimated to be sufficient to provide the benefits to which the participant is entitled. The principal sums required for such purchase or transfer normally come out of the

---

[4]ERISA §407.

[5]ERISA §406; IRC §4975.

[6]In a small plan with some participants close to retirement at the time the plan is established, terminal funding may require larger contributions in the early years than would be required if funds were being set aside in accordance with one of the conventional actuarial cost methods, under which supplemental liabilities could be amortized over many years. In this situation, especially if annuities are purchased for participants as they reach retirement, the employer will contribute the larger terminal funding amounts.

operating revenue of the employer, since by definition the employer makes no advance provision (unless the employer has created a special reserve) for the accumulation of the sums needed. The annual contribution required for terminal funding will tend to increase each year, both absolutely and as a percentage of payroll, until a stable population is achieved, after which it will level off (in the absence of inflation). In small- to medium-size companies, terminal funding costs can vary considerably from year to year since the number of employees retiring in a given year fluctuates greatly. Even large companies can see significant fluctuations due to reductions in force or to uneven hiring patterns many years before. Thus in practice terminal funding produces the least stable annual cost pattern. Like the current disbursement approach, terminal funding is no longer an acceptable method of meeting the cost of qualified pension plans and other plans subject to the funding provisions of ERISA.[7]

The remaining discussion of funding concentrates on those budgetary arrangements that have as their objective the orderly accumulation over a period of years of the sums needed to provide benefits to retiring employees. These arrangements are sometimes referred to as *advance* funding, meaning the setting aside of funds before the date of retirement.[8]

Purposes of Funding

Security of Benefits

The primary purpose of funding is to enhance the security of the benefit rights of the plan participants. In the absence of funding, the participants are completely dependent upon the employer's future willingness and ability to honor their claims, except to the extent that such benefits are guaranteed by the Pension Benefit Guaranty Corporation (described later in this chapter). Moreover, the employer's ability—and perhaps even willingness—to meet the burden of pension claims will be weakened with the addition of each new name on the pension roll. On the other hand, if a funding program is in effect, the employees can look to a segregated fund, irrevocably committed to the payment of benefits and administered by an independent third party, for the satisfaction of their claims. The higher the ratio of assets in the fund to the actuarial liabilities of the plan, the greater the assurance that the claims of the participants and pensioners will be satisfied. If each dollar of actuarial liability is matched by a dollar of assets in a segregated fund or the promise that a life insurer will pay, there will be a high degree of assurance about the benefit rights that have been created at any given time.

Protection of the Pension Benefits Insurance Program

A related purpose of funding is to protect the pension benefits insurance program against abuse. Under ERISA, the PBGC insures the vested benefits of plan

---

[7]ERISA §3(31).

[8]For the sake of completeness, the concept of postretirement funding should be mentioned. Under the practices of some insurers, the benefits of employees at or near retirement at the date of plan inception or liberalization may be spread over a period extending 5 to 10 years beyond retirement. The same technique may be used in trust fund plans.

participants subject to certain limits (see Chapters 33 and 34). If an insured event occurs and the plan assets are less than the actuarial present value of the insured benefits, the PBGC must make good on the deficiency. It clearly would be impracticable to insure the vested benefits of a pension plan if the employer were under no obligation to set aside funds in a systematic manner to meet the accruing costs of the benefits. The employer could promise any permissible level of benefits, make no contributions other than those necessary to pay benefits to retired participants or their beneficiaries, and eventually terminate the plan with no further financial obligation. To prevent this type of abuse and to instill a sense of responsibility when setting benefit levels, ERISA requires pension plans to conform to specified minimum funding schedules. These funding standards are benefit security devices in themselves, but they are also an essential element in a feasible program of plan benefits insurance.

Enforcement of Fiscal Responsibility

A third purpose of funding is to ensure the fiscal responsibility of those who design and administer pension plans. In other words, funding forces employers to face up to the costs of their pension plans. Before the accounting profession adopted the principle of accrual accounting for pension plan costs, the only way in which such costs were reflected in the financial statements of the firm was through the funding process. If in a particular fiscal year no contribution was made to the plan, no pension cost appeared in the operating statements. This of course distorted the operating results of the firm and affected the apportionment of pension costs over different generations of shareholders, employees, consumers, and taxpayers. With accrual accounting, pension costs of business firms are reflected in operating statements somewhat independently of funding, but for plans of governmental agencies and organizations not affected by accounting standards, funding still serves as the primary force for cost recognition and fiscal discipline.

Advance recognition of pension costs is especially critical for state and local governments. If a plan were to be operated on a current disbursement basis, its initial cost and that of any benefit improvements would become apparent only over a long period of years. There would be a strong temptation for elected officials to seek political gain by granting excessively liberal pension benefits, since it would not require a current increase in taxes or other revenue, as an increase in wages and salaries might. On the other hand, if granting pension benefits must be accompanied by appropriate funding contributions, the pension demands of employees are more likely to receive critical scrutiny.

Reduction of Employer Outlay

One of the most persuasive arguments in favor of funding, from the standpoint of the employer, is that it will reduce the ultimate out-of-pocket cost of the plan. If an employer were to provide $600 a month to an employee who retires at age 65 and lives 15 years thereafter, it would pay $108,000 on the current disbursement basis ($600 times 12 months times 15 years). However, if the sum required to provide the benefit were to be accumulated through a series of level annual installments, extending from age 30 to age 65 discounted for interest at 5 percent but not for mortality, the outlay would aggregate only $28,322 (about $809 per year for 35 years) or about one-fourth of the cost under the current disbursement basis.

The difference in the outlay under the two methods of financing is, of course, wholly attributable to the interest factor. Under the current disbursement method, the employer's contributions obviously earn no interest, and the total cost is the sum of the individual payments. Under the advance funding scheme, each annual installment is credited with interest (5 percent in the above example) from the date of payment until the time it is disbursed as a retirement benefit. Over the years, the sums contributed to the plan are credited with $79,678 in interest. If the funding agency earns more than the assumed 5 percent, the employer's outlay would be reduced to an even greater extent than that indicated.

Although investment earnings on the funds set aside to pay benefits reduce the employer's outlay for pensions, they should properly be viewed as part of the true cost of the pension plan. They represent money that presumably would have been earned if the funds transferred to the plan had been invested elsewhere. In fact, the counter argument for nonfunding is that such funds will earn more in the employer's business than in the hands of a separate funding agency. While this may be true on a gross yield basis, allowance must be made for the tax-deferred status of the investment income of a qualified pension plan. An employer would have to enjoy an earnings rate, before taxes, substantially higher than that of the funding agency to net the same rate.

Disadvantages of Funding

From the standpoint of the employees, there appear to be no disadvantages to funding unless the financial burden involved would discourage an employer from adopting a pension plan at all or would lead an employer to provide less generous compensation and benefits than would otherwise be provided. From the standpoint of the employer, however, there are possible disadvantages, which in a given case may or may not be important.

The most obvious potential disadvantage of funding is that the agency to which the funds are transferred may earn a lower investment return than the employer could have obtained by retaining and investing the funds in its own business (or a return less than what the employer pays as interest on borrowed funds), even after income taxes. This situation has undoubtedly prevailed in a number of cases in years gone by and may still prevail to some extent.

A second possible disadvantage of funding is that the accumulation of large sums of money in the hands of the funding agency may create such an aura of affluence that the participants will demand liberalization of the pension plan. Financially unsophisticated employees do not understand why a pension plan must accumulate large sums of money, and they tend to equate a large buildup of assets with the ability to provide higher benefits. Some groups interpret an excess of plan income over plan outgo as grounds for plan liberalization. An employer with a well-funded plan must be prepared to explain to its employees, or to their bargaining agents, why such a large accumulation of assets is necessary.

A third possible disadvantage of funding is that the accumulation of the large pools of wealth necessary to fund pension plans may provide a tempting target for politicians. Outright confiscation is perhaps less likely in the United States than in many other countries, but the last decade has seen various proposals offered in Congress for special taxes on pension plans or for government-directed "social investments" drawn from pension funds. As the total amount of money in pension funds grows, the gains from expropriation in this manner also grow.

A fourth disadvantage, of a minor nature, is that a funded plan involves more actuarial, legal, and investment expenses than a plan operated on a current disbursement basis.

Statutory Funding Standards

Congress has long imposed *upper* limits on the amount of pension plan contributions that an employer can deduct as an ordinary and necessary business expense for federal income tax purposes.[9] These limits are designed to prevent an employer from timing contributions to minimize the employer's income tax liability over the years. Before ERISA, Congress never set any *lower* limits on plan contributions, although the IRS promulgated rules through PS 57 that some construed as requiring a minimum level of funding. ERISA articulated new guidelines for both *maximum* and *minimum* contributions. The minimum standards are especially significant and are described first.

Minimum Standards

The plan's supplemental liability or liabilities must be amortized over a specified time, in addition to the funding of the normal cost.[10] The amortization period depends upon whether the plan was already in existence on January 1, 1974. There are separately articulated amortization schedules for experience gains and losses and for liabilities created by plan amendment or change in actuarial assumptions. Changes in the actuarial liability of an integrated pension plan attributable to changes in Social Security benefits or the wage base subject to Social Security taxation are treated as experience gains or losses.

The requirement to amortize the supplemental liability applies only to defined benefit plans, since a pure money purchase plan cannot have a supplemental liability. The minimum amount that is to be contributed under a money purchase plan is the amount called for by the plan formula. A collectively bargained multi-employer plan that calls for a specified level of contributions and an agreed level of benefits during the contract period is considered to be a defined benefit plan. On the other hand, a target benefit plan is to be treated as a money purchase plan for purposes of the minimum funding rules.

For defined contribution plans, compliance with minimum funding requirements must be demonstrated on the annual report form, Form 5500. For defined benefit plans, compliance must be demonstrated on Schedule B, which is prepared by the enrolled actuary and attached to Form 5500.

[9]IRC §404.
[10]ERISA §302(b); IRC §412(b).

To meet minimum funding standards, the liabilities of a plan are to be calculated by and large on the basis of actuarial assumptions and actuarial cost methods that individually offer the actuary's best estimate of anticipated experience under the plan or that in aggregate would produce similar results as generated by individually reasonable assumptions.[11] Requirements for the valuation of assets are discussed in Chapter 30.

Unless the employer elects to meet the alternative minimum funding standard as described later in this chapter, the same actuarial assumptions and cost method must be used for determining the minimum annual contribution to the plan and the maximum amount that can be currently deducted for federal income tax purposes.[12] The funding requirements for multiemployer plans differ in certain respects from those applicable to all other plans. In this chapter all plans other than multiemployer plans are referred to as "single-employer plans," although the category actually includes multiple-employer plans that are not multiemployer plans as defined by law.

Basic Amortization Periods

Unfunded actuarial liabilities in existence on the effective date of the minimum funding standards must be amortized in equal annual installments over a period of years that take into account both interest and principal.[13] For purposes of the minimum funding requirements, the amortization period for each portion of the unfunded actuarial liabilities depends on its source. The amortization periods for new unfunded liabilities and changes in unfunded liabilities with amortization periods commencing after January 1, 1988, are shown in Table 27-1.

Amortization periods for unfunded liabilities were longer when the amortization commenced on certain earlier dates, and these longer amortization periods continue to apply to such amounts. This shorter amortization period for actuarial losses was prescribed to encourage realism in the choice of actuarial assumptions. Actuarial valuations must be made at least once a year and should include the determination of experience gains and losses unless a spread gain method is used.[14]

Neither statutes nor regulations define the amortization period applicable to changes in unfunded liabilities resulting from changes in actuarial cost methods and asset valuation methods, though expired revenue procedures exist that detail the amortization of these items. Amounts to be amortized under the various schedules may be combined (with offsets for any amortizable credits) into a composite amortization schedule, weighted by the amounts and remaining years associated with each schedule.[15]

Funding Standard Account

Each plan subject to the minimum funding standards must set up and maintain a special account called the "funding standard account," which provides a cumula-

[11]ERISA §302(c)(3); IRC §412(c)(3).
[12]IRC §404(a)(1)(A); Treas. Reg. 1.404(a)-14(d)(1).
[13]ERISA §302(b)(2), (3); IRC §412(b)(2), (3).
[14]ERISA §§103(d), 302(c)(9); IRC §§412(c)(9), 6059(a).
[15]ERISA §302(b)(4); IRC §412(b)(4).

TABLE 27-1   Amortization Periods for Unfunded Liabilities

Initial unfunded liability, plans established after January 1, 1974	30 years
Plan amendments	30 years
Actuarial gains and losses	
Single-employer plans	5 years
Multiemployer plans	15 years
Changes in actuarial assumptions	
Single-employer plans	10 years
Multiemployer plans	30 years

tive comparison between actual contributions and those required under the minimum funding standard.[16] The primary purpose of the funding standard account, apart from its record-keeping function, is to provide some flexibility in funding by allowing contributions greater than the required minimum, accumulated with interest, to reduce the minimum contributions required in future years.

Each plan year the funding standard account is charged with the normal cost for the year and the share of the actuarial liabilities that must be amortized annually under the rules set forth above. The account is credited each year with the current year's amortization of any decreases in the unfunded actuarial liabilities resulting from experience gains, changes in actuarial assumptions or methods, or plan amendments. Some special rules apply to multiemployer plans.[17] Interest is added to all charges and credits from their effective date to the end of the plan year (see Chapter 25).[18] If the contributions to the plan, adjusted for actuarial gains and losses, exactly meet the minimum standards, the funding standard account will show a zero balance. If the contributions exceed the minimum requirements, at the end of the year the account will have a credit balance available to reduce the minimum requirement for the following year. If the contributions for a plan year are less than the minimum requirement, the account will show a deficiency, called the "accumulated funding deficiency," which will accrue interest at the valuation rate.

Full Funding Limit

Despite the foregoing rules, the employer is under no obligation to contribute more than required to satisfy the full funding limit. The full funding limit is the excess of the lesser of the plan's actuarial liability determined for funding purposes or 150 percent of its *current liability* over the value of plan assets. Pension Reform Legislation added another condition, effective in 1995, that the full funding limit cannot be less than the excess of 90 percent of the *new current liability* over plan assets.[19] If the actuarial liabilities cannot be directly determined on the basis of the

[16]ERISA §302(b)(1); IRC §412(b)(1).
[17]ERISA §302(b)(6),(7); IRC §412(b)(6),(7).
[18]ERISA §302(b)(5); IRC §412(b)(5).
[19]ERISA §302(c)(6),(7); IRC §412(c)(6),(7).

actuarial cost method used for regular valuations, the liabilities are to be calculated on the basis of the entry-age normal cost method.

For this purpose the current liability is the plan's liability determined on a plan termination basis. The interest rate used to determine the current liability must fall within a permissible range. The permissible range is between 90 percent and 110 percent of the weighted average yield on 30-year Treasury securities during the 4-year period immediately preceding the plan year, except that regulations may extend the lower bound of the range to 80 percent. The new current liability defines the assumption slightly differently by requiring the use of the GAM 83 mortality and restricts the upper bound of interest rates to 109 percent of the weighted average. This upper restriction is graded from 109 percent to 105 percent in 1999. The interest rate is also required to be a reasonable estimate of the interest rate that is implicit in the price of deferred and immediate annuities available to discharge the current liability. However, this second requirement must not cause the interest rate used to fall outside the permissible range.

If either the actuarial liability for funding purposes or 150 percent of the current liability has been used to determine the full funding limit, the asset value used must be the lesser of the fair market value of plan assets or the actuarial value of the plan assets. But if the new current liability has been used, the asset value must be the actuarial value of the plan assets without an offset for the credit balance in the funding standards account.

To whatever extent use of the current liability reduces required contributions below the level that would have been required if the full funding limit had been determined on the basis of the regular actuarial liability of the plan, regulations may require increased contributions in future years.

Additional Funding Requirements for Single-Employer Plans

Beginning in 1995 additional funding requirements for *deficit reduction contributions* apply to a single-employer plan with more than 100 participants that has an *unfunded current liability* for a year.[20] A plan's unfunded current liability is the excess of 90 percent of a plan's new current liability over the actuarial value of plan assets, using the highest interest rate in the range. Exceptions apply to plans that are at least 80 percent funded on this basis and that have been 90 percent funded for two consecutive years in the last three years.

For this purpose the current liability is determined as described above except that for anyone who became a participant after 1987 and has less than five years of participation, a stipulated percentage of the participant's service prior to participation may be disregarded in determining his or her accrued benefit. As a result, every new plan that provides accrued benefits on its effective date for prior service will have an unfunded current liability during its first plan year.

The additional funding requirement ordinarily equals the excess, if any, of the deficit reduction contribution over the plan's net charges and credits for amortization of unfunded liabilities arising from establishment of the plan, plan amendments, net of funding waivers, or the switch back from the alternative minimum

---

[20]ERISA §302(d); IRC §412(l).

TABLE 27-2   Deficit Reduction Contribution

Regular minimum funding requirement	
Normal cost	$250,000
Amortization amount (30-year amortization of $3 million)	205,606
Total	$455,606
Additional funding requirement	
Deficit reduction contribution plus (30 percent of $2 million)	$600,000
Current liability service cost	$300,000
Less total amount above	455,606
Additional funding requirement	$444,394
Total minimum funding requirement	$900,000

funding requirement (described later in this chapter). But this contribution should not exceed the amount necessary to increase the new current liability funded status to 100 percent.

The deficit reduction contribution consists of three parts: the unfunded *old* liability amount, the unfunded *new* liability amount, and the expected increase in the new current liability due to benefits accruing in the plan year. The unfunded old liability amount is the annual amount required to amortize over 18 years the unfunded current liability as of the beginning of the plan year starting in 1988, in accordance with the plan provisions in effect on October 28, 1987. In addition, the unfunded old liability includes the increasing current liability attributable to new changes in interest rates and mortality assumptions introduced by the new 1995 legislation. This amount is treated as the "additional unfunded old liabilities amount" with amortization over 12 years. The unfunded new liability amount ordinarily is a percentage of the excess of the unfunded current liability over the unamortized portion of the unfunded old liability amount. The applicable percentage is 30 percent for a plan that is 60 percent funded on this basis, grading down to as little as 18 percent as the funded ratio of the current liability increases to 90 percent.

The required deficit reduction contribution is illustrated in Table 27-2 for a new plan that, as of its effective date, has a normal cost of $250,000, current liability normal costs of $300,000, an actuarial liability for funding purposes of $3 million, a current liability of $2 million, and plan assets of $0. There is an extensive transition process that grades from the current method of calculating deficient reduction contributions to the method described here. The transition period is from plan years beginning in 1995 through plan years beginning in 2001.

This additional funding requirement may discourage employers from establishing plans that provide accrued benefits as of the effective date with respect to prior service.

The additional funding requirement may be increased if an *unpredictable contingent event* occurs. Such an event is one that is not reasonably or reliably predictable and that is not contingent upon the age, service, compensation, or disability of participants. An example of an unpredictable contingent event might be a plant closing that, under the terms of the pension plan, triggers an increase in benefits.

The additional funding requirements do not apply to plans with fewer than 100 participants. For plans with fewer than 150 participants, the additional requirement is reduced. In determining the number of participants for this purpose all defined benefit plans of the same employer and of other employers in the same controlled group must be aggregated. In addition, special rules apply to certain collectively bargained plans and certain steel industry plans. A multitude of transitions and phase-in rules also apply.

If a plan is amended to increase the current liability by more than $10 million and the plan assets are less than 60 percent of the current liability at the end of the year of the amendment, requirements for bonding or other security apply.[21] Also, PBGC-covered single-employer plans sponsored by the controlled group with more than $50 million in aggregated unfunded vested benefits cannot change assumptions for determining current liability without IRS approval if the change in assumptions decreases the unfunded current liability by more than $50 million or more than $5 million and at least 5 percent of current liability. If a plan is subject to deficit reduction contributions and is required to pay variable premiums during the year, plan participants must be notified of the plan's funded status and the limits of PBGC guarantees.

Shortfall Method

Special provision has been made for plans, usually of the multiemployer type, that are maintained pursuant to collective bargaining agreements that call for a predetermined level of contributions over a period longer than a year, such as a specified dollar amount per hour of covered service by an employee or a specified dollar amount per ton of coal mined.[22] The purpose of the exception is to permit employers to base their contributions on the terms of the labor agreement during the agreement period (but generally not longer than three years), irrespective of any experience gains or losses that might emerge during the period. If the actuarial assumptions were reasonable and the actuarial calculations were correct at the beginning of the labor contract period, and the agreed-upon contributions were made when due, no deficiency in the funding standard account would develop during the term of the collective bargaining agreement. This would be the case even if the contributions turned out to be less than was reasonably expected at the beginning of the contract term, because of a decline in employment, for example, or a reduction in output. In that event, any difference between anticipated and actual contributions would be treated as an actuarial loss, to be amortized in 20 equal annual dollar installments. At the option of the plan, amortization of the contribution "shortfall" may be deferred for 5 years and then amortized over 15 years. An excess of actual over anticipated contributions would be treated as an actuarial gain, to be amortized in the same manner as an actuarial loss.

[21]ERISA §307; IRC §401(a)(29)
[22]Treas. Reg. 1.412(c)(1)-2.

Overriding Minimum Funding Standards for Multiemployer Plans

A special minimum funding standard applies to a multiemployer pension plan in *reorganization,* as defined below. Referred to as the minimum contribution requirement (MCR), this provision stipulates that the annual contributions to the plan must be sufficient to fund the benefits of all *retired* participants over a period of 10 years and *all other vested benefits* over a period of 25 years.[23] This requirement becomes operative whenever it would produce larger annual contributions to the plan than would be required under the basic funding standard (essentially, normal cost plus 30-year amortization of supplemental liabilities). The plan is deemed to be in reorganization whenever the annual contributions under the MCR would exceed those under the normal funding standard.

If for a plan in reorganization the number of *pay status participants* (participants receiving retirement benefits) in a given year (the base year) exceeds the average number of active participants in that year and the two preceding years, the plan is said to be "overburdened" and is entitled to an *overburden credit* against the contribution called for by the MCR.[24] The amount of the credit is one-half of the average guaranteed benefit (the average annual benefit insured by the Pension Benefit Guaranty Corporation) multiplied by the *overburden factor.* The factor is simply the excess of the average number of pay status participants over the average number of active participants for the base year and two preceding years. In effect, the plan is credited with one-half of the average insured annual benefit payable in respect of an unidentified group of retired participants considered to be excess to a normal cohort of retired persons. "Normal" is implicitly defined as a number equal to the average number of active participants. This is obviously a crude measure of an overburden, but it was not intended to be anything more than that. The credit merely reduces the contribution required in the plan year in question and does not relieve the participating or signatory employers of their obligation ultimately to fund all insured benefits. Moreover, an overburden credit is not available for any plan year when the contribution base was reduced through collective bargaining, unless there was a corresponding reduction in the plan's unfunded vested benefits attributable to pay status participants.

A multiemployer plan in a reorganization mode is permitted to reduce accrued benefits retroactively to the level of benefits guaranteed by the PBGC, subject to a number of restrictions safeguarding the interests of the participants.[25] Benefits must not be proportionally reduced more for inactive participants (retired and terminated vested) than for active participants.

As explained in Chapter 33, a plan sponsor may not terminate a single-employer plan before all benefit commitments (generally vested benefits) are funded unless the employer is in "distress."[26] Even in a distress termination the employer is required to continue funding certain benefit commitments.

Alternative Minimum Funding Standard

Some plans that use the entry-age normal cost method for the regular funding requirements may use an alternative funding standard.[27] In this case, the minimum

[23]ERISA §§4241, 4243; IRC §418B.
[24]ERISA §4244; IRC §418C.
[25]ERISA §4244A; IRC §418D.
[26]ERISA §4041.
[27]ERISA §305; IRC §412(g).

annual contribution to the plan would be the normal cost plus the excess (if any) of the actuarial value of the benefit accruals over the fair market value of the assets. Under this standard all assets, including equities and fixed-income instruments, would be valued at their actual market value on the date of valuation, without benefit of averaging or amortization. The normal cost for this standard would be the lesser of the normal cost generated by the actuarial cost method used for the plan and the normal cost that would be developed under the traditional accrued benefit cost method. Compliance with this standard would ensure that the plan would at all times have assets, valued at market, at least equal to the actuarial value of all accrued benefits, whether vested or not. This provision was added because many persons maintain that there is no need for a plan to hold assets in excess of its liabilities for accrued benefits, computed on a plan termination basis, and that there is no justification for the law to require a more rapid buildup of assets than that needed to meet the accrued benefits, realistically valued. The law restricts the alternative standard to plans that use the "entry-age normal" actuarial cost method (to use the language of the law).

Having elected to use the alternative method, a plan must maintain an alternative funding standard account. The account will be charged each year with the normal cost plus the excess of the actuarial value of accrued benefits over plan assets (but not less than zero) and will be credited with contributions. There is not a carryover of contributions over the required minimum from one year to the next, since the excess contributions become part of the plan assets for the next year's comparison of assets and liabilities. On the other hand, any shortfall of contributions will be carried over from year to year, with interest, and an excise tax will be payable on the cumulative deficiency (or on the funding deficiency existing in the basic funding standard account, if smaller).

A plan that elects the alternative funding standard must maintain both an alternative funding standard account and the basic funding standard account. The basic account is credited and charged under the usual rules, but an excise tax will only be levied on the smaller of the accumulated funding deficiencies of the two accounts, if any. A plan making this choice is required to maintain both accounts since the minimum required contribution is the lesser of the contributions called for by the basic and alternative standards.

The required contributions under the alternative standard may exceed those required under the basic method for a particular year or period of years, if there is a substantial decline in the market value of the plan assets or a substantial increase in liabilities, as through a plan amendment. If the minimum required contributions under the basic standard become lower than those under the alternative standard, the employer is likely to switch back to the basic standard.

If a plan switches back from the alternative to the basic funding standard, it is generally given five years in which to amortize the excess of charges over credits that may have built up in the basic funding standard account over the years during which the alternate standard was being used. However, if there should be a funding deficiency in the alternative funding standard account in the year before the switchback, it must be paid off immediately (not over a period of five years). Such a deficiency would have to be corrected within the permissible period whenever it occurred, not only at the time of the switchback.

Whenever an employer switches back from the alternative to the basic funding standard, it is relieved of the obligation of maintaining the second account. If in some subsequent year the employer should return to the alternative standard, it would have to establish a new account with a zero balance.

Variances from the Prescribed Standards

If an employer would otherwise incur substantial business hardship,[28] and if enforcement of the minimum funding requirements would be adverse to the interests of plan participants in the aggregate, the Internal Revenue Service may waive for a particular year payment of part or all of the plan's funding requirements.[29] This type of waiver can be made for both single-employer and multi-employer plans. For single-employer plans, no waiver will be granted unless the business hardship is expected to be temporary. Security may be required if the waiver exceeds $1 million. If a waiver is to be granted for a multiemployer plan, there must be a finding that 10 percent or more of the employers contributing to the plan would suffer a substantial business hardship if required to make the funding contributions for the year in question. No more than three (five for multiemployer plans) waivers may be granted to a plan within any consecutive 15-year period. The amount waived, plus interest, must be amortized not less rapidly than ratably over 5 years (15 years for multiemployer plans). Of course, the contributions waived by the IRS increase the exposure of the PBGC, a matter of some concern since the waivers are generally granted to the weaker plans and plan sponsors.

A plan may also request an extension of up to 10 years in the amortization period for unfunded actuarial liabilities.[30] In practice, this extension is rarely if ever requested, since the waiver previously described provides more effective relief.

During the time that a variance is in effect, whether it be in the form of a year-by-year waiver of funding contributions or an extension of the time to amortize unfunded actuarial liabilities, there can be no plan amendments that increase the benefits or accelerate the rate of vesting, except as noted below.[31] Under exceptions to the general rules, amendments that increase plan liabilities may be permitted if (1) they are *de minimis* in nature, as determined under regulations of the Secretary of Labor; (2) they are required as a condition for the plan to retain its qualified status; or (3) they merely repeal, in whole or in part, a previous decrease in benefits.

Contributions

For plan years beginning after 1988, contributions to single-employer plans to satisfy the minimum funding requirements must be paid in four quarterly install-

---

[28]The law provides that the factors to be taken into account in determining business hardship shall include, but not be limited to, whether or not (1) the employer is operating at an economic loss, (2) there is substantial unemployment or underemployment in the trade or business and in the industry concerned, (3) the sales and profits of the industry are depressed or declining, and (4) it is reasonable to expect that the plan will be continued only if the waiver is granted.

[29]ERISA §303(a); IRC §412(d)(1).

[30]ERISA §304(a); IRC §412(e).

[31]ERISA §304(b); IRC §412(f).

ments, similar to the estimated payments for income tax. The *required annual payment* is the lesser of 90 percent of the amount required to satisfy the minimum funding requirements for the current plan year or 100 percent of the amount required to satisfy the minimum funding requirements for the prior plan year. If the plan year is a calendar year, 25 percent of the required annual payment must be paid by April 15, July 15, and October 15 of the plan year and by January 15 of the following year. Comparable dates apply when the plan year is not a calendar year.

Contributions made after the close of the plan year may be credited to that year to satisfy the minimum funding requirements. They may be retroactively credited if made within 8½ months after the end of the year.[32] Starting in 1995, plans 100 percent funded on the basis of the new current liability definition are exempt from quarterly contribution in the following year. A liquidity requirement is added to the quarterly contribution requirement, as an additional minimum required quarterly contribution. Plans sponsors must make liquidity contributions if the plan's cash and marketable securities do not equal at least three years' worth of benefit disbursements. Benefit disbursements include annuity contract purchases, single sum and annuity distributions, and administrative expenses.

Enforcement

Any accumulated funding deficiency in the Funding Standard Account is subject to an excise tax of 10 percent for single-employer plans and 5 percent for multi-employer plans (100 percent in both cases if not "corrected" or paid off within a limited period).[33] In addition to the excise tax, the employer may be subject to civil action in the courts for failing to meet the minimum funding standards.[34]

Exemptions from the Prescribed Standards

In general, the funding requirements apply to qualified pension plans, as well as to nonqualified plans of private employers in interstate commerce and non-qualified plans of employee organizations with members in interstate commerce.[35]

Other plans specifically exempt from the funding standards are (1) those established and maintained outside the United States primarily for the benefit of persons substantially all of whom are nonresident aliens; (2) those maintained primarily to provide deferred compensation to a select group of highly compensated employees; (3) those that provide supplemental benefits on an unfunded, nonqualified basis; and (4) those to which the employer does not contribute.

---

[32] ERISA §302(c)(10); IRC §412(b)(4).
[33] IRC §4971.
[34] ERISA §502(b).
[35] ERISA §301(a); IRC §412(h). Courts have interpreted interstate commerce so broadly as to include almost all businesses and industry.

Maximum Deductible Contributions

An employer can deduct for income tax purposes only such contributions to a pension plan as fall within the permissible limits set forth in the law.[36] The most general rule on deductibility of employer contributions is that the firm may deduct any amounts that were required to meet the minimum funding standards. Beyond this general rule there are two specific limits for defined benefit plans that have long been part of the tax law on pensions.

Under the first rule, sometimes called the "straight-line" rule, the employer is permitted to deduct any sum necessary to provide all plan participants with the remaining unfunded cost of their past and current service credits distributed as a level amount, or a level percentage of compensation, over the remaining future service of each such employee. This simply means that each year an employer can deduct such sum, computed in accordance with applicable regulations, as is needed to provide on a level contribution basis (dollars or percentage of covered payroll) the total projected benefits payable under the plan. The calculation can be made for each participant or for the employee group as a whole.

The second rule, known as the "normal cost" or "normal cost plus 10-year" rule, permits the employer to deduct annually an amount equal to the normal cost of the plan, plus, if there are supplemental liabilities, an amount necessary to amortize such supplemental liabilities in equal annual dollar installments over 10 years. Obviously, deductions for contributions toward the amortization of the supplemental liabilities are available only as long as there are unamortized amounts. Both the normal cost contributions and the amortization payments must be determined in accordance with relevant regulations.[37]

The tax deduction for any particular year cannot exceed the amount needed to bring the plan to a fully funded status. That is, no deductions can be taken for contributions that would raise the plan assets to a level above the actuarial value of plan liabilities. It follows, of course, that no deductions could be taken for contributions made while a plan was in a fully or overly funded condition. Full funding for tax deduction purposes is determined in the same way as full funding under the funding requirements.

If an employer covers more than 100 employees under one or more defined benefit pension plans, the maximum deductible limit for each plan is not less than the plan's unfunded new current liability. Using the lowest interest rate at the presented range, this rule can result in substantially larger deductible contributions than the rules described above. This provision even applies if this amount exceeds the full funding limit described above.

As explained in Chapter 7, a 10 percent excise tax is imposed on all employer contributions for a year that exceed the maximum deductible limit, unless the employer is otherwise tax-exempt. In addition, a penalty is imposed if it is determined that an employer's deduction exceeded the deductible limit because of an error in the actuarial computations or because the actuarial assumptions used

---

[36]IRC §404(a).
[37]Treas. Reg. 1.404(a)-14.

were too conservative. Limits on the deductibility of contributions to profit-sharing and stock bonus plans and limits that apply when an employer maintains both a defined benefit plan and a defined contribution plan covering the same employees are described in Chapter 12.

Patterns of Funding

As a normal practice, an employer will not make contributions to a pension plan in any year in excess of the amount that can be deducted as an ordinary and necessary business expense for federal income tax purposes. Yet, in order to avoid penalties, the amount to be contributed must comply with the minimum funding standards described in the preceding pages. Within these parameters, the actual amount of the employer's annual contributions will depend upon the actuarial cost method that it chooses to use and, in certain circumstances, on the funding instrument employed. As a matter of fact, the minimum and maximum constraints are themselves expressed in terms of the actuarial cost method used by the employer, except for the alternative minimum standard and the full funding limit.

Any of several actuarial cost methods may be selected if the actuary certifies that the method and assumptions are reasonable in the aggregate. ERISA lists six acceptable actuarial cost methods,[38] but additional methods may be designated as acceptable by the Internal Revenue Service. Any change in the method used may be made only with prior IRS approval.[39] The choice of method will be influenced by the nature of the benefit formula, the type of funding instrument, and the degree of funding flexibility desired. These factors are interrelated, and a decision with respect to one may dictate the course of action with respect to the other two. The choice of funding instrument may even dictate the actuarial cost method, as well as the type of benefit formula and the degree of funding flexibility. Having selected (consciously or indirectly) the actuarial cost method, the employer must set aside funds on a cumulative basis equal to the normal (or annual) cost of the plan and the statutorily prescribed portion of the supplemental liability, if any. Thus the actuarial cost method and the funding policy are inextricably intertwined.

The interplay between the actuarial cost method, the funding instrument, the benefit formula, and the funding policy is briefly explained below.

Benefit Allocation Actuarial Cost Methods

Benefit allocation actuarial cost methods assume that the normal cost of a pension plan for any particular year is precisely equal to the present value of the benefits allocated to the participants for service during that year. These methods are best suited to the type of benefit formula that attributes a specifically identifiable unit of benefit for each year of credited service, including service prior to inception of the plan.

---

[38]ERISA §3(31); Treas. Reg. 1.412(c)(3)-1.
[39]ERISA §302(c)(5); IRC §412(c)(5). Rev. Proc. 85-29 grants automatic approval for certain changes in funding methods.

If a plan's funding policy is geared to a benefit allocation cost method, the cost of each dollar of future service benefit (actual or estimated) will be met in full in the year in which it accrues by a contribution to the pension plan. This is especially true of the traditional accrued benefit cost method, which allocates benefits on the basis of actual, realized benefit accruals, without projections. Benefits attributable to service prior to establishment of the plan are funded in accordance with a policy especially adopted for that purpose by the employer or dictated by an insurer. Because of the statutory limits discussed earlier, past service benefits are seldom funded in full at the inception of the plan; instead, contributions for past service are generally spread over a number of years. The sharp differentiation between past and future service benefits, with the former giving rise to a supplemental liability, provides a desirable degree of financial flexibility.

The traditional accrued benefit cost method of funding is virtually always used in connection with group deferred annuity contracts and may be used with other types of arrangements. It is equally appropriate for a benefit formula that provides a definite benefit and one that utilizes the money purchase concept. From a structural standpoint, it is not well suited for a plan that provides a flat composite benefit or one that provides for the deduction of Social Security benefits. Some observers question whether the accrued benefit cost method is appropriate for a plan that bases benefits on the earnings of some future period, such as the last five years of service, because of its structural inability to take future salary increases into account. The complications associated with all such formulas can be accommodated by the other two forms of benefit allocation cost methods, since they project or estimate benefits.

If the traditional accrued benefit cost method is used in connection with a group deferred annuity contract, the periodic contributions are applied to the purchase of single premium deferred life annuities; the contributions cover not only the present value of the deferred benefits but also the charge levied by the insurer to take care of its expenses and to accumulate a contingency reserve. The future service contributions are allocated to the participants on the basis of the benefits earned during the time interval involved. Past service contributions are allocated in accordance with a formula prescribed in the contract, annuities generally being purchased in the order of nearness to normal retirement date.

Under trust fund plans and group deposit administration annuity contracts, contributions are determined in respect of specific individuals for specific units of service; but deferred annuities in the appropriate amounts are generally not purchased for such individuals. Consequently, in the event of termination of the plan, the previous contributions plus interest would be allocated among the pensioners[40] and participants in accordance with the termination formula set forth in the plan or the provisions of ERISA.

Since the present value of each dollar of benefits to be paid at retirement increases with the attained age of the participant, there is a tendency for future service contributions for the plan as a whole to rise each year until the employee

---

[40]In the case of a deposit administration plan, annuities for pensioners would already have been purchased.

group matures. However, this tendency is offset to some extent by new entrants to the plan, withdrawals, deaths, and retirements. As a result, the average cost per dollar of annuity credited may show only a slight percentage increase or, under certain circumstances, an absolute decrease. If the initial past service liability is liquidated over the first 20 or 30 years, as is generally the objective, the total contributions will level off after maturity of the plan at a rate equal to the cost of future service benefits. Under a group deferred annuity contract, the initial past service liability must be fully funded upon attainment of normal retirement age by the youngest participant with prior credited service.

Cost Allocation Actuarial Cost Methods

Cost allocation cost methods can be used with any type of benefit formula, and are especially adaptable to the type of formula that provides a composite benefit (as opposed to a series of unit benefits). Within this family of methods, procedures exist that are suitable for any type of funding instrument, with the possible exception of the conventional group deferred annuity. Likewise, procedures are available that provide a high degree of flexibility in funding policy. The specific approaches within the family of cost allocation cost methods have such diverse characteristics, however, that it is necessary to consider each one separately.

A. INDIVIDUAL LEVEL PREMIUM COST METHOD   The individual level premium cost method is closely identified with plans funded exclusively by individual and group permanent contracts of life insurers. Under these arrangements, the contract or certificate for a particular participant is written in an amount exactly adequate to provide the benefits that would be payable to the participant if his or her rate of compensation remains unchanged to normal retirement age and the payment of premiums on the contract meets the funding requirements. As is true of all insurance or annuity contracts, the premium is calculated as of the attained age of the employee on the effective date of the contract or certificate. If the rate of compensation increases, with an attendant change in benefits, an adjustment in the amount of coverage is made in the manner described in Chapter 24, and the funding of the increase in benefits is accomplished by a separate and additional level premium, payable from the date of increase.

Inasmuch as the insurance contracts are written in amounts designed to provide benefits for the entire period of credited service, no distinction is made between past and future service costs. The sums necessary to amortize the initial actuarial liability are merged distinguishably into the annual premium and are not identifiable as past service contributions. The total amount funded each year is simply the sum of the premiums on all contracts issued under the plan, less dividends and surrender credits, if applicable.

In the event of termination of the plan, all participants would be entitled to take over the contracts (individual) being maintained on their lives. They could continue the contracts in full force by assuming premium payments or could surrender them pursuant to their terms. The degree to which the anticipated retirement benefits would be funded as of any given date would depend upon the age at which the employee became a member of the plan; the amount of past service benefits, if any; and the length of time during which premiums have been paid. If no portion of the benefits of a particular employee is attributable to service prior to establishment of the plan, the "accrued" benefits on any given date would tend to be overfunded to some extent because of the leveling out of costs that would otherwise be increasing each year. After a point, the cost of each year's "unit of benefit," if the total benefit can be so apportioned, will exceed the annual premium and the degree of overfunding will begin to decline. At retirement, the assets (represented by the reserve under the contract) will be in exact balance with the present value of the benefits payable. Any benefits attributable to past service will be fully funded only upon maturity of the insurance contract. Benefits for participants at or beyond normal retirement age at inception of the plan can be funded with a single-sum payment equal to the present value of future benefits plus an allowance for the insurer's expenses, or through a series of contributions extending beyond actual retirement.

This pattern of funding is not confined to individual and group permanent insurance contracts or to insurance contracts in general. It can be, and frequently is, used to fund trust fund plans. If it is used with a group deposit administration annuity contract or trust fund plan, the annual level cost may be determined and funded as a level percentage of payroll, rather than as a level dollar amount. With these unallocated funding instruments, the prospective benefits payable to specific individuals serve only as a measuring rod to determine the sums of money to be set aside periodically. The sums are paid into an unallocated fund, and an individual participant has no vested interest in, or prior claim to, the contributions attributable to his or her benefit expectations. In the event of early termination of the plan, the assets might, and in all likelihood would, be distributed among the employees in a manner quite different from the pattern by which contributions were computed. Once, however, the implicit initial actuarial liability is funded as these methods contemplate, there should be enough assets upon termination to meet the accrued benefit claims of all participants.

Irrespective of the funding agency employed, contributions under this approach to funding will be relatively high during the early years of the plan, especially under the level *dollar* cost method, when the initial actuarial liability is being amortized at a rapid rate. The amortization of the initial actuarial liability slows down gradually with the retirement of employees who had large past service credits (or whose period of future service was relatively brief), and after the retirement of the last employee with prior service the contributions level off at a rate equal to the cost of future service benefits.

B. INDIVIDUAL ENTRY-AGE NORMAL COST METHOD   The individual entry-age normal cost method serves as the funding guide for many trust fund plans and deposit administration contracts, and it sets the funding pattern for plans that cover a large number of employees. The rationale of this funding policy is that the prospective benefits of a participant should be funded at a uniform percentage of compensation or in uniform annual increments over an entire working lifetime. With respect to any particular pension plan, the individual's working life span is usually assumed to extend from the earliest date of employment recognized for benefit purposes to the normal retirement age, or, alternatively, the average age at which the participants under the plan are expected to retire. Thus the "normal" cost of benefits for any specific participant is conceived to be that uniform annual amount or percentage of compensation that would have to be paid from the earliest date of credited service to the assumed age of retirement to accumulate the capital sum needed to provide the anticipated benefits. In practice, the funding contributions are sometimes based on an assumed age or ages of entry into the plan rather than the actual age or ages, but the underlying principle is the same.

If the individual enters the service of the employer after the effective date of the plan, the annual funding payments with respect to the employer could, depending upon the assumptions, be identical to those under the individual level premium cost method. If, however, the employee's actual or assumed credited service occurred before the plan was established, the funding contributions would be smaller than under the aforementioned method and a supplemental liability would be created—for reasons explained earlier.

The employer has great flexibility in deciding how to fund the initial actuarial liability generated under this approach. It can be funded over a period as short as 10 years or over a period as long as 30 or 40 years, depending upon the effective date of the plan. Supplemental liabilities associated with plan liberalizations can be funded over a period of 30 years, while those arising out of actuarial losses must be funded within a 5- or 15-year period.

Normal cost contributions under this method tend to be fairly level, changing slightly if the average entry age changes. Total contributions depend upon the funding policy adopted in relation to the initial actuarial liability and subsequently emerging supplemental liabilities. This funding approach may be used with any type of benefit formula and any type of funding instrument that does not allocate contributions to individual participants before retirement.

C. AGGREGATE LEVEL COST METHOD   The aggregate level cost method is analogous to the individual level cost method, except that it calculates costs and contributions on a collective rather than individual basis. If the annual cost accruals are computed on the basis of total anticipated benefits, including those attributable to past service, there is no supplemental liability and a portion of each annual contribution will in effect go toward funding the benefits credited for service prior to inception of the plan. This makes for a higher initial level of contributions than might otherwise be necessary and deprives the employer of the flexibility associated with a supplemental liability. In this form, the aggregate cost method dictates a rather inflexible funding policy.

To provide more flexibility in funding and to lower the level of contributions in the early years of the plan, the actuary may create a supplemental liability under this approach. This liability may be produced in various ways, such as calculating the first-year costs on the basis of either the accumulated plan benefit method or one of the individual level cost methods (with supplemental liability, of course). The resulting supplemental liability can then be funded at a pace consistent with the employer's overall financial policy and applicable law.

This approach to funding has found its widest use among trust fund plans. It is equally adaptable to group deposit administration annuity contracts. It is not appropriate for use with allocated funding instruments.

Critique of Funding Regulations

Since the early 1980s, a number of regulatory changes have jeopardized the retirement income security of many workers. These laws have gradually chipped away at the tax preferences accorded employer-sponsored retirement plans by limiting the amount employers can set aside in tax-qualified retirement plans. For example, the Tax Equity and Fiscal Responsibility Act of 1982 and the Tax Reform Act of 1986 reduced or froze temporarily the funding and benefit limits for defined benefit plans and the contribution limits for defined contribution plans. Furthermore, changes in the accounting rules affecting pensions forced sponsors of pension plans to alter the funding methods for their defined benefit plans.

The net result of these regulatory changes has been to slow down or stall the funding of workers' retirement benefits. The ensuing risk is that plan sponsors may not be able to meet the promises that their current plans hold out to covered workers. The current benefit formulas in many defined benefit plans imply significantly higher future contributions than plan sponsors are currently making. These higher contributions are the result of two factors: the aging of the work force and the ways in which plan sponsors have responded to the changing regulatory environment.

A 1980 survey of large plans revealed that nearly two-thirds of defined benefit plans that based benefits on salaries of covered workers—that is, either final or career average plans—funded benefits on the basis of the *entry-age normal cost method.* As described in Chapter 28, the Financial Accounting Standards Board (FASB) in the late 1980s promulgated accounting rules requiring that accruing pension benefits be accounted for by a uniform method known as the *projected unit credit actuarial cost method.* Changing from the entry-age normal method of calculating costs to the projected unit credit method results in lower costs early in a worker's career and higher costs later in the worker's career. An employer's pension costs for a hypothetical worker under the two actuarial cost methods is shown in Figure 27-1.

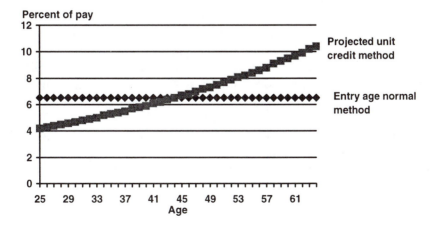

Figure 27-1. Pension costs under alternative actuarial cost methods, 25-year-old worker over a 40-year career. Source: Watson Wyatt.

TABLE 27-3   Percentage of Large Final Pay Plans Using
Projected Unit Credit Method

Year	Percentage of Firms
1983	10
1984	19
1985	25
1986	36
1987	44
1988	50
1989	49
1990	52
1991	54
1992	60
1993	63

Source: Watson Wyatt.

The FASB change technically affected how pension expenses are reported on financial disclosure documents but not the actual funding of plans. However, many plan sponsors, particularly sponsors of final pay plans, wanted to keep their accounting and funding methods the same and so moved to a projected unit credit funding method (see Table 27-3).

The baby boom generation ranged in age from 20 to 40 as the FASB rules were discussed and ultimately issued. Looking back to Figure 27-1, shifting from an entry-age normal funding method to a projected unit credit funding method for a large group of workers of such a young age inevitably slowed the funding of their retirement benefits. The net effect of this shift toward projected unit credit funding was to delay the funding of the baby boom generation's retirement benefits from the first half of their career to the second half.

Another significant change was introduced by the Omnibus Budget Reconciliation Act of 1987 (OBRA87), which reduced the full funding limits for defined benefit plans from 100 percent of projected plan liability to the lesser of that value or 150 percent of benefits accrued at the time of each annual valuation. When the funding limit was based solely on projected plan liability, plan sponsors could take into consideration expected pay increases for workers covered by the plan between the time of the annual valuation and their expected date of retirement. In basing the funding limit on benefits that already have been accrued, anticipated pay increases could no longer be considered.

Consider the funding pattern of a plan that uses projected pay increases, as is done in the projected unit credit funding method, in comparison with a plan that funds the benefit on the basis of the annual increments in accrued benefits (see Figure 27-2). In the case of a worker beginning a 40-year career job at age 25, the accrued benefit contribution rates would be less than the projected unit credit contribution rates over the first half of the career. Under OBRA87, the plan sponsor could fund for up to 150 percent of the accrued benefit. But for workers under age 40, in many cases 150 percent of the accrued benefit was less than

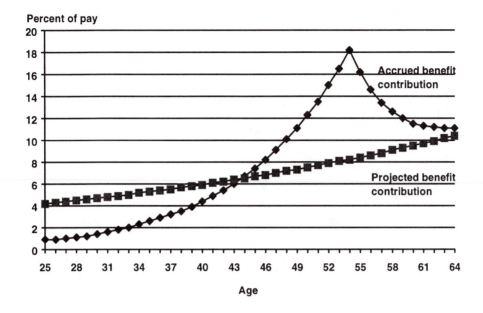

Figure 27-2. Pension funding perspectives under alternative actuarial cost methods, 25-year-old worker over a 40-year career. Source: Watson Wyatt.

100 percent of the projected benefit. When this legislation was passed in 1987, the baby boom generation ranged in age from 23 to 41. At that time we estimated that 47 percent of the large plans in the United States would be affected by the new funding limits in OBRA87.

The situation that OBRA87 created may have been worse in many cases than Figure 27-2 suggests. OBRA87 pushed many employers who had been contributing to their plans under the entry-age normal funding method or the projected unit credit method into an excess funding position. This meant that they could not contribute to their plans until the accruing liabilities caught up with the assets that they had put into the plan under the earlier rules. So rather than continue to contribute to their plans at the rates implied by the accrued benefit contribution line in Figure 27-2, they enjoyed contribution "holidays," during which their plans required no funding at all for some years. These contribution holidays may ultimately be the death knell of some defined benefit plans. It is one thing for a company to see its annual contributions to its pension program rising gradually over a decade as its work force ages. It is quite another to have the contribution rate jump from zero to 7 or 8 percent of payroll. That is the impact OBRA87 will have on some plans. With such precipitous changes in plan funding requirements, some sponsors simply will not continue to support their plans.

Data on employer contributions to pension plans illustrate the impact of pension legislation on contribution levels. Employer contributions to private plans increased throughout the 1970s, but beginning in the 1980s contributions began to decline. Employer inflation-adjusted contributions in the early 1990s were 15 percent below contribution levels in the early 1980s (see Figure 27-3). Despite the 1974 passage of ERISA—the federal law designed to improve the funding and

Billions of 1993 Dollars

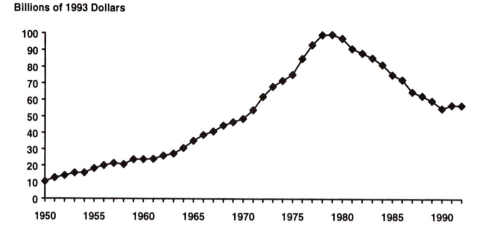

Figure 27-3. Inflation-adjusted employer contributions to private pension and profit-sharing plans, 1950–92. Source: U.S. Department of Commerce, *National Income and Product Accounts* for selected years.

security of employer-sponsored retirement plans—contributions in 1990 adjusted for inflation were at the same level as in 1970. Per capita contributions adjusted for inflation were at the level of the early 1960s.

Despite the fact that plan sponsors had cut back on their contributions to their retirement plans in the 1980s, the assets in private plans continued to grow because of the favorable rates of return realized during that decade (see Figure 27-4). Some observers point to the growth in these assets as an indication that everything is fine with the pension system. But anyone feeling secure in the size of current accumulations is ignoring the claims that the baby boomers will ultimately place on these plans. Moreover, anyone taking solace in the good financial performance of pension assets during the 1980s as a potential solution to the continual

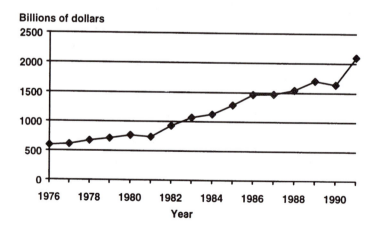

Figure 27-4. Assets in private retirement plans (in CPI-adjusted dollars), 1976–90. Source: The Employee Benefit Research Institute, *EBRI Quarterly Pension Investment Report* (Washington, D.C.: EBRI, June 1993).

restrictions on pension funding is ignoring the longer-term prospective claims on the system and the reality that the value of assets in retirement plans should have grown even more than it did over this period. The move from the entry-age normal cost method of funding to the projected unit credit method in response to FASB rules and then the move toward funding accrued benefits rather than projected benefits have skewed our perceptions of the adequacy of funding levels.

Because of the pension funding changes implemented in the 1980s, employers ultimately will have to put considerably more into their plans in the future than they are putting into them today. The work force covered by pension plans is aging, and Americans will have to pay the price for the slowdown in funding during the 1980s and early 1990s. Some employers will pay that price by accelerating their funding later in the baby boomers' careers, but some will not be able or willing to make the added contributions that will be required and will simply curtail the benefit promises of their current plans.

Despite growing concerns about the baby boomers' retirement security, the government continues to enact laws that curtail the funding of tax-qualified retirement plans. For instance, the Omnibus Budget Reconciliation Act of 1993 reduced the level of individual employees' compensation that can be considered in funding and contributing to tax-qualified plans. The effects of OBRA93, like those of OBRA87, will limit the funding of employer-sponsored retirement programs even more.

The Tax Reform Act of 1986 limited compensation for purposes of retirement plan contributions to $200,000. It further provided that the limit would be indexed for increases in the consumer price index. By 1993 the compensation limit had risen to $235,840. OBRA93 reduced the compensation limit for tax-qualified retirement plans to $150,000 beginning in 1994. Two important points are raised by these changes. First, although reducing the compensation limits from $235,840 to $150,000 might appear to affect only highly paid employees, the impact reaches much further down into the ranks because of the effect of assumed future salary increases. Second, although the reduction in the compensation limits affects both defined benefit and defined contribution plans, the impact is somewhat different depending on the type of plan.

In the case of defined contribution plans, the new limits can affect workers earning less than $100,000 per year more than it affects those earning between $150,000 and $235,840 per year. This is because the plans have to ensure that the average contribution levels of higher-paid workers are only modestly higher than the average contribution levels of lower-paid workers. In terms of the new pay limits, workers covered by 401(k) plans can continue to contribute the same dollar amount to the plan as they did previously, but their actual contribution rate will be higher because it will be based on the lower compensation limit. This will raise the contribution rate for all "highly compensated" workers. If the new contribution rate among the highly compensated workers results in the plan's noncompliance with the actual deferral percentage test, overall contribution rates among the highly compensated will likely be reduced. If historical experience is a gauge, the reductions in contributions required to comply with the compensation limits will fall most heavily on individuals just above the Social Security wage base—namely, workers earning $65,000 to $85,000 per year.

TABLE 27-4   Impact of Compensation Limit Reductions on 401(k)
Contributions (dollars)

	Worker 1	Worker 2
Annual pay	80,000	230,000
401(k) contributions	6,400	8,998
Contribution percentage	8.00	3.91
New pay limit under OBRA93	80,000	150,000
New contribution percentage	5.95	5.95
New contribution level	4,760	8,925
Percentage change in contribution level	25.6	0.8

Source: Watson Wyatt.

Consider a hypothetical firm in which only two workers were in the class of workers designated highly compensated in 1993. Assume the contribution amounts the non–highly compensated workers made allowed the highly compensated workers to contribute up to 5.95 percent of their salary under the compensation limits. In the example, we assume that the higher-paid worker's annual salary was $230,000 and the lower-paid worker's was $80,000. Table 27-4 shows how contributions to the company's 401(k) plan are affected by reductions in the compensation limit.

Prior to the change in the compensation limit, assume that Worker 1 contributed $6,400 or 8.0 percent of pay to the plan. Assume Worker 2 contributed the maximum amount allowed in 1993, that is, $8,998, which amounted to 3.9 percent of pay. Between the two, they complied with the ADP because their average contribution was 5.95 percent (i.e., [8.0 + 3.9] ÷ 2 = 5.95). Now assume that their respective pay levels remain the same in 1994 when the new contribution limits apply. If Worker 2 attempts to contribute as much to the plan in 1994 as in 1993, the contribution rate would now be 6.0 percent of salary, which when averaged with the contribution rate of Worker 1 would produce a combined ADP of 7 percent (i.e., [6.0 + 8.0] ÷ 2 = 7.0). This would fail the ADP test, given the contribution rates of lower-paid workers. A common way that companies force their plans into compliance with the ADP tests is to limit the contribution rates that highly compensated workers can make to their plans. In this case, the plan could be brought into compliance with the new limits by restricting the two workers to contribution rates of 5.95 percent of covered pay. If that were to occur, the worker earning $80,000 per year would see his or her contribution reduced by slightly more than one-quarter, while the higher-paid worker would suffer a reduction of less than 1 percent (see Table 27-4).

The effects of the reduced limits for defined contribution plans would be known almost immediately by anyone affected. The "immediate notice" should give such workers time to adjust their other saving behavior to make up for losses in their retirement programs. In the case of defined benefit plans, however, the effect could be felt by a much broader group of workers, and its full force might not be known for some years. Tax law does not allow retirement plan sponsors to anticipate expected increases in the salary limit for pension funding purposes. With reason-

TABLE 27-5   Funding Shortfall Resulting from Compensation Limits (dollars)

Age	Salary	Maximum Considered for Funding	Salary over Compensation Limit
35	35,000	31,752	3,248
36	36,925	34,838	2,087
37	38,956	38,224	732
38	41,099	41,940	0
39	43,359	46,017	0

Source: Watson Wyatt.

able assumptions about future salary growth, an employee expected to retire 30 years from now who is earning $30,000 to $35,000 today would likely be subject to the new pension funding limits. Consider a worker who is 35 years of age today, earning $35,000 per year. In the calculations that the Social Security Administration does for purposes of estimating the future costs of Social Security, it assumes an average future worker will receive wage increases of 5.5 percent per year in an economy that will experience 4 percent inflation per year.

For the 35-year-old earning $35,000 today, 5.5 percent wage increases until retirement at age 65 would imply a final year's salary of $165,342. This salary exceeds the proposed compensation limit by $15,342. An employer sponsoring a pension for this worker would be required to reduce the funding of the pension below the amount allowed by current law in any year in which projected final earnings exceed the compensation limits.

Table 27-5 shows the pay levels and maximum compensation that could be considered for funding the pension of the hypothetical 35-year-old worker earning $35,000 in the first year under the new funding limits. In the first year, slightly more than $3,200 of the worker's pay could not be considered for funding a pension benefit under the plan. The table also shows that the amount of compensation that cannot be included in terms of pension funding declines each year using the Social Security wage-growth assumptions. After three years, full funding of the benefits promised to the hypothetical worker can be resumed. But the funding shortfall that occurred during the three years between ages 35 and 38 for this worker has to be made up over the remaining 27 years before retirement if the benefits promised under the plan are to be paid.

The funding slowdown suggested by Table 27-5 appears to be relatively moderate for the hypothetical worker, and the shortfall would not be so significant that it would create a huge problem to overcome by accelerating funding later in this worker's career. Rather, the problem is that the $31,752 compensation limit that applies to a $35,000 worker is the same compensation limit that will apply to a worker with $40,000, $50,000, or $100,000 in current salary. For 35-year-old workers earning $40,000 per year, the new limit means that $8,200 of their earnings during the first year cannot be considered in funding the promised pension benefit. For the $40,000 worker, it will take *six years* before the compensation on

TABLE 27-6   Years of Reduced Funding due to New
Compensation Limits

Salary at Age 35 (dollars)	Years of Reduced Contributions	Remaining Years until Retirement
40,000	6	24
50,000	12	18
60,000	17	13
70,000	21	9
80,000	24	6
90,000	27	3
100,000	30	0

Source: Watson Wyatt.

which funding will be based can catch up with actual earnings. In this case, the employer will have only 24 years left to make up the underfunding that would occur because of the new compensation limit.

Table 27-6 shows the number of years in which funding would be reduced under the new compensation limits compared with the current limits for workers with age-35 salaries ranging up to $100,000 per year. For workers earning $50,000 per year, funding would be reduced over a period amounting to 40 percent of their remaining career. For workers earning $90,000, funding would be reduced for 90 percent of their remaining career. For workers earning $100,000 per year, the new limit would reduce the funding of their promised pension benefit over the entire remainder of their career.

Pension plan benefit formulas are essentially promises to provide some level of benefits, generally in relation to a worker's earnings and years of coverage under the plan. If these promises are to be met, funds must be put aside to pay the benefits by the time they fall due. ERISA recognized and established by law the desirability of employers funding benefit promises during a worker's active work career. Because ERISA recognized the importance of these promises to individual workers, it established the Pension Benefit Guaranty Corporation to put the weight of a government insurance program behind them. Deferring the funding of promised benefits from early until later in a worker's career creates a variety of risks.

For workers whose actual pay levels ultimately fall below the compensation limits, it will still be possible for a pension plan sponsor to make up the initial limitations in funding. But if the plan sponsor speeds up funding later to offset current reductions because of the lower compensation limit, it will create larger tax deductions and smaller tax collections in the future. For some participants, such as the workers earning $70,000 or more per year cited in Table 27-6, some promised benefits cannot be funded in the remaining years until retirement. These benefits will have to be funded after the worker retires and is no longer contributing to the productivity of the firm. Prior experience shows, however, that firms sometimes fall on hard times and cannot fulfill prior unfunded promises. In these cases, benefits may become the government's obligation through the PBGC.

Regrettably, the PBGC does not always assume responsibility for the entire amount that the plans had promised to participants. Middle-income employees and retirees lose benefits in these cases.

Even if employers should be able to make up for funding delays, lower compensation limits would force them to delay the funding of pension promises until later in workers' careers. These delays will make plan funding far more expensive in the future than under current policy. In particular, it will make funding the baby boom generation's retirement benefits even more expensive than currently anticipated. Some employers will have to curtail their plans or possibly terminate them altogether.

If benefits are reduced in the future because of the higher expense, it is unlikely that the cuts will be limited to highly paid workers, as detailed above. In most firms, people earning incomes in the ranges most heavily hit by this proposal are the ones responsible for the design and management of the pension plans sponsored by their employers. Regrettably, human nature being what it is, these individuals often suggest their employers reduce the benefits going to others when their own benefits are reduced.

Summary

In the not-too-distant future, corporate pension plans clearly will face the tough choice of higher contribution costs or lower pension benefits, the same prospect now facing the Social Security program.[41] What will make this choice even more difficult is that many employers may have become too accustomed to the low contributions they have been making to defined benefit plans in recent years because of regulatory changes and the extraordinary performance of financial markets. But these low contribution rates are not going to be sustainable because the work force is aging and regulatory changes have already had the effect of reducing early contributions to the baby boomers' retirement accruals. In addition, the high rates of return that retirement plan sponsors have realized over the last decade are likely to begin moderately. When all of these forces converge, employers may choose to cut back benefits rather than increase contribution levels.

What is particularly troubling is the possibility that the funding shortfalls of Social Security and employer-sponsored plans will occur simultaneously, forcing both systems to pare down promised benefits. That will leave the baby boomers in a tenuous financial position as they enter their golden years.

---

[41]It should be noted that this discussion focuses on defined benefit plans. The defined contribution system is not expected to run out of assets; in fact, it could be a modest net source of saving even when the largest number of baby boomers retire.

Chapter 28
Pension Accounting

Historically, pension accounting has been concerned with measuring the impact of a pension plan on the earnings and financial condition of the sponsor of the plan. More precisely, it has been concerned with measuring and recording the cost of accruing pension benefits and with recognizing the unfunded actuarial liabilities of the pension plan, especially those arising out of the granting of benefit credit for service prior to the inception or amendment of the plan.

A succession of committees of the American Institute of Certified Public Accountants and its predecessor organizations have grappled with the problem of developing an acceptable set of principles to guide the actuarial profession in accounting for pension costs and liabilities and to bring about uniformity in practice. Each of these committees has issued authoritative, officially endorsed statements of recommended practice, all of which are reviewed briefly in this chapter. With the passage of the Employment Retirement Income Security Act of 1974, certain reporting and disclosure requirements were imposed on the pension plans subject to its jurisdiction, and the accounting profession was charged with certifying the appropriateness and accuracy of the financial information in the reports. Thus it became necessary for the profession to develop generally accepted accounting principles for the plans themselves, quite apart from to their sponsors. In response to this challenge, the Financial Accounting Standards Board, the current arbiter of accounting practices and standards, launched two projects, one to develop generally accepted accounting principles for pension plans themselves and the other to develop such principles for the business and nonprofit entities that sponsor the plans. The result of these projects is examined in this chapter.

Unless otherwise indicated, the discussion focuses on *defined benefit* plans, since pension cost accounting is concerned primarily with such plans. For any given accounting period, the employer's expense for a defined contribution plan is usually known with exactitude. Some defined contribution plans have a formula that specifies precisely how much must be contributed by the employer for the period in question. Other defined contribution plans give the employer complete discretion; but by the time the financial statements for the period are prepared, the contribution ordinarily has been paid, or at least has been determined. For defined contribution plans, the employer's charge to expense for a period is the actual amount contributed to the plan for the period. Any portion of the required contribution not paid by the end of the period is shown on the employer's balance sheet as an amount payable. Since the employer makes no benefit commitment, there is no basis for showing any other pension liability on the employer's balance sheet.

Accounting for the Plan

Form 5500 and Related Forms

Titles I and IV of ERISA and the Internal Revenue Code require a pension plan sponsor or plan administrator to submit certain information about the plan to the Department of Labor (DOL), the Pension Benefit Guaranty Corporation, and the Internal Revenue Service.[1] To help plan administrators and sponsors comply with this requirement, the three regulatory agencies developed a joint annual report form, designated Form 5500. Form 5500 is filed with the IRS, which provides a copy to the Department of Labor and transmits certain extracted data to the PBGC. Simplified Form 5500-C was developed for plans with fewer than 100 participants,[2] and an even more abbreviated Form 5500-R may be filed by these small plans for two out of every three years. Form 5500 and Form 5500-C include a statement of assets and liabilities and a statement of changes of fund balance, and they require that certain additional financial information be attached.

Form 5500 and Form 5500-C show the plan assets and liabilities as of the beginning and end of the plan year. Assets are generally shown at current value,[3] which is the market value of an investment if an active market exists, as it does for most pension plan investments. The value of any portion of an allocated annuity or insurance contract that fully guarantees any benefit payments is excluded from the assets shown. Thus the assets shown generally exclude the value of any annuities that have been purchased for retired employees, as well as any amounts individually allocated under an annuity contract to guarantee benefits for active employees. The liabilities shown on Form 5500 include liabilities for amounts payable, including any benefit payments currently due and unpaid, but they do not include any actuarial liabilities for benefits that will become payable in the future. These liabilities are subtracted from the total assets to produce the net assets available to pay future benefits and expenses.

Form 5500 and Form 5500-C include a statement that reconciles the net assets at the beginning and end of the year. This provides a summary of income, expenses, and other changes in net assets, including the change in unrealized appreciation and depreciation of assets.

Form 5500 requires a number of attachments:

- Schedule A, Insurance Information: This schedule provides financial information concerning any insurance or annuity contracts used to fund the plan.
- Schedule B, Actuarial Information: This schedule, prepared and signed by the enrolled actuary for any defined benefit plan subject to ERISA's funding requirements, presents information concerning compliance with the funding

[1] ERISA §§103, 4043; IRC §6058.
[2] ERISA §104(a)(2)(A).
[3] An exception applies to annuity contracts with unallocated funds, other than separate accounts, which may be shown at their contract value.

requirements, as well as the present value of vested and nonvested accrued benefits as of the beginning of the plan year.[4] For this purpose, "accrued benefits" generally means the retirement benefits earned to date as defined by the plan. It must also include, if significant, the value of subsidized early retirement benefits, death benefits, and disability benefits related to the accrued benefits. Each significant actuarial assumption used to calculate the value of accrued benefits is required to "reflect the best estimate of the plan's future experience solely with respect to that assumption."

- Schedule SSA, Annual Registration Statement Identifying Separated Participants with Deferred Vested Benefits: This schedule is used when participants who will be entitled to benefits in future years terminate. A copy of Schedule SSA is forwarded to the Social Security Administration, which reminds participants of their benefits when they become eligible for Social Security benefits.
- Schedule of all investments: Not required with Form 5500-C.
- Schedule of any party-in-interest investments.
- Schedule of any loans or leases in default.
- Schedule of all transactions exceeding 3 percent of the current value of plan assets: Not required with Form 5500-C.
- Opinion of an independent qualified public accountant: Not required with Form 5500-C. While the law apparently permits the accountant to express an opinion on the financial statements included on the form, almost all accountants actually prepare an additional balance sheet and income statement as part of their report.

Except for Schedule B, all of the above requirements apply to both defined benefit and defined contribution plans.

Almost all plans with at least 100 participants[5] are required to have an annual audit by an independent qualified public accountant. The audit must follow generally accepted auditing standards. This audit provides the basis for the accountant's opinion referred to above.

The financial statement and schedules required for the annual report of a plan with 100 or more participants must be examined by an independent qualified public accountant retained by the plan on behalf of its participants.[6] The accountant must render an opinion on whether the financial statements and supporting schedules are presented fairly, in conformity with generally accepted accounting principles. Such an opinion has to be based on an examination carried out in accordance with generally accepted auditing standards.

Generally Accepted Accounting Principles

Since there were no generally accepted accounting principles for pension plans at the time that ERISA imposed this statutory responsibility on the accounting profes-

---

[4]This value of accrued benefits may be omitted for plans with less than 100 participants if it has not been calculated.

[5]An exception applies to certain plans funded exclusively with allocated insurance or annuity contracts. 29 CFR §2620.104-44.

[6]ERISA §103(a)(3).

sion, FASB launched a project, referred to above, to develop a set of accounting principles for pension plans as soon as possible. After several years of discussion, debate, and consultation with all interested groups, FASB in March 1980 promulgated *Statement of Financial Accounting Standards No. 35, Accounting and Reporting by Defined Benefit Pension Plans,* and made it effective for plan years beginning after December 15, 1980.[7] Financial statements for defined benefit plans must be prepared in accordance with Statement 35 if they are to receive an unqualified opinion from the plan auditor.[8] Information developed in accordance with the principles of Statement 35 is acceptable for related items on Schedule B of Form 5500.

In developing Statement 35, the Board and staff focused on the information needs of plan participants, with an eye on the needs of others, such as investors, creditors of the plan sponsor, and those who advise or represent participants. The primary function of the financial statements prepared on the basis of Statement 35 is to provide financial information useful in assessing the plan's present and future ability to pay plan benefits when due. While Statement 35 is based on the assumption that the plan is ongoing, the intent is to portray the financial condition of the plan at a given moment as realistically as possible. The result is a series of cross-sectional snapshots of the plan over time, as contrasted with a longitudinal long-run view of the financial needs of the plan as reflected in funding decisions of the plan sponsor.

Statement 35 stipulates that the financial statement for a defined benefit plan must include information about

- Net assets available for benefits as of the end of the plan year.
- Changes during the year in the net assets available for benefits.
- Actuarial present value of accumulated plan benefits.
- Significant effects of factors such as plan amendments, plan merger or spin-off, and changes in actuarial assumptions on the actuarial present value of accumulated plan benefits.

The benefit information may be presented as of either the beginning or end of the plan year. If a beginning-of-year date is chosen, the statement must show net assets as of that date (in addition to net assets at the end of the year), and the changes in net assets for both years.

Plan assets must be reported on the accrual basis of accounting. They must include contributions receivable as of the reporting date, if they are payable pursuant to a formal commitment or a legal or contractual requirement. Most

---

[7]The background of this statement is set out in a FASB Discussion Memorandum, "Accounting and Reporting for Employee Benefit Plans" (Stamford, Conn., October 1975). See also the FASB Exposure Draft, "Accounting and Reporting by Defined Benefit Plans," issued in July 1979.

[8]Statement 35 applies to all ongoing defined benefit pension plans, including plans not subject to ERISA and plans not qualified under the Internal Revenue Code, other than social insurance programs. However, FASB Statements 59 and 75 have indefinitely deferred the effective date of Statement 35 for pension plans of state and local governmental units, in the expectation that the Governmental Accounting Standards Board will publish standards for these plans. Statement 35 does not apply to plans to be terminated.

assets must be presented at their "fair value," which is basically the same as "current value" (i.e., market value) used by ERISA. Unlike the IRS asset valuation rules for funding, Statement 35 does not authorize any smoothing or averaging of asset values. This, of course, makes for sharp variations in year-to-year reported values, which may be partly or fully offset by changes in the actuarial present value of plan obligations. Insurance and annuity contracts are valued on the same basis as for Form 5500. This is generally the contractual account balance for a group deposit administration or IPG annuity contract and the contractual cash value of individual contracts. For contracts that provide for the purchase of annuities for some or all participants, the value of the purchased annuities is excluded from both the plan assets and the accumulated plan benefits. Operating assets owned by the plan, such as buildings and equipment employed in the administration of the plan, are valued at cost less accumulated depreciation or amortization.

In developing Statement 35, the Board concluded that accrued benefits should be measured in a uniform manner, irrespective of the type of benefit formula contained in the plan document. In pursuit of this objective, the Board stipulated that plan benefits should be measured on the accumulated plan benefits basis. As noted earlier, accumulated plan benefits are benefits reasonably expected to be paid under the provisions of the plan in exchange for services already rendered by the participants. Measurement of the accumulated benefits is based primarily on the participant's pay history, service, and other appropriate factors as of the date of measurement. Future salary changes are not considered (a decision that has been roundly criticized by some pension actuaries and others), and future years of service are considered only in determining expected eligibility for particular types of benefits such as early retirement, death, and disability benefits. *Automatic* cost-of-living adjustments are taken into account, but a mere expectation of such adjustments on an ad hoc basis without a prior contractual commitment is not recognized. In summary, accumulated plan benefits include vested and nonvested benefit accruals, as determined by plan provisions, and a pro rata portion of other benefits, such as supplemental early retirement benefits, death benefits, and disability benefits.

The accumulated plan benefits are valued on the assumption that the plan is ongoing. This means the various decrements that affect the probability of payment of the benefits—death, disability, withdrawal, and retirement—are taken into account. The resulting values are reduced to present values through the use of a realistic interest assumption. Under Statement 35 guidelines, the assumed rate(s) of investment return must reflect the expected rates of return during the periods for which benefit payment is deferred, and the return must be consistent with returns realistically achievable on the type of assets held by the plan and with the plan's investment policy. Many plans use a higher interest assumption for Statement 35 purposes than for funding purposes, to reflect among other things the fact that the average deferral period for benefits already *accrued* is shorter than the average deferral period for *projected* benefits, which are usually used in funding computations. Stated differently, the actuarial present value of accumulated plan benefits is more heavily weighted toward those participants already retired and those close to retirement, for whom the deferral period is shorter, than is the value of all projected benefits used for funding purposes. This relationship between the interest rates used for accrued versus projected benefits implicitly relies on a downward-sloping yield curve.

Under Statement 35, the actuarial present value of accumulated plan benefits must be shown separately for three categories: benefits in payment status, other vested benefits, and nonvested benefits. Accumulated employee contributions for active participants must be separately identified.

Statement 35 also requires that a defined benefit plan's statement include a description of the significant actuarial methods and assumptions used to determine the actuarial present value of accumulated plan benefits, as well as any significant changes in those methods and assumptions. A brief, general description of the plan agreement must be provided, as well as the funding policy for the plan. Statement 35 also lists other items that must be disclosed where applicable.

Statement 35 values may differ substantially from those developed for other purposes, especially the values used for funding in the valuation balance sheet and Schedule B of Form 5500 because of different asset valuation rules, interest assumptions, or measures of benefit accruals. Even though the two sets of values serve different purposes, the uninitiated may be confused by the discrepancies between the two balance sheets. Many actuaries and others question the value of the FASB's Statement 35 exercise, while others, conceding some value to the approach, question whether the benefit to the users equals the extra cost and effort of preparing a second financial analysis.

Statement 35 does not apply to defined contribution plans. These plans are subject to the generally accepted accounting principles that apply to all financial statements.

Accounting for Pensions by Employers

Employer accounting is concerned with the impact of a pension plan on the financial statements of the entity that sponsors the plan. A separate question is how the asset and liability values of the plan itself are determined and presented, although some common issues and subissues are involved. Thus the central task of employer pension accounting is to determine the proper charge against operations for pension expense and to decide whether the obligation assumed by the sponsor of a defined benefit plan is of such nature that it should be reflected on the balance sheet of the sponsor, and if so, how it should be reflected. Several philosophical, legal, and accounting questions are involved in resolving these two controlling issues.

Practice Prior to Opinion No. 8

Before Opinion No. 8 was published by the Accounting Principles Board of the American Institute of Certified Public Accountants in 1966, the prevailing practice was to treat the contribution to a pension plan in any given year as the pension expense for that year. This was the accepted practice, despite the fact that the contributions to the plan reflected financial and tax judgments more than accounting considerations. This was a form of *cash* accounting, in contrast to *accrual* accounting used for most business transactions. The accounting treatment of the contribution was the same, whether it represented normal cost only, normal cost plus interest on the unfunded supplemental liability, or normal cost and a portion of the supplemental liability. Similarly situated businesses could show widely varying pension expense solely because of differences in actuarial assumptions, actuarial cost methods, or funding policies. A business could improve its earnings statement for a given year simply by omitting or reducing its contribution to the pension plan. Over the years many firms, some of them prominent, showed no pension expense in their financial statements for a year or two, despite the fact that pension benefits continued to accrue in the normal manner. On the other hand, a firm could understate its true earnings by making a disproportionately large contribution to its pension plan in a particular year, to take advantage of a favorable cash or tax position. All this obviously impaired the comparability of financial statements and the validity of any analyses based on the statements.

The accounting treatment of costs associated with benefits credited for service prior to inception of a pension plan or retroactive benefit liberalizations was a subject of continuing study and debate within the accounting profession. In theory, there were three ways in which these costs could be handled: (1) they could be charged to retained earnings (then called earned surplus) as payments for services performed in the past; (2) they could be charged to income in the year of the plan's inception (or benefit liberalization) as a current cost of establishing or liberalizing the plan; or (3) they could be amortized by charging them to operations over a period of future years on the assumption that the plan sponsor will receive *future* benefit from plan benefits bestowed in recognition of *past* service. The third approach was the only one recognized by the IRS for tax-deduction purposes.

Accounting Research Bulletins

The first authoritative pronouncement on this subject was issued by the Committee on Accounting Procedure of the American Institute of Certified Public Accountants in 1948 in Accounting Research Bulletin No. 36 *Pension Plans: Accounting for Annuity Costs Based on Past Services.* In paragraph 4 of ARB 36, the committee expressed its opinion as follows:

> The committee believes that, even though the calculation is based on past services, costs of annuities based on such services are generally incurred in contemplation of present and future services, not necessarily of the individual affected but of the organization as a whole and, therefore, should be charged to the present and future periods benefited. This belief is based on the assumption that although the benefits flowing from pension plans are intangible, they are nevertheless real. The element of past services is one of the most important considerations of most pension plans and costs incurred on account of such services contribute to the benefits gained by the adoption of a plan. It is usually expected that such benefits will include better employee morale, the removal of superannuated employees from the payroll, and the attraction and retention of more desirable personnel, all of which should result in improved operations.

The Committee went on to say in paragraph 5:

(a) Costs of annuities based on past services should be allocated to current and future periods; provided, however, that if they are not sufficiently material in amount to distort the results of operations in a single period, they may be absorbed in the current year. (b) Costs of annuities based on past services should not be charged to surplus.

The Committee had nothing to say about normal costs and the practice of treating plan contributions for a period as the pension expense for that period.

In 1953 the Committee on Accounting Procedure issued ARB No. 43 *Restatement and Revision of Accounting Research Bulletins.* Chapter 13A of that Bulletin carried forward the language and content of ARB 36 unchanged.

In 1956 the Committee on Accounting Procedure issued ARB No. 47, *Accounting for Pension Costs.* This was the first official publication of the accounting profession to address the entire subject of pension cost accounting, the previous bulletins having dealt solely with accounting for past service costs. In ARB 47, the Committee reaffirmed the previous opinion that past service benefit costs should not be charged to earned surplus *at the inception of the plan,* but indicated that it might be appropriate for an *existing plan* to charge to earned surplus that portion of the initial past service liability that should have been charged to income since plan inception but for any reason was not so charged.

The Committee recognized two prevailing but conflicting views as to the proper basis for accounting for pension costs. One view held that the accrual of pension costs should not "necessarily" be dependent upon the funding arrangements of the plan or be governed by a strict legal interpretation of the sponsor's obligations under the plan. According to this view, normal costs should be systematically accrued during the expected period of active service of covered employees, and the cost of past service benefits should be charged off in a systematic and rational basis over some reasonable period without distorting the operating results of any one year. The second view was that accruing pension costs in excess of plan contributions could lead to a recorded pension liability in excess of the amount that the plan would have to pay in benefits if the plan should terminate. Some holding this view expressed concern that "in the case of an unfunded or partially funded plan the accumulation of a substantial accrual would lead to pressure for full funding, possibly to the detriment of the company and its security holders, and that the fear of this might deter management from entering into pension arrangements beneficial to employees."[9]

APB Opinion No. 8: Accounting for the Cost of Pension Plans

Notwithstanding the preferences expressed in ARB 47, accounting for pension costs continued to vary widely among plan sponsors and sometimes resulted in wide year-to-year fluctuations in the provision for pension costs of a particular plan sponsor.

[9]ARB Bulletin No. 47, Par. 6.

Because of the growing importance of pensions and continuing lack of uniformity in their accounting, the Accounting Principles Board commissioned a study by Ernest L. Hicks, a partner in the Arthur Young accounting firm, that led to the publication in 1965 of a book by Hicks, *Accounting for the Cost of Pension Plans*, and the issuance in 1966 of APB Opinion No. 8 of the same title, which was based on the reasoning and recommendations in the Hicks treatise.

Opinion No. 8 was a landmark development in the quest for comparability in pension cost accounting and served as the official guide to pension accounting by plan sponsors for 20 years, until it was superseded by FASB Statements 87 and 88 (described later in this chapter). It established the principle that accounting for pension costs should not be discretionary for the plan sponsor and that the cost should be recognized annually, whether funded or not. It set the parameters for a basic accounting method, identified actuarial cost methods acceptable for determining pension costs, prescribed the accounting treatment of actuarial gains and losses, and identified the employees who should be included in the cost calculation. It also required footnote disclosure of many important aspects of the pension plan, including its major features, the funding policy, the annual charge to operations for pension expense, the basis for determining the annual charge, and the plan amendments.

Opinion 8 took the position that the entire cost of benefit payments ultimately to be made should be charged against income subsequent to adoption or amendment of the plan, and that no portion of the cost should be charged directly to surplus. The APB members held such differing views on how to measure the cost of ultimate benefit payments that they settled for merely *narrowing* the range of practices by establishing rules for determining *minimum* and *maximum* pension cost accruals that bracketed their differing views.

The basic charge to expense for pension cost under Opinion 8 equaled the sum of the annual normal cost, an amount equal to interest on any unfunded prior service cost, and, if indicated, a provision for vested benefits. No provision for vested benefits was required if the benefits were fully funded or if the unfunded value of vested benefits decreased at least 5 percent during the year. If a provision for vested benefits was required, the minimum provision for vested benefits was the lesser of the amount needed to bring about a 5 percent reduction in the unfunded vested benefits or the amount needed to amortize the entire unfunded prior service cost over 40 years.

The minimum *funding* requirement for a year, before recognizing any credit balance in the funding standard account, usually equals or exceeds the minimum *charge to expense* for accounting purposes under Opinion 8. But a credit balance could reduce or eliminate the minimum funding requirement, resulting in a minimum charge to expense that exceeded the minimum funding requirement. The basic maximum charge to expense was the sum of the normal cost plus 10 percent of any initial past service cost or any prior service cost arising from plan amendments.

Opinion 8 allowed the minimum and maximum charge to expense to be determined on the basis of any reasonable set of actuarial assumptions and any reasonable actuarial cost method not specifically banned in Opinion 8. The Opinion specifically banned the terminal funding and pay-as-you-go approaches. The employer's discretion as to choice of actuarial cost method and actuarial assumptions was clearly at odds with the objective of uniform treatment of pension costs. The Opinion's approach to this critically important aspect of pension accounting represented a compromise between the actuary's (and plan sponsor's) desire for flexibility and the accountant's desire for comparability.

As noted in Chapter 23, some actuarial cost methods automatically spread actuarial gains and losses over the future working lifetimes of employees through an adjustment in the normal cost. If such a spread-gain method was not being used, actuarial gains or losses had either to be spread over a period of 10 to 20 years or merely added to the unfunded liability and made subject to whatever amortization procedure was being used.But if a gain or loss arose from a single occurrence not directly related to the operation of the plan, and not in the ordinary course of the employer's business (e.g., a plant closing), the entire gain or loss had to be recognized immediately.

As a general proposition, unfunded actuarial liabilities did not have to be shown on the balance sheet as a liability. There were two exceptions to this general rule. If the plan sponsor had a legal obligation to provide the benefits under the plan and if the actuarial value of the accrued benefits exceeded the amounts paid or accrued, the excess had to be shown in the balance sheet as both a liability and a deferred charge. Likewise, if the actual contributions paid to a plan during a given year were less than the charge to expense for pension cost for that year, the difference had to be included in the balance sheet as a liability for accrued pension cost. On the other hand, if the contributions exceeded the charge to expense, the excess was reflected on the balance sheet as an asset for prepaid pension cost.

As with all accounting standards, deviations were allowed without disclosure if they were deemed not material. When Opinion 8 was adopted, the maximum deductible contribution for past service was 10 percent of the past service base. ERISA changed this to allow amortization of the past service base over 10 years, which, with interest, may allow contributions of 13 or 14 percent. Subsequent IRS regulations changed the methods used in determining the base itself. Accountants usually considered any contribution that was within the deductible limits to be acceptable as a charge to expense, even if it exceeded the amount described by Opinion 8. This difference was allowed either because the accountant determined that the difference was not material or because he or she believed, rightly or wrongly, that Opinion 8 could reasonably be interpreted to allow past service liabilities to be amortized at the same rate at which they could be funded on a tax-deductible basis. For whatever reason, there was usually little difference between the pension expense for an accounting period and the contributions to the plan for the period.

FASB Statement 36: Disclosure of Pension Information

Pending completion of the project on employer accounting for pensions (described later in this chapter), FASB issued Statement No. 36, *Disclosure of Pension Information*. Statement 36 amended Opinion 8 to require plan sponsors to disclose in notes to their financial statements much of the same information that Statement 35 requires of the plans themselves. If the employer maintained more than one plan, the information could be reported in total for all plans, separately for each plan, or combined in useful groupings. For both defined benefit and defined contribution pension plans the following items were required:

a. A statement that a pension plan existed, identifying or describing the employee groups covered,
   b. A statement of the company's accounting and funding policies,
   c. The provision for pension cost for the period, and
   d. The nature and effect of significant matters affecting comparability for periods presented, such as changes in accounting methods (actuarial cost method, amortization of past and prior service cost, treatment of actuarial gains and losses, etc.), changes in circumstances (actuarial assumptions, etc.), or adoption or amendment of a plan.

For defined benefit plans, the notes also had to disclose the actuarial present values of vested and nonvested accumulated plan benefits, the interest rates used in determining them and the date as of which they were determined, and the plan's net assets available for benefits. Statement 36 made no change in the basic provisions of Opinion 8 that governed measurement of pension cost and pension liabilities.

FASB Statement 87: Employers' Accounting for Pensions

Despite the fact that Opinion 8 was a major step forward in the evolution of rational accounting for pension costs by sponsors of defined benefit pension plans, the financial community and certain segments of the accounting profession gradually grew dissatisfied with it. The principal criticisms of the opinion were that it

- accepted a variety of actuarial cost methods and amortization practices,
- permitted artificial leveling or smoothing of pension expense,
- failed to recognize certain obligations as liabilities of the plan sponsor,
- provided too much latitude in the choice of actuarial assumptions,
- ignored postretirement benefits not provided within the framework of a pension plan.

Recognizing these perceived flaws in Opinion 8, the FASB undertook a broad project to develop a new set of pension accounting principles for plan sponsors that would be acceptable to all segments of the business and financial communities, especially the accounting and actuarial professions. Over a period of several years the FASB produced a background paper on the subject,[10] a discussion memorandum,[11] a set of tentative conclusions entitled *Preliminary Views*, an exposure draft,[12] and finally, in 1985, Statement of Financial Accounting Standards No. 87, *Employers' Accounting for Pensions*. At various stages in the long drawn-out process, public hearings were held, and interested constituents and knowledgeable profes-

[10]FASB, "Accounting for Pensions by Employers: A Background Paper" (Stamford, Conn., March 1980).
[11]FASB Discussion Memorandum, "Employers' Accounting for Pensions and Other Post-retirement Benefits" (Stamford, Conn., February, 1981).
[12]FASB, Exposure Draft, "Employers' Accounting for Pensions" (Stamford, Conn., March 1985).

sionals were consulted extensively. Many persons and groups have criticized the final document or portions of it.

Underlying Propositions

Certain fundamental concepts or propositions underlie Statement 87.

A. DEFERRED COMPENSATION   The first proposition is that pensions are a form of deferred compensation. Plan participants exchange a portion of their service to the employer for the latter's promise to pay them certain benefits at a later date, if certain conditions are met. By participating in the plan, the participants implicitly (or, in certain collective bargaining situations, *explicitly*) agree to accept lower current compensation in return for the promise of pension plan benefits, subject to the terms and conditions of the plan, and the employer incurs a parallel obligation independent of any contributions that the employer may be making to the plan.

B. OBLIGATION TO INDIVIDUALS   The second proposition is that the employer's obligation for ultimate payment of the "deferred wages" runs to the employees, as individuals, rather than to the plan or to the plan participants collectively. Under this view, the plan and its associated trust are merely the vehicles or instrumentalities through which the employer discharges its obligation to the individual employees. This view rejects the notion that the employer discharges its obligation by making the required contributions to the plan trustee. Despite the fact that the employer can recapture its contributions to the plan only under severely restricted conditions, the employer retains a financial stake in the plan assets. If the total return on the assets exceeds the assumed rate of return, the employer can reduce future contributions to the plan; if the investment experience of the plan is unfavorable, the employer must make larger contributions to the plan than anticipated. Indeed, in the long run the employer must make up any loss of principal that the assets may suffer.

Because of the contingencies involved in qualifying for a benefit, notably employee turnover and deaths, some respected observers believe that the employer's obligation under the plan is to the covered employees, as a group. As a practical matter, the difference between the two views may be more conceptual than real.

C. INDEFINITE CONTINUANCE   The third proposition is that the plan will continue indefinitely. The significance of this assumption is that all the benefits that accrue under the plan will ultimately have to be paid, subject to the actuarial experience. The employer cannot look only to the benefits that have vested as of a given point in time. If the plan were to terminate, some nonvested benefits might not be paid; but if the plan continues, both vested and nonvested benefits will qualify for payment, again subject to diminution through population decrements.

D. BENEFIT EARNED PROPORTIONATELY   The fourth proposition is that a plan participant earns a pro rata proportion of his or her total prospective benefit with each year of service. This has to do with the *measurement* of benefit accruals. It is also an essential element in the venerated accounting concept of matching *revenue* and *expense*. Presumably an employee's service during a given accounting period produces revenue to the employer. The pension cost component of the total compensation package of the individual for that period should be recognized and charged to operations in the same manner as cash wages and current fringe benefits. Thus it is necessary to determine on some rational basis the rate at which employees earn their total pensions over the various accounting periods of their employment.

The actuarial profession has generally preferred to allocate or attribute the total prospective pension in such a manner as to produce a level annual *cost,* in dollars or as a percentage of compensation, the *benefit* allocation being grossly distorted in many cases. In theory, the employees should earn their pension at the same rate at which they earn their wages or salary. This would mean that the dollar amount of prospective pension benefit allocated to each accounting period should constitute a *level percentage of pay.* For practical reasons, the FASB chose to prorate the total pension over the total years of service, which obviously produces a constant *dollar* amount of benefit accrual for each year of service.

E. FUTURE VALUE OF PRIOR SERVICE BENEFITS   The fifth proposition is that granting benefit credits for service prior to inception or amendment of the plan will produce future economic benefits to the firm through reduced employee turnover, improved productivity, lower cash compensation, and enhanced prospects for attracting additional qualified employees. This proposition provides the rationale for charging the cost of such "prior service benefits" (which may include postretirement cost-of-living benefit increases) to future earnings, rather than to retained earnings, and for recognition of an intangible asset offsetting the future cost of such benefits. It is further presumed that the economic benefits from prior service benefits will be realized from the future efforts and attitudes of the employees with the firm at the time the benefit credits are bestowed. Thus it follows that the intangible asset should be amortized or written off over the average remaining service period of the active employees.

F. PENSION PLAN AUTONOMY   The sixth and final proposition is that a pension plan is a sufficiently autonomous legal entity that it would be inappropriate to include its assets and liabilities on the balance sheet of the business firm or other organization that sponsors the plan. The plan participants have first claim to the assets of the plan, and those assets are not available to the plan sponsor as long as the plan is in existence. The assets, however, are properly regarded as an offset to the plan's benefit obligations. Thus the FASB has concluded that the net difference between the plan's assets and liabilities should be reflected in the sponsor's balance sheet, in the manner described hereafter.

Provisions of FASB Statement 87 [13]

A. MEASUREMENT OF BENEFIT OBLIGATION   Statement 87 uses several measures of the value of benefits attributable to the past, which it calls the "benefit obligation."

---

[13]Statement of Financial Accounting Standards No. 87, *Employers' Accounting for Pensions* (Stamford, Conn.: FASB, 1985). It is essential to study including the illustrations in Appendix B, to fully understand its provisions. This text uses various phrases from the Statement without indicating their quotation.

The term "accumulated benefit obligation," is essentially the same as the term "actuarial present value of accumulated plan benefits" of FASB Statement 35 and the term "present value of accrued benefits" used by Form 5500. It is the actuarial present value of benefits attributed by the pension plan's benefit formula to employee service rendered before a specified date, based on employee service and compensation prior to that date. The "vested benefit obligation" is the actuarial present value of vested benefits. This is the vested portion of the accumulated benefit obligation.

The "projected benefit obligation" is the actuarial present value as of a specified date of benefits attributed by the pension plan's benefit formula to employee service rendered prior to that date. Unlike the accumulated benefit obligation, the projected benefit obligation utilizes salary projections to estimate the amount of benefits that will ultimately be payable and to determine the proportion of those projected benefits that are related to service to date. For a plan in which benefits are not related to pay, the accumulated benefit obligation and the projected benefit obligation are the same.

The "service cost" is the actuarial present value of projected benefits attributable to the single year (or other fiscal period) for which the financial statement is prepared. Like the projected benefit obligation, the service cost is based on projected future salaries.

If future increases in benefits have been contractually promised, as under a collective bargaining agreement for hourly employees, such increases must be reflected in both the accumulated benefit obligation (assuming retroactive application of the benefit increases) and the projected benefit obligation, as well as in the service cost. This means the participants' expected year of retirement must be recognized.

If an employer has a history of regular increases in non-pay-related benefits or in the past service benefits under a career-average-pay plan, this may indicate that the employer has a present commitment to make future amendments and that the substance of the plan is to provide benefits attributable to prior service that are greater than those described by the plan document. If so, the substantive commitment must be used in determining the projected benefit obligation and the service cost.

B. MEASUREMENT OF PLAN ASSETS   Statement 87 uses two measures of plan assets, "fair value" and "market-related value." Fair value is the amount that a pension plan could reasonably expect to receive for an asset in a current sale between a willing buyer and a willing seller, that is, other than in a forced or liquidation sale. If an active market exists for the asset, fair value is the market value. Plan assets used in the operation of the plan, such as buildings and equipment, are valued at their cost less accumulated depreciation or amortization.

The "market-related value of plan assets" may be either the fair value or a calculated value that recognizes changes in fair value over not more than five years, such as a five-year-average-market-value method.

Plan assets include amounts held in a trust or annuity contract to provide benefits but do not include other employer assets or reserves that may have been designated for pension funding but not effectively restricted to such use.

C. ANNUITY CONTRACTS   A number of special rules apply to annuity contracts under which the insurer has guaranteed to provide specified benefits to specific participants. Benefits funded through such contracts are generally excluded from all three measures of benefit obligation, and the value of such contracts is excluded from the plan assets. For participating annuity contracts under which future dividends are anticipated, however, the excess of the purchase price over the cost of a comparable nonparticipating contract is treated as the purchase of a right to future dividends. The statement provides rules for valuing such an asset in future years.

The treatment of annuity contracts described above does not apply to annuity contracts that do not guarantee specified benefits to specific participants or to annuity contracts under which the employer remains subject to all or most of the risks and rewards related to future experience. Such contracts are treated as investments and are valued at fair value. The contract's cash surrender value or conversion value, if determinable, is considered its fair value.

D. ASSUMPTIONS   Each significant assumption used in calculating the benefit obligations and the service cost must reflect the best estimate of anticipated experience solely with respect to that specific assumption. The salary increase assumption should reflect estimated compensation changes for present participants, including changes related to price inflation, productivity, seniority, promotions, and other factors. Projected Social Security benefits used to calculate benefits in Social Security offset plans should reflect estimates of the future increases in price and wage levels that affect Social Security benefits. Projected benefits should be based on the assumptions that any automatic future increase in the maximum limits on benefits under Section 415 of the Internal Revenue Code will occur (to the extent the plan document reflects such future increases), in contrast to the Code's requirement that these increases be ignored for minimum funding purposes.

The interest assumption used to calculate each of the benefit obligations and service cost, called the "discount rate," must reflect the rates at which the pension benefits could be effectively settled. In estimating these discount rates, the actuary would find it appropriate to consider information about interest rates used in current annuity purchase rates (including rates published by the Pension Benefit Guaranty Corporation). The PBGC periodically surveys annuity purchase rates and publishes regulations stating the interest rates implied in the annuity purchase rates. The computations required by Statement 87 and their explanation are simplified if the employer uses a single interest rate as the discount rate, but the PBGC rates consist of one interest rate for retired participants and a series of rates applicable to different years for participants not yet retired. Some plan sponsors have adopted either the PBGC rate applicable to retired employees or a composite level rate that would approximately reproduce the service cost generated by the series of PBGC rates. Instead of using interest rates reflecting annuity purchase rates, employers may look to rates of return on high-quality fixed-income investments currently available and expected to be available during the period to maturity of the pension benefits. Such fixed-income rates are generally higher than the PBGC rates and other annuity purchase rates. Material changes in long-term interest rates may not be ignored. Thus if interest rates fluctuate, it could be necessary to change the discount rate almost every year.

In addition to the discount rate used to calculate benefit obligations and service cost, Statement 87 requires an investment return assumption to be used to estimate the expected return on plan assets. This investment return assumption, called the "expected long-term rate of return on plan assets," may or may not be the same as the discount rate. In selecting this rate, the plan sponsor must consider the returns currently being earned by the plan assets and rates of return expected to be available for reinvestment. Because of the extreme volatility of common stocks as a class, past rates of return on the common stock component of a pension plan investment portfolio may be an unreliable guide to future performance. Long-term bond rates may be a better indicator of future portfolio returns. Some employers have adopted the discount rate as the expected long-term rate of return on plan assets, and illustrations included in Statement 87 indicate that using the same rate for both purposes is acceptable, at least in some circumstances.

E. RECOGNITION OF NET PERIODIC PENSION COST   The "net periodic pension cost" (which Opinion 8 termed "annual provision for pension cost") to be charged as an expense against income for a year (or other fiscal period) consists of six components:

- service cost,
- interest cost,
- actual return on plan assets,
- amortization of unrecognized prior service cost, if any,
- gain or loss (including the effects of changes in assumptions) to the extent recognized,
- amortization of unrecognized obligation at the date of initial application of Statement 87.

As a result of the combination of these six elements, the net periodic pension cost may be negative, although it will usually be positive. Each of the six elements needs explanation. For simplicity, this text assumes that the fiscal period is a year.

1. SERVICE COST   The service cost is the cost associated with the benefits attributable to the particular year for which the financial statement is prepared. It is the actuarial present value of benefits attributed to services rendered by employees during that period, calculated as of the last day of that period. Pension benefits are to be attributed to particular years in accordance with the plan's benefit formula, except that, like the projected benefit obligation, benefits are to be based on projected salaries rather than actual compensation prior to the statement date. If the plan benefit formula is the same for all years of service, the benefit attributed to any particular year would equal the participant's anticipated benefit calculated on the basis of projected salary and service, divided by the projected years of service.[14] But if the benefit formula is not the same for all years, such as 1 percent

---

[14]This is comparable to the unit credit actuarial cost method with benefits prorated by years of service, also called the "projected unit credit" method. Unlike IRS minimum funding regulations for plans using the unit credit method, Statement 87 requires that career average pay plans, like final average pay plans, use projection of benefits with projected salary increases.

of pay per year of prior service and 1.5 percent of pay per year of future service, the allocation of the projected benefit among the years of service would be similarly prorated. Special rules apply to benefits not related to years of service, such as death, disability, or supplemental early retirement benefits that are not a function of service.

2. INTEREST COST   The interest cost component represents the amount by which the projected benefit obligation is expected to grow during the year because of interest. It normally represents the discount rate multiplied by the projected benefit obligation at the beginning of the year, perhaps adjusted to reflect interest on benefits paid during the year.

3. ACTUAL RETURN ON PLAN ASSETS   The actual return on plan assets is the total investment income for the year, including realized and unrealized appreciation and depreciation of the fair value of plan assets. It equals all of the increase in the fair value of plan assets during the year except the portion resulting from the excess of contributions over benefits.

Under Statement 87 the *expected* return on plan assets is to be based on the expected long-term rate of return on plan assets and the market-related value of plan assets. As noted below, the net periodic pension cost includes a credit equal to the excess of the actual return on plan assets over the expected return on plan assets. Thus while the net periodic pension cost appears to include the actual return on plan assets, the effect of this offsetting credit is that the net periodic pension cost actually includes only the expected return on plan assets. This enables the net periodic pension cost to be predicted at the beginning of the year, before the actual return on plan assets is known.

The actual return on plan assets is a negative element, to be subtracted from the positive elements of the net periodic pension cost. If the interest rate used for the expected return on plan assets (a negative element) is the same as the discount rate applied to the projected benefit obligation (a positive element), the net effect of these two elements of net periodic pension cost is that interest will be charged on the unfunded portion of the projected benefit obligation, just as interest on the unfunded liability is required under Opinion 8. But the two interest rates may differ.

Statement 87 applies to unfunded nonqualified plans, such as excess benefit plans, as well as to funded plans. For an unfunded plan, of course, there is no actual return on plan assets.

4. AMORTIZATION OF UNRECOGNIZED PRIOR SERVICE COST   A new pension plan usually credits benefits based on service prior to the effective date, creating a projected benefit obligation on the effective date. Plan amendments frequently increase the projected benefit obligation. Such an increase is termed "prior service cost." Occasionally an amendment can decrease the projected benefit obligation; in this case the prior service cost will be negative. Amounts of projected benefit obligation established before the effective date of Statement 87 are not treated as a prior service cost, but are accounted for separately.

The entire prior service cost is not included in the net periodic pension cost in the year that it is created. Rather, it is amortized over the expected future period of service of present active participants expected to receive benefits under the plan.[15] By using rates of death, retirement, disability, and other forms of withdrawal, the actuary can project the periods of service expected to be worked in future years by present participants.

For example, for 1,000 participants expected to receive benefits under the plan at the beginning of a year when a prior service cost is created, the actuary may project that 980 years of service will be credited during that year, that 940 will be credited the following year, and so forth. Totaling these projections for all future years, the actuary may determine that the total number of years of service to be credited in all future years is 15,000 years of service. Of these 15,000 years, 980, or 6.53 percent of them, will be credited during the first year. Therefore 6.53 percent of the prior service cost would be included in the net periodic pension cost for the first year as amortization of unrecognized prior service cost. The next year the amount of unrecognized prior service cost included in the net periodic pension cost would be 6.27 percent (940/15,000) of the amount of prior service cost that was determined at its creation.

This complex approach to amortization can be avoided by adopting an alternative approach that amortizes the prior service cost more rapidly, such as straight-line amortization over the average remaining service period. In the above example, the average remaining service period is 15 years (15,000/1,000); thus one-fifteenth of the prior service cost could be treated as the amortization amount each year.

Note that the amortization amount does not include any interest. Interest on the prior service cost has already been included as part of the interest cost based on the total projected benefit obligation described earlier.

5. GAIN OR LOSS (INCLUDING THE EFfECTS OF CHANGES IN ASSUMPTIONS) TO THE EXTENT RECOGNIZED   For purposes of Statement 87, a gain or loss is a change in the amount of projected benefit obligation or plan assets resulting from actual experience different from that expected or from changes in assumptions. This differs from funding requirements and traditional actuarial practice, which do not treat changes in assumptions as gains and losses.

The gain or loss component included in net periodic pension cost consists of two parts, (1) the difference between the actual return on plan assets and the expected return, and (2) the amortization of the unrecognized net gain or loss from previous years. The first of these, the difference between the actual return on plan assets and the expected return, has the effect of removing from the net periodic pension cost the current year's gain or loss on assets that is included in the component for actual return on plan assets.

The second part of the gain or loss component, the amortization of the unrecognized net gain or loss from prior years, is determined in several steps. The total net gain or loss for all prior years after the effective date of Statement 87 is adjusted by the amount of such gain or loss recognized in prior years. This unrecognized net loss (negative if a net gain) is then increased by the excess of the

---

[15]If all, or almost all of the participants are inactive, their remaining life expectancy is used instead of the remaining service period for this purpose and other requirements of Statement 87.

fair value of plan assets over the market-related value of plan assets (a negative amount if the fair value is smaller), thus deferring asset gains not yet included in the market-related value. The amortization amount to be included in the gain or loss component can be based on this adjusted unrecognized net gain or loss, but it is permissible to first reduce its magnitude by 10 percent of the larger of the projected benefit obligation or the fair value of plan assets, basing the amortization on the excess, if any. If amortization is required, this net amount is divided by the average remaining service period of active employees who are expected to receive plan benefits to obtain the amortization amount included in the gain or loss component of the net periodic pension cost. The amortization amount of the gain or loss component is positive if there is a net loss and negative if there is a net gain. With this process of determining the gain or loss component, the recognition of gains and losses is substantially deferred and cost fluctuations are smoothed out between years.

6. AMORTIZATION OF UNRECOGNIZED OBLIGATION AT THE DATE OF INITIAL APPLICATION OF STATEMENT 87   At the beginning of the first year to which Statement 87 applies, there exists an unrecognized obligation equal to the excess, as of the end of the previous year, of (a) the pension benefit obligation over (b) the fair value of plan assets plus any accrued pension cost included in the liabilities of the employer's balance sheet (or less any asset for prepaid pension cost included in the employer's balance sheet). The component for amortization of unrecognized obligation is determined by dividing this difference by the average remaining service period for active employees expected to receive plan benefits. The employer may elect to use 15 years if this is longer than the average remaining service period. The component for amortization of unrecognized obligation at the date of initial application of Statement 87 is a positive element of the net periodic pension cost if the initial projected benefit obligation exceeds the fair value of plan assets adjusted for balance sheet accruals; otherwise it is a negative element of the cost.

F. RECOGNITION OF LIABILITIES AND ASSETS   The amount of employer contributions to the plan will ordinarily differ from the net periodic pension cost. The cumulative difference between these two is recognized on the employer's balance sheet as an asset for prepaid pension expense if employer contributions exceed the net periodic pension cost, and as a liability for unfunded accrued pension cost if less.

An additional liability may be required on the employer's balance sheet if there is an "unfunded accumulated benefit obligation" which means the excess, if any, of the accumulated benefit obligation over the fair value of plan assets. This additional liability equals the excess, if any, of the unfunded accumulated benefit obligation over the unfunded accrued pension cost, increased by any asset for prepaid pension expense. Thus the combination of this additional liability and any prepaid pension expense or unfunded accrued pension cost produces a net liability on the employer's balance sheet that is equal to the unfunded accumulated benefit obligation. Any such additional liability is generally offset by adding an "intangible asset" of equal amount to the balance sheet.[16]

[16]However, the intangible asset may not exceed the unrecognized prior service cost plus the unrecognized net obligation arising before the effective date of Statement 87. If the additional liability exceeds this amount, the net worth on the balance sheet will show a decrease.

G. DISCLOSURES   Statement 87 describes extensive disclosures required in the employer's financial statements regarding the employer's pension plans, their funding, and their accounting. The net periodic pension cost must be broken down between the service cost component, the interest cost component, the actual return on assets for the period, and the net total of other components. All three measures of benefit obligation must be shown. A detailed schedule is required reconciling the funded status of the plan with amounts reported in the employer's balance sheet. Statement 87 provides examples of such disclosure statements.

H. EMPLOYERS WITH TWO OR MORE PLANS   If an employer sponsors more than one defined benefit plan, the net periodic pension cost, asset, and liability items for the employer's financial statement must be calculated separately for each plan. The employer's financial statement combines amounts for all such plans in the statement, but it does not offset them. Thus an excess of plan assets over the accumulated benefit obligation for one plan cannot reduce the unfunded accumulated benefit obligation of another plan, and the prepaid pension cost of one plan does not offset the unfunded accrued pension cost of another. For purposes of the required disclosures, all of an employer's defined benefit plans may be aggregated or they may be aggregated in groups to provide the most useful information. However, plans with unfunded accumulated benefit obligations may not be aggregated with other plans for purposes of the required schedule reconciling the funded status of the plan with amounts reported in the employer's balance sheet.

I. DEFINED CONTRIBUTION PLANS   Statement 87's requirements for defined contribution pension plans are quite simple: the net periodic pension cost equals the required employer contributions to the plan. Any difference between the net periodic pension cost and the actual employer contributions results in either a liability for unfunded accrued pension cost or an asset for prepaid pension cost, the same as under defined benefit plans. The disclosure requirements for defined contribution plans are brief and simple.

J. MULTIEMPLOYER PLANS   The requirements for accounting for the costs of a multiemployer plan in the financial statement of a contributing employer are usually comparable to the requirements with respect to defined contribution plans. However, if it is either probable or reasonably possible that the employer will withdraw from a multiemployer plan with resulting withdrawal liability, other requirements apply (see chapter 34 for a description of withdrawal liability under multiemployer plans).[17]

K. OTHER RULES AND EffECTIVE DATES   Special rules apply to non-U.S. pension plans and to a variety of special situations not described herein. Statement 87 is generally effective for financial statements for fiscal periods beginning after December 15, 1986. But for a business whose securities are not publicly traded and that does not sponsor any defined benefit plan with more than 100 participants, the Statement is effective for fiscal periods beginning two years later. That later effective date also applies to foreign plans, and to all plans with respect to the requirement that any unfunded accumulated benefit obligation be shown on the balance sheet.

---

[17]Requirements in this case are determined by FASB Statement No. 5.

Earlier application was encouraged for all employers, and many decided to comply early. The advantages and disadvantages of adopting the new rules before the mandatory dates differ from employer to employer. That is why employers reached differing decisions concerning early adoption.

FASB Statement 88: Plan Terminations, Settlements, Curtailments, and Termination Benefits

Under FASB Statement No. 88, an employer's financial statements are required to indicate the effect of certain special events in defined benefit plans, such as a plan termination or curtailment, settlements of benefit obligations by purchase of annuities or lump-sum payment, and the provision of certain termination benefits. Statement 88 describes the amount of gains and losses that must be recognized immediately in the employer's financial statements for these events. These requirements supplement the requirements of Statement 87 and become effective at the same time as Statement 87. Thus a decision to adopt Statement 87 early will automatically trigger the early adoption of Statement 88.

Settlements

Statement 88 defines a settlement as "a transaction that (a) is an irrevocable action, (b) relieves the employer (or the plan) of primary responsibility for a pension benefit obligation, and (c) eliminates significant risks related to the obligation and the assets used to effect the settlement." A settlement will occur if a plan's obligation to provide benefits is discharged by paying a lump-sum distribution or by purchasing a nonparticipating annuity contract.

If a participating annuity contract is purchased, this constitutes a settlement only if the employer is no longer subject to all or most of the risks and rewards associated with the annuity. But if a purchase of a participating annuity is a settlement, the portion of the premium that exceeds the cost of a similar non-participating annuity is treated as an investment in the asset of future dividends.

Even discharging the benefit obligation for a single participant by paying a lump-sum distribution or purchasing an annuity constitutes a settlement, but the employer may elect not to recognize settlements if the total of all settlements in a year is less than the sum of the service cost component and the interest cost component of net periodic pension cost for the year. Thus in a large plan the settlements resulting from routine benefit distributions will not ordinarily require recognition, but in a small plan the retirement of a single participant may require recognition as a settlement.

Curtailments

A curtailment is an event that significantly reduces the benefits that would ordinarily be expected to be earned in the future by present participants. Any event that significantly reduces the expected years of future service, such as a plant closing that results in a significant number of terminations of employment, would constitute a curtailment. A plan amendment reducing or eliminating benefits to be accrued in the future would also be a curtailment.

Plan Terminations

A plan termination usually involves both a curtailment and a settlement. Therefore it is usually subject to the requirements for both events.

Termination Benefits

Some pension plans provide special termination benefits triggered by a particular event such as a plant closing. Other employers have agreed to provide such benefits outside the pension plan under the terms of a collective bargaining agreement. Statement 88 includes both types in its definition of "contractual termination benefits" and establishes requirements for accounting for them.

In a temporary effort to encourage early retirements, some employers have offered special termination benefits to certain employees if they retire or terminate employment during a limited period of time, often called a "window period." Statement 88 establishes rules for accounting for these "special termination benefits."[18]

---

[18]Accounting for such special termination benefits prior to the effective date of Statement 88 is governed by FASB Statement No. 74.

Section V
Assets and Insurance

Chapter 29

Management of Pension Plan Assets: Policy

The funding of a pension plan, whether in response to regulatory requirements or the dictates of sound financial management, leads to the accumulation of assets dedicated to the payment of plan benefits and administrative expenses. Productive deployment of these assets reduces the direct cost of a defined benefit plan and increases the benefits that can be paid under a defined contribution plan. For example, if the assets of a fully funded defined benefit plan can be invested in a manner that earns on average a total rate of return of 6 percent in a stable economic environment, about 70 percent of the plan's benefits will be paid from investment earnings, leaving only 30 percent to be met from contributions to the plan. With a given level of contributions, investment earnings play a comparably significant role in generating benefits for participants in a defined contribution plan. Plan assets and their capacity to generate future investment earnings are the primary source, at any given time, of benefit security—the assurance that the accrued benefit rights of the plan participants will ultimately be honored. Thus the management of pension plan assets is a major concern for plan sponsors and those regulatory authorities responsible for protecting the interests of plan participants and their beneficiaries.

Regulatory Constraints

The management of pension plan assets is subject to regulation and oversight at both the federal and state level. Federal constraints are found primarily in the statutory prescriptions of Employment Retirement Income Security Act and the implementing regulations promulgated by the Department of Labor and the Internal Revenue Service. State constraints are contained in the statutes, regulations, and court decisions relating to the investments of life insurance companies, banks, trust companies, and fiduciaries of various sorts. The general preemption of applicable state law by ERISA does not extend to state laws regulating the investments of banks, trust companies, and life insurance companies.

Federal Regulation

The rules and regulations of various federal agencies have some relevance to the investment of pension plan assets; but the primary regulatory responsibility in this area lies with the Department of Labor, the Internal Revenue Service, the Securities and Exchange Commission (SEC), the Federal Reserve System, and the Comptroller of the Currency. The authority of the DOL and IRS derives mainly from ERISA.

ERISA

The constraints imposed by ERISA on the management of pension plan assets are an integral part of the basic fiduciary responsibilities the act transmits to all persons who exercise any discretionary authority or control over the management of a pension plan.[1] Full responsibility for all aspects of the plan's operations, including the management of its assets, ultimately rests with the directors and senior management of the sponsoring entity. For operating purposes, that responsibility will usually be vested in a specific individual or a committee, known as the retirement, pensions, or benefits committee. Either the plan sponsor[2] or such person or committee is usually designated as the plan administrator.[3] ERISA requires the plan to have a named fiduciary,[4] which is typically either the plan administrator or the plan sponsor. Some technical and administrative functions may be contracted out to specialists, but the ultimate responsibility for the overall operation of the plan and compliance with applicable law rests with the plan sponsor.[5] Under an individual account plan that permits individual participants and their beneficiaries to exercise control over their own accounts, no fiduciary is liable for the actions of participants or beneficiaries.[6]

A. SEGREGATION OF PLAN ASSETS   Both ERISA and the Internal Revenue Code require that the assets of a pension plan be held in trust or under a comparable arrangement.[7] There are at least three reasons for this requirement: (1) to remove the assets from the control of the plan sponsor and to ensure that they are ultimately used to pay plan benefits and the reasonable expenses of administering the plan; (2) to prevent the commingling of plan assets with the assets of other plans (except under approved conditions) or the assets of the institution or individual providing trust or investment services; and (3) to facilitate the identification, management, and control of plan assets by the trustee or trustees.

Qualified pension plans funded through insurance or annuity contracts issued by a domestically licensed life insurance company have always enjoyed a statutory exemption from the general requirement that their assets be held in trust.[8] This is true whether the insurer guarantees all funded benefits through individual or group annuity contracts or merely holds the assets in unallocated fashion in its general asset account or in one or more separate accounts. The assets of the insurer issuing such contracts are likewise exempt from the trust requirement.

---

[1] ERISA §3(21).
[2] ERISA §3(16)(B).
[3] ERISA §3(16)(A).
[4] ERISA §402(a).
[5] ERISA §§402(b), 405(c).
[6] ERISA §404(c).
[7] ERISA §403; IRC §401(a)(1).
[8] ERISA §403(b)(1); IRC §403(a); Treas. Reg. 1.403(a)-1(d).

Assets in individual retirement accounts held in certain custodial accounts[9] are also exempted from the trust requirement, as are any assets invested in mutual funds or other regulated investment companies and held in custodial accounts in respect of Section 403(b) annuity contracts (individual tax-deferred annuities, or TDAs).[10] Section 403(b) annuities funded through life insurers have been exempt from the trust requirement from their inception. There are exemptions for other less common arrangements,[11] and the Secretary of Labor has authority under ERISA to grant other exemptions.

In an important ruling[12] with general application, the Secretary of Labor has held that registering the securities of a pension plan in the name of a nominee or its street name ("street name" registration) does not violate the trust requirement if the securities are held on behalf of the plan by a bank, trust company, broker-dealer, or clearing agency or by the nominees of any of these entities. The plan trustee or trustees must maintain control over such securities and evaluate the safeguards against loss from such an arrangement, including the financial stability of the nominees, adequacy of insurance, and so forth.

The plan sponsor appoints the trustee or, if the plan is to be funded through a life insurer, selects the insurer and the contractual arrangement.[13] The trustee or trustees must be named in the plan document or the trust instrument or appointed by the named fiduciary for the plan.[14] After the trusteeship is accepted and their fiduciary status is acknowledged in writing, the trustee or trustees have exclusive authority and discretion to manage the assets of the plan, unless (1) the plan document or trust instrument expressly provides that the trustee or trustees are subject to the direction of a named fiduciary (not a trustee in this sense), or (2) the authority to manage, acquire, or dispose of assets of the plan is delegated to one or more asset managers.

Investment responsibilities can be legally delegated only to an investment adviser registered under the Investment Advisers Act of 1940, a bank (as defined in that act), or an insurance company qualified under the laws of two or more states to provide investment management services.[15] To be qualified, an asset manager must acknowledge in writing that it is a plan fiduciary, as defined by ERISA. The plan sponsor must exercise prudence in selecting and retaining asset managers. When authority to manage some or all of the plan assets is delegated to other investment entities, such assets retain their identity as plan assets, and the title to them remains with the plan trustee or trustees.

B. DEFINITION OF PLAN ASSETS   Identification of plan assets has crucial significance in fixing the scope of the trustee's authority and responsibility. One issue that arises

---

[9]IRC §408(h).

[10]ERISA §403(b)(5); IRC §403(b)(7).

[11]ERISA §403(b).

[12]29 CFR2550.403a-1.

[13]Under a negotiated multiemployer pension plan, the plan sponsor is the board of trustees, composed of an equal number of labor and management representatives, which is responsible for the plan's operation and determines investment policy and chooses asset managers.

[14]ERISA §403(a).

[15]ERISA §§3(38), 402(c)(3), 405(d).

when a plan invests in another entity is whether the plan's asset consists only of its investment in the entity itself or whether the underlying assets of the entity are also considered plan assets. For example, if the plan purchases shares of a mutual fund, the issue is whether the plan assets consist only of the shares of the mutual fund or whether the plan assets include an undivided interest in the underlying investments of the mutual fund. The manager of such a pooled investment vehicle would be a plan fiduciary if retained directly by the plan to invest a portion of the plan assets, and arguably it should make no difference that the manager is retained indirectly through the acquisition of an ownership interest in the pool.

In attempting to discern and implement the will of Congress in this matter, the Department of Labor[16] has embraced the general proposition that where a pension plan invests in an equity interest of another entity, the underlying assets of that entity are properly viewed as plan assets and must be managed in accordance with the fiduciary responsibility provisions of ERISA, unless there are circumstances that make these provisions unnecessary or inappropriate. As a practical matter, it is argued, the plan is retaining the manager of the other entity, generally a pooled investment vehicle, to manage the portion of the plan's assets that is so invested.

Whenever a plan invests in any entity, if the underlying assets of the entity are construed to be plan assets, the manager of the entity will be a fiduciary with respect to the pension plan, and the plan fiduciaries will have fiduciary responsibility for the prudent investment of the underlying assets. Congress recognized the importance of this issue and included a provision in ERISA that was intended to clarify the status of a pension plan's contractual arrangements with investment companies and life insurance companies.[17] That provision declares that the underlying assets of a mutual fund or other investment company registered with the SEC under the provisions of the Investment Company Act of 1940 are *not* to be construed as assets of a pension plan holding securities of the investment company. Congress reasoned that the supervision of the investment company by the SEC provides sufficient protection to the pension plan and its participants. This conclusion does not relieve the plan trustee from the obligation of exercising prudence in the acquisition and retention of investment company shares, which constitute plan assets. Regulations have extended this relief to all publicly offered securities that are freely transferable, widely held, and registered under federal securities laws.[18]

The same ERISA provision states that the assets of a life insurer's general account, against which most contractual guarantees and other general obligations are enforceable, shall not be construed to be assets of a plan that owns a guaranteed benefit contract. Rather, only the contracts or policies issued to the plan trustee by the life insurer are to be treated as plan assets. The rationale for this exemption, apart from its inherent logic, is that the general account operations, including its investment activities, are adequately supervised by state regulatory authorities.

---

[16]29 CFR 2510.3-101.
[17]ERISA §401(b).
[18]29 CFR 2510.3-101(a),(b).
[19]29 CFR 2510.3-101(i).

The same issue arises when a pension plan acquires certificates or securities backed by mortgages that are guaranteed or insured by various housing agencies of the federal government, such as GNMA, FNMA, or FHLMC. The question is whether the plan assets include the mortgages in the government-backed pool or only the certificates that evidence a pro rata ownership of the pool. Concluding that the real security behind these pass-though certificates is the government guarantee rather than the individual mortgages in the pool, the DOL has taken the position that only the certificates are the plan assets, and not the underlying mortgages.[19] Thus the sponsor or manager of a governmental mortgage pool would not be a fiduciary of a plan merely by reason of the plan's investment in the pool.

Under another rule, if a plan has an equity interest in an operating company that is primarily engaged, directly or through majority-owned subsidiaries, in the production or sale of a product or service, the underlying assets of the operating company, such as property and equipment, are not deemed to be plan assets.[20]

The rule for operating companies described above also applies to certain equity investments in a venture capital operating company (VCOC). Generally a limited partnership or corporation, a VCOC raises money through the sale of its own securities or participation shares and then invests the money in selected securities of small operating companies. As part of the investment arrangements with portfolio companies, the VCOC management may participate or be given the right to participate in the management of the portfolio companies. By regulation[21] the Department of Labor has stipulated that a pension plan's investment in a VCOC will not cause the the VCOC's assets to be classified as plan assets so long as certain conditions are fulfilled. The same principle applies to a real estate operating company that satisfies certain criteria.[22]

Apart from the special rules explained above, the underlying assets of an entity in which a plan has an equity interest are deemed to be plan assets unless the equity participation in the entity by all benefit plan investors is less than 25 percent of the particular class of equity interests. In the case of any plan investment in a group trust or a common or collective trust of a bank that pools the investments of more than one plan, or any investment in a separate account of an insurance company, the plan assets are deemed to include the underlying assets of the entity, except where the entity is a registered investment company, regardless of any other rules.

In summary, unless the entity is a registered investment company, plan assets will always be deemed to include the underlying assets in the following situations:

- a group trust,
- a common or collective trust fund of a bank,
- a separate account of an insurance company.

Otherwise, if a plan has an equity interest in an entity, the underlying assets will be treated as plan assets unless less than 25 percent of the equity interest of the

---

[20]29 CFR 2510.3-101(a)(2),(c).
[21]29 CFR 2510.3-101(d).
[22]29 CFR 2510.3-101(e).

company is held by benefit plan investors or unless the entity is one of the following:

- a registered investment company;
- a publicly offered security that is freely transferable, widely held, and registered;
- an operating company, including a venture capital operating company or a real estate operating company;
- a governmental mortgage pool.

C. STATEMENT OF INVESTMENT POLICY   Some observers believe that the plan sponsor is under a fiduciary obligation to develop and adopt a set of written policy guidelines for the investment of the plan assets. It should keep the guidelines under continual review and make appropriate modifications as economic and plan circumstances warrant. The guidelines should be communicated to the asset managers and reasonable efforts made to ensure that the managers comply with the guidelines.

D. DIVERSIFICATION OF INVESTMENTS   The plan sponsor and its investment managers are under specific mandate to diversify plan assets and thereby minimize the risk of large losses, unless under the circumstances it is clearly prudent not to do so.[23] The degree of diversification must be determined by the facts and circumstances of the particular case, including the purposes of the plan, the amount of plan assets, and financial and industrial conditions. A highly diversified portfolio might reflect diversification by (1) type of investment—stocks, bonds, mortgages, and the like; (2) geographic location; (3) industrial sector; and (4) dates of maturity of fixed-income instruments.

If the assets are allocated to more than one asset manager, with each manager being instructed to hold specific classes of investments, such as common stocks only or bonds only, the managers are not liable for failure to diversify their holdings by type. Instead, the diversification test is applied to the deployment of plan assets as a whole. The diversification requirement can be satisfied by placing all the plan assets in a pooled investment account, if the latter is itself properly diversified. Thus the plan assets can be held in a pooled trust fund, a pooled separate account of a life insurance company, or in shares of a mutual fund. Alternatively, the assets may be invested wholly in insurance or annuity contracts guaranteed by a life insurance company or wholly in the securities of the federal government or its agencies, since these require no diversification to minimize the risk of large losses. In addition to the general diversification requirement, defined benefit plans and most money purchase pension plans are prohibited from acquiring or holding more than 10 percent of plan assets in the securities or real property of the employer.[24]

E. PRUDENCE STANDARD   In managing the assets of a qualified pension plan, an individual or organization must act "with the care, skill, prudence, and diligence

[23]ERISA §404(a)(1)(C).
[24]ERISA §407.

under the circumstances then prevailing that a prudent man acting in a like capacity and familiar with such matters would use in conducting an enterprise of like character and with like aims."[25] This is a variation of the "prudent man" standard that derives from the classic rule first enunciated in 1830 by the Supreme Judicial Court of Massachusetts in the famous case of *Harvard College v. Amory*. The original rule was enunciated as a standard for a trustee in managing the assets of a personal trust or an institutional endowment. The new federal standard, which applies to all pension plan fiduciaries, whether or not they have investment responsibilities, is intended to measure the behavior of a pension plan asset manager against the behavior of other such managers, rather than against the investment behavior of individuals managing their own funds or professional managers handling the assets of personal trusts or other aggregation of funds not associated with a pension plan. This has caused some observers to characterize the new benchmark as the "prudent expert" standard. Another purpose of the standard is to ensure that the overall investment performance of the portfolio is judged, rather than the performance of specific portfolio holdings.

The federal courts have the ultimate responsibility of determining the meaning and full ramifications of this standard of prudence for pension plan fiduciaries. The Department of Labor has promulgated a regulation[26] to provide some guidance on the interpretation of "prudence" in the ERISA context. The regulation was not intended to serve as the exclusive method for satisfying the prudence rule but as a "safe harbor" approach, namely, one officially sanctioned method of complying with the law.

The regulation is couched in general language and provides little additional guidance as to the suitability of a particular course of investment conduct. The primary contribution may well rest on its support of risk/return trade-off and other tenets of modern portfolio theory. The regulation's preamble states that no specific investment or investment course of action is prudent per se or imprudent per se but must be judged by the role that it will play within the overall plan portfolio. In determining the prudence of a particular investment or investment course of action, an asset manager must consider the following items pertaining to the portion of the total plan portfolio that he or she manages:

- the composition of the portfolio, with regard to diversification,
- the liquidity and current return of the portfolio in relation to the cash flow requirements of the plan,
- the projected return of the portfolio in relation to the funding objective of the plan.

In assessing these factors, an asset manager may rely and act upon information provided by or at the direction of the appointing fiduciary, if the manager does not know and has no reason to know that the information is incorrect. This is an especially important provision from the standpoint of an asset manager who manages only a portion of the plan portfolio.

[25] ERISA §404(a)(1)(B).
[26] 29 CFR 2550.404a-1.

While endorsing the concept of total portfolio performance, the DOL notes in the preamble of the regulation that no relevant or material attributes of a contemplated investment may properly be disregarded and no particular investment may be deemed prudent solely by reason of the propriety of the aggregate risk/return characteristics of the overall portfolio. The DOL approves the use of an index fund if the fund filters out the securities of companies subject to adverse financial developments and the use of the fund is consistent with the plan's needs and investment objectives. It also states that "prudence" does not require that every item in a plan portfolio be income-producing under all circumstances. In effect, the DOL accepts the "total return" concept of portfolio performance.

Federal Securities Laws

The investment operations of a pension plan (and other employee benefit plans of the asset accumulation type) are subject to the Securities Act of 1933, the Securities Exchange Act of 1934, and the Investment Company Act of 1940, as these important pieces of legislation have been interpreted by the SEC and federal courts.[27] The Securities Act of 1933, which regulates the offer and sale of securities, is most relevant, especially its registration (disclosure) and antifraud provisions. A critical question, which has generated much disagreement and controversy, is whether any aspect of pension plan operation gives rise to an interest that might be characterized as a "security" and hence should enjoy all the investor safeguards embodied in the 1933 act and other securities laws. To be more specific, has a participant in a pension, profit-sharing, or similar plan made an investment, and is the acquisition by the plan of a fractional interest in a pool of assets managed by a bank or insurance company tantamount to the purchase of a security?

With respect to the first issue, the Securities and Exchange Commission has long applied a test first enunciated in the landmark case of *SEC v. W. J. Howey Co.*[28] Under the *Howey* test, an investment contract (security) requires (1) the investment of money (or its equivalent in goods or services), (2) in a common enterprise, (3) with an expectation of profit (a return in excess of the cash contribution), (4) from the managerial efforts of others.

Since 1941 the SEC has held the general view that the interests of employees in pension, profit-sharing, and similar plans are investment contracts in the generic sense, since such plans are capital accumulation vehicles designed to produce a "profit" to the employees in the form of retirement benefits or a cash distribution.[29] However, with the exception noted below, the Commission has taken the position that the plans need not be registered and need not comply with all relevant provisions of the 1933 act.[30]

The SEC has consistently maintained that a voluntary, contributory pension or profit-sharing plan meets all the *Howey* tests of an investment contract and should

---

[27]Much of the material for this section was drawn from *SEC Release no. 33-6188* (February 1, 1980) (45FR8960); and SEC Release no. 33-6281 (January 15, 1981) (46FR8446).

[28]328 U.S. 293 (1946).

[29]Opinion of Assistant General Counsel, CCH Fed. Sec. L. Rep. 1941–44.

[30]This administrative practice was affirmed by Congress in 1970 and codified in §3(a)(2) of the 1933 act.

be registered if employee contributions are to be invested in employer securities, as they frequently are in profit-sharing plans and may be in a pension plan. It contends that when an employee elects to participate in a voluntary, contributory pension, or other similar plan, he or she has made an investment decision motivated by an expectation that the ultimate return on his or her contributions in the form of cash or retirement benefits will exceed the return on alternative investment opportunities. The need for full disclosure is magnified when employer securities are to be acquired. The SEC position was ratified by Congress in the 1970 amendments to Section 3(a)(2) of the 1933 act. When participation in the plan is involuntary, no investment contract is involved, even though employee contributions are required, since the expectation of profit or gain is not a motivating factor.

The applicability of federal securities laws to employee interests in pension and profit sharing plans has been before the federal courts on various occasions—one case, *International Brotherhood of Teamsters v. Daniel*,[31] reached the U.S. Supreme Court. This case involved a noncontributory multiemployer plan in which participation of eligible employees was automatic and hence involuntary. The Court held that the interest of the employee, Daniel, in the plan was not a security because Daniel had no choice as to participation, made no contribution other than his labor, and had no realistic expectation of profit at the time of plan entry in view of the 20-year service requirement for vesting. This was a rather narrow case and the courts have yet to speak on some of the broader issues.

The question of registration of pooled asset accounts maintained by banks and insurance companies for the investment of pension plan assets was largely resolved by the aforementioned amendments to Section 3(a)(2) of the 1933 act, which were proposed by interested banks and insurance companies. The amended Section 3(a)(2) exempts from registration bank collective trust funds and insurance company separate accounts maintained for the exclusive use of qualified pension, profit-sharing, and stock bonus plans. The justification for this broad exemption, which the SEC staff interprets to include interests of the plan participants themselves, is that these pooled investment vehicles are available only to plan trustees who are presumed to possess sufficient financial sophistication to assess the investment characteristics of the pooled funds. These unregistered funds are prohibited from dealing directly with the public. Pension plans may acquire shares in investment companies that offer their investment services to the general public, but such funds must be registered with the SEC and must comply with the Investment Company Act of 1940.

The amended Section 3(a)(2) also exempts any security arising out of a contract issued by an insurance company to qualified plans. This provision is broad enough to encompass guaranteed income contracts, annuity contracts, and any other security relating to an insurance company contract issued to an employee benefit plan.[32]

The SEC deems the interests of participants in voluntary, contributory Keogh plans and IRAs to be securities but does not require separate registration of the interests. Most such plans can rely on an exemption from registration for the offer

---

[31]99 S. Ct. 790, *International Brotherhood of Teamsters v. Daniel* (1979).
[32]SEC Release no. 33-6281 (January 15, 1981) (46 FR 8446).

and sale of employee interests. Securities acquired by these plans must meet the usual requirements of the 1933 act, no special exemptions being available.

Banking Laws

Pension plans that utilize the investment facilities of banks and trust companies may be affected by the laws and regulations pertaining to national banks, member banks of the Federal Reserve System (FRS), and members of the Federal Deposit Insurance Corporation (FDIC). These laws are administered by the Comptroller of the Currency, the Board of Governors of the FRS, and the FDIC, respectively. They are designed to ensure the general soundness of the banking system and the solvency of individual banks.

Pension plans deal primarily with the trust departments of commercial banks and trust companies and would tend to be most affected by the laws regulating the trustee functions of those institutions, including the investment of trust assets. Both the Federal Reserve authorities and the Comptroller of the Currency have issued regulations pertaining to collective trust funds, which are widely used by small- and medium-size plans for the investment of the total plan assets. Specialty collective trust funds are commonly used for a portion of the assets of larger funds, especially money market funds utilized for cash management. In combination with the securities laws administered by the SEC, these regulations are designed to ensure that collective trust funds are operated in a sound and equitable manner.

State Regulation

ERISA preempts state law with respect to most matters that directly apply to the operation of a pension plan. State laws that regulate banks, trust companies, and insurance companies are an exception to this preemption. Nevertheless, there may be overlapping jurisdiction in the investment of assets that fall into the DOL classification of "plan assets."

Trust Investments

All states have laws that regulate the investment of assets held in a fiduciary capacity. These laws tend to be rather restrictive and may limit investments to a so-called legal list of fixed-income instruments. The more enlightened laws prescribe standards to be observed and permit the fiduciary to acquire and hold any assets that fall within those standards. The laws of many states permit a portion of the assets to be invested in common stocks, sometimes under the discretion afforded by the prudent man test. In all states, these statutory restrictions can be set aside for trust assets by agreement if the trustee and the person or entity creating the trust agree. It is common practice for the parties to a pension trust agreement to waive the statutory restrictions and to confer on the trustee whatever discretion the grantor is willing to grant and the trustee is willing to accept. However, the plan trustee and any persons or institutions providing advice on how to invest or manage plan assets are fiduciaries under the plan and must conduct their investment operations in accordance with the federal prudent man standard enunciated in ERISA.

The common law of trusts, frequently codified in state statutes, requires that the assets of any given trust be held separate and apart from the assets of every other trust administered by the trustee and from the assets of the trustee itself. To provide greater diversification of risk and operating economies, most states have modified the common law doctrine to permit commingling of trust assets, at the direction of the trust grantors involved. The laws may provide for one commingled pool for small personal trusts and estates, generally called a *common trust fund* and required to observe a 10 percent limit on participation by one entity, and another such pool for employee benefit plans, called a *collective trust fund* and not restricted as to the amount of plan assets that may be placed in the pooled trust. Federal banking authorities have granted permission for the pooling of trust assets in respect of banks subject to their jurisdiction.

Insurance Company Investments

Investments of the general asset account of a life insurer are regulated by the laws of the state in which the company is domiciled and, if it does business in the state of New York, by the laws of that state. The standards vary greatly from state to state. The proportion of the general asset account that can be invested in common stocks is limited in most states, although beginning in the late 1980s the restrictions have been relaxed somewhat in a number of states, including New York. Indeed, investment restrictions in some important states have been relaxed enough to permit insurers to take advantage of new investment instruments, strategies, and markets and to pursue more aggressive investment policies. The general asset account of an insurer is not subject to ERISA's investment standards, since the assets therein are usually not regarded as plan assets.

Life insurer separate accounts are also subject to regulation by state insurance authorities, but they are free of the limits on common stock holdings and certain other strictures that apply to the general asset account. The assets in these accounts are regarded as plan assets by the Department of Labor and must be managed in accordance with federal prudence standards.

Investment Characteristics of Pension Plans

Pension plans have a number of distinctive characteristics that influence investment policies and strategies. These characteristics vary by sponsorship and type of plan. Thus it is useful to distinguish between defined benefit plans, which promise a determinable retirement benefit and usually commingle the plan assets, at least for active employees, and defined contribution plans, which make specific contributions on behalf of plan participants that accumulate, with investment earnings, in individual accounts, and whose benefits at retirement are then determined by the individual account balances.

Defined Benefit Plans

A dominant feature of the investment policy of a defined benefit plan is that the plan sponsor bears most of the investment risk. As noted earlier, ultimate contributions of the plan sponsor are reduced by investment earnings on the plan assets. Contributions are calculated initially on the assumption that plan assets will earn a certain rate of return. If the return is greater than assumed, future contributions will be smaller than anticipated. If the return is smaller than assumed, contributions will be greater. The amount of benefits payable to plan participants or their beneficiaries is not affected by investment experience, except in the event of plan termination, and only then under certain circumstances (see Chapters 33 and 34). It follows that a plan sponsor (employer or employers) can pursue riskier investment strategies without breaching its fiduciary obligations than if unsatisfactory investment results were going to diminish the benefits of the participants.

A second important feature of the investment environment is that the plan assets can be invested with a long time horizon. Corporate pension plans are usually established as permanent undertakings, and except in the case of employees near retirement, the obligations of the plan will not mature for many years. Thus investment managers have the option of ignoring short-term convolutions in the financial markets and concentrating on long-term results. Of course, the plan may have a strategy of active, aggressive asset management that would call for efforts to anticipate interest rate movements and short-term developments in the stock market. Moreover, the asset managers may feel that they are under pressure to show favorable performance (as compared with the performance of other managers) for each review period, which is sometimes as short as a calendar quarter. The point is that under normal circumstances the cash flow and liability characteristics of a plan provide investment managers with the latitude to pursue any strategies that seem to be called for, including investing for the long term.

A related characteristic is that under normal circumstances a plan has a positive cash flow and can invest its assets with only minimal regard for liquidity. Since the bulk of its obligations are deferred to the participants' retirement and then consist of income payments spread over the individual's remaining lifetime, and since contributions to finance the distant benefit payments are made throughout the employees' period of employment, large accumulations of assets are amassed. Current contributions, investment earnings on the plan assets, and maturing investments exceed benefit and expense disbursements for many years. There may be a minor need for liquid assets within each plan year because of the timing of cash flows (many employers make their contribution for the entire year at the end of the year, for example), but this need can be met through money market instruments. A contributory plan requires somewhat more liquidity than a non-contributory plan, since a terminating participant is entitled to a lump-sum refund of his or her contributions with interest. Plans that provide lump-sum death benefits and permit a cash-out of accrued benefits at retirement obviously need more liquidity than those without those features, but the payments can generally be made out of cash flow. An exception might occur with a small plan that has to make a large lump-sum settlement to a terminating or retiring employee. Another exception would be an old plan with few if any new entrants for the last several years. The plan population could become so mature that its benefit payments could exceed its income from all sources. Finally, a unique liquidity need would arise if the plan should be terminated and closed out through lump-sum distributions or the purchase of paid-up annuities for all active and retired employees.

Another significant investment characteristic of a qualified pension plan is that its investment earnings are exempt from federal income taxation. This is true not only of dividend and interest income but also of capital gains. This means that tax-exempt securities should not be attractive to a pension plan, since the lower yields usually associated with such securities have no offsetting tax advantage. Moreover, the plan need have no tax preference, as among dividend and interest income, realized gains and losses, and unrealized appreciation. A decision as to whether to invest in low-dividend growth stocks or higher-dividend securities with little growth potential need not be influenced by tax considerations, as it must be for tax-paying entities. Similarly, a decision to sell or hold a security with unrealized appreciation or depreciation can be made strictly on the basis of investment merit, since there is no tax effect from realizing the gain or loss. Despite this tax neutrality, it has been observed that most plans subject to public scrutiny are reluctant to realize losses, although such action might offer distinct investment advantages through asset redeployment.

A final characteristic is that the plan trustee need not distinguish between *principal* and *income* beneficiaries in the investment of plan assets and the allocation of investment earnings. The trustee of a personal trust must balance the conflicting interests of the trust beneficiaries who are to receive the current income and who naturally want to see the income maximized, even if the principal is jeopardized, and the parties—individuals or organizations—who are to receive the trust corpus upon termination of the trust. The dominant interest of the latter is to see the trust corpus preserved and even enhanced by investment in growth stocks and other assets that offer the potential of capital gains but may generate relatively low levels of income. In a pension plan, all trust beneficiaries are of the same class and, if the plan is of the defined benefit type, have no direct interest in or claim to the investment returns. This provides much more flexibility to the asset managers than if they had to deal with conflicting interests. In a contributory plan, the trustee may perceive a duty to invest employee contributions in a more conservative fashion than employer contributions, but that is a relatively minor consideration.

Defined Contribution Plans

In a defined contribution plan, the participants bear the investment risk, in that their ultimate benefits vary directly with the plan's investment results. The employer's contributions are not at all affected by the plan's investment experience, at least in the short run. The plan trustee invests the plan assets on behalf of the participants and may feel a keener sense of fiduciary responsibility than if it was investing for the employer's account. Whether the trustee in fact has a heavier fiduciary burden when investing for the accounts of individual participants has not been tested in the courts. As a practical matter, the trustee is more vulnerable to class action suits and to derivative and individual suits from disgruntled participants unhappy over investment performance.

There may be conflicts of interest among the plan participants comparable to those found in personal trust situations. There will almost certainly be differences among the participants' risk aversion and degree of financial sophistication. Participants nearing retirement may prefer a more conservative investment policy than those just entering the plan. Those who anticipate a lump-sum settlement may be more interested in preserving the book value of the assets than do those who expect to have their interests liquidated over a long period of time. Some plans accommodate these differing objectives by allowing each participant to allocate his or her own account balance among two or more investment funds with different objectives, such as an equity fund and a fixed-income fund.

Many individual account plans permit terminating or retiring employees to take their account balances in lump sums. This increases the liquidity requirements of the plan and may affect investment policy.

Investment Policy and Strategy

Many plans, especially larger ones, develop a statement of investment policy for the plan and communicate that policy to the managers of the plan assets. It is customary to review the policy regularly and to make whatever modifications seem appropriate in the light of economic and capital market developments. Not all plans have adopted a formal statement of investment policy, and some of the statements adopted have been rudimentary in scope and substance. Many sponsors delegate development of the investment policy to the trustee or insurer.

It is not sufficient that a statement of investment policy be developed, whether thoughtfully or purely for the record. The ways to accomplish the stated objectives must also be considered. Implementation of policy goes under the rubric of strategy. What follows in this section is not a comprehensive and theoretically rigorous treatment of investment policy and strategy but an outline of the factors that should be considered and some of the alternatives available—all described in nontechnical terms.[33]

Elements of Investment Policy

As a minimum, a statement of investment policy must have three components: a rate-of-return objective, acceptable risk parameters, and liquidity requirements. A fourth component, diversification, is frequently included in deference to the ERISA mandate that investments be diversified. The statement may also specify the types of investments that are to be included or excluded from the portfolio.

Rate-of-Return Objective

The rate-of-return objective may be stated in various ways. One is to state it in very general terms without quantification, for instance, to maximize the return consistent with the preservation of principal and the need for liquidity. Few could disagree with that formulation as a statement of principle, but it provides little guidance to the asset managers. Most statements attempt some quantification of

---

[33]The literature on investment policy and operations is voluminous, much of it highly technical and statistical in nature. Two very readable but authoritative books that can be consulted on various investment topics treated in this volume are Sidney Cottle et al., *Pension Asset Management: The Corporate Decisions* (New York: Financial Executives Research Foundation, 1980); and Arthur Williams III, *Managing Your Investment Manager* (Homewood, Ill.: Dow Jones–Irwin, 1980).

the return objective. The simplest, but perhaps least satisfactory, approach is to state the goal in terms of a specific nominal rate of return on the aggregate investment portfolio. This ignores the asset allocation formula as well as the projected rates of return on different types of investment instruments and in various sectors of the capital markets. This approach is sometimes refined by setting separate return objectives for the equity and fixed-income segments of the portfolio. A similar—and equally simplistic—approach is to set as a target an overall nominal rate of return equal to that assumed in the actuarial valuation of the plan's liabilities. This obviously should be the minimum aggregate rate of return over the long run but, under normal circumstances, it does not represent a challenging target to the investment managers.

A more enlightened and more common approach is to express the income goal in relative terms. For example, the target for the cash equivalent segment might be the index of returns on 90-day Treasury bills, which is designed to serve as a proxy for the risk-free return available to investors. The target for the equity portion of the portfolio might be the return on the Standard & Poor's 500 Composite Stock Index, while the target for the fixed-income segment might be the return on the S&P High-Grade Corporate Bond Index or the Salomon Brothers High-Grade Long-Term Bond Index (these indices and others are described in Chapter 30). Such goals would signal a willingness to accept investment results equal to that of the "market," which could be obtained from investment in appropriately structured stock and bond index funds with greater certainty and a lower outlay for investment management services. In the hopes of enjoying an incremental return from active portfolio management, many plans specify a return objective somewhat higher than that of the designated indexes, possibly 200 basis points (2 percent) higher for the equity and fixed-income segments of the portfolio, which, of course, entails greater risk.

A more sophisticated approach sometimes used is to establish a goal in terms of the anticipated return on a "benchmark" or baseline portfolio, reflecting a supposedly optimal mix of stock, bond, and short-term securities characterized by a particular risk/return relationship. The asset managers for the plan would participate in the construction of the baseline portfolio, an indexlike fund, which would reflect and be consistent with the plan's broad investment objective. Performance would be measured against this standard.

Finally, disheartened by years of *negative real* rates of return on pension portfolios, a plan sponsor may establish an objective of earning a *real* rate of return of a specified magnitude. Operationally, the policy statement would stipulate that the portfolio should be managed so that it produces a *nominal* rate of return of 2, 3, or 4 percent over and above the long-term rate of inflation. Alternatively, the goal might be stated in terms of an index, such as the S&P 500, which is assumed to reflect an inflation component.

Risk Tolerance

A second task of investment policy is to determine the amount of portfolio risk that the plan sponsor is willing to tolerate. Risk in connection with a common stock portfolio is generally viewed as the variation between actual return and expected return. Return variance may be due to broad economic forces, such as recession, unemployment, and inflation, which can cause unexpected results in the entire universe of common stocks, or it may be attributable to causes that are peculiar to the individual portfolio companies. The first type of variance is called *market* or *systematic* risk, while the second is generally referred to as *residual* risk, although it is sometimes known as *specific, nonmarket,* or *nonsystematic* risk.

The most common measure of systematic risk is "beta," which is a measure of the price volatility of a stock or entire portfolio in relation to the overall market, with Standard & Poor's Composite 500 Index generally being treated as a proxy for the market.

A beta of 1.0 signifies that the variability of return or riskiness of the portfolio is the same as that of the market—that volatility, up or down, in the market will be reflected in the portfolio. A beta of less than 1.0 indicates that the portfolio in general is less sensitive to broad economic forces than the market, while a beta of more than 1.0 indicates it is more sensitive than the market. By definition, this element of risk is endemic to investment and cannot be eliminated by diversification. Since systematic risk cannot be eliminated, economic theory postulates that an investor should be rewarded for assuming it. The expected systematic return of a portfolio is the portfolio beta times the expected market return.

That portion of the total variability or risk not explained by beta is termed *residual risk.* Residual risk is present in any portfolio that deviates from the market portfolio. Since this form of risk usually arises from an asset manager's making a "bet against the market" by holding a portfolio different from the market, it can be considered the risk of *active management.* One theory holds that in the aggregate there is no reward for assuming residual risk. This means that the positive incremental returns from the assumption of residual risk by successful active managers must be offset by negative relative returns of unsuccessful managers. Residual risk can be reduced through diversification and in fact can be effectively eliminated in an index fund.

The extent to which residual risk has been diversified away in a given stock portfolio is designated by R^2, the coefficient of determination. R^2 indicates the proportion of the total variance in a portfolio's return accounted for by market moves. A portfolio with an R^2 of 1.00 will have all of its variability explained by market movement. It would be perfectly diversified, as exemplified by an index fund. A portfolio with an R^2 of .90 will have 90 percent of its volatility explained by market forces.

Residual risk can be further subdivided into the risk of investment strategy (extra market covariance risk) and the risk of security selection (specific risk). Extra market covariance risk refers to the observed tendency for the returns on certain groups of securities to move in tandem, apart from overall market variability. For example, price changes of international oil stocks tend to move in a uniform direction, creating an element of nonmarket risk for a portfolio holding such securities. Other examples might include pharmaceutical stocks, consumer product stocks, and interest-sensitive stocks. Investment managers assume this form of risk when, for reasons of strategy, they overweight or underweight certain groups of securities with common characteristics, as compared with the weighting of these securities in the market portfolio. This risk element would be present, for example, if a particular group of securities made up 12 percent of a given port-folio, while on a capitalization basis that group constituted only 8 percent of the market portfolio.

Variability in return resulting from changes in the circumstances surrounding an individual firm exposes a portfolio holding stock of that firm to specific risk, the risk associated with selection or "stock picking." Examples of events that might affect the specific risk associated with the holding of the stock of a particular firm would be a change in management, a change in ownership (as through a merger or acquisition), a technological breakthrough by a major competitor, a prolonged work stoppage, and so on.

The relative importance of these various components of risk depends upon the body of assets involved. In terms of an individual stock, specific risk is the most important component, possibly accounting for more than half of the total risk, followed by systematic risk and extra market covariance, in that order. As the number of securities in a portfolio increases, the levels of extra market covariance and specific risk diminish from the diversification effect—the combining of stocks with varying risk characteristics that are negatively correlated. Thus for an entire portfolio, especially one assembled by an institutional investor, systematic risk is by far the dominant element, with extra market covariance and specific risk following in that order. As an extreme, the residual risk component is virtually eliminated from a well-designed index fund, leaving only market or systematic risk.

There is a theoretical relationship between risk and expected return at any given time that can be represented in optimal terms by an upward-sloping line (the efficient frontier) when risk is shown on the horizontal axis and return on the vertical axis. A plan sponsor can express portfolio objectives quantitatively by identifying the point along the efficient frontier at which it would like to have the common stock portfolio located. Its decision reflects its risk aversion. The more risk (volatility or beta) it is willing to assume, presumably the greater the expected return. The policy statement should indicate the common stock beta that the plan sponsor favors. This, of course, should be consistent with other elements of invest-ment policy, especially the rate-of-return objective for the entire pension portfolio. The statement might also quantify the degree of diversification sought by setting an R^2, or market correlation, target.

The beta and R^2 concepts are as relevant to fixed-income securities as they are to common stocks, but they are more difficult to implement. Fixed-income securities are subject to three basic types of risk: (1) credit risk or the risk of default (or delay) on principal and interest payments; (2) the risk of interest rate changes, which affect the market price of a fixed-income security and the rate at which cash flows can be reinvested; and (3) the risk of nonparallel changes in bond yield curves on both maturities and market sectors (e.g., Treasuries versus corporates), which could reduce (or enhance) the attractiveness of a given bond or portfolio of bonds.

Generally speaking, there is no systematic attempt to quantify the total risk associated with a portfolio of fixed-income securities. The credit risk of bonds and commercial paper is rated by a number of rating organizations. It is customary for the investment policy statement to speak to the quality of the fixed-income securi-ties that are to be held in the portfolio. The statement may set a quality floor below which the managers are not to venture, or it may designate a weighted-average quality rating as a general target or guideline.

Like common stock volatility, credit risk and a portion of interest rate risks can be reduced by judicious diversification. Likewise, the risk of nonparallel yield curve shifts can be reduced by diversifying the portfolio in market sector, quality, and maturity. Thus the policy statement may contain directions on diversification of the fixed-income portfolio. This would normally be done by specifying portfolio holding limits by issuer and issue. The statement may also set a duration target for the portfolio. (Duration is explained later in this chapter.)

Liquidity Requirements

As noted earlier, the typical pension plan has only minimal liquidity needs, which can usually be met out of the plan's cash management program. If there are any special liquidity needs, the asset managers should be alerted through an appropriate provision in the investment policy statement. If the asset managers are not constrained by liquidity considerations, the policy statement and instructions to the managers should so indicate.

Diversification

Many policy statements contain a reference to diversification, in part because of the explicit mandate in ERISA that the plan assets be diversified. Diversification is one method of attempting to achieve the three substantive objectives of portfolio management: acceptable return, preservation of principal, and adequate liquidity. Thus in a sense it is inappropriate to regard diversification as a goal of *investment policy*. It may be more properly regarded as a strategy consideration. In that regard, there is a trade-off between the stabilizing effect of diversification and the promise of higher risk-adjusted returns from more highly concentrated stock and bond selection. The diversification component of a policy statement may be no more than a generalized commitment to the principle, or it may contain specific guidelines as to diversification by types of assets, sectors, quality ratings, and the like.

Elements of Investment Strategy

Investment strategy is that complex of approaches, techniques, tools, and devices used to achieve the investment goals of the pension plan—as determined by the plan sponsor, trustee, and insurer. There are many factors to consider in developing an overall strategy for the investment of a pension plan portfolio, and the alternatives are becoming increasingly more complex and challenging. The major decisions involved in the implementation of any given investment policy are set out below, proceeding from the general to the specific.

Active Versus Passive Portfolio Management

The most fundamental decision is whether the portfolio will be actively or passively managed. Active portfolio management implies asset concentration, frequent trading, and risk-and-return objectives higher than those of the market portfolio. Passive management connotes a well-diversified portfolio with infrequent trading and market-level risk-and-return expectations. The ultimate in passive management is investment in index funds of various types, a subject treated in Chapter 30.

The common stock component of any institutionally managed portfolio has traditionally been actively managed. Implicit in this approach is the belief that at any given time some stocks are overpriced and some are underpriced in terms of the capital-asset pricing model. While the issues of some dominant blue-chip companies are sometimes held indefinitely, with little thought being given to their replacement, most portfolio companies are kept under periodic if not continual review to determine their suitability for retention, not only in absolute terms but in comparison with other issues available for acquisition. In a volatile business environment, a third or half of a common stock portfolio may turn over within a one-year period. In the process, the portfolio may become "unbalanced" in the sense that certain groups of stocks may be overweighted or underweighted, as compared with their representation in the market portfolio. This is an almost inevitable result of identifying underpriced and overpriced stocks and abandoning the concept of perfect diversification.

Until the mid-1960s, the bond component of an institutional portfolio was typically managed according to a different concept, characterized as *buy* and *hold*. In an era of low and stable interest rates, debt instruments of financially strong, well-entrenched corporations promised the preservation of capital, a modest but predictable cash flow, and ample liquidity. The only risk in holding a debt instrument was the probability of delay or default on payment of interest and principal, the so-called credit risk. With a normal, upward-sloping (as to maturity) yield curve, long-term debt instruments were attractive because of their higher yields. Long-term bonds—and the buy-and-hold strategy—seemed especially well suited to the needs of pension plans. The liabilities of the latter were expressed in nominal terms, were highly predictable, and were, on balance, long term in nature. Coupon income and the proceeds of maturing bonds were reinvested at prevailing interest rates that did not vary much from year to year. If the plan sponsor was dissatisfied with the long-term bond yields available, it could seek higher returns through investment in common stocks.

The profound changes in the capital market interest rate structure that accompanied the virulent inflation of the late 1960s and 1970s wrought drastic changes in the investment characteristics of fixed-income securities, especially long-term bonds. Spiraling interest rates for all maturities produced a general decline in the prices of all outstanding debt securities, the sharpest declines being associated with the longest maturities. While coupon payments and proceeds of maturing securities could be reinvested at the higher interest rates, the bulk of the bond portfolio could not be switched to higher-yielding securities without unacceptably large capital losses. Inflation was eroding the purchasing power of the coupon payments to such an extent that the *real* return on bond investments turned negative. In the meantime, the benefit obligations of pension plans were beginning to assume real, as opposed to nominal, character as they kept pace with inflation through final-averagesalary formulas and ad hoc cost-of-living adjustments for retired participants. These concurrent developments focused attention on the need for a *real* return on the pension portfolio and a strategy that would produce such a result.

By 1970 active bond management was well on the way to supplanting the buy-and-hold philosophy. It was developed more as a response to unprecedentedly *volatile* interest rates than to unprecedentedly *high* interest rates. Sharp and rapid changes in the level and structure of interest rates create opportunities as well as challenges for bond managers. While active bond managers rely on a number of stratagems and techniques to achieve better results than those of an unmanaged portfolio, success depends primarily on the ability to forecast future interest rate movements. There is little evidence that any manager can do so consistently. Nevertheless, there is a widespread belief that active bond managers as a group will over time outperform the long-term market indices on a cumulative basis.

In-House Versus External Management of Portfolio

The plan sponsor must decide whether the pension plan assets are to be managed "in-house"—by the financial staff of the plan sponsor—or by outside money managers. In the early days of pension programs, there was a natural tendency for the plan sponsor to invest the pension plan assets within the organization. As the industry grew and the asset accumulations became sizable, banks, trust companies, insurance companies, and investment counseling firms developed special staffs and facilities to manage the assets, and external management became common. Today an overwhelming proportion of the vast accumulation of pension assets is managed by professional money managers.

However in response to the mounting sums paid to outside firms for investment services and the unimpressive performance of the investment community over the last decade or so,[34] more and more firms are evaluating the situation, and many have taken some or all of the pension portfolio management back in-house. Another response to the same phenomenon is to place some or all of the plan assets in an index fund or funds. A significant number of large plan sponsors perform cash management services for their pension plans with the staff that performs that corporate function.

Allocation of Assets

A third strategy decision that must be made or affirmed at each meeting of the pension investment committee or similar body is whether to allocate assets among (1) cash or cash equivalents (instruments with original or remaining maturity of less than one year), (2) intermediate and long-term fixed-income instruments, and (3) equities, predominantly common stocks and real estate holdings. In some respects, this is the most challenging investment decision that the plan sponsor must make, and it must continually be reevaluated as the economic and financial outlook changes. It involves a judgment about the relative investment merits of

---

[34]In any given period, a substantial percentage of investment managers fail to match the performance of the market indices, and very few *consistently* outperform the market when transaction costs and management fees are taken into account.

equities and fixed-income securities over the near term under a projected economic scenario. Cash and cash equivalents provide flexibility in investment decision making and a hedge against unforeseen developments. They maximize liquidity and minimize the risk of principal loss. Of course, they may be held for their own investment merit, as in recent years when they outperformed every other category of investment. A common reason for holding cash equivalents today is to enable the plan sponsor to postpone an allocation decision until it can be made with increased insight and confidence. Under "normal economic circumstances," with a normal yield curve, cash and cash equivalents will be held primarily for market-timing purposes.

At present, a typical allocation of assets might be 10 percent in cash equivalents, 30 percent in intermediate and long-term bonds, and 60 percent in equities. An alternative approach is to make a basic allocation between equity and fixed-income managers and let them decide how much "cash" to hold. A 60-40 split between equities and fixed is common. Some plans allocate all the assets to equities, realizing that some proportion will be held in cash equivalents at any given time, while others want all assets in debt securities, even obligations of the federal government or its agencies.

An adjustment in the asset allocation can be accomplished through transactions and through the channeling of cash flow. The latter is the preferred method, if it can accomplish the purpose, since one set of transaction costs can be avoided. Depending upon the time available, a major shift in allocation may have to be carried out through dispositions and new acquisitions.

There is a difference in philosophy with respect to distortions in the allocation formula produced by market action. For example, a decision may be made to hold 60 percent of the portfolio assets in equities at a time when somewhat less than that percentage is in that form. What if a bull market develops and the *market value* of *existing* equity holdings causes the proportion to rise to 65 or 70 percent of the total portfolio? Some plan sponsors take the position that under such circumstances no part of current cash flow should be allocated to the equity component as long as it exceeds the specified target, but that no holdings should be disposed of to bring the allocation back into balance. Others would instruct the equity managers to sell enough stock to restore the target ratio, on the theory that this form of discipline ensures that some of the gains associated with the market rise will be captured.

The asset allocation may extend beyond the broad divisions discussed above and may direct assets into various sectors of the capital markets. Typically, however, sector decisions are left to the asset managers, since they are paid to exercise their judgment on such matters.

Choice of Sector and Quality

The capital markets are stratified into various sectors and subsectors, each of which issues securities of varying quality. The fixed-income market sectors generally recognized are transport, telephone, utility, financial, industrial, and government (including agencies). Aggregations of common stocks, such as Standard & Poor's Composite 500 Index, and those listed on the New York Stock Exchange, are also broken down into a number of sectors by industry. Portfolio managers typically spread their investments among sectors in order to lessen extra market covariance.

Fixed-income securities and common stocks are classified by their investment characteristics, which may strongly influence the terms on which they are traded in the capital markets. Bonds and commercial paper are rated by such organizations as Moody's and Standard & Poor's, which publish the quality ratings according to certain standardized classifications. Asset managers and brokerage houses may, for internal purposes, classify common stocks by their investment characteristics, such as growth, income, speculative possibilities, and so on.

There are yield differentials among fixed-income securities that reflect sector, quality, maturity, call feature, and so on, and from time to time these differentials spread in such a manner as to create trading or swapping opportunities for capital gains or higher yields. Likewise, the attractiveness of a common stock issue in the marketplace may change overnight with an unfavorable development or a disappointing earnings report. For these and other reasons, allocation of assets by sector, quality, and so forth is generally left to the asset managers who can be expected to follow financial developments closely and act promptly when circumstances require.

Maturity Spacing

The question of maturity spacing is unique to fixed-income instruments. It is a function of that most difficult of all investment exercises—predicting future interest rate behavior and the term structure of interest rates. If the asset manager concludes that interest rates for intermediate and long-term bonds are going to rise, he or she will want to hold most of the fixed-income portfolio in cash or cash equivalents to minimize the effects of price erosion and to maximize the quantity of assets available to "go long" near the peak of the interest rate climb (price decline). A portion of the portfolio may be allocated to other maturities as a partial hedge against a forecasting error. If intermediate and long-term interest rates are expected to decline, the portfolio manager will want to "lock in" the existing yields and maximize capital gains by committing most of the portfolio to long-term bonds, unless it thinks that the interest rate decline is only temporary and that rates will shortly soar to new heights.

Some bond portfolio managers, as a hedge against unpredictable interest rate behavior, utilize a "laddered" approach—allocating assets in some systematic fashion, possibly proportionally, to various available maturities. This approach sacrifices the probability of great gains from a major commitment to the "right" maturity (in retrospect) and avoids the probability of a serious loss from a bad timing decision. It is also useful in meeting any liquidity needs of the pension plan. The same objectives can be pursued by applying the immunization concept. Maturity spacing and other timing decisions are generally left to the fixed-income managers.

Selection and Trading of Securities

The most specific and operational phase of investment strategy is the selection and trading of the portfolio securities. In a sense, it is the "bottom line" of the whole operation. It must be carried out within the framework of the broader policy and strategy decisions examined above. The asset managers select the securities to be acquired or sold and normally execute the trades. In some situations, depending upon the nature of the asset manager(s) and the entire investment apparatus, the trades may be executed by a master trustee upon instructions from the asset manager. The *timing* of purchases and sales is a critical element of portfolio management and is the responsibility of the asset manager or managers. How well this function is carried out has a vital bearing on the overall performance of the investment manager.

Nontraditional Investment Objectives

Various groups have sought to have pension plan assets invested in a manner that will promote certain economic, social, and political goals, some of which are in conflict with the traditional objective of maximizing return within acceptable risk levels. These interest groups are diverse in nature—they include labor unions, church organizations, state and local governments, and ethnic constituencies—and their goals are diverse.

The American Federation of Labor and Congress of Industrial Organizations and certain of its constituent international unions are on record as favoring the investment of "union" pension funds in ways intended to create jobs, promote unionism, provide housing, and increase the pool of funds for mortgage lending. By and large, organized labor takes the position that pension assets are "owned" by the plan participants (since they represent deferred wages) and should be invested in a manner that supports their general welfare and, as a minimum, does not directly conflict with their interests. Labor argues that its general investment goals can be achieved with little or no loss of investment return; but some international unions, the Teamsters union being one, advocate investing pension funds below market rates for certain purposes, especially for residential mortgages.

Various church groups, working through the Interfaith Center for Corporate Responsibility, oppose investing pension funds (and other institutional portfolios, such as university endowments) in companies that produce socially questionable goods (e.g., liquor and tobacco products), engage in certain marketing practices in Third World countries, have discriminatory employment practices (against women and African-Americans, in particular), or manufacture certain military equipment (especially nuclear components).

Many state and local government officials favor investing the assets of their public employee retirement systems in ways that will stimulate the local economy, rebuild inner cities, reduce borrowing costs, and achieve other local goals. Several states have modified their investment statutes to make it lawful for public retirement systems to respond to some of these capital needs. New York City provides a dramatic example of the use of retirement system assets to help solve a particular problem: not long ago the city retirement systems were asked to purchase a special issue of New York City bonds of questionable investment merit.

Corporations sometimes employ the assets of their pension plans to achieve corporate goals that are only tenuously related to the interests of the plan participants.

An example is the use of plan assets to purchase outstanding common stock of the plan sponsor to ward off a takeover by another corporation.

Whether the assets of pension plans should be invested to achieve these collateral goals involves a number of issues. The first is where legal and beneficial ownership of the plan assets lies and what authority should attend such ownership. A second issue is whether ancillary investment objectives should be pursued only if they do not conflict with the primary investment objectives, or whether they should be followed even if they involve a potential reduction in yield or an increase in risk. If there is a known or potential cost, a third issue is which party will bear the direct loss and whether there are to be any cost trade-offs. A fourth issue is how will decisions be made about the nontraditional goals that will be pursued and at what cost to the parties involved. A fifth issue is whether ancillary investment goals are compatible with the prudent man standard and with the ERISA mandate that the plan assets be employed for the sole and exclusive benefit of the plan participants and their beneficiaries.

The answer to some of these questions is known. Legal title to the plan assets is vested in the plan trustee (or insurer, if no trustee is used), while the equitable title (or beneficial ownership) is shared by all the plan participants and their beneficiaries. The legal relationships are similar to those of an irrevocable personal trust. The plan sponsor relinquishes title to its contributions the moment they are paid to the trustee or insurer, and it can recover them, with certain minor exceptions, only if the plan is terminated and the accumulated plan assets are more than adequate to satisfy all claims against the plan. No plan participant or beneficiary has legal claim to any particular plan assets. Participants and beneficiaries have certain claims, ripened or unripened, against the plan as a legal entity and thus fall into the creditor classification. The status of plan assets under defined contribution individual account plans may be different, but the question of nontraditional investments is largely, if not entirely, confined to defined benefit plans.

Under a defined benefit plan, the plan sponsor is the primary risk bearer. It commits itself to contribute whatever sums are needed, along with investment earnings, to provide all benefits that accrue under the plan. Earnings on the plan assets are a direct offset to the plan sponsor's contributions, and any change in investment policy or strategy that would reduce that stream of income to the plan would have to be made up by additional contributions. Since the plan sponsor can normally deduct its pension contributions for federal income tax purposes, it follows that taxpayers as a body bear much of the cost of an investment policy that diminishes the rate of return on plan assets. If the plan continues indefinitely, the plan sponsor and the general body of taxpayers absorb any cost of a nontraditional investment policy. If the plan were to terminate with inadequate assets because of diminished investment income, the Pension Benefit Guaranty Corporation would sustain the initial loss but would ultimately recoup the loss from the sponsor or through higher premium payments from other sponsors of defined benefit plans. In some cases the loss of investment income would fall upon plan participants whose benefit claims exceed the amount insured by the PBGC.

Clearly, the parties who stand to lose from a course of action that would impair the flow of income to pension plans—plan sponsors, plan participants, taxpayers, and the general corporate community—should have something to say about whether such a course is to be pursued. In theory, an employer could negotiate a curtailment of benefits, a wage cut or freeze, or some other type of trade-off in exchange for its willingness to forgo some investment income through targeted investments. Under collectively bargained multiemployer plans, employees have a voice, weak though it may be, in investment policy through union representatives on the joint board of trustees. The only way that taxpayers and other plan sponsors (which support the PBGC) can make their voices heard on this issue is through the legislative process.

The Department of Labor, which has the primary responsibility under ERISA for safeguarding the interests of plan participants and beneficiaries, has not provided much guidance on this delicate issue. It has reaffirmed the primacy of the interests of plan participants and beneficiaries. On the other hand, the DOL has endorsed the concept of targeted investments of a social nature if such investments do not adversely affect earnings or the level of risk. The DOL distinguishes between "exclusionary" and "inclusionary" investment policies, finding the former acceptable if it does not unduly restrict the pool of eligible investments and the latter objectionable because it may become too restrictive, making it difficult to achieve proper diversification and a proper balance among investment criteria. In a nutshell, the DOL's present position seems to be that socially motivated and regionally focused investments are in conflict with the congressional mandate that pension plans be managed for the sole and exclusive benefit of plan participants and their beneficiaries if they reduce portfolio earnings or increase portfolio risk. It interposes no objection to the consideration of social and related benefits in choosing among investment alternatives that satisfy the prudence standard and other traditional criteria. It is worth noting that if a proposed investment meets standard criteria for risk and expected return, there is no special benefit to the socially desired project. If the capital market functions the way it is supposed to, socially desirable projects can gain only at the expense of present and prospective pensioners or of all plans through the operations of the PBGC. It seems likely that the twin issues of who shall control pension plan assets and how they are to be invested will continue to be debated over the next decade or so.[35]

---

[35]For a comprehensive and rigorous analysis of the issues involved in the broad topic, see Dan M. McGill, ed., *Social Investing of Pension Plan Assets* (Homewood, Ill.: Richard D. Irwin, 1984).

Chapter 30
Management of Pension Plan Assets: Operations

Pension plans invest in a wide array of tangible and intangible assets. Under the prudent man concept and the current philosophy of judging investment performance in terms of the total portfolio, rather than its individual components, there are few *classes* of assets that are not suitable for a pension plan portfolio. Trustees are generally freed of the strictures of fiduciary investment statutes, and the separate accounts of life insurers offer a variety of investment approaches. Competition among investment managers and the desire of plan sponsors to hold portfolio assets that will outperform inflation (and hence produce a real return) have broadened the search for productive investments and boosted the tolerance of plan sponsors to investment risk and unconventional holdings.

Forms of Investment

Despite periodic publicity concerning various "exotic" investment opportunities, the great bulk of pension plan portfolios remain invested in common stocks, intermediate and long-term bonds, money market instruments, group annuity contracts, and other conventional investments. Modest percentages may be found in real estate equity and mortgages, oil and natural gas properties, collectibles, options, futures contracts, foreign securities, and other innovative investment opportunities believed to offer the prospect of higher-than-average returns.

Common Stocks

Since common stocks have historically offered a higher rate of return than fixed-income securities, they have occupied a prominent place in the portfolios of most pension plans over the last 25 to 30 years. Many plans have a long-term program of holding at least half of their assets in common stocks. There is a broadly held opinion that in the long run common stocks will outperform inflation, giving the plan a real rate of return. That faith is shaken from time to time by depressed conditions in the common stock market, but many plan sponsors believe that in the long run common stocks will outperform fixed-income securities. Some plan sponsors are committed to 100 percent investment in common stocks, except for cash equivalents held for market-timing purposes. At the other extreme, some plans have never invested in common stocks, relying entirely on fixed-income securities, sometimes only obligations of the federal government or its agencies.

Intermediate and Long-Term Debt Instruments

Along with common stocks, intermediate and long-term debt instruments (especially long-term bonds) have served as the foundation of pension plan portfolios. If call or refunding features are not exercised, long-term bonds offer the chance of locking up a high level of steady cash flow for the life of the bond, as well as an opportunity to garner extraordinary capital gains if interest rates decline. Furthermore, long-duration bonds may be used to immunize pension liabilities for relatively long periods, as discussed later in this chapter. These bonds may become less attractive in periods of volatile and rising interest rates.

Intermediate bonds, especially those in the 4- to 10-year maturity range, are more appealing to investors than long-term bonds during periods of high and gyrating interest rates. Their price is less volatile than longer-term bonds, and they offer more stable income than the short-term alternative. Some of these bonds have been issued with very low or zero interest coupons to reduce or eliminate the coupon reinvestment risk. Such bonds are issued at a substantial discount, the purchase price determining the yield to maturity date of the bond, which sometimes extends as far as 30 years. Some bonds of this type permit the issuer to call, or the holder to redeem, the bond at par at specified intervals. Called "extendibles," these bonds, if called or redeemed, are usually reissued at current coupon rates, the intent and effect being to make them variable coupon bonds, protecting both the issuer and investor against adverse changes in the interest structure.

Most corporate debt instruments are publicly traded and hence are marketable—at a price. Many plans hold some privately placed securities, directly or through participation in pools of such instruments managed by insurance companies or banks. Private debt instruments usually command a somewhat higher yield than comparable public debt, partly because of limited marketability. The limited marketability of privately placed debt instruments is partly offset by a more rapid and systematic return of cash to the investor through scheduled interest and principal (sinking-fund) payments.

Pension plans also hold sizable quantities of debt issued by the federal government or its agencies. Much of the debt is represented by Treasury bills or certificates, but some is in Treasury notes and bonds. The major appeal of government debt instruments is that they carry no risk (no default risk) and they are liquid. Their liquidity is heightened by the very active futures market that utilizes Treasury issues as the underlying or deliverable securities.

Some pension plans have acquired holdings in the foreign bond market. Bonds issued by foreign governments or business concerns may be denominated in dollars or in foreign currencies. American pension plan sponsors have been primarily interested in Eurobonds and Yankee bonds. Eurobonds are bonds issued by one country in a second country and denominated in the currency of a third country, usually the United States. Yankee bonds are dollar-denominated bonds issued by foreign concerns and registered with the Securities and Exchange Commission for sale in the United States. These foreign bonds appeal to some portfolio managers as a way of achieving greater diversification of risk and earning a superior return because of perceived inefficiencies in the foreign bond market. Some plans prefer bonds denominated in selected foreign currencies to have an opportunity of gains from currency fluctuations. (Of course, there is also the chance of loss from currency fluctuations.)

Short-Term Debt Instruments

In recent years, short-term debt instruments, those with maturities of less than one year, have been significant components of many pension plan portfolios. Domestic short-term debt instruments are issued by corporations, financial institutions, and the federal government. Collectively these are referred to as money market instruments.

U.S. Treasury bills, generally 90 days or 6 months in maturity, are auctioned each week. T-bills, as they are generally known, are quoted on a discounted basis, with selected government security dealers essentially bidding for an effective yield. They provide no interest payments but at maturity pay a lump sum at par value.

A variety of short-term instruments can be purchased from banks. Certificates of deposit (CDs) are receipts for short-term time deposits in a bank, which may be issued in negotiable or nonnegotiable form.[1] Interest and principal are generally paid in a lump sum at maturity. CDs normally mature in one to five years. Some pension plans buy dollar-denominated CDs from European banks or European branches of American banks, which yield a slight margin over domestic CDs because of reserve requirement differentials and different risk perceptions. Some plans buy CDs payable in foreign currencies to take advantage of currency fluctuations. Most CDs are issued at fixed interest rates, but some longer-term CDs of both the domestic and Eurodollar variety are offered on a floating rate basis.

Bankers' acceptances are time drafts drawn on a bank by a customer to be used to settle a domestic or international commercial transaction. The bank accepts the draft for a fee and honors it at maturity, thus substituting its credit for the customer's credit. The bank is reimbursed by the customer for assuming its obligation. The bank, which will collect the trade debt from its customer at the maturity of the time draft, may retain the instrument as an earning asset or may realize cash on the instrument before its due date by offering it for sale in the secondary market at the going discount rate for the period involved. Bankers' acceptances generally sell at a slight risk premium above the T-bill or CD rate.

In a repurchase agreement (a REPO), the purchaser, normally an institutional investor, acquires ownership of a debt security and the seller, usually a security dealer, agrees at the time of the sale to repurchase the obligation at a mutually agreed upon time and price, thereby determining the yield during the purchaser's holding period.[2] This results in a fixed rate of return insulated from market fluctuations during the period. Any security can serve as the basis of the repurchase

---

[1]Nonnegotiable CDs are usually issued in amounts not exceeding $100,000. They are attractive to many small pension plans because in those amounts they are fully insured by the Federal Deposit Insurance Corporation.

[2]Many people describe a repurchase agreement as a loan from the investor (purchaser) collateralized by the underlying security. The distinction between a purchase and a collateralized loan can be significant in case of the seller's default or bankruptcy.

agreement, but T-bills and GNMA certificates are generally used. If the seller defaults on its promise to repurchase the security, the purchaser can sell the security to other investors. The risk to the purchaser is that its recovery under the transaction will be less than it would have been under the repurchase agreement, because of a decline in the market price of the underlying security and legal costs involved in enforcing its rights. Repurchase agreements are usually for short periods, such as one week or even one day, but they may be longer. REPOs of 15 or fewer days' duration are characterized as "short" and those of 16 or more days' duration are termed "long." Reverse REPOs are agreements under which lending institutions themselves borrow from security dealers or other institutions by means of a sale and repurchase of a particular security.

Many large corporations, including financial institutions, raise money in the capital market by selling their negotiable, short-term unsecured promissory notes, known as commercial paper. Creditworthy firms avail themselves of this source of funds in lieu of more expensive bank loans. The paper is usually sold at a higher rate than that payable by T-bills, but lower than the prime rate of banks. Maturities run from 30 to 270 days. Moody's and Standard & Poor's rate the credit quality of this commercial paper, using three investment grade classifications.

Predictably, in a portfolio of short-term debt instruments, maturities produce a high rate of turnover. As each instrument matures, it is usually replaced by another of short-term maturity. The yield on the portfolio reflects recent and current capital market conditions and may fluctuate substantially, unlike the current yield on a portfolio of long-term bonds. But the fluctuation in yield of a short-term portfolio has only a minimal effect on market values, particularly if the portfolio is limited to instruments having a remaining maturity of 90 days or less. The instruments themselves are generally marketable, with only minimal risk of capital losses. Such a portfolio is well suited to a defined contribution plan that seeks to provide participants both liquidity and preservation of principal. It is also useful as a temporary haven for pension assets when the manager is awaiting more favorable investment opportunities in stocks or bonds.

A number of major banks have established collective trust funds invested in money market instruments. These funds are used both for regular investment of a portion of the portfolio and as a temporary investment to facilitate cash management. All cash in the trust—which originates from contributions, investment income, and sale of securities—may be swept into the money market fund daily to be kept there temporarily until it is permanently invested, in order to keep the trust assets fully invested at all times. Other banks use money market mutual funds for this purpose.

Historically, long-term debt instruments have typically provided a higher return than short-term instruments. At various times, notably during the 1980s, however, an "inverted" yield curve has prevailed, meaning that short-term investments of the types described above have generally yielded higher rates of return than those available from longer-term, and thus presumably riskier, investments. Investment in these instruments also provided a "safe harbor" for principal in periods of high market volatility and protected the plan against the price hazards of taking a "long" position in the debt sector before interest rates had peaked. In periods of high short-term interest rates, this "hedge" against interest rate volatility costs the investor little or nothing in forgone returns. Of course, the investor takes the risk of matching long-term liabilities with assets having short-term maturities. Many plans hold a fourth or third of their portfolio in these short-term debt instruments, and some have at times had all their money invested in that manner.

Real Estate Investments

Real estate equity investments became popular during the 1960s and 1970s, stimulated by rising real estate values and the success of certain real estate pools of life insurers. This was somewhat reversed in the 1980s and early 1990s because of illiquidity and market downturn. Money may be placed in specific real estate properties (frequently through limited partnerships) or in real estate pools managed by life insurers, banks, and trust companies. The great preponderance of pension plan real estate equity investments, which still constitute a relatively small percentage of total pension assets available for investment, is in commercial properties—office buildings, industrial parks, and shopping centers. Some investment managers are touting investment in farmland and farm properties, offering their management services for such properties.

A growing (but still small) percentage of pension plan assets is invested in real estate mortgages. These investments tend to be concentrated in large commercial properties. Some insurance companies offer separate accounts for mortgages, and the general account of insurance companies often includes substantial mortgage investments. In many quarters there is a strong interest in channeling pension funds into residential mortgages to stimulate the housing industry and to relieve the growing shortage of living accommodations. Legislation has been introduced into Congress from time to time to force pension plans to invest a stipulated percentage of their assets in residential mortgages, possibly at interest rates below the market. As might be expected, building contractors, materials suppliers, mortgage bankers, and organized labor—especially the building trades unions—have supported such legislation, none of which has been enacted yet.

Pension plans have been reluctant to go into individual residential mortgages because of the administrative problems involved in originating and servicing the mortgages. They have also wished to be insulated against direct dealings with borrowers, especially their own plan members. Some plans have been attracted to pass-through certificates of participation in government-insured pools of residential mortgages or bonds backed by such mortgage pools. These certificates or bonds offer yields somewhat higher than those available from competing investments and minimize the administrative problems, but they lack marketability, which accounts for the higher yield. As noted earlier, the Department of Labor has tacitly approved investment in these mortgage pools and has issued a regulation designed to encourage investment in the pools. Real estate investments in general tend to be illiquid and cannot prudently dominate a plan's portfolio.

Leased Property

Some pension plans purchase or acquire tangible assets of various sorts and then lease them to industrial and commercial users. Examples of assets acquired for the purpose of leasing include offshore drilling rigs, aircraft, and railroad rolling stock. These arrangements are usually subject to approval by the IRS (via private letter rulings), since the leasing or rental income might otherwise be subject to taxation as unrelated business income. As mentioned in Chapter 27, some airlines have made their pension plan contributions in the form of aircraft, which they subsequently leased back from the plan. The investment return on these leasing activities of pension plans has generally been much higher than that on more traditional investments.

Tangible Personal Property

When it became apparent during the 1970s that common stocks once again were not a satisfactory hedge against inflation, except inflation with a long lag, investment managers began searching for assets with the potential to appreciate in value at a greater rate than the rate of inflation. This search led to so-called collectibles—tangible personal property such as precious metals, jewelry, oriental rugs, art objects, coin and stamp collections, and antiques of various kinds. Enterprising dealers sometimes assembled pools of such items and offered shares in the pools. Other dealers offered individual items as investments. Some pension plans invested a small portion of their portfolio in these objects in the interest of diversification and as a modest hedge against inflation. When the prices of many collectibles declined and their tax treatment changed adversely,[3] pension plans seemed less interested in them.

Options and Interest Rate Futures Contracts

During the 1980s, pension plan sponsors became interested in *options* and *futures*, two risk-management vehicles that serve the same general purpose for pension plan sponsors. An option is the right to buy or sell a security at a specified price (the "striking" price) during a stipulated period, generally not exceeding one year. The right to buy is a *call* option, while the right to sell is a *put* option. A call option is purchased when the investor believes that the price of the security will rise, whereas a put option is purchased when he or she believes that the price of the security will decline. A put can be used to lock in a portion of an unrealized capital gain on a portfolio holding, whereas a call gives the investor an opportunity to realize a capital gain in an up market with a minimum investment of funds. Thus an option can be viewed as a hedge or as a speculation. An investor may *sell* call options against certain securities in its own portfolio ("covered" call options), realizing earnings from the option price at the risk of giving up some capital gains, or it may buy a put as a hedge against sustaining some capital losses. The options market is not only highly developed but also complex and sophisticated.

When authorized and disposed to use options, pension portfolio managers generally write (sell) calls and buy puts against certain of their equity holdings as a means of

---

[3]If the investment of individual accounts under a defined contribution plan is individually directed, for tax purposes investment of such individual accounts in collectibles is generally treated as though the investment had been distributed to the participant; this effectively precludes collectibles from individually directed accounts. IRC §408(m).

reducing the variability of returns or earning incremental returns. Such portfolios are sometimes considered bond substitutes because they are expected to show returns that are 30 to 40 percent less variable than a common stock portfolio without giving up all of the potential excess return. Options may also be written in the course of liquidating positions in individual stocks, or they may be written in the expectation that the underlying security will not be "called" away (i.e., the option will expire unexercised, the option premium serving as incremental income).[4] It remains to be seen whether the Barings bankruptcy will lead pension plan sponsors to move away from options.

The futures market originally developed to serve the needs of suppliers and users of various types of commodities. The concept has been adapted to fixed-income securities as a mechanism for reducing the impact of anticipated interest rate changes on a bond portfolio.

Futures trading takes place in certain standardized securities, namely, long-term U.S. Treasury bonds, GNMA modified pass-through mortgage-backed securities, 90-day T-bills, and 90-day commercial paper. A futures contract *sale* obligates the seller to deliver a specified amount of one of the foregoing types of instruments (as specified in the contract) at a specified future time and at a specified price. A futures contract *purchase* obligates the buyer to take delivery of the specified instrument at a specified future time at a specified price. Although futures contracts by their terms call for the actual delivery or acceptance of securities, it is customary for the contract to be closed out before the settlement date by an offsetting transaction, without actual delivery or receipt of the securities. Thus closing out a futures contract *sale* is effected by the original seller entering into a futures purchase contract for the same aggregate amount of the stipulated security and the same delivery date. If the price in the sale exceeds the price in the offsetting purchase, the seller realizes a gain. If the sale price is less than the offsetting purchase price, the seller sustains a loss on the transaction. A *purchase* contract is settled by an offsetting *sale* contract.

When commodity futures contracts are traded, both buyer and seller are required to post margins with the brokers handling their transactions as security for the performance of their undertakings to buy and sell and to offset losses in their trades due to daily fluctuations in the market. The *initial* margin, posted at the time of the trade, is in the nature of a good-faith deposit, and must not be smaller than the minimum amount specified for that size and type of transaction by the commodity exchange through which the trade was made. The broker may permit certain customers to deposit Treasury bills or other securities, rather than cash, as margin. The traded security is marked to market daily, and the "loser" must post an additional margin with the broker equal to the change in market value. Called the *variation* margin, this deposit is always made in cash.

Since the only current commitment of funds is that involved in the maintenance of the required margins, futures transactions are highly leveraged. Consequently, any movement in the market price of the leveraged security produces a disproportionate immediate gain or loss to the investor. The risk of loss can be minimized if

---

[4]For a comprehensive treatment of options, see Lawrence G. McMillan, *Options as a Strategic Investment* (New York: New York Institute of Finance, 1980).

futures contract sales are restricted to those made against existing portfolio hold-ings. This practice treats the futures contract as a hedge rather than a speculation.

Futures contract *sales* are made when the owner of the securities believes that interest rates may rise, while *purchase* contracts are entered into when the buyer believes that interest rates may decline. If futures operations are not used (or cannot be used), a portfolio manager, expecting an interest rate rise and wishing to position the portfolio to take advantage of the change, would shorten the maturity structure of the portfolio and then reverse the move when the interest rate rise appeared to reach its peak. With a normal yield curve, this type of portfolio shift would cost the portfolio income during the time the proceeds were being held in short-term instruments, and large transactions costs would be in-curred. With a futures market and the assumption that yield differentials in the "cash market" among various securities will continue at approximately the same levels in the near term, the same general objective could be achieved by agreeing to sell a particular type of security or securities at some specified future date. Futures contracts can also be used to smooth the commitment of funds to the capital markets when cash flows, principally contributions, are excessively uneven.

Foreign Securities

As mentioned earlier, pension portfolio managers are often interested in the bonds of foreign governments and foreign business firms. There is parallel interest in the common stock of foreign corporations, especially those in Western Europe and Japan, that have an aggregate dollar value greater than that of the common stock in U.S. corporations. Extending the geographical boundaries for investment activities expands the universe of available securities, affording an opportunity to earn higher returns, achieve a broader diversification of risk, and capture foreign exchange gains from strong currencies. These potential advantages of foreign investing must be evaluated against the additional risk of currency fluctuations.

If selected in accordance with normal investment criteria, foreign investments do not violate the prudence standard of the Employment Retirement Income Security Act. The more prevalent the practice becomes among pension plan investors, the more consistent it will be with the ERISA definition of prudence, which is a relative rather than absolute standard.

Valuation of Assets

The basis used for valuing the assets of a pension plan has both operational and public policy implications. The value placed on the assets has an effect on the funding standard account and the required contributions to the plan. To measure portfolio performance on a total return basis, it is necessary to find a consistent and uniform method of determining asset values. A realistic basis of asset valuation is also needed to disclose of the financial condition of the plan to its participants, the business community, and the regulatory agencies. The basis of valuation may depend upon the purpose for which the valuation is being made.

Assets are valued at fair market value for many purposes. It may be difficult or impossible, however, to determine the fair market value of some assets that are not traded in an organized market, such as insurance and annuity contracts, privately placed fixed-income securities, real estate, and collectibles. In these cases, an approximation or alternative value must be used. For individual insurance and annuity contracts, the cash value is the market value. Group annuity contracts such as the deposit administration (DA) type or the immediate participation guarantee (IPG) generally use the contractual account balance. Separate accounts under annuity contracts use market value.

Funding Defined Benefit Plans

For purposes of funding a defined benefit plan, it can be argued that the most appropriate asset value is the fair market value. This is the true value of the assets in the sense that it generally represents the value for which the assets could be sold. As indicated above, for some assets fair market value is difficult or impossible to determine.

But even when fair market value is known exactly, there may be problems in using it for purposes of funding. Fair market value is subject to sharp fluctuations that can disrupt funding patterns and budgetary projections. And changes in asset values attributable to shifts in the interest structure would have to be offset by compensating or commensurate changes in the actuarial interest assumption, a practice at variance with American actuarial tradition. In recognition of these practical difficulties, pension actuaries have tended to use asset values other than fair market value in preparing actuarial balance sheets and determining funding contributions.

One alternative approach is to value all assets at cost. This has the advantage of being simple and of stabilizing asset values. But if market values differ substantially from cost, the cost value may be unrealistic. And if market values are rising, the plan may be forced to sell assets to realize the appreciation and reflect it in plan costs.

A modification of the cost approach is sometimes used for bonds and other debt instruments purchased at a premium over, or a discount under, their maturity value. The current book value of the bond may be obtained by amortizing the premium or discount over the period between its purchase date and its maturity date or earliest call date.

Such methods can smooth the fluctuation of asset value and gradually recognize appreciation and depreciation in market values. Over the years, actuaries have developed a number of approaches to stabilizing the market value of assets for actuarial purposes. The most common approach is to use a moving average of year-end market values for a specified period, typically five years. Another approach is to capitalize at a realistic discount rate the anticipated stream of dividend income from the equity assets. Still another approach is to increase the initial cost of an equity asset by an assumed rate of long-term growth. A variation of that approach is to assume asset growth equal to actual inflation plus a subjectively determined real rate of return. One other approach is to increase the aggregate value of the equity assets at the previous year-end, adjusted for changes in the portfolio, by the percentage change in some designated stock index. With any of these procedures, the actuary may set upper or lower limits on the percentage variation from the actual market value that would be acceptable.

Any asset valuation method other than *actual* fair market is termed an *actuarial* valuation method, and the values derived thereunder are called *actuarial* values to distinguish them from actual values. For purposes of the minimum funding standard, ERISA requires that the value of the plan assets be determined on the basis of a "reasonable actuarial method of valuation which takes into account fair market value" and is permitted under regulations.[5] These asset valuation procedures were designed to mitigate the effect on the funding standard account of short-run changes in the fair market value of plan assets.

In due course, the Internal Revenue Service promulgated a regulation[6] stipulating that the asset valuation method must take account of fair market value, either directly in the calculation of the value itself or indirectly in determining the outside limits of the value. The method must be consistently applied and must produce an actuarial value falling within a corridor of 80 to 120 percent of the fair market value of the assets as of the applicable valuation date. Fair market value is defined as "the price at which the property would change hands between a willing buyer and a willing seller, neither being under any compulsion to buy or sell and both having reasonable knowledge of relevant facts." Alternatively, prior to 1989 a plan could use a procedure that produces an aggregate value falling within a corridor of 85 to 115 percent of the *average value* of the assets as of the valuation date.

The asset valuation method cannot be designed to produce a result consistently above or below fair market value or average value. The method has to be applied on a consistent basis and cannot be changed without advance IRS approval.[7]

The plan administrator for a multiemployer plan may elect to value all bonds and other evidence of indebtedness (e.g., mortgages, notes, and the like) at amortized cost, rather than under the general rule described above. The election is made by a statement attached to Schedule B of Form 5500 and must apply to all bonds and evidence of indebtedness not in default. Once elected, the election may be revoked only with IRS consent. Most plans have not made such an election.

Regulations may allow use of an alternative approach for single-employer plans with a dedicated bond portfolio (discussed later).

The method of asset valuation affects the amount of the gain or loss from investment return each year. This becomes part of the plan's total actuarial gain or loss. The method must be specified in an attachment to Schedule B of the plan's annual actuarial report and be described in such detail that another actuary employing the method would arrive at a reasonably similar result.

---

[5] ERISA §302(c)(2)(A); IRC §412(c)(2)(A).
[6] Treas. Reg. 1.412(c)(2)-1.
[7] The IRS takes the position that an asset valuation method is an actuarial cost method (a view contested by some) and that advance approval is therefore required for any change. However, a change in the method to reflect a type of asset not previously held by the plan is not construed to be a change of actuarial cost method and thus does not require IRS approval.

Funding Defined Contribution Plans

Under defined contribution plans, the fair market value of plan assets is used to determine the value of each participant's individual account. Valuations must be made at least annually.[8]

Accounting Requirements

The valuation of plan assets for accounting purposes must be determined under generally accepted accounting principles (see Chapter 28).

Other Uses of Asset Valuation

For purposes of determining the financial condition of a terminated pension plan, the Pension Benefit Guaranty Corporation values all assets at fair market value and the liabilities on the basis of the current interest rate structure. For internal management purposes, a plan sponsor may value the assets and liabilities of the plan on any basis that it chooses. It is customary to use different assumptions for funding purposes than for reporting in accordance with the FASB prescriptions.

Asset Managers

As noted earlier, the assets of a pension plan may be managed by the staff of the sponsoring firm or by outside firms that specialize in providing investment services. The decision should be made by the plan sponsor. As a practical matter, only firms with a large and sophisticated financial staff can safely undertake the investment of pension assets. The sponsoring firm may manage certain types of assets in which it has special skills, such as cash equivalents, leaving the remaining assets to external managers. Assets managed in-house must still be held in trust, but an individual or group of individuals may be designated as the plan trustee under the trust agreement. The remainder of this section concentrates on external asset managers.

Bank or Trust Company

Trust companies and banks with trust powers manage a substantial proportion of all pension plan assets. They may perform this function as a trustee of the pension plan or as a professional asset manager engaged by the trustee to manage a portion of the pension portfolio. Whatever the role, the function falls within the purview of the trust division of the bank.

Traditional Functions

As a trustee-investment manager, the bank or trust company performs the traditional services of a trustee, all in accordance with the trust indenture entered into between the plan sponsor and the trustee. It receives contributions from the

---

[8]Rev. Rul. 80-155.

plan sponsor, invests and reinvests the accumulated assets, and renders periodic accounting of its stewardship to the plan sponsor. As a minimum, the trustee provides the plan administrator with all the financial information called for in governmental reports, notably Form 5500. It may make benefit payments on instructions from the plan sponsor.

The trustee is under legal obligation to invest the funds received under a pension plan. In the absence of any specific instructions in the trust instrument, the trustee would have to invest the funds in accordance with any applicable state statute governing fiduciary investments. It is customary, however, for the plan sponsor to free the trustee from the constraints of the state fiduciary investment statute and to bestow on the trustee varying degrees of authority over the investments of the trust. Many trust agreements give the trustee complete discretion in the performance of its investment function, with the trustee being held to a commensurate degree of responsibility for the investment results. It is common for the trust indenture to contain some limitations on the trustee's investment behavior, especially on the proportion of the portfolio to be invested in broad classes of assets. In practice, instructions of this sort may come from the plan sponsor in periodic written form.

In acting as an asset manager but not as plan trustee, a bank or trust company would perform all the conventional services of a trustee except the disbursement function. Benefits are paid by the trustee or by the plan sponsor, acting as the trustee's agent. Under these circumstances, of course, the bank is responsible only for the assets entrusted to it but is a fiduciary under ERISA with respect to those plan assets.

As an asset manager, a bank is subject to the basic principle of trust law that the assets (or the records of ownership of the assets) of each trust must be segregated from the assets of all other trusts administered by it and from its own assets. This feature of trust administration makes it difficult for a small pension plan to adequately diversify its investment risks without some relief. To make the advantages of diversification available to small plans, all states have modified the common-law rule as to segregation of trust assets by authorizing the pooling of plan assets, subject to certain restrictions. Banks active in the pension field offer one or more commingled trust funds designed for the special needs and exclusive use of pension plans, with no limit on the extent of participation. The investment of plan assets in a commingled trust must be specifically authorized by the plan sponsor. Further information on the trustee's function is provided in Chapter 32.

Master Trusteeship and Custodianship

A trust company or a bank with trust powers may perform other trust services that support the investment function. The plan trustee, usually a bank or trust company, must hold legal title to and possession (or "indicia" of ownership) of specifically identifiable plan assets. Holding and accounting for plan assets is a custodial function that is not the exclusive jurisdiction of a trustee but is frequently combined with the trustee function.

With the growth of multiple investment managers for the assets of a single pension plan (see page 692) has come the need for a master trustee and custodian, a service offered by many large banks in money market centers. Such a fiduciary may offer a broad range of services logically associated with that function, but the plan sponsor need not avail itself of all the services. As a minimum, the master trustee holds legal title to, and effective possession of, all plan assets. In practice, it (and any other plan trustee) may choose to delegate the custodial function to a central depository, such as the Depository Trust Company in New York City, that would hold the indicia of ownership of registered securities in the United States under an agency agreement and would issue electronic records against them. Subcustodians may have to be appointed to hold foreign securities. It is generally immaterial to the plan sponsor who performs this ministerial function, as long as the entity is efficient and surrounded by sufficient safeguards. Upon instructions from the plan sponsor, the master trustee allocates plan assets and cash flow among the various asset managers and monitors their activities. The master trustee makes timely collection of dividends, interest, and proceeds from sales, redemptions, and maturities; settles securities transactions; often computes and compares the investment performance of the asset managers; and submits consolidated (as well as detailed) financial results to the plan sponsor.

The master trustee may perform cash management services for the plan. Located in a financial center and in receipt of the plan's cash flow, the master trustee is the logical party to see that cash balances are continuously and favorably invested and that the cash needs of the plan are met. The master trustee normally disburses benefits for the plan on instructions from the plan sponsor. If the plan sponsor has authorized the lending of securities to brokers and to other capital market participants—a low-risk activity (if done properly) that may produce enough income to meet the total fee of the master trustee and custodian—the master trustee will perform that function.

The master trustee may manage some of the plan assets but does not usually do so. The trustee can perform its other functions more objectively if it is not competing with the other managers on the very case that it is monitoring. Some master trustees do not offer asset management services to pension plans.

Immunization of Portfolio against Risk of Interest Rate Changes

In an effort to match the popularity of insurance company guaranteed income contracts (discussed later) and to meet a perceived need of many plan sponsors, a number of banks offer a bond management service usually described as the immunization of plan liabilities or dedication.[9] The basic objective of the technique is to eliminate the interest rate risk associated with reinvesting the income (and the proceeds of maturing investments) from a fixed-income portfolio.[10] More broadly, it is an attempt to match the assets of the portfolio to the liabilities of the pension plan (or other financial entity). Since for various technical reasons it is

---

[9]The concept of immunization was introduced into the economic literature in the late 1940s. The pioneering paper on the subject in the context of pension plans was F. M. Redington, "Review of the Principles of Life Insurance Valuation," *Journal of the Institute of Actuaries*, vol. 78 (1952): pp. 286–340.

[10]Another approach to this objective is the purchase of zero coupon bonds, which provide no payoff until maturity and sell at a deep discount. There is no income to be reinvested until maturity, and the purchase price determines the yield to maturity, which is ensured—barring credit risks.

usually not possible to immunize the entire portfolio, the asset manager "partitions" the liabilities into various subsets having identifiable time horizons that lend themselves to the immunization technique. In the pension field, the technique has been largely confined to the actuarial liabilities of a closed group, such as the already retired segment of the plan population.

There are two basic approaches to immunization: the laddering of maturities and duration management.[11] Under the first approach, the asset manager constructs a dedicated portfolio that will throw off a cash flow (including the proceeds of maturing investments) approximately equal to that of the immunized liabilities. In the case of retired lives, the portion of the portfolio dedicated to that segment of actuarial liabilities is expected to generate a cash inflow to the plan that matches the highly predictable cash outflow for benefit payments to the retired participants. There is no reinvestment risk of any consequence, since the cash inflow goes out with a short time lag to the benefit recipients.

Under the second approach, the asset manager constructs a dedicated portfolio with a duration such that, with no change in the yield curve, a given nominal return will be realized over a particular time horizon, related to the "partitioned" liabilities to which the assets are dedicated. If the future reinvestment rate of return deviates from what is implicit in the current yield curve, the increase or reduction in reinvestment income, as the case might be, would be precisely offset by capital losses or capital gains, respectively—unless there are nonparallel shifts in the yield curve. If there are nonparallel shifts in the yield curve, the dedicated portfolio must be reimmunized to achieve the desired balance of yields and maturities, as measured by the duration. This approach requires sophisticated computer programming and active management.

According to some analysts, immunization appeals to the plan sponsor because it may permit the use of a higher interest rate in valuing the immunized liabilities of the plan, thus lowering required contributions to the plan over the immunized holding period. This is simply not true. Immunization stabilizes expense, although at a higher level, but does not stabilize contributions. An additional drawback of the technique, apart from its complexity, is that it may produce a duration or maturity structure that is not optimal in terms of expected or actual interest rate behavior. In effect, the liability structure dictates the asset structure, which might not be the one that the portfolio manager would have preferred in the light of its interest rate forecasts. Furthermore, actual results from immunization may deviate from expectations because of nonparallel shifts in the yield curve, calls, and other

[11] "Duration" is one of the most frequently used concepts in fixed-income markets. It has two meanings. First, it denotes the (present value-weighted) average time until cash payments are received from an asset. As a measure of time until payment, duration is a more comprehensive concept than maturity, because maturity is the time until the final payment only; and the final payment may represent a small fraction of the asset's total present value. With zero coupon bonds and synthetics, the maximum duration of financial instruments in the marketplace today is at least 30 years. Second, duration is a gauge of interest sensitivity. The "longer" the duration of an asset, the greater its price reaction to a movement in interest rates. The duration of a bond is shorter than the remaining period to maturity, since it recognizes intervening coupon payments. The longer the maturity of a bond, the lower its coupon rate; and the lower the current level of market interest rates, the longer the duration of the bond and the greater the rate of return volatility of the bond. Thus duration is a measure of bond return volatility and as such is a proxy for risk.

unexpected events. This risk can be minimized through frequent reimmunization, a technique involving burdensome administrative procedures and some transactions costs. An intermediate approach is to pursue an active management strategy, unless the return on the portfolio declines to a predetermined level. At that point, the portfolio would be immunized as promptly as feasible. This approach or strategy is called *contingent immunization.* In effect, a "safety net" is placed under an actively managed portfolio to ensure that the return will not drop below a preselected floor. In the meantime, the portfolio manager can pursue the added returns potentially available from active management.

Life Insurance Companies

Life insurance companies compete head-on with banks and trust companies for the management of pension plan assets. They offer a number of contractual arrangements (to be described later), under which the insurer assumes legal responsibility for the payment of all plan benefits that have been fully funded with the insurer. Insurance or annuity contracts representing the insurer's obligations become assets of the pension plan. The investments of the insurance company are not assets of the plan, although under certain contractual arrangements they may be deemed plan assets for purposes of fiduciary responsibility under ERISA. The insurer, not the plan sponsor, has all rights to possession, control, and disposition of the investments acquired with the sponsor's contributions. Life insurers offer certain contractual arrangements that do not contemplate the purchase of annuities for vested or retired employees and are designed to be purely investment vehicles for pension plan assets. The assets under these contracts may be held in the general asset account of the insurer or in one or more separate accounts. In some cases, the assets are placed in the general asset account of a fully owned subsidiary.

General Asset Account

Under a life insurer's traditional mode of operation, all of its assets are held in one commingled account and are available for the satisfaction of any and all obligations of the company, regardless of their nature or source. The account is not labeled since it consists of all the insurer's assets, which are not earmarked for any particular obligations or segmented in any way. Traditionally, net investment income has been allocated to the various lines of business on a pro rata basis, without regard for the timing of the cash flows or for the rate of return at which particular cash flows are invested. This composite rate of return, computed in accordance with the rules of the National Association of Insurance Commissioners on the basis of amortized book values, is referred to as the *portfolio rate of return.* It serves as the basis for the crediting of interest to participating individual insurance and annuity contracts, under the insurer's dividend formula, and the crediting of investment earnings to group insurance and annuity contracts for experience rating purposes.

The portfolio basis of crediting interest is a generally equitable, simple, and satisfactory way of allocating investment earnings when interest rates are stable and funds remain with the insurer over a long period of time, encompassing any interest rate cycles that might develop. However, in a period of volatile interest rates with large pools of money seeking the highest rate of return, the portfolio basis of allocating investment earnings becomes inequitable and possibly even impracticable, except for individual lines of insurance. Thus in the early 1960s life insurers active in the group insurance and pension business introduced the investment generation method of allocating such earnings in order to (1) allocate investment earnings more equitably, (2) eliminate adverse financial selection, and (3) meet competition. Each company has its own distinctive procedure for this exercise, but the general objective is to allocate investment earnings in such a way as to recognize the rate of interest at which the net cash inflows are invested and reinvested. Since the method generally keeps track of cash flows and investment returns by calendar year generation, it is called the "investment year method" (IYM); but some companies have used a longer accounting period, especially for individual lines of insurance. The general approach is commonly described as the "new money" method.[12]

Even with a more equitable and realistic basis for allocating investment earnings, the companies found that the general asset account (or general account)—as the general purpose commingled account has become known to distinguish it from various special or separate accounts—was not a completely satisfactory vehicle for the investment of pension plan assets. In the first place, the general asset account is subject to the investment constraints imposed by state law, which, among other restraining features, frequently imposes severe limits on the amount of common stock that can be held. Second, the general asset account is subject to the liquidity requirements of the company's individual insurance and annuity business, particularly those imposed by policy loans and cash surrenders. Third, as the residual repository of assets, the general asset account holds various types of low-yielding assets, such as old real estate mortgages, the company's home office and regional office buildings, and policy loans that were frequently made at what today seem to be unrealistically low contractual interest rates. Fourth, the investment earnings on assets backing the benefit obligations of qualified pension plans held in the general asset account of an insurer must bear a share of the insurer's federal income tax. Fifth, a portion of the investment earnings of the general asset account must be set aside in the Mandatory Security Valuation Reserve. Finally, the investment policy appropriate for the mix of business backed by the general asset account may not be appropriate for pension plans or may not meet the objectives of particular pension plans.

Separate Accounts

Because of the foregoing drawbacks of the general asset account as a vehicle for the investment of pension plan assets, particularly the limitation on the use of common stock, a number of insurers, under the authority of special legislation or administrative interpretation of existing law, took the momentous step in the early 1960s of establishing separate accounts for investing pension assets. The companies

[12]The investment year method is described in detail on pp. 726 ff.

continued to make their general asset account available to those plans that wanted traditional insurance company interest and annuity rate guarantees or simply found the investment services of the general asset account suitable for their purposes, even when annuity purchases were not contemplated.

In the beginning, most of the insurers considered establishing only one separate account, which would commingle the assets of a number of pension plans. In response to the widely held view that common stocks were an excellent inflation hedge, the account would be invested exclusively in common stock (and cash equivalents). As the full capabilities of the separate account approach became apparent, many insurers set up more than one separate account for common stocks, each having a different investment objective and assets of varying risk characteristics, as well as separate accounts for other types of assets. Today there are separate accounts for publicly traded bonds, direct placement bonds, real estate mortgages, real estate equity, oil and natural gas properties, money market instruments, and perhaps other classes of assets. The largest pension insurers operate 10 or 12 separate accounts, covering a wide range of investment objectives, each tailored to meet a specific objective. These accounts are pooled accounts, the assets being commingled on a basis similar to that of a collective trust fund.

Contributions to a pension plan are placed in a separate account only upon written agreement with the plan sponsor or the plan trustees. The agreement may specify the percentage of plan assets and future contributions to be allocated to the various accounts, or it may permit the plan sponsor to give directions for the allocation of each individual contribution. The agreement may permit the plan sponsor to reallocate past contributions and associated investment earnings from time to time. The plan sponsor is under no obligation, of course, to allocate contributions to all of the separate accounts.

Under some agreements the insurer may be authorized to provide total management of the plan assets, with the right to distribute the assets among the various accounts. Under none of these arrangements does the insurer make any guarantee of its investment performance. It promises neither preservation of principal nor a minimum rate of return. It is obligated, however, to invest the assets in accordance with applicable law[13] and the stated investment objectives of the account. The account is maintained on a market value basis, and the actual investment experience (including realized and unrealized capital gains and losses) is reflected directly and immediately in the status of the account.

Transactions between the plan sponsor and a pooled separate account are carried out in terms of units, which are identical in principle to those used in connection with equity-based annuity contracts and mutual funds. When the plan sponsor makes a contribution to the separate account, its plan is credited with an appropriate number of units (determined by dividing the dollar value of the contribution by the current market value of one unit). When funds are withdrawn from the separate account for benefit payments or transfer to the general account,

---

[13]In general, a separate account of a New York–licensed insurer is subject to the same investment restrictions as the general account. However, all separate accounts are permitted to invest up to 10 percent of their assets in a manner not authorized for the general account, and an equity separate account may be invested entirely in common stocks and other equity interests.

another separate account, or another funding agency, an appropriate number of units are redeemed. The same procedure is followed when the insurer, under its discretionary authority, reallocates plan assets. Investment earnings operate to increase the *value* of the unit rather than the *number* of units credited to the participating plans.

If the plan assets are large enough to permit an appropriate degree of diversification, the sponsor or trustee may arrange to have all the assets managed in an individual account, independent of the general account and any other separate account. Such an arrangement is known as an "individual customer" separate account. It permits a closer working relationship between the sponsor and the asset manager than is possible under a pooled separate account. As an example, the plan sponsor may specify that assets are to be allocated among broad classes of investments and levels of quality. In all cases, however, the choice of specific assets to be acquired and held rests with the insurer.

The assets in a separate account may be held by the insurer under a group annuity contract that obligates the plan sponsor to purchase annuities for retiring participants from an unallocated contractual fund as long as the contract remains in effect. Alternatively, they may be held under a type of contract that merely offers the plan sponsor the opportunity to purchase annuities in accordance with a stipulated schedule of annuity rates but does not obligate it to do so. If fixed-income annuities are purchased under either arrangement, the sums required are transferred to the general asset account, which normally underwrites all guarantees of the insurer. Sums set aside for asset-based (variable) annuities are held in a separate account maintained for the writing of such annuities. If the plan holds funds in the general asset account, the purchase payments may be taken from that source, or they may be drawn from one or more of the separate accounts to which contributions have been made. Transfers between and among the various accounts, including the general account, are made in cash (obtained through the redemption of units in the case of separate accounts) rather than in kind. Transfers from a single customer separate account to another separate account of the same insurer can be made in kind if permitted by state law and if the securities are acceptable to the insurer.

Funds under these contracts can usually be withdrawn by the plan sponsor upon relatively short notice, usually 90 days. Withdrawals from separate accounts (other than guaranteed income contracts, which are described below) are on a market value basis and are generally payable in a single sum. Withdrawals from the general asset account, if large in amount, may have to be spread ratably over a period as long as 10 years. If paid in a single sum from the general asset account, the book value is adjusted (upward or downward) to a "market value" equivalent determined by a bond-yield calculation, reflecting the average period to maturity and the yields currently available on new money invested in securities of a quality comparable to that of the securities in the general account portfolio.

A separate account is considered to be an investment company by the Securities and Exchange Commission, and in the absence of special statutory or administrative exemptions it would have to be administered in conformity with the Investment Company Act of 1940, the Securities Act of 1933, the Securities and Exchange Act of 1934, and the Investment Advisers Act of 1940. However, through a series of SEC administrative rulings and eventually a statutory enactment (the Investment Company Amendments Act of 1970), separate accounts available only to qualified pension plans (other than Keogh plans) have been given an exemption from the most burdensome provisions of the foregoing laws and implementing regulations. This exemption applies to all qualified plans, irrespective of size and the presence of employee contributions and irrespective of whether the plans provide fixed-income annuities or asset-based (variable) annuities.

Guaranteed Income Contract

As one facet of its asset management services, the insurer may accept a block of funds and guarantee a rate of return that reflects the yields currently available on the type and quality of assets acquired with the funds. Contracts containing such an interest guarantee have various appellations, depending upon the insurer, but they tend to be known under the generic name of "guaranteed income contract." This approach to crediting investment earnings is a variation of the investment year method. Under the latter, interest is credited to contract experience accounts in accordance with the composite rate at which monies were invested by the insurer during the entire calendar year. Under a GIC, the insurer may guarantee a rate of return for a specified time period only slightly lower than the rate currently obtainable in the capital market. The insurer bases its guarantee on the bonds or other securities that are purchased with the new funds and are in effect earmarked for the plan's account. The insurer seeks call protection for the period during which its interest guarantee will be in effect, but depending upon the contract terms, it may assume the risk of not being able to reinvest the investment income at the guaranteed rate. The insurer's commitment may take the form of a series of interest rate guarantees, the rates declining with the length of the guarantee. The insurer may accept a series of deposits over a period of years, in contrast to a single-sum (presumably one-time) deposit, in which case the interest guarantee is graded downward over time, because of the insurer's uncertainty over the interest rate structure that may prevail in the future, beyond the period for which loan commitments have been made.

The guaranteed income contracts on the market vary greatly, often in their crucial features. The most important feature, of course, is the minimum rate of interest to be credited.

A second feature is the time over which the guarantee is to apply. Perhaps the most common period is 5 years, but some insurers offer guarantees, albeit cautiously fashioned, that extend up to 20 years.

A third factor, related to the term of the guarantee, is the timing of the insurer's repayment of the funds to the contract-holder or other disposition of the assets. Under some contracts, the original sums deposited plus accumulated interest are paid in a lump sum at the end of the guarantee period or are otherwise disposed of in accordance with instructions from the plan sponsor. Other contractual arrangements call for the deposited sums and accumulated interest to be paid to the plan sponsor in monthly or annual installments throughout the term of the contract. This type of arrangement reduces the reinvestment risk of the insurer. The contract-holder may be permitted to specify the pattern of the payout.

A fourth factor to be considered is whether the interest income that is accruing at a guaranteed rate can itself be reinvested at the guaranteed rate during the term of the contract. Some insurers provide for the compounding of interest at the guaranteed rate, while others credit the accruing interest with the new money rate applicable to the period during which the interest accrued. In some cases the interest is paid out annually, to be reinvested by the plan sponsor on the best terms available or applied to the payment of benefits.

A fifth consideration is whether the contract-holder is credited with its share of investment earnings in excess of the guaranteed rate. In technical parlance, the question is whether the contract is participating or nonparticipating. Some insurers guarantee the highest rate of interest that their circumstances can justify but make no provision for participation by the plan sponsor in excess investment earnings. If positive, the margin between the guaranteed and actual rate of return may be viewed as the price or penalty paid for the guarantee feature. When the contract is nonparticipating, there is no explicit charge for the guarantee. Some insurers prefer to "hedge their bets" by offering conservative interest guarantees while providing for participation in excess investment earnings.

A sixth factor is the nature and magnitude of the charge made for the guarantee. The "charge" may take the form of nonparticipation in excess investment earnings, a conservative (favorable to the insurer) algorithm for computing excess interest earnings, or an explicit charge. Normally, the charge, expressed as a percentage of the assets and ranging up to 25 basis points, is applied as a deduction from the excess investment earnings that would otherwise have been credited to the contract. Under some contracts, the charge can reduce the effective yield on contract assets below the minimum rate guaranteed.

A seventh area in which practices may differ is the manner in which the market value is computed for partial withdrawals under the contract. Under the terms of most contracts, no market value adjustment is made for sums deposited in the first year of the contract or for sums withdrawn to pay benefits in any year. Under all other circumstances, a market value adjustment is usually made. Some insurers assume that the sum withdrawn was spread pro rata over all investment year cells, producing a "coupon" rate for the withdrawn segment equal to the composite rate on all the investment year cells. Other insurers assume that the funds are withdrawn from the most recent investment year cells, beginning with the cell for the immediately preceding year. This procedure is generally referred to as the last in, first out (LIFO) method. Still other insurers assume that all withdrawals are made from the current year's cell, even if this creates a negative balance for the cell and causes the cell to be credited with negative interest thereafter. This procedure avoids the need for a market value adjustment. At least one insurer computes the market value on the assumption that the withdrawn amounts came from the oldest investment year cells, starting with the first. Quite logically, this is known as the first in, first out (FIFO) method. Some companies apply the LIFO concept to withdrawals in a given calendar year not in excess of a specified limit, such as 10 percent of the contract-holder's beginning balance, with amounts in excess of that limit being spread ratably over all investment year cells.

Another aspect of this same question is whether the algorithm permits a market value in excess of book value. In theory, the market value of the withdrawn sums should be greater than book when the "coupon" rate on that segment of the investment portfolio from which the withdrawn funds were assumed to come is higher than the rate at which funds are currently being invested or committed. Most companies let the adjustment go in either direction, but there are some that do not recognize a market value in excess of book value.

Another aspect alluded to earlier is whether interest earnings accumulated at a guaranteed, minimum rate of interest can be withdrawn or transferred at the end of the contract term without a market value adjustment. This would be a concern only if interest rates were higher at the end of the term than the rate at which interest was credited. There is also the question of whether the principal can be withdrawn or transferred intact (i.e., at book value) at the end of the contract period.

A final issue is whether the guarantee of principal and interest is funded through the general asset account or a fixed-income separate account. Guarantees have traditionally been associated with the general asset account, but a few insurers are in a position to offer them through a separate account, passing along certain federal income tax savings and a potentially higher yield. The separate account may be an attractive mechanism for this purpose, but the plan sponsor should assure itself that the guarantee has the ultimate backing of the general asset account.

For a plan sponsor with a substantial body of retired participants, the guaranteed income contract may be an appealing alternative to the purchase of single-sum immediate annuities for the retired employees. Under this alternative, the plan sponsor deposits with the insurer a single sum calculated to be the approximate equivalent of the actuarial value of the retirement benefits in pay status, at the rate of interest proffered by the insurer. The insurer credits the deposit with a fixed, guaranteed rate of interest and returns the money over a period of years in monthly or annual installments that roughly "track" the pattern of benefit payments to the retired persons. In this way, the plan sponsor avoids the charge that the insurer would justifiably make for its mortality guarantee and the disbursement of monthly checks. Of course, the plan sponsor will incur a benefit disbursement expense in one form or the other. A GIC used for this purpose is a form of liability immunization from the standpoint of the plan sponsor.[14] The ultimate form of immunization is the actual purchase of annuities for the retired lives, or some other segment, of the plan population.

The total volume of outstanding GICs has reached such proportions that a secondary market for the instruments has developed. There are firms that specialize in the active management of GICs; indeed, some do nothing else. GICs are being actively managed to guard against credit risk, achieve broader diversification, smooth out cash flows and thus minimize the reinvestment risk and meeting liquidity needs, and enhance the rate of return. Some of these firms hold out the possibility of adding 20 to 30 basis points to the net return while achieving some of the other goals of active management. These various goals are pursued through such strategies as renegotiating maturities, which stretch out payments from the

---

[14]The insurer may, in turn, immunize its own liability created by the sale of the GIC.

GICs into smaller units such as $1 million to $5 million denominations. Smaller units, or denominations, can create a broader market, fill in gaps in plan liquidity, and achieve other purposes.

Segmentation of the General Asset Account

It was stated earlier that by law and tradition all assets of a life insurer are available to meet the contractual and other obligations of the insurer. This concept was breached when pension insurers, with the approval of regulatory authorities or state legislatures, dedicated certain assets of the company to particular contract-holders through the device of legally constituted separate accounts, established by action of the insurer's board of directors. Since the SEC views these separate accounts as investment companies, certain formalities must be observed to avoid the full burdens of registration and regulatory oversight that attaches to a full-fledged investment company. These formalities themselves can be burdensome and restrictive.

The same objectives could be achieved through the creation of a series of fully owned subsidiaries, but they pose their own administrative, financial, and regulatory burdens. Nevertheless, a number of companies have established subsidiaries to offer investment services or to service particular kinds of pension plans.

Recently, several pension insurers have obtained regulatory approval to partition their general asset account without going through the legal formalities of establishing separate accounts or chartering fully owned subsidiaries. This procedure is called *segmentation*. By this device, the insurer can allocate general account assets to various lines of business or to defined classes of contract-holders by merely setting up and maintaining *memorandum* accounts. The segmentation must be carried out and maintained on an equitable and consistent basis. The claims of a particular segment of contract-holders are not limited to assets dedicated to that segment but are enforceable against the entire general asset account.

Segmentation is a powerful and flexible tool for the management of assets and the allocation of investment earnings. It permits the matching of assets and liabilities in a way not possible under other approaches. Assets can be segmented to meet the differing investment objectives of various groups of contract-holders, or to introduce the investment year method of allocating investment earnings when the insurer does not want to do it in a formal fashion or for all purposes. In the hands of unscrupulous management, it could become an instrument of gross favoritism of one class over another or unfair discrimination among the various classes of contract-holders.

The issuance of a GIC based on a particular lending transaction, a common-place occurrence, is an extreme form of portfolio segmentation. The GIC is supported by an identifiable set of securities, with a claim against the insurer's surplus if the two sets of cash flows do not mesh. It may also be argued that a GIC is an extreme form of the new money approach to allocating investment earnings.

Registered Investment Advisers

Hundreds of firms and individuals provide investment advice to pension plans, institutional endowments, financial institutions, and other individuals. The adviser may be an individual operating under his or her own name or a business name, or it may be a firm with dozens or hundreds of specialists and supporting staff and the most sophisticated computer hardware and software. It may be an independent entity or a subsidiary of a bank, insurance company, or other financial institution. Often the investment adviser is also the designated *investment manager* for part or all of a plan's assets, with authority to make investment decisions as long as they observe investment policy guidelines. Any investment manager of a pension plan who is neither a trustee nor a named fiduciary of the plan must be registered under the Investment Advisers Act of 1940. Like a bank or insurer managing pension assets, the manager must acknowledge in writing that it is a fiduciary under ERISA.[15]

Many of these firms, large and small, offer their services to qualified pension plans. Some specialize in one sector of the capital market. One firm may specialize in common stocks, one in conventional bonds, and another in convertible bonds. There may be specialization within a sector. Thus one firm may be a specialist in growth stocks, while another emphasizes stocks with superior dividend performance.

Some investment advisers offer a full range of investment services, including execution of trades. Others merely advise the plan sponsor or trustee on investment policy, investment strategy, and stock or bond selection but leave execution, custodianship, and record keeping to the trustee. Some advisers also manage stock or bond mutual funds or an index fund, which can be used by pension plans. In one form or the other, investment advisers play an important role today in the management of pension plan assets.

Use of Multiple Managers

When a pension plan has accumulated assets of a certain size, such as $50 to $100 million, it may employ more than one investment manager. Many large plans use as many as 20 or 25 managers; at one time, AT&T used more than 100. Many plan sponsors are reluctant to entrust more than $50 million to any one manager. On the other hand, many managers are unwilling to manage less than $5 or $10 million for any one account.

A plan sponsor might decide to use more than one manager for three basic reasons, all related. The first, and most obvious, is to broaden the diversification of risk. Since successful investing is very much an art and not a science, and since it involves a high degree of subjective judgment, risk can be reduced by reflecting the judgment and skills of more than one firm. A portfolio put together by three investment managers, even when operating under the same guidelines, will inevitably be different and more diversified than if it had been assembled by one manager.

A second reason for using multiple managers is to have the benefit of the research resources, contacts, and innovative ideas of several firms. These things are reflected, of course, in the stock and bond selections that make up the portfolio.

---

[15]ERISA §§3(38), 402(c)(3).

A third reason is to blend the investment styles and strategies of several managers in such a way as to reduce risk and take advantage of the special skills that they may have. As indicated above, many investment advisers choose to concentrate their research and resources in a particular sector of the capital market, and they become extremely knowledgeable and adroit in that area. The only way that a plan can avail itself of this special expertise is to use a number of such specialists, perhaps mixed in with some generalists. Some managers may be selected for distinctive types of investments—such as common stocks, bonds, or convertibles—or all managers may be permitted to invest in all types of investments. The strategies developed by some investment advisers work better in one kind of market environment than another; if some of these conflicting strategies are reflected in the same portfolio, the portfolio is insulated to some extent from unexpected movements in the market. It will be recognized that this blending of styles and strategies is a form of diversification.

As might be expected, there are certain disadvantages in using multiple managers. For one thing, the total annual fee paid for investment services is almost certain to be larger for multiple managers than it would have been for one manager. In standard practice, the investment management fee is expressed as a percentage of the assets under management, with the percentage declining as the size of the portfolio increases. The annual fee, which is customarily paid in monthly or quarterly installments, generally is applied in accordance with a sliding scale that declines with the magnitude of assets under management. For example, the fee often starts at $\frac{1}{2}$ percent and declines to $\frac{1}{10}$ percent, but for some asset managers the scale starts at $\frac{3}{4}$ percent or even higher. The highest percentage is often applied to the first $5 million, and the minimum is often paid on amounts in excess of $100 million. The fee of each manager is based on its share of assets and may never reach the lowest percentage if the plan assets are divided among too many managers.

The second disadvantage is that multiple managers place an administrative burden on the plan sponsor, who is responsible for monitoring the performance of the various managers and making allocation decisions. The monitoring may be delegated to a master trustee or some other firm, but then a fee must be paid for this service. This, of course, adds to the cost disadvantage of using several managers. The additional cost may be offset many times over by better investment performance, but again it may not be. Those who allocate net cash flow of the plan to the various managers must make frequent judgments about relative performance and possibly emotionally upsetting reallocations of assets.[16] If only one

---

[16]There is no prescribed formula for deciding how to allocate new contributions among existing managers. The simplest procedure is to give each manager an equal amount, but that would change the proportions of the portfolio allocated to each manager. To maintain existing proportions, each manager could be given a pro rata share of new money. The cash flow could be apportioned in terms of performance; but, depending on market conditions and anticipated changes, this philosophy could lead to favoring the *best* performer or the *worst performer*. Another basis of allocation is to maintain or achieve a preferred mix of asset categories, particularly if the various managers invest in different types of assets. Another is to assign a disproportionate share to the manager or managers whose asset category appears to be undervalued. Under some conditions, assets are allocated on the basis of a pattern designed to create a baseline portfolio over some time period. Finally, the allocation may be done on the basis of pure judgment. The reverse process, liquidating assets to meet benefit payments or choosing assets to transfer to a new manager, involves many of the same judgments.

manager is employed, there are no subsequent allocations to consider. Since cash flow allocations involve both policy decisions and delicate business relationships, they should be given considerable top-management attention.

The third disadvantage may be the most serious of the three. This is the possibility that the strategies and investment decisions of the various managers may work at cross-purposes and cancel each other out. This possibility becomes all the more likely if the managers are chosen because of the diversity of their styles and strategies, as is becoming more common. The greater the number of managers and variety of styles, the greater the possibility that their special skills will be neutralized and the overall performance will approach that of an index fund. Some practitioners believe that this neutralizing effect becomes serious when more than three or four managers are employed.

There are investment consultants whose primary or even exclusive service is evaluating the qualifications of other investment counselors and asset managers. In effect, they are investigative firms. They make in-depth studies of the portfolio managers, research staff, and traders of the leading firms, looking for distinctive philosophies, strategies, market specializations, and decision-making processes. For a fee, they assist plan sponsors in selecting a coordinated group of outside managers whose special expertise and interests are optimally suited to the invest-ment goals and objectives of the plan sponsor. They may also advise the plan sponsor on policy and strategy. Some firms' services include the monitoring and continuing evaluation of the outside managers engaged on their recommendation to manage a portion of the plan portfolio.

Index Funds

Disillusioned by the apparent inability of active money managers to consistently outperform (or even equal) the market averages and desiring to reduce invest-ment management fees and transaction costs, a few years ago a number of plan sponsors developed a strong interest in the concept of an index fund. An *index fund* is a portfolio of securities constructed in such a manner that its risk-and-return patterns are identical to or closely replicate those of a selected market index or some other standard. In its pure form, an index fund holds every security in the index in the same proportion as its weight in the index. To reduce the cost and inconvenience of holding all securities in the index in the proper proportions, some index funds hold only those securities selected by a sampling procedure intended to replicate the risk-and-return patterns of the whole market index.

By placing assets in an index fund, an investor enjoys perfect diversification within the marketplace bounded by the index and is reasonably assured of a rate of return equal to that of the marketplace less transaction costs and the manage-ment fee. Both the transaction costs and management fees for an index fund are much lower than for a comparable actively managed portfolio.[17] For these advan-tages, the investor forgoes the opportunity of earning a higher rate of return than that of the market and may give up some flexibility in adapting the overall invest-

17Nevertheless, these and other costs have caused many "sample" index funds to underperform the "market" to a noticeable degree.

ment program to its needs. Investment in an index fund is the extreme manifestation of a passive investment strategy with respect to the assets so deployed.

In theory, the ideal index fund would be one that holds all the stocks, bonds, and other financial instruments in the marketplace, and in the precise proportions in which they appear in the marketplace. In practice, such a fund could not be created or maintained. It would be too cumbersome to operate, and most of the advantages of such a comprehensive fund can be obtained from a much smaller and narrower set of assets. If an investor had a large enough body of assets under its management, it could construct and maintain its own index fund, at considerable expense and inconvenience. In reality, investors have turned to the index funds operated by professional money managers—banks, brokerage houses, and investment advisers.

The index fund concept is applicable to both common stocks and bonds, but it is much more difficult to construct and maintain a bond index fund.[18] Hence most index funds in operation at the present time are stock funds. While a number of common stock indices are available, the vast majority of index funds attempts to track the returns of the Standard & Poor's Composite (S&P) 500 Index, including reinvested dividends. The companies included in the S&P 500 Index are so dominant in the economy that an index fund patterned after the S&P 500 Index is considered to be an acceptable proxy for the entire universe of U.S. common stocks.

The largest proportion of pension plan indexed assets are in pooled funds. Because of economies of scale, these permit the manager to charge lower management fees than any other arrangement. The plan sponsor decides what proportion of plan assets should be in the index fund and then purchases shares or participation units in the fund. The manager of the pooled index fund assumes the responsibility of maintaining the proper balance of common stock by capitalization through appropriate sales and purchases. Management fees on the order of $\frac{1}{10}$ percent of assets under management and transaction costs are charged to the fund and will probably cause the overall return to be slightly less than that of the S&P 500. Fortunately, index fund portfolio turnover tends to be extremely low, rarely exceeding 5 percent per year, compared with 25 to 30 percent for a conventionally managed stock portfolio.

Some index fund managers will operate an individual customer index fund for a minimum-size fund, possibly as low as $10 million but usually closer to $25 million. The management fee for a separately managed index fund is somewhat higher than for a similar pooled fund. The plan sponsor might want a separate fund for a number of reasons. One reason, often used by church denominational plans, is to exclude stocks of companies that engage in controversial business

---

[18]Owing to the dynamic nature and size of the fixed-income securities universe, it is not possible to hold all the issues in a fixed-income index fund in their capitalization weighted proportions relative to the bench mark, such as the Shearson Lehman Government Corporate Index or the Salomon Brothers Broad Investment Grade Index. This means that a sampling strategy must be utilized, the index fund being constructed of a large number of "cells" that in combination reflect the risk/return characteristics, duration, and weights of the targeted universe. Constant monitoring of these cells and their interdependence is necessary to replicate the results of the selected index. The first bond index fund was introduced in 1983, and today a number are in operation.

practices or in manufactured products of questionable social utility. Another reason is to exclude the stock of companies known or believed to be in serious financial condition.[19] An index fund that has been purged of such stocks is known as a "filtered" fund and may have a better chance of meeting the prudence standard of ERISA than one that has done no screening. A third reason for a separate index fund is to save administrative transaction costs by reducing the number of stocks in the portfolio. Studies have shown that a capitalization weighted portfolio of 250 of the largest capitalization securities should track the S&P Index within 50 basis points (0.5 percent) on an annual return basis before transaction costs. The 25 largest companies by capitalization account for 40 percent of the S&P Index, and the smallest 200 companies have such minimal impact that many index funds exclude them. It must be recognized, of course, that any "tinkering" with the S&P Index on the basis of social considerations, investment judgment, or transaction cost control weakens the link to the S&P Index and erodes to some extent the reason for utilizing the index approach.

Few pension plans invest all of their assets in an index fund. Such a fund is viewed as another vehicle in the total range of investment alternatives. The marketing pitch of firms merchandising their index funds is that a pension plan should use an index fund to achieve the desired degree of portfolio diversification and to ensure that the plan has a market rate of return on a portion of the portfolio (the so-called passive core) so that it is free to pursue a more venturesome and presumably more remunerative active investment policy with respect to the remainder of the portfolio. To the extent that risk is rewarded by higher returns, this combination of passive and active investment strategy would produce a composite return in excess of market indices. Correspondingly, it also dampens return volatility in relation to a totally active portfolio.

The index fund concept can be applied to various subsets of capital market instruments, and a number of specialized funds in operation, such as "dividend tilt" funds, cater to the tax motivations of broad classes of investors and to funds containing stocks of foreign corporations. The case for indexing international equity investments rests on the assumption that it is more difficult to add value from selection in those markets.

Accountability for Investment Results

As pointed out earlier, a pension plan sponsor has a fiduciary responsibility to invest the plan assets in a prudent manner and for the sole benefit of the plan participants and beneficiaries.[20] If it delegates the investment function, as is the custom, it has a fiduciary responsibility to use prudence in selecting the asset managers and in continuing their services after the original selection process is completed. This means that there must be a system by which the various asset

---

[19]Most pooled index funds engage in such purging, the practice not being confined to individually managed funds.

[20]For a more detailed and technical analysis of this subject, consult Arthur Williams III, *Managing Your Investment Manager* (Homewood, Ill.: Dow Jones–Irwin, 1980), pp. 117–40; or Sidney Cottle et al., *Pension Asset Management: The Corporate Dimensions* (New York: Financial Executives Research Foundation, 1980), pp. 229–58.

managers account periodically for their investment results and the plan sponsor can evaluate their absolute and relative performance. This is something that a prudent and concerned plan sponsor would do in the absence of a legal obligation purely out of self-interest if for no other reason.

Time Horizon

When an investment manager is engaged, there is generally a tacit understanding that it will be retained for a sufficiently long period to demonstrate its competence (or lack thereof). In most cases the parties are thinking of a time horizon that encompasses a number of up markets and down markets. This period seems reasonable since it allows for differences in risk postures and investment styles. The market does not favor, or go against, all investment strategies or risk postures at the same time. Instead, there is a different market environment in each cycle, during which different types of stocks and bonds may perform differently. Over the years, market cycles have averaged four to five years in duration. Thus the time horizon is usually at least four years, but often in the ranges from three to five years. These time horizons undoubtedly reflect the parties' consciousness of market cycles and are intended to relate to them.

Time horizons are informal understandings and not at all in the nature of a contractual commitment. The plan sponsor can terminate the arrangement at any time, with reasonable notice. Termination before the end of the contemplated time horizon would normally occur only because of dismal, if not calamitous, results clearly attributable to the manager or because of changes in the organization or professional staff of the asset manager that presage changes in the nature and quality of the investment services that could be expected in the future. There is much turnover of skilled performers in the investment community, and the character of a particular firm, especially a small one, may change overnight with the departure or death of one or two key persons. Thus the plan sponsor must at all times be capable of adapting to changed circumstances.

Frequency of Reporting

Investment managers report periodically on their stewardship of the assets entrusted to them. The most common reporting frequency is quarterly, although some joint trust pension plans review results annually. The managers report in a format that either shows various performance measurements or permits the plan sponsor to make its own calculations. For larger plans, performance data are generally submitted to a firm that provides performance measurement services, and the analysis and comparative performance data will be furnished by the latter in connection with the periodic review. If the assets under management are sizable, the portfolio manager and supporting staff will generally present the results in person, explaining why the portfolio performed well or poorly during the period under review. These presentations usually include economic and market forecasts and an explanation of the strategies to be pursued during the next few months. The presentations and their accompanying economic analysis may cause the plan sponsor to revise its overall strategy, especially the mix of assets.

Measurement of Investment Performance

As noted, the investment results are generally presented in a format that allows one to compare the return on various stock and bond indices, and possibly other pension portfolios. Two measures of performance are critical to these comparisons: the *dollar-weighted* rate of return, and the *time-weighted* rate of return.

Both of these measures are based on the *total* rate of return; that is, they reflect not only dividend and interest flows but *realized* and *unrealized* capital gains and losses. Both measures require that the market value of the portfolio be known as of the beginning and end of the time period for which the rate of return is being computed.

The *dollar-weighted* rate of return for a given period is the percentage rate of change (positive or negative) in the market value of the portfolio assets during the period, when recognition is given to the timing and magnitude of external cash flows. It is the rate that will discount the end-of-period value of the portfolio back to the beginning-of-period portfolio plus interim contributions and less withdrawals. It is logically identical to the interest rate at which the beginning portfolio and all net cash flows must be invested to arrive at the ending value of the portfolio. This measure is also known as the *internal* rate of return and as the *discounted cash Xow rate of return*. It is a measure of the actual performance of the portfolio during the period, since it reflects both the skills of the portfolio manager and the timing effect of contributions to, and withdrawals from, the pension fund.

The *time-weighted* rate of return is the percentage change in the market value of a unit of assets (e.g., $1 or $100) invested continuously for the entire measurement period. More simply, it is the rate at which a dollar invested at the beginning of a period would have compounded during that period, regardless of interim cash flows. To compute this rate, it is necessary to use "units" or "shares" and to determine the net asset value per unit at the beginning and end of the measurement period and on any date when a cash flow transaction occurs. To account for a contribution or withdrawal during the year, units are "bought" or "sold" at the then-prevailing net asset value per unit. Investment income (dividends and interest) is not converted into units but serves to increase the net asset value of existing units. At year-end, the ending portfolio value divided by the outstanding units gives an ending net asset value per unit that can be compared directly with the beginning value or with any interim value. The concept is identical to that used in mutual fund accounting.

The essential contribution of the time-weighted rate of return is that, contrary to the dollar-weighted rate of return, it eliminates the effect on return of the *timing* of external cash flows (i.e., contributions and withdrawals).[21] The two measures of return are identical for any period when there are no external cash flows or, irrespective of cash flows, when the rate of return throughout the period is constant. The two rates differ only when additions to the portfolio are invested at a different yield from that of the existing assets or when net withdrawals force the

---

[21] For a comprehensive and technical explanation of the time-weighted rate of return, see Bank Administration Institute, *Measuring the Investment Performance of Pension Funds for the Purpose of Inter-Fund Comparison* (Park Ridge, Ill.: BAI, 1968).

liquidation of assets having a different return from the remaining assets. Since the portfolio manager has little, if any, control over the external cash flow of the portfolio, the time-weighted rate of return is considered to be the better measure of the *manager's* performance. The *dollar-weighted* return is the better measure of the *portfolio's* performance. If the portfolio manager, under a discretionary grant of authority, has control over the cash flow of a particular segment of the portfolio, such as the equity component or the bond component, the dollar-weighted rate of return is the appropriate measure of the manager's performance for the segment of the portfolio. Each measure is significant and makes a distinctive contribution to the evaluation of investment results.

It was noted above that to compute a time-weighted rate of return for a portfolio, or segment of a portfolio, the market value of the relevant assets must be known on the date of each external transaction. This would create no difficulties if transactions occurred only at the end or beginning of calendar quarters, at which point portfolio valuations usually take place. In reality, contributions and withdrawals can occur at any time during the calendar year. To overcome this practical problem, an approximation of the time-weighted rate of return can be derived by determining the *internal* rate of return for each period between portfolio valuations and linking the results to obtain an annual (or annualized) rate of return.[22] This modification of the pure method assumes that the return within the period (quarter) is uniform, which will not be true if there are significant cash flows within the period. The shorter the period between valuations, the less the approximation violates the pure rate.[23]

The investment results of each of the asset managers are combined to produce dollar-weighted and time-weighted rates of return for the entire pension portfolio, as well as for each of its major components: equities, bonds, and short-term instruments. Some problems in definition and differences in custodian accounting practices may cause the computed rates of return not to be precisely comparable to those of other pension plans and market indices.

Performance results are more meaningful if they can be related to the total risk of the portfolio. There is a theoretical relationship between risk and return for all types of capital assets. Some observers contend that if one portfolio outperforms another only because it took greater nonsystematic risk, no credit is due the portfolio manager. They assert that the real measure of a manager's performance is whether it was able to earn a superior return when recognition is given to differences in risk and that it is necessary to look at *risk-adjusted* rates of return.

---

[22]This linking is accomplished by multiplying the separate internal rates of return times each other, with equal weight being assigned to each period. For example, if the internal rate of return per quarter for four quarters were 2 percent, 8 percent, 5 percent, and –6 percent, the time-weighted rate of return for the year would be 8.73 percent ($1.02 \times 1.08 \times 1.05 \times .94 - 1.00$, converted to a percentage).

[23]Some measurement services estimate the market value of the portfolio at each month-end by regression analysis and then compute monthly internal rates of return. The estimation is carried out by applying the portfolio's beta to the rate of return on the market during the monthly subinterval. There are technical problems with the estimation process, but this approach can produce more accurate results than the linking of quarterly returns.

For a common stock portfolio, a statistical measure of "value added" from active management is called alpha. It is the intercept of the regression line of return on the portfolio and that of the market when the market return is zero. Both are adjusted for the return on a risk-free asset. If the alpha is equal to 0.0, there is a zero risk-adjusted rate of return, and the manager has added no nonsystematic value from its efforts. If the alpha is greater than 0.0, there is a positive risk-adjusted rate of return. An alpha of less than 0.0 indicates that there is a negative risk-adjusted rate of return. There may be a *negative* risk-adjusted return even when the nominal rate of return is *positive,* and vice versa. As with beta, it is possible to measure the statistical significance of the derived values, and this item is included in some performance analyses.

The alpha factor is not a wholly satisfactory measure of the value added from active bond management, primarily because the risk characteristics of a bond or aggregation of bonds continually change as the maturity date approaches. However, an approximation to the alpha can be derived by the same statistical techniques used to determine the alpha for common stock portfolios. The risk level and rate of return are compared with a "market line" portraying various percentage combinations of riskless Treasury bills and a slice of the overall bond market. The line reflects various combinations of risk and return, and any combination of risk and return for a particular portfolio above that line suggests a positive risk-adjusted return, or value added from active management. Any point below the line indicates a negative risk-adjusted return.

The impact of active management on a bond portfolio can also be ascertained, with some limitations, through the duration model. Duration, it was noted earlier, is a measure of the average time to receipt of discounted cash flows from a fixed-income instrument. It is a measure of the sensitivity of a bond's price to changes in interest rates. With this information for all the portfolio securities, it becomes possible to attribute the sources of the portfolio's return to the market, the policy effect, the interest rate anticipation effect, the analysis effect (the selection of issues with better-than-average long-term prospects), and the trading effect (the difference between the total management effect and the effects attributable to analysis and interest rate anticipation). This is a complex process and the rates of return must be precisely measured to attribute return to various effects. Moreover, duration is not a measure to the total portfolio risk, since it ignores the quality factors. There are other conceptual flaws that limit the usefulness of this approach.

A more recent approach to determining value added to a bond (or stock) portfolio by management is to compare actual investment results with market results and with the results that would have been obtained had the beginning portfolio been held without change throughout the measurement period, the so-called naive alternative. The difference between the rate of return on the market and the theoretical return on the beginning portfolio is considered to be the management differential, as reflected to the beginning of the period. The yield on the beginning, or buy-and-hold, portfolio will equal its beginning yield to maturity if nothing else changes. However, interest rates may change during the period, and sector and quality differentials may broaden or narrow, with unequal effects on the market portfolio and the buy-and-hold portfolio. The difference between the total rate of return on the beginning portfolio and the sum of the beginning yield to maturity, the interest rate effect, and the sector/quality effect is called the "residual" or "other selection" effect. Finally, the difference between the return on the beginning portfolio and the return on the actual portfolio is called the "activity" or "swapping" factor. It measures the effect of active management during the measurement period.

The total riskiness of an equity or bond portfolio when the asset manager has discretionary control over cash flow may be estimated by the mean absolute deviation (MAD) of the time-weighted rate of return. The MAD is the average of the absolute difference in the time-weighted rate of return on each portfolio holding and the time-weighted return for the entire portfolio. In this context, "absolute" means without regard to sign, a deviation of −3 having the same value as +3. The MAD is a useful value to have when comparing investment results with market indices and other portfolios.

Rates of return and risk factors are computed not only for the latest measurement period but for various time intervals and on a cumulative basis. It is customary to show results for the most recent calendar year; the last 2-, 3-, 4-, and 5-year periods; the last 10 years; and for individual managers, the whole period of their stewardship on a cumulative basis. Rates of return may be shown separately for principal (changes in market value) and income (or principal and income combined).

Comparisons with Other Pension Portfolios and Market Indices

Absolute rates of return, especially internal rates of return, have important implications for a pension plan sponsor's investment goals and objectives and actuarial interest assumption. However, their impact can be better understod if they are compared with the investment results of appropriate market indices and other pension plans with similar investment objectives. This is especially important when the rates of return are disappointing or even negative, as they have been in some years.

It is customary for asset managers to include comparisons with widely recognized market indices in their periodic reports of investment performance. The best-known common stock indices are those maintained by Standard & Poor's, Dow Jones, the New York Stock Exchange, the American Stock Exchange, Value Line, Wilshire Associates, and Frank Russell Company. These indices differ in composition, the weighting of the stock issues, changes in the list of securities, the treatment of income, and the frequency and timing of index available. The most widely used stock indexes for comparison purposes is Standard & Poor's Composite 500 Index, which, as its name suggests, contains the common stock of 500 large corporations, weighted by the market value of the outstanding shares of the constituent companies (referred to as capitalization weighted). Standard & Poor's also maintains an index of the stock of *industrial* corporations, also weighted by market capitalization. The second most frequently cited index is that maintained by Dow Jones for 30 industrial stocks (actually the stocks of 29 industrials and AT&T). The stocks are weighted by price, and the published value is derived by dividing the aggregate market value of the outstanding stock by a constant that was originally 30 but has been adjusted downward over the years to reflect stock splits and other changes in capitalization. The denominator is published each Monday in the *Wall Street Journal.* Thus, strictly speaking, the resulting value is an *average* not an *index.* Dow Jones also computes separate averages for 15 utilities and 20 companies in transportation and then combines the 65 companies into a composite average.

The indices of the two stock exchanges contain the stocks of all listed companies, weighted by market capitalization. The Wilshire index reflects the market value of about 5,000 stocks, with changes in the group being made monthly. The Value Line index contains about 1,700 stocks, which are given equal weighting, and reflects the geometric mean of daily price relativities.

There are a number of bond indices. The index of returns on 90-day Treasury bills is designed to serve as a proxy for the risk-free return available to investors. The returns are computed on the assumption of continuous reinvestment on a tax-free basis in 90-day T-bills. Standard & Poor's High Grade Corporate Bond Index is widely used for long-term bonds. In effect, this is a hypothetical high-quality bond portfolio with a 20-year maturity and 4 percent coupon rate, priced to reflect current interest rates. The Salomon Brothers High-Grade Long-Term Bond Index and the Lehman Brothers Kuhn Loeb Corporate Long-Term Bond Index each reflect the coupon rates and current prices of a broad group of outstanding bond issues (almost 4,000 issues), weighted by market capitalization. They are regarded as superior indicators of market return and are widely used for evaluative purposes. Their primary drawback is that they consider only bonds with a remaining maturity of at least 20 years. The Lehman Brothers Kuhn Loeb Bond Index is a capitalization weighted return index on more than 4,000 issues of more than one-year maturity. Moody's, Merrill Lynch, and Dow Jones also publish a number of specialized bond indices. An investor can construct its own hybrid index by combining several of the published indices with weightings reflecting the composition of its own bond portfolio.

Comparisons of the investment results of a particular pension portfolio with certain market indices can be misleading if the investment objectives of the plan are significantly different from those implicit in the market results. It may be more meaningful to compare results with those of other large pension plans that are pursuing investment policies similar to those of the plan under review. A number of firms in the financial field offering investment performance and analysis services have created and maintained a data bank that contains performance data on several hundred pension plans of various types. These firms offer risk-and-return comparisons not only with standard market indices but with the pension plans in their data bank, and possibly with the commingled funds of banks and insurance companies operated for qualified pension, profit-sharing, and savings plans. These comparisons are becoming very sophisticated in that they reflect several risk/return measures and show the relative ranking of the client plan against all other plans in the universe by quartile or quintile groups. Risk-and-return measures are given by broad categories of assets—equities, bonds, and short-term securities—and possibly by sector groupings. Performance data are furnished for past periods of varying duration and for various ending dates, which of course can be crucial. There are reasons to believe that these performance analyses are helping plan sponsors to reassess their investment objectives and strategies on a continuing basis and to evaluate the performance of their asset managers against that of their peers.

Chapter 31
Allocated Funding Instruments

As noted in earlier sections of this volume, the assets of a qualified pension plan must either be held in trust or be transferred to a life insurance company in exchange for its promise to pay the plan benefits when they become due or to provide stipulated investment services. The financial institution—bank, trust company, or life insurer—to which plan contributions are paid is called the *funding agency.* The legal document that defines the obligation of the funding agency is called the *funding instrument.* The funding instrument serves as a conduit through which contributions intended for benefit payments are channeled to the ultimate recipient—the participants or their beneficiaries. It also provides the legal and institutional framework in which accumulated plan assets are invested.

Funding instruments may be broadly classified according to whether they represent agreements with life insurance companies or with trustees, normally banks and trust companies. A more meaningful classification for many purposes can be derived from how plan contributions to the funding agency—and accumulated plan assets—are applied to satisfy individual benefit claims. Within this context, funding instruments can be classified as *allocated* funding instruments or *unallocated* funding instruments.

In an *allocated funding instrument,* all past and current contributions are credited to individual plan participants in a way that gives them a legally enforceable claim to the benefits that can be provided by cumulative contributions. This claim is contingent on the satisfaction of certain stipulated conditions. In an *unallocated funding instrument, some or all* of the current and accumulated contributions are held by the *funding agency* in a pooled account until they are disbursed in benefit payments or applied to purchase paid-up annuities at retirement or on earlier termination of employment with vested benefits. This distinction is of crucial significance to plan design, the administration of plan assets, and the security of benefit expectations.

General Characteristics

As a practical matter, only certain types of insurance and annuity contracts issued by life insurance companies can satisfy the above definition of an allocated funding instrument. The assets of a defined benefit plan funded through a trust are commingled and are allocated to individual participants only when paid to them in lump sums or income benefits, or when they are used to purchase annuities in the names of terminated vested or retired employees. Under a money purchase pension plan funded through a trust, the *plan sponsor* maintains individual *memorandum* accounts on behalf of the participants to which contributions and associated investment income are currently credited, but these individual accounts are not funding instruments. The funding instrument is the trust agreement, and the trustee does not ordinarily[1] partition the trust fund into subaccounts, one for each participant, against which the participants would have legally enforceable rights, including the right of a periodic accounting. The trust fund instead is a pooled account held and invested for the collective benefit of the participants and their beneficiaries.

Sometimes a bank, in addition to acting as trustee, provides record-keeping services for the employer and maintains the individual accounts on behalf of the employer. In such instances, however, the bank is acting as administrative assistant to the plan sponsor rather than performing its role of trustee.

Premiums and annuity considerations paid to the insurer under allocated funding instruments generally flow into the general asset account and lose their identity as pension assets, except for tax apportionment purposes. This is in accordance with the general principle and tradition that all contractual guarantees of a life insurer are obligations of the general asset account. The guarantees are fixed-dollar obligations, payable without adjustment for fluctuations in the market value of the underlying assets. The premium rates for individual life insurance contracts remain fixed throughout the premium-paying period of the contracts. The annuity purchase rates under group contracts, however, are normally guaranteed for only the first five years of the contract and are subject thereafter to the risk of adverse rate changes that would apply only to *future* annuity purchases. Group annuity rates may be adjusted downward for favorable experience, and the nominally fixed premiums of participating individual life insurance contracts are adjusted annually through so-called dividends, which are refunds of a portion of the premiums for favorable experience.

The primary appeal of an allocated funding instrument to the plan sponsor is that it transfers risk to the insurer—that is, the life insurer will assume the legal responsibility of paying part or all of the benefits under the plan on behalf of the sponsor. Every dollar paid to a life insurer under an allocated funding instrument carries with it the insurer's unconditional guarantee that a retirement benefit of a specified amount will be paid pursuant to the terms of the plan. The risk transferred to the insurer is that there might be unfavorable deviations from assumed experience with respect to mortality, investment earnings, and expenses of administration. To the extent that the benefit obligations of the plan have been funded by allocated funding instruments and thus have been assumed by the insurer, the participants look to the insurer, rather than to the sponsor, to pay their benefits. It is an unsettled question whether, under the Employment Retirement Income Security Act, the plan sponsor retains a residual, contingent liability for the benefit claims under the plan if the insurer, because of insolvency, cannot meet its contractual obligations.

---

[1]Trust assets are partitioned in the case of participant-directed individual accounts, as described in Chapter 32.

An important corollary to the risk transfer that occurs under an allocated funding instrument is that as of any given time the plan sponsor's cost for benefits accrued to that date is *known* and fixed. The accrued benefits and their maximum cost are fixed at all times. As noted above, the nominal cost may be reduced retroactively through dividends and experience rate credits.

Another appeal of the allocated funding approach to the sponsor is that the insurance or annuity contract may be part of a comprehensive package of services needed to establish and maintain a pension plan. In addition to assuming responsibility for benefit payments, the insurer may provide all actuarial, investment, disbursement, accounting, and reporting services associated with a plan. The insurer may either prepare or supply the information for reports going to regulatory authorities and participants. It generally keeps the plan sponsor informed about all legislative, legal, or tax developments that may affect the operation of the plan. A representative of the insurer usually does the designing of the plan, which is not always an objective exercise. The only service that the sponsor may have to seek from other external sources is legal and tax advice.

Finally, the allocated funding approach appeals to some plan participants, a factor that may contribute to the overall morale of the work force, with resulting benefits to the employer. Plan participants may respond favorably to the idea of individual insurance or annuity contracts (or units of paid-up annuities, under a group deferred annuity contract) being issued in their name, even though they cannot take possession of the contracts until they leave the service of the employer with vested rights. Except for past service benefits under group deferred annuity contracts, the benefits are at all times fully funded and are usually not subject to divestment through reallocation of assets upon termination of the plan. In other words, the allocation of plan contributions that takes place when each contribution is made usually remains in effect when the plan terminates and the ERISA allocation formula becomes applicable to previously unallocated plan assets. The owner-participant in a small plan may find this feature of an allocated funding instrument particularly appealing. If the allocations under a group deferred annuity conflict with the plan termination allocation formula of ERISA (an unlikely occurrence), deferred annuities and those in pay status might have to be cancelled or reduced in amount.

There are two major disadvantages to the allocated funding approach: it is inflexible and rather costly. The contracts used by life insurers to accommodate allocated funding are highly structured. The individual and group permanent insurance contracts were designed for other purposes and were adapted with minor modifications, if any, to funding pension plans. The other contract used for allocated funding, the group deferred annuity contract, was developed specifically for pension plans but utilizes a rigid system of contribution allocation. Under defined benefit plans funded solely with allocated funding instruments, the plan must be designed to fit the contract forms, rather than the other way around. The benefit formula, in particular, is highly constrained. It is not feasible, for example, to utilize benefit formulas that recognize final pay, offset benefits by Social Security, or provide early retirement benefits not based on full actuarial equivalence. Final-pay formulas may produce an undesirable cost pattern. (Some plans that employ a final-pay formula do not recognize pay increases that occur within five years of the individual's normal retirement age.) Contributions are shaped by schedules of premium and annuity purchase rates and do not recognize anticipated turnover, retirements at other than the normal retirement age, and other developments that might affect the amount of contributions. Transfer of the accumulated funds to another funding agency is awkward, if not impossible.

The cost per unit of benefit is likely to be higher under an allocated funding instrument than under an unallocated funding instrument for a number of reasons. The first, which is not the fault of the instrument, is that allocated funding tends to be used with small groups; this limits the opportunity to spread fixed costs. Furthermore, distribution costs associated with marketing individual contracts are incurred, the principal costs being commissions to the soliciting agent or broker. Of course, any type of pension plan incurs installation costs, and commissions to agents or brokers under individual contracts may be offset to some extent under other funding instruments by payments to an actuarial firm or to an employee benefit consultant. State taxes have to be paid on premiums on individual insurance contracts and may be payable under group annuity contracts. Administrative expenses are higher when individual contracts are issued or individual annuity accounts must be maintained; this source of expense is not found under unallocated funding contracts. Finally, the cost may be higher in the long run because the plan is funded through the general asset account and does not have access to the potentially higher investment returns of the various separate accounts maintained by the insurer. In some circumstances, the purchase of individual contracts may be determined to be a breach of fiduciary responsibility by the plan sponsor, the trustee, or other fiduciaries because of the higher costs.[2]

These disadvantages of allocated funding instruments are so serious that their use is largely confined to small plans and situations in which the sponsor believes that the advantages of the approach may outweigh the disadvantages. Individual insurance or annuity contracts are extensively used to fund small defined contribution plans, Section 403(b) annuities, individual retirement accounts, and other individual account arrangements. These arrangements are typically operated on a *money purchase* basis, which does not require the degree of adaptability that a defined benefit plan does.

The following sections briefly explain these allocated funding instruments and the reasons that life insurers found it necessary to develop more flexible funding instruments.

Individual Insurance or Annuity Contract

General Characteristics

The primary characteristic of this form of allocated funding is that individual insurance or annuity contracts are purchased on the lives of persons eligible to participate in the plan. The contracts may be held by the employer or by a trustee or custodian acting under the terms of a trust or custodial agreement executed by the employer. If a trust is used, the provisions of the plan are usually incorporated

---

[2] *Brock v. Shuster*, Civil no. 87-2759 (D. DC, filed Nov. 3, 1987).

in the trust agreement, and the trustee—frequently an officer of the employer firm—is charged, along with the plan administrator, with the responsibility of administering the plan.

Many insurance companies have developed a master or prototype plan that the employer can adopt by executing a joinder agreement.[3] Under this arrangement, all ownership rights to carry out the terms and conditions of the plan are vested in the trustee or the employer, but the participants retain the right to name a beneficiary to receive the death benefit and to specify the manner in which the benefit will be paid. The master or prototype plan may permit the employer to select various options relating to such basic provisions as employee coverage, contributions, benefit schedules, and vesting. A master or prototype plan must be approved by the Internal Revenue Service, which assigns a serial number to it; but such approval does not constitute a ruling or determination on the qualification of the plan of a particular employer who adopts the master or prototype plan.

The plan usually calls for the purchase of insurance policies or annuity contracts similar to the individual policies or contracts offered to the general public. If an insurance policy is used, evidence of insurability satisfactory to the insurer may be required. The more common practice, though, is to underwrite the plan on a "guaranteed issue" basis, which means that no evidence of individual insurability is required, subject to certain limits determined by the nature of the group and the aggregate amount of insurance involved. The *no-evidence* basis of underwriting must be distinguished from the *nonmedical* basis, under which an individual health statement is always required and a medical examination may be requested at the option of the insurer. A minimum number of five lives is usually required for guaranteed issue underwriting, and there may be other requirements as well. Amounts of insurance in excess of that provided under the guaranteed issue formula will be made available, subject to the normal underwriting requirements of the insurer. If the insurer employs regular underwriting procedures, a medical examination or other evidence of insurability is required for each participant as he or she enters the plan or becomes entitled to another policy because of an increase in benefits. If the participant who has to show evidence of insurability cannot qualify for insurance at standard rates, the contract may be issued on a substandard or classified basis, with the extra cost being borne by either the employer or the employee, or shared in some proportion. Alternatively, substandard risks may be issued policies providing the same retirement benefits at standard rates but with reduced death benefits, called "graded death benefits." When the participant is not insurable on any basis, a retirement annuity contract may be used in lieu of an insurance policy.

To permit more flexibility in plan specifications and a more liberal underwriting approach, as exemplified by the guaranteed issue device, some companies have developed special policy series for pension plans. These policies usually contain provisions specifically adapted to the needs of a pension plan and their actuarial treatment is different from that accorded policies in conventional series.

---

[3]There is a technical distinction between a master plan and a prototype plan. See Rev. Proc. 84-23. Master and prototype plans have also been developed by banks, investment companies, and trade or professional associations.

Premiums, cash values, settlement options, and other features under the contracts must not permit plan benefits to differ by sex. Their commission scales are lower, their cash values and death benefits are different, and they have special dividend classifications.

The plan may be contributory or noncontributory. In either case, the employer periodically pays the premiums on the insurance or annuity contracts, either directly or through a trustee. Benefit payments are generally made directly by the insurance company, upon certification of entitlement by the employer, plan administrator, or trustee.

Types of Contracts

A plan sponsor can choose from among many different types of insurance or annuity contracts.

Level-Premium Retirement Annuity Contract

Under a level-premium retirement annuity contract, level annual premiums are used to accumulate a cash value that may be converted into annuity payments at retirement. The guaranteed cash value under a retirement annuity is the equivalent of the premiums paid less a charge for expenses, accumulated with interest at a guaranteed rate, sometimes reduced by a surrender charge. Frequently, dividends or interest in excess of the guaranteed rate are added to increase the cash value.

Upon retirement or earlier termination of employment (or earlier if permitted by the plan), the contract may be surrendered for its cash value, or the cash value may be applied to provide a monthly annuity to the participant. The amount of monthly annuity that can be provided for each $1,000 of cash value depends upon the form of the annuity and, if payments are contingent on the survival of the annuitant, upon the age of the annuitant. It was formerly common practice to have the amount of monthly annuity differ by sex to recognize the longer average lifetime of females, but this practice is no longer allowed under employee plans. The settlement option provisions of the contract specify the minimum guaranteed monthly income per $1,000 applied. Under the provisions of one leading company, each $1,000 applied is guaranteed to provide a monthly life income of $5.61 to an annuitant aged 65, with payments guaranteed for 10 years.

For many companies, if the annuity rates associated with insurance and annuity contracts that are currently being issued for immediate annuities under qualified plans are lower than those guaranteed in the settlement options provision of the policy, these more favorable *current* rates are substituted for the guaranteed *contract* rates. Should the participant die before the contract has been surrendered or before he or she applied for an annuity, a death benefit equal to the cash value, but not less than the considerations paid, is available.

flexible-Premium Retirement Annuity

flexible-premium retirement annuities function in essentially the same way as level-premium retirement annuities, except that they have great flexibility in their ability to vary the premium from year to year. As under the level-premium retirement annuity, the guaranteed cash value under a flexible-premium retirement annuity equals the premiums paid less a charge for expenses, accumulated with interest at a guaranteed rate, sometimes reduced by a surrender charge. Dividends or interest in excess of the guaranteed rate increase the cash value.

If a plan wants to increase the amount of contributions for a participant using level-premium retirement annuities, it is necessary to issue an additional contract. If flexible-premium annuities are used instead, the amount of premium under the existing contract is simply increased. While a plan funded with level-premium contracts may have many contracts on the life of one participant, only one flexible-premium annuity contract is needed. This reduces the administrative costs of both the insurance company and the employer. The commissions payable are also reduced because there are fewer first-year premiums, with their higher commission rate. Likewise, the cash values generally increase because a lower expense charge is deducted from renewal premiums than from first-year premiums in determining the cash value. In view of the disadvantages of level-premium annuity contracts, many plans have turned to flexible-premium retirement annuities or some other funding instrument.

Variable Annuity Contracts

Under individual variable annuity contracts, the assets representing the contract reserves are invested in a separate account or in a unit investment trust, which in turn is invested in common stocks or mutual funds (variable annuities are described in more detail in Chapter 21). The benefits provided by the contract depend upon the investment performance of the underlying assets.

During the accumulation years before benefit payments begin, the variable annuity contract is similar to a mutual fund. The premiums, less an expense charge, are applied to purchase units. The value of the unit reflects the total investment return of the underlying assets, including investment income and realized and unrealized appreciation and depreciation of market values, reduced by a charge for expenses. When benefits become payable, the value of the units may be paid as a lump sum or may be applied to provide a fixed annuity or a variable annuity. Individual variable annuity contracts may be used in any of the ways that flexible premium annuities are used.

Retirement Income Policies

The retirement income policy is identical to the level-premium retirement annuity contracts, except that the former incorporates an insurance feature.[4] The retirement annuity contract only returns the premiums paid or the cash value (whichever is larger) if the participant dies before retiring. The retirement income policy, on the other hand, pays $1,000 for each $10 unit of monthly income that

---

[4]Technically, the retirement annuity contract contains a minor insurance element during the first few years after issue, measured by the excess of the accumulated premiums over the cash value of the contract.

would have been provided under the policy at age 65, or the cash value (whichever is greater) if the participant dies before retiring. The excess of the death benefit over the cash value represents the insurance element. The amount of insurance protection decreases as the cash value increases, and it eventually declines to zero when the cash value equals or exceeds the face amount of insurance under the policy. The type of insurance involved is decreasing term, since it is both limited in duration and reducing in amount. After the term insurance has expired, the contract in effect becomes an annuity contract, and its cash value continues to increase until at maturity the proceeds are sufficient to provide the stated amount of monthly income.

Term Life Insurance

Term life insurance usually provides a level amount of death benefit protection for a limited period. The term of the policy may be a single year, a period of years such as five years, or a period of years extending to some stipulated age such as 65. At the end of the term the policy expires with no value.

Traditionally, the premium remains level during the stipulated period. At the end of the period most policies provide for automatic renewal for a new period of the same length. Many policies do not allow a renewal to extend the insurance beyond some maximum age such as 70, but since 1986 any such limit on the right of active employees to continue coverage violates age discrimination requirements. The premium for the new period will be higher than for the original period and will be based on the attained age of the insured. Many policies include the right to convert the policy to another form of insurance without evidence of insurability.

Term life insurance has lower initial premiums than any other form of life insurance. However, future increases in premiums produce higher annual premiums than other forms in later years.

Whole Life Insurance

A whole life policy, sometimes called a "straight life" policy, provides a level amount of death benefit throughout the lifetime of the insured, with premiums that continue for life. Traditionally, the premiums remain level for all years, although some insurers offer a modified form with reduced premiums for the first few years.

Whole life insurance develops a cash surrender value. If the policy is surrendered prior to the death of the insured, the cash value may be paid in a lump sum or may be applied under the settlement options of the policy to provide a monthly annuity. Some whole life policies also allow additional amounts to be added to the cash value at the time of retirement to increase the amount of monthly annuity that can be provided.

Limited-Payment Life Insurance

A limited-payment life insurance policy is the same as a whole life policy except that premium payments are limited to a certain number of years, although the insurance continues throughout the remaining lifetime of the policyholder. Many pension plans have used limited-payment life policies with premiums payable to age 85, 90, or 95. Such policies are essentially whole life policies.

Universal Life Insurance

A universal life insurance contract functions somewhat like a savings account plus term life insurance. Premiums paid are deposited in an account. Each month the account is increased by interest and is decreased by an expense charge and the cost to purchase term insurance. The account balance may be called the "gross cash value," or simply "cash value." If the policyholder surrenders the contract, he or she will receive the "cash surrender value," which equals the gross cash value less any surrender charge. After the early policy years any surrender charge is generally reduced to $0. Some contracts have no surrender charge at any time.

The initial face amount of insurance will be the amount that was applied for, provided the insurance company agrees to insure this amount. Thereafter the face amount of insurance will generally remain the same, except that the policyholder will have the option to reduce the amount of insurance at any time. The policy-holder may also increase the amount of insurance if evidence of insurability (i.e., good health) is provided.

Universal life insurance offers two alternative patterns of death benefits, often called "level death benefit" and "increasing death benefit." Under the level death benefit method, the death benefit generally equals the face amount of insurance. This level death benefit includes the policy's cash value plus a pure term insurance element. Thus each month term insurance is purchased that equals the face amount of insurance less the cash value. The cost of insurance that is deducted from the account is the cost to purchase this amount of term insurance.

Under the alternative method of "increasing death benefits," the death benefit equals the sum of the face amount of insurance *plus* the cash value. Here, term insurance is purchased each month for the full face amount of insurance, and the cost of insurance is determined accordingly. Since more insurance is purchased under this method than under the level death benefit method, less of the premium is available to add to the savings element of the policy. The total death benefit will increase or decrease with any increase or decrease in the cash value.

The premium payable under a universal life policy is usually completely flexible. The first premium must be at least sufficient to pay the expense charge and cost of term insurance for the first month. Thereafter the policyholder may pay any amount desired, as long as the amount paid each month plus the surrender value is sufficient to pay the monthly expense charge and the cost of insurance.

Although the amount of premium payable is flexible, a level "target premium" or "planned premium" is usually established. Sometimes the target premium is established at a level that would be expected to be sufficient to maintain the cost of insurance until some advanced age such as 90 or 100 and to gradually increase the cash value to equal the face amount of insurance at that age. However, many other ways to determine the target premium are also used. Thus the purchaser has great flexibility in determining the premium level for any particular face amount of insurance. Federal regulations establish a maximum on the ratio of premiums to face amount that is required to prevent adverse tax consequences.

The level of costs and benefits under universal life are controlled by four cost elements:

1. the expense charge specified in the policy,
2. the rates used to calculate the cost of insurance,
3. the rate of interest credited,
4. the surrender charge.

The cost of insurance is based on a set of rates. The insurance company maintains two sets of rates, current rates and guaranteed rates. The current rates are the rates actually used to determine costs of insurance under the contract. The current rates do not appear in the contract and may be changed by the insurance company without prior notice. The guaranteed rates are rates specified in the contract that place a guaranteed maximum on the current rates. The guaranteed rates are established on a conservative basis. One would not ordinarily expect the current rates to ever rise to the level of the guaranteed rates.

The interest credited is also subject to two rates, a current rate and a guaranteed rate. The current rate is the rate actually used, while the guaranteed rate is a minimum guarantee. The guaranteed rate is specified in the policy. The current rate generally reflects currently available interest rates and may be changed from time to time. Any expense charges and surrender charges are stated in the policy and are guaranteed.

Benefit Structure and Funding

Some defined benefit plans and some defined contribution plans are funded entirely with individual insurance and annuity contracts. In this case the benefit structure and funding of the plan are shaped by the characteristics of the contracts used. In other cases individual contracts are used to fund part of the benefits under the plan; in these plans the characteristics of the contracts may also have a significant effect on the benefit design and the funding of the plan.

Defined Benefit Plans Fully Funded with Individual Contracts

In earlier years it was common to fully fund defined benefit plans with retirement income policies, retirement annuity contracts, or both. The level-premium retirement annuity contract may be used to accumulate through the payment of level annual contributions a maturity value at a stipulated age that is sufficient to provide a life income of a specified amount. The income objectives are usually expressed in units of $10 per month. Under the actuarial assumptions of one leading company, a maturity value of $1,828.18 is needed to guarantee a monthly life income of $10 to a participant aged 65, with payments guaranteed for 10 years. If a participant in a pension plan should be entitled to a retirement benefit of $100 a month at age 65, with 120 guaranteed payments, an insurance company using the rates cited would have to have $18,281.80 on hand when the participant reaches retirement age. Theoretically, it would be immaterial to the insurer whether the $18,281.80 was paid to it in a lump sum at the time of the employee's retirement or was accumulated over a period of years by a series of payments. If, however, a retirement annuity should be purchased for the participant at age 45, an annual deposit of $557.66 with the insurer would be guaranteed to accumulate to the required sum of $18,281.80 when the participant reaches age 65. At that time annuity payments would begin at the normal rate of $100 per month, unless the participant elected an option with a more generous refund feature.

Dividends or interest credits exceeding the guaranteed interest rate could be applied to reduce the required employer contributions. If the *current* annuity purchase rates are substituted for the *contract* rates stated above, the maturity value of the policies would be *larger* than the sum needed to provide the plan benefits. In that event, the excess maturity value may be credited to the employer to reduce its future contributions under the plan or be applied to increase the amount of monthly pension.[5]

The retirement income policy could be used in the same manner as indicated above for the retirement annuity contract. The only differences would be the slightly higher premiums under the retirement income policy and the higher death benefit.

Retirement income policies were once commonly used as the sole funding instrument for many defined benefit plans. They are no longer commonly issued, but many previously issued policies remain in force, either on a premium-paying or paid-up basis, continuing to fund part of the benefits under plans.

The retirement benefits of a defined benefit plan fully funded through individual insurance or annuity contracts are typically expressed as a flat percentage of salary or as a percentage of compensation for each year of service. Under plans funded with level-premium retirement annuities and retirement income policies, the benefit formula is often designed to produce units of benefit commensurate with those of the underlying contracts, partly to avoid issuing additional contracts for very small increments of benefit. If the benefit is expressed as a flat percentage of compensation, salary brackets may be set up and the stipulated percentage applied to the midpoint of each bracket to produce benefit units in multiples of $10, or whatever sum is envisioned in the benefit formula. If the benefit formula provides for a percentage of compensation for each year of service, the projected benefit may be rounded off to the highest, or nearest, multiple of the basic benefit unit.

Under both types of formula, the participant's compensation at any given time is assumed to continue at the same level until normal retirement age, and the premiums or considerations are adjusted to the total anticipated benefit. For example, the initial contract for a participant is issued in an amount guaranteed to provide the monthly benefit that would be payable to the participant should he or she remain on the payroll at his or her current salary until he or she reaches retirement. If a subsequent increase in compensation should entitle the participant to an increase in his or her projected retirement income, a premium increase is made in the case of a flexible-premium retirement annuity, or an additional level-premium policy in the appropriate amount is purchased for him or her. Each such increase is assumed to remain in effect until normal retirement age. If

[5]Rev. Rul. 78-56.

level-premium policies are used, over a period of years the trustee or employer may purchase half a dozen or more policies for a single participant. Each one, after the original, represents an additional increment to the employee's retirement income.

Benefits payable to a participant upon his or her withdrawal from the plan prior to retirement are derived from the cash values of the contracts on his or her life at the time of termination. If the cash values are less than the benefit required to be vested by ERISA, a supplemental amount must be provided by the plan. If the vested benefit is not paid as a lump-sum distribution, the deferred vested benefit must satisfy the qualified preretirement survivor annuity requirements.

Under ERISA, a defined benefit plan funded exclusively with individual level-premium insurance and annuity contracts is defined as an "individual contract plan," provided no premiums are in default and there are no policy loans or other security interests against the contracts. Such a plan is not subject to the usual rules defining the required amount of accrued benefit, if the accrued benefit at least equals the policy cash value. In such a case, the cash value must be determined on the assumption that there are no premiums in default and no policy loans.[6] Because of the general decline in the use of level-premium retirement annuity and retirement income contracts, combined with the problems of complying with sex discrimination and qualified preretirement survivor annuity requirements, few if any plans still meet the requirements for "individual contract plans" as defined in ERISA.

The terminating participant may be given the right to continue, on a premium-paying basis, that portion of the life insurance policy or annuity contract represented by the vested cash values. Some plans permit the former employee to continue the contract or contracts in full force by paying to the trustee a sum of money equal to the nonvested cash values. To prevent the former employee from converting his or her vested benefits into cash (through surrender or assignment of the paid-up policy vested in him or her), some plans stipulate that the paid-up policy will be retained by the trustee, as an earmarked trust asset, until the individual attains the normal retirement age, at which time the contract will be released to the prospective annuitant. Another means of achieving the same objective is to turn over the vested policy to the terminating employee, but with an endorsement prohibiting surrender of the policy for cash or assignment of the policy as collateral until the individual reaches the normal retirement date specified in the plan. The endorsement may provide that upon maturity of the policy the proceeds are to be paid to the employee only in the form of a life income.

It is customary for the individual contract pension plan to provide for the payment of a death benefit in the event that the participant should die before retirement. Such a benefit is inherent in the types of contracts used to fund the retirement benefits. If the deceased was covered under a level-premium or flexible-premium retirement annuity contract, the death benefit would be equal to the gross considerations paid, without interest, or the cash value, whichever is greater. The death benefit under a retirement income insurance policy is even more generous. This type of policy typically provides a minimum death benefit of $1,000

---

[6]ERISA §§204(b)(1)(F), 301(b); IRC §§411(b)(1)(F), 412(i).

for each $10 unit of monthly life income, the cash value being paid if greater. This is a definitely planned death benefit, clearly intended to supplement the arrangement for retirement benefits.

Death benefits after retirement depend upon the form of annuity specified by the plan or elected by the participant. The normal annuity form for most individual contract pension plans is a life income with payments guaranteed for 120 months; but the insurer offers a number of other forms with an actuarially equivalent amount of benefits for the participant to elect. Pursuant to ERISA, the actual retirement benefits for married participants must be paid in the form of a qualified joint and survivor annuity, regardless of the normal form of retirement income, unless the participant elects in writing, with spousal consent, to have them paid in some other available form. In the event of a participant's death before his or her actual retirement date, the policy proceeds may be applied to satisfy the requirements for a qualified preretirement survivor annuity (see Chapter 11).

Various arrangements are made to protect a participant who becomes totally disabled before reaching the normal retirement age. A minimal step is to vest the cash values in the participant and make them available for withdrawal. Retirement benefits would be diminished by any sums withdrawn by the participant. A somewhat more generous arrangement is to include a waiver of premium provision, at an extra premium, in all contracts issued under the plan. This would preserve all accumulated values in the contracts of the disabled participant and, through annual increments to the cash values, would ensure that the participant, if still alive at the normal retirement age, would receive full retirement benefits.

Funding a defined benefit plan exclusively through conventional individual insurance and annuity contracts is inextricably tied to the premium structure of the contracts. If the plan remains in operation and premiums are paid on time, all participants are assured of receiving all of their benefits in full. Current service benefits are fully funded at all times, and all past service and other retroactively granted benefits are ultimately funded in full if the contracts remain in force. Thus there is a high degree of benefit security associated with this funding instrument. Insurance contract plans are exempt from the minimum funding requirements.[7]

Individual insurance or annuity contracts used to fund pension benefits are kept in force through level-dollar contributions payable during the participant's continued employment until normal retirement age. While called "premiums" (in the case of life insurance contracts) or "annuity considerations" (in the case of annuity contracts), these payments are derived in accordance with the principles of the individual level-premium cost method. The leveling of costs is characteristic of this method, along with the absence of withdrawal assumptions in the premium computations.

As is true of all individual insurance and annuity contracts, the premium and annuity purchase rates of any particular contract are guaranteed for the lifetime of the contract. The plan sponsor knows at the outset the maximum cost of providing the set of benefits in effect under the pension plan at any given time. The insurance company, however, makes no guarantee about the rates that will apply to contracts

---

[7]ERISA §301; IRC §412(h)(2), (i).

issued in the future to new participants or to current participants who qualify for additional retirement benefits. Such contracts are subject to the rate basis currently being applied by the underwriting insurer.

All pension plans underwritten by a life insurance company provide for certain credits (actuarial gains) to the employer, which, under the requirements of the Internal Revenue Code, cannot be paid in cash but must be applied against future premiums or contributions. If the pension plan is funded through "participating" contracts, policy dividends will become payable within a few years after they are issued. Companies that use a special policy series for pension plans set up separate dividend classifications for such policies. This practice is dictated by the special actuarial and underwriting treatment accorded the policies.

Whenever a participant terminates service with the employer before all cash values have vested, the nonvested values are applied to reduce future premiums. This, of course, means surrendering the portion of the insurance or annuity contract represented by the nonvested cash values.

As under any type of pension plan, the participant in an individual contract pension plan may continue in service beyond the normal retirement date, but the normal retirement benefits must become payable to the participant no later than April 1 following the year the participant reaches age 70½, even if he or she is still working.

The most common arrangement is to defer starting the annuity payments until the participant actually retires, subject to the age 70½ limit. The proceeds of the matured policies are credited with interest, which may be accumulated for ultimate distribution to the retired pensioner in the form of augmented annuity payments or may be applied to reduce future premiums. At actual retirement, the participant may become entitled to a retirement benefit that reflects his or her attained age and the retained policy proceeds, possibly augmented by accumulated interest. If larger, the participant must receive a benefit calculated using the plan's benefit formula, but recognizing his or her service and compensation after normal retirement age in the same manner as service and compensation before normal retirement age. The employer is credited with any difference between the accumulated cash value and the sum required for an annuity for the amount of benefit specified in the plan. This credit is allowed in one sum at the date of actual retirement, rather than in a series of annual adjustments.

flexible premium annuities have sometimes been used as a substitute for individual retirement income insurance policies. The traditional death benefit under a defined benefit plan of 100 times the projected monthly pension will exceed the cash value of the annuity contract. To fund this death benefit, a yearly renewable term insurance contract is issued to each participant. The amount of death benefit under the term insurance fluctuates each year and equals the death benefit provided for under the plan, less the death benefit payable under the flexible premium annuity as of the beginning of the year. The insurance contracts may be issued to the trust as part of the pension plan or may be purchased outside the pension plan.

This combination of flexible-premium annuity and yearly renewable term insurance separates the funding of the pension and the funding of the death benefit. Compared with retirement income insurance, this approach allows for greater flexibility in designing the amount of death benefit. Death benefits do not have to be a multiple of the amount of retirement income. But if the term insurance is issued to the pension trust, the usual rules concerning incidental death benefits apply.

Defined Contribution Plans Fully Funded with Individual Contracts

Some defined contribution plans are fully funded through individual contracts. flexible-premium retirement annuity contracts or variable annuity contracts may be used for this purpose. If one wants to provide life insurance under the plan, a combination of flexible-premium retirement annuity contracts and either whole life policies or term insurance policies may be used. It is possible to allow the individual participant to elect what portion, if any, of the contributions to his or her account are to be invested in insurance contracts, subject to the limits on incidental death benefits described in Chapter 12.

Plans Partly Funded with Individual Contracts

Some small defined benefit plans and defined contribution plans are funded by a combination of individual insurance policies and an unallocated funding instrument. The insurance contracts used are usually whole life policies, limited payment life policies, or universal life policies, although term insurance is also sometimes used. Such combinations of funding instruments are discussed in Chapter 32.

Group Permanent Insurance Contract

General Characteristics

Pension and profit-sharing plans normally restrict the use of individual contracts to a group of employees that is not large enough to qualify for coverage on a group basis. Many large plans that were originally funded through individual contracts are now being funded through group contracts issued by life insurers or by trusts administered by banks. The group approach that most closely resembles the individual contract approach—and into which some individual contract pension trusts have been converted—is known as the group permanent plan. It originated with group life insurance outside of pension plans in an attempt to provide life insurance protection beyond the working years of the participants. It derived its name from the fact that so-called permanent forms of insurance, such as retirement income insurance and whole life, were substituted for the more conventional group term insurance. Since these contracts developed cash values, which could be used for retirement benefits, it was a logical and simple step to adapt the mechanism of the group permanent life insurance plan to the funding of pension benefits.

A group permanent whole life, universal life, or retirement income insurance contract is very similar to the collection of individual insurance contracts of the same type it was designed to replace. Similarly, group-level premium annuity contracts, sometimes called group permanent annuities because of their similarity to group permanent insurance, are essentially a collection of individual-level premium annuities.

Plans fully or partly funded through group permanent insurance or annuity contracts tend to have the same general characteristics and design features as those utilizing individual contracts. A group permanent insurance contract under a defined benefit plan can be adapted to any type of benefit formula, but it is most widely used with a formula that relates the benefit to compensation, either as a flat percentage of earnings or as a unit of benefit for each year of service. The benefits are normally payable under a life income option with payments guaranteed for 5 or 10 years. Vesting provisions are similar to those found in plans funded through individual contracts and must meet the minimum standards of ERISA.

For profit-sharing plans, group permanent insurance may be used to replace individual insurance contracts for employees who elect to have part of their account invested in permanent insurance. Disability benefits can be provided in the form of accelerated vesting, early retirement provisions, waiver of premium, or even disability income payments independent of sums accumulated for retirement.

Funding

The partial or total funding of a pension plan through a group permanent insurance contract may be determined by the premium structure of the contract, as in the case of plans funded through individual insurance or annuity contracts. Premiums tend to conform to those for individual insurance contracts, except that the expense component may be smaller because of economies of scale and a lower commission. Premium and annuity rates are guaranteed for the lifetime of each amount of insurance or annuity. As with a plan funded through individual contracts, certain credits, or cost offsets, are generated and credited against future employer contributions to the plan.

Group Deferred Annuity Contract

General Characteristics

The earliest contractual arrangement made available by life insurance companies for funding pension benefits on a group basis was the group deferred annuity contract. Few new group deferred annuity contracts have been issued in recent years to fund ongoing plans, but many still remain in force, usually on a paid-up basis. However, many group deferred annuity contracts have been issued to fund benefits in terminating defined benefit plans. While utilizing the group approach, this type of contract is not subject to the statutory rules that regulate the writing of group life insurance.

The underlying legal document of the group deferred annuity is the master contract. This document—along with the application, if attached—constitutes the entire contract between the employer and the insurer. Each employee receives a certificate setting forth in substance the rights and benefits to which the employee and his or her beneficiaries are entitled. This certificate is merely evidence of participation in the plan and in the eyes of the law is not regarded as a contract between the employee and the insurer. Nevertheless, the employee is considered to be a third-party beneficiary under the master contract and, as such, can enforce his or her rights created thereunder. Since no life insurance mortality risk is involved, no evidence of insurability is required for participation in the plan.

Benefit Structure

The group deferred annuity contract is designed for the funding and payment of retirement benefits, any other benefits being incidental. For ongoing plans, it was best suited to (and was usually used with) a formula that provides a unit of benefit for each year of service. The benefit may be expressed as a flat amount for each year of service or as a percentage of earnings. The typical group deferred annuity contract provided a specified percentage of current earnings for each year of service. For purposes of administrative convenience, a schedule of salary classes was frequently established, and the percentage was applied to the midpoint of the appropriate salary bracket.

The benefits are provided through the medium of a deferred life annuity. Under this type of annuity, the income payments do not commence until a specified period has elapsed. The typical period of deferment extends from the date of purchase to the attainment of a specified age by the annuitant. A *pure* deferred life annuity refunds no part of the purchase price if the annuitant should die before reaching the specified age, since the rates charged make allowance for anticipated mortality. The *refund* deferred life annuity, on the other hand, returns the purchase price, with or without interest, if the annuitant should die before the annuity payments commence.

When a pension plan that has not been funded with allocated funding instruments is terminated, plan assets are often applied to purchase deferred annuities under a deferred annuity contract for part or all of the accrued benefits. The amount of annuity is the amount that was accrued at the time of plan termination under the plan's benefit formula. The normal form of annuity as well as the qualified joint and survivor annuity must be in accordance with the forms in effect at the time of termination. In addition, the deferred annuity contract must guarantee early retirement benefits, lump-sum distributions, and other options as generous as those in the plan just before termination, and it must provide for the qualified preretirement survivor annuity. Immediate annuities are purchased under the same group contract for participants and beneficiaries for whom the annuity commencement date has already occurred.

Funding

Annuity Purchase Rates

For any given group of participants and set of benefits, the amount of the periodic consideration is determined by reference to a schedule of *annuity purchase rates* that determine, for each attained age in the group, the amount of money that must be paid to the insurer for each $1 of monthly benefit payable at normal retirement age under the normal annuity form. These rates reflect assumptions about mortality, interest, and expenses, including an allowance for contingencies and profit (or contribution to surplus, in the case of a mutual insurer). Mortality assumptions are based on the observed experience of individuals covered under group annuity contracts, with margins for deviations and allowance for future reductions in mortality.

Interest assumptions used in the derivation of group annuity rates to purchase annuities upon plan termination reflect the rates of return that can be obtained at the time of purchase. An explicit allowance ("loading" in insurance terminology) for expenses, contingencies, and profit (or contribution to surplus) is usually made.

Experience Accounting

All group deferred annuity contracts issued to fund ongoing plans and some contracts issued to fund terminated plans provide for an adjustment in the plan contributions if experience warrants it. In a mutual life insurance company it is usually described as a "dividend," and in a stock life insurance company it is referred to as a "rate credit." Except for the smallest plans, the amount of the refund depends primarily on the experience of the plan in question. This is accomplished through the maintenance of a noncontractual memorandum account, generally called the "experience account," for each group annuity contract.

During any particular contract year, including the first, this experience account is credited with all contributions under the contract for that year. The accumulated balance, including contributions for the current year, is credited with a rate of interest or a series of interest rates designed to reflect the actual investment earnings of the various segments of the fund, determined by reference to the year in which the funds were invested and reinvested (see Chapter 32 for an explanation of the rationale and technique for allocating investment earnings in accordance with the calendar year in which the plan assets were invested or reinvested). The account is charged with benefit disbursements under the contract during the current year, as well as with all expenses allocable to it under accepted cost accounting techniques. It may be credited or charged, as the case may be, with a "mortality adjustment," which has the effect of smoothing mortality fluctuations (1) over the years of the particular contract, and (2) among all group annuity contracts written by the company. A "risk charge" is also deducted from the experience account, as a contribution to the insurer's profits or surplus.

At the end of the contract year, the insurer calculates the present value of the benefits that are payable under the annuities that have been purchased and are still in force. The minimum basis for this valuation may be specified in the contract; but the actual valuation may be more stringent than the minimum and may include various contingency reserves. Nevertheless, whatever basis is used is normally applied to all group deferred annuity contracts, regardless of when they were issued.

The difference between the amount shown in the experience account and the contractual liabilities, as revealed by the periodic valuation, reflects the gain or loss under the contract. After appropriate amounts have been allocated to the contingency reserve, and in some companies to the reserve for future expenses, the gain, if any, may be returned to the plan sponsor in the form of a dividend or rate reduction. The insurer is under no contractual obligation to pay a dividend, if earned, and the sponsor has no legal right to an accounting.

Strictly speaking, a group annuity contract is not terminated until the insurer has fulfilled all its obligations under the contract. Therefore in the usual circumstances the contract will not be fully terminated until the last annuitant dies. If a situation arises in which there is no entity to act as the contract-holder, however, the contract may be terminated, and thereafter the insurer's obligation regarding for the benefits purchased to the date of termination will be to serve the covered employees directly.

Chapter 32
Unallocated Funding Instruments

The term *unallocated funding* is applied to any arrangement under which contributions are held in an undivided fund until they are used to meet benefit payments as they come due or are used to purchase deferred or immediate annuities. There are two general types of unallocated funding instruments: *unallocated group annuity contracts* and *trust agreements* with banks and trust companies (or, in some cases, natural persons). There are several types of unallocated group annuity contracts, but they all have certain basic characteristics in common.

General Characteristics

The distinguishing characteristic of an unallocated funding instrument is its flexibility. It accommodates any policy or practice permitted by law. Subject only to legal constraints, it provides almost complete flexibility in benefit structure, actuarial assumptions, and funding procedures, and often in investment policy as well. Any type of benefit formula can be used, since the amount of benefit to be paid to a participant need not be determined until he or she retires or terminates with vested benefits. Thus it can accommodate a final average pay formula, with such otherwise complicating features as integration with Social Security, subsidized early retirement benefits, alternative normal retirement ages, and minimum benefits.

Actuarial assumptions can be more flexible than those underlying the insurance and annuity rates of a life insurer shouldering the legal responsibility for paying the plan's benefits and in the process offering guarantees that extend 50 to 75 years into the future. The unallocated funding instrument can make allowances for anticipated withdrawals, staggered retirements, and salary progression, and the mortality and interest assumptions can be set more realistically. Contributions to the plan need not be linked to a presumed, unchangeable pattern of benefit accruals but can be geared to one of a wide range of actuarial cost methods, with their varying presumptions as to the pattern of benefit or cost accruals. Finally, unallocated instruments permit broad latitude in investment policy and strategy through the use of life insurance company separate accounts and the various investment vehicles of banks, trust companies, investment advisers, and mutual funds.

Group Deposit Administration Annuity Contract

The term *deposit administration* may be broadly applied to any type of group annuity contract under which contributions are not currently used to purchase single premium-deferred annuities for individual participants. Group annuity contracts embodying this concept were made available as early as 1929 but did not achieve much popularity until after World War II, when plan sponsors began to seek more flexibility in plan design, funding procedures, and investment policy than was available under conventional insured arrangements. The use of group annuity contracts spread until the deposit administration contract and its variants—the immediate participation guarantee contract and the guaranteed investment contract—became the standard contractual form for funding large- and medium-size plans through the facilities of life insurance companies.

The original or basic deposit administration contract has been modified over the years to try to match the flexibility of the trust arrangement. The integrated package of traditional insurance company guarantees and services has been "unbundled" to give plan sponsors the opportunity to forgo the purchase of annuities while taking advantage of the investment services of the insurer. Today many large plans are using only the investment services of the insurer, typically, one or more of the separate accounts or a guaranteed income contract (see Chapter 30). These investment services are provided within the conceptual and contractual framework of the group deposit administration contract, although for product differentiation purposes the contracts may bear distinctive names.

General Characteristics

The central concept of the *conventional* deposit administration arrangement is that all funds intended to pay benefits to participants still on the active rolls of the plan sponsor are held in an undivided account, variously called the "active life fund," "annuity purchase fund," or "deposit administration fund." The money in the account is commingled with the other assets of the insurer and held in the general asset account. The account is credited with all contributions and interest at the rate specified in the contract; it is charged with the purchase price of all annuities provided for retired participants (and possibly vested participants), and with any ancillary benefits (death, disability, and withdrawal) disbursed directly from the account. No expenses are charged against the account, except for the administration or contract charge, expense assessments against cash distributions, and the expense component in the annuity purchase rates.

An amount sufficient to provide an immediate annuity for the retiring participant, pursuant to the terms of the plan and the group annuity contract, is withdrawn from the active life fund as that participant reaches retirement. The purchase price includes an allowance (the loading) for expenses and contingencies. The group deposit administration annuity contract is usually issued directly to the employer, but it may be issued to a trustee or board of trustees, as under a multiemployer pension plan.

Benefit Structure

The deposit administration arrangement can accommodate any set of benefits, any type of benefit formula, and any form of annuity. Preretirement death and disability benefits are payable directly from the active life fund and do not need to have any particular link to retirement benefits. Postretirement death benefits are a function of the annuity form under which benefits are being paid. Disability benefits are sometimes paid directly by the employer until the disabled person reaches retirement age, at which time an immediate annuity in the proper amount is purchased for the disabled participant with money drawn from the active life fund.

A withdrawing participant will normally be given a refund of employee contributions, with interest; this amount is charged directly to the active life fund. Depending upon the terms of the plan, a terminating vested participant may be given a paid-up deferred annuity in the appropriate amount or retain a claim against the plan to be discharged in the normal manner at retirement.

Funding

The funding of a group deposit administration annuity contract, unlike that of the allocated funding instruments, is not tied to a premium structure. It can be funded through any of the traditional actuarial cost methods. The required contributions can be determined by the actuarial department of the life insurer or by an actuarial consulting firm retained by the plan sponsor.

The deposit administration contract sets out a schedule of annuity purchase rates and an interest rate at which the money in the contractual fund (the active life fund) will be accumulated; both rates are guaranteed for the first five years of the contract. Yet the contributions to the plan need not bear any fixed relationship to the annuity purchase rates, other than being sufficient in the aggregate to accumulate a fund capable of providing an immediate annuity in the appropriate amount for each participant as he or she reaches retirement. Moreover, the cumulative contributions must be no less than those called for under the minimum funding standards of the Internal Revenue Code.

The specified (and guaranteed) rate to be credited to the active life fund tends to be well below prevailing rates, and the annuity purchase rates are computed on a very conservative basis. Moreover, after the contract has been in effect for five years, the rates for future contributions can be changed from year to year. These rate guarantees are intended to put a *ceiling* on the cost of benefits already accrued and funded. The minimum interest rate and the rate schedules in effect at the time a dollar is paid to the insurer apply to that dollar regardless of when it is withdrawn from the active life fund to provide an annuity. The actual cost of the accrued benefits is determined by experience, and downward adjustments are made through the dividend process.

These adjustments are made through the maintenance of a memorandum experience account that reflects all facets of the plan's operations. It should be distinguished from the contractual active life fund, which, with the exception of dividends on immediate annuities, reflects only those transactions under the contract pertaining to active participants, up to and including the purchase of paid-up annuities. Like its counterparts, the deposit administration experience account is credited with all contributions to the plan, whether originating with the plan sponsor or the participants, and the plan's proper share of the insurer's investment earnings. It is charged with the actual benefit disbursements to date (not with the purchase price of annuities), with the expenses and taxes allocable to the plan under accepted cost accounting techniques, and with a "risk charge," which is a contribution to the insurer's surplus. The balance in the account at the end of any accounting period, less the estimated present value of the insurer's liabilities under the plan—including the obligation to provide annuities at fixed rates out of the sum in the active life fund—is theoretically available for dividend or rate credit.[1] In determining such credits, however, the insurer generally applies a "credibility formula" to smooth out mortality fluctuations and withholds a reserve for expenses and contingencies.

The interest rate credited to the accumulated balance in the experience account has a significant impact on the size of the dividend or rate credit and hence on the cost of the plan to its sponsor. For many years, the standard practice was to credit the account with the net interest rate earned on the insurer's total investment portfolio (or, in some companies, the net rate of return on all investments other than policy loans). This was a natural, but not necessarily inherent, consequence of the commingling of insurer assets for investment purposes.

The yield on the composite portfolio reflects the condition of the capital markets at the time the various assets were obtained, and only by coincidence will it ever equal the rate of return currently obtainable on new investments. It may be higher or lower than the new money rate. If the rate of asset growth among all classes of contracts is approximately the same, and if no class is in a position to take advantage of the spread between the composite portfolio yield and the return on new investments, the use of an average rate produces no complications and achieves an acceptable degree of equity among the various kinds of contract holders. In many companies, however, funds generated under pension plans have been growing more rapidly than the general assets of the insurer; and under group annuity plans, especially of the deposit administration type, the plan sponsor is able to exercise considerable control over the flow of funds to the insurer and may have the contractual right to withdraw funds already paid to the insurer (but not committed to pay benefits to persons already retired). When the new money rate is lower than the portfolio rate, as it was during the 1940s, for example, the channeling of pension (and all other kinds of) money to the insurer dilutes the investment return to all classes of contracts. When the opposite condition prevails, the flow of pension money to insurers is impeded, since the funds that might otherwise have gone to life insurers are diverted to bank trustees to invest at current rates of return. Moreover, funds on deposit with insurers may be withdrawn to transfer them to bank trustees.

To deal with these problems and to compete with banks for pension money, group insurers in the early 1960s adopted procedures designed to credit each block of pension money with the interest rate at which the funds were actually

---

[1]As pointed out in connection with group deferred annuity contracts, the insurer, in valuing its liabilities, may use assumptions more conservative than those underlying the rate guarantees. This is also true of the liabilities attaching to the sums in the active life fund. If the insurer should conclude that the assumptions underlying its rate guarantees are too optimistic, it might place a higher value on its obligations to active participants than the sum credited to the active life fund. Normally, however, the reserve liability with respect to active lives is exactly equal to the amount in the active life fund, less the portion intended for expense reserves and contingencies.

invested. This approach is referred to as the "investment year," or "new money," method of allocating investment earnings.[2]

Investment Year Method of Allocating Investment Income

Under the investment year,[3] or new money, approach to allocating investment earnings, the net calendar year increase in the assets of a life insurer is treated as a separate cell or component of the general asset, subject to investment year accountability.[4] (Under one method discussed later in this chapter, the rollover of investments of previous calendar years is also treated as a separate cell.) The net investment income, including realized capital gains and losses, derived from the assets in that calendar year cell is credited to the cell as long as the assets are held by the company. Each year there will be changes in the composition of the cell's assets, because of maturities, repayments, redemptions, sales, and exchanges. This, of course, affects the rate of investment return credited to the cell. The effect depends upon whether these developments are being treated in accordance with the "declining index" method or the "fixed index" method of accounting.

Under the *declining index method*, the portion of a calendar year cell that rolls over in a subsequent year because of maturities, repayments, redemptions, sales, and exchanges goes into the cell for the calendar year in which the reinvestment takes place. Likewise, the investment income from the assets that remain in the cell will be placed in the successive calendar year cells corresponding to the years in which the income is invested. After each annual rollover, the rate of return is adjusted to reflect the yield on the remaining assets. The balance in the original cell (and all other cells) declines as the portfolio turns over and eventually, perhaps in 20 or 30 years, approaches zero.

Under the *fixed index method*, the amount of assets associated with a particular calendar year cell remains constant from year to year, being equal to the sum originally credited to the cell. Reinvestments arising from sales, repayments, redemptions, and maturities are placed back in the cells from which the rolled-over assets came. The interest rate at which the rolled-over portions of the cell are reinvested is monitored. The rate credited to an entire cell is the weighted average of the rates of return at which its various segments were invested and reinvested. If the trend of interest rates is upward, the weighted rate will rise each year, reflecting reinvestment of the cell assets in higher-yielding securities and mortgages. If the trend is downward, the opposite result will occur. Investment income credited to

---

[2]For a development of the rationale of the approach and a general description of the various procedures that may be used, see Edward A. Green, "The Case for Refinement in Methods of Allocating Investment Income," *Transactions of the Society of Actuaries*, vol. 13 (1961): pp. 308–19, and the discussion on pp. 320–52.

[3]Some insurance companies use investment generation periods shorter than a year, owing to the volatility of new money interest rates within a year.

[4]Not all investment income is allocated in accordance with the investment year method. It is customary to exclude the income from real estate, stocks, policy loans, short-term notes and bills, and bank deposits. In other words, the method is used primarily for bonds and real estate mortgages, which, because of definite maturities and repayment schedules, lend themselves more readily to investment year accounting.

the various cells in any given year is treated as new money for that year and goes into the cell for that year.

Two Methods for Allocating Investment Income: An Illustration

The specific manner in which these two methods allocate investment income among investment years may be grasped from the following simplified illustration of the treatment of the new money received in one particular year, T. The money received in subsequent years is ignored. It is assumed that the investable funds generated in a particular year are received at the end of the year and are all invested or reinvested at that time. In reality, of course, investment income and proceeds from portfolio turnover are being received and reinvested throughout the year, the transactions occurring on average at midyear. Actual investment year allocation formulas also allow for the timing of the cash flows. Moreover, the illustration ignores outflows due to benefits and expenses.

Assumptions

Year T new money, including investment income $1,000,000

Interest Rates Credited to New Money

Year of Investment	Year of Crediting			
	T	$T+1$	$T+2$	$T+3$
T	8.50	8.48	8.45	8.40
$T+1$	—	8.60	8.52	8.44
$T+2$	—	—	8.56	8.51
$T+3$	—	—	—	8.58

Rate of Portfolio Rollover

Year of Investment	Percentage of Assets Rolled Over			
	T	$T+1$	$T+2$	$T+3$
T	—	4	5	6
$T+1$	—	—	6	7
$T+2$	—	—	—	6

Declining Index Method

A: Interest credited in year $T+1$

$$\$1,000,000 \times .0848 = \$84,800$$

Distribution of total fund at end of year $T+1$

$ 960,000	Year T cell ($1,000,000 less 4% rollover)
124,800	Year $T+1$ cell ($40,000 rollover in Year $T+1$ plus $84,000 interest credited in year $T+1$)
$1,084,800	

B.   Interest credited in year $T+2$

$960,000 \times .0845 = \$81,120$ interest on year T balance
$124,800 \times .0852 = \underline{\quad 10,633}$ interest on year $T+1$ balance
Total $91,753

Distribution of total fund at end of year $T+2$

$ 912,000	Year T cell ($960,000 less 5% rollover)
117,312	Year $T+1$ cell ($124,800 less 6% rollover)
147,241	Year $T+2$ cell ($55,488 rollover from T and $T+1$ cells in year $T+2$ plus $91,753 interest credited in year $T+2$)
$1,176,553	

C.   Interest credited in year $T+3$

$912,000 \times .0840 = \$76,608$ interest on year T balance
$117,312 \times. 0844 = \quad 9,901$ interest on year $T+1$ balance
$147,241 \times .0851 = \underline{\quad 12,530}$ interest on year $T+1$ balance
Total $99,039

Distribution of total fund at end of year $T+3$

$ 857,280	Year T cell ($912,000 less 6% rollover)
109,100	Year $T+1$ cell ($117,312 less 7% rollover)
138,407	Year $T+2$ cell ($147,241 less 6% rollover)
170,805	Year $T+3$ cell ($99,039 interest credited in year $T+3$ plus $71,766 rollover from cells T, $T+1$, and $T+2$ in Year $T+3$)
$1,275,592	

Fixed Index Method

A.   Interest credited in year $T+1$

$1,000,000 \times .0848 = \$84,800

Distribution of total fund at end of year $T+1$

$1,000,000	Year T cell
84,800	Year $T+1$ cell
$1,084,800	

B. Interest credited in year $T+2$

$1,000,000 \times .084528^* = \$84,528
$84,800 \times .0852 = \underline{\quad 7,225}$
$91,753
$^*(.96)(.0845)+(.04)(.0852) = .084528$

Distribution of total fund at end of year $T+2$

$1,000,000	Year T cell
84,800	Year $T+1$ cell
91,753	Year $T+2$ cell
$1,176,553	

C.   Interest credited in year $T+3$

$$1,000,000 \times .08407048* = \$84,070$$
$$84,800 \times .084442** = \quad 7,161$$
$$91,753 \times .0851 = \quad \underline{7,808}$$
$$\$99,039$$

$*(.96)(.95)(.0840)+(.04)(.94)(.0844)+[1-(.96)(.95)-(.04)(.94)](.0851) = .08407048$
$**(.94)(0844)+(.06)(.0851) = .08442$

Distribution of total fund at end of year $T+3$

$1,000,000	Year T cell
84,800	Year $T+1$ cell
91,753	Year $T+2$ cell
99,039	Year $T+3$ cell
$1,275,592	

This illustration shows that the two methods produce identical results and are, in fact, only different ways of looking at the same investment phenomena. The investment income allocation under both methods depends upon the assets that become available for investment in each calendar year, as depicted under the declining index method. In the example, it is assumed that $1 million of new money is received in year T and is initially invested in that year. It is further assumed that the money earned 8.48 percent in year $T+1$, producing investment income of $84,800. This income and the 4 percent of the year T new money that turns over in the year $T+1$ are placed in the $T+1$ cell and, under the simplifying assumptions of the example, become available for investment at the end of year $T+1$. In the meantime, the turnover on year T investments has reduced the yield on those assets slightly, and the $960,000 remaining in the year T cell is credited with a rate of 8.45 percent in year $T+2$, or $81,120 in income. The $124,800 in the $T+1$ cell is credited with a return of 8.52 percent in year $T+2$, resulting in an allocation of $10,633. The $T+2$ investment income and the rollover from the T and $T+1$ cells are placed in the new cell $T+3$ and the process continues, becoming quite involved when the number of accounting cells reaches 20 or 25, as they have in some companies. With the computer, however, the computations are manageable.

The fixed index method assumes that the original inflow of money remains in cell T with the investment income generated by the funds being placed in the cell for the year in which the income is credited. The problem then becomes one of determining the weighted rates of return to be applied to the various cells, each of which has a balance equal to the original input. The weights come from the asset allocations of the declining index procedure and are shown in parentheses in juxtaposition to the rates of return. The weights are simply the percentage of the cell balance invested at the various rates of return. This process is continued beyond the point where any of the original assets remain in cell T. In the allocation formula, that calendar year cell, as well as any subsequent cells that no longer contain any derivative assets from Year T, is assigned a weight of zero. Nevertheless, as long as the derivative assets remain with the company, they will be credited with interest in accordance with this principle.

Any assets acquired by the insurer before the effective date of the investment year method may be credited with an aggregate interest rate appropriate for a generalized "year" or cell consisting of all investments made before the effective date of the investment year method. The aggregate rate represents the average yield on all assets not subject to the investment year method, adjusted to reflect the use of "new money" rates for the other assets. Whenever the balance in any calendar year cell becomes unduly small, or the spread between the aggregate rate and the new money rate for the cell becomes significant, the cell may be closed out and the remaining assets transferred to the segment of the general account subject to the aggregate rate. Such closeouts are likely to be in the sequence in which the cells were created. Some companies merge all investment years that originated at least 10 years in the past.

The investment year method can be used to allocate investment income among the major product lines of an insurer (e.g., ordinary life insurance, group life insurance, group annuities, individual annuities, and debit life insurance), as well as among the various classifications of contracts within each major line of business. In New York, if the method is to be used *within* any line of business, it *must* be used to distribute investment income *to* the major annual statement lines of business.[5] To the extent feasible, the same method must be used to allocate investment income to each line and within each line. The companies have generally found it feasible to apply the method within only the group lines and the individual immediate annuity line, where the largest and most mobile accumulation of assets is found. The method is of critical importance to the group annuity line of a company.

The concept works the same way for an individual group annuity contract as it does for the entire life insurance company or the group annuity department of the company. In the case of a group annuity contract, the experience account (or fund) serves as the focal point and is divided into investment year components, or cells. Under the fixed index method, the new money for any particular calendar year cell is the net increase in the experience fund for that year; under the declining index method, the new money is the net increase in the experience fund plus the rollover of investments associated with the experience fund. A new cell comes into existence each calendar year. The investment income and portfolio rollover associated with the original assets of each cell can be accounted for on either the declining index or fixed index basis, the same procedure being used for all cells—and all contracts. This approach is a feature of the experience rating process and does not affect any rate guarantees in the contract. The total amount of investment income credited to group annuity contracts for experience rating purposes in respect of each calendar year cell should correspond to the investment income available to that calendar year cell for the entire group annuity line.

Having once adopted the investment year method, an insurer licensed in New York cannot revert to the portfolio average method—except on a gradual basis and in accordance with a plan approved by the New York Superintendent of Insurance six months prior to its effective date. Any deviations from the rules laid down for

[5]Regulations of the New York Insurance Department, §91.5(2).

the investment year method in the regulations of the New York Insurance Department require the prior approval of the department and must be necessary for reasons of feasibility. These rules, and those of other state insurance departments, are designed to ensure equitable treatment of all classes of policyholders, both old and new.

Discontinuance of the Plan

The discontinuance of a pension plan funded through a deposit administration contract has no effect on the annuities already purchased, except perhaps to accommodate the asset allocation procedure of the Employment Retirement Income Security Act.[6] The money in the active life fund must be allocated.

If the plan itself is not terminated but is to be continued through some other funding instrument, the plan sponsor may wish to transfer the unallocated funds to the new funding agency. This is normally permitted by specific contract provision, and even when the contract does not specifically grant the transfer privilege, some insurers may be willing to consider a transfer on a basis negotiated at the time of discontinuance. In either event, the assets to be transferred are subject to a market value adjustment. This adjustment, which may be positive or negative, reflects the difference between the fund balance and the market value of assets purchased with deposits to the fund. This adjustment will usually be negative if interest rates are higher at the time of transfer than at the time of investment and reinvestment, and positive if lower.

Immediate Participation Guarantee Group Annuity Contract

Compared with allocated funding instruments, the conventional deposit administration contract is an enormously flexible funding vehicle. Yet many plan sponsors, keenly sensitive to cash flow considerations, find certain features of the instrument objectionable. They particularly object to the insurer's control over the experience rating process through which net actuarial gains are credited to the active life fund or against future contributions. They also object to the insurer's holding a contingency reserve, which defers the crediting of a portion of the cumulative actuarial gains. Finally, some feel that investment returns are unduly constrained by the necessity of maintaining the active life fund in the insurer's general asset account, whose characteristics were described earlier.

To meet these objections, life insurers modified the conventional deposit administration contract, variously labeled *immediate participation guarantee, pension administration,* or *direct rated* deposit administration contract. Like the basic contract, the modified version—hereafter called the IPG contract—calls for the creation and maintenance of a contractual account into which all contributions to the pension plan are deposited. The account is credited annually with interest at the rate applied to all group annuity experience accounts, the rate generally being determined by applying the investment year method to the insurer's actual investment experience. The account is charged directly with its allocable share of insurer

---

[6]ERISA §4044.

expenses and taxes, with a risk charge and, under the practices for some insurers, with all benefit payments, including those to retired participants. In other words, some insurers do not withdraw from the contractual account the sum required to provide annuities for individual participants, although they guarantee the benefits of retired participants and provide evidence of such undertaking with individual certificates. In the practice of other insurers, as each participant retires the IPG account is debited with the actuarial value (or gross single premium) of the annuity benefits to be paid to the individual. In this case, provision is made (usually through annual cancellation and reissue of all outstanding annuities) for an adjustment in the IPG account that has the net effect of fully and currently reflecting the experience of retired lives with respect to all relevant cost factors.

Contributions to the IPG account can be determined by the plan sponsor in accordance with any IRS-approved cost method and must meet ERISA minimum funding standards. The contract usually requires the plan sponsor to maintain the account balance at a level sufficient to provide full benefits to all participants who have retired, plus a specified margin, on the order of 5 percent. This means that the account must at all times be at least equal to the actuarial present value of all benefits payable to retired participants, computed on the basis of the schedule of annuity purchase rates in effect at the time the participants retired. The valuation is based on a gross premium to ensure that the annuities will be self-sustaining if the contract is discontinued. The contract usually stipulates that if the account balance should ever fall to a level the insurer has actuarially determined to be necessary to pay guaranteed benefits in full to retired participants, plus the afore-mentioned margin (a contingency reserve), the contract will become a conventional deposit administration group annuity contract, participating in dividends in the normal manner. Except for very mature plan populations, this insurer-imposed level of funding is likely to be exceeded by that flowing from compliance with ERISA minimum funding standards.

The practical effect of this modus operandi is that the insurer is not able to accumulate a contingency reserve (except for the margin in respect of obligations to retired participants and the margin implicit in conservative rate schedules), and net actuarial gains are reflected directly, fully, and immediately in the IPG account, rather than through the noncontractual dividend or experience rating formula of the insurer. Furthermore, the plan sponsor may elect to have some or all of the IPG account invested in one or more of the insurer's separate accounts, which are maintained on a market value basis (separate accounts are described in Chapter 30).

Some IPG contracts offer no guarantee of the rate of investment return or the preservation of principal, while others guarantee principal and provide a minimum guarantee of interest, similar to a traditional deposit administration contract. The IPG account is credited with its pro rata share of investment earnings, adjusted for capital gains and losses (only *realized* gains and losses, if the account is invested entirely in the general asset account). The older contracts contain a schedule of annuity purchase rates, guaranteed against an adverse change during the first five years of the contract, and they require that the benefits of retired participants be underwritten by the insurer in the form of annuities. Later versions of the IPG contract omit the requirement that annuities be purchased but include a schedule of annuity purchase rates in the event the plan administrator *elects* to purchase annuities for retiring participants.

Certain "investment-only" arrangements, such as the guaranteed income contract (discussed in Chapter 30), while written in the form of an IPG contract, make no pretense of offering annuities. Furthermore, the contract contains no reference to annuity purchase rates.

Trust

The second major category of unallocated funding instruments is that of trusts.

General Characteristics

A trust is the most flexible of all funding arrangements. Its flexibility stems from the nature of the trust concept and the fact that the trustee, unlike an insurer, makes no long-term guarantees that must be circumscribed by contractual conditions and limitations.

In essence, in a trust fund arrangement the contributions used to provide pension benefits are deposited with a trustee—usually a bank, but sometimes a natural person or group of persons—who invests the money, accumulates the earnings, and pays benefits directly to eligible claimants or makes funds available to the plan administrator to pay benefits. The trustee also renders periodic accountings to the employer or to other sponsoring organizations and to the plan administrator. The rights and duties of the trustee are set forth in the trust indenture, which is a formal, written agreement between the plan sponsor and the trustee. The indenture may, but usually does not, incorporate the terms and conditions of the pension plan itself.

The plan sponsor remits all contributions to the trustee, whether they originate with the participants or the firm. If the plan is noncontributory, contributions may be paid over to the trustee only once a year, although some sponsors prefer to make more frequent payments of smaller size. If the plan is contributory, however, the sponsor may remit after each pay interval the sums withheld from the participants' paychecks. It is not customary for the trustee to distinguish between money contributed by the sponsor and by the participants or to record the amounts contributed by, or on behalf of, a particular individual. The employer maintains a record of participant contributions and, if circumstances should demand it, can certify to the trustee the amount contributed by any particular person.

In acting as a funding agency for a pension plan, the trustee is subject to the basic principle of trust law, which is that the assets of each trust must be segregated from the assets of all other trusts administered by it and from its own assets. This requirement stems from the fact that the relationship among the parties to a trust is essentially fiduciary rather than contractual in nature. However, recognizing the need to diversify investments, regulatory authorities have granted permission to bank trustees to operate commingled trust funds for the exclusive use of qualified pension and profit-sharing plans, subject to certain safeguards. Diversification may also be achieved through investment in mutual fund shares.

The trustee is legally obliged to invest the funds received under a pension plan. In the absence of any specific instructions in the trust agreement, the trustee has to invest the funds in accordance with any applicable state statute governing fiduciary investments. It is customary, however, for the plan sponsor to free the trustee from the restraints of the state fiduciary investment statute and to bestow on the trustee varying degrees of authority over the investments of the trust. Many trust agreements give the trustee complete discretion in the performance of its investment function, and the plan sponsor holds the trustee to a commensurate degree of responsibility for the investment results. Such sponsors want to take full advantage of the investment skills of the trustee and to relieve their own officers of the burden of participating in the investment decisions associated with the trust. At the other extreme, some trust agreements stipulate that the trustee shall buy and sell only those investments selected by the plan sponsor or by the person or persons designated by the sponsor, and only on written instructions from the sponsor or such person or persons. In such cases, the bank or trust company is not performing the traditional function of a trustee and, except for holding legal title to the assets of the trust, is little more than a custodian. Some plan sponsors charge the trustee with the responsibility of managing the investment portfolio but require the written approval of the pension board, or some other representative of the sponsor, before any transactions can be carried out. A variation of this approach, applicable especially to common stocks, is for the plan sponsor to approve a trustee-recommended list of securities eligible for the portfolio, with names being periodically added and deleted upon recommendation of the trustee. Other sponsors specify the classes of investments to be purchased, as well as the percentage of the total fund to be invested in each class, and permit the trustee to select the specific assets to be bought and sold.

In some defined contribution plans the trustee maintains two or more separate portfolios with differing objectives, for example a common stock fund and a fixed-income fund. Participants are allowed to designate the proportion of their accounts to be invested in each portfolio.

Some plans allow each participant to direct the investment of his or her own account.[7] The plan may restrict the allowable investments to certain types, such as mutual funds or securities listed on a major stock exchange, or it may allow any legal investment. Under this approach the trustee performs only custodial functions. This self-directed approach involves substantial administrative problems.

As has been pointed out, the plan sponsor may delegate the investment function to more than one asset manager. In that event, the trustee may be one of several asset managers or may perform only a trustee and custodial function, managing no assets itself except possibly overnight cash balances.

The disbursement function is strictly routine and involves minimal discretion on the part of the trustee. No benefits are disbursed, except upon written instructions from the pension board or plan administrator. Whenever a participant becomes entitled to benefits, the pension board or plan administrator certifies that fact to the trustee, along with the amount and duration of the payments and mailing

[7]ERISA §404(c).

instructions. Some plans provide for the purchase of immediate annuities for employees as they become entitled to retirement benefits. In such event, the trustee, upon written instructions from the pension board or plan administrator, transfers a sufficient sum of money to the insurer named in the instructions to purchase an immediate annuity of the proper size for the retiring employee. In many instances, the pension board or plan administrator, acting as agent for the trustee, disburses the benefits directly, requisitioning from the trustee, from time to time, the funds needed to finance the benefits. The payor must withhold federal income tax from the benefit payment unless the payee has directed otherwise and in any case must report the amount of payment to the Internal Revenue Service (see Chapter 7).

Periodically—at least once a year—the trustee presents accounts to the employer or other sponsoring organization and to the plan administrator for the administration of the trust. The completeness of the accounting will, of course, vary from trustee to trustee; but as a minimum, the report will show the balance in the trust at the beginning and the end of the accounting period; the contributions received; the investment earnings, reflecting realized capital gains and losses; the sums disbursed in the form of benefits; the charges against the fund, including the trustee's fee; the assets acquired and disposed of during the period; and a listing of the specific assets owned by the trust, with such details as the date acquired, cost, and current market value. The plan administrator incorporates the pertinent portions of this accounting in the annual report Form 5500 and in the summary annual report provided. The trustee's report will also provide other information needed for any schedules to be attached to Form 5500.

Thus the role of the trustee in a trust fund pension plan is normally confined to managing and disbursing the funds accumulated under the plan. It usually does not participate in the development of the plan or in the various activities incident to inauguration and administration of the plan.[8] Finally, it generally does not provide any actuarial services, either before or after the plan is established.

The trustee under a trust fund plan generally levies two types of fees: investment and remittance. The fee for investment services is the principal charge levied by the trustee. It is levied annually or quarterly and is usually expressed as a graded percentage of the market value of the trust fund. The fee is graduated downward as the size of the fund increases and may be adjusted to the responsibilities placed upon the trustee. The fee for preparing and mailing checks to pensioners and other benefit claimants is usually a specified amount per check, subject to a minimum annual charge.

The trust agreement usually stipulates that the trustee shall be entitled to reimbursement for reasonable expenses, including counsel fees, incurred in the administration of the trust. This would be in addition to the investment and remittance fees discussed above. The employer may pay the trustee's fees and reimbursable expenses directly or may authorize the trustee, usually in the trust agreement, to charge such items against the trust fund.

---

[8]Banks in the largest financial centers may aggressively solicit pension funds and actively participate in the development of plans. Some banks employ—or maintain an affiliation with—actuaries to help develop new pension business.

Benefit Structure

Funding a pension plan through a trust imposes no constraints on its benefit structure that are not already found in relevant law. Any type of benefit formula can be used, no matter how complex. The plan can also provide benefits that vary, after retirement, by linking them with a specified price or wage index or through changes in the market value of plan assets. The plan may provide for a single normal retirement age, or it may permit retirement without actuarial reduction at any age within a specified range of ages, subject to minimum service requirements. Benefits may be provided in the form of an annuity or a single-sum payment. Under trust fund defined benefit plans, the normal annuity form is typically the straight-life annuity, without a refund feature (except for participant contributions). Most plans, however, provide the same optional annuity forms as those available under plans funded through life insurers. Plans are subject to ERISA's requirements concerning provision of a joint and survivor annuity.

Some trust fund plans stipulate that the trustee shall purchase an immediate annuity in the appropriate amount for each participant as he or she reaches retirement. This practice is most common where the number of participants is relatively small and where the sponsor wishes to avoid the risks of providing lifetime benefits out of plan funds.

Participants who terminate before becoming eligible for retirement are usually entitled to a refund of their own contributions, with interest; if they have satisfied the vesting requirements, they have a nonforfeitable right to all accrued benefits. The plan may permit the actuarial value of the vested benefits to be paid in a lump sum or to be transferred to an IRA or to the pension plan of a successor employer (with the latter's consent). Under defined benefit plans, the terminated vested participant is entitled to retain a claim against the plan for deferred benefits.

The plan must provide a qualified preretirement survivor annuity benefit, if applicable, and it may provide other death benefits in any amount deemed "incidental" to the retirement benefit by the IRS. Any such benefits may be paid directly from the trust fund. Disability benefits of any kind can be accommodated. Claims are adjudicated by the plan administrator and benefits are paid from the trust fund.

Funding

The funding of a defined benefit plan through a trust is identical in all material respects with funding under an insurer's deposit administration contract. Actuarial costs and liabilities are determined by an actuarial consultant who is retained and paid by the plan sponsor (directly or out of the trust fund), but who acts on behalf of the plan participants by mandate of ERISA. The actuarial assumptions are likely to be similar to those used with any unallocated funding instrument, any differences being attributable more to the judgment and temperament of the actuary than to the funding instrument employed. Any allowable actuarial cost method can be used. As under any form of unallocated funding, the suitability of the actuarial assumptions and the cost method must be attested to by an enrolled actuary, one whose professional qualifications have been certified by the Joint Board established by ERISA.

Actuarial gains or losses are reflected directly and immediately in the level or size of the trust fund. Depending upon the actuarial cost method and other considerations, these gains and losses may be amortized over several years to determine annual contributions to the plan. For purposes of the funding standard account, actuarial gains and losses must be spread in equal dollar installments over a period of years.

Discontinuance of the Plan

Whenever a trust fund plan terminates, the assets in the trust must be allocated among the active participants, terminated vested participants, retired participants, and other persons in benefit status in accordance with the priorities set out in ERISA (see Chapters 33 and 34). Within the latitude permitted by regulations, the plan may establish more refined priority classes than those set forth in the law. The employer or plan administrator may, of course, terminate a trust agreement pursuant to its terms and transfer the plan assets to another trustee without terminating the plan.

Combination of Funding Instruments

The funding instruments already described may be combined in various ways to accumulate the funds needed to meet the obligations of a defined benefit pension plan. One of the most prevalent blends, often used under small plans, is that produced by combining life insurance contracts with an unallocated fund of assets, often called a "side fund" or "auxiliary fund." Another type of blending is achieved by funding a portion of the benefits through a group annuity contract and the other portion through a trust fund. These combinations of instruments are referred to as *split-funding* or a *combination plan*.

Life Insurance and Side Fund Under Defined Benefit Plans

The core of a combination defined benefit plan is an individual contract pension trust or group permanent life insurance contract that provides life insurance protection until the date of retirement and accumulates cash values that become a part (usually about one-third) of the principal sum needed to provide the retirement benefits. The additional sums required for the retirement benefits are accumulated in an unallocated fund administered by a bank under the terms of a trust agreement or by the insurer on the deposit administration principle. At the direction of the plan sponsor, the unallocated money held by the insurer may be placed in the general asset account or in a separate account. The insurance contracts contain a provision that permits them to be converted into annuity contracts at (or immediately prior to) the participants' normal retirement dates, at annuity rates guaranteed on the original date of issue, or, if more favorable, at current annuity rates. The sums in the side fund are also convertible into immediate annuities on the same basis as the cash values of the affiliated life insurance contracts. Upon retirement, these conversions may be made, or the policies may be surrendered and all benefits paid directly from the trust in the form of a life annuity or a single-sum payment. The plan combines the rate guarantees of the life insurance contracts with the funding and investment flexibility of the auxiliary fund. Funding flexibility is provided, whether the unallocated fund is administered by a trustee or the life insurer, but investment latitude is provided only under a trust arrangement or separate accounts of life insurers.

Any type of life insurance contract that promises protection to the date of retirement, accumulates a cash value, and is contractually convertible into an annuity contract can be used with a combination plan. In practice, some form of whole life or universal life policy is usually used. The policy may be one of the types available to the general public, or it may be the type that is specifically designed for combination plans. The coverage may be made available through individual contracts, if the number of employees is small, or through a group permanent contract, if the number of participants is large enough to qualify the plan for group coverage. Individual contracts may be made available on a guaranteed issue basis, as is the case under individual contract plans funded with retirement income or retirement annuity contracts.

The benefits under a combination plan are essentially the same as those under a fully insured individual contract or a group permanent plan. Retirement benefits are frequently payable in units of $5 or $10 per month, and payments are usually guaranteed for 120 months. The death benefit prior to retirement is generally $1,000 for each $10 of monthly life income; unlike the death benefit under a retirement income or retirement annuity contract, it remains level up to the normal retirement date. No part of the side fund is usually paid out as a lump-sum death benefit—all such benefits are provided through the related insurance policies.

Withdrawal benefits must conform to the requirements of ERISA and, depending upon the circumstances, may be met out of the cash value of the insurance policies on the life of the terminating participant or out of the policy cash values and some of the money in the side fund. The amount of vested benefit must satisfy ERISA's vesting requirements, regardless of whether this is more or less than can be provided by the policy cash values. The amount of benefit must be definitely determinable under the plan's provisions, independent of the amount of contributions or assets in the side fund. Contributions to the side fund are not premiums in the technical sense, but they do carry with them insurer guarantees as to the rates at which they may be converted into retirement benefits. The actual amount of annual contributions to the fund is subject to the discretion of the employer but must meet ERISA's minimum funding requirements. Actuarial valuations for the plan may be performed by an actuary employed by the insurance company or by a consulting actuary.

The employer is free to adopt any funding pattern for the side fund that suits its desires and circumstances and meets the requirements of ERISA. The funding usually results in the accumulation by the participants' retirement dates of the necessary funds to convert the policies on their lives to annuities of the appropriate amount or to provide the benefits from the trust. The insurer has no responsibility for the management of the side fund, unless the money is held under a deposit administration arrangement. If the side fund is invested in the general asset account of the life insurer, the assets are guaranteed against loss of principal and are credited with a guaranteed rate of return, plus such excess interest as may be earned and declared on such assets. If the side fund is invested in the insurer's equity separate account, of course, it will reflect increases and decreases in market value. Under no circumstances is the insurer responsible for the adequacy of the fund. The purchase of life insurance under defined contribution plans is discussed in Chapter 12.

Group Annuity and Trust Fund

Split-funding with a group annuity contract and trust fund may be entered for several reasons. The employer may want to take advantage of certain insurer guarantees and the investment latitude of a trust. Some employers believe that insurance companies can earn a higher rate of return on fixed-dollar investments than a bank or independent investment manager but are less effective with equity investments. Annuities may be purchased for retirees at a cost less than the plan's calculated liability for them in order to reduce the plan's unfunded liability and thus reduce the current employer contribution and pension expense. Or split-funding may occur because of a change in strategy, with new contributions being placed in one funding medium and old contributions in another. In defined contribution plans, participants may be given a choice between two or more investment media.

The insurance vehicle for split-funding may be either a group deferred annuity contract, a group deposit administration annuity, an immediate participation guarantee contract, or a guaranteed investment contract. The group annuity contract may be issued directly to the plan sponsor or to the trust. If the latter, the contract becomes, in effect, an asset of the trust.

Under a defined benefit plan, the allocation of pension contributions between the group annuity contract and trust may be determined by the extent to which equity investments are to be held. Contributions to the insurer are usually placed in the general asset account of the insurer, where they are invested predominantly in fixed-income securities; contributions to the trust may be channeled almost exclusively into common stocks. In practice, the plan administrator may decide what proportion of each employer contribution should go into common stocks, with the remainder going to the insurance company. Under such circumstances, the payments to the insurer would tend to be residual in nature. Participant contributions, if any, may be paid to the insurer, where they enjoy a contractual guarantee as to the preservation of principal and the minimum rate of return.

The arrangement may contemplate disbursement of retirement benefits by both the insurer and the trustee, by the trustee only, or by the insurer only. If the latter, as each participant reaches retirement the trustee may purchase from the insurer holding the other assets an immediate annuity of the appropriate amount. The insurer might or might not provide guarantees on rates at which the annuities can be purchased by the trustee. The normal rate and other guarantees would apply to the funds held by the insurer. Split-funding is primarily concerned with how plan assets are administered, and it need not affect the substantive features of the plan.

Chapter 33
Single-Employer Plan Termination and Plan Benefits Insurance

There are many reasons why an employer might terminate a pension plan. The entire operation may go out of business and have no more employees, or the facility in which all of the plan participants were employed may be closed. The business may be sold to another firm that intends to cover all employees under its own plan. The employer may decide to combine two or more plans or may decide to replace the plan with another type of plan. The employer may not be able to afford to continue funding the plan. A number of statutory and regulatory requirements affect whether and how a plan may be terminated, and a system of plan benefits insurance guarantees the payment of part or all of the benefits earned to date under covered plans.

Internal Revenue Code Requirements Affecting Plan Termination

Permanence Requirement and Discrimination upon Early Termination

In invoking the right to terminate its pension plan, an employer must abide by a series of rulings and regulations of the Internal Revenue Service. Like most other rules of the IRS, these are intended to prevent discrimination in favor of highly compensated employees. In the absence of appropriate constraints, a firm with a small core of officers and permanent employees would be able to establish a plan, make tax-deductible contributions for all employees for several years, and then discontinue further contributions, with only the favored few participants ever qualifying for retirement benefits. This sort of scheme would be especially attractive during years of high profits and large tax liabilities.

In order to forestall such practices, the IRS has taken the position that the term "plan" implies a permanent, as distinguished from a temporary, program.[1] If a plan were to be terminated within a few years after it was established for any reason other than business necessity, such action would be construed as evidence that the plan from its inception was not a bona fide program for the exclusive benefit of employees in general. If the IRS concludes from all the facts that a plan from its inception was not intended to be a permanent and continuing program for the

---

[1] Treas. Reg. 1.401-1(b)(2); Rev. Rul. 69-25. But see *Lincoln Electric Co. Employees Profit-Sharing Trust*, 51-2 USTC, 190 F2d 326 (1951).

exclusive benefit of employees in general, employer contributions toward the plan are disallowed as federal income tax deductions for all open tax years.[2] Some of the motivating forces for termination that the IRS has recognized as valid business reasons include bankruptcy, insolvency, change of ownership, change of management, and financial inability to continue contributions to the plan.

Limit on 25 Highest-Paid Employees

Another expression of the IRS's concern that early termination of a defined benefit plan could lead to discrimination in favor of highly compensated employees is seen in the limit on the benefits payable to the 25 highest-paid employees within either 10 years of the effective date of the plan or 10 years of an amendment increasing benefits under the plan.[3] Before these restrictions were originally adopted in 1956, it was possible to establish a plan and collect only enough contributions to provide large benefits for one or more highly compensated employees retiring in the first few years and to leave few if any assets available to fund the benefits of other employees in the event of early plan termination.

The restriction places limits on annual payments to the 25 most highly compensated employees and former employees (determined as a single group) arising from the accrued benefit and other benefits to which an employee is entitled under the plan. The limit applies to benefits paid in a form other than a single life annuity, plus a Social Security supplement.[4]

Every qualified defined benefit plan is required to set forth intricate provisions containing the above restrictions. Plan provisions may define the group of employees subject to the restriction in any manner, provided that the group includes the 25 most highly compensated employees and former employees. If there are fewer than 25 highly compensated employees and former highly compensated employees, the plan is not required to reach into the non–highly compensated employee group to restrict distributions.

The restrictions on distributions apply at all times prior to plan termination unless any of the following requirements are satisfied:

- the value of the benefits payable to an employee whose benefits are restricted is $3,500 or less;
- current liability is at least 110 percent funded after payment of all benefits payable to the employee whose benefits are restricted;
- the value of the benefits payable to an employee whose benefits are restricted is less than 1 percent of the value of current liability before the distribution.[5]

Unless one of the stated exceptions applies, distribution of amounts in excess of the single life annuity (plus social security supplement) is permitted only if the plan requires adequate security to guarantee repayment. An amount in excess of

[2]Generally, taxes must be assessed within three years after the original return is filed. IRC §6501(a).
[3]Treas. Reg. 1.401-4(c).
[4]Treas. Reg. 1.401(a)(4)-5(b)(3)(i)(A) & (B).
[5]Treas. Reg. 1.401(a)(4)-5(b)(3)(iv).

the single life annuity payment (an amount also known as the "restricted amount") can be distributed if the employee agrees to promptly secure repayment of the restricted amount. Three methods of securing repayment are available:

- make a deposit in escrow with an acceptable depository property having a fair market value equal to at least 125 percent of the restricted amount,
- post a bond (issued by an insurance company, bonding company, or other Treasury-approved surety for federal bonds) equal to at least 100 percent of the restricted amount,
- provide a bank letter of credit in an amount equal to at least 100 percent of the restricted amount.[6]

Other security arrangements may also be possible. For example, the repayment agreement may be secured by the assets in the employee's IRA.[7]

Vesting Upon Plan Termination

Upon termination or partial termination of any qualified plan, whatever the cause, the accrued benefit rights of all participants must vest to the extent funded.[8] Under a defined contribution plan all accrued benefits are funded, so this rule results in the full vesting of all accrued benefits. Under a defined benefit plan this rule results in the vesting of nonvested accrued benefits to the extent that plan assets are sufficient to fund them.

Nondiversion and Exclusive Benefit Requirements

The trust of a pension plan must be established for the exclusive benefit of participants and their beneficiaries.[9] It must be impossible, at any time prior to the satisfaction of all liabilities with respect to employees and their beneficiaries, for any part of the trust assets to be used for or diverted to purposes other than the exclusive benefit of employees and their beneficiaries.[10] Regulations interpret this statement generally to prohibit any reversion of plan assets to the employer prior to the termination of the plan and related satisfaction of liabilities.[11] In a defined contribution plan, the plan assets are ordinarily exactly equal to the sum of the individual accounts, which represent the liabilities to participants and their representatives. But in a defined benefit plan it is not uncommon for plan assets to substantially exceed the liabilities. Upon plan termination, any excess assets may in general be allocated to increase benefits for participants and beneficiaries or, if the plan so provides, may revert to the employer. If the employer maintaining a plan with such excess assets wishes to recover the excess assets, the only way to do so is to terminate the trust.

[6]Rev. Rul. 92-76.
[7]Private Letter Ruling 8801060.
[8]ERISA §411(d)(3).
[9]IRC §401(a).
[10]IRC §401(a)(2).
[11]Treas. Reg. 1.401-2(b).

Reestablishment Terminations and Spin-off Terminations

Some employers, desiring to recover the excess assets under a defined benefit plan but also desiring to continue the operation of the plan, have adopted one of two permissible devices to accomplish this result.[12] One of these is called a "reestablishment termination." Under a reestablishment termination, the plan is terminated, annuities are purchased from a life insurance company to satisfy all liabilities to participants and beneficiaries, and the residual assets revert to the employer. Simultaneously the employer adopts a new pension plan, usually identical to the plan just terminated except that it specifies that the benefits determined under the plan's benefit formula will be offset by the amount of annuity purchased under the terminated plan.

The second device is called a "spin-off termination." Under a spin-off termination, the plan is split into two plans: one is for retired participants and beneficiaries receiving payments, and the other is for active participants. Annuities are purchased to guarantee all accrued benefits under both plans. All of the excess assets are initially placed in the plan for retirees, which is then terminated, with the excess assets reverting to the employer.

In both a reestablishment termination and a spin-off termination, participants and beneficiaries generally receive the same benefits that they would have received if there had been no termination at all. However, all accrued benefits become vested and have annuities purchased for them at the time of the event, with the result that benefit payments are made to those participants who would have terminated employment prior to vesting.

Taxation of the Reversion

Any reversion of excess assets to the employer upon plan termination is included in the employer's taxable income in the year received. If the employer is subject to federal income tax, this results in either current taxation or a reduction of any tax loss carried forward from prior years.

If the employer is subject to federal income tax, a special excise tax is payable by the employer on the amount of the reversion in the year in which it is received.[13]

See Chapter 7 for a full discussion of the excise tax on reversions.

Plan Benefits Insurance

Inasmuch as most pension plans begin operations with a supplemental liability and additional layers of supplemental liability may be created from time to time by plan amendments, actuarial experience losses, and changes in actuarial assumptions—and since the funding of the supplemental liability is generally spread over a long period—there is no assurance that the accrued benefits of a typical defined benefit plan could be paid in full if the plan should terminate. Over the years, thousands of plans have terminated, many with the loss of some benefits to the participants as

---

[12]Implementation Guidelines adopted by the Department of the Treasury, the Department of Labor, and the Pension Benefit Guaranty Corporation.
[13]IRC §4980

a group. To deal with this situation and to assure participants that their vested benefits will be paid, up to a limit, irrespective of the funded status of the plan at the time of termination, Title IV of ERISA established a program of plan benefits insurance, officially known as "plan termination insurance."

The provisions concerning plan benefits insurance for multiemployer plans, which are described in Chapter 34, differ substantially from those for other plans. Except as noted, this chapter describes the provisions applicable to plans other than multiemployer plans. These other plans are generally referred to as "single-employer plans," although in fact they include many multiple-employer plans that do not fit into the definition of "multiemployer plan."

Administering Agency

The plan benefits insurance program is administered by a self-financed public corporation named the Pension Benefit Guaranty Corporation.[14] It functions under a board of directors consisting of the Secretaries of Commerce, Labor, and the Treasury, with the Secretary of Labor serving as chairman. The board of directors establishes general policies of the Corporation, while its day-to-day operations are under the direction of an executive director. The employees of the Corporation are nonpolitical government employees and are appointed in accordance with federal civil service regulations.

An advisory committee counsels the Corporation on matters of broad policy, especially the investment of funds.[15] It consists of two representatives of employee organizations, two representatives of employers, and three representatives of the public.[16] The members, who serve staggered three-year terms, are appointed by the President, upon the recommendation of the board of directors. The committee must meet at least six times a year and may meet at other times determined by the chairman or requested by any three members of the committee.

Plans Covered

The insurance program covers, with certain exceptions, all qualified defined benefit pension plans and all other defined benefit pension plans affecting interstate commerce that, for the preceding five years, have in practice met all the requirements of a qualified plan.[17] A plan once determined by the IRS to be qualified continues to be a covered plan with respect to all accrued benefits, even if the determination is subsequently deemed to have been unwarranted or if the plan loses its qualified status because of a subsequent amendment. However, benefits accruing after the disqualification are not insured.[18]

Among the classes of plans specifically excluded from coverage are individual account plans (such as money purchase pension plans, profit-sharing plans, thrift

---

[14]ERISA §4002.
[15]ERISA §4002(h).
[16]Dan McGill was the first chairman of the advisory committee and served on the committee for two terms.
[17]ERISA §4021(a).
[18]ERISA §4022(b)(6).

and savings plans, and stock bonus plans), governmental plans, church plans that have not elected coverage and meet other specified conditions, plans of fraternal societies to which employers of the participants do not contribute, plans for a limited group of highly paid employees, plans that only provide for benefits or contributions in excess of the limitations in the Internal Revenue Code, plans established and maintained outside the United States primarily for nonresident aliens, plans maintained by a "professional service employer" covering not more than 25 active participants, and qualified plans exclusively for "substantial owners" (a substantial owner being a person who owns a sole proprietorship, has more than 10 percent interest in the capital or profits of a partnership, or at least 10 percent of either the entire stock or the voting stock of a corporation).[19]

Plan Termination as the Insured Event

The objective of the plan benefits insurance program is to ensure the ultimate payment of vested benefits, within defined limits, irrespective of the funded status of the plan at the time of its termination or the dissolution of the business entity that sponsored the plan. If one accepts the proposition that the sponsor of a pension plan has a moral and legal obligation to fund the benefits that have accrued to date under the plan, it follows that the insured event (i.e., the event or circumstance that triggers the insurance mechanism) should be the liquidation or dissolution of the sponsoring firm. Under this philosophy, the plan sponsor should continue funding the plan on some stipulated basis as long as it continues in operation, even though the plan has been terminated and no additional benefits are accruing or vesting.

This view of the sponsor's obligation was not originally embodied in ERISA. Instead the act provided that a plan termination would activate the insurance mechanism, even though the sponsor continued in business and perhaps established another plan. This meant that the insured event was *plan termination*. The sponsor and all members of its control group were liable to the PBGC for any unfunded insured benefits up to 30 percent of its net worth at the time of plan termination. If the unfunded insured liability exceeded 30 percent of the sponsor's net worth, the PBGC had to absorb the excess and spread the loss over all insured plans.

Prior to the enactment of the Single-Employer Pension Plan Amendments Act of 1986 (SEPPAA), plan sponsors generally had an unrestricted right to terminate a pension plan at any time, on the condition that they provide 10 days' advance notice to the PBGC. An exception to this applied (and still applies) to plans subject to collective bargaining, which generally may not be terminated or modified during the period of the collective bargaining agreement without the union's consent.

This was a flawed concept. Contrary to sound insurance principles, the insured event was largely under the control of the plan sponsor, an interested party. Coupled with this, the law created an incentive for a plan sponsor to terminate the

[19]ERISA §4021(b).

plan at any time the unfunded insured liability exceeded 30 percent of its net worth. It also created a disincentive to fund at the maximum tax-deductible level, since there was always the potential of terminating the plan at some future date under circumstances that would relieve the sponsor of some of its unfunded insured liabilities. Many such plan terminations occurred, and they created large liabilities for the PBGC. Some of the firms that terminated their plans were ongoing employers, and some of these immediately set up other pension or profit-sharing plans.

SEPPAA substantially restricted the ability of plan sponsors to terminate plans with unfunded guaranteed benefits, as described later in this chapter. While plan termination is still the insured event, an employer is no longer free to terminate a plan with unfunded accrued benefits except in a "distress" situation, a term generally used to describe the looming insolvency of the plan sponsor. If an employer that is not in a distress situation desires to terminate a plan with unfunded accrued benefits, it may need to first freeze the accrual of benefits and continue funding the plan until all accrued benefits are funded, at which time it could terminate the plan. Thus plan terminations with unfunded accrued benefits are now limited to distress situations. The Omnibus Budget Reconciliation Act of 1987 further restricted a plan sponsor's ability to transfer plan benefit liabilities to the PBGC by eliminating the 30 percent limit on the plan sponsor's liability.

An employer can effectively terminate a plan for some participants and continue it for others. For example, the plan can be effectively terminated for employees at a particular plant or facility and yet be continued for employees at all other locations if the coverage requirements continue to be met. The IRS may regard this as a *partial termination*, but it is not considered to be a termination of any kind for purposes of the plan benefits insurance provisions of Title IV of ERISA. This leaves the plan sponsor with full liability under ERISA's funding rules.

Reportable Events

The administrator of any covered pension plan is required to report to the PBGC certain specified developments or changes in circumstances that might indicate a deterioration in the financial condition of the plan and hence might portend plan termination.[20] These reportable events are (a) a loss of qualified status under the Internal Revenue Code; (b) a determination by the Department of Labor that the plan is not in compliance with Title I of ERISA; (c) a plan amendment that decreases the benefits of the participants or discontinues the accrual of future benefits; (d) a decrease in active participants to 80 percent of the number at the beginning of the plan year, or 74 percent of the number at the beginning of the previous plan year; (e) an IRS determination that there has been a complete or partial plan termination for tax purposes; (f) a failure to meet the minimum funding standards; (g) an inability of the plan to pay benefits when due; (h) a distribution from the plan of $10,000 or more within a 24-month period to a "substantial owner," for reasons other than death, if there are unfunded vested liabilities after the distribution; (i) a merger or consolidation of the plan with

---

[20]ERISA §4043; 29 CFR 2615.

another plan, or the granting by the Labor Department of an alternative method of compliance with any requirements;[21] and (j) any other event that the Corporation determines may indicate a need to terminate the plan, such as the closing of a plant or the cessation of benefit accruals.

The law gave the PBGC authority to waive the reporting requirement for some or all of the specified events and to add new events. Under this authority, the PBGC added two new events: (1) the granting of a waiver of the minimum funding standards; and (2) certain changes in the plan sponsor's ownership or financial condition, including a sale of the business or a portion thereof, voluntary liquidation, and bankruptcy. ERISA stipulated that reportable events were to be reported within 30 days after their occurrence, but the PBGC has waived this requirement for most events.

Certain contributing sponsors must notify the PBGC at least 30 days before the event occurs. A contributing sponsor is subject to the advance notice requirement if it and members of its controlled group maintain plans subject to Title IV (excluding plans without unfunded vested benefits) with (1) aggregate unfunded vested benefits in excess of $50 million, and (2) an aggregate funded vested benefit percentage of less than 90 percent.[22]

However, the 30-day advance notice requirement does not apply if the contributing sponsor or the member of the contributing sponsor's controlled group to which the event relates is subject to the reporting requirements of section 13 or 15(d) of the Securities Exchange Act of 1934, or is a subsidiary of a corporation subject to such requirements. Thus advance reporting is generally not required if the contributing sponsor or the controlled group member to which the event relates is a publicly held corporation.[23]

Recent legislation added four new reportable events:[24]

1. when a controlled group member ceases to be a member of the controlled group as a result of some event, such as the sale of a subsidiary (notice of a change in the controlled group was previously required only in cases of significant underfunding);[25]
2. when a contributing sponsor or a member of the contributing sponsor's controlled group liquidates in bankruptcy (previously, plan administrators were not required to report a related employer's bankruptcy liquidation);[26]
3. when a contributing sponsor or a member of a contributing sponsor's controlled group declares an extraordinary dividend or redeems 10 percent or more of the total value or total combined voting power of a controlled group's stock in any 12-month period;[27]

---

[21]The PBGC does not consider a change in the plan's funding instrument or funding agency a reportable event.

[22]ERISA §4043(b)(1).

[23]ERISA §4043(b)(2).

[24]The Retirement Protection Act, included as part of the Uruguay Round of the General Agreement on Tariffs and Trade. The new provisions become effective for events occurring on or after February 6, 1995.

[25]ERISA §4043(c)(9).

[26]ERISA §4043(c)(10).

[27]ERISA §4043(c)(11).

4. when an aggregate of 3 percent or more of a plan's benefit liabilities are transferred out of the controlled group in any 12-month period.[28]

The PBGC has waived the new postevent reporting requirements for fully funded plans. In addition, multiemployer plans are exempt from all reportable event requirements. However, privately held companies subject to the advance reporting rules must report all transactions 30 days in advance, including those involving fully funded plans.[29] The Secretaries of Labor and the Treasury are obligated to report to the PBGC any other events or developments that raise questions about the soundness of the plan.

Liability of Plan Sponsor

To foster a sense of prudence and discipline on the part of the plan sponsor in setting benefit levels and meeting the cost of accruing benefit credits to discourage termination of underfunded plans, to help finance the insurance program, and to provide accrued benefits in excess of those insured, ERISA requires that the sponsor of a terminated single-employer plan pay the PBGC the amount of any unfunded benefit liabilities.[30]

General Nature and Determination of the Liability

The obligation to reimburse the PBGC attaches not only to the plan sponsor but to all members of its controlled group, as defined in the law. In fact, the plan sponsor and the members of its controlled group are *jointly* and *severally* liable for any such obligation, so each can be held responsible for the entire liability. The amount of the potential obligation is the excess of (1) the actuarial value of the plan's accrued benefits as of the date of plan termination over (2) the fair value of the plan's assets on the date of plan termination.

The plan sponsor's obligation to the PBGC is payable in a lump sum upon demand from the PBGC, except that any obligation in excess of 30 percent of the sponsor's net worth is to be paid under commercially reasonable terms prescribed by the PBGC. However, by written agreement with the PBGC, the firm can arrange to meet the obligation over a period of years. The terms of the installment settlement vary with the circumstances.[31]

The net worth of the plan sponsor and controlled group members is determined as of a date chosen by the PBGC within a corridor bounded by the date of plan termination and a date not more than 120 days prior to plan termination. The law requires the PBGC to determine net worth on whatever basis best reflects, in its judgment, the current status of the firm's operations and economic prospects. It is computed without taking the PBGC claim into account. It is increased by any asset transfers made by the plan sponsor prior to plan termination, and by any assump-

---

[28]ERISA §4043(c)(12).
[29]PBGC Technical Update 95-3.
[30]ERISA §4062.
[31]ERISA §4067.

tion of liabilities deemed by the PBGC to have been improper. Since the balance sheet net worth is greatly affected by the methods and basic assumptions used by the firm in valuing its assets and liabilities, the PBGC does not use balance sheet values. If the firm is in the process of dissolution, the net worth may be determined in terms of its liquidation value.

In effect, the employer liability provisions of ERISA supersede certain contract law principles that would allow a plan sponsor to limit its financial obligation for pensions to the amounts already contributed to the plan. Thus, an exculpatory provision in the plan document limiting the employer's liability under the plan, or a provision in a collective bargaining agreement obligating an employer to contribute only specified amounts to the plan, does not modify, substitute for, or extinguish the employer's statutory liability to the PBGC under Title IV of ERISA. Moreover, the discharge of an employer's obligation to the PBGC does not override any contractual rights that the plan participants may have against the employer for benefits payable but not insured by the PBGC. For example, there may be contractual rights to vested noninsured benefits under a collective bargaining agreement. These benefit rights would normally be treated as general unsecured claims in a Title 11 or a similar state proceeding.

If two or more sponsors that are not under common control have contributed to the same multiple-employer plan (other than a multiemployer plan) that terminates, ERISA provides a method of allocating the liability to the PBGC among the employers.[32] If an employer withdraws from such a plan while the plan continues, it may be required to place in escrow the amount that its liability would have equaled had the plan then terminated.[33] The escrowed amount is to be held to offset any liability that the plan incurs in the event it is terminated during the following five years and is returned to the withdrawing employer at the end of the five years if there has been no plan termination in the interim. In lieu of the escrow, a withdrawing employer may post bond for 150 percent of the amount required for escrow. In some situations, the plan may be treated as if it was split into two plans, with the plan of the withdrawing employer being treated as terminated.

PBGC Claim Against the Assets of the Plan Sponsor

The PBGC must have legal recourse against the assets of a plan sponsor or controlled group member with primary or secondary liability if it is to enforce its claim for reimbursement in respect of benefits paid by the PBGC on behalf of a terminated plan. The legal status of that claim is important to all parties concerned, especially the other creditors of the plan sponsor or other controlled group members, both current and potential. Through the years, there has been concern in various quarters about the impact of the PBGC's potential claim on the availability of credit to the sponsor of defined benefit plans. This impact is affected not only by the potential magnitude of the claim but also by its relationship to the claims of other creditors in insolvency or bankruptcy proceedings.

[32]ERISA §4064.
[33]ERISA §4063.

Conceptually, the PBGC could be treated as a preferred creditor vis-à-vis other unsecured creditors, a general creditor, or a subordinated creditor—one whose claim is subordinate to those of all other creditors but superior to those of preferred and common shareholders. As a preferred creditor, the PBGC would have a prior claim to any assets available after satisfaction of the claims of secured creditors and other unsecured creditors with a higher priority. As a general creditor, it could seek an active role on the creditors' committee in the proceedings but would have to settle for its pro rata share of the assets available to that class of creditors. As a subordinated creditor, it would have only a remote chance of realizing on its claim in reorganization or bankruptcy proceedings and would have minimal influence in trying to protect its interests in competition with other creditors.

If a plan sponsor or its controlled group does not pay or make acceptable arrangements to pay its liability to the PBGC, other than any liability exceeding 30 percent of the sponsor's net worth, the PBGC automatically acquires a lien against all the assets and property rights of the controlled group.[34] The lien remains in effect for six years after termination of the plan, or for the duration of any collection agreement entered into between the plan sponsor (or members of its controlled group) and the PBGC. During that period, the PBGC may bring a civil suit in a U.S. district court to collect its claim or to enforce its lien on the plan sponsor's property. In the event that the plan sponsor becomes insolvent or bankrupt before liquidating its debt to the PBGC, the latter's claim is treated as a judgment lien; that is, it has the same priority as a judgment lien of the federal government for unpaid taxes. The only claims with higher priority are those of secured creditors (only with respect to the collateral), mechanics' liens, and a few other special claims.

The PBGC may have other types of claims against the plan sponsor or the plan, such as unpaid contributions and expenses connected with the takeover of the terminated plan. Unpaid contributions are generally treated as *wages due*, which enjoy a limited priority, the balance being general unsecured creditor claims. Any claims for unpaid contributions that arise after the plan sponsor files a bankruptcy petition are accorded the status of *administrative expenses*, a priority category. Expenses incurred by the PBGC in taking over a terminated plan are treated as an offset to the plan assets and thus are recovered directly. The offset, however, increases the asset insufficiency, which the PBGC may not be able to recover because of the net worth limitation, the sponsor's insolvency, or other reasons.

IRS Claims Against the Assets of the Plan Sponsor

In addition to the claims of the PBGC, the IRS may often have claims against the plan sponsor for excise taxes, particularly excise taxes for not making required contributions to the sponsor's pension plan. An excise tax of 10 percent is levied on an employer whose defined benefit plan has a funding deficiency.[35] If the funding deficiency is not corrected within a specified period, an additional excise

---

[34]ERISA §4068.
[35]IRC §4971(a).

tax of 100 percent of the outstanding funding deficiency is imposed.[36] Since the 100 percent excise tax can be waived by the IRS upon a contribution to the plan to eliminate the funding deficiency, the 100 percent tax is used as negotiating leverage by the IRS to induce the plan sponsor to contribute to the plan.

When a plan sponsor enters bankruptcy, the excise taxes become a claim of the IRS against the bankruptcy estate. However, how those excise taxes are characterized significantly affects the priority of the claim. Taxes are generally accorded administrative priority under bankruptcy law,[37] while nonpecuniary penalties are given much lower priority. The IRS, unsurprisingly, has attempted to enforce payment of the 10 percent and 100 percent taxes as excise taxes in bankruptcy, on the basis of the simplistic argument that administrative priority is afforded "excise taxes"[38] under the bankruptcy code, and the underfunding taxes are clearly labeled by the Internal Revenue Code as such. The IRS has had some limited success with this argument[39] but for the most part has experienced difficulty in obtaining priority status for underfunding excise tax claims.

Bankruptcy courts have tended to look past the label on the assessment to determine whether the amount is actually a tax, using the standard of whether the assessment is a pecuniary burden laid upon individuals or their property regardless of their consent, for the purposes of defraying expenses of government or undertakings authorized by it.[40] The analysis usually centers on whether the assessment is for public purposes, including defraying expenses of government or undertakings authorized by it. Many courts have determined the underfunding excise tax to be a legislative penalty intended to induce employers to meet the minimum funding requirements and not a tax, thereby assigning lower priority to the underfunding excise tax in bankruptcy.[41]

Benefits Insured

The law provides that the PBGC shall guarantee payment of all basic benefits of a terminated pension plan, subject to certain limits, that become nonforfeitable (or vested) by the terms of the plan. Since all accrued benefits, to the extent funded, vest upon plan termination by virtue of the termination, it is significant that the insurance coverage is limited to benefits that vested prior to termination through satisfaction of the service (or age and service) requirements of the plan. Basic benefits so vested are insured, with limits, even though they achieved that status by more liberal plan provisions than those required by the minimum vesting standards of ERISA.

Basic Versus Nonbasic Benefits

The Corporation is authorized to provide insurance coverage for both *basic* and *nonbasic* benefits. Coverage of basic benefits is mandatory if the benefits are

---

[36] IRC §4971(b).
[37] Bankruptcy Code §§503(b)(1)(B), 507(a)(7)(E) & (G).
[38] Bankruptcy Code §507(a)(7)(E).
[39] *U.S. v. Mansfield Tire and Rubber Co.*, 942 F2d 1055 (6th Cir. 1991), cert. denied sub nom *Krugliak v. U.S.*, 112 S.Ct. 1165 (1992).
[40] *City of New York v. Feiring*, 313 US 283 (1941).
[41] *In re Chateaugay Corp.*, 15 EBC 1237 (Bankr. SDNY 1992), and *In re Airlift International, Inc.*, 97 Bankr. 664 Bankr. (SD fla. 1989).

otherwise eligible for protection, whereas insurance of nonbasic benefits is optional with the Corporation. The two types of coverage are to be kept separate and distinct from a financial standpoint through the use of separate trust, or guaranty, funds.[42] The law does not define the terms *basic* and *nonbasic*, leaving the matter to regulations.

In a nutshell and as an oversimplification, the PBGC has defined a basic benefit as any type of retirement benefit that was nonforfeitable on the date of plan termination and any death, survivor, or disability benefit that was owed or was in payment status at the date of plan termination.[43] For this purpose, a benefit is nonforfeitable if, by the date of plan termination, the participant has met all of the plan's substantive conditions for entitlement.[44] The fact that a participant had not applied for his or her benefit or had not completed a waiting period (for a disability benefit, for example) would not be disqualifying. A benefit is not considered *forfeitable* even if entitlement ceases if and when the recipient remarries, reaches a specified age, or recovers from disability, although the PBGC would treat the recipient's continued eligibility to receive guaranteed benefits in accordance with the terms of the plan. Moreover, by an explicit provision in ERISA, a retirement benefit is not considered *forfeitable* merely because it can be suspended if the participant returns to active employment with the employer or, in the case of a multiemployer plan, if he or she returns to work in the same industry, trade, or craft, and in the same geographic area covered by the plan.[45]

The Corporation regards as "basic" only that portion of the normal retirement benefit payable in level monthly installments for the remaining lifetime of the participant.[46] This excludes lump-sum and special supplemental monthly benefits provided under some plans to encourage early retirement or to ease the participant's transition from an active to a retired status. Benefits earmarked for the payment of medical insurance premiums or other purposes are not basic benefits, unless the participant may elect to take them in the form of retirement benefits payable to her or himself. An otherwise basic benefit is deemed to satisfy the requirement that the basic benefit be one payable in level installments, even though the level of payments may change at some time as a result of (1) the application of a Social Security, Railroad Retirement, or workers' compensation offset; (2) a joint and survivor annuity option; or (3) cost-of-living adjustments or other increases for retired participants.

A basic benefit may reflect cost-of-living adjustments for active, terminated vested, and retired participants effective prior to termination of the plan. These adjustments may have been on an ad hoc basis or in accordance with a formula escalation factor or a specified cost-of-living index. Such benefit increases that have become effective pursuant to plan provisions prior to termination of the plan are entitled to insurance protection, subject to the phase-in rules; but any increases that take effect after the termination date are not insurable.

[42] ERISA §4005(a).
[43] 29 CFR §§2618.2, 2613.3.
[44] 29 CFR §2613.6.
[45] ERISA §203(a)(3)(B); IRC §411(a)(3)(B).
[46] 29 CFR §§2613.2, 2613.4.

The insurance payments of the Corporation are to be made in the form of monthly benefits, even though the terminated plan may have made provision for the participant to take some or all of the normal retirement benefit in a lump sum.[47] As an exception, the PBGC will pay in a lump sum the value of a participant's guaranteed benefit attributable to his or her mandatory employee contributions, if the participant so elects and if such payment is consistent with the plan's provisions. The benefit may be paid under any of the annuity forms made available by the Corporation, including joint and survivor annuity options, provided the election is made a specified period prior to retirement. The benefits under the optional annuity forms are to be the actuarial equivalent of the normal annuity form, as computed by the Corporation, using its own mortality and interest assumptions.[48] This principle is to be applied even though one or more of the optional annuity forms made available by the terminated plan is subsidized by the employer. However, any elections of optional annuity forms executed by participants prior to termination of the plan will be honored by the Corporation, the benefit payments being those that would have been made under the terms of the plan.

The normal retirement benefit is regarded as a basic benefit by the Corporation regardless of the age of the participant at the time the income commences. Thus if the plan provides that the full amount of accrued retirement benefits will become payable upon the participant's retirement after 30 years of service, irrespective of his or her attained age, such benefits of participants who have elected early retirement prior to plan termination will be insured by the Corporation, up to the applicable limits. The same is true if eligibility for full, unreduced benefits (for service rendered to date of retirement) is conditioned on the total of the participant's attained age and years of credited service equaling some specified number, such as 90. Under both of these types of eligibility requirements, retirement with full, unreduced benefits may (and probably will) take place before age 65, which is regarded by many as a standard normal retirement age. Note that the limit on the amount of basic monthly benefits that can be insured (discussed below) is actuarially reduced if the normal retirement benefit becomes payable before age 65. Thus persons retiring before age 65 may suffer a reduction in insured benefits.

Some negotiated plans provide that if an employee loses his or her job because of the closing of a plant or facility, he or she will be permitted to retire with full, unreduced benefits for service rendered to date with less service or at an earlier age than employees who remain in employment until they satisfy the other eligibility requirements. The Corporation would not regard a benefit payable under these circumstances as a basic benefit unless it was in pay status at the time of plan termination, and even then the amount insured could not exceed the dollar amount of basic retirement benefits accrued for normal age retirement.

The Corporation regards as basic benefits all early retirement benefits in pay status payable in level monthly installments for the remaining lifetime of the participant, even though they may be greater than the actuarial equivalent of the

---

[47]29 CFR §2613.8.
[48]29 CFR §2621.4(a).

normal retirement benefit.[49] It does not insure as basic benefits temporary supplemental benefits paid from the early retirement date to the normal retirement date, or for some other temporary period. An exception is made for benefits payable under the so-called Social Security adjustment option, in connection with which the participant's normal retirement benefit is permanently reduced to provide a temporary life annuity during the early retirement period equal to the estimated Social Security benefit payable at age 65.

In all these cases, the benefits must be vested and nonforfeitable by the terms of the plan before they become insurable. However, the qualified preretirement survivor annuity benefits that have not yet matured are not generally regarded as vested, even though the participant has become vested in his or her retirement benefits. Thus, if a vested participant dies or becomes disabled after leaving the service of the employer, no benefits other than the qualified preretirement survivor annuity are payable. The PBGC has concluded that other preretirement death and disability benefits not in payment status before termination of the plan are not basic benefits and are not currently entitled to insurance protection unless the benefit constitutes a return of the employee's mandatory contributions to the plan. If, at the time of the plan termination, there are pending death claims payable in a lump sum, the Corporation will honor such claims and pay them in a lump sum.

Nonbasic benefits would presumably include death and disability benefits not treated as basic benefits, monthly retirement benefits in excess of the amount that can be insured as basic benefits, medical insurance premiums and benefits, and other more unusual benefits that might emerge from the collective bargaining process. Thus far the PBGC has made no arrangements to insure nonbasic benefits, and there is no indication that it intends to do so.

Limitation on Amount of Monthly Benefits

ERISA imposes a limit on the amount of basic benefit that can be insured by the PBGC. The statutory ceiling for single-employer plans is linked to changes in the Social Security contribution and benefit base. Originally $750 per month, the limit had risen to $2,573.86 by 1995.[50] The benefit to which the ceiling applies is a single life annuity (popularly known as a "straight-life annuity") commencing at age 65. If the benefit is payable at a lower age than 65, or in any annuity other than the straight-life form, the limit is actuarially reduced on the basis of actuarial factors prescribed from time to time by the PBGC. The applicable reduction can be substantial in respect of disability income benefits, survivor income benefits, or retirement benefits payable after a stipulated period of service, such as 30 years, irrespective of attained age, since recipients of such benefits may be young at plan termination. The limit is not actuarially *increased* when the participant retires at an age later than 65.

The limit relates to the basic benefits that the PBGC is permitted to guarantee in respect of any one individual, regardless of the number of plans in which benefits

---

[49]The Corporation does not insure any portion of early retirement benefits in excess of the dollar amount of basic retirement benefits accrued for normal age retirement.
[50]ERISA §4022(b)(3)(B).

might have been earned.[51] The benefit ceiling in effect on the date the plan terminates is the controlling factor, irrespective of when the participant begins to receive benefits. In no event can the benefit guaranteed to a given participant be greater than this average gross income from the plan sponsor during the five consecutive years of highest earnings (or, if the period is shorter, the time during which the employee was an active participant).[52]

Phase-In of Insurance Coverage

To make the plan benefits insurance program less vulnerable to abuse, Congress stipulated that *full* coverage of basic benefits was to be available only after the benefits have been in effect for five years or more. This restriction was aimed not only at newly established plans but also at amendments to existing plans that increase benefits. However, provision was made for the coverage of single-employer plan benefits to take effect in graduated steps during the five-year period, unless the Corporation found substantial evidence that the plan was terminated not for a reasonable business purpose, but rather for the purpose of taking advantage of the insurance. Specifically, the law states that 20 percent of the basic benefit, up to the specified limit, shall be insured at the end of the first year, with an additional 20 percent of the benefit becoming insured at the end of each subsequent year until full coverage is available. The first 20 percent of coverage becomes effective 12 months after the later of the adoption date or effective date of the plan (or plan amendment). The successive increments become effective each 12 months thereafter.

To prevent too rapid a phase-in of benefits that exceed the statutory maximum guarantee ($2,573.86 in 1995), the amount of coverage phased in each year is the lesser of 20 percent of the new benefit (or benefit increase) or 20 percent of the statutory maximum guarantee.[53] For example, a plan is amended July 1, 1993, to increase a straight-life annuity commencing at age 65 from $2,200 to $2,600 per month and is terminated two years later on July 1, 1995. The increase guaranteed is $149.54 (40 percent of the excess of $2,573.86 over $2,200).

The law provides a more rapid phase-in of the guarantee of small benefits (under $100 per month) by insuring $20 of the benefit each year, irrespective of the 20 percent limitation, until the full benefit is guaranteed. Thus, a benefit increase of $50 per month would be fully insured after three years.

The law provides a special phase-in rule for substantial owners because they have the greatest incentive to abuse the program. The insurance coverage of the basic benefits of a substantial owner is phased in at the rate of $1/30$ per year, without application of the minimum benefit of $20 per month discussed above. This rule applies not only to the benefits of a newly established plan but also to those provided by a plan amendment. The insurance coverage of each set of newly created benefits must be phased in over a 30-year period beginning with the date of the amendment (or, if later, the effective date of the increase).[54]

[51]29 CFR §2621.3(b).
[52]ERISA §4022(b)(3)(A).
[53]ERISA §4022(b)(7); 29 CFR §2621.5-6.
[54]29 CFR §2621.7.

If a new pension plan covers substantially the same persons that an earlier plan covered and provides essentially the same benefits, the years of existence of the predecessor plan are added to those of the successor plan in determining the insurance coverage of any particular set of benefits.[55] Any increase in the value of the plan benefit, such as that arising out of a liberalization of vesting or a reduction in the normal retirement age, is subject to the same phase-in rules as those applicable to an explicit benefit increase. Benefits provided under a plan provision calling for automatic cost-of-living adjustments are subject to the phase-in feature, as are ad hoc adjustments in the benefits of retired persons.

Allocation of Single-Employer Plan Assets

Since not all benefits under a pension plan are insured, it was necessary for ERISA to provide a procedure for allocating the assets of a single-employer plan that has become subject to an insured event between the benefits that are insured and those that are not insured. The allocation procedure is important to plan participants since it can affect the amount of benefits they receive. It also is important to both the PBGC and the employer, and they both profit from maximizing the proportion of assets going to insured benefits. The more assets that are assigned to insured benefits, the smaller the amount of PBGC resources that must be applied to the payment of insured benefits. On the other hand, the more plan assets that are allocated to insured benefits, the smaller the amount of noninsured benefits that will be paid from plan assets.

Priority Classes

It might have been assumed that the law would give first priority against the plan assets to insured benefits. However, Congress decided that the benefits payable to participants who had been retired for at least three years on the date of the insured event, or who could have been retired for three years, should be given priority over employer-financed benefits of other insured participants, even for amounts in excess of the insurance limit. This meant that some uninsured benefits were to have a higher priority than other insured benefits, making it necessary to establish priority classes even among the insured benefits.

The statutory allocation formula establishes six classes of benefits, in descending order of priority, with the assets for the first four classes being allocated on a pro rata basis, if necessary, within each successive class:[56]

1. Benefits attributable to voluntary employee contributions. For participants not yet retired, the claim would be for assets in an amount equal to the balances in the individual accounts. These benefits are not insured by the PBGC, since they are almost invariably provided on a money purchase basis. Because they have first claim to all plan assets; their payment is virtually assured.
2. Benefits attributable to mandatory employee contributions, taking into account those paid out before the date of the insured event.

[55]ERISA §§4021(a), 4022(b); PBGC Opinion Letter 86-9.
[56]ERISA §4044.

3. Benefits of a participant or beneficiary that had been in a pay status for at least three years on the date of the insured event, and the benefits that would have been in pay status for three or more years if the participants had retired with normal benefits three years prior to the insured event. In each case, the priority attaches only to the lowest benefit level under the plan during the five years prior to retirement; and for those already retired, the priority attaches only to the lowest benefit level of the three-year period of benefit payments. These restrictions are designed to withhold this high priority from general benefit increases provided within five years prior to the insured event and from participants who become eligible to begin receiving benefits within the three-year period preceding the insured event. Within the limits described, this priority attaches to all benefits falling within this class, irrespective of the amount of the monthly benefit. Thus uninsured benefits may enjoy this priority.
4. All other benefits up to the applicable limits that would be insured but for the aggregate limit of $750 (indexed) per month on insured benefits from two or more plans and the special limitation on the coverage of a "substantial owner." The waiver of these special limits has the effect of giving certain uninsured benefits a priority over other uninsured benefits.
5. All other vested benefits, meaning the *uninsured* vested benefits not falling within one of the higher-priority classes. Assets allocated to this category must be applied first to benefits offered by the plan five years before the occurrence of the insured event and then to benefits added later, in the order in which they were made available.
6. All other benefits under the plan.

A benefit that could be placed in more than one priority category, such as the vested benefit of a person who retired four years before the insured event, is assigned the highest priority for which it qualifies and is not included in more than one category. A PBGC regulation permits plans to provide for limited subclasses within each priority category—advanced age, seniority, and disability being permissible bases for preference in asset allocation.[57]

The statute is silent about the allocation of plan assets between the insured and uninsured benefits of a participant whose benefit claims fall within one of the priority classes. Obviously, the financial burden on the PBGC would be minimized if the insured benefits were to be given first claim to the plan assets. If the plan assets were sufficient to cover the insured portion of the participant's benefits, there would be no drain on the Corporation's resources. By the same token, the proportion of the participant's benefit claims that would be satisfied by the combination of plan assets and insurance payments would be maximized if the uninsured portion of his or her benefits were to be given first claim to the assets. ERISA requires plan assets to be prorated among participants on the basis of the value of their total insured and uninsured benefits in the category. The PBGC has made a policy decision that the assets allocated within any category to a particular participant are assigned first to the participant's insured benefits in the category, and the

[57] 29 CFR §2618.17.

remaining assets are assigned to the participant's uninsured benefits in the category.

The statutory formula supersedes the allocation procedure set forth in the plan, except possibly for any assets that might remain after satisfaction of all vested benefits. The superimposed procedure applies both to previously allocated assets and to assets still unallocated at the time of termination. In that connection, the amended law states that life insurance or annuity contracts issued by life insurers are plan assets and as such are subject to the statutory allocation formula. This could force a life insurance company to reduce or cancel some life insurance and annuity contracts.

Recapture of Benefit Payments

Not only does the statutory allocation formula give priority, with the exceptions noted, to insured benefits, including assets previously allocated, but the trustee is authorized to recapture from a retired participant certain payments made during any 12-month period within the three years prior to the occurrence of the insured event.[58] The intent of this provision is to permit the trustee to recover any amounts substantially in excess of the stipulated limits paid out by the plan administrator in the form of a lump sum or in accelerated pension payments in anticipation of the insured event. There is no recapture threat if the participant's entire interest in the plan is taken in the form of a conventional life annuity, but the amount of future annuity payments is subject to reduction in accordance with the asset allocation rules. If benefits were not paid as a life annuity, the trustee may recover any excess of the actual payments during the three years over the sum of (1) the payments that would have been paid in the life annuity form (or if larger, the lesser for each 12-month period of $10,000 or the actual payments) plus (2) the present value at the time of termination of the participant's future guaranteed payments that would have been payable if benefits were paid as a life annuity.

The trustee is not authorized to recover any amounts paid by reason of the death or disability of the participant, provided that the disabled participant is also receiving disability benefits under the Social Security program. The PBGC is authorized to waive any recovery that would cause substantial economic hardship, which, of course, could increase the plan sponsor's liability for unfunded insured benefits.

Plan Termination Initiated by the Plan Sponsor

The virtually unlimited right of plan sponsors to terminate plans contributed to very large liabilities being placed upon the PBGC, thereby creating substantial deficits in the benefits insurance program. SEPPAA was enacted to ameliorate the situation. It amended ERISA to limit the sponsor's right to terminate a defined benefit plan. A defined benefit plan may not be terminated voluntarily unless it meets the condition of a *standard termination* or a *distress termination*.[59]

[58]ERISA §4045.
[59]ERISA §4041(a).

Standard Termination

A standard termination is a plan termination in which the plan assets are sufficient to cover all *benefit liabilities* for benefits earned to date, and to protect participants from the loss of such benefits without imposing any liability on the PBGC.[60] Benefit liabilities include all accrued benefits.[61] Benefit liabilities also include early retirement supplements and subsidies such as early retirement reduction factors, which are more liberal than actuarial equivalent factors, as well as special benefits that become payable only upon plant shutdown or certain other special events. However, they are included in benefit liabilities only if at the time of plan termination the participant has satisfied all the conditions required under the provisions of the plan to establish entitlement to the benefits, other than submission of an application for benefits and similar administrative requirements. Benefit liabilities always equal or exceed the amount of guaranteed benefits.

Sixty days prior to the date of a proposed standard termination the plan administrator must send a notice of intent to terminate to each participant and beneficiary and to any labor union representing participants. The notice of intent to terminate must state the proposed termination date.[62]

As soon as practicable after the notice of intent to terminate is provided, the plan administrator must provide a notice to the PBGC. This notice must include a certification by an enrolled actuary stating, as of the proposed termination date, the projected amount of plan assets and the actuarial present value of the benefit liabilities. The notice must also state that the plan assets are projected to be sufficient to satisfy the benefit liabilities. The notice to the PBGC must also include certification by the plan administrator that the data used by the actuary in preparing the actuarial certification were complete and accurate.[63]

No later than the date that the above notice is sent to the PBGC, the plan administrator must provide another notice to each participant and beneficiary. This notice must state the amount and form of the individual's benefit entitlement and the data, such as length of service and compensation, on which this information is based.[64]

Unless the PBGC issues a notice of noncompliance within 60 days of receiving its notice from the plan administrator, the plan administrator generally must begin distributing the plan assets as soon as practicable after the 60-day period. If the plan administrator fails to make a timely distribution, the termination is void, and the plan is treated for all purposes as an ongoing plan. Thus the employer is always able to abandon a standard termination before its completion. After the distribution has been completed, a final notice must be provided to the PBGC.

Method of Distribution of Plan Assets

All benefits that were payable as an annuity under the provisions of the plan must be provided in the form of an annuity after plan termination unless a

[60]ERISA §4041(b).
[61]ERISA §4001(a)(16); IRC §401(a)(2); Rev. Rul. 85-6.
[62]ERISA §4041(a)(2).
[63]ERISA §4041(b).
[64]Ibid.

lump-sum distribution is allowed under one of several exceptions.[65] A lump-sum distribution is permissible if the present value of the benefit is less than $3,500 or if the benefit is smaller than the smallest monthly benefit normally provided by an insurer. A lump sum may also be provided if the plan provided for this form of distribution and if the participant elects it.

The benefit liabilities to be provided as annuities generally must be provided under one or more annuity contracts issued by a life insurance company. This may include any annuities that had been purchased in the normal course of the plan's funding and any additional contracts purchased at the time of termination.

The benefit liabilities include benefits payable immediately to some participants and beneficiaries and benefits payable commencing at some deferred date for others. The right to a deferred annuity often includes the right to elect early retirement, with reduced benefits determined on either an actuarially equivalent basis or some subsidized basis. Under some circumstances the plan administrator may not be able to purchase deferred annuities that include the early retirement benefits and have rates that reasonably take account of the probability of early retirement. In this case the PBGC may provide the early retirement benefits if the plan administrator pays the PBGC the value of the benefits. Any benefit liabilities to be provided in the form of a lump sum must equal the present value of the benefit liabilities, determined in accordance with regulations.[66]

Allocation of Excess Assets

If the plan assets are more than sufficient to satisfy the allocation requirements for all benefit liabilities, the residual assets are allocable to either the plan sponsor or to participants and beneficiaries.[67] Unless the plan document provides otherwise, all such residual assets are to be allocated to participants and beneficiaries. This allocation must be in proportion to their other allocations of plan assets (other than any allocations for voluntary employee contributions) unless that would be discriminatory. Any plan amendment creating or increasing the amount of reversion to the employer may not become effective until five years after its adoption.[68] If the plan provides for a reversion to the employer, it is first necessary to determine the amount of residual assets that must be allocated to mandatory employee contributions if the plan is contributory;[69] any remainder of the residual assets may revert to the employer.

Distress Terminations

If plan assets are less than the benefit liabilities, a plan may not be terminated voluntarily unless each contributing employer (and each member of a controlled group with such employers) satisfies the requirements for a distress termination.[70] An employer is in distress if it satisfies any one of four criteria:

[65]29 CFR §2617.4.
[66]29 CFR §2619.26.
[67]ERISA §4044(d); 29 CFR §2618.30-32.
[68]ERISA §4044(d)(2).
[69]IRC §411(c); ERISA §4044(d)(3).
[70]ERISA §4041(c).

1. A petition for liquidation of the employer has been filed under bankruptcy laws.
2. The employer is in the process of reorganization under bankruptcy laws, the bankruptcy court determines that the employer will be unable to pay its debts under reorganization and to continue in business outside reorganization, and the court approves the termination.
3. The employer demonstrates to the PBGC that it will be unable to pay its debts when they come due and will be unable to continue in business unless the distress termination occurs.
4. The employer demonstrates to the PBGC that its pension costs have become unreasonably burdensome solely as a result of a decline in the employer's work force.

To initiate a distress termination, the plan administrator must provide a notice of intent to terminate to plan participants and beneficiaries and union representatives as for a standard termination, except that for a distress termination the notice of intent must also be sent to the PBGC.[71]

As soon as practicable after providing the notice of intent to terminate, the plan administrator must provide the PBGC with the information it needs to determine whether the criteria for a distress termination have been satisfied. In addition, the information must include a certification by the enrolled actuary including, as of the proposed termination date, the projected value of plan assets, the present value of all benefit liabilities, and the present value of the portion of benefits guaranteed under the plan benefits insurance program. The certification must state whether the plan assets are sufficient for benefit liabilities or for guaranteed benefits, or for neither. The information must also include the name and address of each participant and beneficiary and the information the PBGC or the trustee needs to pay future benefits to them. In addition, the plan administrator must certify the completeness and accuracy of the information on which the actuary's certification is based and the completeness and accuracy of all other information provided.

Unlike a standard termination, a distress termination does not require that participants and beneficiaries be provided with any information concerning their individual benefits. In a standard termination the plan administrator may proceed with the termination unless the PBGC provides a notice of noncompliance, but under a distress termination the plan administrator may not terminate the plan until the PBGC notifies the plan administrator of its determination.

In a distress termination, if the PBGC determines that the assets exceed the benefit liabilities, the termination is thenceforth treated as a standard termination. If the plan assets are less than the benefit liabilities but the allocation of plan assets results in all guaranteed benefits being fully funded, the plan administrator must proceed to distribute all of the plan assets in the same manner as for a standard termination.

Any payments received by the PBGC for unfunded nonguaranteed benefits (the excess of a plan's unfunded benefit liabilities over its unfunded guaranteed benefits) will be applied to provide the unfunded nonguaranteed benefits of

[71]Ibid.

participants.[72] If a plan's unfunded nonguaranteed benefits exceed $20 million, any such payments received will be applied to provide unfunded nonguaranteed benefits under the particular plan. Otherwise, any such payments received will be pooled to provide unfunded nonguaranteed benefits under all other such plans.

If the plan assets are insufficient to provide for all guaranteed benefits, the plan must be brought under the control and administration of a "termination trustee." The termination trustee may be the PBGC, the plan administrator, or an individual appointed by a federal court, possibly from a list of persons submitted by the PBGC. The administrator and the PBGC may agree that the latter is to be the termination trustee. Court approval is not required for such an agreement. It is the policy of the PBGC to seek trusteeship status for itself in virtually all cases, in the interest of uniform administration and operating efficiencies. With few exceptions, the plan sponsor usually agrees to the arrangement. When the PBGC has found it necessary to go to court to be appointed trustee, its petition has generally been approved.

As termination trustee, the PBGC assumes responsibility for the further administration and eventual winding up of the plan. It maintains plan records, processes applications for retirements, issues checks to benefit recipients, and responds to inquiries from plan participants and their beneficiaries.

Under present policy, the assets of the plan are transferred to a commingled trust fund maintained by the PBGC for purposes of investment diversification and efficiency. These assets are managed for the PBGC by private sector investment managers, selected by competitive bidding on the basis of past investment performance and future potential performance. The assets are invested in the private sector under a set of guidelines laid down by the PBGC, with the counsel of the Advisory Committee.

Plan Termination Initiated by the PBGC

A pension plan is generally terminated at the initiative of the plan sponsor. Under ERISA, however, the PBGC was given the authority to petition an appropriate federal district court to terminate a plan irrespective of the plan sponsor's wishes in certain specified circumstances.[73] Basically, involuntary termination is authorized when necessary to protect the interests of plan participants or the PBGC. The latter is interested in protecting itself against unreasonable increases in its exposure to loss through continued operation of the plan, against continued accruals of benefit obligations, and against possible deterioration of the sponsor's net worth. The PBGC may institute judicial proceedings to terminate a pension plan if it finds that

- the plan is not in compliance with the minimum funding standards of the Internal Revenue Code;
- a reportable event has occurred;
- the ultimate loss to the PBGC with respect to the plan may reasonably be expected to increase unreasonably if the plan is not terminated forthwith;

[72]ERISA §4022(c).
[73]ERISA §4042.

• the plan is unable to pay benefits when due (in which case termination by PBGC is mandatory).

After approval by the court, an involuntary termination proceeds in much the same way as a distress termination that has been approved by the PBGC.

Liability for Accumulated Funding Deficiencies and Waived Funding Deficiencies

At the time of plan termination the amount of any accumulated funding deficiency plus the amount of any previously waived funding deficiencies becomes immediately due and payable to the plan trustee.[74]

Amendment to Reduce or Freeze Plan Benefits

At times a plan sponsor may desire to make a plan amendment to reduce or discontinue all future benefit accruals, but without terminating the plan. Such a step may be taken for many of the same reasons that a plan termination is undertaken, generally in order to reduce plan costs or to make changes where reduction or elimination of accruals is appropriate, as in a change to a different type of plan for future service or in a plant closing.

The least disruptive of such courses of action would be a plan amendment (effective only with respect to service thereafter) to reduce the rate at which pension benefits accrue, to decrease or eliminate ancillary benefits (such as those payable upon death or disability), or to cut back on other attractive but costly plan features. This type of action is called a plan *curtailment* and does not involve any official response (other than IRS approval) or penalty.

A more drastic form of action would be a plan amendment to discontinue all future benefit accruals, but with the recognition of future service for vesting and phase-in purposes and with the continuation of contributions for the funding of benefits already accrued. With no further change of policy, all accrued benefits of continuing employees would eventually become fully vested and fully funded. This type of action is referred to as *freezing* of the plan or, in IRS terminology, as a "suspension" of the plan. In some circumstances—for example, when it creates or increases a potential reversion of assets to the employer—the IRS may regard a suspension as a *partial termination* requiring all accrued benefits to vest to the extent then funded.[75]

If a plan is frozen without a plan termination, the employer avoids any immediate assessment of liability to the plan's trust for previously waived funding deficiencies, or to the PBGC for unfunded guaranteed benefits. The employer is required to notify participants and beneficiaries at least 15 days before the effective date of any amendment that eliminates or significantly reduces future benefit accruals.[76]

[74]ERISA §4043.
[75]IRC §411(d)(3); Treas. Reg. 1.4111(d)-2(b)(2).
[76]ERISA §204(h).

Financial Structure

The PBGC is intended to be a self-financed entity that is not dependent on the federal government for support. The PBGC receives no appropriations from the Congress but has its own sources of revenue, which can be utilized for corporate purposes. However, its budget is subject to the budgetary processes of the federal government, and its revenue and disbursements are included in the totals of the federal budget.

The PBGC has five main sources of funds: premium income, investment earnings, levies against plan sponsors subject to liability for unfunded insured obligations, money borrowed from the U.S. Treasury, and assets of terminated insufficient plans. Under present practices, premium payments and Treasury borrowings, if any, flow into two statutory guaranty funds, while assets from insufficient terminated plans and employer liability collections are held in trust funds managed by or for the PBGC. Investment earnings are added to the assets that generated them.

Guaranty Funds

ERISA originally provided for four revolving funds, but only two of these have been established.[77] One fund is operated to insure basic benefits of single employer plans, while the other fund holds the money accumulated to insure basic benefits of multiemployer plans. Representatives of multiemployer plans insisted upon a separate guaranty fund—and a lower scale of premiums—in the belief that such plans rested on a firmer financial foundation than single-employer plans and offered a lower probability of termination. Statutory provision was made for another revolving fund for each of these two categories of plans to account for money associated with the insurance of nonbasic benefits. Since no programs have yet been established for nonbasic benefits, these guaranty funds have not been activated.

Amendments to ERISA have added three more funds, two related to multiemployer plans and the other to segregate premiums for single-employer plans resulting from premium increases taking effect after 1987. Having two separate funds for single-employer plans has the same practical effect as having only one fund.

Premium payments by pension plan sponsors are credited directly to the appropriate revolving funds.[78] Benefit payments by the PBGC to participants in terminated plans and operating expenses of the Corporation are initially charged to the revolving funds, with periodic reimbursement from the trust funds for their pro rata share of benefit payments and expenses.

Each revolving fund is intended to be self-sufficient, except that transfers will be made from the newer single-employer fund to the older single-employer fund as needed, with this exception: the resources of one fund are not to be used to pay the insurance losses or expenses of another fund. The overhead expenses of the

[77]ERISA §4005(a).
[78]ERISA §4005(b).

Corporation are allocated to the funds in accordance with accepted cost accounting procedures. Any amount borrowed from the Treasury must be allocated to one or more of the funds and must be repaid by money withdrawn from the same funds.

ERISA states that the Corporation *may* invest any money in excess of its current needs in obligations issued or guaranteed by the federal government. The Treasury Department has taken the position that the money in the guaranty funds, derived essentially from premium payments and investment earnings thereon, *must* be invested in government securities. The Treasury at one stage argued that the assets of terminated plans taken over by the Corporation as trustee should also be invested in government securities; but a compromise was eventually worked out under which the trusteed assets are invested in the private sector in the expectation of higher yields and thus lower premiums for plan sponsors.

The financial officers of the PBGC manage the investments of the revolving funds within the scope permitted. At their discretion, they may negotiate with the Treasury for the purchase of special nonmarketable securities, or they may acquire and dispose of government securities in the open market. The maturity structure of the securities held by the revolving funds reflects cash flow projections and anticipated interest rate behavior.

Trust Funds

The PBGC operates two commingled trusts, one for single-employer plans and the other for multiemployer plans. These are maintained for plans for which the PBGC is trustee. For accounting and fiduciary purposes, all the assets of terminated plans under the administration of the PBGC are regarded as part of the financial resources of the Corporation. Through periodic transfers to the revolving funds, plan assets held in PBGC trusts will ultimately be used up in payment of benefits and expenses.

Premiums

If the PBGC is to be self-supporting, as intended, its premium income, supplemented by investment earnings and employer liability payments, must be sufficient to underwrite the unfunded benefit obligations that it assumes. However, Congress has imposed some rigid constraints on setting the premium rates for basic benefits.[79]

As a first principle, ERISA states that separate premium schedules must be developed and maintained for single-employer and multiemployer plans. This mandate, along with the corollary requirement that the premiums be accumulated and held in separate revolving funds, reflects Congress's acceptance of the argument by multiemployer plan representatives that multiemployer plans have different risk characteristics from single-employer plans and are, in fact, subject to a lower probability of termination.

[79]ERISA §4006.

The second principle is that the Corporation can change premium rates or change the basis on which premiums are computed only with the advance approval of Congress, acting through a joint resolution. This provision reflects the fact that the Corporation, an insurance agency, is not subject to state insurance regulations and should be accountable to some public body. The prior approval requirement parallels that applicable at the state level to various forms of insurance, except that the approving authority at the state level is an administrative agency.

The PBGC has adopted a third principle, not expressly articulated in the law, that premium rates for all types of benefits and coverages should be set at such a level as to produce annual revenue sufficient to amortize over a period of years any unfunded actuarial liabilities associated with plans terminated during prior years. Of course, this revenue stream is augmented by investment earnings and employer contingent liability payments, and must also cover the unfunded actuarial liabilities associated with plans terminating during the year to which the premiums relate. This concept is in contrast to an approach known as the pay-as-you-go principle, under which the premium and other revenues would be sufficient only to pay benefits as they become due. The fundamental issue here is whether to distribute the social costs of plan terminations over successive generations of plan sponsors. The PBGC has taken the position that the full cost of each year's plan terminations should be borne by the plans subject to the risk of termination during that year, rather than be spread over a period coterminous with the future lifetimes of the participants and beneficiaries whose benefits were insured under the terminated plans. Implementation of this principle means that the PBGC must collect premiums each year that are expected to equal the actuarial present value of all unfunded benefit payments that it will make in future years in respect of the plans that terminate in that year and that are expected to amortize its unfunded liabilities arising in prior years. This will inevitably lead to a substantial accumulation of assets in the guaranty funds. When the PBGC periodically requested an increase in the premium rate, this principle came under attack from certain members of the business community, who questioned the need for short-term amortization of the Corporation's cumulative operating deficit, which at the time of this writing is estimated at $2.7 billion in the single-employer guaranty program, owing to claims well in excess of projections. These critics presumably would prefer, or at least tolerate, a system of financing closer to pay-as-you-go than to full funding. Currently, the PBGC is resisting any additional increases in the premium rate, or at least the flat rate premium rate discussed below, as a disincentive to the formation or maintenance of defined benefit plans.

Premium rates for the insurance protection provided by the PBGC should, in theory, reflect the statistical probability of the occurrence of the insured event and the amount of loss that would be sustained if the insured event should occur. The probability of occurrence of an insured event would be importantly related to the risk characteristics of the plan sponsor, such as the size and financial stability of the firm, the nature of the industry in which the firm operates and the firm's competitive standing in the industry, and the future prospects of the firm and the industry.

The amount at risk would be largely represented by the *unfunded* actuarial liability in respect of insured benefits, reduced by recoveries from plan sponsors under ERISA employer liability provisions. This amount is subject to wide fluctuations because of changes in the market value of accumulated plan assets, the value of guaranteed benefits, and the amount of the employer's net worth.

In view of the complexities involved in developing a theoretically correct scale of premium rates and the lack of reliable data on the actuarial status of the insured plan universe, Congress decided that the program should start with a very simple, even crude, premium structure, namely, a flat per capita levy. The initial premium, set forth in the statute, was $1 per participant per year for single employer plans and $.50 per participant under multiemployer plans. This simple approach was easily understood and administered, had the capability of generating a reasonably predictable flow of premium income, and would not produce gross inequities among plan sponsors if the initial burden of the program proved to be light, as was expected. Congress anticipated that a more sophisticated premium structure would eventually be needed and indicated that the premiums under such a revised structure could be based on (1) the number of plan participants, (2) the present value of insured benefits, or (3) the excess of the present value of insured benefits over the plan assets, or some combination of the three.

The initial per capita levies proved to be inadequate and, with congressional approval, the PBGC raised the premium for single-employer plans to $2.60 per participant per year, effective with plan years beginning after 1977, and to $8.50 per participant per year for plan years beginning after 1985.

For plan years beginning after 1987, the premium was increased to $16.00 per participant per year, with a subsequent increase for plan years after 1990 to $19 per participant, plus an additional amount for plans with unfunded vested benefits.[80] The interest rate used to determine the value of vested benefits for this purpose must be 80 percent of the annual yield for 30-year Treasury bonds for the month preceding the plan year for plan years beginning before July 1, 1997, and increasing to 85 percent for plan years beginning after June 30, 1997, and before 2000, and finally increasing to 100 percent of the annual yield of 30-year Treasury bonds for plan years beginning after 1999. This additional amount per participant equals $9.00 for each $1,000 (or fraction thereof) of unfunded vested benefits as of the end of the preceding plan year, divided by the number of participants at the end of such prior year.[81] However, this additional premium may not exceed $53.00 per participant.[82] Recent legislation[83] eliminated the $53.00 cap on the risk-related premium.[84]

If, for example, a plan had 10 participants at the end of the preceding plan year and had unfunded vested benefits equal to $1,700, the additional premium per participant would be $1.20 (2 times $6.00 divided by 10), making the total premium $17.20 ($16.00 plus $1.20). This premium rate would be applied to the number of participants at the end of the preceding plan year.

[80]ERISA §4006(a)(3)(A)(i).
[81]ERISA §4006(a)(3)(E)(ii).
[82]ERISA §4006(a)(3)(E)(iv).
[83]Retirement Protection Act of 1994.
[84]The variable premium is commonly referred to as a risk-related premium since the amount of the premium reflects the amount of underfunding in the plan and therefore the potential risk to the PBGC.

Proponents of this new approach argue that it assesses the costs of the system more equitably among those plans creating the risk of loss. Some opponents argue that it increases administrative costs for both employers and the PBGC, and that it assesses the higher premiums against employers for whom there is no risk of loss since they are not eligible for a distress termination or since they have net worth sufficient to reimburse the PBGC for any unfunded guaranteed benefits. Others have expressed concern that the approach will discourage the granting of past service credits and cost-of-living adjustments for retirees under plans in which such benefits could reasonably be expected to amortize without loss to the plan benefits insurance system.

Premiums for the basic benefits component of the plan benefits insurance program can be paid out of plan assets, but in many cases payment is made directly by the employer. The premiums in respect of a particular plan for a plan year must be paid not later than seven months after the beginning of the plan year, but plans with 500 or more participants must pay estimated premiums within two months after the beginning of the plan year.[85] Failure of the plan administrator to make timely payments of the premium does not affect the insurance protection, but it subjects the plan to interest charges and late payment penalties. This penalty for late payment may be waived by the PBGC upon a finding of substantial hardship.

For purposes of determining a plan's premium, the plan administrator must count as a "participant" (a) an individual currently accruing benefits or earning or retaining credited service, (b) a retired employee or a terminated vested employee, (c) a deceased participant whose survivors are entitled to benefits, and (d) anyone else defined as a participant under the plan's terms. A former employee with no vested rights who has incurred a break in service of at least one year's duration is not counted as a participant, nor is a retired or terminated vested employee whose guaranteed benefits are fully and irrevocably insured by a life insurance company.

A plan's premium obligation is based on the number of participants in the plan as of the last day of the preceding plan year. If an individual is a participant in more than one single-employer plan covered under the insurance program, each plan must include the participant in its premium computation.

Recoveries from Plan Sponsors

Recoveries from firms primarily or secondarily liable for the unfunded insured benefits of terminated pension plans, described earlier, are another source of revenue for the PBGC.

Borrowing Authority

The final potential source of funds for the Corporation is borrowing authority. The Corporation is authorized to borrow $100 million from the U.S. Treasury through the issuance to the Secretary of the Treasury of notes or other obligation in such forms and denominations, bearing such maturities, and subject to such

---

[85]Form PBGC-1 must accompany the premiums.

terms and conditions as the secretary may prescribe.[86] The obligations are to bear interest at a rate determined by the secretary, taking into consideration the current average market yield on outstanding marketable obligations of the United States with comparable maturities during the month preceding the issuance of the obligations. They must be repaid, of course, since the Corporation is intended to be self-financing. Initially, the Corporation borrowed $100,000 to finance its organizational expenses, and the loan was repaid out of the first premiums received.

[86]ERISA §4005(c).

Chapter 34
Multiemployer Plan Withdrawals and Plan Benefits Insurance

A multiemployer plan is a plan maintained according to one or more collective bargaining agreements and requires more than one employer to contribute to it.[1]

Plans Covered

As originally enacted, the Employment Retirement Income Security Act provided that the plan benefits insurance program for multiemployer defined benefit plans would be basically the same as the program for single-employer plans, with some exceptions. On the theory that multiemployer plans are less likely to terminate than single-employer plans, the law provided for separate trust funds and different premium rates, with the rate for multiemployer plans being just half that of single employer plans.

   The coverage of multiemployer plans became effective for purposes of premium payments on the date that ERISA was enacted, but the Pension Benefit Guaranty Corporation was not *required* to insure benefits of multiemployer plans that terminated before July 1, 1978. However, it had the authority to insure the benefits of terminated multiemployer plans on a discretionary basis, subject to certain conditions designed to safeguard the solvency of the multiemployer plans guaranty fund and to avoid premium increases.[2] Benefits were paid to the participants of several terminated plans under this discretionary authority.

   As the deadline for mandatory assumption of the unfunded insured obligations of terminated multiemployer pension plans approached, many policy makers saw that it would be impracticable to extend the program in its original form to multiemployer plans. At the heart of the difficulties was the procedure specified in the law for the allocation of the unfunded actuarial liabilities of a multiemployer plan, especially the procedure for allocating the liabilities between those employers who withdraw from the plan before it terminates and those who remain until the date of termination. To permit the PBGC staff and others to devise solutions to the perceived problems, Congress extended the deadline for mandatory coverage several times. Finally, on September 26, 1980, the Multiemployer Pension Plan

---

[1] ERISA §§3(37), 4001(a)(3); IRC §414(f).
[2] ERISA §4402(c)(2).

Amendments Act (MPPAA) was enacted. Its provisions fundamentally changed how the insurance program treats multiemployer plans.[3]

Liabilities of a Withdrawing Employer to a Multiemployer Pension Plan

Under the original Title IV provision for multiemployer plans—which, except for a few terminated plans insured by the PBGC under its discretionary authority, was effective for only about two months immediately prior to the enactment of the MPPAA—an employer could withdraw from a plan without any further financial obligation if the plan continued for another five years.[4] Upon eventual termination of the plan, all employers who were still members of the plan and all those who had withdrawn during the preceding five years had to assume their pro rata share of the plan's then unfunded insured liabilities. The proration was based on the required contributions to the plan during the preceding five years. This arrangement, if permitted to become operative, would have created a powerful incentive for employer members of a financially troubled plan to withdraw before its ultimate collapse and would have discouraged new employer affiliations, both of which would have exacerbated the problems of the plan and hastened its demise. The MPPAA repealed the original provisions in their entirety and substituted an approach under which employers withdrawing from a multiemployer plan must generally assume their allocable share of the plan's unfunded vested liabilities.

Definition of Withdrawal

For purposes of assessing withdrawal liability, the law distinguishes between a *complete* withdrawal from the plan and a *partial* withdrawal. A *complete* withdrawal occurs whenever an employer (1) permanently ceases to have an obligation to contribute to the plan or (2) permanently ceases all covered operations under the plan, including the sale of all assets.[5] The first circumstance is generally associated with decertification of the union that cosponsors the plan, with the employer operating thereafter with a nonunion work force or one affiliated with another union. The second circumstance generally occurs when an employer discontinues the operations that were subject to the collective bargaining agreement under which the plan functions.

Subject to the exception noted below, a partial withdrawal of a signatory employer occurs if *any one* of the following three conditions is present on the last day of a plan year:

1. the employer's contribution base units (e.g., hours worked) during each of the three consecutive plan years ending with the current plan year are 30 percent

---

[3]Publ. Law 96-364, 29 USC 1001.
[4]This was not true for a "substantial" employer, as defined in the law, which upon withdrawal was required to post a surety bond or place assets in escrow for the full amount of its allocable share of the plan's unfunded liability to discharge its obligation in the event that the plan would terminate within the next five years.
[5]ERISA §4203(a).

or less of the employer's contribution base units for the "high base year" (defined below);

2. the employer permanently ceases to have an obligation to contribute under one or more, but not all, of the collective bargaining agreements under which the employer has been obligated to contribute to the plan, but the employer continues to perform other work under the jurisdiction of the collective bargaining agreement(s) similar to the type for which contributions were previously required, or transfers such work to another location;

3. the employer permanently ceases to have an obligation to contribute under the plan with respect to work performed at one or more (but fewer than all) of its facilities, but the employer continues to perform work at the facility (or facilities) of the type for which the obligation to contribute ceased.[6]

In the construction industry, a partial withdrawal does not occur unless an employer continues to have an obligation to contribute for only an "insubstantial" portion of its work within the craft and the area of jurisdiction of the applicable collective bargaining agreement. Presumably, the responsibility of the plan trustees is to define "insubstantial."[7] Plans in the retail food industry may elect to define a partial withdrawal as a 35 percent reduction in contribution base units (as compared with the otherwise applicable 70 percent reduction).[8] There is no liability for partial withdrawal from a plan in the entertainment industry, except under the conditions and to the extent prescribed by PBGC regulations.[9]

The partial withdrawal test couched in terms of the reduction in contribution base units needs further explanation. Contribution base units are the units on the basis of which the employer is required to contribute to the plan, for example, hours worked, compensation, tons of coal produced.[10] The three-year period during which the decline in contribution base units must occur is designated as the "test period." Contributions during the test period are measured against those for the "high base year," which is defined as the average number of the employer's contribution base units during the *two* plan years for which such units were the highest during the five plan years immediately preceding the beginning of the three-year testing period.[11] For example,

Plan Year	Employer's Contribution Base Units	Plan Year	Employer's Contribution Base Units
1	19,000	5	17,000
2	20,000	6	15,000
3	20,000	7	10,000
4	18,000	8	5,000

During this eight-year period, the employer's contribution base units declined from a high of 20,000 to a low of 5,000; this amounts to an overall decline of

[6]ERISA §4205(a).
[7]ERISA §4208(d)(1).
[8]ERISA §4205(c)(1).
[9]ERISA §4208(d)(2).
[10]ERISA §4001(a)(11).
[11]ERISA §4205(b)(1)(B).

75 percent. Yet this overall decline does not determine whether a partial withdrawal has occurred. To determine whether a partial withdrawal occurred during
year 8, the contribution hours for plan years 6, 7, and 8 must be compared with the
contribution hours for plan years 2 and 3, the two years of highest contributions
during the five plan years preceding the three-year test period. Thus

$$\frac{\text{Plan year 6 contribution hours}}{\text{High base year's hours}} = \frac{15,000}{20,000} = 75 \text{ percent}$$

$$\frac{\text{Plan year 7 contribution hours}}{\text{High base year's hours}} = \frac{10,000}{20,000} = 50 \text{ percent}$$

$$\frac{\text{Plan year 8 contribution hours}}{\text{High base year's hours}} = \frac{5,000}{20,000} = 25 \text{ percent}$$

Inasmuch as the ratio was 30 percent or less for only one of the plan years in the
test period, a partial withdrawal has not occurred. The ratio would have had to be
30 percent or less for *each* of the three plan years for a partial termination to occur.
Operations at the reduced level would have to continue for another two years
before a partial withdrawal becomes a possibility, but then the high base year hours
would drop to 19,000—an average for plan years 3 and 4.

Except for a sale of assets (which is discussed later in the chapter), a withdrawal
is not deemed to have occurred merely because of a change in the employer's
corporate structure (or a change to an unincorporated form of business enterprise) if the change causes no interruption in the employer's contributions or
obligation to contribute under the plan.[12] Nor does a suspension of contributions
during a labor dispute constitute a withdrawal.[13] A successor or parent corporation
or other entity resulting from a change in business form is considered to be the
original employer.

In the building and construction industry (and certain segments of the entertainment industry), there is a complete withdrawal only if the employer remains in
the area (or returns within five years and does not renew its obligation to contribute) and performs work (presumably with nonunion labor) that would have been
covered by the plan.[14] A trucking employer who withdraws from a plan in the
trucking, household goods moving, or public warehousing industries may post a
five-year surety bond or escrow assets in an amount equal to 50 percent of its
withdrawal liability until the PBGC can determine whether cessation of the
employer's obligation to contribute did not result in "substantial damage" to the
plan's contribution base.[15] If the PBGC determines that there was no substantial
damage to the contribution base, no withdrawal liability is assessed, and the surety
bond or escrowed assets are returned to the employer. On the other hand, if the
contribution base was substantially damaged, withdrawal liability is assessed, the
surety bond or escrowed assets are paid to the plan, and the employer must
commence making payments to discharge the remainder of its obligation. These

---

[12]ERISA §4218.
[13]Ibid.
[14]ERISA §4203(b),(c).
[15]ERISA §4203(d).

exceptions to the general rule are based on the premise that withdrawal liability can be prudently waived if the withdrawals in the aggregate do not significantly erode the contribution base, which would be the case if the overall employment level in the industry and locality covered by the plan remains reasonably constant, with new signatory employers (e.g., contractors) replacing those who withdraw. Indeed, the PBGC is authorized to prescribe regulations under which plans in industries other than construction and entertainment may provide for special withdrawal liability rules, if the PBGC determines that the industry characteristics make such rules appropriate and that the rules would not pose a significant risk to the PBGC.[16] The term *industry characteristics* relates primarily to whether the amount of work (contribution base units) in the jurisdiction of the plan is or is not substantially affected by the movement of union employers out of and into the jurisdiction of the plan.

A plan may provide that an employer can become a member for up to six years and then withdraw without any liability for the plan's unfunded vested benefits.[17] This is the "free look" provision of the MPPAA that is intended to help overcome an employer's reluctance to become a member of the plan. An employer can take advantage of the provision only one time. This rule applies to an employer only if its contributions are less than 2 percent of the total contributions to the plan during each of the six years. A plan can extend this privilege only at a time when its assets are at least eight times its annual benefit payments. This free look is not permitted for plans in the building and construction industry.

Withdrawal liability and the statutory definitions of withdrawal not only bolster the financial condition of multiemployer plans but also serve as a strong deterrent to signatory employers to discontinue participation in the plan when withdrawal liability would be assessed, especially to "go nonunion." It was presumably not the intent of the legislation to place this roadblock in the path of nonunionization, but it certainly is one of the results.

A critically important component of the definition of a withdrawal pertains to the sale of assets by a signatory employer. Many small employers, especially family-operated businesses, eventually sell out to larger firms. If the seller's business is an incorporated entity, it is the corporation that is deemed to be the employer, and sale of the stock of the corporation to a new owner will not trigger a withdrawal by the employer. But if an owner of an unincorporated business sells it, or if a corporation sells part or all of its operations (e.g., sells the factory, equipment, and business as a going concern) to a new owner, the seller (who was the employer) has ceased its obligation to contribute to the plan and withdrawal liability would ordinarily be assessed.

The seller's withdrawal liability under a multiemployer plan can be a serious impediment to the transaction. As a form of relief, the MPPAA provides that an employer whose obligation to contribute to the plan is terminated through the sale of its assets in a bona fide, arm's-length transaction with an unrelated party within the meaning of the Internal Revenue Code shall not be required to make liability payments if the purchaser of the assets becomes obligated to contribute to the plan

[16]ERISA §4203(f).
[17]ERISA §4210.

in respect of the operations for substantially the same number of contribution base units (typically, hours of covered employment) for which the seller was obligated to contribute.[18] However, this relief is available only if the purchaser posts a surety bond or escrows assets equal to the greater of (1) the average annual contribution required to be made by the seller for the three plan years immediately preceding the plan year in which the sale of assets occurs, or (2) the seller's required contribution for the last plan year before the assets were sold; *and* the contract of sale provides that if the purchaser withdraws from the plan with respect to the acquired operations within five years, the seller will be secondarily liable for any withdrawal liability it would have had to the plan (in the absence of this relief provision) if the purchaser fails to meet its liability payments. If the seller goes out of business during the five-year period, it must escrow assets or post a surety bond in an amount equal to the present value of the withdrawal liability it would have had in the absence of this exception.

Allocation of Unfunded Liability for Vested Benefits

Conceptually, there are two general approaches to allocating a plan's unfunded liability for vested benefits: (1) the liabilities can be pooled and allocated to the participating employers on some equitable basis, and (2) the liabilities can be allocated to individual participants in the plan and then attributed to their various employers on the basis of periods of service with those employers. The first approach may be characterized as *pool attribution* and the second as *individual* or *direct* attribution.

MPPAA recognizes both approaches and sets out three acceptable methods of allocating pooled liabilities.[19] It has also directed the PBGC to prescribe by regulation a procedure by which a plan may, by amendment, adopt some other method of determining an employer's allocable share of unfunded vested benefits, subject to approval by the PBGC on the basis of its determination that adoption of the method by the plan would not significantly increase the risk of loss to the plan participants and beneficiaries, or to the PBGC.

Attribution of Pooled Liabilities

The pool attribution methods sanctioned by MPPAA have certain common characteristics, the most important being the use of plan contributions as the basis for liability allocation. In each case, the numerator of the prorating fraction is the *required* contributions of the withdrawing employer and the denominator is the total *actual* contributions to the plan for the period involved, reduced by the contributions of withdrawn employers. The numerator uses *required* contributions to ensure that the withdrawing employer will not be permitted to profit from any delinquency in its contribution obligation. (Contribution delinquency is a perennial problem in most multiemployer plans.) The denominator uses actual contributions because of the difficulty and expense of determining the required

[18]ERISA §4204(a)(1).
[19]ERISA §4211(b),(c), and (d).

contribution for all signatory employers. In each case, the basis of allocation is contributions to the plan for a period of five plan years. Finally, the determination of the unfunded portion of the vested benefits takes into account all outstanding claims for withdrawal liability that can reasonably be expected to be collected by the plan.

The principal differences among the methods relate to (a) the period or periods for which the unfunded liabilities are pooled, (b) the group of employers assumed to be responsible for the allocable liabilities, and (c) the rate at which the unfunded vested liabilities are assumed to be amortized.

1. THE PRESUMPTIVE METHOD   The MPPAA specifies the method to be employed, unless the plan trustees adopt another approved method. The specified procedure is called the *presumptive* method, which, by explicit mandate of the MPPAA, must be used by the building and construction industry.[20] The presumptive method distinguishes between the unfunded liabilities for vested benefits (UVB liabilities) for plan years ending before April 29, 1980, and those arising in plan years ending on or after that date. Responsibility for that first pool of liabilities, which includes the unfunded obligations left behind by employers who withdrew over all the years of the plan's existence, is assigned to that group of employers still participating in the plan during the first plan year ending after April 28, 1980. Any employer in that group who withdraws before these unfunded liabilities are fully amortized must assume a proportion of the unamortized amount as a withdrawal liability. This liability is determined by multiplying the unamortized unfunded liabilities by the ratio of the employer's required contributions over the last five plan years (ending prior to April 29, 1980) over the total plan contributions for that period by the group of employers specified above. For the purpose of this allocation, it is assumed that 5 percent of the original amount of the UVB liability is funded each year over a 20-year period beginning with the first plan year ending on or after April 29, 1980.

The UVB liabilities arising in plan years ending on or after April 29, 1980, are segregated by the plan year in which they arise and are prorated among the employers having an obligation to contribute to the plan as of the end of that year. For each plan year ending on or after April 29, 1980, the net change in the UVB liability is computed and prorated over the then participating employers on the basis of contributions for that year and the four preceding plan years. The net change in the UVB liability for a given plan year is affected by (a) experience gains and losses; (b) retroactive plan liberalizations, especially benefit increases; (c) reallocation of withdrawal liabilities of earlier plan years that could not be collected or were not assessed because of various relief provisions; (d) assumed amortization of the prior year's liability; (e) any change in the actuarial assumptions; (f) the level of employer contributions for the year; and (g) the value of new vested benefits created by employees becoming vested and earning another year's benefit accrual.

As with the pre-April 29, 1980, UVB liability pool, each plan year's UVB liability is assumed to be reduced by 5 percent (or the original amount) per year through contributions. Thus each pool has a life of 20 years. This produces a "rolling"

[20]ERISA §4211(b).

liability attribution with a "piece" of the total potential liability of an employer expiring after the lapse of 20 years. Stated differently, this method provides for 21 distinct UVB liability pools: the pre-1980 pool and one for each of 20 plan years. By the year 2000, the pre-1980 pool will have been completely funded, according to the assumptions, and thereafter as of any given year there would be only 20 pools.

It is worth emphasizing that, under the presumptive method, employers joining the plan after April 28, 1980, are not liable for any portion of the pre-1980 UVB liabilities. They are required to assume only a pro rata share of the UVB liabilities arising for the plan years in which they participate.

2. THE MODIFIED PRESUMPTIVE METHOD   A second method of allocating pooled liabilities is the *modified* presumptive method.[21] The principal modification introduced by this method has to do with the treatment of unfunded liabilities arising in plan years ending on or after April 29, 1980. These liabilities are pooled without reference to the plan years in which they arise and are allocated among the participating employers on the basis of contributions to the plan over the preceding five years, irrespective of when the employers became signatories to the plan. (Proration by contributions and annual recomputation of the unfunded liability moderate the potential inequity in this broad type of pooling.) Thus, there are only two pools of UVB liabilities under this method, in contrast to the 21 under the presumptive method. The pre-1980 pool of UVB liabilities is assumed to decline in a pattern reflecting 15-year amortization in equal annual installments, beginning with the first plan year ending on or after April 29, 1980. This is, of course, a faster rate of amortization than that implicit in the 5 percent annual reduction assumed under the presumptive method. The UVB liability for all plan years ending on or after April 29, 1980, is recomputed each year, taking into account collectible withdrawal liability payments. A withdrawing employer is assessed its pro rata share of that UVB liability computed as of the end of the plan year preceding the plan year when the withdrawal occurs.

3. THE ROLLING-FIVE METHOD   A third method of allocating pooled liabilities is the so-called rolling-five method.[22] This method makes no distinction between the pre-April 29, 1980, UVB liabilities and those arising thereafter. All UVB liabilities, irrespective of the plan year or years of origin, are pooled and allocated to withdrawing employers on the basis of contributions over the preceding five years. Thus there is only one pool under this method. The UVB liability is recomputed each year by taking into account past amortization payments and withdrawal liability payments. There is no assumed rate of amortization, the computation reflecting actual experience. This is clearly the simplest method to administer, but it may discourage new employers from joining the plan.

Under any of the pooled attribution methods, the employer can be assessed withdrawal liability even though the plan has no UVBs as of the end of the preceding plan year. Since the attribution methods consider the UVBs for years prior to the year preceding the employer's withdrawal from the plan, the lack of

[21]ERISA §4211(c)(2).
[22]ERISA §4211(c)(3).

UVBs in the year prior to withdrawal does not determine if an employer is assessed withdrawal liability.[23]

Direct Attribution Method

The alternative to pooling the UVB liabilities of a multiemployer plan and allocating them on a basis that achieves only rough equity is to identify the source of the actuarial liabilities and attribute them (with matching assets) to the employers in respect to whom they arose. This is called the "direct attribution" method and, as noted above, its use is sanctioned by the MPPAA.[24]

In concept, this is the most equitable method of allocating unfunded liabilities. Unfortunately, it is feasible only for plans in industries that enjoy reasonably stable employment relationships. For most multiemployer plans, the method would be completely impracticable. Even when it is possible to associate a given body of unfunded liabilities with a given employer, it is usually more expensive and more cumbersome to attribute liabilities in this manner than to allocate them by contributions, which are the most accessible and verifiable information maintained by a multiemployer plan.

There is some pooling of liabilities in the direct attribution method, as prescribed in the MPPAA. A withdrawing employer is assigned, in addition to its own attributable liabilities (and matching assets), its pro rata share of the unattributable liabilities of previously withdrawn employers. The proration may be based on either attributable liabilities or contributions.

Partial Withdrawal

An employer's obligation for a partial withdrawal is determined by multiplying the withdrawal liability for a complete withdrawal by the ratio of contribution base units in the year following the withdrawal to the average contribution base units during the five years preceding the withdrawal. In the event that an employer who has a partial withdrawal one year has a complete or partial withdrawal in a subsequent year, an appropriate adjustment is made.[25]

Reductions in Withdrawal Liability

The MPPAA contains several provisions designed to to reduce the withdrawal liability determined according to the allocation methods described above.

---

[23]The PBGC took this position after changing its mind twice. In 1983 the PBGC issued Opinion Letter 83-19, which assessed withdrawal liability even if the plan had no UVBs as of the year prior to withdrawal. This position was upheld by the Eighth Circuit Court of Appeals in *Ben Hur Construction Co. v. Goodwin*, 784 F2d 876 (8th Cir. 1986). Later, the PBGC issued a Notice of Interpretation (at 51 FR 47342) that reversed this decision and indicated that it would no longer follow Opinion Letter 83-19, a position that was upheld in *Bershire Hathaway, Inc. v. Textile Workers Pension Fund*, 874 F2d 53 (1st Cir. 1989). However, when *Wise v. RufWn*, 914 F2d 570 (4th Cir. 1990), *cert. denied* Feb. 25, 1991, declined to follow the Notice of Interpretation, the PBGC revoked the Notice and returned to applying Opinion Letter 83-19 (56 FR 12288).

[24]ERISA §4211(c)(4).

[25]ERISA §4206.

Under the *de minimis* rule, enacted for the relief of small employers, especially those wishing to sell their assets or go out of business, an allocable withdrawal liability of $50,000 or less (or 0.75 percent of the plan's UVB liabilities, if less) is waived.[26] The first $50,000 of any assessment of $100,000 or less is waived for any employer, but $1 of the waiver is forfeited for each $1 that the assessment exceeds $100,000, so there is no relief for assessments of $150,000 or more. The law permits the plan trustees to amend the plan to waive instead the first $100,000 of assessments (or 0.75 percent of the UVB liabilities, if less), with the offset beginning at $150,000. The *de minimis* rule is not applicable when all employers withdraw from the plan within a three-year period (a mass withdrawal).

In the case of a bona fide sale of all or substantially all assets of any employer other than an employer undergoing *reorganization* under Title 11 of the Bankruptcy Code or state bankruptcy laws, the unfunded vested benefits otherwise allocable to the employer are limited to the greater of two amounts, the unfunded vested benefits attributable to employees of the employer or a proportion of the liquidation or dissolution value of the employer.[27] The alternative related to benefits attributable to the employer applies regardless of whether the plan otherwise uses the direct attribution method, but presumably does not apply if it is not feasible to calculate the unfunded vested benefits according to that method. If the liquidation or dissolution value of the employer is $2 million or less, the proportion used as the limit is 30 percent, increasing to 80 percent of liquidation value in excess of $10 million. For a liquidation value of $10 million, the proportion is 43.5 percent, while for a value of $20 million the proportion is 61.75 percent. As the liquidation value goes up, the proportion asymptotically approaches 80 percent.

In the case of an insolvent employer undergoing *liquidation* or *dissolution*, the amount of unfunded vested benefits otherwise allocable to the employer is limited to the greater of 50 percent of the amount or the liquidation or dissolution value of the employer. For this purpose an employer is deemed to be insolvent if its liabilities, including its withdrawal liability before this adjustment, exceeds its assets.[28] If, after a complete withdrawal, the employer resumes covered operations or renews its obligation to contribute, its withdrawal liability originally assessed may be adjusted or waived.[29]

Withdrawal Liability Payments

A withdrawing employer discharges its allocable share of the plan's UVB liabilities through annual level installment payments to the plan. The amount of the installment payment is determined by the contribution *base* and the contribution *rate*.

The contribution base is unique to the withdrawing employer. As stipulated in the MPPAA,[30] the base is the *average* annual number of contribution base units for

[26]ERISA §4209.
[27]ERISA §4225(a).
[28]ERISA §4225(b),(d).
[29]ERISA §4207.
[30]ERISA §4219(c)(1)(C)(i).

the 3 consecutive plan years for which the employer's contributions were the *highest* during a period of 10 consecutive plan years ending before the plan year when the withdrawal occurs. For most plans, a contribution base unit is an hour of covered employment. This rather stringent definition of the contribution base was intended to discourage employers from deliberately winding down operations before withdrawal to minimize their UVB liability payments. It may create a hardship for an employer who has suffered a genuine, unavoidable decline in operations during the last few years before withdrawal, a not unlikely circumstance. The formula would cause the employer to have to make larger withdrawal payments than the contributions it was making to the plan during its last few years of membership, at a time when it may be experiencing general financial difficulties.

The contribution rate of a multiemployer plan is negotiated by the collective bargaining representatives. The contribution rate has usually been increased with each new labor contract. The rate to be used in calculating an employer's withdrawal liability payment is the *highest* rate at which the employer was obligated to contribute during the 10-year period *ending with the plan year* in which the withdrawal occurs. The plan year of withdrawal was included in the 10-year period since, under recent experience, the highest contribution rate is likely to be found in that year.

The employer's annual withdrawal liability payment is arrived at by multiplying the contribution rate times the contribution base, both components being derived in the manner described above. The employer is obligated to make a payment of this amount each year until its withdrawal liability is fully amortized, but in no event for a period of more than 20 years even though the liability is not fully amortized.[31] Because the higher contribution rate of the final year is often multiplied by a higher number of contribution base units for an earlier period, the required amortization payments may be substantially greater than the level of the employer's contributions had ever been. Partly for this reason, the withdrawal liability will frequently be amortized over a period shorter than 20 years. This has led to criticism that the 20-year cap on installment payments is a meaningless limit. Payments by an employer to amortize its withdrawal liability are generally deductible for federal income tax purposes when paid.[32]

Assessment and Collection of Withdrawal Liability

Having been notified or having determined that a partial or complete withdrawal has occurred, the trustees of a multiemployer plan ascertain the amount of the withdrawing employer's liability (in accordance with the principles and rules outlined above), inform the employer of the amount of its liability, and demand payment.[33] Determining the withdrawal liability is a complex matter, involving, among other things an actuarial valuation of the plan's vested liabilities and assets, and it is carried out by the plan's enrolled actuary under the direction of the plan

[31]The law specifies that each annual payment shall be payable in equal *quarterly* installments unless the plan states otherwise. ERISA §4219(c).

[32]IRC §404(g).

[33]ERISA §4219(b)(1).

trustees. The actuary must use actuarial assumptions that, in the aggregate, are reasonable and represent the actuary's best estimate of future experience, and he or she must use actuarial techniques or methods that are appropriate to the task.[34]

The employer has 90 days after receipt of the notice of assessment in which to contest the amount of the liability or the schedule of payments.[35] However, within 60 days the employer must make its first quarterly payment, even though the amount or legitimacy of the payment is in dispute.[36] If the employer questions the amount of the assessment, the schedule of installment payments, or the legitimacy of any assessment, and if the differences cannot be resolved by the two parties, the disputed matters must go to arbitration.[37]

The arbitration must be conducted in accordance with procedures prescribed in PBGC regulations, unless the parties agree to use alternative procedures that have been approved by the PBGC.[38] An arbitrator is selected in accordance with the procedures, usually from a list prepared by the American Arbitration Association.

For the arbitration proceeding, the MPPAA states that the plan's determination of the amount of withdrawal liability and the schedule of payments is presumed to be correct unless the employer shows "by a preponderance of evidence that the determination was unreasonable or clearly erroneous." The Third Circuit ruled that the presumption of correctness accorded the plan trustees' determination of withdrawal liability was unconstitutional in violating the withdrawing employer's right to a fair hearing. Courts in other jurisdictions have held to the contrary. By an evenly divided four-to-four vote, the Supreme Court upheld the Third Circuit.[39] The effect of this evenly divided vote is that the decision is not binding outside the Third Circuit. Further litigation of this issue is expected.

Determining the installment payments does not involve actuarial judgments (other than an interest discount rate), and hence these payments are not likely to be in dispute. Thus it is usually the *amount* of the assessment that is in dispute and that may involve nonactuarial matters such as the determination of the employer's required contributions. If the dispute involves actuarial considerations, in order to have the liability assessment itself set aside or modified the employer must prove that the actuarial assumptions and methods employed in the determination of the liability were unreasonable or that the plan's actuary made a significant error in applying the actuarial assumptions or methods.

The arbitrator's decision may be appealed to the federal courts by either party within 30 days.[40] In the appeal process, the arbitrator's *findings of fact* are given a rebuttable presumption of correctness.

---

[34]ERISA §4213.

[35]ERISA §4219(b)(2).

[36]ERISA §4219(c)(2).

[37]ERISA §4221(a)(1).

[38]29 CFR §2641. The only procedures approved by the PBGC are those of the American Arbitration Association and the New Jersey Mediation Board Multiemployer Withdrawal Liability Arbitration Rules and Regulations.

[39]*United Retail and Wholesale Employees Teamsters Union Local No. 115 Pension Plan v. Yahn & McDonnell, Inc.*, 787 F2d 128 (3d Cir. 1986) aff'd by an equally divided court, 107 S.Ct. 2171 (1987).

[40]ERISA §4221(b).

As indicated earlier, withdrawal liability payments are made quarterly, unless the plan specifies a different pattern. The employer may prepay the outstanding amount of unpaid liability at any time. If a payment is not made when due, interest at the prime rate (as published by the PBGC) can be charged from the due date to the date of payment.[41] In the event of default, the plan after 60 days' notice may require immediate payment of the outstanding amount of liability (a penalty known as "acceleration").[42]

Reimbursement for Uncollectible Withdrawal Liability

The MPPAA directed the PBGC to establish a supplemental insurance program by May 1, 1982, that would reimburse the multiemployer plan for withdrawal liability payments that proved to be uncollectible because of the employer's bankruptcy or other reasons considered appropriate by the PBGC.[43] Participation in the program was to be voluntary, with an additional premium being charged for the coverage. Because of budget limits, the PBGC has not established such a program and has recommended that the statutory mandate be repealed.

The law also authorized the sponsors of multiemployer plans acting in concert to establish a *withdrawal liability payment fund*, dubbed by some a "super trust fund," that would reimburse a signatory plan for that portion of a withdrawn employer's liability that is unattributable to any given employer, is waived, or is proven to be uncollectible.[44] It could also, at the option of the sponsors of the fund, provide for payment of an employer's attributable liability if the fund provides for the payment of both the attributable and unattributable liability of the employer in a single sum and the fund is subrogated to all rights of the plan against the employer.

No such super trust funds have been established as yet. However, some private insurers are now offering reimbursement for uncollectible or waived liability payments. Moreover, at least one organization, Lloyd's of London, offers an insurance contract designed to protect an employer who is forced to withdraw from a multiemployer pension plan for reasons beyond its control. The contract, subject to a deductible and coinsurance, will reimburse an insured employer for up to $1 million of withdrawal liability and, for an additional premium, will provide additional payments to help defray legal and actuarial expenses involved in evaluating withdrawal liability claims and possible arbitration and lawsuit expenses. The policy insures employers against withdrawals caused by the discontinuance of a major product line, a change in collective bargaining representative pursuant to an election conducted by the National Labor Relations Board, a physical destruction of an employer's business, a mass withdrawal of all employers in a multiemployer plan, or other unintentional events.

Reorganization

If a multiemployer plan is financially troubled, as defined by the MPPAA, it is in a state known as "reorganization." If a plan is in reorganization, it is subject to more

[41] 29 CFR §2644.3.
[42] ERISA §4219(c)(5).
[43] ERISA §4222(a).
[44] ERISA §4223.

stringent minimum funding requirements than those applicable to plans not in that condition,[45] and it is also subject to certain notification requirements.[46] Such a plan may be amended to reduce certain nonguaranteed accrued benefits, irrespective of the usual requirement forbidding amendments that reduce accrued benefits.[47] In addition, if a plan is in reorganization, all benefits must be paid in the form of an annuity, except that lump-sum distributions of less than $3,500 are permitted.[48] To determine whether a multiemployer plan is in reorganization for a plan year, the *vested benefits charge* and the *net charge to the funding standard account* must be determined and compared.[49]

The *vested benefits charge* is the annual amount required to amortize a plan's unfunded vested benefits as of the end of the *base plan year* over certain specified periods. The base plan year is the plan year preceding the plan year for which the vested benefits charge is to be determined or, under specified circumstances, an earlier year.

The value of vested benefits must be determined separately for persons in pay status and for other participants. The amount of unfunded vested benefits is determined for each group by subtracting the applicable plan assets from the value of vested benefits for each of these two groups, allocating plan assets first to the value of vested benefits for participants in pay status and, if assets are more than sufficient for that purpose, allocating the remainder of plan assets to the remaining participants. In some circumstances the amount of unfunded vested benefits is subject to adjustment. Next, the *vested bene*fits charge for the year is determined as the amount required to amortize the unfunded vested benefits for persons in pay status over 10 years and to amortize the unfunded vested benefits for other participants over 25 years.

The *net charge to the funding standard account* for the plan year is the sum of all charges to the funding standard account for the year under the regular minimum funding requirements reduced by all amortization credits to the funding standard account for the year. This net charge is generally equal to what the regular required minimum funding requirement for the year would be if the funding standard account had no credit balance resulting from having received more contributions than required by the funding requirements in prior years.

The *reorganization index* is determined as the excess, if any, of the vested benefits charge over the net charge to the funding standard account. If the reorganization index is greater than 0, that is, if the vested benefits charge exceeds the net charge to the funding standard account for the year, the plan is in reorganization.

Plan Benefits Insurance

Multiemployer plan withdrawal liability is only part of the PBGC's coverage for such plans. The government's benefits guarantee program also operates for

---

[45]ERISA §§4243, 4244; IRC §§418B, 418C.
[46]ERISA §4242; IRC §418A.
[47]ERISA §4244A; IRC §418D.
[48]IRC §418(c).
[49]ERISA §4241.

multiemployer plans in a manner similar to the single-employer plan program, with certain benefits guaranteed upon the occurrence of an insured event and the requirement of a per participant premium.

Insured Event

Under ERISA's original provisions, the insured event that triggers the PBGC's guarantee of benefits under a multiemployer plan was plan termination. The MPPAA changed the insured event from plan termination to plan insolvency. The insured event occurs when it is determined that the plan assets will not be sufficient to pay the plan benefits expected to become payable over the next three years. Under the amended law, a withdrawn employer must continue to make its withdrawal liability payments until its obligation is fully discharged. The procedure for making the resources of the PBGC available to a multiemployer plan is complex.

Liability of a Plan Sponsor to the PBGC

Under the original provisions of ERISA, both the sponsor of a terminated *single-employer* plan and the employer's signatory to a multiemployer plan were required to reimburse the PBGC for any loss that it incurred in meeting the benefit obligations of the terminated plan, up to 30 percent of the employer's net worth. Amendments to ERISA have removed the 30 percent limit for both single-employer plans and multiemployer plans—in effect imposing liability up to the full amount of the employer's net worth.[50] However, the PBGC only has authority to impose a lien on the employer's assets in an amount of 30 percent of the employer's net worth.[51]

Benefits Insured

The type of benefits insured for multiemployer plans is the same as for single-employer plans: that is, they are basic benefits.

Limits on Amount of Monthly Benefits

ERISA limits the amount of basic benefits that can be insured by the PBGC. The limit for multiemployer plans, promulgated by the MPPAA, is the sum of 100 percent of the first $5 of monthly benefit per year of credited service and 75 percent of the next $15 of monthly benefit.[52] The benefit to which the ceiling applies is a single life annuity (popularly known as a "straight-life annuity") commencing at

---

[50]ERISA §§4062(b), 4063(b), and 4064(b).

[51]ERISA §4068(a). In addition, a lien can be imposed on the employer's assets if the employer fails to make a required contribution under the minimum funding rules and the unpaid balance of missed funding contributions exceeds $1 million. The amount of the lien can generally only be the amount by which the missed funding contributions exceed $1 million. ERISA §302(f). The PBGC estimates that no more than 10 employers per year will meet these requirements.

[52]For plans becoming insolvent before the year 2000, the 75 percent is reduced to 65 percent. ERISA §4022A(c).

the designated normal retirement age. If the benefit is payable at a lower age than the normal retirement age, or in any annuity form other than the straight-life annuity, the limit is actuarially reduced.

Phase-in of Insurance Coverage

For multiemployer plans, benefits are not guaranteed until the plan (or amendment) has been in effect for five full years. In other words, there is no phase-in of the coverage for benefits of multiemployer plans.[53]

Implementation of the Guaranty

The process by which the resources of the PBGC are made available to pay the benefits of multiemployer plans is more complex than the process that applies to single-employer plans. The added complexity is attributable to the nature of the multiemployer plan.

A plan need not terminate to qualify for financial assistance from the PBGC. The latter's assistance depends on the plan's inability to meet its basic benefit obligations, whether it is ongoing or terminated.

Actually, the plan must be *insolvent* under the MPPAA definition before the PBGC comes to its rescue. A plan is insolvent when its available resources are not sufficient to pay the plan benefits for the plan year in question, or when the sponsor of a plan in reorganization reasonably determines, taking into account the plan's recent and anticipated financial experience, that the plan's available resources will not be sufficient to pay benefits that come due in the next plan year.[54] The term *available resources* means the plan's cash, marketable assets, contributions, withdrawal liability payments, and investment earnings, less reasonable administrative expenses and any amounts owed to the PBGC for the plan year by reason of financial assistance previously provided.

Another concept involved in this process is the *resource benefit level*.[55] This is the estimated level of benefits that can be paid in a given plan (insolvency) year on the basis of the plan sponsor's reasonable projection of the plan's available resources and its payable benefits. If the resource benefit level is below the level of the basic benefits guaranteed by the PBGC, the payment of all benefits other than basic benefits must be suspended for the year, and the reduction in benefits must be accomplished equitably in accordance with IRS regulations.[56] If it appears that available resources will not support the payment of all basic (i.e., insured) benefits, the PBGC will provide the additional resources needed *as a loan*.[57] If, by the end of an insolvency year, the plan sponsor determines that the plan's available resources could have supported benefit payments above the resource benefit level for that year, the plan sponsor must distribute the excess resources to plan participants and beneficiaries receiving benefits in that year.

[53]ERISA §4022A(b)(1).
[54]ERISA §4245(b)(1),(3).
[55]ERISA §4245(b)(2).
[56]ERISA §4245(c).
[57]ERISA §§4245(f), 4261.

At least three months in advance of each "insolvency year," the plan sponsor of a plan in reorganization must determine the resource benefit level for that insolvency year and inform all interested parties.[58] The PBGC may provide loans to the plan year after year. In the event that the plan recovers from its insolvency status, it must begin repaying the "loans" on reasonable terms in accordance with regulations.

A plan administrator or the PBGC may petition a U.S. court to appoint the PBGC trustee of a multiemployer plan to protect the interests of plan participants. The court must agree to the PBGC's appointment if the plan is in reorganization or if all employers have withdrawn and the appointment is in the interest of participants. As trustee, the PBGC would take over the plan and attempt to recover all amounts owed to the plan. If the available resources of the plan are insufficient to pay all insured benefits, the PBGC would provide financial assistance.

Premiums

The initial premium, set forth in ERISA, was 50 cents per participant per year for multiemployer pension plans and $1 per participant per year for single-employer plans. The MPPAA raised the premium for multiemployer plans in stages to $2.60 per participant. The full amount of the increase took effect in 1989, and the premium rate has not been increased since then.[59]

Plan Termination

A multiemployer plan terminates when it is amended to stop the accrual of further benefits or credit of any kind under the plan or to convert it to an individual account plan. It is also terminated when all member employers withdraw from the plan or no longer have an obligation to contribute to it.[60] In addition, the PBGC may initiate an involuntary termination if the plan fails to satisfy the minimum funding requirements or is unable to pay benefits when due, if there has been a reportable event, or if the corporation determines that continuation of the plan may reasonably be expected to increase its losses.[61] The procedures to be followed in order to implement the termination of a multiemployer plan and the requirements that apply to the plan's operation after its termination are specified in ERISA.[62]

[58] ERISA §4245(d)(3).
[59] ERISA §4006(a)(3)(A)(iii).
[60] ERISA §4041A(a).
[61] ERISA §4042.
[62] ERISA §§4041A, 4042.

Appendix A
Basic Actuarial Functions and Values for Derivation of Pension Plan Costs and Liabilities

TABLE A-1   Mortality, Disability, and Termination Rates and Related Probabilities of
Surviving in Service to Age 65 (percent)

Age	Mortality Rate	Disability Rate	Termination Rate	Probability of Surviving in Service to Age 65
20	0.0005	0.0013	0.1494	0.0888
21	0.0006	0.0013	0.1394	0.1046
22	0.0006	0.0013	0.1294	0.1218
23	0.0006	0.0014	0.1194	0.1402
24	0.0007	0.0015	0.1093	0.1595
25	0.0007	0.0016	0.0993	0.1796
26	0.0007	0.0017	0.0933	0.1999
27	0.0008	0.0017	0.0872	0.2210
28	0.0008	0.0019	0.0812	0.2428
29	0.0008	0.0020	0.0751	0.2650
30	0.0009	0.0021	0.0691	0.2874
31	0.0009	0.0022	0.0650	0.3097
32	0.0009	0.0023	0.0610	0.3324
33	0.0009	0.0025	0.0569	0.3552
34	0.0009	0.0027	0.0528	0.3780
35	0.0009	0.0029	0.0487	0.4006
36	0.0009	0.0031	0.0446	0.4228
37	0.0010	0.0033	0.0405	0.4444
38	0.0010	0.0037	0.0364	0.4653
39	0.0011	0.0040	0.0323	0.4852
40	0.0012	0.0043	0.0281	0.5040
41	0.0012	0.0046	0.0260	0.5215
42	0.0013	0.0049	0.0237	0.5387
43	0.0015	0.0054	0.0214	0.5553
44	0.0016	0.0060	0.0191	0.5715
45	0.0017	0.0065	0.0167	0.5871
46	0.0019	0.0070	0.0142	0.6020
47	0.0020	0.0075	0.0117	0.6162
48	0.0023	0.0085	0.0092	0.6296
49	0.0025	0.0096	0.0066	0.6425
50	0.0028	0.0106	0.0040	0.6547
51	0.0031	0.0116	0.0013	0.6662
52	0.0035	0.0126	0.0000	0.6770
53	0.0039	0.0144	0.0000	0.6881
54	0.0043	0.0163	0.0000	0.7009
55	0.0048	0.0181	0.0000	0.7156
56	0.0053	0.0199	0.0000	0.7323
57	0.0060	0.0218	0.0000	0.7513
58	0.0068	0.0230	0.0000	0.7727
59	0.0076	0.0242	0.0000	0.7965
60	0.0086	0.0255	0.0000	0.8227
61	0.0097	0.0267	0.0000	0.8517
62	0.0109	0.0280	0.0000	0.8838
63	0.0123	0.0280	0.0000	0.9195
64	0.0139	0.0280	0.0000	0.9581
65	0.0156	0.0000	0.0000	1.0000

TABLE A-2   Immediate Annuity Values for Single Male Life Annuity of
$1 per Year Payable Monthly, Ages 55–65

Age	Values (dollars)
55	11.4683
56	11.2890
57	11.1028
58	10.9103
59	10.7177
60	10.5072
61	10.2969
62	10.0816
63	9.8620
64	9.6389
65	9.4131

TABLE A-3 Temporary Life Annuity Values to Age 65 at 7 Percent
Compound Interest and Survival Probabilities from Table A-1

Age	Temporary Employment-Based Life Annuity of $1 per Year to Age 65	Temporary Employment-Based Life Annuity of 1 unit per Year Increasing Annually at Total Salary Scale to Age 65
20	13.9449	49.5443
21	13.8908	46.8892
22	13.8334	44.4062
23	13.7723	42.0804
24	13.7073	39.8996
25	13.6384	37.8519
26	13.5651	25.9263
27	13.4870	34.1125
28	13.4040	32.4317
29	13.3156	30.9007
30	13.2211	29.5058
31	13.1203	28.2358
32	13.0127	27.0800
33	12.8977	26.0297
34	12.7746	25.5290
35	12.6429	24.1442
36	12.5017	23.2766
37	12.3507	22.4259
38	12.1894	21.5909
39	12.0173	20.7709
40	11.8338	19.9644
41	11.6381	19.1702
42	11.4296	18.3870
43	11.2074	17.6137
44	10.9706	16.8487
45	10.7181	16.0907
46	10.4488	15.3385
47	10.1620	14.5910
48	9.8564	13.8470
49	9.5311	13.1053
50	9.1844	12.3645
51	8.8151	11.6231
52	8.4216	10.8799
53	8.0024	10.1334
54	7.5550	9.3820
55	7.0786	8.6237
56	6.5696	7.8486
57	6.0261	7.0634
58	5.4454	6.2597
59	4.8244	5.4364
60	4.1594	4.5968
61	3.4461	3.7337
62	2.6797	2.8451
63	1.8546	1.9286
64	0.9641	0.9822
65	0.0000	0.0000

TABLE A-4   Present Value of Sums Payable in Future Years at 7 Percent
Compound Interest

	Present Value of $1		
Years	Payable in Years Hence	Per Annum Payable for n Years	Per Annum Increasing 4 Percent per Year Payable to n Years
1	0.935	1.000	1.000
2	0.873	1.935	1.972
3	0.816	2.808	2.917
4	0.763	3.624	3.835
5	0.713	4.387	4.727
6	0.666	5.100	5.595
7	0.623	5.767	6.438
8	0.582	6.389	7.257
9	0.544	6.971	8.054
10	0.508	7.515	8.828
11	0.475	8.024	9.581
12	0.444	8.499	10.312
13	0.415	8.943	11.023
14	0.388	9.358	11.714
15	0.362	9.745	12.385
16	0.339	10.108	13.038
17	0.317	10.447	13.673
18	0.296	10.763	14.289
19	0.277	11.059	14.889
20	0.258	11.336	15.471
21	0.242	11.594	16.037
22	0.226	11.836	16.588
23	0.211	12.061	17.123
24	0.197	12.272	17.643
25	0.184	12.469	18.148
26	0.172	12.654	18.639
27	0.161	12.826	19.117
28	0.150	12.987	19.581
29	0.141	13.137	20.032
30	0.131	13.278	20.470
31	0.123	13.409	20.896
32	0.115	13.532	21.310
33	0.107	13.647	21.713
34	0.100	13.754	22.104
35	0.094	13.854	22.484
36	0.088	13.948	22.854
37	0.082	14.035	23.213
38	0.076	14.117	23.562
39	0.071	14.193	23.902
40	0.067	14.265	24.231

TABLE A-5 Total Salary Scale: Merit Scale Plus 3.5 Percent Annual Inflation and
.05 Percent Productivity Increase

	Annual Salary Increase				Ratio of Salary at Attained Age to Salary at Age 20
Age	Inflation	Productivity	Merit	Total	
20	0.035	0.005	0.068	0.108	1.000
21	0.035	0.005	0.066	0.106	1.108
22	0.035	0.005	0.064	0.104	1.225
23	0.035	0.005	0.062	0.102	1.353
24	0.035	0.005	0.060	0.100	1.491
25	0.035	0.005	0.058	0.098	1.640
26	0.035	0.005	0.056	0.096	1.801
27	0.035	0.005	0.053	0.093	1.974
28	0.035	0.005	0.049	0.089	2.157
29	0.035	0.005	0.045	0.085	2.349
30	0.035	0.005	0.041	0.081	2.549
31	0.035	0.005	0.037	0.077	2.755
32	0.035	0.005	0.033	0.073	2.967
33	0.035	0.005	0.030	0.070	3.184
34	0.035	0.005	0.027	0.067	3.407
35	0.035	0.005	0.025	0.065	3.635
36	0.035	0.005	0.024	0.064	3.871
37	0.035	0.005	0.023	0.063	4.119
38	0.035	0.005	0.022	0.062	4.379
39	0.035	0.005	0.021	0.061	4.650
40	0.035	0.005	0.020	0.060	4.934
41	0.035	0.005	0.019	0.059	5.230
42	0.035	0.005	0.018	0.058	5.538
43	0.035	0.005	0.017	0.057	5.860
44	0.035	0.005	0.016	0.056	6.194
45	0.035	0.005	0.015	0.055	6.540
46	0.035	0.005	0.014	0.054	6.900
47	0.035	0.005	0.013	0.053	7.273
48	0.035	0.005	0.012	0.052	7.658
49	0.035	0.005	0.011	0.051	8.056
50	0.035	0.005	0.010	0.050	8.467
51	0.035	0.005	0.009	0.049	8.891
52	0.035	0.005	0.008	0.048	9.326
53	0.035	0.005	0.007	0.047	9.774
54	0.035	0.005	0.006	0.046	10.233
55	0.035	0.005	0.006	0.046	10.704
56	0.035	0.005	0.005	0.045	11.197
57	0.035	0.005	0.005	0.045	11.700
58	0.035	0.005	0.005	0.045	12.227
59	0.035	0.005	0.004	0.044	12.777
60	0.035	0.005	0.004	0.044	13.339
61	0.035	0.005	0.004	0.044	13.926
62	0.035	0.005	0.004	0.044	14.539
63	0.035	0.005	0.003	0.043	15.179
64	0.035	0.005	0.003	0.043	15.831
65					16.512

Appendix B
List of Case Citations

Appendix C
List of Statutes, Rules, and Regulations

Employee Retirement Income Security Act of 1974 (ERISA)

Internal Revenue Code of 1986

Tax Reform Act of 1986 (TRA)

Other Statutes

Code of Federal Regulations

Treasury Regulations

Proposed Treasury and Labor Regulations

Revenue Rulings

Index

See also Appendix B: List of Case Citations and Appendix C: List of Statutes, Rules, and Regulations

The Pension Research Council

The Pension Research Council of The Wharton School of the University of Pennsylvania is an organization committed to generating debate on key policy issues that affect pensions and other employee benefits. The Council sponsors interdisciplinary research on the entire range of private and social retirement security and related benefit plans in the United States and around the world and seeks to broaden public understanding of these complex arrangements through basic research into their social, economic, legal, actuarial, and financial foundations. Members of the Advisory Board of the Council, appointed by the Dean of The Wharton School, are leaders in the employee benefits field, and though they recognize the essential role of Social Security and other public sector income maintenance programs, they share a strong desire to strengthen private sector approaches to economic security.

Executive Director

Olivia S. Mitchell *International Foundations of Employee Benefit Plans Professor,* Department of Insurance and Risk Management, The Wharton School, University of Pennsylvania, Philadelphia

Institutional Members

Bankers Trust Company
Ford Motor Company
John Hancock Mutual Life Insurance Company
Hay/Huggins Company, Inc.
Loomis, Sayles & Company, Inc.
William M. Mercer Companies, Inc.
Merck & Company, Inc.
Metropolitan Life Insurance Company
Mutual of America Life Insurance Company
Northwestern Mutual Life Insurance Company
KPMG Peat Marwick
Price Waterhouse
The Principal Financial Group
The Prudential Foundation

Pension Research Council Publications

Concepts of Actuarial Soundness in Pension Plans. Dorrance C. Bronson. 1957.

Continuing Care Retirement Communities: An Empirical, Financial, and Legal Analysis. Howard E. Winklevoss and Alwyn V. Powell with David L. Cohen, Esq. and Ann Trueblood-Raper. 1983.

Corporate Book Reserving for Postretirement Healthcare Benefits. Edited by Dwight K. Bartlett. 1990.

Demography and Retirement: The Twenty-First Century. Edited by Anna M. Rappaport and Sylvester J. Schieber. 1993.

An Economic Appraisal of Pension Tax Policy in the United States. Richard A. Ippolito. 1990.

The Economics of Pension Insurance. Richard A. Ippolito. 1989.

Employer Accounting for Pensions: Analysis of the Financial Accounting Standards Board's Preliminary Views and Exposure Draft. E. L. Hicks and C. L. Trowbridge. 1985.

Fundamentals of Private Pensions (Seventh Edition). Dan M. McGill, Kyle N. Brown, John J. Haley, and Sylvester J. Schieber. 1996.

The Future of Pensions in the United States. Edited by Raymond Schmitt, 1993.

Inflation and Pensions. Susan M. Wachter. 1987.

It's My Retirement Money, Take Good Care of It: The TIAA-CREF Story. William C. Greenough. 1990.

Joint Trust Pension Plans: Understanding and Administering Collectively Bargained Multiemployer Plans Under ERISA. Daniel F. McGinn. 1977.

Pension Asset Management: An International Perspective. Edited by Leslie Hannah. 1988.

Pension Mathematics with Numerical Illustrations (Second Edition). Howard E. Winklevoss. 1993.

Pensions and the Economy: Sources, Uses, and Limitations of Data. Edited by Zvi Bodie and Alicia H. Munnell. 1992.

Pensions, Economics and Public Policy. Richard Ippolito. 1985.

Providing Health Care Benefits in Retirement. Edited by Judith F. Mazo, Anna M. Rappaport, and Sylvester J. Schieber. 1994.

Proxy Voting of Pension Plan Equity Securities. Edited by Dan M. McGill. 1989.

Retirement Systems for Public Employees. Thomas P. Bleakney. 1972.

Retirement Systems in Japan. Robert L. Clark. 1990.

Search for a National Retirement Income Policy. Edited by Jack L. Van Derhei. 1987.

Securing Employer-Based Pensions: An International Perspective. Edited by Zvi Bodie, Olivia S. Mitchell, and John A. Turner. 1996.

Social Investing. Edited by Dan M. McGill. 1984.

Social Security (Fourth Edition). Robert J. Myers. 1993.